D0816431

NEW OXFORD HISTORY OF MUSIC

VOLUME IV

THE VOLUMES OF THE
NEW OXFORD HISTORY OF MUSIC

THE AGE OF
HUMANISM
1540–1630

EDITED BY

GERALD ABRAHAM

LONDON

OXFORD UNIVERSITY PRESS

NEW YORK   TORONTO

Oxford University Press, Ely House, London W. 1

GLASGOW NEW YORK TORONTO MELBOURNE WELLINGTON
CAPE TOWN IBADAN NAIROBI DAR ES SALAAM LUSAKA ADDIS ABABA
DELHI BOMBAY CALCUTTA MADRAS KARACHI LAHORE DACCA
KUALA LUMPUR SINGAPORE HONG KONG TOKYO

ISBN 0 19 316304 7

© *Oxford University Press 1968*

First published 1968
Third Impression 1974

*Printed in Great Britain
at the University Press, Oxford
by Vivian Ridler
Printer to the University*

GENERAL INTRODUCTION

THE present work is designed to replace the *Oxford History of Music*, first published in six volumes under the general editorship of Sir Henry Hadow between 1901 and 1905. Five authors contributed to that ambitious publication—the first of its kind to appear in English. The first two volumes, dealing with the Middle Ages and the sixteenth century, were the work of H. E. Wooldridge. In the third Sir Hubert Parry examined the music of the seventeenth century. The fourth, by J. A. Fuller Maitland, was devoted to the age of Bach and Handel; the fifth, by Hadow himself, to the period bounded by C. P. E. Bach and Schubert. In the final volume Edward Dannreuther discussed the Romantic period, with which, in the editor's words, it was 'thought advisable to stop'. The importance of the work—particularly of the first two volumes—was widely recognized, and it became an indispensable part of a musician's library. The scheme was further extended in the new edition issued under the editorship of Sir Percy Buck between 1929 and 1938. An introductory volume, the work of several hands, was designed to supplement the story of music in the ancient world and the Middle Ages. New material, including two complete chapters, was added to volumes i and ii, while the third volume was reissued with minor corrections and a number of supplementary notes by Edward J. Dent. The history was also brought nearer to the twentieth century by the addition of a seventh volume, by H. C. Colles, entitled *Symphony and Drama, 1850–1900.*

Revision of an historical work is always difficult. If it is to be fully effective, it may well involve changes so comprehensive that very little of the original remains. Such radical revision was not the purpose of the second edition of the *Oxford History of Music*. To have attempted it in a third edition would have been impossible. During the first half of the present century an enormous amount of detailed work has been done on every period covered by the original volumes. New materials have been discovered, new relationships revealed, new interpretations made possible. Perhaps the most valuable achievement has been the publication in reliable modern editions of a mass of music which was previously available only in manuscript or in rare printed copies. These developments have immeasurably increased the historian's opportunities, but they have also added heavily to his responsibilities. To attempt a detailed survey of the whole history of music is no longer within the power of a single writer. It may even be doubted whether the burden can be adequately shouldered by a team of five.

The *New Oxford History of Music* is therefore not a revision of the older work, nor is it the product of a small group of writers. It has been planned as an entirely new survey of music from the earliest times down to comparatively recent years, including not only the achievements of the Western world but also the contributions made by eastern civilizations and primitive societies. The examination of this immense field is the work of a large number of contributors, British and foreign. The attempt has been made to achieve uniformity without any loss of individuality. If this attempt has been successful, the result is due largely to the patience and co-operation shown by the contributors themselves. Overlapping has to some extent been avoided by the use of frequent cross-references; but we have not thought it proper to prevent different authors from expressing different views about the same subject, where it could legitimately be regarded as falling into more than one category.

The scope of the work is sufficiently indicated by the titles of the several volumes. Our object throughout has been to present music, not as an isolated phenomenon or the work of a few outstanding composers, but as an art developing in constant association with every form of human culture and activity. The biographies of individuals are therefore merely incidental to the main plan of the history, and those who want detailed information of this kind must seek it elsewhere. No hard and fast system of division into chapters has been attempted. The treatment is sometimes by forms, sometimes by periods, sometimes also by countries, according to the importance which one element or another may assume. The division into volumes has to some extent been determined by practical considerations; but pains have been taken to ensure that the breaks occur at points which are logically and historically justifiable. The result may be that the work of a single composer who lived to a ripe age is divided between two volumes. The later operas of Monteverdi, for example, belong to the history of Venetian opera and hence find their natural place in volume v, not with the discussion of his earlier operas to be found in volume iv. On the other hand, we have not insisted on a rigid chronological division where the result would be illogical or confusing. If a subject finds its natural conclusion some ten years after the date assigned for the end of a period, it is obviously preferable to complete it within the limits of one volume rather than to allow it to overflow into a second. An exception to the general scheme of continuous chronology is to be found in volumes v and vi, which deal with different aspects of the same period and so are complementary to each other.

The history as a whole is intended to be useful to the professed student of music, for whom the documentation of sources and the bibliographies are particularly designed. But the growing interest in the music of all periods shown by music-lovers in general has encouraged us to bear their interests also in mind. It is inevitable that a work of this kind should employ a large number of technical terms and deal with highly specialized matters. We have, however, tried to ensure that the technical terms are intelligible to the ordinary reader and that what is specialized is not necessarily wrapped in obscurity. Finally, since music must be heard to be fully appreciated, we have given references throughout to the records issued by His Master's Voice (R.C.A. Victor) under the general title *The History of Music in Sound*. These records are collected in a series numbered to correspond with the volumes of the present work, and have been designed to be used with it.

J. A. WESTRUP
GERALD ABRAHAM
ANSELM HUGHES
EGON WELLESZ
MARTIN COOPER

CONTENTS

V. LATIN CHURCH MUSIC ON THE CONTINENT—1

VI. LATIN CHURCH MUSIC ON THE CONTINENT—2

ILLUSTRATIONS

INTRODUCTION TO VOLUME IV

THE title of the present volume of the *New Oxford History of Music* has already been explained in the Handbook to the accompanying volume of gramophone records in *The History of Music in Sound*: 'It was mainly during this period that music changed its orientation from the divine to the human. There had been plenty of secular music before . . . but the secular forms had been subordinate forms. Throughout the period covered by the present volume more and more importance is assumed by secular vocal forms—above all, the madrigal and, later, monody—and by instrumental music; the musical form in which Renaissance thought and the Renaissance spirit enjoyed their fullest flowering—opera—actually appeared only at the turn of the century.' And it may be worth while to emphasize that humanism generally, not merely its manifestation in music, did not saturate European thought (outside Italy) until long after it had impressed outstanding European minds. Italy led the way but even in Italy the universities were still organized on medieval lines and still using medieval textbooks at the beginning of the sixteenth century. The new influences of Italian thought made themselves felt in Germany in the fifteenth century but only in a few small circles, while France—above all the University of Paris, with its enormous international prestige—was still more conservative. So were England and Scotland. The position in England during the early decades of the sixteenth century is typical; one can point to the names of the great humanists, Colet and More and Skelton, and to Erasmus teaching at Cambridge, but scholasticism remained firmly entrenched at Oxford and the Scottish universities held out even longer. Professor H. W. Lawton concludes his survey of 'Vernacular Literature in Western Europe, 1493–1520' with the comment that 'the full impact of the revival of ancient learning (even in Italy itself) and of the Italian example was yet to reach the rest of Europe and then usually modified and in some cases limited by the effect of the Lutheran and Calvinist Reformations'.[1] The full humanist penetration of European thought and feeling, to such depth that musical composition became affected and later actually conditioned by it, was a long and slow process continuing throughout the sixteenth century.

[1] *The New Cambridge Modern History* i (Cambridge, 1957), p. 193.

The extent to which this process had not yet fulfilled itself musically even towards the end of the century is proclaimed by the fact that almost every country from Portugal to Poland justly claims the latter part of the century as the golden age of its polyphony. The essential manifestation of humanism in music is the domination of the word; it is not a mere coincidence that the essentially homophonic *frottola* 'flourished chiefly in the courts of northern Italy, especially in Mantua, Ferrara, Venice, Urbino, and Florence . . . the very ones in which Pietro Bembo . . . was influential'[1] and that the even more word-dominated Latin odes of the German composers originated in humanistic circles.[2] Polyphony—at any rate, 'golden age' polyphony—resists domination by the word; in its finest and purest forms it merely uses and absorbs and dissolves words; it is one of the supreme forms of absolute music. 'Golden age' polyphony is in fact the final flowering of that fourteenth-century *ars nova* which was 'the first full manifestation of pure musical art, freed from the service of religion or poetry and constructed according to its own laws'[3] and which Dufay and his contemporaries had drastically refined and purified yet essentially continued. It could, after all, continue to serve religion so long as religion remained beyond the grasp of human reason, the magic of sound matching the magic of faith; but when religion became 'reasonable' its music began to submit to the word.

Much of the present volume is devoted naturally to this 'golden age'. We may no longer think of the later sixteenth century as, above all, 'the age of Palestrina' nor even be as confident as our fathers that Palestrina's music represents the acme of pure polyphony, but the highest musical achievements of the period were polyphonic, based on techniques evolved through centuries and now brought to that perfection which is in any art a sign of inner decadence. For artistic styles are like political empires, nurturing always within them the forces which are to bring about their decay, and never more strongly than when they themselves appear to be at the height of their power. The greatest Masses and motets of Palestrina and Lassus and Victoria are unsurpassable in their kind, but the study of these masterpieces is additionally fascinating to the historian because within their very perfection he detects the symptoms of that which was (temporarily) to supersede them. The domination of the word makes itself felt, in homophonic, note-against-note passages, in a large proportion of this 'polyphonic' music. And this is very

---

[1] See vol. iii, p. 394.   [2] Ibid., pp. 370–1.   [3] Ibid., p. xvii.

different from the occasional, exceptional note-against-note passage in Machaut or Dufay; nor has it anything to do with the Council of Trent or the Commission of Cardinals. The humanistic subordination of music to text, the insistence that music shall have meaning through carrying words or shall simply heighten the effect of words, is as evident in religious music as in *frottola*, madrigal, and *chanson*. And in the religious music both of the Catholics and of every variety of Protestant: Lutheran hymn and Calvinist psalm, Cranmer's 'as near as may be, for every syllable a note', and the injunctions of the Council of Trent, all point in the same direction. The problem was really simpler in religious music where homophony or near-homophony, allowing the text to be clearly audible, was often an adequate solution. Secular composers attempted a number of quite different solutions: the verse scansion of the German ode-composers and the French practitioners of *musique mesurée*, the symbolic illustration of the text practised by the madrigalists, the supposedly Greek recitative of the Florentine monodists, the empirical matching of words and music in the English lute ayres. With historical hindsight we see that *musique mesurée* was a blind alley and that recitative was the 'right' solution, but can we deny that much of the charm of the madrigal springs from the incongruous crossing of polished polyphony with naïve symbolism or point to more perfect marriage of verse and music than in the best of the English ayres? (For that matter, *musique mesurée* also has its masterpieces.)

Instead of 'art constantly aspiring towards the condition of music', as Pater put it, music aspired towards the condition of poetry. It surrendered a part of its magic, its purely musical sense, for the sake of extra-musical sense. But there is one kind of music, besides vocal polyphony, which finds it difficult to take on extra-musical sense: independent instrumental music. All through the Middle Ages instrumental music had been essentially indistinguishable from vocal music, imitated from it, or elaborated from it in terms of some peculiar instrumental technique (lute or keyboard music); until the middle of the fifteenth century music arising out of the very nature of an instrument was infinitesimal in quantity and negligible in artistic quality. Independent instrumental music was bound to develop on its own lines, but it seems probable that its more intense cultivation during the period of the present volume was a species of compensation for the increasing rationalization of vocal music. From the first, lute and keyboard music had led the way in technical emancipation and, broadly speaking, technical emancipation—emancipation of idiom—preceded structural emancipation, which was made fully possible only through the replacement of modality by tonality, or (rather) by the conception of organized modulation and key-structure arising out of tonality.

The gradual mutation of modality into tonality, making itself felt first in performance (use of *musica ficta*) rather than in notation, was a subtle, long-drawn, and still not clearly and completely understood process, but there can be little doubt that it was closely connected with the undermining of polyphony by homophony—notably in the *frottole*, though its beginnings were a good deal earlier. The development of the ideas of tonal unity and variety-within-unity can be traced through the familiar masterpieces of the sixteenth century from Josquin to Palestrina and beyond, but 'the evolution of tonal awareness in the sixteenth century does not proceed in a straight line. The chromaticists [Willaert, Rore, Lassus, Marenzio, Gesualdo] cause a switch of direction leading to phenomena that one might well define as "triadic atonality".'[1] All the same, sixteenth-century chromaticism is usually a form of 'symbolic illustration of text' rather than a purely musical phenomenon; its quasi-atonal extremes are aberrations in the sense that *musique mesurée* is an aberration.

Willaert's pupil Zarlino, the last great theorist to concern himself with the modal system and the first to advocate equal temperament, was also the first to differentiate consciously between major and minor harmonies and to associate them with cheerfulness and sadness: 'quando si pone la Terza maggiore nella parte grave l'Harmonia si fa allegra et quando si pone nell'acuto si fa mesta' (*Istitutioni harmoniche*, 1558).[2] Consequently progressions of minor chords 'will make the harmony very melancholy' (farebbe il concento molto maninconico). Zarlino recognized not only the expressive power of harmony, and hence the necessity of relating it to the verbal context, but the literally fundamental function of the bass and the importance of letting it move slowly (per movimenti alquanto tardi)—though he reveals that composers at the middle of the century were still writing the tenor first, the soprano next, and the bass only in the third place. The stage was already set for the *bassus pro organo* thirty years later and the *basso continuo* of the turn of the century.

[1] Edward Lowinsky, 'Awareness of Tonality in the 16th Century, *Report of the Eighth Congress of the International Musicological Society* (Kassel, 1961), p. 44. See also the same author's *Tonality and Atonality in Sixteenth-Century Music* (Berkeley, 1961).

[2] Zarlino, *Tutte l'opere*, i (Venice, 1589), p. 221.

The appearance in 1600 of Peri's *Euridice* and Caccini's, and of Cavalieri's *Rappresentazione*—followed by Caccini's *Nuove musiche* and Viadana's *Concerti ecclesiastici* in 1602—has lent that year the factitious importance of a dividing-line, like 1066. Palestrina and Lassus were six years dead; the mature work of Monteverdi was soon to come. Parry, like many others, was misled into declaring that 'the change in the character and methods of musical art at the end of the sixteenth century' was 'decisive and abrupt'.[1] But the old polyphonic style did not die with its greatest masters; it lived on in the 'silver age' of the Anerio brothers and the *prima prattica* of Monteverdi himself, while on the other hand his *seconda prattica* in which 'l'oratione sia padrona del armonia e non serva'[2] had its roots deep in the past. The present volume chronicles the rise of one and the heyday and decline of the other.

PUBLISHER'S NOTE

We record with regret the deaths of Edward J. Dent, Henry Coates, Théodore Gérold, Gerald Hayes, and Charles Van den Borren prior to the publication of this volume.

Acknowledgements are due to the following for their work of translation: Mr. Edward Lockspeiser (Chapter 1), Mr. Basil Lam (Chapter 3), Mr. Norman Suckling (Chapter 5a and b), Mrs. Ann Livermore (Chapter 7), and Miss Elizabeth Mercer (Chapter 8).

The bibliography has been largely compiled by Dr. John D. Bergsagel, the index by Miss Margaret Dean-Smith. The editor gratefully acknowledges the help of Dr. Nigel Fortune in reading proofs and suggesting emendations.

As is usual in publications of this kind, there has inevitably been a considerable gap between the final establishment of the text and the volume's appearance. Thus it has not been possible to incorporate references to the most recent publications—notably of sources—relating to the period.

[1] *Oxford History of Music*, iii (Oxford, 1902), p. 1.
[2] Giulio Cesare Monteverdi, 'Dichiaratione' appended to his brother's *Scherzi musicali* (Venice, 1607).

I

THE FRENCH *CHANSON*

By CHARLES VAN DEN BORREN

ORIGINS OF THE *CHANSON*

THE French polyphonic *chanson* of the Renaissance was a highly original form which in its day enjoyed unprecedented fame throughout Europe. Its influence in Italy led to the creation of the *canzon francese*, a favourite instrumental form which in turn was the original of the seventeenth-century *sonata da chiesa*.

In French-speaking countries the word *chanson* had for centuries been used in a general way to describe any kind of monodic or polyphonic song composed on a vernacular text. From the thirteenth century onwards, however, when the words of vocal music were first treated contrapuntally, pieces composed in this manner were also known by the names of the poetic forms, *rondeaux, ballades*, and *virelais*, used as texts by musicians.[1] These terms are used to describe the great majority of the secular *chansons*, both polyphonic and monodic, dating from the periods of Machaut and Dufay. The main feature of these pieces is that their musical form was determined by the poetic form; the same musical phrases were used for different lines according to a pre-established scheme of repetitions. This scheme varied according to the lines set, but it allowed no kind of development. Such technical restrictions in the manner of setting words to music apply similarly to the madrigals and *ballate* of the Italian fourteenth-century *ars nova*, and also to the *frottole, strambotti*,[2] and other Italian forms of the end of the fifteenth and beginning of the sixteenth centuries.[3]

The publication at Venice in 1501 of the collection of *chansons* known as the *Odhecaton* shows that the early years of the sixteenth century were a transitional period in which, though the ties with the past were still strong—the *Odhecaton* contains a large number of *rondeaux*—the more forward-looking musicians were beginning to abandon the rigid medieval forms. Freer forms inspired by the realism

---

[1] See Vol. II, Chap. VII.
[2] See Vol. III, Chap. II.
[3] Ibid., Chap. XI.

of popular poetry rather than by the conventional urbanities of the preceding generation began to take the place of the staid *rondeaux*, *ballades*, and *virelais*. The new spirit was expressed even in the old fixed forms by such composers as Loyset Compère[1] (d. 1518) who cultivated a light contrapuntal style and whose lively rhythms were calculated to convey a suggestion of humour quite unknown to the traditional courtly art. A similar tendency is noticeable in the Italian forms of this period, the *frottole*, *villotte*, and *canti carnascialeschi*; and doubtless there were reciprocal influences.

An exceptional place was held in this transitional period by Josquin des Prez[2] (d. 1521), in that he was a precursor endowed with genius in all the forms. His French *chansons* and Italian *frottole* are touch-stones, as indeed are his Masses and motets, revealing all that the sixteenth century owes to the wealth and range of his inventive mind. Josquin's vast technique and rare sensibility are illustrated in a wide variety of *chansons*, from the powerfully constructed examples in five or six parts with their blossoming of free counterpoint over a two-part canon in the bass, to the delicate pavane 'Mille regretz' and such light transparent trifles as 'Basiez-moi', 'Bergette savoyène', 'El grillo', and 'Scaramella'. And so it came about that the new French *chanson* which began to appear just before 1530 was naturally inspired by the secular works of Josquin and especially by those in which the composer, having broken away from the complexities of Flemish counterpoint, had cultivated a simpler and more humble art designed to match the lucidity of the poetic texts.

The earliest collections of French *chansons* were published in Paris by Pierre Attaingnant: *Chansons nouvelles en musique a quatre parties*[3] (1528), *Trente et quatre chansons musicales a quatre parties* (1529), *Quarante et deux chansons musicales a troys parties* (1529), *Trente et une chansons musicales a quatre parties* (1529), and the succeeding volumes. Of these collections, the *Trente et une chansons*[4] is the easiest to study; it contains examples by various composers. The most gifted were genuine Frenchmen. Cadéac, Claudin de Sermisy (represented in this collection by no fewer than eleven pieces), Gascongne, and Janequin (five pieces) form a group whose work in this field repre-

[1] See Vol. III, p. 291.

[2] Ibid., pp. 270–2, and Howard M. Brown, 'The Genesis of a Style: The Parisian *Chanson*, 1500–1530', in *Chanson and Madrigal 1480–1530*, ed. James Haar (Cambridge, Mass., 1964).

[3] See Maurice Cauchie, 'Les deux plus anciens recueils de chansons polyphoniques imprimés en France', *Revue de musicologie*, v (1924), p. 72.

[4] Republished by Henry Expert as vol. v of *Les Maîtres musiciens de la Renaissance française* (Paris, 1897).

sents the French tradition of precision, grace, and vivacity, and displays a sense of texture quite different from that of works in this form by their Flemish contemporaries.

CHARACTERISTICS OF STYLE

Looking at the main features of the earlier *chansons*, one may say that they are for the most part completely free in form. There are no signs of any tenor or *canto fermo* in the old, strict sense, though there are occasional borrowings from earlier melodies. Imitation is not unknown, but is used less frequently than in the motets and Masses, and imitations are woven into the robust rhythmic patterns characteristic of these *chansons*—patterns which are essentially opposed to the more ethereal style of contemporary church music. This homorhythmic sense is most strikingly displayed in vertical writing, in ornamented or slightly ornamented chord-progressions, and is highly symptomatic of the separation of the secular from the sacred style. It is a feature in complete accord with the spirit of the Renaissance, and originated mainly in the Italian *frottole* of *c.* 1500.

The French *chansons* of 1529 are not concerned with musical development for its own sake. They therefore make only a restricted use of repetitions of words and phrases. Repetition generally occurs at the end of pieces, so as to provide a gradual, discreet close with no pretension to lyricism. On the other hand, purely musical repetitions often occur at the beginning of *chansons*, recalling the earlier *ballades* with their two *pedes*.[1]

In short, in freeing itself from the age-long servitude to poetic structure, the French *chanson* did not submit to any kind of arbitrary form. Details of the form vary according to circumstances, though in the main the *chansons* follow certain general schemes of which the most common may be roughly set out as follows: *A A* (different texts) *B C C* (same text). This holds good not only for the *chansons* of 1529, but for the greater number of the *chansons* of the Renaissance. Other distinctive features are: (1) a comparatively rare use of *da capo*; (2) the replacing of poems with refrain by various forms of *rondeaux à couplets*; and (3) the use for many *chansons*, at any rate up to the middle of the century, of dance forms, particularly the pavane. From all of this it will be seen that from first to last the French *chanson* conformed to structural concepts which perfectly corresponded to its particular needs.

The grace and lightness of touch of so many of the *chansons* may in

[1] See Vol. III, p. 14.

the last analysis be said to derive from the use of rapid melismata
which are either unfurled on a single syllable or act as support to an
animated declamation in which each note corresponds to a syllable
of the text. In the latter, when the syllabic declamation, instead of
following the free curves of musical arabesque, consists of the repetition of one and the same note, the result is a *quasi parlando* style, foreshadowed in Compère's 'Et dont revenez vous', and sometimes rather
like the recitative of *opera buffa*.

THE 'THIRTY-ONE *CHANSONS*'

Among the lighter of the *Trente et une chansons* those by Claudin
de Sermisy and Clément Janequin are specially conspicuous by reason
of their vivacity, gaiety, and picturesque effects. The fashion at this
period was to set to music poems in which licentious humour was
sometimes frankly revealed, sometimes disguised by ambiguities perfectly familiar to the contemporaries of Francis I. Of this type are
pieces such as 'En entrant en ung jardin' by Claudin de Sermisy—
characterized by homorhythmic writing almost devoid of any kind of
figuration, by buoyant syllabic declamation and by little symmetrical
repetitions more or less analogous to those of dance forms—and
Janequin's 'Au joly jeu du pousse avant', a piece that admirably
displays this composer's inventive genius, with its expressive imitative
stretti, its division of the voices in pairs according to Josquin's principle, and the regularity of a form ideally conceived to underline the
salient features of the text. Less bawdy, and artistically no less accomplished, are Janequin's rustic *chansons* 'Ce moys de may' and
'Au verd boys'. The first of these is a sort of homorhythmic *villanella*
with no trace of figuration, in which trochees in triple time fleetingly
alternate with iambics, with the most charming effect; the second is
a fresh and naïve *ronde* in which Janequin shows the extraordinary
grace with which he was able to manipulate his peculiar melodic gifts.
To the same vein belongs Claudin's Bacchic *chanson* 'Hau, hau, hau
le boys', the nimble counterpoint and free rhythms of which belong
to the tradition of Josquin and Compère while at the same time foreshadowing the style of Lassus.

But while high spirits, sometimes expressed with Rabelaisian frank-
ness, are brilliantly represented in the *Trente et une chansons*, the more
serious side of life is by no means neglected. Sohier's authentically
French miniature 'J'ay cause de moy contenter' expresses the rapture
of love in a delightful polyphony built from the imitative play of
serene and intimately happy melismata. In melancholy vein such

songs as Cadéac's 'Je suis désheritée' (sometimes attributed to Lupi),[1] Gascongne's 'Mon povre coeur' and 'Je ny sçaurois', Claudin de Sermisy's 'Au joly bois' and 'C'est une dure départie'—describe love's deceptions or the pangs of separation in a musical language unparalleled in nobility and expressive intensity. The French composers of the time of Francis I possessed the very rare gift of ability to express elementary feelings with the maximum simplicity and concentration.

It is noteworthy that several of these *chansons*, especially those of Sermisy, are composed in the rhythm and form of pavanes. The *pavana dolorosa* and the *pavana lachrymae*, dear to Dowland, have in fact antecedents here, showing how apt was this grave, ceremonious court dance to express the emotions of pain, grief, and resignation. The pavane was, moreover, quite frequently used up to the middle of the century not only in France but in the Netherlands, where feelings of this kind had to be expressed. It was often used, too, for the setting of moralizing texts or others whose emotional content was not particularly inspiring, where the insignificance of the poem was sometimes compensated by the purely musical value of the setting.

No sooner had the *chanson française* been published and made known in the Attaingnant editions than arrangements appeared, showing the liberties allowed to performers at this period in the matter of interpretation. The *Tres breve et familiere introduction*,[2] printed in October 1529 by the same publisher, gives transcriptions for solo voice and lute of *chansons* by Claudin de Sermisy and a number of anonymous pieces, all of which appeared in their original vocal forms in the Attaingnant collections of 1529 and 1530.[3] We need not dwell on these arrangements, which are discussed in a later chapter; they perpetuate a practice which had been common for many years. We need only note here that such arrangement was facilitated by a 'vertical' style of writing which throws into relief the highest voice while the remaining parts are confined to the role of accompaniment.

Sermisy was the composer of most of the *chansons* of this collection and the poet who most often and most happily inspired him was

---

[1] As in *Das Chorwerk*, xv, p. 22.   [2] See Vol. III, p. 450, n. 2.

[3] One of these songs by Sermisy, 'Il me suffit' (reprinted by La Laurencie, Mairy, and Thibault, *Chansons au luth* (Paris, 1934), p. 35, had a particularly eventful future. Clemens non Papa used the melody for his setting of Psalm 128 in the *Souterliedekens* (see p.230) (Antwerp, 1557); it became popular in Germany to the secular words 'Beschaffens Glück' and provided the model for a parody-Mass by Lassus (pub. 1574); in 1572 Joachim Magdeburg published it in his *Christeliche und Tröstliche Tischgesenge* to the words 'Was mein Gott will, das gscheh alzeit', with which it passed into the Protestant chorale-repertory and was employed by Schein, Schütz, J. S. Bach, and many others.

Clément Marot, above all in 'Tant que vivray en âge florissant',[1] a miracle of elegance in the expression of amorous gallantry.

THE DESCRIPTIVE *CHANSON*

The French *chanson* of this period was generally written in four parts, more rarely in three. The ideal balance of this combination answers perfectly to the demands of an intimate art devoid of all grandiosity or solemnity. Aware of this, the French composers resorted only exceptionally to a larger number of parts, and were thus able to maintain the essentially modest and intimate style of the *chanson* throughout the whole period of its development.

There was, however, one particular type in which they abandoned this ideal. This was the descriptive *chanson*, of which the supreme master was Janequin. 'La guerre', 'Le chant des oyseaux', 'La chasse'[2]—the hunt of the stag and not of the hare, as has erroneously been stated—'L'alouette', 'Le caquet des femmes', 'Les cris de Paris':[3] such are the titles of these pieces, composed throughout the reign of Francis I and even later. With their predilection for the picturesque in music, exemplified again and again in the later Middle Ages, the French during the Renaissance transformed what had been mere miniatures into highly developed musical frescoes which have nothing in common with the classical conception of the *chanson* except a tendency to gracefulness, to 'highly seasoned' diversion. The enlargement of the form of the *chanson* was not always to its advantage. There are no modulations and the monotony of the harmony is hardly compensated by the onomatopoeic effects and by the singers' opportunities to hold the listener's attention by the lively rendering of the amusing mosaic constructed from these little tricks (drum-rolls, military or hunting fanfares, the chirping of birds, and so on). Janequin's 'La guerre' was written to celebrate Francis I's victory at Marignano in 1515. It has a pendant in the 'Battaglia italiana'[4] in which the Flemish *maestro di cappella* of Milan Cathedral, Matthias

---

[1] Recorded in *The History of Music in Sound* (H.M.V.), iv; Sermisy's 'Vivray-je tousjours en soucy?' in the version for voice and lute is also recorded in the same volume.
[2] All three, with 'Chant de l'alouette' and 'Las povre cœur', printed by Attaingnant in *Chansons de maistre Clement Janequin* (1528?: cf. Cauchie, op. cit.), which Expert reprinted in *Les Maîtres musiciens de la Renaissance française*, vii (Paris, 1898). There are a number of modern editions of 'La guerre'.
[3] 'L'alouette' is given in Davison and Apel, *Historical Anthology of Music* (London, 1946), i, p. 109, and 'Les cris de Paris' in Expert, *Florilège du concert vocal de la Renaissance*, iii (Paris, 1928). Complete edition of Janequin's *chansons*, ed. François Lesure and A. T. Merritt (Paris, 1965–).
[4] Published by Tirabassi (Brussels, 1931).

Hermann Werrecoren, depicted in no less appropriate manner the various episodes of a defeat of the French king—perhaps at Pavia in 1525.[1]

Janequin's descriptive pieces enjoyed a brilliant success, as one gathers from the numerous editions which appeared up to 1559 not only in France, at Paris and Lyons, but at Venice and Antwerp, and from the instrumental transcriptions and various adaptations of them made by distinguished composers. Among the last are the five-part version of 'La guerre' made by Philippe Verdelot and the three-part version of 'Le chant des oyseaux' by Nicolas Gombert. The latter is particularly interesting because of Gombert's double contraction of the original score: the number of bars is reduced from 209 to 178 and the number of voices from four to three; the musical texture is thus made much lighter and much more appropriate to the effect one might expect from a concert of birds. (Despite the contrary opinion of Michel Brenet,[2] the Janequin version must be earlier than the Gombert.) Mention may also be made here of the two 'Chasses du lièvre' ('Or escoutez, gentilz veneurs') published by Susato at Antwerp in 1545, the first anonymous and the second under the name of Gombert. Both composers used the same text, but with certain modifications in the second which point to the fact that the first was written in France for a French public and the second in the Netherlands, possibly for the Court of Charles. V. It seems extremely likely that the anonymous composer of the first version was none other than Janequin, for one cannot imagine who else in France at that time could have written such lively and realistic music (notably the setting of the disconnected conversation between the huntsmen). The following passage is specially characteristic:

Ex. 1

---
[1] On this 'Battaglia', see Rudolf Gläsel, *Zur Geschichte der Battaglia* (Leipzig Diss., 1931), pp. 48, 86–87, and 115–16. But the identification of Werrecoren with Matthieu Le Maistre is erroneous: see *Grove's Dictionary* (2nd ed., 1910), article 'Werrecore'.
[2] *Musique et musiciens de la vieille France* (Paris, 1911), p. 175.

(Come, good huntsmen, I pray you. Let's drink our fill. Lead on, keepers, sound the *curée*. . . .)

Less light-hearted and witty, Gombert's piece is none the less remarkable for its ingenuity of detail—a quality often found in the work of this incomparable melodist.

The descriptive *chanson* of Janequin and his contemporaries attracts one first and foremost by its picturesque qualities. But it is equally notable for its well-balanced form. Sometimes the introduction, with its formal expression of joyousness, is recalled in the course of the work or at the end like the refrain of a rondo; sometimes the whole piece is divided into two, three, or four sections. Clearly the composers were striving toward an ideal of symmetry as a means of avoiding the dangers of a purely rhapsodic conception. There was no question of such dangers in the smaller forms, such as the 'Guerre de Renty'[1] in which Janequin recalled the victory of Henry II over Charles V at Renty on 13 August 1554. In this work of his old age, in which the onomatopoeic element is hardly perceptible, Janequin is at his best from beginning to end, though chiefly in the introduction ('Croisez vos piques, soldats') and in the conclusion, a beautiful and peculiarly arresting prayer.

LATER *CHANSON* COLLECTIONS

The immediate success of the *chanson* encouraged publishers in France and later in the Netherlands to multiply collections. Attaingnant himself set an example by printing several dozen books of *chansons* between 1529 and 1549. He was followed by other French publishers, notably Jacques Moderne at Lyons and Nicholas du Chemin in Paris, and in 1543 he found an important rival in the person of Tielman Susato, an Antwerp publisher who issued an imposing series of collections over a period of about ten years. In Paris Attaingnant had founded a tradition carried on during the second half of the century by Adrian Le Roy in association with Robert Ballard; while after Susato's death (*c.* 1550) the firm of Phalèse, established first at Louvain (from 1551) and later at Antwerp (under the name of Phalèse et Bellère), produced numerous collections of *chansons* unmistakably showing the vogue of the form long after its first appearance. The *Répertoire international des sources musicales— Recueils imprimés, XVIᵉ–XVIIᵉ siècles*, i (Paris, 1960), shows that the main publishers brought out thousands of *chansons*, to say nothing of the numerous editions of minor firms.

The Attaingnant editions from 1530 onwards reveal, as one can see from the numerous extracts published by Eitner,[2] Henry Expert,[3] Maurice Cauchie,[4] François Lesure,[5] and others, an astonishingly varied range of *chansons* which persistently maintain the original tradition. All that has been said regarding the form, spirit, and technique of the original form equally applies to the *chanson* of the following twenty years. Reticence, concision, and polished form are

---

[1] Modern edition by Vincent d'Indy (Rouart, Lerolle & Cie.)

[2] *Publikation älterer praktischer und theoretischer Musikwerke*, xxiii (Leipzig, 1899).

[3] In the series *Les Maîtres musiciens de la Renaissance française* and *Florilège du concert vocal de la Renaissance*, and separate numbers (*Collection Henry Expert* and *Anthologie chorale*).

[4] *Quinze chansons françaises du XVIᵉ siècle* (Paris, 1926).

[5] *Anthologie de la chanson parisienne du XVIᵉ siècle* (Monaco, 1953).

the main features of the vast number of *chansons* which appeared between 1530 and 1550.

Very often the pavane provided the minor masters not only with a ready-made pattern but with an idiom suitable for the dignified, sometimes even profound, expression of mournful sentiments or grave thoughts of more abstract origin. Composers such as Jacotin ('Mon triste cœur'), Mittantier ('Tel en mesdit'), Sandrin ('Doulce memoire',[1] 'Voyez le tort', and 'Puisque de vous'),[2] P. de Villiers ('Je n'oserays le penser') rival Claudin de Sermisy ('Qui se pourrait plus désoler', 'Vous perdez temps') in the art of adapting the ceremonial rhythm and inherent melancholy of the pavane for such expressive purposes.

THE LEADING COMPOSERS

Among the major composers who successfully cultivated the serious or semi-serious *chanson* must be mentioned Pierre de la Rue.[3] Although he died in 1518 he is represented in the collections printed in the second quarter of the sixteenth century by pieces which show him —if the attributions to him are correct—to have been a real precursor. Thus 'Au feu d'amour'[4] is almost the classic type of the future French *chanson* in its more tender and graceful aspects: and 'Ma mère, hélas, mariez moi' discloses beneath the simplicity of its ternary homo-rhythm a disturbing mixture of sadness, sweet emotion, and intimate happiness. No less appealing in both emotional and musical qualities are the *chansons* of the Cambrai composer Johannes Lupi ('Il n'est trésor',[5] 'Reviens vers moy', 'Plus revenir') where the most delicate harmonic refinements are accompanied by a breath of archaism which takes one back to the days of Josquin. Less severe, Arcadelt[6] is seen in his *chansons* 'Quand je me trouve auprès de ma maîtresse' and 'Quand je vous ayme ardentement' (on a poem by Marot) to be the same suave melodist as in his Italian madrigals.[7] A little-known musician, Bourguignon, reaches in 'Continuer je veux' the perfection of grace and delicacy, slightly tinged with melancholy. Another minor master, Passereau, cultivates the vein of popular humour with astonishing verve and sense of comedy in 'Il est bel et bon',[8] while his 'Au joly son du sansonnet' is notable for the delightfully childlike freshness and grace of its contrapuntal devices.

[1] See Ex. 143. [2] Cauchie, *Quinze chansons françaises*, no. 5.
[3] See Vol. III, p. 289. [4] Eitner, *Publikation*, p. 68.
[5] Hans Albrecht, *Johannes Lupi: Zehn weltliche Lieder* (*Das Chorwerk*, xv), p. 8.
[6] *The Chansons of Arcadelt*, i, ed. Everett B. Helm (Northampton, Mass., 1942).
[7] See Chap. II, pp. 39 and 41 ff.
[8] Recorded in *The History of Music in Sound*, iv.

But the composer who brought the *chanson* to its highest stage of
development was undoubtedly Janequin, who turned out masterpieces with almost inexhaustible fecundity and spontaneity. 'Au joly
mois de may' with its *da capo* is a model of gaiety and childlike grace.
'Ce tendron est si doulce' ('This tendril is so sweet a thing'), the
opening of which may be quoted, is a completely successful combination of rhythmic variety with polyphonic facility:

Ex. 2

(This tendril is so sweet that it almost makes me lose my senses. It is red as
a rose . . .)

'Petite nymphe folastre' is a model of the Renaissance *chanson*, the fineness of its touch prompting a comparison with the paintings of the Fontainebleau school. In 'Si j'ay esté vostre amy' the most charming sense of freedom is ideally matched by the invention of happily devised detail. 'Il n'est plaisir ne passe temps' evokes with exquisite skill the mood of lovers who enjoy '*en chantant, dansant, riant*' the happiness of being together '*par boys et par champs*'. And the beautifully finished 'Du beau tétin' might have been monotonous on account of its length, but for the freedom of the writing, in syllabic chords in diverse rhythms: a perfect medium for the interpretation of the frank but piquant audacity of Marot's verses.

This last piece is an example of the licence which appears so disconcertingly in the Attaingnant collections. Renaissance listeners, accustomed as they were to pungent language, would not have been offended and apparently the poets felt themselves able to take even greater licence under cover of a musical setting. The interesting point is that while the words are generally coarse enough, their musical translation is by no means so; from which we may conclude that the composers, who included ecclesiastics, found in these *puantises* (as they were called in 1576) sources of inspiration in the directions of gaiety, humour, and satire but not of sensuality. Indeed, we find unknown or little-known composers displaying in this inferior form of the *chanson* imagination of a high order: Jean Courtois in 'Faisons un coup' with its piquant effects of quick repeated notes; Garnier in his delightful aubade, 'Réveillez-moi, mon bel ami' in rondo form; Pierre Hesdin in 'Ramonez-moy ma cheminée'[1] in which a *da capo* brings back, with insistent *stretti*, unbelievably pretty themes; René in 'Gros Jehan', a narrative *chanson* in which the racy language mingles with a tragic element that neither poet nor musician seems to have taken very seriously, however. All these pieces have many features in common with the contemporary Italian *villanella*, though the contrapuntal refinements of the French school were not known to the Italians until later.

Side by side with these minor composers appear better-known figures such as Pierre Certon whose 'Ung bon vieillard' and 'La, la, je ne l'ose dire'[2] are characterized by homorhythm—rather heavy, though appropriate to the subjects; the Netherlander Jachet Berchem, who in his gay, bustling 'Jehan de Lagny' also approached the style

---

[1] Eitner, *Publikation*, p. 55.
[2] Ibid., p. 28, and Einstein, *A Short History of Music* (London, 5th ed., 1948), p. 228. Ten other *chansons* by Certon have been edited by Albert Seay, *Das Chorwerk*, lxxxii (Wolfenbüttel, 1962).

of the *villanella*; and Clemens non Papa who found in 'Une fillete bien
gorrière' and 'Frisque et gaillard'[1] unparalleled pretexts for the display of both Rabelaisian humour and contrapuntal virtuosity.

SUSATO'S COLLECTIONS: THE LARGER PIECES

The Brussels Conservatoire Library possesses modern manuscript
scores[2] of the thirteen books of *chansons* published at Antwerp by
Susato between 1543 and 1550. These manuscript scores make it easy
to study a repertory of *chansons* which, in addition to those by
Josquin to whom the seventh book is devoted, contains no fewer than
342 examples, very few of which duplicate those available in modern
publications. Obviously, the Antwerp publisher was in closest contact with composers whose main field of activity was the Netherlands,
as distinct from the Parisians around Attaingnant. Composers such
as Certon, Sandrin, and Sermisy are included but have a subordinate
place in these collections, just as—conversely—important Netherland
composers have in the Attaingnant collections.

Particularly striking in the Susato collections is the considerable
number of compositions in more than four parts, mainly in five and
six. The Flemish musicians had undergone a more severe training in
the complexities and refinements of counterpoint than the French
and it was only natural that they should be inclined to exploit to the
extreme limit their own technical resources. In this they were, however, not always successful. The over-elaborate settings of 'D'amour
me plains' and 'Tant seulement' in eight real parts by Jean Guyot
(known as Castileti),[3] are out of proportion with the unpretentious
poems. Writing in six and particularly in five parts is less exposed
to this danger, especially when it is handled by major masters. The
most prominent of these was Charles V's Master of the Choristers,
Nicolas Gombert (d. *c.* 1556), the supreme virtuoso of the imitative
syntactic style and, all in all, with Willaert and Rore, the greatest
musician of the generation between Josquin's and that of Lassus and
Palestrina. Gombert's five- and six-part *chansons* show us in all their
plenitude his gift for the invention of original plastic melodies and
his skill in treating them polyphonically so as to deploy their expressive powers to the full. Five-part pieces such as 'Le berger et la bergère'
and 'Quand je suis auprez de ma mye' in gay or playful vein, the five-
part 'Souffrir me convient' and the six-part 'Tous les regretz' in

[1] Eitner, *Publikation*, p. 33.   [2] Made by Wotquenne.
[3] On this composer see E. Wauters, *Jean Guyot de Châtelet, musicien de la Renaissance;
sa vie et son œuvre* (Brussels, 1944).

austere style, are among the most precious jewels that have come down
to us from the second quarter of the sixteenth century. A fragment
(Ex. 3 on opposite page) from 'Souffrir me convient' will give an
idea of this spacious and by no means superficial style.

Quite different from the aristocratic Gombert, Clemens non Papa
was at his best able to combine somewhat boisterous popular verve
with unusual inventive power. His talent is equally evident in the
amusing and the severe. Examples of his five- and six-part *chansons*
are 'Sans lever le pied', in which wantonness is expressed with
malicious and racy naïveté; 'Languir me fais', in which the highest
voice amplifies the corresponding part of the setting of the same
words by Sermisy; and 'C'est à grand tort', a solidly constructed
piece in popular style by a master in the handling of materials.[1]

This trio of Netherlanders is completed by Charles V's later *maître
de chapelle*, Thomas Créquillon (d. *c.* 1557), a composer of great sensibility and elegance, whose *chansons* are peculiarly fascinating. He is
at his best in his four-part pieces, such as 'Puis que vous ayme', of
which the opening is reprinted in the *Oxford History of Music*, ii
(Oxford, 1905), p. 284, but there are also some charming examples
among those in five and six parts: for instance, the five-part 'Belle,
donne-moi un regard', an exquisite essay in the light style, and the six-
part 'Si me tenes tant de rigueur', a sort of large-scale *villanella*, in a
galant style, graceful and spontaneous.

Among other famous musicians represented by five- and six-part
pieces in the Susato collections is Adrian Willaert (d. 1562), who
delights in using canons in the manner of Josquin in pieces of vast
dimensions, such as the six-part 'De retourner, mon ami, je te prie',
'Mon cœur, mon corps', and others, in which his impeccable technique is displayed in sound-fabrics of the purest crystal. Nearer perhaps to the spirit of the French *chanson* is the six-part 'Qui veut
aymer', though the influence of the Italian *frottola* and the *villanella*
may easily be discerned through the mesh of this light polyphony with
its firm balance and its quite new sense of harmony.

Finally a few anonymous pieces in five and six parts must be
mentioned, some of which are worthy of the greatest masters: for
instance 'Si vous n'avez ma dame' (*à* 5), remarkable for its sense of
line and development; 'Verdure le bois' (*à* 6), popular in style, in
which repeated *stretti* on fragments of scale in the form of rapid
syllabic declamation produce a most amusing effect; and 'Mon petit

[1] Reprinted in *Jacobus Clemens non Papa: Opera Omnia*, x (American Institute of
Musicology, 1962), pp. 113, 130, and 135.

Ex. 3

cœur' (*à* 6), in which the charming poem is set with refinement and sensibility to a polyphony that is lightened and aerated by ingenious division and distribution of groups of voices.

A number of the *chansons* in more than four parts published by Susato were written by secondary figures, though they show qualities far above the average. Thus, treating a *galant* subject with an undercurrent of melancholy in 'Je prends en gré la dure mort' (*à* 6), Josquin Baston shows his technical prowess by introducing a mirror canon into what is essentially a charming and graceful piece. Benedictus Appenzeller, Master of the Choristers of Mary of Hungary, though uneven in achievement, occasionally shows admirable refinement and expressive precision, as in 'Fors vous n'entends jamais' (*à* 6), 'Je perds espoir' (*à* 5, with canon), 'Si je me plains' (*à* 5, with noteworthy intertwinings between three tenors and a baritone), and 'Peine et travail' (*à* 6). The resigned grace associated with the key of F is happily exploited by Eustatius Barbion in his 'Adieu celle que j'ay servi' (*à* 5).

SUSATO'S FOUR-PART BOOKS

The greater number of the Susato *chansons* are, however, in the traditional four parts. Of the thirteen books, seven contain only pieces in this category, two being devoted to single composers, the Third to Créquillon and the Ninth to Pierre de Manchicourt (d. 1564). In general the composers of the Susato publications, mostly Netherlanders, conform to the models of the Attaingnant composers. Though often hampered by very poor poems, an unfortunate heritage of the decadent rhetoric of the preceding age, they got out of the difficulty by setting these verses in ready-made musical forms, chief among which was the pavane. Susato's collections contain a great number of these vocal pavanes, which as the titles indicate—'Chansons . . . convenables tant à la voix comme aux instruments'—could be performed instrumentally if so desired. Among the very beautiful examples are the anonymous 'Je prends en gré la dure mort' (First Book, No. 24), the themes of which were used by Josquin Baston in his 6-part setting, and 'Si pas souffrir' (Fourth Book, No. 12). Composers of the second rank, such as Susato himself, were often able to use the noble pavane as a happy means of escape from the colourless platitudes in which they were inclined to indulge when imitating French models, whose wit and natural elegance were beyond their reach.

It is impossible to examine here, however summarily, all the four-part *chansons* in the Susato collections. But those of Créquillon and Manchicourt, by their numerical importance, demand a general con-

Ex. 4

(Pretty, dainty little flower, tell me if you love me.)

sideration. Créquillon was a master of refinement in every sense of the word, equally successful in dealing with tender emotions, with the elegiac, and with Gallic wit. He usually practised what the Germans call *Kleinarbeit*, but with an elegance, lightness, and moderation that exclude excessive complication. His pieces in pavane form ('Par trop souffrir', 'Pour plaisir', 'Toutes les nuits') are models of their kind, and he was also an admirable interpreter of the humour of such pieces as 'Ung gay bergier' and 'Alix avait aux dents'. In the *galant* vein he shows a delicacy of touch recalling the suavity of the madrigal, notably in 'Si pour aimer' and 'Petite fleur cointe et jolie', the opening of which is shown in Ex. 4.

Though not as original as Créquillon's, Manchicourt's best achievements—notable for their tenderness and melancholy—include such delightful little things as 'Pourquoy m'es tu tant ennemie', 'Voyant souffrir celle', 'D'amour me vient', and 'Un doux regard'. In more playful vein, inclining to satire or bawdiness, as in 'Jeune galant qui d'envieux effort' and 'Celle qui a fâcheux mari', he excels in syllabic declamation to quick notes, with light and fluent counterpoint, in the authentic French manner.

Of the other well-known composers whose four-part *chansons* appear in the Susato collections, Gombert and Clemens non Papa are outstanding; some of their pieces rank with the finest examples in this genre. One need only mention Gombert's 'Or suis-je prins' in which, by the novelty and boldness of his themes and his contrapuntal skill, he shows himself a true precursor of Lassus. Unlike Créquillon and Gombert, Clemens was not remarkable for delicacy of touch, but he was unsurpassed in the expression of broad humour. Pieces such as 'Entre vous, filles de quinze ans', the Bacchic song 'La, la, la, Maître Pierre', and the *chanson de table* 'Jouons, jouons beau jeu' are unsurpassed models of the latter kind.

In a less popular vein Clemens has moments of inspiration surprising in such an interpreter of bawdy realism. An exquisite freshness inspires his evocation of spring in 'Rossignolet qui chantez' which opens thus:

Ex. 5

(Nightingale singing in the greenwood)

Again, in 'Pour une, las, j'endure', 'Coeur langoureulx', 'Incessamment suis triste', and 'Mais languirai-je toujours' elegiac sentiment is expressed with a naturalness and intensity free from every kind of conventional formula.

Beside these princes of music Susato also found room in his anthologies for a number of lesser nobles, room which they well deserve for the taste with which they handle the musical miniature. Among them is Guyot (Castileti) whose four-part pieces 'L'arbre d'amour', 'Je l'ayme bien', 'Joyeusement', 'Je suis amour' are marked by a real originality due largely to a mosaic-like counterpoint, singularly rich in charming effects. Corneille Canis resembles Créquillon both in technical accomplishment and in aristocratic refinement. He was equally successful with serious subjects such as 'Mal et souci' and 'Pour vous seule la mort m'assault', where he sometimes seems to stand in the line of Josquin and Pierre de la Rue, with pieces of lighter character ('En désirant que je vous voie', 'Quand je suis où les aultres sont', 'Coeur prisonnier'), and with songs in humorous or popular style ('Il estait une fillette'; 'Ma mie a eu de Dieu'; 'Mariez-moi, mon père'), the verve of which recalls Clemens. Jean Lecocq (known also as Gallus) does not reach this level, though such a piece as 'Si tu voulais' shows that he was capable of great delicacy, and 'Las me faut-il' is the work of a man who had mastered every secret of craftsmanship.

Antoine Barbé provides a fine example of the animated, picturesque style in his narrative song with refrain, 'Ung capitaine'. Josquin Baston contributes pieces in a noble and refined style, such as 'Si loyal amour', 'Fors seulement rigueur', 'C'est à grand tort', and the beautiful pavane 'Si mon languir'. Christian Hollander sounds a somewhat severe, archaic note—but with fine effect—in the elegy 'Plaisir n'ay plus'. In the exquisite little piece 'On a mal dit de mon ami', Jean de Hollande provides the musical equivalent, in light, transparent counterpoint with delightful imitations, of an exceptionally good poem. And Rocourt gives us in the elegiac note of 'Plaindre ne vaut' an unrivalled miniature of unpretentious delicacy.

Just as Attaingnant had almost from the first published *chansons* arranged for solo voice and lute, so Phalèse issued at Louvain in 1553, in the second part of the *Hortus Musarum*, a collection of similar arrangements containing pieces by the most popular composers, chief among whom were Créquillon and Clemens non Papa.[1]

THE *CHANSON* IN THE LATER SIXTEENTH CENTURY

It is clear from the foregoing that the French *chanson* enjoyed a remarkable efflorescence between 1530 and 1550. During the second half of the century this development was slowed down and the style became rather less individual: partly because of the influence of the Italian madrigal, partly by reason of the appeal of poems of a different nature from those which had inspired the composers of the earlier period. The latter had not usually been very happy in their choice of words; apart from Clément Marot,[2] most of their poets were inferior writers. Only the texts of the bawdy or popular *chansons*, while of no great literary distinction, were at any rate less trite. Bawdiness was to persist for some time in the French *chanson*, as

---

[1] See Chap. IV, p. 185.
[2] On settings of Marot see Jean Rollin, *Les Chansons de Clément Marot* (Paris, 1951).

we shall see from the secular works of Roland de Lassus, though Lassus clearly preferred subtly humorous poems to crudely realistic ones. But this was in accordance with a general tendency to set poems of greater distinction. It was Ronsard, the poets of the Pléiade, and later Desportes, who now inspired the *chanson* composers. The winds of humanism blew among them; their literary taste grew more and more refined.

This greater refinement coincided with an Italian influence deriving from the madrigal—a form which avoided all crudity, every tendency to vulgarity. In striking opposition to the French *chanson*, the Italian madrigal developed a harmonic and melodic style founded on suavity and contemplative lyricism. On the other hand, the madrigal in the course of its evolution developed those devices, known to musicologists as 'madrigalisms', which before long proliferated in innumerable forms to produce an idiom of hitherto unsuspected musical and expressive richness.

Like the *chanson*, the Italian madrigal had at first utilized no more than four voices, but soon enlarged its scope to five. During the first twenty-five to thirty years of their common existence *chanson* and madrigal followed parallel lines of evolution without any obvious influence of the Italian on the French form.[1] It was only during the last thirty years of the century that the *chanson* became in many instances practically indistinguishable from the madrigal.

THE CONTRIBUTION OF LASSUS

Under the influence of the madrigal, the *chanson* undoubtedly lost some of the characteristics it had possessed during the second third of the sixteenth century. On the other hand, it acquired a new lease of life, as is evident from the *chansons* of Lassus (1532–94) whose vast production consists of one *chanson* in three parts, 67 in four, 55 in five, 5 in six, and 5 in eight.[2] Here, as in the motet and madrigal, Lassus assimilated all extraneous influences and created a world entirely his own. In sheer originality none of his contemporaries can

[1] See, however, Daniel Heartz, 'Les Goûts Réunis, or the Worlds of the Madrigal and the *Chanson* Confronted', in Haar, op. cit.

[2] Most of these were originally published by Susato in *Le Premier livre de chansons à quatre parties* (Antwerp, 1564), or by Le Roy of Paris in the *Livre de chansons nouvelles à cincq parties* (1571), *Les Meslanges d'Orlande de Lassus* (1576), (reprinted by Expert in *Les Maîtres musiciens de la Renaissance française*, i (Paris, 1894), and the *Continuation du Mellange* (1584). These are printed complete by Sandberger in the *Sämtliche Werke*, xii, xiv, and xvi (Leipzig, n.d.). Further *chansons*, overlooked by Sandberger, are published by Wolfgang Boetticher in *Orlando di Lasso: Sämtliche Werke*, i (Kassel and Basle, 1956).

be compared with him; he reconciles extreme variety of detail with the spirit of synthesis which characterizes the work of genius.

We need not dwell on questions of form. Here Lassus took over the framework used by his predecessors, only filling it with ampler total conceptions, with a greater wealth of melodic, rhythmic, and harmonic invention. Absolute master of his craft, he employs in his *chansons* for more than four voices a polyphony the lightness and clarity of which derive from delicately adjusted distribution of voices and judicious alternation of true counterpoint with homorhythmic passages. He makes little use of chromaticism in his *chansons*, though some of them give an impression of striking modernity, especially those in a major key such as 'Un jeune moine', 'Beau le cristal', and 'Gallans qui par terre',[1] all in four parts and all written after 1570.

Like Dufay, Lassus throughout his life wrote *chansons* which, although they reflect the successive stages of his career, in no way suggest a steady ascent towards an ideal perfection. The most one can say is that his most brilliant work in this field dates from between 1560 and 1575, notably in the two great collections of 1564 and 1571. Yet as early as 1555, the year when his first *chansons* appeared,[2] the four-part 'Las voulez-vous qu'une personne chante'[3] sums up all that is best in the elegiac style at that period. The master's personality is fully revealed in this little piece despite the affinity of its inspiration with the ethos of Johannes Lupi and its technical affinity (in the division of the voices) with Josquin. The imitative vocalizations on the word 'chanter' and the uncommon modulation in the passage 'Et me laissez' show Lassus's forward-looking mind.

These early works foreshadow all the main features of his later evolution, which branches out in three directions. There are the *chansons* in which the traditional spirit persists unchanged; those in which it is renewed and enriched by elements from the madrigal; and those in which it is completely superseded by the spirit of the madrigal. Obviously the traditional form was best suited to the lighter type of *chanson*, whether bawdy or semi-serious. 'Quand mon mari vient de dehors' and 'Un jour je vis un foulon' (both *à* 4)[4] are typical examples of the vitality and boldly stylized realism displayed by Lassus in dealing with subjects of this order. In the interpretation of licentious humour, bordering on profanity in 'Il estoit une religieuse' (*à* 4) and on bawdiness in 'Si par souhait' (*à* 4),[5] he hesitated at nothing. In the

---

[1] *Sämtliche Werke*, xii, pp. 89, 94, and xvi, p. 111.
[2] In the volume of *Madrigali, Villanesche, Canzoni francesi, e Motetti a quattro voci* published at Antwerp by Susato.   [3] *Werke*, xii, p. 3.
[4] Ibid., pp. 23, 39.   [5] Ibid., pp. 74, 12.

semi-serious vein he piled masterpiece upon masterpiece: 'Bonjour mon coeur' (à 4) is an exquisite homorhythmic rendering of Ronsard's poem, while 'Et d'où venez-vous, madame' (à 5)[1] is based on melodic motives of an originality of which Lassus alone was capable. The five-part 'Bon jour et puis quelle nouvelle',[2] on a rondeau by Marot, bathes the words 'bon vespre, bonne nuit, bon soir' in an atmosphere of quasi-impressionistic vesperal poetry produced by vocal grouping and unexpected modulations for which it would be difficult to find parallels at this period. The quodlibet, 'Las je n'iray plus jouer au bois',[3] in free rondo form captivates at once by its dotted rhythms and delicate, interlaced counterpoint.

The spirit of the *chanson* is happily mated with the technique of the madrigal in a number of instances, above all in 'En un chasteau, madame'[4] (à 4) where the licentious humour is lightly tinged with humanism. In 'Quand un cordier' (a four-part setting of a poem by Alain Chartier)[5] the rope-maker's long strands are suggested by means of thread-like arabesques, in the true madrigal style. Other examples of this fusion of madrigal and *chanson* include the five-part 'Mon coeur ravi d'amour',[6] a passage from which is given on page 24. 'Le rossignol', a most sensitive and elegant piece, belongs to the same category, as does 'Hélas, j'ay sans merci'[7] where the charming turns of phrase and harmonic progressions suggested by the various flowers are almost Schubertian in their freshness and spontaneity.

Among the French *chansons* which are completely madrigalian in style may be mentioned 'Si je suis brun' (à 4), where the parody of the Song of Songs ('Nigra sum') explains and justifies this tendency; 'La nuit froide et sombre' (a four-part setting of a poem by Joachim du Bellay), another impressionistic essay, bathed in an atmosphere in full accord with the cosmic naturism of the words; 'J'endure un tourment' (à 5), depicting with great harmonic subtlety the pangs of secret love; 'Je ne veux plus que chanter de tristesse' (à 5), in which the lyrical intensity of the music throws into relief a poem of almost romantic qualities; and 'Paisible domaine',[8] which celebrates Renaissance Paris in an atmosphere of dreamy serenity and with such perfection of style that one is almost tempted to place this music in a class by itself high above both *chanson* and madrigal. The same may

[1] Ibid. xii, p. 100, and xiv, p. 68.   [2] Ibid. xvi, p. 53.
[3] Ibid. xvi, p. 126.   [4] Ibid. xii, p. 14.
[5] Ibid. xii, p. 108.   [6] Ibid. xiv, p. 22.
[7] Ibid. xiv, p. 107, and xvi, p. 132.
[8] Ibid. xii, pp. 30, 34, xiv, pp. 38, 88, and xvi, p. 50.

Ex. 6

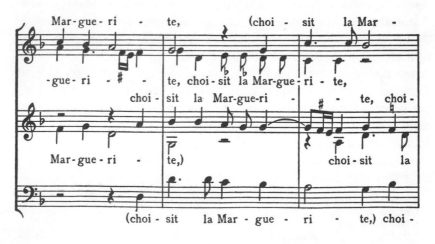

be said of the dialogue for double quartet (à 8) 'Que dis-tu, que fais-tu' (on a poem by Ronsard)[1] where the turtle-dove, deprived of its mate by a cruel bird-catcher, mourns its loss in tones of other-worldly tenderness. 'Hélas, mon dieu' (à 5) owes much of its effect to the Phrygian mode, an appropriate choice for the contemplative expression of the poem's Petrarchan pessimism; while 'O, faible esprit' (text by du Bellay)[2] describes the torments of love in a madrigal-like style, divorced from all earthly associations.

FLEMISH CONTEMPORARIES OF LASSUS

Lassus eclipses all his French and Flemish contemporaries in this genre. Several other figures among the Flemish composers certainly deserve consideration, but so far as our knowledge of their work goes at present, it is far below the level of that *thrésor de musicque* which Lassus accumulated. The relatively small number of *chansons* by Philippe de Monte (1521–1603) is itself an indication that this master of church music and the madrigal was not particularly attracted to the form. Essentially of a meditative disposition, he was able to work with ease in this sphere only when he came upon a text peculiarly suited to his temperament, such as 'Sortez regrets'[3] (à 4); indeed, he was so possessed by the spirit of the madrigal that none of his *chansons* preserves anything of the usual conception of the form. Nevertheless his 'Comme la tourterelle' (à 5)[4] and 'Que me servent mes vers' (a five-part setting of Ronsard) are, of their kind, models of noble suavity; and 'La déesse Vénus' (à 5),[5] a long piece in three sections, displays the beauties of the madrigal manner in purest Renaissance style.

Hubert Waelrant (1517–95) shows his alert mind in a piece of advice to musicians, 'Musiciens qui chantez' (à 5)[6] which is a lively and attractive synthesis of *chanson* and madrigal. The five-part *chansons* of André Pevernage (1543–91), so far as one can judge from Maldeghem's transcriptions,[7] with their unfortunate travesties of the texts, show his deficiencies in piquancy and sense of the picturesque; serious-minded and highly skilled, he had less affinity with the *chanson* style than with those of the motet and madrigal.

[1] *Werke*, xiv, p. 142. [2] Ibid. xvi, pp. 46, 34.
[3] Reprinted by G. Van Doorslaer, *Philippe de Monte: Opera*, xx (Malines, 1932), p. 9.
[4] Reprinted by Henri Lammers, *Collection de musique ancienne*, i (Paris, 1948), p. 10.
[5] *Opera*, xx, p. 66.
[6] Reprinted by Barclay Squire, *Ausgewählte Madrigale*, ii (Leipzig, n.d.).
[7] *Trésor musical: Musique profane*, vols. of 1865, 1869, 1870, 1871, 1872, and 1886 (Brussels).

There is no need to dwell on that fertile composer Jean de Castro, except to mention his *Sonnets, chansons à deux parties*, published at Antwerp in 1610. They are strange pieces, these *bicinia*, with their platitudinous and affected texts set to facile, rather dry music marked by an endless flow of madrigalisms. Yet the archives of the Antwerp publisher, Plantin, reveal that at the beginning of the seventeenth century Jean de Castro was, with Lassus, his best-selling composer.

GUILLAUME COSTELEY

Having considered the Flemish contribution, we must now turn to the purely French musicians who maintained the *chanson* tradition during the second half of the sixteenth century. Here there was a most interesting late flowering which took on various aspects, all characterized by an aristocratic tendency which contrasts with both the realism and the poetic melancholy of the earlier *chansons*. Even where traces of the tradition of the 1530–50 period persist, the popular vein is coloured with delicate pastel shades which soften its harshness without harming its freshness and spontaneity, as may be seen, for example, in such a piece as de Bussy's 'La rose fleurie',[1] a little masterpiece of rustic naïvety without a trace of sophistication in its melodic inspiration. But the outstanding *chanson* composer under the last of the Valois was Guillaume Costeley (born *c.* 1530–1).

Costeley's four-part *chansons*[2] are not all of the highest quality; but his three books contain a certain number of pieces which are among the most precious jewels of the second half of the sixteenth century. In the exquisitely delicate 'Mignonne, allons voir si la rose'[3] Costeley finds the perfect musical counterpart of the three stanzas of Ronsard's poem; 'Allons au vert boccage'[4] is a delightful May song, a model of its kind; the imaginative 'Las, je n'iray plus jouer au boys'[5] is in every way the equal of the setting of the same words by Lassus; 'Je voy des glissantes eaux'[6] uses the technique of homorhythm for the controlled expression of unhappy love; and 'Puisque ce beau mai'[7] is another May song in which the melodic inspiration anticipates, in 1570, the merriment of the English madrigalists of the

[1] Published by Cauchie, *Quinze chansons françaises*.
[2] Most of them published by Le Roy and Ballard in *Musique de Guillaume de Costeley* (Paris, 1570); republished by Expert in *Les Maîtres musiciens de la Renaissance française*, iii, xviii, and xix (Paris, 1896–1904).
[3] Expert, op. cit. iii, p. 75.
[4] Ibid. xviii, p. 19; recorded in *The History of Music in Sound*, iv.
[5] Ibid. xviii, p. 1.
[6] Ibid., p. 56.
[7] Ibid. iii, p. 85.

end of the century—the Batesons and Morleys—as may be seen from this excerpt:

Ex. 7

que rendray content mon a-my tant gay

(which will please my gay lover)

THE INSPIRATION OF RONSARD

We have seen that from the middle of the sixteenth century onwards the poems of Ronsard (1524–85) were frequently used as texts for *chansons*. Ronsard loved music and sang its praises in prose and verse,[1] so it is not surprising that many of his poems were composed by his contemporaries. Ronsard settings by Janequin, Lassus, Philippe de Monte, and Costeley have already been mentioned. Nor were these the only composers attracted to Ronsard. The serious-minded Goudimel, famous for his Psalms, wrote masterly settings of the sonnet 'Quand j'apperçoy ton beau chef jaunissant' (*à* 4) and of the ode to Michel de l'Hospital, 'Errant par les champs de la grâce', deeply felt pieces in every way worthy of the poet's graceful images or lofty thought. Nicolas de La Grotte's settings are better known in the solo versions with lute, described in a later chapter.[2] Ronsard's reputation was such that his name often figured prominently in the titles of publications containing only a few of his pieces, such as *Sonetz de P. de Ronsard mis en musique . . . par Philippe de Monte* (Paris, 1575) and *Poésies de P. de Ronsard et autres Poëtes mis en musique par M. François Regnard* (Paris, 1579).

The general level of the four-part *chansons* of Regnard[3] is not high. Among his settings of Ronsard, 'Je suis plus aise que les dieux' shows, however, that he was not devoid of subtlety in a style more akin to the madrigal than to the *chanson*. Ronsard's vogue was such that even a large part of his *Les Amours* was set to music by such composers as Jehan de Maletty, Guillaume Boni, and Anthoine de Bertrand, and published by Le Roy and Ballard (Paris, 1578).

---

[1] See *infra*, p. 184.   [2] See *infra*, p. 186.
[3] Published by Expert in *Les Maîtres musiciens de la Renaissance française*.

We may form some judgement of the stature of Anthoine de Bertrand from the modern edition of his four-part pieces.[1] This composer of gentle birth, from Auvergne, certainly showed some temerity in approaching Ronsard. Not only are most of the poems of *Les Amours* hardly suitable for music; their lack of variety and the preciosity that characterizes many of them must make their setting all the more difficult. All the same, one cannot deny the refinement of Anthoine de Bertrand's sixty little pieces, which one almost hesitates to describe as *chansons*; they are so much more nearly madrigals—yet French, not Italian, in their discretion and understatement and the moderation with which the composer employs Italian chromaticism. Considered as a complete cycle, these settings of *Les Amours* may be monotonous; yet one or two pieces are worth singling out, particularly 'Je suis tellement amoureux', the end of which is remarkable for the use of *ad libitum* microtones to modify the chromatic texture in the manner advocated by Nicola Vicentino in his *L'antica musica ridotta alla moderna* (Rome, 1555):

Ex. 8

Et si mon cœur ne peut s'ar - mer Con-

- tre l'œil qui le navre à tort, Car plus

il luy don - ne la mort, Plus il est con - traint de

<hr />

[1] Edited by Expert, *Monuments de la musique française au temps de la Renaissance,* iv–v (Paris, 1926–7).

[The crosses show where microtones may be introduced.]

(And so my heart is defenceless against the eye that playfully wounds it, for the more mortal the wound, the more it is obliged to love.)

There is a real sensitiveness in the details of 'Plus que jamais je veux aymer'; while 'Je meurs, hélas', 'Las, sans espoir', and 'Douce beauté' show uncommon intelligence in the employment of the simplest means to match Ronsard's verses with adequate music. It is in his third *Livre de chansons*, however, that de Bertrand gives overwhelming proof of his innate artistic sense. Here, unconstrained by a somewhat unvaried cycle of poems, he was able to give much freer rein to his inspiration. In this book 'Cest humeur vient de mon oeil', 'Las, ô pauvre Didon', 'O doux plaisir', and 'Pucelle, en qui la triple grâce' with its pendant 'Devant les yeux' are among the most polished and significant examples of this particular phase in the development of the French *chanson*, the phase of marked affinity with the madrigal and *villanella*.

VERS MESURÉS

The new manner of Ronsard and the Pléiade was not the only influence which diverted the French *chanson* from the course on which it had been set in the days of Francis I. The *vers mesurés* in the style of classical antiquity brought into fashion by the poets of the Académie du Palais (founded by Jean-Antoine de Baïf) awakened the lively interest of musicians, who experimented with settings in the same sense.[1] Claude Le Jeune was the most prominent of the composers who occupied themselves with this poetico-musical idea. It is questionable whether the principle of quantity is suited to the French language, but there is no denying that the poets and musicians who championed it—despite the ultimate sterility of their experiment—produced a body of work which occupies a by no means insignificant

---

[1] On the rather similar German settings of Horatian odes earlier in the century, see Vol. III, pp. 370–1. On Baïf's Academy, see *infra*, p. 805.

place in the history of the music of the Renaissance. Indeed, according to the plausible theory of Henry Prunières,[1] the *canto alla francese* which inspired Monteverdi to write his *Scherzi musicali* of 1607 was none other than this *musique mesurée à l'antique* of Le Jeune, Mauduit, and du Caurroy.

Le Jeune also wrote *chansons* of the ordinary kind in addition to his experiments with *musique mesurée*. The four-part songs in the *Livre de mélanges* (1585)[2] are rather unequal in value. A variety of subjects is dealt with in refined and intelligent—perhaps too intelligent—music. Despite this suggestion of artificiality, some of them are undoubtedly charming and original: for instance the aristocratic 'Si dessus vos lèvres de rose', the virginal grace of which is brought out by the key of F, and 'Villageoise de Gascogne' (the text of which is in dialect) with its dotted rhythm suggesting a gigue or a *morisque*, a particularly successful essay in the style of popular dance music.

The *musique mesurée à l'antique* was bound to remain very simple. Obliged by its very nature to renounce the devices of counterpoint, it consisted essentially of simple successions of chords. But in order to avoid monotony certain figurations of the chords were allowed on condition that each syllable of the text was sung simultaneously by all the voices. Such restrictions could be counterbalanced only by outstanding melodic invention or by exquisite taste in the contrivance of melismatic figuration, and it is astonishing to see what Le Jeune was able to accomplish with such limited resources in both his secular pieces and his French Psalms in *vers mesuré*. Here we are concerned only with the former category,[3] which are all contained in the posthumous collection of 2-, 3-, 4-, 5-, 6-, 7-, and 8-part pieces entitled *Le Printemps*, published by Ballard in 1603.[4] Reading through the whole collection, one cannot escape a feeling of monotony, despite the constant changes of metrical schemes and the variety in the number of voices. Moreover Le Jeune's inspiration, fettered by his system, seems to flag after the earlier pieces, reviving only when he comes upon a particularly stimulating text.

Le Printemps opens with a piece in *vers rimés*, 'Voicy du gay printems' (on a poem by Desportes), a delightful synthesis of the suavity of the madrigal with the polish and concision of the *chanson*. Next comes the first *mesuré* piece, 'Revecy venir du Printans', with a

---

[1] *La Vie et l'œuvre de Claudio Monteverdi* (Paris, 1924; English translation, London, 1926), pp. 46 ff. of the English edition.
[2] Partially republished by Expert, *Les Maîtres musiciens*, xvi.
[3] For Le Jeune's Psalms, see p. 446.
[4] Reprinted by Expert, *Les Maîtres musiciens*, xii–xiv (Paris, 1900).

five-part *rechant* (refrain) between the repeats of which are couplets for 2, 3, and 4 voices respectively. The total effect is delightful, thanks to the grace and verve of the melody and the simple charm of the figurative ornamentation:

Ex. 9   *Rechant à 5*

Re-ve-cy ve-nir du Prin-tans L'amoureuz' et bel - le sai - son.

(See, Spring comes again, season of beauty and love)

But such dainty miniatures are rare in this collection; other examples worth attention are 'Cigne je suis de candeur' (no. 17), 'La brune-lette violette' (no. 26), and 'Pastourelles jolietes' (no. 29), in which Le Jeune's very distinctive melodic inspiration is fully manifest.

We need not linger over the *Chansonettes mesurées à l'antique* (twenty-three four-part settings of poems by Baïf) by Jacques Mau-duit (Paris, 1586),[1] though 'Vous me tuez si doucement' (no. 1), 'Voicy le verd et beau may' (no. 5), and 'Vostre tarin je voudrois estre' (no. 9) are the work of a delightful musician worthy of an honourable place alongside Le Jeune. The same may be said of Eustache du Caurroy, whose *Meslanges* (Paris, 1610)[2] include eight pieces *mesurés à l'antique*. Of these, 'Déliette mignonette' (*à* 4) is memorable for the graceful line of a *superius* already heavily indebted to the accompanied monody.[3]

SWEELINCK

This survey of the French polyphonic *chanson* would be incomplete without mention of the contributions of the Dutch master J. P. Sweelinck (1562–1620). A truly international figure, Sweelinck derives his fame mainly from historic importance in the evolution of organ music.[4] Though he has no such claim to pre-eminence in the field of vocal music, he nevertheless stands out at the end of the sixteenth and beginning of the seventeenth centuries as one of those superior minds who were able to turn to personal ends everything

---

[1] Ibid., x.   [2] Ibid. xvii.
[3] See Chap. IV.   [4] See pp. 635 ff.

acquired by their vast knowledge and exceptional powers of assimilation. In his *Chansons a cinc parties*[1] he showed what he had learned from the simultaneous study of *chanson* and madrigal. There is nothing very original in this first collection; but some years later, in his five-part 'Tu as tout seul, Jan, Jan' (text by Marot) (published in a collection *Le Rossignol Musical*, Antwerp, 1597) he produced a masterpiece of light-hearted good humour, highly accomplished and full of interesting detail. His *Rimes françoises et italiennes* (Leyden, 1612)[2] conclude with a four-part piece in four sections, 'Rozette, pour un peu d'absence' (poem by Desportes), in the true tradition of the French *chanson* with many felicitous touches and employing all the resources of the polyphonic technique of the late sixteenth century. In sharp contrast with the spontaneity of these two *chansons*, the two- and three-part *Rimes françoises*[3]—all, with one exception, on poems by Desportes—show Sweelinck's 'madrigalizing' tendency: they are beautifully wrought pieces and extremely ingenious, but more cerebral than inspired and calculated to please the mind and the eyes rather than to satisfy the ear and the heart.

[1] The date 'En Anuero ce XXVIII de May 1584' in Phalèse's preface led even Van Sigtenhorst Meyer to believe in an edition of that date, but no copy is known and 1584 may well be a misprint for 1594 (see Äke Davidsson, *Musikbibliographische Beiträge* (Upsala, 1954), p. 17). The edition of 1594 is the basis of Seiffert's reprint, *Werken van J. P. Sweelinck*, vii (The Hague and Leipzig, 1899), and was probably the first.

[2] Reprinted by Seiffert, ibid., viii (1900).

[3] Ibid.

II

THE SIXTEENTH-CENTURY MADRIGAL

By E. J. DENT

CARNIVAL SONGS AND *FROTTOLE*

The secular music of the Italian Renaissance may be said to begin with the *canti carnascialeschi* of Florence.[1] Considered as music, these are not very attractive. Their melodies, such as they are, are curiously primitive, and it is sometimes difficult to guess whether the tune is in the uppermost part or in the tenor. Their chief interest lies in the words, which are extremely amusing and characteristic of popular life. They are all strophic, generally with a refrain. The music is mainly homophonic and in four parts, sometimes with a middle section for two voices which is more contrapuntal. We must imagine them bawled in the streets with riotous gusto. Popular they certainly were, for a great many of them were adapted to religious words and sung as *laudi spirituali*; the collections of these are most valuable sources for popular Italian song.[2]

It is difficult for us to realize now the extraordinary delight that singers of the Renaissance derived from the mere sound of the simplest block harmony in four parts. We catch a glimpse of it in the macaronic poems of Teofilo Folengo, known as Merlinus Coccaius (1496–1544). Folengo was educated at the University of Bologna and became a Benedictine, but he left his monastery in 1524 for the life of a wandering goliard, returning to the order ten years later. His mock epic *Baldus*, first published in 1517, as well as his other poems, contains many allusions to music and paints the peasant life of the period in vivid colours. He describes (canto xx) Baldus and his three friends singing together as they ride on a journey:

> Quattuor in voce post haec cantare comenzant.
> Arripit ut gracili sopranum voce Rubinus,[3]
> Falchetti firmum suscepit bocca tenorem,
> Gorga tridans notulas prorumpit Cingaris altum,
> Trat contrabassum extra calcanea Baldus.
> Quattuor hi varios pergunt cantando sonettos.

. . . . . .

[1] See Vol. III, Chap. XI.
[2] See Vol. III, p. 389.
[3] Rubinus would have sung in falsetto.

Plus auscultantum sopranus captat orecchias.
Sed tenor est vocum rector, vel guida tonorum.
Altus Apollineum carmen depingit et ornat,
Bassus alit voces, ingrassat, firmat et auget.
Cantus Italicos, Francesos atque Spagnolos
Cantabant, nam sic facientes tempora passant.

They would appear to be improvising their harmony, judging from lines not quoted here, but their methods are much the same as those laid down later by Zarlino,[1] who compares the four voices to the four elements—the bass being earth, the tenor water, counter-tenor or alto air, and soprano or *canto* fire. The tenor sings the subject, which decides the mode; the bass proceeds in slower notes—'it nourishes and fattens the music'—the alto decorates the subject with more movement and the soprano is the most active voice and the one which owing to its penetrating quality reaches the ear first. Zarlino actually quotes the lines of Folengo as a final illustration. Zarlino was a priest writing mainly for church composers, and his views are conservative; but he cannot have failed to see that by the beginning of the century the leading melody, at any rate in secular music, had shifted from the tenor to the uppermost voice.

The carnival songs were succeeded by the *frottole*,[2] of which eleven books were printed by Petrucci (1504–14). The original home of the *frottola* was Mantua, where the court of the Gonzagas carried on a peaceful and highly cultivated life under the aegis of the Duchess Isabella d'Este, whose copious correspondence shows her to have been passionately devoted to music and poetry; she was herself a performer on the clavichord or spinet. (Tromboncino and Marchetto Cara were her favourite composers.) But the vogue of the *frottola* spread very soon from Mantua to Ferrara, Florence, and Venice. Venice had already established itself as the great centre of music-printing. Tromboncino seems to have died there about 1535, but by that date the *frottola* had gone completely out of fashion; its place was being taken by the new madrigal, and the first composers of madrigals were nearly all Netherlanders. Musicians from France and the Low Countries had found employment in large numbers all over Europe from Lisbon to Warsaw, and, just as the Italians did in the eighteenth century, they pushed the native composers into obscurity. Every Italian prince made a point of securing a Netherlander for the direction of his chapel, and in this the princes followed the example of the Pope.

[1] Gioseffo Zarlino, *Le istitutioni harmoniche* (Venice, 1562), pp. 238 ff.
[2] See Vol. III, pp. 390–405.

FROTTOLA AND MADRIGAL

The new madrigal of the sixteenth century, which has no connexion with the Italian madrigal of the fourteenth, emerged from the contact of Netherland composers with Italian poets. It is impossible to ascribe it to any one composer. The words *frottola* and *madrigale* were originally names for clearly defined forms of versification, like *sestina, canzone, ottava, sonetto,* &c. but after about 1500 they become musical terms and lose their literary sense. Petrucci's eleven books of *frottole* include many different verse-forms, even sonnets among them; the 'madrigal' as set to music became equally various. Petrarch, the favourite poet of the madrigalists, wrote actually very few *madrigali*, and though his sonnets and other poems were set to music over and over again, his real madrigals were never set at all.

The fundamental difference between the *frottola* and the madrigal was that the *frottola* was a strophic song in several verses, while the madrigal was a short poem seldom exceeding twelve lines and generally content with less. The *frottola* therefore had a straightforward tune with an accompaniment; it seems that although it was printed in four separate parts on facing pages, it was more often sung by a solo voice to the accompaniment of the lute.[1] The bass part moves in slow notes and merely supports the harmony all the way through; the two middle parts (which cross frequently) often look contrapuntal, but are in reality mere filling up. The written and printed lute transcriptions generally leave out one of them. The singers of *frottole* were sometimes the composers as well, but in any case hired professionals; they would no doubt perform from memory and would have no need to look at the music-book.

Contemporary pictures often show three or more people singing and playing from one single book of this type; one can only wonder how they ever managed it. In 1525 Pierre Hautin of Paris invented the method of printing music in one impression; a few years later this method was adopted by the Venetian printers, who at the same time began the issue of part-music in separate part-books which made reading much easier and the production much cheaper. Moreover, notes could be more widely spaced than in the tightly packed pages of Petrucci, and words could be printed under them with more accurate adjustment. Madrigal-singing could not become a practical possibility until this had been accomplished.

The transition from *frottola* to madrigal must have begun with the

[1] See Vol. III, p. 398.

practice, however awkward and uncomfortable it may have been, of performing *frottole* by a quartet of voices. We have already noted in Folengo's *Baldus* the new pleasure which this gave to the singers. The solo singer to the lute was not by any means ousted, although the *frottola* died out altogether and was considered quite old-fashioned by about 1530. Many madrigals could be sung, and undoubtedly were sung, in this way,[1] but the composers intended them mainly, if not always, for voices either unaccompanied or doubled by melodic instruments, and for that reason each part was regarded as of equal importance. The madrigals, except those intended for ceremonial occasions, were composed for the enjoyment of the singers, for their enjoyment both of music and of poetry; each singer had to feel that he was contributing his part to the intensification of the poet's words, and that is the real reason for the elaborate contrapuntal treatment of them. As the madrigals became more and more elaborate, complaints were made by critical writers of the 'laceration of poetry' brought about by this entangled polyphony. But what killed the madrigal at the end of the sixteenth century was not the exaggeration of counterpoint and chromatic harmony, but the general spread of musical enjoyment and appreciation to a public which had learned to want to listen to music rather than to sing it themselves. The finest of the madrigals, the most sensitive and artistic, were composed for a limited *élite*, the numerous 'academies' of highly cultivated amateur singers; a larger and more middle-class public had by this time learned to read music at sight and wanted entertainment of a more frivolous type, and simultaneously there developed a class of virtuoso singers who found their true vocation in the opera of the following century. It is therefore not so paradoxical as it may seem that the expression of words, the ideal which first inspired the madrigal, led to its destruction.

THE LITERARY LANGUAGE OF THE MADRIGAL

The transition from *frottola* to madrigal coincided with the new literary movement in Italy of which Pietro Bembo was the leader and

---

[1] In which case the solo part might be ornamented by improvised coloratura. Ernest Ferand gives 'diminutions' of the highest part of Rore's, 'Signor mio caro' from Girolamo dalla Casa's *Il vero Modo di diminuir* (Venice, 1584) and Bassano's *Ricercate, passaggi et cadentie* (Venice, 1585) in *Die Improvisation* (Cologne, 1956), p. 63; parallel diminutions of Palestrina's 'Vestiva i colli' are given by Robert Haas in *Aufführungspraxis der Musik* (Potsdam, 1934), p. 117. Another example from Bassano, with diminutions of the tenor of Rore's 'Quando signor' is printed by Max Kuhn, *Die Verzierungskunst in der Gesangsmusik des XVI. und XVII. Jahrhunderts (1535–1650)* (Leipzig, 1902), p. 110. On similar ornamentation of church music, see *infra*, p. 332.

dictator. Spoken Italian was then (as indeed it is still to a large extent) a large number of local dialects often quite unintelligible to Italians outside their own area. Dante, early in the fourteenth century, had stressed the necessity of a uniform vernacular for cultivated intercourse and literary employment that should be understood throughout the peninsula, and at that date it indeed needed all Dante's faith and courage to defend the vernacular against the claims of Latin for serious prose and poetry. Petrarch himself thought that his Latin epic *Africa* was far superior to the Italian poems which have made his name immortal. Dante, Petrarch, and Boccaccio, being all Tuscans, wrote in their own Tuscan dialect and thereby established Tuscan as the basis of standard Italian; it is in fact the dialect which comes nearest to Latin. But the revival of learning which marked the early Renaissance gave a new impetus to Latin owing to the new study of the great classical authors and the beginnings of real classical scholarship. Bembo again took up the defence of Italian, but had to admit that the Tuscan of Dante, Petrarch, and Boccaccio was by now archaic and not practicable for the usage of his own time. He was a poet himself, though not a great one, and perhaps more interested in poetry than in prose; he decided that for poetry the infallible model was Petrarch, and his followers not only imitated Petrarch but borrowed lines from him openly and unashamedly. A knowledge of Petrarch is thus indispensable to all students of the Italian madrigal. Petrarch is the poet of introspection and sensibility; he requires to be studied intimately and savoured line by line, word by word; it is with this intention and method that the madrigal has to be approached, for this lingering enjoyment of the beauty of words and thoughts accounts at once for the unhurried leisureliness of both the simplest and the most sophisticated musical settings of his poems.

How far Bembo was interested in music is uncertain, but there must have been some contact between the musicians and the members of his circle. We must not suppose that the composers of that time chose their own texts; Isabella d'Este would obtain a poem from someone and would then ask Tromboncino to set it to music. All music was written to order. The Netherlanders dominated the music of both the courts and the churches; in the Pope's chapel there was only one Italian, Costanzo Festa, and he is also the only Italian of distinction among the first group of madrigalists. It may seem astonishing to us today that there is no evidence of the slightest jealousy or chauvinism on the part of the Italian musicians; they accepted the music of the Netherlanders, admired it cordially, and in many cases were on terms of personal friendship with the composers. But another question arises in connexion with the madrigals: how much Italian did those Netherlanders really know? In our own times many foreigners have made their home in England; but legal naturalization does not confer a full knowledge of the adopted language. Poetry is the test; some can learn to write quite correct English prose, but only rarely good English poetry. Only a few acquire a really good English accent in speaking, and though they may have a keen appreciation of English poetry, they betray themselves when they set it to music. Was that the case with the Netherland composers of Italian madrigals? We have to remember that even for the Italians their language had not yet acquired the background of a long-established classical style, which in our case goes back to Shakespeare and the English Bible; but we cannot follow the course of the sixteenth century without noticing that the madrigals acquire a new fluidity of movement and sensitivity of expression as soon as Italians themselves take complete possession of them.

THE EARLIEST MADRIGAL-COMPOSERS

It is uncertain whether Costanzo Festa or Philippe Verdelot is to be regarded as the first composer of madrigals; in any case Festa stands by himself among a crowd of Netherlanders. Verdelot was not a Netherlander by birth but a Frenchman from the south of France, possibly from Carpentras. He may have been born about 1490 or even later; Attaingnant printed two motets by him in 1529 under the name of Philippe Deslouges, and the name Verdelot was possibly a pseudonym. From about 1525 onwards he appears to have divided his time between Florence and Venice and to have died (probably at Florence) about 1538. His career as a madrigalist was therefore a very short one.

Costanzo Festa must have been about the same age. He came from the diocese of Turin and was a member of the papal chapel under Leo X. He died at Rome in 1545, but although chiefly working in Rome he seems to have had some contact with Florence. He is mentioned with great admiration by various contemporaries, including Folengo in *Baldus*, where he is placed on a level with Josquin himself.[1]

---

[1] *Macaronea vigesima:*

> O Josquine Deo gratissime, nascere mundo
> Compositure diu, quem clamat Musica patrem,
> Iannus motonus, Petrus de robore, Festa
> Constans, Iosquinus qui saepe putabitur esse.

The date of Jacques Arcadelt's birth is often given as about 1514, but was more probably earlier; in any case he was some years junior to Verdelot and Festa. He is mentioned as 'Flandrus' as a member of the Cappella Giulia in Rome in 1539; for some time previously he had lived in Florence, and there is some evidence for a stay in Venice even earlier, though in the early prints it is often very uncertain whether madrigals are attributed to their true composer. In 1557 he was in Paris as a member of the royal chapel; he is mentioned by Rabelais along with Janequin and Claudin, and is supposed to have died in Paris some time later.

BEGINNINGS OF THE MADRIGAL STYLE

The earlier madrigalists approached their new task with some timidity. The madrigal was intended to be a reaction against the frivolity of the *frottola*; its texts, though still mainly amorous, were more decorous and more sentimental. But it continued the style of the *frottola*[1] in having a recognizable 'tune' in the uppermost voice, and it was a long time before this principle was discarded. The tune created the main shape of the madrigal; the lower voices were for a long time merely an accompaniment in block harmony, though enlivened by short passages of free imitation here and there. This technique was adopted from the earlier French *chanson*. In the interval between the short vogue of the *frottola* and the first emergence of the new madrigal, Attaingnant had published collections of the new type of French *chanson*[2] represented most conspicuously by Janequin, and these soon crossed the frontier into Italy and influenced the madrigalists in various ways, notably by the habit of beginning a four-part *chanson* with a double canon. Strict canon is quite foreign to the general madrigal technique, though it occurs occasionally, as with Arcadelt. What the first madrigalists, both Flemish and Italian, did was to start with two voices together followed by a repetition of the phrase by the other two; as the first pair rested at the end of the phrase determined by the sense of the words, the canon became more obvious to the ear, but it was not continued systematically and gave place to block harmony and fragmentary free imitations. The middle parts of the *frottole* had been generally contrapuntal, but not imitative; the madrigal preferred imitation, because it was definitely vocal and thus each voice could contribute to the expression of the words,

---

[1] In the transition from *frottola* to madrigal, see further Claudio Gallico, *Un canzionere musicale italiano del cinquecento* (Florence, 1961).   [2] See p. 2.

though at first large portions were in simultaneous harmony. These early madrigals are agreeable and interesting to sing because the chords formed are almost all common chords in root position, thereby compelling the composer to make his parts move. In the later madrigals of Marenzio and others, where the most extraordinary chromatic chords appear, sometimes going through the entire circle of keys, this strong preference for root positions is very remarkable.

The close affinity to the *frottola* which still persisted is shown by the fact that in 1536 Willaert arranged twenty-two of Verdelot's madrigals for solo voice with lute accompaniment. But we may note a small difference in the short codas which almost invariably conclude these madrigals. After the uppermost voice has made its last cadence, the final note is held for two or three bars (as we should now say) while the lower voices sing little imitations before coming to rest altogether with a cadence which is invariably plagal. The *frottole* have similar codas, obviously instrumental, and very often plagal endings too; but these codas have a natural function because they are interludes between the stanzas of the song. The words of the madrigal are often no longer than one stanza of a *frottola*, though the imitations may make them longer to sing; but the madrigal is self-contained and not repeated for several stanzas. The music ought to be complete in itself, and in fact is so in most of the later madrigals. The plagal-ending coda is a mannerism of church music; in 'modal harmony' (if this is not a contradiction in terms) general tonality was so vague that an extension of the last note was a necessity, to show that this was the real end of the piece. Even when a madrigal begins and ends on the same chord and ends with a dominant cadence, the intermediate tonality is still quite vague and there is no strong sense of finality. One may often wonder whether even the most accomplished of the madrigalists ever started to write a madrigal with a definite conception of how it was going to end.

In reading these early madrigals we must beware of supposing that the notation in white notes, with the minim as unit of the beat, necessarily implies a slow tempo. Very soon the crotchet was adopted as the unit in general practice with the time-signature C instead of ₵ (while the church music continued *alla breve*), but it made little difference to the actual speed of performance, which in the last resort always depended on the sense of the words. Whether singers in practice employed any sort of rubato, rallentando, or accelerando we do not know; but they are never indicated, and any change of pace, or pause, takes place automatically according to the lengths of the notes and rests themselves, the beat remaining the same. The words are paramount; all depends on them.

RISE OF THE FIVE-PART MADRIGAL

The four-part madrigal was soon superseded by that in five parts, which became the standard arrangement for the most elaborate and consciously artistic style, but four and three parts were by no means abandoned altogether, and for ceremonial occasions the five parts were increased, sometimes to quite large numbers. Ceremonial madrigals can almost always be identified with certainty from the words; they may have been needed for weddings (the poetic allusions to places, rivers, armorial bearings, and so forth often give clues to the families concerned), receptions, and elegies on deceased persons, as well as incidental music to plays. The last category appears quite early and generally in four-part block harmony. They are not anticipations of opera, but simply prologues, entr'actes, and epilogues, in which it is essential that the words should be understood as clearly as possible; we find examples by Arcadelt and Corteccia at Florence about 1538–9. One by Arcadelt, evidently for an old Latin comedy, shows us incidentally that in these plays the female parts were acted by men—

> Et quest' in gonna
> Fu si leggiadra donna
> Ch'ancor molti di qua par ch'inamori.

(This man in a skirt was such a pretty lady that many fell in love with him.)

This also shows that the actors, presumably students, were able to sing too.

Verdelot composed several madrigals in five parts; Arcadelt preferred four, as in the well-known 'Il bianco e dolce cigno',[1] a good example of the elegantly erotic text. The advantages of the five-part texture were many. It provided a richer harmonic sonority and a more widely extended compass, although sometimes for male voices only; it enabled the composer to break up the ensemble into smaller sections of two or more generally three voices, which was useful in madrigals suggesting a dialogue. In such cases the middle voice (generally the *quintus*) was kept at work all the time as he had to do duty in both groups; the *quintus* is a tiresome problem for modern madrigal groups, as it can be solved only by a counter-tenor. To

[1] Published in his *Primo libro di madrigali* (Venice, 1539) and reprinted by Barclay Squire in his *Ausgewählte Madrigale* (Leipzig, n.d.), no. 22.

what extent the upper parts were sung by women it is difficult to say: in some cases perhaps boys sang them, and in later years we know that they were sung by women who were highly trained professional singers, generally of the *meretrix honesta* class. The moral dangers of musical studies for young women of good family were a matter of common knowledge and comment down to quite modern times, above all in Italy.

Festa preferred four parts and even three;[1] before writing his madrigals he had also composed several three-part motets. His three-part writing is masterly in its clarity, and in four parts he is more melodious and airy in texture than Verdelot, whose melody moves within a narrower range and with shorter phrases. Verdelot seldom uses *melismata* except at a cadence, and they are generally no more than an ascending or descending scale of about five notes:[2]

Ex. 10

Ma - don - na qual cer-tez - za Ha-
-ver-si puo mag-gior del mio gran fuo - co Che
ve - der con-su - mar - mi a po - - - co a
ve - der con-su - mar - mi
ve - der con-su - mar - - - mi, con -

¹ For a five-part example by Festa, see *Das Chorwerk*, lviii (Wolfenbüttel, 1956), p. 13.
² *Primo libro de Madrigali* (Venice, 1537); reprinted in Einstein, *The Italian Madrigal*, iii, p. 21 (Princeton, 1949).

(My lady, what stronger evidence could you have of my fire than to see me consume myself little by little.)

Festa shows more invention and his melody has more movement, suggesting that he is more at his ease in the setting of Italian poetry:

Ex. II

(So pleasant is the fire and sweet the knot with which love burns and binds me.)[1]

[1] First printed in Arcadelt's *Quarto libro di Madrigali* (Venice, 1539); reprinted in Einstein, op. cit., p. 36.

Arcadelt also wrote mainly in four parts; the most famous of all his madrigals is the already mentioned 'Il bianco e dolce cigno' to words by Alfonso d'Avalos, often reprinted in the sixteenth century. We associate it at once with 'The silver swan' of Gibbons, as it has the same utter simplicity of harmony; but Gibbons's madrigal is a cynical epigram, whereas Arcadelt's is a sentimental love-song. Yet it has no perceptible passion in its music; it simply clothes the words with agreeable sound, and at this time that was what the poets, the singers, and their audience wanted—what they meant by their favourite words *dolcezza e soavità*.

THE MADRIGAL POEMS

The madrigal (as a poetical form) is a short composition, and so are the *sestina* and the *ottava* which also become 'madrigals' in the musical sense; but composers now began to attempt much longer works, choosing for this purpose the *canzoni* of Petrarch, the best-known of which is 'Chiare, fresche e dolci acque' (no. 27 *in vita di Madonna Laura*). The *canzone* is a long poem in several stanzas, and all *canzoni* end with the *commiato*, a coda of three lines. The stanzas are variable in metrical scheme, though uniform for any one *canzone*; each stanza is in fact a madrigal, free in its number of lines—some have six, others twenty ('Chiare fresche' has thirteen)—and the lines are a mixture of eleven or seven syllables, but each stanza ends with two rhyming lines. The musicians set them as a sequence of madrigals, with different music to each stanza, generally obtaining variety by alternating between five, four, and three voices, and alternating time-signatures also. Arcadelt was the first to adopt this plan and was followed by many others.

These developments point to the growth of a new attitude towards the madrigal; it was no longer written for one occasion only, but for circles of persons who appreciated it as a work of art in its own right. Groups, sometimes dignified by the name of academies, were formed in various places, notably at Venice and Verona, of highly cultivated amateurs who met regularly for the study of madrigals. An audience may have been present or not, but the madrigals were written primarily for the enjoyment of those who sang them. Such persons were doubtless thoroughly familiar with the poetry of Petrarch and Ariosto, to say nothing of other poets, before they began to sing the musical settings; there would be no singing through the notes first and then puzzling out the words (or not) afterwards, and it thus follows that the natural and effortless recitation of the words would dictate the shaping of the musical phrases—a condition most important for singers who read from single part-books without barlines and without a conductor. The frequent cross-rhythms and syncopations, indicated in some modern editions by bars of varying lengths, would fall into place quite spontaneously and the music would sound much less stiff and more elastic than it looks in a printed score. Modern singers are easily tempted to put a sharp accent on the first beat of each bar, but it may be doubted whether the old Italian singers ever made sharp accents of this kind unless the words compelled it. A sharp accent is unnatural to the voice altogether; that style of performance must have come into music gradually through instrumental music and through association with an initial up-beat. An initial short up-beat is extremely rare in serious madrigals; even when the words are iambic, the first note, whether for one voice or more, is always a long one, as if the singer required a little time to make sure of it.

THE WORK OF WILLAERT

Few musicians of this period received so much admiration as Adrian Willaert, both during his lifetime and after his death.[1] Born at Roulers about 1490, he was trained in Paris under Jean Mouton; shortly before 1520 he went to Italy and in that year entered the service of Ercole I, Duke of Ferrara. In 1527 he succeeded a Frenchman as *maestro di cappella* at St. Mark's in Venice, where he remained until his death in 1562. In what year he began composing madrigals is uncertain; the earliest is doubtfully ascribed to 1536,[2] but this seems a late date, for we must not assume that madrigals were always published as soon as they were written. He continues the style of Verdelot, of whom he was a devoted admirer, but from the first he shows more breadth of treatment and a more elaborately contrapuntal style. He makes a point of setting long poems, among them several sonnets of Petrarch which he divides into two movements each, quatrains and sestet, with a definite pause between them—a practice followed by all the later composers.

A general characteristic of Willaert is his leisurely treatment of the words, which are spaced out with rests of some length between the phrases in all the voices; this adds considerably to the expressiveness,

---

[1] Einstein quotes several of these eulogies, both in prose and in verse, op. cit., i, p. 323.

[2] Announced by Marcolini in the preface to Francesco da Milano's *Intavolatura di Liuto* in that year; if published, no copy is known to survive.

because the texture thereby becomes much more translucent and
each voice gets the chance of being heard separately. At the same
time this treatment adds a good deal to the length of the madrigal;
another cause of length is his partiality for semibreves (he always
uses the white-note *alla breve* notation), and crotchets are quite
rare. The monotony which we cannot escape feeling in these early
madrigals is due not to the white notes as units of time but to the
fact that practically not more than two kinds of time-value are
employed at all, whereas in the following generations we shall find
time-values ranging from the semibreve to the semiquaver, with the
crotchet as main time-unit.

THE ADVENT OF CHROMATICISM

In the four-part madrigal 'Amor mi fa morire'[1] we notice a good
many accidentals, some original, some suggested by the editor on the
principles of *musica ficta*. If we try the experiment of singing this
madrigal through, first without the accidentals and then with them
all, we shall at once notice a complete change of general feeling. To
anyone moderately at home in madrigal-singing—and we cannot be
even moderately at home in madrigals without singing in them ourselves—the diatonic version may seem a little archaic, but not un-
pleasantly so, but the chromatic version will bring us at once into a
new and almost Mendelssohnian world of expression, though we can
have little doubt that some contemporary singers did sing the work
like that: it is no abominable anachronism of style. Chromaticizing of
that kind was simply a matter of individual taste; conservative minds
preferred modalism, progressive ones inclined towards tonal harmony,
though they certainly had no idea then of the direction in which they
were moving. We have reached the moment when the appearance of
the word 'chromatic' indicates a new emotional attitude to music in
general.

The word *cromatico*, which now begins to appear frequently on
title-pages, bears two quite separate meanings. *Croma* and *biscroma*
are the Italian names for quaver and semiquaver; in many cases
madrigali cromatici simply means madrigals with a liberal use of
these time-values. But it may also mean the use of chromatic intervals,
and here we must distinguish three different usages. First, there is the
common sharpening of the leading note at a cadence, and then of any
note which is a temporary leading note in any key whether at a cadence

---

[1] From *Madrigali a quattro voci* (Venice, 1563); reprinted in Einstein, op. cit., iii, p. 59
(see also i, pp. 326–7.)

or not; the same principle applies to the use of a flat analogously to the medieval *b molle* in any key. Secondly, there is the use of melodic steps by semitone either upwards or downwards, whether the melody takes one step only or as many as a dozen, producing a complete chromatic scale. Thirdly, there is the employment of chromatic notes taken by leap as well as by step for the purpose of what we should now call modulation to new keys and leading eventually to a practical, if not theoretical, recognition of the complete 'circle of fifths'. These three forms of chromaticism need to be considered separately.

Musica ficta is generally supposed to have begun as an instinctive or even subconscious act on the part of singers. The writings of the medieval theorists are here irrelevant, except for giving a more or less definite guarantee for the official recognition of this practice and indeed for many others; the theorists may allow or forbid this and that, but they merely codify what composers and singers (generally the same persons) have been doing for some time and they do not explain what inward urge induced these men to do it. It may be suggested that even the very first instinctive practical use of a sharp or a flat had for the singer some faintly emotional or expressive value. This seems to be corroborated by the terms *alzar la voce* and *abbassar la voce* used by a rather later composer, Francesco Orso,[1] in the sense of sharpening or flattening a note; for although *voce* here certainly means 'note' the two expressions can equally well mean singing louder or softer, and Kroyer[2] suggests that some of these chromaticisms did imply a slight *crescendo* and *diminuendo*.[3]

The melodic use of the chromatic scale in melody, at first for only a few notes, is certainly expressive in intention and suggested by the sense of the words. Church music as a rule avoided it, as it did the notation in black notes—though Rore wrote a *Missa a note negre*.[4] The church authorities were always hostile to innovations and regarded chromatics as effeminate and immoral. Yet in the madrigal period the semitone does not seem to have had systematically erotic associations. As an element in harmony it produced a leading-note (or its converse) moving towards a new key, sharp-wards or flat-wards, and it also emphasized the contrast between major and minor. We associate these now mainly with cheerfulness or melancholy, but in Purcell's time they are 'masculine' and 'feminine',

[1] In the dedication of his *Primo libro de Madrigali* (Venice, 1567).
[2] T. Kroyer, *Die Anfänge der Chromatik im italienischen Madrigal des XVI. Jahrhunderts* (Leipzig, 1902), pp. 83–84.
[3] As perhaps in Luzzaschi's 'Quivi sospiri' (*Secondo libro*, Venice, 1576), recorded in *The History of Music in Sound* (H.M.V.), iv.   [4] See pp. 288 and 290.

military and amorous, *la gloire* and *l'amour*; this attitude, however, became possible only after the quite definite establishment of the key-system. Chromatic fugue-subjects and ground basses, too, needed a firm sense of general tonality to make them safe; in the sixteenth century chromatics were a tentative and perhaps dangerous exploration of unknown country. The revival of Greek learning led a few musicians to futile speculations on the ancient diatonic, chromatic, and enharmonic *genera*, but their musical experiments were of no practical value. The keyboard, stabilized in its present form by about 1470, was no doubt a further stimulus to chromatic exploration; as late as 1603 G. M. Trabaci of Naples was still fumbling about for *consonanze stravaganti*, as he called them.[1]

CIPRIANO DE RORE

The chromatic movement in the madrigal begins with Willaert, but he did not go very far, though he probably suggested the idea to his pupils, notably Cipriano de Rore. Rore was born *c.* 1516, probably of poor parents at Antwerp; nothing is known of his early life until he brought out a book of five-part madrigals at Venice in 1542.[2]

Rore's reputation as a chromatic innovator rests mainly on a curious composition for four bass voices to Latin words by some humanist imitator of Catullus, 'Calami sonum ferentes', printed in 1555 as the last item in a collection of madrigals and other songs, Italian and French, by Lassus at Antwerp. Lassus also contributed to this the Latin chromatic madrigal 'Alma Nemes' which was obviously an answer to the challenge of Rore. Both works[3] were probably written for some learned academy, though Lassus's is for a normal group of S.A.T.B. They are too accomplished to be called experimental; we must regard them as demonstrations of the chromatic principle.

Despite this reputation of a chromatic innovator, Rore's madrigals on the whole are not particularly chromatic. Einstein prints[4] a sonnet of Petrarch, 'Per mezz' i boschi', which he curiously calls 'a direct anticipation of the Prelude to the third act of *Parsifal*';[5] it

[1] See p. 642.

[2] For biographical particulars, see p. 286. The first two books of Rore's five-part madrigals are reprinted in his *Opera Omnia* (American Institute of Musicology, 1959–   ), i, ed. Bernhard Meier, the Third Book, ibid. iii.

[3] They are both printed in full by Burney, *General History of Music*, iii, pp. 317–20. See also Kroyer, op. cit., pp. 66–72; R. von Ficker, 'Beiträge zur Chromatik des 14. bis 16. Jahrhunderts', *Studien zur Musikwissenschaft*, ii (Leipzig and Vienna, 1914), pp. 28–29; and Einstein, op. cit., i, pp. 414–15.

[4] Op. cit. iii, p. 92; from the 1562 edition of Rore's *Madrigali cromatici a cinque voci*.

[5] Ibid. i, p. 398.

is much longer than that Prelude, 155 bars, and contains hardly a single accidental. It is in the key of F and only rarely demands a B natural or an E flat. The interest of it is sustained first by the poem itself, which dictates its form, and secondly by the beauty and expressiveness of its unusually long vocal phrases. There is variety of rhythm, following the sense of the words, but no conspicuous contrasts; the madrigal is contrapuntal all the way through, with no sign of those marked alternations of counterpoint and block harmony characteristic of later madrigalists. Themes enter in imitation, but the imitation is quite loose and never more than barely indicated for a bar or two, though each voice has a very melodious part and every opportunity of enjoying the language of the poet. Rore is not much concerned with metrical form, but aims always at the most intense expression of words and ideas.

In his later years Rore is certainly chromatic in a new way; he modulates to strange keys to express gloomy and painful words, as in this passage from 'O morte, eterno fin':[1]

Ex. 12

[1] From *Il quarto libro di Madrigali a cinque voci* (Venice, 1557); reprinted in Einstein, *The Golden Age of the Madrigal* (New York, 1942), p. 13.

(Haven of blind and wretched mortals.)

In these cases he is mainly homophonic and uses the chromatic chords nearly always in root positions.

NEW TENDENCIES AFTER THE MID-CENTURY

About 1550–70 we come across a large number of minor composers —Pietro Taglia, Francesco Manara, Hettore Vidue, and many others —experimenting with chromatics, some of them perhaps noble amateurs. Modern theorists are often much puzzled by the various notations and technical terms which they employ;[1] obviously each man was trying to find his own method. It is curious that it took so many years for composers and printers to discover the practical advantage of what we now call the 'natural', a sign no less useful in music than the nought in arithmetic.

Another device which now begins to make its appearance gradually is rhythm and syncopation as a means of passionate expression, often misunderstood by modern scholars. Reacting rightly and violently against the nineteenth-century 'tyranny of the bar-line' and the habit of assuming a thump on the first beat of every bar, they were led to an odd extreme of mixing (in modern reprints) bars of three, four, five, or six crotchets helter-skelter, and even one part barred differently from another. The old composers did not print bar-lines in their separate parts, but they expected singers to count silently, or with a touch of finger and thumb, 'one two one two', and it is quite clear that they had a definite sense of syncopation, i.e. the entry of a note or sometimes a full chord a beat before it is expected, suggesting some emotional excitement. Madrigal-singers are thoroughly familiar with the syncopation always associated with 'sighing', and it is by no means confined to that one idea, either in English or in Italian. For

[1] Ficker, op. cit., pp. 15 ff. should be read as a corrective to Kroyer on chromatic notation.

modern singers regular four-beat barring is a positive help, provided
that they sing without a separate conductor and that they know the
words (whether English or Italian) thoroughly from the very first
reading, as the Italians of those days must have known their Petrarch
and Ariosto. It is this sense of conscious syncopation that gives a new
vitality to the madrigals of about 1550 onwards as contrasted with
the pedestrian monotony of Verdelot and Arcadelt. Einstein quotes[1]
various passages from madrigals by Pietro Taglia of Milan; his comment on one of them is:

Harmonically and metrically, this piece seems in a state of wild disorder,
yet there is order just the same; on the rhythmic side, too, Taglia is constantly alternating between rest and motion, yet in the end he is always
careful to even out this fluctuation.

The following extract shows a bold and original use of chromatic
harmony, but its vitality and excitement arise mainly from syncopation, intensified, as always, by the contrapuntal movement of the
parts producing syncopations that are not simultaneous:

---

[1] *The Italian Madrigal*, i, pp. 426–8. Bernhard Meier has reprinted two of Taglia's
madrigals in *Das Chorwerk*, lxxxviii (Wolfenbüttel, 1962).

(Evil oppresses me and I fear the worst.)

A lively and outspokenly amorous little madrigal by Jachet Berchem (1555) printed by Einstein in full[1] amusingly illustrates the contrast between syncopated and 'straight' declamation of the words.

THE *VILLANELLA* AND KINDRED FORMS

At this time a considerable invigoration of the madrigal by the infusion of fresh blood from popular sources is noticeable. The madrigal was no longer the music of a small group of intellectuals and experimenters; it had become an established musical form like the concerto and the sonata in later centuries through its appeal to much wider circles, especially in Venice, where music of all kinds was in constant demand. The Netherlanders still continued to be the chief providers of madrigals and the occupants of the most lucrative posts under the Venetian Republic and at the princely courts of Italy, for which they had to supply church music as well as music for entertainment; but from Willaert onwards they began more and more to enter into the appreciation of what had originally been the art of the humbler classes. Parallel with the *frottola* of north Italy there appeared the *canzone villanesca* or *villanella* at Naples, the popularity of which soon spread to the north as well. The exact dates at which collections of

[1] *The Italian Madrigal*, iii, p. 123.

these were printed is of little importance, as we may be sure that the
actual composition dates much further back; it suffices to say that
they belong to the first half of the century. (The vogue of the nearly
related *canzonetta* came later, from *c.* 1565 onward.)[1] The leading
composers of Neapolitan *villanelle* were Giovan Tommaso di Maio[2]
and Gian Domenico da Nola.[3] The *villanella* is generally in three parts
and homophonic; its main characteristic is plentiful use of consecutive triads. Scholars have speculated variously on the origin of this
most unorthodox harmony in consecutive fifths, as indeed they have
speculated on the reasons for their prohibition in serious music. The
most sensible explanation would seem to be that singing in fifths,
with or without an intermediate third, comes naturally to uneducated
singers, as may be heard sometimes in the streets of London at the
present day; it was probably forbidden simply because it was vulgar,
and its reappearance in the 'art-music' of modern composers has been
intended as a deliberate (and salutary) gibe at conventional good
taste. The same thing took place in the sixteenth century; the *villanelle*
and their analogous forms in north Italy were taken up by the serious
composers as a reaction against the pedantic orthodoxy of the
Petrarchistic madrigal. It may be suggested that the classical madrigal
eventually died of an indigestion of Petrarch and the *petrarchisti*; the
exaggerated cult of Petrarch in the sixteenth century was an out-of-
date, unnatural and constipating diet.

The popular forms, which, it is needless to say, were as keenly
enjoyed by the highly cultivated classes of society as by those from
which they sprang—we may compare the aristocratic success of *The
Beggar's Opera* in Hogarth's England—spoke the plain language of
their local dialects instead of the affected speech of the *petrarchisti*;
we might call it 'dialectical materialism'. Such a passage as this

---

[1] See Einstein, *Italian Madrigal*, ii, pp. 582 ff.

[2] Two examples are printed in ibid. iii, pp. 78–79.

[3] Two examples, ibid. pp. 80 and 86; others, with *villanesche* by other composers in
Erich Hertzmann, *Volkstümliche italienische Lieder* (*Das Chorwerk*, viii) (Wolfenbüttel,
1930).

(and like the ivy or the acanthus to the trunk)

from Marenzio's wedding madrigal 'Scendi dal Paradiso'[1] shows that
the most accomplished masters thoroughly enjoyed the effect of consecutive fifths even when they ingeniously evaded a technical breach
of rule. Similar examples can be found in Monteverdi, who also
emphasizes the fifths by the same dancing and obviously accentuated
rhythm. In the three-part *villanelle* there was no need for hypocritical
evasions. The fundamental popularity of singing in fifths can be seen
too in the collections of *laudi spirituali* right into the following century.[2]

A more vital stimulus to artistic composition was provided by the
dance-rhythms of the popular forms, for square-cut dance-rhythms
inevitably led to the emancipation of music from the tradition of the
medieval modes so reverently perpetuated by the theorists and the
church composers and so cheerfully disregarded by the practitioners
of secular music. Folksong in fifths naturally emphasized the medieval
habit of juxtaposing scales a tone apart,[3] which survives in many
British folksongs, and in popular dance-music of the sixteenth century
we can find this combined (in one and the same piece of music) with
an unmistakably clear definition of diatonic harmony.

Interesting and attractive oddities among these three-part popular
songs are the Venetian *giustiniane*, the name of which is derived from
the Venetian patrician poet Leonardo Giustiniani,[4] but which in the
period under discussion are grotesque presentations of the aged and
senile Venetian patrician in general, the type symbolized by Pantalone
of the *commedia dell'arte* with his characteristic stammer. Venetian,
too, are the *greghesche*, with words mainly by Antonio Molino

---

[1] From his fourth book of *Madrigali a cinque voci* (Venice, 1584). Printed complete
in W. Barclay Squire's *Ausgewählte Madrigale*, no. 16, Einstein's *Publikationen älterer
Musik*, vi (Leipzig, 1931), p. 12, and Lavinio Vergili's *Madrigalisti italiani*, i (Rome,
1952); recorded in *The History of Music in Sound*, iv.

[2] See Edward J. Dent, 'The *Laudi spirituali* in the XVIth and XVIIth centuries',
Proceedings of the Musical Association, xliii (1917).

[3] See W. H. Frere, 'Key-relationship in early mediaeval music', ibid., xxxvii
(1911).

[4] See Hermann Springer, 'Zu Leonardo Giustiniani und den Giustinianen', *Sammelbände der internationalen Musikgesellschaft*, xi (1909–10), p. 25.

(Manoli Blessi), merchant, poet, and composer too, in a comical mixture of Venetian, Istrian, and Greek (as then spoken); another product of both Venice and Naples was the *moresca*, caricaturing the negro slaves (generally female) imported from Africa. It is difficult to separate all these from the *mascherate* composed to be sung by people dressed up in various costumes, always in groups of three, who (as we learn from contemporary documents) appeared at banquets and other festivities to entertain the guests; they resemble the *canti carnascialeschi* of Florence in that they nearly always begin by saying 'we are' this or that and proceeding to address the spectators with the usual obscene impertinences.[1] The admission of the *villanelle* to polite society is oddly illustrated by the practice of such Netherland composers as Willaert and Lassus, who took soprano parts from Nola and set them for four voices instead of three with Nola's melody in the tenor, which completely destroys their primitive charm even when some of the consecutive fifths are retained:[2]

---

[1] Einstein prints a copious and linguistically fascinating anthology of *villotte, moresche,* and so on, *Italian Madrigal*, iii, pp. 78–91.   [2] Ibid., pp. 86 and 88.

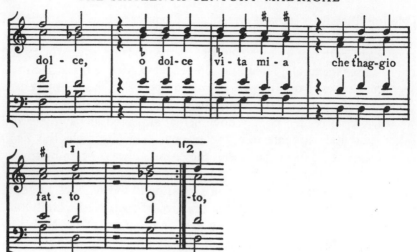

(O my sweet life that has brought you to me)

THE TRANSALPINE MADRIGAL

In the last quarter of the century the Italian madrigal became widely popular beyond the Alps. It was much cultivated at the court of Bavaria and by the wealthy Fugger family at Augsburg; Italian madrigals were printed at Lyons and Paris and above all at Antwerp and Louvain by the publisher Pierre Phalèse from 1574 onwards. Madrigals had reached England some years earlier. The ambiguously titled *Musica Transalpina* was published by Nicholas Yonge in 1588, but this was a collection of Italian madrigals translated into English.

The two great Netherlanders of this period, Roland de Lassus[1] and Philippe de Monte, came to Italy in their youth and attained their musical maturity there, but most of their later life was spent in the service of German princes—Lassus at Munich, de Monte at Prague and Vienna. Lassus's life is a distressing story. He was taken to Naples at the age of sixteen and became choirmaster at the Lateran in Rome soon after he was twenty; he was called back to Antwerp almost immediately, visited England, and in 1556 entered the choir of Duke Albrecht V at Munich, where he remained until his death in 1594. He paid several visits to Italy during these years, and seems always to have regarded Italy as his spiritual home, but although his first publication (Antwerp, 1555) included lively *villanesche* as well as madrigals, French *chansons*, and Latin motets, the last of which is 'Alma Nemes' followed by its model Rore's 'Calami sonum

[1] As a supplement to Einstein's study of Lassus's madrigals, op. cit. ii, p. 477, consult Wolfgang Boetticher, 'Über einige neue Werke aus Orlando di Lassos mittlerer Madrigal- und Motettkomposition (1567–1569)', *Archiv für Musikwissenschaft*, xxii (1965), p. 12.

ferentes', he came under the gloomy influences of the Counter-Reformation and ultimately under those of the Jesuits in Munich, and his last years were overclouded by an ever-deepening melancholia. His last work, published after his death at Munich was the *Lagrime di San Pietro*, a cycle of twenty *madrigali spirituali*[1] by Luigi Tansillo, a poet who had followed the same path from exuberant lasciviousness to morbid religiosity. Lassus's favourite poet throughout his career was Petrarch, and Petrarch led very naturally to the *madrigali spirituali* of the religious *petrarchisti* such as Gabriele Fiamma, a canon at the Lateran. He ignored the pastoral poets of the new generation, such as Tasso and Guarini, but his court duties obliged him to write a certain number of ceremonial madrigals for weddings and state occasions, and as late as 1581 he published (with an apologetic preface) a collection of *villanelle, moresche*, and other items which was printed in Paris. This set contains two very well-known and still popular pieces, 'Matona mia cara' and 'O la che bon echo'. A curious episode took place in 1568 when on the occasion of the marriage of Albrecht's son, Duke Wilhelm, it was suddenly decided during the festivities to improvise an amateur *commedia dell'arte* performance in which Lassus took the part of Pantalone; Massimo Trojano's description of it in his *Discorsi* is actually the first definite record of any such play, although it was given outside Italy and by amateurs, not by the professional comedians from whom the *commedia* took its name (*arte* meaning the trade guild of actors).

As compared with Rore, Lassus is much more concise and energetic. He prefers short motives for imitative treatment rather than long melodies; beauty of melody such as we find in Marenzio and others is indeed conspicuous by its absence. He is keenly concerned to express the sense of the words, yet at the same time often awkward in the declamation of them; he possesses all the Netherland skill in counterpoint, but for expression he tends to rely more on harmony and is a much more 'vertical-minded' composer than most of his contemporaries. At the same time he shows no sense of tonal harmony and prefers the modal system; he understands chromaticism but makes very little use of it. His most attractive pieces are his *villanelle* and *moresche*; he had an abundant sense of humour which was liable to break through in his copious correspondence even at a time when his *melancholia hypochondriaca*, as his friend Dr. Mersmann called it, led him into penitence and pessimism.

[1] Reprinted by H. J. Therstappen, *Das Chorwerk*, xxxiv, xxxvii, and xli (Wolfenbüttel, 1935–6).

De Monte was ten years older than Lassus and lived ten years longer; the first half of his productive life was spent in various Italian cities, the second at Vienna and Prague. The mere fact that he wrote well over a thousand madrigals makes him the representative composer of his age[1] and that perhaps more for the outside world than for Italy. His music is accomplished, well-mannered, and agreeable—the typical conventional classical madrigal; it often has great melodic charm but more good taste than originality or intensity of feeling. He was particularly successful with the *madrigale spirituale*,[2] a typical product of the Counter-Reformation, approximating to the motet, but always remaining a madrigal in style because it is set to Italian poetry and not to Latin prose; it was in fact a derivation from Petrarch and his *Rime in morte di Madonna Laura*. A typical example is the third madrigal from the first six-part book:

Ex. 16

---

[1] See Einstein, *The Italian Madrigal*, ii, pp. 498 ff.

[2] See P. Nuten, *De 'Madrigali Spirituali' van Filip de Monte (1521–1603)* (Brussels, 1958) with appended re-editions of the first book of *Madrigali Spirituali a cinque voci* (Venice, 1581) and the second book *a sei & sette voci* (Venice, 1589). The *Primo Libro de madrigali spirituali a sei voci* (Venice, 1583), has been reprinted by Georges Van Doorslaer (Bruges, 1928).

(Pure virgin, may you enjoy eternal day from the warm rays of the true sun)

De Monte's later books of madrigals were not reprinted and he himself began to realize that he was being left behind. At the age of sixty-five he made a final effort to rejuvenate his style in a collection dedicated to Count Mario Bevilacqua,[1] the famous and enthusiastic patron of music at Verona, and turned from Petrarch and Bembo to the elegant and voluptuous pastorals of Tasso and Guarini.

The transition to the new style is still more apparent in Giaches de Wert, another Netherlander associated with Mantua and Ferrara. He is admirably represented by 'Chi salirà per me', to a stanza of Ariosto:[2]

[1] *L'undecimo Libro delli Madrigali à cinque voci* (Venice, 1586).
[2] From *Il Primo Libro de Madrigali a quattro voci* (Venice, 1562); reprinted in Barclay Squire's *Ausgewählte Madrigale*, no. 19.

(Who will ascend for me into heaven, my lady, to bring back my lost wits?)

and by 'Io non son però morto';[1] both of them exhibit a gaiety and charm of melody seldom achieved by the earlier Netherlanders.

PALESTRINA AND THE MADRIGAL

Palestrina, as a composer of madrigals, is of very minor importance. He is always conservative in outlook; his early madrigals, mostly settings of Petrarch and his imitators, are mainly homophonic, declaiming the words with great care, but with no feeling either for melody or for musical expression. He is scrupulous in the accuracy of his imitative counterpoint, monotonously conjunct in melodic motion with an unfailing sense for beauty of mere vocal sound. In the dedications of his motets he twice repudiates his madrigals,

[1] From *L'Ottavo Libro de Madrigali a cinque voci* (Venice, 1586); reprinted in Einstein, *Italian Madrigal*, iii, p. 301. Wert's first five books of five-part madrigals are reprinted in his *Opera Omnia* (American Institute of Musicology, 1961–), i–v, ed. Carol MacClintock.

saying that he regrets them and blushes for them, though as a matter of fact his amorous madrigals have very innocent words—'*unschuldige Mondschein-Poesie*', as his devout editor Haberl calls it. Einstein frankly accuses him of hypocrisy. In 1584 he published his motets on the Song of Solomon with the penitential dedication to Pope Gregory XIII; Gregory died in April 1585 and in 1586 Palestrina brought out another collection of madrigals. In 1592 he contributed to *Il Trionfo di Dori*, a collection of madrigals by various hands which was the prototype of the English *Triumphs of Oriana*. As one might expect, his ceremonial madrigals,[1] in which he exploits his masterly skill in handling large masses in plain chords and extended sonorities, are his best works in the secular style. He naturally cultivated the *madrigale spirituale*.[2]

FIN DE SIÈCLE TENDENCIES

During the last quarter of the century the output of madrigals, including minor forms, such as the *balletti* of the Mantuan composer Gastoldi,[3] becomes enormous, especially in Venice, where music was always in demand both for the academies of connoisseurs and for festivities of every kind. The composers were now all of them Italians; the Netherlanders gradually died out and were not replaced by a younger generation. As a result the madrigal music of this period (which some scholars have called the decadence of the madrigal) acquires a new freedom of technique and expression; both poets and musicians show a new sensibility and variety of styles associated with a much more subtle and intimate understanding, on the part of the composers, for all aspects of the Italian language. In the first half of the century we see Netherlanders setting poems mostly of a serious cast to the order of courtly patrons; in the second the social circle has been greatly widened, and the musician has become so important a personage that poetry is now written for the express purpose of

[1] A variety cultivated with outstanding success by the Venetians, notably Andrea and Giovanni Gabrieli: for instance, such magnificent double-choral pieces as Andrea's 'A le guancie di rose' and his nephew's 'Lieto godea', both originally published by Gardano in a volume of *Concerti* (Venice, 1587) and both reprinted by Torchi, *L'arte musicale in Italia*, ii (Milan, 1897), pp. 129 and 193.

[2] His two books of five-part spiritual madrigals (Venice, 1581, and Rome, 1594) have been reprinted by Franz Xaver Haberl, *P. da Palestrina's Werke*, xxix (Leipzig, 1883) and R. Casimiri, *G. P. da Palestrina: Le opere complete*, ix and xxii (Rome, 1940 and 1957).

[3] *Balletti a cinque voci, con li suoi versi per cantare sonare et ballare* (Venice, 1591). Examples reprinted in Einstein, *Italian Madrigal*, iii, p. 246; Einstein, *A Short History of Music* (5th ed., with music), (London, 1948), p. 243; Johannes Wolf, *Music of Earlier Times* (New York, 1946), p. 105; Davison and Apel, *Historical Anthology of Music*, i (Cambridge, Mass., and London, 1947), p. 179. Some of Gastoldi's three-part *balletti* have been reprinted by W. Herrmann (Berlin, 1927).

musical setting. Music has become the predominant partner, but it still follows both the form and the sense of the words with ever more elaborate intensity and subtlety of interpretation; the poetry may sink to triviality and commonplace, but it is always respected. There is a great variety of poetic forms, but a general tendency to assimilation in musical style; rhythmical figures from the more frivolous types find their way into serious madrigals, and sentimental phrases into the *villanelle* and *canzonette*. Music thus acquires a huge vocabulary of conventional clichés, and poetry does the same, but we find exactly the same situation in the days of Handel, Mozart, Cherubini, and Beethoven, who all operate with conventional material and yet create works of supreme greatness.

We are indebted to Einstein[1] for pointing out a new factor in musical style at this date which was to lead eventually to important developments in the following century after the true madrigal had practically ceased to exist. At the court of Ferrara there were three ladies whose vocal accomplishment was equalled only by their personal beauty and their accomplishment in the arts of love, Tarquinia Molza, Laura Peperara, and Lucrezia Bendidio,[2] for whom several composers wrote madrigals in which the three sopranos could show off their virtuosity to the accompaniment of two or more lower voices which sang quite subordinate parts. Luzzasco Luzzaschi went even further and wrote duets and trios for them[3] which he caused to be engraved, not type-set, with a fully written-out accompaniment for the harpsichord. These look forward at once to the duet-cantatas of Alessandro Scarlatti and Handel, and many of the duet-cantatas of the seventeenth century are actually entitled *madrigali*. The three ladies named were probably not the only ones who could sing such music, for we find vocal virtuosity, especially in soprano parts, anticipated in many madrigals of this period.

LUCA MARENZIO

The outstanding master of the madrigal is Luca Marenzio (1553–99), perhaps the greatest Italian composer of the century,[4] and indeed the greatest in Europe with the possible exception of William Byrd. He possesses all the techniques, contrapuntal, rhythmical, and

---

[1] *Italian Madrigal*, ii, p. 825.   [2] See p. 144.

[3] *Madrigali . . . per cantare et sonare a uno, e doi, e tre soprani* (Rome, 1601). See pp. 144–6 and Kinkeldey's study in *Sammelbände der internationalen Musikgesellschaft*, ix (1908), pp. 144–6. A complete example is reprinted in Schering, *Geschichte der Musik in Beispielen* (Leipzig, 1931), p. 176; for an excerpt from it see Ex. 52.

[4] On Marenzio generally, see Hans Engel, *Luca Marenzio* (Florence, 1956) and Denis Arnold, *Marenzio* (London, 1965).

chromatic, and knows exactly how to use them; there is nothing tentative or experimental about his work. His most immediate attraction lies in his invention of melody arising from his recognition of the complete major scale and the interval of the octave which is a frequent feature, as at the beginning of the wedding madrigal 'Scendi dal Paradiso', mentioned on p. 54.

Another characteristic is his variety of rhythm, ranging in the course of a single madrigal from semibreves to semiquavers. His melodic line is sometimes curiously instrumental especially in his bass parts, and we see that although he is always scrupulously attentive to the sense and rhythm of words he gradually comes more and more to regard a madrigal as a purely musical composition, no longer subservient to a poetic form. In this passage from 'Il vago e bello Armillo'[1]

(and said: O blessed waves that mirror so much glorious beauty . . .)

[1] From *Il Nono libro de madrigali a 5 voci* (Venice, 1599); reprinted Torchi, op. cit., ii, p. 215.

note how ingeniously the burst of emotion (Armillo is standing on
a high rock contemplating the sea) is obtained by the delayed and
syncopated entry of all five voices in harmony, with a high A at the
top—a note used only once before to suggest the 'cima' (top) of the
rock—then by the clear declamation of 'beate' and the picture of
the sea with its almost Handelian waves, alternating again as the
passage settles down to the entry of the next musical motive.

How syncopated rhythm combined with quickly rising fifths and
octaves can contribute to intensify emotion may be seen in 'Giunto
alla tomba'[1] (Tancredi at the tomb of Clorinda, from Tasso's
Gerusalemme Liberata):

Ex. 19

(Take these kisses)

As an example of Marenzio's chromatic entanglements we may
take this from 'O voi che sospirate':[2]

Ex. 20

(Change once that old style of yours)

[1] From *Il Quarto Libro de Madrigali a cinque voci* (Venice, 1584).
[2] From *Il Secondo Libro de Madrigali a cinque voci* (Venice, 1581).

which in modern notation is perfectly simple:

Ex. 21

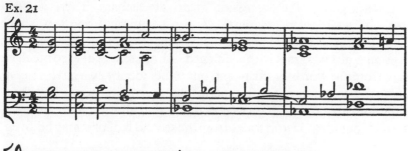

The consummate art of Marenzio is best seen in 'Solo e pensoso' (1599), a complete sonnet of Petrarch.[1] It falls into two parts, the quatrains beginning in G and ending in D, the tercets beginning on A and ending in G again. The soprano leads off with a chromatic scale of semibreves from G to high A and down again to D against imitations of a descending triad in crotchets; the harmony is really quite simple and logical. When the soprano descends, the harmony is in semibreves too. Philip Heseltine[2] rightly praises 'the magnificent shape and structure of the whole passage which illustrates with such perfection the spirit of the words which inspired it':

> Solo e pensoso i più deserti campi
> Vò misurando a passi tardi e lenti.
> (Alone and thoughtful, I pace the empty fields with slow and loitering steps.)

Marenzio's madrigals, like those of every other Italian composer except perhaps the few amateurs, were all written to order, whether ceremonial or not. Even the most advanced and elaborate ones such as 'Solo e pensoso' were written for private academies like that of Count Bevilacqua at Verona, where *musica reservata* was understood and appreciated. Scholars have made many attempts to define this curious technical term, but Einstein makes it clear that it signified simply 'music for connoisseurs'.[3] Composers may have had their

[1] From *Il Nono libro de madrigali a 5 voci* (Venice, 1599); reprinted in Torchi, op. cit., p. 228, in Virgili, op. cit. i, p. 20, and in Schering, op. cit., p. 174.
[2] Cecil Gray and Philip Heseltine, *Carlo Gesualdo, Musician and Murderer* (London, 1926), p. 115.
[3] *Italian Madrigal*, i, p. 228; but see also *infra*, p. 348, n. 3.

personal preferences for certain poets, but we have no right to regard
their madrigals as the expression of private feelings. There is, however, one madrigal of Marenzio, and a ceremonial one too, which
seems to hint at a more personal emotion, 'Filli, l'acerbo caso',[1] an
elegy on a girl who met with a violent death at a tender age; so much we
learn from the words of the poem, but to her identity we have no clue,
nor to the occasion of the first performance, which cannot have been
in the course of a church service as there is no allusion in the poem to
any religious idea. Two extracts from the second half of it may be given:

Ex. 22

[1] From the *Libro quarto de madrigali a cinque voci* (Venice, 1584).

(i) (Thou, dying innocent . . .)
(ii) (Nor did thy death extinguish all its glory)

Note in (i) the choking sob of the rest after 'Tu' and the beautiful long line of the soprano to the half-close, imitated in all the voices, and in (ii) the treatment of the words 'ogni sua gloria estinse'. The madrigal would have been sung by male voices with a falsetto alto for the *canto* or soprano. A Netherlander would have brought the elegy to a quasi-religious end with an elaborated plagal cadence in full harmony. Marenzio knows that for such griefs there are no consolations; the mourners just go away without formality and the music is 'extinguished'.

GESUALDO DA VENOSA

The private life of Carlo Gesualdo, Prince of Venosa (1560 ?–1615) does not concern us; his madrigals[1] are enough to tell us that he was a man of violent passions and it is obvious that he composed for his own pleasure, and presumably for the expression of his own private emotions. His technique is based on that of Marenzio and Luzzaschi. He cannot be called an inventor or a pioneer; he does no more than push to extremes devices that are already available as part of the common stock. We notice them with more of a shock because he prefers

[1] See Ferdinand Keiner, *Die Madrigale Gesualdos von Venosa* (Leipzig, 1914) and Einstein, *Italian Madrigal*, ii, pp. 688 ff. The six books of five-part madrigals have been republished by Francesco Vatielli and Annibale Bizzelli (Rome, 1942–58); there are a number of separate modern reprints. A complete edition of Gesualdo by Wilhelm Weismann and Glenn Watkins is in progress (Hamburg, 1957–   ).

short poems and a compressed treatment of them instead of spreading
his music over the length of a Petrarch sonnet. The originality of
Gesualdo lies in his rhythms, not in his harmony. His discords are due
sometimes to mere clumsiness of part-writing, more often to double
suspensions and to the expressive value of chromatic intervals which
in contrapuntal movement lead to the augmented triad, e.g. G B D
sharp, already frequent in Rore and Lassus. A short example from his
Libro VI (Genoa, 1611) will show some of his characteristics.

Ex. 23

(Cease to vex me, cruel and false thought)

Gesualdo often begins an entry with a syncopation as if choking
with rage against frustration. The chromatic chord on the second
syllable of 'noia' is the inevitable common chord harmonization of
the rising semitone of the melody, but also intensifies its 'annoyance'.
This rising semitone was a characteristic of French singing too, sometimes called *plainte*, but indicated at most by a sign, as an ornament;[1]
we can find it in Verdi's *Falstaff*, too, though sometimes exceeding
a semitone. In several of Gesualdo's madrigals these passages of close
harmony and strange chords are alternated with sudden bursts of
quick contrapuntal writing. Marenzio works on the same principle of
alternating harmony and counterpoint, but the one glides gently into
the other and the alternations are spread over long continuous movement. Gesualdo's themes are short, chopped up by rests, and he
makes his contrasts as violent as possible; his passion pours itself out

[1] Théodore Gérold, *L'Art du chant en France au XVIIe siècle* (Strasbourg, 1921).

in torrents of semiquavers and even of demisemiquavers which require very accomplished singers to execute them.

Gesualdo is a pathological case—the first Romantic. Along with Claudio Monteverdi he marks the end of the madrigal as a standard form, though madrigals continued to be written down to the days of Alessandro Scarlatti and Lotti. Who sang them and where we do not know; perhaps they were composed as academic exercises. We may note that G. B. Martini in his *Saggio di contrappunto* (Bologna, 1774–6) analyses madrigals of various composers with evident admiration, but treats them exclusively as studies in counterpoint and fugue.

MONTEVERDI

Monteverdi[1] hardly belongs to the sixteenth century at all; he was violently attacked in 1600 by Artusi[2] for his improper use of dissonance in 'Anima mia, perdona' and 'Che se tu se'il cor mio', later published in his *IV Libro dei Madrigali* (Venice, 1603) and 'Cruda Amarilli' and 'O Mirtillo' (later printed in the Fifth Book, 1605); one of the passages to which Artusi took exception was the end of 'Anima mia':

Ex. 24

(of thy own sorrow.)

Monteverdi's early madrigals[3] follow the example of Marenzio; with Gesualdo he seems to have had no contact. What is notable in these is not so much the free treatment of dissonance which shocked Artusi, but a further development of certain expressive devices already anticipated by Marenzio and Giaches de Wert. Verdelot and Arcadelt had

---

[1] This section, left unfinished by Professor Dent, has been completed by the Editor.

[2] *L'Artusi, ovvero delle Imperfettioni della musica moderna* (Venice, 1600; 2nd part, 1603). The relevant chapter is translated in full in Oliver Strunk, *Source Readings in Music History* (London, 1952), pp. 393–404, where it is followed by a translation of Monteverdi's reply—in the form of a 'declaration' by his brother, appended to the *Scherzi musicali* (Venice, 1607).

[3] His first four books were published in 1587, 1590, 1592, and 1603 respectively.

never expected professional singers, least of all professional female singers; anyone would suffice who could read their notes in time and in tune. The ladies of Ferrara, as we can see from the madrigals written for them, were not solely *coloratura* singers, as we should now call them; they knew how to make music sound passionate. Wert in his 'Cruda Amarilli'[1] made them leap up a tenth to a high note to illustrate 'i monti'; Monteverdi frequently gives his voices exclamatory themes in which we foresee the style of the opera, as in the opening of 'Vattene pur crudel' from the Third Book:

Ex. 25

(Go then, cruel one, with such peace [of mind] as you leave me)

Another favourite device is the recitation of a phrase on one note, sometimes in one voice, sometimes in imitation and also chordally, like the intoning of a psalm, as in the famous opening of 'Sfogava con le stelle' in the Fourth Book:

[1] From his *L'Undecimo Libro* (Venice, 1595).

Ex. 26

(The lover in his agony cried out to the stars, under the night sky, telling of his sorrow)

In all these devices Monteverdi is guided by the principle stated in his brother's *Dichiaratione*: that in what he calls the 'Second Practice, or Perfection of modern music', initiated by Rore and followed by Gesualdo, Cavalieri, Ingegneri, Marenzio, Wert, Luzzaschi, Peri, Caccini, and others whom he names, 'the words are the mistress of the harmony'—as opposed to the *prima prattica* of the Netherlanders, 'finally perfected by Messer Adriano [Willaert] with actual composition and by the most excellent Zarlino with most judicious rules', in which music is 'not the servant but the mistress of the words'.

Besides boldly dissonant harmony and declamatory vocal writing, other significant tendencies are perceptible in the Fourth Book. One may not agree with Prunières[1] that whereas 'the most revolutionary madrigals of Gesualdo or Marenzio are written for voices, it seems that from the Fourth Book onward Monteverdi composed for strings. . . . Such madrigals as "Sfogava con le stelle" or "A un giro sol" suggest fantasias for viols such as Giovanni Gabrieli might have written rather than madrigals to be sung by human voices'; yet there are many passages whose intonation is very difficult without instrumental support.[2] 'A un giro sol' opens with duetting upper parts and a purely harmonic bass, and is quite instrumental in feeling:

[1] *Monteverdi* (Paris, 1924), p. 34.
[2] When in 1615 Phalèse republished the Third and Fourth Books at Antwerp, he provided them with *basso continuo* parts.

Ex. 27

(At a single turn of those radiant eyes, the air around smiles)

The five parts are no longer equally important; the highest part, or two highest parts, tends to be more important, the bass to become a harmonic support.

In his Fifth Book (Venice, 1605), prefaced by a brief, provisional reply to Artusi, Monteverdi took the decisive step of issuing it '*col basso continuo per il Clavicembano, Chitarrone, od altro simile istrumento; fatto particolarmente per li sei ultimi et per li altri a beneplacito*' (with thorough-bass for the harpsichord, *chitarrone* or other similar instrument, made particularly for the last six pieces and *ad libitum* for the others). The *basso continuo* had already appeared in other fields of composition[1] and even in the madrigal proper Monteverdi had been anticipated by Salomone Rossi in his *II. libro de Madrigali a 5 voci . . . con il Basso continuo per sonare in Concerto* (Venice, 1602), to say nothing of Luzzaschi's already mentioned *Madrigali per cantare et sonare* with written-out keyboard accompaniments.[2] Of the six pieces with obbligato *continuo*, the most striking pointers to the future are 'Ahi come a un vago sol' and 'Questi vaghi concenti': the first essentially a duet for tenor and *quinto*, with the line 'Ah che piaga d'amor non sana mai' set as a refrain and all five voices used together only at the end, the second with nine voices treated as antiphonal choirs in canon and introduced and interrupted by nine-part instrumental *symphoniae*, all very much in the style of Giovanni Gabrieli.

Four more *libri de madrigali* by Monteverdi were published in 1614, 1619, 1638, and 1651, the last posthumously, as well as the two volumes of *Scherzi musicali* (1607 and 1632). He did not at once forsake the polyphonic madrigal; the Sixth Book, for instance, contains the celebrated five-part version (1610) of the monodic 'Lamento d'Arianna' (1608); but the true madrigals are exceptions among the '*altri generi de canti*'. And these are essentially monodies, chamber duets, *madrigali concertati*, often constructed on ostinato basses, often with obbligato instrumental parts; they have nothing in common with the classical madrigal.

THE MADRIGAL COMEDY

One other type of Italian madrigal flourished towards the end of the century, for the most part humorous and sometimes composed in sets, which some scholars have classified as 'dramatic', regarding

[1] See pp. 149 ff. and 574.
[2] See p. 62.

them as precursors of comic opera. But we may be quite sure that not one of them was written for the stage. The most notable ancestor of these is Janequin with his numerous descriptive *chansons*.[1] Another is the *caccia* of the *trecento*;[2] its music had been long forgotten, but the poems had been printed and were available to later composers. There are numerous madrigals describing battles, generally for eight or more voices, which may have been sung in *intermedii* or in connexion with tournaments at court festivities.[3]

In 1567 Alessandro Striggio[4] published 'Il cicalamento delle donne al bucato',[5] a composition for seven voices in a prologue and four scenes representing the chatter of women at the wash. First the poet describes how he came upon them; they begin with greetings and talk about their lovers and their mistresses. A kite swoops down and carries off a chicken while the women shriek at it; one of them tells about a ghost she saw, while the others laugh at her. Another is accused of stealing a handkerchief; there ensues a quarrel; finally some of the women induce them to make peace and sing a popular song, after which they all go home. The music is vivacious and realistic and the interwoven popular songs have great charm, but the counterpoint is so complicated that it makes little effect as a musical whole; it is music for the enjoyment of singers rather than for listeners. The same can be said of Striggio's 'La Caccia' (published with the 'Cicalamento') and his 'Gioco di Primiera'.[6] *Primiera* was a fashionable card game and the singers go through it in detail; the same happens in Giovanni Croce's 'Gioco dell' Oca', The 'goose game' is probably the original of all games of the 'race game' type played with dice on a map of the course; it is still a favourite with Italian children. We can deduce practically all the rules of it from Croce's madrigal, which is included in his *Triaca musicale* (Venice, 1595).[7] Another collection of Croce's is his *Mascarate piacevole et ridicolose per il carnevale* (Venice, 1590); it is difficult to separ-

---

[1] See p. 6.

[2] See Vol. III, pp. 61 ff.

[3] The fine example in eight parts by Andrea Gabrieli is printed in Benvenuti, *Istituzioni e monumenti dell'arte musicale italiana*, i (Milan, 1931), p. 203, and (second part only) in Torchi, *L'arte musicale*, ii, p. 139. A list of Italian vocal *battaglie* is given in Rudolf Gläsel, *Zur Geschichte der Battaglia* (Diss. Leipzig, 1931), pp. 91–94.

[4] Alessandro Striggio the elder, composer, must be distinguished from his son Alessandro Striggio the younger, poet and author of the *Orfeo* set to music by Monteverdi.

[5] Reprinted by Solerti in *Rivista musicale italiana*, xii (1905) pp. 822–38 and xiii (1906), pp. 91–112 and 244–57; practical editions by Perinello (Milan, 1940) and Somma (Rome, 1947).

[6] Published 1569; reprinted in Einstein, *Italian Madrigal*, iii, no. 86.

[7] Reprinted by Schinelli (Rome, 1942), the 'Gioco dell' Oca' separately by Torchi, op. cit. ii, p. 245.

ate the *mascherate* from the many other types of music written for private entertainment. But we can easily distinguish between these and the court music; the *intermedii* were meant for spectators and listeners, the others primarily for musical parties at home. The *Festino della sera del giovedi grasso* of Adriano Banchieri (Venice, 1608)[1] gives us a good idea of them; we can imagine the guests arriving to be received by a *compère* with a long humorous discourse (spoken); there follows a whole evening of singing, with perhaps other friends to listen too. Perhaps some of the singers dressed up for the various parts that they represented; but it would all have been more or less impromptu and informal, and Banchieri leaves us in no doubt that there was plenty to eat and drink. The music of all Banchieri's publications (see pp. 80–81) is dull and trivial to a modern reader; the humour turns very largely on dialects and the imitation of characters from other countries and provinces—we have to put ourselves in the mood for it, feel that we belong to Bologna, that we are welcome guests and enjoy meeting friends and singing with them; one thing we may be sure of— Bologna is a great place for food and wine.

VECCHI'S *AMFIPARNASO*

By far the most original work of this type is the *Amfiparnaso* of Orazio Vecchi (Venice, 1597).[2] Lassus's last book of *villanelle* (1581) included an eight-part dialogue between Pantalone and his servant Zanni, and we remember that in 1568 Lassus had himself played the part of Pantalone in an impromptu comedy of masks at the Bavarian court; but although this madrigal was probably written long before the performance, it cannot possibly have been a quasi-operatic part of it on this occasion. It is quite possible, however, that this madrigal was known to Vecchi; but what was certainly Vecchi's own and completely new idea was to set a whole comedy of masks to music in a series of fourteen madrigals. It has been generally assumed that Vecchi wrote the words himself; but he seems to have discussed it previously with Giulio Cesare Croce, the Bolognese comic poet, and their correspondence (in verse) at any rate hints at a collaboration.[3]

It is really not a matter of much importance whether Vecchi wrote the words of the *Amfiparnaso* himself or with the help of Croce. Much of the text can be traced to Croce's innumerable little

[1] Reprinted by Somma (Rome, 1939).
[2] Carlo Perinello's edition, 2 vols. (Milan, 1938), gives a facsimile of the original edition as well as a transcription. There are a number of other modern editions.
[3] E. J. Dent, 'Notes on the *Amfiparnaso* of Orazio Vecchi', *Sammelbände der internationalen Musikgesellschaft*, xii (1911), p. 330.

chapbooks, and probably these are hardly more than transcripts of
the common stock of stereotyped backchat talked by the itinerant entertainers of the *commedia dell'arte*. The *Amfiparnaso* was preceded
by the *Selva di varia ricreazione* (Venice, 1590), a miscellany of
humorous madrigals for from three to ten voices which includes a
capriccio (five voices) that is clearly a preliminary study for the *Amfiparnaso*, Pantalone knocking 'tich toch' at the door answered by
Zanni who is in the kitchen. The *Amfiparnaso*, which Vecchi calls
comedia harmonica, is in three acts, preceded by a prologue in which
he tells us quite plainly that his 'comedy' is for the ears alone and not
for the eyes—that is the novelty of it. The characters are the familiar
masks, Pantalone, the Doctor, three *zanni* (comic servants), the
Spanish Captain Cardon, the conventional lovers Lelio and Nisa,
Lucio and Isabella, with the courtesan Hortensia; there is also a
chorus of Jews. (The Jews, numerous and long established in north
Italy—at Mantua there was a Jewish University, the students of which
sometimes acted plays before the court—are frequently made fun of in
Croce's chapbooks.)

The text of the *Amfiparnaso* is actually the first existing text, and
possibly the only one, of a complete *commedia dell'arte* play; but it
seems to have been ignored altogether by the historians of the Italian
theatre. The characters speak their appropriate languages, Venetian,
Bolognese, Bergamask, Spanish, and mock-Hebrew; the lovers solilo-
quize or converse in literary Italian. The musical technique throughout is that of the dialogue madrigal, the *quinto*, as always, having to
do duty for both sexes, and the soprano and alto singing for males as
well as for females if required.

The opening scene gives a good idea of the style:

Ex. 28 PANTALONE

(T.) O Pie-ru - lin, dov' es - tu? dov' es - tu, Pie-ru -

- lin, Pie-ru-lin, Pie-ru-lin? (Q.) Me - sir, no poss ve - gnì ch'a su'n cu -

PANT.: Pierulin, where are you?
PED.: I can't come, sir. I'm in the kitchen.
PANT.: Thief! Dog! What are you doing in the kitchen?
PED.: I'm stuffing myself with such as used to sing *pipiripi cucurucu.*

We note at once the melodic interest as well as the natural vigour of the first entry, as Pantalone shouts to his servant Pedrolino, who is in the kitchen, stuffing himself, needless to say, with all the food he can find—in this case, chickens and pigeons. The *zanni* are always great eaters. How lively and full-blooded it is compared with the anaemic recitation of Peri's *Euridice*! The intonations of the dialects, especially the stuttering Venetian of Pantalone and the curt pomposity of the Doctor's Bolognese are very cleverly brought out. Noises on or off the imaginary stage have all to be made by the singers; when Francatrippa knocks at the Jews' door he sings 'tich tach toch, tiche tache toch' and rattles away most realistically. When Hortensia empties her slops on Pantalone's head, we hear them fall 'plop plop plop' (*flo flo flo*). The chorus of Jews, who refuse to let Francatrippa pawn a diamond because it is the sabbath day, are heard singing within while he knocks; it is supposed to be a synagogue service, but their 'Hebrew' is pure gibberish. Its counterpoint is very complicated and one Italian critic has suggested that Vecchi was here satirizing the Catholic polyphony of his own time.[1]

In another scene Pantalone asks the Doctor to sing a serenade to his daughter, whom the Doctor is to marry. The Doctor sings a very well-known madrigal by Cipriano de Rore, 'Ancor che col partire', but he makes complete nonsense of the words which Vecchi's singers and audience would no doubt have known by heart. This is in four parts, and Rore's soprano is reproduced exactly, apart from negligible variants,[2] but the three lower parts are quite different. It is obvious from the distorted words that Vecchi must have intended some sort of a joke here, but the musical joke is obscure, and it is odd that no learned scholar has attempted to elucidate it.[3] The frequent syncopations and the little scale-passages in quavers here and there might perhaps suggest that Vecchi meant to caricature a rather incompetent lutenist improvising the accompaniment of a *frottola*.

The *Amfiparnaso* as a complete work of art stands unique in the history of music. We can trace its ancestors and its descendants, but the former are primitive and tentative, the latter mere imitations, mostly trivial and puerile. It is absurd to call it a precursor of comic opera and link it up with Mozart and Rossini; there is no continuous line to join them. It is impossible to classify it, except in Einstein's very comprehensive category of 'music in company'. Although no more than a series of sketches, as the composer himself said, it is a beautifully balanced whole, ending with the ensemble which brings all the characters together (except Hortensia) to present wedding gifts in turn to Isabella. Nisa brings her a little dog, 'to keep her

---

[1] Gino Roncaglia in *Orazio Vecchi, Contributi nel 4° centenario* (Modena, 1950).

[2] Rore's madrigal is printed in Einstein, *Italian Madrigal*, iii, p. 112.

[3] But cf. Ferand, '"Ancor che col partire": Die Schicksale eines berühmten Madrigals', *Festschrift Karl Gustav Fellerer* (Ratisbon, 1962), p. 137.

faithful to Lucio'—perhaps with a sly innuendo, for we learn from other sources that a dog was a favourite wedding present:

Che ai ladri abbaia ed a gli amanti tace.
(He'll bark at thieves and shut his mouth at lovers.)

Ridiculous as all the offerings are, she acknowledges each in the same incomparably gracious phrase:

(I thank you, sir)

(Great hand-clapping, cries of praise)

Pantalone says briskly 'Entriam hor tutti in casa' (let us all go in now to the wedding breakfast); the company turns to its imaginary audience of 'courteous and illustrious spectators' to express the hope that they have enjoyed the play and to ask for the applause which they themselves have to sing (see Ex. 30 on previous page.

The epilogue and applause balance the introductory prologue and bring the entertainment to a brilliant and well-planned conclusion. But the audience, even if present, is negligible; if we are to understand and enjoy the *Amfiparnaso* we must sing in it ourselves.

BANCHIERI AND GUASPARRI TORELLI

Adriano Banchieri's *Festino* has been described above; his *La Pazzia senile* (Venice, 1598)[1] is a direct imitation of the *Amfiparnaso*, but for three voices only, two tenors and bass; the tenors have to sing soprano in falsetto when they represent women. It is all very slight and unpretentious, but certainly shows plenty of direct and unsubtle humour. Banchieri, like Vecchi, gives us a serenade, parodying in this case Palestrina's early madrigal 'Vestiva i colli'; it is interesting to see that even at this date it was still evidently a popular old favourite. Banchieri frames it in imitations of lute accompaniment, like the *don don don diri diri don* of Lassus's drunken German's serenade 'Matona mia cara'. Imitations of musical instruments of all kinds, as well as of birds and animals, were a favourite feature of all the 'music in company'. Banchieri also includes *intermedii* of street cries, which are quite amusing to sing.

Guasparri Torelli (1600) produced another imitation, *I Fidi amanti,*[2] for four voices. The story is a pastoral, feebly imitated from *Aminta* and *Il Pastor Fido*, with *intermedii* for the Magnifico (Pantalone) and the Doctor and a Nymph who is something like Hortensia. The work, both in its serious and its comic scenes, is tedious and monotonous. Banchieri followed up his *Pazzia senile* with *La Prudenza giovenile* (Milan, 1607), reprinted twenty years later under the title of *La Saviezza giovenile* (Venice, 1628).[3] He gives some directions as to their performance. Before the music begins, one of the singers is to read the heading of each scene, the names of the characters represented, and the tercet which gives the argument; behind the singers there is to be a consort of lutes, harpsichords, or other instruments. The second edition has one of Banchieri's sarcastic prefaces pouring scorn on the modern *atto scenico rappresentativo*. 'Anyone who sticks to the good

[1] There is an unreliable reprint in Torchi, op. cit. iv, p. 281; excerpts, ed. Vatielli, in *I Classici della musica italiana*, ii (Milan, 1919).   [2] Torchi, op. cit. p. 73.
[3] Excerpts, ed. Vatielli, in *I Classici della musica italiana*, iii.

old rules of counterpoint is now struck off the rolls of the musicians and relegated to the antiques. What is *atto scenico rappresentativo*? An old man, a young man, a maidservant, a girl, and such like, sometimes in soliloquy, sometimes in dialogue, with *balletti* and *mascherate* in between; such is the music of today. You hear a bass, an alto, a tenor, a soprano, and so forth singing alone and together as in *intermedii*, airs, and symphonies, and that is called the modern style; and here is a specimen of it so modern that the good school of musical lawgivers would never have dreamed of it, and it proves the old adage

> Che il buono non è buono
> Ma buono quel, che piace.
> (That the good is not good,
> but good is whatever pleases.)

The following *Saviezza giovanile* (Youthful Wisdom) is also in the *scenico rappresentativo* style. Observe it, gentle reader, and you will find the old style coupled with the modern, as many of understanding practise, even today; the design is dramatic and a mixture of grave and gay. Be pleased with the one, enjoy the other; sing away merrily and good luck to you.'

There can be no doubt here that Banchieri is presenting *commedia dell'arte*, but not on the stage; what he calls the 'modern' style is the reaction against Netherland counterpoint—homophonic declamation; and we should note that he addresses his 'gentle reader' not as a listener but as a singer. All these collections, Croce's *Triaca*, Vecchi's *Selva* and *Veglie di Siena*, Banchieri's *Barca di Venezia per Padova*, may be tedious stuff as modern concert music or as illustrations to learned lectures—but they are all great fun to sing. *Canta allegramente e vivi felice*.

THE MADRIGAL OUTSIDE ITALY

The classical madrigal, peculiar to Italy throughout the century, was created by the Netherlanders and destroyed by the Italians. Up to about 1600 the whole of European music, both sacred and secular, was dominated by the Netherlanders; after that date—except for Sweelinck—they disappear altogether. The Italians, Marenzio and Gesualdo, had perfected the madrigal and transfigured it, but its existence depended almost entirely on Petrarch, Ariosto, Tasso, and Guarini, poets whom the seventeenth century was content to forget. The Petrarchan madrigal was smothered in its Italian undergrowth, the jungle of popular music that began with the Neapolitan *villanelle*.

By the end of the century northern musicians were travelling to

Italy not to teach the Italians but to learn from them. The northern publishers at Nuremberg, Antwerp, and other places, were printing enormous quantities of Italian music, but it was only in England that a native school of real madrigalists was able to develop. The Netherlanders had begun to infiltrate into Germany, including Prague and Vienna, but (owing probably to the Reformation) they never established themselves in England. It must be remembered that the Netherlanders were primarily church musicians, and that the export of church music from Italy, whether by Netherlanders or Italians, through the northern publishers, far exceeded that of secular music. A few madrigals of various types with Italian words were written by other non-Italians, but no northern country except England developed a real madrigal school based on its own language.

The main reason for this is that no country except Italy had ever possessed a Petrarch. The madrigal was rooted in the Italian language, and its style resisted adaptation to any other, even to French. The French, as in the subsequent history of opera, never submitted wholeheartedly to Italy, and (as we have seen in the previous chapter) the polyphonic *chanson*, though influenced by the madrigal, went its own way. The outstanding French madrigalist of the last period, Jean (Giovanni) de Macque, lived in Italy and set Italian words.[1] The Spaniards, too, had an indigenous type of polyphonic song in the *villancico*,[2] which continued to flourish throughout the sixteenth century[3] and indeed even in the seventeenth,[4] making increasing use of imitative techniques. The outstanding master of the *villancico* was Juan Vázquez, who published collections of *Villancicos y canciones* and *Sonetos y villancicos* in 1551, 1559, and 1560;[5] his works show no traces of madrigalian influence. The *Canciones y villanescas espirituales* (Venice, 1589) of Francisco Guerrero[6] are more Italianate, and by Morales we actually have two Italian madrigals.[7] Mateo Flecha the

---

[1] Cf. Suzanne Clercx, 'Jean de Macque et l'évolution du madrigalisme à la fin du XVIe siècle', *Festschrift: Joseph Schmidt-Görg zum 60. Geburtstag* (Bonn, 1957).

[2] See Vol. III, p. 378, and *infra*, p. 135.

[3] See, for instance, the collection of *Villancicos de diversos Autores, a dos y a tres y a quatro y a cinco bozes* (Venice, 1556), reprinted by Mitjana as the *Cancionero de Uppsala* (Uppsala, 1909; fresh transcription by Jesús Bal y Gay, Mexico, 1944).

[4] Cf. the *Cancionero musical y poético del siglo XVII*, ed. D. J. Aroca (Madrid, 1916) and the *Romances y letras a tres vozes* transcribed by Miguel Querol (Barcelona, 1956).

[5] His collection of 1560 has been republished complete by Higini Anglès in *Monumentos de la música española*, iv (Barcelona, 1946).

[6] Reprinted by Vicente Garcia in Guerrero, *Opera Omnia*, i (Barcelona, 1955).

[7] The opening of 'Ditemi o si o no', originally published in Arcadelt's Fourth Book of four-part madrigals (Venice, 1539), is printed by Mitjana in Lavignac and La Laurencie, *Encyclopédie de la musique*, 1ère partie, iv (Paris, 1920), p. 2003. Cf. also the comment on Mudarra's *canciones*, *infra*, p. 129.

younger published a book of madrigals at Venice in 1568, including one with Spanish text, but he and his uncle are deservedly better known for their *ensaladas* or quodlibets.[1] Both Spanish and Catalan, as well as Italian, texts are set in the *Madrigales* of Joan Brudieu (Barcelona, 1585)[2] and the *Odarum* (*quas vulgo Madrigales appellamus*) ... *lib. I* of Pedro Vila (Barcelona, 1561); it is significant that one of Brudieu's poets is Ausias March, one of the leading imitators of Petrarch in Spain. Other Spanish madrigalists—such as Sebastiàn Raval and Pedro Valenzuela (Valenzola)—published in Italy and set only Italian texts.[3] The *Parnaso español de madrigales y villancicos* (Antwerp, 1614) of Pedro Ruimonte, who composed Spanish texts in the style of Marenzio and Monteverdi, marks the end of the Spanish madrigal.

Like France and Spain, Germany had its own tradition of secular song (which will be discussed in the next chapter) and the only German composers of importance as madrigalists were Hans Leo Hassler and Heinrich Schütz.[4]

THE MADRIGAL IN ENGLAND

In England conditions were more favourable to the cult of the madrigal. England had never had a Petrarch, but it was the moment when English literature was absorbing all that it possibly could from the Italians. Castiglione's *Il Cortegiano* (1528) had been translated into English in 1561; there appears to have been no German translation before 1960.[5] England welcomed everything that was Italian; the literary friendship between the two countries dates back indeed to Chaucer, who was personally acquainted with Petrarch. The earliest evidence for the singing of Italian madrigals in England is provided by two manuscript collections, the first belonging to the period of Verdelot, who is well represented in it; Alfredo Obertello[6] suggests that it was presented to Henry VIII by Alfonso d'Este, as it contains a motet in the king's honour. The second manuscript, dated 1564, is in the library of Winchester College, and includes a large number of madrigals by Hubert Waelrant, whose works had been published only at Antwerp and not in Italy. Tradition makes Elizabeth I the first

[1] *Las Ensaladas de Flecha* (Prague, 1581); reprinted by Higini Anglès (Barcelona, 1954); see pp. 407–8.
[2] Republished by Pedrell and Anglès (Barcelona, 1921); complete example in André Mangeot, 'The Madrigals of Joan Brudieu', *The Score*, no. 7 (1952).
[3] Valenzuela's 'La verginella' was republished by Barclay Squire, *Ausgewählte Madrigale*, no. 36. [4] See pp. 112 ff. and 119 ff.
[5] Translated and annotated by Fritz Baumgart (Bremen, 1960).
[6] *Madrigali italiani in Inghilterra* (Milan, 1949). The manuscript was acquired in 1935 by the Newberry Library, Chicago.

owner of it; the manuscript certainly shows that it was put to much practical use.

Part-singing was quite well known in England at that date. We know of the *XX Songes* of 1530,[1] and Thomas Whythorne published his *Songes to three, fower, and five voyces* in 1571.[2] These are all mainly homophonic and not very interesting. A typical example of this period (not later than 1564) is the well-known 'In going to my naked bed' by Richard Edwards.[3] It employs what we may call the international Netherland technique of plain harmony with occasional little contrapuntal imitations; but if we compare it with Arcadelt's 'Il bianco e dolce cigno' we shall see at once the difference of style due solely to the rhythm produced by the English masculine (monosyllabic) rhymes.

BYRD AND *MUSICA TRANSALPINA*

The year 1588 saw the issue of two important collections—the *Psalmes, Sonets & songs*[4] for five voices by William Byrd, and *Musica Transalpina*, a collection of Italian madrigals with words translated into English (together with one original English madrigal, Byrd's 'The fair young virgin'). The composer most strongly represented in *Musica Transalpina* is Alfonso Ferrabosco the elder, a competent but rather dull and very conservative musician who had served at Elizabeth's court from *c.* 1562 to 1578 and was more highly regarded in this country than in his own. From this date onwards there was a continuous output of madrigals in English by native composers until 1627 when the madrigal school came to an end with the *Ayres or Fa Las* of John Hilton.[5] Byrd's songs of 1588 are not madrigals at all. He tells us himself in his preface that they were composed for a solo voice accompanied by a quartet of viols,

[1] See Vol. III, p. 348.

[2] See also p. 200. Twelve of Whythorne's songs were reprinted by Peter Warlock (London, 1927).

[3] First printed by Hawkins in his *General History of Music* (London, 1776); modern reprints in Fellowes, *The English Madrigal School*, xxxvi (London, 1924), and, without words, in *The Mulliner Book* (*Musica Britannica*, i) (London, 1951), p. 60. Other examples of English part-song preserved in Thomas Mulliner's transcriptions (ibid. i)—e.g. Edwards's 'By painted words' ('O the silly man') and 'When griping griefs', Johnson's 'Defiled is my name', Tallis's 'O ye tender babes', 'Like as the doleful dove', and 'When shall my sorrowful sighing slake', and Sheppard's 'O happy dames'—have been reconstructed by Denis Stevens and published separately.

[4] Reprinted by Fellowes, op. cit. xiv (London, 1920), and *The Collected Vocal Works of Byrd*, xii (London, 1948). See also Dent, 'William Byrd and the Madrigal' in *Festschrift für Johannes Wolf* (Berlin, 1929), p. 24.

[5] Reprinted in *Publications of the Musical Antiquarian Society*, xiii (London, 1844). In discussing the English school it is difficult to avoid using the word 'madrigal' in a very free sense.

and this is quite evident from their technique. It is further confirmed by a manuscript of about 1581 at Christ Church, Oxford,[1] in which words are written in for the 'first singing part' (as Byrd calls it in the edition of 1588) alone. As with the Italian *frottole*, we shall see that in the English school there was often the same latitude as regards vocal or instrumental accompaniment. In Byrd's songs the music of the solo voice (not always the uppermost) is clearly cut up into lines by rests, and it hardly ever repeats words, whereas the other parts go on continuously like instruments and repetition of words becomes a necessity. What we note conspicuously is the English rhythm of the verse and the strongly tuneful character of the vocal melody; in the madrigals of the Netherlanders real tunefulness is a great rarity. The constructive principle of the song-tune persists through Byrd's second publication, the *Songs of Sundry Natures* (1589);[2] the 'first singing part' is not named, but can almost always be picked out, as it generally is the last to enter. The English squareness of the verse naturally affects the music, however contrapuntal, and this accounts for Byrd's sturdy sense of major or minor tonality. The majority of the *Songs* are strophic, but as Byrd (at this time) never goes in for Italian word-painting the music is adequate for all the stanzas, and he aims more at expressing the general idea of the whole poem.

Musica Transalpina was a miscellany, and for that reason the English madrigal school was a miscellany too; it had no tradition behind it and imitated what it happened to like, struggling at first to reproduce Italian rhythms and then going its own way to the natural rhythms of English, with its own English sense of humour. Obertello has shown that *Musica Transalpina* was made up out of various Italian miscellanies for export,[3] and he has also shown that a great many English madrigal poems were actually translations, paraphrases, or free imitations of Italian originals which he has identified. They can generally be recognized by their preponderance of feminine rhymes, but there are also many which have no feminine rhymes at all; English translators of the Italian classics have always been forced to abandon any attempt to reproduce the normal Italian feminine endings. Another set of *Italian Madrigalls Englished* followed in 1590, edited by Thomas Watson, the large majority being by Marenzio;[4] it also includes two of Byrd's few genuine madrigals, settings *à* 6 and *à* 4 of 'This sweet and merry month of May', of which he republished the

---

[1] Christ Church, 984–8.   [2] *The English Madrigal School*, xv (London, 1920).
[3] The contents, with their sources, are listed in Joseph Kerman, *The Elizabethan Madrigal* (New York, 1962), pp. 53–55. The Marenzio madrigals have been published by R. A. Harman (London, 1955).   [4] Sources listed Kerman, op. cit., p. 59.

four-part composition in his *Psalmes, Songs, and Sonnets* of 1611. Nicholas Yonge's sequel to *Musica Transalpina* did not come out until 1597.[1] As far as the Italian influence was concerned, the elder Ferrabosco,[2] Marenzio, and Gastoldi were the prime favourites with the English madrigalists. Obertello, however, suggests that Watson, who was something of a poet, chose his Italian madrigals more for their poetical than for their musical value.

THOMAS MORLEY

The first English madrigal publication after 1588–9 was Thomas Morley's *Canzonets to three voices* (1593), followed by four-part madrigals[3] in 1594, ballets (five voices), and canzonets (two voices) in 1595; two years later came his canzonets for five and six voices. That is the total of Morley's output, of polyphonic song.[4] Even if we take into account his editorship of *The Triumphs of Oriana* (1601),[5] it may seem small reason for regarding him as the unquestioned head of the English school, the more since the ballets, always his most popular works and those by which he is chiefly remembered, are barefaced imitations of Gastoldi's,[6] while his canzonets are closely modelled on *canzonette* by Felice Anerio.[7] But the ballets brought something new into English music; they were imitated by Morley's followers and given new and original interpretations; the 'fa la', as it was often called, was combined with the serious madrigal and used for serious and ironic ends. The Italian *canzonetta* was the other form which attracted Morley. His own canzonets have a fascinating airiness and gaiety, besides accomplished contrapuntal ingenuity. In this he set the example to his compatriots of treating counterpoint as the ideal vehicle for wit and grotesque humour. This is very characteristic of the English. The

---

[1] Sources, Kerman, op. cit., pp. 62–63.

[2] On Ferrabosco's madrigals and their influence on the English school, see ibid., pp. 78 ff. G. E. P. Arkwright published fifteen of them in his *Old English Edition*, xi and xii (London, 1894).

[3] The first English collection actually so called. 'Ho! who comes here', from this set, is recorded in *The History of Music in Sound*, iv.

[4] Reprinted in *The English Madrigal School*, i, ii, iii, iv.

[5] *The English Madrigal School*, xxxii. On this collection, see Kerman, op. cit., pp. 194 ff.

[6] See, in particular, Denis Arnold, 'Gastoldi and the English Ballett', *Monthly Musical Record*, lxxxvi (1956), p. 44, and Frank Zimmerman. 'Italian and English traits in the music of Thomas Morley', *Anuario musical*, xiv (1959).

[7] In 1595 Morley published a volume of two-part Italian canzonets with English and Italian texts, and in 1597 a volume of Italian canzonets with English words only; he himself also set or adapted four of these translated texts.

Italians certainly enjoyed the grotesque, and had the further advantage of their various dialects (music of this type is always in some dialect), but their settings of it were almost invariably homophonic. And Morley, like Byrd, has the advantage of English monosyllables, with their tendency to square-cut rhythms and vigorous staccato utterance, making for firm tonality.

WEELKES AND WILBYE

Thomas Weelkes (1575?–1623) was not much over twenty when he published his first set of madrigals in 1597.[1] He must have been already familiar with the Italian style, though we have no knowledge of how he was educated. At this time he was organist of Winchester College, and he may have found there other singers of madrigals. His knowledge of Marenzio and other Italians could have been acquired only by actually singing them, as no scores were then available. His melody is smoother than Morley's and his chromatic effects, quite unknown to Morley, are very surprising, all the more so from their extreme rarity. In no. 3, 'In black mourn I', which is in plain G major, we suddenly find

Ex.31
(My curtall dog that wont to have played)

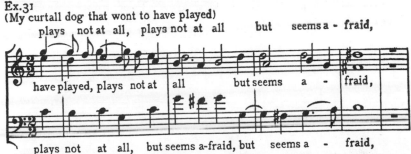

No. 6, 'Cease sorrows now' ends with a passage which is remarkable in many aspects and must be quoted at length:

Ex.32

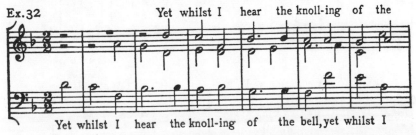

---

[1] *The English Madrigal School*, ix. On Weelkes's madrigals generally, see Kerman, op. cit., pp. 223 ff., and Arnold, 'Thomas Weelkes and the Madrigal' *Music and Letters*, xxxi (1950), p. 1.

We notice first the descriptive 'knolling' of the bell; then the imitative treatment of a chromatic scale subject and in the fourth bar from
the end the clash of C sharp and C natural. The same false relation
(C sharp, C natural, or in one case F sharp, F natural) occurs three
times more in Weelkes's madrigals, always standing out as an inten-
tional expression of grief.

Weelkes's ballets for five voices (1598)[1] are a great advance on
those of Morley. The ballet (so Morley suggests) was not actually
danced in England; it had become simply a musical form in which
the composers introduced 'fa la' episodes alternating with the lines
of the original poem. These 'fa las' are completely free in treatment
and are often contrapuntal, contrasting with a homophonic and
sometimes more dance-like setting of the words. Being half-way
between madrigal and dance the ballet naturally enjoyed great
popularity. How much Weelkes had learned from Marenzio may be
seen in the madrigal for five voices, 'O Care, thou wilt despatch me'.[2]
Like many of Marenzio's (generally sonnets) it is in two sections
which ought never to be sung separately, though they are numbered
separately in Weelkes's publication: a deeply serious work in which
the poet calls on Music to relieve his misery. Music is here symbolized
by 'fa la' episodes, but they are in a minor key and sometimes sung
to slow notes. This idea is certainly Weelkes's own and has no parallel
in the Italians; but the two chains of slow modulations, the first
going through flat keys, the second through sharp ones, is a direct
imitation of Marenzio. The effect is most striking, and the emotional
conception extremely moving; but it was an experiment which the
English composer did not repeat, though there are some effective
chromatic harmonies in 'The Andalusian merchant' (the second part
of 'Thule, the period of cosmography', for six voices, 1600) describing 'how strangely Fogo burns'. It must, however, be admitted that
if we compare the total output of the English and Italian schools in the
last ten years of the century, the percentage of extreme chromatic
cases to normal diatonic usage may not be very different.

John Wilbye (1574–1638) published his first set of madrigals in
1598 and his second in 1609.[3] He tries no strange experiments, but on

[1] *The English Madrigal School*, x.
[2] From the set published in 1600, reprinted ibid. xi. 'O Care' is recorded in *The History of Music in Sound*, iv.
[3] *The English Madrigal School*, vi and vii. 'Ye that do live in pleasures', from the second set, is recorded in *The History of Music in Sound*, iv. On Wilbye's madrigals generally, see Kerman, op. cit., pp. 233 ff., and Hugo Heurich, *John Wilbye in seinen Madrigalen* (Augsburg, 1931).

the whole he is the most accomplished and also the most expressive of the English madrigalists. He had the advantage of setting poets more skilful in language than those of his predecessors; the poems are obvious imitations (some identified by Obertello) of Italian ones and nearly all in double rhymes. This makes it easier for Wilbye to set lines in long phrases, and he escapes, too, the awkwardness involved by words which are unstressed but long by quantity. (The interrelation of stress and quantity in Italian and English poetry is a highly important factor in the differentiation of national styles in madrigal music, but it is too complicated for discussion here.) It is obvious that these two young Englishmen, Weelkes and Wilbye—Weelkes especially—absorbed more of the music of the Italian madrigals that they sang and studied than of the words and the way they were set. The Italian madrigal, early or late, was always dictated by its words, even when they were no more than *poesia per musica*, and at the lowest it was always *poesia* with a certain standard of literary elegance which the English poets, caring less for sound than for sense, did not often achieve. The English composers, appreciating the Italian madrigal mainly as musical sound, did not always grasp the basic principle of its composition. Modern singers and listeners, anxious to find some native quality in this music, find it most naturally in its rusticity and humour. The Italian literary pastoral was classically bucolic but never rustic; that was possible only in dialect.

Weelkes's *Ayeres or Phantasticke Spirites* (1608)[1] for three voices are what Morley would have called 'tavern music'; it is odd that they should have been printed as for two trebles and bass, unless intended for boys, as they seem much more appropriate for men, though their words are quite decent. They are spirited and lively as well as highly skilful in humorous counterpoint, with words full of grotesque rhymes. These are peculiarly English and quite inconceivable in Italian music. Indeed, throughout the English school humour constantly breaks out, often in unexpected places.

BYRD'S *PSALMES, SONGS, AND SONNETS*

In 1611 Byrd, after a silence of twenty-two years, published what he called his *ultimum vale*, a miscellany of *Psalmes, Songs, and Sonnets*[2] probably containing items written much earlier. Byrd was always conservative and adapted himself with some effort to the madrigal style. The three-part songs which begin the volume may well

---

[1] *The English Madrigal School*, xiii.
[2] Ibid., xvi and *The Collected Vocal Works of Byrd*, xiv.

have been written for boys, as they are all on moral texts, rather
schoolmasterish in diction. More than half the collection is sacred
and serious; there are also two 'fantazias' for viols, and sacred songs
accompanied by four and five viols. Very little of this volume can be
called madrigalian in character; the serious and sacred pieces (Byrd
calls them all 'songs' and never uses the word 'madrigal') have no
affinity with the Italian *madrigali spirituali*. The stiffness of Byrd's
counterpoint, masterly as it is, matches the sententiousness of his
texts. The most interesting number is the five-part 'Come, woeful
Orpheus', which is evidently intended as an old man's protest against
'modern music', as it speaks of 'strange chromatic notes', 'sourest
sharps and uncouth flats', which Byrd illustrates with complete
command of chromatic technique, as if to show that although he
finds the new style detestable he can write in it just as easily as the
youngsters. The serious madrigals of Byrd are, however, interesting
as leading eventually to those of Orlando Gibbons.

MINOR ENGLISH MADRIGALISTS

Between Wilbye and Gibbons, whose one set of twenty madrigals
appeared in 1612, there are several minor composers, all of whom contributed to the formation of a definitely English style. This English
style arose mainly from the natural rhythms of English poetry with its
preference for masculine line-endings and for a prosody based more
on stress than on quantity. Morley and Weelkes are thus tempted to
fall into a slightly monotonous rhythm of jog-trot crotchets which
may be agreeable and appropriate in any single madrigal but becomes
wearisome if we sing too many. The suppleness, fluidity, and variety
of Marenzio could never be reproduced in English words. By the time
the English took over the madrigal, music had already become the
predominant partner in Italy itself. The English composers keenly
appreciated the sense of the words they set, but not—as the Italians
could not help doing—the musical sound of them; they were skilful
contrapuntists, but what attracted them more was the richness, the
'linkèd sweetness long drawn out' of full five- or six-part harmony
which resulted from contrapuntal movement of the individual parts.
This probably accounts for their love of gliding dissonances and unusual suspensions; the music, although 'expressive', becomes an end
in itself and often suggests that the composers were influenced by
organ-playing or perhaps more probably by the chest of viols, since
this was also the great age of instrumental chamber music in England.

Kirbye, Bateson, and Ward[1] are the chief exponents of this serious style in the early seventeenth century and show a marked partiality for writing madrigals of considerable length. Others preferred the lighter style and often show a very original charm in this vein.[2]

GIBBONS AND TOMKINS

The secular songs of Orlando Gibbons (1612), which he described on his title-page as *Madrigals and Mottets*,[3] are nearly all of a serious cast which might be called ethical or philosophical. As Kerman remarks (op. cit., p. 123), they are 'neither madrigals nor motets, but mature compositions in an individual idiom which Gibbons developed to great lengths from the basic abstract polyphonic style practised by Byrd, as well as by a number of second-rate composers' (such as John Mundy, Richard Carlton, and Richard Alison). The words were selected by Sir Christopher Hatton. One is an epigram translated either from the Greek Anthology or from a Latin version of it, and various others have a similar epigrammatic shape. The first, 'The silver swan', beloved of all English madrigal singers, might at first suggest an English version of 'Il bianco e dolce cigno', but no Italian would have ended with the cynical words

More geese than swans now live, more fools than wise.

The finest of these pieces is 'What is our life?', the grimly austere words of which are by Sir Walter Raleigh.[4] What we must admire in Gibbons, in addition to his habitual grave serenity, is his complete command of tonality and his power of constructing very long madrigals on a strictly diatonic system. No madrigalist repeats his words so often as Gibbons; a stanza of six lines may be spread over some seventy bars. He is never chromatic, and modulates only to the keys so near the tonic that he seems hardly to leave it at all, yet without monotony and with a strong sense of building up to a climax. A poem by Joshua Sylvester, 'I weigh not Fortune's frown nor smile', forms a sequence of four six-lined stanzas, all in G major, the first four lines of each being plain statements like the first; the general subject is equanimity and contentment, and the metrical scheme suggests the monotony of a brick wall, but Gibbons seizes on every detail that he can utilize, rejecting all chromatics or startling discords, and ends

---

[1] *The English Madrigal School*, xxiv, xxi and xxii, and xix.
[2] See, for instance, Thomas Greaves's ballet 'Come away, sweet love', recorded in *The History of Music in Sound*, iv.   [3] *The English Madrigal School*, v.
[4] Kerman argues ingeniously that this is an arrangement of a consort song for solo voice and instruments.

with a climax so simple and so skilfully contrived as to suggest the majestic assurance of Handel:

Ex.33
(A- mind content and conscience clear)

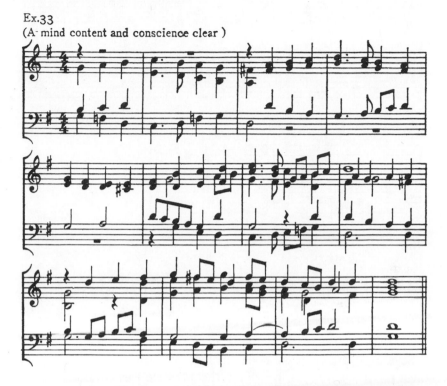

Thomas Tomkins (1573 ?–1656) is the last of the greater madrigalists and a link with the instrumental school of the seventeenth century. His madrigals (1622)[1] make a great contrast to those of Gibbons; on the one hand he is full of pathos, on the other bursting with energy and vitality. Several of his madrigals include 'fa la' episodes; these have long since lost any suggestion of the dance and they often suggest that they were intended for viols, especially as the bass part often goes down to low D. Some of the rhythmic figures are most original and new for the period, at any rate in vocal music:

Ex.34
(i)
(See, see, the shepherds' queen)

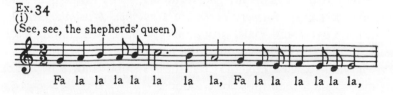

Fa la la la la la la la, Fa la la la la la la,

[1] Ibid. xviii. See Denis Stevens, *Thomas Tomkins* (London, 1957), pp. 95 ff.

(ii)
(Phyllis, now cease to move me)

Fa   la la   la   la   la la   la   la   la la
Fa   la la   la la   la la, Fa   la   la la   la la

(iii)
(Fusca, in thy starry eyes)

Fa   la la, Fa   la la, Fa la la   la   la,   Fa la la, Fa   la la   la la   la

'APT FOR VIOLS AND VOICES'

Several of the madrigal books include solo songs with accompaniment for three, four, or five viols;[1] this practice was continuous from before the time of Byrd. Weelkes, in 1600, was the first to describe his madrigals as 'apt for the viols and voices'; Wilbye in 1609 writes 'apt both for voyals and voyces'. Michael East's 'Fifth set of Books' (1618) contained 'Songs full of spirit and delight, so composed in 3 parts that they are as apt for Vyols as Voyces'; in these only the opening words of each are printed and the lyrics are lost. Scholars have not always agreed in their interpretations of such directions (which appear in almost all of the publications), but E. H. Fellowes[2] seems to take the view that madrigals were performed sometimes by voices alone, and also either with viols or other instruments, or by instruments alone. Martin Peerson's *Mottects or Grave Chamber Musique* (1630) are 'all fit for Voyces and Vials, with an Organ Part' (which may alternatively be played on the virginals, bandora or Irish harp); the *basso continuo* had reached England; but these secular 'mottects' are even less madrigalian than those of Gibbons.

---

[1] These are discussed in Chapter IV.
[2] E. H. Fellowes, *The English Madrigal Composers* (Oxford, 1921), pp. 77–79.

The transition was easy from pure vocal music to instrumental chamber music, which was already flourishing in the earlier years of the reign of Elizabeth I.[1] This close association of the madrigal with autonomous instrumental music is historically most important, for without it the madrigal style would have perished altogether in the reign of Charles I without leaving any trace of influence on the subsequent music of England. Singers had turned to the polyphonic form of ayre.[2]

Compared with the Italian madrigal school,[3] that of England is a very small affair; the total number of madrigals published amounts to about a thousand or less over a period of about twenty-five years. Twenty-seven composers wrote madrigals, but few issued more than one set, and wrote no more even when they lived for many years afterwards. The collapse of the madrigal was in no way due to the Puritans; the madrigal was simply out of date, its vogue had passed. The Italian madrigal had disintegrated about the time that the English school was just coming to birth.

[1] See Chap. XI.   [2] See Chap. IV.
[3] In which we must include one Englishman, Peter Philips, resident for half his life in the Netherlands, where he published two books of six-part madrigals (Antwerp, 1596 and 1603), and one of eight-part (Antwerp, 1598).

III

GERMAN SECULAR SONG

By KURT GUDEWILL

DURING the hundred years 1530–1630 German secular song consisted almost exclusively either of polyphonic treatments of existing melodies or of free polyphonic compositions. Solo songs performed either to the lute, in the sixteenth century, or, at the end of the period, with figured bass accompaniment, are exceptional, though by 1630 the solo song[1] had so far superseded the polyphonic type that this date may be taken to some extent as a 'natural boundary'. On the other hand, the earlier date, 1530, marks not so much a fresh beginning as the culmination of the 'tenor song' period[2] which began at the time of the *Lochamer Liederbuch* (1452–60).[3] Around 1560 this style was in decline as composers, in the field of secular song at least, had lost interest in polyphonic settings built round a *canto fermo* generally in the tenor, and preferred to set texts *ad hoc*, with the result that scarcely any complete self-contained song melodies were produced. This development was the concomitant of a basic change in style, so that the period 1530–1630 presents a far from unified picture. This change was far less evident in sacred music, where the method of building a composition round a tenor *canto fermo*, also employed in the hymn compositions of the Reformation period,[4] persisted into the age of Bach. The numerous collections containing both secular and sacred pieces (the latter not always intended for liturgical use) show how closely the two kinds were associated in the sixteenth century; after 1600 a sharper division is evident.

A survey of the whole period under consideration raises three fundamental issues. The first concerns the extent to which external influences worked upon the German song, the second how far the designation 'song' belongs in the strict sense to the diverse kinds of composition broadly included under that name.[5] The third question concerns the social assumptions and conditions of song composition and performance.

[1] See pp. 122 ff.
[2] Ibid., p. 372.
[3] Cf. Vol. III, p. 373.
[4] See Chap. VIII.
[5] See Kurt Gudewill, article 'Lied' (A I), *Die Musik in Geschichte und Gegenwart*, viii (1960), col. 746.

The tenor song is perhaps the most essentially German creation; yet some Netherland influence, especially in the use of imitation, must be recognized, as well as that of the Italian *frottola*.[1] Practically all the German *canto fermo* pieces are song-like inasmuch as their form is determined by an already existing melody. However, the picture changes with the revolution in style. The falling-off in song-production by native composers is particularly striking. Instead, Netherlanders resident in Germany took over and, being themselves under Italian influence, employed not only the technique of the motet, but elements also of *chanson*, madrigal, and *villanella* in the setting of German song-texts. Thus, when German composers began to renew their activity about 1570 they were familiar with two national styles. From the end of the century direct Italian influence increased, not so much through the few Italians working in Germany as through the many Italian compositions which had been circulating in Germany since the middle of the sixteenth century, and through German composers such as Schütz and Hassler who studied the new style at its source. However, this absorption of foreign elements rarely produced mere imitation of foreign models, and the development of German song up to 1630 is marked by a creative synthesis of non-German elements with the native tradition.

After the change of style, tendencies foreign to the *Lied* proper predominated at first, notably in the adoption of procedures derived from the motet; for motet and song are opposed in principle, just as are madrigal and song, not least because the asymmetrical form of madrigal texts is unsuited to the song. Conversely, the essential features of the 'song' (in the narrowest sense) are the formal coincidence of the melody with a symmetrically designed text and the setting of a number of stanzas to a single melody. The repetition of phrases or single words disturbs this symmetry, but it belongs to the very essence of motet and madrigal to which a continuously composed text is far more suited than the strophic principle. Although later on there was an increased number of songs with freely invented melodies—which, in contrast with those of the 'tenor song' period, lie in the highest part—the influences of motet and madrigal were still potent. About 1620 the influence of the vocal concerto[2] may be detected.

It is true that the polyphonic *Lied* has features in common with the *chanson*, which, however, rarely served it as a direct model—unlike the *villanella* with its tuneful highest voice and its systematic

---

[1] Cf. Herbert Rosenberg, 'Frottola und deutsches Lied um 1500. Ein Stilvergleich', *Acta Musicologica*, xviii–xix (1946–7), p. 30.   [2] See Chap. X.

three-part repetitive form. Midway between these stands the canzonet, combining the form of the *villanella* with the polyphony of the madrigal. The canzonet has also elements of the *balletto* and of the predominantly homorhythmic chordal 'dance-song', one of the genres of this period in which the song principle is most strongly pronounced.

The questions, which classes of society the song composers sprang from, for what purposes they wrote, and in what circles their songs were sung, can be answered only in particular cases. While we know that some compositions come from court circles, others from middle-class circles, it would not always be easy to decide on internal evidence to which social class they belong. The writing of polyphonic songs was cultivated by court musicians and *Kapellmeister*, by municipal cantors, organists, and town musicians, and also by amateurs. The growth of music-printing in the sixteenth century led to an exchange of song-repertory between court and town, and each performed the works of the other. All that can be said of the composers' public is that whereas the more exacting types, such as the madrigal and song-motet, may be considered as intended for performance to an audience, the popular dance-songs and drinking songs and the humorous quodlibets were primarily intended for use in sociable gatherings. One gets some idea of the dissemination of song in these forms throughout Germany from the large number of printed song-books issued between 1530 and 1630, besides numerous manuscript copies. It is the more remarkable that the production of these publications was scarcely affected during the last decade of the period, which coincides with the earlier part of the Thirty Years War.

CLIMAX AND DECLINE OF THE TENOR SONG

The tenor song played a decisive part in that first blossoming of German music in the sixteenth century which gave Germany a claim to an important place among the musical nations of Europe. Polyphonic songs on tenor *canti fermi* were admittedly cultivated in other countries, but to a much lesser extent than in Germany, where more than 1,500 examples have come down to us, the majority with several stanzas. The essential part of this tradition is to be found in the song-books issued between 1534 and 1556 by printers, publishers, and collectors, which are separated by a considerable interval of time from the three court-repertory collections of the printers Oeglin, Schöffer, and Arnt von Aich, which appeared in the second decade of the sixteenth century. It is remarkable that the years 1534-45 saw the appearance not only of the two collections of the publisher Johann Ott, containing 236 songs, and the first two parts of the *Frische teutsche Liedlein* (containing, together, 380 songs) of the Nuremberg town physician Georg Forster, but also the song books of Egenolff, Formschneider, and Schöffer-Apiarius, Georg Rhaw's *bicinia* and *tricinia*, and Wolfgang Schmeltzl's quodlibets.[1] Such activity is an impressive documentation of the predominantly bourgeois musical culture found at the beginning of the hundred-year period we are considering. With the exception of Caspar Othmayr's *Reutterische und Jegerische Liedlein* (Nuremberg, 1549), the earliest example of a collection comprising only works by a single composer, the publications mentioned consist of collections of compositions by a number of masters, though in some collections certain composers feature more prominently than others. For example, Ott's two collections of 1534 and 1544 contain, respectively, 82 and 64 pieces by the greatest German song-composer of the day, Ludwig Senfl. After the heyday of the tenor song, the miscellaneous collection gave place to the publication of compositions by single composers. Of the numerous composers of the tenor song, active mainly in south Germany and Austria, Adam of Fulda, Heinrich Finck, Stoltzer, Grefinger, and the Netherland master Heinrich Isaac were all dead by 1530. Thomas Sporer and Paul Hofhaimer died in 1534 and 1537, Senfl (born *c.* 1490) in 1543. Senfl was then at the height of his powers, as were his contemporaries Arnold von Bruck (d. 1554), Lemlin (d. *c.* 1549), Greiter (d. 1550), together with the members, all born about 1510, of the Heidelberg circle, Othmayr (d. 1553), Forster (d. 1568), Jobst vom Brandt (d. 1570), and Zirler (d. *c.* 1576). The state of development at this period is most clearly seen in the song-books of Johann Ott, in Othmayr's *Liedlein*, and in the last three parts of Forster's collection (1549, 1556, 1556),[2] which are the chief sources for the songs of the Heidelberg circle. Nor should we ignore Forster's second part (1540) in which more than half the pieces are anonymous.

By far the majority of the tenors in the polyphonic songs are so-called *Hofweisen* or court tunes,[3] related to *Minnesang* and *Meistergesang*; only a minority come from popular song. The words of the *Hofweisen* differ from those of popular song, with their spontaneity and wealth of content, by a certain restriction to a few subjects, by a leaning to the didactic and moralizing, and by formality of

[1] See the bibliographies to this chapter and Vol. III, Chap. X.
[2] A selection of ten songs from these three parts has been published by Gudewill, *Das Chorwerk*, lxiii (Wolfenbüttel, 1957).
[3] See Vol. III, p. 374.

verse-structure. Musically, the *Hofweise* is distinguishable from popular song by wide melodic range, by a certain melodic formality connected with specific modes or keys,[1] and by a preference for *Bar* form: *AAB*. By far the commonest mode is Ionian on F. A highly characteristic example of the *Hofweise* is this tenor, used and perhaps invented[2] by Forster:

Ex. 35

(The scholar nowadays lives without fame and favour; the only thing that counts is self-interest . . .)

It is surprising that the three court-repertory collections mentioned above contain hardly a single piece based on popular song. But this should not lead us to suppose that no popular songs were sung at the princely courts. Senfl, who spent his active life in the service of courts, showed, especially in his Munich period, a marked preference for popular song.[3] Rather, we may suppose that the increased representation of popular song in the printed collections, beginning with Ott's first book, reflects contemporary taste both at the courts and among the middle-classes. However, the collection in which popular song is most prominent, Forster's second book of *Liedlein*, belongs to a different category, since it presents a repertoire of students' songs.

Certain other features characterizing the development of the tenor

---

[1] See Gudewill, 'Beziehungen zwischen Modus und Melodiebildung in deutschen Liedtenores', *Archiv für Musikwissenschaft*, xv (1958), p. 60.

[2] *Das Erbe deutscher Musik, Reichsdenkmale*, xx (Wolfenbüttel, 1942), p. 27.

[3] Cf. Arnold Geering and Wilhelm Altwegg, *Das Erbe deutscher Musik, Reichsdenkmale*, xv (Wolfenbüttel, 1940), p. vi.

song from 1530 onward may be noted. Pieces in more than four parts begin to appear. Although four-part writing remains the general rule, the number of parts is often increased, as in Senfl and Brandt, notably in the 'simultaneous' quodlibets which combine several tunes,[1] while 'successive' quodlibets where the same text is used in all voices, as in Schmeltzl (1544), and Forster's second book, keep generally to four parts. The free handling of the added parts in tenor songs of the older type is increasingly replaced by a more homogeneous texture produced by means of imitation:[2]

(The world will pay you back, and so you'll find)

or by pairing the voices. But it must be remembered that chordal pieces, sometimes with coincidence of caesuras in all the parts, are to be found at all stages of the development of the tenor song.[3]

Whereas in the older song-books only the tenor was underlaid with text, after 1536 the other parts, until then presumably intended for instruments, were provided with words and occasionally reshaped so as to make them suitable for singing.[4] As the newer composers

---

[1] See Vol. III, p. 375, Ex. 161.   [2] From *Reichsdenkmale*, xv, p. 53.
[3] See Vol. III, Ex. 160 and 162, and cf. Ludwig Senfl, *Deutsche Lieder*, iii (Wolfenbüttel, 1949), pp. 20 and 66.   [4] Cf. Gudewill, *Reichsdenkmale*, xx, pp. vii ff.

adopted syllabic declamation and moreover preferred shorter note-values, underlaying no longer presented a problem. In this effort to elucidate the words, as in the simplification of strophe-forms,[1] one recognizes humanistic influences. But this was not yet equivalent to adopting purely vocal writing; on the contrary, the greatest variety of tone-colour[2] is suggested by the prefaces and titles, such as that of Forster's fifth volume (1556): 'not only to be sung, but to be played on all kinds of instruments' ('. . . nicht allein zu singen | sonder auch auff allen Instrumenten zu brauchen . . .').

As often occurs when styles change, the new style was fore-shadowed before the end of the tenor-song period. The transition from the song with tenor *canto fermo* to the song-motet was effected not in the field of *Hofweise* arrangements but on the basis of popular song. In handling the *Hofweise* composers were conservative, taking care to maintain the congruence of text and *canto fermo*, whereas the popular song was much more freely treated.[3] This is partly true of Senfl, but especially so of Othmayr, Brandt, and the as yet unidenti-fied anonymous composers of Forster's second part.[4] Melodic lines and phrases are repeated, sometimes with transposition, free inter-polations are made, or the song melody is completely broken up in the manner of the motet. Although it is not certain that no. 28 of Forster's Second Part, 'Mein' Mutter zeihet mich', is based on a song-melody (it could well be a free setting of a sixteen-line poem), such a possibility may be excluded in the cases of nos. 10 and 31, especially the latter—the through-composed 'Wohl auf'—as the song form has here been entirely lost; these must be called 'song motets'. It may be asked whether we can conjecturally attribute these and other anonymous pieces in the collection to Netherland com-posers. In this connexion it is worth remembering that Heinrich Isaac, who died in 1517, had already written a piece on the song 'Mein Mütterlein'[5] which shows all the symptoms of dissolution of the *canto fermo*. It is also significant that Forster's Second Part, in many respects the most 'modern' collection of the period, was printed for the fourth and last time in 1565; that both *chansons* and madrigals by Netherlanders appear in Ott's second collection (1544);

---

[1] Cf. Gudewill, 'Zur Frage der Formstrukturen deutscher Liedtenores', *Die Musik-forschung*, i (1948), pp. 116 ff.

[2] Geering, 'Texterung und Besetzung in Senfls Liedern', *Archiv für Musikforschung*, iv (1939), p. 1.

[3] Cf. Gudewill, 'Zur Frage der Formstrukturen', pp. 114 and 118 ff.

[4] Ed. Robert Eitner in *Publikation älterer praktischer und theoretischer Musikwerke*, xxix (Leipzig, 1905).

[5] Ibid. i p. 106.

and that the last two parts of Forster's collections (1556) were issued once only. Evidently the German composers' interest in polyphonic secular pieces on a *canto fermo* was flagging by 1560. The two posthumous publications of Caspar Glanner (d. *c*. 1577), which appeared in 1578 and 1580, were the final products of this period.

THE NETHERLANDERS AND GERMAN SONG

Two considerations account for the ascendancy of Netherland composers in the field of German song after 1560.[1] For one thing, Germany at this period was poorly endowed with native creative talent; for another, Netherlanders occupied the leading positions in several south German courts and in the Imperial Chapel, which was at Prague towards the end of the century. This was a consequence of the political situation which, since the reign of Charles V (1519–56), had produced a close cultural bond between the House of Habsburg and the Netherlands. We either possess or have knowledge of about a thousand German songs, both sacred and secular, which are the work of some thirty Netherland composers, of whom the most influential and celebrated were Lassus (*c*. 1532–94) and Jacob Regnart (*c*. 1540–99). From 1556 until his death Lassus worked at Munich under the Dukes Albrecht V and Wilhelm V, for the greater part of the period as *Hofkapellmeister*. Regnart, who entered the Habsburg service in 1560, ended his career as assistant *Kapellmeister* to Rudolf II in Prague. Just as Lassus had continued, with the warm encouragement of the ducal family, the song tradition established in Munich by Senfl, he, like most of his compatriots and like many German masters, employed the old texts of the tenor-song period. Even after Regnart, Hassler, and Haussmann had put song poetry on a new basis suggested by Italian models,[2] composers continued to set the *Hofweise* texts, although the melodies belonging to them were no longer used. Not even in the work of Le Maistre (1505–77), whose *Geistliche und Weltliche Teutsche Geseng* (Wittenberg, 1566) contain tenor songs with *Hofweise* texts as well as sacred *canto fermo* settings, does one find any borrowing of old melodies except in two quodlibets. That reflects his position in a period of transition. The markedly conservative outlook of this particular Netherlander is revealed by the fact that, ten years after the appearance of Forster's fifth volume,

---

[1] Helmuth Osthoff, *Die Niederländer und das deutsche Lied* (Berlin, 1938). This has a musical appendix with 22 songs.
[2] R. Velten, *Das ältere deutsche Gesellschaftslied unter dem Einfluß der italienischen Musik* (Heidelberg, 1914).

he was still attached to the secular tenor song, though with *canti fermi* probably of his own composition. Le Maistre, who came to Munich before Lassus and took charge of the Dresden court chapel in 1554, showed his awareness of the new trends only in the occasional use of madrigalian elements and the three-sectional *villanella* form.

The new chapter in the history of German song began not, as used to be assumed, with Le Maistre but with the great cosmopolitan Lassus, who consummated 'a stylistic revolution going to the foundations of the *Lied*'.[1] Lassus was a master of French, Italian, and German, which he mingled freely in his correspondence, and was able to bring to bear on German song the experience gained in the composition of *chansons*, *villanelle*, and madrigals on texts in other languages. None of his compatriots attained this universality, but of none could it be said to the same extent that German song was merely one field amongst many. For Lassus the madrigal came first,[2] offering, as it did, the richest opportunities for interpretation of the text. However, he did not simply employ the madrigal style unaltered in his German songs—the old German texts were ill suited to such handling—nor can his songs be regarded as *villanelle* or *chansons* with German words. It would be truer to say, rather, that he turned the elements of these types to account in various ways in the setting of German texts, with the result that his *Lieder* show much greater stylistic variety than his secular compositions with Italian or French texts.

Altogether Lassus published ninety-three German songs in from three to six parts, in seven publications between 1567 and 1590.[3] Forty-nine of these have religious words, but, with the exception of the three-part *Geistliche Psalmen* (1588), they are interspersed among the secular compositions; most of them are based on the *canto fermo* principle. The collection of 1576 even contains a few secular tenor songs with freely invented *canti fermi*. In contrast to the conservative Le Maistre, Lassus, however, did not adopt the amorous texts of the old *Hofweisen*, but was more attracted by realistically coarse popular songs, drinking songs, and comic incidents which he loved to expand into entertaining stories in several sections.[4]

The foundation of Lassus's song style is polyphony; chordal

---

[1] Osthoff, op. cit., p. 207.   [2] See p. 56.

[3] Reprinted by Adolf Sandberger, in *Orlando di Lasso: Sämtliche Werke*, xviii and xx (Leipzig, 1909–10).

[4] Cf. ibid. xx, p. 31: 'Ich hab ein Mann, der garnichts kann.'

writing is rarely found at any length and serves generally for contrast, as in the 1583 collection which shows the greatest element of influence from the *villanella*.[1] The repetition of whole sections for musical reasons derives equally from the *villanella* and the *chanson*, while the repetition of themes and phrases on account of the literary content is taken over from the madrigal, as are themes based on word painting and expressive harmonic details.[2] A feature of Lassus's secular songs, as distinct from sacred ones, is syllabic declamation in short notes, a method of word-setting most marked in those pieces influenced by the style of the *villanella* and in the *chanson*-like drinking songs, with their pregnant opening themes:

---

[1] Ibid., p. 28: 'Ich weiß mir ein Meidlein hübsch und fein.'
[2] Ibid. xviii, p. 82: 'Ein Meidlein zu dem Brunnen ging.'
[3] Ibid., p. 44.

(A good wine is praiseworthy above all)

Yet, despite many song-like traits, Lassus's secular compositions to German words are 'song motets' rather than 'songs' in the more narrow sense.

The motet principle is still dominant in the work of Christian Hollander (c. 1540–1568/9) who, uninfluenced by Lassus, adopted in his posthumous collection of 1570 the double-choir technique of the Venetians,[1] and in two of Lassus's pupils, Anton Gosswin (c. 1540–98) and Ivo de Vento (1544?–75), the short-lived court organist at Munich. Gosswin is known only by his *Neue teutsche Lieder* (Nuremberg, 1581)[2] which consist largely of skilful three-part arrangements or *contrafacta* of five-part pieces from Lassus's similarly named collection of 1567, but Vento, Lassus's most important pupil, rivalled the productivity of his master as a song-composer. Like Lassus, Vento produced no fewer than seven books of *Teutsche Lieder* ranging from three to six parts, which appeared in rapid succession between 1569 and 1575. His preface to his four-part collection of 1572, where he objects to textual illustration on the lines of the madrigal, shows him as more conservative than his master; in further contrast with Lassus, he stood in close relationship to the old German love-song. More forward-looking in style are his three-part songs of 1572 where, four years earlier than Regnart, he borrows the form and style of the Italian *villanella* and thus comes close to the *Lied* principle.

To regard Jacob Regnart merely as a composer of *villanelle* would be to misjudge his significance, for in these, as he made clear in the preface to his First Part (1576), he did not aim very high. These were

[1] See pp. 276 ff.
[2] Reprinted by K. G. Fellerer, *Das Chorwerk*, lxxv (Wolfenbüttel, 1960).

merely the popular counterpart to the more important part of his output, in which, like Lassus in the majority of his songs, he addressed himself to connoisseurs. To this latter category belongs his first publication, the five-part *Canzoni italiane* of 1574, to which a second part appeared in 1581. Whereas in these the polyphony of the madrigal is combined with the *villanella* form, in his five-part *Teutsche Lieder* (Nuremberg, 1580)[1] Regnart goes further than Lassus in adopting the madrigal style, at least in his love-songs. The collection contains also some through-composed pieces in several sections, in Lassus's manner. The three parts of Regnart's *Kurtzweilige teutsche Lieder zu drei stimmen nach Art der Neapolitanen oder welschen Villanellen* appeared in the transition period (1576–9).[2] Nine editions of separate issues and eight of the whole set testify to the unusual popularity of this work, with which Regnart, the first Netherland specialist of the secular *Lied*, gave—though in a different way from Lassus—a new and lasting impulse to German song. What was decisive in Regnart's work was that he did not merely adopt the three-sectional musical *villanella* form on the patterns *AABBCC* and *AABBC* (with repetition of text as well as of melody), but also assimilated his (doubtless original) texts in content and form to the Italian pattern. He preferred stanzas either of three lines of eleven syllables or of six lines on the plan (6+6) (7+7) (7+7), as in Ex. 38. Admittedly, in his first three books there is a tendency towards the German popular style in the content and on the musical side a tendency to homophony and to shortening of the dimensions. Small melodic range, syllabic setting, and identical rhythm in all parts predominate, and the highest part is decidedly the most important. In this way the song principle reasserted itself for the first time since the change of style, though not everywhere in the collection so unmistakably as in the following example, which served also as model for many religious *contrafacta*:

Ex. 38

---

[1] Five songs from this collection have been published by Osthoff (Kassel, 1928). See Bibliography.

[2] Ed. Eitner, op. cit. xix (Leipzig, 1895).

(Venus, you and your child are both blind—and apt to blind him who turns
to you, as I found in my youth.)

The last Netherland contribution to German song came at a time
when the German composers had generally reasserted themselves. It
consisted of the four-part *Teutsche Liedlein* (Vienna, 1602) in canzonetta style, of Lambert de Sayve (*c.* 1549–1614),[1] who ended his
career as Imperial *Oberkapellmeister* in Prague and obviously worked
under the influence of Regnart, who contributed two pieces to the
collection. Michael Praetorius held de Sayve's songs in sufficient
esteem to reissue them nine years later.

Lastly, three Italians must be mentioned, who worked at German
courts during the Netherland ascendancy and set Italian as well as
German texts. They were two of Le Maistre's successors at Dresden—
Antonio Scandello (1517–80) and Giovanni Battista Pinello—with
Gregorio Turini, who was active in Prague in the latter part of his
career. In his *Neue und lustige weltliche teutsche Liedlein* of 1570
Scandello significantly foreshadows Hassler's *Canzonette*.[2]

[1] Reprinted complete by Friedrich Blume, *Das Chorwerk*, li (Wolfenbüttel, 1938).
[2] See p. 112.

THE REVIVAL OF NATIVE COMPOSITION IN THE 1570's

Although Jakob Meiland (1542–77) published his *Newe außerlesene teutsche Liedlin* in 1569 it was not until six years later that a true revival began. In 1575 Meiland published a second book (*Teutsche Gesäng*) which was the first of a close succession of publications by German composers. At the head stood two of Lassus's pupils, Leonhard Lechner (*c.* 1550–1606) and Johannes Eccard (1553–1611). The fact that the native song-composers born between 1540 and 1560 are too numerous for all to be mentioned here is a sufficient indication of the extent of German song-production during the last third of the sixteenth century.

As in the time of the tenor song, Nuremberg was the chief publishing centre. Now, moreover, it became a centre of composition as well, as is testified by the names of Brechtel, Lechner, and Hassler. The tradition was continued in Heidelberg by Johann Knöfel and Nicolaus Rosthius, whose two books of *XXX newer lieblicher Galliardt* (1593 and 1594) are the first examples of dances intended for both singing and playing. Bavaria and Austria now fall behind while other regions come into prominence: East Prussia with Eccard, Thuringia (Eccard's homeland) with Steuerlein and Henning Dedekind, Lower Saxony with Hagius and Mancinus, Silesia with Elsbeth, and Frankfurt-on-Oder with Gregor Lange, a notable exponent of the three-part *villanella*-like *Lied* (two books, 1584 and 1586). Other composers, such as Meiland, who sometimes held fast to the *canto fermo*, sometimes borrowed elements from the *balletto*, changed their residence from time to time. There is no evidence that Meiland was ever in Italy.

If we examine in its entirety the song output of the period it becomes evident that in many instances the number of parts bears a close relation to style and form. Song-motets and madrigalian songs are mostly in five parts, canzonets and dance-songs in four, while for the *villanella* type three-part writing is the rule. Often, though not always, one can draw inferences from the titles when they point to Italian models.

Leonhard Lechner, who came from the Tyrol and was a schoolmaster at Nuremberg from 1575 to 1583, ended his life as *Hofkapellmeister* at Stuttgart. He enjoyed the tuition of Lassus and was also a pupil of Ivo de Vento, but made use in a highly individual way of both these formative influences. Lechner composed some 150 songs, in which strophic pieces and those in motet style are roughly equal in

number, though admittedly the latter are largely sacred songs which
in some editions are mingled with the secular works. In Lechner's
time there were in Nuremberg three patrician and bourgeois music
societies[1] for which a number of his songs were written. All his work
shows a leaning toward polyphony though his strophic pieces reveal
an increasing tendency to song-like treatment of the upper parts. Also
noteworthy is Lechner's preference for serious secular texts. His first
collection, which appeared in 1576 (the year that also saw the publication of Regnart's first set of German *Villanellen*), comprised
three-part songs; a second collection followed in 1577. However, the
resemblances in style between him and Regnart are insignificant.
Lechner was not concerned with popular effect, or he would hardly
have brought out in 1579 masterly five-part versions of *villanelle* by
Regnart,[2] in which the 'popular' character of the originals is completely lost. His *Newe teutsche Lieder mit vier und fünff stimmen*
(1577)[3] are of greater intrinsic and historical significance; here he
goes even further than Regnart in his 1580 collection towards the
absorption of the madrigal style, so that the secular pieces may well
be called German madrigals. Some Italian madrigals of his have also
been preserved. Although the poetic form of no. 12, 'O Lieb, wie
süß und bitter',[4] is admittedly non-madrigalian, this cannot be said
of the content, the sonority, or the interpretation of the text:

Ex. 39

[1] Cf. Konrad Ameln, article 'Lechner', *Die Musik in Geschichte und Gegenwart*, viii
(1960), col. 430.
[2] Ed. Eitner, op. cit. xix (Leipzig, 1895).
[3] Ed. Uwe Martin in *Leonhard Lechner: Werke*, iii (Kassel, 1954).
[4] Ibid., p. 58.

(O Love, how sweet and bitter, a burning, anxious need, full of sorrow)

Of similar significance are the four-part *Neue lustige Teutsche Lieder nach Art der Welschen Canzonen* of 1586[1] in which Lechner adhered very closely to the model of the canzonet, which was to be repeatedly followed in the period immediately following. The term 'Canzonette' was first used in Germany by Joachim Brechtel in 1590. In the last year of his life Lechner composed the impressive *Deutsche Sprüche von Leben und Tod*,[2] a cycle of madrigalian motets on song-texts of a religious nature which, in their expressive power, are comparable with the *Cantiones Sacrae* of Heinrich Schütz.

The conservative Johannes Eccard was far less successful than Lechner in freeing himself from the influence of his master Lassus. He differs also from Lechner in that the greater part of his work in song form was expressly intended for use in church,[2] and his publications of 1578 and 1589[3] contain only a few secular pieces in four

[1] Ed. Ernst Fritz Schmid, *Lechner: Werke*, ix (Kassel, 1958).
[2] See p. 452.
[3] *Newe teutsche Lieder mit fünf und vier Stimmen* (Königsberg, 1589), ed. Eitner, op. cit. xxi (Leipzig, 1897).

or five parts. The majority are song-motets. Here again Eccard introduces madrigalian elements and his drinking songs reveal the influence of the *chanson*, though one never finds the forms of the *villanella* and *canzonetta*.

HANS LEO HASSLER

With Hans Leo Hassler (1564–1612) we come to a song composer whose influence on his contemporaries—especially with his *Lustgarten neuer teutscher Gesäng*—was almost without parallel. He was active at Nuremberg (where he was born and where he was inspired by Lechner's example), Venice, Augsburg, and Dresden. From 1602 to 1604 he was again in Nuremberg as city *Oberkapellmeister*. With Hassler, a pupil of Andrea Gabrieli, begins the real 'Italian period' of the German *Lied*, though he provided also the basis for a synthesis of styles by combining the Italian *balletto* with the German dancesong which had been cultivated, particularly in Nuremberg, from the early decades of the sixteenth century. Further, he was, with Schütz and Lechner, one of the few important Germans to compose secular music on Italian texts, and it is significant that he turned to the *Lied* only after the publication of his *Canzonette a quattro voci* (Nuremberg 1590).[1] These differ from Lechner's canzonets by their chordal texture and the sparing use of madrigalisms, thus acquiring the stamp of the *Lied*. Most are in the three-part form *AABCC*, though some employ a modified two-part *AABB*. A complete contrast to the canzonets is provided by the highly wrought polyphony of Hassler's Italian madrigals in from five to eight parts,[2] which appeared in 1596, the same year as the *Neue teutsche Gesäng nach Art der welschen Madrigalien und Canzonetten* (for four to eight voices).[3] Whereas the first two collections are each in a single style, the third, as the title implies, displays the opposing tendencies of madrigal and *Lied;* Hassler profits here from his experience in setting Italian texts. Unlike Lechner he makes no use of texts from the tenor-song period, but in most cases writes his own poems after Italian models. No. 17, 'Ich scheid von dir mit Leide', is a true madrigal, even as regards the seven- and eleven-syllable lines of the text. Homophonic canzonets are represented by nos. 3 and 4, in which the highest voice shows melodic traits characteristic of the allemande, and by no. 24, the

[1] Ed. Rudolf Schwartz, *Denkmäler der Tonkunst in Bayern*, v (2) (Leipzig, 1904).
[2] Ed. Schwartz, ibid. xi (1) (Leipzig, 1910); revised in *Sämtliche Werke*, iii (Wiesbaden, 1961), by C. Russell Crosby, Jr.
[3] Ed. Schwartz, op. cit. v (2) (Leipzig, 1904).

eight-part 'Mein Lieb will mit mir kriegen', in which interchange of
parts and groups of voices produces novel sound effects. On the whole
these canzonets are richer in madrigalian features than those in the
1590 collection.

In 1601 Hassler brought out his *Lustgarten neuer teutscher Gesäng
Balletti Galliarden und Intraden* (for four to eight voices);[1] this is
based on similar texts to those of the *Neue teutsche Gesäng* and remained until about 1630 the pattern for collections of dances with and
without text. The most important dance forms, which now reappeared
for the first time since the days of the tenor song, if we except Rosthius
and Haussmann, were the *Tanz* in common time, identical with the
allemande:

Ex. 40

[1] Ed. Friedrich Zelle, *Publikation älterer praktischer und theoretischer Musikwerke*, xv
(Leipzig, 1887).

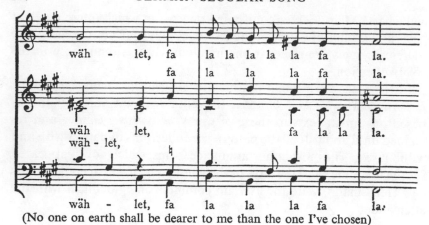

(No one on earth shall be dearer to me than the one I've chosen)

occasionally provided with a *proportio*, and the galliard:

Ex.41

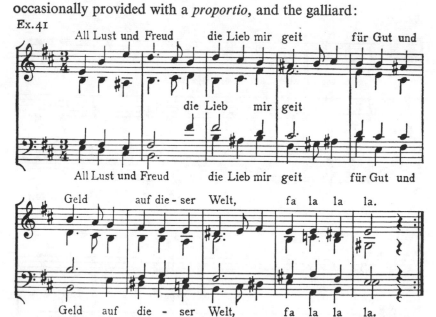

(Love gave me all happiness and joy before worldly goods and wealth)

Many such pieces have 'fa-la-la' refrains like Gastoldi's *balletti*.

The historical importance of the homorhythmic chordal dance-songs in the development of the solo song lies in the fact that the song-principle appears in its purest form in their highest parts; very probably even in Hassler's time, the highest parts of these songs were sung as solos, the lower ones being reduced to a sort of *continuo* accompaniment.[1] In one of Hassler's most beautiful songs, 'Mein

---

[1] Cf. Walther Vetter, *Das frühdeutsche Lied*, i (Münster, 1928), pp. 3, 6, 33.

Gmüt ist mir verwirret', the dance rhythm is polymetrically transformed in accordance with the verbal accent. Madrigalian pieces play
only a small part in the *Lustgarten* as Hassler was here aiming above
all at popular effect, though not in the same way as Regnart. The
trend towards the popular was, of course, characteristic of the
period; echoes of popular melodies occur frequently. It is not yet
known to what extent actual popular melodies were the bases of the
dance-songs and instrumental dances, but it seems likely that this was
frequently the case.[1]

Nuremberg continued to be an important centre of song composition in the period which took its character from the work of the composers born between 1560 and 1590, yet the centre of gravity began to
change. Saxony and Thuringia, where solo song was to flourish later,
became increasingly important in the field of choral song—a term
which may at any rate be correctly applied to the dance-song. It was
here that Heinrich Schütz worked, and Johann Hermann Schein, the
greatest polyphonic *Lied* composer after Hassler.

In 1601, the year in which Hassler's *Lustgarten* appeared, the
organist of St. Sebald's in Nuremberg, Hans Christoph Haiden
(1572–1613), a relative of Hassler, brought out a collection containing four-part dance-songs and instrumental dances of which both
music and texts—the composer's own—show a definitely 'popular'
character. (A second volume appeared in 1614.) The *Neue teutsche
Lieder* of Johann Staden (1581–1634), published in 1609, are related
both in style and content to Haiden's collection. That a conscious
striving after artistry can diminish the value of an artist's work is
shown by Staden's *Venuskränzlein*, which followed his first collection
a year later, for in this work, written with an eye to the post of
organist in Nuremberg, he avoided the popular style.[2] Johann
Andreas Herbst (1588–1666), whose activity was divided between his
birthplace, Nuremberg, and Frankfurt-on-Main, showed no interest
in the dance-song but made a valuable contribution to the five-part
German madrigal with his *Theatrum Amoris* (1613).

A greater variety of types is found in the songs of Christoph
Demantius (1567–1643) who was employed as cantor in the Saxon
towns of Zittau and Freiberg. Admittedly the pieces in his first publication (1595) are all of one type; five-part writing is applied not in
the madrigal style but exclusively to strophic songs in the canzonet

---

[1] Cf. Walter Wiora, *Europäische Volksmusik und abendländische Tonkunst* (Kassel, 1957), p. 99.
[2] Cf. Vetter, op. cit., p. 73.

form *AABCC*, with a chordal but not homorhythmic texture. On the other hand, a more varied picture, as the title and subtitle suggest, is presented by his *Convivalium concentuum farrago* for six and eight voices,[1] which appeared in 1609, and was intended for social occasions. The phrase 'In welcher deutsche Madrigalia, Canzonette und Villanellen . . .' does not refer to the typical formal elements and characteristic number of voices; Demantius seems rather to have wished to indicate that he had mixed the stylistic elements peculiar to these varieties. *Gruppenformen* more or less disappear, though the strophic principle predominates. Noteworthy also is the appearance for the first time of mythological turns of phrase and fashionable foreign words, such as *inficiret* and *probiret* (no. 12), for which Schein was later to display a special liking. Demantius published not only German, but also Polish dances, with and without words, in three books (1607, 1608, and 1613).

The voluminous body of songs by Valentin Haussmann (*c.* 1570–1611/14) remains almost unexplored. About 1600 he was organist in the Saxon town of Gerbstädt but travelled extensively through Germany to gain support for his music; from a sociological point of view, this is one of the most interesting phenomena of the period. Between 1592 and 1604, Haussmann published no fewer than eleven books comprising canzonets, dance-songs, and instrumental dances, the last (as with Demantius) including Polish dances. In the following period Haussmann, who had considerable literary ability, busied himself with the publication of canzonets and *balletti* by Marenzio, Orazio Vecchi, Gastoldi, Capilupi, and Morley, for which he provided German texts, part free translation, part paraphrase. Haussmann played a decisive role in the dissemination of Italian music in Germany.

While it is not known that Hassler had any personal contact with Demantius and Haussmann, there can be no doubt that the Coburg *Hofkapellmeister* Melchior Franck (*c.* 1580–1639), a Saxon, was a pupil of Hassler, whose influence is unmistakable in Franck's secular songs, published in fourteen collections during the period 1602–23. All kinds are represented here, from the polyphonic (though rarely madrigalian) song to the plainly harmonized dance, the number of parts ranging from three to eight. Half of them are vocal and instrumental dances. In two respects Franck holds a unique position

---

[1] This collection and Demantius's *Neue deutsche weltliche Lieder* (Nuremberg, 1595), have been edited by Kurt Stangl, *Das Erbe deutscher Musik* (*Sonderreihe* i) (Kassel, 1954).

in the history of German song. He was the only composer since the tenor-song period who made polyphonic settings of the older popular songs, his principal publications being *Reuterliedlein* (1603) and the *Neues teutsches Convivium* (1621). And he produced the richest and most noteworthy contribution to the quodlibet since Senfl and Schmeltzl; Franck wrote ten of these pieces, which were published separately and then collected in his *Musicalischer Grillenvertreiber* of 1622.[1] With the exception of one very highly polished polyphonic composition in six parts, unique in the whole literature, this collection consists of four-part 'successive' quodlibets, full of spirit and wit and quoting from numerous popular songs.

Two other composers, related by many common factors, who worked mainly in Franconia and Württemberg, were Erasmus Widmann (1572–1634) from Schwäbisch-Hall, and Johann Jeep (1582–1634) who came from Lower Saxony and was Widmann's successor as *Hofkapellmeister* at Weikersheim. Both were especially notable for their contributions to the polyphonic student song, Jeep in his *Studentengärtlein* (for three to six voices) which appeared in two parts in 1605 and 1613–14, and Widmann with his *Studentenmut* (for four or five voices) of 1622.[2] With his songs, which met with unusual success, Jeep initiated a line of both vocal and instrumental publications of student music leading to Adam Krieger's *Arien* of 1657 and 1667, and Johann Rosenmüller's *Studentenmusik* of 1654. The *Studentengärtlein* consists almost exclusively of strophic songs, mostly love-songs; the continuous texture of the madrigal is entirely lacking. Equally notable by its absence is the typical student element of the drinking song, a type which appeared first in the work of Widmann. Widmann's songs, which in contrast with Jeep's went into several editions, are marked by a 'popular' quality rather old-fashioned in nature; at the same time they are topical, for the *poeta laureatus* Widmann, more than almost any of his contemporaries, refers in his songs to politics, particularly to the events of war.[3] Mention must also be made here of the numerous songs written to order, a field in which, beside many others, the Austrian Andreas Rauch appeared with his *Musikalisches Stammbüchlein*.[4]

[1] Three quodlibets from this collection edited by Gudewill, *Das Chorwerk*, liii. See also Gudewill, 'Ursprünge und nationale Aspekte des Quodlibets', *International Musicological Society: Report of the Eighth Congress: New York, 1961*, i (Kassel, 1961), p. 41.

[2] Jeep's *Studentengärtlein*, ed. Rudolf Gerber, *Das Erbe deutscher Musik*, xxix (Wolfenbüttel, 1958); selection from Widmann's *Studentenmut* and other song-books, ed. G. Reichert, ibid. *Sonderreihe* iii (Mainz, 1959).

[3] Cf. Vetter, op. cit., pp. 106 ff.

[4] Ibid., pp. 137 ff.

K

It is pleasant to see how Nicolaus Zangius (*c.* 1570–*c.* 1620), in his *Geistliche und weltliche Liedlein*, while writing in three parts, preferred the older German strophic scheme to Regnart's *villanella* form. Zangius, a Brandenburger, whose career took him to Berlin by way of Danzig and Prague, published this collection in three volumes in 1594, 1611,[1] and 1617. His volume of five-part sacred and secular songs, which appeared in 1597,[2] shows similarly conservative tendencies. He was succeeded as *Kapellmeister* at the Marienkirche at Danzig by a Pomeranian, Andreas Hakenberger (*c.* 1574–1627), whose *Neue deutsche Gesänge nach Art der welschen Madrigalien* (for five to eight voices) (Danzig, 1610), are noteworthy because, with one exception, they show the strophic continuous composition of Lassus and Regnart raised to the level of an accepted principle.

The Baltic city of Rostock has a place in the history of German song, thanks to the works of a Thuringian, Daniel Friderici (1584–1638), who was strongly influenced by Hassler—and who, among other things, produced an edition of Morley's three-part canzonets (Rostock, 1624). Especially noteworthy among his six books of songs (in three to six parts) published between 1617 and 1633, is the *Hilarodicon* of 1632[3] which contains five-part choruses entitled 'Vinetten' and set to humorous texts with dedications to various wine-merchants. Such pieces were intended as diversions for the consuls and the Rostock students. That Hassler's influence extended to other parts of North Germany is shown by the five-part *Neue teutsche weltliche Madrigalien und Balletten*[4] (1619) of the Holsteiner Johann Steffens (*c.* 1560–1616) who was organist at Lüneburg. The title gives a good idea of the contents, which consist in roughly equal numbers of madrigals and dance-songs, some of which have 'fa-la-la' refrains. Also active in Lower Saxony was Otto Siegfried Harnisch (*c.* 1568–1627), whose three-part songs (two books, 1587 and 1588) are closer in style to the canzonet than to the *villanella*. In 1622 the Brunswick-Lüneburg court organist at Dannenberg-on-Elbe, Johannes Schultz (1582–1653), brought out a collection of vocal and instrumental pieces entitled *Musicalischer Lüstgarte*,[5] which in its motley nature must be almost unmatched, at any rate among the

---

[1] The *Ander Theil Deutscher Lieder* (Vienna, 1611), ed. Hans Sachs and Anton Pfalz, *Denkmäler der Tonkunst in Österreich*, lxxxvii (Vienna, 1951).

[2] *Geistliche und weltliche Lieder mit fünf Stimmen* (Cologne, 1597), ed. Fritz Bose (Berlin, 1960).

[3] See Hans Joachim Moser, *Corydon* (Brunswick, 1933), i, p. 33, ii, p. 58.

[4] Ed. Gustav Fock, *Das Erbe deutscher Musik*, xxix (Wolfenbüttel, 1958).

[5] Ed. Hermann Zenck, *Das Erbe deutscher Musik. Landschaftsdenkmale Niedersachsen*, i (Wolfenbüttel, 1937).

publications of the seventeenth century. It is a typical collection of
practical music, for two to eight voices, for the most varied occasions
and includes Latin motets, fugues, and fantasias. The settings of
German secular texts are partly chordal dance-songs, partly polyphonic pieces, with much use of imitation. To distinguish these from
the dance-songs Schultz almost always calls them 'madrigal', though
several stanzas of each poem are printed. These songs have little in
common with the through-composed Italian madrigal:

Ex. 42

(With your modesty, my dearest . . .)

SCHÜTZ AND SCHEIN

Rarely have two German composers produced under the name of
'madrigal' compositions as contrasted in style as those in Schultz's
Lüstgarte and the brilliant *Opus primum*[1] of Heinrich Schütz, the

[1] *Sämmtliche Werke*, ix, ed. Philipp Spitta (Leipzig, 1890); *Neue Ausgabe sämtlicher
Werke*, xxii, ed. H. J. Moser (Kassel and Basle, 1962).

Primo Libro de Madrigali (Venice, 1611). In their expressiveness, their wealth of figures, contrast-motives, and harmonic boldness, Schütz's five-part Italian madrigals are among the finest of their kind:

Ex. 43[1]

(O bitterest sweetness of love)

[1] *Sämmtliche Werke*, ix, p. 9; *Neue Ausgabe*, xxii, p. 9.

Furthermore, they bear the stamp of Schütz's unique personality and are far from copies of Italian models. It is significant that this particular work should stand at the very beginning of Schütz's career. In this field he was able to explore the possibilities of interpreting the text, a matter of the first importance later when he had to set biblical prose. Schütz stood in no very close relationship to either church-song or secular song in the narrowest sense; all the more important was the influence which his style of musical declamation, the 'monodic principle', exercised on song-composition. This influence, however, was more effective in the development of solo song and polyphonic vocal chamber music with *basso continuo*,[1] for the choral song as such had nearly reached its end.

As in the decade 1620–30 the boundary between choral song and solo song becomes somewhat vague, thanks to the possibility of reducing polyphonic pieces to solos with accompaniment, so the terms 'madrigal' and 'canzonet' undergo a similar change of meaning, reflected in the eight books of Monteverdi's madrigals with their development from the polyphony of the *prima prattica* to the style of the vocal concerto and solo cantata. If Schütz set his German madrigals[2]—written between 1620 and 1630 and left in manuscript—mostly for two voices, two obbligato instruments, and *basso continuo*, it was doubtless because he took Monteverdi's Seventh Book (1619) as his model. The texts are taken from the leading poet of the day, Martin Opitz, whose *Buch von der teutschen Poetery* appeared in 1625, and this partnership is a milestone in the history of German song, for composers now increasingly turned to such poets as Simon Dach, Paul Fleming, and Johann Rist.

Schütz's contributions to German secular song, though of great value, are thus few in number. It was in the work of Johann Hermann Schein (1586–1630), cantor at St. Thomas's, Leipzig, from 1616 until his death, that once more all the formal possibilities were explored.[3] Schein was responsible for all the texts of his works; they are of literary merit, and, despite the Italian titles of two collections, are entirely German. In the *Venuskränzlein* (1609), written for the bicentenary of Leipzig University, Schein composed five-part choruses modelled on Hassler's dance-songs, the homorhythmic principle being even more strongly stressed, though the rigid dance-rhythms

---

[1] See Moser, op. cit.
[2] *Sämmtliche Werke*, xv, ed. Spitta (Leipzig, 1893).
[3] *Johann Hermann Scheins Werke*, i, ii, iii, ed. Arthur Prüfer (Leipzig, 1901 ff.). On Schein generally, see Prüfer, *Johan Herman Schein* (Leipzig, 1895) and *Johann Hermann Schein und das weltliche deutsche Lied des 17. Jahrhunderts* (Leipzig, 1908).

are usually modified for the sake of better declamation. The 'monodic principle' is adapted to polyphony:

Ex. 44

Heu - len | und schmerzlich's | Wei - nen | jetz-un-der | hö-ret auf,

weil wie-der-|um   tut |schei-nen | die Sonn' mit | fröhl'- chem | Lauf,'

(Wailing and sorrowful weeping now cease, as the sun shines again joyfully.)

As regards form, the binary scheme of Hassler's canzonets predominates.

Whereas the texts of these songs are simple and popular in style, Schein adopts in his *Musica boscareccia* (three parts, Leipzig, 1621, 1626, and 1628) the newer type of pastoral poetry. According to the sub-title, these songs are written in *villanella* style, but this refers mostly to the three-part writing. In other respects Schein almost completely forsook the model of Regnart's *villanelle*, not merely by adding a doubtless optional *continuo* or by his employment of the binary scheme *AABB*, but by so crowding his work with imitations, word-repetition, madrigalisms, and passage-work as frequently to produce a discrepancy with the strophic principle. Of great importance are the six suggestions for vocal and instrumental performance in the preface to the First Part—particularly the last one, for performance by a solo soprano with *basso continuo*. A year later, in 1622, Schein published one of the first true solo *Lieder*, the 'Jocus nuptialis' for tenor and *basso continuo*.

If the *terzetti* of the *Musica boscareccia* are scarcely designed for choral performance, the same is even more true of the *Diletti pastorali* (1624), if we ignore the chordal endings of some of the pieces. These are five-part *continuo* madrigals with instruments. Not only has Schein, like Schütz, taken Monteverdi's Seventh Book as model, he has also written texts which, based chiefly on mythology, are completely madrigalian in style. As in the *Musica boscareccia*, contrapuntal and chordal writing are intermingled, but the dimensions are bigger and the madrigalisms still more numerous. If Schein moved furthest from the *Lied*-principle in the *Diletti*, he made a complete return to it in his last secular vocal work, the *Studentenschmaus* of 1626, which strikes the same popular note as the *Venuskränzlein*, here carried into the world of a convivial 'Compagni de la Vino-biera' (as the sub-title tells us). These five-part pieces are among the finest examples of student music in the last phase of the secular polyphonic *Lied* of the baroque period.

THE DECLINE OF THE POLYPHONIC SECULAR *LIED*

The two Dresden court musicians, Johann Nauwach (*c.* 1595–*c.* 1630) and Kaspar Kittel (1603–39), studied in Italy and were decidedly influenced by their master Schütz, whereas Thomas Selle (1599–1663),[1] who came from central Germany, followed Schein. Selle was active from 1624 onwards as cantor in several Holstein towns until, in 1641, he was appointed music-director of the five principal churches in Hamburg.

The work of Schütz's two pupils clearly shows that the German solo song did not originate primarily in adaptation of Caccini's monody but was rooted much more in the polyphonic tradition. The polyphonic pieces in Nauwach's *Teutsche Villanellen* of 1627 (for one to three voices with *continuo*)[2] and in Kittel's *Arien und Kantaten* (for one to four voices with *continuo*), published in 1638, are not only closer in style to the *Lied* proper, but musically superior to the pieces modelled more on Caccini.

Much more comprehensive is Selle's secular vocal music, largely determined by the *Lied* principle, in which the development from polyphonic or optionally solo performance to pure monody can be traced more clearly than in the work of any other composer of the period. In the four books of songs published between 1624 and 1636 Selle nowhere went beyond the three parts of the *villanella*, one part being represented by the *basso continuo*. He began with the three-part *Deliciae Pastorum Arcadiae*, still far from unified in style. The suggestions for vocal and instrumental performance remind one of Schein's and also apply to the two following books; the possibility of reduction to a solo song is always kept in mind. In 1634 appeared

[1] A number of songs by Nauwach, Kittel, and Selle are reprinted in Vetter, op. cit., ii.
[2] On Nauwach's solo songs, see *infra*, p. 183.

the *Deliciae Juvenilium* for two voices, followed a year later by the three-part *Amores musicales*, one of Selle's best works, largely because he mainly chose popular rather than mythological texts:

Ex. 45

Möcht ich jetzt mild dei - ne Gunst spü - - ren
ad - li - ches Bild, wollt ich be - rüh - - ren

(Now fain would I enjoy thy favour . . .)

Whereas up to this point it had been quite possible for all the parts to be sung, in the *Monophonetica* of 1636 Selle took the decisive step to solo song with *continuo*; this is the earliest collection of German songs in which this principle is employed exclusively.

Johann Rist, the founder of the Hamburg school of song-writers, who began to publish in 1641, had no doubt that the composers who used his poems should set them as solo songs. But the position is less clearly defined in the *Arien* which Schütz's cousin and pupil, Heinrich Albert, published at Königsberg between 1638 and 1650. In these we find from the beginning monodic and polyphonic compositions side by side, though true *Lieder* predominate; however, in the later issues the proportion of polyphony actually increases, for the solo song did not at first make much headway in Königsberg. On the whole, though, by 1650 the solo song—using the word 'song' in its narrower sense—had conquered the polyphonic type, though vocal chamber music on the pattern of Schütz's German madrigals and Schein's *Diletti pastorali* was still being written up to about 1680 by Rubert, Knüpfer, Theile, and Horn.

IV

SOLO SONG AND CANTATA

By NIGEL FORTUNE

ARRANGED SONG

THE history of the surviving vocal music of the sixteenth century is
to a great extent the history of ensemble music. Except for the songs
of the Spanish *vihuelistas* it was not until the end of the century that
large numbers of songs were composed expressly as solos. This is not
to say that countries other than Spain managed without a literature
of solo song. The tendency towards monody exists in the *frottole* of
the beginning of the century;[1] as Alfred Einstein has pointed out, the
later 'trend towards the *a cappella* ideal seems like a deviation' from
this conception of monody and the eventual 'trend away from it
a return. But this is not the whole story, for even in the sixteenth
century the flow of monody never ceased; it went underground, as it
were, and continued to run parallel to the *a cappella* forms.'[2] The art
of solo song in the sixteenth century was, as we have seen in Chapter
I,[3] very largely an art of arrangement. It was also undoubtedly an art
of improvisation, and improvised music rarely survives. We must
bear in mind, then, that the sixteenth-century songs discussed here
represent perhaps not even a half of those known at the time.

A typical piece of about 1550 might be performed in several forms
other than its original one for, let us say, four voices (if indeed such
a version always was the original one): for example, in an elaborate
arrangement for a keyboard instrument; as a keyboard piece with
a florid counterpoint for a viol; as a dance for instrumental ensemble;
as a lute solo; or—the form that concerns us in this chapter—with
the top part sung as a solo to an instrumental accompaniment consisting of two or all three of the lower parts. The *frottole* of Tromboncino and Cara could easily be sung in this last form; indeed, from
1509 onwards Petrucci had published *frottole* in Venice as solos to
the lute, with the original alto parts suppressed.[4] In Paris in 1529

---

[1] See *supra*, p. 35, and Vol. III, pp. 398 and 400.
[2] *The Italian Madrigal* (Princeton, 1949), ii, p. 836.　　　　[3] See pp. 5 and 20.
[4] See Vol. III, p. 440, and Benvenuto Disertori, *Le frottole per canto e liuto intabulate
da Franciscus Bossinensis* (Milan, 1964). Examples also in Hans Dagobert Bruger, *Alte
Lautenkunst aus drei Jahrhunderten* (Berlin and Leipzig, [1923]), i, p. 18, and *Schule des
Lautenspiels* (Wolfenbüttel, 1925), i, p. 16; Ernest Ferand, *Die Improvisation in der Musik*

Attaingnant had, as we have seen in Chapter I, printed voice-and-lute versions of twenty-four polyphonic *chansons*.[1] In Germany the native tenor-songs were adapted in this manner, in printed books at least, much less often than for lute alone (possibly because of printing difficulties): almost the only examples are those that the lutenist Sebastian Ochsenkuhn published at Heidelberg in 1558 in his *Tabulaturbuch auff die Lauten*,[2] and later in the century there are the rather dull arrangements in Adrian Denss's *Florilegium* (Cologne, 1594) of polyphonic *Lieder* by Leonhard Lechner and other composers. However, the two melodic strands of many pieces that appear to be simple lute solos turn out to be subsidiary lines of four-part songs; if the main melodies of the original versions are sung to them as solos a new, hitherto unsuspected song-repertory is arrived at.[3] Nevertheless, Germany began again to play an important part in the history of solo song only about 1620: there will therefore be few more references to German music in this chapter.

THE SPANISH *VIHUELA*-BOOKS

This is the most convenient point at which to interrupt the account of arranged song in order to survey the solo songs of the *vihuelistas*.[4] After this the way will be clear for a survey of all the possible types of solo song in Italy (both composed as such and arranged), one or two of which eventually merged into the 'new music' towards the end of the century; sixteenth-century songs in England and France will be treated in a similar fashion, though more briefly.

Music-printing in sixteenth-century Spain was not the flourishing trade that it was in France and Italy. Spain had no printer who devoted himself exclusively to the printing of music, as several Frenchmen and Italians did, and only seventeen volumes of music

---

(Zürich 1938), pp. 382–5; Oswald Körte, *Laute und Lautenmusik bis zur Mitte des 16. Jahrhunderts* (Leipzig, 1901), pp. 158–61; and Johannes Wolf, *Handbuch der Notationskunde*, ii (Leipzig, 1919), pp. 60–61.

[1] See p. 5. Reprinted in Lionel de la Laurencie, Adrienne Mairy, and Geneviève Thibault, *Chansons au luth et airs de cour français du XVIᵉ siècle* (Paris, 1934), pp. 2–51, with facsimile of a specimen page of music on p. xxxiv. Other reprints and facsimiles include Körte, op. cit., pp. 156–7, Frits Noske, *The Solo Song outside German-speaking Countries* (Cologne, 1958), p. 18, Wolf, op. cit., ii, pp. 77–78, and *Musikalische Schrifttafeln* (Bückeburg and Leipzig, 1923), p. 61. The arrangement of Sermisy's 'Vivray-je toujours en soucy' is recorded in *The History of Music in Sound* (H.M.V.), iv.

[2] Examples of arrangements of tenor-songs by Senfl and Isaac in Bruger, *Alte Lautenkunst*, i, pp. 8–13.

[3] Cf. Denis Stevens, *A History of Song* (London, 1960), pp. 94–95.

[4] Much the best general survey of these songs is to be found in John Ward, *The Vihuela de mano and its Music* (Diss., New York, 1953, unpub.).

are known to have been published there during the whole of the century.[1] Yet seven of the surviving volumes, published between 1536 and 1576—a much higher proportion than in other countries at this period—include songs for a solo voice; these are accompanied in all but a handful of cases by the *vihuela de mano*, a six-stringed cross between lute and guitar, which was the favourite instrument of elegant Spanish society. The short titles of the seven books are:

Luis Milán, *Libro de Música de vihuela de mano intitulado El Maestro* (Valencia, 1536: this is the date of the colophon—the title-page says 1535).[2]

Luis de Narváez, *Los seys libros del Delphin de música* (Valladolid, 1538).[3]

Alonso de Mudarra, *Tres libros de música* (Seville, 1546).[4]

Enrique Enriquez de Valderrábano, *Libro de música de vihuela intitulado Silva de Sirenas* (Valladolid, 1547).[4]

Diego Pisador, *Libro de música de vihuela* (Salamanca, 1552).

Miguel de Fuenllana, *Orphenica lyra* (Seville, 1554).[5]

Esteban Daza, *El Parnaso* (Valladolid, 1576).[6]

These books all contain much instrumental music[7] as well as vocal music. Nor does the vocal music consist only of songs. Starting with Narváez's *Los seys libros*, these Spanish books, like those in other countries, include solo arrangements of ensemble music, even of motets and mass-sections, by Flemish, French, and Italian, as well as Spanish composers. Milán's *El Maestro* is secular and largely

[1] Cf. Ward, 'The Editorial Methods of Venegas de Henestrosa', *Musica Disciplina*, vi (1952), p. 106.

[2] Reprinted complete as *Musikalische Werke*, ed. Leo Schrade, in *Publikationen älterer Musik*, ii (Leipzig, 1927). The disadvantage of this edition is that it does not always show clearly enough the polyphonic movement of the *vihuela* part.

[3] Reprinted complete, ed. Emilio Pujol, in *Monumentos de la música española*, iii (Barcelona, 1945). Three songs also in Eduardo Martinez Torner, *Composiciones escogidas de El Delphin de Música (1538)*, in *Colección de vihuelistas españoles del siglo XVI* (Madrid [1923]), pp. 12–19.

[4] Reprinted by Pujol in *Monumentos*, vii and xxii–xxiii (Barcelona, 1949 and 1965).

[5] For facsimiles, lists of contents, descriptions, and transcriptions cf. Hugo Riemann, 'Das Lautenwerk des Miguel de Fuenllana (1554)', *Monatshefte für Musikgeschichte*, xxvii (1895), p. 81, and Felipe Pedrell, *Catàlech de la Biblioteca Musical de la Diputació de Barcelona*, ii (Barcelona, 1909), pp. 125–55. One song in Daniel Heartz, 'A Spanish "Masque of Cupid"', *Musical Quarterly*, xlix (1963), p. 62.

[6] The principal modern anthology of songs from these books is Guillermo de Morphy, *Les Luthistes espagnols du XVIᵉ siècle*, 2 vols. (Leipzig, 1902). The transcriptions are, however, very unreliable. Smaller collections include Jesús Bal y Gay, *Romances y villancicos españoles del siglo XVI* (Mexico, 1939) and Luis de Villalba Muñoz, *Diez canciones españolas de los siglos XV y XVI* (Madrid, n.d.). The poetical texts have frequently been studied and anthologized: cf. the list of publications in Daniel Devoto, 'Poésie et musique dans l'œuvre des vihuelistes', *Annales musicologiques*, iv (1956), pp. 86–89. This paper is a valuable starting-point in an attempt at co-ordinating the work of musical and literary historians on the songs of the *vihuelistas*.

[7] This is discussed in a later chapter, pp. 682 ff.

Spanish in character and consists solely of his own music; only eleven years later Valderrábano's book is, on the other hand, a completely cosmopolitan collection of all kinds of music, both sacred and secular, original and arranged, which reflects the widening interests of Spanish music-lovers. Fuenllana's volume is almost entirely made up of arrangements of other men's music, more of which are for voice and *vihuela* than for *vihuela* alone as in some of the other books. It should also be pointed out that many of the apparently original songs in these books, Milán's and Mudarra's certainly excepted, are possibly arrangements of no longer extant polyphonic, or even instrumental, originals. Milán's volume also differs from the later books in being overtly didactic: the very title *El Maestro* stamps it as a book of instruction, and indeed the music it contains, stated in the preface to be for beginners, is arranged in order of difficulty and interspersed with instructions as to its performance.

The handsomely produced *El Maestro* stemmed from the brilliant and cultivated court of the Vicereine Germaine de Foix at Valencia; the high-born Milán was himself a courtier and the author of a handbook on court life modelled on Castiglione's *Il Cortegiano*.[1] This book must have been intended for the same public as *El Maestro*; like the Italian sonnets and dances included in the latter work, it reflects the increasing influence of Italian literature, music, and manners at the Valencian court, an influence further stimulated no doubt by Germaine de Foix's choice of an Italian as her third husband and paralleled in Spanish literary life in general by the assured Petrarchan manner of poets like Boscán and Garcilaso de la Vega. The music in *El Maestro* is remarkably assured, too, and—despite the differences mentioned above—this volume set the pattern, so far as secular song is concerned, for most of the later *vihuela*-books. Apart from the sonnets, the solo songs consist of twelve *villancicos* and four *romances*, two of the principal Spanish song-forms. The totals are still similar in the books of Valderrábano and Pisador; Narváez and Mudarra published markedly fewer *villancicos*, but Mudarra included instead a handful of Latin songs, Spanish and Italian sonnets, and *canciones*. The later *vihuelistas* came from a humbler social environment than Milán; many of them were clerics or professional lutenists, sometimes, like Narváez or the blind Fuenllana, achieving great technical brilliance.

Before discussing the actual music, mention must be made of a matter concerning its performance, upon which there seems to have

[1] Cf. J. B. Trend, *Luis Milan and the Vihuelistas* (London, 1925), pp. 1–12 and 69–81.

PLATE I

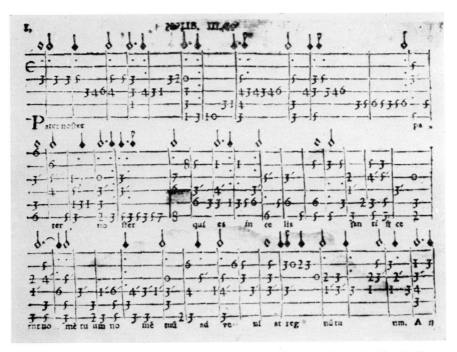

(*a*) The first page of Libro III of Mudarra's *Tres libros de música* (Seville, 1546)

(*b*) The first page of piece No. 12 from Francesco da Milano's *Intavolatura de Lauto libro primo* (Venice, 1546). See pp. 691 (Ex. 348(i)) and 778. In this tablature the lowest line represents the highest string.

been no agreement even among the composers themselves. Even when the vocal line is printed separately in mensural notation (as in all the books except *El Maestro*), the *vihuela* part, which is always printed in tablature, invariably includes figures representing the vocal line, either printed conspicuously in red, as in the books of Milán, Narváez, Valderrábano, Pisador, and Fuenllana, or indicated by adjacent comma-like dashes, as in those of Mudarra and Daza.[1] The question arises: should the vocal part be doubled on the *vihuela*? Milán merely says that the songs should first of all be tried over on the *vihuela* and that when the player gets the feel of them he should sing the notes indicated by red figures.[2] Narváez is ambiguous, but Valderrábano says unequivocally that the *vihuela* should not double the voice.[3] Evidence from Fuenllana's songs, on the other hand, suggests that both voice and *vihuela* should perform the disputed notes; of several possible reasons for this the most persuasive is that their omission from the *vihuela* part would seriously disrupt the logical flow of the polyphony.[4] It is reasonable to assume that on the whole the vocal part was more often doubled than not, though, supposing that singer and player were not the same person, it would, as Trend says, 'have been a positive insult to a good singer to play his part for him on an instrument'.[5] But good singers were often good players too: Milán, for instance, both sang and played his songs.

The songs of the *vihuelistas* display one basic texture: plangent vocal lines, divided into well-defined phrases corresponding to the lines of the text, proceed relentlessly in long note-values against instrumental backgrounds that are mainly polyphonic though occasionally chordal or decorative. Mudarra's through-composed *canciones* are the closest parallels in the *vihuela*-books to early Italian madrigals. His Italian sonnets also emphasize the growing Italian influence in Spain already noticeable in *El Maestro*. Milán repeats musical phrases to new lines of a sonnet in no particular order (and sometimes in his sonnets, too, musical and poetic phrases do not coincide). But Mudarra makes a clear distinction between octave and sestet. In his setting of 'O gelosia' from Sannazaro's famous pastoral *Arcadia*[6] the second halves of both octave and sestet are set to the

---

[1] Facsimile of a typical page shown in pl. I (*a*). For other facsimiles cf. the complete editions and the anthologies mentioned on p. 127, n. 6; also Noske, op. cit., p. 12, and Wolf, *Handbuch*, ii, pp. 107–10, 113, 161.   [2] Cf. Milán, op. cit., p. 71.

[3] Cf. Narváez, *Los Seys libros*, ed. Pujol, introduction, pp. 43–45.

[4] The evidence is well summarized in Bal, 'Fuenllana and the transcription of Spanish lute-music', *Acta Musicologica*, xi (1939), p. 16. Also cf. *infra*, p. 689, and Ward, *The Vihuela de mano and its Music*, pp. 95–100.   [5] Trend, op. cit., p. 46.

[6] Mudarra, *Tres libros de música*, ed. Pujol, no. 68.

same music as the first halves, as, for example, in the sonnets published in Petrucci's second book of *frottole*. The octaves of Petrarch's 'La vita fugge' and of the Castilian sonnet 'Qué llantos son aquestos'[1] are set in similar fashion; the sestets are through-composed and contain reminiscences of musical phrases from the octaves.

SPANISH *ROMANCES*

Granted that the *vihuela*-books contain many intrusions of music from abroad, there are some respects in which they remain thoroughly Spanish in character. No vocal form, for instance, is more representative of the Spanish genius than the *romance*. It is the one with the longest and most continuous history, from the Middle Ages to the present day. It is, moreover, the property of prince and peasant alike.[2] Melodies inspired by deeply moving events are wedded to the resourceful invention of brilliant instrumentalists: it is not surprising that the resulting songs are among the finest of their time. Famous collections of *c.* 1500 like the *Cancionero musical de Palacio*[3] and the *Cancionero musical de la Casa de Medinaceli*,[4] Francisco Salinas's *De musica libri septem* (Salamanca, 1577) and the books of the sixteenth-century polyphonists and *vihuelistas* provide a rich store of some seventy old *romance* melodies with their traditional words, most of them in vocal or instrumental settings. They may be conveniently split up into five classes: historical, Carolingian, Romanesque, lyrical, and biblical.[5] As befits their epic origins, the melodies of most *romances* are sombre, solemn, and a little remote, and they are rarely lyrical. They include melodic fragments widely found in Spanish folk-music; these frequently fall through the space of a fourth (e.g. C, B, A, G, or E flat, D, C, B, and, particularly at cadences, A, G, F, E).[6] The most universal of all *romances*, 'Conde Claros' (a genuine folk-melody, no doubt, rather than a popular one like most other melodies), enjoyed wide popularity because so many other *romances* could be sung to it and because the very monotony of its melody was a challenge to composers to exercise their talents for variation-

---

[1] Mudarra, op. cit., nos. 66 and 59, respectively.   [2] See Vol. III, p. 379.

[3] Printed complete, ed. Higini Anglès, in *Monumentos de la música española*, v and x (Barcelona, 1947 and 1951).

[4] Printed complete, ed. Miguel Querol Gavaldá, in *Monumentos de la música española*, viii–ix (Barcelona, 1949–50). Also cf. the earlier work of F. Asenjo Barbieri, *Cancionero musical de los siglos XV y XVI* (Madrid, 1890).

[5] Cf. Querol Gavaldá, 'Importance historique et nationale du romance', *Musique et poésie au XVIe siècle* (*Colloques internationaux du Centre National de la recherche scientifique: sciences humaines*, v) (Paris, 1954), pp. 306–19, for a detailed catalogue.

[6] Ibid., p. 305.

writing.[1] In fact 'the variation form seems to have arisen in Spain, through the necessity for relieving the monotony of the lute-accompaniment during the recitation of a long *romance*'.[2] The oldest and commonest practice was to write music for only one verse of a *romance*; this is what Narváez did. Mudarra provided accompaniments for two verses; in 'Durmiendo yva el Señor'[3] they are linked by polyphonic treatment of the *romance* melody on the *vihuela*. Mudarra and Valderrábano are two composers who round off their *canto-fermo*-like treatment of the popular melodies with long, expressive cadences on the *vihuela* under pedal points in the vocal parts; Pisador and Fuenllana wrote instrumental introductions to some of their *romances*.[4] The following are the openings of three different settings of the same *romance*, by Narváez, Pisador, and Fuenllana respectively (Fuenllana's setting is for voice and guitar):[5]

Ex. 46
(i)

Pa - se - á - - - ba - se el Rey
mo - - - - ro por la ciu - -
- dad de Gra - na - - - - da,

---

[1] Ibid., pp. 321–2.

[2] Trend, *The Music of Spanish History to 1600* (London, 1926), p. 105. Also cf. idem, *Luis Milan*, pp. 54–56.   [3] Mudarra, op. cit., no. 53.

[4] Cf. Querol Gavaldá in *Musique et poésie* (Paris, 1954), pp. 323–4.

[5] Narváez, op. cit., no. 36 (without '8' to the clef); Pisador, *Libro de música de vihuela* (Salamanca, 1552), fo. v^v (adapted from Morphy, op. cit., p. 179); and Fuenllana, *Orphenica lyra* (Seville, 1554), fo. clxiii^v (taken from Wolf, *Handbuch*, ii, pp. 162–3), respectively. Other reprints of Fuenllana's setting include Archibald T. Davison and

(ii)

Pa - se - á - - - ba - se   el

rey   mo - ro   por la ciu - dad de

Gra - na - - - da,   Cuan - do le

(iii)

Pa - se - á - ba - se el rey mo - ro por la ci - u - dad de Gra - na - da, car -

(The Moorish king walked through the city of Granada . . .)

It is the *romances* of Milán, however, that show off the form to its greatest advantage: later composers may have introduced innovations, but none quite attained to the artistic perfection of his four examples. Of these, three are in two parts: the melody of the first is popular; that of the second is Milán's own, though it is related to the first. The second part of his 'Durandarte', for example, develops the last phrase of the first; this phrase reappears unchanged at the end. Ex. 47 shows the end of the first part and the beginning of the second:[1]

Ex. 47

Willi Apel, *Historical Anthology of Music*, i (London, 1947), p. 132; Trend, *Luis Milan*, pp. 114–16; Albert Lavignac and La Laurencie, *Encyclopédie de la musique et dictionnaire du conservatoire*, 1ère partie, iv (Paris, 1920–2), pp. 2022–3; Pedrell, *Cancionero musical popular español*, iii (Barcelona, 1920), p. 148; and Wolf, *Handbuch*, ii, pp. 162–4.

[1] Adapted from Milán, op. cit., pp. 77–78. Other reprints include Bal y Gay, *Romances*

(. . . of that good time past. Words are flattering . . .)

The powerful effect of music as gravely beautiful and elemental as this is enhanced if the melodies are sung, as Milán directs, in a free and spacious manner and not too fast and if the instrumental passages between the vocal phrases are played as quickly as possible.[1] (The tempo directions of Milán and Valderrábano, incidentally, are among the earliest recorded ones.)

THE *VILLANCICOS*

The other important group of songs to be discussed here are the *villancicos*.[2] Here 'court and city art met in a form that charmed all classes, furnishing writers and composers with a national touchstone'.[3] Once again the music is typically Spanish in feeling; it is popular, not folk music. In earlier times courtly love had been a favourite theme for *villancicos*;[4] 'the melody and the verse were originally composed for each other and often by the same person'.[5] In the later fifteenth century a more popular tone invaded *villancicos*; many of those in the *vihuela*-books are strictly popular; and those that are not 'are less strained and artificial than those of the *Cancioneros*'.[6] *Villancicos*, like *romances*, could be historical; they might pay homage to a city or important personage or comment upon trivial incidents at court. But love, at a more homely level, remained the most popular subject of all. The increasing number of religious *villancicos* found in the sixteenth century points towards the transformation of the form in the seventeenth century into an extended sacred cantata.

y villancicos, pp. 14–15; Asenjo Barbieri, op. cit., pp. 612–14; Bruger, *Schule des Lautenspiels*, iv, p. 161; Lavignac and La Laurencie, op. cit., pp. 647–9 and 2018–19; Pedrell, op. cit. iii, p. 86; and Arnold Schering, *Geschichte der Musik in Beispielen* (Leipzig, 1931), p. 91.　　　　　　　　　　　　　　　　　　[1] Milán, op. cit., p. 179.

[2] See vol. III, p. 378, and *supra*, p. 82.　　　　　　[3] Ward, *The Vihuela*, p. 150.

[4] Sister M. P. St. Amour, *A Study of the Villancico up to Lope de Vega* (Washington, D.C., 1940), pp. 10–13.

[5] Isabel Pope, 'Musical and metrical form of the villancico', *Annales musicologiques* ii (1954), pp. 190–1.　　　　　　　　　　　　[6] St. Amour, op. cit., p. 14.

The traditional scheme of the *villancico* is illustrated by this one set by Milán[1] (the number of lines and the number of syllables to a line vary from song to song):

> Toda la vida vos amé,
> Si me amais, yo no lo sé.
>
> Bien sé que teneis amor,
> Al desamor y al olvido.
> Sé que soy aborrecido,
> Ya que sabe el disfavor.
>
> Y por sempre vos amaré.
> Si me amais, yo no lo sé.

(All my life I have loved you. If you love me I do not know it. I well know that you hold love in unlove and forgetfulness. I know that I am hated, since I have experienced disfavour. And I shall always love you. If you love me I do not know it.)

The first section (the *estribillo*) is sung to a melody which is then modified for the second section (the *vuelta*); the last section is sung to the original melody, the last line, with the repetition of earlier words, being in the nature of a refrain. Sometimes this monothematicism results in a certain monotony, as in Milán's 'Falai miña amor' (one of a number of *villancicos* to Portuguese words).[2] Elsewhere, as in 'Toda la vida' or in Ex. 48, the first phrase of the *vuelta* is sufficiently different to appear as the logical continuation of what has gone before, thus giving the song greater momentum. 'Toda la vida' is one of several *villancicos* that Milán wrote in two ways, the first simple, the second characterized by brilliant running passages in the *vihuela* part. A *villancico* existing in only one version contains elements of both of the styles found in the paired settings:[3]

Ex. 48

ESTRIBILLO

A - go - ra vi - nie - sse un vien -
Y me hi - zie - sse tan con - ten -

---

[1] Milán, op. cit., p. 72. Other reprints include Trend, op. cit., pp. 101–3. Recorded in *The History of Music in Sound*, iv.

[2] Milán, op. cit., p. 76. Other reprints include Bal y Gay, op. cit., p. 19; Bruger, *Alte Lautenkunst*, i, p. 32; Pedrell, op. cit. iii, p. 81; Schering, op. cit., p. 92; and Trend, op. cit., pp. 103–4.   [3] Adapted from Milán, op. cit., p. 74.

(Oh! that a wind would now come to carry me over there, a wind as favourable as I wished, that would carry me to the arms of my mistress and give me so much pleasure.)

While Mudarra set his melodies against a skilfully constructed web of delicate polyphony, the rather less lively Narváez followed Milán in his use of variation. His complete setting of 'Si tantos halcones' is preceded by two settings of the *estribillo* only; Ex. 49 shows the opening of each setting:[1]

Ex. 49

[1] Narváez, op. cit., nos. 37–39 (without '8' to the clef).

(The hawk fought with so many falcons . . .)

Several of Fuenllana's pieces call for the four-stringed gittern instead of the *vihuela*.[1] From about this time the so-called Spanish guitar with five strings became more and more popular, and with the waning popularity of polyphonic music it gradually supplanted the *vihuela* as the favourite instrument at all levels of society. No more music-books like those of the *vihuelistas* appeared after 1576. But even if it died out in Spain, it is surprising that a form of the perfection of the polyphonically accompanied lute-song should at this time have remained an isolated phenomenon peculiar to Spain: not until the songs of the English lutenists and the psalms of Gabriel Bataille is its like seen again.

ARIOSTO AND POPULAR ITALIAN SONG

The famous Venetian theorist Gioseffe Zarlino advised musicians to turn to Ariosto if they wanted texts for narrative songs to be sung to the lute.[2] Now the appearance of *Orlando furioso* in 1516 had in fact stimulated composers to set its stanzas in a variety of ways; as with the other contents of Petrucci's publications, the same setting might appear in versions for one voice and for four voices. A good example is Tromboncino's 'Queste non son più lagrime' (xxiii, 126), which appeared as a solo in 1520,[3] three years after being published for four voices. A similar song is his 'Acqua non è l'humor' (1514),[4] though the text is actually not by Ariosto. The bass here resembles the *folia*. In popular, improvised singing of *ottave* from *Orlando furioso* the same tune was used for each of the four pairs of lines, a principle occasionally adopted by professional composers.[5] Before long it became the custom to sing long series of successive stanzas in this manner. We can see at once that such performances must soon become exceedingly monotonous unless the singers varied their lines. This is in fact what they began to do, at least in courtly circles, and certain standard basses became established which were the simplest forms of basses resulting from typical harmonies used by the *improvvisatori*.[6] The *folia* was one of them. Roman singers had the *romanesca*, those in the north the *aria di Genova*, southern Italians the

[1] Cf. Adolf Koczirz, Die Gitarrenkompositionen in Miguel de Fuenllana's *Orphenica lyra* (1554)', *Archiv für Musikwissenschaft*, iv (1922), p. 241.
[2] *Le Istitutioni armoniche* (Venice, 1562), p. 75.
[3] Reprinted in Einstein, op. cit. iii, p. 317   [4] Reprinted, ibid., p. 318.
[5] Cf. ibid. i, p. 285, and iii, p. 49, for Francesco Corteccia's 'Io dico e dissi e dirò' (*Orlando furioso*, xvi, 2).
[6] Cf. Claude V. Palisca, "Vincenzo Galilei and some links between "Pseudo-Monody" and Monody', *Musical Quarterly*, xlvi (1960), pp. 352-4.

ruggiero, whose very name came from Ariosto's stanza beginning 'Ruggiero, qual sempre fui, tal' esser voglio' (xliv, 61), and so on. These basses soon found their way into written-down 'art music' in many parts of Italy and later appeared frequently as basses in settings of *ottave* composed by the monodists of the first decades of the seventeenth century. By the second half of the sixteenth century improvised singing founded on these stock basses was all the rage, as Montaigne, for one, testifies: in 1581 he saw 'peasants with lutes in their hands and even the shepherdesses with Ariosto on their lips. *But one sees this everywhere in Italy* . . .'.[1] Untutored singers like these were probably not very ambitious in devising variations on the basic patterns. At the very end of the century and on a higher plane, we find Giovenale Ancina, in the preface to his *Tempio armonico*, praising the 'unequalled' art of Giovanni Leonardo dell'Arpa and saying that 'some *laude* at the end of the book are purposely left plain, with only the words and without the music; these are reserved for him alone, so that he may accommodate various *arie* (basses) to them in his fashion . . .'.[2]

Castiglione, in *Il Cortegiano*, not only praises the 'lamenting sweetness' of the singing of Marchetto Cara[3] but observes that 'singing to the lute with the ditty (methink) is more pleasant than the rest, for it addeth to the words such a grace and strength that it is a great wonder'.[4] The gay ladies of Florentine society also liked to sing solos to the lute.[5] They can hardly have confined their performances (any more than the singers heard by Castiglione did) to songs with noble or heroic words, if indeed they bothered with them at all. It is no surprise, then, to find solo arrangements of other forms, such as madrigals and *ballate*. Significant features of one such song, Tromboncino's setting of a *ballata* by Sannazaro, include the slight ornamentation of the top part, which would make it especially suitable for arrangement as a solo, a quaver figure that would not be out of place in the songs of a century later, a steadily moving bass, and the rather instrumental nature of the inner parts. The opening shows some of these features:[6]

[1] Michel de Montaigne, *Journal de voyage*, ed. Louis Lautrey (Paris, 1909), p. 391, quoted in Einstein, op. cit. ii, p. 848.
[2] Cf. Einstein, loc. cit.
[3] Cf. ibid. i, pp. 106–7.
[4] Sir Thomas Hoby's translation. Cf. Oliver Strunk, *Source Readings in Music History* (London, 1952), p. 284.
[5] Cf. Einstein, op. cit. i, p. 78.
[6] Petrucci, *Frottole, libro undecimo* (Venice, 1514), no. 6. Adapted from reprint in Einstein, op. cit. iii, p. 14, where the note-values are quartered.

Ex. 50

(If, Lady, because of your haughty disdain the grief that afflicts me leads me to the black Styx . . .)

Nothing could better illustrate the 'trend towards the *a cappella* ideal' than a comparison of this narrative solo with Arcadelt's serene setting of the same words, published in 1539.[1] All the parts are now of equal importance, and all are equally vocal. Again, it is significant that when Willaert arranged madrigals by Verdelot for voice and lute he chose only those madrigals with a well-defined melody in the top part;[2] and Arcadelt's setting (1556) of some of Dido's last words from the fourth book of the *Aeneid* is a good example of a madrigal published in the heyday of the *a cappella* style that was doubtless conceived as a solo to the lute.[3]

MONODIC TENDENCIES IN *VILLANELLA* AND CANZONET

At this period the tendency towards monody was 'less marked in madrigals and motets than in the many kinds of composition that made no claims to artistic and technical mastery but that set out to give ready enjoyment and yet were not inelegant: villanellas, the new villottas, and canzonets. Basically these songs continued the tradition of the frottola (clarified and refreshed, perhaps, by renewed contact with popular music); but the melody in the highest part was now still more conspicuous and it was discreetly supported by the other voices, whose parts were very often played on instruments instead',[4] just as in the *frottole* of the early years of the century. It is noteworthy, in fact, that the first solo songs that Vincenzo Giustiniani mentions in his manuscript survey, *Discorso sopra la musica de' suoi tempi*,[5] are not those of Caccini and other composers of the 'new music' but the homophonic *villanelle alla napoletana* that he had heard sung in his youth about 1575 by the Neapolitan singers Giovan Andrea and Giulio Cesare Brancaccio and by Alessandro Merlo, a Roman bass with a range of three octaves; these men, we are told, all modified the original music, in the Neapolitan fashion, 'with a variety of passage-work new and pleasing to the ear of all'.[6] Giovanni Leonardo dell'Arpa and Caccini's teacher Scipione del Palla also sang in Naples. Brancaccio lived from 1577 to 1583 at the Este court at Ferrara, and Giovanni Leonardo sang there in 1584.[7] But it was not they who

---

[1] Reprinted in Einstein, op. cit. iii, p. 41.   [2] Example in ibid., p. 319.

[3] Cf. ibid. ii, p. 838. The piece is reprinted in *Fünf Vergil-Motetten*, ed. Helmuth Osthoff (*Das Chorwerk*, liv) (Wolfenbüttel, 1956), p. 13.

[4] Nino Pirrotta, 'Temperaments and Tendencies in the Florentine Camerata', *Musical Quarterly*, xl (1954), pp. 173–4.

[5] Printed by Salvatore Bongi (Lucca, 1878). Reprinted in Angelo Solerti, *Le origini del melodramma* (Turin, 1903), pp. 98–128, and translated by Carol MacClintock in *Musicological Studies and Documents*, ix (American Institute of Musicology, 1962), p. 63; differently translated extract in Nigel Fortune, 'Giustiniani on instruments', *The Galpin Society Journal*, v (1952), p. 48.

[6] MacClintock's translation, p. 69.

[7] Cf. Pirrotta, 'Tragédie et comédie dans la Camerata fiorentina', *Musique et poésie* (Paris, 1954), pp. 290–1.

made Ferrara famous for its dazzling musical life; the ecstatic tributes of a thousand poets, composers, and courtiers were not for them. These plaudits were reserved for three brilliant sopranos, who made Alfonso d'Este, musically speaking, the most envied ruler in all Italy.

THE LADIES OF FERRARA

Lucrezia Bendidio, Tarquinia Molza, and Laura Peperara had all settled at Ferrara by about 1580.[1] Night after night they enchanted the court with their solos, duets, and trios. Tasso and the principal court composer, Giaches Wert, and who knows how many lesser men, were infatuated with them. Hundreds of sonnets and madrigals celebrated their splendour. In a letter written from Ferrara in 1584, Alessandro Striggio, composer to the rival court of the Medici, says: 'these ladies sing excellently, both to accompaniment and from part-books; they are sure-footed in improvisation. The Duke is kind enough to be continually showing me in manuscript everything that they sing by heart, with all the runs and passages as they perform them. . . .'[2] Striggio wrote some music for the three ladies and sent it to Florence with the suggestion that Caccini sing the solo pieces. The following year, Alfonso, who for some years had guarded his ladies with especial jealousy from envious Medici eyes, actually allowed them to sing in the masques produced in Florence for the wedding of Cesare d'Este and Virginia Medici. Ottavio Rinuccini, librettist to the *Camerata*, wrote five poems for them, which were probably set to music by Striggio.

It is evident that as more and more singers sang solo the polarity between the top part of a composition and the bass would become more marked: this was true whether the music were basically polyphonic as in madrigals, or homophonic as in canzonets, and it is an important step in the development towards the monodic music of the next century. Moreover, in five-part madrigals actually sung as such, the upper voices tended to stand out against the lower ones. Certain madrigals of this type—some of Wert's, for example—were almost certainly sung by the ladies of Ferrara. Similar madrigals, while perhaps not composed with them in mind, may well have been influenced by those that were. Ex. 51, which is the opening of a madrigal by Monteverdi, published in his third book in 1592, begins,

[1] Cf. p. 62. The best accounts of these ladies and their art are in Solerti, *Ferrara e la corte estense* (Città di Castello, 1899), pp. cxxix–cxl, and in Einstein, op. cit. ii, pp. 825–35 and 844–7.

[2] Cf. Riccardo Gandolfi, 'Lettere inedite scritte da musicisti', *Rivista musicale italiana*, xx (1913), p. 530, translated in Einstein, op. cit. ii, p. 846.

moreover, with a turn of phrase common in the monodies of the next thirty years (the voices shown are the three highest ones—tenor and bass enter some bars later):[1]

Ex. 51

(O what great suffering it is to conceal one's desire when with pure faith. . .)

It was not, however, until 1601, when the childless Duke Alfonso had been dead four years, his state handed over to the Church and the splendour of his court a mere memory, that the world was shown the kind of music that had made the ladies really famous: in that year there were engraved in Rome the *Madrigali di Luzzasco Luzzaschi per cantare et sonare a uno, e doi, e tre soprani. Fatti per la Musica*

---

[1] Claudio Monteverdi, *Opere*, ed. Gian Francesco Malipiero, iii (Bologna, 1927), p. 8.

del Già Ser. Duca Alfonso d'Este.[1] Luzzaschi was court organist at
Ferrara, and he must often have accompanied the three ladies at the
harpsichord. We can be fairly sure that he had composed all the
songs in his book by 1585; it includes three solo madrigals, which
are so similar to the elaborate madrigals performed in the Florentine
intermedii of 1589[2] that their influence on the later music cannot be
denied. This is part of one of them, 'O primavera':[3]

Ex. 52

---

[1] Cf. p. 62 and Otto Kinkeldey, 'Luzzasco Luzzaschi's Solo-Madrigale mit Klavierbegleitung', *Sammelbände der internationalen Musikgesellschaft*, ix (1907–8), p. 538.

[2] See p. 793.

[3] Schering, op. cit., p. 176, where the note-values are quartered. The others are
reprinted complete in Kinkeldey, *Orgel und Klavier in der Musik des 16. Jahrhunderts*
(Leipzig, 1910), pp. 286–92. For the opening of a madrigal of 1589 by Caccini, 'Io che
dal ciel', see Ex. 384.

([O spring, the year's youth,] fair mother of flowers, new green shoots and new loves. . .)

They are basically four-part madrigals played on a keyboard instrument with the top part doubled by the voice in decorated form. As Einstein says, 'not one is particularly expressive; all swing back and forth in the somewhat neutral territory midway between *parlando* and the rambling mechanical coloratura of the virtuoso'.[1] The gentle, unobtrusive ornamentation of a song like the Venetian Baldisserra Donato's 'Dolce mio ben' is surely much more appealing.[2]

THE ART OF DIMINUTION

The excessively elaborate madrigals of Luzzaschi and the 1589 masques are among the most extreme examples of the rather tiresome sixteenth-century art of diminution, which by this time was being applied in Italy to all kinds of vocal music. Handbooks were printed instructing performers how this should be done—usually by applying deadening chains of semiquavers and demisemiquavers to all voices of a composition indiscriminately (even to the bass, though some sensible writers protested against this meddling with the foundation

---

[1] Einstein, op. cit. ii, p. 845.
[2] Reprinted in ibid. iii, p. 322.

of a composition);[1] it became quite impossible to tell from the confused polyphonic uproar of voices and instruments performing in resonant buildings whether a piece was supposed to be sad or joyful. In the monodies of the seventeenth century these inexpressive diminutions survive as ornamentation mainly in the works of Roman composers.[2] That they were not more widespread may well have been due to the efforts of Caccini, who, however, alongside many that are more subtle and capricious, continued to write roulades that are indistinguishable from those in the handbooks: there really is no very sharp division between late sixteenth- and early seventeenth-century practice (cf. pp. 157-8).

SONGS IN THE *INTERMEDII*

The only sixteenth-century Italian songs that remain to be discussed are those that were actually conceived as accompanied solos. A few, by the singer-lutenists Cosimo Bottegari and Hippolito Tromboncino, survive in a large manuscript song-book compiled by the former from 1574 onwards.[3] Other simple solo songs were sung in the sumptuous *intermedii* (or masques) presented between the acts of plays on festive occasions at the Florentine court. The earliest solos are two that Francesco Corteccia wrote in 1539 for the wedding of Duke (later Grand Duke) Cosimo I:[4] the few brief roulades in 'Vatten', almo riposo', in particular, help the vocal line to stand out against the darker background of keyboard instruments and trombones (employed to underline the entry of Night towards the end of the piece).[5] Very little of the later masque-music (most of it composed by Striggio) has survived, but from descriptions of the performances

---

[1] For good general accounts cf. Max Kuhn, *Die Verzierungs-Kunst in der Gesangs-Musik des 16.-17. Jahrhunderts (1535-1650)* (Leipzig, 1902), and Imogene Horsley, 'Improvised embellishments in the performance of Renaissance polyphonic music', *Journal of the American Musicological Society*, iv (1951), p. 3. Some convenient recent reprints of complete pieces 'diminished' are in Ferand, *Improvisation in Nine Centuries of Western Music* (Cologne, 1961), especially pp. 57-74. An interesting contemporary account is a letter in *Delle Lettere del Sor Gio. Camillo Maffei da Solofra* (Naples, 1562), reprinted, complete with examples, in Nanie Bridgman, 'Giovanni Camillo Maffei et sa lettre sur le chant', *Revue de musicologie*, xxxviii (1956), p. 10.

[2] Also cf. Ignazio Donati's deliberately 'diminished' solo motet 'O admirabile commercium', in Ferand, *Improvisation*, p. 100.

[3] Cf. MacClintock's edition (Wellesley, Mass., 1965) and her 'A Court Musician's Songbook: Modena MS. C311', *Journal of the American Musicological Society*, ix (1956), p. 180.   [4] See pp. 788-9.

[5] Cf. Einstein, op. cit. ii, pp. 840-1, and iii, p. 321 (opening of the song quoted). Also cf. Robert Haas, *Die Musik des Barocks* (Potsdam, 1928), pp. 19-20. The other song, 'O begli anni d'oro', may be consulted in Haas, *Aufführungspraxis der Musik* (Potsdam, 1931), p. 118, and in Schering, 'Zur Geschichte des begleiteten Sologesanges im 16. Jahrhundert', *Zeitschrift der internationalen Musikgesellschaft*, xiii (1912), p. 191.

and from the stage directions in the librettos it is clear that a good
deal of it must have been monodic. We are told that in a masque
produced for the marriage of the Grand Duke Francesco I to Bianca
Cappello in 1579 a hush of amazement fell over the audience when a
singer in the guise of Night awoke to sing two songs to the sound of
his own viol and of many others hidden behind the scenes. The
singer was Giulio Caccini (*c.* 1545–1618). The songs that he sang
were by Piero Strozzi, an aristocratic dilettante who was a member of
the Florentine *Camerata* and one of the interlocutors in Vincenzo
Galilei's *Dialogo*.[1] Fortunately the vocal line and bass of the first
madrigal have been preserved in a Florentine manuscript:[2]

Ex. 53

Fuor dell' hu-mi-do ni-do, Us-ci-ta con le
mie pre-sa-ghe schie-re Di fan-tas-mi, di so-gni e di chi-
-me-re, La Nott' io so-no, la Nott' io so-no;

(Arisen from my dank home, with my attendant flocks of dreams, ghosts and
illusions, Night am I. . .)

This madrigal seems to be the earliest surviving song to strive after
the kind of expression that Caccini and other monodists were later
to achieve. It is true that the missing accompaniment may have been

[1] Cf. Federico Ghisi, *Feste musicali della Firenze medicea (1480–1589)* (Florence,
1939), p. xxxvi.

[2] Corrected from Ghisi, *Alle fonti della monodia* (Milan, 1940), p. 46 (from Florence,
Biblioteca Nazionale, Codici Magliabecchiani, xix. 66, no. 46). It is also printed by
Ghisi in Roland-Manuel (ed.), *Histoire de la musique*, i ([Paris], 1960), pp. 1423–4.
Facsimile in Ghisi, *Feste musicali*, facing p. 88.

polyphonic, that the bass is not seen as a slowly moving support for the voice and that the song as a whole is hurried and not at all expansive like the best seventeenth-century solo madrigals.[1] Yet the frequent cadences are the very simplest forms of those that frequently punctuate the flow of monodies, and the expressive vocal phrase of bars 13–14 would not be out of place in the songs of the mature Caccini.

The same manuscript contains another important, though not very expressive, song, composed for the production in Florence in 1590 of Rinuccini's *Maschere di bergiere*: it is not known who wrote it, but we do know that Lucia Caccini, Giulio's first wife, sang it, and on grounds of style Caccini himself could have been the composer.[2] Ex. 54 shows the start of the song: the declamatory opening phrase is a simple version of one of the favourite openings of solo madrigals during the next thirty years; the bass is beginning to move more slowly and (except in the fourth bar) independently; and the roulade is more expressive than many contemporary ones. We are well on the way, in fact, towards *Le Nuove musiche*.[3]

Ex. 54

(Most serene lady, whose great name, adorned with a thousand honours, resounds on high . . .)

[1] Cf. Schrade, 'Les Fêtes du mariage de Francesco dei Medici et de Bianca Cappello', *Les Fêtes de la Renaissance*, i (Paris, 1956), pp. 120–1.
[2] Cf. his *intermedio* song of the previous year, of which the opening is printed as Ex. 384.
[3] Ghisi, *Alle fonti della monodia*, p. 47, from Florence, Bib. Naz., Codici Maglia-

THE *CAMERATA FIORENTINA*

Caccini has been mentioned a number of times now, and it is time to turn to his musical environment and to his music itself. Of Roman origin and sometimes referred to in his day as Giulio Romano, he was the protégé of Giovanni de' Bardi, Count of Vernio, the moving spirit behind the *Camerata*. Now, even though they are usually referred to in the singular, there were really three *camerate* in Florence. The one that interests us here is the first, the typical Renaissance academy—a kind of learned club or *salon*—that met in Bardi's house probably from about 1576 to 1582. Bardi himself was a typical, cultivated Renaissance nobleman, conservative, munificent, and erudite in many branches of thought. His principal associates included Caccini, Vincenzo Galilei, composer, and father of the astronomer, and Girolamo Mei, who was much the most learned of them all in matters relating to antiquity and whose hand may be detected behind the writings of both Galilei and Bardi himself.[1] This *Camerata*, it cannot be too strongly emphasized, was not in the least interested in the development of stage-music and certainly did not envisage anything in the nature of opera. These matters, on the other hand, absorbed the attention of the two later, more practical *camerate*: the one that met under the protection of the young nobleman Jacopo Corsi after Bardi left for Rome in 1592; and one which can perhaps be seen as a rival group, led by the lively composer and dancer Emilio de' Cavalieri, whom the new Medici Grand Duke, Ferdinando I (1587–1608), had known in Rome during the exile imposed upon him by his predecessor—with the support of, among others, Bardi's family. There can have been no love lost, therefore, between Bardi on the one hand and the new ruler and his favourites on the other, and it is not surprising that Bardi should have left for Rome within five years of Ferdinando's return. Caccini, too, would have had to try to escape from the consequences of having been Bardi's secretary: it was not in his nature to accept for long the humble place that he occupied even in such an all-embracing affair as the masques of 1589.[2]

becchiani, xix. 66, no. 49. The song is also found in Florence, Conservatorio Cherubini, Barbera MS., fo. 65, and in Brussels, Conservatoire Royal de Musique, MS. 704, no. 122.

[1] Cf. Palisca, 'Girolamo Mei, mentor to the Florentine Camerata', *Musical Quarterly*, xl (1954), p. 1, and his editionm of Mei's *Letters on Ancient and Modern Music to Vincenzo Galilei and Giovanni Bardi* (American Institute of Musicology, 1960).

[2] Cf. p. 793. Further on the *Camerata*, see Solerti, *Gli albori del melodramma* (Milan, 1905), i; Pirrotta, 'Temperaments and Tendencies in the Florentine Camerata', *Musical Quarterly*, xl (1954), p. 169, and in *Musique et poésie* (Paris, 1954), p. 287.

The main concern of Bardi's *Camerata* was to reform the dominant musical language of the time: to substitute for the iniquities (as they saw it) of counterpoint a means of expression holding fast to the Platonic dictum that the purpose of music is to uplift the listener. Uplift must not be synonymous with pleasure. It was no use for Aristotle to say that music is 'one of the pleasantest things':[1] Galilei insisted that 'any pleasure the listener might experience was not merely a subsidiary advantage, but that it was actively harmful. . . . It was harmful because it occupied the listener's attention and thus prevented him being influenced morally or emotionally.'[2] One of the troubles about counterpoint was that it afforded sensuous pleasure. Now Greek music, said the *Camerata*, tamed wild beasts and produced all kinds of other marvellous effects which are quite beyond the power of all this contrapuntal music today. Greek music, however, was monodic: surely this must have been the reason for its excellence? Our kind of music, then, must be monodic, too—a judicious combination of melody, harmony, and rhythm that will enable every word to be clearly heard and expressed in the appropriate fashion. Here is the kernel of their argument, though it is not a particularly original one: after all, Glareanus had recognized the expressive power of Greek monody, and the Reformers of the middle of the century had urged the expulsion of counterpoint from church music in order to make the words audible.

VINCENZO GALILEI'S POLEMICS

Galilei, in his *Dialogo . . . della musica antica e della moderna* (Venice, 1581),[3] one of the principal manifestos of the *Camerata*, speaks for them all when he defines 'the noblest, most important and principal quality of music' as 'the expression of the concepts of the mind by means of words, and not, as present-day practical musicians say and believe, the consonance of the parts'. He also tells of some musician of old who was admired because he fashioned his music 'to the subject of the words with the utmost nicety and expressed with marvellous art all the effects that the poet had displayed in them', and he adds: 'this most important and principal function of the art of music means nothing to the practical musicians of today'.[4] It will be

---

[1] Aristotle, *Politics*, vii. 5, quoted from Strunk, op. cit., p. 18.

[2] D. P. Walker, 'Musical Humanism in the 16th and early 17th Centuries', *Music Review*, iii (1942), p. 64.

[3] Facsimile editions have been published in Rome (1934) and Milan (1946). Extract translated in Strunk, op. cit., pp. 302–22.

[4] Galilei, *Dialogo*, pp. 83 and 79, respectively, quoted in Italian by Walker, *Music Review*, ii (1941), p. 289.

seen that the *Camerata* argue from the point of view of the listener, and they are among the first writers to do so. They forget that most sixteenth-century composers wrote their madrigals for the enjoyment of performers, who had the words in front of them; these singers did not expect to find a petulant Galilei sitting at the back of the room abusing the counterpoint for obscuring the words.[1] It should not be assumed that those people who sang madrigals arranged as solos did so because they or their audiences shared the views of the *Camerata*—indeed Caccini, as we shall see, actually objected to 'arranged' music of this kind. Such people may well have been prompted simply by man's natural urge to sing a song and may have sung these arrangements because there were no ready-made songs. Yet we cannot be too sure, for in the following passage from that part of *Il Cortegiano* already quoted from, Castiglione, for one, advances at the beginning of the century an argument that, but for its moderate tone, would hardly be out of place in Galilei's *Dialogo*:[2] 'Methink . . . pricksong [counterpoint] is a fair music, so it be done upon the book surely and after a good sort. But to sing to the lute is much better, because all the sweetness consisteth in one alone, and a man is much more heedful and understandeth better the feat manner and the air or vein of it when the ears are not busied in hearing any more than one voice.' Zarlino, who was no ally of the *Camerata*'s, seems to have thought along similar lines.[3]

No one outdid Galilei in the purely destructive matter of attacking counterpoint, but when it comes to the more important matter of how the new music was to sound he is not helpful. It is unfortunate that his two works in the alleged new style are lost, though we may have clues to their nature in his manuscript arrangements of madrigals and similar pieces for bass voice and lute.[4] One was a setting of part of the Lamentations and Responds for Holy Week, the other of Count Ugolino's lament from the *Inferno* (xxxiii, 4–75); his setting Dante at this time shows, however, that he was either out of touch or at least out of sympathy with contemporary musico-literary trends and lends weight to the opinion that much of his polemic was remote from practical affairs. Pietro de' Bardi, Giovanni's son, says in his letter of 1634 to Giovanni Battista Doni (the leading Italian musical theorist of the first half of the seventeenth century) that Galilei's two

---

[1] Cf. Fortune, 'Italian Seventeenth-century Singing', *Music and Letters*, xxxv (1954), p. 218.
[2] Cf. Strunk, op. cit., p. 284.
[3] Cf. Zarlino, loc. cit., quoted in Einstein, op. cit. ii, pp. 837–8.
[4] Cf. Palisca in *Musical Quarterly*, xlvi (1960), p. 344.

pieces were 'intelligibly sung by a good tenor and precisely accompanied by a consort of viols' and that they 'aroused considerable envy among the professional musicians' but adds that, compared with the later songs and operas of Caccini and Peri, they suffered from 'a certain roughness and excessive antiquity'.[1] Perhaps they were similar to the song by Strozzi shown in Ex. 53, especially as Strozzi knew Galilei and may have written his song under the influence of the *Camerata*.

CACCINI AND *LE NUOVE MUSICHE*

In practical matters Giovanni de' Bardi is more helpful than Galilei. Yet even his *Discorso . . . mandato a Giulio Caccini sopra la musica antica e'l cantar bene* (MS., *c.* 1585?)[2] contains advice (such as that about the setting of different poems to music only in what Bardi considered the appropriate modes)[3] that a hard-headed professional musician like Caccini could afford to ignore. Bardi is sounder on singing[4] and may well have fostered certain features of Caccini's performances that helped to make him one of the finest singers of his day. Bardi echoes the ideals of the *Camerata*, conditioned by their conception of Greek music, when he repeatedly reminds Caccini not to spoil the words, that his 'chief aim is to arrange the verse well and to declaim the words as intelligibly as you can', that 'just as the soul is nobler than the body so the words are nobler than the counterpoint'.[5] Moreover, Bardi's insistence 'that music is pure sweetness and that he who would sing should sing the sweetest music and the sweetest modes well ordered in the sweetest manner'[6] is reflected, whether by chance or design it is impossible to say, in Caccini's songs: he may have cashed in with his *Euridice* on the new vogue for opera, his singing may have been passionate and his embellishments lively, yet beside Peri and Monteverdi he is seen as an essentially lyrical, undramatic, and 'sweet' composer.

Caccini's epoch-making preface to *Le Nuove musiche* (Florence, 1602)[7] presents the fullest statement we have of the aims of a

[1] Cf. Strunk, op. cit., p. 364. Strunk translates the complete letter on pp. 363–6; the Italian text is printed in Solerti, *Le origini del melodramma*, pp. 143–7.
[2] Printed in Doni, *De' trattati di musica*, ed. Antonio Francesco Gori (Florence, 1763), ii, pp. 233–48, and translated in Strunk, op. cit., pp. 290–301.
[3] Cf. Strunk, op. cit., pp. 295–6.   [4] Ibid., pp. 298–300.
[5] Ibid., p. 295.   [6] Ibid., p. 300.
[7] Facsimile reprints of the complete book, ed. Francesco Mantica (Rome, 1930) and Francesco Vatielli (Rome, 1934). The preface is reprinted in Solerti, *Le origini del melodramma*, pp. 55–70, and there is a complete translation in Strunk, op. cit., pp. 377–92.

composer in the new style, prompted by his association with Bardi's *Camerata* and by his own experiences as singer, instrumentalist, and composer. He denounces two of the principal kinds of solo song of his time: (*a*) (by implication and even though he had written some himself) elaborate madrigals weighed down with long embellishments, which 'have been invented, not because they are necessary unto a good manner of singing, but rather for a certain tickling of the ears of those who do not well understand what it is to sing passionately . . . there being nothing more contrary to passion than they are'; and (*b*) solo performances of madrigals composed for several voices, which were unsatisfactory because 'the single part of the soprano, sung as a solo, could have no effect by itself, so artificial were the corresponding parts'.[1] Yet even Galilei, as has been mentioned, had arranged contemporary madrigals as solos to the lute,[2] and Doni, an enthusiast for monodies, recommends for their accompaniment that same 'artificiosa testura' of a consort of viols that Caccini deplores; in Doni's view such an accompaniment would throw the vocal line into sharper relief.[3]

It is probable that, taking as his point of departure songs like those quoted in Ex. 53 and 54, Caccini began in the late 1580's to compose solo madrigals on the lines of Ex. 384 that were later included in *Le Nuove musiche*; dedicating his *Euridice* (Florence, 1600) to Bardi he mentions three that were probably composed about that time (he says 'many years ago') in a manner that Bardi had 'declared to be that used by the ancient Greeks when introducing song into the representations of their tragedies and other fables'.[4] In the preface to *Le Nuove musiche* he maintains that these songs 'had more power to delight and move than the greatest number of voices singing together'.[5] He sang them, he says, in Rome (probably in 1592 or 1593), and their 'power to move the passion of the mind' delighted his noble audiences.[6] It is significant that one of the songs, 'Perfidissimo volto', begins with a slightly embellished version of the figure applied to identically stressed words at the beginning of Ex. 54.[7] No doubt the earliest versions of the songs were rough and unpolished compared with the final versions. Several such plain versions exist in manu-

---

[1] Strunk, op. cit., pp. 380 and 379, respectively.

[2] Cf. Einstein, 'Vincenzo Galilei and the Instructive Duo', *Music and Letters*, xviii (1937), p. 361.

[3] Cf. Doni, *Compendio del trattato de' generi e de' modi della musica* (Rome, 1635), pp. 123–4.   [4] Strunk, op. cit., pp. 370–1.

[5] Ibid., p. 379.   [6] Cf. loc. cit.

[7] Caccini, *Le Nuove musiche* (Florence, 1602), p. 8. Opening quoted in Eugen Schmitz, *Geschichte der weltlichen Solokantate*, 2nd ed. (Leipzig, 1955), p. 59.

scripts;[1] these are almost certainly 'maimed and spoiled'[2] copies
sung by those who were baffled by the unfamiliar style of the final
versions, yet they are possibly similar in texture to Caccini's own early
experiments. Ex. 55 shows the beginnings of the vocal line of one of the
three early madrigals Caccini mentions, in (i) what may well have
been something like its earliest version and (ii) the published version:[3]

Ex. 55

(i)
Ved - rò'l   mio   sol,   ved - rò'l   mio

(ii)
Ved - rò'l   mio   sol,   ved - rò'l   mio

sol, ved -   rò   pria   ch'io muo - - -

- sol,   ved - rò pri - ma ch'io muo - - - - -

- ia.

- ia, Quel sos-pi - ra - to   gior - - - no

(I shall see my sun before I die. That sighed-for day. . .)

Caccini divided the songs in his book into two main groups:
madrigals and arias. These remained the main classes of Italian song
for the next twenty-five years. The novelty of his manner is much
more evident in his madrigals. His fundamental innovation was to

[1] e.g. Florence, Bib. Naz., Codici Magliabecchiani, xix. 66, and Conservatorio Cherubini, Barbera MS.; Modena, Biblioteca Estense, MSS. Mus. F. 1526–7; and Tenbury, St. Michael's College, MS. 1018. On these manuscripts cf. Ghisi, *Alle fonti della monodia, passim*; idem, 'An early seventeenth century MS. with unpublished Italian Monodic Music by Peri, Giulio Romano and Marco da Gagliano', *Acta Musicologica*, xx (1948), p. 46; and Fortune, 'A Florentine Manuscript and its Place in Italian Song', *Acta Musicologica*, xxiii (1951): postscript, p. 134.

[2] Cf. Strunk, op. cit., p. 377.

[3] (i) Tenbury, MS. 1018, fo. 38ᵛ; (ii) Caccini, op. cit., p. 10.

'bring in a kind of music by which men might, as it were, talk in harmony, using in that kind of singing . . . a certain noble neglect of the song'.[1] Caccini's word for this is *sprezzatura*; it is significant that Castiglione had used this very word to define the effortless grace of manner of the ideal courtier.[2] Caccini was thus using a kind of *rubato* to express both nobility and spontaneity. The arioso of his vocal lines is a type of song midway between the recitative found in operas and the clearly defined melodies of arias. The accompaniment was to be played, for preference on a *chitarrone* (a large archlute with a double neck and extra bass strings, which was Caccini's own instrument), from the recently invented *basso continuo*; monodies could also be accompanied on the harpsichord, clavichord, harp, double harp, theorbo, or other similar instruments, but no monodist specially asks for a bass viol to double the *basso continuo*.[3] (The accompaniment of Monteverdi's solo madrigal 'Con che soavità', published in 1619, is exceptional in being for various stringed and continuo instruments set out in three groups.[4]) Caccini says that he passed 'now and then through certain dissonances, holding the bass note firm, except when I did not wish to observe the common practice, and [played] the inner voices on an instrument for the expression of some passion, these being of no use for any other purpose'.[5] The accompaniment was distinctly subsidiary, although, as harmonic support to a harmonically conceived melody, it was, as can be seen, essential to Caccini's conception of monody. It might continually vary in fullness and be heightened by little flourishes between the vocal phrases; it was more capricious and less sustained and uniform than that of the earlier consort of viols or of vocal polyphony transferred to the lute.

Caccini further heightened the emotional effect of the words by embellishments of the vocal line, which, melodically and rhythmically, are often more subtle and appropriate to vocal music than those commonly found in the sixteenth century. Sometimes, however, for all his proud claims to be an innovator, his roulades are indistinguishable from, say, Luzzaschi's.[6] Even he, moreover, constantly employed two stereotyped ornaments which originated in late

[1] Strunk, op. cit., p. 378.
[2] Cf. Pirrotta in *Musique et poésie*, p. 293.
[3] Cf. Fortune, 'Continuo Instruments in Italian Monodies', *The Galpin Society Journal*, vi (1953), p. 10.
[4] Monteverdi, op. cit. vii (Bologna, 1928), p. 137.
[5] Strunk, loc. cit.
[6] Cf. the illuminating parallel in Edward J. Dent, 'Italian Chamber Cantatas', *Musical Antiquary*, ii (1910–11), pp. 146–7.

sixteenth-century practice and might be considered 'contrary to passion': (i) the *gruppo* and (ii) the *trillo*:[1]

Ex. 56
(i)

(ii)

From the very earliest solo madrigals the *trillo* was continually applied to long penultimate notes at cadences that fall by step to the final notes; so common was it that it was rarely written out but was indicated either by the sign 't.' or else not at all. (In Ex. 59, for instance, it should clearly be applied in bars 8, 16, and 21). Caccini writes at length of the devices that he used as aids to *sprezzatura*. Exclamations, for instance: these involve diminishing and increasing the tone on descending phrases beginning with a long dotted note; they were termed 'languid' in conjunct motion and 'livelier' in phrases like the first one in Ex. 51. Like other composers, Caccini also introduced uneven and contrasting note-values into his vocal lines (cf. Ex. 55 (ii)), in vivid contrast to the typically smooth lines of sixteenth-century music. Caccini's preface includes specimen songs with full directions as to their interpretation in his new manner.[2] Ex. 57 shows the beginning of a typically bland madrigal from *Le Nuove musiche*:[3]

Ex. 57

Dol - cis - si - mo sos - pi - - - ro,

Ch'es-ci da quel - la boc - ca O - ve d'a - mor, O - ve d'a-

---

[1] Cf. Strunk, op. cit., p. 384.   [2] Ibid., pp. 386–90.
[3] Caccini, op. cit., p. 4, where there is no sharp in the key-signature.

(Sweetest sigh, from that mouth whence pours all the sweetness of love. . .)

Another one is 'Amarilli, mia bella',[1] famous now as when it was the
international favourite of the early seventeenth century; the repetition emphasizing the last line is another splendid example of ornamentation crowning a song.

THE POETS OF THE SOLO MADRIGAL

The poems used for solo madrigals were similar to those used for
polyphonic madrigals. Composers underlined the final 'point' either
by embellishments, as in 'Amarilli', or else by repetition, as in many
a polyphonic madrigal. Caccini, like other monodists, favoured at
first the lively, concise, and elegant verses of such poets as Rinuccini
(cf. Ex. 57) and Battista Guarini, whose pastoral drama *Il Pastor
fido* (1590) in particular was ransacked by musicians.[2] Beneath the
apparently innocent surfaces of many pastoral poems erotic secondary meanings lie concealed. Within ten years or so the song-books
began to mirror the growing attractions of the less consciously elegant
verses of Giambattista Marino and his followers, whose heart-
rending poems of absence and parting (cf. Ex. 58) and candid and
voluptuous delineation of physical passion are heightened by cunning
use of antithesis, paradox, hyperbole, and oxymoron. Hardly a song-
book published between 1610 and 1625 lacks a Marinist text; in
Caccini's *Nuove musiche e nuova maniera di scriverle* (1614) Guarini
hardly appears at all—nearly all the poems are the products of

---

[1] Ibid., p. 12. It has been many times reprinted; cf., for the best version, Knud
Jeppesen, *La Flora* (Copenhagen, 1949), i, p. 12.
[2] Cf. Arnold Hartmann, Jr., 'Battista Guarini and *Il Pastor Fido*', *Musical Quarterly*,
xxxix (1953), p. 415.

Marinism. As in the songs of other countries and of other times, love in all its aspects is by far the predominant subject of poems set by the monodists. The most popular verses of a really popular poet like Guarini might be set by as many as thirty different composers.

SIGISMONDO D'INDIA AND OTHERS

In Italy between 1602 and 1635 over a hundred composers published more than two hundred music-books containing anything from one to fifty secular monodies; many of them were reprinted, some more than once.[1] This is by far the largest body of song to be dealt with in this chapter. Very few of these books contain nothing but monodies: even Le Nuove musiche includes a six-part chorus. Many of them contain a few duets or trios or sacred songs, practically all with continuo, but monodies are in the majority in most books. It was through monodies, which could be easily bought, and performed at home, rather than through operas, performed before aristocratic audiences at court and sometimes not published, that the new style founded on the basso continuo was disseminated through Italy. Every kind of composer took to composing monodies. Amateurs like the Sienese gentleman Claudio Saracini and the lawyer Domenico Maria Melli (or Megli),[2] and those professional composers such as Sigismondo d'India, Marco da Gagliano, Domenico Belli, and Jacopo Peri who were employed, often as singers, at flourishing centres of secular music like the courts of Florence, Mantua, and Savoy, were on the whole more successful at capturing the essential qualities of the new manner than were those composers, such as Stefano Landi, Gian Domenico Puliaschi, and Francesco Severi, who worked in a centre of church music like Rome or those, such as Antonio Cifra and Giovanni Ghizzolo, who were choirmasters of cathedrals and churches in unsophisticated provincial towns. The songs of these latter composers lack lyrical warmth and are frequently burdened with otiose embellishments reminiscent of the diminutions of the sixteenth century.

[1] For fuller accounts of the monody-books than can be given here cf. Fortune, 'Italian Secular Monody from 1600 to 1635: an introductory survey', Musical Quarterly, xxxix (1953), p. 171; Schmitz, op. cit., pp. 11–74; idem, 'Zur Frühgeschichte der lyrischen Monodie Italiens im 17. Jahrhundert', Jahrbuch der Musikbibliothek Peters, xviii (1911), p. 35; and August W. Ambros, Geschichte der Musik, iv, 3rd ed., rev. Hugo Leichtentritt (Leipzig, 1909), passim, but especially chap. x. An extensive unpublished source is Fortune, Italian Secular Song from 1600 to 1635: the Origins and Development of Accompanied Monody (Diss., Cambridge, 1954). The fullest list of the monody-books is idem, 'A Handlist of printed Italian secular Monody books, 1602–1635', R.M.A. Research Chronicle, iii (1963), 27.

[2] Melli was so early in the field that he published two books in 1602, the first of which probably appeared two months before Le Nuove musiche.

Solo madrigals are in common time. Their form is free: they are unified and organized by the repetition of short phrases or of rhythmic figures or by snatches of imitation between vocal line and bass (even in those of the avowedly anti-contrapuntal Caccini: cf. Ex. 57, bars 8–9). The bane of the solo madrigal in the hands of lesser men is the tendency to introduce too many perfect cadences coinciding with the end of each line of the poem. The joins could no longer be concealed by counterpoint, and the most successful monodists are those who wrote their arioso in expansive phrases stressing only the more important poetic cadences. Sighing, trembling, silence, laughter, and all the other stock-in-trade of madrigal verse are still represented by the naïve illustrative formulae that Galilei and others had ridiculed in the polyphonic madrigals of the previous century (cf. the treatment of the words 'tremble' and 'remain' in Ex. 58, bars 15 and 18–21 respectively). Caccini's madrigals, as can be judged from the extracts already quoted, are essentially diatonic and must, in this respect, have been applauded by Bardi, who, no doubt in his insistence upon 'sweetness', bade him reject 'the improper practices employed today by those who search for unusual sounds'.[1] Some later monodists, such as the Mantuan court singer Francesco Rasi, wrote in the same vein.[2] Other monodists took up quite a different attitude. For example, in the preface to his *Musiche* (Milan, 1609) d'India actually draws attention to his 'unusual intervals' and the way in which he passes 'with the utmost novelty from one consonance to another', at the same time censuring the songs of other composers—was he thinking of Caccini?—for the monotony of their harmony and declamation.[3] Chromatic writing was indeed new to solo madrigals in 1609, but of course there had been plenty of it in polyphonic ones.

The more radical monodists—men such as d'India, Belli, Pietro Benedetti (another Florentine and a priest), Lodovico Bellanda (a Veronese amateur), and above all Saracini[4]—frequently match the

---

[1] Strunk, op. cit., p. 299.

[2] Example quoted by Fortune in *Musical Quarterly*, xxxix (1953), p. 183. Further on Rasi, cf. MacClintock, 'The Monodies of Francesco Rasi', abstract of lecture, *Journal of the American Musicological Society*, ix (1956), p. 242, and 'The Monodies of Francesco Rasi', ibid. xiv (1961), p. 31.

[3] Cf. Federico Mompellio, 'Sigismondo d'India e il suo primo libro di *Musiche da cantar solo*', *Collectanea Historiae Musicae*, i (1953), p. 121, and Fortune, 'Sigismondo d'India: an introduction to his life and works', *Proceedings of the Royal Musical Association*, lxxxi (1954–5), p. 33.

[4] There are several complete songs, and quotations from other songs, by these composers (not all of them 'unusual') in Ambros, op. cit., *passim* (not very reliable); Mompellio, *Sigismondo d'India* (Milan, 1956), *passim*; idem, *Collectanea Historiae Musicae*, i (1953), pp. 122–8; Noske, op. cit., p. 31; and Bence Szabolcsi, *Benedetti und Saracini*

exaggerated and vivid pathos of Marinism with music abounding in
acrid clashes, irregularly resolving suspensions, wide leaps and other
'unusual sounds'. The wayward passion of their mannered settings
often pays no regard to the structure of a song as a whole. They dart
off impulsively into foreign keys (returning at the end with difficulty,
if at all, to the original one)—a procedure at the opposite pole to
that of Caccini, who sometimes (as in the piece quoted in Ex. 57)
stays in the same key for almost the whole of a madrigal; they indulge in violent contrasts of mood and dynamics and linger with
anguished fascination on all the poignant words and phrases. The
unbridled emotionalism of many of their songs is well illustrated by
the following extract from Saracini's lugubrious setting of one of
Marino's madrigals; both poet and composer provide a parallel to
the dramatic contrasts of light and shade in the paintings of their
contemporary Caravaggio:[1]

Ex. 58

(Diss., Leipzig, 1923, unpub.), appendix, and *A History of Melody* (English ed.,
London, 1966), pp. 82–83. Saracini's *Le Seconde musiche* (Venice, 1620) has been reprinted in facsimile (Siena, 1933).
    [1] Saracini, *Le Seste musiche* (Venice, 1624), p. 24.

(Alas! you depart, and my heart leaves me at your departure. And as I tremble and weep, ravaged by doubt and anguish, a mute lover I remain.)

In d'India's disciplined, professional hands the excitability of a Saracini is generally tempered with the urbanity of a Caccini, to result on occasion in songs of great power and distinction. Consider the variety of mood, declamation, and pace in these opening bars of one of his madrigals, a setting of words from Act 3 of *Il Pastor fido*:[1]

Ex. 59

[1] D'India, *Le Musiche* (Milan, 1609), p. 44. Reprinted complete by Mompellio, *Collectanea Historiae Musicae*, i (1953), p. 123.

(O most bitter sweetness of Love, how much harder it is to lose you than never to have tasted or possessed you! What a happy state love would be if one were not to lose the already-enjoyed beloved!)

D'India's five long laments to his own texts are especially impressive: in particular, Dido's lament, published in 1623, is the work of a composer of incontestable imagination, invention, and staying-power, and a serious rival to Monteverdi's famous operatic lament of Ariadne,[1] which was also printed as a continuo-monody in 1623, nine years after the five-part version appeared. D'India set his laments as recitatives, which at this time are found only very rarely outside opera. Two comparatively accessible examples are Monteverdi's long and somewhat monotonous *lettere amorose*, 'Se i languidi miei sguardi' and 'Se pur destina', which he published in his Seventh Book of madrigals in 1619.[2] The musical 'love letter' attracted a few other composers too, while the lament, alone of non-strophic song forms and perhaps prompted by the fame of Monteverdi's example, came into its own after about 1625.

Saracini, d'India, and similar composers have above been called radicals, and that, at first sight, is what they seem to be. But their 'progressive' path was in fact a cul-de-sac. In the early seventeenth century chromatic madrigals were a dead end—as, indeed, were all madrigals, both solo ones and the polyphonic ones that continued to be written, in some cases by the same composers, alongside them.

[1] On d'India's lament cf. Fortune in *Proceedings of the Royal Musical Association*, lxxxi (1954–5), pp. 42–44 (including a musical example).

[2] Monteverdi, op. cit. vii (Bologna, 1928), pp. 160–75. In the first edition of Monteverdi's Seventh Book the second *lettera* is called *partenza amorosa*.

The popularity of solo song injected new life into a dying form at the turn of the century. But by 1625 the stimulus provided by the injection had worn off, and the song-books now contained only a handful of madrigals: the madrigal in whatever guise was to all intents and purposes dead. The seeds of the development of Italian song lay in the aria, which indeed influenced the madrigal in its later stages before finally overwhelming it (cf. p. 178).

The earlier song-books of those composers, such as Benedetti and Ghizzolo, who published several books over a number of years consist mainly of madrigals, while the later ones consist mainly of arias. The year 1618 is the real watershed in the history of Italian song at this period. In this year there were published: (a) the last song-book (d'India's third) but one (an unimportant book of 1626) in which all the monodies are madrigals; and (b) the first in which all the monodies are arias—this was the Venetian Giovanni Stefani's *Affetti amorosi*, which was popular enough to go into five editions by 1626.[1] 1618 is also the first year in which song-books containing more arias than madrigals outnumber those containing more madrigals than arias. The proportion is eight to three; and it is reproduced, often more markedly, in the figures for succeeding years, until madrigals finally disappear.

THE ARIA

We must now consider the various types of song covered by the general term 'aria'. All arias are settings of strophic poems. The commonest type in the first twenty years of the seventeenth century, and the one offering the greatest contrast to the madrigal, is the short, light canzonet in triple or common time, in which, to quote Caccini again, 'there is to be used only a lively, cheerful kind of singing which is carried and ruled by the air itself':[2] no room here for 'languishment', chromaticism, passionate exclamations, or winding embellishments. The bass, far from being a slow-moving support for the vocal line, keeps time with it. Of the ten arias in *Le Nuove musiche*, however, only one is strictly of this type; the cheerless nature of the words suggests that the form rather than the content of a poem determined the kind of music a composer wrote for it:[3]

---

[1] Reprinted, not quite complete, by Oscar Chilesotti in *Biblioteca di rarità musicali*, iii (Milan, 1886).
[2] Strunk, op. cit., p. 384.
[3] Caccini, op. cit., p. 33. Reprinted in Jeppesen, op. cit. i, p. 7.

Ex. 60

(Hear, lovers, hear, wild wandering beasts, O heaven and stars, O moon and sun, women and maidens, hear my words! And, if I do right to grieve, weep at my grief.)

Songs like this continue the tradition of the sixteenth-century canzonet for several voices; their only 'new' feature is that they were conceived as solos, the inner parts being improvised at sight by the accompanist. The lively, anacreontic rhythms of Gabriello Chiabrera, a poet influenced by Ronsard and the Pléiade,[1] stimulated the composition of many delightful canzonets; as he himself says in his dialogue *Geri*, composers 'readily admit that the variety of the lines makes it easier for them to woo the listeners with their notes'.[2] None of these settings is more enchanting than the following example, with its bouncing melody and hemiola rhythm (reminding one of 'Vi ricord', o boschi ombrosi' in *Orfeo*), by Vincenzio Calestani, a musician in the service of the Medici at Pisa:[3]

Ex. 61

1. Da-mi - gel - la Tut - ta bel - la, Ver-sa, ver-sa quel bel vi - no;

Fa che ca - da La ru - gia - da Dis-til - la - ta di ru - bi - no!

(Pour out that good wine, my pretty girl; make the ruby-distilled dew fall!)

The composers of the Florentine school excelled at this type of song; they often employed popular dance-rhythms such as galliard and courante, adopted the procedure of the variation-suite, and wrote instrumental ritornellos that are usually variations on the tunes of the songs themselves. Many canzonets contain stereotyped formulae, of which the figure in the first half of bars 2 and 5 of Ex. 62 is the commonest and, as we shall see on p. 177, perhaps the most significant. This song is by Raffaello Rontani, who published it after he had moved to Rome; but on the whole, the canzonets of Roman composers are, like their madrigals, much less attractive than those of the Florentines. The way Rontani conceals the ends of the lines of the poem is especially skilful:[4]

[1] Cf. Ferdinando Neri, *Il Chiabrera e la Pleiade francese* (Turin, 1920), pp. 53–88.
[2] Quoted, ibid., p. 96.
[3] Calestani, *Madrigali et arie* (Venice, 1617), p. 35, where there is no sharp in the key-signature. Quoted by Fortune, *Musical Quarterly*, xxxix (1953), p. 186. Ritornello omitted.   [4] Rontani, *Le Varie musiche*, op. 7 (Rome, 1619), p. 8.

Ex. 62

1. Vag-hi rai di ci-glia ar-den-ti,
Più lu-cen - - ti Che del sol non
son i ra - i; Vin-ti al-

(Fair beams of burning eyes, than which sunbeams are not brighter . . .)

It will be gathered that, in contrast to both the sudden key-changes and the absence of key-change in the more amorphous madrigals, there is in songs of this type a simple, convincing scheme of modulation characteristic of music whose form is organized and whose rhythms are clear-cut. Their well defined tonality is indeed their most important 'progressive' feature.

Several of the other arias in *Le Nuove musiche* are unrepresentative of Italian arias as a whole in that they are virtually strophic madrigals. There is, for instance, little difference in mood and technique between 'Occhi immortali'[1] and Ex. 57. In three of these arias Caccini introduced the principle of 'strophic variation', for which he was admired by Doni.[2] Such Roman composers as Landi and Gregorio Veneri, writing between about 1618 and 1625, were particularly fond of this form: in their strophic variations, which occasionally have a grave, sonorous beauty all their own, a madrigalian vocal line is varied from verse to verse, while the bass, moving mainly in crotchets,

[1] Caccini, op. cit., p. 34. Reprinted in Jeppesen, op. cit. i, p. 10.
[2] Cf. Doni, *Compendio*, p. 118.

remains more or less unchanged.[1] Caccini's modifications are almost too slight, as in 'Fere selvaggie',[2] or too great, as in 'Io parto, amati lumi',[3] to justify calling his songs strophic variations.

OTTAVA AND SONNET SETTINGS

Two other groups of early seventeenth-century 'sectional' songs may be briefly considered here in parenthesis: settings of *ottave* and of sonnets. A few *ottave* were set over static basses as recitatives (to some of which, following a popular Renaissance custom, several poems might be sung), but the majority continued to be set in four sections in madrigalian style over the stylized basses that were first used for them in the sixteenth century, two lines of text corresponding to one statement of the bass. Many of the texts were taken now from Tasso's *Gerusalemme liberata* and from poets influenced by Tasso, rather than from Ariosto and his imitators. It is true that Tasso's epic was more in harmony with the age than Ariosto's, yet the settings of its *ottave* doubtless improvised by the ladies of Ferrara may well have contributed to the popularity it won among musicians at the expense of the earlier poem. Like madrigals and sonnet-settings, *ottava*-settings virtually died out in the 1620's, when arias and cantatas by Venetian composers became all the rage. Venetian monodists showed practically no interest in *ottave* and stylized basses, just as they published very few madrigals: their attitude is in marked contrast to that of Florentine and Roman composers and provincial choir-masters, who published many settings of *ottave*, especially over the *romanesca*. Cifra alone composed thirty.[4]

Some fifteen sonnets by Petrarch were still set by the monodists; many of the others that they chose are in the modish manners of Guarini or Marino, though some set by Roman composers are sacred sonnets of austerer cast. They were rarely composed straight through as madrigals. Instead they were usually split up into two or more sections corresponding to the octave and sestet or to sub-divisions of them. Most of them were written by the same groups of composers as wrote *ottave*; Monteverdi's 'Tempro la cetra' is one of the few examples from Venice.[5] Sonnets were usually composed in

---

[1] Examples of typical basses by Landi in Riemann, *Handbuch der Musikgeschichte*, ii. 2, 2nd ed. (Leipzig, 1922), pp. 51–54.

[2] Caccini, op. cit., p. 31. Reprinted in Jeppesen, op. cit. i, p. 8.

[3] Caccini, op. cit., p. 25. The differing vocal lines are reprinted one above the other in Riemann, op. cit., p. 25.

[4] Cf. Einstein, '*Orlando Furioso* and *La Gerusalemme Liberata* as set to music during the 16th and 17th centuries', *Notes*, viii (1950–1), p. 623.

[5] Monteverdi, op. cit. vii (Bologna, 1928), p. 1. (The *sinfonia* on p. 1 is part of it.)

madrigalian style and, in the hands of Belli and Landi, resemble
strophic variations when passages of the bass used in the first section
are repeated in later sections in support of a varied melodic line.[1]
The form can be well represented here by one of the greatest Italian
songs of the time, Gagliano's setting of 'Valli profonde' by the sixteenth-century poet Luigi Tansillo. Gagliano, one of the leading
musicians of his day, was eminent alike as a composer of operas
and other stage music, church music, polyphonic madrigals, and
monodies. No madrigal is quite as arresting as this, nor does any
madrigalist achieve Gagliano's variety within a single mood; the
reappearance at the end of a melodic idea from an earlier part of the
song is also a unique unifying stroke. Ex. 63 shows part of the
octave:[2]

Ex. 63

[1] Landi's 'Superbi colli e voi, sacre ruine', in praise of Rome, is quoted in Riemann,
op. cit., pp. 46–47.
[2] Gagliano, *Musiche* (Venice, 1615), p. 20. Reprinted in Jeppesen, op. cit. i, p. 14.

(Deep valleys, enemies of the sun, proud rocks threatening the sky, caves where silence and darkness reign undisturbed, winds that cover the sky with black clouds, falling stones, high cliffs, unburied bones, overgrown and broken walls. . . .)

THE CANTATA

The word 'cantata' (or 'cantada') was first used to denote songs
in which a lyrical, un-madrigalian vocal line, varied from verse to
verse, unfolds over repeated statements, either strict or free, of the
same bass, moving mainly in crotchets. This is clearly a development
of the principle of strophic variation and is in fact adumbrated in one
or two songs in that form by Belli. It may also owe something to
those parts of madrigals that have 'walking' basses, prompted in
some cases by word-painting (e.g. bars 19–20 in Ex. 58). The
earliest so-called cantatas are by Alessandro Grandi, who from 1620
was Monteverdi's principal assistant at St. Mark's, Venice, and they
overlapped with the more cumbersome madrigalian strophic variations still being composed in Rome. The second edition of Grandi's
first set of *Cantade et arie* appeared in Venice in 1620; the first edition
is lost, and the one known extant copy of the second edition is in-
accessible in private hands. Two of Grandi's cantatas are settings of
sonnets.[1] One at least is still rather like a set of strophic variations,
but in some of his other cantatas he seems to have achieved the
greater smoothness typical of the new genre. The genuine strophic-
bass cantata is seen at its best in 'Oh con quanta vaghezza' by
Giovanni Pietro Berti, who also worked at St. Mark's. The first half
of each verse is shown in Ex. 64; there is great variety in the ways in
which the different vocal lines unfold over an identical bass, ranging
from the imaginative use of rests in verses 3 and 5 to the commanding
yet graceful sweep of the long-breathed phrases of the last verse. This
cantata is one of several in which a ritornello separates one verse
from another.[2]

---

[1] Example in Manfred F. Bukofzer, *Music in the Baroque Era* (London, 1948), p. 32.
Other cantatas by Grandi are quoted in Lavignac and La Laurencie, op. cit. ii (Paris,
1925–31), pp. 3395–6; Henry Prunières, 'The Italian Cantata of the XVIIth century',
Music and Letters, vii (1926), p. 41; Riemann, op. cit., pp. 39–45; and Schmitz, *Geschichte
der weltlichen Solokantate*, p. 67.

[2] Berti, *Cantade et arie* (first set) (Venice, 1624), pp. 61–65.

Ex. 64

-ti, Spi- ran dol - ce piè - tà quei sos- pi-

-si; E pur per al - tra vi - - a mo-ve

-no. Ec - co, pe - rò, mi pen - -

-to. Quel -la don - na si - gnor che m'ha tra-

-ga; Ris- cal-dai pre-ghi pur;

-quȩa ra - gio - ne, Ec - co, pe - rò, ri -

(O how fondly, O how softly, Love, you entice me . . . / My heart knows from experience that your road, Love, leads to Death. And yet another way . . . / I resolved never again to set foot in your kingdom. See though. . . . / Ah! do not redouble my pain because I have fled from your chains. That proud lady. . . . / Weep on; she enjoys it; sigh; she does not hear you and relents not. Redouble your prayers. . . . / O! forgive my heart if thus I fled from prison to Reason.)

The few remaining strict strophic-bass cantatas are almost all by composers connected with Venice. Monteverdi's 'Ohimè ch'io cado', published in Carlo Milanuzzi's *Quarto Scherzo delle Ariose Vaghezze*, is perhaps the finest.[1] (Monteverdi, alone of the more eminent composers of the time, arrived at monody solely through the disintegration of the polyphonic madrigal; his surviving songs,[2] though not negligible, occupy as unimportant a place in his output as, for example, Mozart's do in his.) The chamber cantatas of the next period of Italian song are patchworks of recitatives, ariosos, and various kinds of aria, including some founded on recurring basses of the type

[1] Monteverdi, op. cit. ix (Bologna, 1929), p. 111. Milanuzzi's book appeared in 1623 or 1624. It is known only from a reprint of 1624; the *Terzo Scherzo* came out in 1623.
[2] In the complete edition Malipiero once or twice prints as separate songs what appear to be sections of one song. See Domenico de' Paoli, *Claudio Monteverdi* (Milan, 1945), appendix, for three songs, in facsimile and transcription, omitted from Malipiero's edition.

we have been considering as well as on the newly introduced chaconne basses; they will be discussed in Vol. VI.

Although more monodies were printed in Venice than anywhere else, few were composed there before about 1620; it began to come into its own as a centre of monody with strophic-bass cantatas, and it did so to a much greater extent with the development of strophic arias beyond the point at which we left them. We have already seen that 1618 was a crucial year in the waning popularity of madrigals and the growing popularity of arias. It was also about this time that strophic songs—those, that is, in which every verse is sung to the same music—began to split into two well-defined groups.

POPULAR STROPHIC SONGS

The less important by far of these groups embraces simple strophic tunes, some of them still similar to the canzonets of previous years, but more of them less sophisticated and of a more artless and folk-like character. They are of no great interest and may be quickly disposed of. Their poems, dealing with the lighter aspects of love, are nearly all contemptible doggerel, full of the wearying rhymes that come so easily in Italian. These songs poured from the presses of Venice in cheap books of the small-quarto size—formerly used exclusively for part-books and henceforward also for more serious songs—first used for this purpose by the enterprising Venetian publisher Giacomo Vincenti in 1618 for Stefani's *Affetti amorosi*; all previous monody-books had been folios. For accompanying these little songs the new modish instrument was the Spanish guitar. In addition to the *basso continuo* these song-books included letters indicating the harmonies to be played by the guitar. (They were sometimes added to more serious songs, too). A few unimportant volumes of verses were also published in which, apart from a few suggestions as to which already popular tunes they should be sung to, guitar-letters provide the sole musical indications. These popular songs were written for the most part by composers who wrote almost nothing else: Milanuzzi, Andrea Falconieri, and Domenico Manzolo are three of them.[1] A few of the more serious composers also included one or two in their song-books. 'Maledetto sia l'aspetto' by Monteverdi (*Scherzi musicali*, 1632) is a delightful example.[2] Even Saracini inserted a few among the pathetic madrigals of his books of *Musiche*.

[1] For representative examples cf. *22 Arie a una voce di Frate Carlo Milanuzzi*, ed. Giacomo Benvenuti (Milan, 1922).
[2] Monteverdi, op. cit. x, p. 76.

A few of the songs of Saracini and Stefani seem to have been based on Balkan folk-tunes.[1]

DEVELOPMENT OF THE CANZONET

The second of our two groups comprises those songs which, parallel to the unambitious popular songs, illustrate the first stages of the development of canzonets into the broad, sensuous arias found in the cantatas of the later seventeenth century. In 1617 Calestani published among his dance-songs and canzonets the following, quite different, song:[2]

Ex. 65

1. Fol - go - ra - te, Sa - et - ta - te,
Oc - chi, pur ch'io v'of - fro il co - re;
Non si mo - re, Non si
mo-re Per fe - rir d'oc - chi lu - cen - ti,

---

[1] Cf. Szabolcsi, *History*, p. 102 (with three examples).

[2] Calestani, op. cit., p. 33, where there is no sharp in the key-signature. Ritornello omitted.

Se ben da guer - ra e tor - men - ti.

(Flash and wound me, eyes, yet I offer you my heart. It does not die from the wounds of bright eyes, though attacked and tormented.)

This song is different because it is more expansive, urbane, and seductive than any previous canzonet; indeed, it can hardly be called a canzonet any more, even though the poem is still typical of the persiflage that composers normally turned to for their canzonets. Henceforward, as madrigals died out, strophic verses began to deal increasingly with the more serious matters that had usually been the concern of madrigals. Not only did their general musical tone become more serious and refined in the direction suggested by Calestani's song: the roulades characteristic of madrigals were transferred to arias in a new guise. Many singers would be reluctant to dispense altogether with vocal display. At the same time, composers were no doubt equally reluctant to sacrifice the smooth flow of their arias to 'static' coloratura. In the new roulades a single syllable is set to a long series of notes, frequently arranged in sequences and moving in the normal note-values of arias at a speed faster than such notes would have been taken in madrigals. Such roulades almost certainly grew out of short figures like the one in bars 2 and 5 of Ex. 62. Ex. 66 shows a typical roulade from the canzonet 'Se muov'a giurar' by Caccini's elder daughter, Francesca:[1]

Ex.66

1. A - mo - re, i ser - vi suoi
go - (verna)

(Love, your servants . . .)

[1] Francesca Caccini, *Primo libro delle musiche* (Florence, 1618), p. 94. Also cf. Fortune in *Acta Musicologica*, xxiii (1951), p. 129.

Calestani and Francesca Caccini worked for the Medici; but with the increasing tendency to religious bigotry at their court after about 1620 the popularity of secular music gradually waned, and, except for the two books of arias published by Frescobaldi[1] during his break with Rome, practically no secular songs appeared there for another fifteen years. Florence, cradle of opera and first home of the 'new music', where even as late as 1620 life at court seemed to be one long carnival, became a desolate musical backwater. Between 1620 and 1630 the main stream of Italian song flowed through Venice.

The songs of Berti are most characteristic of Venetian songs of this decade. They are nearly all in triple time. He constructs his melodies in broad, sweeping phrases, generating great emotional power, and he supports them with firm basses and straightforward, stereotyped harmonies within a simple scheme of modulations in which chromaticism plays next to no part (cf. Ex. 67). His arias, and those of other Venetian and north Italian composers such as Grandi, the blind Martino Pesenti, and Giovanni Felice Sances, sometimes breathe too a gentle, languishing melancholy that is a perfect match for their elegant, though scarcely momentous and nearly always anonymous, verses.

ARIA WITH RECITATIVE

It was just before 1620 that the verses of strophic songs began to be split up with increasing frequency into two parts, one set as a recitative, the other to aria-like movement in triple time. At the same time the movement of madrigals was becoming increasingly discontinuous as passages of triple time intruded upon the prevailing common time; Falconieri's uniquely constructed song 'Deh! dolc' anima mia' (1619)[2] is an excellent example of such a madrigal. Madrigals and arias were drawn together again into a common style: those in Benedetto Ferrari's *Musiche varie* (Venice, 1633) are musically indistinguishable from each other. This time arias proved finally and indisputably to be the stronger magnet; in Caccini's strophic variations madrigals had won a temporary victory. Peri and d'India are among the first composers to set strophic texts as recitatives and arias. In his delightful 'Torna il sereno zefiro' (1623) d'India writes in three successive styles—those typical of madrigals, recitatives and

---

[1] His *Primo libro d'arie musicali* (Florence, 1630) has been edited by Felice Boghen (Rome, 1933) and by Helga Spohr, *Musikalische Denkmäler*, iv (Mainz, 1960).
[2] Reprinted in Guido Adler, *Handbuch der Musikgeschichte*, 2nd ed. (Berlin, 1930), pp. 438–9, and in Suzanne Clercx, *Le Baroque et la musique* (Brussels, 1948), pp. 106–8.

arias[1]—in order to conform exactly to the poet's feelings. Unexpectedly few of the earliest recitatives and arias of Venetian composers are settings of texts like, for instance, Rinuccini's madrigal 'Sfogava con le stelle', in which a scene could be set in recitative and the expression of a lover's feelings treated as an aria. In his setting of this poem in *Le Nuove musiche*[2] the undramatic Caccini seems merely to be groping towards this kind of setting: Monteverdi's five-part setting[3] is much more prophetic. In the arias of Berti and other Venetians the last line or so of a verse is often treated as a refrain and repeated over and over again. The next step was for this section of an aria to become more conspicuous than ever, to develop into an aria in its own right, while the words of the main part of the verse were crowded into an introductory recitative. The following song by Berti illustrates this procedure as well as turns of phrase typical of recitative and of the long, flowing lines characteristic of Venetian arias:[4]

Ex. 67

1. Da gra-ve in-cen - dio op-pres - so, Chia - mo soc-cor-so e la pie-ta - de in - vo - co; E in suon fu-nes-to e spes-so Gri-da il cor pal-pi - tan-do al fo-co, al fo - -

---

[1] All quoted by Fortune in *Musical Quarterly*, xxxix (1953), p. 191.
[2] Giulio Caccini, op. cit., p. 13. It is reprinted in Davison and Apel, op. cit. ii (London, 1950), p. 3, where it is incorrectly called an aria.
[3] Monteverdi, op. cit. iv (Bologna, 1927), p. 15.
[4] Berti, *Cantade et arie* (second set) (Venice, 1627), p. 5. The music is modified for the last of the four verses.

(Oppressed by a relentless burning, I cry for help and invoke Pity, and with dreadful, choking sounds my palpitating heart calls to the fire. And although my life burns with a living ardour no one comes to my aid. And so, my eyes, relieve me with ample tears, for my heart demands it.)

CHAMBER DUETS

Two kinds of two-part vocal music of the early seventeenth century really belong to spheres other than solo song: (a) two-part polyphonic madrigals and canzonets of a type going back to the midsixteenth century, in which the lower part may be treated also as an instrumental *basso seguente*; and (b) dialogues, sacred and secular, whose connexions are mainly with dramatic music, masques, and the early stages of the oratorio. This leaves the Italian chamber duets of the early seventeenth century as the only significant body of vocal duets analogous to the solo songs in any country in the period covered by this volume. In these duets the relationship of the two voices to the *continuo* is exactly the same as that of the solo voice in monodies, just as in later years the duet cantata parallels the solo cantata.

As has been mentioned above (cf. p. 160), several of these duets were published in books containing monodies, but one or two composers, such as d'India (*Le Musiche a due voci*, Venice, 1615) and Giovanni Valentini (*Musiche a doi voci*, Venice, 1622), published collections of duets alone. The outstanding collection on musical grounds is Monteverdi's significantly named *Concerto: settimo libro de Madrigali* (Venice, 1619),[1] which was reprinted four times up to 1641: sixteen of its twenty-nine items are duets.

Most of the types of solo song discussed in the foregoing pages occur, handled in the same ways, in the duets. There are far fewer duets than monodies, but in one group—settings of *ottave* over stylized basses—they outnumber monodies. The figures given by Einstein[2] thirteen settings of Ariosto and Tasso as solos and twenty-three as duets—are paralleled in the more numerous settings of other *ottave*. Cifra is again a prominent composer here, and the bulk of d'India's book of 1615 consists of music of this kind. The outstanding example is Monteverdi's 'Ohimè, dov'è 'l mio ben'.[3] Here the characteristic layout of nearly all duets is seen on the highest artistic level: homophonic writing, with the voices moving mainly in thirds, alternates with imitative passages involving the use of suspensions, none more painful than the one at the beginning of Monteverdi's piece. Sonnet settings include Monteverdi's 'Interrotte speranze',[4] which is remarkable for its 'static', mysterious kind of incantatory

---

[1] Edited complete as Monteverdi, op. cit. vii.
[2] *Notes*, viii (1950–1), pp. 628–30.
[3] Op. cit., p. 152; the last part in Jeppesen, op. cit. iii, p. 74. There is another example, by Filippo Vitali, in ibid., p. 86.
[4] Monteverdi, op. cit. vii, p. 94, and Jeppesen, op. cit. iii, p. 76.

writing for the voices, which do not break into imitation until the last line of the text.

The first outstanding vocal piece on a chaconne-bass is Monteverdi's magnificent 'Zefiro torna, e di soavi accenti',[1] published in 1632. The contrasts of mood in Rinuccini's text, another sonnet, are exactly the same as those in d'India's 'Torna il sereno zefiro' (cf. p. 178), a popular type going back to Petrarch, whose sonnet 'Zefiro torna e'l bel tempo rimena' Monteverdi himself set as a five-part madrigal in his sixth book. Over a free bass Monteverdi breaks into passionate declamation of the poet's sadness, and this is in violent contrast to the vernal freshness of the rest of the piece as it pursues its course over the constantly repeated two-bar bass. This duet represents the ultimate stylistic fusion of madrigal and aria mentioned on p. 178. Several of Monteverdi's earlier duet settings of madrigals contain passages in triple time, e.g. 'Dice la mia bellissima Licori' and 'Non vedrò mai le stelle',[2] not necessarily at points in the poems that demand such a change: these are often purely musical changes indicating the growing dominance of the triple-time aria. His 'O come sei gentile'[3] is an example of the earlier kind of elaborately ornamented madrigal wholly in common time; yet even here the roulades tend not to be static but to move with the basic pulse, as in the triple-time canzonet quoted in Ex. 66.

There are no important strophic duets by Monteverdi or other composers before 1630 comparable with the broad triple-time arias of Berti and other Venetian composers: as has been pointed out, the composers approached this style in duets mainly through through-composed madrigalian texts. Most strophic duets correspond to the simpler kind of solo canzonet, sometimes, as in Monteverdi and Valentini, with ritornellos for violins. Monteverdi's charming 'Chiome d'oro' is the most familiar example of a piece of this kind.[4]

SOLO SONG IN GERMANY

From the Italian music of this period grew a vocal style that was to sweep Europe during the next two centuries. At first, however, Italian monody travelled slowly to other lands; not unexpectedly, there is no trace in the period under review of the influence of the Venetian arias of the 1620's. So far as Germany is concerned the

---

[1] Monteverdi, op. cit. ix, p. 9.
[2] Op. cit. vii, pp. 58 and 66 respectively.   [3] Ibid., p. 35.
[4] Ibid., p. 176. There are further examples, by Marco and Giovanbattista da Gagliano, Cifra and Frescobaldi, in Jeppesen, op. cit. iii, pp. 82, 84, 88, 85, and 89 respectively.

slowness of the penetration of monody may have been due to the fact
that the Italian music best known there seems to have been Venetian
music, and Venice in the early years of the seventeenth century was
famous not for monodies but for the choral music of Giovanni
Gabrieli and for sacred chamber music on a smaller scale; German
publications of this period show that these were the only potent
Italian influences.[1]

The only significant German composer of solo songs before 1630
was Johann Nauwach, a musician in the service of the Elector of
Saxony; he studied in Italy for six years[2] and in 1623 published at
Dresden his *Libro primo di arie passeggiate*, entirely to Italian texts.
The title may have been suggested by the book of tedious *Arie
passeggiate* that the expatriate German, Johann Kapsperger, had
engraved, complete with tablature for the *chitarrone*, in Rome in
1612. (He published another set in 1623.) Nauwach may also have
met Saracini, either during his own stay in Florence between 1614
and 1618 or while the latter was in Germany, or at least have seen
Saracini's *Musiche* of 1614, since nearly all the poems he set to music
also appear there. But his settings are dry and mechanical compared
with Saracini's. He also included in his book a version of Caccini's
'Amarilli' deprived of its exquisite final cadence and subjected
throughout to arid and tasteless divisions that replace Caccini's
elegant embellishments and drain it of all sentiment and expressiveness.[3] Nauwach is seen at his best in his four Italianate canzonets:
Einstein quotes one that is very similar to Ex. 62.[4] The eight solo
songs in Nauwach's *Teutsche Villanellen* (Dresden, 1627),[5] especially
'All Leut und Thier', are in the main similar to these canzonets.
About half the poems found in this book are by Martin Opitz, who
had fashioned a new kind of German verse, more elegant than that
of his predecessors. The collaboration of Opitz and Nauwach, which
may be said to have created the German *continuo* song, can be seen

[1] Cf. the lists in Otto Ursprung, 'Der Weg von den Gelegenheitsgesängen und dem
Chorlied über die Frühmonodisten zum neueren deutschen Lied' ('Vier Studien zur
Geschichte der deutschen Lieder', iv), *Archiv für Musikwissenschaft*, vi (1924), pp. 283–90.

[2] Cf. Hans Volkmann, 'Johann Nauwachs Leben', *Zeitschrift für Musikwissenschaft*,
iv (1921–2), p. 554.

[3] Cf. the comparison of the two settings in Einstein, 'Ein unbekannter Druck aus der
Frühzeit der deutschen Monodie', *Sammelbände der internationalen Musikgesellschaft*,
xiii (1911–12), pp. 294–5.

[4] Ibid., p. 296.

[5] Reprinted in Walter Vetter, *Das frühdeutsche Lied* (Münster, 1928), ii, pp. 44–50.
For a discussion of them cf. ibid. i, pp. 141–55, and R. Hinton Thomas, *Poetry and Song
in the German Baroque* (Oxford, 1963), pp. 39–42; also cf. Haas, *Die Musik des Barocks*,
pp. 99–100. One song is reprinted in Hans Joachim Moser, *The German Solo Song and
the Ballad* (Cologne, 1958), p. 16.

at its most fruitful in 'Ach liebste, lass uns eilen'. Johann Hermann Schein, an altogether bigger figure than Nauwach, has been discussed in the previous chapter.[1]

THE LUTE SONG IN FRANCE

The verses of the leading French poets of the sixteenth century—Ronsard, Desportes, Amadis Jamyn, Étienne Jodelle, and several others—abound with references to the lute and lyre and to singing to these instruments.[2] Ronsard, for example, writes in the twelfth of his first book of odes (published in 1550):

> Premier j'ay écrit la façon
> D'accorder le luth aux odes.

(I was the first to show how the lute should be matched to odes.)

And these lines open the third ode in his second book (also 1550):

> Viens à moy, mon luth, que j'accorde
> Une ode, pour la fredonner
> Dessus la mieux parlante corde
> Que Phoebus t'ait voulu donner. . .

(Come to me, my lute, that I may compose an ode and sing it to the best-speaking string that Phoebus has wished to give you.)

We should not take these references too seriously; no doubt many of them are merely poetic gestures, sometimes vague and unexpected (as when Ronsard speaks of a lute played with a bow), which were products, perhaps, of the *mystique* concerning the union of music and poetry created to a great extent by the prose writings of Ronsard himself and of such men as Pontus de Tyard, who anticipated the opinions of Bardi's *Camerata* in considering ensemble-singing 'un vulgaire usage' inferior to solo singing as a vehicle for fine poetry.[3]

It is nevertheless true that, in France and elsewhere, there must have been a public who enjoyed singing French *chansons*—the most popular musical representatives of the internationally dominant French culture—as solos to the lute;[4] in the middle years of the century a number of volumes were published, on the lines of Attaingnant's collection of 1529,[5] in response to this demand. The first was actually published in

---

[1] See p. 122.

[2] For a comprehensive selection of them cf. La Laurencie, Mairy, and Thibault, op. cit., pp. xxvii–xxx.

[3] Cf. François Lesure, *Musicians and Poets of the French Renaissance* (New York, [1956]), pp. 56–57, and Henri Quittard, 'L'*Hortus Musarum* de 1552–53 et les arrangements de pièces polyphoniques pour voix seule et luth', *Sammelbände der internationalen Musikgesellschaft*, viii (1906–7), p. 274. Ronsard's important dedication of his *Livre de mellanges* (Paris, 1560) is translated in Strunk, op. cit., pp. 286–9.

[4] Cf. La Laurencie, *Les Luthistes* (Paris, 1928), pp. 56–57.   [5] See p. 5.

Antwerp by another of the leading publishers of the time, Pierre Phalèse. His *Hortus musarum*, consisting of arrangements of *chansons* and other vocal music, appeared in two parts, the first, for lute alone, in 1552, the second, for voice and lute, in 1553. The bulk of the second part consists of twenty *chansons*,[1] nine of them by Créquillon and five by Clemens non Papa. Whereas the solos in Attaingnant's book were arrangements of *chansons* that had been published already, nearly all of those in Phalèse's book antedate by a year or two the publication of the purely vocal versions. It is not known who made the arrangements. Many of them are literal even to the retention in the lute part of imitative entries (cf. Clemens's 'Puis que voulez'), though others, such as Créquillon's 'L'ardant amour', are better adapted to the capabilities of the lute.

LE ROY'S PUBLICATIONS

Adrian Le Roy, the famous printer and a past master at arranging vocal music for the lute, was more sensible of the differences between vocal and instrumental techniques. The second and fifth of his *Livres de guiterre* (1551 or 1552—only the second edition of 1555 is known—and 1554, respectively) contain a total of forty-two *chansons* to be sung to the four-stringed gittern; Arcadelt is the most frequently named composer (in the fifth book only). Le Roy also published arrangements by himself and by the lutenist Guillaume Morlaye of psalms by Certon.[2] But his most celebrated publication in this genre is his *Livre d'airs de cour* of 1571,[3] written for the clever and cultivated Claude-Catherine de Clermont de Vivonne, Comtesse de Retz, who gathered around her a brilliant circle of poets and musicians. Le Roy had already dedicated to her his *Instruction de partir toute musique facilement en tablature de luth*, a volume known now only from English translations of the second part (1568) and of the complete work in three parts (1574). In his *Instruction* Le Roy shows in detail how vocal works should be set for the lute, taking as his principal examples

---

[1] Reprinted complete in La Laurencie, Mairy, and Thibault, op. cit., pp. 53–131, with facsimile specimen page of music on p. [xlvi]. Two reprinted by Quittard in *Sammelbände der internationalen Musikgesellschaft*, viii (1906–7), pp. 280–5, and one in Noske, op. cit., p. 20.

[2] Cf. Morlaye, *Psaumes de Pierre Certon réduits pour chant et luth*, ed. Richard de Morcourt (Paris, 1957). Other reprints include Bruger, *Schule des Lautenspiels*, i, p. 46, iii, p. 94, and iv, p. 145, and Morcourt, 'Adrian le Roy et les psaumes pour luth', *Annales musicologiques*, iii (1955), pp. 201–11.

[3] Reprinted as complete as possible (the only surviving copy is imperfect) in La Laurencie, Mairy, and Thibault, op. cit., pp. 133–75 and lxvi–lxxii, with facsimile of specimen page of music on p. liv. Other reprints in Janet Dodge, 'Les Airs de cour d'Adrian le Roy', *Mercure musical et Bulletin de la S.I.M.*, iii (1907), pp. 1136–43.

a number of *chansons* by Lassus. But the *chansons* of Lassus, he says
(in the dedication of the *Livre* of 1571), are 'difficiles et ardues', and
so, by way of contrast, he has put into this new book *chansons* that
are 'beaucoup plus legieres', of the kind formerly known as *voix de
ville* and now called *airs de cour*.[1] This is the first use of a term, *vaudeville*, that (along with *airs*, first used in Costeley's *Musique* of 1570)
was to become general for this kind of lighter song, in both solo and
ensemble versions: the *précieux* of the court embraced the music of
the streets.

Of the twenty-two *chansons* in Le Roy's collection thirteen are
taken from the settings of verses by Ronsard, Desportes, and other
leading poets published the previous year by Nicolas de La Grotte, an
admired performer on keyboard instruments. Le Roy may have been
influenced in his choice by the simple, clear-cut melodies and homophonic texture of La Grotte's *chansons*. His songs are not 'straight'
transcriptions and are indeed often more expressive than the originals.
He doubled the vocal lines in his lute parts. But he introduced variations into both the lute and voice parts as well; his lute parts (as in La
Grotte's 'Las! que nous sommes misérables') sometimes look forward to the *style brisé* of the Gaultiers, and he introduced into them
little flourishes to underline key words. He published two versions of
four of the *chansons*, one with a simple lute part, the other, 'plus
finement traitée', with a rather more elaborate one, though not so
elaborate as the second versions of Milán's songs.[2] Ex. 68, showing
the opening of a *chanson* (i) in its original form and (ii) as treated by
Le Roy, illustrates his art of arrangement. The music is by La Grotte
and the poem by Ronsard; it was almost certainly performed in the
second form in a sumptuous masque staged at Fontainebleau in 1565:[3]

Ex. 68
(i)

1. Je   suis A - mour,   le grand mai - stre   des Dieux,

<hr />

[1] The dedications of the *Livre* of 1571 and of the 1574 translation of the *Instruction*
in La Laurencie, Mairy, and Thibault, op. cit., pp. xxv–xxxvi and lvi–[lvii], respectively.
[2] See p. 136.
[3] (i) *La Fleur des musiciens de P. Ronsard*, ed. Henry Expert (Paris, 1923), p. 62;
(ii) La Laurencie, Mairy, and Thibault, op. cit., p. 167. Alsa cf. Prunières, 'Ronsard et
les fêtes de cour', *Revue musicale, numéro spécial; Ronsard et la musique* (May, 1924),
pp. 34–37.

(I am Love, great master of the gods, I am he.)

FRENCH SONG IN THE EARLY SEVENTEENTH CENTURY

It is curious that no more solo songs were published in France until 1608. The civil wars that rocked France during the earlier part of the intervening period cannot alone have been the reason for this, since more than five hundred ensemble *airs* were published between 1576 and 1600.[1] It is possible, however, that publications involving lute-tablatures were temporarily abandoned because of their expense. It is also possible that, as a result of Le Roy's publications, people could now be expected to arrange their own solos at home if they wanted to. That musicians, at least, continued to think in terms of tunes separable from lower parts is shown by the publication in 1582 of

[1] Cf. Kenneth Jay Levy, 'Vaudeville, vers mesuré et airs de cour', *Musique et poésie* (Paris, 1954), p. 189, with a list of books in n. 19.

Airs de plusieurs musiciens réduits à quatre parties,[1] in which tunes by other composers are re-set for four voices by Didier Le Blanc, and by the way in which the top parts stand out against a homophonic background in the *airs* of such men as Jehan Planson and Charles Tessier (the latter published by Thomas Este in London in 1597). There is also the evidence of Jehan Chardavoine's *Recueil des plus belles et excellentes chansons en forme de voix de ville* (1576), which consists of 190 unaccompanied tunes probably sung by the ordinary townsfolk; their more popular tone is well illustrated if Chardavoine's symmetrical melody for Ronsard's celebrated poem 'Mignonne, allons voir si la rose' is compared with the top part of Costeley's 'learned' four-part setting published in 1570.[2] Finally, Pierre Cerveau provides a link with the practice in other countries when he remarks in the preface to his four-part *Airs* of 1599 that 'according to the most learned musicians of this time' the top part only of an *air* could be sung, with the lower parts played on instruments.

The first French solo songs of the seventeenth century are the twenty-six *airs de court* (*sic*) in that huge international rag-bag of lute-music, the *Thesaurus harmonicus* (Cologne, 1603) of Jean-Baptiste Besard, a Frenchman trained as lawyer and lutenist and living in Germany.[3] Most of these songs, too, have clear-cut melodies of a popular cast; in 'Si jamais mon âme blessée',[4] on the other hand, the movement is completely held up by embellishments as indiscriminately applied as in Nauwach's 'Amarilli' (see p. 183).

After a curious six-year hiatus, during which no *airs* of any kind appeared, solo song eventually got under way in France in 1608 with the publication of *Airs de différents autheurs mis en tablature de luth par Gabriel Bataille*. This is the first of a series of sixteen such volumes that continued until 1643. Bataille, a fine lutenist himself, intabulated the songs in the first six (to 1615); the arrangements in the next two (1617–18) are by the composers 'eux mesmes'; and those from the

---

[1] Reprinted complete by Expert in *Monuments de la musique française* (Paris, 1925).

[2] Both reprinted in *La Fleur des musiciens de P. de Ronsard*, pp. 74 and 44, respectively. Or cf. Julien Tiersot, 'Ronsard et la musique de son temps', *Sammelbände der internationalen Musikgesellschaft*, iv (1902–3), pp. 132–3, where the same comparison is made. Also cf. Claude Frissard, 'A propos d'un recueil de "chansons" de Jehan Chardavoine', *Revue de musicologie*, xxx (1948), p. 58.

[3] These songs have been reprinted in several different places. The largest selections are those of Chilesotti in *Biblioteca di rarità musicali*, vii (Milan, 1914) (eleven *airs*) and in 'Gli airs de cour di Besard', in *Atti del Congresso Internazionale di Scienze Storiche*, viii, for 1900 (1905), pp. 131 ff. (nine of the same *airs* and one additional one). There are three *airs* in *Airs de cour pour voix et luth* (*1603–1643*), ed. André Verchaly (Paris, 1961), pp. 4–9. Cf. Lavignac and la Laurencie, op. cit. i, p. 670, for a facsimile of an *air*.

[4] Reprinted in *Biblioteca di rarità musicali*, vii, p. 14. Facsimile reprint in Georg Kinsky, *A History of Music in Pictures* (London, 1930), p. 135.

ninth book (1620) onwards are by Antoine Boësset, who from 1626 was superintendent of chamber music at court. Other song-books of this time include five (1624–35) by the admired singer Étienne Moulinié and eight (1615–28) brought out by the printer Pierre Ballard and consisting of tunes only.[1] The books are quartos, often running to seventy folios. Most of the songs they contain are still arrangements of ensemble music, and the mainly chordal lute parts[2] generally keep pace with the vocal lines; the *basso continuo* is not found in French music of this date. There are no bar-lines.

The songs fall into four main groups. (1) *Airs de cour* proper: most of the more serious secular songs belong to this group; although even drinking songs are occasionally called *airs*, it is true on the whole to say that this type of song became more *précieux* and less popular over the years. (2) The more light-hearted *chansons*, with squarer and catchier tunes and sometimes based on specific dance rhythms. They seem to have become more popular towards 1630 at the expense of *airs* proper. (3) Psalms: these are strictly outside the range of this chapter. The eleven psalms in Bataille's books, nearly all composed by him, are, however, among the noblest French songs of the period; their melodies, resembling those in the Huguenot psalter, are set against lute accompaniments richer and more polyphonic than those of the other songs. The psalms are among the few French songs of the time actually conceived as solos.[3] (4) *Récits*: these form an essential part of *ballets de cour*.[4]

GUÉDRON AND THE *RÉCIT*

The *récits* are the only French songs of this period to show even a semblance of Italian influence. Pierre Guédron, the leading French composer of the age, is the only one who seems to have studied Italian music, and it was he who composed most of the known *récits*. Like the psalms they are written expressly as solos. In their lute parts

[1] For fuller surveys than can be given here cf. Théodore Gérold, *L'Art du chant en France au XVII* siècle* (Strasbourg, 1921), pp. 1–95, Verchaly, 'Poésie et air de cour en France jusqu'à 1620', *Musique et poésie* (Paris, 1954), p. 211, and idem in Roland-Manuel, op. cit., pp. 1532–43. The most important selection of reprinted *airs* is Verchaly, *Airs de cour* (with introduction and detailed commentaries), which contains 90 *airs*; there are 24—all but two different—in Peter Warlock, *French ayres from Gabriel Bataille's Airs de différents autheurs (1608–1618)* (London, [1926]). Verchaly's volume appeared after this chapter had been written.

[2] On the lute parts, see Verchaly, 'La Tablature dans les recueils français pour chant et luth (1603–1643)', in *Le Luth et sa musique*, ed. Jean Jacquot (Paris, 1958), p. 155.

[3] Cf. 'Tous ceux qui du Seigneur ont crainte', reprinted in Verchaly, 'Gabriel Bataille et son œuvre personnelle pour chant et luth', *Revue de musicologie*, xxix (1947), pp. 19–20.

[4] See p. 806.

there are chords only on the strong beats, supporting fairly free and declamatory vocal lines. But even a typical *récit* such as Guédron's 'Quel espoir de guarir'[1] is comparatively un-Italian. The short embellishments of *récits* are much less incisive and passionate than the longer ones found in Italian madrigals. The French tended to add short, pliable flourishes to many syllables (even mute 'e') without regard to their emotional significance: the occasional flourish of this kind, resembling the one at the beginning of Caccini's 'Perfidissimo volto' (cf. p. 155), affords one of the few points of contact between the two nations. Again, French exclamations usually rise through a *port-de-voix* or *coulé*, whereas Caccini's nearly always fall.[2] The later, more extravagant elaborations of the vocal lines of *airs de cour* by Boësset, Moulinié, and the singer Henry Le Bailly include many passages in even note-values that resemble the diminutions of the previous century rather than the roulades of the finest Italian monodists. We are fortunate in knowing the embellishments that they added to Boësset's song 'N'esperez plus';[3] while they are typically un-Italian, it is significant that, as in Italian arias, the section of the song in triple time is much less florid than that in duple time. Embellishments of this nature were probably introduced not merely to gratify the vanity of virtuosos but to compensate for the narrow range of the melodies of all airs except *récits* and to bring variety to the singing of a song with several verses.

Most of the features of *airs* that I have mentioned are symptomatic of a general attitude to music, paralleled in other aspects of cultural life, that is peculiarly French. The French agreed with Descartes that the objects of music are to please and to represent human feelings in a simple, graceful manner conforming to the ideals of *précieux* society in its avoidance of passionate exaggeration. In his *récits* Guédron merely took over a few gestures from the Italian style. He never attempted to adapt that style to French taste. Marin Mersenne, the greatest musical theorist in France and an ardent champion of solo as opposed to ensemble music, attacked French composers for this unwillingness to enliven the soft, undemonstrative French style with a strong dose of Italian passion.[4] (There was, as we have seen, more 'sweetness' in Italian music than Mersenne seems

---

[1] Warlock, op. cit., p. 26.

[2] Cf. examples in Gérold, op. cit., p. 90. Gérold, on pp. 80–92, gives a very good account of this subject.

[3] Printed in Marin Mersenne, *Harmonie universelle* (Paris, 1636), ii, 'Traitez des consonances', pp. 411–14. They are reprinted in Ferand, *Improvisation in Nine Centuries*, p. 107.   [4] Cf. Mersenne, op. cit., pp. 198 and 356.

to have allowed). Yet his views on Italian music are not typical of
French thought. The French and the Italians were antipathetic to
each other's music, and they were to remain so until well into the
eighteenth century. The literary and musical ties between France
and Italy in the later sixteenth century, resulting perhaps in as yet
unexplored links between *airs de cour* and the lighter Italian forms such
as the *villanella*, weakened with the vogue for the more passionate
solo madrigals in Italy. The one Italian song—an arrangement of
a *villanella* by Ruggiero Giovanelli—and the settings by Frenchmen
of Italian words in the books of solo *airs de cour* are quite unlike
Italian monodies.[1] Caccini and his family seem to have made no
impression on French composers when they sang at the French court
during the winter of 1604–5; and the French and the Italians blamed
one another for the same 'faults' in their singing.[2]

AIRS DE COUR

The words of *airs de cour* are mainly by poets of the second rank,
who perpetuated Petrarchan themes and vocabulary in amorous,
passionless poems covering a wide range of forms and metres; the
verses of most are either four or six lines long. The influence of
Spanish poetry is also marked. All the songs are strophic, and many
fall into two repeated halves. The songs of the lighter type, with their
well-defined outlines and regular rhythms, are well represented by the
following *bergerette* by Bataille:[3]

Ex. 69

1. Ma ber - gè - re, Non lé - gè - re En a-
-mours, Me fait re - çe - voir du bien tous les jours, Ma ber-
jours: Je la mei-ne La pour-mei-ne Par les champs, Où nous prenons en-

[1] Several are reprinted in Verchaly, 'Les Airs italiens mis en tablature de luth dans les
recueils français du début du XVIIe siècle', *Revue de musicologie*, xxxv (1953), p. 59.

[2] Cf. Fortune in *Music and Letters*, xxxv (1954), p. 214, and Verchaly in *Revue de
musicologie*, xxxv (1953), p. 50.

[3] Bataille, *Airs de différents autheurs*, iv (Paris, 1613), fo. 10ᵛ. Taken from reprint in
Warlock, op. cit., p. 20, where it is anonymous and the repeats are written out; the bar-
lines are Warlock's. Also in Verchaly, *Airs de cour*, p. 52.

-sem-ble de doux pas - se - temps,   Je la -temps.

(My shepherdess, not fickle in love, makes me receive good things every day.
I lead her through the fields, where we pass the time pleasantly together.)

Very different from these *chansons*, and most characteristically French
of all, are the *airs de cour* in the first of the four groups listed on p. 189.
They are of three distinct rhythmic types, though all have peculiarities of rhythm that render the time-signatures, when they have any,
meaningless. It is probable that the first type was consciously influenced by *musique mesurée à l'antique*,[1] large quantities of which
were published only in the early years of the seventeenth century,
some thirty years after Baïf founded his academy. In these songs the
metre of the text is underlined by long notes at the *coupes* and at the
ends of the lines.[2] In ten-syllable lines the *coupe* comes after the fourth
syllable, in alexandrines after the sixth. Octosyllabics are commoner
than these in *airs de cour*, and they normally have no *coupe* at all: in
all these songs, however, a *coupe* is inserted after the fourth syllable,
sometimes even on mute 'e'. In songs of this type a certain monotony
and hesitancy are inevitable. Here is a strict example:[3]

Ex. 70

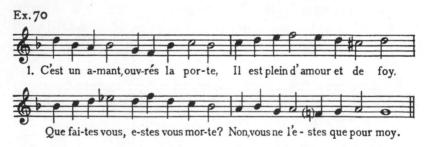

1. C'est un a-mant, ouv-rés la por-te,   Il est plein d'amour et de foy.

Que fai-tes vous, e-stes vous mor-te? Non, vous ne l'e - stes que pour moy.

(It is a lover, open the door; he is filled with love and faith. What are you doing,
are you dead? No, you are dead only for me.)

D. P. Walker considers that the smaller number of *airs* of the second
type were unconsciously influenced by *musique mesurée*. They have the
same 'unbarrable' rhythm in minims and crotchets, but 'no attempt
is made to follow the real or imaginary metre of the text', which 'is set

---

[1] See p. 29.
[2] Cf. D. P. Walker, 'The Influence of *musique mesurée à l'antique*, particularly on the
airs de cour of the early seventeenth century', *Musica Disciplina*, ii (1948), p. 141.
[3] Bataille, *Airs de différents autheurs*, ii (Paris, 1609), fo. 10ᵛ. Taken from Walker's
quotation in *Musica Disciplina*, ii (1948), p. 151; the complete song is in Verchaly, *Airs
de cour*, p. 24.

with a complete disregard for natural verbal rhythm'.[1] In some later *airs* changes of rhythm are shown by rapidly changing time-signatures, but the irregularity is sometimes only imaginary, because the changes at cadences from triple to duple time can be regarded as written-out ritardandos. Ex. 71 shows two typical lines of a song of this nature:[2]

Ex. 71

1. Vostre hu-meur est par trop vol - la - ge, Bel - le,

pour pos - se - der mon cœur, Cher-chés donc si vous

(Your humour is too fickle, fair one, to possess my heart. . . .)

There remain songs of a third type whose rhythm is like that of *musique mesurée* except that it is based on no metrical scheme. The following is the opening of such a song by Guédron:[3]

Ex. 72

1. Heu-reux qui se peut plain-dre Li - bre-ment, Heu-reux qui se

(Happy he who can lament freely. . . .)

[1] Walker, op. cit., p. 152.

[2] Bataille, op. cit., fo. 20ᵛ. Taken from reprint in Warlock, op. cit., p. 4. Also cf. Walker, op. cit., p. 154, for three versions of the final cadence in this example.

[3] Bataille, *Airs de différents autheurs*, iii (Paris, 1614), fo. 44ᵛ. Taken from reprint in Warlock, op. cit., p. 13.

The most noteworthy feature here is the distortion of the rhythm that allows insignificant words and syllables like 'se' and '—dre' to be set to long notes. Edward Filmer, who in 1629 published English versions of some *airs de cour*[1] for four and five voices, mentions this point in his preface and rightly observes that such apparently eccentric stressing is less offensive in French because tonic accents there are weak and versification is syllabic. In couplets, which composers of *airs de cour* set to music much more frequently than did earlier composers, the latter feature results in misplaced accents. Another influence was no doubt the stressing that we have already noticed of the fourth syllables in octosyllabics. Although some of them may seem rather etiolated, many of these most typically French songs, if they are not sung in too rigid or literal a manner, will be found to have an elusive, subtle charm that puts them among the most appealing lyrical creations of the time; they bear something of the same relation to the songs of other countries as do the songs of Fauré and Debussy to those of the great German song-writers.

ENGLISH SOLO SONGS OF THE MID-CENTURY

As in France and Italy, so too in England there seem to have been few secular solo songs in the sixteenth century. But in England two important differences must be noted. Firstly, more of the surviving songs seem to have been conceived, rather than arranged, as solos than in the other two countries. Secondly, in pronounced contrast to the situation in France and Italy, comparatively little secular music of any kind has survived, at any rate from the fifty years before madrigals first appeared, and almost none of it in printed form. I use the word 'survive' deliberately because the loss or the lack of sources is probably the main reason for the apparent scarcity of native secular music. For one thing a great deal of singing, notably of the more popular kind, must surely have been improvised—a supposition borne out by the appearance in English manuscripts from the second half of the century of basses associated with improvised singing in Italy. Moreover, in more sophisticated circles, the long and hard-dying tradition of French culture at the English court, lack of opportunities for music-making there, and a general air of austerity after the Reformation may, at one time or another during this period, have prevented the development of a strong native secular tradition.

A few four-part songs, probably sung around the middle of the

---

[1] Cf. example by Antoine Boësset, with the original French version, in Noske, op. cit., p. 29; facsimile reproduction of the French version, ibid., p. 13.

century, survive in scattered manuscript sources. Although some are more imitative in texture than the three-part songs of Henry VIII's reign, it would not have needed much adjustment to sing, say, Richard Edwards's 'When griping grief' as a solo to instrumental accompaniment.[1] Other manuscripts include lute pieces associated with verses by such famous poets as Wyatt and Surrey. In one source, for instance, there is a lute piece bearing the title 'In winter's just return'; these are the opening words of a poem by Surrey printed in Tottel's celebrated *Songes and Sonettes* in 1557.[2] The music, which seems complete in itself, fits two lines of the poem, which has eighty-two lines altogether. The bass resembles the *passamezzo antico*, the oldest of the stylized Italian basses. Was the music, then, sung over and over again until the poem was finished, the top part being varied as *ottave* were in Italy? Such a performance must have become intolerably tedious, but the possibility cannot be ruled out. Other similar pieces in the same manuscript may originally have been treated in the same fashion. 'Blame not my lute' is the opening of a poem by Wyatt, and a lute piece with this title and a bass which is that of the *caracossa* type of *folia* in triple time was inexpertly scribbled into another important manuscript, probably in 1559 or shortly after.[3] It is difficult to see this jog-trot music as an apposite setting of Wyatt's words. The poem, however, is probably one of those that Wyatt appears to have written to already existing tunes, thus transferring a popular fifteenth-century practice to the higher sphere of lyric poetry and helping to initiate what became a popular ballad repertory. At the same time we must not assume that, conversely, his other lyrics—the great majority—required music to complete them: his allusions to music, like those of Ronsard, are surely no more than conventional poetic gestures, not necessarily calling for complementary music.[4]

[1] Cf. Denis Stevens, 'La Chanson anglaise avant l'école madrigaliste', in *Musique et poésie* (Paris, 1954), p. 125, and 'Tudor part-songs', *Musical Times*, xcvi (1955), p. 362.

[2] The poem is in *Tottel's Miscellany*, ed. Hyder E. Rollins, i (Cambridge, Mass., 1928), pp. 16–18, and the music, in Brit. Mus. MS. Royal App. 58, fo. 52, is reproduced in Ivy L. Mumford, 'Musical settings to the poems of Henry Howard, Earl of Surrey', *English Miscellany*, viii (1957), between pp. 16 and 17, and transcribed in Arthur W. Byler, *Italian Currents in the Popular Music of England in the 16th Century* (Diss., Chicago, 1952, unpub.), p. 127. Also cf. Mumford in *English Miscellany*, viii (1957), p. 10, and Byler, op. cit., pp. 47–48.

[3] The poem is in *The Collected Poems of Sir Thomas Wyatt*, ed. Kenneth Muir (London, 1949), p. 122. The music is in Washington, Folger Shakespeare Library, MS. v.a. 1. 59, fo. 4ᵛ. Its reconstruction in Byler, op. cit., p. 137 (also cf. ibid., p. 58) is printed in Mumford, 'Musical settings to the poems of Sir Thomas Wyatt', *Music and Letters*, xxxvii (1956), p. 318. The preposterous reconstruction in John H. Long, 'Blame not Wyatt's lute', *Renaissance News*, vii (1954), p. 129, was commented upon by Otto Gombosi and Bukofzer in *Renaissance News*, viii (1955), pp. 12–14.

[4] Cf. John Stevens, *Music and Poetry in the Early Tudor Court* (London, 1961).

The last-mentioned manuscript and a few others contain other lute pieces associated with courtly verse. On a less sophisticated level, too, such popular miscellanies as *A Handefull of Pleasant Delites* (1566?—known only from an edition of 1584)[1] and *A Gorgious Gallery of Gallant Inventions* (1578) are filled with verses, many of them rather perfunctory, that were written to existing tunes. That one such tune is that of the exquisite song 'The poor soul sat sighing',[2] the best-known of the 'willow songs', indicates the high quality of the popular music that might be associated with these collections. Like Wyatt several decades earlier, even the most sophisticated poets did not scorn to write poems to such music; to quote only one example, Sidney wrote 'The time hath been' to 'Greensleeves'.[3] Italian basses such as 'rogero' (= *ruggiero*: cf. p. 141) continued to be used, and it is a striking fact that exactly a quarter of the pieces in the large Dallis lute-book in Trinity College, Dublin (begun in 1583) are based on them;[4] they may originally have been introduced into England by travellers or by the Italian musicians at court.

SONGS FOR THE CHOIRBOY PLAYS

A number of the English songs of the second half of the sixteenth century are either known, or (from the nature of the words) may be assumed, to have been written for plays. These were usually the choir-boy plays performed by the boys of chapels in and near London—those of the Chapel Royal, for example, under such men as Richard Edwards and William Hunnis, or those of St. George's, Windsor, under Richard Farrant.[5] The Masters of the Children were versatile men: Edwards, for instance, was accomplished as playwright, lyric poet,

pp. 135–9, which gives the most judicious account of this subject and warns against the more injudicious assumptions of Mumford. See also Mumford, 'Sir Thomas Wyatt's Songs: a trio of problems in manuscript sources', *Music and Letters*, xxxix (1958), p. 262.

[1] Cf. Ward, 'Music for *A Handefull of pleasant delites*', *Journal of the American Musicological Society*, x (1957), p. 151.

[2] Brit. Mus. Add. MS. 15117, fo. 18. Facsimiles in Warlock, *The English Ayre* (London, 1926), p. 127, and in Frank H. Potter, *Reliquary of English Song* (New York, [1915]), facing p. ix, with transcription on pp. 20–21. Other transcriptions by John P. Cutts in 'A Reconsideration of the *Willow Song*', *Journal of the American Musicological Society*, x (1957), pp. 21–23, and, the best, by F. W. Sternfeld, *Music in Shakespearean Tragedy* (London, 1963), which contains the fullest account of the subject.

[3] Printed in Pattison, op. cit., p. 175. See also William A. Ringler, Jr.'s edition of *The Poems of Sir Philip Sidney* (Oxford, 1962), pp. 423–34.

[4] Dublin, Trin. Coll. D. iii, 30. Cf. Byler, op. cit., p. 61.

[5] For a full account of these plays cf. G. E. P. Arkwright, 'Elizabethan choirboy plays and their music', *Proceedings of the Musical Association*, xl (1913–14), p. 117.

and composer. Several of the songs that probably they, and colleagues like Robert Parsons, composed for their plays survive mainly in two sets of part-books.[1] The opening of theatres in the 1580's and the appearance of more literate and exacting audiences produced by the expanding grammar schools led to a demand for full-time professional dramatists served by adult companies, and the functions of playwright and composer ceased to be combined in the same man. Shakespeare, just such a dramatist, satirized the choirboy plays, especially their absurdly contrived alliterations, in the play scene in *A Midsummer Night's Dream.*

One or two of the play-songs are found in manuscripts set for voice and lute. Such a one is 'O death, rock me asleep',[2] a very beautiful song interesting for being constructed over a kind of ground bass. It is one of numerous 'death songs' that were especially popular. Sentimental legend has it that Anne Boleyn wrote at least one of them in prison, but it is much more likely that they are all stage-songs, dramatic rather than historical. Another song known only as a lute-song is 'Awake, ye woeful wights',[3] which was accompanied by regals when it was sung at court, probably in 1564, in Edwards's play *Damon and Pithias.*[4] This song, then, could easily be accompanied by any instrument that happened to be handy. But the accompaniments of most of these songs and of others of the time seem definitely to have been conceived for a consort (usually a quartet) of viols; some, however, are also found adapted to the lute alongside arrangements of madrigals. They belong, therefore, to the type of monody recommended by Doni (cf. p. 155). It is possible that they were influenced by the German tenor songs (cf. Vol. III, p. 373, and *supra*, p. 98), which may have been introduced to England by Flemish musicians in the royal service, while the string textures no doubt owe a good deal to native forms such as the 'In nomine'. Now, however, the vocal part is usually the highest or the second highest line in the

---

[1] Brit. Mus. Add. MSS. 17786–91 and Oxford, Christ Church, MSS. 984–8. For a fuller account of these and of later songs in the same tradition (discussed *infra*, pp. 198 ff.), cf. Philip Brett, 'The English Consort Song, 1570–1625', *Proceedings of the Royal Musical Association*, lxxxviii (1961–2), p. 73. On the songs in the choirboy plays only, also cf. Arkwright, 'Early Elizabethan stage music', *Musical Antiquary*, i (1909–10), p. 30, and iv (1912–13), p. 112. The definitive collected edition of all types of consort song (excluding Byrd's and some others) is *Consort Songs*, transcr. and ed. Brett, *Musica Britannica*, xxii (London, 1967).

[4] Brit. Mus. Add. MS. 15117, fo. 3 v. Printed in William Chappell, *Old English Popular Music*, 2nd ed., rev. H. E. Wooldridge (London, 1893), i, p. 111, and in Arnold Dolmetsch, *Select English Songs and Dialogues of the 16th and 17th Centuries*, ii (London, 1912), p. 1.   [3] Brit. Mus. Add. MS. 15117, fo. 3.

[4] Cf. Denis Stevens, 'Plays and Pageants in Tudor Times', *Monthly Musical Record*, lxxxvii (1957), p. 8.

texture (as in few of the German songs), thus affording further evidence of the increasing prominence of upper parts, which we have seen as one of the most significant developments in ensemble music in the later sixteenth century. These songs are scarcely different in texture from Byrd's *Psalmes, Sonets & songs* of 1588, which, as he states in his well-known preface, were 'originally made for instruments to express the harmony, and one voice to pronounce the ditty' and had words added in the printed versions to what had been string parts. Byrd still calls the original solo part 'the first singing-part'.[1]

LATER CONSORT SONGS

Byrd was easily the most prolific composer of string-accompanied consort songs.[2] In addition to those printed by Fellowes (either as solo songs or in Byrd's revisions published in 1588 and indeed in his collections of 1589 and 1611 too) a few others have lately come to light that are almost certainly by Byrd—on grounds of style, because they are so distinguished, because of connexions through some of the texts with Sidney's circle (to which, almost alone among musicians, Byrd seems to have had access), or because of the overtly Catholic or politically dangerous nature of these and others of the texts, which only a privileged Catholic like Byrd would have dared to set to music.[3] His songs are of several kinds, and there are both sacred and secular ones. He seems to have written very few of them for plays, and these not for choirboy plays but for those staged probably by undergraduates and lawyers. They are of many different kinds, including elegies, 'death songs', lullabies and carols, and one or two, such as the beautiful Christmas carol 'From Virgin's womb',[4] were published. The melodies of some songs resemble metrical psalm-tunes, embedded in the polyphony of independent string parts. In other

---

[1] Cf. pp. 84–85 for a fuller discussion of this volume. Also cf. Dent, 'William Byrd and the Madrigal', *Festschrift für Johannes Wolf* (Berlin, 1929), p. 26, David Brown, 'William Byrd's 1588 Volume', *Music and Letters*, xxxviii (1957), p. 371, and Joseph Kerman, *The Elizabethan Madrigal* (New York, 1962), pp. 102–5.

[2] Cf. the account of them, with a catalogue, in Edmund H. Fellowes, *William Byrd*, 2nd ed. (London, 1948), pp. 160–72. Many are reprinted in *The Collected Vocal Works of William Byrd*, ed. Fellowes, xv (London, 1948), three incorrectly, with words added to more than one part. Also cf. Brett in *Proceedings of the Royal Musical Association*, lxxxviii (1961–2), pp. 81–85.

[3] See Brett and Dart, 'Songs by William Byrd in Manuscripts at Harvard', *Harvard Library Bulletin*, xiv (1960), p. 343, which not only lists the contents of the important MS. Harvard Mus. 30 but links them through handwriting, etc. with several other important manuscripts in England and the U.S.A. One of these songs, almost certainly by Byrd, 'Out of the orient crystal skies', has been arr. Dart (London, 1960).

[4] In *Songs of Sundrie Natures* (1589), reprinted in *The Collected Vocal Works*, xiii, rev. Brett (London, 1962), p. 135.

songs, such as 'Ye sacred muses' (written on Tallis's death in 1585),[1] vocal and instrumental parts share the same material in imitative fashion, just as in madrigals. Ex. 73 shows the opening of another song of this kind and may serve as an illustration of the kind of texture commonly found in string-accompanied songs:[2]

Ex. 73

[1] *The Collected Vocal Works*, xv, p. 141.
[2] Ibid., p. 135; expression marks, etc., omitted. The original words were a threnody for Mary, Queen of Scots, beginning 'The noble famous queen'.

The vocal parts are often rather square, slow-moving, and of narrow range, but they may have been ornamented in performance; the words are generally set one syllable to a note in an 'unliterary' manner characteristic of Byrd; hardly any of them are repeated; and the musical and poetic stresses coincide. Byrd also devised progressive tonal schemes, little of his writing in these songs being modal.[1] There is evidence that songs of this type went on being popular, at least in some circles, through the heyday of madrigals and lute-songs in the early seventeenth century. Their style was perpetuated, moreover, in verse anthems, in a few ayres, and in one or two other kinds of music.[2]

Most viol-accompanied songs are serious in tone, but a few, such as those by one William Wigthorpe and by Richard Nicholson (who in 1627 became the first Professor of Music at Oxford) are sprightly and homophonic. A song in similar vein is 'Buy new broom',[3] the only one of the *Songes to three, fower, and five voyces* (1571) by Whythorne[4] in which the lower parts lack words: this little piece, based on a street-cry, is therefore the only printed sixteenth-century English solo song before 1596, as the volume in which it appears is the only secular one printed in England between 1530 and 1588.

THE ENGLISH AYRE

It was in 1596 that William Barley included in *A New Booke of Tabliture*[5] four unimportant anonymous songs, accompanied by the guitar-like bandora, which may have been adapted from polyphonic originals. The following year was much more auspicious, for it was then that John Dowland published the first of his four books of ayres. This volume marks the inception of the English school of lutenist song-writers. The printed English ayres resemble the songs of French and Spanish composers in that they underwent scarcely any stylistic development;[6] Dowland's first songs are as masterly and mature as, *mutatis mutandis*, those of Milán, the first of the *vihuelistas*; and the songs of John Attey, published in 1622, would not have been anachronistic in 1597. During the quarter-century bounded by these dates some thirty volumes devoted wholly or partly to ayres were published

[1] Cf. Franklin B. Zimmerman, *Features of Italian Style in Elizabethan Part Songs and Madrigals* (Diss., Oxford, 1955, unpub.), pp. 127–36 and 264–70.
[2] Cf. Brett and Dart, op. cit., pp. 345 and 343.
[3] Reprinted in Warlock, *The Second Book of Elizabethan Songs* (London, 1926), p. 20.
[4] See p. 84.
[5] Ed. by Wilburn W. Newcomb as *Lute Music of Shakespeare's Time* (London, 1966).
[6] See p. 211 for the new declamatory songs of the 1610's, few of which were printed.

by a score of composers. All but half-a-dozen had appeared by 1612;[1] the slow rate of publication after this was possibly due to the innovation of declamatory songs. These are small figures compared with those for Italian songs, but they nevertheless reflect a lively interest in the medium. Robert Jones published five books, usually with far-fetched excuses for doing so; Thomas Campion, like Dowland, published four on his own, and he also shared one with Philip Rosseter; nearly all the other composers issued only one each. A book containing only ayres would consist of upwards of twenty items.

Ayres, like English madrigals and Italian monodies, attracted all kinds of composers. Most of them lived in London, where all the songs were published. Dowland, the greatest composer of ayres, encompassed the emotional range of Monteverdi but specialized in only two branches of composition, songs and lute music. Alfonso Ferrabosco the younger and Thomas Ford, like Caccini or d'India, were court musicians. Rosseter was a man of the London theatre. John Bartlet and Thomas Greaves belonged, like Wilbye, to the musical retinues of noblemen. Michael Cavendish was himself of noble birth, like Saracini, and dabbled with equal success in this new kind of fashionable English music. The very modishness of ayres may well have attracted composers who seem, whether by training or temperament, to have been ill at ease in them: Giovanni Coperario and Tobias Hume, for instance, were much more at home in instrumental music. Thomas Morley was the only master of the vocal ensemble to publish ayres, and, with one or two splendid exceptions,[2] they are not among his finest music; although, unlike monodies in Italy, ayres were not self-consciously advertised as 'new'—and indeed they were not at all new in the same way—the other great English madrigalists, such as Wilbye, Weelkes, and Ward, nevertheless published none at all.

[1] Most are reprinted in *The English School of Lutenist Song-writers*, ed. Fellowes (32 vols. in two series, London, 1920–32). These volumes are unnumbered; for easy reference they are numbered in footnotes to this chapter in the order in which they appeared. However, both series are now being re-issued, revised by Dart, as *The English Lute-songs* (London, 1959 ff.). These revised volumes are numbered. The pagination of their revised material remains unchanged, but it should be noted that they may contain additional songs and one or two entire volumes consist of songs not published by Fellowes. Many of these songs, including several not in Fellowes's edition, are reprinted in Warlock and Wilson, *English Ayres, Elizabethan and Jacobean*, 6 vols. (London [1927–31]). The standard work on the ayres is Warlock, *The English Ayre*. Other useful accounts include Morrison Comegys Boyd, *Elizabethan Music and Musical Criticism* (2nd ed., Philadelphia, 1962), pp. 127–52, and Pattison, op. cit., pp. 113–40. On the relation of words and music in ayres, see also Imogen Holst, *Tune* (London, 1962), pp. 79–90, Henry Raynor, 'Framed to the Life of the Words', *Music Review*, xix (1958), p. 261, and especially Wilfrid Mellers, *Harmonious Meeting* (London, 1964), Chaps. 7–9.
[2] Such as 'Thyrsis and Milla', recorded in *The History of Music in Sound*, iv.

Neither did Byrd or Gibbons. The verses of which ayres are settings are consistently of high quality and admirably suited to musical setting: the serious ones the equal of the finest Italian ones, the lighter ones considerably more refined than their Italian counterparts.[1] Nearly all are anonymous; only a small proportion are Italianate or known to be translations of Italian poems. Very few were set more than once, as so many Italian verses were.

Ayres, again like madrigals and monodies, seem to have been so popular that very few were allowed to remain in manuscripts unprinted. Although the myth has been exploded that used to see every literate person in Elizabethan England as an accomplished singer or lutenist, capable of adequately performing at sight the music of composers who must, from the point of view of difficulty, have been regarded as the Stravinskys or Hindemiths of their day, the fact remains that many members of the middle classes must have bought ayres to sing and play at home. Certainly the aristocracy were continually sending to London for new ones as they appeared.[2] There must have been plenty of copies available, for the surviving records of a lawsuit show that the edition of Dowland's Second Book of Ayres ran to 1025 copies;[3] but Dowland was a famous man, and the editions of lesser composers' ayres may well have been smaller.

We do not know whether the clearly defined preferences of many composers for either madrigals or ayres were reflected in their customers' tastes. Cavendish and Greaves included both ayres and madrigals in their only publications, which suggests that perhaps they were not. On the other hand, ayres need not be treated exclusively as solos: several composers provided their ayres with three lower vocal parts so that they could be sung if desired as quartets. These vocal parts are set out on the open folio page, as shown in pl. II, in such a way that four performers could all sing from the same copy, with or without a lute as appropriate. Such ayres are the only songs discussed in this chapter that were explicitly intended by their composers to be performed in two quite different ways. Thus did the composers set out to attract as wide a public as possible: that Dowland at first succeeded in doing so the five editions of his first song-book testify. Campion has this to say about the matter in the preface to his *Two Bookes of*

---

[1] They are reprinted in Fellowes, *English Madrigal Verse, 1588–1632* (3rd. ed., rev. and enlarged Sternfeld and David Greer, Oxford, 1967), pp. 337–676.

[2] Cf. Walter L. Woodfill, *Musicians in English Society* (Princeton, 1953), especially Chap. ix and Appendix B.

[3] Cf. Margaret Dowling, 'The Printing of John Dowland's *Second Booke of Songs or Ayres*', *The Library*, 4th ser. xii (1932–3), p. 367.

PLATE II

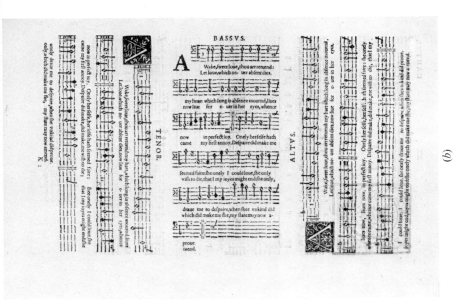

(b)

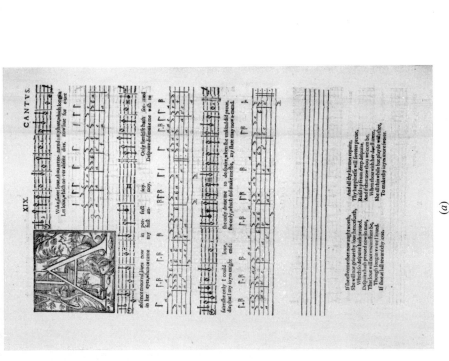

(a)

'AWAKE SWEET LOVE', A FOUR-PART AYRE FROM DOWLAND: *THE FIRST BOOKE OF SONGES*

(London, 1597). (See Ex. 76)

Ayres (c. 1613): 'These ayres were for the most part framed at first for one voice with the lute or viol, but upon occasion they have since been filled with more parts, which who so please may use, who like not may leave. Yet do we daily observe that when any shall sing a treble to an instrument the standers-by will be offering at an inward part out of their own nature. . . .' Better by far to give such enthusiasts parts to sing from than to allow their inexpert improvisations to ruin the harmony. Dowland started this fashion in his first song-book (1597); the following is part of the title-page: 'The First Booke of Songs or Ayres of foure parts with Tablature for the Lute. So made, that all the parts together, or either of them severally, may be sung to the Lute, Orpherian, or Viol de gambo. . . .' (This means, incidentally, that Cavendish's *14 Ayres in Tabletorie to the Lute* . . . (1598) are the earliest English ayres printed expressly as solos without alternative four-part versions; six others in his book are set for four voices.)

The phrase 'or either of them severally' is clearly absurd—nobody was expected to sing an alto part, for instance, as a solo. This clumsy phrase, invented no doubt by the publisher (as may be deduced from its reappearance on the similarly worded title-page of Jones's First Book in 1600), merely means that the *top* part may be sung by itself to an instrument. The lute was the really popular household instrument of the time and the one, presumably, to which ayres were most frequently sung. The wire-strung orpharion was a kind of cittern. Two popular instruments of the time not mentioned on Dowland's title-page are the virginals and the lyra-viol. The virginals is recommended only by Martin Peerson for his *Private Musicke* in 1620 as an alternative to the now equally rare consort of viols. The bass viol played lyra-way from tablature found an enthusiastic champion in the eccentric Hume (who was later quite mad). 'Henceforth', he cries in the preface to his *Musicall Humors* (1605), 'the stateful instrument *Gambo Violl* shall with ease yield full various and as deviceful music as the lute.'[1] In the preface to *A Pilgrimes Solace*, published seven years later, Dowland, with sustained indignation appropriate to the greatest lutenist of his time, rebuked him for his impudence.

Dowland's own idiomatic writing for the lute, born of his skill as a performer, was indeed an important factor in shaping the English ayre. The various other elements, not all of them English, that went to form the ayre are best studied in his songs, not simply because he was also the greatest song-writer of his time—indeed one of the

[1] The complete preface is reprinted in Warlock, *The English Ayre*, p. 83. (The songs in Hume's volume are among those not reprinted by Fellowes.)

greatest of all time—but also because he spent so much of his life abroad and must have been unusually well aware, for a composer of that time, of musical activity outside his own country. The evidence of his songs will be supplemented with briefer consideration of the more personal aspects of the songs of other composers.

THE WORK OF DOWLAND

One influence upon ayres, though not the most important, was that of the consort songs already discussed. This influence can perhaps be seen in three wonderfully expressive songs in Dowland's last song-book, *A Pilgrimes Solace* (1612), the most passionate and contrapuntal of them all.[1] Instead of alternative four-part versions these songs have parts for a gamba and obbligato parts for a treble viol, which plays a role similar to that of the highest part in those consort songs whose second-highest lines are the vocal ones. The legacy of these songs is also to be seen in certain pages of the less familiar *Songs for the Lute Viol and Voice* (1606) by John Danyel, brother of the poet Samuel Danyel. Danyel deserves to be ranked second only to Dowland if only because of the tragic power of his two lamenting song-sequences, in which his passion burst through the confines of the strophic form and demanded fresh music for each verse. In one of these works, 'Can doleful notes',[2] he boldly and imaginatively employs the chromatic writing beloved of the madrigalists. The following example shows a characteristic passage from the other, 'Grief, keep within':[3]

Ex. 74

And on-ly let my heart, and on-ly let my heart, my

---

[1] *The English School*, 1st ser. xii, pp. 36–51.
[2] Ibid. 2nd ser. viii, p. 36.
[3] Ibid., p. 24. This extract is from pp. 25–26; expression marks, etc., omitted.

heart, my heart That knows the rea - son why Pine,

fret, con - sume, swell, burst and

die, swell, burst and die.

A second, more widespread influence was that of dance music, which plays a conspicuous role in Dowland's influential first song-book in particular. Dowland's dances for lute were among the most popular of the time both at home and abroad. Several of his songs certainly, and others presumably, were created by the simple expedient of adding words to these dances,[1] a practice that would undoubtedly have horrified the Florentine purists but (as we have seen from *A Gorgious Gallery*) was popular in England. These songs may be gal-liards, almans, or corantos; they are made up of the usual four-bar phrases and are in the usual ternary (or sometimes binary) form, with each section repeated; usually, like most ayres, they are unambigu-

[1] Cf. Diana Poulton, 'Dowland's Songs and their Instrumental Forms', *Monthly Musical Record*, lxxxi (1951), p. 175.

ously in major or minor keys;[1] and the rhythms are of course clear-cut. For example, the melody of the familiar 'Now, o now I needs must part'[2] is a coranto, which was widely but mistakenly known in its instrumental form as 'The Frog Galliard'.

It may be no accident that a *voix de ville*, 'Hélas, que vous a fait', in the already-mentioned *Recueil* (1576) of Jehan Chardavoine has the same persistent trochaic rhythm as this song of Dowland's and that all the dance-forms that Chardavoine lists in his preface are found in the English song-books.[3] Dowland says, moreover, in the preface to his book of 1597 that he had written most of its contents some years previously. Now in the early 1580's, while in the service of the English ambassador, he had, to quote the same preface, 'travelled the chiefest parts of France, a nation furnished with a great variety of music'. He may well have met composers of *airs de cour* like Planson and the Tessiers; certainly he must have known their music. That the French edition of Guillaume Tessier's *Premier livre d'airs* (Paris, 1582) was dedicated to Queen Elizabeth I and Charles Tessier's *Premier livre de chansons et airs de court* (1597) was published in London by Thomas Este, one of Dowland's publishers, may have been due to his efforts. It would not be surprising, then, to find French influence in his own songs: in fact it is possible to say that, through them, 'the English ayre was a vigorous offshoot of the French *air de cour*'.[4] The very term 'ayre' is literally taken over from the French. Dowland's ayres are strophic; he seems to have preferred poems with eight- and ten-syllable lines; the range of his melodies is almost invariably that of an octave or less: these are some of the regularly recurring French features of his songs. The setting of the words here is also clearly indebted to French practice:[5]

Ex. 75

Come a - way, come, sweet love! The gol-den morn - ing breaks;

Campion, himself an eminent poet, interested in versification, was, however, the only English song-writer to experiment with *musique*

---

[1] On the tonal aspects of Dowland's ayres, cf. Edward E. Lowinsky, *Tonality and Atonality in Sixteenth-century Music* (Berkeley and Los Angeles, 1961), pp. 54–61.

[2] *The English School*, 1st ser. i, p. 22; *Musica Britannica*, vi (2nd. ed., London, 1963), p. 10.

[3] Cf. Dart, 'Rôle de la danse dans l' "ayre" anglais', *Musique et poésie* (Paris, 1954), pp. 207–8.

[4] Translated from Dart, in *Musique et poésie* (Paris, 1954), p. 205.

[5] *The English School*, 1st ser. ii, p. 42; *Musica Britannica*, vi, p. 18.

mesurée—in the song 'Come, let us sound with melody', published in Rosseter's *Booke of Ayres*.[1] The four-part versions of Dowland's ayres resemble the French *airs*, with an injection of the counterpoint that he must have studied during his later journeys in Germany and Italy; from Marenzio, whom he knew personally, he may also have learned how to handle chromatic harmony. As an illustration of a four-part ayre, the first half of one in short galliard form from his First Book[2] is reproduced on pp. 208–9 (Ex. 76). The lute part does not always follow the vocal parts so closely as it does in this song.

Sometimes the words fit the inner parts rather clumsily, just as in many ayres the words of later verses have to be adjusted to fit the music that the composers wrote with only the first verses in mind. It is often possible to say with a fair degree of certainty whether the solo or the four-part version of an ayre was the original one. Dowland's 'Burst forth, my tears',[3] for instance, evidently originated as a solo. On the other hand, the dignified songs at the end of *A Pilgrimes Solace* and songs as different in mood as the madrigalian 'Go, crystal tears' and the canzonet-like 'Wilt thou, unkind, thus reave me'[4] seem to have been conceived as contrapuntal ensemble music and are less expressive as solos.

CAMPION AND ROSSETER

In many of the tripping lighter ayres counterpoint was out of place. Campion and Rosseter pay it scant attention in the preface—probably written by Campion—to their ayres of 1601: Campion here equates ayres only with this lighter kind and likens them to epigrams, 'then in their chief perfection when they are short and well seasoned'. But he is quick to point out that 'a naked ayre without guide or prop or colour but his own is easily censured of every ear, and requires so much the more invention to make it please'. One is reminded of Doni's rejoinder to those adherents of counterpoint who scoffed at monody as being easier to write than counterpoint: is it easier, he asked, to paint a nude than a clothed body?[5] Of the ayre-composers, Campion, with his leanings towards humanism, came closest to the Florentines in denouncing word-painting and the exclusive cultivation of music 'which is long, intricate, bated with fugue, [and] chained

---

[1] *The English School*, 1st ser. xiii, p. 25.
[2] Dowland, *Ayres for four voices*, transcr. Fellowes and ed. Dart and Fortune, in *Musica Britannica*, vi, p. 30. Cf. pl. II.
[3] Ibid., p. 13, and *The English School*, 1st ser. i, p. 30.
[4] Dowland, *Ayres for four voices*, pp. 15 and 24, respectively, and *The English School*, 1st ser. i, p. 34, and ii, p. 58, respectively.　　　　[5] Cf. Doni, *Compendio*, p. 124.

Ex. 76

now   in   per - fect joy.
came   my first   an - noy.

lives now in   per - fect   joy.
whence came my first   an - noy.

now   in   per-fect   joy.
came   my   first an - noy.

now   in   per - fect joy.
came   my first   an - noy.

On - ly   her - self   hath
Des - pair did   make   me

On - ly   her - self, her - self
Des - pair did   make,   did make

On - ly   her - self,   her - self
Des - pair did   make, did   make

On - ly   her - self   hath
Des - pair did   make   me

with syncopation'. Many of his songs reflect his views, and even in the most intense ones he is careful to preserve the original poetic metre and to avoid repeating even the most emotional words—quite the opposite of Dowland's methods. In fact, in the work of the lutenists as a whole, really imaginative serious songs are easily outnumbered by light songs of comparable invention, enchanting settings—sometimes suggested by popular music[1]—of what Campion calls 'ear-pleasing rhymes, without art', supported by a lightly sketched-in lute accompaniment. Jones wrote many songs in this vein. The Dowland who plumbed the depths of passion and despair displays equal genius in less weighty songs ranging from the resigned tranquillity of 'Me, me, and none but me'[2] (one of the most heartbreakingly beautiful of all ayres), through the elegance of 'Sleep, wayward thoughts'[3] to the engaging artlessness of 'Fine knacks for ladies'.[4] But it is Rosseter who is the real master of the airy nothing. It is often tempting to overestimate serious music at the expense of lighter music just because it is serious. Let us give his due, then, to a composer who can sustain this level through twenty songs:

Ex. 77[5]

1. What then is love but mourn-ing? What de-sire but a self - -burn - ing? Till she that hates doth love re - turn,

---

[1] Cf. the illuminating remarks on songs by Jones and Rosseter, with comparative examples, in Greer, ' "What if a day"—an Examination of the Words and Music', *Music and Letters*, xliii (1962), pp. 313–14 and 316–18.

[2] *The English School*, 1st ser. x, p. 17; *Musica Britannica*, vi, p. 56.

[3] *The English School*, 1st ser. ii, p. 50; *Musica Britannica*, vi, p. 21. Recorded in *The History of Music in Sound*, iv.

[4] *The English School*, 1st ser. vi, p. 48; *Musica Britannica*, vi, p. 39.

[5] *The English School*, 1st ser. ix, p. 64; phrasing omitted.

Thus will I mourn, Thus will I sing:

Come a-way, come a-way, my dar - ling.

ITALIAN INFLUENCES IN THE AYRE

Dowland and Ferrabosco are two composers of ayres whose song-books include songs written for plays and masques. They are also—apart from Nicholas Lanier and one or two others who wrote a few unpublished declamatory masque-songs[1]—the only two who wrote ayres at this period showing the influence of recent developments in Italian music, a limited influence, in fact occurring mainly in masques.[2] (The songs of Coperario are sometimes said to be Italianate, too, but they are nothing of the kind, although some of them do fore-shadow the continuo-songs of the next generation of English com-posers.)[3] They show this influence more authoritatively than do the songs of any of their non-Italian contemporaries. *A Musicall Banquet* (1610), edited by Dowland's son Robert and including Italian, French, and Spanish, as well as English, songs, is in this context a 'key' publication, for not only the presence of the four Italian songs but even more noticeably the style of two of its three songs by John Dowland seem to argue a lively interest, on the part of some influential musicians at least, in the newest Italian music; and there was also the

[1] See p. 815.

[2] Cf. Ian Spink, 'English Cavalier Songs, 1620–1660', *Proceedings of the Royal Musical Association*, lxxxvi (1959–60), pp. 61–65. There are some good examples in *Songs and Dances for the Stuart Masque*, ed. Andrew J. Sabol (Providence, Rhode Island, 1959).

[3] Coperario's complete songs, not reprinted by Fellowes, have been edited by Gerald Hendrie and Dart (*The English Lute-songs*, 1st ser. xvii, London, 1959).

example of the admittedly rather feeble Italian songs that Angelo
Notari, an Italian musician at the English court, published in his
Prime Musiche Nuove in 1613.[1] The Italian songs in *A Musicall Ban-
quet* include three from the earliest monody-books—a madrigal by
Melli, and 'Amarilli', and 'Dovrò', dunque, morire' from Caccini's
Le Nuove Musiche, each with an instructive chordal accompaniment in
tablature. Dowland wrote songs both in the urbane diatonic style of
Caccini and, more successfully, in the dramatic, pathetic style of such
men as d'India and Saracini. In 'Far from triumphing court'[2] he uses
Caccinian arioso for a strophic poem, and it is therefore a type of
song found, in Italy, almost exclusively among the 'arias' of *Le Nuove
Musiche*, which may have influenced it (see p. 168). Ferrabosco's
setting of Donne's 'So, so, leave off' (from his *Ayres* of 1609) is a
similar, slightly tentative hybrid. In the following example the opening
bars are compared with those of a solo madrigal by d'India. If they
are sung expansively and not 'rather fast' (as Fellowes directs) it will
be seen how far an Englishman (albeit one with an Italian composer
for father) assimilated the new Italian style; his weakest moment is
his tame harmonization of the potentially passionate cadence in bars
4–5:

Ex. 78[3]

(i) 1. So, so,   leave off   this last la - ment - ing kiss, which sucks two

(ii) O   ben mi - o,   do-ve se - i,   do-ve sei tu,

[1] Cf. Spink, 'Angelo Notari and his "Prime Musiche Nuove" ', *Monthly Musical
Record*, lxxxvii (1957), p. 168.
[2] *The English School*, 1st ser. xiv, p. 104.
[3] (i) Ibid. 2nd ser. xvi, p. 13 (expression marks, etc., omitted); (ii) d'India, *Le
Musiche . . . libro terzo* (Milan, 1618), p. 12.

ben mi - o? Per-chè non di - co͜ohi-me͜, per-chè non di - co

((ii) O my beloved, where are you? Why do I not say 'alas!'?)

Dowland's 'Welcome, black night',[1] a masque-song from *A Pilgrimes Solace* existing only in solo form, is, especially at the beginning, like Italian monody seen through unwilling, half-comprehending French eyes. (It is perhaps from France, in fact, rather than from Italy that there came the main foreign influence on English songs of the next generation—just, as has been shown, as French influences were important in shaping the ayre at the end of the sixteenth century.) But there are no half-measures about the two great songs in which Dowland adopted the passionate accents of the more intense Italians. One is a setting of an Italian poem, 'Lasso, vita mia'.[2] The other is 'In darkness let me dwell'.[3] This magnificent song, published in his son's anthology, is the nearest thing to a solo madrigal in England, where madrigals were never composed as solos; the poem is not in fact a madrigal, but it has one verse only. Dowland's free, stylized declamation vividly translates into musical terms the heightened tones of emotional speech, the pace being adjusted to the mood of the moment with a mastery paralleled in Italy only in the pages of d'India and very few other composers. Here is the last part of this neurotically intense song, where, it will be noticed, the composer calls for passionate use of Caccini's 'livelier exclamation' (cf. also Ex. 51) and returns with original and telling effect at the end to the mood of the opening:[4]

Ex. 79

$[\textstyle \frac{1}{2} = d]$

Thus wed - ded to my woes, And bed - ded

---

[1] *The English School*, 1st ser. xiv, p. 91.   [2] Ibid. xiii, p. 46.
[3] Ibid. xiv, p. 116.   [4] Ibid. pp. 119–20; phrasing omitted.

ORNAMENTS IN MANUSCRIPT VERSIONS

The comparatively small number of Jacobean songs surviving only in manuscript includes the justly famous setting of Ben Jonson's 'Have you seen the bright lily grow',[1] which is probably by Robert Johnson.[2] Several manuscripts include versions of ayres by the lutenists, notably Campion, whose words and music differ widely from those in the printed song-books.[3] Such manuscripts are valuable for one reason in particular: they record the ornaments with which singers embellished the original plain versions.[4] Not only ayres were treated in this way. A manuscript at Cambridge contains, as well as ayres by Dowland, Morley, and other lutenists, a florid, complete version in two long sections for voice and bandora of one of the

[1] Brit. Mus. Add. MS. 15117, fo. 17ᵛ and other MSS. Facsimile in Potter, op. cit., facing p. x, with transcription on pp. 28–29. Other transcriptions in Dolmetsch, op. cit. i (London, 1898), p. 6, and Robert Johnson, *Ayres, Songs and Dialogues*, transcribed and edited by Spink, *The English Lute-Songs*, 2nd ser. xvii (London, 1961), p. 64.

[2] Cf. Spink's note, ibid., p. 75.

[3] Cf. especially Brit. Mus. Add. MS. 24665 ('Giles Earle's book', dated 1615). On the later, different treatment of an ayre by Campion as a *continuo* song cf. Vincent Duckles, 'The Gamble Manuscript as a Source of *Continuo* Song in England', *Journal of the American Musicological Society*, i. 2 (1948), pp. 26–28.

[4] For a fuller account of these embellishments, see Duckles, 'Florid Embellishment in English Song of the late 16th and early 17th Centuries', *Annales musicologiques*, v (1957), p. 329.

loveliest of the late sixteenth-century songs for voice and viols, 'Pour down, you pow'rs divine' ('Pandolpho'), probably by Robert Parsons.[1] Italian songs, too, were treated in this way. The ubiquitous 'Amarilli' turns up twice more,[2] as does the anonymous song 'O bella più',[3] also, like 'Amarilli', printed in *A Musicall Banquet*. That Caccini's *Le Nuove Musiche* was known at first hand, however, seems to be proved by the presence in one source of 'Dolcissimo sospiro'[4] (original version quoted in Ex. 57). Sometimes only the cadences are ornamented to any great extent, but in other decorated songs one finds more repetitive, indiscriminate embellishment, the product of the singers' delight in stylized decoration for its own sake. The following example shows the opening of a song by Campion (i) in its published form and (ii) with the addition of typical roulades of this second kind and with a typical textual variant:

Ex. 80[5]

(i) 1. Shall I come, sweet love, to thee When the eve-ning beams are set? Shall I not ex-clud-ed

---

[1] Cambridge, King's College, Rowe Library, MS. 2. Cf. Philippe Oboussier, 'Turpyn's Book of Lute-Songs', *Music and Letters*, xxxiv (1953), pp. 147–8. First part printed as a consort song in Warlock, *The Second Book of Elizabethan Songs*, p. 16, and [by Arkwright] in *Musical Antiquary*, i (1909–10), pp. 35–40; printed complete—the first part as a consort song, the second with bass lute—in *Musica Brittannica*, xxii, p. 10.

[2] Brit. Mus. MS. Egerton 2971, fo. 28ᵛ, and Brit. Mus. Royal App. 55, fo. 7ᵛ.

[3] Brit. Mus. MS. Egerton 2971, fo. 22ᵛ, and Brit. Mus. Add. MS. 29481, fo. 13.

[4] Brit. Mus. MS. Egerton 2971, fo. 24ᵛ.

[5] (i) *The English School of Lutenist Song-writers*, 2nd ser. x, p. 32; (ii) Brit. Mus. Add. MS. 29481, fo. 20.

As the century wore on there was a tendency in England to use ornaments to intensify expression. But this development and indeed the study of the English *continuo* songs that began to appear in the second decade of the century are best left, for the sake of continuity, until a later volume.[1] The real dividing-line (though not a very marked one) between the old style and the new occurs in the early 1620's. The great composers of the Jacobean age nearly all died at this period within a few years of one another, and the development of English music passed into the hands of young men who were virtually unknown before 1620.

[1] See Vol. VI.

V

LATIN CHURCH MUSIC ON THE CONTINENT—1

(a) THE FRANCO-FLEMINGS IN THE NORTH

By NANIE BRIDGMAN

JOSQUIN'S SUCCESSORS

The Franco-Flemish school did not die out with Josquin, and the style of which this great master had been so brilliant an exponent was continued by a whole generation of musicians throughout the sixteenth century, until the appearance of Lassus. But whereas the earlier school had evinced the boldness and progressiveness characteristic of great ages, the later made no innovations, and indeed was content to practise—often with great talent—the strict Netherland style, quite unaffected by influences from Italy. It should be understood, however, that these remarks apply only to those composers who did not settle away from their Northern homes—and who should therefore be regarded as the true representatives of Netherland art in the sixteenth century, whereas the art of such a man as Willaert, for example, is inconceivable apart from Italy.

As with the preceding generation—and in contrast with what was happening in France at the same time—church music dominated musical life. For all these musicians, secular *chansons* seem to have been no more than an amusement, and their church music is superior in both quantity and quality. Moreover, as they were often churchmen themselves, all more or less connected with the Imperial court, it was to be expected that they should devote themselves chiefly to religious music. What encouraged them all the more to do so was the fact that often enough they were in a position to hear excellent performances of their works, not only in church but on the occasion of diplomatic conferences and ceremonial entries of the Emperor into cities, when the singing of at least a motet was a recognized part of the proceedings. The choirs, most carefully recruited, were still the only professional organizations capable of overcoming the difficulties of so complicated an art; and these were to be found not only in churches, for—as the Venetian ambassador himself admitted—the Emperor had 'the fullest and most excellent choir in Christendom'.[1] The Regent of the Netherlands—Margaret of Austria at Mechlin and afterwards Mary of Hungary at Brussels—also maintained a private chapel.

The forms in use were still, therefore, those of the Catholic liturgy: Masses, motets, Magnificats, and Lamentations. The Masses were for the most part *missae parodiae*, in which the *canto fermo* technique was abandoned in favour of the newer style where all voices were equally important. If in these works the composers showed more evidence of erudition than of inspiration, they tried in their motets, on the other hand, to make the music suit the words—encouraged no doubt by the more varied texts, and thus developing a tendency already adumbrated by Josquin which was to find its chief representative in Lassus. Although Josquin was closer than they were to the Renaissance spirit, and had a stronger sense than they had of plastic beauty and expressiveness, they were none the less his direct disciples, much more so than the French composers of the same period. But whereas Josquin was not the slave of any one procedure and varied his musical language, trying any experiment that might lead to a beautiful result, his successors on the contrary all worked in the same style, the style so aptly described by Charles Van den Borren as 'the imitative syntactic style',[2] and in no other. What was only occasional with Josquin became, with them, a 'sovereign principle'. The method consisted in the provision of each verbal phrase with its own musical theme, stated by each voice in free imitation, the continuity of the musical argument never being interrupted by a cadence. The musical phrases interlock in a closely knit web, with an almost complete absence of the two-part episodes typical of the previous age; nor is there any tendency toward the new style of accompanied monody. This is what Hermann Finck meant when he said of Gombert: 'Is enim vitat pausas et illius compositio est plena cum concordantiarum tum fugarum'[3] ('For he avoids pauses and his composition is filled not only with full chords but with imitations'). This style was certainly the best suited to the *a cappella* performance which was becoming more and more common, but it hindered the understanding of the words, since these musicians sacrificed the text to purely musical considerations. Their art, while it was the logical and inevitable conclusion of all that had been done in the previous age, could not on the other hand be very fruitful for the future; it led to a dead end and provoked the Palestrinian reaction.

---

[1] André Pirro, *Histoire de la musique de la fin du XIVe siècle à la fin du XVIe* (Paris 1940), p. 308.
[2] 'Quelques réflexions à propos du style imitatif syntaxique', *Revue belge de musicologie*, i (1946), p. 14.   [3] *Practica musica* ... (Wittenberg, 1556).

NICOLAS GOMBERT

Many musicians of that time found their destinies linked with that of Charles V or some other member of the Habsburg family. This Emperor, very musical himself (the Netherland organist Bredemers had been his tutor), attracted to his domestic chapel at least two of the greatest musical figures in the first half of the sixteenth century: Gombert and Créquillon.

We know neither the date nor the place of birth of Nicolas Gombert, described by Finck as 'Jusquini piae memoriae discipulus'[1]— which would explain why he wrote an elegy on that master's death.[2] He is known to have been 'maistre des enffans de la chapelle de nostre empereur'; he appears in a list of payments for 2 October 1526, but in none later than 28 December 1540.[3] He afterwards lived at Tournai, but it is not known when or where he died. The chief events of his life are the travels he undertook in Spain, Italy, and Germany as the Emperor's *maître de chapelle*. Of all musicians of that age he was undoubtedly the most brilliant exponent of the style which we have defined in general terms. It is at the same time worthy of note that he deliberately avoided any display of learning and was able to achieve the greatest simplicity. His motet 'Diversi diversa orant',[4] in which each of the four parts has a different liturgical melody allotted to it, each plainsong theme being varied after its first simple statement, will suffice to show the extent of his erudition and his skill in combining with ease a number of pre-existent themes. But he set no great store by such academic exercises, and would seem to have been more concerned with inventing melodies of a new type, suited to the words, and thus with laying the foundations of a new musical language. His themes have a plastic and expressive value which makes him both a worthy disciple of Josquin and a forerunner of Lassus. His works, which reflect the tendency of his age in that they include no more than 60 *chansons*[5] as against 10 Masses, 8 settings of the *Magnificat*, and 160 motets, appeared in print at various dates between 1529 and 1600.[6]

All his ten Masses, except the 'Missa tempore paschali', are composed in the manner of *missae parodiae*, one being based on the simple plainsong 'Da pacem', two on *chansons* and the remaining six on motets. The Mass 'Je suis déshéritée'[7] provides a good example of the

---

[1] Op. cit.

[2] Published in *Werken van Josquin des Prés*, ed. Albert Smijers, i (Amsterdam, 1921).

[3] Joseph Schmidt-Görg, *Nicolas Gombert, Kapellmeister Karls V: Leben und Werk* (Bonn, 1938), p. 73.   [4] Published ibid., p. 23.   [5] Cf. p. 13.

[6] Complete edition edited by Schmidt-Görg, *Nicolai Gombert: Opera Omnia* (Rome, 1951–   ), in progress.   [7] Ibid. i, p. 81.

composer's technique, for this very expressive *chanson* by Cadéac[1] was very well suited to Gombert's sensitive talent, and he made admirable use of it: for instance, the employment of the theme with a leap of a fourth to express supplication in the 'Miserere' of the *Agnus Dei*. The whole melody of the *chanson* is to be found in each section of the Mass, and it is frequently recalled by quotation of its opening phrase. A Mass of this type enables us to understand why well-known *chansons* were chosen for such a purpose: on the one hand, the choirboys would find it easier to sing melodies which they already knew by heart, and on the other, the congregation would take a greater interest in following a ritual in which a familiar tune played so important a part. Contrary to his usual practice, Gombert here uses the *canto fermo* technique, in that he has the entire melody of the *chanson* sung unaltered in the *superius* in the first section of the *Credo* and in the last, six-part, *Agnus Dei*.

Like most of his contemporaries Gombert usually laid out his motets[2] for five voices. It is in his motets that the characteristics of his art stand out most clearly: simplicity and clarity, which by no means excludes elegance, and a fondness for stretching out his themes, which are very flexible and often inspired by Gregorian chant. Unlike his predecessors, when Gombert used a plainsong melody he did not reduce it to a long-note *canto fermo*, but allowed it to appear in its own character, as it were, applying the same technique of variation as with a melody of his own invention, as in the five-part motet 'Inviolata'. Nevertheless *melismata* are infrequent in his work; his melodic line employs quite small intervals, and his rhythms are very simple, nearly always in *tempus imperfectum*, hardly ever in the *tempus perfectum* so much used in the previous period. Despite his observance of the sovereign principle of systematic imitation, Gombert also employed the homophonic style for particular passages of the text; but he never adopted the dry syllabic style of French music. He was very skilled in the use of dissonant suspensions, as Palestrina was later; like all his contemporaries he usually avoided note-against-note dissonance. He shows a certain fondness for chords of the sixth, and the progressions of the two outside parts in tenths, which he still introduces sometimes, recall the principles of Gafurius. What is especially

[1] Published by Attaingnant in 1533 as the work of Lupi, but attributed to Cadéac in numerous later sources. Reprinted by Eitner in *60 Chansons* (*Publikation älterer praktischer und theoretischer Musikwerke*, xxiii) (Leipzig, 1899), p. 20, and in Schering, *Geschichte der Musik in Beispielen* (Leipzig, 1931), p. 115.

[2] On the motets, see particularly Hans Eppstein, *Nicolas Gombert als Motettenkomponist* (Würzburg, 1935).

noteworthy about him is his knowledge of the art of singing (he was, after all, by profession a singing-master), and the moulding of his themes shows him to have been a musician who understood the voice. No better examples of this could be found than the motet 'Gaudeamus omnes'[1] or the final 'Alleluia' of the motet 'Inter natos mulierum'.[2] The *Benedictus* of his Mass 'Je suis déshéritée', where the melodic line of the *superius* tends toward the top of the register, and the elegy on the death of Josquin, in which the bass descends to the low E and D, show the range of vocal resources that he explored. Gombert, 'qui omnibus musicis ostendit viam', as Finck said,[3] was certainly the greatest musician of his generation, and has the merit of having been the first to perfect the style followed by all his contemporaries. Of these at least two— Créquillon and Clemens non Papa—showed marked originality of mind.

THOMAS CRÉQUILLON

Thomas Créquillon, who like Gombert was *maître de chapelle*—or, at least, master of the choristers—to Charles V, may for various reasons be compared with his predecessor, whom he almost equalled in talent. All the remarks of general character just made about Gombert can also be applied to Créquillon, so completely do these two masters sum up in their work all the characteristics of the music of the time. We know as little of Créquillon's life as of Gombert's, whom he succeeded as master of the *enfants de la chapelle* in 1540. (Apparently he died in 1557 at Béthune, where he had held a canonry since 1555.) A churchman himself, Créquillon wrote best for the Church, although he was the only Netherland musician of his generation who composed more *chansons* (192)[4] than motets (116); to the latter category, however, must be added settings of the Lamentations, for four and five voices, and five psalms in French. His first motet was published in 1545 by Kriesstein at Augsburg, his earliest Masses in 1546 by Susato at Antwerp, and his works appeared in the printed collections as late as 1636. Créquillon was always held in the highest esteem by his contemporaries even after his death: Pietro Cerone quotes him as an example alongside Willaert and Cipriano de Rore,[5] Sweertius calls him 'musicus excellens',[6] and still later, in 1689, Berardi considered him a worthy representative of the older school of composers.[7] In his own day his works were copiously transcribed for instruments and his *chanson* 'Un gay bergier' was one of the most

[1] Schmidt-Görg, *Nicolas Gombert*, p. 36.   [2] Ibid., p. 16.
[3] Op. cit.   [4] Cf. p. 16.   [5] *El Melopeo y maestro* (Naples, 1613), p. 89.
[6] *Athenae Belgicae* (Antwerp, 1628), p. 693.
[7] *Miscellanea musicale . . .* (Bologna, 1689), p. 40.

famous of the century. He has, however, been unjustly neglected in our time, and very few of his works have been reprinted.

Fifteen of Créquillon's sixteen Masses are *missae parodiae*, eight of them based on *chansons* and seven on motets—among them three *chansons* and two motets by the composer himself. The remaining one is built, in accordance with the old *canto fermo* method, on the German song 'Kein Adler in der Welt'.[1] All these Masses are written in a more or less freely imitative style, with short homophonic passages set to certain important parts of the text (often for 'Et incarnatus est'), and keep more or less close to the model on which they are based. Sometimes the composer borrows only a few short passages from his model, with which the Mass will then have only a very remote connexion. This is the case, for example, with the Masses 'Domine Deus omnipotens' and 'Mort m'a privé'—even though the models are the composer's own works. The 'parody' technique is basically a matter of variations; variations not only in melody but also in harmony and rhythm, as in the *Credo* of the Mass 'Se dire je l'osoie',[2] which is founded not so much on the *chanson* as on a theme suggested by the *chanson*:

Ex. 81

[1] W. Lueger, *Die Messen des Thomas Crecquillon* (Bonn dissertation, 1948. Unpublished).   [2] Munich Staatsbibl. 40; transcribed, Lueger, op. cit., p. 102.

Créquillon's fondness for square-cut motives often has the effect of making the over-long periods of his music somewhat cold; but when he imparts greater vigour to them—making a real musical motive out of a simple theme by the device of syncopation, for example—his art takes on an energetic character very personal to him. The most remarkable section of his Mass 'Domine Deus omnipotens' (for six voices) is the final *Agnus Dei*; though written in eight parts, it does not give the impression of a double chorus—rather is it a compact body of sound, sustained by an idea in the bass which sounds like an instrumental theme.

His Lamentations, published in 1549 by Montanus and Neuber with a dedication written by the poet and historian Caspar Bruschius, have much dramatic vigour and great expressive power. In the first, for five voices, on the word 'convertere' the *discantus* enters with a rising semitone, the *altus* and *primus tenor* with a fourth, the *secundus tenor* with a third and the *bassus* with an octave, thus making the exhortation stand out strongly.

In his motets Créquillon shows the full measure of his talent and employs all the resources of his art in the service of the words. His transparent counterpoint is best suited by long, calm, well-balanced themes, with octave leaps providing the opportunity for vocal expansiveness, as in 'Parasti in dulcedine tua' (the second part of 'Unus panis'):[1]

Ex. 83

Like Palestrina he had a feeling for scale passages, and in the motet 'Sed melius est' (the second part of 'Ingemuit Susanna')[2] he uses three series of scales to make a fine peroration.

[1] *Liber septimus cantionum sacrarum*, published by Phalèse in 1559.
[2] Ibid.

Ex. 84

He tries to suit his opening theme to the general feeling of the words; and often, after announcing it, he will restate it in a varied form and prolong it with a second phrase set to the same words, a procedure which enables the hearer to grasp the general tone of the whole work from the outset. Like Gombert, Créquillon uses dissonant suspensions, sometimes even for expressive purposes, as in the opening of 'Verbum iniquum et dolosum':[1]

Ex. 85

Many examples could be given to show the plasticity and scope of Créquillon's themes. If his art seems rational and intelligently planned rather than spontaneous, the purity of his melodic gift and the clarity of his counterpoint earn him a very honourable rank among his Netherland contemporaries and justify Ambros's eulogistic verdict.[2]

In 1548 three other musicians in the service of Charles V joined with Créquillon in bringing out a collection of four-part motets (*Cantiones selectissimae*), in which they were described by their publisher, Ulhard of Augsburg, as 'eximii et praestantes Caesareae majestatis capellae musici'. Only Créquillon, however, really deserved such praise. The organist Jean Lestainnier died too young to leave any very significant work.[3] Nicolas Payen doubtless enjoyed a great reputation, since he was entrusted with the writing of an eight-part motet on the death of the Empress Isabella, 'Carole, cur defles Isabellam, curve requiris?' A more important body of work has come down to us from Cornelius Canis, who was *maistre des enffans* in 1542 and left the Imperial chapel in 1556;[4] we have a six-part Mass and twenty-six motets by him.

CLEMENS NON PAPA

Standing rather apart from the official world, and not apparently awarded many honours, lived one of the greatest composers of this generation: Jacobus Clemens 'non Papa'. His religious music—16

[1] *Liber tertius ecclesiasticarum cantionum*, published by Susato in 1553.
[2] *Geschichte der Musik* (Leipzig, 2nd ed., 1881), iii, p. 311.
[3] G. Van Doorslaer, *Jean Lestainnier organiste-compositeur* (Malines, 1921).
[4] Schmidt-Görg, *Nicolas Gombert*, p. 63.

Masses, 15 settings of the *Magnificat*, and 230 motets, to which may be added his 158 *Souterliedekens*—is of great importance. Of his personal life little is known. Although he composed some of his motets to the glory of Charles V, he does not seem ever to have been in the Imperial service. (In 1544–5 he was *succentor* at Saint-Sauveur at Bruges, and an account-book of the Onze Lieve Vrouwe-Broederschap at 's Hertogenbosch refers to him in 1550 as 'sanger ende componist'. He died about 1556.)[1]

Fifteen of his Masses are based on polyphonic compositions, seven on *chansons* and eight on motets, according to the principle of the *missa parodia*.[2] The remaining one, a 'Missa pro defunctis' built on the Gregorian melodies, was long thought to be partially lost, and was reprinted only in 1959.[3] All the Masses are written in the systematically imitative style, but the Mass 'Miséricorde',[4] based on two of the composer's own *chansons*, shows a special concern with textual clarity, most of the main sections opening with a distinct statement of the words in the strictest homophonic style. The variation-technique which the composer applies to his chosen themes is always original and interesting. He adds to them themes of his own invention, returning to his basic material only at significant points of the text as if to emphasize their importance.

Clemens non Papa left a considerable number of motets, set for the most part to Biblical words. Although the texts are short, his motets are often long—even too long, for he was fond of repeating the words to fresh musical ideas; in 'Erravi sicut ovis',[5] for example, the first sentence is sung three times, each time to a different melody in the *superius*:

Ex. 86

[1] For biographical details see K. Ph. Bernet Kempers, *Jacobus Clemens non Papa und seine Motetten* (Augsburg, 1928), and the notice prefaced to his Clemens bibliography, *Musica Disciplina*, xviii (1964), p. 85; also R. Lenaerts, 'Voor de biographie van Clemens non Papa', *Tijdschrift der Vereeniging voor Nederlandsche Muziekgeschiedenis*, xiii (1929), p. 178.

[2] J. Schmidt[-Görg], 'Die Messen des Clemens non Papa', *Zeitschrift für Musikwissenschaft*, ix (1926–7), p. 129.

[3] By Bernet Kempers in *Clemens non Papa: Opera Omnia* (Rome, 1951–), viii.

[4] Ibid. i, p. 1.   [5] From Scotto's *Motetti del laberinto* (*Libro secondo*) (Venice, 1554).

Although his themes are well chosen, he contented himself too readily
with the formulae of a musical language which he had evolved for
himself at an early date—a fact which helps to explain his high productivity. To produce expressive effects he seldom had recourse to dissonance, but rather to certain melodic intervals, such as the minor
sixth at the beginning of 'Delicta juventutis' (the second part of

'Erravi sicut ovis') or of 'Vox in Rama'.[1] Noticeable in his work is a special treatment of the upper voice which sets it apart from the rest. To it he entrusted certain *ostinato* motives such as that of the bells in 'Angelus Domini'.[2] Similarly, in the 'Domine Deus' of the Mass 'Languir my fault', the *superius* persistently repeats the first four notes of Claudin de Sermisy's *chanson*.[3] His rhythm is more lively than Gombert's, and his melodic line more sinuous, moving more readily by leap than by step. It was from a study of the works of Clemens non Papa, among others, that Edward Lowinsky argued that there had been, in the performance of motets, a practice of *musica ficta* which became a highly organized chromaticism that probably had to be kept as a secret craft for religious and political reasons.[4] It is possible that the audacities of this kind to be found in Clemens non Papa's motets were tolerated from one of his modest social status, whereas the official positions of Gombert and Créquillon obliged them to keep to traditional ways.

Although they belong to the religious side of Clemens non Papa's output, the *Souterliedekens* published by Susato in 1556–7 do not come within the scope of this chapter, as they were not intended for use in church. They are three-part harmonizations of popular tunes adapted to the Dutch version of the psalter, and were meant to be sung in the home.[5]

RICHAFORT AND SOME LESSER FIGURES

Among the musicians in the service of the House of Habsburg were also those employed by Mary of Hungary: Jean Richafort, 'prêtre et chantre de la reine' in 1531, Benedictus Appenzeller, who was in charge of her chapel from about 1540 to 1550, and Roger Pathie, her organist. Those of the Imperial Chapel in Vienna included Jean Guyot de Chatelet, known as Castileti, who was *Kapellmeister* for a few months in 1563–4, and his successor Jacob Vaet, who in his turn was followed in this post by Philippe de Monte. And, finally, there was Pierre de Manchicourt, who was in the service of Philip II until 1564, in which year he died at Madrid.

---

[1] *Opera Omnia*, ix, p. 105; also reprinted in A. T. Davison and Willi Apel, *Historical Anthology of Music*, i (Cambridge, Mass., 1946), p. 134, and Bernh ard Meier, *Das Chorwerk*, lxxii (Wolfenbüttel, 1959), p. 6.   [2] *Opera Om nia*, ix, p. 99.
[3] Ibid. v, p. 69, with the *chanson* on p. 103.
[4] *Secret Chromatic Art in the Netherlands Motet* (New York, 1946).
[5] Reprinted in *Opera Omnia*, ii; see also Bernet Kempers, 'Die Souterliedekens des Jacobus Clemens non Papa', *Tijdschrift der Vereeniging voor Nederlandsche Muziek-geschiedenis*, xii (1928), p. 261; xiii (1929), pp. 29 and 126.

Of these, Jean Richafort deserves special mention. He was *magister cantus* to the church of Saint-Rombaut at Malines from 1507 to 1509, but all trace of him is then lost until 1531, when his name is found in the household records of Mary of Hungary. May he not perhaps, in the interval, have been drawn into the orbit of the French court? The cathedral organist at Angers, Jean Daniel, known as Mitou, did in fact refer to him, along with other musicians who were all in the king's service, in a *Noël* written about 1525:

> En ce petit hostelet
> Richard fort ne fut saulvaige
> Deschanta ung motelet
> Dieu scet s'il estoit ramaige.[1]

He died about 1548. His earliest motet was published in 1519, and although the bulk of his work is not great—4 Masses, 3 Magnificats, 35 motets, and 17 *chansons*—it is enough to prove that he had a very personal style.[2]

His six-part Requiem Mass is evidence of his command of complicated technique. It complies with two conditions: on the one hand the *superius* sings the proper liturgical text, a free treatment of Gregorian melody, on the other Josquin's canon 'Circumdederunt me dolores mortis' is sung by the two tenors almost throughout. This double *canto fermo* is twice replaced by a canon of Richafort's own on a phrase ('C'est douleur non pareille') from Josquin's *chanson* 'Faulte d'argent'; the double reference to Josquin—whose pupil Richafort is said to have been—suggests an association with Josquin's death. Despite these technical pre-conditions, Richafort's Requiem is both expressive and plastic; the Entombment is suggested by descending scales, and the words 'non timebo' are sung by men's voices only. The Mass is a sombre and touching work, in which the bass states each intonation before the other parts take it up.

In his *Magnificat quinti toni*[3] Richafort manages to alternate the sharply cut motives so dear to the French with the longer-breathed lines of the Flemish composers. The two-part 'Fecit potentiam' section is reminiscent of similar episodes in Josquin, and Richafort emphasizes the words 'Dispersit superbos' by setting them to a scale-passage in the *altus* while the upper voice recites on a monotone in syncopated rhythm:

[1] *Les Noëls de Jean Daniel dit Maître Mitou* (ed. by H. Chardon, Le Mans, 1874), p. 9.
[2] G. Van Doorslaer, *Jean Richafort maître de chapelle-compositeur* (Antwerp, 1930).
[3] From *Magnificat omnitonum cum quatuor vocibus* (Venice, 1562).

Ex. 87

Richafort's motets found much favour with his contemporaries, and were frequently chosen as models for *missae parodiae*. His 'Christus resurgens' inspired a Mass by his contemporary, Van Pulaer, and a Mass by Palestrina based on the same theme has been discovered in a Mexican library.[1] 'Quem dicunt homines'[2] was used for Masses by Josquin, Divitis, Mouton, Morales, and Palestrina; while Gombert, Claudin de Sermisy, and Lupi each composed a Mass on 'Philomena praevia temporis ameni'. This secular motet,[3] to a Latin text about the nightingale heralding the spring, has been printed in collections of religious motets; in it the composer introduces numerous melismatic passages which sometimes stray beyond the limits of the mode. The supple line of the final section, to the words 'Avis predulcissima, ad me, queso, veni', is worthy of notice:

Ex. 88

[1] R. Stevenson, 'Sixteenth and Seventeenth Century Resources in Mexico', *Fontes* (1955), p. 13.

[2] From *Motetti del fiore, liber primus* (Lyons, 1532); opening portion reprinted in *Oxford History of Music*, ii (Oxford, 1905), p. 269.

[3] Cambrai, Bibl. de la Ville, Ms. 125–8.

as is also the melodious opening of the second part, in which the bass
has a different theme from the other three voices.

Benedictus Appenzeller has left us, among other things, a four-part
motet on the death of Josquin. 'Musae Jovis ter maximi',[1] in which
the expressive contrast between two low and two high voices shows
him as a worthy disciple of the master. His double canon 'Sancta
Maria', dedicated to Mary of Hungary, was once worked into the
design of a tapestry; and his church music (thirty-five motets, a Mass,
and an *Agnus Dei*) appeared in print between 1532 and 1569.

Although the textbooks do not devote much space to him, the work
of Jacob Vaet, standing between Gombert's and that of Lassus, is by
no means inconsiderable; it includes 9 Masses, 8 Magnificats, and 76
motets, and consists almost entirely of church music, to which, as he
said, he had devoted himself from his earliest years: 'Ego itaque cum
prima mea aetas sacrae Musices studio addicta fuisset.'[2] Only three
chansons by him are known. Vaet was a transitional composer, as may
be observed from the evolution that took place in his style. For,
whereas his motets in three, four, or five parts are still mostly written
in accordance with the principle of continuous imitation in Gombert's
manner, those for six or eight parts show new tendencies and we are
confronted with a progressive undermining of this sovereign principle
by the various devices of free imitation already employed, though
more timidly, by Clemens non Papa and his contemporaries. Vaet's
later style is marked also by a bolder use of dissonances and by a
freer use of accidentals, tending towards the supersession of the old
modal system. Whereas Gombert's influence can be detected in his
earliest motets, those of his later period certainly show that of Lassus,
as witness his motet 'Vitam quae faciunt beatiorum', written in 1559;
'darinnen hatt er des Orlando "Tityre tu patulae" wollen imitiren',
as was remarked by Dr. Seld, the vice-chancellor of Albrecht V of
Bavaria.[3] It was Vaet also who composed an elegy on the death of
Clemens non Papa, 'Continuo lachrimas', in which, in accordance
with tradition, he used the Introit of the Mass for the Dead as *canto
fermo*.[4]

Pierre de Manchicourt, on the other hand, belonged to the more
conservative branch of the Netherland school, and remained faithful
to the style of his predecessors. His contrapuntal learning seems too

[1] Printed in *Werken van Josquin des Prés*, i, and in R. J. Van Maldeghem's *Trésor
musical*, xiv (1878), p. 34.
[2] Milton Steinhardt, *Jacobus Vaet and his Motets* (East Lansing, Mich., 1951), p. 5.
[3] Ibid., p. 10.
[4] On Vaet, see also *infra*, p. 267.

often to have served him instead of inspiration; the value of his motet
'Ave virgo Cecilia'[1] lies chiefly in the skill with which he uses constant
double counterpoint in the imitative treatment of two themes in each
section. Nevertheless, such things as the *Benedictus* of his Mass 'Gris
et tanné' suggest that a better knowledge of his work would enable us
to do his musicianship better justice. In any case, his preface to the
Ars versificatoria of Petrus Pontanus (Paris, 1520), concerning the
accentuation of Gregorian chant, shows clearly that he was held in
high esteem by the humanists of his day.

To give a correct picture of Netherland music at this period, we
should, instead of limiting ourselves to the most illustrious names,
cite in addition the host of composers whom we now regard as of
secondary rank, either because very little of their work has come down
to us or because they were less prolific. Some of them enjoyed, none
the less, a great reputation with their contemporaries and filled important posts in the great chapels. Such were Jean Courtois, *maître de
chapelle* at Cambrai, who, for a visit of Charles V to that town on the
20 January 1540, composed a four-part motet 'Venite populi terrae',[2]
performed by thirty-four of the cathedral singers before the bishop's
palace; Jean de Hollande, choirmaster of Saint-Sauveur at Bruges in
1541; Gheerkin de Hondt, whose career was spent at 's Hertogenbosch; Lupus or Lupi, a name which may stand for two composers
whose works, since their names were similar, are not always easy to
distinguish—Lupus Hellinck (d. 1541), who is known to have been at
Utrecht and afterwards at Bruges, and Jean Lupi (d. 1539), who lived
at Cambrai;[3] Laurent de Vos, brother of Martin de Vos the painter,
who was hanged at Cambrai in January 1580 for writing a motet with
a political significance; Pevernage, active at Antwerp; and Hubert
Waelrant, who was not only a composer and teacher but a music
publisher of Antwerp, where he died in 1595. Sweertius described
Waelrant as 'novorum appetens', and indeed study of his work shows
him to have been a musician with a great love of novelty who has
hitherto been unjustly neglected.[4] Later still, but by no means the
least of the Netherlanders, stands the isolated figure of Sweelinck—

---

[1] Printed by J. Delporte in 'L'Ave virgo Cecilia de Pierre de Manchicourt', *Revue
liturgique et musicale* (1936–7), p. 113.

[2] Published by N. Bridgman in 'La participation musicale à l'entrée de Charles Quint
à Cambrai le 20 janvier 1540', *Les Fêtes de la Renaissance*, ii (Paris, 1960), p. 235.

[3] See Gustave Reese, *Music in the Renaissance* (London, 1954), pp. 306–7, and the
articles on these composers by Hans Albrecht and Ludwig Finscher, *Die Musik in
Geschichte und Gegenwart*, vi, col. 105, and viii, col. 1315. Hellinck's motet 'Panis quem
ego dabo' has been published by Schmidt-Görg as a supplement to *Kirchenmusikalisches Jahrbuch*, xxv (1930).   [4] Lowinsky, op. cit., p. 70.

essentially an instrumental composer and a Protestant, though his *Cantiones sacrae* (Antwerp, 1619), with organ *continuo*,[1] are an imposing contribution to Latin church music.

CONCLUSION

The musicians whom we have been considering lived in a country whose political and geographical structure was somewhat peculiar, having been artificially produced by the accidents of royal marriages and premature deaths. Although national schools, in the strict sense, did not yet exist, it was during the course of the sixteenth century that each European country began to manifest an artistic style with qualities of its own. But can any such unity be recognized in the musical art of the empire of Charles V, who had recently added Spain to his family dominion of Burgundy and the Netherlands? The Emperor often journeyed to Spain, and while there he was always accompanied by his Flemish chapel. His musicians therefore lived for frequent periods in Spain; and since music in that country had not only reached a high stage of development but possessed a very individual character, marked by 'Mediterranean' respect for the words (shown in a homophonic style far removed from the elaborate erudition of the Netherlanders and nearer to popular music, as is shown by the contents of the *Cancionero de Palacio*),[2] one might be tempted to suppose that the mutual influence exerted by these two tendencies would have given rise to a new form of art, constituting a quasi-national music for the dominions of Charles V. In fact, it did nothing of the kind.

It has often been said that a decisive stamp was set upon Spanish music by Northern polyphony, and it is indeed true that Morales and Guerrero employed Netherland technique.[3] Further traces of the Franco-Flemish musicians' visits to Spain are to be found in the numerous manuscripts of their works still reposing in the libraries of that country.[4] Manuscripts containing Netherland compositions are to be found as far afield as Mexico, where Charles V sent as first teacher of music a Fleming, Fray Pedro de Gante. The Franco-Flemings also bulk largely in the collections of instrumental music put together in Spain during the sixteenth century. On the other hand, the Northern-

---

[1] Edited by Max Seiffert, *Werken van Jan Pieterszn. Sweelinck*, vi (Leipzig and The Hague, 1899); many motets published separately, notably by Bank (Amsterdam).

[2] Printed by Higini Anglès in *La Música en la Corte de los Reyes Católicos*, ii and iii (Barcelona, 1947–51). See Vol. III, pp. 352 and 377 ff.

[3] See Chap. VI.

[4] See, for instance, Lenaerts, *Nederlanse Polyfonie uit Spaanse Bronnen* (*Monumenta Musicae Belgicae*, ix), (Antwerp, 1963).

ers do not seem to have been in any way influenced by Spanish music, and neither Gombert nor Créquillon shows any sign of having been affected by his sojourn in Spain. Gombert's only Spanish *chanson*[1] is written in the purest imitative style, and neither he nor his fellows built any of their Masses on Spanish melodies. They remained faithful to the style they had devised for themselves, and one cannot even detect any evolution in their work. This conservatism, maintained by the various social and political factors which inevitably arise in such circumstances, was doubtless encouraged by the personal taste of Charles V, who always retained an affection for his native Flanders. The facts that no Spaniard was a member of his chapel and that none but Netherland works were sung at official ceremonies are enough to show that he also was unmoved by the music of his new domain. While Northern sculptors and painters were strongly affected by Spanish influence, so that one can speak of a 'Hispano-Flemish' school of painting, nothing similar can be detected in the field of music, where influence operated in one direction only and no new style attested to the reality of an empire which had no underlying unity.[2] These musicians, sometimes described paradoxically as 'the Spanish Court composers', actually upheld to the last the cause of Netherland music and demonstrated the supremacy which it still enjoyed.

(b) FRANCE IN THE SIXTEENTH CENTURY
(1520–1610)

By FRANÇOIS LESURE

ORIGINS OF THE FRENCH STYLE

It is still difficult to distinguish the main lines along which church music developed in sixteenth-century France, because of the lack of modern reprints[3] and musicological studies.[4] The following is there-

---

[1] Printed by R. Mitjana and J. Bal y Gay in the *Cancionero de Upsala* (Mexico City, 1944), p. 125.

[2] N. Bridgman, 'Les échanges musicaux entre l'Espagne et les Pays Bas au temps de Philippe le Beau et de Charles-Quint' (*La Renaissance dans les provinces du nord* (Arras, 1955)).

[3] Henry Expert has published modern editions of Masses by Certon and Goudimel in *Monuments de la musique française au temps de la Renaissance*, ii and ix (Paris, 1925 and 1928), and a separate edition of Janequin's Mass 'La Bataille' (Paris, 1947). Albert Smijers began and A. Tillman Merritt completed a new edition of the thirteen books of motets published by Pierre Attaingnant in 1534–5 (Paris and Monaco, 1934–1963).

[4] The most important—and even so it is not concerned with vocal music—is Yvonne

fore no more than a preliminary inquiry, a provisional synthesis intended to indicate the possibility of detailed analyses rather than to sum up the results of any already in existence.

While we cannot speak of a specifically 'French' music before the death of Josquin, yet after this date (1521) the characteristics of a national style appeared almost at once. Throughout the first half of the century the figure of Josquin seems nevertheless still to be hovering in the background: a precursor whose works were no longer very much sung but to whose example one referred because of the roads he had opened up. Even Ronsard, in 1560, included the majority of contemporary French composers in an imaginary list of his pupils, although not one of them perhaps had ever been acquainted with his supposed teacher. Adrian Le Roy, who as late as 1555 published a collection of his motets, wrote of him in the highest terms in a dedication to the patron, Jacques Aubry, speaking of him as a hero who had 'omnes omnium modulationum et cantum ideas in animo impressas atque insculptas'. In the reign of Louis XII and at the beginning of that of Francis I, the influence of musicians from the northern provinces (such as Brumel, Févin, Gascongne, and Mouton) was predominant at the Court, at Notre-Dame, and at the Sainte-Chapelle; but the composers of the next generation in Paris came from a much wider range of districts. Whatever the reasons, a sharp change of style followed. When Louis Van Pulaer, a native of Cambrai, left Notre-Dame in 1527,[1] his departure marked not only the end of the wave of Northern musicians coming south, but above all a break in stylistic tradition. The true successors of Josquin were henceforth unmistakable Flemings, while the French school of church music was to develop along its own lines.

Doubtless the vogue, after 1520, of the Parisian type of *chanson*, with its forceful rhythm and its absolute control by the words, partly explains the nature of this change: a lack of both breadth and tension in the melody, obsession with the declamatory style yet at the same time an absence of expressiveness—such were the new features which religious art in France inherited from the *chanson*. This style, which owed so little to that of neighbouring lands, was to enjoy a certain success in Europe, which will be referred to later, and which was

Rokseth's *La Musique d'orgue au XVᵉ et au début du XVIᵉ siècle* (Paris, 1930); see also for a very rapid sketch of the subject François Lesure, 'La Musique religieuse en France au XVIᵉ siècle', *Revue musicale*, no. 222 (1953–4), p. 61, with a chronological table of works.

[1] F. L. Chartier, *L'ancien chapitre de Notre-Dame de Paris* (Paris, 1897), p. 76. There is a modern edition by J. Delporte of Van Pulaer's Mass 'Christus resurgens' (cf. p. 232) in the *Collection de polyphonie classique*.

perhaps due to 'that French simplicity which does not tax the listener, but persuades him that he perfectly understands the musician, will have no trouble in following him, and will know at once where he is going'.[1] In other words, composition means an honest craft in which masterpieces were the exceptions, but which was perfectly in place in a society that knew nothing of mystical passion and had lost the serenity of a deep-seated faith.

Moreover, one can detect a decadence in the art of singing in the choir-schools. Claudin de Sermisy put this very plainly in a letter to the Duke of Ferrara: 'It is difficult at present to find good children in France. I think their mothers must be dead.'[2] The French had retained an even dimmer memory of Latin accentuation than their neighbours; so that when Ammerbach, of Basle, sent his two sons in 1501 to study in Paris, he warned them against the bad prosody current in that city, urging them not to lengthen short syllables.[3] Peter Wagner has noted a number of passages from French Masses of the sixteenth century which fully justify such a warning.[4]

FRENCH TENDENCIES IN MASS AND MOTET

The form most cultivated was the setting of the complete Ordinary of the Mass, though one still finds a few isolated Credos, reminiscent of the days, not so far distant, when Petrucci had published a collection of Mass-fragments. Such are the eight-part *Credo* by Jean Maillard (published in 1557) and the '*Patrem* de la Bataille', also for eight voices, by Jean Larchier (preserved in manuscript).[5] French Masses were nearly always for four voices, but usually included sections for two, three (*Benedictus*), or five voices (*Agnus*). They are short works, both in those sections where the text is of some length and also in the *Kyrie*[6] and *Agnus*, where few melismata are to be found and the imitation is rudimentary. All these features distinguish them from the kind of Mass then in favour among the Netherlanders or in Italy. Finally, apart from a very few Masses *ad placitum* (by Cadéac, Sermisy, and Le Jeune), they are all parody-Masses, their themes

---

[1] André Pirro, *Histoire de la musique de la fin du XIVe siècle à la fin du XVIe* (Paris, 1940), p. 239.

[2] Undated letter (probably to Ercole II) printed in Henry Prunières, *L'Opéra italien en France avant Lulli* (Paris, 1913), p. xv.

[3] Quoted by Pirro, 'L'enseignement de la musique aux universités françaises', *Acta Musicologica*, ii (1930), p. 47.

[4] *Geschichte der Messe* (Leipzig, 1913), p. 253.

[5] K. W. Hiersemann's Catalogue 392 (Leipzig, 1911), p. 18.

[6] There is a *Kyrie* of only six bars in a Mass by Cléreau quoted by Wagner, op. cit., p. 250.

borrowed from motets or *chansons*, even from some with decidedly uninhibited texts (e.g. the Masses 'M'amie un jour' by Maillard and 'O gente brunette' by Nicolas de Marle). When a Mass was based on a Gregorian chant, the composer might use the liturgical material very briefly (as in the Mass 'Veni sponsa' by J. Leleu) or almost in its entirety. Lastly, the Proper of the Mass was sometimes given a polyphonic setting; thus, in the first printed collection of polyphonic church music ever to appear in France, the *Contrapunctus seu figurata musica* published by Guaynard at Lyons in 1528, there are four-part Introits, Offertories, and Graduals for solemn festivals, with *canti fermi* generally in the tenor.[1]

In motets the composers preferred to base their work on the Gregorian melodies of psalms, antiphons, or sequences; one no longer finds anything like the *chanson*-motets with Latin tenors by Compère or Agricola in the *Odhecaton*. The text of the motet was generally divided into two sections—into still more at the end of the century. It was not so regularly set for four voices as the Mass; often there were five or more parts. But the most distinctive feature of the French motet was the way in which the words were treated; sixteenth-century French composers attached more importance to clear comprehension of the words than to strictly musical elaboration. This technique seems to have arisen in the earliest years of the century; probably the earliest dated examples of it are two three-part motets by Brumel, 'Mater patris' and 'Ave ancilla Trinitatis', published in Petrucci's *Odhecaton Canti B*, in which the text is set syllabically almost throughout.

Finally one might regard as a separate genre the polyphonic Passions of the dramatic type, as distinct from those motets on Passiontide texts which are found with other motets in the collections of the period. Two of these were published in 1534 by Attaingnant in the *Liber decimus* of his series of motets: one anonymous, the other by Claudin de Sermisy.[2] The latter, a Passion according to St. Matthew, is constructed entirely on a single melody, that of the *turba*. It is written for low voices and only the crowd passages are set consistently in four parts, while the words of Judas, St. Peter, or Pilate may be set for two or four voices. In this genre may also be included the Lamentations of Jeremiah, at which Sermisy, Dominique Phinot,[3] Leleu,

---

[1] Georg Eisenring, *Zur Geschichte des mehrstimmigen Proprium Missae bis um 1560* (Düsseldorf, 1913), and Walther Lipphardt, *Die Geschichte des mehrstimmigen Proprium Missae* (Heidelberg, 1950), p. 45.

[2] Otto Kade, *Die ältere Passionskomposition bis zum Jahre 1631* (Gütersloh, 1893), pp. 121 and 127.

[3] Edited by Mason Martens (Brooklyn, N.Y., 1961).

Genet,[1] and Cadéac tried their hand, and in which homophonic passages were traditionally of great importance.

THE LYONS SCHOOL

The two principal centres at which composers published their works were, in the first half of the century, Lyons and Paris. Only a few of the most representative figures of this earlier generation can be mentioned here.

Lyons occupied a unique position by reason of its favourable situation between Italy and the Netherlands. Parisians were less influential there than Italians and Northerners, generously welcomed by the printer Jacques Moderne. But there also existed a Lyons school proper, one representative of which was François Layolle, organist at Florence, who died about 1540. Layolle published three Masses (one of them on Josquin's *chanson* 'Adieu mes amours') and a score of motets,[2] in which he displays a very keen sense of colour and effective contrast, as in 'Veni in hortum meum'.[3] These works enjoyed a lasting success, if we may judge by the number of foreign manuscripts in which they are included. Another Lyonnais was Pierre Colin, Moderne's most notable discovery, who published 10 Masses, 15 motets, and 8 settings of the *Magnificat*; he was later in charge of the music at Autun Cathedral, and when Lyons ceased to be a centre of music-printing he entrusted his works to Nicolas du Chemin. It is curious that we find two of his Masses ('Christus resurgens' and 'Beatus vir') in an Italian publication side by side with Palestrina's 'Missa Papae Marcelli' and a Mass by Gastoldi.[4] A third was Pierre de Villiers; his three-part canonic Mass 'De Beata Virgine', whose affinities are rather with the Northern style, justified that reproach of 'science fantastique' mentioned by Charles de Sainte-Marthe in a poem written in the musician's honour.[5] Lastly, the most important of this school, apart from Layolle himself, was certainly Dominique Phinot, who lived at Lyons where the printer Beringen issued his motets and *chansons*, dedicated to leading personages of the district such as César Gros, sieur de Saint-Jouaire, or François Bonvalot. Among his motets, some

---

[1] On Genet's Lamentations, see Vol. III, pp. 298–9.

[2] Two specimens printed in Ambros–Kade, *Geschichte der Musik*, v (Leipzig, 1889), pp. 201 and 204; opening of 'Noe, noe' in *Oxford History of Music*, ii (Oxford, 1905), p. 264.

[3] G. Tricou, 'Les deux Layolle et les organistes lyonnais du XVIe siècle', *Mémoires de la Soc. litt., hist. et archéol. de Lyon*, 1896–7, p. 229; J. Killing, *Kirchenmusikalische Schätze der Bibliothek des Abbate F. Santini* (Münster, 1908), p. 39.

[4] A collection, without date or title-page, in the library of Milan Cathedral.

[5] *La Poésie françoise* (Lyons, 1540), p. 97.

ninety in all, are five for double choir (published in 1548) which derive from the Venetian style and testify to a feeling for effect which ensured him a great influence on his age.[1]

With this group should also be included Elzéar Genet, of Carpentras,[2] who, after a brilliant career in the papal chapel, retired to Avignon, where Jean de Channey printed five of his Masses on French *chansons*, Lamentations which were to enjoy a lasting success at Rome, and hymns and motets. Most of these have not, unfortunately, been republished. The comparatively severe style of 'Carpentras' greatly diminishes the value of the still current semi-legend of the 'Palestrinian reforms'. As a further proof of the close links binding the south of France with Rome we may mention the presence of Jean Lhéritier at Avignon in 1540 as '*maître de chapelle* to the Cardinal-Legate'.[3]

THE PARIS SCHOOL

The style of music in Paris was much more uniform and much more typical of what foreigners normally regard as the French style. Willaert and Verdelot were certainly known there, for Attaingnant published their works, but for a long time composers seemed almost impervious to the development of church music in Italy and the North. On the other hand, foreigners sometimes welcomed the work of such men as Claudin and Certon (Morales was later to write a Mass on his motet 'Si bona suscepimus'), though the publishers of Venice and Nuremberg seem to have done so only for the sake of including specimens of all kinds in their collections.

Claudin de Sermisy (though he died as late as 1562) was, thanks to his Italian connexions, the first 'Parisian' composer to be published in Italy, even before Attaingnant had begun printing. He wrote, as early as 1529, a 'Praeparate corda vestra' in the typical form of the French motet: it follows its text closely, without any very unexpected features, and is constructed on a rhythmical theme and with a repeat of the last phrase as in a *chanson*. Claudin remained faithful to this form throughout his motets—some seventy in all, for three, four, five, or six voices, in which he treats the Gregorian melodies with care and sets himself 'to interpret accurately the saddest of liturgical texts'. In general he shows more contrapuntal sense than other Frenchmen of his day, especially in his thirteen Masses which mark 'the sum of his

[1] On Phinot, see Gustave Reese, *Music in the Renaissance* (New York, 1954), p. 349, and Lesure's article in *Die Musik in Geschichte und Gegenwart*, xii, col. 1210.

[2] See Vol. III, p. 298.

[3] Lesure, 'Notes pour une biographie de J. Lhéritier', *Revue de musicologie*, xli (1958), p. 219.

achievements',[1] although one feels an ever-present tendency to return to syllabic treatment. (The Mass 'Domine quis habitavit', which makes important concessions to the Northern tradition, is an exception.) Not only does Claudin quite often make use of canonic writing; he shows many other signs of deep musicianship, such as the extended vocalizations on 'Amen' in 'Regi seculorum', his happy use of sequence in 'Nisi Dominus', the rhythmic alternations of 'Veni Sancte Spiritus' and 'Lava quod est sordidum', and, in general, the interest of his melodic lines. The writing of a three-part *Magnificat*, preserved in manuscript in the Milan Library, is so closely knit that one might take it for an instrumental fantasia.

Clément Janequin (d. 1558)—a whole volume of whose motets has probably been lost—left only two Masses (on the themes of two of his *chansons*) and one motet. Although he held the posts of master of the choir-school and composer-in-ordinary to the king, he does not seem to have been suited to church music. His Mass 'La Bataille' follows too closely the various sections and themes of his *chanson* 'La guerre'.[2] Listeners could not fail to recognize 'Avanturiers bons compagnons' behind 'Quoniam tu solus sanctus', and there is more expressiveness in 'Bruyés, bonbardes et canons' than in 'Cujus regni non erit finis' which is note for note the same. However, his motet 'Congregati sunt'[3] shows more sense for motet style, in its most French form with a natural tendency to rapid declamation.

It would need the discovery of a very great masterpiece to redeem Pierre Certon, master of the children of the Sainte Chapelle (d. 1572) from Pirro's merciless, indeed over-severe, judgement on his church music:[4] sketchy structure, monotony of device, over-indulgence in two-part passages, imitation loosely constructed and too soon given up, accentuation constantly faulty. Pirro goes so far as to wonder whether he was trying to 'turn the Roman liturgy to ridicule'. Certon's technique may be studied in the opening of his Mass 'Dulcis amica',[5] the basis of which is one of his own motets;[6] the first *Kyrie* makes use of the first section of the motet, the *Christe* of the second, and the second *Kyrie* of the last; and the same procedure is followed in the

[1] Pirro, *Histoire*, p. 319, and Lesure's article in *Die Musik in Geschichte und Gegenwort*, xii, col. 562.   [2] See p. 6.

[3] Ed. Lesure (Monaco, 1949). Expert's edition of the Mass 'La Bataille' (Paris, 1947) was his last publication.

[4] Pirro, *Histoire*, p. 320.

[5] The Masses 'Sur le pont d'Avignon', 'Adjuva me' and 'Regnum mundi' have been published by Expert, *Les Monuments de la musique française au temps de la Renaissance*, ii.

[6] Printed, with *Kyrie* I of the Mass, in Peter Wagner, op. cit., p. 246.

Credo, as if the composer were afraid to abandon his ready-made framework for a moment.

Perhaps when all the remaining material is published we shall find that the three great *chanson*-composers just discussed are *not* also the best French composers in the domain of church music. And, knowing this, we may find that Pierre Vermont, the elder, a musician of the Sainte Chapelle from 1509 to his death in 1532 (except for a short stay in Italy) stands out as one of the most interesting of the Parisian group. In his 'Ave Virgo gloriosa' he writes with ease in six parts on a *canto fermo* ('O pia, o clemens'), and indulges in long vocalizations in 'Benedicat nos Deus noster', following up this invocation with 'Deus misereatur nostri', a work whose equal one may seek in vain in the music of his Parisian contemporaries. For the purposes of the Chapelle Royale he wrote a motet in five parts in honour of St. Denis.[1] His brother, Pierre Vermont the younger, also composed motets which it is often difficult to distinguish from those of his senior; his model appears to have been Prioris, whose serene Requiem Mass he desired should be performed at his own funeral.

Another outstanding personality was Hesdin (Nicolle des Celliers) (d. 1538), master of the choir-children in the cathedral at Beauvais, whose ease of writing has caused a Mass of his, 'super Benedicta', to be taken for the work of Willaert.[2] His three motets in Attaingnant's Fourth Book, on texts in honour of the Virgin, are written in a pellucid and varied style which sets them apart from the Parisian manner.[3]

Guillaume Le Heurteur, a much later successor of Ockeghem at St. Martin's, Tours, was one of those sixteenth-century churchmen who made fun of their colleagues in their *chansons*, as, for example, when he described the adventures of a priest who sang an '*Agnus grignoté*', or those of the 'white monks' with whom Rabelais also concerned himself in the same district. Whether he wrote for four, five, or six voices, his motets on the Antiphons of Our Lady (published in 1545) all follow the same pattern, and he seems to have had no idea of the resources of polyphony. The little vocalizations which he scattered through his works serve only a decorative purpose, as it might be in a *chanson*. Once indeed, in 'In te Domine speravi', he sets the text syllabically, perhaps because it is a verse of a psalm forming part of the Office for Holy Thursday. But when the

---

[1] In Smijers, *Treize livres de motets parus chez P. Attaingnant*, iii (Paris, 1938).

[2] Myroslaw Antonowytsch, *Die Motette 'Benedicta es' von Josquin des Prez und die Messen 'super Benedicta' von Willaert* ... (Utrecht, 1951), p. 11, attributes this Mass to Willaert on stylistic grounds.

[3] Reprinted in Smijers, *Treize livres de motets*, iv (Monaco, 1960), pp. 103, 157, and 182.

liturgical text calls for rejoicing he still subordinates his music to the
words, as in 'Noe, Noe, natus est Christus'.

Ex. 89

Marked by more varied resources is the four-part 'Christum ascen-
dentem' in which the choir frequently divides antiphonally and the
composer uses triple time in the final section to indicate the Christian's
hope in the Holy Spirit on Ascension Day.

Of the life of Jean Maillard we know nothing; which is perhaps the
reason why none of his motets (some seventy-five in all) and none of his
four Masses have so far been republished.[1] His first collection, dating

---

[1] The portrait generally accepted as his looks more like that of a magistrate. Unfortunately the name is not uncommon: there were two men named Jehan Maillart living
in Paris in 1541; one of them procurator in the Ecclesiastical Court, the other first
usher in the Chambre des Requêtes (Archives nationales, Minutier central, viii, 69).

from 1555, contains only motets in one section; at the end are two six-part motets in canon, 'Surrexit Dominus' and 'Fratres me elongaverunt'. Lassus, who made new versions of several of his motets on Antiphons, knew his work well; so did the lutenists such as Adrian Le Roy, who were doubtless attracted by his rather short rhythmic units with hardly any continuous movement, as at the beginning of the five-part motet 'Domine si tu es'.

Ex. 90

In his Mass 'Je suis déshéritée' the references to Cadéac's *chanson* are positively obsessive, the culmination coming in the first *Agnus*, where the whole *chanson* is introduced unchanged; in the 1553 edition, in case anyone should be unfamiliar with fashionable songs, Maillard even prints the whole text of Cadéac's profane work under the words of the *Agnus*.

Pierre Cadéac himself, master of the choristers at Auch Cathedral, first made a name as a writer of *chansons* and then published a whole book of motets in four, five, and six parts (1555), and six Masses in which he shows a certain originality in the thematic treatment. And he employs alternation of imitative with note-against-note writing.[1]

Of the six Masses by Pierre Cléreau, master of the choristers at Toul Cathedral—all published in Paris by Nicolas du Chemin—the most valuable are the Requiem, which strictly carries out the liturgical intentions, and the Mass 'Caecilia Virgo', in which he purposely uses black notation.[2] The rest of his work gives the impression of having been composed somewhat hurriedly.[3]

---

[1] See Reese, op. cit., p. 341. [2] See p. 290.
[3] Peter Wagner, op. cit., p. 250.

CLAUDE GOUDIMEL

It is impossible to discuss here all the French composers of repute during the first two-thirds of the century. One can only mention the names of the Parisians Mathieu Sohier and Jean Hérissant, and the provincials Jean Guyon (Chartres), Simon de Bonefond (Clermont-Ferrand), Vulfran Samin (Amiens), Nicolas de Marle (Noyon), Barthélemy Beaulaigue (Marseilles), or refer in passing to such isolated figures as Antoine de Mornable, private musician to the Duc de Laval, whose motets and Masses are found in the publications of Attaingnant, Nicolas du Chemin, Adrian Le Roy, and Robert Ballard.[1]

But special attention must be given to Claude Goudimel (d. 1572), whose famous settings of the Huguenot Psalter[2] have obscured the rest of his achievement. Actually he contributed with equal distinction to the music of the Catholic liturgy, with his five Masses, five motets, and three settings of the *Magnificat*, all composed before he left Paris. In 1553, when he was in charge of Nicolas du Chemin's publishing house, he noted three *chansons* in the *Quart livre* of his rivals Le Roy and Ballard, and based on them his Masses 'Tant plus je mets' (the theme by Maillard), 'De mes ennuys' and 'Le bien que j'ay', both by Arcadelt.[3] ('De mes ennuys' had already inspired the lutenists.) The choice of these models, fairly broad and not too rhythmical, shows him as a musician determined to treat the Mass as a truly religious composition and at the same time to reconcile French brevity with depth. When the need arose, he would modify one of his sources ('De mes ennuys') or use only a very short element of the *chanson* ('Le bien que j'ay'), and in any case never regarded his borrowed themes otherwise than as points of departure. The serenity of his writing explains how he was for a time supposed to have been the teacher of Palestrina; and in the latter's 'Missa brevis'[4] the three-part *Benedictus* may even have been inspired by that of Goudimel's Mass 'Audi filia':[5]

---

[1] For details of the composers here referred to, see François Lesure and Geneviève Thibault, 'Bibliographie des éditions musicales publiées par N. Du Chemin', *Annales musicologiques*, i (1953), p. 269, and *Bibliographie des ouvrages publiés par A. Le Roy et R. Ballard* (Paris, 1954). Beaulaigue's 14 motets have been published by A. Auda, *B. Beaulaigue, poète et musicien prodige* (Woluwe-St. Pierre, 1958).

[2] See p. 443.

[3] The Masses, 'Tant plus je mets' and 'De mes ennuys' have been republished by Expert, *Monuments de la musique française au temps de la Renaissance*, ix (Paris, 1928), 'Le bien que j'ay' by Charles Bordes, *Anthologie des maîtres religieux primitifs, Livre des Messes*, ix (Paris, 1894).   [4] See pp. 320 ff.

[5] Pirro, *Histoire*, p. 297. The Mass 'Audi filia' has been republished by Expert, *Monuments*, ix, and separately in *Répertoire des maîtres musiciens de la Renaissance française* (Paris, 1929). Several complete movements from Goudimel's Masses are printed in Wagner, op. cit., p. 260.

Ex. 91

All the same one must not credit him with miracles; the big twelve-part 'Salve Regina' for three choirs is a forgery, due to nineteenth-century enthusiasm for his personality.[1]

THE ADVENT OF LASSUS

The year 1564 saw the publication in Paris, by Le Roy and Ballard, of the earliest religious works of Lassus; this is a cardinal date, marking the beginning of an almost absolute hegemony. The success of this new composer was considerable from the first, and seemed to eclipse the activities of the French school. For, although until about 1570 the older generation—the generation of Certon, Maillard, and Marle—and a few younger composers such as Claude Le Jeune were fairly active, no more than five or six religious publications by French composers between 1570 and 1582 have been preserved, and none after that date. It is perhaps symbolic that the old *Missae tres* of Sermisy should have been reprinted in 1583. Lassus himself was so careful to cultivate the French public that in 1571 he empowered his friend Le Roy to print for the first time a score of recently completed motets,[2] and in 1587 entrusted the same publisher with the manuscripts of two Masses ('Locutus sum' and 'Beatus qui intelligit') which had not yet been printed. He even composed Masses *à la française*, keeping very close to his models (Certon's 'Frère Thibault' and Sermisy's 'La, la,

[1] The fanciful attribution of this work to Goudimel is repeated by Reese, op. cit., p. 502, though he had himself cast doubts on it in *Notes*, vi (1948), p. 99.

[2] *Moduli quinis vocibus* (Lesure and Thibault, *Bibliographie . . . Le Roy et Ballard*, no. 151).

maître Pierre') and sometimes hardly modifying their counterpoint at all.[1] Moreover, he did not disdain to compete in the *puy de musique* at Evreux, where motets of his carried off the prize in 1575 and 1583.

'RONSARD'S MUSICIANS'

All the same, it would be an exaggeration to speak of a decline in the French school. Publishing was adversely affected by the terrible internal upheavals that the country was undergoing, but there was no real break in the tradition of the choir-schools. The list of awards at the Evreux *puy* from 1575 to 1589 proves this; every year a prize was awarded for a motet by some Parisian or provincial master, and various newcomers won their spurs there: du Caurroy (1576), Mauduit (1581), Blondet (1583), Paschal de L'Estocart (1584), and many others who never attained the dignity of print, such as Michel Nicole, Michel Malherbe (of Coutances), Adrian Allou (of Tours), Jean Boette (of Evreux), and others.[2]

The generation of composers known as 'Ronsard's musicians' was far from neglecting church music. The Toulouse master, Guillaume Boni, applied his slightly mannered technique to the most challenging liturgical texts; if he set the words 'Terribilis est' in his motet 'Amen dico vobis' in madrigal style and indulged in melismas like those of the plainsong Alleluias, he was very well able on the other hand to represent the idea of death in 'Tristis es'. Like Costeley (to whom also we owe a few motets), he widely exploited the resources of chromaticism, which Claude Le Jeune had perhaps been the first to employ for religious purposes in a three-part motet published in 1565.[3] More interesting still are the motets by Fabrice Marin Caietain, who lived at the court of Lorraine in the service of the Guises; they have unfortunately not yet been reprinted; in them the quest for expressiveness manifests itself sometimes in curious vocalizations (as in 'Ave verum') and constantly in chromaticism. Such a work as 'Estote fortes in bello', for example, in which the composer follows the melody of the antiphon for the Common of Apostles, cuts completely across the French tradition in its narrower aspect and is a work of great value.

[1] Pirro, *Histoire*, p. 338, and Peter Wagner, op. cit., p. 359. On Lassus's church music generally see *infra*, pp. 333 ff.

[2] Th. Bonnin and A. Chassant, *Puy de musique, érigé à Evreux, en l'honneur de madame Sainte-Cécile* (Evreux, 1837).

[3] 'Nigra sum sed formosa', in *Modulorum ternis voc.* (Lesure and Thibault, *Bibliographie . . . Le Roy et Ballard*, no. 98).

THE POST-TRIDENTINE REFORMS

Let us now consider the basic problems set by the reactions of musicians to the post-Tridentine reforms. The instructions issued by the Council of Trent in the sphere of music amounted to hardly any-thing;[1] and it does not seem that there was in the minds of the reformers any more specific intention than to put an end to anarchy and deca-dence in the liturgy. This intention was given quite a different turn by Palestrina (or, more probably, his son Iginio under his name), Zoilo, and Guidetti, who dealt a severe blow to the traditional chant by their application of mensural values and other mutilations.[2] (Unfortunately the revised *Pontificale Romanum* issued in 1596 by order of Clement VIII served as a model for French publications.) But a return to something like liturgical purity in polyphonic church music may be observed long before that date: for example, in the four-part *Litaniæ in Alma Domo Lauretano* entirely in note-against-note style (1578), in the *Psaumes et Cantiques qu'on chante en la Chapelle de la Congrégation* (1583)—the only evidence of interest in liturgical song shown by Le Roy and Ballard—and finally in the *Instruction pour apprendre à chanter à 4 parties selon le plain chant les Pseaumes et Cantiques* (1582) in which an obscure Caen musician, Laurens Dandin, contented himself with harmonizing the *Magnificat* in note-against-note style in each of the eight tones, and 'In exitu'.

The Jesuits did not wait for the completion of the post-Tridentine reforms before severely regulating the old forms of 'learned' music. Consider, for example, the result of visitations carried out between 1576 and 1587 in a Parisian Jesuit college by the Provincial of the Order: the function of instruments and the importance of polyphonic music were prescribed with great strictness; works in which there was too much musical development, or excessive repetition of words, were rejected; the Masses and motets of Lassus were prohibited; moreover, 'motets shall be discontinued altogether unless by permission of the Rector; in their place an Antiphon of the Virgin shall be said, with fauxbourdons'. Finally there was a renewal of the prohibitions which the Church had never really succeeded in imposing since the thirteenth century: 'Ad rationem cantus attinet, illud generatim omnino caveatur, ne quippiam cantetur compositum ad leves cantiunculas seculares,

---

[1] See p. 317.
[2] See Augustin Gatard, *La Musique grégorienne* (Paris, 1913), pp. 86 ff. or Otto Ursprung, *Die katholische Kirchenmusik* (Potsdam, 1931), p. 198; the standard work is Raffael Molitor, *Die Nach-Tridentinische Choralreform zu Rom.* 2 vols. (Leipzig, 1901–2). Also *infra*, pp. 368 and 394.

multoque lascivas, aut etiam ad cantionum belli, ut vocant, cum in cultu divino hujusmodi profana minime deceat, sed tota musica gravis sit, tempori accommodata, non prolixa; quaque pietatem redeleat, et excitet devotionem.' (As concerns song in general let all beware not to sing anything fitted to trivial secular—much less light-minded —ditties or to songs of war as they are called, since in divine worship profanity of this kind is specially unbecoming; but let all music be serious, suited to the occasion, not prolix; by which piety may be restored and devotion excited.)[1]

CATHOLIC PSALM-SETTINGS

For a long time non-Huguenot musicians did not hesitate to set the Marot–Bèze Psalter[2] to music. Here there was still no clear distinction between Catholic and Calvinist music. About 1542 there was a craze for the psalms at Court, and, as de Villemadon remarked in 1559, musicians occupying the most strictly official posts, 'indeed all the musicians of our country, vied with each other in setting the aforesaid psalms to music'[3]—a remark aimed at Certon, Janequin, Thomas Champion, Mornable, Arcadelt, and others, who do not appear at any time to have attached themselves to the new religion. And Villemadon adds that both Francis I and Henry II had a great liking for psalms. The mere act of translating the psalms into the vulgar tongue was thus not an offence in itself. But once the critical period was over, the Catholics wanted their own vernacular texts. One of the earliest was Pibrac's *Quatrains*, set to music by Boni, Planson, L'Estocart, and Lassus himself: a naïvely pious version whose popularity lasted well into the seventeenth century. Then, most important of all, came the new translation of the psalms by Philippe Desportes. And in 1607 the Jesuit Michel Coyssard, in his *Hymnes sacrez*, published even French paraphrases of the *Credo*, 'Pangue lingua', 'Conditor alme', 'Stabat mater', &c., to be sung to the original plainsong. He protested against those who reproved him for translating the doctrine into the vulgar tongue by reminding them of the terms in which the Cardinal in charge of the Inquisition at Rome had approved of his work in 1597; and in the course of his arguments he wrote in defence of popular hymns and Christmas carols, the music of Antoine de Bertrand (a posthumous book of *Airs spirituels*), and the Psalms of Desportes.[4]

---

[1] Bibl. nat., lat. 10989. [2] See p. 442.
[3] O. Douen, *Clément Marot et le psautier huguenot*, i (Paris, 1878), p. 284.
[4] The rise in popularity of Desportes's psalms may be studied in a bibliographical article by André Verchaly, 'Desportes et la musique', *Annales musicologiques*, ii (Paris, 1954), p. 271.

There were musicians who had preceded Coyssard in this field; as early as 1587 Le Long had composed *Nouveaux cantiques spirituels* for four voices, containing vernacular translations of 'Veni Creator' and 'Veni Sancte Spiritus',[1] and in 1592 Virgile Le Blanc published, in his native city of Lyons, a *Paraphrase des hymnes et cantiques spirituels*, consisting of nine four-part airs to words from Coyssard's translations of the *Credo*, 'Ave maris stella', and the *Te Deum*; they could also be sung to the superius alone.

Finally, in the early years of the seventeenth century, theatrical performances, mostly favoured by the Jesuits, called for musical collaboration, often of considerable importance. One such was the *Céciliade* staged in 1606 by Soret, into which Abraham Blondet, *maître de musique* at Notre-Dame, introduced a large number of four-part choruses in very 'vertical' style, including not only the hymn sung by St. Cecilia in her boiling cauldron but also the song of Valerianus, for which one might justifiably have expected a solo voice.[2] But the monodic style was still identified with profane purposes, even though Gabriel Bataille, Denis Caignet, and others set several of Desportes's psalms for solo voice with lute accompaniment.

NEW TENDENCIES IN CHURCH MUSIC

The music of the traditional Latin rite was gradually developing towards the style employed a little later by Nicolas Formé (1567–1638) and Henry du Mont (1610–84). One of the initiators of this style was Jacques Mauduit (1557–1627), whose Requiem Mass, sung at the Collège de Boncourt in 1586 for the funeral of Ronsard, called for the participation of instruments. Of this work unfortunately only the Introit, for five voices, has been preserved. Mauduit also introduced instrumental parts into the 'grands concerts des Ténèbres' which he organized every year in Holy Week at the Abbaye Saint-Antoine.[3]

The device of the double choir appeared in France first in the work of Eustache du Caurroy (1549–1609), composer of about fifty motets and four Masses, only one of which has been preserved. It took firm root by the end of the sixteenth century; for example at Notre-Dame in Paris the musicians of the Household and those of the Chapelle Royale performed a kind of dialogue in the course of the peace

[1] There is a copy in the library of the Brussels Conservatoire.

[2] K. G. Fellerer, 'N. Soret's "La Céciliade" mit Musik von A. Blondet (1606). Ein Beitrag zur Geschichte der französischen Oper', *Festschrift Joh. Biehle zum 60. Geburtstag* (Leipzig, 1930), p. 47.

[3] Michel Brenet, *Musique et musiciens de la vieille France* (Paris, 1911), p. 233.

celebrations of 1598. In his *Preces ecclesiasticae* du Caurroy varies the layout of his vocal parts considerably; his motets may be in three, four, or even six parts (e.g. 'In exitu Israel'), while passages for three, four, five, and seven voices may occur in the same piece ('Virgo Dei genetrix'). His motets for double choir are for five, seven, and eight voices.[1] His sense of effect is equally keen in his five-part Mass 'Pro defunctis', which was to enjoy lasting popularity and in which he turned his learning to much more felicitous uses than in his secular works. The only place in this Mass[2] where he literally—and very happily—quotes a Gregorian melody is in the 'Lux aeterna'.

French church music thus developed in the sixteenth century quite continuously but almost in a closed compartment until the appearance of Lassus, who soon became the most frequently performed composer in the country. The formation of a 'national' style coincided fairly closely with the end of the hegemony exerted by French composers along with the older Netherlanders. There are still too few texts available, too many essential problems still unexamined (such as the study of liturgical usages and of the provincial choir-schools, and the clearing-up of the uncertain boundaries between Catholic and Protestant music) for us to be able to pick out the most significant personalities and works of the last two-thirds of the century, or to describe with any precision the evolution of the religious style in France. But the most striking feature appears to be its parallel development with that of the *chanson*.

(c) CENTRAL EUROPE

By H. F. REDLICH

ISAAC AND HIS SCHOOL

The overwhelming influence of the Emperor Maximilian's court composer, Heinrich Isaac, on music in Germany in the early sixteenth century has been described in Vol. III.[3] He founded a whole school of composers and his disciples disseminated the principles of his style throughout the sixteenth century. The majority of them served under him as choirboys and members of the Imperial Court Chapel or as singers in the cathedral choir at Constance. The older group, who display the psychological and religious peculiarities of the German mind at the time of Luther's advent, include Ludwig Senfl, Benedictus

---

[1] D. Launay, 'Les motets à double chœur en France dans la première moitié du XVIIe s.', *Revue de musicologie*, xxxix–xl (1957), p. 173.

[2] Modern edition by E. Martin and J. Burald (Paris, 1951).   [3] See pp. 279–84.

Ducis, Balthazar Resinarius, Sixtus Dietrich, and Adam Rener. Their religious music reflects the split in the German soul which more or less coincides with the announcement of Luther's theses, publicly exhibited on the church-door of the Court Chapel of Wittenberg in the very year of Isaac's death (1517).

Although Isaac's masterpiece, the *Choralis Constantinus*[1]—or *Choralis Constantiensis* as it should perhaps be called[2]—had been begun as early as April 1508, it was still incomplete when he died. The various manuscript parts were copied under Senfl's supervision in 1530–1 and completed by him; in 1537 the Nuremberg publisher Formschneider announced his intention of publishing it but many more years passed before it was actually published, in three books, in 1550 and 1555. The differences of style in the use of dissonance, in the employment of the third at cadences, in the variety of sequences, &c., to which Louise Cuyler,[3] Gustave Reese,[4] and others have drawn attention, are easily explained not only by the long period of composition but by Senfl's contribution. This is undoubted at the very end of Book III, but he may have brought his editorial influence into play throughout the whole work. It is almost certain that the later part of the St. Ursula sequence was written by him.[5]

LUDWIG SENFL[6]

As with Isaac, there is some uncertainty concerning the dates of Senfl's life. He was born at Zürich *c.* 1490 and may have lived there until about 1504. Shortly after that date he became a pupil of Isaac at Constance.[7] His attachment to Isaac as man and artist is expressed in the fifth and seventh stanzas of his autobiographical song 'Lust hab' ich ghabt zur Musica', of which the initials of each stanza form an acrostic on his own name:

[1] See Vol. III, p. 282.

[2] See Walther Lipphardt, *Die Geschichte des mehrstimmigen Proprium Missae* (Heidelberg, 1950), p. 35. Lipphardt gives particulars of four German manuscripts of 1500–20 containing polyphonic settings of the Proper of the Mass (Jena, Universitätsbibl. 30, 33, and 35; Weimar, Stadtkirche, Codex A) which may be regarded as precursors of the *Choralis Constantinus* or are closely related to it.

[3] *The Choralis Constantinus, Book III (1555)* (Rochester, New York, unpublished dissertation, 1948).

[4] *Music in the Renaissance* (London, 1954), p. 217.

[5] Cf. the facsimile of the original edition of the St. Ursula sequence in Cuyler, op. cit., p. 21. It bears the marginal printed note: 'Additio Ludovici Senfl's quia hic Isaac obyit morte'. Cf. Dr. Cuyler's edition of Book III (Ann Arbor, 1950), pp. 452 ff.

[6] The name is also spelled Senffl, Saenftli, Senfel; he is sometimes called 'Schweizer'.

[7] Thürlings believes that Senfl had become his pupil as early as 1497: see *Denkmäler der Tonkunst in Bayern*, iii (2), pp. xxvii ff.

PLATE III

(a)

(b)

THE TWO SIDE-PANELS OF THE ORGAN CASE IN THE ANNAKIRCHE AT AUGSBURG

Showing in the left-hand picture Heinrich Isaac (marking the notes of the hexachord), and in the right-hand picture Ludwig Senfl (pointing to (a)

Jzac das war der name sein,
halt wol es werd vergessen nit,
wie er sein Compositz so fein
vnd clar hat gsetzt, darzu auch mit
Mensur hat gziert, dardurch probiert,
noch heuttigs tags sein lob vnd kunst,
verhanden ist, Herr Jhesu christ,
tail Im dort mit göttlichen gunst.

.   .   .   .

Sein vleyß der ward an mir erkennt,
deßhalb trug mir der kayser huld:
dann weyl man mich sein schuler nent,
Must ich erfüllen on mein schuld,
den Chorgsang sein, wie wol da mein,
Erlernte kunst was vil zu schwach. . . .[1]

Senfl, who began his career as a male alto in the choir of the
Imperial Chapel at Augsburg,[2] Innsbruck, Vienna, and Constance
under Isaac, became in time his trusted assistant and—possibly in
1515—his official deputy in the direction of the choir. He must have
been appointed court composer to Maximilian I shortly after Isaac's
death (cf. the second of the stanzas quoted above). After the Emperor's
death in 1519 and the subsequent dissolution of the court chapel,
Senfl remained at Augsburg where he completed and edited the
Choralis Constantinus; here he also issued the *Liber selectarum cantionum* (1520) as a memorial volume dedicated to the late Emperor[3] and
the collection of Horatian odes (*Harmoniae poeticae*) by his later
friend Paul Hofhaimer. In 1523 Senfl was appointed *Musicus into-
nator* at the Bavarian Court *Cantorei*, a post which may have combined the office of choirmaster with that of court composer, and
which he may have held until after 1540. During Senfl's years in
Munich he married and had a daughter, but the last fifteen years of
his life are shrouded in darkness. He certainly had died by 1556; he
may have died long before that date and probably not in Munich.
His known sympathy with Luther and the cause of Protestantism
may be partly responsible for this total obscurity; his sympathies
may well have cost him the patronage of the Bavarian court.

Senfl's relations with Luther are symptomatic of the age. They anticipate the religious and psychological dualism characteristic of nearly

---

[1] Complete text reprinted ibid. Appendix, p. cii; the music in *J. Wolf-Festschrift*
(Berlin, 1929).
[2] Cf. the reproduction of Jörg Breu's paintings on the side-panels of the organ-case
of the Annakirche at Augsburg, with the supposed portraits of Isaac and Senfl (pl. III).
[3] Cf. H. J. Moser, article 'Senfl' in his *Musiklexikon* (Berlin, 1935).

all Isaac's pupils. Luther, who was an admirer of Senfl, wrote him a letter on 4 October 1530, asking him to compose a motet on the tenor 'In pace in idipsum'. This letter[1] was written during the greatest personal and political crisis of Luther's life (that is, shortly after his official clash with Imperial authority at the diet of Augsburg); it elicited a sympathetic response and also some music from Senfl.[2]

SENFL'S MASSES

Senfl's contemporary and posthumous fame rests chiefly on his achievement as a master of the polyphonic *Tenorlied*[3] and on his compositions of Horatian odes.[4] His church music has become accessible only in comparatively recent years. As a composer of Masses[5] he cannot compare with Isaac in fertility or with Josquin in originality. The fact that only seven of his Masses exist may or may not prove that the species as such held but little attraction for him and that the motet with its affinity to the *Tenorlied* was more congenial to his creative temperament. Senfl's reliance on Isaac's methods is underlined by the somewhat archaic character of the three *Missae Dominicales*, based on the plainsong Ordinary of the Mass. *Missa I* combines plainsong and *chanson* tenors in typically Flemish fashion:[6]

Ex. 92

[1] Printed in F. A. Beck, *Dr. M. Luthers Gedanken über die Musik* (Berlin, 1828), p. 58.

[2] The motet 'Non moriar sed vivam' (the text of which amounted to a concealed declaration of sympathy with Luther's cause) and later on the motet 'In pace' (which has been rediscovered in recent years): cf. Friedrich Blume, *Evangelische Kirchenmusik* (Potsdam, 1931), p. 46; also *Denkmäler der Tonkunst in Bayern*, iii (2), pp. lii ff. On his vernacular church music, see p. 431.   [3] See pp. 98 ff.

[4] *Varia carminum genera* (Nuremberg, 1534), based on the melodies of Petrus Tritonius (cf. Vol. III, p. 371).

[5] Reprinted in *Sämtliche Werke* i (*Das Erbe deutscher Musik*, v), ed. Edwin Löhrer and Otto Ursprung (Basle, 1937). See also Löhrer, *Die Messen von Senfl: Beitrag zur Geschichte des polyphonen Messordinariums um 1500* (Lichtensteig, 1938). H. Birtner 'Sieben Messen von Ludwig Senfl', *Archiv für Musikforschung*, vii (1942), p. 40; Peter Wagner, *Geschichte der Messe*, i, (Leipzig, 1913), pp. 317 ff. and W. Heinz, *Isaaks und Senfls Propriumskompositionen in HSS der Bayrischen Staatsbibliothek, München* (Diss., West Berlin, 1952). Wagner prints the Kyries of the *Missa ferialis* and the second *Missa Dominicalis* complete, with long excerpts from the *Gloria* of the latter and the *Gloria* of the 'L'homme armé' Mass.

[6] Reese, op. cit., p. 689, points out that such double *canti fermi* are usually confined to the *Credo* sections of Netherland Masses.

- - ra pax

with the plainsong melody (Vatican XII) in the *cantus* and 'L'homme armé' in the lower parts. Equally archaic is the instrumental manner in the polyphonic tissue of the *Kyrie* of the *Missa Dominicalis II*, which seems to have been conceived in the sense of Dufay's *Gloria ad modum tubae*[1] and may well have required the support of wind-instruments. These may have woven garlands of sound based on a trumpet-like theme round the plainsong melody in the descant:

Ex. 93

In contrast with these features which link Senfl strongly to the fifteenth century, certain progressive traits may be observed, especially the employment of arpeggios of triads and also a tendency to clear-cut diatonic tonality, as in the *Missa Dominicalis II*:

[1] See Vol. III, p. 221.

Ex. 94

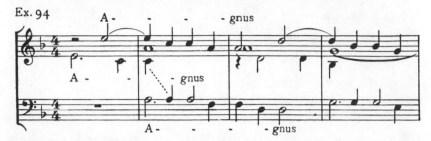

Two *missae parodiae*, 'Nisi Dominus' and 'Per signum crucis', were most probably composed in 1530 and 1540 respectively. To Ursprung[1] they seem to indicate a deliberate change of style from the archaic *canto fermo* technique, with alternating unison sections of plainsong, to the continuously polyphonic motet style with canonic imitation.

SENFL'S MOTETS

The *canto fermo* technique of five of Senfl's Masses also plays a determining part in his numerous motets, some of which—'Ave rosa sine spinis'[2] (Nuremberg, 1537) and 'Ave Maria virgo serena'—were evidently influenced by Josquin's 'Stabat mater'. They too are composed around secular tenors, as in the case of 'Ave rosa':

Ex. 95

[1] Cf. Preface to *Sämtliche Werke*, i.
[2] Reprinted in Ambros-Kade, *Geschichte der Musik*, v (Leipzig, 1889), p. 385, and by Walter Gerstenberg—with 'Mater digna Dei'—in *Das Chorwerk*, lxii (Wolfenbüttel, 1957).

which is based on Agricola's *chanson* 'Comme femme', on which Josquin had composed his 'Stabat mater'.[1]

Senfl's motets are now accessible in two critical editions, which between them offer a good cross-section through his prodigious output. The *Magnificat octo tonorum* (Nuremberg, 1537) and twelve Latin motets (mainly taken from the two publications of 1520 and 1537) appear in *Denkmäler der Tonkunst in Bayern*, iii (2)[2] (Leipzig, 1903) and motets and psalms in the *Sämtliche Werke*, iii (1) and viii (Basle, 1939 and 1965). Of the occasional pieces, the funeral motet supposedly for the Emperor Maximilian I, 'Quis dabit oculis',[3] generally attributed to Senfl, is probably a composition by Costanzo Festa.[4] The psalms, clearly modelled on Josquin, divide into two groups: one of free invention, the other (though less frequent) revolving round a *cantus prius factus*, sometimes from one of the psalm-tones, as in the case of 'Deus in adjutorium', from the *Liber selectarum cantionum*, which may be quoted as an example of Senfl's earlier motet-style:

Ex. 96

ISAAC'S OTHER DISCIPLES

Isaac's other disciples form a compact generation of partly German-born composers, following stylistically in the wake of the earlier

[1] See Vol. III, p. 270.

[2] From which 'Salutatio prima' is reprinted in Davison and Apel, *Historical Anthology of Music*, i (Cambridge, Mass., 1947), p. 113.

[3] Reprinted in *Sämtliche Werke*, iii, p. 17, and Schering, *Geschichte der Musik in Beispielen* (Leipzig, 1931), p. 72.

[4] See Alexander Main, 'Maximilian's Second-hand Funeral Motet', *Musical Quarterly*, xlviii (1962), p. 173.

generation represented by Isaac himself, Heinrich Finck, and Paul Hofhaimer. The younger generation differs from these pioneers by the ambiguity of its relations to the Roman Church and the chief among them may be conveniently divided into two groups:

(a) Sixtus Dietrich (c. 1492–1548)
   Benedictus Ducis (c. 1485?–1544)
   Balthasar Resinarius (Harzer) (c. 1480–after 1549)
   Adam Rener (c. 1485–1520)
(b) Thomas Stoltzer (c. 1480?–1526)[1]
   Arnold von Bruck (c. 1490–1554)
   Stephan Mahu (fl. c. 1540).

Both groups provided the Roman Church with music for its liturgy, yet only the second group were definitely Catholics. As for the first group, three of the four direct pupils of Isaac were definitely Protestants.[2] The different shades of half-concealed sympathy for Luther among group (b) are well known, although they may not always be as conclusive as in Senfl's case.

The religious ambiguity of the church music of both groups is due to the fact that the Lutheran Church continued to use Latin Kyries and Glorias, and often Latin settings of the *Credo* and *Agnus*, as well as Latin motets and Magnificats; consequently a great deal of service music was interchangeable in use. German-born composers of both faiths throughout the greater part of the sixteenth century published their religious music in an interconfessional atmosphere.[3] Each member of the second group at some time entertained relations with leaders of the Lutheran movement, yet apparently without forfeiting his position as a composer for the Roman rite. This seems to have been notably the case of Arnold von Bruck who—although an ordained priest at Laibach (Ljubljana) and Court *Kapellmeister* of the bigoted Emperor Ferdinand I from at least 1527—could with apparent impunity compose polyphonic settings of some of Luther's most celebrated songs, published in 1534 by Ott and in 1544 by Rhaw, both open supporters of Luther.[4] Georg Rhaw's famous collection *Newe deudsche geistliche Gesenge* (Wittenberg, 1544)[5] contains, side by side,

---

[1] On problematic points in Stoltzer's life, see Lothar Hoffmann-Erbrecht, *Thomas Stoltzer: Leben und Schaffen* (Kassel, 1964).

[2] The fourth—Resinarius—was originally a Catholic but turned Lutheran and became minister at Böhmisch-Leipa (Česká-Lipá) in 1534. He had had no connexions with the Hussites, as has been suggested: cf. Inge-Marie Schröder, *Die Responsorienvertonungen des Balthasar Resinarius* (Kassel, 1953), pp. 16–17, 43 *et passim*.

[3] Cf. Blume, op. cit., pp. 46 ff., 61 ff.   [4] Cf. ibid., p. 47.

[5] Reprinted by Johannes Wolf, *Denkmäler deutscher Tonkunst*, xxxiv (Leipzig, 1908).

settings by Catholics such as Isaac, Finck, Stoltzer, and Resinarius and compositions by such belligerent Protestants as Ducis and Dietrich. This remarkable lack of religious prejudice marked also the choice of texts. In the latter half of the century Protestants still wrote many motets with Latin texts, and some Catholics (including Lassus himself) set Lutheran texts.[1]

SIXTUS DIETRICH

A native of Augsburg, Sixtus Dietrich[2] was educated in the choir school at Constance and at the universities of Freiburg in Breisgau and Strasbourg. In 1517 he was appointed prefect of the choir of Constance Cathedral where he came at once into contact with Protestant ideas; he fully shared the struggle of the cathedral chapter in favour of Zwinglian Protestantism. He became an open and militant Protestant and died at St. Gall (21 October 1548), fleeing from the approaching army of Charles V.[3] Although one of the most prominent Lutheran composers, he also entertained relations with the humanist Bonifacius Amerbach and with the Swiss reformer Zwingli, whose poems he set to music. He was also a friend of Glareanus, to whose *Dodecachordon* he contributed. Dietrich's music consists chiefly of *canto fermo* settings in the great Netherland tradition. We have no setting of the Ordinary of the Mass by him, but a number of his works are still related to the Roman liturgy.[4] That links with the world of Josquin and Isaac had not yet snapped is shown by the quotation of 'L'homme armé' in the *Magnificat VII toni*. Flemish polyphony had ceased to be an artistic conviction for Dietrich and his generation, but it was still cherished as a tradition.[5]

BENEDICTUS DUCIS AND ADAM RENER

Ducis, Rener, and Resinarius all began their careers as choristers in the court chapel of Maximilian I, directed by Isaac. Benedictus Ducis[6] (*c.* 1480–1544) was a militant Protestant like Sixtus Dietrich,

---

[1] Reese, op. cit., p. 685. Hans Leo Hassler wrote such motets as late as 1600.

[2] See Hermann Zenck's study, *Sixtus Dietrich* (Leipzig, 1928).

[3] Cf. Blume, op. cit., pp. 47 ff. and Zenck, op. cit.

[4] His Magnificats were published at Strasbourg in 1535 and 1537; the hymns of his *Novum opus musicum* (Wittenberg, 1545) have been reprinted by Zenck partially in *Das Erbe deutscher Musik*, xxiii (Leipzig, 1942), and complete (St. Louis, 1960), the antiphons by Walter Buszin (Kassel, 1964).

[5] On Dietrich's German church music, see p. 434.

[6] A Latinized form of Duch, not 'Herzog'. See Hans Albrecht, 'Benedictus Ducis', *Die Musik in Geschichte und Gegenwart*, iii, col. 858. On Ducis further, see p. 433.

but evidently a less forceful character. At one time he was believed to be identical with two other composers, Benedictus Appenzeller and Benedictus de Opitiis, but more recent research has exploded these theories.[1] It seems almost certain that he was a German from the neighbourhood of Constance. This is also borne out by his contacts with Isaac and his pupils and by his composition of whole cycles of the Proper of the Mass (evidently taking his cue from Isaac's *Choralis Constantinus* and from Dietrich's cycles of antiphons and hymns). Much of his music is lost[2] and the little that has become accessible in modern reprints does not include his Latin church music.

Even less is known about Adam Rener, who seems to have been a chorister of the Imperial Chapel at Innsbruck around 1498 and may have received his first musical instruction in the company of both Dietrich and Ducis. He was born at Liège between 1480 and 1485 and was attached to the Imperial court at Augsburg in 1503 as court composer. After that he was appointed director of the *Cantorei* at Torgau (1507–20) during the reign of Frederick the Wise, Elector of Saxony, as successor to Adam of Fulda. This appointment suggests that Rener may have become a Protestant in later years. Nevertheless he composed numerous Masses, motets, and Magnificats, one of which has become famous;[3] some of them were published by Rhaw in the 1540's. As the author of most of the ninety-three *Proprium* compositions of Jena Universitätsbibl. 33 (see p. 254, n. 2) he anticipates the style, aims, and liturgical connotations of Isaac's *Choralis Constantinus*.[4] A *missa parodia* of his, based on Josquin's 'Adieu mes amours', was published by Rhaw in his *Opus decem Missarum* of 1541.[5] The fact that the *canti fermi* in Rener's *Proprium* collection lie in the treble links him stylistically with Dietrich and Ducis.

RESINARIUS (HARZER)

Another presumed pupil of Isaac and one-time colleague of Dietrich, Ducis, and Rener, was Balthasar Resinarius (*c.* 1480–after 1549)

[1] Cf. Albrecht, op. cit. and Dénes Bartha, *Benedictus Ducis und Appenzeller* (Wolfenbüttel, 1930).

[2] Among it the *Proprium* cycles which at one time had been lodged in the Heidelberg court chapel to which Ducis may have been attached *c.* 1522.

[3] See T. W. Werner, 'Die Magnificat-Kompositionen Adam Reners', *Archiv für Musikwissenschaft*, ii (1920), p. 195.

[4] Cf. Lipphardt, op. cit., p. 34.

[5] Cf. Willi Schulze, *Die mehrstimmige Messe im frühprotestantischen Gottesdienst* (Wolfenbüttel, 1940), p. 23.

or Harzer. His most important contribution to Latin church music of undeniable Roman associations is his *Responsorium Numero octoginta*,[1] published in 1543 by Rhaw with a typically Lutheran commentary. The same publisher had issued during 1540–4 a whole series of music for Vespers, beginning with the *Vesperarum precum officia* of 1540; and Resinarius also appeared here, in the *Hymnorum sacr. Lib. I* (1542), though this time under his German name, 'Harzer'. The collection contains so many hymn texts rejected by the Lutheran Church that Rhaw felt obliged to explain that he had included them not because of their texts but because of their beautiful music.[2] Resinarius's *Responsorium* contains a *Summa Passionis*, a 'motet-Passion' in the manner of Longueval's.[3]

HÄHNEL, BRUCK, AND MAHU

Among the lesser lights of this generation of Isaac's pupils who seem to have specialized in the composition of Latin church music (even if published by the Lutheran, Rhaw) were Johannes Galliculus (= Hähnel, alias Alectorius) and Stephan Mahu. Galliculus (born *c.* 1490; *fl.* 1520–55) composed two Latin but Protestant Easter Masses *a* 4, each containing Introit, *Kyrie*, *Gloria*, Alleluia, and the Easter sequence 'Agnus redemit oves' (from 'Victimae paschali laudes'), *Evangelium*, *Sanctus*, *Agnus*, *Communio*.[4] The first[5] was published by Rhaw in his *Officia paschalia* of 1539. *Kyrie*, *Gloria* and the *Proprium* pieces are based on plainsong melodies, either as long-note *canti fermi* or treated freely and imitatively; but the melody and German words of the chorale 'Christ ist erstanden' are woven into the 'Prosa de Resurrectione' as tenor and, later, ostinato bass, and again quoted in the *Agnus Dei*: a telling aural symbol of the ambivalent position in which such composers as Hähnel found themselves:

[1] Modern edition in two volumes by Inge-Maria Schröder, *Georg Rhau: Musikdrucke*, i and ii (Kassel and Basle, 1955 and 1957).

[2] Cf. Blume, op. cit., p. 64.

[3] See Vol. III, p. 276. Resinarius's Passion is described in Kade, *Die ältere Passionskompositionen bis zum Jahre 1631* (Gütersloh, 1893), p. 23; it has been reprinted by Blume and Schulze, *Das Chorwerk*, xlvii (Wolfenbüttel, 1937). For Resinarius's Protestant compositions, see p. 432.

[4] Cf. Blume, op. cit., p. 63. Only *Credo*, Gradual, Offertorium, and part of the *Gloria* are missing; otherwise it would make a complete Roman Mass. Cf. Albrecht, article 'Galliculus', *Die Musik in Geschichte und Gegenwart*, iv, col. 1293.

[5] Reprinted by Blume and Schulze, *Das Chorwerk*, xliv (Wolfenbüttel, 1936). Cf. also Schulze, *Die mehrstimmige Messe*, pp. 58 ff; Lipphardt, op. cit., p. 50; Reese, op. cit., p. 681.

Ex. 97

A much more important composer than Galliculus was Arnold von Bruck (Arnoldus de Bruck), who served for many years in the Imperial Chapel of Ferdinand I at Vienna.[1] But although he was probably a Catholic and a master hardly inferior to Senfl or Stoltzer, he composed remarkably little for the Roman rite.[2] Not a single Mass by him has come down to us, but we have from him one of the earliest polyphonic settings of 'Dies irae', a four-part composition preserved in Munich, Bay. Staatsbibl. Mus. 47, beside Pierre de la Rue's 'Missa pro defunctis' (see Vol. III, p. 289):[3]

Ex. 98

[1] See Albrecht, article 'Arnold von Bruck', *Die Musik in Geschichte und Gegenwart*, col. 660, for the problems of his biography.

[2] On his Protestant compositions see p. 433.

[3] Quoted from P. Wagner, op. cit., who gives a substantial excerpt, pp. 313–17.

It is difficult to determine the exact relationship of Stephan Mahu to the cause of Protestantism. He can hardly have been a professing Protestant,[1] although the fact that his works were published by Ott and Rhaw and the choice of some of his texts suggest that he may have been secretly in sympathy with the new faith. Very few of Mahu's motets, Lamentations, or Magnificats have been reprinted.[2] Stylistically he stands between Arnold von Bruck and Resinarius.

THOMAS STOLTZER

Next to Senfl, the most talented German composer of his generation was Thomas Stoltzer, court *Kapellmeister* to the King of Hungary (1522–26). Stoltzer was for the Hungary of the early sixteenth century what Heinrich Finck had been for the Poland of the late fifteenth.[3] His relation to the religious cleavage is not easy to determine; he may have remained a professing Catholic all his life, but it is nevertheless a fact that he composed in 1526, the year of the disastrous battle of Mohács (in which it is commonly believed that he himself perished) psalms in Luther's translation. One of them, Psalm 37, was composed for Duke Albrecht of Prussia, on the suggestion of the

---

[1] Mahu must have been a Catholic while he occupied the posts of trombonist and *Vizekapellmeister* at the Court of Ferdinand I between approximately the years 1528 and 1540: cf. Hellmut Federhofer, 'Biographische Beiträge zu Erasmus Lapicida und Stephan Mahu', *Die Musikforschung*, v (1952), p. 37.

[2] The only easily accessible example of his Latin church music is the motet 'Accessit ad pedes', from Rhaw's *Symphoniae jucundae* (1538), in Schering, op. cit., p. 105.

[3] See Vol. III, p. 286. Fresh biographical information is given by Hoffmann-Erbrecht, op. cit.

Queen of Hungary, and Stoltzer's letter accompanying this composition is the only personal document we have.[1] It is particularly
interesting because in it the composer points out that in composing
it he had thought of the 'Khrumphörner':[2] an indication that much
of the polyphony of this period was probably meant to be executed
partly or wholly with instrumental support. Of Stoltzer's Latin
church music, only a little of which is available in modern reprints,[3]
special mention should be made of the antiphon 'Admirabile commercium'[4] as one of his most felicitous works; also of the plainsong
Masses (Missale 1543, Königsberg MSS. 1968) of which the second
and third are headed 'Duplex per totum annum St. Thomas Stoltzer'.[5]
This Latin church music of Stoltzer's is more austere and linear-
polyphonic than his music based on German words; it is stylistically
related to Isaac and Finck.

Stoltzer was also drawn on by Rhaw in his *Hymnorum sacr. lib. I*
of 1542, which contains thirty-seven hymns by him. His motets and
Latin psalms were published between 1538 and 1569.

VAET, REGNART, AND BUUS

After the generation of Isaac's pupils, Catholic church music in
central Europe was dominated by the giant figure of Lassus at the
ducal court of Bavaria, from 1556 onward, and that of de Monte at
the Imperial Court in Vienna or Prague from 1568. The work of these
very great masters is discussed separately in a later chapter,[6] but their
stature should not distract attention completely from the other distinguished musicians who served the Habsburgs and the princes of the
Empire—mostly Franco-Flemings, like Lassus and de Monte, but
including also native composers such as Aichinger and Blasius Amon.

Arnold von Bruck's successor as *Hofkapellmeister* to Ferdinand I
was a colourful character but mediocre and unprolific composer
named Pieter Maessins (Massenus),[7] who had served Charles V as a

---

[1] Reprinted by Otto Gombosi in his preface to *Das Chorwerk*, vi (Wolfenbüttel,
2nd ed., 1953).

[2] Krummhorns: see p. 740.

[3] *Thomas Stoltzer: Sämtliche lateinische Hymnen und Psalmen* (ed. Albrecht and Gombosi), *Denkmäler deutscher Tonkunst*, lxv (Leipzig, 1931); *Thomas Stoltzer: Ausgewählte Werke* (ed. Albrecht), *Das Erbe deutscher Musik*, xxii (Leipzig, 1942); *Missa
paschalis* (ed. Hoffmann-Erbrecht), *Das Chorwerk*, lxxiv (Wolfenbüttel, 1958.)

[4] *Das Erbe deutscher Musik*, xxii, no. 12.

[5] Cf. Schulze, *Die mehrstimmige Messe*, pp. 50 ff.

[6] See pp. 333 ff. and 350 ff.

[7] Othmar Wessely, article 'Maessins', *Die Musik in Geschichte und Gegenwart*, viii,
col. 1466.

condottiere before serving his brother as a musician. He held the post from 1546 probably till his death in 1563, and was succeeded for a short while by Jean Guyot de Chatelet and then by a much more distinguished figure, Jacob Vaet, who died in the prime of life on 8 January 1567 and was followed the next year by de Monte. A native and choirboy of Courtrai, where Maessins had been the drunken, neglectful, and duelling master of the choristers for two or three years (1540–3), Vaet seems to have been recruited by his old master for the service of the Habsburgs in 1553.[1] After some years in the court chapel at Prague under Maximilian he was appointed *Obrister Kapellmeister* of the Imperial Chapel in Vienna on 1 December 1564. His eminence is underlined by the fact that his death was commemorated in three notable elegies, one of which, 'Defunctum charites Vaetem moerore requirunt', was composed by his pupil Jacob (or Jacques) Regnart.

As has been shown in an earlier section,[2] Vaet represents with special clarity the development of the Netherland technique after Gombert. And he made one major essay in the double-choir technique of the Venetians: his *Te Deum* for double choir, possibly composed shortly before his death and published posthumously in Pietro Giovanelli's *Novus thesaurus musicus* (Venice, 1568).

An interesting feature of Vaet's motets[3] is the occasional employment of the technique of 'parody'; thus one of his settings of 'Salve Regina' was composed 'Ad imitationem iay mys mon coeur' and his 'Huc me sidereo', 'Justus germinabit', and 'Aspice Domine' 'are parodies of like-named compositions by Josquin des Prés, Eustatius Barbion, and Jachet de Mantua respectively'.[4] Most of his nine Masses are likewise 'parodies' on sacred or secular models by Mouton, Clemens non Papa, Lassus, Créquillon, and himself.

Vaet's friend Jacob Regnart (c. 1540–99), one of a Douai family of five musical brothers, held various posts in the court chapels at Innsbruck, Prague, and Vienna. He was best known for his secular songs, such as the *Kurtzweilige teutsche Lieder nach Art der Neapolitanen oder welschen Villanellen*,[5] but he was a copious composer of church music. His 150 motets were published as *Sacrae cantiones* (1575 and 1577), *Mariale* (a collection of Marian motets), and in a

---

[1] Milton Steinhardt, *Jacobus Vaet and his Motets* (East Lansing, Mich., 1951), p. 4.
[2] See p. 234.
[3] Modern editions include six motets edited by E. H. Meyer, *Das Chorwerk*, ii, three printed complete in Steinhardt, op. cit., two hymns (ed. Steinhardt), *Musik alter Meister*, viii (Graz, 1958), and 'Rex Babylonis' (with the *missa parodia* on it by Johannes de Cleve), ibid. xii (Graz, 1960). The reprints in Commer, *Collectio operum musicorum Batavorum* (Berlin, 1844–58), are unreliable.
[4] Steinhardt, *Jacobus Vaet*, pp. 56–57.   [5] See p. 107.

third book of *Sacrae cantiones* prepared by his widow, who also published three books containing twenty-nine of his Masses, some of which are based on German popular songs.

Another Flemish musician in the Imperial service at this period was Jacques Buus (Bohusius), court organist at Vienna from 1551 till his death *c*. 1564. Buus was essentially an instrumental composer,[1] but he published a number of motets as well as secular vocal music. However, as an associate of Willaert's in Venice and first organist at St. Mark's from 1541 to 1550, he may be more appropriately considered in a later section.[2]

JOHANNES DE CLEVE

Of the same age as Vaet was Johannes de Cleve who was born *c*. 1529, probably at Cleve, near the Dutch frontier, and who died on 14 July 1582 at Augsburg.[3] He was active in Vienna, Graz, and Augsburg. Cleve's reputation is chiefly based on his Masses, which (like de Monte's)[4] represent a late flowering of the *missa parodia* at the very end of the polyphonic period. Two of these Masses, the six-part 'Dum transisset sabbatum' and the five-part 'Tribulatio et angustia',[5] are based on Responsories of his own. The four-part *chanson* Mass on Claudin de Sermisy's 'Vous perdes temps',[6] though more homophonic, similarly testifies to the conservatism of this composer whose music harks back to the days of Josquin and Pierre de la Rue, without, however, rivalling their contrapuntal ingenuity or melodic inventiveness.

Cleve's motets,[7] which follow in the wake of Vaet, like his Masses, express an evident desire to capture the stylistic conditions and austere atmosphere of earlier Flemish polyphony. Outstanding among them are the eight-part 'Erravi sicut ovis', the five-part 'Domine Jesu Christe' and 'Domine clamavi' and the four-part 'In nomine Jesu'

[1] See pp. 552 and 603.
[2] See pp. 292–3.
[3] Cf. Osthoff, article 'de Cleve', *Die Musik in Geschichte und Gegenwart*, ii, col. 1504.
[4] See pp. 355 ff.
[5] Reprinted in Maldeghem, *Trésor musical* for 1878, p. 15, and 1879, p. 3 respectively. Peter Wagner, *Geschichte der Messe* (Leipzig, 1913), pp. 209 ff., gives an interesting analysis of Cleve's peculiar parody technique.
[6] Reprinted by Federhofer, *Musik alter Meister*, i (Graz and Vienna, 1949). See also Federhofer, 'Zur Neuausgabe der vierstimmigen A cappella-Messe "Vous perdes temps" von Johannes de Cleve', *Aus Archiv und Chronik (Blätter für Seckauer Diözesangeschichte)* ii (1949), p. 52.
[7] See Leichtentritt, *Geschichte der Motette* (Leipzig, 1908), pp. 90 ff. Cleve's first two books of *Cantiones sacrae* (1559) were reprinted complete by Maldeghem, *Trésor musical* (1865–80).

and 'Filiae Jerusalem', the opening of which may be quoted as typical:

Ex.99

The treble entry on 'filiae' at the end of the quotation is the beginning of a statement of the theme in augmentation.

CHARLES LUYTHON

The Antwerp-born Charles Luython (Luthon, Leuthon, Luyton) (*c.* 1557–1620) belongs to the next generation. He studied in Vienna under Vaet and de Monte, and spent his life chiefly in the service of Maximilian II (1576–7) and Rudolf II (1577–1612). He was appointed third court organist at Prague on 1 January 1582, succeeded de Monte as court composer in 1593, became first organist there on 30 June 1596, and was finally dismissed with his colleagues in 1612 on the death of Rudolf. Luython was distinguished as a composer of Masses (six preserved, five reprinted by Commer), three of which[1] belong to

[1] *Musica sacra*, xvii (1877) and xix (1878).

the curious genre of the *missa quodlibetica*. Vaet also composed a *Missa quodlibetica cum quinque vocibus*[1] and a still earlier example is Isaac's 'Missa Carminum' (see Vol. III, p. 281). But according to Schletter's catalogue of the City Library of Augsburg[2] two of these Masses are based on Italian madrigals, 'Amorosi pensieri' and 'Tirsi morir volea', and Peter Wagner,[3] who quotes the complete first Kyries of all three, shows that they all appear to be straightforward 'parody' Masses; he also draws attention to their brevity and compression. Wagner believed that these *Missae quodlibeticae*—two in four parts, the third in only three—were deliberately written in a simple style and designed for modest choral conditions, or alternatively that this simplicity indicates the beginning of decadence from a higher artistic ideal. It is possible that the type of *missa quodlibetica* presented here may anticipate the *missa brevis* (with its telescoping of liturgical text and its grotesque simultaneity of different lines of text) which became so popular in the church music of the Austrian provinces in the mid-eighteenth century.

Luython's Masses, including the ones just discussed, were first published in 1609 by Nikolaus Strauss in Prague. Their music is of remarkable nobility and technical finish, but conservative in its Palestrinian idiom. It is the music of a latecomer on the scene who managed to remain untouched by *basso continuo* technique or the harmonic innovations of the generation of Marenzio and Monteverdi, although as an organist he did not remain untouched by progressive tendencies, and his 'Fuga suavissima' on three themes[4] is not unworthy to be compared with similar experiments by Sweelinck and Frescobaldi. He also possessed an *archicembalo* (mentioned by Michael Praetorius in his *Syntagma*) with special keys for sharps and flats.

As a prolific composer of motets,[5] most of them in six parts (Prague, 1603), he remained—as in his Masses—intrinsically a traditionalist, occasionally influenced by the homophonic tendencies of the post-Palestrinian Italians. Among his best-known ecclesiastical compositions are his *Lamentationes* (Prague, 1604).

NATIVE GERMAN COMPOSERS

The native composers of the Empire at this period seem specially linked with Italy. Gregor Aichinger (1564–1628) in his youth studied in Venice with Giovanni Gabrieli, and Blasius Amon (*c.* 1560–90) may

---

[1] Nuremberg, Lorenzkirche Bibl., MS. sign. 227 (dated 3 September 1573).
[2] Berlin, 1878: supplement to *Monatshefte für Musikgeschichte*, x and xi.
[3] Op. cit., pp. 230–7.   [4] See p. 657.
[5] See Albert Smijers, *Karl Luython als Motettenkomponist* (Amsterdam, 1923).

have been a pupil of Andrea; their liturgical music clearly shows the influence of contemporary Italian methods of choral polyphony. Born at Ratisbon, Aichinger spent most of his life in the service of the Fuggers at Augsburg. He was one of the first German composers to adopt the *basso continuo*:[1] in his *Cantiones ecclesiasticae* (Dillingen, 1607). His earlier works are related on the one hand to the Italians, on the other to Lassus. His beautifully clear textures are illustrated by his five-part 'Maria uns tröst'[2] which he contributed to a set of thirty-three pieces by various composers—including Hassler, Erbach, Regnart, and Luython—on the same musical theme, set by the Augsburg *Kapellmeister* Bernhard Klingenstein (1545–1614) and published by him in 1604 under the title *Rosetum Marianum*.

Blasius Amon seems to have been the first German composer to adopt the technique of *cori spezzati* in his ecclesiastical music.[3] A Tyrolese by birth, Amon had a typically Austrian career. He was a member of the court chapel of Archduke Ferdinand I at Innsbruck, and joined the Franciscan monks there in 1578, becoming cantor of the Cistercians of the Heiligenkreuz Monastery in 1585. In 1587 he entered the Franciscan monastery in Vienna. Perhaps his most significant publication is the *Sacrae cantiones* (Munich, 1590) which contains both motets for double chorus in the Gabrieli manner and motets in which six parts are manipulated so as to give an impression of two four-part choirs. Even the earlier *Liber cantionum* (Vienna, 1582)[4] shows Venetian influence in its harmonic, rather than linear, writing. Organ tablatures of some of Amon's choral compositions, preserved in manuscript,[5] indicate that they must have been accompanied on the organ. When Johannes Donfried included works by Amon in his *Promptuarium musicum*, iii (Strasbourg, 1627), he added *continuo* parts. In Amon's four-part Masses (Vienna, 1588), the predilection for writing in few parts suggests a relationship with the *Missae quodlibeticae* of Luython.

---

[1] See *infra*, p. 545.

[2] Edited by Joseph Funk in the series *Musica orans*, xxiv (München-Gladbach, n.d.), Aichinger's 'Missa paschalis', ibid. xxiii. A quantity of Aichinger's church music has been reprinted, notably in Proske, *Musica divina*, ii, iii, and iv (Ratisbon, 1855–63), Commer, *Musica sacra*, xvi (1875) and xxviii (1887), and Theodor Kroyer, *Denkmäler der Tonkunst in Bayern*, x (1) (Leipzig, 1909). Aichinger's four-part 'Factus est' is easily accessible in Davison and Apel, op. cit. i, p. 188.

[3] See Arnold Geering, article 'Amon', *Die Musik in Geschichte und Gegenwart*, i, col. 429, and Coecilianus Huigens, 'Blasius Amon', *Studien zur Musikwissenschaft*, xviii (Vienna, 1931), p. 3.

[4] Both these volumes reprinted by Huigens, *Denkmäler der Tonkunst in Oesterreich*, xxxviii (1) (Vienna, 1931).

[5] Munich, Bay. Staatsbibl. Mus. 263; Vienna, Minoritenkloster, Mus. 8.

JACOBUS DE KERLE

Another important musician, active at Augsburg and Prague, was Jacobus de Kerle, whose affinities are with Palestrina and the Roman school. De Kerle was born *c.* 1532 at Ypres and died on 7 January 1591 at Prague. He went early to Italy, was appointed *magister cappellae* at Orvieto in 1555, and published hymns and Vesper psalms (Rome, 1558) and Magnificats (Venice, 1561). In 1562 in Rome he entered the service of the Bishop of Augsburg, Cardinal Otto Truchsess von Waldburg, whom he eventually accompanied to Germany and Spain. In 1582 he entered the Emperor's service and finally held the position of court chaplain to Rudolf II at Prague until his death.

Through his connexion with Cardinal Truchsess von Waldburg he became involved in the activities of the Council of Trent.[1] Although not yet director of the Cardinal's private chapel, he was already commissioned by him in the autumn of 1561 to compose for the Council his famous *Preces speciales*[2] (Venice, 1562), which were repeatedly performed at Trent and influenced the decision to permit the continued use of polyphony in church music, albeit in simpler form and with special emphasis on clarity of declamation. The ten *Preces* are responsorially constructed prayers, each closing with doxology and *Kyrie*. The music shows a striking similarity to certain deliberately simple Masses and motets by Palestrina, as may be seen from the opening of no. 6, 'Pro remissione peccatorum':

Ex. 100

[1] See pp. 250 and 317.
[2] Reprinted by Otto Ursprung, *Denkmäler der Tonkunst in Bayern*, xxxiv (Jg. 26) (Augsburg, 1926). See also Ursprung, *Die katholische Kirchenmusik* (Potsdam, 1931), pp. 184–5, and *Jacobus de Kerle. Sein Leben und seine Werke* (Munich, 1913).

Kerle's Mass 'Regina coeli'[1] (for two tenors and two basses), with its passages of simple homophony such as the following:

Ex. 101

in a style intent on clarity of declamation and subservience to the liturgical words, was in Ursprung's opinion probably the earliest 'reform-Mass', composed after the *Preces*, whereas the rest of the *Sex Missae* (Venice, 1562) must have preceded them. As Peter Wagner points out,[2] Kerle's other Masses reveal old stylistic traits as well as 'reforming' tendencies. Among these the four-part Mass on the hexachord theme 'Ut re mi fa sol la'[3] certainly shows strong links with the style of the old Flemish Mass, particularly in the *Kyrie* and *Agnus*. In all the other Masses plainsong themes are used. Yet the simplification of polyphony and the insistence on verbal clarity clearly anticipate the style of Palestrina's 'reform' Masses, such as the 'Missa Papae Marcelli' which was probably composed in the winter of

---

[1] Maldeghem, *Trésor*, xxiii (1887).
[2] Op. cit., pp. 212 ff.
[3] Maldeghem, op. cit. xxiv (1888).

1562–3[1] and, if so, is antedated by Kerle's work by a whole year. In that case, the title of 'Saviour of Church Music', awarded to Palestrina for several centuries, should be transferred to Kerle.

Kerle's 'Responsoria' and hymns as well as his motets are notable for similar qualities of style. Outstanding among the motets is 'Exsurge', in two sections,[2] in which the predilection for parallel chords of the sixth reminds one of Palestrina. The splendid eight-part 'Si consurrexit' ends with actual double-choral writing.

'HANDL, GALLUS VOCATUS'

One of the most interesting Austrian composers of the end of the century was 'Jacobus Handl, Gallus vocatus, Carniolanus' as he calls himself in the prefaces to his four books of Masses (Prague, 1580). Born in 1550, he was a member of the Imperial Chapel in Vienna in 1574 and *Kapellmeister* to the Bishop of Olmütz (Olomouc) from 1579 to 1585 when he went to Prague. There he remained, as cantor in the church of St. Johannis in Vado, till his death in 1591.

Handl is a strikingly individual figure, yet at the same time very characteristic of his period. As Paul Pisk has put it,[3] his technique is 'a completely individual fusion of the Netherland style with the Venetian'. His employment of double choirs is Venetian; his preference for major-minor tonality to the modes and his occasional boldly expressive chromaticism stamp him as 'baroque', and as such he will be referred to in a later chapter.[4] Yet he also looks back to much earlier practices. Nearly all his Masses are *missae parodiae*[5] and the models include not only motets, five of them his own, but German songs, Créquillon's 'Ungaybergir' (as he spells it), and madrigals. Some are *missae breves*, sometimes almost as melodious and perfunctory as the earlier French *chanson*-Masses[6]—the first *Kyrie* of his Mass on Lassus's 'Im Mayen' is just four bars long—but really closer, as Peter Wagner says, to Luython's *missae quodlibeticae*. And he employs the Netherland devices of a hundred years before: in the 'Pleni' of his

---

[1] See Knud Jeppesen, 'Marcellus-Probleme', *Acta Musicologica*, xvi–xvii (1944–5), p. 11, but particularly pp. 34–38.

[2] Reprinted by Proske, *Musica Divina*, Annus I, ii (1854), p. 88; second section in Davison and Apel, op. cit., p. 163.

[3] Preface to *Jakob Handl (Gallus): Sechs Messen, Denkmäler der Tonkunst in Oesterreich*, xlii. 1 (Vienna, 1935), p. iv.

[4] See p. 545.

[5] See Peter Wagner, op. cit., ff. 330–41, and Paul Pisk, 'Das Parodieverfahren in den Messen des Jacobus Gallus', *Studien zur Musikwissenschaft*, v (Leipzig and Vienna, 1918), p. 35.

[6] See *supra*, pp. 239–40.

six-part Mass 'Elisabeth Zachariae' he develops three parts out of one marked 'Trinitatem in unitate veneremur'.

More important than Handl's Masses are his motets,[1] above all the collection of 374, for the entire liturgical year, in the four volumes of his *Opus musicum* (Prague, 1586–91).[2] These range from the simplest four-part chordal pieces, such as the lovely arrangements of 'Resonet in laudibus'[3] and the well-known 'Ecce quomodo'[4] to psalm-settings for twenty-four voices (in four choirs), but between these extremes lie a great number of four- and five-part pieces of normal 'late Netherland' polyphony.

(d) THE VENETIAN SCHOOL

By H. F. REDLICH

BEGINNINGS OF THE VENETIAN SCHOOL

It was only at the outset of the cinquecento that Venice became one of the musical nerve-centres of northern Italy. Although San Marco had been completed by 827, it was only *c.* 1312 that a large organ was installed[5] and in 1316 that the appointment of an organist (one Zucchetto) was recorded.[6] Nearly a hundred years later still—in 1403 —a singing school was founded. Organ and choir became the natural media for the special devotional music composed by the later so-called 'Venetian school' of the seicento.

Approximately in 1470 organ pedals were installed and *c.* 1490 a second organ with pedals was built by the Venetian Fra Urbano. Starting with 20 August 1490, a 'second organist' was regularly appointed at St. Mark's,[7] the first being Francesco d'Ana (died

---

[1] On Handl's motets, see Leichtentritt, op. cit., pp. 290–7, and Edward W. Naylor, 'Jacob Handl (Gallus) as Romanticist', *Sammelbände der internationalen Musikgesellschaft*, xi (1909), p. 42; also Dragotin Cvetko, *Gallus, Plautzius, Dolar et leur œuvre* (Ljubljana, 1963).

[2] Reprinted by E. Bezecny and J. Mantuani, *Denkmäler der Tonkunst in Oesterreich*, vi (1); xii (1); xx (1); xxiv; xxvi (1899–1919); many of Handl's motets are published separately by Bank (Amsterdam). See also *infra*, p. 545.

[3] Various modern reprints.

[4] Often reprinted, e.g. in Davison and Apel, op. cit. i, p. 174.

[5] See Vol. III, p. 34.

[6] *Istituzioni e monumenti dell'arte musicale italiana*, i (1931), p. xix.

[7] Lists of the organists are given by Carl von Winterfeld, *Johannes Gabrieli und sein Zeitalter* (Berlin, 1834), i, pp. 198–9, and Fr. Caffi, *Storia della musica sacra nella già cappella ducale di San Marco in Venezia dal 1318 al 1797* (Venice, 1855; facsimile reprint, Milan, 1931), pp. 53–55. See also *Istituzioni*, i, pp. xxxix and lxiv.

c. 1502–3) who had earlier been organist of San Leonardo in Venice. He was an early frottolist whom Einstein calls 'the only Venetian musician of any importance as a productive artist'.[1] A 'Passio sacra' of his was printed by Petrucci after 1501.[2]

Petrucci's activity as a music-printer naturally gave a great impetus to musical production in Venice from 1501 to 1511, when he transferred his business to his birthplace, Fossombrone, near Ancona, and his printing works in Venice was taken over by Scotto and Niccolo de Raffael. After the death of Pope Leo X (1521) and still more after the sack of Rome (1527), Venice—though past her political prime—became ever more important as a centre of European music. After the catastrophe, Rome gradually became 'more a centre of church music, while in Venice even church music takes on a secular colouring'.[3] It is typical that Verdelot, who was a singer at St. Mark's—Vasari actually says *maestro di cappella*,[4] though this cannot be correct—in the early part of the century, is famous as a madrigalist while his church music[5] lies in oblivion.

It was at this period—the late 1520's—that the greatest personality in the history of Venetian music first entered the city: Adrian Willaert.

WILLAERT AND THE *CORO SPEZZATO*

For many years Willaert was regarded as the chief founder, if not the actual inventor, of the technique of so-called *coro spezzato* or *coro battente* which became the chief characteristic of Venetian church music of the seicento. However, research has shown that Willaert, in his famous *Salmi spezzati* of 1550, only perfected an already existing choral practice, especially at home in northern Italy.[6] The

---

[1] *The Italian Madrigal* (Princeton, 1949), i, p. 41.
[2] Two motets by him are reprinted in Torchi, *L'arte musicale in Italia*, i, pp. 13 and 17.
[3] Einstein, op. cit. i, p. 319.
[4] Ibid., p. 155.
[5] On Verdelot's church music, see Ambros, iii, pp. 293–4. Some of his motets have been reprinted by Maldeghem, *Trésor musical*, ii, xxiii, and xxviii, and by Smijers and A. Tillman Merritt in their edition of *Treize Livres de motets parus chez Pierre Attaingnant*, i, ii, iii, iv, x, xi (Paris, 1934–63).
[6] Cf. Hermann Zenck, 'Adrian Willaerts "Salmi spezzati" (1550)', *Die Musikforschung*, ii (1949), p. 97; Giovanni d'Alessi, 'Precursors of Adriano Willaert in the practice of *Coro spezzato*', *Journal of the American Musicological Society*, v (1952), p. 187; Manfred Bukofzer, *Studies in Medieval and Renaissance Music* (New York, 1950), pp. 180 ff. Bukofzer refers here to two MSS. (Modena, Bibl. Estense, a. M I. 11–12, *olim* lat. 454–5) dating from the middle of the fifteenth century, that 'call for two choirs which sing, polyphonically, alternate stanzas of the hymns or alternate lines of the psalms'.

original title of the *Salmi* is as follows: *Di Adriano et di Jachet i Salmi Apertinenti Alli Vesperi Per tutte le Feste Dell'anno, Parte a versi, et parte spezzadi* [sic], *Accomodati da cantare a uno et duoi Chori, Novamente posti in luce et par Antonio Gardane con ogni Diligentia ristampati et Corretti in Venetia Appresso di Antonio Gardane 1557.* The collection, which includes compositions by Phinot, Giovanni Nasco ('Maistre Jhan'), and Heinrich Scaffen, in addition to the psalms by Willaert and Jachet (da Mantova) to which the title refers, contains three different types of antiphonal setting of the psalms:[1]

1. *Salmi spezzati*, i.e. psalms composed for double choir.
2. *Salmi a versi con le sue Risposte*, i.e. psalms in which the separate verses, in four-part settings based on the Gregorian tones, may be sung by one or by two choirs.
3. *Salmi a versi senza Risposte*, i.e. psalms in which monophonic plainsong intonation alternates with simple four-part harmonization of the psalm-tone.

It is the first group, consisting of only eight pieces by Willaert, which earned special fame for its composer and to which Zarlino's description[2]—long misinterpreted—must have referred. They differ essentially from earlier psalm compositions for double chorus by Fra Ruffino Bartolucci d'Assisi (*maestro di cappella* at the Cathedral of Padua from 1510 to 1520) and by his assistant Francesco Santacroce (also called Patavino, i.e. from Padua),[3] which seem to have been composed in 1524 or earlier. While the great Fleming strictly preserves the unity of each psalm verse, his Italian predecessors frequently split up the verse into short dialogue exchanges between both choral groups, regardless of its unity. The excerpts on ff. 278–9 from settings of Psalm 112, 'Laudate pueri',[4] demonstrate the intrinsic difference between Ruffino's vivacious, syllabic, and declamatory choral dialogue, pointing towards the Gabrielis, and Willaert's choral antiphony.

The *Salmi spezzati* were the result of more than twenty years of choral practice at St. Mark's, where Willaert had succeeded to the post

[1] Cf. Zenck, op. cit., p. 98.
[2] *Istitutioni harmoniche* (Venice, 1558), iii, chap. 66. The whole paragraph is quoted in English translation in d'Alessi, op. cit., p. 188.
[3] Excerpts printed by d'Alessi, op. cit. Gustave Reese, *Music in the Renaissance* (London, 1954), p. 285, mentions a Mass 'Verbum bonum', for two four-part choirs, by Ruffino.
[4] Quoted from d'Alessi, op. cit., pp. 196 and 201.

(i) RUFFINO

of *maestro di cappella* on 12 December 1527. (The Doge Andrea
Gritti forced his election upon the Procurators, who favoured Lupato,
the assistant of Willaert's predecessor, the Frenchman Pietro de Ca'
Fossis.)[1] Between Willaert's appointment to St. Mark's and the date
of his death (7 December 1562) lie thirty-five years of impressive
activity, during which he was distinguished not only as director of a
famous ecclesiastical choir, but as a composer of Masses, motets, and
vesper psalms,[2] in addition to his achievements as a composer of
chansons, madrigals, and instrumental music which are discussed elsewhere in this volume.[3]

At the time of his appointment, Willaert (born at Roulers in Flanders or perhaps at Bruges, *c.* 1490, and therefore in his late thirties)
was at the summit of his creative powers and already well acquainted
with musical life in the north of Italy. He was a pupil of Mouton.[4]
After a period of legal study at the University of Paris, Willaert
seems to have gone to Italy by 1518. He may have stayed in Rome[5]
but he was certainly attached to the ducal house of Este in Ferrara
from 1522 to 1525, and subsequently to Cardinal Este at Milan from
1525 to 1527. In the latter year Willaert became *cantor regis Ungariae*,
but a stay of his in Hungary, then mostly in Turkish hands, seems
very unlikely.[6] Apart from a small number of early works, such as
the Mass 'Mente tota' written *c.* 1517, four motets (Bologna, Codex
Rusconi), a St. John Passion, and 'Lamentationes Jeremiae' (both
in Bologna manuscripts), the bulk of Willaert's religious music was
written during his tenure of office in Venice.

WILLAERT'S MASSES

Only nine of Willaert's Masses are known at present, and only one
is available in a modern critical edition.[7] Five four-part Masses are

---

[1] Cf. Einstein, op. cit. i, p. 320.

[2] Yet, according to Gerstenberg in his preface to the *Opera Omnia*, v (Rome, 1957),
Willaert, unlike so many of his colleagues, was never given ecclesiastical status.

[3] See pp. 14, 45, and Chap. XI.

[4] See Vol. III, pp. 297–8.

[5] He certainly composed his famous *duo cromatico*, 'Quidnam ebrietas' for Leo X:
cf. Ambros, *Geschichte der Musik*, iii (Leipzig, 3rd ed., 1893), p. 524, and J. S. Levitan,
'Adrian Willaert's famous Duo, "Quidnam ebrietas"', *Tijdschrift der Vereeniging voor
Nederlandsche Muziekgeschiedenis*, xv (1938), p. 166. The title of this textless piece
appears to be a playful allusion to Horace, *Epistolae*, i. 5. v. 16 and 18.

[6] Cf. Otto Gombosi's review of Erich Hertzmann, *Adrian Willaert in der weltlichen
Vokalmusik seiner Zeit* (Leipzig, 1931) in *Zeitschrift für Musikwissenschaft*, xvi (1934),
p. 54. Gombosi believed that Willaert was for a time a member of the chapel of Ferdinand I, then titular King of Hungary.

[7] The doubtfully authentic 'Benedicta es', edited by Anton Averkamp, *Vereeniging*

preserved in the original Venetian edition of 1536: 'Quaeramus cum pastoribus', 'Gaude Barbara', 'Christus resurgens', 'Laudate Deum', and 'Osculetur me'.[1] Of the other surviving Masses two five-part Masses, 'Benedicta es' and a nameless one, two in six parts—'Mente tota' and 'Mittit ad virgmem'—are preserved in various manuscript sources.[2] They are practically all 'parody' Masses. 'Mente tota' is based on the fifth section of Josquin's motet 'Vultum tuum'; Lenaerts[3] describes its completely canonic construction which, he says, 'moves in a sphere quite different from that of Josquin's motet'. The other six-part Mass, 'Mittit ad virginem', a very late work, is modelled on a motet by Willaert himself.[4] 'Queramus cum pastoribus', 'Laudate Deum', and 'Gaude Barbara' are based on motets by Mouton, 'Christus resurgens' on one possibly by Mouton but more probably by Richafort. The five-part Mass based on Josquin's 'Benedicta es' by either Willaert or Hesdin is preserved in eight manuscripts,[5] of which two give it to Willaert, three to Hesdin, and three are anonymous. The case for ascription to Hesdin was put by Smijers,[6] but Antonowytsch gives it on stylistic evidence to Willaert.[7] It is particularly unfortunate that this is the only Willaert Mass at present available in print.

Antonowytsch's detailed study of 'Benedicta es', of which the Hertogenbosch manuscript[8] dates from c. 1530, shows the surprising degree to which the mature Willaert—if it was he—still depended on the concepts of style established by Josquin. Its parody-technique, absorbing literally large tracts of Josquin's motet, and also its close thematic adherence to the original plainsong, underline the retrospective character of this Mass, conceived in the spirit of Ockeghem and

voor Nederlandsche Muziekgeschiedenis, xxxv (Amsterdam, 1915). The extant Masses will be published in vols. ix and x of the Opera Omnia, edited by Zenck and Gerstenberg, (American Institute of Musicology, 1950–   ).

[1] Cf. Hermann Beck, 'Adrian Willaerts Messen', Archiv für Musikwissenschaft, xvii (1960), p. 215; R. B. Lenaerts, 'The 16th century Parody Mass in the Netherlands', Musical Quarterly, xxxvi (1950), p. 410; F. X. Haberl, 'Messen Adrian Willaerts, gedruckt von Franc. Marcolini da Forlì', Monatshefte für Musikgeschichte, iii (1871), p. 81.

[2] See Beck, op. cit., for location of the manuscripts.

[3] Op. cit., p. 416. See also his 'De zesstimmige mis "Mente tota" van Adriaen Willaert', Musica Sacra, lxii (1935), p. 153.

[4] Printed in Opera Omnia, v, p. 173.

[5] Cf. Beck, op. cit., p. 222.

[6] 'Hesdin of Willaert', Tijdschrift der Vereeniging voor Nederlandsche Muziekgeschiedenis, x (1915), p. 180.

[7] Die Motette 'Benedicta es' von Josquin des Prez und die Messen 'super Benedicta' von Willaert, Palestrina, de La Hèle und de Monte (Utrecht, 1951).

[8] Hertogenbosch, MS. 72 A, fo. 1.

Josquin rather than reflecting Willaert's own novel style. It is instructive to compare the opening with the model:

Ex. 103

and with the parallel passage in de Monte's later working.[1] Typical
of the archaic flavour of the whole work is the use of fauxbourdon-like
chords of the sixth (so popular with Dufay and his contemporaries)
as they occur in the *Agnus Dei III* of this Mass:

[1] See Ex. 163.

Ex.104

The conservative approach to Mass composition in general seems to have been characteristic of Willaert. But there is little doubt that these nine Masses of his represent only a fraction of his compositions of the Ordinary; indeed Haberl[1] believed that a whole book of Masses once in the archives of St. Mark's has been lost. If these lost Masses represent compositions of the composer's later years, as seems likely, they may well show new traits of style and thus, if recovered, compel scholars to revise their assessment of Willaert as a Mass-composer.

WILLAERT'S MOTETS

The figure of Willaert as a composer of church music is clearly discernible only through the medium of his motets. These were mainly published in a series of collections between 1539 and 1559: two books for four voices (1539: revised edition, 1545), one for five (1539: revised edition, 1550), one for six (1542), and motets in from four to seven parts in the *Musica Nova* (which also included twenty-five madrigals) of 1559.[2] Hermann Zenck has made a convincing appraisal of the motets in general;[3] according to him, Willaert continued to compose as a Fleming in the Venetian environment, adopting the Venetian cult of harmony and colour without sacrificing the northern polyphonic element.

In accordance with the tradition of Josquin and his chief disciple Jean Mouton, Willaert composed sacred and secular motets, based usually on plainsong tenors; but he is specially notable for his expressive declamation with marked accentuation. The standard form of the four-part 'tenor'-motet predominates until the late *Musica Nova*. In the occasional use of secular texts (such as Dido's lament 'Dulces exuviae', which dates from 1542 at latest,[4] and the story of Susanna

---

[1] Op. cit.
[2] *Opera Omnia*, i–v; vol. vi, not yet published (1967), will contain miscellaneous motets, such as the three published by Walter Gerstenberg in *Das Chorwerk*, lix (Wolfenbüttel, 1957).   [3] Preface to *Opera Omnia*, i.
[4] Reprinted by Osthoff, *Das Chorwerk*, liv (Wolfenbüttel, 1956), p. 9.

from the Apocrypha, and also the Wenceslas motet and the two
Sforza motets[1] which bear testimony to Willaert's service under the
house of Habsburg) one is conscious of an affinity with the Italian
madrigal—to the expressive development of which Willaert contributed so much.[2] The severity of much of Willaert's ecclesiastical
music is typified by such works as the four-part 'Pater noster',[3] with
its tendency to low sonorities and its insistence on the liturgical tenor,
and the late six-part 'Aspice Domine' (from *Musica Nova*) with its
gloomy C minor tonality—itself a strikingly novel effect:[4]

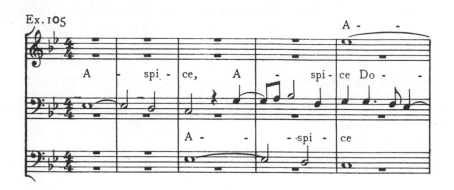

[1] *Opera Omnia*, iii, pp. 78 and 90.
[2] See p. 45.
[3] *Opera Omnia*, ii, p. 11, and easily accessible elsewhere: e.g. Ambros–Kade, *Geschichte der Musik*, v, p. 538, and Davison and Apel, *Historical Anthology of Music* (Cambridge, Mass., 1946), i, p. 80 (where it is misattributed to Obrecht).
[4] *Opera Omnia*, v, p. 144. The original key-signatures are: cantus, altus and second bass, three flats; tenor and first bass, two flats; vagans—the 'resolutio' of the canon, which only just begins in the quotation—one flat.

It is in the *Musica Nova* that the changing musical climate of Venice in the sixteenth century becomes noticeable in Willaert's motet writing. Einstein suggested that the very title contains an artistic programme, the hidden meaning of which is revealed in the dedicatory letter from its editor Francesco Viola (Willaert's pupil and friend) to Duke Alfonso d'Este of Ferrara, Willaert's former employer. Einstein interprets that letter and with it the original title as implying 'new in its literary uniformity, new as an attempt to reflect the changing moods of the soul as expressed in the sonnets of a single great poet'. (All but one of the madrigals in the *Musica Nova* are Petrarch settings.) However, according to Viola himself, the title simply meant that all the contents were being printed for the first time, and Armen Carapetyan[1] sees the peculiar novelty of the publication in other features. (Among other things, it was unusual for motets and madrigals to be published in one volume.) Among the thirty-three motets for four, five, six, and seven parts (some *a voci impari*, or S.A.T.B. as we should say, some *a voci pari*, for higher or lower voices only, and some *a voci mutate*, without soprano but with two altos or two tenors), a few—like 'Aspice Domine'—seem to point towards chromaticism and expressiveness in the sense of Cipriano de Rore, who continues where Willaert leaves off. Their dark and melancholy colour forms a telling contrast to the luminosity and brilliance of the younger Venetians.

However, in the six-part motets of 1542 Willaert had already anticipated the later practice of Andrea and Giovanni Gabrieli in their *Concerti* of 1587; in the dedicatory preface to this volume of 1542 he suddenly focuses attention on the combination of voices and instru-

---

[1] 'The *Musica Nova* of Adriano Willaert', *Journal of Renaissance and Baroque Music*, i (1946), p. 200.

ments: 'Dove ogni sorte di stromenti musicali in buona quantità tenete, e . . . i piu perfetti Musici cantate e suonate.' Nevertheless, even these modernistic motets are chiefly based on the principle of canonic imitation and on the *cantus prius factus* of the Franco-Flemish tradition. In the same volume, incidentally, Willaert also published works by colleagues such as Loyset, Jachet Berchem, Verdelot, and 'Maistre Jhan' (Giovanni Nasco).

Willaert's achievement as a composer of church music in the Franco-Flemish tradition, enriched in the musical climate of the city of his adoption, is matched by his achievement as the musical preceptor[1] of a whole generation. Among his pupils—in addition to Cipriano de Rore who succeeded him at St. Mark's upon his death—were Parabosco, Vicentino, Andrea Gabrieli, Costanzo Porta, Gioseffo Zarlino, Leonardo Barré, Jacques Buus, Francesco Viola, Anton Berges, Alessandro Romano, and Hubert Waelrant.

CIPRIANO DE RORE

On 1 May 1563 Willaert was succeeded by his most brilliant pupil, Cipriano de Rore, who had been born *c.* 1516 at either Malines or Antwerp and may—like Willaert himself—have received a first introduction to music at Notre Dame in Paris. The life and music of this highly original, obstinately self-centred, and fascinatingly progressive composer have so far been but little explored, and while the outlines of Rore the madrigalist are fairly clear,[2] it still remains difficult to assess his achievement as a composer of sacred music.

As in Willaert's case, the greater part of Rore's short life (which ended in or about October 1565 at Parma) was spent in Italy, whither he may have gone as a prospective pupil of Willaert's in Venice. He presented himself to the world as a fully matured artist with his two earliest publications, the First Book of five-part *Madrigali cromatici* (1542) and the First Book of five-part Motets (1544), both published by Gardano in Venice. The greater part of his remaining years was spent in Ferrara, Parma, and Venice. During his apprenticeship in Venice as a singer in the choir of St. Mark's he had as colleagues and fellow pupils Porta, Vicentino, Andrea Gabrieli, Viola, Verdelot, Maître Jachet, Zarlino, and his German friend Hieronymus Uttinger, to whom the First Book of five-part motets was dedicated by the

---

[1] Willaert seems to have been employed as a teacher at the Accademia of Messer Marco Trivisano (to whom the six-part motets of 1542 are dedicated) and also as *maestro* and composer at the academy of Polissena Pecorina.

[2] See p. 48.

printer, Gardano. Rore seems to have gone as early as 1547 to Ferrara, where he entered the service of Duke Ercole d'Este and became the teacher of the madrigalist Luzzasco Luzzaschi, later the master of Frescobaldi. In 1549 or 1550[1] he was appointed choirmaster there, in succession to Vicentino, and remained in office until 1557 (or 1558 at latest). It was for Ercole d'Este and his private chapel that Rore's two famous 'Hercules' Masses were composed, one of which, 'Praeter rerum seriem' *à* 7, was sent in 1557 to Albrecht V, Elector of Bavaria, who greatly admired Rore's art and subsequently ordered the compilation of the famous Rore codex of Munich, lavishly illustrated by the miniatures of the Bavarian court-painter Hans Mielich, son-in-law of Lassus, which contains *inter alia* twenty-six of his motets.[2] On the way back to his native Antwerp, Rore travelled via Munich where he sat for his only extant portrait (by Mielich) in April 1558.[3] 1558 and 1559 were spent partly in Antwerp, partly in Ferrara. At the end of 1559 Rore received an appointment from Margaret of Parma, at that time Governor of the Netherlands in Brussels, but transferred himself to Margaret's husband Ottavio Farnese at Parma by 26 January 1561, and there he seems to have spent one of the most fruitful periods of his life, until he was appointed *maestro di cappella* of St. Mark's in 1563. Rore's tenure of office there was disappointingly short. He must have offered his resignation in the spring of 1564, for by 1 August of that year he was back at his old post in Parma. The reasons for Rore's dislike of his Venetian appointment are succinctly enumerated in a letter:

l'uno, la gravezza del' servitio,
l'altro, il disordine per la divisione della Capella in due,
terzo, la poca provisione . . .

The second point refers to the division of the choir into a 'cappella magna' and a 'cappella piccola' which had come into effect two months before Willaert's death, in order to ease the ageing master's burden. The third point, 'meagre salary', must also have played its part and a whole year passed before Rore's successor was appointed: Gioseffo Zarlino (1517–90), like himself one of Willaert's trusted disciples. At the end of September or in early October of 1565, Rore died at Parma.

---

[1] Josef Musiol, *Cyprien de Rore, ein Meister der venezianischen Schule* (Halle, 1932) and Einstein, op. cit. i, p. 385, disagree on these dates. See Alvin Johnson, 'Rore', *Die Musik in Geschichte und Gegenwart*, xi, col. 897, for further biographical and bibliographical details.
[2] The Codex (Bay. Staatsbibl., Cim. 52) was completed in December 1559; in 1564 the humanist Samuel Quickelberg added a learned commentary.
[3] Reproduced in Einstein, op. cit. i: plate facing p. 383.

Although Rore's secular compositions—all madrigals—outnumber his sacred ones by almost two to one, the latter represent an important contribution to the development of the Franco-Flemish polyphonic tradition in northern Italy.

RORE'S MASSES

Rore is known to have composed a number of Masses and 112 motets,[1] though not all of them have been preserved. Of his Masses two only were published in his lifetime or soon after his death and only five survive altogether.[2] The two printed in Rore's lifetime are both five-part 'parody' Masses: a *Messa . . . a voci pari* published in the *Secondo Libro de le Messe a cinque voci* of Jachet da Mantova (Venice, 1555), an immature work of the early 1540's, based on Josquin's *chanson* 'Vous ne l'aurez', and one published by Gardano in a miscellaneous volume of Masses (Venice, 1566), probably based on Sandrin's 'Doulce memoire', though so remotely that the matter is open to doubt.[3] The other three are two 'Hercules' Masses composed in Ferrara between 1550 and 1557, in homage to Ercole II d'Este, 'Vivat felix Hercules' *à* 5 and 'Praeter rerum seriem' *à* 7, and a five-part *Missa a note negre* preserved at Munich.[4] Munich also has the manuscript of 'Vivat felix Hercules'[5] which was probably suggested by Josquin's 'Hercules' Mass of seventy years earlier, dedicated to the duke's grandfather, Ercole I. Like Josquin's Mass, Rore's is based on a *soggetto cavato*, a theme derived from the vowels of a verbal motto through the equivalent solmisation syllables; but whereas Josquin's subject consists of notes of equal value and passes from one part to another (cf. Vol. III, Ex. 99), Rore's is not only longer but rhythmically varied, confined to a single part, the first tenor, and the words of the motto are actually sung to it (see Ex. 106 opposite).

Rore's other 'Hercules' Mass, 'Praeter rerum seriem', is also connected with Josquin, being a *missa parodia* on a six-part motet by the older master.[6] Here the words 'Hercules secundus dux Ferrariae

---

[1] If their *seconda, terza, &c. . . . parte* are counted separately.

[2] Cf. Alvin Johnson, 'The Masses of Cipriano de Rore', *Journal of the American Musicological Society*, vi (1953), p. 227. The Mass discussed by Peter Wagner, op. cit. pp. 199–202, as the work of Rore is really Janequin's 'La Bataille' (see p. 243). Musiol thinks that three were published in the composer's lifetime.

[3] Cf. the opposite conclusions arrived at by Van den Borren in his *Geschiedenis van de muziek in de Nederlanden* (Antwerp, 1948), i, p. 273, and in *La Musique en Belgique* (Brussels, 1950), p. 113.   [4] Bay. Staatsbibl. Mus. 45.

[5] Bay. Staatsbibl. Mus. 9.

[6] Printed in *Josquin: Werken* (ed. Smijers), *Motetten*, ii, p. 21, and *Das Chorwerk* (ed. Blume), xviii, p. 23.

Ex. 106[1]

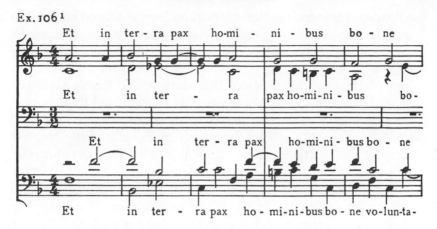

[1] Bay. Staatsbibl. Mus. 46.

quartus, vivit et vivet' are sung throughout by the second alto, not to a *soggetto cavato* but to the first line of the *canto fermo* used by Josquin—a poem and melody which can be traced back to the thirteenth century.[1]

The *Messa a note negre* is so called because, like Rore's *Madrigali cromatici* it is written with the crotchet as the unit in $\frac{4}{4}$ time, instead of with the minim in $\frac{4}{2}$. Alvin Johnson believes it to be a *missa parodia*,[2] since 'the entire Mass is a continuous reworking of a limited number of melodic ideas'. The opening of the *Christe* (Ex. 107) well illustrates Rore's colourful vocal scoring.

'All in all', concludes Johnson, 'the five extant Masses of de Rore show a wide divergence of stylistic characteristics. The rigorously methodical imitative polyphony of the *Missa a voci pari*, i.e. the

Ex. 107

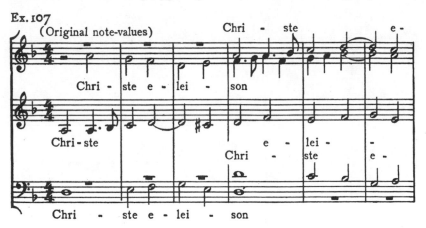

---

[1] There is a two-part setting in Wolfenbüttel, Herzogl. Bibl. 677.
[2] 'The Masses', p. 237.

parody Mass on the Josquin *chanson* "Vous ne l'aurez", may be contrasted with the harmonically controlled polyphony of the *Missa a
note negre* or the "Doulce memoire" Mass. These are stylistic poles
between which the two Masses in honour of Hercules stand. In the
short space of time from about 1540 to 1565 . . . de Rore made such
rapid and radical changes in the concept of polyphony that Monteverdi, years later,[1] could point back to de Rore as the inaugurator of
the *seconda prattica*.'

RORE'S MOTETS

Rore's motets survive mainly in the following sources: three books
of motets *à* 5 (published 1544, 1545, and 1549 respectively),[2] the
already mentioned Rore codex at Munich, *Cipriani de Rore et aliorum
auctorum Motetae a 4* (Venice, 1563), and *Sacrae Cantiones seu Moteti
ut vocant, non minus instrumentis quam vocibus aptae* (published in two
sets, Amsterdam, 1573 and 1595). Josef Musiol expresses the view that
the motets show an evolutionary curve not dissimilar to that described
by Rore's madrigals—leading from the tradition of Franco-Flemish
polyphony to more homophonic structure and to greater subjectivism
in the sense of the tendencies of the Italian Renaissance. In Book I
of the five-part motets only seven out of twenty-three pieces are by
Rore himself; here, as well as in Book II (1545), occasional syllabic
declamation, as in the madrigals, shows the influence of Willaert's
later Venetian manner. Both books, however, abound in traditional
Netherland polyphony. The Munich codex contains twenty-six sacred
motets and five secular compositions on Latin texts, including a
superb setting of Virgil's 'Dissimulare etiam sperasti' (*Aeneid*, iv.
305–19).[3]

---

[1] In the 'Dichiarazione' of 1607, issued by Giulio Cesare Monteverdi, in his brother's
Scherzi musicali of that year.

[2] Edited by Bernhard Meier, *Cipriano de Rore: Opera Omnia*, i (American Institute of
Musicology, 1959).

[3] Published by Osthoff, *Das Chorwerk*, liv, p. 17.

The six motets *à* 4 (for the lower sonorities of male choir), first published by Scotto in Venice in 1563, revert to stricter polyphony. The thirty-four *Sacrae Cantiones a* 4–7 include fifteen items published earlier in the three books of five-part motets, six from the Munich codex, and thirteen which here appeared for the first time.[1] Among them 'Exspectans exspectavi Dominum'[2] is specially indicative of Rore's growing predilection for bold experiments in chromatic harmony:[3]

Ex. 108

Mi - se - re - re   no - stri   Do - mi - ne,   mi-

- se - re - re   no - stri   Do - mi - ne

A Passion according to St. John,[4] published by Le Roy and Ballard (Paris, 1557), is modelled on an earlier St. Matthew Passion by Maistre Jhan and belongs to the so-called motet-Passion type initiated by Longueval.[5] Finally, a book of Psalms, published in 1554 in collaboration with Jachet of Mantua, may be mentioned.

OTHER ASSOCIATES OF WILLAERT

Willaert's associates and disciples at St. Mark's included a number of distinguished organists who were also held in high esteem as composers of sacred music: Buus, Annibale Padovano, Merulo, Verdelot, Zarlino, Andrea Gabrieli.

Jacques Buus (Jacobus Bohusius, van Paus),[6] a Fleming from

[1] Musiol believes two of them may be spurious.
[2] Quoted in Musiol's ex. 35.
[3] Comparable to his famous ode 'Calami sonum ferentes' (cf. p. 48).
[4] Reprinted by Arnold Schmitz in *Oberitalienische Figuralpassionen des 16. Jahrhunderts* (*Musikalische Denkmäler*, i) (Mainz, 1955), p. 59. Kade discusses both the Maistre Jhan Passion and Rore's in *Die ältere Passionskomposition bis zum Jahre 1631* (Gütersloh, 1893), pp. 27 and 33.   [5] See Vol. III, p. 276.
[6] See Joseph Schmidt-Görg, article 'Buus', *Die Musik in Geschichte und Gegenwart*, ii, col. 542, and Hedwig Kraus, 'Jacob Buus, Leben und Werke', *Tijdschrift der Vereeniging voor Nederlandsche Muziekgeschiedenis*, xii (1926), p. 35, (1927), p. 81, and (1928), p. 221.

Ghent, born *c.* 1500, was the successor of Baldassare da Imola who had been appointed first organist of St. Mark's in 1533.[1] Buus, a pupil of Willaert, was appointed on 15 July 1541, but his salary seems to have been disappointingly small and he broke his contract in the winter of 1550–1 by going to Vienna, where he died probably *c.* 1564. In his church music—mostly four-part motets (*Libro de Motetti,* Venice, 1549)—Buus seems indebted to Gombert's technique of imitative polyphony based on plainsong themes. Several single motets, among them a six-part wedding motet 'Qui invenit mulierem bonam', were published in the collections of Montanus (Berg) and Neuber (Nuremberg, 1555, 1556, and 1564).[2]

Buus's successor at St. Mark's in 1551 was Girolamo Parabosco (*c.* 1524–57), who also called himself a 'discipulo di Messer Adriano', while Annibale Padovano (*c.* 1527–75) was appointed to the second organ in November of the following year and remained till 1564. Both were, like Buus, essentially instrumental composers, but Annibale published a book of motets in 1567 and a book of five-part Masses in 1573.

The keyboard music of Claudio Merulo (1533–1604), who served from 1557 to 1564 at the second, and from 1564 to 1584 at the first organ of St. Mark's, is discussed elsewhere in this volume.[3] His rich production of sacred vocal music has been rather overlooked. He published a book of five-part Masses in 1573—two others appeared posthumously in 1609—and six books of four-, five-, and six-part motets (between 1578 and 1605).[4] Some of the motets are for two antiphonal choirs, as in the *missa parodia* on Wert's 'Cara la vita mia', while that on Andrea Gabrieli's 'Benedicam Dominum' is for three.

Yet another of Willaert's chief disciples, Gioseffo Zarlino (1517–90), his personal pupil, who succeeded Rore as *maestro di cappella* of St. Mark's in the summer of 1565, won his chief fame outside the sphere of church music. His *Istitutioni armoniche* (Venice, 1558) established him as the foremost musical theorist of his age, whose writings were ultimately issued in a complete edition of four volumes in 1589 shortly before his death. They are indeed of more than

---

[1] See Giacomo Benvenuti, preface to *Istituzioni e monumenti dell'arte musicale italiana,* i (Milan, 1939), pp. xxxix–xl.

[2] Reprinted by Commer, *Collectio operum musicorum Batavorum saeculi XVI,* viii, p. 76.

[3] See p. 608.

[4] On Merulo's motets see Leichtentritt, op. cit., pp. 216 ff. Examples have been reprinted by Commer, *Musica Sacra,* xvi, xxiii, xxv, xxvii, and xxviii (1875–87) and Torchi, *L'arte musicale in Italia,* i (1897).

theoretical value, for they give us practical information, e.g. that the 'beat' in music is measured by the human pulse, and on the correct way of underlaying a verbal text. Of his compositions, however, but few have been preserved. Much of his sacred music composed during his long appointment, such as the Mass for the foundation of Santa Maria della Salute in 1577, seems to have perished. One four-part Mass has been preserved in manuscript[1] and a few motets printed in different collections; a few of the latter have been reprinted in modern times.[2] As a composer Zarlino seems to have lacked the quality that distinguishes his theoretical writings: originality of thought. It remains to be seen, however, whether the discovery of more of his liturgical music would seriously challenge that verdict.

THE GABRIELIS[3]

The Venetian School culminated in the work of an uncle and nephew, · Andrea and Giovanni Gabrieli, both native Venetians. Andrea (c. 1520–86) succeeded Merulo as second organist at St. Mark's in 1564, and as first organist in 1585. His nephew and pupil Giovanni (1557–1612) spent four years at the court of Munich under Lassus (1576–80)[4] and actually held the post of first organist of St. Mark's for a short period in 1584 until his uncle was appointed; he then became second organist—and was not promoted when Andrea died shortly afterwards.[5] (Andrea's successor was another of his pupils, Vincenzo Bell'Haver, madrigalist and keyboard composer.)

Although, like Annibale Padovano, Merulo, and the rest, the Gabrielis were distinguished instrumental composers and madrigalists, their church music towers above that of all the other Venetians except Willaert and perhaps Rore. Andrea is relatively conservative, particularly in his Masses, though the title-pages of both his five-part motets (1565) and his six-part Penitential Psalms (1583) expressly mention the use of instruments ('tum viva Voce, tum omnis generis Instrumentis . . .' and 'tum Omnis generis Instrumentorum, tum ad vocis . . .'), while Giovanni not only carried the polychoral technique to an unsurpassed peak but in his later church compositions introduced striking 'affective' writing and independent obbligato parts for

---

[1] Bologna, Liceo Mus.
[2] In Torchi, op. cit. i, pp. 69 and 79, and by Roman Flury, *Das Chorwerk*, lxxvii (Wolfenbüttel, 1961). See Flury, *Gioseffo Zarlino als Komponist* (Winterthur, 1962).
[3] By the Editor.
[4] Benvenuti, op. cit., p. lxxxiv.
[5] Ibid., p. lxxiv.

instruments.[1] Andrea's motets are much more numerous and important than his Masses,[2] and Giovanni left no complete setting of the
Ordinary at all.

Even in his most modest and conservative church compositions, the
four-part motets of 1576,[3] Andrea shows his sense of choral scoring,
as in this excerpt from 'Maria Magdalena' which also illustrates his
often essentially harmonic style and syllabic setting of the text:

Ex.109

[1] See pp. 523 ff. where this 'baroque' aspect of Giovanni Gabrieli's church music is
discussed.

[2] Proske reprinted 'Pater peccavi', one of the four six-part Masses of 1572, *Selectus
novus missarum*, ii (Ratisbon, 1861), p. 525, and a four-part *Missa brevis*, *Musica
Divina*, Ann. 1, i, p. 165: a separate edition of the latter is published by Bank (Amsterdam). Three separate Mass-movements à 12 from the *Concerti* of 1587 are reprinted by
Giovanni d'Alessi, *A. Gabrieli: Messe e mottetti* (*I classici musicali italiani*, v) (Milan,
1942). On the Masses, see P. Wagner, op. cit., p. 408.

[3] Eleven of them in Proske, *Musica Divina*, 1. ii, from which Ex. 109 is taken (p. 146);
other examples in Charles Bordes, *Anthologie des maîtres religieux primitifs*, i–ii (Paris,
1893–4), and elsewhere. Two five-part motets and a Penitential Psalm are reprinted in
Torchi, op. cit. ii; one five-part motet and one Psalm in Benvenuti, op. cit. i. Three
four-part motets, one five-part, and two Psalms are available separately in the Bank
edition. Motets for larger combinations, from the 1587 *Concerti*, are reprinted in d'Alessi,
A. Gabrieli. On the motets generally, see Leichtentritt, op. cit., pp. 218 ff. and Reese,
op. cit., p. 496.

Perhaps the finest of the Penitential Psalms is the sixth, 'De profundis clamavi',[1] which makes much use of antiphony between the three upper and three lower voices, an antiphony as effective in its different way as the more obvious antiphony of such big motets as the twelve-part 'Deus misereatur nostri' with its three choirs: high, middle, and low.[2]

In that field—polychoral composition—Andrea was, however, surpassed by his famous nephew. Giovanni's motets[3] are nearly all polychoral or at least antiphonal within a single choir of at least six parts. Most of them were published in three collections: five of them in Andrea's 1587 volume of *Concerti*, the rest in two books of *Sacrae symphoniae* (1597 and 1615); the *Ecclesiasticae cantiones* of 1589 are less important. Even the pieces in the volume of 1587 include such a masterpiece as 'O magnum mysterium'[4] with its characteristic 'Alleluias' in triple time, which in itself demonstrates that Gabrieli did not always use antiphonal choirs for effects of splendour and brilliance—as he does in 'Angelus ad pastores' in the same volume.[5] Often antiphony is employed to contrast light and shade or height and depth, as in the wonderful opening of 'O Domine Jesu Christe'[6] from the first book of *Sacrae symphoniae*. Another striking effect of which Gabrieli was fond is the crescendo of volume and pitch, if not of dynamics, as in the six-part 'Beata es virgo'[7] of 1597:

[1] Benvenuti, op. cit., p. 13; Arnold Schering, *Geschichte der Musik in Beispielen* (Leipzig, 1931), p. 130; Bank edition.

[2] On Gabrieli's polychoral motets, see Denis Arnold, 'Andrea Gabrieli und die Entwicklung der "cori-spezzati"-Technik', *Die Musikforschung*, xii (1959), p. 258.

[3] Published by Denis Arnold, *Opera Omnia* (American Institute of Musicology, 1956–   ). Thirteen complete works and a number of substantial excerpts were printed by Winterfeld in the third volume of *Johannes Gabrieli und sein Zeitalter* (Berlin, 3 vols., 1834); six motets by Heinrich Besseler and Christiane Engelbrecht in *Das Chorwerk*, x (1931) and lxvii (1958); there are numerous separate reprints. On the motets see Winterfeld, op. cit. i and ii, Leichtentritt, op. cit., pp. 221 ff., and Denis Arnold, article 'Gabrieli', *Die Musik in Geschichte und Gegenwart*, iv, particularly cols. 1200 ff.

[4] *Opera Omnia*, i, p. 10, and Einstein, *A Short History of Music* (London, 5th ed., 1948), p. 236.

[5] *Opera Omnia*, i, p. 34; Torchi, op. cit. ii, p. 177.

[6] *Opera Omnia*, i, p. 93; Winterfeld, op. cit. iii, p. 11; *Das Chorwerk*, x, p. 4.

[7] *Opera Omnia*, i, p. 57; Winterfeld, op. cit. iii, p. 29.

Ex. 110

a passage which follows an opening for three high voices only. The 'crescendo' is heard at its most dramatic in the twelve-part *Magnificat*[1] of 1615:

---

[1] *Opera Omnia*, iv, p. 133.

Ex. III

The indication 'Capella' for the middle choir here is explained by Praetorius[1] as meaning *chorus vocalis*: all parts to be sung, not given to instruments.

It is in this posthumously published Second Book of the *Sacrae symphoniae* that Gabrieli appears most strikingly as an innovator.[2] The First Book had been described as 'tam vocibus quam instrumentis', but the instrumental parts are not differentiated from the vocal and one need only compare the *Magnificat primi toni* of 1597[3] with Ex. 111, or the first few bars of the two settings of 'O Jesu mi dulcissime', both for two four-part choirs,[4] to see how Gabrieli stepped into a new world during the last decade of his life:

[1] *Syntagma Musicum*, iii (Wolfenbüttel, 1618–19), part 3, ii, p. 133.
[2] See pp. 523–5.
[3] *Opera Omnia*, ii, p. 44; Winterfeld, op. cit., p. 18.
[4] 1597 setting in *Opera Omnia*, i, p. 167; 1615 version, ibid. iii, p. 30, and *Das Chorwerk*, x, p. 20.

Ex 112

(e) EASTERN EUROPE

By GERALD ABRAHAM

POLAND

The Polish historian Zdzisław Jachimecki dated the 'golden age of Polish music' from the foundation of the royal chapel of the Rorantists at Cracow in 1543:[1] rector, nine chaplain-singers, and clerk, all native Poles. Side by side with it existed the king's private chapel and these two bodies were naturally a focus for creative activity. From the archives of the Rorantists and an inventory of the music in the royal chapel, compiled in 1572,[2] we know something about their repertories which included a great deal of French and Italian music; the royal chapel possessed motets and psalms by Willaert, Rore, and Phinot, and Masses by Gombert and Morales; the Rorantists sang Gombert, Certon, Cadéac, Goudimel, Sermisy, Lassus, Victoria, Giovanelli and, above all, Palestrina. But native compositions were not neglected; the Rorantist repertory included music by Sebastjan z Felsztyna,[3] Marcin Leopolita (c. 1540–c. 1589), royal compositor cantus from 1560 to about 1564, Tomasz Szadek (c. 1550–c. 1611), who entered the royal chapel in 1569 but left it for the Rorantists six years later, and later still became a vicarius of the cathedral, and such minor figures as Krzysztof Borek, Walentyn Gawara, and Marcin Paligonus.

By Leopolita we have a five-part 'Missa paschalis'[4] or 'Missa de resurrectione', which has the distinction of being the earliest complete setting of the Ordinary by a Polish composer that has survived. It is based on four Polish Easter songs, three of them really German in origin—for the most part on 'Chrystus Pan zmartwychwstał' (Christ the Lord has risen from the dead) which opens every movement except the Benedictus—which also appear together in a pseudo-plainsong Credo ('Patrem super Christus jam surrexit') found in Polish sources of the seventeenth and eighteenth centuries. The style is late Netherland, with much close imitation: see, for instance, the opening of the Kyrie.[5] The Agnus Dei I (repeated as III) is in six parts: the only

[1] See Vol. III, p. 301, and Adolf Chybiński, *Materiały do dziejów królewskiej kapeli rorantystów na Wawelu, i: 1540–1624* (Cracow, 1910). (The edict of foundation dated from 1540 but the chapel did not actually come into being till three years later.)

[2] Printed by Chybiński, *Kwartalnik Muzyczny*, i (1912), p. 253.

[3] See Vol. III, p. 301.

[4] Published by Józef Surzyński, *Monumenta musices sacrae in Polonia*, iii (Poznań, 1889), and Hieronim Feicht, *Wydawnictwo dawnej muzyki polskiej*, xxxv (Cracow, 1957). See also Feicht, 'O mszy wielkanocnej Marcina Leopolity', *Kwartalnik Muzyczny*, vi–vii (1930), p. 109.

[5] Quoted from Surzyński in *Oxford History of Music*, ii (Oxford, 1905), p. 302; the pitch should be a fourth higher.

piece of Polish six-part polyphony that has come down to us from the sixteenth century. Two other Masses by Leopolita, a 'Missa Rorate' and another 'Missa de resurrectione', are lost and his motets have been preserved only in organ transcription.[1]

Szadek's two Masses, 'Officium Dies est laetitiae'[2] and 'Officium in melodiam moteti Pisneme'[3] (i.e. 'Puis ne me peult venir', perhaps by Créquillon who also wrote a Mass on it), dated respectively 1578 and 1580 on the manuscripts, are both four-part works. The former, a *canto fermo* Mass with the theme in long note-values in the first bass, was written specifically for the Rorantists whose choir was limited to men's voices; the *Agnus* is missing.

A more notable figure than Szadek or even Leopolita was the rather earlier Wacław z Szamotuł (Szamotulczyk, Szamotulski) (*c.* 1526– *c.* 1560),[4] who entered the royal chapel on 6 May 1547 *pro componista* only to leave it eight years later for the court of 'Black' Michael Radziwiłł, the Protestant *wojewoda* of Lithuania, at Vilna, where he remained for the rest of his short life. At Vilna Wacław turned from Latin church music to the composition of religious songs with Polish words. We must estimate his stature not so much from his surviving compositions as from contemporary esteem and the fact that two of his four-part psalm-motets were published by Berg and Neuber at Nuremberg—'In te Domine speravi'[5] in *Psalmorum selectorum . . . . tomus quartus* (1554) and 'Ego sum pastor bonus'[6] in *Thesaurus musicus* (1564)—side by side with the work of the greatest French and Netherland masters. Even his reputed masterpiece, the eight-part Mass probably composed for the wedding of King Sigismund Augustus in 1553, is lost, together with other works mentioned in the inventory of 1572; of his Lamentations, published at Cracow in 1553, only the tenor part has survived; another motet, 'Nunc scio vere', has been preserved only in organ tablature. Yet from what little we have of

---

[1] Facsimile of 'Cibavit eos' in tablature in Zygmunt Szweykowski (ed.), *Z dziejów polskiej kultury muzycznej — I: Kultura staropolska* (Cracow, 1957), facing p. 97.

[2] Published by Feicht, *Wydawnictwo*, xxxiii (Cracow, n.d.)

[3] Published by Surzyński, *Monumenta*, i (Poznań, 1885); first *Kyrie* in *Oxford History of Music*, ii, p. 305.

[4] See Chybiński, 'Wacław z Szamotuł', *Kwartalnik Muzyczny*, xxi–xxiv (1948), nos. 21/22, p. 11; 23, p. 7; 24, p. 100, and 'O motetach Wacława z Szamotuł', *Przegląd Muzyczny* (Poznań, 1929), no. 3; also H. Przybylski, *Wacław z Szamotuł, nadworny kompozytor króla Zygmunta Augusta* (Szamotuły, 1935).

[5] The earliest Polish composition to be published outside the country. Reprinted by Maria Szczepańska and Henryk Opieński, *Wydawnictwo*, ix (Warsaw, 1930), and by Józef Chomiński and Zofia Lissa in *Music of the Polish Renaissance* (Cracow, 1955), p. 234.

[6] Reprinted by Surzyński, *Monumenta*, ii (1887); opening in *Oxford History of Music*, ii, p. 304.

Wacław's music[1] one can see, for instance, from the long flowing lines of 'In te Domine speravi':

Ex. 113
(i)

(ii)

[1] Complete list of works in Szweykowski, op. cit., p. 280; this volume lists the works of all the composers mentioned in this section.

that he deserved his contemporary reputation.

Although Wacław is said to have introduced melodic material from Polish devotional songs in his motets—for instance, the phrase 'In justitia tua libera me' in Ex. 113 (ii), borrowed from a Christmas song[1]—his style is essentially late Netherland. Poland at this period, unlike Russia, only recently freed from 'the Tatar yoke', and unlike Hungary, under the Turkish heel since Mohács (1526), belonged in every respect to the European cultural community; she even had her Protestant minority. The general style of Polish church music was that of Catholic church music all over the Continent and, as the Franco-Flemish style became Italianized generally, Italian influence became strong in Poland.[2] At the end of the century, beside the conservative works of Gawara and Paligonus, we find the Silesian Johannes Polonus (Hans Pohle) publishing *Cantiones aliquot piae* (1590) in the Roman style. Roman influence reached its height under the fanatically Catholic Sigismund III who, having moved his capital and the court chapel from Cracow to Warsaw, persuaded Marenzio in 1595–6 to come there, giving him Polish nobility and offering a handsome salary. Marenzio appears not to have stayed very long or to have become master of the royal chapel; indeed it is not clear whether Sigismund's first master of the chapel, the composer Krzysztof Klabon, held the post till 1603 or whether he was succeeded in 1595 by Alessandro Cilli; but from 1603 to 1623 the chapel was directed by Asprilio Pacelli,[3] who was succeeded by Giovanni Francesco Anerio, and he in turn in 1628 by Marco Scacchi who held the post for twenty years.

In a collection of *Melodiae sacrae* made by the Roman Vincentius Lilius (Vincenzo Gigli), published at Cracow in 1604, consisting

[1] Zdzisław Jachimecki, *Historja muzyki polskiej* (Warsaw, 1920), p. 55.

[2] Jachimecki, *Wpływy włoskie w muzyce polskiej — I: 1540–1640* (Cracow, 1911).

[3] Mateusz Gliński, *Asprilio Pacelli, insigne maestro di cappella alla corte di Polonia* (Rome, 1941). Gliński has also edited a complete edition of Pacelli's works (Rome, 1948–   ).

almost entirely of compositions by Italian members of the court chapel, one work by a Pole, Andrzej Staniczewski's 'Beata es virgo Maria', suggests Venetian influence; only three parts have survived but they suffice to show that it was an eight-part piece for double chorus. And it is clear, not only from the nature of the other pieces in this collection and of Pacelli's work, that the king himself favoured the brilliant Venetian polychoral style; Sigismund even tried to entice Giovanni Gabrieli to Warsaw. It is possible also that the king persuaded the Primate of Poland to send his organist and choirmaster Mikołaj Zieleński to Venice to study with Gabrieli; at any rate Zieleński published in Venice in 1611 two great collections of *Offertoria totius anni* and *Communiones totius anni*,[1] in eight part-books and *partitura pro organo*, which entitle him to be considered one of the outstanding masters of early baroque church music. His twelve-part *Magnificat*[2] is worthy to stand beside Victoria's, Giovanni Gabrieli's, and Merulo's. All the pieces in the first collection—forty-four Offertories, two Communions, nine motets, and the *Magnificat*—are for two choirs, except the *Magnificat* which is for three. In eight numbers trombones are indicated; the *partitura pro organo* is not a *continuo* part but gives the unfigured bass and highest voice of each choir: thus at the beginning of the *Magnificat*[3] (see Ex. 114).

The *Communiones* are much more varied in style; they include 15 solos for various voices; 8 duets (soprano and bass); 40 pieces in late-sixteenth-century style for from three to seven voices, some with, some without, instruments in addition to the organ, and with a considerable amount of written-out ornamentation; and three instrumental fantasias, the earliest known Polish examples of this genre. 'In monte Oliveti' and 'Domus mea'[4] are good examples of the older style. But even the solo pieces are not true monodies like those among

---

[1] Full titles and complete lists of contents in *Grove's Dictionary* (5th ed., London, 1954), ix, pp. 415–16. For the *Offertoria*, see *Zieleński, Opera Omnia* (ed. Władysław Malinowski), i–iii (Warsaw, 1966–); about a dozen pieces from the *Communiones* are available in Surzyński, op. cit. i and ii; ed. Chybiński, B. Rutkowski, and Szczepańska, *Wydawnictwo*, xii, xxxi, xxxvi, xli, and xlv; and ed. W. Gieburowski in *Cantica selecta musices sacrae in Polonia* (Poznań, 1928). Surzyński also printed one of the two 'Haec dies' motets complete in his article 'Ueber alte polnische Kirchenkomponisten und deren Werke', *Kirchenmusikalisches Jahrbuch*, v (1890), p. 67.

[2] See particularly Szczepańska, 'O dwunastogłosowem *Magnificat* Mikołaja Zieleńskiego z r. 1611', *Polski Rocznik Muzykologiczny*, i (1935), p. 28; and for biographical correction, J. J. Dunicz, 'Do biografji Mikołaja Zieleńskiego', in the *Rocznik* for the following year, p. 95. Dunicz points out that Zieleński's visit to Venice is purely hypothetical.

[3] The small notes show the inner voice-parts omitted from the organ-score, which is of course wordless. The original edition abounds in inaccuracies: see facsimile, Jachimecki, *Historja*, p. 82.

[4] Published in Surzyński, *Monumenta*, ii, and *Wydawnictwo*, xxxi, respectively.

Ex. 114

Viadana's *concerti*; the organ part is fully written out and the vocal
line is part, if an ornamented part, of a polyphonic complex; the
opening of the Communion 'Si consurrexistis'[1] may be quoted as
typical:

Ex. 115

Si con - sur - re - xi - - stis cum

Chri - - - sto,

After Zieleński, Polish music lay for some time becalmed under the
Italian ascendancy. Of the members of the royal chapel, Adam
Jarzębski (before 1590–1648), a man of all-round talents, violinist,
architect, poet, composed only instrumental music, Franciszek Lilius
(*c.* 1600–57), choirmaster of the cathedral at Cracow from 1630,
was the son of Vincentius Lilius (cf. *supra*, p. 304) and therefore at
least half-Italian, though he published devotional songs with Polish
words as well as composing Latin service music;[2] and the music of
Scacchi's successor, Bartłomiej Pękiel (d. 1670) belongs to a later
period. The most considerable church composer of the period between
Zieleński and Pękiel was Marcin Mielczewski (d. 1651), known to
have been a member of the Rorantist chapel at Cracow in 1617, later
a member of the court chapel and in 1643 composer to Ladislas IV;

---

[1] *Wydawnictwo*, xxxvi.   [2] A motet, ibid. xl.

practically nothing of his fairly copious output was printed in his own day and very little has been published since. The great bulk of it consists of *a cappella* Masses and psalm-motets but he also wrote a dozen or so solo *concerti* and *motetti concertati*[1] with independent instrumental introductions—styled *symfonia* or *sonata* according to the length—and accompaniments. One of these, 'Deus in nomine tuo', for bass solo, two violins, bassoon, and basso continuo, was published in the collection *Jesu Hilf! Erster Theil Geistlicher Koncerten* (Berlin, 1659).[2] Some of the *motetti concertati* are scored for impressive forces: for instance, 'Benedictio et claritas'[3] for six voices, two violins, four trombones, and continuo, 'Audite et admiramini' for eight vocal and six instrumental parts.[4]

BOHEMIA

Although just as closely integrated with the culture of Western Christendom as Poland was, Bohemia at this period made a much less valuable musical contribution—particularly in the field of Catholic church music. For this there were two reasons. Protestantism, both Hussite and Lutheran, struck much deeper roots in Bohemia than it ever did in Poland. And the election in 1526 of a Habsburg prince (Ferdinand I) to the Bohemian throne led to a fatal identity or near-identity of king and emperor; the king of Bohemia was either Holy Roman Emperor or heir to the Emperor and usually preferred Vienna or Innsbruck to Prague. Ferdinand I founded a court chapel at Prague in 1564 but filled it almost entirely with Netherlanders.[5] The art-loving Rudolf II's preference for Prague as a residence gave it a period of unexampled musical brilliance during his reign (1576–1612); the Imperial Court Chapel spent much of its time there, yet the presence of such masters as Philippe de Monte, Jacobus Kerle, Regnart, Luython, and Gallus (Handl) proved even more oppressive to native talent than the contemporary Italian ascendancy at the court of Sigismund III.

Nevertheless, there was native talent and, although most of it was employed in the service of the Protestant churches or the Bohemian

---

[1] See Chybiński, 'O koncertach wokalno-instrumentalnych Marcina Mielczewskiego', *Kwartalnik Muzyczny*, i (1928), p. 34, ii (1929), p. 144, iii (1929), p. 246, v (1929), p. 10, viii (1930), p. 306.

[2] Reprinted by Chybiński and Sikorski, *Wydawnictwo*, ii. Two of Mielczewski's instrumental *canzoni* have been published in the same series, vi and xxix, and his 'Vesperae dominicales', ibid. xlii.

[3] Berlin, Deutsche Bibl., Mus. MS. 30184, fo. 119.

[4] Danzig, Bibl. miejska MS. Cath. q. 7 (nr. 2).

[5] Walter Senn, *Musik und Theater am Hof zu Innsbruck* (Innsbruck, 1954), pp. 65 ff.

Brothers, a certain amount of Latin church music was written by Czech composers. Thus Jiří Rychnovský (c. 1545–1616), whose works consist for the most part of Czech motets, also left a 'Missa super Maria Magdalena' and the same manuscript[1] contains a four-part Officium 'Dunaj, voda hluboká', of which all five movements are based on a (now lost) Czech song as *canto fermo*.[2] This has been attributed to Jan Trojan Turnovský,[3] who similarly based his Czech motets on national songs and published three-part arrangements of Czech devotional songs in 1577. Jan Simonides Montanus (d. 1587) essayed eight-part composition and Pavel Spongopaeus Jistebnický (*fl. c.* 1598) eight-part double choruses in Venetian style in his Office settings. A more substantial figure than any of these, and the most considerable Czech master of late sixteenth-century polyphony, was the Catholic nobleman Kryštof Harant z Polžic (1564–1621)[4] who in his youth spent eight years (1576–84) at the court of Innsbruck, where he studied singing and counterpoint with Gerhard van Roo, a member of the Hofkapelle. Harant was a man of many parts: humanist, soldier, politician, and traveller. In 1608 he published an account of his travels in the Middle East[5] with many observations on the music of the eastern peoples and a musical supplement in the form of a six-part motet, 'Qui confidunt in Domino',[6] which he had written in Jerusalem ten years earlier. Harant, like other Czech nobles of the time, notably Vilém and Petr z Rožmberka, maintained a private chapel of his own at his castle of Pecka. He enjoyed the favour of Rudolf II and Matthias, but went over to the Utraquists (moderate Hussites), took the patriotic side against Ferdinand II, and after the Battle of the White Mountain was imprisoned and executed on 21 June 1621 with the other Czech leaders.

Although he was an amateur, there is nothing amateurish about the few compositions by him which survive complete, of which the most

[1] Prague, Národní a universitní knihovna, XI B 1. Two passages from an Office, 'super Vias tuas Domine', dated 6 July 1577, in the same manuscript, possibly Rychnovský's work, are printed in Jitka Snížkova, *Musica Polyphonica Bohemiae* (Prague, 1958), pp. 52 and 53; the Introit 'Gaudeamus omnes' celebrates 'Sanctus Johannes Hus'. A simple, mainly note-against-note motet by Rychnovský, 'Decantabat populus', is printed ibid., p. 50.

[2] *Kyrie* printed in Jaroslav Pohanka, *Dějiny české hudby v příkladech* (Prague, 1958), p. 49.

[3] See Karel Konrád, *Dějiny posvátneho zpěvu staročeského od 15. věku do zrušení literátskych bratrstev* (Prague, 1893), p. 248.

[4] See Rudolf Quoika, 'Christoph Harant von Polschitz und seine Zeit', *Die Musikforschung*, vii (1954), p. 414.

[5] Republished by K. J. Erben in 1854.

[6] Reprinted by Karel Stecker (Prague, 1910) and by Jiří Berkovec in his complete edition of Harant's compositions, including the fragments (Prague, 1956), p. 25.

important is a five-part Mass on Marenzio's madrigal 'Dolorosi martir, fieri tormenti', published in Weissensee's *Opus melicum* (Magdeburg, 1602).[1] The style is not far removed from that of Marenzio himself:

Ex. 116

[1] The Mass was reprinted in original notation by Zdeněk Nejedlý, *Časopis Českého musea* (1905); there are editions in modern notation by J. C. Sychra (Prague, 1910) and Berkovec, op. cit., p. 45. The 'Qui tollis' is printed in Pohanka, op. cit., p. 54.

but Czech critics also detect in it the melodic influence of Czech popular devotional song 'for it is close to the contrapuntal tradition of the Czech polyphonic school of the late sixteenth century (Trojan Turnovský)',[1] that is to say, less richly complicated than that of the Netherlanders, Italians, or English.

Extreme simplicity also marks some of the earlier Czech essays in the 'new style': for instance the *Magnificat* of Jan Sixt z Lerchenfelsu (d. 1629), printed at Litoměřice in 1626.[2] In his youth Sixt had sung in the court chapel of Rudolf II; later he became court chaplain and held various appointments in Prague, and was finally dean of the cathedral at Litoměřice. As a staunch Catholic, he celebrated the Habsburg victory at the White Mountain in a *Te Deum* and *Magnificat*. In the latter[3] the short phrases of a soprano voice supported by three viols are continually responded to by a choir *cum tubis et organis*, all in the simplest possible four-part harmony.

[1] Jan Racek, *Česká hudba* (Prague, 1958), p. 76.
[2] Cf. Robert Haas, 'Ein leitmeritzer Musikdruck von 1626', *Auftakt*, iii (1923), p. 106.
[3] Opening printed in Pohanka, op. cit., p. 74.

VI

LATIN CHURCH MUSIC ON THE CONTINENT—2

THE PERFECTION OF THE *A CAPPELLA* STYLE
By HENRY COATES AND GERALD ABRAHAM

THE final perfection of the *a cappella* 'Netherland' style in church music was reached in the work of four composers: Palestrina (*c*. 1525–94), Lassus (1532[1]–94), de Monte (1521–1603), and Victoria (*c*. 1548–1611) (whose work is discussed in the next chapter). Although there are numerous passages in their music which might pass for the work of any one of them, each shows an unmistakable individuality within the common style, the almost universal language of European church music of the late sixteenth century. Palestrina and Victoria achieved a mystic impersonality, with utmost smoothness of counterpoint; Lassus is always more personal, more vivid and realistic; de Monte often reflects in his work a genial vigour and simple serenity.

These men lived very different lives, a fact which had some influence in shaping their musical destinies. Palestrina's was spent almost entirely in Rome, in daily association with its great churches, though he seems to have felt the need for some counterpoise to ecclesiastical routine, in later life eagerly entering into commerce, managing his second wife's furriery business, buying and selling property. Lassus as a young man travelled far and wide in Europe, even (according to one source)[2] visiting England. His stay in Rome, where he was for a time master of the music at St. John Lateran (1553–5),[3] undoubtedly had a considerable influence on his style, which assimilated so much from the Italian madrigal. De Monte is known to have stayed in England (as the only Netherlander in Philip II's Spanish chapel)[4] in 1554–5; both he and Lassus eventually settled down at secular courts.

---

[1] On the date of Lassus's birth, see Charles Van den Borren 'En quelle année Rol. de Lattre est-il né?' *Bulletin de la société Union musicologique*, vi (1925), p. 51.

[2] Samuel Quickelberg, 'Orlandus Lassus', in H. Pantaleon, *Prosopographia heroum . . . totius Germaniae* (Basle, 1565–6), iii, p. 541.

[3] Raffaele Casimiri, *Orlando di Lasso, maestro di cappella al Laterano nel 1553* (Rome, 1920).

[4] See G. Van Doorslaer, *La Vie et les œuvres de Philippe de Monte* (Brussels, 1921), p. 6,

THE PALESTRINA STYLE

The ultimate refinements of the *a cappella* polyphonic style are to be found in the more mature works of Palestrina. As a Roman church musician he inherited a tradition of smoothness, euphony, and un-adventurousness from both native Italians such as Costanzo Festa, a member of the Sistine Chapel from 1517 till his death in 1545, and Italianized Netherlanders like Arcadelt, master of the Chapel from 1539 or 1540 to 1545 and again 1547–52: cf. the opening of Arcadelt's five-part motet 'O sacrum convivium':[1]

Ex. 117

It may be mentioned in passing that a similar style was employed in Florence at the same period by Verdelot and Corteccia, and in Mantua by Jachet.[2] The characteristics of Palestrina's later style are smoothness of the contrapuntal strands (with a marked partiality for movement by step), their essentially melodic character, and their comparative simplicity as compared with the earlier, more florid style exhibited by himself and his predecessors in the liturgical field. Always a supreme craftsman, he used all the devices of counterpoint—such as canon and fugue—with the greatest of ease and skill, in his later days, however, showing a preference for a style of free melodic imitation. Harmonically this is based upon the concord of three notes, with a smooth systematization of the embellishments—carefully prepared suspensions, passing and auxiliary notes—which constitute the

---

[1] Reprinted by Maldeghem, *Trésor musical*, xx (Brussels, 1884), p. 3; three Masses are published in *Jacobi Arcadelt Opera Omnia*, i (American Institute of Musicology, 1965), ed. Albert Seay. For Festa's Masses, see his *Opera Omnia*, i (American Institute of Musicology, 1962), ed. Alexander Main. Motets by Festa have been reprinted by Torchi, *L'arte musicale in Italia*, i (Milan, 1897), p. 49, by E. Dagnino in *Monumenta Polyphoniae Italicae*, ii (Rome, 1936)—a collection of fifteen motets, two hymns, and a Magnificat—and separately by Bank (Amsterdam, n.d.). Three volumes of little-known Italian church music of the first half of the century have been published by Knud Jeppesen, *Italia Sacra Musica* (Copenhagen, 1962).

[2] On Verdelot, see p. 276, n. 5. Torchi gives Corteccia's five-part 'Benedictus Dominus', op. cit. i, p. 121. Jaquet or Jachet of Mantua, a Frenchman, has often been confused with other composers of the same name (see K. Huber, 'Die Doppelmeister des 16. Jh.', *Sandberger-Festschrift* (Munich, 1918), p. 170; on wrongly ascribed reprints see Gustave Reese, *Music in the Renaissance* (London, 1954), footnotes on pp. 366–8. His four-part *missa parodia* 'Quam pulchra es' (Paris, 1554) has been reprinted by Bank.

contrapuntal movement. The play of rhythms is almost solely governed by the relationship of one note to another in time value, one phrase to another in balance; this produces a constantly varying rhythmic tension, tightening or slackening according to the musical or aesthetic requirements of the moment. Such a delicate poise of rhythmic accents gives the feeling of equilibrium, the sense of repose rather than of movement forward, the lightness of textural effect which are the marks of the finest work of the period. Another characteristic of the Palestrinian style is the subtle rhythmic variation of the motives as they pass from one voice to another, thus giving a soft richness to the sonorities.[1] But Palestrina's artistic stature is much more than that of a master of technique: it represents in its finest aspects a quality of liturgical music such as no other composer has ever surpassed. He was almost purely a church composer, and it is easy to understand why his music has been generally regarded as a model of church style, so perfectly does it fit and adorn the sacred text. His art has its roots deep in the liturgical soil, the Gregorian chant which is used not merely as a *canto fermo* against which to weave elaborate counterpoint: its contours are infused into every one of the contrapuntal strands. As Richard Wagner expressed it,[2] Palestrina's music gives us 'a picture almost as timeless as it is spaceless, a spiritual revelation throughout that rouses unspeakable emotion, as it brings us nearer than aught else to a notion of the essential nature of religion'.

PALESTRINA'S MASSES

It is in his 105 Masses that Palestrina's genius soars to its highest point.[3] His design for the Mass as shown in his later works is to treat the *Credo* mostly as a majestic declamation, the *Gloria* and *Sanctus*

---

[1] Among the most important studies of the 'Palestrina style' in general are: Karl Gustav Fellerer, *Der Palestrinastil und seine Bedeutung in der vokalen Kirchenmusik des 18. Jahrhunderts* (Augsburg, 1929) and *Palestrina* (Ratisbon, 1930; rev. and enlarged ed. Düsseldorf, 1960); Knud Jeppesen, *Der Palestrinastil und die Dissonanz* (Leipzig, 1925; 2nd Eng. ed., rev., *The Style of Palestrina and the Dissonance*, Copenhagen and London, 1946); H. K. Andrews, *An Introduction to the Technique of Palestrina* (London, 1958).

[2] 'Beethoven', *Gesammelte Schriften und Dichtungen* (4th ed., Leipzig, 1907), ix, p. 61. Quoted here in Edward Dannreuther's translation.

[3] On the Masses, see particularly Peter Wagner, *Geschichte der Messe* (Leipzig, 1913), pp. 432 ff.; Fellerer, *Palestrina, passim*; Gustave Reese, *Music in the Renaissance* (London, 1954), pp. 469 ff.; Joseph Samson, *Palestrina ou la Poésie de l'exactitude* (Geneva, 1940); Johannes Klassen, 'Untersuchungen zur Parodiemesse Palestrinas', *Kirchenmusikalisches Jahrbuch*, xxxvii (1953), p. 53, 'Die Parodieverfahren in der Messe Palestrinas', ibid. xxxviii (1954), p. 24, 'Zur Modellbehandlung in Palestrinas Parodiemessen', ibid. xxxix (1955), p. 41; Knud Jeppesen, 'The Recently Discovered Mantova Masses of Palestrina', *Acta Musicologica*, xxii (1950), p. 36; and 'Pierluigi da Palestrina,

as hymns of praise, the *Kyrie*, *Benedictus*, and *Agnus Dei* in a motet-like and more lyrical style. Homophony largely prevails in both *Credo* and *Gloria*; in the others the polyphonic strands generally show more movement, especially in the *Sanctus*.

The Masses naturally vary in merit, but a large proportion of them are certainly masterpieces. As Palestrina spent the whole of his life in the service of three Roman basilicas—St. Peter's, Santa Maria Maggiore, and St. John Lateran—doubtless some of his Masses and motets had to be hastily written to order for special occasions. One may recall the story told by Baini,[1] that in 1585 Palestrina hurriedly composed a motet and parody Mass 'Tu es pastor ovium'[2] as an offering to a newly elected Pope (Sixtus V); the latter is said to have remarked that the music hardly lived up to the standard of the 'Papae Marcelli', and there may have been some truth in this, for Palestrina himself withheld the music from publication, and his son Iginio has been criticized for bringing it out soon after his father's death. The Masses differ not only in quality but in style, according to the liturgical needs they serve, from those written for the great festivals of the Church to those of smaller calibre for everyday use. To the former class belong the great works in eight and six parts, to the latter those in four parts. Palestrina's first published work, *Missarum . . . liber primus*, appeared at Rome in 1554, when he was about twenty-nine years of age. As he brought out this publication, and most of his later ones, at his own expense he may have had to wait until he could afford to do it. We may therefore hazard a guess that part, at least, of the contents of this book had been written some years previously: for example the Mass 'Ecce sacerdos magnus',[3] no doubt a youthful act of homage to his patron the Bishop of Palestrina, who, elevated to the See of St. Peter as Julius III in 1551, soon appointed the composer as *maestro di cappella* of the Cappella Giuliana. (The whole volume of Masses is dedicated to Julius III.) This is an old-fashioned *canto fermo* Mass on the melody of the Vespers antiphon for the feast of a

Herzog Guglielmo Gonzaga und die neugefundenen Mantovaner-Messen Palestrinas', *Acta Musicologica*, xxv (1953), p. 132; Wilhelm Widmann, 'Motette und Messe "Dies sanctificatus" von Palestrina', *Kirchenmusikalisches Jahrbuch*, xxi (1908), p. 77, and 'Sechsstimmige Messen Palestrinas', ibid. xxv (1930), p. 94, xxvi (1931), p. 59, xxvii (1932), p. 110, xxviii (1933), p. 10; Michael Haller, 'Analyse der Missa "O admirabile commercium" von G. P. da Palestrina', ibid. ix (1894), p. 69.

[1] Giuseppe Baini, *Memorie storico-critiche della vita e dell'opere di Giovanni P. da Palestrina* (2 vols., Rome, 1828), ii, p. 160.

[2] *Werke*, ed. F. Espagne, F. X. Haberl, and others (33 vols., Leipzig, 1862–97), vi, p. 21, and xvi, p. 85. Lavinio Virgili, Knud Jeppesen, and Lino Bianchi: *Opere complete*, ed. Raffaele Casimiri (Rome, 1939–), Mass only, xxiii, p. 115.

[3] *Werke*, x, p. 3; *Opere complete*, i, p. 1.

confessor. It constantly recurs, sung in long notes to the original words:

Ex. 118

The third *Agnus Dei* is purely 'Netherland' in its ingenuity, the two higher voices singing in *tempus perfectum minor*, the tenor in *tempus perfectum major*, and the bass in *tempus imperfectum* and *prolatio*

perfecta. Comparison with such a Mass as the 'Aeterna Christi munera',[1] written some thirty or more years later, will show how very far Palestrina's style developed.

THE 'MISSA PAPAE MARCELLI'

Palestrina's patron, Julius III, was succeeded in 1555 by Marcellus II, who died only a few weeks after his elevation to the Holy See. On the third day of his very brief pontificate (Good Friday, 12 April) he summoned to his presence the Papal choir, of which Palestrina at this time was a member, and commanded that in future the music for Good Friday should be more in character with the solemnity of the day. The sudden death of the Pontiff soon afterwards may have deepened the impression made by his speech, and it is reasonable to assume that Palestrina later resolved to commemorate the Pope by writing a Mass which endeavoured to put into practice the latter's precepts. Although there may be no truth in Baini's story[2] that the 'Missa Papae Marcelli' 'saved church music', the Council of Trent's recommendations in 1562, and the ensuing sittings of the commission of cardinals in Rome, had their influence upon composers, and modern research suggests that the Mass does date from this period.[3] The Council's recommendations[4] amplified Marcellus's *audiri atque percipi*, by insisting upon the essential requirements for church music: dignity and restraint, the exclusion of secular tunes, and textual clarity with no troping. Composers, indeed, began to advertise their church music as fulfilling these precepts. At St. Peter's, Giovanni Animuccia issued Masses and motets described by him as 'seconda la forma del Concilio di Trento' (Rome, 1567).[5] Vincenzo Ruffo at Milan followed suit with similar works 'composto secondo la riforma del Concilio Tridentino'.[6] Costanzo Porta at Ravenna says much the

---

[1] *Werke*, xiv, p. 1; *Opere complete*, xv, p. 1.   [2] Op. cit. i, pp. 216 ff.

[3] See Jeppesen, 'Marcellus-Probleme', *Acta Musicologica*, xvi–xvii (1944–5), p. 11.

[4] See Karl Weinmann, *Das Konzil von Trient und die Kirchenmusik* (Leipzig, 1919); K. G. Fellerer, 'Church Music and the Council of Trent', *Musical Quarterly*, xxxix (1953), p. 576; Lewis H. Lockwood, 'Vincenzo Ruffo and Musical Reform after the Council of Trent', *Musical Quarterly*, xliii (1957), p. 342; Hermann Beck, 'Das Konzil von Trient und die Probleme der Kirchenmusik', *Kirchenmusikalisches Jahrbuch*, xlviii (1964), p. 108. Haberl's 'Die Kardinalskommission von 1564 und Palestrina's *Missa Papae Marcelli*', *Kirchenmusikalisches Jahrbuch*, vii (1892), p. 82, is valuable but needs correction from later studies.

[5] The *Kyrie* and *Gloria* from Animuccia's Mass 'Conditor alme siderum' in this volume are printed by Torchi, op. cit. i (Milan, 1897), pp. 159 and 165.

[6] Robert J. Snow has published a 'Missa sine nomine' from Ruffo's third book of Masses (surviving only in its second edition, Brescia, 1580) (Cincinnati, 1958); *Gloria* and *Credo* from the same book in Torchi, op. cit., pp. 193 and 197. On Ruffo, see Lockwood, op. cit., and Luigi Torri, 'Vincenzo Ruffo, madrigalista e compositore di musica sacra del sec. XVI', *Rivista musicale italiana*, iii (1896), p. 635, and iv (1897), p. 233.

same in the preface to his *Missarum liber primus* (1578). Palestrina, without openly making a similar declaration, stated, in the preface to his Second Book of Masses (Rome, 1567)[1] (which includes the 'Papae Marcelli') that he had 'endeavoured to adorn the Mass with music of a new order in accordance with the views of the most serious and religious-minded persons in high places'.

The 'Missae Papae Marcelli' has often been spoken of as Palestrina's greatest work. This is perhaps an overstatement of its merits, although it must rank among the best of his Masses because of its fine proportions and its admirable design. It has also been characterized as austere, a mistaken view of its dignity: solemn it may be, for it is perhaps in the nature of an elegy upon the Pope whose name it bears. To some extent it does inaugurate a new style on its composer's part, a comparatively simple type of contrapuntal writing, sometimes note against note, with effects made by skilful grouping and regrouping of the voices, their various entries and re-entries, thus relying more upon vocal colour, refreshing the ear with new combinations. The choice of the particular voices to be employed and the use of the various registers of those voices became an aesthetic problem which Palestrina often solved with remarkable skill. His use of vocal tone-colour, indeed, might well be termed choral orchestration. The *Christe eleison*[2] affords an excellent example: cantus and altus, with the second bass, begin, then there are successive entries of first tenor parallel with altus, second tenor parallel with first bass.

Ex 119

[1] Reprinted in *Werke*, xi, and *Opere complete*, iv.
[2] Borrowed from the passage 'Qui sedes' in the *Gloria* of the Mass 'Benedicta es' on Josquin's motet, *Werke*, xxiv, p. 72; *Opere complete*, xxviii, p. 222: see Jeppesen, 'Marcellus-Probleme', pp. 26–27.

Another striking instance of this employment of particular tone-colour for a special effect is to be found in the 'Ave Maria, gratia plena' for three soprani and tenor.[1] Here the close texture, as the voices enter successively at the same pitch, and the bright vocal tone, give a luminous duality to this music, which is based upon the plainsong melody of the Vespers antiphon for the Feast of the Annunciation, sung by the tenor:

Ex. 120

[1] *Werke*, v, p. 164; *Opere complete*, xi, p. 63.

The 'Papae Marcelli' Mass is freely composed, with no plainsong basis so far as is known. One motive of the *Kyrie*:

Ex 121

Ky - rie e - lei - - - son,

which reappears in the *Credo* at the words 'Patrem omnipotentem', in the second *Agnus Dei*, and elsewhere, happens to be identical with 'L'homme armé', but it is very common in Palestrina.[1]

LATER MASSES

If the 'Papae Marcelli' represents to some extent an experiment, it was one that certainly had an influence on Palestrina's future style. The exquisite four-part 'Missa Brevis', published in the third Book of Masses (Rome, 1570)[2] shows, for example, the employment of homophonic passages in *Gloria* and *Credo*, and the grouping and re-grouping of voices. Its thematic material is insignificant; Baini[3] conjectured that this was taken from Goudimel's Mass 'Audi filia'[4] but it might have been derived equally well from fragments of plainsong; indeed one or two motives are unquestionably taken from that source. But what is most significant is the use made of these short motives: for example, the theme with which the *Christe* begins seems to be employed as a symbol of the Saviour:

Ex. 122

and is beautifully transformed in the 'Qui tollis' of the *Gloria*:

Ex. 123

---

[1] See Jeppesen, 'Marcellus-Probleme', pp. 24–25.   [2] *Werke*, xii; *Opere complete*, vi.
[3] Op. cit. i, p. 363.   [4] See p. 247 and Ex. 91.

and again in the 'Crucifixus' of the *Credo*:

Ex. 124

In addition to such constructional features, the 'Missa brevis' has many beauties, one of which is the strikingly melodic character of the tenor part. The three-part *Benedictus* is a movement of exquisite delicacy, with decorative counterpoints such as this:

Ex. 125

and the *Agnus Dei*[1] founded on a soaring four-note theme, the polyphony woven in close imitation, is one of the finest parts of the Mass:

Ex. 126

[1] The second *Agnus Dei*, its two *cantus* parts in canon at the unison, is recorded in *The History of Music in Sound* (H.M.V.), iv.

The style thus created is continued later in such four-part masses as those founded upon the office hymns from which they derive their names: 'Jesu nostra redemptio',[1] 'Iste confessor', and 'Aeterna Christi munera',[2] the last one of the simplest but most perfect ever written by Palestrina. It has usually been cited as the most typical example of Palestrina's later style, with its melodic movement smooth almost to the point of cloying, and its perfectly balanced part-writing. Based on a Matins hymn in Mode XI, identical with the modern major mode, it naturally manifests a leaning towards the diatonic. Such passages, for instance, as the opening of the *Gloria* and the

---

[1] Originally published in the Fourth Book of Masses (Venice, 1582); reprinted in *Werke*, xiii, p. 29; *Opere complete*, x, p. 30.

[2] Both published in the Fifth Book (Rome, 1590); *Werke*, xiv, pp. 54 and 1; *Opere complete*, xv, pp. 72 and 1.

Sanctus[1] are undeniably diatonic in feeling, rather than modal, and might easily belong to a work written in a later age.

PALESTRINA'S PARODY MASSES

Among the Masses in six or more parts there are at least three master-pieces besides the 'Papae Marcelli': the rarely beautiful work written for the feast of the Assumption, 'Assumpta est Maria',[2] the magnificent Mass for All Saints, 'Ecce ego Joannes',[3] and the festal 'Laudate Dominum'.[4] The first-named is founded on Palestrina's own six-part motet[5] which in turn is based on the antiphon for the day; it is perhaps the finest of all his parody Masses. There is some exquisite contra-puntal writing, the music being characterized by a delicate brilliance, especially remarkable if sung by a choir no larger than that for which it was written. This is largely due to two technical effects: the frequent employment of the upper registers of the voices, the six parts con-sisting of two sopranos, alto, two tenors, and bass, and the frequent close weaving and crossing of the parts, particularly between the sopranos and the tenors. This last device gives a soft richness to the musical texture, as at the end of the *Gloria*:

Ex. 127

---

[1] Recorded in *The History of Music in Sound*, iv.

[2] Published separately in Rome after 1611, but composed before 1585. Printed in *Werke*, xxiii, p. 97; *Opere complete*, xxv, p. 209.

[3] First published in 1887 in *Werke*, xxiv, p. 129; *Opere complete*, xxix, p. 197.

[4] Published posthumously (Venice, 1601); reprinted, *Werke*, xxii, p. 1; *Opere complete*, xxx, p. 1.

[5] *Opera Omnia*, vi, p. 28.

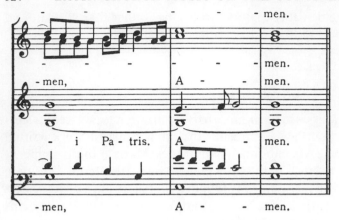

The passage should be compared with the brilliant end of the first part of the motet, on which it is, of course, based:

Ex. 128

There are many other felicitous touches of craftsmanship in this Mass. For instance, after the brightness, appropriate to a festal occasion, of the first *Kyrie*, there comes a sudden hush at the *Christe* where the four lower voices quietly intone a solemn phrase, as if to remind the listener that, after all, this music is a prayer for mercy.

The similarity in style between the Mass for the Feast of All Saints, 'Ecce ego Joannes', and the 'Missa Papae Marcelli' has been remarked by more than one commentator. There is the same dignity, almost austere in its remote atmosphere, heightened in the former by the insistence upon the typical cadences of the Mixolydian mode in which it is written. Another resemblance is in the comparatively insignificant thematic material, the music making its effect through the superb polyphonic texture as a whole. The brilliant festal Mass 'Laudate Dominum' is another parody Mass, based on the eight-part motet 'Laudate Dominum omnes gentes'.[1] Like the motet, it is written for double choir in eight parts in the Venetian style which Palestrina did not adopt until late in life.

Before leaving the subject of Palestrina's parody Masses, it must be pointed out that, despite the Council of Trent and the commission of cardinals, he by no means confined himself to liturgical models. Apart from posthumously printed works, he published in his lifetime not only two 'L'homme armé' Masses (1570 and 1582)[2] but Masses on Domenico Ferrabosco's very popular madrigal 'Io mi son giovinetta' (1570),[3] on Leonardo Primavera's madrigal 'Nasce la gioia mia' (1590),[4] and on the *chanson* 'Je suis désheritée' (1594).[5] 'Nasce la gioia' actually appeared with this title but Palestrina was usually more cautious; he styled the second, four-part 'L'homme armé' simply 'Missa quarta', 'Io mi son', 'Primi toni'—though the title was betrayed in the Venetian edition of 1599—and 'Je suis désheritée', 'Sine nomine'. Moreover he took some care to conceal the model musically. For instance, in 'Io mi son giovinetta' the two-part passage which— hardly varied at all—opens each section of the Mass:

[1] Published in Palestrina's *Motettorum . . . liber secundus* (Venice, 1572); reprinted, *Werke*, ii, p. 164; *Opere complete*, vii, p. 219.

[2] *Werke*, xii, p. 75, and xiii, p. 45; *Opere complete*, vi, p. 97 and x, p. 60.

[3] *Werke*, xii, p. 26; *Opere complete*, vi, p. 30. This is in four parts; another Mass on the same model, in six parts, was published by Haberl in 1892, *Werke*, xxxii, p. 10. Ferrabosco's madrigal is printed in Alfred Einstein, *The Italian Madrigal* (Princeton, 1949), iii, p. 56.

[4] *Opera Omnia*, xiv, p. 118; *Opere complete*, xv, p. 161.

[5] *Werke*, xv, p. 44; *Opere Complete*, xxi, p. 52. On the *chanson* see p. 5; modern reprints in Hans Albrecht, *Johannes Lupi: Zehn weltliche Lieder* (*Das Chorwerk*, xv) (Wolfenbüttel, 1931), p. 6, and Arnold Schering, *Geschichte der Musik in Beispielen* (Leipzig, 1931), p. 115.

Ex. 129

is not too easily recognizable as a derivation from Ferrabosco's opening:

Ex. 130

the madrigal cantus being at first—though only at first—masked by the higher part in the Mass. The *Christe* comes much nearer to Ferrabosco's 'Io vo per verdi prati' but the real shock to propriety comes in the *Credo*, where the words 'Et incarnatus est de Spiritu sancto' are sung to Ex. 130 with hardly a note changed.

PALESTRINA'S MOTETS

It has been said that in his motets[1] Palestrina must yield place to Lassus. Taken as a whole they may not have quite the vividness and variety, the richness of effect which characterize the latter's motet style, yet it might be fairer to say that each had a sphere in which he was pre-eminent: Lassus in the setting of texts emphasizing the human element, Palestrina in those of a mystical or symbolical character. Regarded from this point of view there is nothing by his contemporary that can surpass such Palestrina motets as the Epiphany-tide 'Surge illuminare',[2] of apocalyptic grandeur, the Pentecostal 'Dum complerentur',[3] full of mystical beauty, the festal eight-part 'Jubilate Deo'[4] a superb hymn of praise, the lovely Nativity 'Hodie Christus natus

---

[1] On the motets, see particularly Hugo Leichtentritt, *Geschichte der Motette* (Leipzig, 1908), pp. 147 ff.; Haberl, 'Die ersten drei Bände der Motetten Palestrina's', *Kirchenmusikalisches Jahrbuch*, v (1890), p. 1; Heinrich Rahe, 'Der Aufbau der Motetten Palestrinas', ibid. xxxv (1951), p. 54.

[2] *Motettorum . . . liber tertius* (Venice, 1575); reprinted *Werke*, iii, p. 134; *Opere complete*, viii, p. 174.

[3] *Motettorum . . . liber primus* (Rome, 1569); reprinted *Werke*, i, p. 111; *Opere complete*, v, p. 149; model for a parody Mass, *Werke*, xvii, p. 85; *Opere complete*, xxiv, p. 117.

[4] From the Third Book; *Werke*, iii, p. 160; *Opere complete*, viii, p. 209.

est',[1] to mention only four of the hundreds of works in motet form that came from the pen of the Roman master, composed for the manifold liturgical occasions of the church's year. The texts, chosen from the Scriptures or medieval prose and poetry, show a great variety of sentiment and there is a corresponding range of style in their musical settings, from modest little movements in three or four parts to large-scale works for double choirs in the Venetian manner. Their thematic origin is sometimes to be found in the plainsong melodies associated with the Proper, though they are more often freely invented. Naturally we find a more vivid style than that employed in the Masses. Instead of unifying themes we generally find that each portion of the text, sometimes even a single word, evokes in turn a musical idea often symbolical or naïvely pictorial, as in the six-part Nativity motet 'O magnum mysterium',[2] where the 'O' is repeated to sustained notes by all the voices in turn, thus suggesting a child-like wonder and awe at the mystery of the Incarnation.

Ex. 131

In 'Surge illuminare' the initial words are illustrated by waves of decorative polyphony which spread upwards in voice after voice,

Ex. 132

CHORUS I

---

¹ From the Third Book; *Werke*, iii, p. 155; *Opere complete*, viii, p. 203; model for a Mass, *Werke*, xxii, p. 40; *Opere complete*, xxx, p. 59.

² From the First Book; *Werke*, i, p. 137; *Opere complete*, v, p. 184; model for a Mass, *Werke*, xiii, p. 110; *Opere complete*, x, p. 150.

and are followed by a magnificent passage of massive homophony in triple time, then another of antiphony between the two choirs. The so-called second part, 'Et ambulabunt'[1], is really a separate movement written some years later, never published by Palestrina himself, and not so striking in quality—the text is perhaps less inspiring—but there is an echo of the first part, especially the use of the 'et gloria ejus' passage:

Ex. 133

[1] *Werke*, vi, p. 90.

for the words 'et laudem Domino'.

There are several other fine examples of the double-choral quasi-Venetian works among the Palestrina motets, for example the already mentioned 'Hodie Christus', a Fra Angelico in music, a simple idyllic picture. Beginning with simple strains punctuated by repeated crics of 'noe' echoed between the choirs, the movement gradually expands into a suave polyphony at the words 'canunt angeli, laetantur arch-angeli', and reaches a fine climax at 'Gloria in excelsis', the whole passage giving the effect of a great hymn sung by the heavenly host. Then, as if suggesting the fading of this vision of celestial choirs, the motet closes simply, with repeated 'noes' in triple time.

The six-part 'Dum complerentur', mentioned above, is another example remarkable alike for its design and its beauty. The quiet impressive opening—at first in three parts only—is doubtless intended to convey the hushed expectancy of the disciples as they await the promised coming of the Holy Spirit:

Ex. 134

Each phrase of the narrative is followed by an exquisite chain of 'alleluias', the finest of which provides a superb climax to the great surge of polyphony at the words 'tamquam spiritus vehementis et replevit totam domum'. These chains of 'alleluias' are constructed upon a downward scale figure, suggesting the descent of the celestial Visitant. The voices chosen—soprano, two altos, two tenors, and bass —impart to them a luminous quality that has already been remarked upon in connexion with other works.

Similarly beautiful and decorative 'alleluias' are to be found in the Ascensiontide 'Viri Galilaei'[1] and the lovely Easter 'Haec dies',[2] both for six parts.

Turning to the four-part motets we find here also some music of outstanding quality. Several of them have become very familiar and have even been fitted with English texts, for example 'Super flumina Babylonis'.[3] As Palestrina has set this psalm lament of the Jewish captivity in simple dignified phrases, it becomes an elegy for a nation in mourning.[4] The central climax comes with the motive accompanying the words 'dum recordaremur tui, Sion', which is twice repeated with the strands more tensely drawn. Another little masterpiece, remarkable for the lyrical quality of its woven melodies is 'Sicut cervus' (for the blessing of the baptismal font on Holy Saturday).[5] Here, in traditional fashion, the tenor voice introduces the principal theme with its charming rhythmic flow.

'STABAT MATER' AND 'SONG OF SONGS'

No survey of Palestrina's art would be complete without some reference to two masterpieces: the eight-part 'Stabat mater'[6] and the five-part settings of passages from the Song of Songs. The former is a work of appealing beauty, much of it having that kind of simplicity which is often the hallmark of genius; for example, the wonderful opening phrases, where a relentless succession of triad harmonies may perhaps be intended to suggest the scene of Calvary. With this may be contrasted the gentle pleading phrases which begin with the words 'Juxta crucem tecum stare' where the melodic line is sung by two sopranos, mostly in thirds, with the support of altos and tenors —another instance of the felicitous 'vocal scoring' to which reference has already been made. And at the end there is a serenely beautiful effect at the words 'paradisi gloria', each voice echoing a simple four-note descending figure.

It may have been a realization of the growing influence of the

[1] From the First Book; *Werke*, i, p. 105; *Opere complete*, v, p. 141; model for a Mass, *Werke*, xxi, p. 111; *Opere complete*, xxix, p. 159.

[2] From the Third Book; *Werke*, iii, p. 114; *Opere complete*, viii, p. 148.

[3] *Motectorum quatuor vocibus . . . liber secundus* (Venice, 1604); *Werke*, v, p. 125; *Opere complete*, xi, p. 14.

[4] Baini attributes its inspiration to grief at the death of the composer's first wife, in 1582, but there is no evidence that it was composed just after that event.

[5] From the Second Book of four-part motets: *Werke*, v, p. 148; *Opere complete*, xi, p. 42. Davison and Apel, *Historical Anthology of Music* (Cambridge, Mass., 1946), i, p. 153.

[6] *Werke*, vi, p. 96; there are a number of separate modern editions. The twelve-part 'Stabat', *Werke*, vii, p. 130, is a work by Felice Anerio.

madrigal style upon polyphonic music that prompted Palestrina to set twenty-nine passages from the Song of Songs,[1] for here was a subject with rich imagery eminently suitable for such treatment, and at the same time the Church's spiritual interpretation of the Canticle made him safe from the charge of writing those secular madrigals for which he apologized in the preface to this work, addressed to Pope Gregory XII. These twenty-nine five-part motets include some of the finest examples of Palestrina's mature style, where the refined melodious polyphony of his later liturgical works is happily modified by some madrigalian elements, bringing a richer warmer quality, while preserving its dignity and spirituality. The invention is freer—there is no plainsong foundation—and the polyphony is always beautifully smooth and polished. The texts were selected to afford due contrast and variety, while preserving enough unity to give the whole the character of a complete work, as the composer intended.

PERFORMANCE OF PALESTRINA

Although instrumental music was excluded from the Sistine Chapel, the Cappella Giulia had an organ[2] and there is no reason to suppose that Palestrina's music was performed unaccompanied. There was no independent accompaniment, but the organ would quietly double the voice parts. Less acceptable to modern minds is the idea that Palestrina's music was ornamented in performance. The practice of ornamenting madrigals with coloratura has been mentioned in an earlier chapter[3] and there is ample evidence that church music was treated in a similar way. Haberl printed twelve such ornamented motet parts in the fourth supplementary volume of his Complete Edition,[4] and it is instructive to compare the unadorned text of the opening of the four-part motet 'Benedicta sit'[5] with a decorated version published in Palestrina's lifetime:[6]

Ex. 136

¹ *Motettorum . . . liber quartus* (Rome, 1584); *Werke*, iv; *Opere complete*, xi.
² Haberl, 'Die römische "schola cantorum" und die päpstlichen Kapellsänger bis zur Mitte des 16. Jahrhunderts', *Vierteljahrsschrift für Musikwissenschaft*, iii (1887), p. 189.
³ See p. 148, n. 1.   ⁴ *Werke*, xxxiii.
⁵ From the *Motecta festorum totius anni* (Rome, 1563); *Werke*, v, p. 33; *Opere complete*, iii, p. 38.
⁶ Giovanni Bassano, *Motetti, madrigali et canzoni francese diminuiti* (Venice, 1591).

The famous nine-part 'Miserere' of Gregorio Allegri (1582–1652),
pupil of Palestrina's friend G. M. Nanino, is a classic example of a
work of this period which depended for its effect almost entirely on
such ornamentation and on the manner of performance.[1]

LASSUS[2]

Lassus is sometimes spoken of as the last great master of the
Netherland School. It is true he was a Netherlander by birth, but at
the period with which we are dealing one can hardly speak any longer
of a 'Netherland school'. The mutual influence of the Romans, Venetians, Netherlanders, and the rest had produced something approaching a pan-European style, at least in church music. But there still
remained the individuality of the composer, and in the case of Lassus
this manifested itself first of all in a certain vigour, then in a search
for more freedom in harmony and modulation; experiments in these
directions can often be found in his music. Thus from the historical
and technical points of view his work perhaps presents a more interesting study than that of his great Roman contemporary.[3]

Lassus was the most prolific composer of the period; the religious
music alone comprises about 500 motets, 53 Masses, and 100 Magnificats. Most of this was written at Munich, where at the ducal court of
Bavaria from 1556 to 1594 he seems to have lived a life of much social
activity, keenly observing the contemporary scene.[4] It is not surprising, then, that it is the human rather than the mystical element in
his church music of which we are so frequently conscious—and not
only in his famous settings of the penitential psalms. The lovely little
'Crucifixus', for example, from the Mass 'Doulce memoire' (see

[1] Charles Burney, *The Present State of Music in France and Italy* (London, 1771);
reprinted in P. A. Scholes, *Dr. Burney's Musical Tours in Europe* (London, 1959), i, p. 232.
See also J. J. Amann, *Allegris Miserere und die Aufführungspraxis in der Sixtina* (Freiburg
dissertation, 1935).

[2] On Lassus generally, see above all Wolfgang Boetticher, *Orlando di Lasso und seine
Zeit* (Kassel and Basle, 1958) and *Aus Orlando di Lassos Wirkungskreis* (Kassel and
Basle, 1963); also Adolf Sandberger, *Beiträge zur Geschichte der bayerischen Hofkapelle
unter Orlando di Lasso*, i and iii (Leipzig, 1894–5); Charles Van den Borren, *Orlande de
Lassus* (Paris, 2nd ed., 1920).

[3] See Boetticher's comparison of settings of the same texts by Palestrina and Lassus,
op. cit., pp. 699 ff.   [4] See pp. 56 ff.

Ex. 145) surely emphasizes, in its touching pathos, the sufferings of the Saviour as a human being.

LASSUS'S STYLE

The range of Lassus's contrapuntal writing is considerable, from madrigal-like liveliness to sedate and dignified polyphony, with a good deal of sonorous homophony where he almost seems to have been thinking in terms of vertical harmony. He had a passion for word-painting and seized every opportunity for indulging in it,[1] even in his Masses where such phrases as 'vivos et mortuos' inspire realistic effects (see Ex. 141). And the whimsicality of such of his letters as have been preserved is also apparent, for example, in the capricious little phrase at the beginning of the motet 'Pulvis et umbra':[2]

Ex. 137

Another individual touch is the exact reiteration of a short phrase several times, either at the same pitch or sequentially, foreshadowing the emotional climaxes of a later age. Lassus, more than his contemporaries, seems sometimes to have realized the value of a striking theme, though he does not always make systematic use of his themes, often employing them merely as points of departure for free writing.

Lassus was not quite so concerned as Palestrina with the problem

---

[1] See Bernhard Meier, 'Wortausdeutung und Tonalität bei Orlando di Lasso', *Kirchenmusikalisches Jahrbuch*, xlvii (1963), p. 75.

[2] Published 1573; ed. Haberl, *Orlando di Lasso: Sämmtliche Werke*, iv (Leipzig, 1894), p. 127.

of tone-colour: the choice of voices and the skilful employment of their various registers. He gains his effects more by dynamic variation, often using a delicate two-part or three-part movement of a highly decorative kind in contrast to a more massive structure in homophonic style.

THE MASSES[1]

If in his Masses Lassus does not quite attain to the high level, in beauty and significance, of the best of his motets, they are yet of fine quality, in some instances achieving in the *Gloria* and *Sanctus* splendid richness and sonority, in the *Kyrie* and *Agnus Dei* touching lyrical tenderness, a quality we also find in the central climax of the *Credo*, the 'Incarnatus' and 'Crucifixus'.

It is not without significance that the thematic material of most of his Masses is drawn from secular sources, from madrigals and *chansons*, occasionally from motets by himself or others, in one case ('Ecce nunc benedicite')[2] a Mass by Ludwig Daser, his predecessor at Munich, and in only six or seven cases directly from plainsong.[3] In his *chanson*-Masses he sometimes surpassed Gombert and the French composers[4] in brevity, perfunctoriness, and failure to conceal secular models with highly unsuitable words—even after the Council of Trent. The first *Kyrie* of the Mass 'Je ne menge poinct de porcq'[5] can easily be quoted in full:

Ex. 138

---

[1] There is as yet no collected edition: Franz Commer reprinted fourteen in *Musica sacra* (Berlin, 1839–1887), v, vii, viii, ix, x, and xii, and Boetticher has begun a complete edition in the *Sämtliche Werke: Neue Reihe* (Kassel and Basle, 1956–   ), iii, iv, and v. On the Masses, see particularly Joachim Huschke, 'Orlando di Lassos Messen', *Archiv für Musikforschung*, v (1940), pp. 84 ff. and pp. 153 ff.; Van den Borren, op. cit., pp. 127 ff.; Peter Wagner, op. cit., pp. 349 ff.

[2] Printed Commer, op. cit. v, p. 63.

[3] See the list in Huschke, p. 177.

[4] See pp. 221 and 239 ff.

[5] *Werke: Neue Reihe*, iii, p. 3.

The *Christe* is seven bars long, and the second *Kyrie* ten. The first *Kyrie* of 'Entre vous filles de quinze ans'[1] hardly does more than elaborate the opening of Clemens non Papa's *chanson* with the addition of a fifth part. Both these Masses are preserved in a Munich choirbook of 1566. But by no means all the parody-Masses on secular models are of this character. The four-part Masses on Lupi's 'Puisque j'ay perdu' and Sandrin's 'Doulce memoire' are typical. The first-named[2] (alternatively known as 'Missa octavi toni' because the first three notes of the melody happen to be also the intonation of the eighth psalm tone) is the best known. Like all these *chanson*-based Masses it is a melodious work, often homophonic, with sonorous harmonic effects. The music shows several characteristics of Lassus's style, such as the use of sequential phrases, as in the second *Kyrie*:

Ex. 139

and this passage from the *Gloria*:

Ex. 140

---

[1] *Werke: Neue Reihe*, v, p. 159.

[2] Originally published by Le Roy and Ballard in *Missae variis concentibus ornatae ab Orlando de Lassus* (Paris, 1577); reprinted in *Werke: Neue Reihe*, iv, p. 23; separate editions by J. A. Bank (Amsterdam, 1950) and Wilhelm Lueger (Ratisbon, 1957). *Benedictus* and 'Osanna' recorded in *The History of Music in Sound*, iv.

His fondness for pictorial treatment of the text finds opportunity in the Mass as well as in the motet; for instance, in the *Credo* at the words 'vivos et mortuos' we have this naïve touch of realism:

and another instance occurs at the words 'et exspecto resurrectionem':

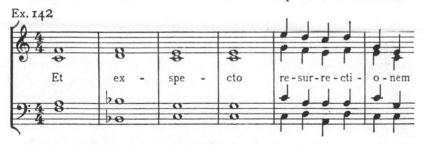

A feature of this Mass is its florid bass part, with an unusual range of nearly two octaves, due perhaps to the circumstance that the ducal choir at Munich possessed a fine bass with a phenomenal compass.

Like 'Puisque j'ay perdu', the Mass on Sandrin's 'Doulce memoire'[1] was first printed at Paris in 1577. It is the most serious of

---

[1] Reprinted in *Werke: Neue Reihe*, iv, p. 3; separate edition by Charles Bordes (Paris, 1952). The model has been reprinted by Eitner in *Publikation älterer praktischer und theoretischer Musikwerke*, xxiii (Leipzig, 1899), p. 103 and by Max Schneider in his edition of Ortiz's *Tratado de glosas* (2nd ed. Kassel, 1936), p. 86.

all Lassus's *chanson*-Masses, thanks to the grave beauty of the model:

Some passages of the Mass have only a faint connexion with the model: for example, the beautiful homophonic 'Quoniam' of the *Gloria*:

Tu so - lus al - tis - si - mus, Je - su Chri - ste.

In the *Credo* occur two exquisite little two-part canons, the first, the
'Crucifixus', of touching tenderness,

Ex. 145

Cru - ci - fi - xus e - ti - am pro no - bis: sub
Cru - ci - fi - xus e - ti - am no - - -

Pon - ti - o   Pi - la - - - - to
-bis: sub Pon-ti - o   Pi - la - to

sung by treble and alto, is clearly inspired by the treble-bass imitation
at 'En plaisir consumée'; the second canon, 'Et iterum', is extended
from the opening phrase of the *chanson*. An almost note-for-note
quotation of 'O siecl' heureulx' is woven into the *Agnus Dei*:

Ex. 146

A - gnus De - - - i A - gnus De - i
A - gnus De - - - i   A - gnus De - i qui
                                           De - i
A - gnus De - - i A - gnus De - i

qui tol - lis pec - - ca-ta mun - - di
     qui tol - lis pec - ca-ta mun - di
tol-lis pec - ca - ta mun - - di
qui tol-lis pec - ca-ta mun - - di

a movement in which the repetition of the final 'miserere', each time at a higher pitch, has a deeply impressive effect.

Some of the other four-part Masses are of the *Missa brevis* type, shorter in dimensions and simpler in texture, perhaps composed for choirs of limited attainments. Such are the 'Missa venatorum'[1] ('Octavi toni') where we find a good deal of simple homophony, with note repetitions such as this, in the French manner, particularly in the *Gloria* and *Credo*:

Ex. 147

and another entitled 'Ad placitum'[2] (a parody Mass on Sermisy's 'La, la, maistre Pierre') where the simple homophony is varied with

---

[1] A species of curtailed Mass: see Siegfried Hermelink, 'Jägermesse', *Die Musik-forschung*, xviii (1965), p. 29. The Mass has been reprinted in *Werke: Neue Reihe*, iv, p. 73, and by Bank (Amsterdam, 1950), Lueger (Ratisbon, 1957), and Georges Renard (Paris, 1953).

[2] Printed in *Werke: Neue Reihe*, iii, p. 27.

some attractive contrapuntal passages. The simplicity of its *Kyrie*, for example, is very different from the flowing counterpoint of the *Agnus Dei*.

Two fine six-part works, among the best of Lassus's Masses, are those on his own motets 'In te Domine speravi'[1] and 'Dixit Joseph',[2] both of which show his flair for picturesque writing, his skilful contrasting of polyphony with homophony, and his wide range of dynamic effect, from such a delicate piece of vocal tissue as the two-part (soprano and alto) 'Pleni sunt' in the *Sanctus* of the first work, an ingenious piece of canonic writing with its reversed themes:

Ex. 148

to the sonorous 'Osanna' which follows. The Mass owes something of its effect to skilful use of two three-part choirs: thus in the first *Kyrie* a combination of soprano and two altos is contrasted against two tenors and bass. The same style is used in much of the *Gloria* and the *Agnus Dei*. The three-part 'Crucifixus' and the superb conclusion ('Et iterum') of the *Credo* are other noteworthy moments in this splendid work.

The finely-proportioned 'Dixit Joseph' has spaciousness and dignity. The fine *Credo* has a four-part 'Crucifixus' of remarkable beauty which offers a contrast to much of the rest of the Mass in its more intimate expression; with a characteristic sense of the dramatic, Lassus writes a two-part passage (soprano and alto) of touching pathos on the word 'crucifixus', to which the tenors and basses add the rejoinder 'etiam pro nobis':

---

[1] Originally published by Phalèse (Louvain, 1570); reprinted *Werke: Neue Reihe*, v, p. 51; the motet is printed in *Sämmtliche Werke*, xvii, p. 87.
[2] Commer, op. cit. viii, p. 65; motet, *Werke*, xv, p. 76.

Ex. 149

A typical instance of the more solid six-part quasi-homophonic writing is the dignified 'Osanna' in triple time from the *Sanctus*.

THE MOTETS OF LASSUS

Lassus is the supreme master of the sixteenth-century motet; he is unsurpassed in this field, where his finest music for the church is to be found. His motets,[1] which owe something to the lighter style of the madrigal, are a literature in themselves, ranging from the miniatures of some of the *Cantiones sacrae* and *Sacrae lectiones*—the familiar little 'Scio enim'[2] and 'Adoramus te'[3] are typical examples—to the greater motets such as the seven-part 'Laudate pueri'.[4]

Within the limits of this chapter only a few of the vast array of antiphons, offertories, offices, psalms, and other pieces for liturgical use can be mentioned. Lassus is at his best when the chosen text presents a vivid picture, where he is able to employ realistic or pictorial effects. An admirable example is the five-part Ascensiontide

[1] Most of the motets, printed in a number of books during his lifetime, were republished—very inaccurately—by his sons in the *Magnum Opus Musicum* (Munich, 1604), which in turn was reprinted by Haberl and Sandberger, *Sämmtliche Werke*, i, iii, v, vii, ix, xiii, xv, xvii, xix, xxi (1894–1926). More motets have been published by Boetticher in the *Sämtliche Werke: Neue Reihe*, and there are numerous separate editions. On them, see particularly Lucie Balmer, *Orlando di Lassos Motetten* (Berne, 1938); Leichtentritt, *Geschichte der Motette*, pp. 96 ff.; Van den Borren, op. cit., pp. 57 ff.; E. Lowinsky, *Das Antwerpener Motettenbuch Orlando di Lassos und seine Beziehungen zum Motettenschaffen der niederländischen Zeitgenossen* (The Hague, 1937).

[2] *Sämmtliche Werke*, iii, p. 105; recorded in *The History of Music in Sound*, iv.

[3] Ibid. i, p. 112; Schering, op. cit., p. 125.   [4] Ibid. xix, p. 94.

'Christus resurgens',[1] where the music is suggestive of the radiant beauty of the scene on which the apostles gazed. Beginning with an exultant theme rising up in free imitation from voice to voice:

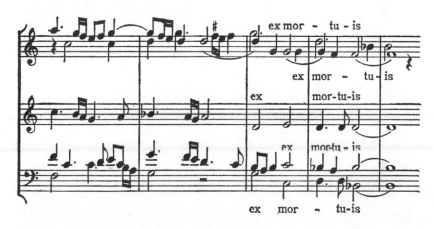

(with a dramatic momentary halt at the words 'ex mortuis') this joyful mood continues and leads to a finely expressive passage—'quod enim mortuus est peccato'—breaking out in joyful mood once more at the thought expressed by the text ('quod autem vivit') and culminating in a chain of 'alleluias', making a most jubilant finale. Here we may notice a fine piece of craftsmanship: the two cantus parts in canon, a bell-like movement in the tenor part, exultant leaps in the bass adding to the general effect:

[1] Ibid. v, p. 54.

Among the motets in six parts one finds Lassus equally inspired by
the Nativity. 'Cum natus esset Jesus'[1] comprises a triptych of little
tone-pictures, music of rare beauty and distinction, the story of the
Magi and their journeyings as related in the Gospel of St. Matthew
read at Epiphany. Part I deals with the appearance to them of the Star
in the East, Part II with their journey to Jerusalem and the learning
of the prophecies; Part III is the arrival at Bethlehem and the adora-
tion of the Holy Child. Each has music of moving simplicity, written
with consummate skill, the three Parts being linked by a 'Bethlehem'
motive especially prominent in the first two Parts, where it is fre-

[1] *Sämmtliche Werke*, xi, p. 141.

quently woven into the general texture with charming effect. It appears
thus in Part II (which is for four voices only) echoed from voice to
voice in free imitation, this repetition doubtless picturing the group
of Jewish priests answering the Magi's query by the quotation of the
prophecy 'In Bethlehem Judeae';

In the Third Part it is less prominent: symbolizing the eager quest of
the Magi, it now fades out from the musical texture, for they have
arrived at their goal, and their sight of the Child is described in a
simple homophonic phrase with a change of rhythm:

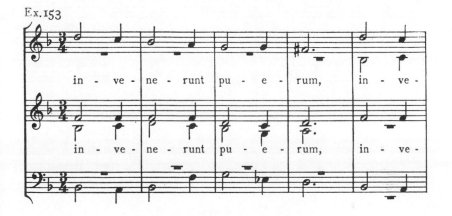

Lassus's predilection for texts taken from the psalms has already been mentioned; among the *Cantiones sacrae* are a number with such texts which inspired some of his best work. A notable example is the four-part offertory 'Exspectans exspectavi'[1] published in the collection issued by the composer at Munich in 1585. Here we have simple melodious strains bringing a feeling of rapt serenity, reflecting perfectly the sentiment of the Psalmist: 'I have waited patiently for the Lord. . . .' The motet begins with the entwined themes (soprano and alto) imitated by tenor and bass in the manner of Netherland composers of an earlier generation:

<hr>

[1] *Sämmtliche Werke*, iii, p. 72.

sinking quietly into homophony at the phrase 'et exaudivit depreca-
tionem meam', and flowering into finely sonorous polyphony suggesting 'the new song, the hymn to the Lord'. Another four-part
offertory, 'Domine convertere',[1] is equally fine, conceived in that
penitential mood which Lassus knew so well how to depict. Here he
achieves an emotional intensity that hardly any other composer of his
time can show, in a passage where the repeated cries of 'salvum me
fac' have a most poignant effect:

Ex. 155

Two other four-part motets may be briefly mentioned as showing
Lassus's genius for choosing thematic material perfectly suited to his
text. The opening of one, 'Pulvis et umbra sumus', which perfectly
suggests the 'dust and shadow', has already been quoted as Ex. 137.

[1] Ibid. iii, p. 17.

The other, 'Pauper sum ego',[1] begins most appropriately with this insignificant phrase:

Ex. 156

THE PENITENTIAL PSALMS

The *Psalmi Davidis penitentiales* of Lassus (Munich, 1584) are generally regarded as among the greatest of his achievements.[2] They were composed about 1560 at the request of his patron Albrecht of Bavaria, a pious prince who on his accession, finding a court given over to worldliness, endeavoured to bring to it a more religious atmosphere; one imagines this to have been a task peculiarly congenial to Lassus. These seven psalm settings are certainly masterpieces. No composer has depicted in more poignant phrases the despair of the sinner, or written music more expressive of the hope for divine forgiveness and grace.[3] The level of inspiration in all seven

[1] *Sämmtliche Werke*, iii, p. 79.

[2] Modern editions by Hermann Bäuerle (Leipzig, 1906) and Bank (Amsterdam, n.d.); excerpts from the third Psalm, 'Domine, ne in furore', in Davison and Apel, op. cit., p. 157.

[3] Quickelberg, op. cit., refers to this expressive quality as an illustration of *musica reservata*, an enigmatic phrase which had first been used some fifteen years earlier by Adrian Petit Coclico both in his *Compendium musices* (Nuremberg, 1552; facsimile, *Documenta Musicologica*, i. ix, Kassel, 1954) and as the title of a collection of motets (modern edition by M. Ruhnke: Lippstadt, 1958). *Musica reservata* most probably means 'music closely expressing the text'. For examinations of this and other views, see M. Van Crevel, *Adrianus Petit Coclico* (The Hague, 1940), pp. 293 ff., Reese, op. cit., pp. 511 ff., and Bernhard Meier, article 'Musica reservata', *Die Musik in Geschichte und Gegenwart*, ix (1961), col. 946, and 'Reservata-Probleme. Ein Bericht', *Acta Musicologica*, xxx (1958), p. 77; also C. V. Palisca, *Acta*, xxxi (1959), p. 133.

is remarkably high and, considering that the sentiments are to some extent the same in each, the variety of treatment is astonishing. This is helped by the design adopted for each psalm: a continuous series of very short separate movements, each a setting of a verse or a part thereof. This procedure has enabled the composer to express the varying sentiments of the text more vividly and swiftly than would have been possible in one continuous movement. The music of each psalm varies from two-part movements to an occasional one in six parts (as in the 'Sicut erat' of each). The two-part movements are very characteristic in their delicate, often florid, texture, possibly showing Lassus's feeling for that intimacy of expression which a later age achieved by the employment of a solo voice. (A similar procedure has been observed in some of his Masses.) One of the most beautiful and interesting of these two-part pieces is the 'Auditui' from the fourth psalm, 'Miserere mei Deus'; another is the canonic duet 'Intellectum' in the second, 'Beati, quorum remissae sunt iniquitates'. Indeed this psalm and the fourth are perhaps the finest of the seven. Some four-part movements of distinctly homophonic character are scattered throughout the series. In similar vein to the penitential psalms are the two series of *Sacrae lectiones ex propheta Job* (Venice, 1565, and Munich, 1582),[1] and the *Lamentationes* (Munich, 1585).[2]

THE MAGNIFICATS

No survey of Lassus's church music would be complete without some mention of the great collection of his Magnificats, published in complete form after his death by his son Rudolf: *Jubilus Beatae Virginis, hoc est centum Magnificat* (Munich, 1619).[3] The settings vary greatly in style and length; there are the simpler *alternatim* ones[4] in which only the even-number verses are set polyphonically, and also the more elaborate settings where every verse is so treated. The *alternatim* settings are based on the eight liturgical tones, elaborated for the most part in simple homophonic style, with the plainsong as *canto fermo*.

It is, however, in those settings, some forty of the total, where Lassus has taken his themes from secular sources—such as Rore's famous madrigal 'Ancor che col partire'—that we find the finest

---

[1] Reprints of two of the 1565 series in Commer, op. cit. vi, p. 40, and vii, p. 47.
[2] Reprinted ibid. xii, pp. 1 ff.
[3] Lassus had published three collections himself in 1567, 1576, and 1587. Nine Magnificats are reprinted in Proske, op. cit. iii, pp. 253 ff., and 22 in Commer, op. cit. x, pp. 102 ff. and xi, pp. 1 ff.
[4] Cf. Vol. III, pp. 307–8.

settings of the canticle, as in the case of the Masses. No doubt he felt that this gave him freer scope in writing, the more so as in them the traditional alternative form was discarded in favour of complete polyphonic settings in five parts. One of the most beautiful of these[1] is composed upon an 'Aria di un sonetto', where the initial phrase of the very graceful melody introduces each verse. Verse 4 is in ternary rhythm, verse 5 a trio:

Ex. 157

PHILIPPE DE MONTE

Lassus's friend de Monte seems to have been a man of considerable culture, speaking and writing not only his native Flemish but Italian, Latin, French, and German. In considering de Monte's church music it is well to remember that he had made a considerable name as a madrigal composer[2] and had already published eight volumes of madrigals, in addition to those printed in miscellaneous collections, before his first volume of church music, the *Sacrarum Cantionum ... Liber Primus* (Venice, 1572). He was then over fifty and had been director of the Imperial Chapel in Vienna since 1568. From this time until his death he produced, according to his principal biographer,[3] 319 motets and 38 Masses, though of this considerable quantity of

---

[1] From the *Patrocinium musices* (Munich, 1587).
[2] See p. 58.
[3] Van Doorslaer, *La Vie et les œuvres de Philippe de Monte* (Brussels, 1921).

work only a small amount was published during his lifetime and not all of it is yet available in modern editions.[1]

It is not surprising, then, that much of his work, especially the motets, has a madrigalian lightness of style, melodic suavity, and grace. And since these and the Masses were all the work of a very mature composer, they show, as we should expect, a perfection of technique unsurpassed by any of his contemporaries. But his contrapuntal mastery is in general subordinated to a simple artistic style which seeks to express the meaning of the text in the most suitable and significant way, often in homophonic passages. As early as 1555 he had been described as the best composer in Flanders 'fürnemlich auf die newest und *musica reservata*'.[2] His music at times has a charming serenity and, when the text allows, is suffused with genial warmth. The thematic material is often more striking than that of his contemporaries.

DE MONTE'S MOTETS

In his motets we find motives of a particularly expressive character, with a certain boldness of outline partly due to his fondness for disjunct, rather than conjunct, movement. An excellent example of the simple but polished workmanship and the melodious character of the moving parts is the five-part 'Ave Virgo gratiosa'[3] built on a *canto fermo* in long note-values:

Ex. 158

---

[1] *Philippe de Monte: Opera Omnia*, ed. Van den Borren, Van Doorslaer and Julius Van Nuffel, 31 vols. (Bruges, 1927–39), is still incomplete.

[2] Van Doorslaer, op. cit., p. 217.

[3] *Opera Omnia*, xv, p. 1.

The six-part 'Lux perpetua lucebit sanctis tuis'[1], which ends with an exquisite chain of 'Alleluias':

Ex.159

[1] Ibid. xvii, p. 125.

is indeed a masterpiece of serene beauty, in which once more one finds that expressive type of melody so characteristic of de Monte: for instance, the opening:

Ex.160

Of equal beauty is the five-part 'Tibi laus, Sancte Trinitas'[1], a sonorous hymn of praise to the Trinity. One piece which may be mentioned here, although it is not a Latin motet, is de Monte's setting of Marot's version of Psalm 107, 'Donnés au Seigneur gloire',[2] with the Geneva psalm-tune[3] in the tenor.

The five-part 'Inclina cor meum' has a special interest, in addition to the attractive simplicity and melodiousness of its music, for it is one of the few of his own motets which de Monte used as models for *missae parodiae*.[4] The opening of the motet:

could be used for both *Kyrie* and *Sanctus* without the alteration of a single note, and the transformations for *Gloria* and *Agnus* are particularly fine (see Ex. 162). The motet itself must rank as one of de Monte's best, showing as it does an intimacy of feeling, a pathos that remind one of such things as Lassus's 'Ego pauper sum' or Palestrina's 'Peccantem me quotidie'.

---

[1] *Opera Omnia*, xvii, p. 95, and separate edition by Bank (Amsterdam, 1960).
[2] Original published by Phalèse in a volume of French *chansons* by Lassus, Rore, and de Monte (Louvain, 1570); reprinted in *Opera Omnia*, xx, p. 23.
[3] See pp. 438 ff.
[4] Both motet and Mass are printed in *Opera*, i.

Ex.162

DE MONTE'S MASSES

De Monte's Masses present an especially interesting study. They show two distinct styles: the 'parody'-Masses and those based on liturgical melodies. The latter, with two exceptions, were the only ones published during the composer's lifetime. The six-part *Missa ad modulum Benedicta es* appeared at Antwerp in 1579; the Mass 'Mon cœur se recommande' appeared in Lindner's *Missae quinque* (Nuremberg, 1590); and the other seven were printed as *Liber I Missarum* in 1587. These show a style more in keeping with Netherland conceptions, more austere and architectural, whereas the *missae parodiae*—at least those based on such madrigals as Rore's 'Ancor che col partire', Giaches de Wert's 'Cara la vita mia', Verdelot's 'Ultimi miei sospiri', and on his own *chanson* 'Reviens vers moi'[1]—reveal their secular origin, in harmony as much as melodically, despite the superb workmanship with which the successive movements are shaped. The *Kyrie* of 'Ancor che col partire', for instance, opens—like 'Inclina cor meum'—with note-for-note quotation of the model in all four parts, and the Mass proceeds by what one might call 'progressive variation' in each movement.[2] The six-part 'Missa sine nomine',[3] in much more note-against-note style throughout than de Monte's other Masses, is also probably a *missa parodia*. Separate movements in note-against-note style do occur here and there—for example, the 'Osanna' of 'Ultimi miei sospiri'—and the eight four-part Magnificats[4] are in the same simple style.

The best known of the Masses based on motet-models is the six-part 'Benedicta es' mentioned above[5], in which de Monte rivalled Willaert[6] and Palestrina in reworking Josquin's beautiful sequence-setting.[7] It is a work of fine proportions and effect, conservative and perhaps deliberately 'learned' in style. The splendid, massively built polyphony of the first *Kyrie*:

Ex.163

[1] Published, each with its model, in *Opera*, viii, xxi, v, and ix.

[2] On this Mass, see Ernest T. Ferand, ' "Anchor che col partire": Die Schicksale eines berühmten Madrigals', *Festschrift Karl Gustav Fellerer* (Ratisbon, 1962), p. 137.

[3] Preserved in Berlin, Deutsche Bibl. 40025, and Loreto, Arch. della Santa Casa 34; published in *Opera*, vii.   [4] *Opera Omnia*, xii.

[5] Reprinted by Van Maldeghem, *Trésor musical: Musique religieuse*, x, p. 5, and Smijers, *Veröffentlichungen der Vereeniging voor Nederlandsche Muziekgeschiedenis*, xxxviii (Amsterdam and Leipzig, 1920); *Benedictus* and *Agnus Dei* recorded in *The History of Music in Sound*, iv.   [6] Or perhaps Hesdin: see p. 281.

[7] See M. Antonowytsch, *Die Motette 'Benedicta es' von Josquin des Prez und die Messen 'super Benedicta' von Willaert, Palestrina, de La Hèle und de Monte* (Utrecht, 1951).

is already a remarkable filling-out of Josquin's opening;[1] the exquisite little 'Christe eleison':

Ex.164

Josquin's motet has been published by Smijers in *Josquin: Werken*, xxxv (Amsterdam, 1954), p. 11, and *Van Ockeghem tot Sweelinck*, v (Amsterdam, 1949), p. 146.

[1] See Ex. 103 (i).

like the 'Qui tollis', 'Et iterum', and *Benedictus*, is based on
Josquin's two-part *secunda pars*, 'Per illud'; and the second *Kyrie*,
'Quoniam', and 'Confiteor' on his *tertia pars* in triple time.

Perhaps the finest moments in the Mass are the eight-part *Sanctus*
(there is an alternative version in six parts) and the second *Agnus Dei*,
also in eight parts: in both cases the additional parts are obtained by
canonic imitation of the highest part a fifth and an octave lower.
There are again massive effects, with a fine sweep of line, as for
instance at the beginning of the *Sanctus*:

Ex. 165

De Monte does not here follow the Venetian practice of dividing the eight parts into two four-part choirs, but employs them all freely. On the other hand, the Mass 'Confitebor tibi' follows its model, an eight-part motet by Lassus,[1] in its double-choral disposition. But perhaps the finest of all his eight-part Masses is the splendid one on his own madrigal 'La dolce vista'.[2] It is a beautifully proportioned work, with a wide diversity of effect, the madrigal themes, melodious and expressive, serving mostly as starting points for a freely developed polyphony. The voices are grouped into the customary four-part choirs, sometimes used antiphonally, often in partial combination, ranging from duos of delicate texture to passages of sonorous eight-part writing, perfectly balanced, the scoring never overloaded. As an example of the former, the exquisite two-part 'Crucifixus' may be quoted.

Ex.166

[1] The Mass is printed in Van Maldeghem's *Trésor musical: Musique religieuse*, ix, p. 24, the motet in *Lasso: Werke*, xxi, p. 56.   [2] Mass and madrigal in *Opera*, xiv.

It weaves its two strands canonically with an effect comparable with
a similar passage in Lassus's Mass 'In te speravi';[1] tenor and bass
reply with equally expressive phrases, and the four voices join together
for the 'Resurrexit'. The following two examples of de Monte's fine
eight-part writing, again with close canonic imitation, are taken from
the *Gloria*:

Ex. 167

(i)

[1] See p. 341.

The Mass 'Confitebor tibi', one of the book of seven published during the composer's lifetime, has already been mentioned. As an example of the vivid, eloquent manner in which the voices are employed, in their grouping and entries, this passage from the *Christe* will serve:[1]

[1] Peter Wagner quotes the openings of the *Kyrie* and *Gloria*, *Geschichte der Messe*, pp. 227 ff.

One of the best of de Monte's four-part Masses is a beautiful little work[1] with no name attached, merely described as 'quaternis vocibus'. It is a *missa brevis*, in which simple polyphony is varied by occasional homophony. The principal theme is a melodious phrase (here shown in the first *Kyrie*) which appears in every part of the Mass.

Ex. 169

[1] *Opera Omnia*, xvi: one of four Masses by de Monte preserved in Cologne, St. Maria im Kapitol, Codex Salvator-Kapelle.

Another four-part 'Missa sine nomine'[1] preserved in the same manuscript may also be cited as characteristic of de Monte's simple but very effective writing in smaller works; in its beautiful 'Crucifixus' we have a further example of his eloquent duos:

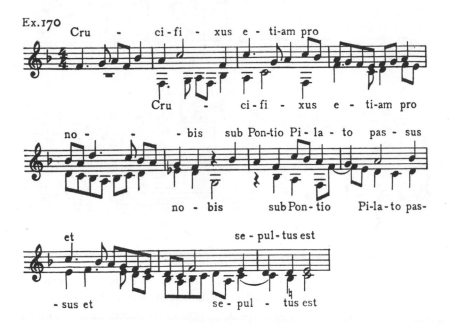

Ex.170

MINOR MASTERS OF THE *A CAPPELLA* STYLE

The greatness of Palestrina and Victoria, Lassus and de Monte should not blind us to the merits of a number of minor masters, both Italians and Netherlanders, who practised the *a cappella* style in its most perfect form. Giovanni Animuccia (1505–71), who succeeded Palestrina at St. Peter's in 1555 and was succeeded by him in 1571, has already been mentioned as a composer of Masses and motets 'according to the reforms ordered by the Council of Trent'. Animuccia is best known, however, for his association with St. Philip Neri and the latter's newly founded Oratory at San Girolamo, for which he composed *Laudi spirituali* (two volumes, published Rome, 1563 and

---

[1] Printed by Commer, *Musica Sacra*, xxiv, and in *Opera Omnia*, xi.

1570) with Italian texts.[1] His simple and suave style is shown in this quotation from the four-part motet 'Ave sanctissima Maria'.

The Milanese *maestro di cappella* Ruffo has also been mentioned on p. 317 as a composer who quickly responded to the demands of the Council of Trent; he had already published in one of the Scotto collections (Venice, 1542) a Mass which appears to be the earliest Italian Mass to get into print, as well as a volume of five-part Masses (Venice, 1557).

Even two celebrated madrigalists wrote church music in the Roman style. Marenzio published several volumes of motets, of which only the first (Venice, 1585) has survived, and his youthful *Sacrae cantiones* were published posthumously (Venice, 1616).[2] His madrigal-like style is evident in such passages as the literal illustration of the words 'sequuntur agnum, quocumque ierit' in the four-part setting of the

---

[1] One example from Animuccia's First Book is printed by Schering, *Geschichte der Musik in Beispielen* (Leipzig, 1931), p. 119. On the *laudi spirituali* of this period generally, see D. Alaleona, 'Le Laudi spirituali italiane nei secoli XVI e XVII e il loro rapporto coi canti profani', *Rivista musicale italiana*, xvi (1909), p. 1, and E. J. Dent, 'The Laudi Spirituali in the XVIth and XVIIth Centuries', *Proceedings of the Musical Association*, xliii (1917), p. 63.

[2] On Marenzio's church music, see Hans Engel, *Luca Marenzio* (Florence, 1956), pp. 198 ff. and Leichtentritt, op. cit., p. 183. The four-part motets have been published collectively or separately by M. Haller (Ratisbon, 1900–3), Engel (Vienna, 1926) and Bank (Amsterdam); Commer printed two pieces for double choir, 'Jubilate Deo' and its second part 'Populus eius', op. cit. xvi.

antiphon for All Saints 'O quam gloriosum', but his church music is generally much more conservative than his secular compositions. The same may be said of Orazio Vecchi (*c.* 1550–1605) a native of Modena and *maestro di cappella* of the cathedral there from 1596 to 1604. Vecchi wrote Masses,[1] three volumes of motets (published 1590, 1597, and 1604) and *Hymni per totum annum* (Venice, 1604).[2] One of his finest motets is a somewhat Venetian 'Beati omnes' for two five-part choirs[3] with chromatic harmony and *quasi parlando* in the final section:

<hr />

[1] Published posthumously in 1607; Proske published an eight-part Requiem from this volume in *Selectus novus missarum*, ii, no. 16.

[2] A number of Vecchi's motets have been reprinted by Proske and Commer in their various collections.

[3] In the 1590 volume; reprinted by Torchi, op. cit. ii, p. 293.

More consistently in the pure Roman style is the work of Ingegneri, Asola, Giovannelli, the Naninis, the Anerios, and Soriano, all connected in some way with Palestrina, some of them his pupils and most of them active in Rome itself. Marc Antonio Ingegneri (*c.* 1547–92)[1], probably a pupil of Ruffo, *maestro* at Cremona Cathedral and teacher of Monteverdi, is best known as the composer of a set of Responses for Holy Week (Venice, 1588) which were long attributed to Palestrina and actually printed, though as a 'doubtful work', in the first collected edition of the latter's compositions.[2] They are dignified and simple, like most of his known work. In the smaller forms he achieved a very finished style, as in the setting of the Vesper hymn 'Lucis creator optime', where stanzas of the plainsong melody, carried from voice to voice, are given simple but most effective fauxbourdons. His Masses (Venice, 1573 and 1587) are partly in the post-Tridentine style of Ruffo, partly in pure Palestrina style.[3]

The Veronese Giovanni Matteo Asola (*c.* 1550–1609), another pupil of Ruffo's, had sufficient reputation in his day to be chosen as the spokesman of the Italian musicians for their tribute to Palestrina in 1592: a volume of settings of Vesper psalms by Asola and others. A laudatory letter accompanying this gift was signed by Asola on behalf of the rest. A four-part Requiem by him[4] shows sound musicianship in its treatment of the plainsong melodies.

Giovanni Bernardino Nanino (Nanini) (*c.* 1560–1623) was one of the first Roman composers to adopt the organ *continuo* (*Motecta*, 1610) but his work is rather overshadowed by that of his elder brother and teacher, Giovanni Maria (*c.* 1545–1607),[5] friend of Palestrina and master-contrapuntist. The elder Nanino showed his friendship in his only known Mass, a double *parodia*[6] on Palestrina's madrigal and Mass 'Vestiva i colli', his contrapuntal skill in his volume of motets (Venice, 1586): thirty canonic settings, for three, four, or five voices,

---

[1] See Haberl, 'Marcantonio Ingegneri. Eine bio-bibliographische Studie', *Kirchenmusikalisches Jahrbuch*, xiii (1898), p. 78.

[2] *Werke*, xxxii, p. 93. A case for considering them as Palestrina's work, after all, has been stated by Julien Tiersot, 'Pour le centenaire de Palestrina', *Rivista musicale italiana*, xxxii (1925), p. 381.

[3] Cf. the five-part *Kyrie* and *Gloria* reprinted by Guido Pannain, *Istituzioni e monumenti dell'arte musicale italiana*, vi (Milan, 1939), p. xxxi.

[4] Printed by Proske, *Musica Divina*, Annus i, i, p. 259; four other Masses are published by Bank. Motets by Asola will be found in the collections of Proske, Commer, Torchi, and Bank.

[5] See Haberl, 'Giovanni Maria Nanino', *Kirchenmusikalisches Jahrbuch*, vi (1891), p. 81.

[6] See H. J. Moser, 'Vestiva i colli', *Archiv für Musikforschung*, iv (1939), p. 129. There is an edition of the Mass by H. W. Frey (Wolfenbüttel, 1935).

of a single *canto fermo*.[1] In addition to these—which are anything but dry technical exercises—such masterpieces as the brilliant five-part 'Haec dies', the joyous four-part 'Hodie Christus natus est', and 'Diffusa est gratia' (also in four parts) have earned Nanino an honoured place in musical history.

PALESTRINA'S PUPILS

Outstanding among Palestrina's own pupils are the brothers Anerio—Felice (*c.* 1560–1614) and Giovanni Francesco (*c.* 1567–1630)[2]—Francesco Soriano (Suriano) (1549–after 1621),[3] and Ruggiero Giovannelli (*c.* 1560–1625).[4] The most gifted of the four seems to have been Felice Anerio, the least Giovannelli—who was Palestrina's successor at St. Peter's. In the work of all four, even in Felice Anerio's which stands closest to Palestrina's, one can trace the gradual impact of innovation on the pure Roman style: not only 'Venetian' choral effects but frequent use of organ *continuo* and occasional madrigalisms. It is characteristic that Giovanni Francesco Anerio arranged the six-part 'Missa Papae Marcelli' for four parts with *continuo*, while Soriano made an eight-part version of it.[5]

'REFORM' OF GREGORIAN CHANT

Another enterprise of Soriano's, in which he collaborated with Felice Anerio, has also brought on him the condemnation of later

[1] The three-part 'Hic est beatissimus' in Davison and Apel, op. cit. i, p. 167, comes from this set; a number of the others have been reprinted by Proske, Commer, Torchi, and others, as well as in cheap separate editions.

[2] On the Anerio brothers and their father, Maurizio, see Luigi Torri, 'Nei parentali di Felice Anerio e di Carlo Gesualdo', *Rivista musicale italiana*, xxi (1914), p. 492; Alberto Cametti, 'Nuovi contributi alle biografie di Maurizio e Felice Anerio', ibid. xxii (1915), p. 122; R. Casimiri, 'Maurizio, Felice e Giov. Franc. Anerio', ibid. xxvii (1920), p. 602; Haberl, 'Giovanni Francesco Anerio', *Kirchenmusikalisches Jahrbuch*, i (1886), p. 51, and 'Felice Anerio', ibid. xviii (1903), p. 28; H. Federhofer, 'Ein Beitrag zur Biographie von G. F. Anerio', *Die Musikforschung*, ii (1949), p. 210. There are numerous reprints of their works, though Giovanni Francesco's are sometimes attributed to his brother, as Felice's own have sometimes been given to Palestrina.

[3] See Haberl, 'Francesco Soriano', *Kirchenmusikalisches Jahrbuch*, x (1895), p. 95. Proske reprinted his four Passions and two of his Masses.

[4] See H. W. Frey, 'Ruggiero Giovannelli: eine biographische Studie', *Kirchenmusikalisches Jahrbuch*, xxii (1909), p. 49; A. Gabrielli, *Ruggiero Giovannelli nella vita e nelle opere* (Velletri, 1926); Carl Winter, *Ruggiero Giovannelli* (Munich, 1935). Motets by Giovannelli have been printed by Proske, Commer and Torchi, his eight-part Mass, 'Vestiva i colli', a *parodia* on Palestrina's Mass (see Moser, op. cit.) by Frey (Berlin, 1909).

[5] Both printed by Proske (Mainz, 1850), though without Anerio's *continuo* part.

purists. The proposed 'reform' of the Gregorian chant, entrusted by Gregory XIII to Palestrina and Zoilo in 1577 but foiled by the intervention of the Spanish composer Fernando de las Infantas, has been mentioned in the previous chapter.[1] But this did not put an end to attempts to purge the chant of 'barbarisms'. In 1582 the Pope's chaplain Giovanni Guidetti, a pupil of Palestrina, published a *Directorium chori* in which the notes were given mensural values—and Palestrina approved of this as 'not only excellent but of its kind unsurpassable'. Guidetti went further in later publications[2] and Cerone describes this practice in his *Regole* (Naples, 1609) as *alla romana*. At about the same time Andrea Gabrieli and Orazio Vecchi published a *Graduale reformatum* (Venice, 1585) which did revise the melodies to some extent but made other objectionable changes. Finally in 1608 Paul V set up a commission to go into the whole question, as the result of which Soriano and Felice Anerio produced a version—printed in 1614 by the Stamperia Medicea (so called from its director, Cardinal Ferdinando de' Medici)—which in the name of reform garbled the melodies worse than before. However, the Pope refused at the last moment to make the version obligatory for the whole church; it existed as a 'private edition' for more than two centuries and its deplorable influence first made itself seriously felt in the nineteenth century when it was officially approved by Pius IX and Leo XIII.

DE WERT AND HASSLER

The Flemish musician Giaches de Wert (*c.* 1536–96), who spent most of his life in Italy, though not one of the 'Roman school', shared its ideals sufficiently to draw the warm praise of Palestrina, who, writing to his friend Guglielmo Gonzaga, Duke of Mantua (in whose service de Wert was) praises him as 'un virtuoso veramente raro'. Like many another Northern musician, de Wert, while assimilating something of the Italian madrigal style, remained at heart an adherent of what might be termed the 'reformed' Flemish school. We may see this in a passage from a fine motet written for the feast of the Assumption, 'Virgo Maria hodie ad coelum assumpta est' from his first book of motets (Venice, 1581):

[1] See p. 250; see also *infra*, p. 394.
[2] See K. G. Fellerer, articles 'Choralreform', *Die Musik in Geschichte und Gegenwart*, ii (1952), col. 1323, and 'Guidetti', ibid. v (1956), col. 1069.

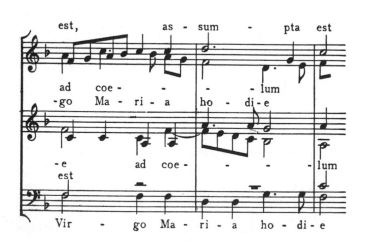

The German Hans Leo Hassler (1564–1612) really belongs to Chapters VIII and X, where his Protestant church music will be considered.[1] But although he studied at Venice with Andrea Gabrieli, some passages in his Masses (Nuremberg, 1599)[2] show more affinity with the Roman than with the Venetian school. As an illustration the exquisite 'Christe eleison' from the Mass 'Dixit Maria'[3] a *missa parodia*, on one of his own motets, may be quoted:

Ex. 174

or the motet 'Quia vidisti me'.[4]

---

[1] See pp. 453 and 544 ff.
[2] Reprinted by Joseph Auer, *Denkmäler deutscher Tonkunst*, vii (Leipzig, 1902).
[3] Ibid., p. 1.
[4] Ibid. ii (ed. H. Gehrmann), p. 31, and Davison and Apel, op. cit. i, p. 186.

VII

LATIN CHURCH MUSIC ON THE CONTINENT—3

SPAIN AND PORTUGAL

By Higini Anglès

INTRODUCTION

THE historical evidence accumulated during recent years shows that the singers and instrumentalists attached to the royal house of Catalonia-Aragon during the fourteenth century were foreigners, as also were some of those who served the courts and royal chapels of Castile and Navarre.[1] Through its singers and religious repertory the royal chapel of Barcelona was connected with the pontifical chapel of Avignon;[2] during the first half of the fifteenth century its musicians and singers continued to be Franco-Flemings and Germans, although in the other peninsular churches native singers and organists predominated.[3]

The Spanish music which has survived shows that peninsular composers of the last ten years of the fifteenth century gradually turned away from the elaborate technique and lofty contrapuntal style of the Flemish school and, like the poets and to some degree the painters,

---

[1] See Higini Anglès, 'Cantors und Ministrers in den Diensten der Könige von Katalonien-Aragonien im 14. Jahrhundert', *Kongress-Bericht Basel 1924* (Leipzig, 1925); 'Gacian Reyneau am Königshof zu Barcelona in der Zeit von 139 . . .–1429', *Festschrift für Guido Adler* (Vienna, 1930); 'El músic Jacomí al servei de Joan I i Martí I durant els anys 1372–1404', *Miscellània: Homenatge a Antoni Rubió Lluch I* (Barcelona, 1936); ' "De cantu organico". Tratado de un autor catalán del siglo XIV', *Anuario musical*, xiii (1958); 'Musikalische Beziehungen zwischen Deutschland und Spanien in der Zeit vom 5. bis 14. Jahrhundert', *Archiv für Musikwissenschaft (Festschrift Wilibald Gurlitt)*, xvi (1959).

[2] Anglès, 'La música sagrada de la Capilla Pontificia de Avignon en la Capilla real Aragonesa', *Anuario musical*, xii (1957); 'El "Llibre Vermell" de Montserrat y los cantos y la danza sacra de los peregrinos durante el siglo XIV', ibid. x (1955).

[3] See Anglès, 'Els cantors i organistes franco-flamencs i alemanys a Catalunya els segles XIV–XVI', *Scheurleer-Gedenkboek* (The Hague, 1925); 'La música en la Corte del Rey Don Alfonso de Aragón, el Magnánimo (años 1413–1420)', *Spanische Forschungen*, 1. Reihe, viii. (1940); 'La música en la Corte real de Aragón y de Nápoles durante el reinado de Alfonso V, El Magnánimo (1421–1458)', *Cuadernos de trabajos de la Escuela Española de Historia y de Arqueología en Roma* (1961); 'Spanien in der Musikgeschichte des 15. Jahrhunderts', *Festschrift für Johannes Vincke* (Madrid, 1963).

sought to create another imperishable form, extremely simple in technical resources and apparently archaic in manner, but nevertheless commanding a highly spiritual evocative power. Such are the Masses of Juan de Anchieta (1462–1523), who was a singer in the choir of Queen Isabella, the Mass by Pedro Escobar (d. 1514), choirmaster at the Cathedral of Seville (especially the *Gloria* and *Credo*), and the three-part Mass by Alonso de Alba.[1] In the same style are the Office hymns of Escobar and Alba[2] and Anchieta's motet 'Clamabat mulier' for four voices.[3] Escobar's setting of the second strophe of 'Veni redemptor gentium' is typical:

Ex.175 (Note-values quartered)

Non ex vi - ri - li - se - - mi - ne sed my - sti - - co spi - - ra - - mi - ne

---

[1] Anchieta's 'Missa de Nuestra Señora' and another four-part Mass, and Alonso de Alba's Mass are printed in *La música en la corte de los Reyes Católicos*, i (Barcelona, 1941; 2nd ed., 1960).

[2] Printed by Rudolf Gerber, *Spanisches Hymnar um 1500 (Das Chorwerk*, lx) (Wolfenbüttel, 1957).

[3] Two motets, 'Domine Jesu Christe' and 'Virgo et mater', are printed by J. B. de Elústiza and G. C. Hernández, *Antología Musical* (Barcelona, 1933).

The more refined style of Francisco de Peñalosa (c. 1470–1528),[1] another member of the chapel of the 'Catholic monarchs', however, suggests Flemish influence.

CHARACTERISTICS OF SPANISH CHURCH MUSIC

Flemish religious polyphony was known and performed in the Iberian peninsula from the fifteenth century onwards; Ockeghem spent some time in Spain in 1469[2] and recent investigations show that Josquin des Prez perhaps visited the peninsula.[3] Philippe le Beau, accompanied by his Flemish chapel, prolonged his visits to Spain in 1502 and 1506. But in spite of the fact that Spanish musicians occupied posts of honour in the pontifical chapel at Rome (as Peñalosa did on the death of King Ferdinand)[4] and in the royal chapel at Naples from the fifteenth century onwards,[5] and later also in the royal chapel of Sicily at Palermo,[6] as well as in the imperial chapel of Vienna,[7] the majority of them worked in isolation at home, content with their native art and in no way concerned to make their work known abroad.[8]

This is surprising when we remember that although the Spanish state made no effort to spread the reputations of native musicians through Europe by such means as assisting them to print their works, nevertheless, when once the New World was discovered, there was

[1] Two Masses, one of them on the famous *villancico* melody, 'Nunca fué pena mayor', in Anglès, *Música en la corte*; other liturgical music in Elústiza and Hernández, op. cit., Gerber, op. cit., and Miguel Hilarión Eslava, *Lira sacro-hispana*, i. 1 (Madrid, 1869). Anglès has prepared an edition of Peñalosa's works, beginning with the motets. Cf. also Gustave Reese, *Music in the Renaissance*, (London, 1954), p. 577, and Robert Stevenson, *Spanish Music in the Age of Columbus* (The Hague, 1960).

[2] Dragan Plamenac, in *Die Musik in Geschichte und Gegenwart*, ix (1961), col. 1828.

[3] Helmuth Osthoff, ibid. vii (1958), col. 195.

[4] Fr. X. Haberl, 'Die römische "schola cantorum" und die päpstlichen Kapellsänger bis zur Mitte des 16. Jahrhunderts', *Vierteljahrsschrift für Musikwissenschaft*, iii (Leipzig, 1887), pp. 189 ff.; E. Celani, 'I cantori della Cappella Pontificia', *Rivista musicale italiana*, xiv (1907), p. 83.

[5] Guido Pannain, *L'Oratorio dei Filippini e la scuola musicale di Napoli*, i (Milan, 1934).

[6] Ottavio Tiby, 'Sebastian Raval: a 16th Century Spanish Musician in Italy', *Musica Disciplina*, ii (1948), p. 217, and 'La musica nella Real Cappella Palatina di Palermo', *Anuario musical*, vii (1952), p. 177.

[7] Albert Smijers, 'Die kaiserliche Hofmusik-Kapelle von 1543–1619, *Studien zur Musikwissenschaft* (Vienna, 1920); G. Van Doorslaer, 'Die Musikkapelle Kaiser Rudolfs II. i. J. 1582', *Zeitschrift für Musikwissenschaft*, xiii (1930–1), p. 481, and 'La chapelle musicale de l'empereur Rudolph II en 1594', *Acta Musicologica*, v (1933), p. 148; Anglès, 'Musikalische Beziehungen zwischen Österreich und Spanien in der Zeit vom 14. bis zum 18. Jahrhundert', *Festschrift für Erich Schenk* (Vienna, 1962), p. 5.

[8] Anglès, 'La polyphonie religieuse péninsulaire antérieure à la venue des musiciens flamands en Espagne', *Report Congrès Liège, 1930* (Burnham, 1931); *Música en la corte*, i, pp. 17 ff.; and 'La musica sacra medievale in Sicilia', *Atti Congresso Palermo 1954* (Palermo, 1959).

official encouragement of teaching there, both artistic and religious, and the state directed the building of magnificent cathedrals and the founding of universities in the colonies, sending innumerable cargoes of musical instruments, books, and pamphlets for use in Mexico and other American regions. Among these shipments were to be found the printed works of religious polyphony by Morales, Guerrero, and Victoria, those of the organists Antonio de Cabezón and Aguilera de Heredia, together with volumes by the Spanish *vihuelistas, cancioneros, romances*, and secular and religious literature; along with these went the dance and popular song, transmitted thus to America.[1]

During the sixteenth century Spain occupied a place of honour in the history of European music. Her religious polyphony of the humanistic age carries an unmistakable and typically national stamp. It is distinguished by its natural and extremely simple technique and for its austerity and dramatic mysticism, which evoke a higher degree of spiritual feeling than that produced by the *a cappella* polyphony of the other European schools. The Spanish composers of the golden age sought to create an art overflowing with emotion and mysticism, expressed with dramatic intensity. Though they were familiar with the technique of the Flemish, French, and Italian artists, they chose to continue their own native tradition, begun at the close of the fifteenth century. In order to appreciate more fully the Spanish character of this religious music, it is important to bear in mind the existence of the traditional popular song of the various regions. In spite of the fact that the Spanish nature is lively, genial, and cheerful, reflecting the nature of the warm sunlight which enriches its soil, this popular song expresses an intimate nostalgia of much depth and therefore more usually employs minor rather than major keys. And just as Spanish songs breathe this atmosphere of intimate experience, ranging from profound sadness to moods of tenderness and optimism, so the religious polyphony reveals these same characteristics with equal emotive power.

The Spanish polyphonists of this century express a religious devotion and mystic fervour parallel to that of the painters and religious

---

[1] See Luis Torres de Mendoza, *Colección de Documentos inéditos . . . . del Archivo de Indias* (Madrid, 1864–   ); Stevenson, *Music in Mexico* (New York, 1952), *The Music of Peru* (Washington, 1959), 'The Bogotá Music Archive', *Journal of the American Musicological Society*, xv (1962), p. 292, and 'European Music in 16th-Century Guatemala', *Musical Quarterly*, l (1964), p. 341; José Torre Revello, 'Algunos libros de música traídos a América en el siglo XVI', *Boletín interamericano de música* (November 1957); Steven Barwick, 'Sacred Vocal Polyphony in Colonial Mexico' (Diss. Harvard, 1949); Jesús Bal, *Tesoro de la música polifónica en México: El Códice del Convento del Carmen* (Mexico, 1952).

poets and prose-writers of the same epoch. The Castilian, Andalusian, Aragonese, and Catalan composers present us with a world entirely unknown in the musical religious atmosphere of that period elsewhere in Europe. Cristóbal de Morales, Pedro Alberch Vila, Rodrigo Ceballos, Francisco Guerrero, and Tomás Luis de Victoria, to mention only the principal ones, are the brothers of Saint Teresa of Avila, Saint John of the Cross, and Fray Luis de León, aesthetically speaking; in their music they evoke those inspired interpretations, both dramatic and realistic, with which we are familiar in the paintings of El Greco, Zurbarán, and Ribera.

The Spanish printing-presses, however, though so rich in the production of other branches of human and ecclesiastical knowledge, were very parsimonious in the printing of polyphonic music during the sixteenth and seventeenth centuries. With the exception of books of songs and music for organ and *vihuela*, music publishing in Spain during the sixteenth century was confined to theoretical treatises,[1] some volumes in Andalusia,[2] and three volumes of polyphony in Catalonia,[3] innumerable theoretical treatises but very little polyphony in Castile during the same period, and only some twelve volumes of religious polyphony in Castile, Aragon, and Navarre from 1598 to 1628.[4] This explains the unfortunate anomaly that, apart from the musicians who lived abroad for many years, relatively few Spaniards could hope to see their works printed. The evidence generally seems to show that much of the music of Spanish composers existed only in manuscript and therefore a great part of it has been irretrievably lost. If the religious music of all those talented men who lacked the means to publish their work had been preserved, the musical output of the peninsula during the sixteenth century would appear even richer and more splendid than it does.

[1] See Anglès, *La música española desde la Edad Media hasta nuestros días* (Barcelona, 1941), pp. 54 ff.

[2] Juan Vásquez, *Villancicos y canciones* (Ossuna, 1551); *Agenda defunctorum* (Seville, 1556); Francisco Guerrero, *Moteta* (Seville, 1556); Vásquez, *Recopilación de Sonetos y Villancicos* (Seville, 1560). See Anglès, *Juan Vásquez, Recopilación de Sonetos y Villancicos*, in *Monumentos de la música española*, iv (Barcelona, 1946), p. 6.

[3] Pedro Alberch Vila, *Madrigales . . . Liber I* and *II* (Barcelona, 1560–1); Nicasio Çorita (Zorita), *Moteta* (Barcelona, 1584); Joan Brudieu, *Madrigales* (Barcelona, 1585).

[4] Anglès, *La música española*, p. 55. The principal are Philippus Rogier, *Missae sex* (Madrid, 1600); T. L. de Victoria, *Missae, Magnificat . . .* (Madrid, 1600); Alfonso Lobo, *Liber Primus Missarum* (Madrid, 1602); Victoria, *Officium Defunctorum* (Madrid, 1605); Sebastián de Vivanco, *Magnificat* (Salamanca, 1607), and *Motetes* (Salamanca, 1610); Juan Esquivel de Barahona, *Missarum . . . lib. I* (Salamanca, 1608), *Motecta* (Salamanca, 1608), *Salmos, Himnos. . . .* (Salamanca, 1613); Miguel el Navarro, *Liber Magnificarum* (Pampeluna, 1614); Sebastián Aguilera de Heredia, *Liber canticorum Magnificat* (Zaragoza, 1618); Stefano Limido (Madrid, 1624); Sebastián López de Velasco, *Libro de Misas* (Madrid, 1628).

CHARLES V AND HIS COURT CHAPEL

The Netherland chapel, known in Spain as the *capilla flamenca*, which always accompanied Charles V during his journeys through Europe and also went with him during his travels and sojourns in the peninsula, was a direct continuation of the chapel he had inherited from the court of Burgundy.[1] Even though he himself showed no interest in having a Spanish chapel served by Spaniards, he was careful to see that his wife, the Empress Isabella.(d. 1539), should have one, and also, on her death, that it should be at the service of their children, Philip II and the princesses Maria (married in 1548 to Maximilian II of Austria) and Juana (married in 1552 to the Portuguese prince Joan Manoel, d. 1554).[2] Moreover, during his stay in the peninsula and even during his journeys through Italy on the occasion of his coronation as Emperor on 24 February 1530 in Bologna by Pope Clement VII, Charles V chose to be served by Spanish instrumentalists.[3]

It was through the *capilla flamenca* that peninsular musicians were able to familiarize themselves with the religious music of Flanders and France, although this contact did not exercise any strong influence on Spanish composers who preferred to follow their own traditions.[4]

On Friday, the twenty-third of October, 1555, there being present in the castle of Brussels king Philip II and many of his servants, among whom figured his musicians and singers, Charles V abdicated in favour of his son. In his speech he recalled that during his reign he had visited Germany nine times, Flanders ten, Spain six, France four, England twice, and twice North Africa. Being still in Brussels on the sixteenth of January in the following year, on this day the emperor renounced his kingdoms in favour of his son and the German empire in favour of his brother Don Ferdinand of Austria.[5]

[1] Anglès, *La música en la corte de Carlos V*, pp. 1 ff.; Joseph Schmidt-Görg, *Nicolas Gombert, Leben und Werk* (Bonn, 1938).

[2] Anglès, *La música . . . Carlos V*, pp. 24 ff.

[3] Ibid., pp. 10 ff. and 35 ff.

[4] Edmond Van der Straeten, 'Les musiciens néerlandais en Espagne', *La Musique aux Pays-Bas avant le XIXme siècle*, vii–viii, 1884–8) and *Charles Quint Musicien* (Ghent, 1894); Georges Van Doorslaer, 'La chapelle musicale de Charles Quint en 1552', *Musica Sacra* (Malines, 1933); Anglès, 'Historia de la música española', in Johannes Wolf, *Historia de la música* (Barcelona, 1934); 'Les musiciens flamands en Espagne et leur influence sur la polyphonie espagnole', *Kongress-Bericht Utrecht 1952* (Amsterdam, 1953) and *Diccionario de la Música Labor*, i (Barcelona, 1954), p. 452; Hellmut Federhofer, 'États de la chapelle musicale de Charles V (1528) et de Maximilien II (1554)', *Revue belge de musicologie*, iv (1950), p. 176; Jean Jacquot (ed.), *Fêtes et cérémonies au temps de Charles Quint* (Paris, 1960).

[5] Anglès, *La música . . . Carlos V*, p. 136 (text).

PHILIP II'S ATTITUDE TO MUSIC

There is historical evidence that it was Philip II, not Charles V, who was the true Maecenas of Spanish music. His musical taste was formed at an early age by the organist Antonio de Cabezón and the clavichord-player Francisco de Soto, between 1539 and 1543. While still a prince, he had no complete musical chapel of his own, since the official organization was at the service of the cardinal Juan de Tavera, who formed part of the Council of Regency and was 'chaplain-general of the imperial chapel'. When Philip was appointed regent of the kingdom in 1543, however, the musicians of this cardinal became part of his chapel. Most outstanding among these was Juan García de Basurto, who was succeeded by Pedro de Pastrana in 1547; Antonio de Cabezón became his organist and Francisco de Soto his musician of the chamber.[1]

On his journey through Italy, Flanders, and Germany in 1548, Philip was always accompanied by the musicians of his chapel, who thus had opportunities to become acquainted at first-hand with the church music of these countries.[2] When Philip came to England in July 1554, on the occasion of his marriage to Mary Tudor—the daughter of Henry VIII and Catherine of Aragon, who had so cared for her daughter's musical education that she was a good singer and player on the lute—he was also accompanied by his artists. During his stay in England, his suite included the royal chapel, consisting of ten chaplains, presided over by the Bishop of Salamanca, twenty-one singers (four basses, six tenors, four altos, seven trebles), besides Antonio de Cabezón and his brother Juan de Cabezón, keyboard player, and Cristóbal de León as official organist. He also brought an orchestra of fourteen *ministriles* (wind players).[3]

During his long stay in Flanders as Archduke of Burgundy, Philip decided that it would be appropriate for him to have not only Burgundian ceremonial but a chapel composed of Flemish musicians. Mary Tudor died in 1558, and when Philip returned to Spain the following year, he took with him singers from Flanders.[4] With his Netherland chapel he wished to pay homage to the memory of his father; the Spanish chapel—perhaps not so rich as the Flemish in singers—was to be a memorial to that other splendid chapel of his ancestors, the 'Catholic Monarchs', and of his mother, the Empress

---

[1] Anglès, *La música . . . Carlos V*, pp. 142 ff.; Jaime Moll, 'Músicos de la corte del Cardenal Juan Tavera (1523–45): Luis Venegas de Henestrosa', *Anuario musical*, vi (1951).
[2] Anglès, *La música . . . Carlos V*, pp. 102 ff.
[3] Ibid., pp. 124 ff.   [4] Ibid., pp. 136 ff.

Isabella. During the sixteenth century the two chapels continued their offices separately, each in its own tradition. The Flemish musicians composed in their particular style and performed the repertory of the Netherlands and the rest of Europe, while the Spanish musicians continued zealously to cultivate their native forms, doubtless more modest in technical resources, but of a more intense, more intimate, and more original religious nature. Nevertheless, in order to show their admiration for the ecclesiastical art of the Flemish and French composers, the Spaniards, in writing their Masses or when compiling their collections for organ or *vihuela*, based their works upon religious pieces of the French-Netherland school, chiefly on those of the masters of Charles V's chapel or of the French royal house, or transcribed these pieces for instruments.

The outstanding musicians of Philip II's Flemish chapel from 1556 were Nicolas Payen, who was transferred with his musicians in office from the service of Charles V to that of his son Philip II; Pierre de Manchicourt[1] (d. Madrid 1564), Georges de La Hèle (Helle), first *cantor* and from 1580 until his death director of the chapel, and Felipe Rogier (Rogerius), the last Netherland master of the chapel (d. Madrid 1596), who was succeeded by the Spaniard Mateo Romero (Maestro Capitán).[2]

Philip II's genuine interest in the preservation of musical treasures is shown by the numerous works, both manuscript and printed, which were placed in the new Escorial library during his reign, and the performance of vocal polyphony in this church was always permitted.[3] That Philip was a most generous patron of Spanish and foreign composers is shown by the series of great collections and editions dedicated to him by Miguel de Fuenllana, Diego Pisador, Francisco Guerrero, La Hèle, Palestrina, and Victoria.[4]

THE PRINCIPAL CATHEDRAL SCHOOLS OF SPANISH MUSIC

From at least the fifteenth century onwards, the more important religious centres were endowed with choirs for the performance

[1] See pp. 234–5.
[2] Van der Straeten, op. cit. vii; Paul Becquart, 'Trois documents inédits relatifs à la Chapelle flamande de Philippe II et Philippe III', *Anuario musical*, xiv (1959), p. 63, and 'Un compositeur néerlandais à la Cour de Philippe II et de Philippe III: Nicolas Dupont (1575–1623)', ibid. xvi (1961), pp. 81 ff.
[3] Samuel Rubio, 'La capilla de música del monasterio de El Escorial', *La Ciudad de Dios*, clxiii (1951), 1, pp. 61 ff.
[4] Isabel Pope, 'The "Spanish Chapel" of Philip II', *Renaissance News*, v, 1–2 (1952); Nicolas Alvarez Solar-Quintes, 'Nuevas noticias de músicos de Felipe II, de su época ...', *Anuario musical*, xv (1960), p. 195; Anglès, *La música ... Carlos V*, p. 83.

of polyphonic music, and during the sixteenth century each had gifted and original musicians. There were three outstanding schools: the Andalusians, heirs to the medieval art of fertile Andalusia which had already seen the musical heyday of the Arabs and Spanish Jews; the Castilians, who continued the polyphonic splendour of the Toledan Church and the court of Alfonso X (the Learned), some of them educated in the universities of Salamanca and Alcala de Henares; and the Catalans, who maintained the ancient artistic prestige of the *Provincia Tarraconensis*, the monasteries of Ripoll and Montserrat, and the royal Aragonese chapel of the fourteenth and fifteenth centuries.

Prominent in the Andalusian school were Pedro Fernández de Castilleja, Cristóbal de Morales, Juan Vázquez, Juan Navarro, Rodrigo de Ceballos, Fernando de las Infantas, Pedro Guerrero, Francisco Guerrero, Ambrosio de Cotes, Andrés de Villalar, Luis de Aranda, Juan del Risco, Alonso Lobo, and Santos de Aliseda; among the Castilians Juan Escribano, Juan Garcia de Basurto, Bartolomé Escobedo, Pedro de Pastrana, Antonio de Cabezón, Andrés Torrentes, Bernardino de Ribera, Pedro Alba, Juan Bernal, Diego Ortiz, Francisco de Montanos, Bernardo Clavijo del Castillo, Tomás Luis de Victoria, Juan Esquivel de Barahona, Ginés Boluda, Mateo Romero (Maestro Capitán), Miguel Gómez Camargo, Sebastián López de Velasco, Sebastián de Vivanco, Juan Ruiz de Robledo; in Catalonia, Antonio Marlet, the two Mateo Flechas (uncle and nephew), Pedro Alberch Vila, Miguel Pedro Andreu, Rafael Coloma, Joan Brudieu, Pedro Riquet, Juan Pujol, Antonio Reig, Juan Verdalet. Nor must we forget the Valencian school with such musicians as Juan Ginés Pérez, Cárceres, Company, Juan Bautista Comes, Francisco Navarro, or the Aragonese with Melchior Robledo, José Gay, Sebastián Aguilera de Heredia, Miguel Navarro, Pedro Rimonte (Ruimonte), and Diego Pontac.[1]

It would be premature to pass a definitive judgement on the achievements of the Spanish polyphonists of this period, since apart from Victoria[2] and seven volumes by Morales,[3] most of the work is still to a great extent unpublished, at any rate in modern editions.[4] But superficial examination suggests that although the Spanish composers

[1] See Henri Collet, *Le Mysticisme musical espagnol du XVI* siècle (Paris, 1913); Joaquin Pena and Anglès, *Diccionario de la Música Labor*, 2 vols. (Barcelona, 1954), for biographies and bibliographies.

[2] *Opera Omnia*, ed. Felipe Pedrell, 8 vols. (Leipzig, 1902–13).

[3] *Opera Omnia*, ed. Anglès (Barcelona, 1952–).

[4] The principal collections of reprints are listed in the bibliography.

do not reveal an altogether unfamiliar musical world, they do, nevertheless, offer special characteristics. In their dedications Morales, Guerrero, and Victoria set forth the principles of their religious musical aesthetic, aims which in some respects differ from those of other composers of the various European schools.

Convinced of the supreme dignity which polyphony ought to show before the altar, as admitted by the Church 'ad cultum divinum ampliandum' (according to Johannes Tinctoris), and at the same time seeking 'to uplift the souls of the listeners to their Creator', the peninsular composers avoided as far as possible the writing of secular music, and dedicated all their powers and talents to enriching the artistic patrimony of the Catholic liturgy. Perhaps only Palestrina himself during the sixteenth century created a devotional music so steeped in mysticism and spirituality as this Hispanic school of the golden age.

The tendency to simplicity of forms and absence of elaborate technique, begun during the fifteenth century, was always the ideal of religious composers in Spain; their aim was to subordinate technique to the musical expressiveness inherent in the text. Apart from Morales, who, in some of his works stood near the art of the Netherlands, this tendency became an obsession in peninsular music during the age of humanism; to it the Spanish composers sacrificed their talent and technical means, even at times fineness of melodic line, and always contrapuntal technique and harmonic effects.

As it is impossible to study here the works of all the above-mentioned musicians, discussion must be limited to the most outstanding, each of whom, however, symbolizes one of the peninsular schools.

CRISTÓBAL DE MORALES

Of the works of Pedro Ferńández de Castilleja, *magister puerorum* at Seville Cathedral from 1514 (d. 1547), the 'maestro de los maestros de España', as his pupil Guerrero called him,[1] only five motets for four or five voices have survived,[2] and it is therefore difficult to judge his artistic merit. But the greatest creative genius of the Andalusian school was undoubtedly Cristóbal de Morales[3] (c. 1500–53).

[1] In the Prologue of his *Viage de Hierusalem* (Seville, 1596).

[2] Two of them, 'Dispersit, dedit' and 'Heu mihi, Domine', published by Eslava, op. cit. i. 1, pp. 157 and 161; Henri Collet printed the four-part motet 'O gloriosa Domina', op. cit., p. 258.

[3] On Morales generally see Pedrell, *Hispaniae Schola Musica Sacra*, i (Barcelona, 1894); Rafael Mitjana, *Estudios sobre algunos músicos españoles del siglo XVI* (Madrid, 1918), pp. 181 ff.; J. B. Trend, 'Cristóbal Morales', *Music and Letters*, vi (1925), p. 11; Anglès, *Morales: Opera Omnia* i, 'Cristobal de Morales en España', *Anuario musical*, viii (1953), p. 70, and 'Cristobal de Morales y Francisco Guerrero', ibid. ix

Musically educated in the same city, perhaps by Francisco de Peñalosa and Fernández de Castilleja, he soon became *maestro de capilla* in the cathedrals of Avila, Plasencia, and Jaen, and went to Rome in 1535 as singer in the papal chapel until 1545. That Morales rapidly made his way in Rome may be deduced from the *Motu Proprio* which Paul III dedicated to him after he had served for a year in the chapel; the Pope was pleased to confer on him the title of 'Count of the Sacred Palace and of Saint John Lateran' in 1536. From the point of view of opportunities for artistic development and the printing of his works, it seems unfortunate that Morales, for reasons unknown, should have decided to leave Rome and return to his own country, where he continued his career at Toledo, Marchena (near Seville), and Málaga.

Morales was the first Spanish composer who succeeded in giving his work an international character; he was the first to break out of that closed circle and isolation in which Spanish musicians lived and to win for himself a place of honour beside the best composers of contemporary Europe. Aware of the obstacle to publication of his works in Spain constituted by the poverty of the peninsular presses, he took advantage of his stay in Rome to show the world what he could do. His earliest printed works were two motets in Moderne's *Motetti del fiore* (Lyons, 1539) and the madrigal 'Ditemi o si o no' in *Il quarto libro di madrigali d'Arcadelt* (Venice, 1539); the following year Scotto of Venice issued three of his Masses and in 1544 the brothers Dorici published two volumes of Masses in Rome. Thanks to these, the name of *Morales Hispanus* soon became celebrated throughout Europe. He himself took care to see that the adjective 'Hispanus' or 'Hyspalensis' (of Seville) was habitually added to his name.

Although Morales in his lifetime was not to see more than a part of his rich musical production in print, there is no doubt that he might easily have had all his works published if he had stayed in Italy; and there is enough of his music extant—printed or in manuscript—to show that he is one of the great masters of the sixteenth century. Of the twenty-two surviving Masses,[1] two are written on the

(1954), p. 56, 'Das sakrale Charakter der Kirchenmusik von Cristóbal de Morales', *Festschrift für Theobald Schrems* (Ratisbon, 1963), p. 110; Stevenson, 'Cristóbal de Morales: a Fourth-Centenary Biography', *Journal of the American Musicological Society*, vi (1953), p. 3, and *Spanish Cathedral Music in the Golden Age* (Berkeley and Los Angeles, 1961), pp. 3 ff.; Reese, op. cit., p. 587.

[1] On the Masses see particularly G. A. Trumpff, 'Die Messen des Cristóbal de Morales', *Anuario musical*, viii (1953), p. 93. Besides the twenty-two Masses we possess the treble of a four-part 'Misa Valenciana', of which nothing more is known.

themes of Castilian songs; the Mass 'Decidle al cavallero', for four voices, perhaps one of his first, and the Mass 'Tristezas me matan', for five.[1] It is curious that both are preserved in Italian manuscripts, the first in Milan (Bibl. Ambrosiana, MS. Mus. E46, fo. 41) and the second in the Sistine Chapel in Rome (Capp. Sist. 17, fo. 80–96). Three other masses are composed on French *chansons*: 'L'homme armé', for four voices, 'L'homme armé', for five, and 'Mille regretz', for six.[2] To assess the proper liturgical worth of his Masses, one must bear in mind that Morales wrote them all before the reforms of the Council of Trent; it explains why he introduced tropes in the *Ordinarium Missae* and why he paid tribute to the Netherlanders, whose technical procedures he had assimilated so well, by writing Masses on French secular *chansons*. In this connexion it should be mentioned that the Roman manuscript Capp. Sist. 17 preserves a version of the *Sanctus, Benedictus*, and *Agnus* of the Mass 'Mille regretz', different from that printed in *Missarum Liber I* and composed in a more elaborate style.[3] This shows how well he could imitate the subtleties and intricacies of the puzzle-canons of the Franco-Flemish masters of the previous generation. The Masses written by Morales on Gregorian themes are six in number: two 'De Beata Virgine', one for four,[4] the other for five voices,[5] composed on the chants of Mass IX of the *Kyriale Romanum*, and preserving the well-known trope 'Spiritus et alme' in the *Gloria*; 'Ave maris stella', on the theme of the hymn, for four notated voices[6] with a counterpoint in the altus sung in *canon subdiatesseron* almost throughout:

Ex.176

---

[1] *Opera Omnia*, vii, p. 86. In a volume of *Villancicos de diversos autores* printed in Venice in 1556 and reprinted by Jesús Bal, *El Colêgio de México*, 1944, nr. 49, there is a composition for five voices by Nicolas Gombert with the same text, 'Tristezas me matan', and similar melodies.

[2] *Opera Omnia*, vi, p. 67, and i, pp. 193 and 238.

[3] See *Opera Omnia*, vii, Appendix, p. 121.

[4] *Opera Omnia*, i, p. 1, and Peter Wagner, *Geschichte der Messe* (Leipzig, 1913), p. 457.   [5] *Opera Omnia*, iii, p. 66.   [6] Ibid. i, p. 104.

'Ave Maria' for four voices,[1] on the theme of the antiphon, written in strict *canto fermo* style, and the 'Missa pro defunctis', for five voices,[2] in a style very different from the rest, profoundly lugubrious in tone, in strong contrast with Palestrina's setting,[3] full of faith and hope, and still more with Brudieu's,[4] all spiritual light and Christian serenity. A 'Missa pro defunctis' for four voices is preserved anonymously in a few manuscripts, though in others till recently unknown it appears under the names of Morales.[5]

Morales cultivated the *missa parodia* with special affection, and eight examples by him are extant: 'Aspice Domine', for four voices,[6] on Gombert's motet; 'Vulnerasti cor meum', for four voices,[7] on an anonymous motet in the *Motetti de la Corona* (Petrucci, 1514, and Jacobus Junta, 1526); three on motets by Mouton, 'Benedicta es caelorum regina',[8] for four voices, on Mouton's motet; 'Gaude

---

[1] *Opera Omnia*, iii, p. 32.   [2] Ibid. iii, p. 114.
[3] Cf. Ambros–Kade, *Geschichte der Musik*, iii (Leipzig, 1893), p. 591, and Mitjana, op. cit., p. 205.
[4] Pedrell–Anglès, *Joan Brudieu: Els Madrigals i la Missa de Difunts* (Barcelona, 1921), p. 213.
[5] Printed by Sister Maria Sagués, *Anonymous, Valladolid Codex, Missa pro Defunctis* (Cincinnati, 1960).   [6] *Opera Omnia*, i, p. 35; model, iii, p. 157.
[7] Ibid. i, p. 70; model, iii, p. 166.   [8] Ibid. iii, p. 1; model, p. 185.

Barbara',[1] for four voices, on another motet by Mouton; 'Quaeramus cum pastoribus', for five;[2] 'Quem dicunt homines',[3] for five, using the four-part motet by Richafort; 'Si bona suscepimus', for six voices,[4] written on the five-part motet by Verdelot; the already mentioned 'Mille regretz', for six, on Josquin's *chanson*, the 'canción del Emperador' (Charles V), as Luis de Narváez writes in his *Delphin de música de cifra para tañer vihuela* (Valladolid, 1538)[5]—Morales gives Josquin's melody great prominence in the highest part throughout. Morales wrote three other Masses using the old strict *canto fermo* technique: 'Tu es vas electionis',[6] for four voices, and the two 'L'homme armé' Masses.[7] Finally, there are a Mass 'Super ut re mi fal sol la', another 'Super fa re ut fa sol fa' and the 'Missa Caça', a markedly canonic Mass;[8] all three are for four voices. Specially noteworthy is the masterly writing in passages of the four-part Masses and in the five-part 'De Beata Virgine' and 'Quaeramus cum pastoribus', and the grandeur of some of the six-part settings of the *Agnus*. Morales composed more Masses than any other Roman musician before Palestrina and in this sphere he is one of the links connecting the Flemish art of Josquin and Gombert with Palestrina.

More than eighty motets by Morales have been preserved.[9] He shows a surprising predilection for Gregorian themes as *canti fermi*, treating them in masterly style, clothing them in austere counterpoint, and cultivating the art of variation as it was known in his day. He also surprises by his choice of dramatic themes which he vitalizes with emotional intensity and descriptive music, thus preparing the way for Guerrero, Ceballos, and Victoria. It is in the motets that Morales reaches the highest peaks of technique and emotion. So we

---

[1] Ibid. vi, p. 34; model, p. 133.   [2] Ibid. i, p. 148; model, iii, p. 172.

[3] Ibid. vii, p. 89; model, p. 142.   [4] Ibid. i, p. 274; model, iii, p. 179.

[5] See the edition by Emilio Pujol, *Monumentos de la música española*, iii (Barcelona, 1945), p. 37.

[6] Ibid. vi, p. 1.   [7] Ibid. i, p. 193, and vi, p. 67.

[8] Ibid. vii, pp. 36, 18, and 1. See Anglès, 'El "Llibre Vermell" de Montserrat', *Anuario musical*, x (1955), p. 61, describing a manuscript containing three pieces with the title 'Caça' (= canon); Barcelona, Bibl. Central, M. 588/2, fo. 48ᵛ, contains an *ensalada* for four voices by the elder Flecha, entitled 'La Caça'.

[9] On the motets, see Ambros–Kade, op. cit. iii, p. 587 and v, p. 595; Pedrell, *Hispaniae Schola*, i; Hugo Leichtentritt, *Geschichte der Motette* (Leipzig, 1908), pp. 368 ff.; Elústiza–Castrillo, *Antología musical*; Morales, *Opera Omnia*, ii (1953) and v (1959); Rubio, *Antología polifónica sacra* (Madrid, 1956), i and ii; and Stevenson, *Spanish Cathedral Music*, p. 94. Stevenson in *Grove's Dictionary of Music and Musicians*, v (5th ed., London, 1954), p. 833, and more recently in *Die Musik in Geschichte und Gegenwart*, ix (1961), art. *Morales*, attributes to Morales 14 anonymous motets of the 1543 and 1546 editions, but the attribution is doubtful. On these editions, see *Répertoire des sources musicales*, i: *Recueils imprimés XVIᵉ—XVIIᵉ siècles*, ed. François Lesure (Munich–Duisburg, 1960).

find Morales austere in the well-known five-part 'Emendemus in melius', in the Escorial Library and reproduced many times,[1] dramatic in 'Lamentabatur Jacob'[2] and 'Job, tonso capite',[3] both for five voices; he knows how to be sweet when in 'Pastores, dicite, quidnam vidistis?'[4] and in 'O magnum mysterium',[5] both for four voices, he sings the Saviour's birth; deeply devotional in 'Per tuam crucem' for four voices and 'O crux, ave, spes unica' for five voices;[6] nostalgic in the six-part 'Veni, Domine, et noli tardare',[7] and full of enthusiasm when he sings Christ's triumph in the five-part 'Christus resurgens ex mortuis'.[8] His sixteen Magnificats,[9] on the eight traditional tones— eight settings of the odd-numbered and eight of the even-numbered— enjoyed unprecedented success; it is significant of the esteem in which they were held that from 1542, when Scotto of Venice published the first five settings, till 1619 at least sixteen editions appeared, and that innumerable manuscript copies have been preserved, all made before the eighteenth century. The Vatican manuscript Capp. Giulia VIII– 39, contains some verses of these Magnificats elaborated by Palestrina.[10] Besides Morales' hymns and antiphons we have his profoundly expressive *Lamentationes* (Venice, 1564), printed simultaneously by Rampazetto and Gardano eleven years after the composer's death:

Ex. 177

---

[1] Escorial, Libro 8 de facistol; printed in Pedrell, op. cit. i, p. 29; Eslava, op. cit. i. 1, p. 109; Davison and Apel, *Historical Anthology of Music*, i (Cambridge, Mass., 1947), p. 138; and elsewhere.

[2] Reprinted *Opera Omnia*, ii, p. 102; Pedrell, op. cit. i, p. 40; Eslava, op. cit. i. 1, p. 119; A. Araiz Martíñez, *Historia de la música religiosa en España* (Barcelona and Madrid, 1942), p. 243.

[3] Reprinted *Opera Omnia*, v, p. 126. [4] Ibid. ii, p. 12.
[5] Ibid. v, p. 7. [6] Ibid. ii, p. 26 and v, p. 103; Rubio, *Antología*, i, p. 92.
[7] Ibid. v, p. 146. [8] Ibid. v, p. 107.

[9] Modern edition by Pedrell, *Hispaniae schola musica sacra*, i, p. 20 (Barcelona, 1894) (Magnificat, VIII tono), and *Opera Omnia*, iv. The setting of the even-numbered verses to the eighth tone is given in Carl Parrish, *A Treasury of Early Music* (New York, 1958), p. 111.

[10] Palestrina's additional parts are printed in *Opera Omnia*, iv; see also Anglès, 'Palestrina y los "Magnificat" de Morales', *Anuario musical*, viii (1953), p. 153.

Morales must be considered as the Roman-Spanish musician who, in advance of his age, anticipated the spirit and liturgical-artistic ideals of the Council of Trent and prepared the way for Palestrina himself. The innumerable manuscript copies of his works and the tributes paid him by the Italian, Spanish, and Portuguese theorists of the sixteenth and seventeenth centuries testify to the veneration in which he was held. In his use of cross-rhythm—one voice singing three notes against two in the other parts—in his earliest Masses, in his employment of sequence and melodic repetition, in his writing for two parts only, in the adaptation of the words to the melody, Morales was still partly following the old style of Ockeghem, Obrecht, and above all of Josquin; but in his handling of suspensions, in his *canto fermo* technique, in the nobility of his style, he shows great originality. In genius and technique he is unquestionably superior to all other Spanish composers of the Golden Age.

In order to understand the spiritual power of Morales, one must remember the moral principles which governed his aesthetic in a period when even the pontifical singers of Rome composed profane songs and madrigals. These principles, expressed by Morales in the dedications of his two books of Masses (Rome, 1544), are those of the theorists of the Middle Ages, for instance the Spaniard Johannes Aegidius Zamorensis and Tinctoris, and of Palestrina in the book of motets dedicated to Pope Gregory XIII (Rome, 1584): 'Music is a gift from God and is given to us to praise the Lord and to give nobility to men.' It is true that Morales was more familiar with the Flemish style than other Spanish composers; yet, while exploring Flemish counterpoint, he always retained the soul of a Spanish artist.

VÁSQUEZ AND PEDRO GUERRERO

Juan Vásquez (d. after 1560) was musically active in the circles of the Andalusian nobility and hence managed to have his works published in Andalusia itself. He was principally a composer of secular music: *villancicos*, songs and *sonetos*.[1] Of his religious music, besides some pieces with Castilian texts, we have his *Agenda defunctorum* (Seville, 1556), in which plainsong alternates with four-part polyphony in Office and Mass; the pleasant sweetness of his secular music is also apparent in his truly spiritual choral music.[2] The name of Pedro Guerrero, elder brother and first teacher of Francisco, appears as *cantor* at Santa Maria Maggiore in Rome from 1560 onward.[3] A series of four-part motets[4] and six Masses, freshly coloured music, transparent in structure, have survived.

FRANCISCO GUERRERO

Next to Morales the most illustrious composer of the Andalusian school was unquestionably Francisco Guerrero (1527/8–99), a *seise* (boy singer) of Seville Cathedral, where he later became cantor; he was a pupil of his brother Pedro, of Cristóbal de Morales, and of Fernández de Castilleja.[5] In spite of the fact that he never lived outside Spain for any length of time, Guerrero managed to get nearly all his works published abroad; this was something unique in sixteenth-century Spain and is *a priori* evidence of his exceptional genius. Only

---

[1] See p. 82.

[2] 'Absolve, Domine' and 'Sana, Domine' are printed in Rubio, *Antologia*, ii.

[3] See Rome, Santa Maria Maggiore, Archives, Reg. 'Cappella 1552–1562', i and ii, July and November 1560.

[4] 'Domine meus' and 'O beata Maria' in Elústiza and Hernández, op. cit.; the latter also in Rubio, op. cit. ii.

[5] On Guerrero generally, see Mitjana, *Francisco Guerrero: estudio crítico-biográfico* (Madrid, 1922); Anglès, 'Cristóbal de Morales y Francisco Guerrero', *Anuario musical*, ix (1954), p. 56; Stevenson, *Spanish Cathedral Music*, pp. 135 ff.

his first book of motets was printed at Seville (by Montesdoca, 1555); his *Magnificat* was printed by Phalèse (Louvain, 1563), the *Liber primus Missarum* by du Chemin (Paris, 1566); another book of motets appeared in Venice (*apud filium Ant. Gardane*) in 1570. His ambition to go to Italy, in order to familiarise himself with musical conditions in Rome and also to print some of his works there, was fulfilled in 1581–2, when his *Missarum liber secundus* was published by Basa (Rome, 1582), who issued his *Liber Vesperarum* two years later. In 1588 he realized his dream of visiting Palestine to see Bethlehem and there 'perform my songs together with the angels and shepherds who first taught us to celebrate the coming of the Messiah'; on this expedition, which he described in his *Viage de Hierusalem*, he was accompanied by his pupil Francisco Sánchez; during his absence no less a person than Zarlino undertook the correction of the proofs of his *Mottecta. Lib. II* and *Canciones y villanescas espirituales* (Venice, 1589). In 1597 the same publisher, Vincenti, published his last collection of motets and the Mass 'Seculorum. Amen'. Pending the appearance of a complete edition of his works,[1] it is difficult to establish a complete and accurate list of his religious compositions.

The volumes printed in Guerrero's lifetime contain about 170 sacred compositions with Latin texts as well as some 68 pieces with Spanish texts, some of which are religious in content.[2] His church music consists of eighteen Masses (strictly speaking, only seventeen since his 'Missa pro defunctis' was printed twice, the second time revised and corrected according to the prescriptions of the Council of Trent), some 115 motets, a series of Psalms and Magnificats, and thirty-four hymns. The Paris edition of 1566 contains four four-part and four five-part Masses; the volume printed in Rome in 1582 includes five Masses for four voices, two for five, and one for six. Other works were preserved only in manuscript: the four-part Mass

[1] The Instituto Español de Musicología is preparing such an edition (Barcelona, 1955–). The second volume of Pedrell's *Hispaniae schola musica sacra* contains a Magnificat, an Office for the Dead, the Matthew Passion, and motets; Eslava reprinted both the Matthew and John Passions (on which see Otto Kade, *Die ältere Passionskomposition bis zum Jahre 1631* (Gütersloh, 1893), p. 153), the four-part Mass 'Simile est regnum' and two motets, op. cit. i. 2. The *alternatim* 'Salve Regina' is reproduced from Pedrell in Davison and Apel, op. cit., p. 150. The five-part 'Ave, Virgo sanctissima', full of verbal and musical references to Marian songs, has been reprinted not only by Pedrell, op. cit., p. 13, and Eslava, op. cit., p. 99, but by Elústiza and Hernández, op. cit., p. 89, Araiz, op. cit., p. 273, and Rubio, op. cit. ii, p. 48. Rubio's two volumes contain seventeen motets and a Magnificat by Guerrero.

[2] *Canciones y villanescas espirituales*. Reprinted by V. Garcia and M. Querol in *Opera Omnia*, i and ii (Barcelona, 1955 and 1957).

'L'homme armé',[1] the Passions and so on. Of his three Masses 'De beata virgine', one contains the trope 'O Paraclite obumbrans corpus Mariae eleison', another the *Kyrie* 'Rex Virginum amator Deus', whereas that of 1582, which paraphrases Mass IX of the *Kyriale Romanum*, is without tropes, in consequence of the Tridentine decrees. His Masses 'Sancta et immaculata virginitas' and 'Inter vestibulum' are 'parody' Masses on motets by Morales. The titles of his Masses show that, apart from 'Dormendo un giorno', on a madrigal by Verdelot, and 'Della batalla escoutez', on Janequin's 'La guerre', and 'L'homme armé', all are based on liturgical themes or motets. They include five on Marian themes, the frequent use of which is one of the characteristics of the Spanish school of this period.[2]

It is interesting to study the later editions in which Guerrero, following the trends of his time, sometimes breaks up ligatures in order to get better settings of the words and prints numerous accidentals which do not appear in the first editions. When Guerrero reprinted his compositions, he by no means always reproduced them identically, but polished and revised them as in the already mentioned case of the 'Missa pro defunctis'; in the 1583 edition of the four-part motet 'Salve Regina', published in 1583, he kept the cantus and altus of the 1570 edition but wrote new parts for tenor and bass, adding accidentals which did not appear in 1570.

Guerrero stated his views on the aesthetics of church music in the dedication (to Philip II) of his Magnificats (1563),[3] in that (to Pius V) of his collection of motets of 1570 and, above all, in the preface to the *Liber vesperarum* which he dedicated to the chapter of Seville (1584): 'I have always endeavoured not to caress the ears of pious persons with my songs, but on the contrary to excite their souls to devout contemplation of the sacred mysteries.' Comparing his music with that of his teacher Morales, one immediately notices a profound difference; Morales is austere, even a little harsh at times, but he can also display an incomparable geniality and his music is always full of character. Guerrero, on the other hand, is a sweet, serene singer both in sentiment and style, faithfully reflecting the Andalusian soul. The opening of the motet 'O Domine Jesu Christe' may be quoted as a typical example of his art:

[1] Three parts only are preserved at Avila in the Monasterio de Santa Ana (the bass is missing) together with three motets and one Magnificat for four voices.

[2] Of the 34 secular pieces by Guerrero that have been preserved, eighteen are transformed 'a lo divino' and printed in his *Canciones y villanescas espirituales*.

[3] Carl-Heinz Illing, *Zur Technik der Magnificat-Komposition des 16. Jahrhunderts* (Wolfenbüttel–Berlin, 1936).

Ex. 178

It is worth noting that in his time the instrumental music of the *ministriles* (wind-players) was used not only in processions at religious festivals, royal and episcopal receptions, coronations, and so on, but also in the performance of sacred music in Seville cathedral and the ten other principal churches in Andalusia, as we learn from their archives.[1] Organ music also enjoyed great importance at Seville during Guerrero's time; he had as colleagues there the eminent organists Rodrigo de Morales, Pedro de Villada, Francisco Peraza, and Diego del Castillo.

JUAN NAVARRO

Juan Navarro (1528–80) (not to be confused with Fray Juan Navarro, of Cadiz, author of the *Liber in quo quatuor passiones Christi Domini continentur*, printed in Mexico, 1604),[2] also figures among the great artists of the Andalusian school. Educated perhaps in Seville itself, he occupied posts at Salamanca (where he became a friend of Francisco de Salinas), Ciudad Rodrigo, Avila, and Palencia. Besides many manuscripts and some other works, we have the well-known *Johannis Navarri Hispalensis Psalmi, Hymni ac Magnificat totius anni*, posthumously printed in Rome in 1590 by his nephew with a preface by Francisco Soto de Langa, the companion of St. Philip Neri, famous for his books of *laudi spirituali*.[3] This preface affirms that Navarro possessed 'artis summam scientiam' and that his music surprised listeners by its 'almost incredible sweetness'. G. B. Martini and other theorists have quoted passages from him as models of polyphony. The quality of his work[4] may be judged by his motets 'Ave Virgo sanctissima' for four voices, 'Laboravi in gemitu' for five, and above all 'In passione positus' for six.[5] Although

[1] For Seville see Anglès, *Anuario musical*, ix (1954), pp. 70 ff.; for León, José Mª Álvarez Pérez, 'La polifonía sagrada y sus maestros en la catedral de León (siglos XV y XVI)' in *Anuario musical*, xiv (1959), pp. 45 ff.; for Granada, José López Calo, *La música en la catedral de Granada en el siglo XVI* (Granada, 1963); for Barcelona, Anglès, *Johannis Pujol: Opera Omnia*, i, p. xl, and *Els Madrigals i la Missa de Difunts d'En Brudieu*, pp. 54 ff.

[2] See Gilbert Chase, 'Juan Navarro *Hispalensis* and Juan Navarro *Gaditanus*', *Musical Quarterly*, xxxi (1945), p. 188; Stevenson, *Spanish Cathedral Music*, p. 242.

[3] Mitjana reprinted one of Soto's *laudi* in Lavignac and La Laurencie, *Encyclopédie de la musique*, 1ᵉ partie, iv (Paris, 1920), p. 1987.

[4] Eslava has reprinted two psalms, motets, and three of the Magnificats, op. cit. i. 2, and there are four examples of his work in Elústiza and Hernández, op. cit.; Pedrell reprinted two psalms in *Salterio sacro hispano*.

[5] All three in Elústiza and Hernández, pp. 116, 119, and 108; 'Ave virgo' also in Rubio, ii, p. 57. The five-part motet 'Ave regina coelorum' published in Morales' *Opera Omnia*, ii, and preserved anonymously in Valladolid (MS. Parroquía de Santiago) is really by Navarro; it is found in *Johannis Navarri Hispalensis Psalmi, Hymni* . . . (Rome, 1590).

nothing is known of his Masses, some of his delightful religious songs with Spanish text have survived.[1]

CEBALLOS AND OTHER ANDALUSIANS[2]

Rodrigo Ceballos, *maestro de capilla* in the cathedral of Córdoba, 1556, and of the royal chapel of Granada in 1561, must be regarded as one of the most brilliant composers of the Andalusian school. His music—it is sometimes difficult to distinguish his works from those of his namesake, and perhaps brother, Francisco Ceballos, *maestro de capilla* at Burgos—remained entirely in manuscript; it consists of four Masses and a series of motets; the Toledo Cathedral MS.7 contains eighteen four-part motets, twenty-two for five voices, and six for six, a four-part 'Salve', and three Masses. To this must be added the pieces preserved in the royal chapel of Granada and at other centres. His motet 'Inter vestibulum et altare'[3] is remarkably bold, dramatic, and awe-inspiring, anticipating the mystical drama of Victoria's *responsories* for Holy Week. Its aesthetic and spiritual emotion comes directly from Morales:

[1] Ed. Miguel Querol Gavaldá, *Cancionero musical de la Casa de Medinaceli siglo XVI*, two vols. (Barcelona, 1949 and 1950).

[2] See José López Calo: *La música – la catedral de Granaden el siglo XVI*, two vols. (Granada, 1963) for further information.

[3] Sometimes printed as the work of Francisco; it is available in Eslava, op. cit. i. 1, p. 102, Araiz, p. 266, Elústiza and Hernández, op. cit., p. 141, and Rubio, op. cit. i, p. 67. Eslava prints two other motets, attributing them to Francisco; Elústiza and Hernández give four more pieces.

Ambrosio Coronado de Cotes, master of the royal chapel of Granada about 1581 (d. 1603, at Seville), belongs to this school and not to the Valencian group, as has been claimed; at Granada there is a fine collection of his motets and other works. Fernando de las Infantas,[1] a great master of academic counterpoint (1534–c. 1608), descendant of a noble family, and favoured by Charles V and Philip II, published three volumes of motets in Venice. *Liber I* for four voices (1578), *Liber II* for five (1578), and *Liber III* for six (1579), as well as his *Plura modulationum genera quae vulgo contrapuncta appellantur* (1579), which contains a rich series of contrapuntal elaborations of Gregorian chant. He achieved fame by his intervention with the Pope and Philip II against the reform of Gregorian chant; Gregory XIII had in 1577 entrusted the revision of the *Graduale Romanum* to Palestrina and Annibale Zoilo, but as a result of Las Infantas's protest

---

[1] See Mitjana, *Don Fernando de las Infantas: teólogo y músico* (Madrid, 1918); Stevenson, *Spanish Cathedral Music*, pp. 316 ff.

this went no further.[1] Of his 189 compositions many are based on plainsong;[2] of his 88 motets at least ten are old-fashioned tenor motets. He wrote a motet-cantata 'Cantemus Domino' after the battle of Lepanto (1571) and another on the victory over the Turks at Memilla (1565). So far as is known, he wrote no secular music. His five-part 'O admirabile commercium' is characteristic:

Ex. 180

[1] See R. Molitor, *Die Nach-Tridentinische Choral-Reform zu Rom*, i (Leipzig, 1901), pp. 36 ff.; Luciano Serrano, *Archivo de la Embajada de España cerca de la Santa Sede*, i (Roma, 1915).

[2] Eslava reprinted his six-part 'Victimae pa   hali', op. cit. i. 2, p. 175; Rubio, op. cit. ii, reprints eleven motets.

Alfonso Lobo (d. 1617) was among the last masters of this school. His *Liber primus missarum* (Madrid, 1602) contains six Masses for four, five, and six voices and seven motets for five, six, and eight voices.[1] A great quantity of his music is preserved at Granada,[2] Toledo[3] (where he became *maestro de capilla* in 1593), and other Spanish archives; he followed the traditional Palestrina style, which remained in common use in Spain right down to the end of the seventeenth century.

THE CASTILIAN SCHOOL

In the number of its composers and the quality of its music the Castilian school stands beside the Andalusian in the front rank of Spanish religious music. As with the Andalusians, one finds distinguished names which mark the culmination of the work of many lesser artists, but with this difference: in Andalusia after Francisco Peñalosa there suddenly appeared a Morales, the stamp of whose genius was set upon those who followed him, whereas in Castile there were various musicians who prepared and matured the polished art which was to culminate in the great figure of Tomás Luis de Victoria. Juan Escribano (*c.* 1480–1557) was one of the Spanish musicians most esteemed in Rome, and one of those to live longest there[4] as a singer of the papal choir, being much favoured by Leo X. His works, relatively few in number, are preserved in the Vatican:[5] a *Magnificat*

---

[1] Eslava reprinted a *Magnificat* for eight voices, op. cit. i, and four motets for four to six voices, ibid. xiii; the four-part 'Credo quod Redemptor' is also in Araiz, op. cit., p. 297; 'O quam suavis' and 'Vivo ego' are in Rubio, op. cit. i.

[2] Capilla Real, Libros de polifonía, 1.

[3] Cathedral, Libros de polifonía, 21 and 24.

[4] See J. M. Llorens, 'La capilla pontificia . . . en Roma durante el pontificado de Paulo III', *Cuadernos. . . . Escuela Española de Historia y de Arqueología en Roma*, viii (Rome, 1956), and 'Juan Escribano, cantor pontificio y compositor', *Anuario musical*, xii (1957).

[5] Capp. Sist. 44, fo. 52ᵛ and 46, fo. 121.

VI toni for four voices, the motet 'Paradisi porta' for six, and some *Lamentationes*, for four to six voices.[1]

Bartolomé Escobedo (d. before November 1563 in Segovia), friend of Morales, was that 'clericus Zamorensis' who because of his great knowledge was admitted to the papal choir without examination, an event which aroused jealous protest from the French singers. On his return to Spain he served the Infanta Juana, daughter of Charles V, as successor to Flecha (1548). It was Escobedo who was entrusted in 1556 with the composition of the six-part 'Missa Philippus Rex Hispaniae' for the coronation of Philip II as king of Spain, a *canto fermo* Mass, in the style practised by Morales, in which one part always sings the words 'Philippus Rex Hispaniae'. Another of his Masses is 'Ad te levavi', also for five–six voices, preserved like the first in the Sistine Chapel,[2] and five motets for four or five voices, one of which, 'Exsurge, quare obdormis,'[3] was printed in *Nicolai Gomberti Motecta* (Venice, 1541), with others by Morales. Of the austere Pedro de Pastrana, singer to Ferdinand V from 1500, chaplain to Charles V from 1527 and *maestro de capilla* to Philip II from 1547, we have music preserved only in manuscript:[4] seven psalms for four voices, three Magnificats, and a series of motets, mostly for four voices. By the Toledan classicist Bernardino Ribera there survives a four-part 'Missa de Beata Virgine',[5] with the usual *Gloria* trope, and a five-part Mass, 'Beata Virgo', as well as various motets for five or six voices and Magnificats.[6]

Most of the Castilian musicians were privileged to serve not only in the papal chapel at Rome but also in the royal chapels of Spain and Italy. One of the most outstanding was Diego Ortiz, *maestro de capilla* to the duke of Alba when he was Viceroy of Naples in 1555 and of the ducal household from 1558; besides the famous treatise on the art of instrumental variation, *Tratado de glosas* (Rome, 1553),[7] he published a *Musicae Liber primus* (Venice, 1565), containing

[1] Rome, Bibl. Vaticana, Capp. Giulia XII 3 (C), fo. 80–97.
[2] Bibl. Vaticana, Capp. Sist. Cod. 39, 13, and 24.
[3] The motets 'Immutemur habitu', 'Exsurge, quare obdormis, Domine?' and 'Erravi sicut ovis' in Eslava, op. cit. i. 1; 'Exsurge, quare obdormis' is also reprinted in Ambros–Kade, *Geschichte der Musik*, v (Leipzig, 1889), p. 584.
[4] Saragossa, MS. with other psalms by Manchicourt and Mouton; Tarazona, Cathedral, MS. 5, three Magnificats for four voices, motets 'Sicut cervus' for three voices, 'In te, Domine, speravi', and 'Miserere mei' for four voices, 'Tibi soli peccavi' for five voices, 'Pater dimitte illis' and 'Benedicamus' for four voices; MS. 17, six-part Mass and one motet for six voices.
[5] Toledo, Cathedral, Libros de polifonía MS. 6; Saragossa, Seo, MS. s.s.
[6] One of the Magnificats and two five-part motets in Eslava, op. cit. i. 1.
[7] Reprinted by Max Schneider (Berlin, 1913; 2nd ed., Kassel, 1936); see *infra*, pp. 560 and 705.

sixty-nine compositions for four to seven voices:[1] thirty-five hymns, eight Magnificats, thirteen motets, &c. and also left a considerable number of manuscript works; the *vihuelista* Valderrábano printed transcriptions of several of his motets in *Silva de Sirenas* (1547).[2] Luis de Narváez, the *vihuelista* of the *comendador mayor* of León, Francisco de los Cobos, is best known for his instrumental music.[3] On the death of his patron in 1547, he entered the service of Philip II during the following year as master of the boy singers and accompanied the king on his journeys in Flanders, Italy, and Germany during 1548–51.[4] Before this, Moderne had printed two of his motets at Lyons: the four-part 'De profundis clamavi' (in *Motetti del fiore, Libr. IV*, 1539) and the five-part 'O salutaris hostia' (in the *Quintus liber Motettorum*, 1542). Of the celebrated teacher and theorist at Valladolid, Francisco de Montanos (d. after 1592), author of a many times reprinted *Arte de música, theórica y práctica* (Valladolid, 1592), who had to give daily lessons in counterpoint to the fifty-five singers, chaplains, and youths of that cathedral, as well as to any *foreigners* who wished to sing, a number of motets have survived;[5] they are perfect in structure and deeply inspired.

TOMÁS LUIS DE VICTORIA

Castilian religious polyphony culminates in the work of Tomás Luis de Victoria (*c.* 1548 near Avila—1611 in Madrid.)[6] When about nineteen years old, Victoria had the good fortune to find discriminating patrons who quickly perceived the young fellow's precocious gifts and 'natural inclination' for music and facilitated his going to Rome in 1565 as *convictor* and singer of the Collegium Romanum. They made sure that in Rome he should continue his studies

---

[1] From which Proske reprinted a Magnificat on the fifth tone, Vesper hymns, a 'Regina coeli', and other pieces in *Musica Divina*, iii and iv (Ratisbon, 1859 and 1862); Eslava reprinted the five-part 'Pereat dies', op. cit. i. 2, and Rubio an *alternatim* 'Benedictus Dominus' (Canticum Zachariae), op. cit. i.

[2] See pp. 687 ff.   [3] See p. 683.

[4] See Anglès, *La Música . . . Carlos V*, pp. 47 and 105 ff.

[5] Two of them are reprinted in Elústiza and Hernández, op. cit. Mitjana prints a four-part canon, showing his technical ingenuity, in *Encyclopédie de la musique*, l. iv, p. 1973.

[6] *Opera Omnia*, ed. Pedrell (Leipzig, 8 vols., 1902–13); a new complete edition in twelve volumes has been begun by Anglès in the *Monumentos* (1965–   ). There are numerous editions of separate works. On Victoria generally, see Pedrell, *Tomás Luis de Victoria Abulense* (Valencia, 1918), a separate edition of the study in *Opera Omnia*, viii; Hans von May, *Die Kompositionstechnik T. L. de Victorias* (Berne, 1943); Raffaele Casimiri, *Il Vittoria: nuovi documenti per una biografia sincera di Tommaso Ludovico de Victoria* (Rome, 1934); Collet, *Victoria* (Paris, 1914); H. Anglès, *Diccionario de la Música Labor*, ii, pp. 2218 ff.; T. N. Saxton, *The Masses of Victoria* (Princeton Diss. 1951); Stevenson, *Spanish Cathedral Music*, pp. 345 ff.

for the priesthood side by side with those of music. For the better understanding of Victoria's work, it is necessary to remember that in 1552 Julius III had founded the Collegium Germanicum, at the request of St. Ignatius Loyola, primarily for the education in Rome of youths from Germanic countries, while the Collegium Romanum —later known as the 'Gregorian University'—had been founded in 1551 by St. Ignatius for the education of youths from other countries. Victoria studied at the Collegium Germanicum, then under Spanish direction, when Palestrina was *maestro di cappella* in the Collegium Romanum, and thus had the opportunity to take lessons from him. The facts that Victoria was put in charge of the music in the Collegium Romanum as successor to Palestrina in 1571 and made *moderator musicae* of the Germanicum in 1573 show that he quickly won the highest esteem of his patrons in Rome.[1]

The work of Victoria, together with that of Morales, constitutes the chief monument of Spanish religious polyphony. Although Pedrell's edition of the 'complete works' needs augmentation,[2] it includes 20 Masses, 44 motets, 34 hymns, a number of Magnificats, an *Officium Hebdomadae Sanctae*, and an *Officium Defunctorum*. In quantity Victoria cannot compare with Palestrina or Lassus; but in quality he is not unworthy to stand beside them, and in expressiveness and depth of religious and dramatic emotion he may be compared with Palestrina himself. Combining the vocations of priest and musician, Victoria created an art of incomparable spirituality.

There are traces in his music of the Florentine monody which was then beginning to develop; Pedrell's lapidary phrase 'In Victoria we glimpse the lyric drama'[3] is fully justified. Studying the relation of text to music, particularly in his motets,[4] we perceive his stature at its most impressive. He had no other aim than to sing of the Cross and the mysteries of the Redemption, using means uncontaminated by profane art. Even when he employed the 'parody' technique he always chose sacred models which he treated in a highly individual manner.

[1] See Anglès, 'Tomás Luis de Victoria und Deutschland', *Festschrift Wilhelm Neuss* (*Spanische Forschungen der Görresgesellschaft*. Erste Reihe, xvi, 1960), p. 174; R. G. Villoslada, 'Algunos documentos sobre la música en el antiguo Seminario Romano', *Archivium Historicum Societatis Jesu*, xxxi (Rome, 1962). The motet-cantata 'Super flumina Babylonis', composed by Victoria in 1573, was sung as a farewell when the Italian *convictores* were separated from the Collegium Germanicum.

[2] See Rubio, 'Una obra inédita y desconocida de T. L. de Victoria: El motete "O Doctor optime... beate Augustine" for four voices', in *La Ciudad de Dios* (El Escorial, 1949), and two unknown motets in *Antología*, ii.   [3] *Opera Omnia*, viii, p. lvii.

[4] On Victoria's motets, see Leichtentritt, op. cit., pp. 372 ff., Gustave Reese, *Music in the Renaissance* (New York and London, 1954), pp. 600 ff., and May, op. cit., *passim*.

Thus Victoria kept to the path traced by his Spanish predecessors, combining the native spirit of his country with those Roman elements which he so thoroughly absorbed in the city of the popes. Faithful to the principles of his ancestors, Victoria continued to use natural and simple forms. He knew how to express himself without recourse to the intricate counterpoint of the Netherlanders. Educated by Palestrina himself, Victoria also imitated, to some extent, the *princeps musicae* of the Roman school, by writing music in praise of God and for the moving and uplifting of the listeners; like the mystical writers and painters of Spanish humanism, he was able to harmonize artistic severity with loving emotion. The secret of this aesthetic achievement lies in the dramatic mysticism with which he infused his works; consider, for instance, the ecstasy of 'Vere languores':[1]

Ex. 181

Ve - re lan - guo - res no - stros, i -
- pse tu - - - lit et do - lo - res
et do - lo - res no-
no - - - stros et do - lo - res no - -

---

[1] *Opera Omnia*, i, p. 24; originally published by Gardano in a volume of Victoria's motets (Venice, 1572).

It is hard to decide which to admire most, the sweetness of the motet 'O magnum mysterium'[1] for the Feast of the Nativity, the moving drama of the Passion which permeates his *Officium*

[1] Ibid. i, p. 11.

Hebdomadae Sanctae,[1] reaching its climax in the *turbae* of the Matthew and John Passions:

Ex. 182   PASSIO SECUNDUM JOANNEM

or the confident piety breathed by the *Officium Defunctorum*.[2] Victoria wrote no madrigals or other secular songs and never departed from the principle that music exists in order to raise men's souls to their Creator.

Of Victoria's nineteen Masses[3] (the 'Missa Dominicalis', published

[1] *Opera Omnia*, v, p. 111. Originally published at Rome in 1585, though some of the numbers—e.g. the six-part 'O Domine Jesu' recorded in *The History of Music in Sound*, iv—had been printed in earlier collections of Victoria's music: the above-mentioned volume of *Motecta*, the *Liber Primus* of Masses, psalms and Magnificats (Venice, 1576), and the enlarged collection of *Motecta* (Venice, 1583). On the Passion-settings, see Kade, op. cit., p. 150.   [2] *Opera Omnia*, vi, p. 124.

[3] On the Masses, see Peter Wagner, op. cit., pp. 421 ff., Reese, op. cit., pp. 605 ff., and May, *passim*.

by Pedrell,[1] is apocryphal),[2] eleven are parody Masses on motets of
his own. His Mass 'Surge propera'[3] is based on Palestrina's four-
part motet;[4] 'Simile est regnum caelorum'[5] seems to be constructed
on a motet by Guerrero. As Peter Wagner observed,[6] when writing
a *missa parodia* Victoria does not simply copy the motet which served
as model, as Lassus and others do, merely adapting it to the text of
the Mass and varying it in successive movements, but uses only the
part of the motet that best lends itself to the purpose. A good example
of this is the Mass 'O quam gloriosum'[7] where Victoria discards the
opening of his own motet[8] and begins the *Kyrie* at 'in quo cum
Christo'; but this passage of the motet is used again only at the end
of the *Credo*:

Ex. 183

[1] *Opera Omnia*, viii, p. 5.
[2] May, op. cit., p. 144; Raffaele Casimiri, 'Una "Missa Dominicalis" falsamente
attribuita a Tommaso Ludovico de Victoria', *Note d'archivio*, x (1933), p. 185.
[3] *Opera Omnia*, ii, p. 119.
[4] Palestrina, *Werke*, v, p. 47; *Opere Complete*, iii, p. 57,
[5] *Opera Omnia*, ii, p. 21; see Guerrero, *Motteta* (1570).
[6] Op. cit., p. 425.   [7] *Opera Omnia*, ii, p. 56.   Ibid. i, p. 1.

(i) *cont.*

(ii) *cont.*

(iii) *cont.*

The *Christe*, part of the *Gloria* ('Filius Patris'), and part of the *Credo* ('non erit finis') are based on the end of the motet ('quocumque ierit'); the second *Kyrie*, part of the *Gloria* ('Tu solus Sanctus . . .'), part of the *Credo* ('Qui propter nos . . .'), and the *Agnus* are evolved from the passage 'sequuntur agnum' in the motet.[1]

The three Marian Masses 'Salve Regina', 'Alma redemptoris', and 'Ave Regina',[2] published in 1600, form a separate group, since they are written for two choirs with organ accompaniment; all three are based on Victoria's own eight-part antiphons.[3] The 'Missa pro

[1] May has analysed Victoria's procedure in all his parody-Masses, op. cit., p. 82, n. 2.
[2] *Opera Omnia*, iv, pp. 72 and 99, vi, p. 1.
[3] Ibid. vii, pp. 120, 73, 85.

Victoria', for nine voices, divided into two choirs, with organ,[1] composed in 1600, is a festal Mass, a *pièce d'occasion*, and for the first time the composer writes in *concertante* style, with a great deal of *parlando*. It is the only work which Victoria based on a secular model, Janequin's 'La Guerre', and, as Reese has remarked, it lacks the mysticism so typical of the rest of Victoria's work. Studying this Mass in 1913, Peter Wagner wondered at its style and actually doubted its authenticity. 'If it is genuine', he wrote, 'we are confronted by the fact that the roots of the *concertante* style go back earlier than we had hitherto supposed.'[2]

As with Palestrina, the basis of Victoria's style is the melodic line; the tension between the melodic and harmonic elements produces incomparable emotive force by means of dissonance. In Victoria's music, as in the classic polyphony of humanism, the melodic and harmonic elements are contrary forces whose union constitutes the typical style. In his music we also find characteristics of the Spanish national school: for instance the ascending interval of the diminished fourth, F$^\sharp$–B$^\flat$, so characteristic of the seventeenth-century organists, and the interval of the augmented second, E$^\flat$–F$^\sharp$, equally typical of certain traditional songs.

LATER CASTILIAN MASTERS

After Victoria came a number of lesser worthies, such as Juan Esquivel Barahona[3] (d. after 1613), composer of three volumes of church music printed at Salamanca, 1608–13: the first with six Masses for four to eight voices, the second containing motets, the third psalms, hymns, antiphons, &c. His music is always deeply religious in character; only his six-part 'Missa batalla'[4] has themes of popular character and military tunes; it is written in *concertante* style like Victoria's 'Pro victoria', and again like that work is thematically related to, though hardly a 'parody' on, Janequin's famous *chanson*:

[1] Ibid. vi, p. 26.

[2] Wagner, op. cit., p. 429.

[3] See Albert Geiger, 'Juan Esquivel: ein unbekannter spanischer Meister des 16. Jahrhunderts', *Festschrift zum 50. Geburtstag Adolf Sandberger* (Munich, 1918), p. 138; Anglès, *Die Musik in Geschichte und Gegenwart*, iii (1954), col. 1538; Stevenson, op. cit. i, pp. 288 ff.

[4] Copious musical examples in Geiger's study. Plasencia Cathedral, Archivo musical, MS. 1, contains 62 motets for four or five parts by Esquivel; see Rubio, *Anuario musical*, v, p. 149.

Ex. 184

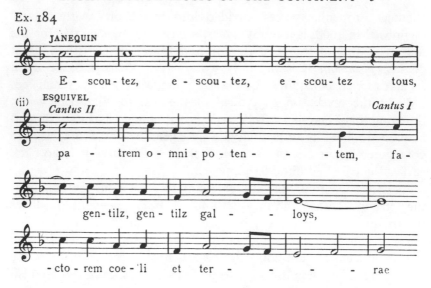

Bernardo Clavijo del Castillo[1] (d. 1626 in Madrid), master of the *cappella palatina* of Palermo from 1569, afterwards organist professor at Salamanca University from 1593, and organist of the royal chapel from 1603, published *Motecta ad canendum tam cum quattuor, quinque, sex et octo vocibus, quam cum instrumentis composita* (Rome, 1588) dedicated to Enrique de Guzman, Duke of Alba; it contains nineteen motets. By the restless Sebastián Vivanco (d. 1622 at Salamanca), *maestro* at Lérida, Avila, Segovia, Salamanca and, in 1612, professor of music in the University of Salamanca, we have a volume of Magnificats (Salamanca, 1607), one of Masses (Salamanca, 1608), one of motets (Salamanca, 1610), and a great quantity of music in manuscript.

Of works by Sebastián López de Velasco (d. after 1648), a well-known *maestro de capilla* at León and teacher of the Infanta Juana in her convent of the Discalced Franciscans of Madrid, we have a *Libro de Misas, Motetes, Salmos, Magnificas y otras cosas tocante al culto divino* (Madrid, 1628) containing five eight-part Masses, one of which is inscribed 'Missa super Bassis Philyppi Rogeri', while the others seem to be written on sacred themes. His style is grandiose; he knew how to combine the contemporary Spanish technique with dramatic-religious fervour, attaining a high degree of expressiveness. By Juan Ruiz de Robledo, *maestro* at León and Valladolid we have

---

[1] Not to be confused with his successor in Madrid, Diego del Castillo.

two books: *Laura de Música Eclesiástica* (Madrid, 1644) and a collection of Masses and psalms (Madrid, 1627).[1] He specialized in
eight-part works for double chorus, broadly conceived, with contrapuntal sections alternating with homophony. Finally we must mention Mateo Romero ('El maestro Capitán') (d. 1647) who in 1596
succeeded Philippe Rogier as chief of the *capilla flamenca* of Philip II.
Although he wrote a great deal of secular music,[2] some of his nine-
part Masses for three choirs have been preserved, as well as psalms for
nine and twelve voices;[3] he specially cultivated polychoral music, and
his contemporaries considered him 'el portento musical de Europa'.

THE CATALAN SCHOOL

After the extinction in Catalonia of the royal chapel of Aragon on
the death of Ferdinand the Catholic in 1516, Catalan musicians were
seldom able to find noble patrons. There were exceptionally talented
men among them, but the limiting of the religious composer's sphere
of activity to the cathedrals and the lack of an encouraging environment had their inevitable consequences. The cathedrals of Barcelona,
Tarragona, Lérida, and La Seo de Urgel could count on musicians
of the first rank. Closely connected culturally with Italy, Naples, and
Sicily, Catalan musicians advanced beyond the Castilians in the
development of the madrigal and secular song. But Catalan composers
seldom went abroad at this period; owing to the lack of patrons and
publishers their work remained in manuscript, and as a result of
continual political struggles many treasures of ecclesiastical music
were lost for ever.

Mateo Flecha the elder (d. 1553), *maestro de capilla* from 1523 at
Lérida, from 1544 to 1548 *maestro* to the royal princesses of Castile,
Doña Maria and Doña Juana, daughters of Charles V, was one of
the most talented Catalan composers. Although none of his liturgical
works have survived, at least some of his *Ensaladas* were printed by
his nephew Mateo Flecha the younger (Prague, 1581). These pieces
are religious quodlibets in which Flecha combines the comic with the
dramatic, the ironic with practical moral instruction, and popular
songs with themes of liturgical origin, mixing texts from Latin, French,

---

[1] On Vivanco, López de Velasco, and Ruiz de Robledo, see Anglès, *Catàleg dels
Manuscrits Musicals de la Collecció Pedrell* (Barcelona, 1921), pp. 7 ff.

[2] See particularly J. Aroca (ed.), *Cancionero musical y poético del siglo XVII* (Madrid,
1916), including twenty-two compositions by Romero; Pedrell, *Teatro lírico español
anterior al siglo XIX* and *Cancionero Musical*, iii, nos. 81–82.

[3] Eslava prints his 'Libera me' for two four-part choirs, op. cit., *serie* 2, i. 1, p. 101.

Italian, Catalan, and Spanish. Such *ensaladas* were widely popular in Spain at that time; they helped materially to create a Christmas atmosphere and to entertain the Court at Christmas and New Year. Flecha's *ensaladas* have a symbolic and doctrinal significance, for they constantly refer to the victory of the newly born Child in the war against Lucifer for the salvation of the human race.[1]

Pedro Alberch Vila (or Villa) (1517–82), of Barcelona, was adviser to all the Catalan cathedrals on matters concerning organs; the finest organists were educated in his school. His motet 'O crux fidelis' for four equal voices, preserved in manuscript,[2] and his Lamentation of Jeremiah 'Lamech: O vos omnes'[3] for three voices, deeply dramatic and mystical, would be sufficient to ensure his fame; his four-part *Magnificat*[4] shows the construction of a master-hand.[5]

Mateo Flecha the younger, educated by his uncle, by Antonio de Cabezón and by Francisco de Soto at the court of the princesses of Castile, was a Carmelite, chaplain from 1564 to the empress Maria in Vienna, court chaplain and cantor to Maximilian II, for whom in 1576 he wrote a Mass which has not survived. Besides a book of *Madrigali* (Venice, 1568), he published *Divinarum completarum psalmi* . . . (Prague, 1581), which is preserved incomplete, three four-part religious *ensaladas* and a *Miserere* for four voices.[6]

Joan Brudieu, born in the diocese of Limoges about 1520, became naturalized among the Catalan uplands, since he lived at La Seo de Urgel from 1539 till his death in 1591. He published a volume of *Madrigales* (Barcelona, 1585),[7] which opens with *Los Goigs de Nostra Dona* (The Joys of Our Lady), and his four-part 'Missa pro defunctis' is one of the finest of its kind. Brudieu adorns the plainsong *canto fermo* with the arabesque melodies and popular cadences typical of his style. His entire Mass is filled with spiritual light and optimism, full of faith and hope in divine pity and eternal life; its contrast with the Masses 'Pro defunctis' of Morales and Guerrero strikingly illustrates the polished art of this modest priest.

[1] See Anglès, *Mateo Flecha, Las Ensaladas* (Biblioteca Central, Publicaciones de la Sección de Música, xvi) (Barcelona, 1955); J. Romeu Figueras, 'Mateo Flecha el Viejo, la Corte literariomusical del duque de Calabria y el Cancionero llamado de Upsala', *Anuario musical*, xiii (1958). Eleven *ensaladas* by Flecha are preserved in print or manuscript. Madrid, Bibl. Medinaceli, MS. 607, contains 'parody' masses 'La bomba' and 'La Batalla' for four voices on *ensaladas* by Flecha.
[2] Barcelona, Iglesia del Palau. s.s.   [3] Barcelona, Orfeó Català. MS. 6, ff. 42ᵛ–43.
[4] Barcelona, Biblioteca Central, Depart. de Música.
[5] On 23 December 1559 Philip II gave permission to 'Pedro Vila, canónico de Barcelona' to publish 'algunas obras de canto llano y de órgano y de misas, motetes y madrigales'; no such book has been preserved. See also p. 616.
[6] See Mateo Flecha, *Las Ensaladas*, new edition by Anglès, p. 37.
[7] See p. 83.

Pedro Riquet, *maestro de capilla* at Urgel from 1598, is notable for a belated four-part Mass 'Susanne un jour', exceptional for its date, especially in the Provincia Tarraconensis, which strove to put into practice the liturgical-musical reforms of the Council of Trent. Pablo Vilallonga, *maestro de capilla* at Santa Maria del Mar in Barcelona, from 1564 at the cathedral of Palma de Mallorca,[1] and Rafael Coloma, at Seo de Urgell (1586),[2] were other masters during the sixteenth century of sacred music in Catalonia.

Until the middle of the seventeenth century Catalan composers continued to cultivate the Palestrina style of the Roman school, with all its mysticism and clarity of form, while at the same time in their psalms, motets, *villancicos* and *chansonetas* they practised the new style which had penetrated every European centre. The religious *villancico*, which had already been known in the sixteenth century despite Philip II's exclusion of it from his chapel, forced its way everywhere.

Various cathedrals and music chapels in Catalonia maintained not only singers but small orchestras of *ministriles* who played the bass, sackbut, *chirimia, vihuela de arco*, harp, *cornetto*, clavichord, and organ.

JUAN PUJOL

The most outstanding composer of religious music during the first quarter of the seventeenth century in Spain was undoubtedly Juan Pablo Pujol (d. 1626).[3] In his youth he was *maestro de capilla* in the cathedral of Tarragona, afterwards in El Pilar at Saragossa, and finally in the cathedral of Barcelona. In the inventory of his works—all in manuscript—made at the time of his death, eighteen collections are enumerated: among them 89 *villancicos* for the Holy Sacraments and Christmas, 120 motets, more than a dozen Masses, psalms, responsories, Passions, &c. His works are always written for four to eight voices, some with *basso continuo*. Pujol's *Officium Hebdomadae Sanctae* has been continuously sung in Barcelona Cathedral from his own day down to our own. While the four-part psalm settings,[4] though in note-against-note style, are remarkable for the ingenuity of their infinite polyphonic embellishments of the Gregorian *canti fermi*, the eight-part Masses astonish by the expressive force and

---

[1] One manuscript with psalms and motets has been preserved in the cathedral of Palma de Mallorca.

[2] Two motets for four voices are preserved at Barcelona, Bibl. Central; Rubio, op. cit. ii, has printed the four-part motet 'Surrexit Pastor bonus'.

[3] Only two of the eight projected volumes of his *Opera Omnia* (ed. Anglès) have so far been published (Barcelona, 1926 and 1932). [4] Ibid. i, p. 1.

mature technique with which Pujol, employing a double chorus, combines the homophonic style with the contrapuntal. His music is not dramatic, like that of some masters of the Castilian and Andalusian schools, but mystical, always severe and profoundly religious, in the tradition of Alberch Vila. It represents an intermediary style between the *a cappella* style of Palestrina and the *basso continuo* style which he generally reserves for settings of Spanish texts. Incidentally, Pujol sometimes strengthens his *canti fermi* with a trumpet.

The boys' choir-school of Montserrat, which flourished during the seventeenth century, was a fertile nursery of distinguished musicians who made their way all over the peninsula. Miguel Andreu, Juan Verdalet, Antonio Reig, Marciá Albareda are among those who continued the tradition of Pujol and his predecessors.

THE VALENCIAN SCHOOL

The city of Valencia, with its Cathedral, the church of Corpus Christi, and the chapel of the dukes of Calabria,[1] was a centre of culture and of religious and secular music during the age of humanism. According to Pedrell the Valencian school during the period 1590–1630 was notable for its *música exultante*, owing to its cultivation of polychoral effects for two, three, or four choirs. Little is known about Cárceres, though it is believed that he came from Gandía; we have a number of five-part Credos, a four-part 'Lamentatio Lamech: O vos omnes', *villancicos* for three to five voices and also some four-part *ensaladas*. Perhaps the sixteenth-century composer Bartolomé Comes was also of Valencian origin; he is known for motets which appear in Gardano's *Motecta quinque vocibus* (Venice, 1547) and Montanus and Neuber's *Tomus tertius evangeliarum* (Nuremberg, 1555) and their *Tomus V* (1556). Juan Ginés Pérez (1548–1612), who had some part in the writing of the music for the *Misterio de Elche*,[2] is one of the most distinguished composers of this school. In addition to works which have disappeared from Orihuela, where he was born and died, and those published by Pedrell in the

---

[1] One of the dukes of Calabria, Don Fernando de Aragón, viceroy of Valencia (d. 1550), married in 1526 Germaine de Foix, widow of Ferdinand V of Aragón; his chapel was, musically, one of the best in Spain, and in 1536 was conducted by Pedro de Pastrana, who was afterwards conductor of the Royal Chapel of Philip II; see José Romeu Figueras, 'Mateo Flecha el Viejo, la corte literariomusical del duque de Calabria y el cancionero llamado de Upsala', *Anuario musical*, xiii (1958), p. 25.

[2] Cf. *Consueta de la Fiesta de Elche*, ed. facs. with an introduction by Eugenio d'Ors (Barcelona, 1941). See also Pedrell, 'La festa d'Elche', *Sammelbände der internationalen Musikgesellschaft*, ii (1900–1), p. 203, and J. B. Trend, 'The Mystery of Elche', *Music and Letters*, i (1920), p. 145.

fifth volume of *Hispaniae Schola Musica Sacra*,[1] some forty compositions by him, all religious, are preserved in the cathedral archives at Valencia; they are for three to six voices; other manuscript works by him are in the Colegio del Patriarca (Valencia), Málaga, the cathedral at Segorbe, and elsewhere. The most famous and characteristic master of this school, however, is undoubtedly Juan Bautista Comes (1568–1643).[2] At Valencia alone there are in manuscript some 230 of his compositions for eight and twelve voices.[3] He was one of the first to devote his talent to the writing of *villancicos* in the form of religious cantatas, with instrumental accompaniment; some seventy-four are preserved in the archives of Valencia Cathedral. Comes must be ranked among the foremost Spanish composers of polychoral religious music; his work is cheerful, optimistic, and technically polished, and he also draws inspiration from popular song.[4]

THE ARAGONESE SCHOOL

One of the first masters of this school was Juan García Basurto (d. 1547), cantor at Tarazona, *maestro de capilla* at the Pilar—one of the two cathedrals—at Saragossa,[5] and finally master of the royal chapel of Philip II; a four-part 'Missa pro defunctis', motets, and other works by him are extant. But the outstanding figure of this school is Melchior Robledo (d. 1586), at one time a singer in the Sistine Chapel and later *maestro de capilla* of the Seo, the other cathedral at Saragossa, who had the distinction of being classed with Josquin, Morales, Victoria, Palestrina, and other classic masters whose music alone might be performed in the Pilar. At least three of his Masses, one for four and two for five voices, survive, as well as a number of motets,[6] and a series of psalms, Magnificats, an eight-part 'Te Deum', *Lamentationes*, and other works.

[1] Rubio prints an *alternatim* 'Miserere mei', op. cit. i, p. 143.

[2] See Manuel Palau, *La obra del Músico Valenciano Juan Bautista Comes* (Madrid, 1944). Selected works ed. J. B. Guzmán, *Obras musicales de J. B. Comes* (Madrid, 2 vols., 1888). Palau has published a separate edition of the four-part Mass 'Exsultet coelum' (Valencia, 1955). The twelve-part 'Hodie nobis' for three choirs is printed by Eslava, op. cit., serie 2, i. 1, p. 1, a simple four-part 'Christus factus est' by Araiz, op. cit., p. 310.

[3] Listed in J. Ruiz de Lihori, barón de Alcahalí, *Diccionario biográfico de músicos valencianos* (Valencia, 1903).

[4] See the editions of Comes's vocal dances for Corpus Christi and his polyphonic *Gozos*, issued by the Instituto Valenciano de Musicología (1952 and 1955).

[5] On music in Saragossa, see Antonio Lozano, *La música popular, religiosa y dramática en Zaragoza* (Saragossa, 1895); *Diccionario de la Música Labor*, i, pp. 91 ff.

[6] Four motets in Eslava, op. cit. i, 1; one in Araiz, op. cit., p. 263, and Rubio, op. cit. i, p. 82, with a Magnificat, ibid. ii, p. 135.

José Gay (d. 1587), Robledo's successor (for only three months), is represented by a number of motets and other religious works. Sebastián Aguilera de Heredia (b. 1570), organist of La Seo, is another distinguished Aragonese. In his Magnificats (*Canticum beatissimae Virginis Deiparae Mariae*) (Saragossa, 1618),[1] for four, five, six, and eight voices in all the eight modes, he works the plainsong contrapuntally according to the tradition of Spanish fauxbourdon; his practice of the art of vocal variation is marked by profound religious feeling and technical austerity:

Ex 185

---

[1] Four-part *Magnificat* in Eslava, op. cit., *serie* 2, i. 1; excerpts in Araiz, op. cit., p. 304, and Mitjana, *Encyclopédie*, iv, p. 2043.

He also wrote some organ pieces[1] which enhance both his own reputation and that of the Aragonese school. Pedro Rimonte (Ruimonte), was first active at Saragossa, but in 1605 entered the service of the Archduke Albert and the Infanta Isabella, governors of the Netherlands, where he published his *Cantiones sacrae* (Antwerp, 1607) and *Missae sex vocum* (Antwerp, 1614), which still await study and a modern edition. Nicasio Zorita (Çorita), *maestro* first at Tarragona, then at Saragossa, is known for his *Liber I Motectorum* (Barcelona, 1584), a collection of thirty-two motets for four voices and twenty for five; there are other works by him in manuscript. Although Cerone, in *El Melopeo y Maestro* (Naples, 1613), chapter xl, treats him as a plagiarist, Zorita's motets have real value and display his masterly technique. Allied to the Aragonese school was Miguel Navarro, *maestro* of the cathedral at Pampeluna, who published a *Liber Magnificarum* for four, six, seven, and eight voices 'et fugis duobus, tribus et quatuor simul concinnatis' (Pampeluna, 1614). Besides Magnificats in all eight modes, this volume also contains seven psalms, a *Salve Regina* and two motets for four voices; other works in manuscript by him have been preserved at Saragossa.

MUSIC IN PORTUGAL[2]

During the greater part of this period, from 1580 to 1640, Portugal was ruled by the kings of Spain. Nevertheless, although Portuguese composers sometimes offered excessive adulation to the Spanish monarchs—as Cardoso did in his 'Missa Filipina'[3] in which one

[1] See p. 679.
[2] The editor is responsible for this section.
[3] Printed by Júlio Eduardo dos Santos, *A polifonia clássica portuguesa*, i (Lisbon 1937), p. 96.

voice or another throughout sings the theme announced by the *cantus* at the outset:

she maintained her artistic tradition, established under Alfonso V (1438–81) and encouraged by the music-loving John III (1521–57); the marked conservatism of her composers must be attributed not to political conditions but to the continuing influence of the Counter-Reformation in a Jesuit-dominated country. And when she regained her independence it was under a king who not only composed but wrote books about music and founded one of the greatest of musical libraries. Of John IV's compositions[1] only two doubtfully authentic four-part motets have survived;[2] of his vast library, destroyed in the Lisbon earthquake of 1755, we have only the catalogue,[3] which he published in 1649; but we possess his two treatises, the *Defensa de la música moderna* (Lisbon, 1649; Italian translation, Venice, 1666) and the *Respuestas a las dudas que se pusieron a la missa 'Panis quem*

---

[1] See L. de Freitas Branco, *D. João IV, músico* (Lisbon, 1956).

[2] Printed in Santos, op. cit. i, pp. 33 and 35; also in Mário de Sampayo Ribeiro, *Cadernos de repertório coral 'Polyphonia'* (Série azul, No. 4) (Lisbon, 1957), and elsewhere.

[3] Published Lisbon, 1649; only two copies are known, at Lisbon (Bibl. nac.) and Paris (Bibl. nat.), but there is a nineteenth-century reprint by Joaquim de Vasconcellos, *Index da Livraria de música do Rey Dom João o IV* (Oporto, 1873).

ego dabo' *del Palestrina* (Lisbon, 1654; Italian translation, Rome 1655), which demonstrate both his learning and the backwardness of musical thought in Portugal.

The earliest Portuguese polyphonist of distinction seems to have been the humanist and traveller, Damião de Goes (1502–74),[1] friend of Erasmus and of Glareanus who printed his three-part motet 'Ne laeteris inimica mea'[2] in the *Dodecachordon* (Basle, 1547); two years earlier Sigismund Salblinger had published his five-part 'Surge propera' in *Cantiones 7, 6, 5 vocum* (Augsburg, 1545). But the most important Portuguese school developed in the Colégio da Claustra and cathedral at Évora[3] under the guidance of Manuel Mendes (d. 1605),[4] whose most distinguished pupils were Duarte Lôbo (*c.* 1563–1646),[5] the already mentioned Manuel Cardoso (*c.* 1571–1650),[6] and Felipe de Magalhães (d. after 1648). Lôbo, director of the music of Lisbon Cathedral for more than forty years, has been generally considered the greatest Portuguese polyphonist; he enjoyed a European reputation in his lifetime and Plantin of Antwerp published four volumes of his work: one containing responsories and an eight-part Mass for Christmas Eve (1602), one of Magnificats (1605), and two of Masses (1621 and 1639); other works were published at Lisbon by Plantin's former apprentice Peter van Craesbeck. Despite the skill of his craftsmanship, his music is sometimes dry and uninspired. The six-part motet 'Audivi vocem' shows him at his best:

[1] See Sampayo Ribeiro, *Damião de Goes na Livraria Real da Música* (Lisbon, 1935).

[2] Several times reprinted: e.g. by Hawkins, *General History of Music*, ii (London, 1776), p. 438, by Thomas Busby, *History of Music*, i (London, 1819), p. 539, and in *Publikation älterer praktischer und theoretischer Musikwerke*, xvi (Leipzig, 1888).

[3] See Freitas Branco, 'Les Contrepointistes de l'école d'Évora' *Actes du Congrès d'histoire d'art, Paris, 1921*, iii (Paris, 1924), p. 846, and A. T. Luper, 'Portuguese Polyphony in the Sixteenth and early Seventeenth Centuries', *Journal of the American Musicological Society*, iii (1950), p. 93.

[4] A 'Missa de feria' and an eight-part 'Asperges' by Mendes have been published by Manuel Joaquim in *Música*, ii (1942).

[5] See M. A. de Lima Cruz, *Duarte Lôbo* (Lisbon, 1937). Of the complete edition by Joaquim, *Composições polifónicas de Duarte Lôbo* (Lisbon, 1945–), only the first volume, containing sixteen four-part Magnificats, has so far appeared. The Masses 'Dum aurora' and 'Ductus est Jesus', with the motet 'Vidi aquam', are reprinted in Santos, op. cit., pp. 40, 57, and 38.

[6] On Cardoso, see Mário de Sampayo Ribeiro, *Frei Manuel Cardoso* (Lisbon, 1961). Proske reprinted two of Cardoso's motets, 'Cum audisset' and 'Angelis suis', in *Musica Divina*, l. ii (Regensburg, 1854), pp. 12 and 98. In addition to the 'Missa Filipina', Santos prints the 'Angelis suis', a 'Tantum ergo', and 'Panis angelicus', op. cit., pp. 75, 77, and 78. J. A. Alegria has published the *Liber Primus Missarum* in *Portugaliae Musica*, v and vi (Lisbon, 1962), and twelve Mass-movements and motets in *Polyphonia*, No. 2 (Lisbon, 1955).

Ex.187

Cardoso,[1] for many years musical director and sub-prior of the Carmelite monastery at Lisbon, was held in high honour not only by the Spanish kings but by John IV, for whom he also wrote an adulatory Mass; his works were published at Lisbon by the Craesbecks—a volume of Magnificats (1613), three books of Masses (1625, 1636, and 1636), and a *Livro de varios motetes, Officio da Semana Santa e outras cousas* (1648); his music is Palestrinian in style. But the favourite pupil of Mendes seems to have been Magalhães (d. 1652), to whom he bequeathed his books. Magalhães became choirmaster of the Capela da Misericórdia at Lisbon and then, from 1623 to 1641, master of the royal chapel. He published a volume of *Cantus eccle-*

---

[1] Not to be confused with an earlier Manuel Cardoso, *archipraecentor* to John III, who published music for Holy Week (Leiria, 1575) and died before the end of the century.

siasticus (Lisbon, 1614; reprinted 1642), a book of Masses (Lisbon, 1631), and *Cantica Beatissimae Virginis* (Lisbon, 1636). He excels in expressive writing, as in the *Sanctus* of his Mass 'De Beata Virgine':

Ex. 188[1]

[1] From a manuscript copy kindly supplied by Mário de Sampayo Ribeiro.

Besides Lisbon and Évora, there were at this period centres of musical activity at Vila Viçosa, where the Dukes of Bragança had a palace,[1] and Coimbra, where a canon, Heliodoro de Paiva (d. 1552)[2] seems to have been the most distinguished of a school of composers at the monastery of Santa Cruz.[3] In the north at Viseu, Estêvão Lopes Morago was choirmaster at the cathedral.[4]

[1] See Joaquim, 'A propósito dos livros de polifonia existentes no Paço Ducal de Vila Viçosa (Portugal)', *Anuario musical*, ii (1947), p. 69.

[2] Manuscript Masses, motets, and Magnificats in Coimbra, Univ. Lib., M.M. 12 and 44.

[3] See Sampayo Ribeiro, 'A musica em Coimbra', *Biblos*, xv (1939), p. 439. Santos prints some anonymous pieces of the Coimbra school, op. cit., pp. 86, 88, and 90. Six compositions by a late Coimbra composer, Pedro de Cristo (c. 1545–1618), are published by Sampayo Ribeiro in *Polyphonia*, No. 3 (Lisbon, 1956).

[4] A selection of his compositions has been published by Manuel Joaquim in *Portugaliae Musica*, iv (Lisbon, 1961).

VIII

PROTESTANT MUSIC ON THE CONTINENT

By THÉODORE GÉROLD

LUTHER'S VIEWS ON CHURCH MUSIC

WHEN various countries adhered to the Reformation in the course of the sixteenth century, music was at once given an important place in their religious life. Two essential trends can be discerned. The countries which adopted the ideas of Luther—a large part of Germany and some Northern lands—retained some connexion with the Catholic faith, and their music had from the beginning a certain richness, which continued to develop and led finally to the creation of masterpieces. In countries which followed the precepts of Calvin— French Switzerland, part of France, some districts of Germany— religious music was confined to a more limited sphere: to more or less elaborated psalm-tunes. But this type of music, also, produced works worthy of admiration and deserving of study. Already in the sixteenth century, and at the beginning of the seventeenth, all this music constituted a vast repertory.

Martin Luther has rightly been called the Father of Protestant music in Germany. Thanks to his fundamentally religious mind, combined with genuine artistic feeling, as well as to his energy and determination, he succeeded in laying the foundations of a type of music which not only became an essential element in the Protestant religion, but also exerted a beneficial influence upon the whole civilized world. He was convinced of the divine origin of music. 'Music,' he said, 'is a gift from God, not from Man.' In opposition to those who, impelled by their hatred of Roman Catholic ceremonies, wished to suppress hymn-singing and organ-playing in religious services, and to destroy the images of saints and other artistic objects, he wrote in the preface to Walther's first collection of hymns (1524): 'I am not of the opinion that all the arts should be stricken down by the Gospel and disappear, as certain zealots would have it; on the contrary, I would see all the arts, and particularly music, at the service of Him who created them and gave them to us.'

The task which he set himself was not easy. He did not wish to suppress the Mass, but only to alter or delete certain passages which, in his opinion, did not conform to the spirit of the Gospel. In addition, he wished the Roman Mass to be translated into German, so that each one of those who attended the service would be able to understand the words of the priest and the choristers, and to grasp the meaning of the ceremonies. But, if the words sung by the celebrant were translated into German, the question arose as to whether the music could be adapted to the new text or whether it would have to be modified. Then yet another problem was raised. In Catholic services, music was entrusted to the priest and his assistants, to the choir, to the organ, and sometimes to other instruments. The congregation did not have to take part; it had only to listen. One of Luther's most ardent desires was that the congregation should take an active part in the service, that they should find in it an opportunity of praising God, of expressing their gratitude towards the Lord, or of confirming their faith and their will to follow the divine precepts. It was, therefore, indispensable to find hymns which could be taught to the congregation. From 1523 onward, Luther was actively occupied with this question, and himself began to write words which could be set to music. On 14 January 1524 he wrote to Spalatin, Councillor of the Elector of Saxony: 'We intend to follow the example of the prophets and the ancient Fathers of the Church, and to make a collection of a certain number of psalms for the people, so that the Word of God may be kept alive in their hearts by song.' Shortly before this, he also expressed his desires and fears in the *Formulae Missae*: 'I would that we had plenty of German songs which the people could sing during Mass, in the place of, or as well as, the Gradual, or together with the *Sanctus* and the *Agnus Dei*. But we lack German poets, or else we do not yet know of them, who could make for us devout and spiritual songs, as Paul calls them.'

THE EARLIEST LUTHERAN SONGBOOKS

However, in 1524, there appeared four collections of religious songs. The first, known as the *Achtliederbuch*,[1] was the work of the printer Jobst Gutknecht of Nuremberg. He collected eight songs, which had been issued on single sheets from various presses during the previous winter, and made a little volume of them. This was soon followed by the two *Enchiridien* printed at Erfurt,[2] and towards the end of the summer the *Gesangk Buchleyn* of Johann Walther was

---

[1] Facsimile edition by Konrad Ameln (Kassel and Basle, 1957).
[2] Facsimile edition (Kassel, 1929).

published, under Luther's direction and with a preface by him. Walther, still a young man, was assistant to the musical director in the chapel of the Elector of Saxony at Torgau, Conrad Rupsch. His volume contains thirty-eight settings of German texts and five of Latin words, and remained the essential foundation of all subsequent publications. They are composed for three, four, or five voices. Walther's essential achievement was the setting of the melodies of the hymns 'to music for several voices'; which of the melodies he himself invented, it is very difficult to say. (The sources of the German Protestant hymn will be dealt with later.) For the moment, let us first of all see how Walther treated the melodies. He employs two methods: in both, the melody is given to the tenor as *canto fermo*, in long notes practically all of equal value. But in a fairly large number of pieces the two upper voices develop above the tenor a very free counterpoint which has very little relation to the melody. Sometimes, at the beginning or towards the end, there is a brief, short-lived access of imitation. In exceptional cases a middle voice also takes the melody of the *canto fermo*, and sings with it in canon. The composition is then for five voices, and again a higher voice and one of the others indulge in supple and lively counterpoint. An interesting example is provided by the composition of the hymn 'Nun komm der Heiden Heiland', by Luther. It is noteworthy that towards the end the *canto fermo* loses its usual rigidity.

The second method is simpler and shows a different point of view; while in the compositions of the first style the musician's aim is evidently to show his skill, in the others he seeks, by very simple means, to make the melody stand out so that it shall be grasped more easily by the congregation. There is no more lively counterpoint; the other voices progress almost as calmly as the tenor, often forming simple chords with it, each line of the verses ending with a cadence. Musically, the verses are often divided into two parts; in the first, lines 3 and 4 repeat the melody of 1 and 2; the second part is generally a little longer. This corresponds closely to a common type of popular song. Later on, this second method was used more than the first; but in both occur obvious attempts, however modest, to vary the form.

[1] On the *Geystliche Gesangk Buchleyn* (1524) (modern edition by Kade, *Publikationen der Gesellschaft für Musikforschung*, Jg. 6 (Leipzig, 1878)) and the compositions of Johann Walther, see the articles by W. Lucke and H. J. Moser in the Weimar edition of Luther's works (1923), xxxv. See also Wilibald Gurlitt, 'Johannes Walther und die Musik der Reformationszeit', *Luther-Jahrbuch*, xv (1933). Examples from the 1524 *Buchleyn* are easily accessible in Davison and Apel, *Historical Anthology of Music*, i (London, 1947), p. 115, Schering, *Geschichte der Musik in Beispielen* (Leipzig, 1931), p. 76, and Jöde, *Chorbuch alter Meister*, ii (Wolfenbüttel, 1948).

In the preface to this collection of 1524, Luther says:

These hymns have been arranged for four voices, for the sole reason that I should like young people, who in any case should and must be instructed in music and in other proper arts, to have at their disposal something which will rid their minds of lascivious and sensual songs, and teach them instead something wholesome, and in this way they may become acquainted with goodness in a joyous manner, as befits the young.

He had already learned to sing as a little boy at school, and later, as a monk, he had found consolation in music at times of sorrow. He had also learned to play the lute and the *flauto traverso*. Above all, he had learned to recognize good church music and had formed his own critical standards. He had become acquainted with the works of Heinrich Isaac, who had spent some time in Wittenberg at the beginning of the century; he esteemed highly the compositions of Josquin des Prez, and corresponded with Senfl, Isaac's favourite pupil.[1]

LUTHER AS COMPOSER

The question whether Luther himself composed the melodies of certain hymns, of which he had written the texts, has often been discussed. He was long believed to be the composer of most of the melodies of his chorales. Then, little by little, doubts arose and for a time no melodies at all were attributed to him. Recent research has made it possible to answer the question more accurately, and there is a fairly general agreement in attributing the melodies of four or five hymns to him.[2] The earliest of these compositions treats the subject of the two martyrs of Brussels: 'Ein neues Lied wir heben an' (1523), simple and scarcely at all narrative in character. The original melody of 'Nun freut euch, lieben Christengmein' may also be by Luther himself. The text is a sort of personal confession, in which the author expresses his joy in the fact that God, through Jesus Christ, has delivered him from the power of the Devil. The mood of the melody is joyous, though hardly of a popular character. The verses have seven lines of 8. 7. 8. 7. 8. 8. 7 syllables. The musical phrases of the first two lines are repeated in the third and fourth; in the second half the melody becomes a little more varied, but the last line returns to the tune of the first:

[1] See pp. 255–6.
[2] See Moser, op. cit.

Ex. 189

Babst's *Geystliche Lieder* (1545)

Nun freut euch lie-ben Christengmein: Und lasst uns frö-lich sprin-gen,
Dass wir ge-trost und all in ein Mit Lust und Lie-be sin - gen

Was Gott an uns ge - wen - det hat   Und sei - ne

süs - se Wun-der-tat   gar teur hat er's er - wor - ben.

(Dear Christians, let us now rejoice. . . .)

The tune of the chorale 'Mit Fried und Freud ich fahr dahin' (based on St. Luke 2, 29–32) is quite different in character. Here again, the feeling of joy and gratitude is expressed, no longer with the idea of new activity, but in a mood of gentle tranquillity. The stanza is a little shorter, six lines of 8. 4. 8. 4. 7. 7. There is no repetition of melodic phrases, the tune goes solemnly on from beginning to end. Here is the first verse (according to Babst's *Geystliche Lieder* of 1545):

Ex. 190

Mit Fried und Freud ich fahr da-hin   In   Gotts Wil - le,

Ge-trost ist mir mein Herz   und Sinn,   Sanft und stil - le.

Was Gott mir   ver-heis-sen hat Der Tod ist mir Schlaf wor - den.

(In peace and joy I now depart. . . .)

It is known that Luther composed a tune for the hymn which paraphrases the Lord's Prayer, 'Vater unser im Himmelreich',[1] and that he subsequently rejected it. But it is not impossible that the hymn, which is in use right up to the present day, is also by him. Finally, he can with certainty be considered the composer of the tune of his most famous hymn: 'Ein feste Burg ist unser Gott'. Something

[1] Published by Karl von Winterfeld, *Der evangelische Kirchengesang*, three vols. (Leipzig, 1843–7).

will be said later about the composition with which he replaced the
Sanctus: 'Jesaia dem propheten das geschah.'

Very soon, too, the reformers began to 'parody' secular texts,
giving them a religious character, while retaining the melodies. So
far as Luther himself is concerned, we have an example in the
charming Christmas hymn 'Vom Himmel kam der Engel Schar'.

Transference of melodies was already fairly frequent at that time.
Take, for example, the very simple melody by an unknown composer
to which Paul Speratus wrote the hymn 'Es ist das Heil uns kommen
her'. It was immediately borrowed by Luther for four different
texts, though these soon acquired tunes of their own. It would also
happen that a text would be set to music in different ways, according to
the part of Germany into which it was introduced, and two musical
versions have sometimes continued to exist right up to the present
day. Luther's fine hymn 'Aus tiefer Not schrei ich zu dir' may serve
as an example. It reflects the words of contrition and hope of Psalm
130. The text is very expressive and impregnated with deeply religious feeling, yet, at the same time, simple and easily understood.
Luther himself seems to have been content with his work, for, in 1524,
writing to Spalatin and asking him for help, and, if possible, to
paraphrase a psalm, he sent him as model this very hymn 'Aus
tiefer Not'. He recommends, moreover, that Spalatin should take
great care to avoid all the new expressions then in fashion and used
in the courts of princes (*neumodische und höfische Ausdrücke*), and that
the words should be simple and popular. The melody admirably
reflects the mood, particularly of the first two verses. It is in the
Phrygian mode, which suits it perfectly. The composer is unknown.
The opinion has been expressed that Luther himself wrote it, borrowing in part from a motet by Josquin des Prez, the first notes of which
are identical with those of the hymn. But the reasons are not conclusive. It will be remembered that in the religious and secular compositions of this period and the preceding one, there are a number
of melodic motives which often recur, each time with different words.
To quote but one example: the five notes which open a fifteenth-
century French song 'Au bois, au bois, Madame', are exactly the
same as those at the beginning of Luther's tune. Now, the year after
the Wittenberg collection appeared and became known in Northern
Germany, the same words were set at Strasbourg to an entirely
different Ionian melody which became very popular in the South. Here,
for comparison, is the first half of each. First, the Wittenberg
melody:

Ex. 191

Aus tief- er Not schrei ich zu dir, Herr Gott, er-hör mein Ru - fen...
(Out of the depths have I cried unto thee, O Lord)

and here is the one which appeared in the *Teutsch Kirchenamt* at
Strasbourg in 1525:

Ex. 192

Aus tief- er Not schrei ich zu dir, Herr Gott, er-hör mein Ru-fen:..

In both melodies, the same notes are repeated for the third and fourth
lines.

LUTHER AND THE MASS

The example set by Luther was soon followed, and bore fruit. But
his musical activities were not limited to the music intended specifically for the congregation. They also extended to other aspects of the
service. The reforms he wished for could not be effected hastily, but
in the meantime certain too impetuous, and at times too drastic,
reformers—Karlstadt at Wittenberg, Thomas Müntzer at Zwickau,
and others—did simplify the service and make various changes. They
introduced hymns in German but kept the original music written for
the Latin words, often with very unfortunate effect. Luther noticed
this at once. In a work published in 1524, *Wider die himmlischen
Propheten*, he declared:

I would very much like now to have a Mass in German, and I am setting
about it. But I want it to have a truly German character. I have allowed the
Latin text to be translated and the Latin melodies preserved, but it sounds
neither agreeable nor right. Both text and music, accentuation, melody and
gait, must come from true mother tongue and voice. Else it is all an
imitation, such as monkeys do.

During 1525 he obtained permission from the Prince Elector to
summon to Wittenberg Conrad Rupsch (or Rupf), the *Kapellmeister*,
and Johann Walther, in order to discuss melodies with them, and the
choice of ecclesiastical modes. For three weeks they worked together,
'Luther trying always to arrange the notes as the rhythm of the
words demanded', said Walther in an account which he made of
these meetings (reproduced by Praetorius in his *Syntagma*). In the
work which appeared in 1526 under the title of *Deudsche Messe und*

Ordnung Gottisdiensts precise instructions, with examples, are given for the different hymns.[1] Thus, for the beginning of the service: 'First of all, we sing an ecclesiastical hymn or psalm in German, in the first mode.' But it will be seen that he still adapts the ancient psalmody. Here, for example, is Psalm 34, of which only the beginning need be given, although it is set to music throughout in the *Deudsche Messe*:

Ex. 193

(I will bless the Lord at all times)

These two phrases are repeated without alteration, save for a few inflexions. Then comes the *Kyrie eleison* sung, not nine times, but only three. For the Epistle, Luther recommends the eighth mode, giving rules and examples, as he does later for the Gospel, for the beginning and ending of the component parts (introitus, comma, colon, full-stop, question, final). He wishes that after the Epistle a hymn should be sung in German, for example: 'Nun bitten wir den heiligen Geist', or another, with the whole choir. He also wishes that in those churches which possess a real choir, the latter should some-times sing with the congregation. He then passes on to the Gospel, which is, he says, *in quinto tono*. This does not quite correspond to what Walther says in his account, already quoted above. According to the latter, Luther said: 'Christ is a kind master and his words are pleasant to hear, therefore let us choose the sixth mode for the Gospel'. But, as Johannes Wolf has remarked, Luther probably had in mind the somewhat dramatic form of the Passion texts, in which the words of the Evangelist, of Christ, and of the other personages have each a different tone: the words of Christ being in the sixth mode, while those of the Evangelist and the others are in the fifth. Here is a short example from the scene of the Last Supper:

Ex. 194

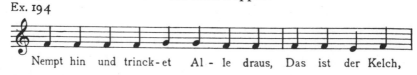

---

[1] *Werke* (Weimar edition), xix; see the edition with music by G. and H. Kawerau (Leipzig, 1926) and Johannes Wolf's facsimile edition (Kassel, 1934).

eyn neu tes - ta - ment in mein - em blut...

(Take and drink of it; this is the cup, a new testament in my blood. . . .)

Later on, the music accompanying these words was to be given much greater expressive force. While the sacrament was being given to communicants, the German *Sanctus* was to be sung. For the latter, both text (based on Isaiah 6, 1–4) and music were composed by Luther. It is in the fifth mode, and it will be noticed how well the words and the melody are suited to each other. It will suffice to quote the beginning:

Ex. 195

Je - sa - ia dem Propheten das geschah, dass er im Geist den Herren sitzen sah

auf eyn-em ho-hen Thron ynn hel-lem Glantz

(It befell the prophet Isaiah that he saw in spirit the Lord sitting upon a high throne. . . .)

Further on, the angels sing three times in succession:

Ex. 196

Hei - lig ist Gott der Her-re Ze - ba - oth

(Holy is God, the Lord of Sabaoth)

Instead of the *Agnus Dei*, the congregation could sing the canticle: 'Christe, du Lamm Gottes'.

Elsewhere, there were some rather remarkable differences. Strasbourg in particular distinguished itself by important modifications in the liturgy. The Preface and *Sanctus* were omitted; after the Lord's Prayer there was sung an arrangement in verse of the same prayer, by Symphorianus Pollio, a rather curious character among the Strasbourg reformers. This hymn begins:[1]

Ex. 197

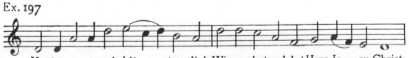

Va - ter un-ser, wir bit - ten dich, Wie uns hat gelehrt Herr Je - su Christ

(Our father, we pray to thee as the Lord Jesus Christ has taught us)

[1] *Gesang und Psalmen, so man singt unter des Herrn Nachtmahl und sonst* (Strasbourg, 1526). (There is a copy in the Zürich Library.)

Compositions on psalms also played an increasingly important part at Strasbourg. Luther did not wish to impose his plan on all the communities which supported him. He left the towns and villages, and the religious institutions of the different states, in complete freedom to organize the liturgy according to the means at their disposal. In the north, as in south and south-west Germany, the services were arranged in different ways.

CONGREGATIONAL PERFORMANCE OF HYMNS

One great difficulty was at once apparent. How would the congregations learn the melodies of the hymns they were to sing? In the polyphonic settings of hymns, like those of Walther's collection of 1524, the melody is given to the tenor, and from these compositions it is often simply transcribed into the collections for single voice.[1] But in the polyphonic hymns the melody, the *canto fermo*, was often subjected to slight alterations, making its rhythm somewhat irregular. Had the people, then, to learn the melodies in the forms in which they appeared in these collections? That can have been hardly feasible. They would obviously sing generally in even note-values adapted to the accentuation of the words. The cantor, or the whole choir in unison, gave the tune to the congregation. Moreover, the tunes were taught in the schools, and the scholars sang in church—as did the members of burial societies and similar organizations.

ARRANGEMENTS

The congregation naturally took no part in the singing of polyphonic arrangements of a hymn tune. The organ did not at this period accompany congregational singing, though it may have played alternate verses of hymns in polyphonic settings in accordance with the Roman practice.[2] But Luther was not in favour of organ-playing during the service; he seldom mentions it in any of his writings. The new organization of the service for the canons of the castle church at Wittenberg, drawn up by Bugenhagen and Justus Jonas in accordance with Luther's advice, prescribes: '*Organa ad missam non debent adhiberi*'. The courts of the princes generally had well-organized chapels and well-trained choirs (*Hofkantoreien*). That at Munich was directed by Senfl; at Stuttgart, at the time of Duke Ulrich, the choir numbered thirty; the chapel of the Prince-Elector Frederick the Wise, at Torgau, under the direction of Johann Walther, was slightly

[1] On this point see particularly Friedrich Blume, *Die evangelische Kirchenmusik* (Potsdam, 1931), pp. 38–39.
[2] See Blume, op. cit., pp. 57–58.

smaller. This last was unfortunately dissolved in 1527 by Frederick's successor, who wanted to economize. Luther protested in vain. But then some citizens of Torgau, musical amateurs, met together and declared that they were prepared to study and sing without remuneration under Walther's direction, and thus the first free choral society was founded. This example was soon followed elsewhere.

THE HYMN-COLLECTIONS

During the first twenty years after 1524, the number of hymn-collections increased considerably, and in different parts of the country various poets and musicians made effective contributions towards the development of the Protestant hymn. At Wittenberg in 1526 appeared the *Enchiridion* of Hans Lufft, which was the first congregational hymn-book. Walther's above-mentioned collection, for choir, had already gone into a new edition in 1525, which was followed by three others, enlarged, in 1537, 1544, and 1551.[1] In 1525 also appeared the Breslau and Zwickau *Gesangbücher*, and the Strasbourg *Teutsch Kirchenamt*. In this last city, the following year, Wolf Köpphel published his *Psalmen, Gebet und Kirchenübung*. In 1530 and 1537 new collections came out at Strasbourg, and in 1538 an entire Psalter, a very important publication by Köpphel.

In Wittenberg in 1529 Josef Klug published a hymn-book under the direction of Luther himself. It is particularly interesting, since it contained, for the first time, the melody of 'Ein feste Burg'. Unfortunately no copy of this work has survived, though it was reprinted with little alteration by Andreas Rauscher of Erfurt as *Geistliche lieder, auffs new gebessert* (1533).[2] Finally, attention must be drawn to the collection of Valentin Babst (Leipzig, 1545),[3] the last to appear under the direction of Luther.

In 1541 there was published at Strasbourg, with a preface by Martin Bucer, a hymn-book printed with special care.[4] Some of the Strasbourg melodies had become known in several districts of Germany and Switzerland. Two composers who must be specially mentioned are Mathis Greiter and Wolfgang Dachstein. The former, precentor of the cathedral, was famous from the beginning of the Reformation for his liturgical compositions; some of his psalms were

[1] The 1551 edition has been reprinted in *Johann Walther: Sämtliche Werke*, i and ii (Kassel and Basle, 1953); pieces omitted from the last edition are printed in iii (1955).
[2] Facsimile edition by Ameln (Kassel and Basle, 1955).
[3] *Geystliche Lieder. Mit einer newen vorrhede D. Mart. Luth.* Facsimile edition by Ameln (Kassel, 1929).
[4] *Gesangbuch, darinn begriffen sind die aller fürnemisten und besten Psalmen, Geistliche Lieder und Chorgeseng.* Facsimile edition by Ameln (Stuttgart, 1953).

highly esteemed by well-known musicians; for example, the melody for Psalm 51, 'O Herre Gott, begnade mich' (see Exs. 199 and 200 on p. 439) was set for four voices by Senfl. The expressive melody which Greiter wrote for Psalm 13 was also used for others:

Ex. 198

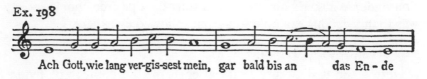

Ach Gott, wie lang ver-gis-sest mein, gar bald bis an   das En - de

(How long wilt thou forget me, O Lord, for ever?)

The most famous of these melodies was that written for the opening of Psalm 119: 'Es sind doch selig alle die . . .'.[1] During the second quarter of the sixteenth century, it was really popular in Strasbourg; the collections from 1538 to 1541 contain something like forty hymns fitted to it. Right into the middle of the seventeenth century, poets were writing lines to this tune. Calvin chose it for Psalm 36 and Théodore de Bèze adapted to it the words of Psalm 68 (see Ex. 201 on p. 440). With Sebald Heyden's words, 'O Mensch, bewein dein Sünde gross', it inspired two beautiful compositions by J. S. Bach, a chorale prelude in the *Orgelbüchlein* and the chorus which ends the first part of the Matthew Passion.

'NEWE DEUDSCHE GEISTLICHE GESENGE'

The collections just mentioned give only a single melodic line. Those with polyphonic settings are much less numerous. One of the best of these is Johann Kugelmann's *Concentus novi trium vocum* (Augsburg, 1540), consisting mainly of three-part hymn-arrangements, many of them by the compiler himself. Kugelmann addressed these compositions to 'the common schools which have only a few pupils', offering them music which could be performed 'by untrained singers'. With the same purpose, Georg Rhaw published in 1544 at Wittenberg his *Newe deudsche geistliche Gesenge für die gemeinen Schulen*.[2] He also wished to develop in young people an understanding of church music and ability to perform it, and thus to help to give church music an increasingly artistic character. The publisher Rhaw was himself a trained musician, who had been cantor of St.

---

[1] On the melodies and words of the first Strasbourg collections, see Gerold, *Les plus anciennes mélodies de l'Église Protestante de Strasbourg* (Paris, 1928).

[2] New edition by Johannes Wolf in *Denkmäler deutscher Tonkunst*, xxxiv (1908). Separate numbers by Stoltzer, Senfl, and Arnold von Bruck are given in Davison and Apel, op. cit., pp. 112, 114, and 115, by Senfl, Mahu, and Bruck in Schering, op. cit., pp. 78, 107, and 108.

Thomas's School, Leipzig, before he founded in 1525 his famous musical printing-press at Wittenberg. In the *Newe deudsche geistliche Gesenge* he gives a valuable selection from the work of a number of musicians who were interested in the Protestant hymn (though five of the most prominent were probably or certainly Catholics). The names of seventeen composers are given: there are twelve anonymous pieces, but it may be assumed that the majority are by Rhaw himself.[1] His choice of works by earlier or contemporary masters enables us to form an idea of the kind of piece that found favour in churches with well-trained choirs.

One of the earliest of the masters represented in this collection is Stoltzer.[2] Two years previously, Rhaw had already published several of Stoltzer's compositions, in his *Liber I Sacrorum Hymnorum*.[3] Five pieces are included in the collection of 1544.

The most famous of the composers in this volume is Senfl. Rhaw's collection contains eleven of his compositions, of varying length and structure. But not one is based on a really Protestant hymn. Despite his correspondence with Luther, his religious vocal works in both this and in other volumes are connected only with tunes of the pre-Reformation period, and we must not assume, as some have done, that he had a real leaning towards Protestant ideas.[4] Rhaw was obviously willing to include in his collection the compositions of a very well-known master, and Senfl was not afraid to see them in a Protestant publication. Some of his pieces are in the old polyphonic style, but new tendencies are manifest in the setting of 'Gelobet seist du, Christe' for five voices. The melody is treated as *canto fermo* in the tenor, while the two lower voices surround it with imitative passages and the upper voices take a freer course. Here already is a foretaste of the *Choralmotette*, of which there is another hint in 'O Herre Gott, begnade mich', where both melody (given to the soprano) and text were borrowed, as already pointed out, from Mathis Greiter of Strasbourg. His most important composition in the volume is 'Da Jakob nun das Kleid ansah',[5] a cry of despair from Jacob when he was shown the blood-stained garments of Joseph, supposed to have been devoured by wild beasts. There are highly expressive and descriptive passages, contrasts of two- with four-part texture and chordal passages with imitative polyphony, and underlinings of

[1] See Werner Gosslau, *Die religiöse Haltung in der Reformationsmusik* (Kassel, 1933).
[2] See p. 265.
[3] Reprinted complete in *Das Erbe deutscher Musik*, xxi and xxv.
[4] See p. 254.
[5] Given in Davison and Apel, op. cit., p. 114.

certain words. Jacob's outburst, 'O weh der großen Not', is expressed almost entirely in chords and low tessitura, in striking contrast with the preceding passage.

Balthazar Resinarius (Harzer) (see pp. 260 and 262) wrote in more traditional style. He was pastor at Leipa in Bohemia, and was on friendly terms with the reformers at Wittenberg. In the preface to a later edition, Rhaw gives some information about the life of this musician-priest. 'As a young boy,' he says, 'he studied music at the court of the Emperor Maximilian, where he had for his master Heinrich Isaac, the most celebrated and learned in the art of music, whose name and magnificent works are known to all musicians. Resinarius skilfully imitated his master's gravity and simplicity; in Austria his harmonies are particularly admired.' The previous year, Rhaw had already published eighty responses arranged by this composer,[1] and devoted in particular to the Evensong of the Protestant churches. In the volume of 1544 his compositions number twenty-six, of different types. Nearly half of them are very short, of from 16 to 25 bars, but their structure is fairly varied. In some, such as 'Christ lag in Todesbanden', the melody is given to the tenor, and the soprano imitates it freely, while alto and bass are quite independent. One setting of Luther's hymn 'Erhalt uns, Herr, bei deinemWort' is written for three voices only, two sopranos and alto; the *canto fermo* is given to the second soprano and the other two voices move in fairly lively counterpoint. It is noteworthy that the text of all three verses is given in its entirety, which is rather rare, and shows how this hymn was sung in the church service. The same text is set a second time in quite a different manner. The melody is given to the tenor in the first verse. But, in the second, separate motives of the melody pass from voice to voice, the soprano consisting mainly of long notes. There is no longer any real *canto fermo* in the third verse; it is distinguished, moreover, by attempts at descriptive music. The word 'Tröster' is vocalised on a somewhat convoluted series of notes, while for the words 'Gib deinem Volk einerlei Sinn' the four voices join in weighty chords in order to stress the value of spiritual unity. After this verse comes one borrowed from another of Luther's hymns, 'Verleih uns Frieden gnädiglich'. But this added verse does not quite correspond in form to the preceding ones. Did the composer allow himself to be guided by free fancy?

Rhaw collected ten melodies by Benedictus Ducis,[2] who died the

---

[1] Modern edition in two volumes by Inge-Maria Schröder in the series *Georg Rhau: Musikdrucke aus den Jahren 1538 bis 1545* (Kassel and Basle, 1955 and 1957).

[2] See pp. 261-2.

very year of this publication. Ducis had led quite an eventful life. In his youth he had been organist at Antwerp and then in London (1516–18); later he spent several years in Vienna, where he associated with the humanists Grynäus, Vadian, and others. Having been converted to Protestantism, he had to leave Austria and finally, in 1535, obtained a position as pastor in a village near Ulm in Bavaria. His works are distinctive in style. In two of them he uses melodies of the Strasbourg church, 'Aus tiefer Not' and 'An Wasserflüßen Babylon' (by Wolfgang Dachstein), the former set in note-against-note counterpoint, the other in more ornate polyphony. As for Luther's hymn 'Nun freut euch, lieben Christen gmein', he treats it in a then unique way. Each phrase of the melody is first sung by the tenor alone, then all four voices repeat the line chordally but with only a suggestion of the original melody. This responsorial method of setting a hymn became very frequent later, but there is no other example in Rhaw's collection.

Seventeen compositions by Arnold von Bruck (see p. 264) were included by Rhaw. This composer's birthplace is not definitely known; some believe he came from Bruck on the Leitha, others take his name to be a corruption of 'Bruges'. Some of his compositions in Rhaw's collection are the prototypes of what came to be called the *Choralmotette*, the hymn-motet. The majority are set to texts by Luther. In some of these ('Vater unser im Himmelreich' and 'Aus tiefer Not') the melody is given first to the tenor, then passes to the soprano, or vice versa. Some are more elaborate. Thus 'Christ ist erstanden' is in three sections, the first of which corresponds to the first verse, with the melody (somewhat amplified by melisma) in the tenor; the second has the *canto fermo* in the soprano; while in the third, which is for five voices, the melody alternates between the second and third sopranos. Some of Arnold's pieces had already been printed in Ott's *Newe Lieder* (Nuremberg, 1534), notably a motet on the Pentecostal hymn 'Komm, heiliger Geist',[1] in which pairs of voices sing each line of the melody in canon.

The Netherlander Lupus Hellinck is another of those concerning whom we do not know to what extent they supported the new doctrine. His settings of hymns by Luther and other reformers appeared only after his death (1541). However, Rhaw gives eleven of them, several of which are quite long, with the melody well developed. In 'Mensch, willtu leben seliglich?', to Luther's words, Hellinck writes long vocalisations on 'seliglich', 'ewiglich', and 'kyrieleison'.

[1] Given in Schering, op. cit., p. 108.

Sixtus Dietrich (see p. 261) twice, in 1540 and in 1545, spent some time at Wittenberg. Schöffer of Mainz published his Magnificats in 1535, but his later works—antiphons and hymns—were published by Rhaw. Among the pieces Rhaw included in his collection of 1544, the most interesting is the setting of Luther's 'Vater unser im Himmelreich'. It is in six sections, one for three voices, the rest for five. In each section the voices, except the bass, sing the whole verse, with the melody in the tenor as *canto fermo*, while the bass repeats one line of the first verse of the text: the first line throughout the first section, the second line throughout the second, and so on.

Of the less important masters, Martin Agricola (1486–1556), cantor of the Latin school at Magdeburg from about 1525, must be mentioned as the author of theoretical and didactic works rather than as a composer. His *Musica instrumentalis deudsch* was published in 1529 and several times later, in 1545 in a revised and corrected edition.[1] In 1528 appeared a *Musica choralis* and in 1532 a *Musica figuralis deudsch*. For these works he composed a great number of examples, and in addition he wrote motets and hymns. Rhaw, in his 1544 collection, gives only three of Agricola's hymn-tune settings. The most developed is that on 'Mit Fried und Freud ich fahr dahin', in which there is a descriptive passage on 'sanft und stille' and, at the end, a long vocalization. Of the works of Stephan Mahu may be mentioned his five-part composition on 'Ein feste Burg',[2] with the *canto fermo* in the second alto, and the two on 'Christ ist erstanden', of which the second, for five voices, is the better.

RHAW AS COMPOSER

There is no point in mentioning all the other composers, but a few words must be said about the compositions supposedly by the publisher himself. As already mentioned, Rhaw (1488–1548), before becoming a publisher, had been *Assessor* at the University of Leipzig (1518) and cantor of St. Thomas's. The following year, at the opening of the disputation between Luther and Eck, he had performed a twelve-part Mass of his own composition which was much admired: 'Missa de Spiritu sancto.' Shortly afterwards he accepted Luther's doctrines, gave up his positions at Leipzig and, after several rather difficult years, went to Wittenberg in 1523, where, soon after his arrival, he founded the most important of the Protestant musical printing presses. The anonymous pieces in his collection of 1544 are

[1] Reprint by Eitner, *Publikationen der Gesellschaft für Musikforschung*, Jg. 24 (Leipzig, 1896).
[2] Schering, op. cit., p. 107.

obviously his own. The objection has been raised that he was in very ill health at the time, but he might well have written them earlier. It has been suggested that Walther helped him; but, in that case, why is he not mentioned? Some of these pieces are short and simple Christmas songs: Luther's 'Gelobet sei'st du, Jesus Christ', the old song 'Dies est laetitiae', the macaronic 'In dulci jubilo, nu singet und seid froh', and others. Rhaw may have felt that songs of this type should not be omitted, and introduced them himself. Others are more developed, such as the paraphrase on 'Vater unser im Himmelreich' and the already-mentioned canticle which Luther substituted for the *Sanctus*: 'Jesaia dem propheten das geschah'.

RHAW'S OTHER PUBLICATIONS

This 1544 collection of Rhaw's is highly important since it shows clearly the various ways in which the Protestant hymn was musically treated by the masters of the second quarter of the sixteenth century. But Rhaw's numerous other publications are equally interesting, above all because they throw light on the—up to a point—interconfessional nature of the religious music of the period. In 1538 Rhaw published compositions for Passion Week (*Selectae Harmoniae*), with a preface by Melanchthon, and fifty-two motets for all the Sundays of the year, with a preface by Luther (*Symphoniae jucundae*)[1]. These two prefaces, written in very elegant Latin, insist that music is of divine origin, a gift of God, and that it is one of the most effective means of making the word of God known among men. They also contain practical instructions on church music and how to execute it. The following year Rhaw issued compositions for the principal festivals of the Church: *Officia Paschalia, de Resurrectione et Ascensione Domini* and *Officia de Nativitate*, &c. These contain not only 'Offices', in the strict modern sense, but Masses; though in the Mass the Gradual, Creed, and Offertory are discarded and passages in German inserted. Besides several Masses there are also motets, and a psalm for Easter by Senfl. In the *Opus decem Missarum* (1541) Catholic composers are found side by side with Protestants. (Six of the Masses are composed on tenors from secular songs.) But Rhaw's dedication to the town of Torgau, *Der besonderen Pflegerin der Musik in den Schulen und der Heimat der besten Musiker*, puts its Protestant purpose beyond doubt. In 1540 he began a new series of the *Vespertini officii opus* with *Vesperarum precum officia*.[2] The psalms

[1] Ed. Hans Albrecht, *Georg Rhau: Musikdrucke*, iii (1959).
[2] Ed. by Moser, ibid., iv (Kassel and Basle, 1960).

are in so-called fauxbourdon style, the hymns, antiphons, and Magnificats in very simple counterpoint. But the contributors include some of the best composers: Isaac, Stoltzer, Walther, Ducis, and others. In 1541 came the 36 antiphons of Sixtus Dietrich, and in 1542 the already mentioned collection of 134 hymns (*Hymnorum sacrorum lib. I*) to which Stoltzer, Finck, Arnold von Bruck, Isaac, Josquin, Walther, Senfl, Resinarius, and others were laid under contribution. The fourth part of the Vesper series consists of the already mentioned Responses by Resinarius (1544), and the last of a number of Magnificats (also 1544). Whereas in all Rhaw's earlier collections, first place was always occupied by the Germans, this time the authors are almost exclusively foreign: Adam Rener of Liège, the Spaniard Morales, Netherlanders of an earlier period such as Pierre de la Rue, Divitis, and Pipelare, the Frenchmen Févin, Richafort, and Verdelot. There is only a single German, Galliculus of Leipzig.

Rhaw died in 1548 and it was left to his successors to print the later, and historically less important, works of the now elderly Johann Walther, such as *Das christlich Kinderlied* (1566).

USE OF THE ORGAN

It is clear that there was a waning of interest in unison congregational singing during the second half of the century. Congregations seem to have grown tired of hymns, and to have lost their old zest for learning new tunes. They preferred listening to the choir. Ecclesiastical ordinances of this time always contain exhortations for animated singing or complaints of lack of enthusiasm among the faithful. The question of how hymns were sung has often been discussed. As already pointed out, we now know that the congregation sang in unison without organ accompaniment, but led by the choirmaster or the choristers. In certain church ordinances it is expressly mentioned that choristers must be placed among the congregation to help them. But the congregation were not usually left to sing an entire hymn; alternate verses were sung by the choir or played by the organist, an old practice long retained by the Lutheran Church. The choir, too, sang practically always without accompaniment and alternating with the playing of the organ. On this subject we have a valuable first-hand account by the Lorraine reformer Wolfgang Musculus of the religious services at which he was present at Eisenach and Wittenberg in 1536. Musculus says: 'Primum ludebatur Introitus in organis succinente choro latine' ('first the choir sang the Introit in Latin, accompanied by the organ'). Then: 'Post Introitum ludebatur in organis et vicissim canebatur a pueris kyrie eleison' ('in the *Kyrie*, the choir and the organ alternated'); similarly in the *Gloria*. After the Gospel the organ plays an interlude and then the choir sings a hymn in German: 'Postea ludebatur in organis et a choro subjungebatur "Wir glauben all an einen Gott"'. The alternation of singing with organ-playing was also effected in other ways. Thus, in the choral hymnbook of Bartholomaeus Gesius (*Geistliche Lieder*: Frankfurt-on-Oder, 1601) we read that it is very pleasant to listen to the alternating verses in *choro et organo* when a boy with à pure, sweet voice sings one verse with the organ and the *chorus musicus* then sings the next; thus, besides hearing all the voices together, everyone can hear distinctly the melody alone and the words, and can thus sing with the others.

Preludes and interludes were to a great extent improvised by the organist.[1] But he might also play the compositions of other musicians, even those of other countries. The only conditions were that they should not be too long, and that they should not savour too much of virtuosity. What the Strasbourg *Kirchenordnung* of 1598 has to say on this subject is of some interest. After a word of praise to figural music and to organ-playing, it continues:

But care must always be taken that this figural music and organ-playing do not interfere with the ordinary singing of the congregation, and do not cause too much delay to the service as a whole. Thus the following procedure should be observed: the organist must begin punctually. Then, during the congregational singing, he must not play pieces or motets which have nothing to do with the service, but only what the people will then sing. In order that the singing and organ-playing should not take up too much time, he should not, after giving the note, play more than once or twice between congregational singing, but when the service is ended and the benediction has been given, then he may play other pieces, or even have a motet sung in Latin.

DIVERGENT TENDENCIES

During the second half of the sixteenth century, there was a certain evolution in Lutheran music, particularly in north Germany. Side by side with the lessening of interest in congregational hymn-singing, composers gradually turned from the fairly simple polyphonic setting of hymn-tunes to the making of complicated arrangements. Moreover, the polyphonic works of Catholic musicians found their way more and more into the Protestant churches. On the other hand, in

---

[1] On organs and organists at the beginning of the sixteenth century, see the very detailed list in Moser, *Paul Hofhaimer* (Stuttgart, 1929), pp. 84 ff. See also Vol. III, pp. 432 ff.

G g

the south and south-west, there was a genuine preference for a very simple form of service and for easier forms of song, particularly psalm-tunes. Here the influence of Switzerland is apparent. In cantons which adhered to the Reformation religious practice became extremely simplified, liturgical music was abolished and organs were suppressed or destroyed. Ulrich Zwingli, though himself a good musician, was compelled to give way on this point. In the preface to Froschauer's *Neues Gesangbüchlein* (Zürich, 1540) written by the Constance Reformer Zwick, the latter says that the psalm-tunes must be developed in the first place, but that other types of song must not be neglected. He adds that no music other than congregational singing should be heard in church. In Strasbourg, too, the singing of psalms had acquired some importance and it was in this town that Calvin produced his first psalter. Calvin's ideas on church music were soon accepted not only in France but also in certain districts of Germany and in. other countries, and we must glance at the birth and development of the Calvinist psalter, and compare its musical value with that of the works of Luther's disciples.

CALVIN AND THE PSALMS

When Calvin, banished from Geneva, took refuge at Strasbourg in September, 1538, he was able to observe that singing was well organized in all the churches of the town. So, having accepted the direction of the little community of French-speaking refugees, he determined as soon as possible to introduce congregational singing. Moreover, he returned to the idea, expounded in the Project presented to the Council at Geneva on 16 January 1537, of congregational psalm-singing (see p. 440). This was in accord with ideas popular in Strasbourg. But where could he find psalms in French, in forms suitable for singing? In France, a young poet, Clément Marot, a protégé of Queen Marguerite of Navarre, had already versified a certain number of psalms and these had become known in various neighbouring countries. Some had evidently reached Strasbourg. Calvin himself set to work and versified a few psalms, so that in the spring of 1539 he was able to produce a little collection, printed by Knobloch, under the modest title *Aulcuns pseaulmes et cantiques mys en chant.*[1] Twelve of the texts were by Marot, five by Calvin. But where did the melodies come from?[2] Marot's psalms were accom-

---

[1] A facsimile reprint was published at Geneva in 1919, with a preface by D. Delétra. See also the English edition, *Calvin's First Psalter*, with critical notes, by R. R. Terry (London, 1932).
[2] The entire corpus of Calvinist psalm-melody from the Strasbourg, Geneva, and

panied by music, but for the others Calvin searched among the religious compositions of Strasbourg musicians. And it must be admitted that he showed much discernment in his choice. It will suffice to mention only a few. The melodies chosen are mostly by Greiter, the finest being that which he wrote for a versification of Psalm 51. The first half is as follows:

Ex. 199

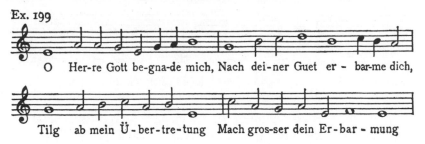

(Have mercy upon me, O God, according to thy loving kindness. . . .)

The next four lines repeat the melody, and the second part begins with a cry of despair:

Ex. 200

(And my sin is ever before me)

Calvin adapted it not to a Penitential Psalm, but to Psalm 91: 'Qui en la garde du Seigneur sa demeure et retraite aura'. The French verses are shorter than the German ones, but by not repeating the melody of the first four lines and by omitting a few notes in the penultimate line of the second half, Calvin skilfully fitted them. When his poetic version was later replaced by Marot's, Greiter's music was not retained. But another melody by the same composer, also chosen by Calvin, has remained in use until the present day; it has merely changed its text. It is the already-mentioned tune written for the first half of Psalm 119: 'Es sind doch selig alle die. . . .' Calvin chose it for Psalm 36, but later Théodore de Bèze adopted it for Psalm 68, 'Que Dieu se montre seulement. . .', to which it soon became well-known as a Huguenot hymn before battle. It will suffice to give the beginning of the melody with the German text, and then Calvin's adaptation with his own words and Bèze's:

Lausanne collections, with all the variants, is given in Pierre Pidoux, *Le Psautier Huguenot du XVIe siècle*, 2 vols. (Kassel and Basle, 1962).

Ex. 201

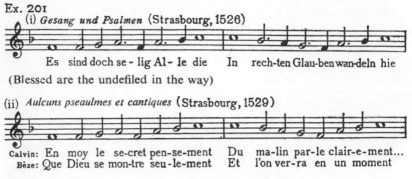

(i) *Gesang und Psalmen* (Strasbourg, 1526)

Es sind doch se - lig Al- le die   In   rech-tenGlau-ben wan-deln hie

(Blessed are the undefiled in the way)

(ii) *Aulcuns pseaulmes et cantiques* (Strasbourg, 1529)

Calvin: En moy le se-cret pen-se-ment   Du   ma-lin par-le clair-e-ment...
Bèze: Que Dieu se mon-tre seu-le-ment   Et   l'on ver-ra en un moment

(Psalm 36: The transgression of the wicked saith within my heart. . . .)
(Psalm 68: Let God arise, let his enemies be scattered)

For Psalm 46, the beginning of which had served as a basis for
Luther's magnificent 'Ein feste Burg', Calvin took the melody which
Wolfgang Dachstein, organist of St. Thomas's Church and Strasbourg Cathedral, had composed for Psalm 15: 'O Herr, wer wird
Wohnung han.' This tune has a tranquil and serious charm, in perfect accord with the words of Psalm 15, but it does not evoke what
Luther read into the first verses of Psalm 46: that absolute trust in
God which gives strength to resist all attacks of the enemy. Calvin
showed better judgement in another case. We have already seen that
for Psalm 130, 'Aus tiefer Not schrei ich zu dir', there was a Strasbourg melody (Ex. 192), the first half of which could hardly be called
austere. Now Calvin chose this tune, not for a song of penitence, but
for the praise to God of Psalm 113: 'Sus, louez Dieu, ses serviteurs.'

Meanwhile the Genevans were trying to persuade Calvin to return;
Farel besought him to resume his activity in Geneva, and, on 13
September 1541, return he did. He immediately resumed work on
the organization of religious music. Before his exile, he had stressed
the value of psalm-singing in the Project of Organisation of the
Church, addressed to the Council: 'Comme nous faisons les oraisons
des fidèles sont si froides que cela nous doit tourner à grande honte et
confusion, les pseaulmes nous pourront inciter à enlever nos cuers a
Dieu et nous esmouvoyr a enlever ung ardeur tant de l'invoquer
que de exalter par louanges la gloire de son nom.' And, like the
Lutherans, he advocated the employment of selected schoolboys to
teach the tunes to the congregations: 'La manière de procéder qui
nous a semblé bonne est, si quelques enfans, auxquels on avait
d'abord appris un chant modeste et ecclésiastique chantent à voix
haute et distincte, le peuple écoutant en toute attention et suivant de
cœur ce qui est chanté de bouche jusqu'à ce que petit à petit, chacun

s'accoutume à chanter ensemble.' Two months after his return to
Geneva, Calvin obtained permission from the Council to introduce
psalms into public worship. He thereupon had a new Psalter
printed by Girard.

At the beginning of 1542 there appeared a printed edition of the
thirty psalms which Marot had offered in manuscript to Francis I of
France some three years earlier. They were greeted with universal
enthusiasm, and the author was favourably received at Court. But
this favour was of short duration. He was once more obliged to leave
France and seek refuge at Geneva. Meanwhile he had made a fresh
translation of a number of psalms and in 1543 a new edition of the
first thirty psalms appeared, with twenty others, under the title of
Cinquante psaumes en français par Clément Marot. It is very probable
that Calvin would have liked Marot to go on to translate the whole
Psalter. He wished also to facilitate the poet's stay in Geneva, and
asked the Council to grant him a subsidy. The Council told him 'to
advise Marot to have patience for the time being'. This refusal
probably decided Marot to leave Geneva and try to re-enter France.
He spent the winter in Savoy; the following summer he crossed the
Alps, but died suddenly at Turin.

LOUIS BOURGEOIS

Meanwhile Calvin had discovered in Louis Bourgeois a good
musician, willing to help him in his task, and the latter published
in 1547 *Pseaumes cinquante de David roy et profète, traduictz en
vers françois par Clément Marot et mis en musique par Loys Bourgeoys à quatre parties à voix de contrepoinct égal consonante au
verbe*. This volume, printed at Lyons by Godefroy and Marcelin
Beringen,[1] was intended to be used for congregational singing during
the service. The melody—often adapted from a popular source—
is given to the tenor, the other voices providing note-against-note
counterpoint. But besides this collection, Bourgeois published another
through the same printers and in the same year. This is shorter,
containing only twenty-four psalms, but more varied. The composer
evidently now had in mind those little meetings often held in the
castles of the nobility or the houses of rich bourgeois; besides being
composed in a different manner, the book is also arranged so that

---

[1] Both collections of psalms by Bourgeois are in the library at Munich. A selection of
thirty-seven Psalms from the *Pseaulmes cinquante* has been published by K. P. Bernet
Kempers (Delft, 1937). Bourgeois's setting of Psalm 1 is given in Davison and Apel,
op. cit., p. 144. The *Premier livre des Pseaulmes* has been edited by P. André Gaillard,
Schweizerische Musikdenkmäler, iii (Basle, 1961).

some of the pieces can be played on instruments, as the title indicates:
*Le premier livre des Pseaulmes de David, contenant XXIV Pseaulmes,
composé par Loys Bourgeois en diversité de musique: à scavoir
familière, ou vaudeville: aultres plus musicales: & aultres à voix
pareilles, bien convenable aux instrumentz.* The compositions pronounced *plus musicales* are those in figural counterpoint, the *familières*,
those in *chanson* style. The words, but not the melodies, are taken
from the previous Psalter. This was hardly the type of composition
to win the approval of Calvin. For, if he said that 'all the arts proceed from God, even those which serve only pleasure and delight,
like the harp and other instruments, which must not be considered
superfluous, let alone be condemned',[1] he declared elsewhere that
'care must always be taken lest the ear be more attentive to the
harmony of the song, than is the mind to the spiritual meaning of
the words'. He opposed all songs 'which are composed solely for
the pleasure of the ear, like all the popish frills and frippery, and
all that they call broken music and *chose faite* [*res facta*] and four-
part songs'.[2]

Before Bourgeois, another French Protestant, Guillaume Franc,
had taken refuge in Geneva. He was appointed cantor by the Council,
who specially ordered him to instruct the children in the singing of
psalms. But, finding his salary insufficient, he left Geneva and settled
in Lausanne, where he again occupied the post of cantor, in 1545.
While there, he also occupied himself with the collection and harmonization of melodies for a Psalter, *Les Pseaumes mis en rime
françoise . . . auec le chant de l'eglise de Lausane* (1565), which was for
some time the rival of the Geneva Psalter. But it does not seem that
Calvin was ever very interested in Franc.

After Marot's departure, Calvin tried to find someone who could
continue the versification of the Psalter. Having learned that Théodore de Bèze, who had been appointed Professor at the Lausanne
Academy, had a real poetic talent, he eagerly engaged him to undertake the translation. Bèze accepted, but was in no hurry. At last,
in 1551, he sent thirty-four psalms which Marot had not versified,
and these were immediately set to music by Bourgeois. Three years
later Bourgeois added five more psalms by Bèze, but in 1557 he left
Geneva to return to France and so ended his collaboration. As Bèze
did not finish his Psalter till 1562, all the remaining psalms had to be
adapted to existing melodies, many of them to other psalm-tunes.

[1] 'Commentarius in Genesim., ch. iv, v. 20', *Opera Calvini*, xxiii.
[2] Calvin, *Institution Chrétienne*, iii, ch. 20, pp. 31–32.

THE PSALM-COMPOSITIONS OF GOUDIMEL AND OTHERS

The name most often mentioned in connexion with the music of the French Psalter is that of Claude Goudimel. It is true that inaccurate claims are sometimes made for him; he never composed psalm-tunes himself. But he made four-part settings of those by Bourgeois and Franc already in use, and these compositions give evidence of exceptional talent. Nor was he, as was once believed, one of the founders of the Roman School of the mid-sixteenth century. Born about 1505 at Besançon, he studied music seriously and his lively mind applied itself to very varied types of music. He published a large number of four-part *chansons* in the collections printed by Nicolas du Chemin at Paris, from 1549 to 1554, and composed two Magnificats, motets, and five Masses. The efforts of the humanists and of the Pléiade to reawaken interest in the poetry and music of antiquity[1] inspired him to set to music the odes of Horace (1555). Then the growing popularity of the Huguenot Psalter incited him to experiment with Marot's psalms. He began by composing eight *en forme de mottetz*, which appeared in 1551 at Paris, published by du Chemin,[2] and in 1557, eight others for 4 or 5 parts, which were published by Le Roy and Ballard.[3] About 1560 he became a Protestant, and when the translation of the Psalter into French verse was completed he made a four-part setting of the whole work. In 1564 there appeared *Les CL. pseaumes de David nouvellement mis en musique a quatre parties* (Paris, Le Roy and Ballard),[4] composed in syllabic counterpoint with the melody generally given to the *superius*. The following year another complete setting—simpler and with the melody usually given to the tenor—appeared at Geneva, published 'by the successors of François Jaqui'.[5] A slightly simpler edition of the 1564 version was printed at Geneva in 1580, after the composer's death (1572) in the St. Bartholomew Massacre at Lyons.[6] Goudimel's settings were intended for domestic use. Some are very simple, note against note, the melody given to the tenor or the highest voice; in

---

[1] See pp. 29 ff.

[2] *Premier livre contenant huyt Pseaulmes de David* (Paris, 1551). Paris, Bibl. Nat. Rés. Vm. 1, 211.

[3] *Tiers livre*, ibid. Rés. Vm. 1, 122.

[4] *Les Cent Cinquante Pseaumes de David* (Paris, 1564). Paris, Bibl. du Conservatoire. Rés.

[5] *Les Pseaumes mis en rime francoise* . . . (Geneva, 1565). Paris, Bibl. du Conservatoire. Facsimile edition by Pidoux and Ameln (Kassel, 1935).

[6] The 1580 edition was reprinted by Henry Expert, *Les Maîtres musiciens de la Renaissance française*, ii, iv, and vi (Paris, 1895–7). On Bourgeois, Goudimel, &c. see Orentin Douen, *Clément Marot et le Psautier Huguenot*, 2 vols. (Paris, 1878–9).

others, note-against-note counterpoint is used only in the first few
bars, after which each of the other three voices develops on its own,
but always quite simply. The two methods may be compared in these
openings of Psalm 25 in the versions of 1565 and 1580:

Ex. 202

(Unto thee, O Lord, do I lift up my soul)

Besides Goudimel, several musicians of lesser importance also set
a certain number of the Marot–de Bèze psalms. In Belgium there was
Jean Louys, who was perhaps *Kapellmeister* of the Emperors Ferdinand I and Maximilian II. He published *Pseaulmes cinquante de*

David, composez musicalement ensuyvant le chant vulgaire par maistre Jean Louys (Antwerp, 1555). He was certainly a Catholic, but Marot's psalms had spread rapidly into several countries. Nor did the famous *chanson*-composer, Clément Janequin, who, toward the end of his life, in 1559, published *Octante deux pseaumes de David, traduit en rhythme françois par Clément Marot et autres . . . composés en musique a quatre parties* (Paris, 1559), renounce the Catholic faith; he even dedicated his psalms to Queen Catherine de'Medici.[1] Another musician, Philibert Jambe-de-Fer, however, was killed, like Goudimel, in 1572, because he was a Huguenot, not before he had set to music the complete Psalter of Marot and de Bèze. Born at Lyons, he spent part of his youth at Poitiers where he made the acquaintance of Jean Poitevin, who, as well as being precentor at St. Radegund, was a man of letters. Poitevin had undertaken to translate into French the hundred psalms which Marot had not published, and Philibert Jambe-de-Fer set them to music for four voices. A complete edition was published at Poitiers in 1558, and at Lyons in 1559.[2] There are a number of psalms which, because of their length, are difficult to adapt to one and the same tune throughout. In such cases Goudimel divided the psalm into groups of two or three verses, giving each a different setting. Jambe de Fer had the same idea. Finally, he set the complete 150 psalms translated by Marot and de Bèze, and his work went through three editions, the last in 1564. In the dedication to Charles IX, at the beginning of the last two editions, the composer insists that he has not had in mind only religious assemblies, but all who like to sing decent songs, even with instruments: 'Et pour autant qu'il y en a plusieurs qui prennent plaisir à chanter les psaumes, non seulement en ce simple chant, duquel on use ordinairement dans les Eglises reformées selon l'Evangile, qui est le plus propre pour l'assemblée publique des fidèles, mais aussi en un chant plus mélodieux selon l'art de musique, hors des assemblées publiques en compagnies particulières, j'ai bien voulu travailler pour ceux-là selon le don que j'ai reçu du Seigneur en cette science'.[3] A still later setting of the complete Marot–

---

[1] See Cauchie, 'Les Psaumes de Janequin', *S. I. M: Premier congrès, Liège: compte rendu* (1930). Janequin had already composed twenty-eight of Marot's psalms (*Premier livre contenant XXVIII Pseaulmes de David*, Paris, du Chemin, 1549) but no complete copy has survived.

[2] On Jambe-de-Fer, see Douen, op. cit.

[3] Pierre Certon's Psalms were arranged by Guillaume Morlaye for voice and lute (1554); a modern edition has been published by François Lesure and R. de Morcourt (Paris, 1957).

de Bèze Psalter, based mostly on Strasbourg and Geneva tunes, is that by Pascal de L'Estocart.[1]

CLAUDE LE JEUNE

A composer who surpassed even Goudimel in certain respects was Claude Le Jeune. Born in 1528 or 1530, at Valenciennes, he became a very active composer in various fields and was appointed Composer of the King's Chamber; in 1598 he became Master of the King's Music. His first religious work: *Dix Psaumes de David nouvellement composés a quatre parties en forme de motets avec un dialogue a sept* (Paris, Le Roy et Ballard, 1564) was certainly not destined for use in church. These are extended compositions. But it was not until much later that Le Jeune became intensively occupied with religious melodies. In 1598 there appeared at La Rochelle a big polyphonic work, the *Dodecacorde contenant douze pseaumes de David, mis en musique selon les douze modes approuvés des meilleurs autheurs anciens et modernes, a deux, trois, quatre, cinq, et six et sept voix.*[2] Here again are very large-scale compositions, each verse being set to different music. The accepted melodies are retained, but differently distributed. The dedication to the Duc de Bouillon, Vicomte de Turenne, is worth reading for the composer's remarks on some of the twelve modes.

Claude Le Jeune died about 1600, and it was left to his sister Cécile to undertake the printing of his remaining works. The most important of these is *Les cent cinquante psaumes de David mis en musique à quatre parties,*[3] which was published by Robert Ballard's widow and son in 1601, and was reprinted several times before 1650. The settings are in simple note-against-note counterpoint, with the melody in the tenor. It had a considerable success, and as late as 1637 Mersenne, in his *Harmonie universelle* (ii, p. 96), recommended its use to Catholics, since these psalms 'serve to incline the mind to the contemplation of things divine'. Three volumes of three-part psalms were printed in 1602–8, and finally in 1606 appeared another remarkable work, the *Psaumes en vers mesurés mis en musique à 2, 3, 4, 5, 6, 7*

---

[1] Facsimile edition by Hans Holliger and Pierre Pidoux (Kassel and Basle, 1954); see also Siegfried Fornaçon, 'L'Estocart und sein Psalter', *Die Musikforschung*, xiii (1960), p. 188.

[2] Paris, Bibl. Nat. Rés. Vm. 1. 41. The first part has been reprinted by Expert, *Maîtres musiciens de la Renaissance française*, xi (Paris, 1900). The setting of the first section of Psalm 35 is given in Davison and Apel, op. cit., p. 136, where it can be compared with Goudimel's 1580 version of the same psalm, p. 135.

[3] Bibl. Nat. Rés. Vm. 1. 46; see also Bibl. Ste Geneviève.

et 8 parties.[1] Here Le Jeune put into practice, as he also did in secular pieces, the theories of Antoine Baïf (see pp. 29–30), and the translation, too, is Baïf's. But Le Jeune's psalms in *vers mesurés* are sometimes surpassed artistically by the *Psaumes mesurés à l'antique de J.-A. de Baïf* (printed belatedly in Mersenne's *Quaestiones Celeberrimae*, Paris, 1623)[2] of his friend Jacques Mauduit, notably by the latter's setting of Psalm 150 ('En son temple sacré').

THE HUGUENOT PSALTER IN OTHER LANDS

The Huguenot Psalter at once aroused much interest in all the countries it reached and quickly inspired attempts at imitation.[3] In Germany a Lutheran Königsberg lawyer, Ambrosius Lobwasser, translated Marot and de Bèze in 1565, and published his version at Leipzig in 1573, with Goudimel's music, slightly adapted. This work had a very favourable reception and went through more than fifty editions in five years. Despite endless criticism of Lobwasser's poetic diction, this edition remained in use until the middle of the nineteenth century. A less successful German Psalter had already been compiled in Württemberg, by Siegmund Hemmel, *Kapellmeister* to the ducal court, who set the whole Psalter for four voices, with melody in the tenor (published posthumously in 1569). The influence of Switzerland, and perhaps also of Strasbourg, is discernible in this Psalter, although the translations are drawn from Hans Sachs and other South German poets, independently of Marot and de Bèze. As we shall see later, the importance of these note-against-note psalm-settings in the history of the Protestant hymn lies in their connexion with the growing practice of accompanied congregational singing. The congregation sang the melody, whether in the tenor or (as became more and more customary) in the highest part, in unison; the other three parts supplied the simplest possible accompaniment.

In 1602 the Landgrave Moritz of Hesse produced a new Psalter, with melodies only, twenty-four of which he wrote himself, and in 1612, after abandoning Lutheranism for Calvinism, published a new edition in four-part harmony. At roughly the same time (1606) Samuel Mareschall of Basle was arranging Goudimel's compositions, to Lobwasser's words, giving the melody throughout to the highest

---

[1] Reprinted by Expert, *Maîtres musiciens de la Renaissance française*, xx, xxi, and xxii (Paris, 1905–6).

[2] Reprinted by Expert, *Florilège du concert vocal de la Renaissance*, vii (Paris, 1928).

[3] The English and Scottish Psalters are discussed in the next chapter (see pp. 501–2).

voice.[1] Finally, Schütz's Psalms of 1628[2] must be mentioned: a rhymed version of the psalms by Cornelius Becker set simply in four parts, with only eleven of the older tunes and ninety-two new ones by Schütz. A second edition (Dresden, 1661) gave melodies for the remaining psalms as well.

Nor were the Catholics to be outdone. In Cologne a convert from Lutheranism, Kaspar Ulenberg, published in 1582 a rhymed German version of the psalms with tunes from various sources—including (as he admitted in the second edition of 1603) Calvinistic ones; a four-part harmonization of the tunes by Conradus Hagius Rinteleus appeared at Düsseldorf in 1589.[3] Two years before Ulenberg, Mikołaj Gomółka brought out four-part settings of the complete Psalter in Polish (Cracow, 1580);[4] again the basic melodies come from various sources, plainsong, popular, and Protestant, and Gomółka's settings—though very simple—are pleasantly varied. Similar, if more modest, collections appeared in Bohemia, where simple vernacular religious song naturally flourished under the Protestant churches and the Bohemian Brethren; for instance, Jiří Strejc's Psalter of 1587, with the Calvinist tunes only, though a four-part harmonization by Daniel Karolides appeared in 1618, and the twelve four-part Psalms which Vavřinec Benedikt Nudožerský published at Prague in 1606,[5] the words in Czech, some at least of the tunes French but *mesurés à l'antique*, like those by Le Jeune printed posthumously in the same year.

All these collections are completely overshadowed in musical interest, however, by the great setting of the Marot–de Bèze translation which Sweelinck published at Amsterdam or Haarlem in four sets: 1603, 1613, 1614, and 1621.[6] (Psalms 3 and 10 had appeared anonymously in 1597, in a volume containing music mostly by Lassus; Psalms 3, 27, and 134 were composed twice.) The compositions are

---

[1] Mareschall's Psalms are in the Library at Basle. Specimens are reprinted in Winterfeld, op. cit.

[2] *Heinrich Schütz: Sämtliche Werke*, xvi (Leipzig, 1894); *Neue Ausgabe sämtlicher Werke*, vi (Kassel and Basle, 1957); two psalms in Schering, op. cit., p. 226.

[3] Modern edition by Johannes Overath, *Denkmäler rheinischer Musik*, iii (Düsseldorf, 1955); see also Overath, *Untersuchungen über die Melodien des Liedpsalters von Kaspar Ulenberg (Köln, 1582)* (*Beiträge zur rheinischen Musikgeschichte*, xxxiii) (Cologne, 1960).

[4] Modern edition by J. W. Reiss (Cracow, 1923) and Mirosław Perz, *Wydawnictwo dawnej muzyki polskiej* (Warsaw, n.d.), xlvii–xlix.

[5] Psalm 82 in Jaroslav Pohanka, *Dejiny ceské hudby v příkladech* (Prague, 1958), p. 63.

[6] Reprinted by Max Seiffert, *Werken van Jan Pieterszn. Sweelinck*, ii–v (Leipzig and The Hague, 1897–8). See also B. Van den Sigtenhorst Meyer, *De vocale muziek van Jan P. Sweelinck* (The Hague, 1948), pp. 108 ff.

extremely varied in every way. Sometimes Sweelinck composes the first verse only, sometimes the whole psalm. Three settings are for three parts only, thirty are for as many as eight, the vast majority being for four, five, or six voices. In almost every case Sweelinck uses the Geneva tune as *canto fermo* but he treats it with the utmost variety; it may appear in any part, though he favours the tenor, and may be rhythmically modified from verse to verse. One finds both sober and florid counterpoint, echo-effects and in Psalm 113 real Venetian *cori spezzati*, chromatic and other madrigalisms, and naïve imitations of instruments (the harp in Psalm 98, and 'tabour' and 'musette' in Psalm 150). Altogether Van den Sigtenhorst Meyer[1] distinguishes five main types: psalm-variations, madrigal-psalms, motet-psalms, echo-psalms, and song-psalms. It may seem strange that Sweelinck based his psalms on the French translation and the Geneva tunes, instead of on the Dutch text and popular tunes of the famous *Souterliedekens* originally published at Antwerp in 1540[2] and many times reprinted; but the latter were intended for domestic, not church, use.

In France itself the Psalter remained in use in the Reformed Church without change until towards the end of the seventeenth century, when the texts of Marot and de Bèze were considered old-fashioned and were adapted by Conrart. But from the beginning and for a long time, these psalms made such a great impression upon many Catholics that the ecclesiastical authorities, as in other countries, sought to counterbalance their influence by new translations and compositions, made by members of their own Church. The first Frenchman to attempt this, towards the end of the sixteenth century, was Philippe Desportes. But the psalms which he versified were not at first set to music. Better was the *Paraphrase des pseaumes de David en vers françois* (Paris, 1659) by Antoine Godeau, bishop of Grasse and Vence, set to melodies by Thomas Gobert, master of music in the King's Chapel.

GERMANY IN THE LATE SIXTEENTH CENTURY

In Germany, after the first flowering of Protestant music, we come to a period which may be described as transitional, in which opposing

---

[1] Op. cit., p. 155.

[2] Modern edition by Elizabeth Mincoff-Marriage (The Hague, 1922); see also D. F. Scheurleer, *De Souterliedekens. Bijdrage tot de geschiedenis der oudste nederlandsche psalmberijming* (Leyden, 1898); P. André Gaillard, 'Essai sur le rapport des sources mélodiques des "Pseaulmes cinquantes" de Jean Louis (Anvers, 1555) et des "Souter-liedekens" (Anvers, 1540)', and Walter Wiora, 'Die Melodien der "Souterliedekens"

trends existed. Compositions on Latin texts once more assumed a very important—even over-important—place, and music by Catholic composers was often included in the Lutheran service, while towards the end of the century the majestic and sumptuous style of the Venetian School was adopted by a number of young German musicians. On the other hand, in certain districts a different trend of ideas is perceptible. The preference for a very simple religious service in the south and south-west of Germany, referred to above, developed further under the growing influence of Calvinism, especially after several German princes had—like Moritz of Hesse—accepted the ideas and ordinances of Calvin both personally and for their states. Calvin influenced even certain Lutheran pastors and musicians. A demand began to arise that Lutheran hymn-music should be made simpler, in the style of the Calvinist psalms. One of the preachers at the Württemberg Court, Hemmel's friend Lucas Osiander, published in 1586 a little volume of *Fünfftzig Geistliche Lieder und Psalmen*[1] containing the principal Lutheran hymns, in the simplest four-part harmony with the melody in the highest part, and this example was soon followed generally. Still, composers preferred to set psalms and other biblical passages in German. Naturally these changes took place only gradually.

The Dresden Court Chapel at this period had a succession of good musicians who, though some were Catholics, all wrote for the Protestant churches. It is curious that none was of German origin. Johann Walther's successor, Matthaeus Le Maistre, was Flemish. He was *Kapellmeister* from 1554 to 1567. He published *Geistliche und Weltliche teutsche Geseng zu 4—5 Stimmen* (Wittenberg, 1566) of which seventy were religious and twenty-two secular. In the year of his death, 1577, there appeared another collection, *Schöne und auserlesene teutsche und lateinische geistliche Gesenge*, for three voices. The composer includes nearly all the hymns sung by Lutheran congregations as well as some from other sources. In his first collection, he follows in general the same style as Walther,[2] in the second it is more akin to that of Kugelmann (see above, p. 430). Besides

und ihre deutschen Parallelen', *Kongress-Bericht . . . Utrecht 1952* (Amsterdam, 1953), pp. 193 and 438. On the most important harmonized edition of the *Souterliedekens*, that by Clemens von Papa, see *supra*, p. 230.

[1] Reprinted by Friedrich Zelle in *Das erste evangelische Gesangbuch* (Berlin, 1903); one example in Schering, op. cit., p. 142.

[2] Le Maistre's setting of 'Hör Menschenkind' is reprinted in Ambros, *Geschichte der Musik*, v (Leipzig, 1889), p. 421; that of 'Aus tiefer Not' in Schering, op. cit., p. 123; two others by Osthoff in *Das Chorwerk*, xxx (Wolfenbüttel, 1934). See also Kade, *Matthäus Le Maistre* (Mainz, 1862).

these compositions, the *Geseng* of 1566 include some more elaborate ones in the style of the hymn- or psalm-motet, such as the outstanding setting of Psalm 90, 'Herr, du bist unsere Zuflucht für und für', for five and six voices.

Le Maistre's successor at Dresden was an Italian, Antonio Scandello (1517–80), some of whose *Newe schöne ausserlesene Geistliche Deudsche Lieder* for five and six voices (1575), remained in use for a considerable time. His Passion music and *Auferstehungshistorie* will be dealt with in Vol. V. Yet another foreigner was Rogier Michael, born at Mons (Hainaut) about 1550, Court *Kapellmeister* at Dresden from 1587 till about 1615. He published a collection of four-part hymn-settings, with the melody in the highest part: *Die Gebreuchlichsten und vornembsten Gesenge Dr. Mart. Lutheri und andren frommen Christen* (Dresden, 1593).[1]

The end of the century was remarkable for a new outpouring of Lutheran hymn-poetry by such writers as Philipp Nicolai ('Wie schön leuchtet der Morgenstern' und 'Wachet auf, ruft uns die Stimme'), Nikolaus Selnekker ('Ach bleib bei uns'), the anonymous author of 'In dir ist Freude', and Ludwig Helmbold of Mühlhausen in Thuringia, whose hymns were first set by his fellow-townsman Joachim a Burck (1546–1610). Burck's compositions,[2] particularly his four-part *Deutsche Liedlein* (of which the first set of twenty appeared in 1575), open a new chapter in the history of Protestant music; as Blume puts it,[3] 'a new relationship between word and note is proclaimed . . . close connection of musician with poet, contact with the artistic bases of Lassus's style'. But Burck himself is overshadowed by his great pupil, Johannes Eccard.

ECCARD AND LECHNER

Born at Mühlhausen in 1553, Eccard as a youth came under the influence of both Helmbold and Burck. From 1571 to 1574, he was a member of the Munich Court Chapel, which was then directed by Lassus. The greater part of his later life was spent at Königsberg (1580–1608) where he became *Oberkapellmeister* and he finally held the same post in the Electoral Chapel at Berlin, where he died in

---

[1] Ambros, op. cit. v, p. 463, reprints the setting of 'Ein feste Burg' from this collection.

[2] On Burck, see Herbert Birtner, 'Ein Beitrag zur Geschichte der protestantischen Musik im 16. Jahrhundert', *Zeitschrift für Musikwissenschaft*, x (1928), p. 457. The *Deutsche Liedlein* of 1575 are reprinted in *Publikationen der Gesellschaft für Musikforschung*, Jg. 26 (Leipzig, 1898).   [3] Op. cit., p. 79.

1611.[1] His early compositions, *Odae sacrae* (1574) and *Crepundia sacra* (1578), were probably written in collaboration with Burck. In 1578 Eccard published *Neuwe teutsche Lieder*, and in 1589 *Newe geistliche und weltliche Lieder*. In these the form is very free; there is no clear-cut melody running right through each piece; very marked contrasts are frequent; 'a man tormented by the world and his sins cries out in his agony, but finally triumphs in the certainty of Divine Grace' (Blume). In 1597 appeared Eccard's famous *Geystliche Lieder, auff den Choral*, based on the familiar hymn-tunes. The melody is given to the upper voice, while the three other parts move rhythmically, giving an impression of polyphony. As Blume says: 'Without them, Bach is unthinkable'.[2] Eccard's last work, the *Preussische Festlieder*, to texts by different authors, composed in collaboration with his pupil, Stobäus, was not published by the latter until 1642–44. These are all long works, for from five to eight voices. The chief melody—usually Eccard's own—is again given to the highest voice, while the other parts freely underline the expression of the words. One of the most expressive is the setting of Helmbold's 'Im Garten leidet Christus Not' where, exceptionally, there is a reference to a traditional tune ('Da Jesus an dem Kreuze stund').

While Eccard was always more or less conservative, another of Lassus's disciples, Leonhard Lechner (*c*. 1553–1606), constantly sought new methods of expression. Born in the Southern Tyrol, he was endowed with a lively and ardent temperament. Besides secular compositions, he wrote numerous religious works, including motets, Masses, eight Magnificats, and a Passion; but it is his last work, *Deutsche Sprüche von Leben und Tod*, which is his greatest. The text consists of rhymed epigrams on death, of considerable literary value, which Lechner underlines with grave music, for four voices, in a highly individual style stamped with genius.[3]

HASSLER AND MICHAEL PRAETORIUS

If Eccard and Lechner were influenced to a certain extent by Lassus, other Protestant musicians were, towards the end of the

---

[1] Eccard's works have often been reprinted separately or collectively, first of all by Winterfeld, op. cit. G. W. Teschner reprinted the *Geistliche Lieder auf den Choral* (Leipzig, 1860), and the *Preussische Festlieder* (Leipzig, 1858). The *Newe geistliche und weltliche Lieder* of 1589 were published by Eitner in *Publikationen der Gesellschaft für Musikforschung*, Jg. 25 (Leipzig, 1897). Part I, *Lieder auf den Choral*, has also been reprinted by Fr. von Baussnern (Wolfenbüttel, 1928). One of the *Preussische Festlieder* is given by Schering, op. cit., p. 167.   [2] Op. cit., p. 85.

[3] The *Deutsche Sprüche von Leben und Tod* have been reprinted by Lipphardt and Ameln (Kassel, 1929). A complete edition of Lechner is being edited by Ameln (Kassel and Basle, 1954–   ).

century, influenced by the Venetian School. One of the most remarkable was Hans Leo Hassler (1564–1612). Son of a Nuremberg organist, he went at the age of twenty to Venice, where he studied under Andrea Gabrieli. If the spirit and methods of this school predominate in his secular compositions and in his religious settings of Latin texts (Masses, motets, *Cantiones sacrae, Sacri concentus*) he also left the Lutheran Church works of value. In 1607 there appeared *Psalmen und Christliche Gesäng, auf die Melodeyen fugweiss componiert*,[1] for four voices; these are genuinely polyphonic compositions, in which the melodic phrases of a hymn are developed successively in free imitation. They show no trace of Italian influence. The following year Hassler published another collection of *Kirchengesäng, Psalmen und geistliche Lieder, auff die gemeinen Melodeyen simpliciter gesetzt*. There are sixty-eight of these:[2] hymns in general use in the Lutheran Church, psalms, and a small number of songs of a more general character. Although very 'simply set' as the title says, they are constructed with great skill. What is so striking about Hassler, and what sets him above most of his contemporaries, is his power of expression and the warm and intimate character of his music.

Important in quite a different way is the colossal work by Michael Praetorius (1571–1621), *Musae Sionae*,[3] in which he explores practically every possible method of treating the Protestant hymn-tune. Published between 1605 and 1610 in nine volumes, it contains 1,244 compositions. Praetorius begins in the first four volumes with sumptuous and majestic pieces for from eight to twelve voices, in the style of the Venetian School; the next volume contains more modest compositions, and the last part consists only of four-part hymns and liturgical songs with the melody in the highest voice, and the whole generally in note-against-note counterpoint. Some of these pieces are not by him, but are borrowed from other composers. He adds *bicinia* and *tricinia*, which are, he says, written in motet or madrigal style, or in a third style invented by himself. This new style is as follows: one voice sings the melody and words of the hymn all through while the two others continuously repeat a different fragment of the text—not a very happy idea. On the other hand, other compositions on hymns, for instruments, three of them in fugal style, are decidedly important. In the ninth volume there are passages which anticipate the concertante style, and experiments with *basso continuo*. The

[1] Ed. C. Russell Crosby in *Sämtliche Werke*, vii (Wiesbaden, 1965); a selection has been reprinted by Ralf von Saalfeld (Kassel, n.d.).
[2] One example in Ambros, op. cit. v, p. 552.
[3] *Michael Praetorius: Gesamtausgabe*, ed. Blume, i–ix (Wolfenbüttel, 1927–42).

different styles adumbrated here in fairly short examples are employed on a much larger scale in the work entitled *Polyhymnia Caduceatrix & Panegyrica* (Wolfenbüttel, 1619).[1] The majority of these are hymn-settings. Praetorius's object in these works is to display the full sonorous richness of vocal or instrumental choirs,[2] methods of varying choral performance by the introduction of instrumental ritornelli, the importance of solo singing, and the principle of the *basso continuo*. But although he accepted a number of Italian innovations, it was always the Lutheran hymn that remained the basis of his works.

LUTHERAN *CANTIONES SACRAE*

Of the numerous Protestant musicians who wrote religious compositions of value, there is space here to mention only those whose works are of special interest or who exercised a notable influence on the development of Protestant music. One important new feature of Lutheran music toward the end of the century was the increasing popularity of the Latin motet (*cantio sacra*), usually based on texts from the psalms or the Gospels. One of those who chose texts in German was Andreas Raselius (*c.* 1563–1602). In 1594 he published fifty-three five-part motets, *Teutsche Sprüche*, settings of verses from the Gospel for each Sunday. The narrative passages are sometimes very vividly composed: for example, the motet entitled 'Navicula fluctuans'[3] (although the text is German), in which the disciples surprised by the storm on the lake of Gennesareth are depicted in a state of extreme agitation. In the preface the composer says that organ, horns, and trombones are to be used in certain motets.

Motets on German Gospel texts were also composed by Christoph Demantius (1567–1643), who was cantor at Freiberg (Saxony) from 1604.[4] His *Corona harmonica* (Leipzig, 1610) contains six-part motets for every Sunday in the year.[5] The one describing the parents of Jesus searching for him in the Temple is especially interesting. Despite the uninterrupted polyphonic texture, the composer knows how to make certain people or words stand out in relief.

An adherent of the Venetian school, Hieronymus Praetorius of

---

[1] *Gesamtausgabe*, xvii (Wolfenbüttel, 1930).
[2] See *infra*, p. 549.
[3] *Denkmäler der Tonkunst in Bayern*, Jg. 29/30, p. 47.
[4] On Demantius, see Reinhard Kade, 'Christoph Demant' in *Vierteljahrsschrift für Musikwissenschaft*, vi (1890), p. 469.
[5] Four of them published by A. A. Abert in *Das Chorwerk*, xxxix (Wolfenbüttel, 1936).

Hamburg (1560–1629)—like his younger namesake—usually wrote for a great number of voices: the *Cantiones Sacrae* (originally published at Hamburg in 1599 but expanded as *Tomus primus* of the *Opus Musicum*, 1622) for five to twelve voices, the *Cantiones variae* (*Opus Musicum*, iv, 1618) for five to twenty, the *Cantiones novae* (*Opus Musicum*, v, 1625) for five to fifteen voices.[1] All the voices have a very wide range and all are handled with extraordinary skill. Most of the motets have Latin texts, but there are a few on Protestant hymns. Compositions of this type could obviously be performed only in towns possessing choirs of numerous well-trained singers, such as Kassel, Stettin, Dresden, and Leipzig.

Melchior Franck (*c.* 1573–1639), *Kapellmeister* to Prince Johann Casimir at Coburg and perhaps a pupil of Hassler, also wrote several difficult compositions for fairly large choir on Gospel texts, but as a rule he contented himself with more modest forces. Thus his *Gemmulae Evangeliorum Musicae* (1623), a Gospel cycle for a year's Sundays and feast days, are written for four voices, some even *ad voces aequales*, perhaps for a choir of boys. Nevertheless, they contain passages very remarkable from the point of view of expression. The majority of Franck's compositions are secular, but among his religious works must be mentioned the *Geistliche Gesäng und Melodeyen* (1608), mostly from the Song of Songs,[2] the *Threnodiae Davidicae*, six-part settings of the seven penitential psalms (1615), and the *Geistlicher musikalischer Lustgarten* (1616) for from four to nine parts.

HERMANN SCHEIN

With Hermann Schein (1586–1630), Samuel Scheidt (1587–1654), and Heinrich Schütz (1585–1672), we come to three masters whose religious works show many different aspects. A great number of them clearly reflect Italian influence; others preserve the spirit of the Reformation. Schein[3] was, as a boy, the pupil of Rogier Michael and singer (soprano) in the court chapel at Dresden; he then studied at the famous Pforta School and in the University of Leipzig. From 1613 to 1615 he was *Kapellmeister* at Weimar, and then became cantor at the Thomas School at Leipzig. His secular compositions were more numerous than his religious works, yet the latter have an importance of their own. His first sacred publication was a collection of

---

[1] A selection from these motets, edited by Leichtentritt, is printed in *Denkmäler deutscher Tonkunst*, xxiii; two edited by Blume in *Das Chorwerk*, xiv (Wolfenbüttel, 1931). See also Leichtentritt's *Geschichte der Motette* (Leipzig, 1908), pp. 309–15.

[2] Five pieces republished by A. A. Abert, *Das Chorwerk*, xxiv (Wolfenbüttel, 1933).

[3] On Schein generally, see Arthur Prüfer, *Johan Herman Schein* (Leipzig, 1895).

quasi-Venetian Latin and German motets for five to twelve voices: *Cymbalum Sionium* (Leipzig, 1615)[1] on texts from the psalms, the Gospels, and the Song of Songs. The forms are those used by earlier composers, and are not developed much further; the sense of the words is underlined by the music, though Schein did not seek new methods. Towards the end of his life he published another conservative work, a *Cantional, Oder Gesangbuch Augspurgischer Confession* (Leipzig, 1627).[2] This collection, for four to six voices, was distinctive for different reasons: for fifty-seven of the hymns Schein composed new tunes; for forty-three, he wrote his own words. (More were added in later editions.) The settings are straightforward harmonizations. But while in these publications Schein showed himself still content with old forms, in others we find him adopting the newest methods of expression. In the *Opella nova / Erster Teil Geistlicher Concerten / Mit 3. 4 vnd 5 Stimmen / zusampt dem General-Bass / auff jetzo gebräuchliche Italienische Invention* (Leipzig, 1618)[3] he arranged the hymn-tunes in Viadana's concerto style[4] usually for one or two voices, with one or two obbligato instruments and *continuo*. There may, for instance, be two soprano voices duetting with fragments of the hymn-tune over the *basso continuo*, while at pauses in this duet the tenor intervenes with the tune in long note-values.[5]

Ex. 203

[1] *Johann Hermann Scheins Werke*, ed. Prüfer, iv (Leipzig, 1911); see also Prüfer, 'J. H. Scheins *Cymbalum Sionium*', *Liliencron-Festschrift* (Leipzig, 1910), p. 176.

[2] Reprinted in Adam Adrio, *J. H. Schein: Neue Ausgabe sämtlicher Werke*, ii (Kassel and Basle, 1963–). On its historical bases, see Walter Reckziegel, *Das Cantional von J. H. Schein* (Berlin, 1963).

[3] *Werke*, v (1914).

[4] See pp. 533 ff. Schein's were the earliest German 'spiritual concertos'.

[5] *Werke*, v, p. 5 and Schering, *Geschichte der Musik in Beispielen*, p. 224.

(Be thou praised, Jesus Christ)

In others, there is no *canto fermo*; two or three voices sing together interchanging fragments of the hymn-tune, often much elaborated. Or a voice sings a new melody to the words, while above it a violin plays another cantilena, the whole being supported by the *continuo*. The second part of the *Opella nova*[1] (1626) is still closer to the monodic type. The texts include not only hymns but prose passages from the Bible: from the Gospels and Epistles for specific days. The voice-part is sometimes in recitative, sometimes resembles an air, and Schein tries to express with the utmost freedom the feeling of the text. Sometimes he calls for choir or specific instruments: for instance in no. 11, the *Dialogo a 6* of the Annunciation, a quartet of trombones plays interludes in the conversation of the angel (tenor) with Mary (soprano), which is accompanied only by the *continuo*. In the Lord's Prayer and the Beatitudes other instruments and choir appear. In these compositions Schein was already foreshadowing Schütz's *Kleine Konzerte* and dialogues. The same bold expressiveness is apparent in a collection of motets with *continuo* which preceded the second part of the *Opella nova*: *Fontana d'Israel* (*Israels*

---

[1] *Werke*, vi and vii (ed. Prüfer and Bernhard Engelke) (Leipzig, 1919 and 1923). On this second part, see Karl Hasse, 'Johann Hermann Schein', *Zeitschrift für Musikwissenschaft*, ii (1920), p. 578.

Brünlein) (Leipzig, 1623).[1] Here, too, we find intensity of expression, chromaticism, and strong contrasts in the 'sonderbar *Italian Madrigalische Manier*', as Schein himself points out. Thus, in the motet 'Die mit Tränen säen werden mit Freuden ernten'[2] ('They that sow in tears shall reap in joy'), the word 'Tränen' is set to a vocalized passage which first rises chromatically, then descends, and 'säen' to another vocalized passage suggesting painful toil; while for 'werden mit Freuden ernten' there is an octave leap and the words 'mit Freuden' are repeated several times in short notes:

Ex. 204

---

[1] Ed. Adrio, *Schein: Neue Ausgabe*, i (1963).

[2] Separate edition by Blume, *Das Chorwerk*. xiv (Wolfenbüttel, 1931), p. 24; see also Leichtentritt, *Geschichte der Motette*, p. 358.

(ii) wer-den mit Freuden, mit Freuden, mit Freuden, mit Freu - den ern - ten,

wer-den mit Freu - den ern - ten,

wer-den mit Freuden, mit Freuden, mit Freuden ern - ten,

-en, wer-den mit Freuden, mit Freu - den ern - ten,

In certain respects Schein recalls Lechner, but sometimes he also makes one think of Monteverdi.

SAMUEL SCHEIDT

Pupil of Sweelinck and friend of Schein, the Halle organist Samuel Scheidt[1] is best known for his keyboard works[2] but he also contributed notably to the choral church music of his day, particularly with motets and concertos on Lutheran hymns. Like Schein, his first publication for church use, *Cantiones Sacrae Octo Vocum* (Hamburg, 1620),[3] consists of *a cappella* motets, both German and Latin, nearly half of them hymn-settings, with a number of psalms. The double-choral technique is employed with great effect, though it is clear that Scheidt acquired it from Sweelinck or his colleague Michael Praetorius, not from Italy. There is no *continuo*, but in no. 15, 'In dulci jubilo', there are *ad libitum* parts for two small trumpets ('vulgo clarien'). However, in his next work, the *Concertus Sacri* of 1622,[4] containing three Magnificats, a Lutheran Mass, and seven settings of Biblical texts—all but one in Latin—Scheidt introduces not only an organ *continuo* but other instruments which sometimes accompany, sometimes play 'symphonies', as in no. 6, 'Angelus ad pastores', which is an arrangement of no. 13 in the *Cantiones Sacrae*.[5]

[1] On Scheidt generally, see Seiffert, 'J. P. Sweelinck und seine direkten deutschen Schüler', *Vierteljahrsschrift für Musikwissenschaft*, vii (1891), p. 145; Arno Werner, 'Samuel und Gottfried Scheidt', *Sammelbände der internationalen Musikgesellschaft*, i (1899–1900), p. 401, and 'Neue Beiträge zur Scheidt-Biographie', ibid. xiii (1911–12), p. 297; Christhard Mahrenholz, *Samuel Scheidt: sein Leben und sein Werk* (Leipzig, 1924).

[2] See p. 666 ff.

[3] Reprinted by Gottlieb Harms and Christhard Mahrenholz, *Samuel Scheidts Werke*, iv (Hamburg, 1933).

[4] See Erika Gessner, *Samuel Scheidts geistliche Konzerte* (*Berliner Studien zur Musikwissenschaft*, ii) (Berlin, 1961).

[5] On Scheidt's arrangements and use of *parodia* technique, first detected by Mahrenholz, see Gessner, op. cit., and Werner Braun, 'Samuel Scheidts Bearbeitungen alter Motetten', *Archiv für Musikwissenschaft*, xix–xx (1962–3), p. 56.

It was not until 1631, when Halle was temporarily freed by the Swedes from Imperialist occupation, that Scheidt brought out *Newe geistliche Concerten* (with German title and all German texts), though the conditions produced by the war obliged him to reduce drastically the forces for which they were originally conceived; in their published forms all are for two or three voices only, with *continuo* but no other instruments. Other sets followed in 1634, 1635, and 1640,[1] and two more are lost; in these, more favourable conditions allowed Scheidt to employ five or even six voices but he was never able to gratify his desire to make public the original forms 'mit. 8. 12 Stimmen/zwey/ drey/vier Choren/mit *Symphonien*, vnd allerley Instrumenten'. In these later 'concertos' the tendency away from the old motet style to the new dramatic one, begun in the *Concertus Sacri*, is carried much further. A typically dramatic effect occurs near the end of 'Kommt her zu mir alle' in the 1634 set, which Scheidt describes as '*Dialogus*, that is a conversation of Christ with the Righteous and the Damned on the Day of Judgment':

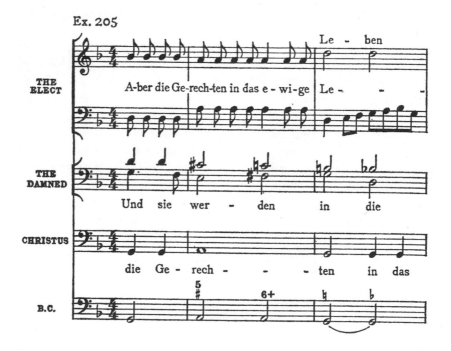

Ex. 205

<hr />

[1] The four sets have been republished in *Werke*, viii–xii (1957–65).

(But the righteous into life eternal)
(And these shall go away into everlasting punishment)

Perhaps the most interesting feature of the later *Concerten* is the way
in which the variation-principle in setting successive verses of a hymn
is developed into a miniature cantata, the precursor of the so-called
'chorale cantatas' of J. S. Bach. Often two or three verses are joined,
so that the whole 'concerto' consists of several sections each embodying two or three variations. Thus 'Wenn wir in höchsten Nöten
sein' in the 1634 set is constructed as follows:

> Verse 1: miniature motet
>   2: duet for soprano and tenor
>   3: variation: hymn-tune in bass
>   ———————
>   4: motet style
>   5: variation: tune in tenor
>   6: duet for soprano and tenor
>   7: note-against-note harmonization of tune

HEINRICH SCHÜTZ

Both Schein and Scheidt have been partially eclipsed in this field
by a still greater figure: their friend Heinrich Schütz.[1] As a boy he was

[1] On Schütz in general, see particularly André Pirro, *Schütz* (Paris, 1913), Hans
Joachim Moser, *Heinrich Schütz: Sein Leben und Werk* (Kassel, 1936; English translation
by Carl F. Pfatteicher, Saint Louis, 1959), and Erich Müller (von Asow) (ed.), *Heinrich*

a protégé of the Landgrave Moritz of Hesse. He sang in the court chapel at Kassel and, when his voice began to break, he was sent to study at Marburg, and finally the Landgrave sent him to Venice, where he worked for three years (1609–12) under Giovanni Gabrieli. In 1617 he was appointed *Kapellmeister* to the Elector of Saxony, a post which he held nominally for the rest of his life, though his service was interrupted by the Thirty Years War and by visits to other courts, notably that of Copenhagen. His first religious publication, *Psalmen Davids sampt etlichen Moteten und Concerten*, appeared in 1619.[1] The majority of these compositions are for eight voices with *basso continuo* 'vor die Orgel, Lauten, Chitaron, &c.', sometimes with other obbligato instruments. In the preface, Schütz gives instructions for performance, on the lines he had learned in Italy. His choirs are divided into two classes: the *coro favorito*, formed of the singers with the finest voices and the most talent, and the *cappella*, employed to enhance the strength and brilliance of particular passages. Like Praetorius[2] he is willing sometimes to replace voices by instruments: for example, in the *cappella*, though one part in each choir should be sung, cornetti may be substituted for the higher voices and trombones for the lower ones. As some psalms are too long to be sung throughout in motet style, he has some verses declaimed 'in stylo recitativo', a style 'almost unknown in Germany at present', by soloists with chordal accompaniment or, more often, by all the voices. He treats some psalms as 'concertos' for a solo voice, and in the psalms of praise he adds obbligato instruments: flute, strings, cornetti, trombones. He tries as far as possible to give a faithful reflection of the text and if he sometimes, like others, indulges in rather puerile word-painting, here too he is only following in his master's steps; thus, as Pirro pointed out,[3] Giovanni Gabrieli in his motet 'Timor et tremor' separates the two syllables of 'timor' by a pause, and Schütz does exactly the same with 'fürchtet' in his Psalm 128.[4] The beginning of Psalm 130, 'Aus der Tief ruf ich, Herr',[5] is particularly impressive; the four voices of the first choir sing in the low register with a dissonance on the word 'Tiefe'; the soprano rises an octave for 'ruf'; and it is only on 'Herr!' that the second choir enters with overpower-

---

Schütz: Gesammelte Briefe und Schriften (Ratisbon, 1931). Schütz's *Sämtliche Werke* were edited in 18 vols. by Philipp Spitta, Arnold Schering, and Heinrich Spitta (Leipzig, 1885–1927); a *Neue Ausgabe sämtlicher Werke* (various editors) was begun by the Neue Schütz-Gesellschaft (Kassel and Basle, 1955–   ).

[1] *Sämtliche Werke*, ii and iii.
[2] See p. 549.
[3] Op. cit., p. 176.
[4] *Sämtliche Werke*, ii, p. 120.   [5] Ibid. p. 47.

ing effect. Schütz is more or less following in Gabrieli's footsteps even in the use of chromaticism:

Ex. 206 (Note-values halved)

(Out of the depths I cry unto thee, O Lord)

The four-part *Cantiones Sacrae* of 1625[1] with Latin texts show us Schütz generally more faithful to the style of the old polyphony; even the 'Bassus ad Organum', he says, was added only because the publisher insisted on it. But here again we find him trying to give special emphasis to certain words; one is stressed by a full chord,

[1] Ibid. iv; *Neue Ausgabe*, viii–ix. The *Historia der Auferstehung* (1623) will be discussed in Vol. V.

another is thrown into prominence by a little melisma. The triptych-like setting of Psalm 6, 'Domine ne in furore tuo',[1] is particularly bold, with its dramatic chromaticism of melody and harmony, its dissonance, and its monodic passages (in which, of course, the *continuo* is indispensable):

Ex. 207

(O Lord, rebuke me not in thine anger)

In 1629 Schütz obtained leave from the Elector and made another journey to Venice. He found that changes had taken place there; Monteverdi had long been *maestro di cappella*; even the second *maestro*, Giovanni Rovetta, who had just succeeded Gabrieli's pupil Grandi, was a disciple of Monteverdi. The first part of Schütz's *Symphoniae Sacrae* (Venice, 1629)[2] shows what Schütz learned during this later sojourn in Italy. But discussion of these, with the other works of the later period, must be left to Vol. V.

[1] *Sämtliche Werke*, iv, p. 124; *Neue Ausgabe*, ix, p. 93.
[2] *Werke*, v; *Neue Ausgabe*, xiii–xiv.

IX

CHURCH MUSIC IN ENGLAND

By FRANK LL. HARRISON

HUMANISM AND LUTHERANISM IN THE ENGLISH REFORMATION

IN the first two decades of his reign Henry VIII showed himself a keen promoter of humanism and of the arts of music, poetry, and pageantry. Later this youthful interest was lost in the maze of controversy which followed his assumption of Renaissance absolutism over Church and State. The 'Oxford reformers' Colet, Erasmus, and More shared a love of humanism but differed in their views of its relationship to Christianity. While Erasmus satirized English choral foundations, Colet sought to put that of St. Paul's on a sounder basis. Though both were revolted by the popular devotion to relics, and Colet preached fearlessly against the luxurious life of churchmen, neither thought of humanism in terms of a Protestant reform. Still less did More, who resisted it to the death on grounds of conscience. Of later humanist churchmen, Pole was the most implacable opponent of the breach with Rome, while Tunstall and Gardiner supported it, but opposed the doctrinal and liturgical Reformation of Edward VI's reign.

The invasion of Lutheran ideas was under way by 1521, when Wolsey ordered the public burning of Lutheran books. Lutheranism, less radical than Wycliffism (which survived into the early sixteenth century), had its groups of proponents at the universities, and produced its martyrs to Henry's determined orthodoxy in matters of faith and ritual. The influence of Lutheran thought, though strong, was indirect until Martin Bucer and Peter Martyr, both of whom came to England in 1549, were called on to help in the revision of the First Prayer Book. However, neither they nor the leaders of the English Reformation took up Luther's explicit direction that choral music, together with the new congregational hymns, should be cultivated in the reformed churches and schools. The influence of Calvinist ideas, which resulted in the printing of the *Psalms in English Metre* (probably in 1548) ensured that the congregational music of the English reformed church should follow the Genevan model.

THE REFORM OF CHURCH AND LITURGY

Erasmus's complaint that the attention of English monks was entirely taken up by music[1] was, of course, a caustic exaggeration, since in almost all cases the polyphonic choir of a great monastery was composed of boys and lay singing-men, under a lay master. The chief losses at the Suppression of 1540–1 were such abbeys as Bury St. Edmund's and Glastonbury, for which there was no place in the reformed church, and those which, like St. Albans and Waltham, were reduced to being parish churches. The secularized communities adopted forthwith the Sarum rite, so that the results of the Suppression were less serious than has sometimes been supposed. The active cultivation of choral polyphony had, in fact, long since passed out of the hands of monastics.

The suppression of chantries in the first year of Edward VI, together with the injunctions of his reign against organs and florid polyphony, were much more significant for the musical life of the Church. Winchester, Eton, and St. George's, Windsor, were exempted from the provisions of the Chantries Act, but other foundations, among them St. Stephen's (Westminster), St. Mary Newark, Fotheringhay, Tattershall, and Higham Ferrers, were suppressed or deprived of their musical establishment. The injunctions for the taking down of rood-lofts and organs and the destroying of Latin service-books were not carried out everywhere with equal rigour, but otherwise the harrowing story of destruction alternating with restoration ran its course for more than a century.

The reign of Henry VIII saw no basic reform of the medieval liturgy. Though the introduction of the vernacular for a lesson at Matins and Vespers in 1543 and for the Litany in the following year was, in principle, a fundamental change, it affected only a small part of the rite and left the main edifice untouched. The Prymer, of which several new translations appeared, was not a liturgical book, and its history belongs to the sphere of private devotions. As such it aroused no controversy, but the First Prayer Book of 1549 was met in Devon and Cornwall with armed resistance, the people refusing to 'receive the new service, because it is but like a Christmas game'.[2] The Western Rebellion was suppressed, and the Second Prayer Book (1552) embodied further changes. In the following year Queen Mary restored

---

[1] Quoted in P. A. Scholes, *The Puritans and Music in England and New England* (London, 1934), p. 216.

[2] F. Procter and W. H. Frere, *A New History of the Book of Common Prayer* (London, 1932), p. 56.

the services as they had been 'most commonly used . . . in the last year of our late sovereign Lord King Henry VIII'.[1] This left the English Litany as a legal form, and it was in fact the only public service in English known to have been printed in her reign.[2]

Queen Elizabeth and her advisers, chiefly Cecil, though rightly anticipating opposition from 'men which be of the papist sect' and, at the other extreme, from those who would 'call the restoration *a cloaked papistry* or *a mingle-mangle*',[3] nevertheless succeeded, by three votes in the Lords, in re-establishing the Second Prayer Book, with some amendments, in 1559. But it was to remain a centre of controversy through the whole of our period. In an Injunction of 1559 the queen desired that in the 'divers Collegiate, and also some Parish-Churches' where there had been 'Livings appointed for the maintenance of men and children to use singing in the Church . . . no alterations be made of such assignments of Living'. The same Injunction allowed that 'in the beginning, or in the end of the Common prayers, either at Morning or Evening, there may be sung an Hymn, or suchlike song to the praise of Almighty God in the best sort of melody and Musick that may conveniently be devised, having respect that the sentence of [the] Hymn may be understanded and perceived'.[4] However, the term 'Hymn or suchlike song' left scope for differences of interpretation, and its performance was a permissive and not an essential part of the rite of Common Prayer.

PURITAN ATTACKS

The atmosphere of disputation and uncertainty in which services were carried on in the early years of Elizabeth may be judged from Bishop Grindal's report in 1565 on the state of affairs in his diocese of London: 'Some say the service and prayers in the chancel, others in the body of the church; some say the same in a seat made in the church, some in the pulpit with their faces to the people; some keep precisely to the order of the book, others intermeddle psalms in metre; . . . the Table standeth in the body of the church in some places, in others it standeth in the chancel', and so on.[5] The petition of the Puritan party in 1563 that 'the psalms appointed at common prayer be sung distinctly by all the congregation . . . and that all curious singing and playing of the organs may be removed' was narrowly defeated, and their Admonitions to Parliament in 1572, attacking the

[1] Ibid., p. 92.   [2] Ibid., p. 94.
[3] H. Gee, *The Elizabethan Prayer-Book and Ornaments* (London, 1902), pp. 196–7.
[4] *Injunctions Given by the Queen's Majesty* (London, 1559), no. 49.
[5] Gee, op. cit., p. 164.

Prayer Book as 'culled and picked out of that Popishe dunghill the Portuise and Masse boke, full of all abominations' and proposing the replacing of the Episcopal system by the Presbyterian,[1] initiated a copious controversy, with Thomas Cartwright as the chief figure on the Puritan side and John Whitgift and Richard Hooker on the Anglican. In the Fifth Book of his *Laws of Ecclesiastical Polity* (1597) Hooker wrote his eloquent defence of the place of music, in church and elsewhere, as

a thing which delighteth all ages, and beseemeth all states; a thing as seasonable in grief as in joy; . . . the reason hereof is an admirable facility which music hath to express and represent to the mind more inwardly than any other sensible mean, the very steps and inflections every way, the turns and varieties of all passions whereunto the mind is subject; . . . There is one [kind] that draweth to a marvellous grave and sober mediocrity; there is also that carrieth as it were into ecstasies, filling the mind with an heavenly joy, and for the time in a manner severing it from the body.

PERSISTENCE OF THE CATHOLIC RITES

In 1560 Walter Haddon's *Liber Precum publicarum*, a Latin translation of the Book of Common Prayer, was printed with a royal Injunction approving its use in the colleges of Oxford and Cambridge, and at Winchester and Eton. There is nothing to show that it was generally used, and Strype's comment that 'most of the colleges in Cambridge would not tolerate it, as being *the Pope's Dreggs*' probably represents the predominant attitude. In some parts of the country Romanism was strong, and there is no doubt that Mass was celebrated regularly in those large households which remained Catholic. In 1564 William Luson, a canon, and the vicars of Hereford entertained priests and some had Mass in their houses.[2] After the abortive rising of the northern Earls in 1569, when the new service books were destroyed and the old rites celebrated in Durham, John Brimley, the master of the choristers, deposed that 'he was twice at High Mass, but he song nott hym selff at them, but played at orgains, and dyd dyvers tymes help to sing Salvaes at Mattyns and Even songe: and plaid on the organes, and went in procession, as other dyd, after the Crosse'.[3] Following Pius V's excommunication of the Queen in 1570 the treatment of recusants became less tolerant, and about the same time

---

[1] Procter and Frere, op. cit., pp. 112–14.

[2] P. Hughes, *The Reformation in England*, iii (London, 1954), p. 124.

[3] *Depositions and other Ecclesiastical Proceedings from the Courts of Durham*, ed. J. Rains (London and Edinburgh, 1845), p. 149.

began the flow of Catholic missionaries from the English College at Douai (founded in 1568), who were received and held services in Catholic houses. That the Queen maintained a personal policy of distinguishing between recusancy and treason, as she did in the case of Byrd, is shown by her description of the Earl of Worcester, one of Byrd's patrons, as 'a stiff papist and a good subject'.[1]

THE JACOBEAN AND CAROLINE RITUALISTS

As soon as James I had shown by his answer to the Millenary Petition that he had no intention of being a Puritan, a new generation of ritual-minded churchmen began to exercise an increasing influence in the larger churches. The first leader of this movement was the saintly Lancelot Andrewes, Dean of Westminster at the accession and later Bishop successively of Chichester (1605), Ely (1609), and Winchester (1618), and also Dean of the Chapel Royal (1619). The adornment of buildings and the restoration of ceremonial and music were fostered particularly by William Juxon at St. John's College, Oxford, from 1621, and at St. Paul's, as Bishop of London from 1633; by John Cosin at Durham as Bishop Neil's chaplain and from 1624 as Canon, and at Peterhouse as Master from 1635; and most actively by William Laud as Juxon's predecessor at St. John's, as Bishop of St. David's (1621), of Bath and Wells (1626), of London (1628), and as Archbishop of Canterbury from 1633.

We have detailed accounts of the 'innovations' at Durham in a sermon delivered there in 1628 and in other writings by Canon Peter Smart,[2] who took a strictly Protestant position based on the Elizabethan Injunctions and Homilies, and was deprived and imprisoned for twelve years. Smart laid the responsibility for bringing in 'pompous ceremonies' at the door of Richard Neil, who from his enthronement in 1617 proceeded to 'countenance, cherish, and maintaine schismaticall, hereticall, and traiterous Arminians and Papists'; and he names here and elsewhere Cosin, Laud, Matthew Wren, and others as introducers of 'Altars, Images, Organs . . . and all manner of Massing furniture'.

[1] Quoted by E. H. Fellowes, *William Byrd* (London, 2nd ed., 1948), p. 36, from Lloyd's *State Worthies* (1670), p. 582.

[2] *The Vanitie & Downe-fall of Superstitious Popish Ceremonies* (Edinburgh, 1628); *A short Treatise of Altars, Altar-furniture, Altar-cringing, and Musick of all the Quire, Singing-men and Choristers . . .* (1629); *A Catalogue of Superstitious innovations . . . Brought into Durham Cathedrall by Bishop Neal . . .* (London, 1642); and *Canterburies Crueltie, coworking with His Prelaticall brethren . . .* (London, 1643). See also J. Buttrey, 'William Smith of Durham', *Music and Letters*, xliii (1962), p. 248.

THEIR MUSICAL 'INNOVATIONS'

Among the changes which so incensed Smart against Cosin in particular were that

the 6. of the clocke Service which was used to bee read onely, and not sung: he chaunts with Organs, Shackbuts and Cornets which yield an hydeous noyse . . . hee enjoynes all the people to stand up at the Nicene Creed . . . which he commands to be sung with Organs, Shackbuts and Cornets and all other instruments of Musicke, . . . He hath brought meere ballads and jigs into the Church, and commanded them to bee sung for Anthems: and among many others, the three Kings of Colen, JASPAR, MELCHIOR, and BALTHASER. Hee will not suffer so much as the holy Communion to bee administred without an hideous noyse of vocall and instrumentall Musicke, (the tunes whereof are all taken out of the Masse-booke).

According to Smart it had been the practice in cathedrals to have early morning prayers 'plainly read by the Minister, with a Psalm in the end, in a vulgar tune, which all the Congregation may sing together', and to sing a metrical psalm before and after a sermon, the preacher remaining in the pulpit. He censures the practice of 'multiplying unlawfull Anthemes, and disallowing lawfull Psalms-singing by the whole Congregation', so that the 'singing of Psalmes in the vulgar tunes within these five years [since 1627] hath quite been banished out of Durham Church, contrary to the practice and custome both of this and all other Cathedrall Churches'. It appears that one of his chief objections was to elaborate music at week-day services, for he admits that David had instruments

at the solemnities of Festivall dayes and Sabbaths. Therefore not every day in the week, nor thrice every day: they did not turn the hours of prayer into solemn services, with piping and chaunting, morning, and evening, and mid-day, as our new-fangled ceremony-mongers of late most audaciously attempted to do in this Church of Durham, and did so indeed the space of two years without authority, contrary to the Injunctions.

Other evidence tends to confirm the impression he conveys of the drabness of services in Elizabethan times, apart from the royal chapel and one or two colleges.[1] The royal choir was maintained at a high level, with about thirty-two gentlemen members, by the system of the monthly course, so that a certain number attended on 'workinge dayes' during their month of 'wayting in the Chappell' and all were

[1] The Mundum Books of King's College show regular payments from 1560–1 onwards for 'pryckyng' sets of 'prycksonge books', including in 1591–2 ten shillings to 'Mro. Hamond Informatori choristarum pro le suit of service De 8 parts ad usum Ecclesie' and the same in 1594–5 to 'Mro. Gibbins [i.e. Ellis Gibbons, elder brother of Orlando] for pricking 3 churche books of ten parts'.

present on Sundays and festivals.[1] Gentlemen who held a local appointment did not provide a deputy for it, as appears, for example, from
the statement of the Dean and Chapter of Rochester in answer to a
direction from Nathaniel Brent, Vicar-General for Laud's Visitation
of 1634: 'Mr. Coton, Mr. Stephens and the said Mr. West have been
dyvers tymes requyred by us to provyde able men to supplye their
places in our quyer, who have alwayes answered, that the deane of
His Majesties chappell did assuer them, that by His Majesties service
there, they were discharged from the servyce of all other quyers,
where they had places.' In this case the Dean and Prebendaries
promised to pay deputies out of their own stipends.[2]

In his Visitation of the cathedrals and colleges in his province, Laud
inquired from each in a series of Articles about the state of buildings
and precincts, the numbers in the Chapter and choir, and the ordering
of services.[3] The articles vary at times in details, so that Salisbury
alone was asked whether 'the voices be sorted every one in his place
soe that there be not more of tenors therein, which is an ordinary
voice, then there be of baces and counter-tenors, which doe best
furnish the quire; and whether have you in your quire a fair and
tuneable pair of organs and a skilfull organist to play thereon?' The
answers give a conspectus of the state of church music, labouring in
some places under the handicaps of insufficient endowments, incompetent singers, and neglected choristers, but also tell of efforts to
improve the standards of music and observance. Thus Rochester had
spent 'of late yeres, upon the fabrick of the church and makeing the
organes . . . above one thousand pounds', and prided itself that 'for
our church bookes . . . no church in England hath newer or fayerer,
for . . . all our pricksong bookes have been pricked newe and trewe,
and fayerlie bound . . . to the great charge of the church'. Christ
Church, New College, King's, and other colleges likewise spent large
sums about this time on paving, woodwork, hangings, and painting
in their chapels,[4] and this but a decade or so before a new wave of
Puritan iconoclasm was to engulf the English Church.

[1] E. F. Rimbault, *The Old Cheque-Book . . . of the Chapel Royal* (London, 1872),
pp. 71–3.
[2] Historical Manuscripts Commission, *Appendix to the 4th Report* (London, 1874),
p. 146.
[3] Ibid., pp. 124–58.
[4] In 1637–8, for example, New College, Oxford, paid 'Richard Hawkins painter for
guilding and painting 62 seates at 4s. 6d. the foote each seate conteyning 9 foote & each
buttresse at 2s . . . £126 3s' and to the same 'for guilding one round bottle in the quire
and 52 Antick seanes 333 starres and the casement about the pictures for pryming and
stopping the wainscott ut per billam £20 3s 5d'. The chapel expenses for that year totalled
£309 odd as compared with £59 odd the previous year (Bursars' Rolls).

ORGANS AND OTHER INSTRUMENTS

The revival of organ-building had begun before the end of the sixteenth century with instruments by John Chappington being installed at Westminster in 1596, at Magdalen in 1597, and at New College in 1598. Thomas Dallam built a new organ for King's in 1605–6, for Christ Church in 1608 and again in 1624–5, for Worcester in 1613, and for Wells in 1620, while Robert Dallam built the organs at Durham (1621), York (1632), St. Paul's, St. John's College, Cambridge (1635), and elsewhere.[1] Charles I had an organ in each of his chapels at Whitehall, St. James's, Hampton Court, Greenwich, and Richmond.[2] The use of other instruments to support the choir seems to have begun about 1600. The chorus of an anthem sung in the royal chapel in 1605 was 'filled with the help of musicall instruments',[3] and in the same year Christ Church bought 'two trebill cornets for the quire', the treasurer adding this precautionary note in the accounts: 'No precedent for the buying of their other instruments; and these 2 are the churches.'[4] There seems to be no direct evidence for the use of stringed instruments in churches, though they may well have been used in the chapels of the royal and other households to which string players were attached. There were cornetts with or without sackbuts in the choir of Worcester in 1619,[5] of Westminster in 1625 (at the funeral of King James),[6] and at Durham in Cosin's time, as we have seen, while the accounts of the Chapel Royal in 1634 have a payment for twelve surplices for wind players, for 'service in the Chappell'.[7] In the same year Canterbury replied to Laud's Visitation Article on the choir that 'in lieu of a deacon and subdeacon . . . are substituted two corniters and two sackbutters, whome we do most willingly maintaine for the decorum of our quire, though with greater charge then we might have done the other'.[8]

---

[1] For details of some of these see W. L. Sumner, *The Organ* (London, 1952), pp. 104, 112–15.

[2] H. C. de Lafontaine, *The King's Musick* (London, 1909), pp. 68–107 *passim*.

[3] Rimbault, op. cit., p. 168.

[4] I am grateful to W. G. Hiscock for this and other references from the Treasurer's Accounts; see also his *A Christ Church Miscellany* (Oxford, 1946), pp. 215–16. The use of cornetts with the *Te Deum* at the Queen's reception in 1566 (ibid., p. 166) conforms to medieval usage.

[5] Ivor Atkins, *The Early Occupants of the Office of Organist and Master of the Choristers of . . . Worcester* (London, 1918), p. 47.

[6] Lafontaine, op. cit., p. 58.

[7] Ibid., p. 90.

[8] Historical Manuscripts Commission (as above), p. 125.

THE END OF AN ERA

The Committee appointed in 1641 by the Long Parliament to consider 'all innovations in the church respecting religion' heard objections to 'singing the *Te Deum* cathedral-wise' and to introducing 'Latin Service in the Communion at Cambridge and Oxford', and a request 'to mend the imperfections of the metre in singing psalms and then to add lawful authority to have them publicly sung before and after sermons, and sometimes instead of the hymns of Morning and Evening Prayer'.[1] As the discussions developed, the Puritan element gained complete ascendancy. This chapter in the history of English church music closes with the Act of 3 January 1645, the day on which Laud's Attainder was passed in the Lords, abolishing the Book of Common Prayer in favour of the *Directory for the Public Worship of God in the Three Kingdoms of England, Scotland and Ireland*.

LAST YEARS OF THE SARUM RITE: MASS AND ANTIPHON

In the last years of the Sarum rite composers seem to have had little interest in writing large-scale *canto fermo* Masses. Almost the only example from this generation, not a felicitous one, is Marbeck's 'Per arma justitiae', which may have been written as early as 1531.[2] The 'Western Wynde' Masses of Christopher Tye and John Sheppard[3] are, like Taverner's on the same melody, sets of choral variations, while Thomas Tallis's 'Salve intemerata' is a *missa parodia* on his own antiphon.[4] The remainder are Lady-Masses or shorter Masses, some with names which do not imply the use of a *canto fermo* (Tye's 'Euge bone',[5] Sheppard's 'French Mass', and 'Be not afraid')[6] or seem to refer to a unifying theme not used in the orthodox *canto fermo* fashion (Sheppard's 'Cantate' and Richard Allwood's 'Praise him praiseworthy Christ full of mercy').[7] The Lady-Masses by

[1] Procter and Frere, op. cit., pp. 152, 154.

[2] Marbeck's polyphonic church music is printed in *Tudor Church Music*, x (London, 1929). He may have been at Windsor in 1531; see ibid. *Appendix* (London, 1948), p. 31.

[3] Both are in Brit. Mus. Add. 17802-5 (Gyffard part-books), almost certainly written during the reign of Queen Mary; see F. Ll. Harrison, *Music in Medieval Britain* (London, 1958), pp. 288-9.

[4] The Latin church music of Tallis is printed in *Tudor Church Music*, vi (London, 1928).

[5] Ed. G. E. P. Arkwright, *The Old English Edition*, x (London, 1893).

[6] In the Gyffard part-books.

[7] In Bodl. Mus. Sch. e. 376-81 (Forrest-Heather part-books), containing eighteen Masses. The last seven, including the two mentioned, were added by William Forrest, chaplain to Queen Mary and minor canon of Christ Church, Oxford. Allwood's Mass, with Thomas Ashewell's 'Ave Maria' Mass, has been printed by J. D. Bergsagel in *Early English Church Music*, i (London, 1963).

Sheppard (called 'Playnsong' because of its restricted rhythms) and Thomas Appleby,[1] and unnamed Masses by Tye[2] and Tallis, have the unifying device of a common opening for some or all of their movements. A Lady-Mass by William Whytbrook and two by William Mundy are based on the common-property melodies called 'squares',[3] used earlier by Ludford and others, while Kyries or Alleluias (or both) for the Lady-Mass were written by most of the composers mentioned, and by John Hake, Robert Okeland, Thomas Knyght, and Hyett.[4] There survive single verses, probably from complete *alternatim* settings, of Lady-Mass sequences by Tallis ('Euge caeli porta' from 'Ave praeclara') and Tye ('Tellus flumina' and 'Unde nostris eya', both canons on the plainsong, from 'Post partum').[5]

The composition of large votive antiphons seems, on the other hand, to have been continued in the last decade of Henry VIII and resumed under Mary. Besides examples in a manuscript of the fifteenforties by such composers as Arthur Chamberlayne, Marbeck, John Mason, Hugh Sturmys (an antiphon of St. Augustine, 'Exsultet in hac die') and Catcott (an Epiphany antiphon 'Trium regum'),[6] there are fine pieces in this genre by William Mundy[7] and Robert Parsons, whose fondness for energetic rhythms is well exemplified in this extract from 'O bone Jesu':[8]

Ex. 208

---

[1] In the Gyffard part-books.

[2] In Cambridge, Peterhouse, 40, 41, 31, 32 (the tenor book is missing), written between *c.* 1540 and 1547; for list of contents see Dom Anselm Hughes, *Catalogue of the Musical Manuscripts at Peterhouse* (Cambridge, 1953), pp. 2–3.

[3] Vol. III, p. 336. See also H. Baillie, 'Squares', *Acta Musicologica*, xxxii (1960), p. 178, and Bergsagel, 'An Introduction to Ludford', *Musica Disciplina*, xiv (1960), p. 118.

[4] The Lady-Mass music is in the Gyffard part-books.

[5] In Christ Church 45, written during the reign of Queen Elizabeth.

[6] In the Peterhouse MSS. The text set by Sturmys is in *Paléographie musicale*, xii (Tournai, 1922–5), pl. 316. For Catcott's text see *Horae Eboracenses*, ed. C. Wordsworth (Surtees Society, York, 1920), p. 74; some editions of the York and Sarum *Horae* have the heading 'An other prayer to the iij kynges of Colen'.

[7] Mundy's Latin Antiphons and Psalms have been printed by Harrison, *Early English Church Music*, ii (London, 1963).

[8] In Christ Church 984–8, which belonged originally to Robert Dow, benefactor of

Robert Whyte set 'Regina caeli' and 'Tota pulchra es' on their own plainsongs in the way normally used for responds.[1] Among the shorter votive antiphons Knyght's 'Sancta Maria', Christopher

the music at Christ's Hospital, and were compiled between 1581 and the early years of James I. The original note-values have been reduced by half in all the musical examples in this chapter.

[1] Whyte's sacred music is printed in *Tudor Church Music*, v (London, 1926).

Hoskins's 'Speciosa facta es' and Thomas Wright's 'Nesciens mater' are also on the homonymous plainsong, while Sheppard's lively 'Gaudete caelicolae' and Robert Johnson's 'Gaude Maria' are in imitative style, and Philip Alcock's 'Salve regina' is in a manner verging on 'playnsong'.[1]

MAGNIFICAT, RESPOND, AND HYMN

Of the seven Magnificats in the Peterhouse collection, only two are by composers whose work did not appear in earlier manuscripts, Appleby and John Dark.[2] Since the tenor book is missing it is impossible to say whether they were based on the plainsong or the faburden. The latter method may have been going out; though Tallis followed it, Mundy, Sheppard, and Whyte used the tone itself, and Stonings used a two-note *canto fermo* which is simpler than any of the tones.[3]

Quite the most vigorous of the liturgical forms in this period was the respond, especially in the hands of Sheppard[4] and Tallis. As foreshadowed by Taverner, the choral parts of responds were treated in elaborate polyphony woven around the plainsong, normally in the tenor.[5] Certain responds of special ceremonial importance were still set in the older fashion, though Sheppard composed 'Inmanus tuas' in both ways.[6] In hymns the work of these two composers is again outstanding, while there are good examples, unfortunately without their tenor parts, by Mundy and Parsons.[7] Hymns were set for *alternatim* performance, the polyphony beginning with the second verse; the melody is usually in the treble, in monorhythm or in a consistent rhythmic scheme, with occasional ornamentation, particularly at cadences.

OTHER RITUAL FORMS

Among other ritual forms in this period is a fine anonymous setting of the St. Matthew Passion.[8] The Lamentations by Tallis and Whyte

---

[1] All these are in the Gyffard part-books.

[2] Hitherto unidentified; he was a vicar-choral of Exeter from c. 1519 to c. 1569.

[3] The settings by Mundy, Sheppard, and Stonings are in the Gyffard books. On the use of faburden in settings of the *Magnificat*, see Harrison, 'Faburden in Practice', *Musica Disciplina*, xvi (1962), pp. 20–2 and 32–4.

[4] A selection of Sheppard's responds is printed by Harrison in *John Sheppard: Sechs Responsorien* (*Das Chorwerk*, lxxxiv) (Wolfenbüttel, 1960).

[5] See Vol. III, p. 340–2.

[6] See Harrison, *Music in Medieval Britain* (London, 1958), pp. 371–2; one of the settings in *Das Chorwerk*, lxxxiv.

[7] In Christ Church 979–83, written in the late sixteenth century; the initials I.B. on the binding may stand for John Baldwin.   [8] In the Gyffard books.

are among the greatest in their kind, Whyte's imposing six-part setting
being designed with three- and four-part sections like the greater Mass
and antiphon, while Osbert Parsley's is unusual in treating the liturgical reading-tone as *canto fermo*.[1] Composition on the plainsong or its
faburden was the almost invariable method of setting other ritual
items. On the plainsong are John Redford's lively 'Christus resurgens',[2] Mason's Lenten antiphon 'O rex gloriose',[3] an anonymous
'Vidi aquam',[2] and Sheppard's six-part *Te Deum* for men, in his best
style, as may be judged from this verse:[4]

Ex.209

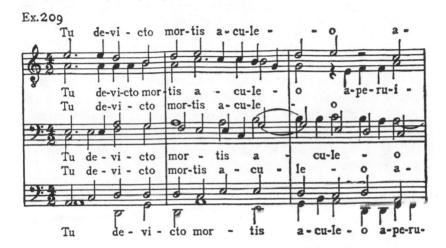

[1] Parsley's sacred music is printed in *Tudor Church Music*, x.
[2] In the Gyffard books.
[3] In the Peterhouse books; the tenor can be supplied from the plainsong.
[4] Christ Church 979–83; tenor supplied from the plainsong.

The first of an anonymous group of four settings of 'Asperges' in the Gyffard part-books is on the faburden, as are Sheppard's psalm 'Laudate pueri' with the Alleluia antiphon, one of his two settings of the antiphon 'Libera nos',[1] and the setting of the psalm 'In exitu Israel' with the Alleluia antiphon made jointly by Sheppard, Mundy, and Byrd (most likely Thomas).[2]

Sacred polyphony in England was more closely related to the ritual and to the votive acts of Mass and antiphon than it was on the Continent. Only two pieces in the Gyffard books cannot be placed in any of the categories which have been mentioned: Philip Van Wilder's 'Pater noster' and Mundy's canonic 'Exsurge Christe',[3] a collect against heresy. The term 'motet' seems not to have been current before Morley defined it, in the *Plaine and Easie Introduction*, as comprehending 'all grave and sober music', and gave a wrong account of its origin.[4] Orlando Gibbons used it in the title of his secular collection of 1612, John Amner applied it to some of the pieces in his *Sacred Hymnes* (1615), while several of Martin Peerson's secular *Mottects or Grave Chamber Musique* (1630) are not what we should normally term 'grave and sober'.

PSALMS

In contrast to the total absence from sources before 1547 of complete Latin psalms (apart from a few special items of the Processional), there is a considerable number among the works of Whyte (with

---

[1] In Christ Church, 979–83.   [2] See Harrison, op. cit., pp. 289, 357.
[3] The anonymous last keyboard piece in the *Mulliner Book* (*Musica Britannica*, i), entitled 'Tres partes in una', is a transcription of this.
[4] Ed. R. A. Harman (London, 1952), pp. 292–3.

twelve), Mundy (with ten), Sheppard, Tye, Tallis, Parsons, and Parsley.[1] Mundy used a special version and the others the Sarum text of the Psalter.[2] It is most unlikely that many of these pieces were written after 1559; most were probably composed in Queen Mary's reign, perhaps under the impulse of a new awareness of their cultivation on the Continent. The surviving examples constitute the largest form of the period, some having the bisectional layout of the greater votive antiphon. This heritage is most apparent in those which have further subdivisions into 'full' and 'solo' sections, and in some of Whyte's and single examples by Parsley and Mundy which keep the convention of triple measure for the first main section and duple for the second. Others follow the more 'modern' method of a continuous full treatment in imitative style with occasional homorhythmic and antiphonal phrases. Whyte has some passages, such as 'et omne consilium tuum confirmet' in 'Exaudiat te Dominus', which rival Taverner in floridity of line, while Mundy is able to achieve intensity of expression without relaxation of linear energy, as in this instance, from his 'Miserere':[3]

[1] See the 'Check List of English Psalm Settings' in Joseph Kerman, 'The Elizabethan Motet: a Study of Texts for Music', *Studies in the Renaissance*, ix (New York, 1962), p. 306. William Mundy's 'In Aeternum' should be added to the list.

[2] Sarum used the 'Gallican' Psalter, i.e. the second, revised, Psalter of St. Jerome, usually known as the Vulgate version. This was officially adopted in the revised Breviary of Pius V (1568). The Psalter in Queen Elizabeth's Latin Prayer Book is yet another version.

[3] Royal College of Music 2035.

Parsley's 'Conserva me' has confident lines, some examples of canonic imitation, and an Amen which begins with the *ostinato* figure which Aston used in his 'Gaude virgo mater Christi'.[1] The psalms of Tallis and Tye, though technically irreproachable, lack the rhythmic vigour and melodic resource of those of Whyte, Mundy, and Parsons. Sheppard, too, adopted a markedly less forceful style in his psalms than in his other Latin works.

LATER LATIN MUSIC: TALLIS AND BYRD

It is clear that one of the purposes of the publication in 1575 of the *Cantiones, quae ab argumento sacrae vocantur*, the first English print of music to Latin texts, was to foster an international reputation for the composers, 'autoribus Thoma Tallisio & Guilielmo Birdo Anglis'.[2] Its dedication to the queen, as one who excelled 'vel vocis elegantia, vel digitorum agilitate', was followed by tributes in Latin verse designed to introduce the leaders of English music to the world of culture and learning. Thus Richard Mulcaster, author of books on education and first headmaster at Merchant Taylors' School, where Edmund Spenser and Lancelot Andrewes were among his pupils, observed that Music, regarded both by antiquity and by the present time as holding the first place in the training of youth and the shaping of the state, and dignified by the pleasure and participation of the Royal Majesty, had already been honoured amongst other nations by the publication of skilful compositions. England, who had suffered her music to remain hidden, now allowed her offspring to see the light and, thanks to the printing-press, to be submitted to the judgement of craftsmen abroad. So Tallis and Byrd, whom she had chosen as her leaders, might earn an honoured name wherever the great fame of

---

[1] *Tudor Church Music*, x, p. 96.

[2] Byrd's contribution is printed in *Tudor Church Music*, ix (London, 1928) and with facsimiles of the preliminary matter in *The Collected Works of William Byrd*, ed. E. H. Fellowes, i (London, 1937).

music extended. Similarly Sir Ferdinand Heybourne (Ferdinand Richardson), a member of the queen's household and himself a composer and with Byrd a fellow-pupil of Tallis, pictures Music honoured among foreign peoples through the work of Orlandus (Lassus), Gombardus (Gombert), Clemens and Alphonsus (Alfonso Ferrabosco) and becoming angry that Britons should prove unworthy of her gifts by being unwilling to publish any books. If the right to judge, he says, were to be given to 'inexperienced youths', he would dare to affirm that these *cantiones* were 'created by inspired pens' and were 'worthy to circulate throughout the world'.

Tallis's contribution to the joint publication is on the whole less uniform in style than Byrd's and more retrospective in its choice of liturgical categories. Since the plainsongs of his hymns and responds agree with the Sarum versions, it may well be that these pieces were composed before 1559. On the other hand the plainsong of Byrd's only *canto fermo* respond here, 'Libera me Domine', differs in significant respects from the Sarum form, which may be seen in the settings by Whyte and Parsons. Tallis's setting of the hymn 'O nata lux' makes a definite departure from earlier practice by treating the first two verses only, as a continuous and virtually homophonic composition independent of the plainsong.[1] He was probably following Byrd in this, for the piece is in a style which Byrd used in a more elaborate form for his hymns 'Siderum rector' and 'O lux beata Trinitas'. The latter is a freely composed setting in *coro spezzato* manner, in which the doxology is cleverly worked out with three canonic parts in such a way as to maintain the overlapping *coro spezzato* effect.

Comparison of the freely composed pieces by the two composers reveals Byrd's abler handling of the imitative style. In several cases, among them 'Absterge Domine' and 'Derelinquat impius', Tallis makes little or no attempt to create a flowing texture by continuing some voices while bringing in a new point; and he is apt to write a literal repeat of the working of a point rather than extend it. The two settings of 'Salvator mundi' come nearest to a continuous texture, the second being a special case, with superius and tenor in close canon. Tallis was not at ease with the technique of through-imitation, probably because of his early training in the differentiated style, of which his 'Gaude gloriosa' is one of the supreme examples. It is difficult to agree with Fellowes's opinion that the 'motets of Tallis published in the *Cantiones sacrae* of 1575 show a marked advance in style

---

[1] The older *alternatim* practice is shown in 'Adesto nunc propitius' (second and fourth verses of 'Salvator mundi') recorded in *The History of Music in Sound* (H.M.V.), iv.

compared with the work of pre-Elizabethan composers'.[1] It would rather seem that Tallis found some difficulty in adjusting his technique to changes in the style and function of church music which took place when he must have been nearing fifty. But of the greatness of his best work there can be no question. In the *Cantiones* there is ample testimony to this in 'In ieiunio et fletu', with its deeply expressive chromaticism, in the ingenious craftsmanship of the canonic essay 'Miserere nostri', and in the lengthy setting of 'Suscipe quaeso', with its contrasts of extended imitative lines and pointed antiphonal dialogue. The towering achievement of 'Spem in alium', where similar contrasts are consummately used in the medium of eight five-part choirs, attests his eventual mastery.

In the Dedication of the first volume of the *Gradualia* (1605) to the Earl of Northampton, Byrd spoke of his feeling for sacred texts, which had, in his experience, 'such a reserve of hidden power that to one who thinks upon divine things and earnestly turns them over in his mind, the fittest possible measures . . . come at once and as if unaided'. This lively response to the inner meaning of sacred words was the motive force behind the subtlety and variety of Byrd's methods. His ability to infuse homophonic writing with linear interest is manifested in the hymns already mentioned and in his first piece in the 1575 collection, the very expressive setting of 'Emendemus in melius'. The immediately striking characteristic of his pieces in imitative style is the apposition of his points and the flexibility of their use. For example, the first point in 'Libera me Domine et pone' illustrates the expressive effect of the reverted point and the free handling of the word 'Domine', which is made a linear accessory to the point. The next motive, on 'et pone me iuxta te', is an unbroken line, and Byrd twice makes a contrapuntal overlap of these two points. He may also devise a relation of 'double descant'[2] between two elements of a single point, as in the first sentence of the second part ('Dies mei transierunt'). The final sentence is worked out in a contrapuntal complex of the three motives arising from the words, in a variety of unions, e.g. Ex. 211 (opposite), and the close is made on a rising form of the 'spero lucem' figure. The pursuit of such contrapuntal relations within sections is an important factor in the unusual length and unflagging interest of Byrd's unfolding of his points. At times his method approaches the effect of subject and regular countersubject, as at the beginning of

---

[1] *Grove's Dictionary of Music and Musicians* (5th ed.), viii (London, 1954), p. 296.
[2] Morley's term for double counterpoint (*Plaine and Easie Introduction*, ed. cit., p. 188).

'Da mihi auxilium', and in its third ('aut aliquid saltem') and final ('ut plangam') sections.

Ex. 211

As counterpoise to such exercises, Byrd has occasional recourse to marked changes in texture, as in this striking passage in the six-part 'Attollite portas':

Ex. 212

and in the chordal antiphony he uses, for example, in 'Tribue Domine', there for a text concerning the Trinity. These and similar sections seem prompted by the words rather than by the special treatment of a liturgical category, as in the hymns which have been mentioned.

Byrd's unit of chordal movement is the semibreve (i.e. minim in the examples as printed here), the normal basis of rhythm at the time, but he is at least as enterprising as any of his contemporaries in his handling of the smaller subdivisions. In the 1575 *Cantiones* he frequently has two quavers, though never more, and only for a special effect (as for 'conturbat' in 'Peccantem me quotidie') the successive dotted rhythms so favoured by Parsons. He is more advanced in his use of the syncopated minim, which may be a feature of a point, as for 'dissipatae sunt' in 'Libera me Domine et pone', and of the minim as the unit, either temporarily, as in Ex. 212 (shown as crotchets), or throughout a piece, as in the hymns.

The most striking examples of dissonance here are the collisions or near-misses between the major and minor third of a chord, an idiom which had a firmly rooted tradition in English polyphony. The collision produces either a diminished octave, as in 'Domine secundum actum', or an augmented unison, as with the first point of 'Attollite portas'. Perhaps more remarkable in their historical context are the diminished fourth in the point on 'Ideo deprecor', the *secunda pars* of 'Domine secundum actum', and the unorthodox treatment of the suspension in the last point of the *prima pars* in the same work:

Ex. 213

BYRD'S *CANTIONES* AND MASSES

Byrd's overt purpose in publishing further books of *Cantiones* was to print a correct text of his works, in view of what he calls the hodge-podge ('farrago') of faulty manuscript copies in circulation.[1] The further object of providing music for Catholic services at home and abroad cannot be doubted, and if the Masses may, on bibliographical evidence, be dated *c.* 1588 or later they too were part of the enterprise at this stage. A ritual purpose for the *Cantiones* is suggested by Byrd's provision of the liturgical return in responds such as 'Laetentur caeli', where it is written out, 'Recordare Domine', where it is given a new setting, and 'Aspice Domine', the plainsong of which deviates considerably from the Sarum form.

The chief developments in style are more frequent recourse to *coro spezzato* treatment, to chromaticism for expressive purposes, and to groups of quavers for appropriate depiction of a text. A special instance of the antiphonal dialogue which occurs in many pieces is 'Infelix ego', where the questioning passages of the text are given particular poignancy, while the brilliant 'Laudibus in sanctis' brings linear and chordal styles into sharp contrast, heightened by hemiola rhythms on two levels. Chromaticism and livelier rhythms are equally manifestations of a deep response to words. The chord on A flat for 'desolata' in 'Vide Domine', the augmented sixth for 'deserta' in 'Ne irascaris', and the many E flats in the context of the first mode in 'Haec dicit Dominus' are examples of the former, the treatment of

---

[1] Dedication of the 1589 set, in facsimile in *The Collected Works of William Byrd*, ii (London, 1937), p. viii. The 1591 *Cantiones* are reprinted ibid. iii.

'exultate et laetemur' in 'Haec dies',[1] of the latter. The word 'repente' in 'Vigilate' and the Alleluia of 'In resurrectione Tua' both have groups of four and five quavers, while the 'exultet' of the latter is one of several instances of a single word set to a brief point in crotchets. Nor did Byrd hesitate to write motives which approach the madrigalesque for such words as 'circuitus', 'persequere', 'exsurge', and 'dormientes'.

The *cantiones* which Byrd allowed to remain in manuscript[2] include his Lamentations, a single lesson in three sections with a remarkable vocalize on the Hebrew letter *Teth*, in the manner of Whyte, though less vocal in style. There are also three complete psalms, two of which, 'Ad Dominum cum tribularer' and 'Domine quis habitabit', are especially fine, and some *canto fermo* settings of responds and hymns.

No title-pages of Byrd's Masses[3] exist, nor do surviving catalogues determine their dates of publication.[4] Nothing in their style or technique makes it impossible that they should have been written well before 1588, though the composer may have been deliberately conservative in his approach. He conforms to earlier practice in the use of common openings, most consistently in the five-part Mass, and departs from it in including the *Kyrie*, hitherto set only in the Lady-Mass.

THE *GRADUALIA*

Byrd's 'carmina cygnea' in the field of Latin music, the two volumes of *Gradualia*[5] (1605, 1607; second edition of both, 1610), were unequivocally for the Catholic rite, and were dedicated to Catholic patrons. Together they provide the Propers for important festivals and for the Lady-Mass for the seasons, some music for the offices, including hymns for the commemorative Office of the Virgin, and several *cantiones*, such as 'Unam petii' and 'Plorans plorabit', which have no special liturgical relevance. Like some of the earlier *cantiones* they have texts which might well express the sentiments of the Catholic community in England. Since neither of the modern editions shows the liturgical categories of the individual pieces, it is not made clear that the direction in the original print for the return

---

[1] Recorded in *The History of Music in Sound*, iv.

[2] Printed *Collected Works*, viii, ix (London, 1939), and *Tudor Church Music*, ix.

[3] Reprinted *Tudor Church Music*, ix, *Collected Works*, i.

[4] See, lower, Peter Clulow, 'Publication Dates for Byrd's Latin Masses', *Music and Letters*, xlvii (1966), p. 1.

[5] Reprinted *Tudor Church Music*, vii (London, 1927), *Collected Works*, iv–vii (London, 1938).

of the introit 'Rorate' after the psalm-verse and 'Gloria patri' must in fact be applied to all the introits, which are of course the only pieces to have the *Gloria*. Byrd seldom made two settings of a text where one would serve; thus he has indicated that the setting of 'Eructavit' as the psalm-verse of 'Salve sancta parens' is to be used, with its 'Gloria patri', both for 'Vultum tuum' and for the Gradual 'Speciosus', where he has supplied the further text 'Lingua mea' to complete the verse. Though not indicated, a similar procedure must be understood in a number of other instances, as in the Proper for the Purification, where the Introit 'Suscepimus' is also to be sung for the Gradual as far as the words 'fines terrae', where a complete stop is provided, after which the verse 'Sicut audivimus' follows. It is evident that Byrd intended each Gradual and Alleluia to be sung as a continuous whole, the repeat of the Gradual after its verse being omitted. In some cases he attached the beginning of the Alleluia directly to the end of the Gradual verse (as in 'Benedicta et venerabilis' with the verse 'Virgo Dei genitrix'), following this with the Alleluia verse (in this case 'Felix es') and the repeat of the Alleluia to new music. In others he wrote the Gradual and Alleluia as a continuous piece, as in 'Timete Dominum' with the Alleluia 'Venite ad me' and 'Oculi omnium' with 'Caro mea'. It goes without saying that all the Alleluia sections are an integral part of the liturgical text; where an Alleluia is used only in the Easter season a separate setting follows, as in the Offertory 'Beata es' and the Communion 'Beata viscera'.[1]

In accordance with their ritual forms, most of the pieces in the *Gradualia* are in relatively short sections, and their points of imitation are not developed to the length of those in the *Cantiones*, so that Byrd's technique of unfolding a contrapuntal complex has little play. With very few exceptions, the verses of Introits and Graduals are for three voices, the other sections being for four, five, or six. Apart from the use at one point in the original of the word 'Chorus',[2] it would be safe to say on liturgical grounds that the verses are to be sung with one voice to a part. They are consistently imitative in style. Contrasts of texture, though on a small scale, are exploited both within and between sections, while *coro spezzato* treatment can have only momentary, but none the less telling occurrence, as in 'Beata virgo', in the respond 'O magnum mysterium', and in the Alleluia 'Ave Maria'.

[1] For a full discussion of the liturgical order of the *Gradualia*, see J. L. Jackman, 'Liturgical Aspects of Byrd's *Gradualia*', *The Musical Quarterly*, xlix (1963), p. 17.

[2] Between the Gradual and Alleluia of the Mass of Christmas Day is printed 'Chorus sequitur'.

And Byrd shows as full an awareness as before of the moving effect of linear homophony, notably in 'Justorum animae' and 'Ave verum'.

Plainsong is rarely an element in the melodic lines, though there is an example of *canto fermo* setting in 'Christus resurgens', and motives derived from the chant are used in its verse 'Dicant nunc' and at the openings of 'Puer natus' and 'Nobis datus'. The most advanced features of the style of the *Gradualia* are the more frequent use of small note-values and the occasional use of melodic sequence. There are many instances of two crotchets or a dotted crotchet and quaver having separate syllables, more particularly in the Second Book and the three-part pieces of the First Book. At first sight the latter group seem very up-to-date in style, with their crisp homophony and short thrusting points, but this impression is somewhat modified by a comparison with Byrd's earlier settings of hymns, the liturgical category of four of these pieces, and with the hymns of Ferrabosco.[1] Byrd also applied this style to good effect in appropriate choruses of the Passion. Both books show a certain development in florid figuration, though it remains a minor element in the melodic style. Groups of four or more quavers are used both for incidental 'ornamentation' and for the depiction of words, as for 'Alleluia' in 'Alleluia: Quae lucescit',[2] for 'velociter scribentis' in 'Speciosus forma' and for 'catenas' in 'Solve iubente'. There seems to be only one instance, probably unique in Byrd's Latin music, of a pair of semiquavers, in 'Hodie Christus natus est'.

In his Latin music, which he certainly considered the most important part of his work, Byrd shows himself endowed to the point of genius with vitality of imagination, wealth of craftsmanship, and a meticulous sense of detail. He was without question the key figure in the continuance of the great tradition of vocal polyphony in England, a path he pursued from firm conviction, both religious and artistic. Though his style is self-sufficient in its mastery, it is tempting to speculate what it may have owed to his continental contemporaries. Music by Lassus, mostly secular, was printed in England in 1570 and later,[3] and there are motets by him and by Clemens non Papa, Gombert, Créquillon, and Palestrina in English manuscripts written in

---

[1] See below, p. 493.

[2] The antiphon to the Magnificat on Holy Saturday; the opening words 'Vespere autem sabbati' are sung by the celebrant. The Alleluia properly belongs to the end of the preceding psalm 'Laudate Dominum'.

[3] See Kerman, 'An Elizabethan Edition of Lassus', *Acta Musicologica*, xxvii (1955), p. 71.

Byrd's lifetime.[1] As a young prodigy he may have met de Monte during the latter's English sojourn in 1554–5, and we are told that in 1583–4 they exchanged compositions, Byrd responding to de Monte's 'Super flumina' with the eight-part 'Quomodo cantabimus', with three parts in canon.[2] The composers whom Heybourne mentioned in 1575 were Lassus, Gombert, Clemens, and Ferrabosco. On the level of mere choice of texts Byrd in 1575 has nothing in common with Gombert or Clemens, but five of his texts in that publication had previously been set by Lassus. Byrd's 'Domine secundum actum' is in part a reworking of Ferrabosco's 'Domine non secundum peccata'.[3] Byrd's relation to Ferrabosco was without doubt one of the closest and most fruitful in his musical life.

FERRABOSCO, MORLEY, AND OTHERS

Alfonso Ferrabosco the elder had entered the service of Queen Elizabeth by 1562 and was in England, apart from a journey of a year or so to France and Italy, until 1578. There is no lack of evidence that Byrd and he pursued musical interests together. Morley tells us that 'in a virtuous contention in love' they both made settings of the 'Miserere' plainsong, 'each making other censor of that which they had done'.[4] Ferrabosco has been judged a routine madrigal composer, though important on the English scene; his church music has been little noticed.[5] Two points only, the solidity and expressiveness of his motets, and the particular style of his hymns, can be briefly touched upon here. He is capable of thematic distinction, as in the opening of 'Ad te levavi', where the first six notes rise through a fifth and seventh to a tenth, and in its *secunda pars*, 'Miserere nostri', where the first point falls by step through a ninth, as well as of the ardent supplication of the beginning of 'Ad Dominum cum tribularer':[6]

---

[1] In 1591 John Baldwin mentions Ferrabosco, Marenzio, de Monte, Lassus, Créquillon, Rore, and Andrea (Gabrieli); see E. H. Fellowes, *William Byrd* (London, 2nd ed. 1948), pp. 237–8.

[2] See ibid., p. 106 (though the evidence dates from the mid-eighteenth century).

[3] See Kerman, 'The Elizabethan Motet', p. 291.

[4] *A Plaine and Easie Introduction*, ed. cit., p. 202. Each wrote forty ways, as appears from the title of *Medulla Musicke*, licensed in 1603, of which no copy is extant (see Fellowes, op. cit., p. 174.)

[5] A working list of sacred music by the two Ferraboscos, with sources, by G. E. P. Arkwright was printed in *The Musical Antiquary*, iv (1912), p. 45; see also Hugo Botstiber, 'Musicalia in der New York Public Library', *Sammelbände der internationalen Musikgesellschaft*, iv (1903), p. 742, and Bertram Schofield and Thurston Dart, 'Tregian's Anthology', *Music and Letters*, xxxii (1951), p. 211.

[6] Christ Church 78–82 and 463–7, written early in the seventeenth century.

Ex. 214

A more surprising aspect of his musical ideas appears in 'Posuisti tenebras', the seventh part of his tremendous setting in eleven sections of the psalm 'Benedic anima mea'. He begins with a point in the modern E major and takes it to F sharp major before making his way back to a cadence on F (Ex. 215 (i)). In the following verse but one he portrays in sound the dawn and the gathering of the 'beasts of the forest' (Ex. 215 (ii)):[1]

Ex. 215
(i)

[1] Christ Church 78–82 and 463–7.

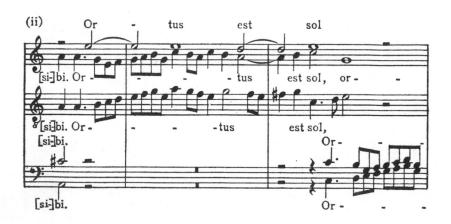

Ferrabosco wrote several settings of hymns in the same style as that used by Byrd for the two in the 1575 *Cantiones* and the five in the *Gradualia*. They are freely composed pieces in a basically chordal style with clearly patterned rhythms, radically different both from the earlier English hymns and from the continental, as exemplified by Palestrina, among others. No precedence as between Byrd and Ferrabosco can be suggested, but the equivalence of method may be judged by comparing the examples by Byrd with Ferrabosco's 'Ecce iam noctis':[1]

Ex. 216

[1] Christ Church 78–82.

Lu - cis au - ro - ra   ru - ti-lans co - ru - scat:

o - mnes

Ni - si-bus to - tis ro - gi - te-mus   o - mnes Cun-

o - mnes

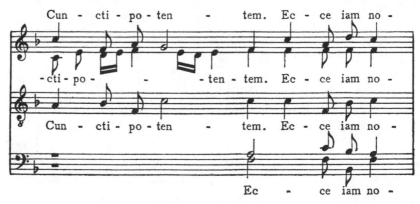

Cun - cti - po - ten - tem. Ec - ce iam no -

-cti - po - ten - tem. Ec - ce iam no -

Cun - cti - po - ten - tem. Ec - ce iam no -

Ec - ce iam no -

-ctis te - nu - a - tur um - bra: Lu - cis au - ro -

-ctis   te - nu - a - tur um - bra:

-ctis   te - nu-a-tur um-bra; Lu - cis   au - ro -

-ctis   te - nu - a - tur um - bra: Lu - cis au - ro -

The effect of such a musician on Byrd cannot have been slight, nor can their combined influence on Morley, whose Latin works,[1] apart from the four illustrative pieces in the *Plaine and Easie Introduction*,[2] may have been written before 1583. It has been suggested that before that date Morley was a Roman Catholic.[3] From 1583 to 1587, however, he was master of the choristers at Norwich Cathedral.[4] Between 1587 and 1590 he moved to London, and began the career which was to make him the champion of the Italian madrigal and the chief English exponent of its style. His 'Domine Dominus noster' and 'Domine non est exaltatum', both written in 1576 at the age of nineteen, are quite cliché- and cadence-ridden, though each is a smooth enough essay in style. In the two Marian-antiphons 'Gaude Maria'[5]

---

[1] *Thomas Morley: Collected Motets*, ed. H. K. Andrews and T. Dart (London, 1959).

[2] Including the fine 'Agnus Dei' recorded in *The History of Music in Sound*, iv.

[3] See David Brown, 'Thomas Morley and the Catholics: Some Speculations', *Monthly Musical Record*, lxxxix (1959), p. 53; Dart, 'Morley and the Catholics: Some Further Speculations', ibid., p. 89; and David Brown, 'The Styles and Chronology of Thomas Morley's Motets', *Music and Letters*, xli (1960), p. 216. Also ibid., xlii (1961), p. 198.   [4] See ibid., xlii (1961), p. 97.

[5] The text is undoubtedly the antiphon, as Brown suggests. The underlay should take account of the gamut-pun *so-la* in the first part, particularly as Morley used the similar, and long-standing, pun *ut sol* in the second part; neither part needs a final Alleluia.

and 'Virgo prudentissima', joined as *prima* and *secunda* parts of one work, there are both exuberance and flow, while in 'De profundis' and 'Laboravi in gemitu' Morley proves himself fully worthy of his master in the pertinence of the themes and his handling of counterpoint and texture.

Among others who composed to Latin words in Elizabethan times were William Daman, John Baldwin, Nathaniel Giles, Nicholas Strogers, and John Mundy. Daman came from the Netherlands between 1561 and 1565 to enter the service of Thomas Sackville, Lord Buckhurst, and was by 1582–3 in the Queen's service. He may have played some part in acquainting English musicians with sacred music from the Netherlands, though his printed works are decidedly Protestant.[1] Nothing is known for certain about Strogers's life, but the others were all in the royal service. To Baldwin as copyist (as composer he was a minor talent) we owe an anthology of Latin music of the century, some otherwise unknown.[2] With the Jacobean revival of ritual practice a few members of the new generation wrote Latin works, among them Alfonso Ferrabosco II and Thomas Lupo, both of the royal household, John Wilbye,[3] Thomas Weelkes, John Milton (father of the poet), and the versatile Thomas Ravenscroft. Ferrabosco was the most productive of these, and could reach to his father's high level of craftsmanship and expression:[4]

Ex. 217

[1] His 'Miserere nostri' was printed by G. E. P. Arkwright in *The Old English Edition*, xxi (London, 1898), p. 35.   [2] Brit. Mus. Royal 24. d. 2.

[3] His 'Homo natus de muliere' and 'Ne reminiscaris' (for solo voice and instruments) are printed in Arkwright, op. cit., pp. 24–34.

[4] Christ Church 78–82 and 463–7; there anonymous, but ascribed to Alfonso II in the Sambrooke MS. in New York (see Botstiber, op. cit., p. 742). Ferrabosco's 'O nomen Jesu' was printed in *The Musical Antiquary*, iv (1912), p. 50.

A conservative style of Latin music was maintained in this and the Caroline period, when the amount of newly composed Latin music was small; there are examples by Martin Peerson, Richard Nicholson, and George Kirby. At Peterhouse during the mastership of Wren (1632) and Cosin (1635) the use of Latin was partly restored, and the choir's part-books, though mainly for the liturgy in English, contain a fair proportion of Latin works by Tallis, Tye, Byrd, Parsons, Strogers, Robert Ramsey,[1] and Thomas Wilson (then organist), among others; and about 1640 William Child composed for Cosin a Latin *Te Deum* and *Jubilate*.

To what extent the Latin music of Peter Philips and Richard Deering, both Catholic emigrés, entered into the musical life of their own country before the Puritan revolution it is hard to say. Philips left England in 1582[2] and his church music was printed at Antwerp from 1612 onwards. Henry Peacham tells us that he 'sent us over many excellent Songs, as well Motets as Madrigals: he affecteth altogether the *Italian* veine'.[3] Though Deering returned in 1625 to serve in the Catholic chapel of Queen Henrietta Maria after publishing sacred music at Antwerp in 1617 and 1618, it is unlikely that his Latin music was much known outside court circles until the Commonwealth and after.[4] In pieces for four and more voices the 'Italian

[1] Ramsey's 'O sapientia' is printed in Hughes, *Musical Manuscripts at Peterhouse*, p. 73.

[2] See A. G. Petti, 'Peter Philips, Composer and Organist: 1561–1628', *Recusant History*, iv, no. 2 (1957).

[3] In *The Compleat Gentleman* (1622); the section on music is reprinted in Oliver Strunk, *Source Readings in Music History* (New York, 1950), p. 331. Philips's 'Ascendit Deus', from the *Cantiones* published at Antwerp in 1612, is reprinted in *Tudor Church Music*, octavo ed., no. 6.

[4] John Playford printed a volume of *Cantica Sacra* for two and three voices, with *basso continuo*, in 1662.

veine' in both composers seems related in style to Giovanni Gabrieli's *Sacrae symphoniae* of 1597,[1] and in those for two or three voices to the work of such composers as Banchieri and Viadana.[2]

THE EARLIEST MUSIC FOR THE ENGLISH LITURGY

The first music directly connected with the English Reformation is in the *Goostly Psalmes and Spirituall Songes* by Miles Coverdale, printed about 1543.[3] Both words and tunes (the book has melodies only) were adapted from Lutheran sources, which proved to be the work's undoing, for in 1546, four months before Henry VIII's death, Coverdale's 'Great' Bible and his *Goostly Psalmes* were among the 'heretical' books burnt at Paul's Cross. Meanwhile, in 1544 Cranmer produced his *Letanie with Suffrages* to a 'devout and solemn note', which replaced the peregrinating processions of the Sarum use.[4] It was printed in the 'playnsong' notation already in use for some fifty years, and was at once provided with settings for three, four, and five voices.[5] Cranmer then set about translating the processions before Mass on some festivals, including their 'Salve festa dies' and verses, the plainsong of which he thought 'sober and distinct enough. . . . Nevertheless, they that be cunning in singing can make a much more solemn note thereto.' But he considered that the other processional items (antiphons or responds) should be set as near as might be 'for every syllable a note', as in the Litany and certain other parts of the ritual.[6] However, in the first Book of Common Prayer (1549) all processions were abolished, and the Litany was ordered to be said or sung on Sunday, Wednesday, and Friday.

Music for the English liturgy survives in two sets of part-books, both incomplete,[7] which show by their texts that they were written between the accession of Edward VI (28 January 1547) and the first Prayer Book.[8] In the Wanley books the liturgical categories include

---

[1] See pp. 296 ff.   [2] See pp. 533 ff.

[3] Reprinted in M. Frost, *English and Scottish Psalm and Hymn Tunes c. 1543–1677* (London, 1953), p. 293.

[4] Facsimile in J. E. Hunt, *Cranmer's First Litany, 1544, and Merbecke's Book of Common Prayer Noted, 1550* (London, 1939).

[5] 'Item for xxiiij latines whereof j dd. noted with playneson of fyve partes at iij s. the dd.vj s' and 'Item paid to the chaunter of Westmynster for pryking the new Latyny in iij, iiij and v partes in prykeson xxd', in 1544; *Durham Account Rolls*, ed. J. T. Fowler (Durham, 1898), iii, p. 726. See also Fellowes, *English Cathedral Music* (London, 1941), p. 25.

[6] Letter to Henry VIII (1544), in Strunk, op. cit., p. 350.

[7] Brit. Mus. Roy. App. 74–76 and Bodl. Mus. Sch. e. 420–2 (the 'Wanley' part-books).

[8] See W. H. Frere, 'Edwardine Vernacular Services before the First Prayer Book' in *Walter Howard Frere: A Collection of his Papers* (London, 1940), p. 5.

morning and evening canticles, the Communion service, with some Offertories and Post-Communions, the Litany and Burial Sentences, the Easter antiphon 'Christ rising again', the hymn 'O Lord the maker of all things' ('Christe qui lux es')[1] and the Introit for Whit-sunday. There are also anthems with prose texts from the psalms or Gospels and a few metrical psalms. The Introit, 'The Spirit of God hath replenished', is interesting in being a direct translation of the Sarum 'Spiritus Domini replevit' with its psalm-verse and *Gloria*; in the 1549 Book the Introits were complete psalms to be said or sung, while in 1552 they were dropped entirely. The Communion services, apart from the Taverner adaptations[2] and an anonymous setting, are syllabic in style—as is the best known of all the very early Anglican services, Tallis's 'Short' or 'Dorian' service—and the same is true in general of the other liturgical items. The anthems and metrical psalms, which allow themselves some brief imitations, include pieces by Tallis, Tye, Sheppard, Johnson, and Okeland.[3] The sacred music in the Royal Library set is confined to prose and metrical psalms and canticles, two anthems, a Litany, a doxology, and a 1552 *Kyrie*.[4] One of the minor mysteries of the Anglican liturgy during its first century or so is the method of singing prose psalms on non-festive days. Here there are four set to plainsong tones in the tenor and six set anthem wise.

On the basis of the first Prayer-Book, Marbeck printed in 1550 his *Booke of Common Praier Noted*, with measured monophonic music for Morning and Evening Prayer, the Communion and the Burial services.[5] He used simplified forms of the Sarum chants for the *Te Deum* and 'Pater noster', but the rest appear to be his own, apart from the psalms and canticles.[6] It is worth noting that his forms of

[1] Printed in *Tudor Church Music*, octavo ed., no. 83, ed. Fellowes, who has added a treble, and changed the first two notes to G from A.

[2] The 'Small Devotion' and 'Meane' Masses (printed, with the help of the originals, in *Tudor Church Music*, iii, London, 1924, pp. 143 and 169); the only other identifiable Communion service is by Heath. This must be Thomas Heath, singer at Westminster in 1540–1 and Master of the Choristers there in 1553 (E. Pine, *The Westminster Abbey Singers*, London, 1953, pp. 42 and 62) and at Exeter in 1557 (*Use of Exeter Cathedral*, ed. H. Reynolds, London, 1891, p. 46) and 1562–3 (Accounts of the Vicars Choral).

[3] Tallis's 'If ye love me' (complete in Day's *Mornyng and Evenyng Praier*) is reprinted in *Tudor Church Music*, octavo ed., No. 69; 'O Lord of Hosts' (complete in Day's *Whole psalmes* of 1563 as by S, for Southerton, but attributed to Tye in Add. 15166, after 1567, and Add. 29289, *c.* 1629) is reprinted in Frost, op. cit., p. 219.

[4] Two composers are named: Johnson for 'Behold brethren how good', set to the seventh tone, and Tallis for a *Benedictus* (not found elsewhere). Tallis's 'Remember not O Lord' (complete in Day's *Whole psalmes*) is reprinted in Frost, op. cit., p. 214.

[5] Facsimile in Hunt, op. cit.

[6] The British Museum MS. 'Add. 34191, a part-book of *c.* 1525, has as later additions a bass part for the English Litany, an English *Te Deum* and Communion Service (all

the fourth, fifth, and eighth psalm-tones are virtually the same as those given by Morley in four-part settings.[1] Morley introduces these settings by remarking that 'the churchmen for keeping their keys have devised certain notes commonly called the Eight Tunes', and in a further discussion he points out that his examples are 'but the forms of giving the tunes to their psalms in the churches which the churchmen (falsely) believe to be the *modi* or tunes'.[2] It is very likely that Morley was referring to the 'churchmen' of his own time, and that psalms were sung to these forms of the tones or to standardized settings of them.[3]

Another famous musical print of this time is Tye's *Actes of the Apostles* (1553), being four-part settings of his own metrical version of fourteen chapters of the Acts, in simple style with some imitation.[4] Tye was an early practitioner of this kind of enterprise, in which William Hunnis also engaged with his *Hyve full of Hunnye, containing the Firste Booke of Moses* (1578) and Marbeck with his versified *Holie History of King David* (1579). Neither of these had music, but Tye's work was anticipated in a paraphrase of the Bible made by the Swiss anabaptist Joachim Aberlin.[5] Tye's book was not intended for church use, but as the title-page puts it 'to synge and also to play upon the Lute, very necessarye for studentes after theyr studye, to fyle theyr wyttes, and also for all Christians that cannot synge, to read the good and Godlye storyes of the lyves of Christ hys Apostles'.

In the second Prayer Book Introits and Post-Communions were eliminated, leaving even less scope for the composer. John Day's *Mornyng and Evenyng Praier and Communion* (1565) included, besides the regular music for those services, the Litany, two Offertories, and the prayer 'Turn thou us' for Ash Wednesday, together with pieces called 'Anthem' or 'Prayer', though they are not otherwise distin-

---

pre-1549 in their texts) which appear to be monophonic settings analogous to Marbeck's, though closer to the original plainsongs than his, and one part of a 1552 *Kyrie* marked at the end 'iij partes'; there are some facsimiles in Hunt, op. cit., pp. 52–9.

[1] *A Plaine and Easie Introduction*, ed. cit., p. 250.

[2] Ibid., p. 304.

[3] Morley has B in the ending of the eighth tone, Marbeck has not; three of the tones in Marbeck are not in Morley. The only music in Robert Crowley's *The Psalter of David . . . whereunto is added a note of four partes*, (London, 1549) is a setting of the seventh tone (printed in *Grove's Dictionary*, 5th ed., vi, p. 958) which omits the intonation but otherwise corresponds to Morley. One of the two four-part settings in Francis Seager's *Certayne Psalmes* (London, 1553) has a form of the sixth tone in the tenor (printed in Frost, op. cit., p. 341).

[4] Reprinted in Frost, op. cit., p. 343.

[5] J. Aberlin, *Ain kurtzer begriff und Innhalt der gantzen Bibel in drew Lieder zuo singen gestellt* (Augsburg?, 1534); each of the three parts (Old Testament, Psalter, New Testament) has a melody at the beginning.

guished. Most of the composers, and some of the pieces, were in the Bodleian part-books, but Tye does not appear, Knyght and a Robert Hasylton do, and Taverner is represented by an adaptation of his 'In nomine', apparently by Thomas Causton, to the metrical version of Psalm 20, 'In trouble and adversity'.[1]

METRICAL PSALTERS

In 1562 and 1563 Day laid the other side of his twin basis for Protestant music with *The Whole Booke of Psalmes, collected into Englyshe metre by T. Sternhold, I. Hopkins & others: . . . with apt Notes to synge them withal*,[2] and the earliest edition of four-part settings of Sternhold's metrical psalter, the *Whole psalmes in foure partes, whiche may be song to all musicall instrumentes*, in which he included some settings of prose texts.[3] In 1567 or 1568 a metrical version of the psalms by Matthew Parker, with nine original tunes (eight of them disposed by modes) set in four parts by Tallis, was printed in a very small edition.[4] Beginning later in the century a series of Psalters using the common tunes appeared, including John Cosyn's in 1585, two by Daman in 1591 with settings in simple imitative style (in one the melody is in the tenor, in the other in the highest part), Thomas East's in 1592 with plain settings by ten composers of the time, Richard Allison's in 1599 with ten tunes set for four voices or solo voice and lute, and Ravenscroft's in 1621 with some new tunes, English and imported, and settings from East and by some of Ravenscroft's contemporaries, including Thomas Tomkins, William Cranford, John Ward, and Peerson.[5] Besides participating in East's and Ravenscroft's Psalters, John Dowland wrote seven settings of texts from the metrical psalter as a 'Lamentation' for Henry Noel (d. 1597),

---

[1] Reprinted in *Tudor Church Music*, iii, p. 199; the only other metrical text is Tallis's 'O Lord in thee is all my trust' (headed 'A Lamentation' in Day's Psalter of 1562; see Frost, op. cit., p. 213), a plain setting of the common tune. See also p. 510 and Ex. 220.

[2] Earlier editions of Sternhold's version, with tunes partly borrowed or adapted from the Geneva Psalter (see p. 441), had been published at Geneva in 1556, 1558, 1560, and 1561.

[3] For example, Tallis's 'Remember not O Lord' (which was in Roy. App. 74–76) and William Parsons's 'Almighty God whose kingdom is everlasting' (reprinted in Frost, op. cit., p. 222). The other composers concerned in Day's Psalter were Causton, Richard Edwards, Richard Brimle (probably the Richard Bramley who was a clerk at King's College 1558–61 and Instructor of the Choristers 1558–60), John Hake (a clerk at Windsor in 1547 and the composer of a *Kyrie* in the Gyffard part-books), and the otherwise unknown N. Southerton.

[4] Reprinted in Frost, op. cit., p. 374.

[5] Examples from these Psalters (except Cosyn's and Allison's) will be found in Frost, op. cit., *passim*.

in four of which he used the common tune.[1] Robert Tailour's *Sacred Hymns Consisting of Fifti Select Psalms of David* (1615) were new versifications 'set to be sung in five parts, as also to the viole, and lute or orpharion'. His settings are fine compositions, homophonically based but with ample linear interest, and with such features of the Jacobean anthem as chromaticism and florid figuration.[2] Though not a psalter, but rather 'the earliest attempt at an English hymnbook',[3] George Wither's *The Hymnes and Songs of the Church* (1623) may be mentioned here, as it had sixteen tunes, each with a bass, by Orlando Gibbons.[4] The Reformation in Scotland produced settings of metrical psalms, both free and on the common tunes, and some devotional songs,[5] the most important Psalters being those of 1564 and 1635.[6]

In England the common tunes were seldom used as bases for more elaborate forms of composition. Among the few examples are an organ setting of 'O Lord turn not away thy face' in the *Mulliner Book*,[7] three anonymous pieces presenting the ingenious combination of psalm-tune and the 'In nomine' *canto fermo*,[8] and an anthem by Peerson.[9]

ELIZABETHAN SACRED MUSIC, AND BYRD'S 1611 *PSALMES*

Given the severely Protestant colour of the episcopal bench and the colleges, it is not surprising that so little music of any greater elaboration than the standard set in Day's publications was written in the Elizabethan period. This is not to ignore the fine quality of such short anthems as Tallis's 'Hear the voice and prayer' and Mundy's 'O Lord the maker of all things'.[10] These are the minor gems of great masters, but much of the music of the new race of composers is simple func-

---

[1] Printed in *Tudor Church Music*, octavo ed., nos. 79, 80.
[2] Reprinted in Frost, op. cit., pp. 468–506.
[3] J. Julian, *A Dictionary of Hymnology* (London, 1907), p. 347.
[4] Reprinted in *Tudor Church Music*, iv (London, 1925), p. 317, and Frost, op. cit., p. 420. The setting of Song 67 is probably not by Gibbons, as the tune had already appeared in the Welsh Psalter of Edmund Prys in 1621 (see Frost, pp. 406 and 421).
[5] Examples in *Music of Scotland 1500–1700*, ed. Kenneth Elliott and H. M. Shire (*Musica Britannica*, xv, London, 1957)
[6] The latter reprinted by R. R. Terry (London, 1935); see also Terry's *A Forgotten Psalter and Other Essays* (Oxford, 1929) and, on Scottish metrical psalms generally, the article in *Grove's Dictionary* (ed. cit.), vi, p. 972.
[7] Ed. Denis Stevens (*Musica Britannica*, i, London, 1951), p. 80.
[8] In Christ Church 984–8; incipits in G. E. P. Arkwright, *Catalogue of Music in the Library of Christ Church, Oxford*, ii (London, 1923), pp. 156, 160, 161.
[9] See below, p. 510.
[10] *Tudor Church Music*, octavo ed., no. 38.

tional service-music. Most of the pieces in which the composer's art is more fully deployed were written by members of the Queen's chapel. Among these are Tallis's five-part *Te Deum*, Tye's 'I lift my heart', Sheppard's four-part service for men, Mundy's 'O Lord I bow the knees of my heart', Whyte's complete psalm 'Lord who shall dwell' (though he is manifestly less comfortable with English than with Latin), and Parsons's service for four to seven parts and 'Deliver me from mine enemies', this last for five voices with an optional canonic sixth part.[1]

Few of Byrd's anthems, apart from the sacred pieces in the prints of 1588 and 1589, can with certainty be dated before the death of Queen Elizabeth.[2] Of those in Elizabethan sources 'How long shall mine enemies triumph' is notable for breadth of style and control of texture, while 'O Lord make thy servant Elizabeth', 'Prevent us O Lord', and 'Arise O Lord' (with second part 'Help us O God') are outstanding examples of the Anglican anthem. There appear to be no Elizabethan sources for Byrd's Preces, Special Psalms, Litany, and Services.[3] Though some of this music must have been used in the Queen's chapel it is very doubtful that it had wider circulation before the seventeenth century, when it appears in choir manuscripts in Durham, St. John's College, Oxford, and Peterhouse, Cambridge. In style the treble part of the homophonic Short Service, like that of similar services in the sixteenth century, is not too far removed from that of the 'composed' pieces in Marbeck. The alternation and combination, without division of parts, of the sides of the choir, *Decani* and *Cantoris*, which was a frequent practice in post-Elizabethan services, is not in this case essential to the music, since there are no overlaps. In the Great Service, however, it is an integral part of a complex scheme of texture with predominantly imitative treatment (except in the Communion items); this, with the amplitude and vigour of the melodic lines, makes the work one of the masterpieces of the Anglican repertory. For his Special Psalms Byrd used an elaborated chant style (as in 'O clap your hands'), or a version of the style of some of his Latin hymns (in 'Save me O God'), or a verse style (in 'Teach me O Lord').

In all three of his publications to English texts—the *Psalmes, Sonets,*

---

[1] The Tallis *Te Deum* is printed in ibid., no. 72; Whyte's psalm in *Tudor Church Music*, v.

[2] The pieces discussed in this paragraph are printed in *Tudor Church Music*, ii (London, 1922).

[3] With the exception of John Baldwin's anthology, which contains sections from the Great Service.

and Songs of 1588, the *Songs of Sundrie Natures* of 1589, and the *Psalmes, Songs, and Sonnets* of 1611[1]—Byrd followed, one is sure not unwittingly, the earlier practice of including both sacred and secular music.[2] Much of the music in these collections is allied both to the pre-Reformation carol and to the contemporary instrumental fantasia, and therefore is historically important for its maintenance of a line of development which led from the court and domestic music of Henry VIII's time to the Jacobean verse-anthem and ayre. All but one ('O God give ear') of the thirteen sacred pieces in the 1588 book are clearly of the kind Byrd referred to in his 'Epistle to the Reader' as having been 'originally made for Instruments to expresse the harmonie and one voyce to pronounce the dittie'.[3] The settings of metrical psalms, comprising all but two of the sacred pieces, are as it were idealized psalm-tunes set in the framework, often of great beauty, of an instrumental fantasia. The words of 'If that a sinner's sighs' are remarkable for their anticipation of the subjective note in Jacobean texts, while 'Lulla lullaby my sweet little baby' is notable both for its expressiveness and its refrain form.

The three-part psalms in the 1589 collection are in quite a different style, being true counterpoint with such devices as double descant and imitation by diminution. Besides three contrapuntal anthems, this book also contains two 'Carowles', one for solo and one for duet with instrumental parts, in each case with a four-part burden (Byrd calls it a 'quire'), and the remarkable setting of the Easter 'anthem' 'Christ rising again' which anticipates a Jacobean characteristic in its disposition of solo voices, instruments, and chorus. The 1611 collection put greater emphasis, numerically speaking, on anthems, now in the rather freer style of the Jacobean full anthem. It also contained two 'Carrolls', one in anthem style, the other, 'O God that guides', having a solo-instrumental *versus* and a burden for *chorus*. A style of solo-instrumental song which comes close to that of the ayre may be seen in such pieces from manuscripts[4] as 'My faults O Christ', 'O heavenly God and Father dear', and 'O that we woeful wretches'. The anthem 'Alack when I look back' seems to be a unique instance of Byrd's using a post-Reformation metrical tune. The words, and the tune on which his setting is based, were printed in William Hunnis's

[1] Reprinted in Fellowes's edition of the *Collected Works*, xii (1948), xiii (1949), and xiv (1949) respectively.

[2] As did John Mundy in his *Songs and Psalmes* of 1594, reprinted complete by Dart and Philip Brett in *The English Madrigalists*, xxxvb (London, 1961).

[3] The original form of two of the pieces may be seen in *The Collected Works*, xv, pp. 1, 35.

[4] Printed ibid.

Seven Sobs of a Sorrowfull Soule for Sinne (i.e. the seven penitential psalms) under the heading 'A Lamentation touching the follies and vanities of our youth'.[1] Byrd turned this into a verse-anthem by making the chorus echo short phrases and the last line of each verse. These settings are significant items in the history of the verse-anthem and of its connexion with devotional poetry.

THE JACOBEAN REVIVAL

The striking features of the Jacobean verse-anthem are its leaning towards 'pietistic' texts and its appropriate treatment of them. Musically, it exhibits at times a vocabulary of 'modernisms' more highly coloured than that of the contemporary ayre or madrigal. For representative examples we may choose from the unpublished anthology called *Tristitiae Remedium*[2] made in 1616 by Thomas Myriell, Precentor of Chichester from 1613 to 1628,[3] supplemented by a set of part-books which has quite a few pieces in common with Myriell.[4] We have here all the signs of a rapid flowering—under the beneficent rays of the King's favour, the interest of churchmen, and the patronage of the higher laity—of the polyphonic verse-anthem anticipated by Byrd and others, and now practised by a sizeable group of composers, some of whom also showed their competence in other fields. The full anthem was widely cultivated too, often in a more 'madrigalian' polyphony than before, and generally to less subjective texts than the verse-anthem. Both are represented in the two collections mentioned and in Sir William Leighton's publication *The Teares or Lamentations of a Sorrowfull Soule* (1614), which contained settings of texts compiled by him, some for four voices and broken consort ('Consort Songs') and some for four or five voices without accompaniment.[5] About one-third of these pieces are also in Myriell's manuscript.[6]

---

[1] See Frost, op. cit., p. 467.

[2] Brit. Mus. Add. 29372–7. Myriell included three of Giovanni Croce's settings of Bembo's sonnets on the Penitential Psalms, originally in Italian as *Li Sette Sonetti Penitentiali* (Venice, 1603, 'novamente ristampati'), Latinized in *Septem psalmi poenitentiales* (Nuremberg, 1599), and 'Newly Englished' in *Musica Sacra* (London, 1608).

[3] See Dart, 'Music and Musicians at Chichester Cathedral, 1545–1642', *Music and Letters*, xlii (1961), p. 224.

[4] Christ Church 56–60; the bass book is missing.

[5] Among the contributions to Leighton available in reprints are those of Byrd, Gibbons, John Milton (in *The Old English Edition*, xxii), and John Wilbye (in *The English Madrigal School*, vi).

[6] There are four full anthems in Tomkins's *Songs* of 1622 (one is dedicated to Myriell and another was in his anthology), and three in Francis Pilkington's *Second set of Madrigals* of 1624 (if we include 'Care for thy soul'). Dowland included four very beautiful sacred songs in his *A Pilgrimes Solace* (1612). All these are available in modern editions.

The subjective element in Jacobean texts undoubtedly reflects the movement to restore poetry to devotion and to assert the place of the senses in religious experience. It took the form of intense contemplation of suffering, as in Edmund Hooper's 'The blessed Lamb', who

> For our sins guiltless on his cross did bleed:
> Mocked, wounded, spit upon, scourged like a slave,

or passionate statement of devotion, as in Matthew Jeffries's full anthem

> My love is crucified, dead and entombed,
> Raised up, ascended, fixed on heaven's high throne
> . . . Christ is my love alone,

or extravagant metaphor, as in Simon Stubbes's 'Father of love':

> Behold thy woeful servant prostrate lie,
> With dreary tears bedewing his sad face,
> The outward map of inward misery.

The keynote of this aspect of the words and of their musical treatment may perhaps be suggested by the openings of Ward's 'Down caitiff wretch' (with second part 'Prayer is an endless chain of purest love') and William Simmes's 'Rise O my soul':[1]

Ex. 218
(i) WARD

---

[1] They are in this order in Christ Church, 56–60, though separated in Myriell.

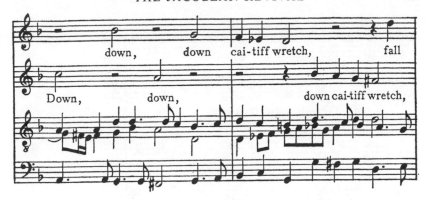

(1)A in Ch. Ch. 57

-fore   the foot-stool of the Lord   of   life

(ii) SIMMES

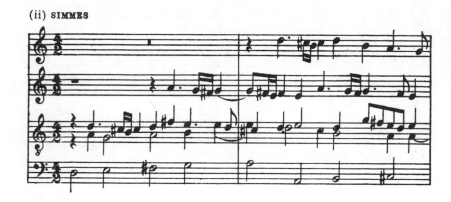

Rise,

Rise,   rise,

And for an extreme case of chromaticism used to express deep penitence we may quote the ending of Thomas Ford's full anthem
'Miserere my maker':[1]

[1] Christ Church, 56–60; I have supplied a bass part.

Ex. 219

Occasionally a special effect is gained by the alternation of very short phrases in voices and instruments, as in Peerson's 'O Lord in thee', a rare instance of an anthem founded on a psalm-tune (the pauses are given exactly as in the manuscript):[1]

[1] Christ Church, 56–60, bass supplied; for the common tune see Frost, op. cit., pp. 213–14. Peerson's setting may be compared with Tallis's in Day's Psalter of 1563 (in the *Yattendon Hymnal*, ed. Robert Bridges and H. E. Wooldridge, Oxford, 1905, no. 57) and with Gibbons's free setting.

Ex.220

The obverse of the subjective texts set as anthems by the Jacobeans are those written for a royal or public occasion or observance, like John Bennet's 'O God of Gods', written for the anniversary of the coronation of James I,[1] 'heaven's darling, England's happiness', which expresses the prayer

> That this triumphant festival
> This holy day Imperial
> To his inauguring consecrated
> May be so often celebrated
> That finally it be not done
> Till the great coming of thy Son.

Other examples of the 'occasional' anthem are Hooper's 'Hearken ye nations', with the lines

> Our King anointed with his blessed seed
> Our sacred prophets that our souls do feed
>
> .　　.　　.　　.　　.　　.　　.　　.
>
> This day our God from fools' bloodthirsty ire
> Hath saved as brands new taken from the fire,

and Edward Smith's 'If the Lord himself', both written for the anniversary of the Gunpowder Treason, Tomkins's 'Know ye not' for the funeral of Prince Henry in 1612, Ward's 'This is a joyful happy day' for the creation of Charles as Prince of Wales in the same year, John Bull's 'God the Father' for the marriage of Princess Elizabeth to Frederick, Elector Palatine, also in 1612, Gibbons's 'Blessed are they' for the marriage of Robert Earl of Somerset and Lady Frances Howard in 1613, his 'Great King of gods' for the King's being in Scotland in 1617, and his 'O all true faithful hearts' for the King's recovery from sickness in 1619.[2]

Probably because they have been in print for some time, Gibbons's verse-anthems have tended to overshadow those of his immediate predecessors and contemporaries.[3] Generally in a more orthodox style than those quoted, they can be vigorous and rhythmically varied, like 'See, see, the Word is incarnate' (the only Gibbons anthem in Myriell),

---

[1] Possibly for the day itself; the text was used for the 'King's Day' under James and Charles I, for Edmund Hooper's setting of it appears in later sources.

[2] Of the three sacred pieces in Richard Allison's *An Howres Recreation in Music* (1606; reprinted in *The English Madrigal School*, xxxiii) the full anthem 'O Lord bow down' is a prayer for the royal family and the verse-anthem 'The sacred choir of angels' (with refrain for chorus) is 'a thanksgiving for the deliverance of the whole estate from the late conspiracie'.

[3] His sacred music is printed in *Tudor Church Music*, iv (London, 1925); new edition of the verse-anthems by D. Wulstan in *Early English Church Music*, iii (London, 1963).

or deeply felt, like 'Behold thou hast made my days',[1] written for Dean Maxsie of Windsor in his last illness in 1618, or merely staid, like 'This is the record of John',[2] composed for Laud during his presidency of St. John's College, Oxford, from 1611 to 1621.[3]

Among other Jacobean composers represented in one or both of the Myriell and Christ Church collections are John Amner,[4] William Corkine, Michael East,[5] Robert Jones, Kirbye,[6] Lupo, John Mundy,[7] Ravenscroft, and Weelkes, the last with full anthems only. The full anthem, whether short and then normally for four voices, or extended and for five or more, kept to the 'madrigalian' version of the traditional polyphonic style, with rather lively rhythms and cogent points. Weelkes could rise to such good examples of the longer type as his 'Alleluia I heard a voice'[8] and 'O Lord arise' (with a splendid closing Alleluia),[9] though in the verse-anthem his restrained style could sound ludicrous when used for such a tricky text as 'If King Manasses',[10] with the lines

> A worthless worm some nice regard may win,
> And lowly creep whose flying threw it down.

Again the full anthems of Gibbons's contemporaries are less widely known than his, both in the larger style, such as 'Hosanna to the Son of David', and the smaller, such as 'Almighty and everlasting God'. The service, which in this period took a very secondary place to the anthem, was like it written in both full and verse forms, and here the

[1] Recorded in *The History of Music in Sound*, iv.

[2] Easily accessible in A. T. Davison and W. Apel, *Historical Anthology of Music*, i (Cambridge, Mass., 1947), p. 195.

[3] The anthem 'Glorious and powerful God' for the dedication of a church, possibly in Gibbons's setting, was sung at the dedication of Sir Henry Willoughby's chapel at Risley in Derbyshire in 1632, after the sermon. There was an organ solo before the *Te Deum*, and before the sermon the psalm 'Lord remember David' was sung with organ, possibly in the metrical form; there is a setting by Jeffries in Myriell. See J. W. Legg, *English Orders for consecrating churches* (London, 1911), pp. 135–6.

[4] Who printed a collection of his own: *Sacred Hymnes of 3, 4, 5, and 6 parts for Voyces and Vyols* (1615).

[5] East included anthems in his *The Third set of Bookes* (1610), dedicated to 'Mr. Henry Wilughby, of Risley, in the Countie of Darby, Esquire; his singular good Master'. *The fourth set of bookes* (1618) contained 'Anthemes for Versus and Chorus, Madrigals and Songs of other kinds to 4, 5, and 6 parts, apt for Viols and Voyces'. *The Sixt set of Bookes* (1624) had only 'Anthemes for Versus and Chorus, of 5 and 6 parts, apt for Violls and Voyces'. Dart and Brett have reprinted the 1610 and 1618 sets complete in *The English Madrigalists*, xxxia and b (London, 1962).

[6] His 'O Jesu look', in Myriell, is printed in *Tudor Church Music*, octavo ed., no. 18.

[7] 'Sing Joyfully', verse-anthem in Myriell, is printed ibid., no. 92.

[8] In the Myriell and Christ Church collections; printed ibid., no. 45.

[9] Ibid., no. 63; there are six further anthems by Weelkes in this series (nos. 9, 17, 35, and 88–90). Other composers represented in it by anthems include John Bull (no. 91), John Hilton the elder (no. 97), Morley (no. 71), and Nicholson (no. 48).

[10] In Royal College of Music, 1045–51.

vein opened up by Byrd and Morley[1] was successfully worked by Weelkes,[2] Gibbons, and Tomkins.[3]

PERFORMANCE OF JACOBEAN AND CAROLINE CHURCH MUSIC

Neither the printed collections of Leighton and Amner nor the manuscript anthologies of Jacobean music were provided with keyboard parts. It seems certain that in Elizabethan times the organ was used at most to set the pitch for psalms and canticles, to accompany anthems and to play voluntaries.[4] From about 1600 it became customary to accompany full choral compositions and to write contrapuntal organ parts to verse-anthems, adapted from or analogous to those written for viols, and an organ-book was eventually provided for each set of part-books.[5] In the surviving specimens from St. Paul's,[6] Durham, Peterhouse, and elsewhere[7] the texture in full sections varies in the course of a single piece from a two-part outline, to be filled in by the player,[8] to the full detail, which is normally given for verses.[9] One of the earliest organ-books has occasional independent ornamentation,[10] but from its general absence (Tomkins's printed compositions being an exception) one assumes that it was left to the taste of the performer. Though it is difficult to gauge the extent of improvised additions in any period, this was probably true also of vocal ornamentation, which would likewise depend on local customs and personalities.[11] That it was considered becoming is suggested by a report on preparations for Charles I's visit to Scotland written at Whitehall in 1631 by Edward Kelley, subsequently (1633) appointed master of the King's Chapel Royal in Scotland. 'Hereupon', he says, 'I carryed

[1] An evening verse-service is printed in *Tudor Church Music*, octavo ed., no. 64.

[2] For an evening service, editorially completed, see the *Evening Service for Trebles*, ed. Peter le Huray (London, 1962).

[3] His Preces, Psalms, and Services are printed in *Tudor Church Music*, viii (London, 1928).

[4] In St. James's Chapel on Easter Day, 1593, when Her Majesty came to Communion, 'Dr. Bull was at the organ playinge the Offertorye' (Rimbault, op. cit., p. 150).

[5] e.g. at New College in 1637–8: 'So for a Sett of Service bookes with Choice Services and Anthemes in number Eleaven with the Organ booke 2 li. 10 s.' (Bursars' Account Roll).

[6] Adrian Batten's Organ-book, with the date 1634; see Fellowes, *The Catalogue of Manuscripts in the Library of St. Michael's College, Tenbury* (Paris, 1934), no. 791 and pls. iii, iv (the captions are reversed).

[7] See *Tudor Church Music*, ii, pp. 26–27.

[8] Cf. Martin Peerson's (secular) *Private Musicke . . . being Verse and Chorus, is fit for Voyces and Viols. And for want of Viols, they may be performed to either the Virginall or Lute, where the proficient can play upon the Ground, or for a shift to the Base Viol alone* (1620).

[9] Both string parts and organ part exist for several of Gibbons's verse-anthems.

[10] Christ Church 1001; see, for example, *Tudor Church Music*, iv, p. 253.

[11] For suggestive passages see ibid., pp. 63, 173, and 181.

home an organist, and two men for playing on cornets and sackbuts, and two boyes for singing divisions in the *versus*, all of whom are most exquisite in their severall faculties.'[1] In 1632 Walter Porter, sometime pupil of Monteverdi, introduced Italian modes of figured bass, ornamentation, and terminology in his *Madrigales and Ayres*.[2] The first, and only sacred, item in this print was a setting of Psalm 147, 'O Praise the Lord', from which a passage may be quoted:[3]

Ex. 221

[1] C. Rogers, *History of the Chapel Royal of Scotland* (Edinburgh, 1882), p. clxvii.

[2] *Of two three foure and five Voyces with the continued Base with Toccatos Sinfonias and Rittornellos to them After the manner of Consort Musique*. No organ-book exists for John Barnard's *The First Book of Selected Church Musick* (1641); though essential to the verse-anthems, it may not have been printed.

[3] The opening is given in *The Musical Antiquary*, iv (1913), p. 247.

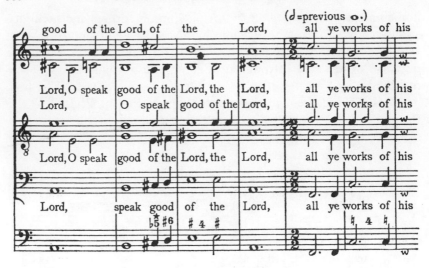

* *sic*

Porter's lead was not followed in organ-books of the sixteen-thirties, nor in the *pars organica* of the posthumous publication of Tomkins's sacred music, the *Musica Deo Sacra* of 1668.[1]

TOMKINS

In their choice of texts Caroline composers[2] and compilers leaned to more exoteric and more definitely liturgical words than did most of the Jacobeans. This is particularly marked in the anthems of Tomkins, whose work covers the whole period from early Jacobean times to the Civil War, and embraces all the forms of Anglican music.[3] Tomkins was in any case a conservative composer, and his church music does not differ from his music of other kinds in showing little progression of style. Indeed some of his most effective anthems are early pieces, like 'When David heard'[4] and 'From deepest horror of sad penitence':[5]

---

[1] *Musica Deo Sacra & Ecclesiae Anglicanae: or, Musick dedicated To the Honor and Service of God, and To the Use of Cathedral and other Churches of England, Especially of the Chappel-Royal of King Charles the First.*

[2] Among the new names are Ramsey, Richard Portman, William Child, Henry and William Lawes, and Christopher Gibbons. A word-book of the anthems used in the Chapel of Charles I (Bodl. Rawl. Poet. 23; printed in *The Musical Antiquary*, ii (1911), p. 109) has 65 full anthems and 152 verse-anthems, here called 'single anthems'.

[3] See Denis Stevens, *Thomas Tomkins* (London, 1957) for a catalogue, with sources, and discussion of the anthems in the *Songs* and the contents of *Musica Deo Sacra*.

[4] 'Perhaps his finest choral work': Bernard Rose, 'Thomas Tomkins 1575?–1656', *Proceedings of the Royal Musical Association*, lxxxii (1956), p. 91. It is in Myriell and the 1622 *Songs*; easily accessible reprint in Davison and Apel, op. cit., p. 191.

[5] Myriell is the only source.

Ex. 222

and at least two of his more elaborate full anthems, the eight-part 'O God the proud are risen' and the seven-part 'O sing unto the Lord', the Alleluia of which is a bold essay in idiomatic dissonance and false relation.[1] Also noteworthy among the full anthems are the twelve-part 'O praise the Lord all ye heathen' and the stern setting of 'O God wonderful art thou'.[2] The organ part of the verse-anthems, which are called 'Songs to the Organ' in *Musica Deo Sacra*, is consistently polyphonic in conception, even at times in strict fantasia style, and in some cases has moments of florid ornamentation,[3] which only rarely appears in the vocal solos.[4] The texture is governed by points of imitation taken from the voice or voices, even in such a case of word depiction as occurs in 'O Lord let me know mine end', undeterred by the implied consecutive octaves, Ex. 223 (opposite).

If one is inclined to regard the treatment of 'nothing' as prophetic of Purcell,[5] the same must be said of the major-minor third changes in the first chorus of 'Hear my prayer O good Lord' (Ex. 224).

---

[1] Both of these are in a part-book dated 1617 (Tenbury 1382) and in two part-books of St. John's College, Oxford, dating from Juxon's presidency, 1621–33. The second is available in an edition by Rose, who has also edited three other Tomkins anthems for Schott (1958), two for Stainer and Bell (1957), and the anthems in *Musica Deo Sacra* in *Early English Church Music*, v (London, 1965–7).

[2] Printed in *Tudor Church Music*, octavo ed., nos. 100, 99 respectively.

[3] See, for example, 'Thou art my King O God' and 'My Shepherd is the living Lord', both ed. Rose (Stainer and Bell).

[4] As on the word 'raise' in 'Above the stars my Saviour dwells'.

[5] In Tomkins's 'Hear my prayer O Lord' the word 'little' is set to a crotchet and a quaver separated by a quaver rest.

Ex. 223

Though by no means all of Tomkins's sacred music is made of as fine
metal as the examples cited, there is no doubt that taken as a whole
his work is the most impressive single contribution to the period of
James I and Charles I, the only age in the history of Anglican church
music which may unreservedly be called 'golden'.

X

EARLY BAROQUE CHURCH MUSIC

By Hans F. Redlich

BAROQUE CHARACTERISTICS

To distinguish what may be called the baroque style[1] in ecclesiastical music, it is only necessary to compare the church music written and published roughly between 1587 and 1630[2] with that of the preceding period—*c*.1550 to 1594—covering the creative life of Palestrina, Lassus, de Monte, and their contemporaries. Whereas the religious music of these latter masters adheres more or less strictly to the style of polyphonic imitation built up by the earlier Flemish masters and their German and Italian followers, keeping well within the structural and sonorous limits of traditional choral polyphony, that of the following generation presents a completely different aspect. New features are discernible at an early date, showing a growing tendency towards a new chordal style of music (coupled with an increasing dislike of polyphonic conception), certainly better fitted to interpret clearly and unequivocally the message of liturgical texts and to enhance their appreciation by enlightened audiences. This revised attitude towards the scriptural text reflects partly a general tendency of the age, partly the combative spirit of the Counter-Reformation, so far as Roman Catholic musicians are concerned. The composers of the reformed churches, by emphasizing the overriding importance of the liturgical word and by enabling its import to be clearly perceived by any listening or singing community, only expressed one of the fundamental articles of their religious conviction.

The chief means employed to establish this new style of musical expression were:

---

[1] On the general conception of 'baroque' in music, see Robert Haas, *Musik des Barocks* (Potsdam, 1932), pp. 5 ff.; Manfred Bukofzer, *Music in the Baroque Era* (New York, 1947), pp. 1 ff.; Suzanne Clercx, *Le Baroque et la musique* (Brussels, 1948).

[2] That is, between the *Concerti di A. e di G. Gabrieli, organisti della Sereniss. Sig. di Venezia, continenti Musica da chiesa, Madrigali ed altro, per voci ed istrumenti musicali* (Venice, 1587), containing for the first time church music with obligatory instruments, and Schütz's *Symphoniae Sacrae I* (Venice, 1629).

(a) A monumental style of combined choirs and orchestra, whereby, for the first time in the history of European music, clearly defined tasks were allotted to the latter.

(b) The invention and practical application of the thoroughbass technique (*basso continuo*), as a way of enabling a single voice or few voices only to perform against a chordally complete background supplied by a keyboard instrument.

(c) The emergence of monody in liturgical music as a logical sequel and complementary feature to (b) and its ultimate crystallization in the solo motet with its subterranean relationship to the *arioso* of the first opera experiments.

(d) Special features introduced by the militant Protestant church in Germany, as opposed to the liturgical tradition of the Roman Church, which it endeavoured to supplant by performing patterns inspired by the vernacular text in contrast to the Latin (hymn and *Geistliches Lied*).

To these dominating tendencies must be added certain derivative features, which came into play only later, such as the German form of *concerto ecclesiastico*, the *geistliches Konzert* which emerged in 1618 with Schein's *Opella Nova*:[1] a combination of the second and third features mentioned above rather than a new formal pattern, but carrying already the seeds of the future Protestant church cantata, notably in Scheidt.[2]

In sharp contrast, a kind of psychological reaction set in (chiefly among the adherents of the equally militant Counter-Reformation) with a deliberate revival of choral polyphony after 1600. This consciously conservative tendency among Catholic composers—which incidentally was shared by prominent representatives from the opposite camp, such as Schütz who continued to compose in the old polyphonic style and stoutly defended it in the preface to his *Geistliche Chormusik* (1648)—resulted in the ultimate petrifaction of the Palestrinian *stile antico*,[3] which artificially survived well into the eighteenth century.[4] All the same, the *stile antico* significantly accepted the most revolutionary feature of the *stile nuovo*, the *basso continuo*; Monteverdi's three conservative Masses (published 1610,

---

[1] See p. 456.   [2] See p. 459.

[3] Cf. the treatises of Marco Scacchi, *Cribrum Musicum* (Venice, 1643); Angelo Berardi, *Miscellanea musicale* (Bologna, 1689); Christoph Bernhard, *Tractatus Compositionis* (reprinted as *Die Kompositionslehre Heinrich Schützens* by J. M. Müller-Blattau); J. J. Fux, *Gradus ad Parnassum* (Vienna, 1725), and G. Paolucci, *Arte pratica di contrappunto* (Venice, 1765–72).

[4] With G. O. Pitoni (1657–1743) as its chief representative in Rome after 1719.

1640, 1651) for instance, are scored for chorus *a cappella* and *basso continuo*. This deliberate ambivalence of style during the whole baroque era found its most convincing expression in Monteverdi's two historic categories: *Prima Prattica* and *Seconda Prattica*.[1]

THE ROLE OF INSTRUMENTS

It is difficult to assess the actual amount of participation by instruments in the ecclesiastical music of the earlier sixteenth century.[2] Contemporary testimony in the form of paintings, prefaces, letters, and financial accounts bears out the fact that much of the choral music of Palestrina, Lassus, and others was performed with the help of instruments. Just how far this collaboration went is still largely conjectural since clearly defined parts for instruments are lacking in publications and manuscripts of that period,[3] but of course instrumentally accompanied church music was well known in the Middle Ages.[4] In the sixteenth century the general practice was based on the principle 'Zu singen oder zu spielen auf allerlei Instrumenten' (to be sung or played on various instruments). Many contemporary descriptions and paintings depict the Renaissance orchestra with its organization 'per choros' (as Praetorius calls it).[5] Schering claimed for the second half of the sixteenth century the existence of a special type of festival Mass, in which instrumental pomp and circumstance must have played a surprising part,[6] and even held that this applied to a great deal of other liturgical music as well. Whether or not we accept his conclusions, we must acknowledge that unaccompanied performance after 1550 may have been the exception rather than the rule; the interchangeable functions of chorus and orchestra may have prevailed between 1550 and 1600 even in the performance of Masses and motets by such composers as Palestrina and Lassus, whose

[1] In the preface to the Fifth Book of madrigals (1605) and in his brother's *Dichiaratione* (see *supra*, p. 71).

[2] Cf. Arnold Schering, *Aufführungspraxis alter Musik* (Leipzig, 1931), Haas, *Aufführungspraxis* (Potsdam, 1934), and Michael Praetorius, *Syntagma Musicum III* (Wolfenbüttel, 1619; reprint, ed. E. Bernoulli, Leipzig, 1916; facsimile, Kassel and Basle, 1958).

[3] Cf. Schering, *Die niederländische Orgelmesse* (Leipzig, 1912) and his *Aufführungspraxis*, in which he even asserts (p. 46) that *a cappella* singing after 1480 was reserved for rare and special occasions, Peter Wagner, *Geschichte der Messe* (Leipzig, 1913), pp. 80 ff., and Denis Arnold, 'Instruments in Church: Some Facts and Figures', *Monthly Musical Record*, lxxxv (1955), p. 32.

[4] Vol. III, pp. 412 ff.

[5] Cf. Schering and Haas, op. cit., and also Hugo Leichtentritt, 'Was lehren uns die Bilderwerke des 14.–17. Jahrhunderts über die Instrumentalmusik ihrer Zeit', *Sammelbände der internationalen Musikgesellschaft*, vii (1906), p. 315, on the conclusions to be drawn from pictorial testimonies.

[6] Op. cit., p. 53.

preserved *res facta* show no traces of orchestral collaboration.[1] The *ad hoc* collaboration of a group of cornetti and trombones in the church music of the sixteenth century may have developed into properly organized collaboration between chorus and orchestra in the Venice of Willaert and Andrea Gabrieli earlier than anywhere else. It certainly asserted itself there in the earliest accessible publication of this kind. It might be claimed already for Andrea Gabrieli's motets of 1565 and his *Psalmi Davidici* (1583).[2] At least equally specific is the title-page of the *Concerti di Andrea e di Giovanni Gabrieli, Organisti . . . . continenti Musica DI CHIESA, Madrigali, & altro, per voci & stromenti Musicali* (Venice, 1587). Giovanni's preface refers expressly to the 'veri movimenti di affetti' and to the 'suoni esprimenti l'energia delle parole e de concetti', as the creative levers of this new type of composition. But the typical baroque grandeur of his music—achieved by the collaboration of several choral groups with a brilliant orchestra of specified wind and string instruments—emerges distinctly only in two later publications exclusively of Giovanni's works: the *Sacrae Symphoniae* I (1597) (discussed in an earlier chapter)[3] and II (pub. 1615, three years after the composer's death). Both contain compositions in 12, 15, 16, and 20 parts, split up into two, three, or four choirs, in which the accumulation of massed harmony alone defeats any lingering tendency to deploy the music on polyphonic lines. But it was only in the Second Book that Gabrieli supplied quite independent obbligato instrumental parts, as in the famous 'In ecclesiis',[4] where he writes for two choirs—one of soloists, the other full—and an orchestra of three cornetti, *violino* (i.e. a viola), two trombones, and organ, or the 'Surrexit Christus' for three-part choir, two cornetti, two violini, and four trombones, which Winterfeld[5] believed to have been written for the entry of the Doge into the church of San Zaccaria on Easter Day:[6]

[1] See Praetorius, op. cit. on the orchestral interpretation of Lassus's motets, p. 122, and on Giaches de Wert's 'Egressus Jesus', p. 134, &c. Cf. also Schütz's instrumental adaptation of Andrea Gabrieli's 'concerto' 'Angelus ad pastores ait' (Schütz, *Sämtliche Werke*, viii, pp. 171 and 191).

[2] In the dedicatory letter to the *Psalmi* Andrea recommends a performance of either vocal or instrumental character: see p. 294 *supra*, *Istituzioni e monumenti dell'arte musicale italiana* (Milan, 1931), p. lxxx, and Giacomo Benvenuti's comment, p. lxxxiv.

[3] See pp. 296 ff.

[4] Reprinted in C. von Winterfeld, *Johannes Gabrieli und sein Zeitalter*, iii (Berlin, 1834), p. 73, and recorded in the *History of Music in Sound*, iv; the only modern edition incorporating the original *basso continuo* part is Frederick Hudson's (London, 1963). See also Hudson, 'Giovanni Gabrieli's Motet *a* 15, "In ecclesiis"', *Music Review*, xxiv (1963), p. 130.   [5] Op. cit. ii, p. 116.

[6] See also Denis Arnold, 'Ceremonial Music in Venice at the time of the Gabrielis' *Proceedings of the Royal Musical Association*, lxxxii (1955–6), p. 47.

Ex. 225

The abrupt modulations of 'In ecclesiis' (e.g. at 'Deus, adjutor noster') anticipate similar passages in Schütz's 'Dialogo per la pascua'.[1]

Gabrieli's revolutionary technique of combining vocal and instrumental 'chori' in great sonorous canvases was for a time unique in its independent employment of obbligato instruments, but he was by no means the only composer at this time of liturgical music conceived in a particularly grand and festive manner. Giovanni Bassano, another musician at St. Mark's, published *Motetti per concerti ecclesiastici a 5, 6, 7, 8, 12* with *bassi per l'organo* in 1598–9, and the *Sacrae Dei Laudes* (Venice, 1605) of Benedetto Pallavicino—successor of Giaches de Wert and predecessor of Monteverdi at the court of Mantua—are marked by effects of doubling at the octave and occasionally written for as many as sixteen parts. Another publication in the new spirit was the volume of *Sacrae Cantilene Concertate a tre, a cinque,*

[1] Schütz, *Sämtliche Werke*, xiv, p. 60.

et sei voci, con i suoi ripieni a Quattro voci et il Basso per l'Organo of
the otherwise conservative Giovanni Croce, *maestro di cappella* at
St. Mark's from 1603 to 1609; this was published in 1610 by a
friend who gives directions for performance in a preface.[1] To
this group may be added Ludovico Viadana's *Salmi a 4 chori per
cantare e concertare nelle gran solennità di tutto l'anno* (Venice, 1612);
here again the preface[2] contains detailed rules for achieving a satisfactory blending of vocal and instrumental combinations. Its ideas
are reflected in Michael Praetorius's *Syntagma Musicum III* (1619)
(especially part III, chap. 8); but with this latter work we reach a new,
post-Gabrielian period, for Giovanni's death in 1612 was soon
followed by Monteverdi's appointment as *maestro di cappella* at
St. Mark's (August 1613).

Pallavicino's use of doubling at the octave is an important principle
of the new style. It had been anticipated as early as 1586 by Monteverdi's later antagonist G. M. Artusi[3] in his demand for unison
intensification of the bass parts in concerti consisting of several 'chori',
and it was eventually embodied in the axiom of Michael Praetorius:
'Octavae in omnibus vocibus tolerari possunt, quando una vox can-
tat, alia sonat.'[4] Unison and octave doubling were the two pillars on
which a completely new principle of distribution of sonorities was to
rest. Praetorius, with his fine sense for the realities of the new style,
justifies unison-doubling by the need of a unifying base for the
columns of harmonies in the different choral entities, and he proves
the logical admissibility of doublings by the fact that some instruments (for instance, the flutes), even when in unison with the cantus,
actually sound an octave higher by virtue of their acoustic peculiarities.[5]

MONTEVERDI'S *VESPRO*

Monteverdi had tentatively tried out in his *Orfeo* the combination of a mixed five-part choir with a colourful orchestra
three years before he published his first volume of church music
since the far-off days of the *Cantiunculae Sacrae* (1582). The collec-

[1] See Arnold. 'Giovanni Croce and the *Concertato* Style', *Musical Quarterly*, xxxix
(1953), p. 37.
[2] See Ambros–Leichtentritt, *Geschichte der Musik*, iv (Leipzig, 1909), p. 239.
[3] *Arte del Contrappunto*, ii, chap. 16.
[4] Op. cit., p. 72 *et passim*.
[5] 'Denn etliche Instrumenta simplicia, als vornemblich die Flöitten . . . seynd
jederzeit eine oder auch zwo Octaven höher nach dem Fussthon zu rechnen, als der
Gesang an jhm selbsten gesetzt ist . . .' (*Syntagma Musicum III*, ed. cit., p. 73).

tion published as *Vespro della Beata Vergine*[1] (Venice, 1610) includes not only experimentally progressive, concerto-like pieces but a conservative *a cappella* Mass on Gombert's 'In illo tempore',[2] in which only the irregular number of vocal parts (seven in the final *Agnus Dei*) and the addition of a *basso continuo* belong to the new century. In the *Vespro*, which includes solo motets and offertory-like movements, as well as the psalms and other pieces proper to Vespers, Monteverdi writes for a six-part chorus:

with an orchestra also in six parts plus *continuo*:

1: Cornetto and *violino da brazzo*
2:    „   „   „   „   „
3: *Viola da brazzo*
4: *Viola da brazzo* and trombone
5: Trombone and *viola da brazzo*
6: Trombone, *contrabasso da gamba*, and *viola da brazzo*
7: *Basso continuo* (organ)

This scheme, which was to be the practical basis of Praetorius's directions,[3] is closely related to Viadana's principles for compositions in massed style (1612) and probably derived from Gabrieli's earlier methods of 1597.

Monteverdi does not stop here, however. He takes a step beyond anything Gabrieli had yet published by introducing the instrumental

[1] *Tutte le opere di Claudio Monteverdi* (ed. G. F. Malipiero), xiv (Asolo, 1932). A number of practical editions have been published. On the problems of performance, see Redlich, *Claudio Monteverdi* (London, 1952), pp. 151 ff. and 'New editions of Monteverdi and Schütz', *Music Review*, xix (1958), p. 72. On certain anticipations of Monteverdi's procedures in the *Vespers*, in Archangelo Crotti's *Primo Libro de' Concerti Ecclesiastici* (Venice, 1608), Banchieri's *Ecclesiastice Sinfonie* (Venice, 1607), and Croce's *Sacrae Cantilenae Concertate* (Venice, 1610), see Arnold, 'Notes on Two Movements of the Monteverdi "Vespers"', *Monthly Musical Record*, lxxxiv (1954), p. 59, and 'Monteverdi's Church Music: Some Venetian Traits', ibid. lxxxviii (1958), p. 83.

[2] Critical edition of Mass and motet by Redlich (London and Zürich, 1963).

[3] Op. cit., chap. vii: 'Welchergestalt ein jedes Concert und Mutet mit wenig oder vielen Choren in der eil und ohne sonderbahre Mühe mit allerley Instrumenten und Menschenstimmen angeordnet und distribuirt werden könne' (ed. cit., p. 121).

ritornello as a completely new feature in the structure of liturgical music. That the appearance of the ritornello within the framework of his ecclesiastical music of 1610 must have been something of special import, appears from Praetorius's commentary (op. cit., p. 84), where his explanation of the ritornello as a new instrumental type is exclusively based on examples from Monteverdi's *Vespro*, and its secular forerunner, the *Scherzi musicali* (1607).

The ritornello, as an independent orchestral interlude surrounded by a mass of vocally conceived music, began to impinge on the strictly vocal character of its surroundings. Praetorius[1] draws attention to the fact that it is quite permissible to perform such works of mixed style in a purely instrumental manner, ignoring the vocal character of the parts (save for one leading melodic part, which should invariably remain vocal) and using the instruments alone 'gleichwie ein Ritornello'.[2] The introduction of the ritornello into church music is specially noticeable in the psalm 'Dixit Dominus',[3] where the *sex instrumenta* may *ad libitum* play four-bar interludes between the sentences of the psalm; they are tentatively introduced with the note: 'Li Ritornelli si ponno sonare et anco tralasciar secondo il volere'. This choice of alternatives in the musical structure—typical of all music of the baroque period—plays a much larger part in Monteverdi's later church music, where polyphonic sections of Masses and the *Magnificat* may be exchanged for concerto-like treatments of the same text. For instance in the 'Et iterum' *a* 3[4] in the *Selva morale e spirituale* (Venice, 1640), 'Concertato con 4 Tromboni o Viole da brazzo quali si ponno anco lasciare, il qual Crucifixus servirà per variatione della Messa a quattro pigliando questo in loco di quello notato tra li due segni. . . .' The two other psalms of 1610, 'Nisi Dominus' and 'Lauda Jerusalem', pay tribute to the Venetian *cori spezzati* technique with their two choirs in seven and ten parts, but the most surprising movement[5] of the whole collection is the 'Sonata sopra Sancta Maria',[6] in which the vocal element has shrunk to a simple *canto fermo* phrase for one voice, monotonously reiterated while a richly coloured orchestra in eight parts plays the Sonata.

---

[1] Op. cit., p. 155.

[2] Op. cit., p. 154: 'Die neunde Art', being part of chap. viii: 'Admonitio und Erinnerung welcher gestalt in meinen Polyhymnis auch andern Operibus die Lateinische und Teutsche Geistliche Kirchen-Lieder und Concert Gesänge angeordnet und angestellet werden können. . . .'

[3] *Opere*, xiv, p. 133.

[4] Ibid. xv, i, p. 187; for the passage of the Mass, cf. ibid., p. 88.

[5] Modelled on one by Crotti published two years before: see Arnold, 'Notes on Two Movements', pp. 60–63.   [6] See also p. 571.

The constitution of the orchestra of the Sonata is another example of Praetorius's 'IXth manner':

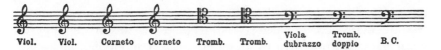

| Viol. | Viol. | Corneto | Corneto | Tromb. | Tromb. | Viola dubrazzo | Tromb. doppio | B. C. |

The hymn 'Ave maris stella', with its *instrumenta lritornello* and its combination and alternation of two choirs, sums up these devices, especially in its final section 'Sit laus' *a* 8 ('senza ritornello inanti'), which is scored for eight-part double choir and *continuo*, and should be executed—according to Praetorius[1]—with instruments and voices together. The hymn is purely chordal in conception, as are so many parts of the *Vespro*, with a gentle, almost 'popular' melody (a beautiful transformation of an original plainsong motive) dominating the whole movement. The differently coloured presentations of this melody appear now in $\frac{4}{4}$, now in $\frac{6}{4}$ time and are invariably shadowed by the same bass. The real happenings are the colour changes in the combination of voices and instruments; melody and harmonic base remain in serene immutability.

Ex. 226
(i)   (Note-values halved)·

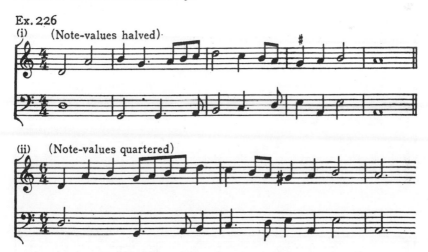

(ii)   (Note-values quartered)

The same principles are applied even more strikingly in the first of the two *Magnificat* settings at the end of the 1610 volume. The *Magnificat* 'septem vocibus et sex instrumentis' is an outstanding example of the new vocal-and-instrumental style in religious music. The liturgical text is split up into twelve separate movements,

---

[1] Ed. cit., p. 84.

abounding in contrasts of style and sonorous combination. To a
certain extent it might be described as a fusion of the two tendencies
in Monteverdi's ecclesiastical music: the *Prima* and *Seconda Prattica*,
the old polyphonic motet style and the new word-interpretative,
instrumentally accompanied style. It includes one movement of purely
vocal eight-part polyphony ('Et misericordia'), monodies, and pieces
for both chorus and orchestra. The 'Quia respexit' expressly asks for
the addition of pairs of 'fifare', flutes, and trombones:

Ex. 227

Ec-[ce]

This is one of the rare cases in the early baroque period where the upper wood-wind are used individually and unequivocally; they were long unpopular in Italy because of their imperfect intonation. Later on in the *Magnificat* ('Deposuit') two solo violins and two solo cornetti are employed in rich coloratura passages and echo-effects.

Neither here nor in the second *Magnificat* (*a 6 voci* with *continuo* but no other instruments) is the organ mentioned by name, but elaborate notes on registration are added in the original to the *continuo* part[1]—perhaps the earliest references to organ stops in any score.[2]

VENETIAN INFLUENCE IN ROME

To complete the picture of the more massive church music of the early Italian baroque period, we must consider the so called 'Roman school' as it came under the influence of Venetian ideas. During Palestrina's lifetime ecclesiastical music in Rome remained within the limits of the *a cappella* style, and his pupils and followers[3] tried hard —especially up to the time of Giovanni Maria Nanino's death in 1607—to keep within the boundaries of this emphatically vocal style. But not for long. Palestrina himself had been so far influenced by the Venetian style as to compose motets for two or even three choirs,[4] and ten years after his death his pupil Giovanni Francesco Anerio was providing some of the Masses, including the 'Missa Papae Marcelli', with organ *continuo*. Giovanni Bernardino Nanino adopted the *continuo* in his *Motecta* (Rome, 1610), and his pupil and son-in-law Paolo Agostini (1593–1629) employed both *continuo* and polychoral effects, as in the famous Mass in forty-eight parts composed for Pope Urban VIII, to say nothing of other works scored for four, six, or

[1] *Opere*, xiv, p. 285.

[2] Monteverdi's spiritual monodies, mostly published between 1615 and 1627, are discussed *infra* (pp. 538–41); his later religious music, the *Selva morale e spirituale* of 1641 and the *Messa a quattro voci et salmi* of 1651, will be dealt with in Vol. V.

[3] See pp. 367–8.   [4] See pp. 327–9.

eight real choirs, which have hitherto remained in manuscript. The older Palestrina disciple Soriano introduced the *basso continuo*. Yet all these composers—even the Cremonese Tiburzio Massaino, who published polychoral motets, *Sacrae Cantiones* with organ (1607), and instrumental *canzoni*—remained reluctant to introduce obbligato instruments in the manner of Gabrieli and Monteverdi. The same may be said of the polychoral motets, Masses, and other liturgical works of Antonio Maria Abbatini (1595–1680), Virgilio Mazzocchi (d. 1646), and Domenico Allegri (*c.* 1585–1629) and their lesser known followers. Despite increasing pomp and numerical splendour, these mammoth choral works show a definite falling off in polyphonic technique and in the general standard of vocal style, which quite naturally relied more and more on block harmonies, without on the other hand achieving the lapidary simplicity and luminous harmony of Giovanni Gabrieli. Nevertheless, in G. F. Anerio's and Soriano's work, as well as in the Masses of Agostini, the traditional arts of Flemish counterpoint and canonic imitation are still very noticeable.

A possible explanation of this expansion of the Venetian style in Rome is that the new principal nave of St. Peter's demanded an increase in sonority. Similarly the imposing proportions of the new cathedral at Salzburg inspired the Roman composer Orazio Benevoli (1605–72) to a festival Mass, which may fittingly be mentioned here as the climax of this style of massed sonorities. Benevoli's Mass[1] (first performed at the consecration of the cathedral on 25 September 1628) is conceived on a truly gigantic scale, with sixteen vocal and thirty-four instrumental parts. This astounding feat of polychoral writing can—as Leichtentritt pointed out—easily be reduced to eight real parts, which are only thrown into gigantic relief by the unison and octave doublings. Although the harmonic conception remains within the compass of the ecclesiastical modes, the embellishments of the instrumental parts as well as the energetic rhythmization of the vocal parts anticipate Carissimi, and even Handel.

ECCLESIASTICAL MONODY

The origins of secular monody have been described in Chapter IV; side by side with it appeared the solo motet with *basso continuo* or

---

[1] Published by Guido Adler, *Denkmäler der Tonkunst in Oesterreich*, xx (Jg. 10 (1)) (Vienna, 1903); facsimile of a page of the score in Haas, *Musik des Barocks*, facing p. 80. On this Mass see particularly Ambros–Leichtentritt, op. cit. iv, pp. 139 ff. Other more

'spiritual concerto'. The actual term 'concerto' had been applied to church music by Andrea Gabrieli in 1587 and again by Adriano Banchieri in 1595, when he published *Concerti ecclesiastici* for eight-part choir with a *basso continuo* part printed under the stave of the treble and containing regular barlines. (It is thus the earliest example of a modern score.) But the decisive step to the concerto for single voice with *continuo* was taken by Costanzo Porta's pupil Ludovico Grossi da Viadana (1564–1627) in his *Cento Concerti Ecclesiastici. A Una, a due, a tre e a quattro voci. Con il basso continuo per sonar nell'organo. Nova inventione commoda per ogni sorte de cantori e per gli organisti* (Venice, 1602).[1] According to the composer's preface, some of these had been composed and publicly performed in Rome as far back as 1596–7. (Praetorius based his explanation of the new 'concerto' idea entirely on Viadana.)[2] Viadana's important preface,[3] in which he explains how he arrived at this new and revolutionary style, ends with instructions for the performance of works of this type. Although he aims clearly at the establishment of a monodic voice-part and quite consciously distinguishes between a choral and a solo part, the artistic results of his effort remain rather modest. The spirit of the older polyphonic motet was still very much alive in his *Concerti*, especially in the numerous settings for two, three, or four voices with *continuo*, in which the older types of *bicinium* and *tricinium* are only thinly disguised by the added instrumental bass. This is specially noticeable in Viadana's 'Missa Dominicalis', in his Second Book of *Concerti*,[4] probably the first attempt at a monodic Mass with *continuo*. Giovanni Gabrieli also composed a *Kyrie*[5] in which the highest part is obviously vocal, with echo-effects and very florid coloratura, while the lower ones are clearly instrumental.

normal works by Benevoli have been published by Laurence Feininger, *Monumenta Liturgiae Polychoralis*, i–ix (Rome, 1950–4).

[1] Despite the title, it contained only fifty-nine pieces; modern edition by Claudio Gallico (Kassell Basle, 1964). The remainder appeared in Books II and III (1607 and 1611). Ten pieces reprinted in Max Schneider, *Die Anfänge des Basso Continuo und seiner Bezifferung* (Leipzig, 1918), pp. 172 ff.; separate examples in Schering, *Geschichte der Musik in Beispielen*, p. 181, Davison and Apel, op. cit. ii, p. 4, Haas, *Musik des Barocks*, pp. 40 ff. On Viadana see F. X. Haberl, 'Lodovico Grossi da Viadana', *Kirchenmusikalisches Jahrbuch*, iv (1889), p. 44, Ambros–Leichtentritt, op. cit. iv, pp. 218 ff.

[2] Ed. cit., p. 17.

[3] Original text and German translation reprinted in Schneider, op. cit., p. 3; English translation in F. T. Arnold, *The Art of Accompaniment from a Thorough-Bass* (London, 1931), pp. 3 and 10, and Oliver Strunk, *Source Readings in Music History* (London, 1952), p. 419.

[4] Reprinted by Peter Wagner, *Geschichte der Messe* (Leipzig, 1913), p. 534, and August Scharnagl, *Musica Divina* (new series), x (Ratisbon, 1954).

[5] Wagner, op. cit., p. 414, and Winterfeld, op. cit. iii, p. 108.

Ex. 228

But it has been pointed out[1] that Viadana's *basso continuo* could have been sung as well as played, considering its stylistic affinity with the motet basses of earlier decades. It is quite possible, then, that both parts were sung, the bass being also doubled by the organist. Sometimes imitation occurs, quite in the old style:

Ex. 229

[1] R. Freymann, *Entwicklungsgrundlagen des deutsch-protestantischen Musikstils um 1600* (MS. 1934).

Discussing Viadana, Blume[1] rightly speaks of the 'pseudo-polyphony', in the spirit of which the majority of these early specimens of ecclesiastical monody were conceived.

Viadana shows himself much more progressive in the following passages also taken from the *Concerti Ecclesiastici*:

Ex. 230

(i) AVE HOSTIA SALUTARIS[2]

(ii) AVE VERUM CORPUS[3]

[1] *Das monodische Prinzip in der protestantischen Kirchenmusik* (Berlin, 1925); see also Adam Adrio, *Die Anfänge des geistlichen Konzerts* (Berlin, 1935), p. 15.
[2] Reprinted complete in Ambros–Leichtentritt, op. cit., p. 223.
[3] Reprinted complete in Schneider, op. cit., p. 188.

In the second of these excerpts chromaticism begins also to influence the harmonic structure and thus anticipates similar passages in Gabrieli, Monteverdi, and Schütz. The passage seems to be conceived in a novel spirit of vertical harmonization. From such insights into the nature of the harmonic bass the younger generation must have derived more encouragement than from the many compositions by Viadana still conceived in the spirit of the polyphonic ideal, even if the notation paid lip service to monody.

The publication of Caccini's *Nuove musiche* and Viadana's *Concerti ecclesiastici* engendered a host of solo motets, which seem to borrow from the early operatic experiments of Peri and Caccini as well as from progressively conceived church music like Banchieri's *Concerti*.

VIADANA'S FOLLOWERS

The repercussions of the new style were particularly noticeable in northern Italy where most of its founders lived and published. Adam Adrio[1] counted no fewer than fifty composers in the territories of the Venetian Republic alone, who took up Viadana's new type of *concerto ecclesiastico*. According to him the main sources for our knowledge of early ecclesiastical monody are three collective publications: Nikolaus Stein's collection[2] of compositions in 1–6 parts by Jacopo Finetti, Pietro Lappi, and Giulio Belli[3] (Frankfurt, 1621); Lorenzo Calvi's *Symbola diversorum · musicorum* (in two volumes, 1620 and 1624), with compositions by forty-five musicians including Monteverdi, Alessandro Grandi, Giovanni Rovetta, Ignazio Donati, and Giovanni Ghizzolo; and Johann Donfried's *Promptuarium musicum* (in three volumes, Strasbourg, 1622, 1623, and 1627), which offers an ample choice among Viadana's immediate followers. Some of these early sacred monodies are not liturgical music but were composed on poems taken from Padre Angelo Grillo's[4] *Pietosi affetti*. (This was the case with the *Motetti e madrigali* (Venice, 1614) of Padre Serafino Patta.) Other composers, such as Ottavio Durante in his *Arie devote* (Rome, 1608), were inspired by secular monodies of the type of Caccini's *Nuove musiche*, while Radesca da Foggia seems

[1] Op. cit., p. 15.
[2] This Frankfurt publisher had reprinted the First Book of Viadana's *Concerti* as early as 1609 and a complete edition in 1620.
[3] Belli's *Concerti ecclesiastici* had already appeared in Venice in 1613.
[4] Whose obituary notice of Monteverdi, reprinted in Malipiero's *Claudio Monteverdi* (Milan, 1930), has saved him from oblivion.

to have modelled his lament of the Virgin 'Anima cara e pia'[1] on Monteverdi's 'Lamento d'Arianna'.

Two members of Monteverdi's choir at St. Mark's, Girolamo Marinoni and Luigi Simonetti, published *Motetti a voce sola* in 1611 and 1613 respectively. To this group of early ecclesiastical monodists also belongs Severo Bonini (organist at Forlì in 1613), who published as early as 1607 *Madrigali e Canzonetti spirituali* (for voice and chitarrone or other *continuo* instrument); Bonini, who calls himself in his preface one of the most ardent imitators of Caccini, proceeded very soon to the imitation of Monteverdi and in 1615 published *Affetti spirituali a 2 voci, parti in istile di Firenze*. (His manuscript *Discorsi e regole sovra la musica*[2] contains important information on both Caccini and Monteverdi.) But whereas some of these early pioneers of spiritual monody—such as Agazzari[3] and Giovanni Francesco Anerio[4]—still adhered to Viadana's basically conservative style,[5] with Ottavio Durante, Marinoni, and others who were partly inspired by Caccini's and Monteverdi's secular monodies, an element of coloratura virtuosity creeps into the hallowed precincts of religious song. The following passage from Durante's 'Angelus ad pastores' in the *Arie devote*:[6]

Ex. 231

---

[1] Cf. Ambros–Leichtentritt, op. cit., p. 424.

[2] Partly printed in Angelo Solerti, *Le origini del melodramma* (Milan, 1903), p. 129.

[3] Agazzari published in 1607 a treatise *Del sonare sopra il basso*; facsimile reprint (Milan, 1933), English translation in Strunk, op. cit., p. 424.

[4] See the 'Adoro te' from the Fifth Book of Anerio's *Sacrae cantiones* (Rome, 1615) printed by Haberl, *Kirchenmusikalisches Jahrbuch*, i (1886), p. 61.

[5] Cf. Leichtentritt, *Geschichte der Motette* (Leipzig, 1908), p. 242.

[6] The piece is printed complete in Haas, *Musik des Barocks*, p. 57.

shows this intrusion.

MONTEVERDI AND THE SACRED MONODY

Monteverdi's *Lamento d'Arianna* (1608) has already been mentioned as an early model for sacred monody. Actually it constitutes, after the monodic portions of *Orfeo* (1607), his earliest contribution to the new style. A year later he composed the first of his *continuo* madrigals,[1] in which this device is only very tentatively employed, but in 1610 he wrote the solo motet 'Nigra sum' (with its continuation 'Audi coelum'), in which the species of ecclesiastic monody seems to be epitomized in one unsurpassable masterpiece. In fact one might boldly assert that 'Nigra sum' and 'Audi coelum', of which the initial stanzas are reproduced here,

Ex. 232

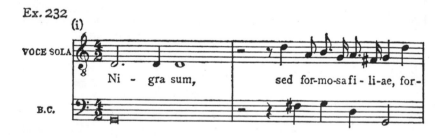

---

[1] 'Una donna fra l'altre', not published till 1614, but composed in 1609 and published the same year as a spiritual parody 'Una es' in Coppini's *Terzo Libro della Musica di Cl. Monteverdi*. Cf. Redlich, *Claudio Monteverdi* (Berlin, 1932), p. 152.

are the most perfect specimens of this new type, uniting secular
vocal artistry with religious fervour and applying the methods of
operatic monody to a religious subject of peculiar emotional tension.
With these two early pieces should be compared the two beautiful
monodies for soprano and *continuo* included in the *Selva Morale e
Spirituale* (1641): 'Jubilet' ('a voce sola in Dialogo') and 'Laudate
Dominum' ('voce sola Soprano o Tenore').[1] These—as well as the
monodies issued separately during Monteverdi's Venetian years—
strike one not only by the particular fervour of their melodic line, as
in the beginning of 'Jubilet',

[1] *Opere*, xv (2), pp. 748 and 753.

Ex. 233

Ju-bi-let, ju-bi-let ... ju-bi-let, ju-bi-let to - (ta)

but also by their inclusion of consciously operatic features of style, as created in the 'genere concitato' of Monteverdi's later years. These features include realistic imitations of particular instruments, as in this passage from 'Laudate Dominum':

Ex. 234

S. or T. ... lau - da - te e - um in cim - ba -

- lis ... in cim-ba - lis

as well as chromaticisms, as in the 'Salve O Regina' 'a voce sola e basso continuo'[1] in the second volume of Calvi's *Symbola*:[2]

Ex. 235

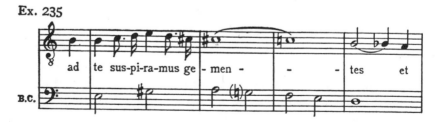

ad te sus-pi-ra-mus ge - men - - tes et

---

[1] Calvi published another 'Salve O Regina' in his 'quarta raccolta' of 1629 for three voices and organ, reprinted in the *Selva Morale* and so in *Opere*, xv (2), p. 741.
[2] Ibid. xvi, p. 475.

flen - tes in hac la-cri-|ma - rum | val - le.

and marked rhythmical affinities to the style of the secular canzonetta
as in 'Currite populi', printed in Leonardo Simonetti's collection
(Venice, 1625):

Ex. 236

Cur - ri - te, curri-te, po-pu-li, cur-ri-te, psal-li-te,

psal-li - te, tim-pa-ni, psal-li - te, di - ci - te, di - ci - te,

vo - ci - bus   di - ci - te   di - ci-te

Various other of Monteverdi's sacred monodies appeared in these
collections of Calvi, Simonetti, and Donfried. Yet another
superb fusion of operatic recitative and religious fervour was achieved
by Monteverdi in the sacred parody of the 'Lamento d'Arianna';
the 'Pianto della Madonna, a voce sola sopra il Lamento d'Arianna'[1]
was to become the model for innumerable plaints of the Blessed
Virgin.

This 'Pianto', issued so late in life, may actually have been composed shortly after the performance of the opera *Arianna* (1608)

[1] Ibid. xv (2), p. 757.

and was certainly widely acknowledged throughout Italy and Germany as a masterpiece of sacred monody.

MONTEVERDI'S DISCIPLES

The generation of Monteverdi's disciples may fittingly close this account of early sacred monody in Italy. Perhaps the most arresting personality among them was Claudio Saracini[1] from Siena, whose 170 preserved monodies[2] are among the most important of the early Baroque period. The highlight among them is undoubtedly 'Il Lamento della Madonna' ('Christo smarrito') 'in stile recitativo',[3]

Ex. 237

(Gasping and weeping, she turned her lovely eyes to heaven)

the chromaticisms of which are clearly derived from Monteverdi's 'Lamento'. Saracini's *Terge musiche* (Venice, 1620) contains a monodic 'Stabat Mater'[4] also in the style of Monteverdi's 'Lamento', which impresses the listener not only by its progressive harmony and bold chromaticism but also by the nobility of its flexible declamation and the inevitability of its vocal contours. All these features show a tremendous improvement on the primitive beginnings of the new style in Viadana.

Among Monteverdi's other disciples, notable for their ecclesiastical monodies, must be mentioned his successor at St. Mark's, Giovanni Rovetta (d. 1668),[5] Ignazio Donati (c. 1585–1638), organist at Urbino

---

[1] See pp. 160 ff.: also Ambros–Leichtentritt, op. cit., pp. 816 ff., and Haas, *Musik des Barocks*, pp. 53 ff.

[2] Published in six books of *Musiche* (1614–24) containing one or two spiritual monodies.

[3] From the *Seconde musiche* (Venice, 1620): facsimile reprint by Count Guido Chigi-Saracini (Siena, 1933).

[4] Excerpt in Ambros–Leichtentritt, op. cit., p. 818.

[5] See the excerpts from his 'Salve Regina', Leichtentritt, *Geschichte der Motette*, pp. 251 ff.

in younger days and ultimately *maestro di cappella* at Milan Cathedral, who published *motetti in concerto, concerti ecclesiastici, motetti concertati, motetti a voce sola*, the nature of which is indicated by their titles,[1] and Alessandro Grandi (d. 1630). The last named, a pupil of Gabrieli, in 1617 one of Monteverdi's *cantori* at St. Mark's, and afterwards vice-*maestro* there, was one of the most successful masters of the *concertato* motet[2] and later, from 1621 onward, of the solo motet. As Arnold says, 'Grandi shows a great flair for making the melodic line flow smoothly and match the emotional emphasis of the words':

Ex. 238

---

[1] See the opening of his 'Languet anima mea', ibid., p. 255.

[2] Three examples reprinted by Blume, *Das Chorwerk*, xl (Wolfenbüttel, 1936). See also Leichtentritt, *Geschichte der Motette*, pp. 259 ff., and particularly Denis Arnold, 'Alessandro Grandi, a Disciple of Monteverdi', *Musical Quarterly*, xliii (1957), p. 171, on Grandi's change of style between the earlier *concertato* motets and the later monodic ones.

THE CHANGE OF STYLE IN GERMANY

In Germany, as in Italy, there were a number of composers who, despite their Lutheran convictions and their consequent attitude to word-interpretation, remained faithful to the old ideals. Outstanding among these was Christoph Demantius.[1] Melchior Franck[2] also eschewed to the last the use of the *basso continuo* and cultivated the motet—even with Latin words, as many Protestants did—from the beginning to the end of his career.[3] Erhard Bodenschatz (c. 1576–1636), the successor of Seth Calvisius at Pforta, is justly famous as the collector of the vocal anthology *Florilegium Portense* (Leipzig, i, 1603; ii, 1621)[4] which was still used by J. S. Bach[5] and in which may be found the most attractive polyphonic compositions of the period, German as well as Italian, including some Latin compositions by the editor himself. The earlier works of Johann Staden (1581–1634), especially his motets (*Harmoniae Sacrae*), of 1616,[6] hark back to the polyphonic style of Clemens non Papa and other Renaissance composers, but Staden later became a progressive and wrote not only motets with *continuo* but sacred concertos with obbligato instrumental accompaniments, 'symphonies', and ritornelli.[7]

THE PROGRESSIVES

The first German composers to be affected by Italian innovations in church music include both Protestants and Catholics. The former are headed by Hans Leo Hassler[8] (1564–1612), Adam Gumpeltzhaimer (c. 1559–1625), Hieronymus Praetorius[9] (1560–1629), Philippus Dulichius (1562–1631), and Michael Praetorius[10] (1571–1621), while the most prominent Catholics are Jacobus Gallus (Handl)[11] (1550–91) and Gregor Aichinger[12] (1564–1628). Among these musi-

---

[1] See p. 454.   [2] See p. 455.

[3] Five German motets from the *Geystliche Gesäng und Melodeyen* (Coburg, 1608), ed. by A. A. Abert, *Das Chorwerk*, xxiv (Wolfenbüttel, 1933).

[4] See Otto Riemer, *Erhard Bodenschatz und sein 'Florilegium Portense'* (Leipzig, 1928) and article 'Florilegium Portense', *Die Musik in Geschichte und Gegenwart*, iv (1955), col. 430. One of Bodenschatz's *Bicinia XC selectissima* (Leipzig, 1615), which Riemer regards as marking an interesting stage between the *bicinia* of Lassus and the two-part concertos of Schütz, is reprinted in Schering, *Geschichte der Musik in Beispielen*, p. 171.

[5] Schering, *Musikgeschichte Leipzigs*, ii (Leipzig, 1926), p. 56.

[6] Examples reprinted by Eugen Schmitz, *Denkmäler der Tonkunst in Bayern*, vii (1) and viii (1).

[7] For instance, in his *Kirchenmusik* (1625 and 1626), *Harmoniae variatae* (1632), and other publications; examples reprinted ibid.

[8] See p. 453.   [9] See pp. 454–5.   [10] See p. 453.
[11] See p. 274.   [12] See pp. 270–1.

cians, born between *c.* 1560 and 1570 and dead before 1630, the influence of Italy is more noticeable in the general sonority of the harmony and choral dispositions than in specially progressive features such as the use of *basso continuo* or obbligato instruments, concerto-like tendencies, or decay of the polyphonic tradition. None of the composers mentioned here composed monodies, yet their debt to the Italians, especially to the Venetians, seems very great.[1] The eldest of this generation, Gallus, appears at his most progressive in his five-part motet 'Mirabile mysterium',[2] famous for its startling chromatic harmonies. Like Hassler, Gumpeltzhaimer, and Hieronymus Praetorius, Gallus excelled in employment of *cori spezzati*, which were cultivated in the second half of the sixteenth century in Germany and Austria, perhaps without any promptings from the Venetians.[3]

In the cases of Hassler and Aichinger the relationship to the Venetian school is unquestionable, as both went to Venice after 1580 (Hassler in 1584, Aichinger perhaps in the same year, but certainly before 1588),[4] there to become pupils of the two Gabrielis. Italian influence is more easily traceable in Hassler's secular compositions than in much of his church music, particularly that to German words. His Italian allegiance is more evident in his Latin motets and Masses, though it appears that he was more impressed by the euphonious motet style of Andrea, or even of the Roman school, than by the experiments of Giovanni Gabrieli.

Very different was the case of the Catholic Aichinger, who became a pupil of Giovanni Gabrieli and won the reputation of being more Venetian than his mentor himself. His most important achievement was his *Cantiones Ecclesiasticae, trium et quatuor vocum . . . cum Basso Generali et Continuo in usum Organistarum* (Dillingen, 1607), the first work by a German composer to pay tribute to Viadana's invention of the sacred concerto, its bassus part containing the earliest German instruction for the use of a *basso continuo*[5] modelled on Viadana's. This publication was followed in 1614 by Book II of

---

[1] This needs the more emphasis because of repeated efforts by German scholars to belittle this influence: cf. Blume, *Evangelische Kirchenmusik*, p. 94.

[2] *Denkmäler der Tonkunst in Oesterreich*, Jg. 6¹ (vol. xii), p. 161; recorded in *The History of Music in Sound*, iv.

[3] Cf. Blume, ibid. It is true that Leonhart Schroeter (1532–c. 1600) published as early as 1571 a German *Te Deum* for eight-part double choir in the latest Venetian manner, reprinted in Ambros–Kade, op. cit. v, p. 465; but *cori spezzati* by Willaert had already been published at Nuremberg in 1564 (cf. *Denkmäler der Tonkunst in Bayern*, v, p. 431).

[4] Cf. *Denkmäler der Tonkunst in Bayern*, x (1), p. xxxii.

[5] Reprinted in Schneider, op. cit., p. 85.

Gumpeltzhaimer's *Sacri Concentus* to which is appended a 'duplicum Bassum ad organistarum usum', thereby turning these motets (originally obviously conceived in terms of traditional polyphony)[1] at one stroke into 'concerti ecclesiastici' in Viadana's sense: a procedure reminiscent of the addition of *continuo* parts to reprints by Phalèse and others of Monteverdi's earlier madrigal-books,[2] and of the *continuo* part in Monteverdi's otherwise completely polyphonic Mass 'In illo tempore'. Hieronymus Praetorius also adopted the polychoral technique of the Venetians in his grandiose choral compositions of up to twenty parts, but like Hassler and Gumpeltzhaimer did not venture on monody or obbligato instrumental parts.

MICHAEL PRAETORIUS

The musicians so far considered remained attached to the traditional motet style except for their contributions to Lutheran congregational song. With Michael Praetorius we reach a composer who was on the one hand positively obsessed by the Lutheran hymn,[3] yet who devoted a great part of his tremendous creative energy to the absorption of every Italian innovation and its fusion with his own characteristically vernacular type of sacred music. In his celebrated *Syntagma Musicum III* he painstakingly collected all the evidence of these Italian innovations of style, from the prefaces and treatises of Italian theoreticians down to oral reports of travellers, fresh from Italy,[4] and reproduced in full translation (enriched by many useful marginal notes) the instructions of Viadana, Strozzi, Agazzari, and Artusi for the practical use of the *basso continuo*. He illustrates the novel use of figures and the art of interpreting the bass harmonically by a curiously angular example from one of his own hymn settings.[5] In explaining every feature of the practical music of his time he shows a thorough knowledge of the progressive side of Italian music in addition to a complete mastery of the style of the Lassus-Palestrina period.

Perhaps the most impressive section of his book is the third part, in which he designs a system of colouring devices for the orchestration of every possible vocal score, whether of the sixteenth century or of his own time, on the basis of Agazzari's and Viadana's suggestions. The *Syntagma III*, written and published in 1619, two years before Praetorius's premature death on his fiftieth birthday (15 February

---

[1] Cf. O. Mayr, introduction to *Denkmäler der Tonkunst in Bayern*, x (2) (Leipzig, 1909), which contains a selection from Gumpeltzhaimer's works.

[2] Cf. Redlich, *Claudio Monteverdi* (Olten, 1949), p. 64, n. 2.

[3] See *supra*, pp. 453–4.   [4] Cf. E. Bernoulli's preface to the modern reprint.

[5] 'Wir glauben', ed. cit., p. 113. See also L. U. Abraham, *Der Generalbass im Schaffen von Michael Praetorius* (Berlin, 1961).

1621), epitomizes the results of a life of remarkable mental energy, almost completely devoted to German religious music—above all in the great collections of compositions on Protestant hymns described in Chap. VIII.

In the vast majority of these works Praetorius contrives to reconcile a true feeling for the style of the traditional motet with a ready acceptance of novel patterns and daring methods of composition. The ideal vehicle for a realization of the new conception of style (closely related to Viadana's type of 'concerto ecclesiastico') seemed the *bicinium* and the *tricinium*, two- and three-part compositions of motet- or hymn-like character, and the *bicinia* and *tricinia*—which had originated in the previous century—helped to undermine traditional polyphony, inasmuch as they fostered a feeling for the true bass properties of the third part. The fact that Aichinger in his *Quercus Dodonae* of 1619 calls his motets for two sopranos and *continuo* '*tricinia*' indicates that a twofold function was still allotted to the bass part. Even Praetorius himself in his *Polyhymnia Caduceatrix* (1619) adds a text to the bass part, which can thus be played and sung as well. The early *bicinia* of Seth Calvisius (1599) and the still earlier *tricinia* of Monteverdi (*Sacrae Cantiunculae*, 1582) point towards a development of deliberate paucity of parts, which culminated in the countless *bicinia* and *tricinia* of Praetorius's *Musae Sioniae*, in which the Lutheran hymn-melodies represent the backbone of the conception. Three methods of interpreting the hymn, in 'motet' or 'madrigalian' manner (according to Praetorius's own terminology) or in a style that anticipates the 'chorale prelude' of the late baroque composers (Lübeck, Pachelbel, Buxtehude, Tunder, and others) were all expounded in the microcosm of the *Musae Sioniae*:[1]

Ex. 239

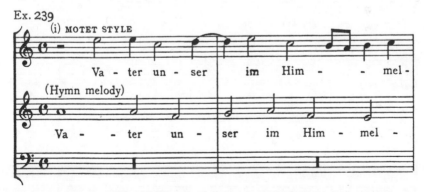

[1] Cf. Blume, *Evangelische Kirchenmusik*, p. 104, and *Gesamtausgabe der musikalischen Werke von Michael Praetorius*, ix (Wolfenbüttel, 1929), pp. 84, 85, and 89.

al - le, der du uns

-le, der du uns al - le

- reich, der

(Our Father which art in Heaven)

They were projected on the much larger canvas of the 'chorale concerto' in the later stages of Praetorius's career, above all in the *Polyhymnia Caduceatrix* (1619),[1] of which the prefatory 'Ordinantz' gives the most remarkable directions for alternative orchestration of the vocal *res facta*. The volume contains elaborate compositions on all the favourite Lutheran melodies. Among these, two are especially notable for their musical value: 'Vom Himmel hoch' (no. 9) and 'Wie schön leuchtet der Morgenstern' (no. 10)[2] for five voices and five instruments, written and published in a kind of 'short score' reminiscent of Monteverdi's *Vespro* and *Magnificat*, which were well known to Praetorius; the real orchestral score has to be constructed on the basis of the prescriptions in the *Syntagma III*, to which the composer expressly refers in a note printed at the head of each item. It is clear that the kind of rich orchestral setting Praetorius had in mind conformed to the pattern of Gabrieli's *Sacrae Symphoniae II* (1615) and Monteverdi's *Vespro* (1610). The *Polyhymnia* also contains a German Mass, 'Die Missa ganz Teudsch',[3] for voices and instruments, with a complete *continuo* part and instrumental 'sinfoniae', strongly reminiscent of the orchestral ritornelli of Monteverdi's *Vespro* (especially 'Dixit Dominus'). Works such as these were at the time unique in their embodiment of Italian stylistic innovations in completely Lutheran and typically German music. Yet Praetorius kept strangely aloof from one Italian innovation, the recitative, with the result that his music—despite its inherently progressive character, despite its acceptance of the *basso continuo* and the Venetian orchestral palette—retains still a sixteenth-century sobriety and austerity, lacking the elasticity and declamatory agility which were to be outstanding features of the following generation: the generation of Schein, Scheidt, and Schütz.[4]

[1] *Gesamtausgabe*, xvii (Wolfenbüttel, 1930).
[2] Ibid., pp. 39 and 45. Redlich's edition of 'Wie schön' (London, 1954) is recorded in *The History of Music in Sound*, iv.
[3] Ibid., p. 664.   [4] On these composers, see *supra*, pp. 455 ff.

XI

CONCERTED INSTRUMENTAL MUSIC

By Ernst H. Meyer

THE GROWTH OF INSTRUMENTAL MUSIC

THE rise of instrumental music during the century of the Reformation is one of the most striking features of comparatively recent musical history. It was brought about by, and itself assisted, the great social changes of that era, changes which signified the end of the Middle Ages and the transition to modern society, the first steps toward the economic, social, political, religious, and cultural emancipation of the peoples of Europe. During the Middle Ages instrumental music in general had been of secondary importance compared with vocal music, owing to the preoccupation of the Church with the latter. The tremendous growth of independent instrumental music during the sixteenth century was a symptom of secularization. By its very nature this type of music was secular rather than religious. Even when sacred polyphony was played on instruments, the general feeling must have been secular, for much of the religious spirit of the vocal originals was lost. Musical gatherings where purely instrumental works were played were intended mainly for pleasure and entertainment.

Towards the end of the Middle Ages the division of music into sacred and profane, in function as well as in ways of performance, had become general in all the main musical countries of Europe. However, the separation of instrumental from vocal music took much longer.[1]

MUSIC FOR VOICES OR INSTRUMENTS

While in lute and keyboard music certain instrumental characteristics had already appeared some time before the sixteenth century, a close relationship in style between vocal and instrumental group music was maintained throughout the sixteenth century. Madrigals, songs, and *chansons* were frequently played by instruments, and

[1] See Vol. III, p. 465.

early instrumental dances were sometimes issued with texts. In all parts of Europe publications[1] appeared with titles such as *Canzoni francese a 2 voci di Antonio Gardane, et di altri autori, buone da cantare et sonare* (Venice, 1539); *Schöne auszerlesene Lieder des Hoch beruempten Heinrici Finckens, lustig zu singen und auf die Instrument dienstlich* (Nuremberg, 1536); *Het ierste musyck boexken mit Vier Partyen . . . Gecomponeert by diversche componisten, zeer lustich om zingen en spelen op alle musicale Instrumenten* (Antwerp, 1551); *Le Recueil des plus belles et excellentes chansons . . . tant de voix que sur les instruments* (Paris, 1576); *Thesaurus musicus Continens selectissimas 8, 7, 6, 5, et 4 vocum harmonias et ad omnis generis instrumenta Musica accomodatas* (Nuremberg, 1564); *Duos or songs for two voyces by Thomas Whythorne, playne and easie to be sung or played on Musicall Instruments* (London, 1590). These pieces could be performed in four different ways: (1) by voices, (2) by instruments, (3) some parts by voices while the other parts were played by instruments, (4) all parts played and sung simultaneously by instruments and voices. In the course of the sixteenth century purely instrumental performances of such works became more and more frequent; after 1600 they became the rule.

In mixed vocal and instrumental performances there was one part which was almost invariably played by instruments: the *canto fermo*. In the middle of the sixteenth century many *Lied* arrangements and compositions in the motet form were still built round a basic tenor, secular or religious. This was especially so in Dutch and German music. As the tenor was often written in very long notes it was generally played on an instrument.

Few principles were laid down for the employment of any particular instruments in preference to others. As a general rule the more powerful types of wind instrument were used wherever instrumental music served the purpose of display in the open air, large halls, or churches. Strings and recorders were preferred for domestic entertainment. Castiglione in his *Cortegiano* (Florence, 1528) speaks of 'musica delle 4 viole da arco, la qual è soavissima et artificiosa' which he recommends for 'una domestica et cara compagnia'. The German composer and theorist Hans Gerle specially demands 'vier Geigen' in a *fuga* contained in his *Musica teusch* (1532). However, these are conventions rather than rules or regulations. Very often

[1] Library references to most of the works listed here and later on in this chapter may be found in Emil Bohn's and Robert Eitner's bibliographies, unless libraries are specially given.

the players must have used whatever instruments happened to be at hand. Only after 1550 can certain standard groupings be found on a larger scale, at first in England where since the days of Tye and Parsons the family of the viols had been very much in fashion.

PURELY INSTRUMENTAL MUSIC

In addition to works published for performance either by instruments or by voices *ad libitum*, leaving the choice to the musicians, collections appeared after the first third of the sixteenth century containing items written solely for instrumental performance and printed without text. Music for lute or organ without vocal implications had already come out considerably earlier, and much of this music for solo instruments capable of playing several parts could also be played by groups of purely melodic instruments. From 1529 onwards purely instrumental publications for groups of players appeared with increasing frequency; some of the more important, composed up to 1580, include Attaingnant's *Six Gaillardes et six Pavanes* (Paris, 1529) and *Neuf basses danses, deux branles, vingt et cinq Pauennes auec quinze Gaillardes en musique à quatre parties* (Paris, 1530);[1] *Trium vocum carmina* (100 pieces without words, Nuremberg, 1538); *Musica Nova* with *ricercari* by Segni, Willaert, Parabosco, and others (Venice, 1540);[2] Buus, *Recercari* (Venice, 1547 and 1549); Tiburtino, *Fantasie et Recercari a 3* (Venice, 1549); Tylman Susato's various publications at Antwerp from 1551 onwards; Padovano, *Il primo libro di Ricercari a 4 voci* (Venice, 1556); Bendusi, *Opera nova de balli* (Venice, 1553); Conforti, *Il primo libro de Ricercari a 4 voci* (Rome, 1558); *Fantasie Recercari Contrapuncti a 3 voci* with works by Willaert, Rore and others (Venice, 1559); Pietro Vinci, *Ricercari* (1560); Lupacchino, *Il primo Libro a note negre a 2 voci* (Venice, 1565); Phalèse's publication *Premier livre de danseries, contenant plusieurs Pavanes, Passomezo, Almandes, Gaillardes, Bransles etc.* (Louvain, 1571); Andrea Gabrieli, *Canzoni francesi* (Venice, 1571); Vicentino, *Madrigali a 5 voci* (fifth book with *canzone da sonare*) (Milan, 1572); Malvezzi, *Il primo Libro de Recercari a 4 voci* (Perugia, 1577); Ingegneri, *Il secondo libro de Madrigali* with two *arie di canzon francese per sonare* (Venice, 1579). A complete list of sixteenth-century instrumental group music would include many more pieces, some in collections of vocal music, among them works

---

[1] The two have been reprinted together by F. J. Giesbert as *Pariser Tanzbuch aus dem Jahre 1530* (Mainz, n.d.).
[2] 'Reconstructed' edition by H. Colin Slim (Chicago, 1965).

by great masters such as Palestrina and Lassus, both of whom wrote instrumental *ricercari*,[1] duos, and other works. Many pieces that have come to us in manuscript would have to be added, too; among others the instrumental *carmina* by late fifteenth- and sixteenth-century composers from Obrecht, Finck, Isaac, Hofhaimer, and Stoltzer to Senfl and Georg Forster. Then again, more instrumental material is contained in theoretical treatises such as Ortiz's *Tratado de glosas* (Rome, 1553).[2]

It is clear from the foregoing that a considerable variety of forms existed from the beginning of the sixteenth century. Two main types can be discerned: dances and 'free' compositions. Greater independence of instrumental performance from vocal practice was first achieved in the dances, but it was in the 'free' forms that the typically instrumental style developed most strongly.

DANCE FORMS

Dances were largely favoured by the rising middle classes. Although this new stratum of society was simpler in its cultural tradition than the nobility and clergy, it had the great advantage of a new optimism, vigour, and vitality. There are few traces of the complex and mystical beauty of the old, essentially ecclesiastical art in the dance collections of Attaingnant, Susato, Phalèse, and others. The intricate art of the masters of cathedral music here met a vital counter-force:

Ex. 240[3]

[1] Palestrina's *Ricercari a 4* are not universally accepted as genuine.
[2] Modern edition by Max Schneider (Kassel, 1913); see pp. 560 and 705–6.
[3] Basse-danse, 'La Brasse', from Attaingnant's *9 basses danses* . . . (1530).

In melody, counterpoint, rhythm, and metrical structure this music is of great clarity, and its character is popular and simple. The influence of folk song is obvious. There is a principal melody which predominates all the time, often (as in Ex. 240) in the top part. There are few syncopations; the accents fall on the main beat. Block harmonies in the manner of the Italian *villotta* and of many French *chansons* replace the intricate network of polyphony. Most conspicuous is the metrical regularity derived from the requirements of the dance: the symmetrical periods of two, four, or eight bars.

This quality of popular clarity and symmetry in formal structure was inherent in the music of all countries from England to Italy and from Spain to Poland; it is equally apparent in the dances of Ortiz, Arena, and the brothers Hesse, the French *danseries*,[1] and collections such as *Etlicher gutter Teutscher und Polnischer Tentz* (Breslau, 1555) and others. It is not clear whether this new simplicity, for which popular forces were responsible, started in the Netherlands, in Italy, or in Spain. But it must have spread soon to other countries where it found imitators and supporters. Nor did it remain confined to the dance literature of the amateur public; the un-named dances of Henry VIII's court have similar square rhythms and an unsophisticated melodic charm.[2]

Among a multitude of dance types the pavane and galliard were the most widely used. In Germany the same forms were often called *Dantz* and *Nachdantz* (*Tripla*, *Hupfauff* or *Proportz*), in Italy, *passamezzo* and *saltarello*. The former was a dance in common time; it was moderately slow in speed and consisted of a number of strains (at first usually two, later three), each of which was repeated. Towards the end of the sixteenth century the pavanes became more elaborate as people ceased to dance to them, and they acquired much of the contrapuntal style of other forms of instrumental and vocal music, especially in Elizabethan England. The galliard was in triple time; it was generally faster and altogether more light-hearted than the pavane.

PAIRS OF DANCES

The pavane and galliard often formed a pair of dances, the galliard following the pavane.[3] If in this procedure of coupling two types of

[1] Expert published a selection from Attaingnant's *Livres de Danseries* (Paris, 1547–50) in *Les Maîtres musiciens de la Renaissance française*, xxiii (Paris, 1908). Three dances from this collection by Claude Gervaise are easily accessible in Davison and Apel, *Historical Anthology of Music*, i (Cambridge, Mass., 1946), p. 148.

[2] See, for instance, the three-part piece by Henry VIII himself, reprinted by John Stevens, *Music at the Court of Henry VIII* (*Musica Britannica*, xviii, London, 1962), p. 41.   [3] Cf. Vol. III, p. 451.

dance we may see an early stage in the development of the suite, we
also find that in many cases the principle of variation is employed,
in that both pavane (*Dantz*) and galliard (*Nachdantz*) are derived
from the same material:[1]

Ex. 241 [2]
(i)

(ii)

The original pair of pavane-galliard from the beginning of the
sixteenth century (Petrucci) was occasionally extended by the addition
of the *piva*, which also existed as an independent dance.[3] (It was

---

[1] The principle had already been adumbrated in the fourteenth century; see Vol. III,
p. 416.

[2] 'De Post', from Susato's *Het derde musyck boexken* (Antwerp, 1551; modern
reprint by F. J. Giesbert, Mainz, 1936).

[3] Cf. Vol. III, pp. 442–3.

already one of the main dances of the fifteenth century, according to Andrea Cornazaro, who in 1465 mentioned it together with the *salta-rello*, *quaternaria*, and *bassadanza*.) It was generally a dance in fast triple time. The *almand* (*allemande*) in common time, the *courante* (*coran-to*) in triple time, the *brando* (*bransle*, brawl) in fast common time, the *volta* (fast triple), the *gigue* in $\frac{6}{8}$, the stately *intrada* in common time, and the variable *ballo* or *balletto*, mostly in common time, were other important dance forms which made their appearance after 1550 and are henceforward met with increasingly often. Some types of the French *basse danse* (*bassadanza* in Italian), the Spanish *danza della muerte*, and the English domp (all before and around 1550) were of particular gravity; they were slow dances and often the mood was sombre.

FREE INSTRUMENTAL FORMS

The other branch of concerted music, the one which has been termed 'free' instrumental music, developed parallel with dance music after the end of the fifteenth century. In form as well as in style this considerable corpus of music was largely modelled on vocal patterns; it grew either out of the music of the Church or out of the musical activities of educated circles. The main types, *ricercar* and fantasia, grew out of vocal forms which were musically the most highly developed of all.

The *carmina*, chiefly cultivated in the Netherlands and in Germany, were closely related both to the elaborate *Lied* arrangements and to the polyphonic motets of early sixteenth-century composers. When handled by the great composers of the time these instrumental movements are often of intense beauty:

Ex.242[1]

[Fairly slow]

[1] *Carmen in La* (c. 1530) by Ludwig Senfl, modern edition in *Nagels Musik-Archiv*, no. 53 (Hanover, 1929).

The melodic life of these instrumental examples of Renaissance music reminds us of the warmth and humanity of the vocal *Lied* arrangements of Forster, Ott, and other sixteenth-century German, Dutch, and Swiss masters. These *carmina* were either composed round a well-known song which was used as *canto fermo* (generally in the tenor) or, less often, built up from freely invented melodic material.

RICERCARI AND FANTASIAS

The *carmina* were superseded by the *ricercari* and fantasias. These forms seem to have been originally confined to organ and lute music,[1] but throughout the sixteenth century there was a continuous interchange between keyboard and lute music on the one hand and instrumental ensemble music on the other. When they developed beyond the stage of mere improvisatory preludes, these pieces were structurally modelled on the motet.

In the motet the various clauses and sentences of the text were generally set to themes based on fragments of the plainsong. Thus the motet consisted of a series of sections, most of which were fugal or semi-homophonic developments of the thematic idea underlying the section. Each section ended in a cadence; but these sections generally overlapped, so that a new section would begin while the cadence of the previous one was still sounding. This is important, for it was largely by this method of overlapping the sections of the motet that the atmosphere of mystic unity and the unbroken majestic flow of the church music of the age were obtained. Moreover, the various thematic lines on which the sections of the motet were based were very similar to one another in character, so that the general effect of this music was contemplative and non-dramatic.

The *ricercari* and fantasias up to the end of the sixteenth century all preserve the principal features of the motet. There is the same sectional work, the same homogeneity of thematic material throughout the various sections; there is indeed little difference between the

[1] See Vol. III, pp. 440–1 and 445 ff.

musical material of the vocal motets and the instrumental *ricercari*
and fantasias.[1] Moreover, a close affinity exists between these forms
and the more polyphonic madrigals and *chansons*.

Ex. 243[2]

[Moderate speed]

The *ricercar* of the sixteenth century has the same continuous flow
and the same overlapping of sections as church music. There are no
heavy emotional accents, no ups and downs of tension and relaxation; the music is entirely non-dramatic and often of a detached
dreaminess, as though it were not quite of this world. Full harmonic
cadences down to the 'earth' of the tonic are infrequent within a
piece and mostly occur only at the very end. Melodic lines in all parts
proceed by step far more often than by third-leaps—just as in vocal
music; fourths and fifths are rarer still; and sixths (generally minor
sixths up, followed by a semitone drop) as well as octaves (generally
up, followed by a small falling interval) are even less frequent. The
melodies are of great length. The instrumental-motet forms of the
later sixteenth century, however, gradually developed greater liveliness and more typically instrumental behaviour of the parts.

The fantasia during the greater part of the sixteenth century
differed from the *ricercar* only in the greater freedom of the melodic
material. This was nearly always freely invented, whereas many
ricercari still used for their thematic material existing vocal melodies,
either sacred or secular. During the second half of the sixteenth

---

[1] On certain differences between motet and *ricercar*, see p. 603.
[2] From Willaert's *Fantasie Recercari Contrapunti a tre voci . . . appropriati per Cantare
e Sonare d'ogni sorte di Stromenti* (Venice, 1559); no. 6 of the modern edition of the
ricercari by Hermann Zenck (Mainz, 1933). No. 7 is recorded in *The History of Music
in Sound* (H.M.V.), vol. iv.

century, however, these differences disappeared, both forms becoming almost identical in structure and general behaviour by the end of the century.

OTHER FREE FORMS

Other instrumental forms of the sixteenth century include the *capriccio* (a freer variety of the fantasia), the *canzona francese*, derived from the vocal *chanson* yet more homophonic in character than the instrumental motet forms—the great historical importance of the *canzon* dates only from the end of the century; it will be discussed in detail later in this chapter—and many others with vague titles such as *trattenimenti, contrapunti*, and innumerable pieces which either have no name at all, or only fanciful titles not alluding to any particular type. There are several pieces named *battaglia* which are early examples of programme music, characterized by repeated notes and chords, and trumpet-like calls. Both instrumental and vocal pieces are found with this title; early examples are those by Janequin and Matthias Werrecoren (both vocal);[1] later there are the well-known ones by Annibale Padovano and Andrea Gabrieli (instrumental, Venice, 1587 and 1590)[2] as well as those by Giuseffo Biffi (*per cantar et sonar*, Nuremberg, 1596), by Adriano Banchieri (instrumental, Venice, 1596), and a collection entitled *Musica de diversi authori, la Bataglia francese et Canzon delli ucelli . . . partite in caselle*, &c. (Venice, 1577). In the seventeenth century, however, there are 'battle' pieces of far greater importance than those mentioned here.[3]

NUMBER OF PARTS

In concerted instrumental music up to the last quarter of the sixteenth century there were combinations of two to seven parts. Pieces for four or five instruments were about equally frequent; six-part works were less popular; and there are only a few examples of instrumental music in more than six parts. However, there is an extensive literature for two and three instruments; these pieces were generally called *bicinia* and *tricinia*, and they were mainly cultivated in Germany and Italy. There are as many *bicinia* for two instruments of equal pitch as there are for one higher and one lower instrument. The form

---

[1] See pp. 6–7.

[2] Reprinted by Benvenuti in *Istituzioni e Monumenti dell'arte musicale italiana*, i (Milan, 1931), pp. 93 and 177.

[3] On the *battaglia* in general see Rudolf Gläsel, *Zur Geschichte der Battaglia* (Leipzig, 1931).

of the *ricercar* was often employed in these pieces. The two or three parts were written in a truly polyphonic, often canonic, style and woven into an intricate pattern in which none is ever the chief melody:

Ex. 244 [1]
(i)

By about 1560 'free' instrumental ensemble music had become such a recognized factor in musical life that many of the greatest composers of all countries contributed to it. Henceforward the names of Palestrina, Lassus, and many others appear regularly as composers of *ricercari*, fantasias, or similar forms.

ORTIZ'S 'TRATADO'

Several features found later in instrumental composition are significantly anticipated in the musical illustrations to the *Tratado de glosas* of the Spaniard, Diego Ortiz (1553),[2] which describes in detail a practice which by that time must have been deeply rooted, at least in Spain. Ortiz deals with the viol (*vihuela*), for which he describes three types of playing: first, entirely free ornamental improvisation, in which the harpsichord strikes chords on which the viol performs a

---

[1] From Lassus's two-part fantasias, *Sämtliche Werke*, i (Leipzig, 1894) and *Hortus Musicus*, xviii and xix (Kassel, 1927), ed. W. Pudelko.
[2] See note 2 on p. 553; also pp. 705–6.

freely invented figuration; second, improvisation on the viol upon a known *canto fermo* (generally a popular or a religious melody) with the harpsichord accompanying; third, the elaboration of a composition in several parts—song, motet, *chanson*, or madrigal—in which the harpsichord plays all the parts while the violist selects any one of them which he adorns with passage-work and other figuration. No doubt much in Ortiz's diminutions and ornamental flourishes was based on early organ and lute figuration; and certainly Ortiz only codified a practice of ornamental improvisation which had been in existence for a long time. Yet, by so doing, he considerably advanced the development of an instrumental style in viol playing.

How advanced Spanish instrumental music had become by about the middle of the sixteenth century is also shown by Tomás de Santa Maria's three- and four-part fantasias (Valladolid, 1565) and by Antonio de Cabezón's *Obras de Música* (published posthumously, Madrid, 1578; reprinted by Pedrell in *Hispaniae Schola Musica Sacra*, vii and viii, Leipzig, 1898). It is also suggested by the instrumental polyphony of Fuenllana's *Orphénica Lyra* for vihuela (Seville, 1554).[1]

Another feature of later instrumental music that appears in Ortiz's treatise is the *ciacona*. As well as variation forms in general, Ortiz, in his 'second type' of playing, visualizes a continuous repetition of the bass motive underlying the composition; this feature anticipates the *basso ostinato* with its variants in different countries (divisions on a ground, passacaglia, &c.).

THE ENGLISH FANCY AND 'IN NOMINE'

With the important exception of England, few countries developed national peculiarities in instrumental music before 1580. The Netherlands had set the standard for all contrapuntal work in vocal music, and the dominating position of Netherland music was maintained in the instrumental field, too. England occupied a unique position in the development of free instrumental music, in that she evolved at an early date—and even more prominently than Spain—a much more independent instrumental style than the other schools and countries. Emancipation from vocal music had already progressed comparatively far by 1570.

The basic forms of English instrumental group music were the fantasia or fancy and the 'In nomine'. The structure of both was

[1] See *infra*, p. 690.

similar and based, on the whole, on that of the continental *ricercari* and fantasias, the 'In nomine' being always built on the plainsong melody of the first antiphon at Vespers on Trinity Sunday, 'Gloria tibi Trinitas':

Ex. 245

and deriving its name from the section 'In nomine Domini' from the *Benedictus* of Taverner's Mass 'Gloria tibi Trinitas'[1] where the *canto fermo* appears clearly, complete, and in notes of equal value.[2] The instrumental *canto fermo* motet was not necessarily of English origin, yet in these two forms—the 'In nomine' and the fantasia— many typically instrumental features developed which advanced beyond anything that had been achieved on the Continent up to that time. Christopher Tye, for instance, in his 'In nomines' as early as 1570 wrote thematic subjects such as:

Ex. 246 [3]

which are obviously unvocal. Simultaneously the compass of the parts grew; there are top and bottom notes in fantasias by Eliza-bethan composers which lie entirely outside the range of voices. Most important, however, in early English instrumental music is the great liveliness of all the parts, which abound in quick passages and figuration. A delicate and intricate polyphonic network, such as this from an 'In nomine' *a* 5 by Byrd,[4] was woven only in early English string music:

[1] See Vol. III, p. 340.
[2] On the 'In nomine' generally, see Robert Donington and R. Thurston Dart, 'The Origin of the "In nomine"', *Music and Letters*, xxx (1949), p. 101; and Denis Stevens, 'The Background of the "In Nomine"', *Monthly Musical Record*, lxxxiv (1954), p. 199. On the keyboard 'In nomine' see the following chapter, p. 622, and Gustav Reese, 'The origin of the English In Nomine', *Journal of the American Musicological Society*, ii (1949), p. 7.
[3] Brit. Mus. Add. 31390.
[4] Ibid., printed in Byrd's *Collected Works*, xvii (London, 1948), p. 58.

Ex. 247

There are many concerted 'In nomines', often full of instrumental
interest, by Taverner, Tallis, Tye, Parsons, Robert White, Parsley,
and others, in addition to those for a keyboard instrument.

INTERACTION OF DANCE AND FREE FORMS

While it is possible, even necessary, to consider dance music and free instrumental compositions separately up to the middle of the sixteenth century, and to treat the various countries on the whole as one family, a different method must be applied in studying the instrumental music of the rest of the sixteenth century and the beginning of the seventeenth. Instrumental dance and 'free' music had so far been distinct from one another, even though a certain amount of interaction between the two did take place. Now both kinds became more akin, a change leading to all the different movements and cyclical forms of seventeenth-century instrumental music. Dance music gradually became artistically contrived and in some cases stylized, while free instrumental music became increasingly secularized and absorbed elements of dance and other popular music. The *rapprochement* of both species in style, and often also in form, is one of the most interesting features of early seventeenth-century instrumental music. On the other hand, more and more national peculiarities appeared towards the end of the sixteenth century. With the progress of the Reformation, the influence of the Catholic Church in matters of culture was correspondingly reduced—and in the Middle Ages this influence had been international in character.

In consequence the development of post-Reformation instrumental music will have to be viewed according to the differences in style and practice from country to country, which now begin to be very marked. It is with what happened in Northern Italy that a new epoch in the history of concerted instrumental music begins.

THE RISE OF ITALIAN INSTRUMENTAL MUSIC

It is curious that Italy's first great age of music opened only after the country's glory in the fields of painting, sculpture, and architecture had already begun to fade. Yet both flowerings, in art and in music, can be traced back ultimately to the same cause—the tremendous social and cultural advance made in Italy towards the end of the Middle Ages. Land tillage—the countryside—had been the basis of medieval Italian life and society. The Church had been the home of art and thought, until trade and commerce gradually broke up its static life. Wealth was being accumulated in the new town-state republics, and the proud merchants and noblemen of Florence, Venice, and Genoa became the patrons of ambitious and thriving cultural activities of a new kind. Long before 1500 the ground was prepared for all the magnificent achievements in the various fields of art. A new standard of musicianship had been growing since the fourteenth century, and the visions, prophecies, and speculations of Italian thinkers during the age of the Renaissance and Reformation heralded bolder and greater achievements in the realm of creative music, too. In the *Nuove musiche* and its instrumental counterparts, emotion and individual expression reached heights never before dreamed of.

THE INSTRUMENTAL *CANZON*

The form through which instrumental music in Italy was revolutionized was the *canzon* (or *canzone*). The term *canzon* existed in early sixteenth-century Italian publications such as *Canzone Sonetti Strambotti e Frottole Libro Primo* (Siena, 1515). Nevertheless, the *canzon* as an instrumental form grew essentially out of the French *chansons* —those spirited settings of light-hearted French poetry which were musically of homophonic or semi-polyphonic structure and which had been popular from the age of Janequin.[1] As early as 1531 Pierre Attaingnant had published instrumental arrangements of *chansons*.[2] At first these were for keyboard instruments, but collections of *chansons* which could be used for voices or for groups of instruments, named or unnamed, followed soon: *Chansons musicales à quattre parties desquelles les plus convenables à la fleuste d'allemant . . .* (Attaingnant, Paris, 1534); *Premier livre des Chansons à quattre parties . . . Tant à la voix comme aux instrumentz* (Susato, Antwerp, 1543), and others.

Italian composers eagerly took over this brilliant new form which was so full of entertaining features, and easily adapted it to their own traditions of *frottole, villanelle,* &c. Gardano's publication of *Canzoni francese a due voci . . . buone da cantare et sonare* (Venice, 1539) was followed by other collections of a similar nature. In 1572 there appeared in the fifth book of Vicentino's *Madrigali a 5 voci* a piece for instrumental ensemble entitled *canzon da sonar*. Henceforward *canzon francese* or *canzon da sonar* signified an *instrumental* piece, and again emancipation from the vocal occurred, as it had before in the other free forms, only much more quickly and radically than in the types derived from the motet (*ricercar*, fantasia, &c.).

In becoming an instrumental form, the *canzon* borrowed characteristics from both the *ricercari* and the numerous dance movements

---

[1] See Chap. I.   [2] See Vol. III, p. 449.

in use at the time. From the former the *canzon* took over the sectional arrangement of the motet described earlier in this chapter: witness the two *Arie di canzon francese per sonare* in Ingegneri's second book of madrigals (1579), the *Canzoni per sonare* by Florentio Maschera (1584),[1] the *Canzoni* by Correggio and Guami (1588), Viadana (1590), Bariola (1594), Metallo (1594), Banchieri (1596, 1603, 1607, &c.), Cavazzio (1597), Stivori (1599), Bonelli (1602), Favereo (1606), and many others. From the dances, especially those in triple time, the *canzon* took over many rhythmic and metrical features, as becomes clear from a study of the *canzoni* by the Gabrielis[2] and a large number of other early seventeenth-century composers.

The initial rhythm characteristic of the vocal *chanson* ♩♩♩♩ was maintained in many instrumental *canzoni* for a long time; yet in all these works less and less was heard of the *legato* style of the earlier vocal music. As in other sixteenth-century forms of light instrumental music, there are shorter melodic phrases and there is greater clarity in the formal structure than in the old motets. Up to the end of the sixteenth century, however, in spite of the new vitality of the *canzoni*, non-harmonic (indeed chiefly polyphonic) interest predominated.

GIOVANNI GABRIELI

The history of the *canzon* (and of instrumental music in general) took a decisive new turn with the appearance of Giovanni Gabrieli's *Sacrae Symphoniae* of 1597, which included sixteen major instrumental movements.[3] For here an element of the most far-reaching importance for the development of instrumental sound was born: the massive, sensuous colour effect, the magic and attraction of *orchestral* music. There had been large-scale performances before Gabrieli,[4] but the works represented in such performances were not *planned* from the point of view of orchestral composition; they could just as well have been played by small ensembles of any instrumental combination, in any other surroundings and without altering a single note. It is the premeditation and calculation of instrumental colour effects which is new in Gabrieli's work of 1597.

This innovation of Gabrieli's occurred at a time of rapid secularization of instrumental music in all spheres, yet it was made within the

---

[1] An example from this set is reprinted in Davison and Apel, op. cit. i, p. 201.

[2] For instance, the very *canzon*-like *Ricercar del duodecimo tuono* by Andrea Gabrieli, reprinted in Benvenuti, op. cit., p. 86, and in Davison and Apel, op. cit., p. 147.

[3] On the subject generally, see Stefan Kunze, *Die Instrumentalmusik Giovanni Gabrielis*. Two vols. (Tutzing, 1963).

[4] See p. 796, for instance.

framework of the Church. Gabrieli and his work, however, must be viewed within the context of the social and cultural scene as a whole. For one thing his church *canzoni* and *sonate* were intended for ostentatious display; they were meant to impress people, even to startle them. It was the aim of the Church of the Counter-Reformation to show its might and splendour and the power of the ideology it stood for by every means available. With immense passion and enthusiasm the two Gabrielis and their colleagues carried out this task, whether inspired by direct commission, by personal conviction, or by purely musical considerations. On the other hand, Gabrieli reaped the fruits of the Renaissance of secular thought and art, and himself continued and intensified it in his works, even though these creations of his were employed in the service of the Counter-Reformation. As an observing and thinking being, he was aware of and filled by the tension in contemporary life, thoroughly alive to the issues of his age in general and to the possibilities of his own art of music in particular. It is these qualities in Gabrieli's music, its topicality, its tension, passion, and breadth, which soon made these works acceptable to both Church and secular circles. They were performed alike in cathedrals, at courts and in the houses of wealthy patricians on all sorts of festive occasions.

The *canzoni da sonar* of the sixteenth century, like the *ricercari*, *capricci*, and other instrumental forms, had been essentially chamber music—music to be played and enjoyed by the players and a small circle around them, rather than music to be listened to by larger audiences. Andrea Gabrieli's eight-part *ricercar*[1] formed the connecting link between the older type of *canzon* and that of his nephew Giovanni. Yet Giovanni Gabrieli's *canzoni* for eight and more instruments were written to be performed to a listening public, and to a large public at that. One can well imagine that in this age of the advancing popularity of sensuous effect, Giovanni's great instrumental works attracted many more people to the church than did the polyphonic *canzoni* of the old type (including his own for four instruments).[2]

So the place of performance had been enlarged from the *camera* to the *chiesa*. And in the *chiesa*, at first in St. Mark's at Venice, architectural possibilities for musical effects were exploited to the full. This is as true of the choice of instruments as of the way in which

[1] Benvenuti, op. cit. i, p. 25.
[2] See the four examples edited by Einstein (Mainz, 1933) from Alessandro Raverii's collection of *Canzoni per sonare* (Venice, 1608) which has been reprinted complete with commentary, by L. E. Bartholomew. Two vols. (Hays, Kansas, 1965).

they were employed. Agazzari in his *Discorso* speaks of stringed instruments as belonging to the *dolci conserti* (the chamber *canzoni* or *ricercari* of the old type), but of wind instruments in the *conserti strepitosi e grandi* (the new large-scale *canzoni* of Giovanni Gabrieli and his school). In the latter type impressive and far-sounding wind instruments, especially *cornetti* and trombones, were organized in several groups of four or five parts each and played off against each other: one chorus of four or five introduced the composition, another followed, until they all united in one mighty symphony. There are up to twenty-two parts in some of these works. Occasionally bowed strings (of the violin family, no longer viols) and even lutes were represented in one or several of the groups; instruments of dark tone-colour and low pitch were set against others of light tone-colour and high pitch in order to intensify the contrast of colours in these 'symphonic oil paintings'.

The contriving of fantastic, sophisticated colour effects is the essence of these works. Problems of form and counterpoint appear as of secondary importance. Novelties in form arise out of the composer's desire for contrast, which certainly is behind the sudden interruptions of slow common time by fast triple time in dance-like periods—as in this passage from a *Canzon per sonar, Primi Toni*, by Giovanni Gabrieli:[1]

---

[1] From *Sacrae Symphoniae* (Venice, 1597); reprinted in Benvenuti, op. cit. ii, p. 1.

There are elements of the form of vocal canzonets and strophic airs; for instance, rondo and da capo forms are frequently used, *A–B–A*, or *A–A–B–B*, or *A–B–A–B–A–B–A*, &c.

The polyphonic character of earlier instrumental works is here much less evident. There is no longer a continuous *fugato* in the two, three or four-chorus *canzon* as there had been in the old single-chorus *canzon*. Among the features that become more important are dynamic contrasts; *forte* and *piano* are introduced, probably for the first time, in playing off instrumental choirs against each other.

Every feature in this music is devised to the same end: the listener is to be overwhelmed with beautiful sound, sound of a magnificence, power, and splendour rarely reached after Gabrieli's death by any other seventeenth-century composer. Nevertheless, some of Gabrieli's contemporaries tried to outdo him in magnitude and amplitude of sound; for instance, Tiburtio Massaini wrote one *canzon* for eight and another for sixteen trombones.[1]

THE SONATA

The other main branch of large-scale Venetian instrumental music, the sonata, was in name and type younger than the *canzon*. The earliest known sonatas were contained in collections by Giovanni Croce, *Sonate a 5* (Venice, 1580), which Fétis mentions,[2] and Andrea Gabrieli, *Sonate a 5 instrumenti* (Venice, 1586), neither of which has so far been rediscovered. Giovanni Gabrieli's two sonatas in the *Sacrae Symphoniae* (Venice, 1597) are the earliest works bearing this title

[1] Both published in Raverii's collection of *Canzoni per sonare* (Venice, 1608).
[2] *Biographie universelle*, ii (Paris, 1861), p. 393.

of which we have the complete text.[1] They were followed by Gussago's *Sonate a 4, 6, et 8* (Brescia, 1608); by publications by Funghetta, Cima, Porta, Riccio, Bernardi, and others; by Giovanni Gabrieli's second great collection of *Canzoni e Sonate* of 1615; and by an ever increasing number of publications during the subsequent decades.

The term 'sonata' signified a 'sounded' piece in general; unlike the *canzon* it was composed without reference to any traditional form, vocal or instrumental. Whereas in the large-scale *canzoni* a certain contrapuntal liveliness was still at least partly maintained, only blocks of chords were left in the sonatas. Praetorius in his *Syntagma Musicum III* (Wolfenbüttel, 1619), described the *canzon* as 'vivid' and 'full of black notes', and the sonatas as 'full of gravity', slow and compact in style; and the contrast may be illustrated by two excerpts from Giovanni Gabrieli, the first from *Canzon Septimi Toni a 8*:[2]

the second from the famous *Sonata pian' e forte a 8*:[3]

---

[1] Reprinted in Benvenuti, op. cit. ii, pp. 64 and 270. The *Sonata pian' e forte* is also reprinted in Schering, *Geschichte der Musik in Beispielen* (Leipzig, 1931), p. 148, and in Davison and Apel, op. cit. i, p. 198.

[2] Reprinted in Benvenuti, op. cit. ii, p. 14.

[3] Ibid., p. 64.

These early sonatas were in the character of improvisations, flowing on majestically.

Of special magnificence and also of greater formal interest than the early Gabrieli pieces is the *Sonata a 8* included in the *Vespro della Beata Vergine* (Venice, 1610)[1] of Gabrieli's great contemporary, Claudio Monteverdi. The most striking feature of this work is the quotation on eleven occasions of a short plainsong phrase:

Ex.251

sung now with serene calmness, now with breathless excitement. This amazingly grandiose composition, scored for cornetts, violins, *viole da brazzo*, trombones, and organ, abounds in effective and thrilling moments such as occur elsewhere only in Monteverdi's operas. It has a dramatic, clear-cut form (the end is a recapitulation of the beginning), and it adopts elements from the *canzon* in that it contrasts several movements of different character.

CONFUSION OF CATEGORIES

Sinfonia or *symphonia* as an instrumental species at first (around 1600) meant a piece little distinguished from the sonata. Often such pieces served as sonorous introductions either to further musical items, vocal or instrumental, or more usually to celebrations, services,

---

[1] Reprinted in Malipiero's edition, *Tutte le opere di Claudio Monteverdi*, xiv (Asolo, 1932), and in numerous 'performing editions'.

or other important ceremonials. Such *sinfonie*, varying in style and form like the sonatas, were written by Viadana, Allegri, Salomone Rossi, and others.[1] In the multitude of forms appearing and disappearing at that time names did not mean very much. There were *scherzi*, as often as not modelled on the vocal form of the same name (Trabaci, Brunelli, Cangiasi), *capricci* (Borsaro), *canti fermi*, *consonanze* (Trabaci), and many others; but these terms were frequently mixed up by the composers themselves, as in Ottavio Bariola's *Capricci overo Canzoni* (Milan, 1594), Banchieri's *Fantasie overo Canzone alla francese* (Venice, 1603), Tarquinio Merula's *Canzoni overo Sonate concertate* (Venice, 1637), and other sets. Forms as well as styles were being moulded at this period; during the first thirty or forty years of the seventeenth century little in the way of tradition was established, and there was little security of style; everything was in a state of flux.

However, thanks largely to the work of the younger Gabrieli and his colleagues the position of instrumental music as the equal of vocal music was established once and for all. During the sixteenth century a few *canzoni* were added to collections of vocal compositions in appendices, sometimes almost apologetically, but after Gabrieli instrumental works were as a rule published independently and in ever-increasing numbers. Some years indeed saw the publication of as many as twenty-five new collections of concerted instrumental music.

GABRIELI'S FOLLOWERS

In the field of the large-scale *canzon* and *sonata* the Gabrielis found enthusiastic supporters among many notable composers in their own city of Venice. The main collection of *canzoni* was issued by the publisher Raverii;[2] it included, among others, pieces by such composers as Marenzio, Luzzaschi, and Merulo. Other publications including *canzoni* for several orchestral choirs contain compositions by Alessandro Marino in his *Primo libro de Madrigali spirituali e canzon a 12* (1597), Radino (1607), Bottaccio (1609), Guami (1612), Usper (1619), and Picchi (1625); Milan followed with works by Beretta (1604), G. D. Rognoni (1605), Cima (1610), Biumo (1627), and Brescia with Canali (1600), Gussago (1608), Lappi (1608), and Mortaro (1610), and they were soon joined by Bologna, Rome, and other cities. In Venice itself few major works for several instrumental

[1] See, for instance, the example from Banchieri's *Ecclesiastice Sinfonie dette Canzoni in aria francese* (Venice, 1607) in Schering, op. cit., p. 155.
[2] See p. 567, n. 2.

choirs appeared after Gabrieli's posthumous publication of 1615 until Neri (1651) and Cavalli (1656) once again took up the mighty forms and style of the great pioneer. But in their hands, progressive though both men were in other fields, and full of inspiring features though their great *sonate a 8* and *12* are, this reintroduction of the Gabrieli style remained an attempted revival which was not followed up elsewhere. Much had happened in the years between Gabrieli and the 'revivalists', Neri and Cavalli.

With the first remarkable successes of the great sonatas and *canzoni*, the road to an unknown and unlimited future was opened for instrumental music. After Gabrieli's death in 1612 it became manifest that his own harmonic conception of instrumental music was only the first step along this road. The 'celestial' calm of medieval church music had gone; the reign of emotion in music, of sensuous sound, of intense and exciting melody, had begun.

The thirty years following the publication of Gabrieli's *Sacrae Symphoniae* were a period dominated by new ideas. Experiment went on in all spheres of music, vocal and instrumental, and certain effects devised by some composers were taken up again only centuries later. It was this 'futurism' in Italian music which led the theorist Artusi to write that the end of music was in sight, since 'its main aim, that of giving pleasure, seemed to fall into neglect'.

The period saw a reduction in the customary number of parts, from 8, 12, 15, or 22 to 2, 3, 4, 5, or 6 instruments. While eight- and twelve-part music was still being composed, playing off one instrumental choir against another, more and more composers took to displaying individual instruments of different tone-colours against each other in smaller ensembles. Definite tone-colour became increasingly important; instruments were named more and more frequently. Viadana demanded a violin, a cornett, and two trombones for a four-part *canzon* published with his *Concerti ecclesiastici* (1602).[1] Ercole Porta, in 1613, asked for the same combination in his *Vaga Ghirlanda*. Giovanni Francesco Anerio at Rome wrote a *canzon* for violin, trumpet, cornett, and lute.[2] Riccio produced some sophisticated instrumental effects in his *Divine lodi* of 1620.[3] Marini sets off two violins against four trombones in his Op. 8 (Venice, 1626), Castello two violins against two trombones (1629). Buonamente's

---

[1] Republished in an unsatisfactory edition by Riemann in *Old Chamber Music*, i (London, 1896).

[2] See F. X. Haberl, 'Giovanni Francesco Anerio', *Kirchenmusikalisches Jahrbuch*, i (1886), p. 59.

[3] See Riemann, *Handbuch der Musikgeschichte*, ii (2) (Leipzig, 1912), p. 114.

sixth book of *Sonate et Canzoni* for two to six instruments (Venice, 1636) includes works for violin, lute, cornett, and three trombones. An unlimited number of combinations is tried out. There are also many works for strings only, with an increasing preponderance of the more penetrating and expressive violin family over the old viol family.

In the long run these instrumental forms on a reduced scale turned out to be more capable of further progressive development than the great Gabrieli works which, like giant marble statues, stood unassailably impressive but, as instrumental forms, proved incapable of modification or expansion.

INSTRUMENTAL MONODY

At the same time the accompanied instrumental solo began to appear. Already in some sixteenth-century *canzoni* (including several by Gabrieli himself) treble instruments had been thrown into prominence by the increasingly homophonic character of the music. These solo-like passages were indicative of a general development. As early as 1553, accompanied solos for the viol had been published by Ortiz.[1] Yet the earliest of the instrumental monodies published shortly after 1600 were clearly based on principles different from those of Ortiz's solos for the *vihuela*, for Italian instrumental monody was modelled on vocal solo melody—which was now subjective, individualistic, and expressive in character—and built on harmonic accompaniment, which gave it colour and emotional emphasis. This harmonic conception of music found its most striking expression with the arrival of the *basso continuo*, described by Viadana in the preface to his *Cento concerti ecclesiastici*[2] which forthwith became the regular attribute of all instrumental music, whether for large or small ensembles.

In the instrumental solos which were always conceived in close contact with developments in the vocal field, the *cantabile* style was established during the first half of the seventeenth century—that 'singing' melody on instruments, elegant, exciting and full of the 'fire and fury' which Roger North admired so much in Italian music.[3]

---

[1] See pp. 560 and 705–6.
[2] Reprinted by Max Schneider in *Die Anfänge des Basso Continuo* (Leipzig, 1918), pp. 3–9, and in translation by F. T. Arnold, *The Art of Accompaniment from a Thorough-Bass* (London, 1931), pp. 3–4 and 10–19, and Oliver Strunk in *Source Readings in Music History* (London, 1952), pp. 419–23.
[3] See John Wilson, *Roger North on Music* (London, 1959), p. 297.

This *cantilena* became characteristic of instrumental music in the same measure that Italy, with the growth of opera, became the country of expressive and dramatic solo vocal melody.

ORIGIN OF THE TRIO SONATA

In the first decade of the seventeenth century a highly important compromise between instrumental solo and instrumental ensemble music was found in the 'trio' of two trebles and one bass part, accompanied by the thorough bass which followed the line of the lowest instrument, as in this excerpt from the second book of Salomone Rossi's *Sinfonie e gagliarde* (Venice, 1608):[1]

Ex. 252

In Gabrieli's *Sonata con tre violini*[2] instruments of equal pitch competed with one another in lively figuration over a harmonic bass. Troilo, Gagliano, Banchieri, Turini, Riccio, Bernardi, Montalbane, and Farina were among the other composers who developed this type of music.

Here again a close connexion existed between vocal and instrumental chamber music: witness the numerous songs, canzonets, madrigals, scherzi, and so on by Monteverdi and his contemporaries which were frequently transcribed for instruments. However, the *sonata a tre* soon became entirely independent of vocal forms and, towards the middle of the seventeenth century, developed into the

---

[1] The three-part *sinfonie* have been reprinted by F. J. Giesbert (Mainz, 1956). Hugo Riemann gives a *Sonata a 3 sopra l'aria della Romanesca*, from the *Varie sonate* (1613), in *Musikgeschichte in Beispielen* (Leipzig, 1921), p. 151.

[2] From the *Canzoni e Sonate* of 1615. There is a good modern text by Werner Danckert, *Hortus Musicus*, lxx (Kassel, 1950).

most popular form of instrumental music in Italy, a position which it held for more than a century. An essential feature of this new form was the great liveliness of all the parts; the empty space between the top parts and the bass was filled by the harmonic accompaniment of the *continuo* player.

Among six-part sonatas and *canzoni* a number of works can be found in which four soprano instruments are joined by two basses, with the obvious intention of setting two trio groups against each other; an early example of such double trio sonatas was written by Salomone Rossi (for four violins and two chitarroni).[1] Another curious variety of the *sonata a tre* is shown in an unpublished *sinfonia* by Frescobaldi[2] which is scored for violin, *spinettino* (this part is fully worked out for both hands) and organ (*continuo*). The bass in trio sonatas, as in works for a greater number of parts, is often strongly reinforced; trombones, *violoni* (bass viols), bassoons and other low-pitched instruments are sometimes added to give weight.

No clear distinction is made in all this music between performance by single or by massed instruments. It is certain that both possibilities occurred in the pieces for two, three, and four choirs (the highest part of the second choir in Gabrieli's *Sonata pian' e forte*, for instance, is marked *violini*, not *violino*), but it seems likely that even such a decidedly chamber form as the *sonata a tre* could be performed orchestrally, as at a later date the composition of Legrenzi's orchestra shows (eight violins, two cornetts, and, for the bass, three *violoni*, four theorbos, one bassoon, three trombones, and an organ).

FORMAL DEVELOPMENTS

Important changes of form took place alike in music *a tre* and in ensemble work for two to six instruments of different pitch. Among all the *canzoni, capricci, ricercari, sonate,* and so on, the last gradually assumed the lead. The term *canzon* lost its importance and disappeared almost completely after 1650; it was probably used for the last time in Italy in Cavalli's *Musiche sacre* (Venice, 1656).

Many early sonatas were built on the 'patchwork' method; a number of small, even minute, episodes, contrasted in type, rhythm, and speed were joined as in a potpourri. Up to twenty such 'patches' can be counted in some of these works, of which Gabrieli's *Sonata con tre violini* and G. B. Fontana's *Sonate a uno, due, tre* (Venice,

---

[1] In his *4 lib. dei varie Sonate* (1636; 1622?), Bibl. Kassel.
[2] Brit. Mus. Add. 34003.

1641)[1] are outstanding examples. This 'patchwork' principle arose on the one hand from the sectional arrangement of the *ricercari*, fantasias, and other motet types from Willaert to Frescobaldi, and on the other from the lighthearted variability of the *canzoni*. However, soon after the beginning of the seventeenth century there developed a tendency to reduce the number of patches and simultaneously to convert 'patches' into 'movements', by increasing the length and specific gravity of each. There is indeed a tremendous wealth of forms in early seventeenth-century Italian chamber music. Yet certain individual types of movement began to develop and to become more and more clearly defined. The change from adagio to allegro (both indications of tempo were now named by the composers) became a leading principle, and generally the adagios were short, solemn and homophonic, while the allegros were longer, more polyphonic and vivacious.

The thematic material of these allegro fugatos was already often laid out in the form of 'thematic lead'+sequences+cadence, which was to be the pattern of melody-building up to the early eighteenth century. This scheme is already to be found in pieces by Giovanni Gabrieli, such as this *Canzon Primi Toni*, reprinted by Benvenuti:[2]

Ex.253

The themes are more and more characteristically shaped. Instead of the lines of the motet we now find bolder melodies made up of shorter elements:[3]

Ex.254

In the same work, as in other earlier pieces, there are beginnings of thematic development:

[1] A posthumous publication, as Fontana died in 1630. Examples have been reprinted in Torchi, *L'arte musicale*, vii, pp. 92 ff.; and Davison and Apel, op. cit. ii, p. 28.

[2] *Istituzioni e monumenti*, ii, p. 1.

[3] From a *Sonata a 5* (1649) by G. Filippi, quoted by A. Schlossberg, *Die italienische Sonate . . . im 17. Jahrhundert* (Diss. Heidelberg, 1932).

Ex.255

From Banchieri and Gabrieli onwards song-like episodes and other symmetrical periods appear, obviously influenced by dance movements. There was a close interplay of elements of style between dance movements and free movements throughout the seventeenth century, despite the fact that both types of instrumental music, separate in the sixteenth century, were again distinguished as separate categories in the late sixteen-thirties. In 1637 Tarquinio Merula deliberately distinguished in his *Canzoni overo sonate concertate* between *sonate da chiesa* ('free' sonatas for use primarily in church) and *sonate da camera* (suites of dance movements), but it should be remembered that the 'church sonatas' were also used as domestic chamber music.

The *sonata da camera* developed gradually out of the pavane-plus-galliard of the sixteenth century. Both dances were still in use in the following century and were joined by yet more types and also frequently by movements in non-dance forms. Antonio Brunelli published a *Ballo in Gagliarda per sonare a 2* (Venice, 1616) consisting of *ballo grave per sonare*, *seconda parte*, *gagliarda*, and *terza parte*, *corrente*, and Lorenzo Allegri's *Primo Libro delle Musiche* (Venice, 1618) contains suites of dances.[1]

INSTRUMENTAL CHARACTERISTICS

After 1600, when instrumental music in Italy first came of age, instrumental characteristics developed rapidly. Violin technique in particular progressed with almost unbelievable speed, both in solo and in ensemble music. There are tremolos (Monteverdi, Filippi,

---

[1] See Hermann Beck's study, *Archiv für Musikwissenschaft*, xxii (1965), p. 99, and his edition of the first suite in *Das Musikwerk*, xxvi (1964).

Farina), wide jumps across several strings (Marini), notes up to the fifth position (Marini), and quick passage-work. Equal liveliness sometimes appears in all parts of works written for instruments of greatly differing character, with apparent disregard of their natural differences, as in this sonata by Giovanni Valentini, scored for violin, *cornettino*, trombone, bassoon, and organ (*c.* 1610):[1]

Ex. 256

VIOLINO
CORNETTINO

TROMBONE
FAGOTTO
+ B.C.

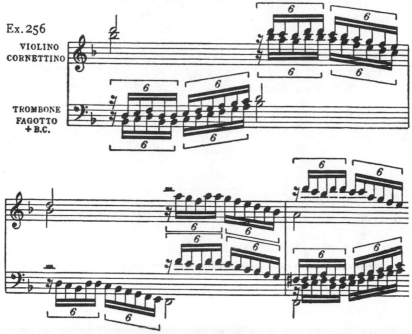

The *concertante* style developed on this basis, i.e. either with several parts competing in lively figuration, or with one solo part exhibiting quick passage-work and expressive melody. In Gabrieli's work the juxtaposition and display of several groups of instruments against each other contain at least one element of the later *concerto grosso*. When O. M. Grandi (1628)[2] wrote for one violin against four trombones, he clearly did so with something like the later concerto principle in mind. Castello, Scarani, and Merula (1621, 1624, and 1631) entitled collections *Sonate concertate*, in which the practices of the vocal concerto with ornamental voice parts are transferred to instrumental music. More evidence of the growth of this style is found in works by Porta (1613), Lappi (1616), Usper (1619), Priuli (1618), Corradini (1624), Picchi (1625), Cavaccio (1626), Buonamente (1636), and Uccellini (1639), to name only some of the more important composers.

---

[1] Bibl. Kassel, MS. Eitner's suggested attribution to Giuseppe Valentini is unfounded.
[2] *Sonate per ogni sorte di stromenti . . . con il B. per l'org.* (Venice, 1628).

ITALIAN EXPERIMENTALISM

Chromatic experiments were made in concerted instrumental music as much as in vocal music. A particularly daring system of key-relationships is employed in another sonata by Giovanni Valentini. A short subject in G minor is immediately repeated as an echo in B minor, and this harmonic alternation continues throughout the work, producing many strange juxtapositions of keys:

Ex.257

In the same piece the echo effect already found in Gabrieli's *Sonata pian' e forte* is extended to a double-echo: piano, pianissimo, and piano-pianissimo (*ppp*).

The Italians were fully conscious of their leading position on the international scene. Valerio Bona called his publication of 1614 *Canzoni italiane da sonare*, no longer *francese*, as the French origin of the form was by then often forgotten, and such composers as Banchieri (1612), Giacinto Merulo (1623), and Castello (1629) add the words *in stile moderno* in the titles of their publications.[1] Yet by the middle of the seventeenth century experiments, with their attendant excitement, had calmed down. New standards of form and style emerged from the creative drive of the first half of the century.

[1] Castello, *Sonate concertate in stile moderno* (Venice, 1629); Banchieri, *Armonia Moderna di Canzoni alla francese*, op. 26 (Venice, 1612); Giacinto Merulo, *Madrigali a 4 in stile moderno* (Bologna, 1623).

CHAMBER MUSIC IN ENGLAND

There is a very striking contrast between Italian and English instrumental ensemble music during the first twenty years of the seventeenth century. Whereas in Italy this new music was performed in halls, in churches, and in the open air, appealing to large bodies of listeners, instrumental music in England was conceived for the homes of well-to-do citizens. The Italian *canzoni* and sonatas were remarkable for glorious colour-effects, the English fancies and pavanes for delicate design. Expressive and exciting violins, cornetts, and trombones dominated the musical scene in Italy; the tender and restrained viols still prevailed in England.

In their own way English composers developed a typically instrumental style even more independent of vocal music than that of their brilliant Italian colleagues. (This applies least to form, most to contrapuntal construction.) At first Italians and English both used, for the most part, the same formal types. The *ricercar* (Italy) or the fantasia (England) reigned supreme until the last years of the sixteenth century. Both of these forms were derived from the vocal motet, and both also had close associations with the lively and usually secular madrigal.

During the earlier part of the seventeenth century, too, the development of form in the instrumental music of both countries proceeded along similar lines. The homogeneous sections of the English fantasia tended to become little movements contrasted in character, style, and often tempo and even time-signature, just as in the Italian *canzon* and early sonata; in fact the English development was in this respect influenced by what happened in Italy. Some of the fantasias of Byrd and Gibbons, for instance, consist of as many as ten little movements: solid fugatos, mostly in common time, gigue-like episodes, tuneful folksong-like sections, severe contrapuntal endings, as in this Fantasia by Orlando Gibbons:[1]

Ex.258
(a)

(b)

[1] Marsh Library, Dublin, MS. Z2. I. 13; printed by E. H. Meyer in *Englische Fantasien aus dem 17. Jahrhundert* (Kassel, 1949), p. 8.

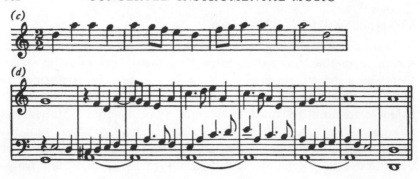

as well as many other types of embryonic 'movement'. Variety was
achieved by a number of means: chromatic contrasted with diatonic sections, homophonic with polyphonic, fast with slow.

Other forms in early English chamber music developed more
independently of Italian influences. The 'In nomine'[1] still played an
important part during the first half of the seventeenth century. Unlike
other 'tenor' motets which appeared in plenty everywhere during the
sixteenth century, the 'In nomine' was a fixed formal type with its
own structural principles. But after 1600 the *canto fermo*, which had
originally been generally confined to the middle parts, began to
appear in the top or bass. Up to Purcell's time the 'In nomine'
appears to have provided a favourite field for experiments of all
kinds: witness the 'In nomines' by John Ward (d. *c.* 1640),[2] Thomas
Tomkins (d. 1656), Thomas Lupo (fl. *c.* 1610), William Lawes
(d. 1645), and others.

English musicians were particularly fond of variation forms; it
may be said that in this field they more than anybody took over the
heritage of the great Spanish masters of the sixteenth century.
'Ground basses' (i.e. ostinatos) abound in early seventeenth-century
English manuscripts, and numerous sets of variations on a popular
song called 'Browning' were composed by some of the best masters.[3]

Among dance forms, pavanes and galliards were still popular as
late as 1650, although by that time people no longer danced to them.
Almans, sarabands, corants, and after 1610 jigs and other dances
had taken their place for actual dancing. All were based, to a lesser
or greater degree, on the sixteenth-century English tradition but were
also influenced by certain foreign models.

[1] See pp. 561–3.
[2] Two examples by Ward in *Musica Britannica*, ix (ed. R. Thurston Dart and William
Coates) (London, 1955), pp. 44 and 148.
[3] Cf. Meyer, *English Chamber Music* (London, 1946), p. 112.

Yet, once again, the most distinctive quality of early English chamber music was not its wealth of forms but its polyphonic life, its reliance on line: the extraordinary melodic independence of all the parts in the score. It is here that its originality lies, and when, around 1600, English chamber music had reached maturity, it was admired and imitated all over Europe because of its contrapuntal vitality and ingenuity.

Two chief methods of performance were the basis of this peculiar style: the 'broken consort' and the ensemble of viols. The term 'broken consort' implies a practice in which a *consortium* of instruments of differing tone-colours co-operate; the sound of the ensemble is split up, 'broken' into such divergent colour units as a viol, a lute, a recorder, a violin, and a cittern. Obviously such a combination of instruments is ideally suited to a polyphonic style in which it is essential that all the instrumental lines of the score should be clearly distinguishable from each other and yet, at the same time, should all be heard equally well. Praetorius in his *Syntagma Musicum*[1] defined the consort as he saw and heard it: 'Several persons with all sorts of instruments, such as harpsichord or large spinet, large lyra, double harp, lute, theorbo, pandora, penorcon, cittern, bass viol, a small descant fiddle, a transverse flute or recorder, sometimes also a quiet sackbut or *Racket*, sound together in one company and society ever so quietly, tenderly, and beautifully, and agree with each other in a graceful symphony.' This is a typically domestic form of music-making, and it was chiefly intended for the educated and well-to-do amateurs who were the mainstay of instrumental performance during the age of Elizabeth I and James I.

Morley's *First Booke of Consort Lessons* (London, 1599),[2] a collection of movements by various composers, some arranged, some original compositions, for treble viol, bass viol, recorder, cittern, lute, and pandora, is a famous collection of music for broken consort. Anthony Holborne, Philip Rosseter, Richard Allison, Tobias Hume, and others published works for similar combinations of instruments of contrasting tone-colour. William Lawes, at a somewhat later date, wrote elaborate pieces for harp, violin, viol, and lute.

The other favourite medium in early English chamber music was the consort of viols, instruments of the same tone-colour. In this type of consort the requirement, as in the broken consort, was for

[1] Part III (Wolfenbüttel, 1619); modern reprint by E. Bernoulli (Leipzig, 1916).
[2] Reprinted by Sydney Beck (New York, 1959); see also Dart, 'Morley's Consort Lessons of 1599', *Proceedings of the Royal Musical Association*, lxxiv (1947–8), p. 1.

audibility of all instruments as well as for clear differentiation of the parts. However, the special tone quality of the viols, tender, slightly thin and somewhat nasal, yet very definite in timbre, enabled each instrumental part to be heard and the polyphonic network to be clearly recognizable.

Works written for ensembles of viols are very numerous. Two-part pieces in the style of the old *bicinia* were composed around 1600 by Whythorne, Morley, East, and others;[1] they show much progress towards freer instrumental writing. There are also large numbers of works for four or five parts. Yet among the various combinations those for a so-called 'chest of viols' became most popular after 1600. A 'chest' included either three or six viols: either one treble, one tenor and one bass, or two of each of these pitches. Playing on viols was extremely fashionable during the early decades of the seventeenth century, and with all this intense cultivation of music for ensembles of viols the style of instrumental writing became the most advanced in all Europe. The technical standard of playing rose quickly, and the liveliness of the parts surpassed anything so far produced in the way of string playing. In many cases the polyphonic vitality of English chamber music was quite extraordinary:

Ex. 259 [2]

Dance music, too, sometimes showed intricate 'polyphonic *concertante*' as in this passage from a six-part pavane[3] by Orlando Gibbons:

[1] See, for instance, Morley's instrumental pieces in his *First Booke of Canzonets to Two Voyces* (London, 1595), reprinted by Fellowes as *Nine Fantasies for Two Viols* (London, 1928) and in D. H. Boalch's complete edition of the *Canzonets* (Oxford, 1950).

[2] Opening of no. 8 of Orlando Gibbons's *Fantasies of Three Parts* (London, *c.* 1610 or later); reprinted by Rimbault (London, 1843) and Fellowes (London, 1924); no. 3 from the same set is recorded in *The History of Music in Sound* (H.M.V.), iv.

[3] Ed. Fellowes (London, 1925).

Ex.260

Instrumental solo playing in early Jacobean chamber music was only a logical consequence of this development of an instrumental style. The treble melody often became the most important part of the ensemble, partly under the influence of vocal airs, canzonets, and madrigals, partly owing to the influx of Italian elements of style. Yet the bass part, too, became increasingly prominent, in particular in combination with a lute, theorbo, pandora, or other plucked instrument. Such combinations can be found in publications and manuscripts by Thomas Ford, Tobias Hume, Francis Pilkington, Daniel Norcombe, and others. In England solo playing developed not as a new expressive and emotional art as in Italy but as a result of the elaborate and delicate instrumental liveliness of polyphonic ensemble-playing. After 1600 the bass viol became the solo instrument *par excellence*, a fact which is reflected in passages or whole virtuoso pieces. Such solos occur either in pieces for a complete 'chest' such as this six-part fantasia by Thomas Lupo, where parts 5 and 6 are for two bass viols:[1]

Ex.261.[1]

[1] Oxford, Christ Church, MS. 2.

or when several bass viols are grouped together. Bass viol duos were composed in plenty by Alfonso Ferrabosco, jr., Michael East, Simon Ives, Richard Deering, John Coperario, and many others. Yet English composers adjusted themselves only very slowly to the idea of the Italian *sonata a tre*. There are works for two treble viols of equal pitch plus one bass viol by Gibbons, Lupo, and others, but at the beginning of the seventeenth century such combinations were exceptional. So are duets for virginals and bass-viol like those in the little volume entitled *Parthenia In-Violata* (*c.* 1625).[1]

The rich and lively figuration in English chamber music did not preclude expressive melody or profound emotion. Perhaps the most telling examples of deep sentiment in early instrumental music are certain pieces by Coperario,[2] Deering, Holborne, and Dowland, especially the famous set of pavanes by the last composer, entitled *Lachrymae or Seaven Teares, figured in Seaven passionate Pavans* (London, 1605). It was this kind of music which must have inspired Spenser, Ben Jonson, and other poets to sing of music and its magic beauty as they did.

As in most sixteenth-century polyphony, the contrapuntal structure of early seventeenth-century English chamber music was largely based on the technique of imitation, with section after section built up in a way which anticipates the classical fugue. Yet the thematic material itself underwent considerable changes: it became more and more characteristically shaped, clearly defined, and altogether more significant from the point of view of invention. Bolder and more individual thematic subjects became frequent in English music after 1600:

Ex. 262
(i) JOHN WARD [3]

[1] Facsimile, and practical edition by Dart (New York, 1961).
[2] For instance, the Fantasia for four viols, Oxford, Christ Church, MS. 2, and Bodl. F. 568–9, printed in Meyer, *English Chamber Music*, p. 262, and recorded in *The History of Music in Sound*, iv.   [3] Fantasia for four viols, *Musica Britannica*, ix, p. 37.

(ii) ALFONSO FERRABOSCO THE YOUNGER

Much of this new life and vigour was inspired by popular music, which had enlivened the style of English composers since the days of Elizabeth. Popular songs and dance tunes were incorporated in many fantasias, pavanes, grounds, and other instrumental pieces. Apart from the 'Browning' mentioned above and literal quotations of popular tunes in works by Gibbons, Byrd, Morley, and Ford, there is a popular strain in the works of many, indeed most, other composers. This appears in their melodic behaviour no less than in their wholesale acceptance of the major and minor keys and in the final elimination of the modes.

The climax of creative activity among English instrumental composers was reached during the years 1605 to 1620. After 1620 the happy unity of musical composition was disrupted—perhaps because the nation's life began to be disrupted by political and social changes. The gap between the art of the common people and that of the educated and privileged classes was widened enormously. Many composers became separated from the wider public, a fact which is manifest in their search for the uncommon, in a certain intricacy and in sometimes extraordinary experiments. Chromatic adventures, for instance, occur in works by Thomas Tomkins, such as this opening of a six-part fantasia:[1]

Ex.263

[1] Ed. Fellowes (London, 1939).

New and strange key-relationships were tried out, and in the hands of some composers contrapuntal science almost recalled the intricacies of late fifteenth-century Netherland polyphony.

The greatest composer of instrumental music of the period 1620–48 and one of the most advanced composers of chamber music anywhere during the seventeenth century was William Lawes, Court composer to Charles I up to his death in 1645. On the one hand his works still maintain some of the vigour and popular flavour of earlier chamber music; on the other, they are characterized by a new and greatly increased contrapuntal liveliness, by a highly original *concertante* style in all instruments, by daring harmonic conceptions, and by impressive melodic invention which covers a wide range of emotion. Some of Lawes's innovations concern the use of instruments; he often wrote for violins instead of viols, chromatic harps instead of lutes and theorbos. His keyboard parts are not always mere bases for improvisation by the *continuo* player, but elaborate, completely worked-out parts, as in this passage from a Fantasia for violin, bass viol, and harpsichord:[1]

Ex.264

[1] Oxford, Bodl. MS. B. 2–3.

Basso continuo parts appear, however, in other works by Lawes. With increasing Italian influence, a more harmonic conception of music developed side by side with the polyphonic style of the fantasias with which so many English composers continued to be occupied.

One of Lawes's most important contributions to the new chamber music was his planning of formal structure; he conceived a work as a whole much more than his predecessors had done. The plan is often dramatic. There are extraordinarily impressive climaxes, sometimes built on pedals. This is also true of some of the works of John Jenkins, who began to compose during Lawes's lifetime, but who really belongs to a later period.

Side by side with the evolved magnificence and brilliance of Lawes, stood the work of another school which inclined to simplify the style of chamber music, in some cases even to oversimplify it. The problematic and profound were avoided by such composers as John Okeover, Richard Mico, Martin Peerson, Henry Loosemore, and Thomas Brewer. Occasionally, fine directness and cheerful vitality were achieved through this homophonic treatment of fantasias and dances, as in this Fantasia for four viols by Simon Ives:[1]

Ex. 265

[1] Ibid. MS. C. 64–69

The influence of English chamber music in continental countries was marked and it was certainly enhanced by the activities of excellent English artists working abroad, among whom William Brade, Peter Philips, Thomas Simpson, and Valentine Flood were outstanding; they made vital contributions to the development of instrumental music particularly in Germany and the Scandinavian countries. Brade especially was a spirited, inventive, and often profound composer, notably in the field of dance music: witness the opening of this allemande from his *Newe auserlesene Paduanen, Galliarden . . .* (Hamburg, 1609).[1]

Ex.266

[1] Brade's *Newe auserlesene Paduanen* have been reprinted in Engelke's *Musik und Musiker am Gottorfer Hofe* (Breslau, 1930); the allemande is printed complete in Schering's *Geschichte der Musik in Beispielen* (Leipzig, 1931), p. 161. A number of pieces by Brade and two dances from Thomas Simpson's *Opusculum neuer Pauanen* (Frankfurt, 1610) are reprinted in the appendix to Günther Oberst, *Englische Orchestersuiten um 1600* (Wolfenbüttel, 1929).

Many compositions by the above masters as well as by Gibbons, Dowland, Holborne, and others were published in continental collections, and their forms and styles were eagerly taken over by composers of the countries where they were issued; for instance, the German composer Lechner (d. 1606) wrote a pavane 'Lachrymae' in homage to Dowland.

FRANCE

Some Frenchmen during the first half of the seventeenth century worked along the same lines as the Elizabethan composers of fantasias. The best known of these are Claude Lejeune, Eustache du Caurroy, Henry de La Voye, Nicolas Métru, Charles Guillet, Louis de Moy, and Antoine de Cousu.[1] None of these achieved great originality; there is a certain scholastic element in their music, perhaps least in some of the *Fantaisies à III, IV, V et VI parties* by du Caurroy (Paris, 1610),[2] which contain some exquisite polyphonic work built around French popular song; by Henri Lejeune of whom Mersenne (1636) quotes a *fantaisie à 5* (it is really more like a pavane); and by Nicolas Métru (1642) whose *Fantaisies à 2* are more advanced than those of other contemporary composers in that they foreshadow the one-subject fugue of the Bach type. The most important composer working in France was the Belgian Henry Dumont whose *Meslanges* (Paris, 1657), containing a few instrumental as well as vocal items, continue and further develop all that is best in the ancient Netherland tradition and the English style. There are some highlights among his almans, notably this piece from the *Meslanges*:

Ex. 267

THE NETHERLANDS

In the Low Countries the times were not favourable to the cultivation of chamber music. The religious and political conflicts of the sixteenth century, with the consequent reshaping of social life,

[1] See Denise Launay, 'La fantaisie en France jusqu'au milieu du XVII siècle', *La Musique instrumentale de la Renaissance* (ed. Jean Jacquot) (Paris, 1955).
[2] Five numbers reprinted by Expert (Paris, 1910).

effected a complete breach of musical tradition. It took two generations before the stage was set, about the middle of the seventeenth
century, for a new flowering of instrumental ensemble music in the
Netherlands, under conditions entirely different from those of the
pre-Reformation Netherland schools.

Between 1600 and 1650 respectable if eclectic attempts to reconcile
the old-style *ricercar* with the more recent Gabrieli type of *canzon*
were made by Cornelius Schuyt, Simon Lohet, Christoph Cornet,
Vredeman, and others. Jean (Giovanni) de Macque, a pupil of de
Monte's, was an exception in so far as he became a pioneer of instrumental coloratura, but he really belongs to Italy as most of his work
as a composer was done there.[1] As in France, music was written for
ensembles of lutes by such men as Thysius, Van den Hove, Valletus,
and Adriaensen.

GERMANY

Instrumental ensemble music was much more alive in all parts of
Germany, although that country by no means represented a single
cultural unit, and some of the innumerable small courts, maintaining
cultural relations with other countries, especially with Italy, Poland,
and England, achieved much higher musical levels than others. The
most advanced centres were the courts of Saxony and Bavaria, and
some of the towns of the Hansa League, especially Hamburg, Lübeck,
and Frankfurt.

The only division recognizable in early seventeenth-century German
music is into regional schools—Northern, Central, and Southern—
each of which developed certain features of its own. Even this division
was anything but rigid; there were numerous cross-currents and
cultural exchanges. On the whole northern Germany, socially and
culturally the most conservative, preserved for the longest time remains of the old Netherland polyphony, but was at the same time the
most open to the influx of elements of English polyphonic music.
Thomas Avenarius, Nikolaus Bleyer, Hans Hake, Antonius Mors,
Bartholomaeus Praetorius, Samuel Scheidt, and Heinrich Utrecht
belonged to this group. In southern Germany there was a greater
fondness for harmonically accompanied melody. Italian influences,
largely entering through Vienna, determined much of the style of
such composers as Hans Leo Hassler, Valentin Hausmann, Paul
Peuerl, Johann Staden, and Melchior Franck. Some of the central
German composers naturally combined in their work elements of

[1] See p. 641.

both north and south, a tendency that culminated in the music of
Johann Hermann Schein.

There are, however, certain features which distinguish German
musical life as a whole from that of other countries. During the first
half of the seventeenth century the *Stadtpfeiffer* (town waits) and
private music-making groups such as students were more important
for the development of instrumental music than were most of the
courts. The Protestant Church, too, assisted in the development of
instrumental music: witness the numerous orchestral establishments
in the larger churches where *canzoni*, sonatas, intradas, and chorale
variations were performed. Popular melody also played an important
part;[1] the incorporation of German popular song in 'art-music' not
only greatly vitalized the work of German masters but also gave it
originality, distinguishing it from the styles of other countries.

Canzon, sonata, and *ricercar* were cultivated by several excellent
musicians of the period about 1600: Michael Praetorius, Hassler,
Hausmann, Aichinger, Valentin Dretzel, Schein, Scheidt, Erasmus
Widmann, and others. These were still living forms with clearly
defined functions in musical life: quite a large number of the non-
dance pieces (and several collections of dances, too, for that matter)
were scored for wind instruments chiefly for performance by town
bands—*Turmmusik* ('tower-music') as it was called later on in the
seventeenth century. The Italian Girolamo Fantini in Dresden,
himself a trumpeter, issued such a collection at Frankfurt in 1638;
the third volume of Johann Erasmus Kindermann's *Deliciae Studiosorum* (Nuremberg, 1643) is for cornetts, trombones, flutes (recorders),
and bassoons; some of the items in Schein's *Banchetto musicale*
(Leipzig, 1617)[2] are for four *Krumbhorns* (cromornes). Matthias
Spiegler's *Olor Solymaeus* (Ravensburg, 1631) includes *canzoni* for
cornetts and bassoons; Valentin Colerus's *Neue lustige liebliche und
artige Intraden Taentze und Gagliarden* (Jena, 1605) include a number
of items for *Zincken* (cornetts).

Some aspects of early German 'free' instrumental music may strike
one as somewhat mechanical compared with the achievements of
other countries. There are, for instance, long chains of sequences
even in instrumental introductions to some of the vocal compositions
of Schütz himself, rows of literal repetitions of quite unimportant
little figures, and a certain tendency towards a too obvious metrical

[1] See, for instance, Meyer, 'L'élément populaire dans les danses instrumentales allemandes jusqu'à la Guerre de Trente Ans', *La Musique instrumentale de la Renaissance*,
p. 139.
[2] Reprinted by Arthur Prüfer, *Johann Hermann Schein's Werke*, i (Leipzig, 1901).

symmetry. Yet, side by side with such products of handicraft rather than art, stand works of great depth and pathos, ranking with the most imposing achievements of early seventeenth-century music.

The most important field of early seventeenth-century German instrumental work, however, was dance music. The forms were those in general use in Europe. Pavane and galliard dominated German dance composition up to 1610, but became gradually less important during the following years. There were, further, allemande, sarabande, corante, tripla, passamezzo, volta, mascarade, saltarello, ballett, bransle (*Brande*), to which must be added a number of marches (some are called *Englisch Marsch*) as well as introductory pieces such as *Auffzug* and *Intrade* (a particularly popular form) and movements called simply German, French, Italian, Spanish, or Polish dance. Many of these dances were published with words and could be either sung or played.

The output of dance music in all parts of Germany at the beginning of the seventeenth century was tremendous. Much more frequently than in other countries, composers grouped several dances together, thus producing suites. This technique, continuing the tradition of the old dance-pairs,[1] was at first at least partly inspired by the work of English composers resident in Germany, such as Brade and Simpson. Yet it became more and more a habit among German composers. The suites of some masters were based on the variation principle, which again had been found in the dance-pairs but was now extended to three, four, five, or even more different movements. Paul Peuerl, for instance, published his *Newe Padouan Intrada Däntz unnd Galliarda* (Nuremberg, 1611)[2] in suites of four dances, all four being based on transformations of the same material.[3] Paul Rivander made up variation suites of *paduan* (pavan), *intrada*, *dantz*, and *currante*, and Schein's suites contain *paduan*, *gagliarda*, *courente*, *allemande*, and *tripla*, all being different versions (in varying rhythms) of the same basic theme, as is shown by the incipits of the tenth suite of the *Banchetto musicale*:

Ex. 268

---

[1] See Vol. III, pp. 416 and 451.

[2] Reprinted by Karl Geiringer in *Denkmäler der Tonkunst in Österreich*, Jg. 36[2] (vol. lxx).

[3] The *padouan* and *intrada* from Peuerl's third suite are recorded in *The History of Music in Sound*, iv.

Block harmonies are characteristic of many of these early German dances, to most of which people still really danced. Stylization of dances was still the exception rather than the rule in Germany, whereas in England and Italy after 1600 dances were often stylized as more or less 'free' forms. Yet polyphonic life there was in plenty, too, in the more ambitious types of dance in Germany, notably the pavanes, galliards, and intradas. There is wonderful vitality and variety in this music, alike in its rich harmonic life, its colourful and often popular melodies, and especially its rhythms, as in this ballet for four instruments by Paul Schäffer:[1]

Ex. 269

[1] From *Pratum Musicale* (Leipzig, 1622).

The development of instrumental ensemble music, as of all other music in Germany, was seriously retarded after 1620 by the Thirty Years War. Ravaged by hordes of foreign mercenaries, its population decimated by murder, starvation, and disease, and the survivors living in constant horror and fear, Germany offered little opportunity for such enjoyments as the playing of musical instruments. Composition stagnated. In the few places where any musicians were still writing, composers right up to the middle of the seventeenth century mostly wrote in the style of the old Gabrieli *canzon* (Paul Siefert (d. 1666) and Thomas Strutius (d. 1678) at Danzig, Hentzschel at Thorn, Johann Klemm (d. 1657) at Zwickau, and others).

Few retained enough of their creative stimulus to keep up the high level of instrumental composition, other than dance music, which had been reached at the beginning of the century. The most important of these were Scheidt (*Symphonien auff Concert-Manier*, Leipzig, 1644),[1] Kindermann (*Deliciae Studiosorum*, Nuremberg, 1640–3), Johann Schop (*Erster (und ander) Theil neuer Paduanen . . .*, Hamburg, 1633) and Johannes Andreas Herbst (*Musica Poetica*, Nuremberg, 1643). The highest degree of originality and artistic perfection was achieved by Johann Vierdanck of Stralsund whose two instrumental collections (both Rostock, 1641) contain dances as well as sonatas, *canzoni*, and *capricci* and include true masterpieces, some of them specially written for wind instruments. All of these are equally remarkable for their flexible contrapuntal writing, their melodic eloquence, and their advanced instrumental style, witness this excerpt from his Sonata for cornett and as trombones, with *basso continuo*:

Ex. 270

[1] Fifteen of which have been reprinted by Hermann Keller (Mainz, 1939), with the editor's hypothetical reconstruction of the lost second treble part.

Another of Vierdanck's compositions, a *Sonata a 5* on an old German students' song ('Als ich einmal Lust bekam'), is unique for its use of instrumental *unisono*; there are several episodes, interrupting fugal developments of the tune, where the tune itself is played in octaves and unison by all the instruments.

If 'free' chamber music fared badly in consequence of the war, the output of dance music, formerly the bulk of German instrumental composition, ceased almost completely in the late 1620's, when Wallenstein's and Tilly's armies swept across Germany and the war began to make itself felt everywhere. Here is indeed a case of a highly developed branch of art being completely destroyed by war—not exhausted or overtaken by more powerful factors within musical history itself but broken off at the height of its flowering. The following lists[1] speak for themselves; the first shows the dates of the often very large collections of dances which appeared in Germany from 1601 to 1628. (It is by no means complete, as it does not include manuscript material):

1601 Demantius, Hassler.
1602 Hausmann, Steuccius (two publications).
1603 Franck, Groh, Hausmann.
1604 Franck, Groh, Hausmann (two publications), Mercker, Steuccius.
1605 Colerus, Franck.
1606 Fritsch, Staden.
1607 Füllsack-Hildebrand.
1608 Demantius, Franck.
1609 Brade, Füllsack-Hildebrand, Lyttich, Mercker, Schein, Staden, Thesselius.
1610 Franck, Hase, Lyttich (two publications), Möller, Staden, Simpson.
1611 Franck, Groh, Otto, Peuerl.
1612 Krumbhorn, Möller, Michael Praetorius.
1613 Demantius, Peuerl, Rivander, Völckel, Widmann.
1614 Brade, Büchner, Franck, Mercker, Selich.
1615 Gesius, Hassler, Lütkemann, Mors, Selich.
1616 Eichhorn, Engelmann, Bartholomaeus Praetorius.
1617 Brade, Engelmann, Hagius, Schein, Schultz, Simpson.

[1] Full titles of all these works may be found in the author's *Die mehrstimmige Spielmusik des 17. Jahrhunderts* (Kassel, 1934).

1618 Posch, Schäffer, Staden, Widmann.
1619 Brade, Christenius (two publications).
1620 Altenburg, Oberndörffer, Peuerl, Bartholomaeus Praetorius.
1621 Brade, Posch, Scheidt, Simpson.
1622 *Amoenitatum Hortulus* (anonymous), Engelmann, Schäffer, Scheidt, Schultz.
1623 Franck (two publications).
1624 Büchner, Roth, Utrecht.
1625 Franck, Peuerl, Schein, Staden.
1626 Farina, Hetz, Posch, Schäffer.
1627 Farina (two publications), Franck, Michael.
1628 Bleyer, Farina (two publications).

Thus 106 publications of dance music were issued during the first twenty-eight years of the century. The second list contains the names of composers who published dance music from 1629 to 1648, the years when the war was at its worst:

1629 Vintzius.
1630 Avenarius, Michael.
1631 Cramer.
1632 ———
1633 ———
1634 Schop.
1635 ———
1636 Hammerschmidt.
1637 ———
1638 Fantini.
1639 Hammerschmidt.
1640 Kindermann.
1641 Vierdanck.
1642 Bleyer, Kindermann (two publications).
1643 Reuffius.
1644–48 ———

Thus only fourteen collections appeared during the last twenty years of the war.

POLAND AND BOHEMIA

There must have been a great deal of instrumental composition in Poland, judging from the large number of Polish dances that appeared in German publications,[1] such as the collections by Christenius, Demantius, Hänisch, Hausmann, Schäffer, and Vintzius.

---

[1] See Alicja Simon, *Polnische Elemente in der deutschen Musik bis zur Zeit der Wiener Klassiker* (Zürich, 1916).

Some of these dances are called *Choreae Polonicae* or simply *taniec polski*. The popularity of early Polish dances in Germany was only partly due to the close political and cultural relations between Saxony, Poland, and Bohemia. The main reason for the widespread cultivation of Polish dances was their popular charm.

The melodic element is very prominent in these pieces. Popular musicians formed themselves into bands of three, four, or five players of fiddles, double basses, Polish zithers, and other plucked instruments, as well as flutes, bagpipes, and even trumpets or shawms, and there must have been plenty of raucous fun in the music-making of these groups. Rhythm in Polish dances is marked too; there is little imitation or syncopated counterpoint which might hide the rhythmic vitality and directness. This 'Polish Dance' from Demantius's *77 Newe außerlesene liebliche zierliche Polnischer und Teutscher Art Tänze* (Nuremberg, 1601) is typical:

Ex. 271

An enormous *Duma* of 1589[1] abounds in extraordinary accents and hiatus:

Ex. 272

The lively rhythms and melodies of Polish folk music reappear in the works of some of the Court composers. The instrumental music of one of the most important of these, Adam Jarzębski, contained in a manuscript collection of *Canzoni e Concerti a due tre e quattro voci cum basso continuo*,[2] contains popular elements, sometimes borrowed from other countries. Jachimecki[3] sees in this *Tamburetta a 3*[4] a 'fiery Spanish dance':

Ex. 273

This *Canzon a 4*,[5] on the other hand, has a marked Polish flavour:

Ex. 274
Vivace

---

[1] Reprinted by Marja Czepańska and Tadeusz Ochlewski, *Wydawnictwo dawnej muzyki polskiej*, viii (Warsaw, n.d.); but it is possible that this is a vocal composition which has lost its text, see Hieronim Feicht, 'Muzyka w okresie polskiego baroku', *Z dziejów polskiej kultury muzycznej* (ed. Z. M. Szweykowski), i (Cracow, 1957), p. 155, n. 82.

[2] Wrocław (Breslau) Municipal Library, MS. Mus. 111, dating from 1627; see J. J. Dunicz, *Adam Jarzębski i jego Canzoni e Concerti* (Lwów, 1938).

[3] *Historja muzyki polskiej* (Warsaw, 1920), p. 88.

[4] *Wydawnictwo*, xi.   [5] *Wydawnictwo*, ibid.

The same is true of some of the fantasias and *canzoni* of Marcin Mielczewski.[1]

In Bohemia and Moravia original Slav elements did not appear conspicuously until after 1648; before that date activity had been centred on the Prague Court which had close associations with Italy and Vienna. Yet there was considerable interchange of elements of style between Czech popular music and German music. It is significant that some of the leading composers of early instrumental music were born and brought up in Bohemia or neighbouring countries (Valerius Otto, Christoph Demantius, Eusebius Bohemus, Isaak Posch, Andreas Hammerschmidt) and their work bears traces of the melodic freshness and rhythmic interest characteristic of Slavonic music; pieces like this Intrada by the Prague composer Valerius Otto:[2]

Ex. 275

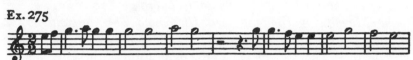

are so strikingly similar to modern national dances such as the first of Dvořák's *Slavonic Dances* (Op. 46, No. 1), that one is tempted to surmise the existence of a common source: Czech folk music.

[1] *Wydawnictwo,* vi and xxix.
[2] From *Newe Paduanen, Galliarden, Intraten und Currenten* (Leipzig, 1611).

XII

SOLO INSTRUMENTAL MUSIC

By WILLI APEL

THE YOUNGER CAVAZZONI

THE history of Italian keyboard music down to 1530, told in Chapter XII of the previous volume, culminates in the work of Marco Antonio Cavazzoni; the present chapter opens with that of his son. In 1542 and 1543 there appeared at Venice two books of far-reaching importance, entitled respectively *Intavolatura cioè recercari canzoni Himni Magnificati composti per Hieronimo de Marcantonio da Bologna, libro primo*, and *Intabolatura d'organo cioè Misse Himni Magnificati . . . libro secondo*.[1] In the dedication of these the author signs as Girolamo Cavazzoni and speaks of himself as 'essendo in giovanissima età' and 'ancor fanciullo'. From these remarks it would appear that Cavazzoni, the son of 'Marcantonio da Bologna,'[2] was born about 1525: he died in or after 1577. Unfortunately no later compositions by him are known.

Cavazzoni's books make him appear as one of the most astonishing examples of youthful achievement in the history of music, perhaps without parallel except for Mozart and Mendelssohn. His compositions show an artistic maturity which one would expect to find at the end rather than the beginning of a creative career. Moreover they indicate an extraordinary advance in style and form over the works of earlier keyboard composers. The Gothic tradition which still lingers on in Schlick and Marco Antonio is completely abandoned by Cavazzoni, being replaced by the harmonious counterpoint, equal participation of all parts, and fully developed imitative technique of Josquin and Gombert. Particularly illuminating in this respect is a comparison of his *ricercari* with those of his father. While Marco Antonio's are vague effusions of a nondescript form, midway between pseudo-imitation and toccata style, those by Cavazzoni are the earliest known examples of the fully developed imitative *ricercar*. This

[1] New editions by Giacomo Benvenuti, in *I classici della musica italiana*, vi (Milan, 1919) and Mischiati (Mainz, 1958); the *Libro primo* only, also by Torchi in *L'arte musicale in Italia*, iii (Milan, 1898).

[2] See Vol. III, pp. 445 ff.

is all the more remarkable as they are no mere copies of the contemporary motet, but represent a type of imitative counterpoint with distinctive characteristics, as will be shown subsequently. It is almost impossible that a composer of only eighteen or twenty years could have achieved this without precedents, and it may be that perhaps Willaert composed organ *ricercari*, now lost, which served as models. It must be pointed out, however, that such models are not to be found among Willaert's *Fantasie et rechercari a tre voci accomodate da cantare et sonare* (Venice, 1549);[1] these are not for organ but for an ensemble of melody instruments or (vocalizing) singers, as is shown by the fact that they were published in part-books. Their principles of style and form differ markedly from those of Cavazzoni's *ricercari*, being much closer to those of the motet. The same remark applies to other sixteenth-century instrumental *ricercari* which have, rather misleadingly, been presented as organ music, e.g. the publications of Tiburtino, Buus, and Annibale Padovano. (This does not exclude the possibility that they were occasionally played on the organ.)

The four *ricercari* by Cavazzoni may be described as compositions in which several themes are treated in successive sections of imitation. In contrast, the motet may be defined as a composition in which several motives are treated in successive points of imitation. In fact, the *ricercar*, though doubtless derived from the motet, differs from it mainly in the fuller imitative treatment of the subjects and, consequently, in the lesser number of subjects, if pieces of comparable length are considered. In a motet a thematic idea is imitated normally four or five times, while the number goes up to eight, nine, thirteen, seventeen, and nineteen in Cavazzoni's *ricercari*. As a result, the motive of the motet becomes a theme, and the passing point of imitation, a fugal section. As a concomitant of this difference (which becomes even more apparent in the later *ricercari*, by Andrea Gabrieli and others), there is a tendency toward full cadential endings in the *ricercar*, as compared with the continuous style of the motet, in which the successive points of imitation usually overlap. Moreover, Cavazzoni repeatedly adds a passage in free toccata style at the end of a section, an element entirely foreign to the motet. On the other hand, sections in chordal style, which are often found in the motets, are absent from the *ricercari* except, occasionally, in the closing bars. Finally, it may be noticed that free part-writing (introduction of an additional part in certain passages, or an extra note in a

[1] Reprinted 1559: see p. 558, n. 2.

chord) is very frequent in the *ricercari* of Cavazzoni, although less so in those of his successors.[1]

The following are diagrams of two *ricercari* by Cavazzoni. A, B, C represent thematic sections, and the figures indicate the number of statements of the theme in each section. A straight dash designates continuation in free counterpoint, without imitation, while a wavy line indicates a passage in toccata style:

Ricercar I   *Ricercar* II

A∥ B∥ C —∥ D —∥ E — ∿ —   A∥ B∥ C∥ D∥ E∥ F∥ G ∿; H ∥ I

5 17 5   4   4   7 7 6 3 4 9 8   13 7

Cavazzoni's first book also contains two *canzoni*, 'sopra Il è bel e bon' and 'sopra Falt d'argens'. The latter is of particular interest, since it uses the thematic material of Josquin's *chanson* 'Fault d'argens', but in a different contrapuntal elaboration.[2] It therefore represents an important step between mere arrangements of *chansons* and entirely independent keyboard *canzoni*.

Apart from his four *ricercari* and two *canzoni*, all the compositions by Cavazzoni are liturgical pieces: three organ Masses ('Missa Apostolorum', 'Missa Dominicalis', and 'Missa de Beata Virgine'), twelve hymns (*inni*), and four Magnificats (*primi, quarti, sexti*, and *octavi toni*). The organ Masses consist of a number of short organ pieces to be used in alternation with plainsong.[3] The first two Masses provide organ music for all five movements of the Ordinary of the Mass, while in the third the *Credo* is omitted. On the other hand, this Mass is amplified by a number of pieces based on *Gloria* tropes, namely, 'Spiritus et alme', 'Primogenitus', 'Mariam sanctificans', 'Mariam gubernans', and 'Mariam coronans'. The 'Missa Apostolorum'[4] is based on the plainsong of Mass IV ('Missa Cunctipotens'). The following diagram illustrates the alternating performance of the organ Mass (organ pieces are represented by italics):

Kyrie Kyrie *Kyrie*. Christe *Christe* Christe. *Kyrie* ('Chirie quartus') Kyrie *Kyrie*.

Gloria in excelsis Deo. *Et in terra pax hominibus bonae voluntatis.* Laudamus te. *Benedicimus te.* Adoramus te. *Glorificamus te.* . . . .

---

[1] For more details see Willi Apel, 'The Early Development of the Organ Ricercar', *Musica Disciplina*, iii (1949), p. 139, which should be consulted also for Andrea Gabrieli and Merulo.

[2] Both compositions are reproduced in Davison and Apel, *Historical Anthology of Music*, i (Cambridge, Mass., 1946), pp. 93 and 126.

[3] See Vol. III, p. 424.

[4] Also reprinted in Davison and Apel, op. cit., p. 123.

Cavazzoni's four compositions of the *Magnificat* generally follow the traditional method of providing organ pieces (versets) for the odd-numbered verses of the chant. For some reason verse 5 ('Et misericordia') is omitted in all the four Magnificats, and verse 11 ('Gloria patri') is missing in the third.

A point of special interest and significance is Cavazzoni's much freer attitude toward the plainsong melodies than that of other composers of the period. While Schlick, Attaingnant, and Cabezón use the Gregorian chants in their entirety and without modification other than the occasional insertion of ornamental figuration, Cavazzoni boldly converts them into new formations by selecting motives from them, adding or discarding notes, modifying the intervals, and making full use of the invigorating resources of rhythm. Another aspect of no small importance is that of the formal structure of the versets for the Mass and the *Magnificat*. The method most frequently used is to divide the *canto fermo* into two phrases, and to present the first of these in a short point of imitation, the second in a single statement in the soprano or another part.

ANDREA GABRIELI

Andrea Gabrieli[1] was the first of a series of composers who made Venice the most important centre of organ music in the second half of the sixteenth century. His organ compositions were all published posthumously between 1593 and 1605, by his nephew Giovanni, so that we have no external evidence as to when they were written, a fact all the more deplorable since his life spanned more than seventy years. Considerations of form and style support the view that, although he was probably somewhat older than Cavazzoni, his *ricercari* are of a later date than the latter's. The tendency, noticed in Cavazzoni, to distinguish the *ricercar* from the motet by the smaller number and fuller treatment of the themes, is carried much further in the works of Gabrieli. Of the seventeen examples contained in his two books of *Ricercari* (Venice, 1595 and 1596)[2] only one has a number of themes comparable with those encountered in Cavazzoni, namely, five. Five have three themes, six have two, and the remaining five are monothematic. Another trait suggestive of a relatively late date

---

[1] See pp. 294 ff. and 566–7.

[2] Reprinted by Pidoux in his edition of Andrea Gabrieli's surviving keyboard works, ii and iii (Kassel, 1941–53); Pidoux's five volumes correspond to Books I–III and V–VI of Gardano's edition. Book IV is completely lost, but three organ Masses, found in a manuscript collection at Turin, have been published by Sandro Dalla Libera (Milan, 1958).

is the extensive use of stereotyped coloratura found in a number of Gabrieli's *ricercari*. Influenced by the late-sixteenth-century method of *diminutio*, Gabrieli frequently applies the standard patterns of this superficial practice, the *trilli, gruppi, minute,* and *tirate,* to the contrapuntal texture of his *ricercari*. The result of this method (which has its counterpart in the excessive decoration in book design, metalwork, and other handicraft of the late Renaissance) can be seen in the following example (*Libro secondo, Ricercare del III° tono*):[1]

Ex. 276

Finally it is important to notice that Gabrieli makes extensive use of those special devices of 'learned counterpoint' which subsequently became one of the most characteristic marks of the *ricercar*: stretto, inversion, diminution, augmentation, simultaneous combination of different themes, double counterpoint. Through the consistent use of such devices Gabrieli strengthened the position of the *ricercar* as a musical type in its own right, removing it even further from the motet. Below is a schematic analysis of some of his *ricercari*. The signs A[s] and A[1] indicate stretto and inversion. The combined use of two themes is indicated thus: A/B.

Libro secondo, No. 5 (Pidoux II, no. 8): A// B[s]// C[s]// D[s]// E[s]
„   *terzo,*   No. 4 („   II, no. 4): A// B
„   „   No. 5[2] („   II, no. 5): A// A/B
„   „   No. 6 („   II, no. 6): A// B// C[s]

The no. 5 of this group is perhaps the most 'progressive'. Since the

---

[1] Pidoux, op. cit. iii, p. 28, and Tagliapietra, *Antologia di musica antica e moderna per pianoforte,* i (Milan, 1931), p. 76.

[2] In Apel, 'The Early Development of the Organ Ricercar', *Musica Disclipina,* iii (1949), p. 147, this *ricercar* is wrongly labelled no. 6.

second theme (B) is hardly more than a characteristic counter-motive, it is essentially monothematic.

Perhaps the most interesting example of contrapuntal elaboration is the *Ricercar del duodecimo tono* of the *Libro secondo*. It opens with a section of fifty-three bars in which a theme consisting of two phrases, A_1 and A_2, is used, A_2 being the counterpoint to the thematic answer of A_1 (Ex. 277, i). Both parts of the theme are exploited in various combinations, the most interesting being that of A_2 with its own inversion, $A_2{}^i$ (Ex. 277, ii). In bar 54 a new theme, B, is introduced and immediately presented in inversion and stretto (Ex. 277, iii), while later on A_1, A_2, and B are combined in various ingenious ways (Ex. 277, iv–vi). It may be noticed that the last two of these examples involve double counterpoint at the lower fifth, in view of the different positions of B^i.

Ex. 277

The method represented by the first of these illustrations (i) will henceforth be referred to as 'duplex theme' ($A_{1, 2}$). It plays an important role in the works of later composers, for instance, Frescobaldi.[1]

[1] A *ricercar arioso* by Gabrieli is recorded in *The History of Music in Sound*, iv.

Passing over Andrea Gabrieli's organ *canzoni*, printed in the *Libro quinto* (1605) and *Libro sesto* (1605),[1] we may turn to a brief consideration of his compositions in free style, the *intonazioni* and the toccatas.[2] The former are liturgical preludes, from twelve to sixteen bars in length, starting with solemn chords, and gradually introducing passage work in faster motion. Despite their shortness, they fully convey the impression of festive pomp which characterizes the Venetian school. In fact, they are a more convincing embodiment of this spirit than are the toccatas which, consisting of the same structural elements but on a considerably larger scale, do not escape the danger of monotony inherent in so limited an idiom.

CLAUDIO MERULO

When Andrea Gabrieli was appointed second organist of St. Mark's, he succeeded a younger man, Claudio Merulo (1533–1604), who had held that position since 1557 and in his early thirties was promoted to the highest place an organist of that time could aspire to, that of the first organist of the same church. If the preference given to the younger man can be taken as a testimony of his outstanding organ playing, his excellence as a composer also appears in his organ works, particularly in his toccatas.[3] These represent a noteworthy advance over those of Andrea Gabrieli. Merulo amplified the formal structure of the toccata by the incorporation of sections in the style of the *ricercar*, usually in the arrangement T R T (T = free toccata; R = strict *ricercar*) or T R T R T. Moreover, he replaced the rigid and patterned toccata style of Gabrieli, Padovano, Diruta, and others by one of much greater subtlety and flexibility, using passage work of greatly varied and often truly expressive design, and dissolving the chordal blocks into contrapuntal progressions. At the same time, he imparted to these toccata sections a new element of strength and cohesion by a fuller realization of the functional significance of the harmonic idiom, often resulting in well-prepared and effective cadences.

In addition to his two books of toccatas (Venice, 1598 and 1604)

---

[1] Pidoux, op. cit. iv and v. The *libro sesto & ultimo* was really a second edition of a volume published originally in 1571.—*Ed.*

[2] Published together by Gardano in the *Libro primo* (Venice, 1593), and reprinted in Pidoux, op. cit. i.

[3] Complete edition, including also some toccatas from the Turin tablatures, by Dalla Libera, 3 vols. (Milan, 1958–9). Separate toccatas have been reprinted in Torchi, op. cit. iii; Tagliapietra, op. cit. ii; Davison and Apel, op. cit. i, p. 168; Schering, *Geschichte der Musik in Beispielen* (Leipzig, 1931), p. 151, and elsewhere.

Merulo published three books of *ricercari*[1] (1567, 1607, 1608), of which only the first needs to be considered here. (The two others contain *ricercari* for four instruments.) In the eight *ricercari* of this book Merulo does not follow Gabrieli's tendency toward a small number of themes. Only one (no. 2) is monothematic, while others employ as many as seven or eight themes (nos. 8 and 1). Here follows a diagram of three *ricercari*:

No. 3: A∥ B/C
No. 6: A∥ A/B∥ C∥ C/D∥ Dˢ
No. 8: A∥ B∥ C∥ Dˢ∥ Eˢ∥ E/F ∥G

In general, Merulo's contrapuntal style tends toward full harmonies, which render it more euphonious than those of Cavazzoni and Andrea Gabrieli but also less interesting from the point of view of true polyphony. His *ricercari*, like Gabrieli's, often suffer from a superabundance of stereotyped coloratura, as in the following example from his *Ricercare del XII tono*:[2]

Ex. 278

Merulo's *Messe d'intavolatura* (*Libro IV*, Venice, 1568) contains a 'Missa Apostolorum', a 'Missa in dominicis diebus', and a 'Missa Virginis Mariae', each with selections for the *Kyrie*, *Gloria*, *Sanctus*, and *Agnus Dei*. In addition, there are three 'Patrem' (Credos), one 'In dominicis diebus', one 'Angelorum,' and one 'Cardinalium'. In these compositions Merulo closely follows the tradition established by Cavazzoni's organ masses. However, a stylistic comparison confirms the impression that he was not a contrapuntist of the first

---

[1] One *ricercar* is printed by Einstein, *A Short History of Music* (5th ed., with music, London, 1948), p. 247.
[2] *Libro primo*, no. 6; reprinted in Tagliapietra, op. cit. ii, p. 17.

order. His three volumes of *Canzoni d'intavolatura d'organo* (Venice, 1592, 1606, and 1611)[1] were long regarded as original keyboard compositions, in which the ornamentation was an essential part of the conception,[2] but some at least are transcriptions of unornamented *canzoni* for instrumental quartet.[3]

GIOVANNI GABRIELI

The last of the chief masters of sixteenth-century Italian keyboard music was Andrea Gabrieli's nephew, Giovanni (1557–1612), who succeeded Merulo in 1586 as first organist of St. Mark's. His *intonazioni*,[4] which he published together with those of his uncle, are very similar to these, though even shorter. His imitative compositions, *ricercari* and *canzoni*, are remarkable mainly for their diversity of formal structure and stylistic means. One gets the impression that Giovanni, dissatisfied with the traditional approach, tried to find new possibilities, without, however, coming to a definite solution. One of his *ricercari*[5] is polythematic, but not polysectional. Its three themes are introduced from the outset and are treated simultaneously, in the manner of a triple fugue. Another *ricercar*[6] uses two themes in repeated alternation, so that the second theme may be said to provide the material for episodic interludes, especially since it is more lively than the first and is treated sequentially:

Ex. 279

Among the organ *canzoni* there is one of particular interest.[7] It consists of nine sections, alternately in duple and triple metre.

[1] *Libro primo* reprinted by Pidoux (Kassel, 1941).

[2] See, for example, Kinkeldey, *Orgel und Klavier in der Musik des 16. Jahrhunderts* (Leipzig, 1910), p. 122.

[3] See Benvenuto Disertori's edition of *Sei Canzoni da sonar a 4* by Merulo (Milan, 1950).

[4] Reprinted in Torchi, op. cit. iii; other compositions in Tagliapietra, op. cit. ii. Complete edition of Giovanni's keyboard music by Dalla Libera, *G. Gabrieli: Composizioni per organo* (2 vols., Milan, 1957). See also G. S. Bedbrook's edition (Kassel and Basle, 1957). Four of these reprinted works (Libera, i, nos. 11, 12, 14, 15; Bedbrook, pp. 14, 22, 26, 30; Tagliapietra, nos. 21–24) are spurious.

[5] Tagliapietra, op. cit. ii, p. 70; Bedbrook, op. cit., p. 4; Libera, i, p. 38.

[6] Tagliapietra, ii, p. 76; Bedbrook, p. 7; Libera, i, p. 19.   [7] Libera, ii, p. 40.

The sections in duple metre are all identical so that the result is a rondo structure: *A B A C A D A E A*. The sections in triple metre are very similar to each other but at the same time sufficiently different to provide variety and change. No less remarkable than the form are details of style, especially the polychoral effects in the refrain. The following is an excerpt from this most attractive composition:

Ex. 280

Giovanni Gabrieli's toccatas are similar to the *intonazioni* of Andrea Gabrieli, both in length and in style. The innovations of Merulo, especially the use of imitative sections, are conspicuously absent, except for one toccata[1] which, however, is anonymous and doubtfully Giovanni's.

MINOR ITALIANS OF THE CINQUECENTO

Side by side with the four chief masters, Cavazzoni, Andrea Gabrieli, Merulo, and Giovanni Gabrieli, there worked numerous others of lesser importance, for instance, Vincenzo Pellegrini, Gioseffo Guami (*c.* 1540–1611, organist at Munich, Venice, and Lucca), Annibale Padovano (1527–75, organist at Venice and Graz), Giovan Paolo Cima (organist at Milan in 1609), Bertoldo Sperindio (*c.* 1530–*c.* 1590, organist at Padua), Luzzasco Luzzaschi (d. 1576, organist at Ferrara), and Costanzo Antegnati (b. 1557, organist at Brescia from 1584 to 1619).[2] Several organ composers who were active in Naples will be discussed later.[3] Brief mention may be made here of Girolamo Diruta's well-known treatise on organ-playing, *Il Transilvano* (Venice, I, 1593; II, 1609) which contains pieces (toccatas and *ricercari*) by Diruta himself, Banchieri, Quagliati, Bell'haver, Fattorini, Mortaro, and Romanini, to mention only names which have not previously been given.[4]

[1] Libera, i, p. 44; Bedbrook, p. 30; Tagliapietra, ii, p. 83.
[2] Examples of their work are reprinted in Torchi, op. cit. iii. Riemann reprinted a *ricercar* by Annibale Padovano, op. cit., p. 94; and Kinkeldey a toccata, op. cit., p. 301.
[3] See p. 641.
[4] A *canzone* by Mortaro and four of Diruta's own compositions are reprinted by Carl Krebs as an appendix to his lengthy study of *Il Transilvano* in *Vierteljahrsschrift für Musikwissenschaft*, viii (1892), pp. 379–88.

CABEZÓN

Although Spain's contribution to our knowledge of sixteenth-century keyboard music is slight in quantity, it is of the highest significance, owing to the artistic greatness of its main—and almost sole—representative, Antonio de Cabezón (1510–66), the famous blind court organist of Charles V and Philip II. The majority of his extant compositions are contained in his *Obras de música para tecla, harpa y vihuela* . . ., published posthumously (Madrid, 1578) by his son, Hernando. Important additions, however, are preserved in an earlier collection published by Luys Venegas de Henestrosa under the title of *Libro de cifra nueva para tecla, harpa y vihuela* (Alcala, 1557).[1] It contains thirty-seven compositions ascribed to 'Antonio', who, no doubt, is Antonio de Cabezón. It is interesting to note that only one of these compositions, an 'Ave maris stella' (no. 85), is duplicated in the *Obras*.[2] Apparently Hernando, who knew Henestrosa's book (in a preserved letter he specified that it should be used as a model for his own publication), deliberately excluded compositions by his father which had already been published. It would be tempting to conclude that at least the majority of the pieces contained in the *Obras* were composed after the date of Henestrosa's book, and there are indeed certain considerations in favour of such a surmise.

Cabezón's keyboard compositions include 29 *tientos*, 32 organ hymns, 9 organ settings for the *Kyrie*, 3 sets of versets, two for the psalmody and one for the *Magnificat*, 9 sets of variations, and several other pieces of various kinds. *Tiento* is the Spanish equivalent of the *ricercar*, as appears clearly from a study of Cabezón's examples. However, such a study shows also that he treated this type in a somewhat different manner from that of the Italian school. Hardly any of his *tientos* show the consistent application of imitative treatment and learned devices found in the Italian *ricercari*, nor do they often contain ornamentations, as in Andrea Gabrieli and Merulo, or toccata passages, as in Cavazzoni; on the other hand, non-imitative contrapuntal sections, which Cavazzoni used modestly and Gabrieli abandoned, are frequent as well as extended in Cabezón. Instead of 'non-imitative' we should perhaps say 'not strictly imitative', because these sections do involve imitation, but imitation of a very

---

[1] New edition of the *Obras* in Felipe Pedrell, *Hispaniae schola musica sacra*, iii, iv, vii, viii (Leipzig, 1895–8); of Henestrosa in Higini Anglès, *La Música en la corte de Carlos V* (Barcelona, 1944). Easily available selections from the *Obras* have been published by M. S. Kastner (Mainz, 1951) and Apel in *Musik aus früher Zeit*, ii (Mainz, 1934). On the notation employed by Henestrosa and Cabezón, see p. 783.

[2] *Obras*, iii, p. 50: presumably a later, revised text.

subtle type which defies description or analysis in hard and fast terms. Motives appear and disappear, are transformed or briefly touched upon, leading to new developments. In their very subtlety of treatment these passages represent the most fascinating display of contrapuntal ingenuity in the entire organ music of the sixteenth century.[1] In most of Cabezón's *tientos* three or four themes are treated in strict imitation, the first in wide spacing, the others usually in stretto, and some or all of the imitating sections are followed by sections in free counterpoint.

Some of the *tientos* in the *Obras* show novel traits which set them apart from the others and which no doubt indicate a later date of composition than that of Henestrosa's publication. While all the *tientos* contained in this book, as well as some of those in the *Obras*, proceed mostly in an unchanging motion of minims and crotchets, others contained in the *Obras* are remarkable for their variety of style and texture, involving quaver figurations, triplet formations, chordal passages, and occasional short ornamentations in semi-quavers. The most impressive example of this group is the *Tiento del primer tono*,[2] with its quadruple diminution of the theme (Ex. 281, iii), its section in 'French' dotted rhythms (iii), and its grandiose peroration (iv) which anticipates the German chorale of the seventeenth century. In compositions like these can be seen the germs of the colourful and discursive style of Spanish organ music in the Baroque period.

Ex. 281
(i)

(ii)

---

[1] See Almonte C. Howell, 'Cabezón: an Essay in Structural Analysis', *Musical Quarterly*, l (1964), p. 18.   [2] Pedrell, op. cit. ii, p. 51.

Cabezón's liturgical compositions, particularly the short versets, contain some of his most exquisite thoughts. An example such as the *Versos del sexto tono*, no. 4,[1] clearly illustrates the spiritual kinship with J. S. Bach which has often been noted.

Cabezón's variations are masterpieces which presuppose a long evolution in the hands of unknown predecessors.[2] It may be noticed that the system of barring used in the original sources and usually taken over by modern editors often obscures the rhythm and the character of the themes and, consequently, of the variations. For instance, in the first set of variations, entitled *Diferencias*,[3] we find the theme given in Ex. 282 as (i). The true nature of this melody appears only if it is realized that it is actually in triple time (*tempus perfectum*), three bars of the original score forming one bar in the modern sense. By using a suitable reduction of the note-values we arrive at the version given as (ii). The notes written underneath the first bar represent the theme in its full and symmetrical form, in which it occurs in all the subsequent variations. Thus reconstructed, it turns out to be a slightly ornamented version of the melody (iii) which, under the name of 'Romanesca' or 'Guardame las vacas', was used by Spanish and Italian composers:

---

[1] Pedrell, op. cit. iii, p. 27, and Davison and Apel, op. cit. i, p. 144.

[2] Kastner has presented a plausible case for the derivation of Cabezón's *fabordones llanos* and *fabordones glosados* from Arnolt Schlick's organ versets: see 'Rapports entre Schlick et Cabezón', *La Musique instrumentale de la Renaissance* (ed. Jean Jacquot) (Paris, 1955), p. 217.—*Ed.*

[3] Pedrell, op. cit. vii, p. 70.

Ex. 282
(i)

(ii)

(iii)

Here is a similar reconstruction of the theme used in the *Diferencias sobre el canto de Cavallero*:[1]

Ex. 283

Original:

Cabezón's method of variation is based on the principles of *canto fermo* treatment and ornamentation, the latter being used when the melody occurs in the top part, the former when it is placed in one of the lower parts. The ornamented soprano melody is usually supported by chordal blocks, while the presence of the theme in one of the lower parts naturally results in a more independent treatment of the surrounding voices. The variations on 'La Pavana Italiana' and 'La dama le demanda'[2] (both on the same theme) may be singled out as

---

[1] Ibid. viii, p. 3; Kastner, op. cit., p. 1; Davison and Apel, op. cit. i, p. 145.

[2] Pedrell, op. cit. viii, pp. 6 and 10. The *Differencias sobre la Pavana Italiana* are also reprinted in Hermann Halbig, *Klaviertänze des 16. Jahrhunderts* (Stuttgart, 1928), p. 16, and Apel, *Masters of the Keyboard* (Cambridge, Mass., 1947), p. 46.

particularly impressive works. In spite of the secular nature of the theme, these compositions are imbued with an almost religious feeling of austerity and dark glowing intensity.

MINOR SPANISH COMPOSERS

Side by side with Cabezón there worked other organ composers known to us through a handful of pieces in Henestrosa's publication. Pedro Alberch Vila (1517–82), famous organist of Barcelona,[1] is represented by two *tientos* (nos. 38, 39) of impressive dignity, in which free counterpoint largely supersedes imitative treatment. A *tiento* by Francisco de Soto (no. 50) and an anonymous *tiento* which has been attributed to him (no. 49) are of particular interest since they show Josquin's paired-imitation[2] technique transferred to the organ, resulting in echo effects which not only anticipate those of Sweelinck by half a century but also surpass them in artistic effect.

Two well-known Spanish theorists, Juan Bermudo (*Declaración de instrumentos musicales*, Ossuna, 1549; enlarged edition, 1555) and Tomás de Santa María (*Arte de tañer fantasía*, Valladolid, 1565), also deserve mention in this account, because of the numerous compositions contained in their treatises.[3] Although these are all instructional pieces, designed to illustrate points in the text, many of them have independent value as examples of sixteenth-century Spanish organ style. Tomás's examples for the different church modes are short fugal compositions in which two subjects are treated in succession. They may be considered as miniature *ricercari* although they are probably more closely related to the sixteenth-century tradition of organ versets, pieces which were traditionally written on a binary plan, in imitation of the structure of the psalm verses of Gregorian chant.

More interesting are the five hymns and four free compositions in Bermudo's *Declaración*. Remarkable for their low range, the frequent use of open fifths, Lydian cadences, and numerous other strange formations, they indicate a composer of great individuality and ingenuity.

---

[1] See p. 408.

[2] See Vol. III, p. 265.

[3] Complete edition by P. Froidebise, *Orgue et liturgie*, xlvii and xlix (Paris, 1960–1). Examples have also been reprinted in Kinkeldey, op. cit., pp. 228–44, Tagliapietra, op. cit. i, and Pirro, 'L'art des organistes' in Lavignac, *Encyclopédie de la musique*, 2ᵉ partie, ii, pp. 1199–1201.

GERMAN KEYBOARD MUSIC

The promising start which German organ music had made in the early part of the sixteenth century under Hofhaimer, Schlick, Kotter, Sicher, Kleber, and Buchner[1] did not lead to continuous growth. Although Buchner's *Fundamentum*,[2] owing to its comprehensive scope and didactic character, might well have become the point of departure for further development in the same direction, there is nothing to indicate that such a development did ensue. Of course, it is difficult to make definite statements, since all sources of German keyboard music between the *Fundamentum* (*c.* 1520) and Ammerbach's *Orgel oder Instrument Tabulatur* (Leipzig, 1571) are lost.[3] Nevertheless, the entirely different scope and nature of Ammerbach's book seem to support the surmise that the early development of German keyboard music had only a short life.

Elias Nicolaus Ammerbach (born 1530?; organist of St. Thomas's Church, Leipzig, *c.* 1570), together with Bernhard Schmid, the elder (1522–92; organist at Strasbourg), Jakob Paix (1556– d. after 1617; born at Augsburg), Augustus Nörmiger (court organist at Dresden), and Bernhard Schmid the younger (born 1548; son and successor of the elder Schmid) represent a late-sixteenth-century school of German keyboard music generally known under the disparaging name of 'the colourists'. This name was coined by A. G. Ritter who, in his valuable work *Zur Geschichte des Orgelspiels* (Leipzig, 1884), was the first to study the books of this period. Comparing their contents with those of the older German sources, notably Schlick, he was struck by their artistic inferiority, particularly by the profusion of meaningless and stereotyped coloratura in the numerous arrangements of motets and *chansons*. There can be no doubt regarding the validity of Ritter's judgement, based on this line of reasoning. However, he overlooked the fact that the 'colouristic' method, although fortunately not employed in the works of the older German masters, is by no means a distinctive trait of the younger German school. Rather was it an inevitable concomitant of the general practice of sixteenth-century arrangements, indeed of still older keyboard practices, and as such it is evident to the same extent in the organ books of Attaingnant, the *canzoni* of Andrea Gabrieli and the Italian, German, and French lute books.

---

[1] See Vol. III, pp. 430 ff.
[2] Ibid., p. 439.
[3] Such as the Breslau tablature of 1565 described by Fritz Dietrich, *Geschichte des deutschen Orgelchorals im 17. Jahrhundert* (Kassel, 1932), p. 14.

Fortunately, the German sources of the late sixteenth century contain not only such colouristic arrangements (although certainly many more than enough) but also, of greater importance, a large and varied repertory of more than 250 dances.[1] Many of these dances (about 110) are Italian types, mostly passamezzos or galliards, and these differ little from the numerous examples found in Italian and other sources. The remaining part of the repertory, however, consists of native dances which offer a very charming picture of German bourgeois culture near the end of the sixteenth century. Of particular interest is Nörmiger's manuscript tablature of 1598 which contains a wealth of attractive examples, 'pageants, passamezzos, galliards, Polish, German, and other dances as well as the customary entrances and exits of Princely Personages when they betake themselves to dance', as we read on the title-page. Here we find dances based upon popular songs, e.g. 'Ach Elselein, du holder Buhle mein', court dances such as 'Churf. Sächs. Witwen Erster Mummerey Tantz' ('First Masque of the Widow of the Elector of Saxony') and character dances like 'Der Heyligen drey Könige Auftzugkh' ('Procession of the Three Holy Kings'), 'Der Mohren Auftzugkh' ('The Moors' Pageant'), and 'Mattasin oder Toden Tantz' ('Dance of Death'). The beginnings of the last two dances are reproduced here.[2]

Ex. 284

(i) DER MOHREN AUFTZUGKH

(ii) MATTASIN

[1] Wilhelm Merian's *Der Tanz in den deutschen Tabulaturbüchern des 16. Jahrhunderts* (Leipzig, 1927) contains many of these dances, though only five by Ammerbach are given. Dances by Ammerbach are also reprinted in Apel, *Musik aus früher Zeit*, i, pp. 11–12, Davison and Apel, op. cit. i, p. 171, Schering, op. cit., p. 136, and Halbig, op. cit., pp. 11–12.

[2] Pieces from Nörmiger's tablature are printed in Merian, op. cit., pp. 229–58, Apel, op. cit. i, pp. 13–14, Schering, op. cit., p. 137, and Halbig, pp. 27–28. Other settings of 'Der Heiligen drey Könige Aufzugk' and 'Der Mohrenn Auffzug' occur in a manuscript

Stylistically these indigenous dances form a unit which is distinguished from the Italian standard dances by simplicity of structure, lack of coloratura, a greater use of 'modern' harmonic progressions, and, above all, more interesting and individually designed melodies.

THE MULLINER BOOK

As has been shown in the previous volume (Vol. III, pp. 458 ff.), English organ music flowered in the first half of the sixteenth century under such masters as John Redford, Thomas Preston, and Philip ap Ryce. One of the main sources for Redford, the *Mulliner Book*[1] of *c.* 1560, contains also the works of a second generation of Tudor organ composers: William Blitheman (d. 1591), master of the choristers at Christ Church, Oxford; Thomas Tallis (*c.* 1505–85), organist of the Abbey of the Holy Cross at Waltham, and later gentleman of the Chapel Royal; Richard Farrant (d. 1580), gentleman of the Chapel Royal under Edward VI; John Sheppard (d. 1563 ?), chorister of St. Paul's; Richard Allwood, and others.

On the whole, these composers followed closely the tradition established by their predecessors. Like Redford, they wrote practically none but liturgical organ pieces, employing for this purpose two strikingly contrasting styles, one derived from vocal polyphony, the other characterized by the use of fairly rapid and, occasionally, 'virtuoso' keyboard figurations. The latter method may be illustrated by excerpts from two compositions on 'Gloria tibi Trinitas' by Blitheman (*Mulliner*, nos. 91, 92), showing most of the devices commonly associated with the virginal style of the late sixteenth century, such as the well-known English sign of ornamentation (Ex. 285, i), figurations in parallel thirds and sixths for the right hand (ii), as well as for the left (iii), and cross-rhythms resulting from the different grouping of the same note-values, for instance three in one part against four in the other (iv):

Ex. 285
(i)

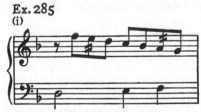

in the Dresden Staatsbibliothek (Msc. Dresd. J. 307*m*) dating from *c.* 1580 (see Halbig, p. 11). They are followed immediately in Nörmiger, and after one other piece in the Dresden MS., by a dance which Nörmiger calls 'Annhaldischer Auftzugkh' and the Dresden compiler 'Einn Ander Auffzug'.

[1] Edited by Denis Stevens, *Musica Britannica*, i (London, 1951).

In compositions of this type the figurative patterns form an effective contrast to the *canto fermo*, which nearly always appears in *cantus planus* style, i.e. in long and equal note-values, one to the bar. In the polyphonic group, on the other hand, the *canto fermo* (most frequently a hymn) is subjected to a process of melodic amplification and rhythmic vitalization, a method ultimately going back to Dunstable and Dufay. In these 'prepared' *canti fermi* the principle of equal note-values is still in operation, since, almost without exception, each half-bar (representing a semibreve of the original notation) contains one note of the chant. This interesting principle is illustrated in Ex. 286, which shows the *canto fermo* of Blitheman's 'Christe qui lux' (*Mulliner*, no. 22) together with the original melody:

Ex. 286

- ne - bras de-ter - gens   lu - ci - fer   lu-cem

As regards the contrapuntal parts added to such a melody, the great majority of the compositions show the use of what may well be called an English national technique of imitation, in which a single motive keeps recurring like an *ostinato*, either in one part or distributed among all of them. Several of Redford's organ pieces are based on the principle of the 'soprano *ostinato*'.[1] A particularly interesting example is an 'In nomine' by Allwood (*Mulliner*, no. 23), the upper part of which consists entirely of repeated statements of a motive, F–G–A–B♭–A, the rhythmic organization of these statements being ingeniously modified (see Ex. 287). This method, interesting in itself, is particularly noteworthy as it is strikingly similar to that employed by Frescobaldi in some of his *ricercari* and capriccios.[2]

Ex. 287

While this composition by Allwood is exceptional, his 'Claro pascali gaudio' (*Mulliner*, no. 18), in which an *ostinato* motive appears in all the parts, is a very typical example of the *ostinato* technique

---

[1] For instance, 'Chorus nove Hierusalem' (printed in music supplement to C. F. Pfatteicher, *John Redford* (Freiburg Diss., 1934), p. 14), 'Eterne rerum conditor' (Pfatteicher, p. 41; *Mulliner*, no. 14), 'Eterne rex altissime' (Pfatteicher, p. 42; *Mulliner*, no. 26). Traces of this style occur also in English vocal music of the period, e.g. in the *Benedictus* of Taverner's Mass 'The Western Wynde'.

[2] See p. 649.

employed in this repertory.[1] The obstinate rigidity of reiteration produces an effect far different from the suppleness of imitative counterpoint as it was practised on the Continent, but certainly not lacking in artistic interest and validity. Another 'Claro pascali gaudio' by the same composer (*Mulliner*, no. 21) has the *canto fermo* in equal, long notes in the upper part, while the lower parts gradually proceed to faster motion, closing with figurations such as are frequently encountered in the repertory of the virginals.

The most representative personality in this group is William Blitheman, known to us by fourteen pieces in the *Mulliner Book*, and one 'In nomine' in the *Fitzwilliam Virginal Book*. The 'In nomine', like the 'Felix namque', is an almost exclusively English species of instrumental music. The 'Felix namque' is always based on the Offertory 'Felix namque' for the Vigil of the Assumption of the Virgin Mary,[2] while the origin of the former has been described in the previous chapter.[3] Not a few of the 'In nomine' pieces exist under the more correct name of 'Gloria tibi Trinitas', among them six compositions by Blitheman (*Mulliner*, nos. 91 to 96). The first four of these are among the most advanced examples of the keyboard-figuration type (see the excerpts in Ex. 285) while the last belongs to the *ostinato*-imitation type.

Blitheman's 'A excellent Meane' (*Mulliner*, no. 32), published as early as 1776 in Hawkins's *General History*,[4] is actually a 'Felix namque'. Here, as in several other examples of this species, the composition starts with the solo section of the Gregorian melody, beginning with 'namque', the choral incipit, 'Felix', being omitted because it was sung by the choir. One of Blitheman's most impressive compositions is his 'Eterne rerum conditor' (*Mulliner*, no. 51)—*melos suave*, as it is called in the manuscript—remarkable for its austere harmonies, pungent dissonances, and typically English false relation (C sharp against C in bar 15), while his 'Te Deum' ('Te Domine' in the manuscript; *Mulliner*, no. 77) shows him at his dullest, at least in the various sections employing the keyboard-figuration style.

Thomas Tallis[5] is represented in the *Mulliner Book* by twelve liturgical compositions, most of which (no. 86 and the entire group

[1] It occurs occasionally in Josquin, e.g. in the *Sanctus* of the 'Missa Hercules Dux Ferrariae'.

[2] See Vol. III, p. 464.

[3] See p. 562. The crucial piece by Taverner is transcribed as no. 35 of the *Mulliner Book*. The previously mentioned 'In nomine' by Allwood (*Mulliner*, no. 23) has no apparent connexion with the species.

[4] Third edition (London, 1875), ii, p. 931.

[5] Complete keyboard works ed. Denis Stevens (London, 1953).

nos. 97–106) belong to the polyphonic type and afford a good insight into the two basic techniques of this type, the ornamentation (one might almost prefer the term 'preparation') of the *canto fermo* and the use of an *ostinato* motive. It may be noticed that nos. 97, 98, and 100 make use of the same (or nearly the same) motives, as do also nos. 101 and 102. Particularly remarkable is no. 106, 'Iste confessor', because its motive, unusual in itself with its downward leaps, occurs in the second half as a real *basso ostinato*, most skilfully combined with the liturgical melody:

Ex. 288

The *Fitzwilliam Virginal Book* contains two 'Felix namque' by Tallis, dated 1562 and 1564.[1] The former opens, according to Van den Borren,[2] with two 'preludes'. Actually, the first 'prelude' is the polyphonic treatment of the choral incipit, 'Felix', while the second is an anticipatory imitation leading to the polyphonic treatment of 'namque es . . .'. This starts in bar 16, each note of the *canto fermo* appearing as a breve (two semibreves) in the soprano: G–F (ornamented)–B♭–C′–D′–C′–&c. The contrapuntal parts proceed in a great variety of figurative patterns, among them such typical virginalistic devices as broken-chord figures (i, p. 430, system 5), patterns with quick alternating notes which have been rather misleadingly termed 'hocket' (p. 432, system 3), and broken octaves (p. 433, system 4). Other patterns, equally virginalistic in character, occur in the second 'Felix namque' (ii, p. 1).

Although the *Mulliner Book* is chiefly a collection of liturgical

[1] Ed. J. A. Fuller Maitland and W. Barclay Squire (Leipzig, 1899), i, p. 427, and ii, p. i.
[2] *The Sources of Keyboard Music in England* (London, 1913), p. 163.

pieces, it contains a number of other compositions, mainly arrangements of songs, dances, and abstract pieces entitled 'Voluntary', 'Poynte', or 'Fansye'. Most of the latter consist of hardly more than single points of imitation, as for instance the 'Voluntary' by Farrant (*Mulliner*, no. 20). The songs include the famous 'In going to my naked bed' by Edwards and 'Fonde youth is a bubble' by Tallis. There are also some pieces that give the impression of being dance songs of French derivation, to judge from such titles as 'La bonnette', 'La doune cella' (La d'où vient cela?), and 'La shy myze' (La chemise?). They are interesting because they appear in a most unusual form: soprano and bass only. Very likely this is a reduction of an original setting in four parts contained in separate part-books. The fact that the two middle parts were considered as dispensable may be regarded as a foreshadowing of a conception which became of universal importance in the seventeenth century.

Dance music proper is represented by only one piece, 'A Pavyon' by Master Newman (*Mulliner*, no. 116), but this is of great interest as a link in a continuous tradition starting with a few rudimentary pavanes of a slightly earlier date and culminating in the splendid examples of the Elizabethan composers. The earliest extant examples of the English pavane are contained in the manuscript Brit. Mus. Royal App. 58. In addition to the famous 'Hornepype' by Hugh Aston and the hardly less interesting 'My Lady Careys Dompe'[1] this source contains two pavanes, 'The Emperors Pavyn' and 'The Kyngs Pavyn'.[2] The former is in slow triple metre, a rhythm not encountered in the later English pavanes, but which occurs in some of the pavanes of the Spanish vihuela composer Milán. Moreover there is a striking similarity between the opening bars of 'The Emperors Pavyn' and those of one of Milán's pavanes, a similarity which one is tempted to interpret as pointing to a common origin, all the more since the title of the English piece suggests a relationship with the court of the Austrian-Spanish emperor-kings:

Ex. 289
(i) THE EMPERORS PAVYN

---

[1] See Vol. III, p. 458; recorded in *The History of Music in Sound*, iv.
[2] Both printed in *Schott's Anthology of Early Keyboard Music*, i (London, 1951).

(ii) LUIS MILÁN

'The Kyngs Pavyn' shows the duple metre normally found in pavanes. It consists of three sections, each of a different design and, very likely, to be repeated. This structure, taken over from French models,[1] was to become the standard form of the pavanes (as well as the galliards) of the Elizabethan composers. In Master Newman's 'Pavyon' this scheme is enlarged to one consisting of four sections; while the first two sections proceed mostly in the steady pulse of full harmonies (Ex. 290, i), the other two show a more intricate texture of imitating figurations. Particularly the fourth section, with its skilful use of a bent-scale motive, approximates to the ingenious treatment found in the pavanes of William Byrd. Newman's 'Pavyon' is also remarkable for its unusual key, C minor, and, in the final cadence, for an early (if not the earliest) example of an augmented sixth chord:[2]

Ex. 290
(i)

---

[1] See, for instance, a pavane from Attaingnant's publication of 1530, reproduced in Davison and Apel, op. cit. i, p. 106.

[2] The sharp for F is omitted in Stevens's edition.

THE VIRGINAL BOOKS

The keyboard music of the Elizabethan period is customarily described as 'virginal music' and usually regarded as the beginning of an idiomatic repertory for the harpsichord, as opposed to that for the organ. From the point of view of musical forms and types, this view is certainly correct. The almost exclusively liturgical repertory of the earlier period is now replaced by one that is almost as exclusively secular, consisting largely of dances and variations. The matter appears different, however, jf considered from the point of view of style. The preceding section has shown that most of the typical ingredients of the virginal style are fully present in the organ music of the Tudor composers. Transferred from liturgical *canti fermi* to dances and secular tunes, from the sustained sound of the organ to the crisp tone of the harpsichord, they grew in number and variety, becoming a store-house of effective devices too well known to be discussed here in detail.[1]

The virginal school includes three generations, represented by the 'three famous Masters William Byrd, Dr. John Bull, and Orlando Gibbons'[2] who were born at intervals of almost exactly twenty years: Byrd in 1542 (43?), Bull *c.* 1563, and Gibbons in 1583. All three died within the same decade, Byrd in 1621, Bull in 1628, and Gibbons in 1625. While Byrd is the only representative of his generation, the second is also represented by Thomas Morley (1557–1603), Ferdinand

---

[1] See the detailed description in Van den Borren, op. cit., pp. 62–152.

[2] As they are called on the title-page of *Parthenia* (London, 1612). Bull is represented in *The History of Music in Sound*, iv, by his jig 'My selfe', Gibbons by an 'almaine', 'The Kings Juell'.

Richardson (*c.* 1558–1618), Giles Farnaby (*c.* 1565–1640), Peter
Philips (1561–1628), and probably John Mundy (d. 1630); and
the third by Thomas Weelkes (*c.* 1575–1623), Thomas Tomkins[1]
(1573–1656), and Benjamin Cosyn (*c.* 1570–*c.* 1644).

Among the few liturgical compositions produced in this period,
John Bull's 'In nomine'[2] may be cited as a further, and final, step
in a direction indicated by the 'Felix namque' of his teacher Tallis:
the use of the Gregorian *canto fermo* as the basis for an enormous
display of technical and intellectual inventiveness. Bull puts the
canto fermo in the bass, extending each of its notes into a pedal-point
of the value of eleven crotchets (two $\frac{4}{4}$ bars plus one $\frac{3}{4}$), which, in the
final section in *prolatio perfecta*, are strictly augmented in the proportion 3:2, resulting in groups of the value of eleven dotted crotchets.
The irregularity of this metrical scheme (which is anticipated in an
anonymous 'Felix namque' in Brit. Mus. Royal App. 56, where each
note covers five beats) greatly contributes to the rhythmic interest
and animation of this composition which, although forbidding in
appearance, is remarkable for the contrapuntal life that unfolds
above its colossal foundation. Of special interest are two passages
(illustrated by the two fragments quoted below), the first of which
shows the use of a playful motive in a manner extensively cultivated by
Sweelinck, while the second illustrates the English propensity for the
'proportional' devices of mensural notation at a time when these
complexities had long been abandoned everywhere else:

Ex. 291

The general reluctance of the English keyboard composers to
accept the methods of imitative counterpoint that were developed on
the Continent is illustrated by the almost complete absence of compositions modelled after the *ricercar*. Instead they cultivated under

---

[1] Although Tomkins is represented in the *Fitzwilliam Book* by five pieces, a large
proportion of his keyboard music dates from the last decade of his life—see Stephen
D. Tuttle's complete edition, *Musica Britannica*, v (London, 1955)—and therefore lies
beyond the chronological limit of this volume.
[2] *Fitzwilliam Virginal Book*, ii, p. 34; *John Bull: Keyboard Music I* (ed. John Steele
and Francis Cameron), *Musica Britannica*, xiv (London, 1960), p. 86.

the name of fantasia or fancy a type which represents an amalgamation of the imitative style with various other elements, ranging from strict counterpoint to the dance. Thomas Morley, in his well-known description of the various musical forms, puts it right at the head of the instrumental forms:

'The most principall and chiefest kind of musicke which is made without a dittie is the fantasie, that is, when a musician taketh a point at his pleasure, and wresteth and turneth it as he list, making either much or little of it according as shall seeme best in his own conceit. In this may more art be showne then in any other musicke, because the composer is tide to nothing but that he may adde, deminish, and alter at his pleasure. And this kind will beare any allowances whatsoever tolerable in other musick, except changing the ayre and leaving the key, which in fantasie may never be suffered. Other thinges you may use at your pleasure, as bindings with discordes, quicke motions, slow motions, proportions, and what you list.'[1]

Usually these fantasias open with a more or less extended section in imitative counterpoint, continuing thereafter with rapid passages, patterned figurations, free imitation of short motives, canons, homophonic sections, song-like tunes, dance-like figurations, &c. One of the most beaùtiful examples is a Fantasia by Byrd (*Fitzwilliam Virginal Book*, i, p. 188) which begins with a Prelude (ibid. i, p. 394) and continues with a truly fascinating variety of formations.

ENGLISH KEYBOARD VARIATIONS

The glorious achievements of the virginalists in the field of keyboard variation are so well known that only a few basic remarks[2] need be made here. Claims for the honour of precedence in this field have been made on behalf of England as well as of Spain. Documentary evidence points to Spain as the home of the variation proper (lute variations by Narvaez, 1538; keyboard variations by Cabezón, c. 1550), to England as that of variations on a ground. Two already mentioned compositions in Brit. Mus. Royal App. 58, the 'Hornepype' by Aston and 'My Lady Careys Dompe', indicate the beginning of an extended development to which many English composers, from Byrd[3] to Purcell, contributed. Like the two early examples, the grounds used by Byrd are mostly harmonically conceived, in contrast

---

[1] *A Plaine and Easie Introduction*, p. 180.

[2] Offered in addition to, and occasionally correction of, the detailed analyses in Van den Borren, op. cit.

[3] For the grounds (and other keyboard works) of Byrd, the following publications should also be consulted: Hilda Andrews, *My Ladye Nevells Booke* (London, 1926) and Tuttle, *William Byrd: Forty-five Pieces for Keyboard Instruments* (Paris, 1939).

to the Italian *ostinatos* which are of melodic derivation. The following illustration shows to what extent the English grounds of the sixteenth century conform to the idea of a harmonic bass:

Ex. 292

Even more remarkable than the English variations on a ground are those based on such tunes as 'The Woods so wilde', 'Walsingham', 'The Maidens Song', 'All in a Garden Greene', 'Goe from my Window', 'Up Tails all', 'Bony sweet Robin', 'Rosasolis', and many others. No other country can boast such a wealth of charming popular sixteenth-century melodies, no other country a group of composers who, recognizing the value of this treasure, cultivated and enhanced it. In the great majority of variations the tune is preserved in one of three ways: in its original form in the upper part, in an inner part, or in the upper part with ornamental figurations. Occasionally, however, the tune is not used at all in a variation, so that the variation is melodically free, being related to the theme either through the bass or only through the scheme of harmonies. William Byrd wrote 15 variation-cycles containing about 130 individual variations. Some 50 of these belong to the first of the types just described, 25 to the second, 10 to the third, and 15 to the fourth. The others represent mixed types in such a way that, for instance, the variation begins with the tune in the upper part and continues with it in the tenor. Byrd's 'Woods so wilde' (*Fitzwilliam Virginal Book*, i, p. 263)

[1] *Fitzwilliam Virginal Book*, i, p. 274.   [2] Tuttle, op. cit., p. 31.
[3] Ibid., p. 13.   [4] Ibid., p. 22.   [5] Ibid., p. 26.
[6] *Fitzwilliam Virginal Book*, i, p. 226; entitled 'Hugh Aston's Grownde' in *My Lady Nevells Booke*, p. 194.

is remarkable for the great number of melodically free variations.
The following illustration shows the beginnings of the theme (var. 1)
and of two variations:

Ex. 293

In var. 9 not only the melody but also the bass of the theme is replaced
by other formations, leaving only the harmonic structure as the
fixed element. As for the variable element, both variations employ
specific motives, a method used by Byrd very often with admirable
ingenuity.

Among the variation cycles of the other virginalists, John Mundy's
eight variations on 'Goe from my window' (*Fitzwilliam*, i, p. 153)
are particularly noteworthy.[1] Immediately after the statement of the

---

[1] The composition appears also (*Fitzwilliam Virginal Book*, i, p. 42) under the name of
Morley, but without the last variation.

theme (var. 1) he introduces (var. 2) a new melody whose soft downward motion and dreamlike quality offer a beautiful contrast to the
charming gaiety of the tune:

Ex. 294

In the last variation the regular phrase-structure of 4+4 bars is
ingeniously modified into one of 3+5; we have here one of the few
examples in which the structural plan of the theme is freely treated.

DANCES IN THE VIRGINAL BOOKS

Not only numerically but also, and mainly, through their refinement and elaboration the pavanes and galliards occupy a place of
much greater importance and artistic significance than the more
recent dance types such as almans, corantos, and jigs. While these

are interesting chiefly as initial steps in the direction of the baroque suite, the pavanes and galliards represent the culmination of the dance music of the Renaissance.

Nearly all the English pavanes and galliards show a tripartite form, *A B C*, in which each section is immediately repeated, usually in figurative variation: *A A' B B' C C'*. A consideration of the structural plans, as indicated by the length of the various sections, is of special interest. The normal structure is one of eight or sixteen bars for each section, and this is found in nearly all the pavanes and galliards of Byrd. Occasionally he increases the length of a section from eight to twelve bars, e.g. in a pavane reproduced in Tuttle's edition on p. 60. The picture changes significantly when we turn to the pavanes and galliards of John Bull and Orlando Gibbons[1] in which irregular phrases prevail. Thus, Bull's 'Pavana of my Lord Lumley' (*Fitzwilliam*, i, p. 149; *Musica Britannica*, xix, p. 181) has eleven bars in its first and second section and one of his galliards (ibid. ii, p. 251; xix, p. 184) shows the extremely irregular scheme of eight, nine, and fourteen bars. In the pavanes and galliards of Gibbons, sections of 7, 9, 10, or 13 bars occur very frequently.

In the numerous cases where a pavane is followed by a galliard, the question of the thematic relationship arises. Among the twenty-one pavane-galliards of Byrd there is only one pair in which the melody of the galliard is derived from that of the pavane (ed. Tuttle, p. 55), and it is of interest to notice that he deliberately avoids the simple transformation of the *proportio tripla*. The following example shows how the eight-bar melodies of the pavane (here shown stripped of their ornamentation) are transformed into melodies of highly irregular lengths:

Ex. 295
(i) PAVANE

GALLIARD

---

[1] Bull's keyboard dances have been edited by Thurston Dart, *Musica Britannica*, xix (1963), the complete keyboard works of Gibbons by Gerald Hendrie, ibid. xx (1962).

(ii)

(iii)

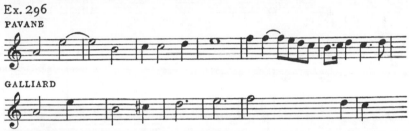

Bull frequently derives the melody of the galliard from that of the pavane, but with very free modifications. Particularly interesting in this respect is his pavane-galliard in A minor (*Fitzwilliam*, i, pp. 124 and 129; *Musica Britannica*, xix, pp. 60 and 64):

Ex. 296

PAVANE

GALLIARD

Some of Byrd's pavanes and galliards are written in that simple and charming style so characteristic of many of his works, while others are filled with an extraordinary emotional tension. The pavanes and galliards of Bull are equally remarkable for their artistic elaboration and for their affective quality which sometimes takes on the expression of violent passion. At the end of the development stands Gibbons's 'The Lord of Salisbury His Pavin' (*Fitzwilliam*, ii, p. 479; *Musica Britannica*, xx, p. 37; also in *Parthenia*); in its expression of deep melancholy and profound grief it stands as a symbol of the impending end of a great period of culture and music:

Ex. 297

FARNABY AND THE GENRE-PIECE[1]

Giles Farnaby (*c.* 1560–*c.* 1620) is of interest particularly for his fantasias, which, together with others written in this period (by Byrd, Bull, Philips, Mundy), provide an insight into the manifold aspects of this elusive type, aspects that range from the strictly contrapuntal to the programmatic (as in Mundy's fantasia, 'Faire Weather').[2] Farnaby's eleven fantasias seem to aim primarily at variety of contents. Thus, one[3] starts out with a tuneful theme treated in imitation in a section which gradually modulates from G major to A major. In a striking contrast of tonality and texture, the second section

---

[1] Farnaby's complete keyboard works have been edited by Richard Marlow, *Musica Britannica*, xxiv (London, 1965).

[2] Farnaby's fantasias are not all so entitled in the manuscript. The piece, ii, p. 330 (*MB*, xxiv, p. 34), is an arrangement of one of Farnaby's canzonets, and the next piece, p. 333 (*MB*, xxiv, p. 20), also gives the impression of being based on a vocal model.

[3] *Fitzwilliam*, ii, p. 82; *Musica Britannica*, xxiv, p. 14.

begins in F major and employs short fragments tossed playfully from one key into another. There follows a dance-like section in a lively $\frac{9}{4}$-metre, the spiritedness of which is increased by figurations, and the piece closes with a section in toccata style; altogether a rather charming composition which Van den Borren extols for its 'delicious perfume of Anglo-Italian sweetness'.[1]

Passing over Farnaby's dances and variations, we must mention briefly some short compositions of his which may well earn him the title of the 'creator of the genre piece'. In such pieces as 'Giles Farnaby's Dreame', 'His Rest', 'His Humour', and 'Farnabye's Conceit' he seems to indicate a trend that was resumed by François Couperin and brought to its fruition in Beethoven's 'Bagatellen' and Schumann's 'Kinderszenen'. By far the most interesting of these is 'His Humour',[2] a whimsical miniature picture of his musical mentality. A little tune, a passage in experimental chromaticism, a few measures filled with a playful motive, and an almost satirical allusion to the pompous ostentation of the hexachord composers: these fragments are combined into a piece unique of its kind.

SWEELINCK

The virginal tradition was transferred to the Continent by composers such as Peter Philips, who went to Belgium in 1590, and John Bull, who followed him in 1612. It was through Jan Pieterszoon Sweelinck (1562–1621), the world-famous organist of Amsterdam, and his numerous German pupils that the achievements of the English masters became a foundation stone of early baroque keyboard music. Hardly second to the English is the Italian influence on the works of Sweelinck. Although the story (based chiefly on a report by Mattheson) of Sweelinck's having studied with Zarlino and Giovanni Gabrieli is now generally discarded, his close acquaintance with the Venetian school appears not only from a consideration of his compositions but also from the fact that his treatise, *Kompositions-Regeln*, is based on Zarlino's *Istituzioni*. It is this combination of two distant and previously unrelated currents which accounts for Sweelinck's key position among the founders of baroque organ music. Of the keyboard composers of his generation (John Bull, Hassler, the younger Gabrieli, Titelouze) he is the only one who signifies the beginning of the seventeenth century rather than the termination of the sixteenth. In this respect he is similar to his most illustrious contemporary, Monteverdi. Sweelinck's influence was felt mainly in

[1] Op. cit., p. 191. [2] *Fitzwilliam*, ii, p. 262; *MB*, xxiv, p. 128; recorded in *The History of Music in Sound*, iv.

Germany through such outstanding pupils or followers as Samuel Scheidt, Jacob Praetorius, Heinrich Scheidemann, and Melchior Schildt. It may be said that Sweelinck unlocked the door through which German organ music entered upon its road to glory.

Sweelinck's keyboard compositions comprise fantasias, some of which belong to the special type of fantasias *op de manier van een echo*; toccatas; variations on secular tunes; variations on church melodies, mostly German chorales; and some dances.[1]

The echo-fantasias are nearly all composed according to a three-sectional scheme, I–E–T, in which I indicates treatment in contrapuntal-imitative style, E echo style, and T toccata style. In no. 15 (10) the last section is missing, while in no. 14 (9) there is another short imitative section between E and T. Ex. 298 shows the beginnings of the three sections of no. 16 (11):[2]

Ex. 298
(i)

(ii)

(iii)

---

[1] New edition by Max Seiffert, *Sweelinck: Werken voor Orgel en Clavicimbel* (Amsterdam, 1943), superseding the incomplete edition in *Werken van Jan Pieterszn. Sweelinck*, i (*Werken voor Orgel of Klavier*, ed. Seiffert, The Hague, 1894). A Supplement was published by A. Annegarn (1958). Seiffert's edition of 1943 contains seventeen compositions which in the sources are anonymous. Some of these, especially the fantasias (nos. 7, 11, 13, 19) may be considered as authentic, while among the anonymous chorale variations (nos 34, 36, 39, 40, 42, 43, 44, 47, 49, 50, 55, 57, and 61) there are several that were probably written by German pupils or followers. In this chapter the compositions are identified by their numbers in the edition of 1943, with the numbers of the earlier edition added in parentheses.   [2] Also reprinted in Davison and Apel, op. cit. i, p. 209.

The motives used in the echo sections show a remarkable variety of form, in their melodic contours and rhythmic patterns as well as in their extension. It is particularly this last element of variety which prevents the hazardous device of echo imitation from becoming dull and monotonous. In spite of this, however, one cannot help feeling that Sweelinck carries the device much too far. In the fantasia no. 14 (9) there are 51 echoes, in no. 17 (12) there are at least 33, and in no. 15 (10) about 28. Only in the two shortest echo fantasias, nos. 16 (11) and 18 (13) is the amount reduced to a bearable minimum.

Among the other fantasias there are four—nos. 9 (7), 11, 12, and 13 (8)—which are probably early works, since they depend heavily upon the English figuration style. They could be termed *ostinato*-fantasias, since the theme is treated not so much in imitation as by frequent repetition. Thus, in no. 12 the theme appears twenty-nine times in succession, always in the upper part. The remaining nine fantasias belong to the field of imitative counterpoint, their most distinctive trait being the use of a single theme—in other words, the consistent rejection of the polythematic method which prevails in the *ricercari* of the sixteenth century. Abandonment of this principle was not, however, accompanied by abandonment of the multisectional treatment. On the contrary, Sweelinck emphasized this treatment by developing it into a fixed scheme of three main sections, each of which often falls into smaller divisions. Each section is characterized by some particular treatment of the main theme. The general principle is to start with a section which presents the theme in its normal form, often also in inversion; to continue with a section using the theme in augmentation (T^2, T^4); and to close with one based on the diminution of the theme ($T\frac{1}{2}$, $T\frac{1}{4}$). This structure is used in all the fantasias except nos. 4 and 6 (5), in which the augmenting middle section is omitted. Within the main sections outlined above there are usually subdivisions based on the use of new counterthemes (c_1, c_2), of stretto (T_s), and other devices. The schematic outline of the Fantasia no. 2 (2) is:

T; T_s; $T+c_1$; ‖ T^2+c_2, fig; T^2+c_3; T^4; $T^{\frac{1}{2}}$; $T^{\frac{1}{2}}_s$; $T^{\frac{1}{2}}$; $T^{\frac{1}{4}}$; T_s

bar: 1   43   60   123   145   168 241 270 276 290 303

The Fantasia no. 13 (8), in which the theme finally appears in sixteen-fold diminution, shows how far playful transformation of the theme may be carried.

Ex. 299

Sweelinck's toccatas resemble Merulo's in their general structure, consisting, as they usually do, of alternating sections in toccata style and in imitative counterpoint. Stylistically, however, they are close to the English tradition, particularly in the toccata sections, in which typically virginalistic figurations abound, for instance in Toccata no. 21 (15):

Ex. 300

Turning finally to the variations, we come to the most outstanding keyboard compositions of Sweelinck. Contrary to current opinion, Sweelinck was a master not of form but of detail. His contributions to the development of musical forms have historical importance, but lack artistic validity, chiefly because they are conceived in much larger dimensions than he was able to fill with significant content. Variations on secular tunes, with their limited and fixed structure, provided him with a much more suitable frame for his imagination, which was inventive rather than formative. The first variation of 'Ich fuhr mich über Rhein' is an admirable example of motive technique:

Ex. 301

Sweelinck's variations on 'Mein junges Leben hat ein End' are among the dozen truly great masterpieces in this genre. An unusually attractive theme is presented with an astonishing exuberance of ideas, which often change within one and the same variation, as, for instance, in variation 4:

Ex. 302

(iv)

The old edition of Sweelinck's keyboard works contained only two liturgical compositions, one on 'Da pacem, Domine' and one on Psalm 140. Recent discoveries have brought to light a great number of chorale variations based on melodies of the German Protestant church, a repertory which shows Sweelinck in a new and surprising role. It is not easy to see what caused him, a Dutch Calvinist, to take an interest in the melodies of the German Lutheran church, melodies which certainly cannot have found a place in the service of a church at Amsterdam. Probably it was Sweelinck the *deutscher Organistenmacher*, the 'maker of German organists', who wrote these compositions for the benefit of his German pupils. The single variations can be roughly grouped into several stylistic categories, such as presentations in four-part counterpoint, in two parts (*bicinia*) with lively figuration against the sustained notes of the chorales (often in semibreves),[1] or in three parts (*tricinia*) with figuration in two parts. In not a few instances the chorale melody itself is presented as *coral colloratus* (ornamented chorale), and examples such as the following show that Sweelinck, ignoring the liturgical dignity of these melodies, subjected them to a treatment no less worldly and playful than he was wont to use when he wrote variations on secular tunes:[2]

Ex. 303

(i) ERBARM DICH MEIN   (var. 6)

(ii) VATER UNSER   (var. 3)

---

[1] Cf. the variations on 'Ach Gott, vom Himmel sieh' darein', recorded in *The History of Music in Sound*, iv.

[2] For further studies of the works of Sweelinck cf. Van den Borren, *Les Origines de la musique de clavier dans les Pays-Bas jusque vers 1639* (Brussels, 1914); B. Van den Sigtenhorst Meyer, *Jan P. Sweelinck en zijn instrumentale muziek* (The Hague, 1946); Robert S. Tusler, *The Organ Music of Jan Pieterszoon Sweelinck* (Bilthoven, 1958).

THE NEAPOLITAN SCHOOL

The central figure in Italian keyboard music of the early seventeenth century is Girolamo Frescobaldi. His musical style is so individual and differs so radically from that of Merulo and the other Venetian composers of the late sixteenth century that he appears as one of the boldest innovators in the history of keyboard music. Indeed, a comparison between a toccata by Merulo of 1598 and one by Frescobaldi of 1615 reveals a most striking contrast. Static breadth is superseded by restless excitement, continuity of thought by multiplicity of figures, even flow by nervous and pressing rhythms, and restrained modal harmonies by abrupt changes into unexpected tonal realms.

Actually, however, Frescobaldi was not entirely without precursors. Many of the surprisingly novel traits of his style are foreshadowed in the works of a school of keyboard composers domiciled at Naples and known to us through four representatives: Antonio Valente, Giovanni Macque, Giovanni Maria Trabaci, and Ascanio Mayone.[1] Valente's *Intavolatura de cimbalo* (Naples, 1576) is written in a curious notation (with figures from 1 to 27 representing the white keys) which is practically identical with a system discussed and recommended by the Spanish theorist Juan Bermudo in his *Declaración de instrumentos* of 1555.[2] (This, by the way, is only one of various traits indicative of a close connexion between the Neapolitan group and the Spanish organ composers of the sixteenth century.) Apart from its notation and some other special points, Valente's book—containing mainly *ricercari, canzoni*, and variations—has little to command interest; the contrapuntal style is very stiff, the variation technique patterned and devoid of interest. Giovanni Macque, a Fleming (born *c.* 1550) who came to Naples in 1586 and died there in 1614, appears in quite a different light.[3] It is in his organ works that for the first time we find those traits of boldness and extravagance which are so typical of Frescobaldi. A short piece entitled 'Consonanze stravaganti'[4] is

---

[1] Cf. Willi Apel, 'Neapolitan Links between Cabezón and Frescobaldi', *The Musical Quarterly*, xxiv (1938), p. 49.   Another important precursor was Ercole Pasquini (*c.* 1560–*c.* 1620), organist of St. Peter's from 1597 to 1608, who left about thirty organ compositions in manuscript (one in Torchi, op. cit., p. 257).

[2] Cf. Apel, *The Notation of Polyphonic Music, 900–1600* (Cambridge, Mass., 1942), pp. 48 ff.

[3] Macque's organ compositions have been published by Joseph Watelet in *Monumenta Musicae Belgicae*, iv (Antwerp, 1938).

[4] Ibid. iv, p. 37; also printed in Davison and Apel, op. cit. i, p. 200.

probably the earliest example in keyboard music of those experiments in daring modulation and unconventional progressions which found a more convincing realization in the madrigals of Gesualdo (whose father Macque had served) and of Monteverdi. The 'Consonanze stravaganti' starts and closes in G but touches, within forty bars, on B flat, A, B minor, C minor, and F sharp minor. An excerpt from the 'Capriccio sopra re fa mi sol' illustrates another aspect of Macque's bold writing:

Ex. 304

Trabaci and Mayone were both pupils of Macque (as was also Luigi Rossi, famous as a composer of early cantatas). Trabaci published at Naples in 1603 a book of *Ricercate, canzone francese, capricci, canti fermi, gagliarde, partite diversi, toccate, durezze, ligature, consonanze stravaganti et un madrigale passeggiato nel fine*, which was followed in 1615 by *Il secondo libro de ricercate ed altri varii capricci, con cento versi sopra li otto finali ecclesiastici*.[1] Both books include examples of practically all the forms of contemporary keyboard music, thus representing an *opera omnia* type of publication similar to Cabezón's *Obras de musica* as well as to Frescobaldi's *Toccate I* and *II*. Mayone's books, entitled *Primo* and *Secondo libro di diversi capricci per sonare* (Naples, 1603 and 1609) contain a similar variety of forms and types: *ricercari, canzoni*, toccatas, variations, and arrangements of madrigals.

The *ricercari* of these composers are based on two or more themes. Trabaci designates them (1603) as *con due, tre, quattro fughe*, indications similar to the *con uno, due, tre, quattro soggetti* of Frescobaldi's

---

[1] Reprints of separate pieces in Torchi, op. cit iii; Tagliapietra, op. cit. v̇; Apel, *Musik aus früher Zeit*, i.

Fantasias of 1608. The contrapuntal treatment is very strict, and shows the intention of crowding the thematic material to the greatest possible extent, a technique which also appears in Frescobaldi's earliest publication, the above-mentioned *Fantasias*. Of particular interest are the *canzoni* by Trabaci, since they include the earliest examples of the variation *canzone*, so extensively cultivated by Frescobaldi. Several of them show the 'cyclical treatment' (i.e. identity or similarity of the first and last sections) found in many seventeenth-century *canzoni*, for organ as well as for ensemble.[1]

Trabaci's toccatas anticipate those by Frescobaldi in their formal structure, which consists of a succession of small sections in contrasting styles, in conformity with the general trend toward disintegration typical of early baroque music.[2] This excerpt from the *Toccata seconda* in his first book:

Ex. 305

---

[1] See the *canzona francese* by Trabaci in Davison and Apel, op. cit. ii, p. 16.
[2] Manfred Bukofzer, in his *Music in the Baroque Era* (New York, 1947), p. 354, aptly remarks that 'sections, parts, and movements are the three units of organization that correspond respectively to the early, middle, and late periods of baroque music'.

illustrates his procedure, so strikingly similar to that of Frescobaldi. Mayone's toccatas are more in the Venetian tradition as regards formal structure, but show interesting innovations of style, particularly in the extensive use of those jerky, restless patterns of figuration which form such a striking contrast to the evenly flowing passage work in the toccatas of the sixteenth century. Not only the *ricercari* and *canzoni* but also the toccatas of Trabaci and Mayone are written in four parts, each printed on a separate stave (*partitura*). The resulting texture is often such as to make one wonder how these pieces were performed, for instance the following bars from Mayone's *Toccata prima*:

Ex. 306

which are manifestly impossible to play on an organ. They are more readily playable on a harpsichord, which requires less attention to holding down the keys, and thus provide internal corroboration of an interesting inscription in Trabaci's book of 1615 which includes the remark that the harpsichord (*cembalo*) 'is the sovereign of all the instruments, and upon it all music can easily be played'.

ITALIAN DANCE MUSIC

Italian keyboard dance literature of the sixteenth century exists chiefly in three collections, an *Intabulatura nova di varie sorte di balli* published by Gardano (Venice) in 1551, *Il secondo libro d'Intavolatura di Balli d'Arpicordo* by Marco Facoli (1588), and *Il primo libro d'Intavolatura di Balli d'Arpicordo* by Giovanni Maria Radino (1591).[1]

[1] For the first, see the edition by William Oxenbury and R. Thurston Dart (London. 1965); the second is available in a new edition by Apel, *Marco Facoli: Collected Keyboard Works* (American Institute of Musicology, 1963); and the third has been

The title of the first refers to *arpichordi, clavicembali, spinette e mana-chordi*; in the others only the harpsichord is mentioned. The Gardano collection, *raccolti da diversi eccellentissimi Autori*, as it proudly states, includes some twenty-four dances, among them, at the very beginning, three *pass'e mezi nuovi*, a type which differs from the *passamezzo antico*, being based on a 'modern' tenor, in the major mode and emphasizing I–IV–V–I progressions:

Ex. 307

Passamezzo nuovo

As the collection also includes three *pass'e mezi antichi*, it affords a neat illustration of this interesting aspect of sixteenth-century dance music. In addition to these, there are numerous galliards with descriptive (or dedicatory?) titles, such as 'El Poverin gagliarda', 'Fantina gagliarda', and 'Comadrina gagliarda'.

Facoli's *Libro d'intavolatura* includes (in addition to a *pass'e mezzo moderno* (with *saltarello*) and four *padoane*) a number of *arie*, short pieces which probably represent instrumental accompaniments that could be used for various poems of identical versification or for the different stanzas of one and the same poem. Several of the *arie* close with a lively *ripresa* which probably served as an accompaniment for a few dance steps. Radino's collection opens with a *pass'e mezo* of such extent that it occupies exactly one-half of the entire publication. It is a *passamezzo nuovo* in five *parti* (variations),[1] followed by a 'Gagliarda del ditto Pass'e mezo' in six variations. As is usual in the *passamezzi* of the late sixteenth century, the *canto fermo* (if it can thus be called) is used in doubled values, each of its notes being expanded to cover four bars ($\frac{4}{4}$) instead of two, as is the case in the Gardano collection. Ex. 308 shows the treatment of the first two notes of the *canto fermo*.

Ex. 308

published, in facsimile and transcription, by Rosamund E. M. Harding (Cambridge, 1949).

[1] Rosamund Harding's remark, op. cit., p. 37, that '*Quarta Parte* should be *Quinta Parte*' is not correct. Actually, the original indication *Quarta Parte* on p. 35 is wrong and should be omitted.

Finally, a Venetian composer of the early seventeenth century may be briefly mentioned: Giovanni Picchi. In his *Intavolatura di balli d'arpicordo* (second edition, 1620)[1] he describes himself as 'organista della Casa Grande in Venetia'. Among the twelve dances contained in this publication, the 'Pass'e mezzo antico di sei parti' (with six variations)[2] is the most interesting, in its brilliant display of ingenious variation patterns. A fascinating sonority (particularly if played on the harpsichord) results from the frequent use of 1–5–8 chords in the left hand, as in the following passage:

Ex. 309

The style of the variations alternates between virtuoso ornamentation and motive technique.

FRESCOBALDI

Gerolamo Frescobaldi[3] was born in 1583 at Ferrara. In 1608 he became organist of St. Peter's at Rome, a position which he held

---

[1] Reprinted by Oscar Chilesotti in *Biblioteca di rarità musicali*, ii (Milan, n.d.), and in Tagliapietra, op. cit. v.

[2] Reprinted in incomplete form in Davison and Apel, op. cit. i, p. 171.

[3] The standard book is Luigi Ronga's *Gerolamo Frescobaldi* (Turin, 1930). Fritz Morel's *Gerolamo Frescobaldi* (Winterthur, 1945), is also important. Most of the keyboard works of Frescobaldi are now available in an edition by Pierre Pidoux (Kassel, 1949–56) in five volumes: i contains the *Fantasie* (Milan, 1608) and the *Canzoni alla Francese* (Venice, 1645); ii the *Capricci, Canzon francese e Recercari* (Venice, 1626), originally published separately as *Recercari e Canzoni Franzese* (Rome, 1615), and *Capricci* (Rome, 1624); iii the *Toccate d'intavolatura, libro primo* (Rome, 1615; reprinted 1628 and 1637); iv *Il secondo libro di Toccate* (Rome, 1627; reprinted 1628 and 1637), and v the *Fiori musicali* (Venice, 1635). The last are also available in editions by Haberl (Leipzig, n.d.), Bonnet (Paris, 1922), and Keller (Leipzig, 1943). In addition to the printed compositions about fifty others exist in various manuscripts; cf. Apel, 'Die handschriftliche Überlieferung der Klavierwerke Frescobaldis', *Festschrift Karl Gustav Fellerer* (Regensburg, 1962).

until his death in 1643. His outstanding role in the development
of organ music has always been recognized, sometimes, however, on
the basis of hearsay or of incorrect evidence. In nearly all collections
published under such titles as *Old Masters of the Keyboard* one finds
four 'Fugues by Frescobaldi'. Actually these fugues are spurious;[1]
they are written in the conventionalized style of the post-Bach
period, possibly by Clementi or some other composer of the late
eighteenth century.

Frescobaldi's first publication for keyboard was *Il primo libro delle
Fantasie* (Milan, 1608), containing twelve fantasias, three each with
one, two, three, and four *soggetti*. They are characterized by the
tendency to derive the entire contrapuntal texture from the thematic
material, with extensive use of the possibilities of variation. In the
fantasias with more than one theme the subjects are not treated in
separate sections, as in the polythematic *ricercar*, but are introduced
more or less simultaneously and employed in this way throughout the
composition, somewhat in the manner of so-called double, triple, and
quadruple fugues. Even in this very early work, Frescobaldi shows his
brilliant imagination in the use of thematic variation. Although he
was not the first to apply it, as we have seen, yet he employed it more
fully and more ingeniously than anybody before or after him. The
Fantasia no. 2, based on *uno soggetto*, is a truly fascinating example
of a contrapuntal 'flight of fancy'. It consists of seven sections, each
of which develops the theme in a different manner:

Ex. 310

¹ See Benvenuti, 'Noterella circa tre fughe attribuite al Frescobaldi', *Rivista musicale
italiana*, xxvii (1920), p. 133.

The idea used in section iii (and reintroduced in vii) is not, as has been suggested,[1] a new motive; Frescobaldi can be trusted not to introduce any new material in a composition which he calls *sopra uno soggetto*; actually this motive is the inversion of the second half of the theme, starting with the fifth note. Of course, the above illustration by no means reveals all the intricate methods which Frescobaldi uses to develop a composition of over a hundred bars from a single theme. A closer study will reveal that practically everything that occurs in the four parts is directly derived from the initial idea, so that the usual distinction between 'theme' and 'counter-theme', to say nothing of 'episodes', loses its significance. Naturally, this method of composition, so closely related in essence to Schönberg's twelve-note technique, is more rewarding to the intellectual faculty than to the ear and the senses. It throws an interesting light upon Frescobaldi's personality that he used this extreme technique most rigidly in his first work, as if to show his mettle to an astonished world. In his later compositions he strikes a much better balance between the two poles which determine his musical individuality: intellectual reflection and exuberant imagination.

Frescobaldi's next essays in imitative counterpoint were the *Recercari et canzoni franzese fatte sopra diversi oblighi, Libro primo* of 1615, which include ten *ricercari* and five *canzoni*. One of the *ricercari*, no. 9, *con quattro soggetti*, is very similar to the fantasias, four themes being developed simultaneously. The *ricercari* nos. 1 and 2 offer good examples of the duplex theme (see p. 607), a method which plays a very important role in Frescobaldi. The following analyses of the *ricercari* nos. 2, 3, and 5 illustrate the diversity of treatment in this publication:

No. 2. $A_{1,2}$// B/C// D/E (each subject is also inverted).
bar: 1   44   79
No. 3. A// B/A// C/B/A
bar: 1   30   44
No. 5. A, B, C// A// B// C// A/B/C
bar: 1   16 38 66 92

The last of these is particularly interesting; in the opening section the three themes are introduced successively in a two-part fabric (soprano and tenor only), while in the closing section they appear in simultaneous counterpoint, thus:

[1] See Tagliapietra, op. cit. iv, p. 1, footnote.

Ex. 311

The *ricercari* nos. 4, 6, 7, and 10 are all based on *oblighi* indicated
by solmization syllables, e.g. *sopra Mi Re Fa Mi* (no. 4). In these there
is a main subject, indicated by the *obligo* which is the basis of the
entire composition, being presented in double, triple or quadruple
augmentation or other rhythmic modifications, while secondary
themes as well as rhythmic variants of the main theme appear in the
counterpoint. For instance, in no. 7, *sopra Sol Mi Fa La Sol*, the main
subject occurs exclusively in the tenor, seven times in semibreves, then
three times in breves, and finally once in double-breves, while the
contrapuntal parts employ two other themes in interesting rhythmic
variants. Probably the most impressive example in this group and, for
that matter, perhaps in all Frescobaldi's contrapuntal compositions,
is no. 10. Here the theme *La fa sol la re* is repeated throughout in the
soprano in a truly amazing variety of rhythmic modifications, with
ever-changing values and accents. There is an obvious similarity (and
possibly, a less obvious historical connexion) between this *ostinato
ricercar* and the *ostinato* organ hymns of the early English masters
such as Redford and Blitheman (see p. 621). Brief mention may be
made of no. 8, an ingenious *tour de force* in which all stepwise motion
is avoided (*obligo di non uscir di grado*).

The five *canzoni* of 1615 are Frescobaldi's first examples of a type
which he cultivated more extensively than any other. The general
characteristics of his *canzoni*, as opposed to the *ricercari*, are a considerably greater rhythmic vitality, a form consisting of clearly distinguishable sections containing some element of contrast but at the
same time bound together by the use of a common theme in rhythmic
variants (variation *canzone*), and in some instances the introduction
of non-imitative idioms adopted from the toccata, from dance types,
or from other contemporary styles.

Most of the *canzoni* of 1615 are in five sections alternately in duple
and triple metre, the former strictly imitative and of moderate length,
the latter in the character of short transitions written in a pseudo-
imitative style and occasionally suggestive of dance rhythms. The
principle of theme-variation is either absent (no. 1) or occurs in a

tentative form through the use of an identical 'head-motive' (first three or four notes) in some or all of the sections.

In the six *canzoni* published twelve years later in the second book of *Toccate* (here briefly referred to as *Toccate II*), the prevailing method of composition is conspicuously different. Theme-variation, which in the earlier group was used sparingly and in a tentative manner, is employed here as a fundamental principle and developed to the highest degree. The following list of themes from the second *canzone* of *Toccate II* illustrates the ingenuity with which seemingly new themes are derived from the same basic material:

Ex. 312

Another characteristic trait of these *canzoni* is the use of a passage in toccata style at the close of almost every single section. The last three *canzoni* of this group all include sections in non-fugal style, a trait which may be said to indicate the transition from the *canzone* to the sonata. This transition is particularly evident in the last two *canzoni*, since here the toccata elements are no longer present.

Passing over the numerous *canzoni* contained in two publications of 1628, entitled *Il primo libro delle Canzoni ad una, due, tre e quattro voci*, because these are destined for ensemble performance, we come to the six liturgical *canzoni* of the *Fiori musicali*. In conformity with their liturgical character, indicated in titles such as *Canzone dopo l'epistola* or *Canzone post il Comunio*, they are somewhat more restrained and quieter than the others, also shorter and free from toccata elements. Apart from the first *Canzon dopo l'epistola*, which is unusually short and anticipates by several decades the fughettas of Pachelbel, Murschhauser, and J. K. F. Fischer, they are variation *canzoni* of the type found in *Toccate II*. A noteworthy trait is the *Adasio* passages in a mainly chordal style which often appear at the

end of a fugal section, thus damming up the motion in a characteristically Frescobaldian manner.

A last collection of keyboard *canzoni* appeared posthumously in
1645 under the title of *Canzoni alla francese in partitura . . . Libro
quarto*. They are, on the whole, similar to those of *Toccate II*, making
ample use of the variation principle and frequently embodying toccata
elements.

Frescobaldi's *Capricci* of 1624 are contrapuntal studies involving
certain peculiarities, problems or tricks. Some of them are based on
popular melodies such as 'Ruggiero', 'La Spagnoletta', or 'La Bassa
Fiamenga'. Others employ traditional subjects such as the hexachord
('Ut re mi fa sol la'), the inverted hexachord ('La sol fa mi re ut')
or 'La sol fa re mi' (= 'Lascia fare mi'), a theme that had been used
by Josquin for a Mass.[1] Some of the *ricercari* of 1615 had also been
based on solmization themes, but there is a noticeable difference of
treatment between the earlier and the later compositions. In the
ricercari the subject is treated more or less on traditional lines, being
presented in various degrees of augmentation, whereas in the capriccios it appears in a fascinating variety of rhythmic modifications,
particularly in the 'Capriccio sopra La sol fa re mi'. The 'Capriccio
di durezze' is a study in dissonances and appoggiaturas which has
served as a model for numerous similar compositions by later masters.
An interesting companion piece is the 'Capriccio cromatico di
ligature al contrario', in which all the dissonances are resolved upwards, in deliberate violation of one of the principal rules of counterpoint. In the 'Capriccio sopra il Cucho' the cuckoo's call is heard
about eighty times in the upper part, and often also in the lower parts.

Although the principle of theme-transformation pervades Frescobaldi's work from beginning to end, the series of variations as a
musical form attracted his interest mainly in his early days. The
Toccate I contain four *partite*,[2] on 'Romanesca', 'Ruggiero', 'Monicha', and 'Folia', as well as another 'Capriccio sopra l'aria di
Ruggiero'. Only two other sets are found in the later publications,
the 'Capriccio sopra l'aria Or chè noi rimena in partite' (*Capricci*,
1624) and the 'Aria detta la Frescobalda' (*Toccate II*, 1627). The
historical relationship of Frescobaldi's variations to those of the
early Neapolitan composers is apparent not only in the selection
of identical themes ('Ruggiero' by Macque, Trabaci, and Mayone;

---

[1] See Vol. III, p. 243. The 'Capriccio sopra un soggetto' is recorded in *The History
of Music in Sound*, iv.
[2] *Partita* is the seventeenth-century Italian term for variations, not for a suite.

'Romanesca' by Mayone), but even more in details of style and treatment. It will suffice to give here the beginnings of Mayone's and Frescobaldi's 'Ruggiero':

Ex. 313

These few bars also indicate to a certain extent Frescobaldi's superiority over his predecessors, particularly in the greater activity of the lower parts and in the progress from strict four-part writing to an idiomatic keyboard style in which parts and chords freely enter and drop out. Among the variations in *Toccate I*, those on 'Romanesca' stand out, because of the superior quality of the theme, which has an extended sweep lacking in the others. The original is notated in common time with four minims to the bar. Actually, however, the tune is in triple metre ($\frac{3}{2}$), starting with an upbeat:[1]

Ex. 314

Thus read, it appears to be what the title suggests: the old sixteenth-century 'Romanesca' melody known to us from Cabezón,[2] to which a *ripresa* is added at the end. Its structural plan is retained in most of the variations, a minor modification being that in the *quinta parte* each note of the 'Romanesca' melody covers two dotted minims, not three plain minims. In 'parts' 8 to 11, Frescobaldi uses a different scheme, in which the *ripresa* is omitted, and the large metrical units consist of six minims for each note of the 'Romanesca' melody, the upbeat being here included in the first group. Moreover, in nos. 10 and 11 the fifth note of the 'Romanesca' tune (the second D) is extended into a unit of eight minims. It will be remembered that such treatment is typical of the *passamezzo antico* variations.[3] It enables the composer to fill the large units with a variety of melodic and harmonious progressions, and Frescobaldi more than anybody else surrounds the skeleton with a fascinating array of ever-changing formations, products of a fertile and restless imagination, of a sensitive and excitable temperament. Nowhere, however, is there a danger of disintegration. Emotional turbulence and intellectual control are in perfect balance, as always in Frescobaldi.

This is also true of Frescobaldi's toccatas, which employ similar elements of style in a different framework. The twelve examples in

[1] See the partial transcription in Davison and Apel, op. cit. ii, p. 17.
[2] See pp. 614–15.　　　　　　　　　　　　　　[3] See p. 645.

Toccate I (1615) reflect the tradition of the sixteenth century in their continuity of metre and tempo, as well as in their basic texture of chords intertwined with figurations, of 'festooned columns', as it were. However, the columns are less regular, the festoons more variegated than in Merulo's toccatas. The sweeping scale passages of the Renaissance are replaced by figurations of a more jagged contour, in motion as well as in rhythm. Frequently short motives appear, are imitated three or four times, and give way to a new motive or to figuration of the type just described. The following example shows a number of such motives used in the *Toccata terza*:

Ex. 315

Particularly striking is the almost complete absence of *ricercar* sections which, it will be remembered, are essential in the toccatas of Merulo, but occur in only one of Frescobaldi's toccatas (no. 9). The toccatas of 1615 are designated *di cimbalo*, but the last two suggest the organ, no. 11 with its pedal points in the opening section, no. 12 with its *durezze e ligature* (dissonances and suspensions).

The eleven toccatas of the second collection (1627) show considerably greater variety of methods and styles. Two of them, nos. 2 and 7, are rather similar to the early works but distinguished by the tendency of the chordal structure to decompose into a thinner texture of interplaying motives. The first and, particularly, the last three toccatas represent the Frescobaldian toccata at its most characteristic. Here the process of disintegration into small sections of contrasting design and different metre and tempo (foreshadowed in some of Trabaci's toccatas) is brought to its final point, especially in the famous *Toccata nona*[1] with its challenging postscript: '*Non senza fatiga si giunge al fine*' (Not without effort is the goal attained). Nowhere in music is the frenzied restlessness of the early baroque period more eloquently expressed than in this toccata, with its multiplicity of formations, constant change of design, jerky motives, bold syncopations, complicated cross-rhythms, unexpected turns of harmony, stubborn and contradictory ostinatos and trills.

Yet the collection containing these hyperbolical compositions also includes some toccatas of an almost diametrically opposed character, the first signposts on the road from uninhibited emotionalism to quiet introspection that finally led to the *Fiori musicali*. They are the four toccatas *per l'organo*, nos. 3 to 6, two of which are marked '*Per sonarsi alla levatione*', while the others bear the inscription '*Sopra li pedali*'. In these the traits of wilful contrast, of variety for variety's sake, are absent or considerably mitigated. This is particularly true of the two toccatas in which the organ pedal is used to produce sustained pedal points, a device which automatically rules out the erratic and capricious elements characteristic of Frescobaldi's earlier toccatas. In no way, however, does it constrain his artistic inspiration, as is the case in the 'pedal toccatas' of later composers such as Pasquini, Pachelbel, and Alessandro Scarlatti. On the contrary, his ability to fill twenty bars over a sustained C with interesting motives and harmonic fluctuations (often including the interchange of major and minor) is one of the most admirable tokens of his genius.

The trend toward liturgical organ composition, noticeable in the above-mentioned toccatas as well as in the organ hymns and Magnificats contained in *Toccate II*, comes to its fulfilment in the celebrated *Fiori musicali* (Venice, 1635). Apart from two capriccios ('Bergamasca' and 'Girolmeta') added at the end, this work consists exclusively of short pieces for the service of the Mass, beginning with a group of the 'Messa della Domenica' (Mass XI of the *Liber*

---

[1] Also reprinted in Davison and Apel, op. cit. ii, no. 193.

Usualis, For Sundays throughout the Year), continuing with a similar one for the 'Messa degli Apostoli' (Mass IV, now for Double Feasts), and closing with one for the 'Messa della Madonna' (Mass IX, For Feasts of the Blessed Virgin). Each group includes a 'Toccata avanti la Messa', a number of versets for the *Kyrie* and *Christe*, and five or six free compositions to be played during the service, for instance a 'Canzon dopo l'Epistola', a 'Recercar dopo il Credo', a 'Toccata per l'Elevazione', or a 'Canzona post il Communio'. The versets are short elaborations of the Gregorian melody, mostly in *cantus planus* style, others in motet style. An unusual treatment is found in the third *Kyrie* of the first Mass, in which the *canto fermo* is stated three times in the alto, against a sustained pedal in the soprano.

The free compositions represent the types which Frescobaldi had cultivated throughout his life, cleansed from arbitrariness and excess. In the *canzoni* the passages in toccata style are replaced by short transitions marked *Adasio*. The *ricercari* are relatively short and remarkable for the clarity of the texture, which frequently includes passages in two or three parts only. One of them (Pidoux's edition, p. 44) is based on a *basso ostinato* which occurs in upward and downward transpositions of the fifth, resulting in modulations (from C) up to E and down to E flat, while another (ibid., p. 57) has an '*obligo di cantare la quinta parte senza toccarla*', similar to one of the capriccios of 1624. Two *ricercari* (ibid., pp. 34 and 57) are preceded by a 'Toccata avanti il Ricercar', an early adumbration of the pre-lude-and-fugue.[1] Finally, the toccatas furnish the most striking proof of Frescobaldi's change of attitude. Completely renouncing the element of capriciousness and surprise, he reduces the form to a short prelude filled with a spirit of devotion, a spirit most impressively embodied in the three 'Toccate per l'Elevazione'.

The *Fiori musicali* indicate the turn from the exuberance of the early baroque to the more restrained expression of the mid-seventeenth century. Here Frescobaldi, at the age of fifty-two, entered a new phase of his life, finding relief from emotional and intellectual turbulence in an all-pervading spirit of devotion and mysticism. Thus matured, he created one of the greatest masterpieces of liturgical organ music, a perfect embodiment of Baroque Catholicism.

[1] Other examples of this combination, e.g. 'Toccata per organo' and 'Canzona che segue la Toccata' are found in a manuscript of the Vatican Library (Codex Chigi Q. IV) containing fourteen organ works by Frescobaldi not included in the printed editions. They have been published as *XIV Composizioni inedite* in the series *Musica Veterum*, ed. Raffaele Casimiri, iii (Rome, n.d.).

THE SOUTH GERMAN ORGANISTS

At the beginning of the seventeenth century German keyboard music rose to a place of equal importance with that of other countries, and soon surpassed these in regard to the number of important masters and the variety of localities in which they worked. Cultural life in Germany has always been decentralized, and this was particularly true in the seventeenth and eighteenth centuries. However this situation may be assessed from the political point of view, it produced most beneficial results in all fields of intellectual and artistic life, leading to a proliferation and dissemination for which there are no parallels in any other country. These results are clearly reflected in the German keyboard music of the baroque period, to such an extent indeed that it is impossible to consider this development under the single classification of 'German keyboard music'. At least three separate lines of evolution must be traced, a south German (including Austria), a north German, and a middle German.

Probably two Netherlanders, Charles Luython (b. Antwerp, *c.* 1557–1620) and Simon Lohet (b. Liège, *c.* 1550–1611) were the first exponents of keyboard music in south Germany. Luython worked at Augsburg and Prague, Lohet at Nuremberg and Stuttgart. Only eight of Luython's organ compositions have survived,[1] among them three extended polythematic *ricercari* (one called 'Fuga suavissima') of which the Ricercar no. 7 is perhaps the most interesting with its skilful, though over-extended, presentation of the three themes in diminution, resulting in a lively interplay of attractive ideas. Lohet's compositions, preserved in Johann Woltz's *Nova musices organicae tabulatura* (Basle, 1617), include twenty *fugae* which foreshadow the fugue not only by their name, hardly ever used before for imitative compositions, but also in their concise form and restriction to one theme. Lohet was the teacher of Adam Steigleder (1561–1633) whose son, Johann Ulrich, played an important role in the later development of keyboard music in south-west Germany.

Hans Leo Hassler (1564–1612), who worked in Augsburg, Prague, Nuremberg, and Dresden, and Christian Erbach (1573–1635) of Augsburg were the first native representatives of the south German

---

[1] Reproduced in *Monumenta Musicae Belgicae*, iv. The 'Fuga suavissima' also in A. G. Ritter, *Zur Geschichte des Orgelspiels*, ii (Leipzig, 1884), no. 29. Four pieces by Lohet are printed in Ritter, nos. 68–71, one by Pirro in ' L'Art des organistes ', in Lavignac, *Encyclopédie*, 2ᵉ partie, ii, p. 1223. The twenty-four fantasias by Charles Guillet included in the *Monumenta* volume are, at least primarily, ensemble music.

school.[1] Erbach's *ricercari* are mostly bithematic, being usually based on a duplex theme whose second half, however, is rarely used separately. In spite of a certain monotony resulting from the unaltered succession of the two parts of the theme, these compositions have sufficient contrapuntal life to hold the listener's attention for the relatively short time they demand. The *ricercari* nos. 3, 4, 7, and 8 are short enough to be considered as early fugues, like those by Lohet. The theme of no. 12 is interesting for its triadic design:

Ex. 316

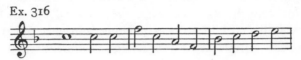

Equally interesting is the character of the themes in Erbach's 'Canzona cromatica', a very remarkable composition of considerable length:

Ex. 317

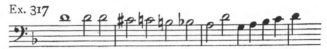

A toccata by Erbach (no. 16) follows essentially the Venetian tradition, except for the occasional use of short motives in quick imitation, in the manner usually associated with Sweelinck. Two *introitus* may be considered as early examples of the prelude and fugue, since the *introitus*, itself something like a short toccata, is followed by a *versus*, that is, a short monothematic fugue. Possibly these *versus* and, as a consequence, the entire compositions, were for liturgical use, like Erbach's Versets for the Mass, the *Magnificat*, and for sequences and hymns.

Hassler cultivated the same forms as Erbach, but on a much larger scale and with more ingenuity, resourcefulness, and grandeur. His *ricercari*, although of excessive length (one of them takes up six pages of the *Denkmäler* edition), are extremely interesting in their details. Most of them employ several themes in separate sections, as, for instance, no. 1 with its several chromatic themes and the following structure: $A_{1,2}$; B; B varied; C (diminution of A_1) with a lively countertheme; close in toccata style. No. 2 starts with an unusually extended theme, A. Later a more concise subject, B, is introduced, and in a final section both themes are employed, B serving mostly for episodic passages as in some of the *ricercari* by Giovanni Gabrieli.

[1] A number of Hassler's and Erbach's keyboard compositions are published in *Denkmäler der Tonkunst in Bayern*, iv²; these represent only a small proportion of what is preserved in manuscript (*c.* 110 pieces by Hassler, *c.* 150 by Erbach).

Ex. 318

In no. 3 three themes are introduced from the outset and treated with great ingenuity throughout a very extended composition:

Ex. 319

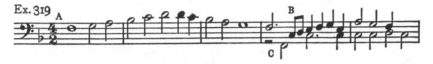

The *introitus* are even longer than the *ricercari* and are marked by the occasional use of homophonic elements and of echo effects.

Hassler's organ compositions are typical products of the late Renaissance, with its tendency toward the utmost pomp and splendour. His *ricercari* may well be said to represent the culmination of those of the Renaissance period. His *introitus* give the impression of having been composed for particularly festive occasions, such as church celebrations in the presence of Emperor Rudolf II.

Johann Ulrich Steigleder (1593–1635), son of the above-mentioned Adam Steigleder, and organist at Stuttgart, published in 1624 a *Ricercar Tabulatura* containing twelve *ricercari*, engraved on copperplate by himself, and in 1627 a *Tabulatur Buch* containing forty organ settings of the Protestant hymn 'Vater unser im Himmelreich'. His *ricercari* show a striking variety of formal structure, stylistic means, and expressive values. Of the four examples reprinted by Ernst Emsheimer,[1] the first (no. 1 of the original collection) fascinates by its baroque flight of fancy and ever-changing variety of formations, while the second (no. 3) is remarkable for its pastoral feeling and pictorial touches (call of the cuckoo). The third (no. 8), although outwardly quiet and restrained, is full of inner tension, and the fourth (no. 12) brings about a fitting close on a note of triumph. There are no *ricercari* before these, and few after them, that reflect so clearly the baroque idea of 'affections', so frequently expressed in the vocal music of that time. The first *ricercar*, although essentially monothematic and of considerable length (240 bars), keeps the interest

---

[1] *Vier Ricercare für Orgel* (Kassel, 1928). Two pieces by Adam Steigleder, taken from Woltz's *Tabulatura* of 1617, are reproduced in Pirro, op. cit., pp. 1223 ff.

constantly alive through an amazing variety of ideas and formations. In its free flight of contrapuntal fancy it is remarkably similar to the contemporary Spanish *tientos* of Aguilera and Correa,[1] a statement which, of course, should not be construed as implying direct influence. Ex. 320 shows some excerpts from this first *ricercar*, which opens with a fugal exposition of a duplex theme ($A_{1,2}$), continues with an extended section in which A_1 is presented with a variety of playful figurations and motives, as well as in inversion, diminution, and variation, and then turns to A_2 for a subject, in two degrees of diminution, until finally A_1 appears again in triumphant augmentation.

Ex. 320

[1] See pp. 679 and 681.

Steigleder's compositions on 'Vater unser' confirm the impression
made by his *ricercari*. The very fact that he wrote forty different
settings of the same melody shows the singular fertility and exuberance of his mind. The collection starts with an extended *Fantasia in
Fugen Manier* and closes with an equally extended composition *Auff
Toccata Manier*. The other pieces are shorter and usually have the
'*Coral*' in one part, either plain or '*colleriert*'. In connexion with three
settings (nos. 4, 5, 6) Steigleder mentions the possibility of having the
chorale melody duplicated by a voice or a suitable instrument, and
adds a remark to the effect that this method of performance can also
be employed with many other pieces of his collection. Of particular
interest is a composition (no. 24) in which the chorale appears '*in
zwo Stimmen zumal*' (in two voices simultaneously) in the following
manner:

Ex. 321

Steigleder pursues this unusual and interesting fauxbourdon method
so consistently that a real fourteenth-century double-leading-note
cadence results—a very unexpected sound in the baroque age:

Ex. 322

The closing toccata is a most interesting composition in the character of a chorale fantasia, and surprisingly similar in many details and
in its bold sweep to the North German toccatas, as may be seen from
the opening bars:

Ex. 323

Steigleder gives the impression of having been a musician of unusual talent, a highly individual composer gifted with a vivid imagination. He died prematurely, a victim of the plague.

NORTH GERMAN ORGANISTS

From as early as the mid-fifteenth century we have one interesting North German manuscript of organ music, the tablature of Adam Ileborgh.[1] Nothing seems to be known about North German organ music during the next century and a half, but about 1600 began an evolution which quickly led North Germany to a most prominent position in the field. The so-called *Celler Tabulatur* of 1601[2] contained about seventy-five organ chorales on such melodies as 'Allein Gott in der Höh sei Ehr', 'Ach Gott vom Himmel sieh darein', 'Ich ruf zu dir, Herr Jesu Christ', and 'Vater unser im Himmelreich'. They are all anonymous with the exception of four signed O. D. (= O. Dithmers?) and two by Johann Stephan, who was organist at Lüneburg and died in 1616. Some of the settings are more or less simple harmonizations, similar to those in the collections of Ammerbach and Nörmiger; others are considerably more extended and elaborate, prophetic of the later development of the North German organ chorale. Thus one of the settings of 'Ach Gott vom Himmel' is a fully developed chorale motet in five parts, in which each line of the chorale is treated in imitation. The four works by O. D. are also chorale motets. His 'Allein Gott in der Höh' (Ritter, op. cit., no. 72) presents the chorale in a serious setting of sombre colours.

Ex. 324

---

[1] See Vol. III, p. 427.

[2] The tablature, though used by Ritter, is now lost. A photographic reproduction has been made available through the kind offices of the Berlin Staatsbibliothek. See Apel, 'Die Geller Orgeltabulatur von 1601', *Die Musikforschung*, xix (1966), p. 142.

Even more elaborate are the two compositions by Stephan, 'Ach Gott, vom Himmel' (beginning ibid., no. 73) and 'Jesus Christus unser Heiland'. The latter is particularly remarkable for traits foreshadowing the free treatment typical of the chorale fantasy: ornamentation, echo-effects, fragmentation, &c. It also shows the change from a 'vocal' to a clearly instrumental style with livelier motion and short motives:

Ex. 325

The main centre of North German organ music at the turn of the century was Hamburg, the working place of Jacob Praetorius the elder (d. 1582), of his son Hieronymus (1560–1629), and grandson Jacob the younger (1586–1651), as well as of Scheidemann (*c.* 1595–1663), Weckmann (1621–74) and Reinken (1623–1722). Hieronymus Praetorius wrote, in addition to motets and Masses, a complete cycle of Magnificats for the organ,[1] preserved in a tablature dated 1611.[2] For each of the eight *toni* he provides three or four verses, fairly extended compositions mostly in five parts, full of grandeur and solemnity. Ex. 326 shows the beginning of the *Primus versus primi toni*:

Ex. 326

Among the few extant organ compositions of Hieronymus's son Jacob, 'Durch Adams Fall' is remarkable as the earliest fully developed example of the chorale fantasy.[3] Lively figurations, interesting

---

[1] Published by C. G. Rayner (American Institute of Musicology, 1963).

[2] Written by Berendt Petri and later owned by Johann Bahr (not Johann Bähr), who added a few pieces. (The designation 'Petri tablature' is preferable to 'Bahr (or Bähr) tablature'.) It is now in the archives of Visby Cathedral. A brief description and a facsimile page are given in J. Hedar, *Dietrich Buxtehudes Orgelwerke* (Stockholm, 1951), p. 18.

[3] Preserved incomplete in the Lynar tablature *B 5*; published in G. Gerdes, *46 Choräle*

motives, numerous echoes, fragmentation of themes, effects of contrast, virtuoso passages in boldly ascending motion, rapid shifts from one manual to another—all these elements combine into a grandiose work of truly dramatic impact. Also of interest are three *praeambula* of Jacob Praetorius because they stand at the beginning of the development leading to the 'prelude and fugue' of Bach; each *praeambulum* consists of a prelude in full chordal style and a fugue based on a single theme.

A contemporary (though not a relative) of Jacob was Michael Praetorius (1571–1621),[1] whose organ works,[2] though few in number, are of the highest significance. They consist (apart from a *sinfonia* which seems to be intended for instrumental ensemble) of six compositions based on Latin hymns and four based on Protestant chorales. The Latin hymns are set in the traditional *cantus planus* style of Schlick and Cabezón, that is, with the melody in long notes of equal value (always in the bass). Three of the Lutheran compositions, 'Ein feste Burg', 'Christ, unser Herr', and 'Wir glauben all', are chorale motets of gigantic dimensions (the second is 410 bars long), while the last, 'Nun lob, mein Seel', consists of two variations, treating the melody ornamentally. It is impossible to do justice to these monumental compositions within the limitations of this survey. They are the works of a master who, more than anybody else in this field, succeeded in combining the great achievements of the sixteenth with the novel ideas of the early seventeenth century. They are admirable for their consummate mastery of the contrapuntal methods of the Renaissance, as well as for their skilful use of baroque figuration in a great variety and constant change of designs. Here follows an excerpt from 'Christ, unser Herr, zum Jordan kam'.[3]

Ex. 327

für Orgel von J. P. Sweelinck und seinen deutschen Schülern (Mainz, 1957). Three *praeambula* from the Lüneburg tablatures are published in Seiffert, *Organum IV*, Heft 2.

[1] See pp. 453 and 546.

[2] Reprinted by Wilibald Gurlitt in *Archiv für Musikwissenschaft*, iii (1921), pp. 135–98, and in a practical edition by Karl Matthäi (Wolfenbüttel, 1930).

[3] Gurlitt's edition, p. 177; Matthäi's, p. 75. Entries of the chorale phrase are indicated by asterisks.

SAMUEL SCHEIDT

Of the German followers and pupils of Sweelinck, the greatest was Samuel Scheidt (1587–1654), organist of the Moritzkirche of his native town, Halle. His *Tabulatura nova* (Hamburg, 1624)[1] is a land-

---

[1] Reprinted in *Denkmäler deutscher Tonkunst*, i (Leipzig, 1892), and in the *Werke* (ed. Mahrenholz), vi and vii (Hamburg and Leipzig, 1953).

mark in the history of German keyboard music, because it was here for the first time that the various forms and styles which had been developed in England, Italy, and the Netherlands made their appearance in a German publication. Variations on secular songs and dances are printed here side by side with organ chorales on Latin and Lutheran hymns, settings for the *Magnificat* and the Mass side by side with courantes and abstract contrapuntal compositions, such as *fugae* and canons. It is worth remark that, like Frescobaldi's *Fiori musicali* and the publications of Trabaci and Mayone, the *Tabulatura nova* was printed in score: each part on a five-line stave.

The methods used in these pieces are mainly of three types: imitative counterpoint of the sixteenth century, figurative counterpoint, and motive imitation. The following three excerpts (from *Psalmus in Die Nativitatis Christi*) illustrate all three:

Ex. 328

With two exceptions, Scheidt's settings of plainsong and Protestant chorale melodies are all sets of variations consisting of a number of *versus*. On the whole, the compositions of Latin hymns are more conservative than those based on Protestant melodies, in which entire *versus* are written in figurative counterpoint or with reiteration and imitation of short motives. Although these latter methods represent the progressive element in Scheidt's style, one cannot help feeling that he does not succeed in transforming them into artistic realities. Their intellectual coldness and rationalistic calculation bespeak the pupil of Sweelinck and contrast sharply with the ingenious inventiveness of Praetorius or the intellectual heat of Frescobaldi. It is perhaps no exaggeration to say that of all the numerous *versus* of Scheidt's chorale compositions only those in truly contrapuntal style (which usually form the beginning of each composition) are real masterpieces.

The two chorale compositions not cast in the form of successive *versus* are a 'Toccata super In te, Domine, speravi' and a 'Fantasia super Ich ruf zu Dir, Herr Jesu Christ'. The former is a rambling and seemingly interminable piece filled with pedantic formations which recall the worst features of the English organ and virginal schools. Its main point of interest is that it is based on the same melody which Scheidt used for what he probably considered the best of his canons (no. 10), since he had it engraved beneath his portrait on the title-page of the *Tabulatura nova*.

The fantasia on 'Ich ruf zu Dir' is the one liturgical composition of Scheidt's which towers high above all others and gives him a place, not only of great historical importance, but also of outstanding artistic achievement in the field of the German organ chorale. Although called a 'fantasia', it is actually a chorale motet, each line of the melody being treated separately in imitative style according to a plan which is as grandly conceived as it is magnificently executed. Each section starts with a fugal treatment of the corresponding chorale line in diminution, an example of the so-called 'anticipatory imitation' which plays so important a role in Bach's chorale motets and which can be traced back in German music to the compositions of Heinrich Finck.[1] After this the chorale line appears once in each part in longer note-values, while the other parts provide a contrapuntal background. Finally, at the end of the section the chorale line is stated in full chords, bringing the presentation to an impressive climax. The following excerpts from the second section illustrate this plan:

[1] See Vol. III, pp. 286-7.

Ex.329
(i)

Among the numerous admirable details of this composition, the extended presentation or, more properly, development, of the fourth line of the chorale—F E D C—may be mentioned:

Ex.330

Scheidt's fantasia is a composition which stands comparison with any of the greatest chorale motets by Bach. How it happened that he wrote only one work of this kind is an enigma.

Shortly before his death Scheidt published a work entitled *Tabulaturbuch 100 geistlicher Lieder . . .*, generally known as the *Görlitzer Tabulaturbuch*,[1] because it is dedicated to the magistrates and town council of Görlitz (Silesia), and may have been written at their request. It contains contrapuntal harmonizations of Lutheran hymn tunes, similar in character to those written by Bach for the close of his cantatas. They are not organ preludes in the proper sense, but simple settings that no doubt served to accompany congregational singing of the hymns. Noteworthy for their skilful combination of the harmonic and the contrapuntal element they are in no way inferior to Bach's harmonizations and may even be preferred by those who feel that Bach's chromatic harmonies and expressive devices overstep propriety. The beginning of Scheidt's second setting of 'Christ lag in Todesbanden' (no. 17*b*):

Ex.331

may be compared with the final chorale of Bach's cantata, no. 4.

---

[1] Modern editions by Gottlieb Harms, *Scheidts Werke*, i (Hamburg, 1923), and Mahrenholz (Leipzig, 1941).

In his variations on secular songs and dance tunes Scheidt used stylistic means similar to those employed in his chorale variations, but with much happier results. Such popular themes, with their pleasant melodies, simple harmonies, and clearly designed phrases of even length, lend themselves more naturally to the figurative treatment which, it should be remembered, had been evolved by the virginalists mainly in connexion with popular songs. Particularly attractive are Scheidt's variations on the *Cantio Belgica* 'Wehe, Windgen, wehe', while those on the *Passamezzo* suffer from the incessant repetition of one and the same figurative pattern.

HEINRICH SCHEIDEMANN

Scheidt is often grouped with Schütz and Schein as one of 'the three great S's' of the early seventeenth century. Actually this trio might be expanded into a quartet by the addition of Heinrich Scheidemann, who is no less worthy of inclusion than Scheidt. Born at Hamburg in 1596, he studied during 1611–14 with Sweelinck and, upon his father's death in 1625, became his successor as organist at St. Catherine's Church in Hamburg, a position he held until his death in 1663. Most of his organ works are preserved in the Lüneburg tablatures, which (together with the Lynar tablatures) are the most important source of North German organ music. His keyboard compositions include 13 preludes, 4 pieces in fugal style, 2 toccatas, 27 organ chorales, an Alleluia, a number of dances, and 8 intabulations of vocal compositions.[1]

Scheidemann's *praeambula* are mostly written in a chordal style interspersed with motivic repeats, echoes, rudimentary imitations, and toccata elements. Two of them consist of prelude, fugue, and postlude, while one (*Organum*, no. 11) takes the 'prelude and fugue' form of the *praeambula* of Jacob Praetorius. In the fugue Scheidemann employs as a counter-subject the descending chromatic tetrachord used by so many composers for the same function. Of particular interest are Scheidemann's compositions on chorale melodies. Only two of them, 'Mensch willst du' and 'Vater unser' I, are chorale variations. In some of the other settings he places the melody without ornamentation in the upper part; in some it appears partly in the soprano, partly in the bass; yet others are ornamented melody

---

[1] The preludes and fugal compositions are published in Seiffert's *Organum IV*, no. 1; other pieces in Fritz Dietrich, *Geschichte des deutschen Orgelchorals im 17. Jahrhundert* (musical supplement) (Kassel, 1932); Gerdes, op. cit.; *Das Erbe deutscher Musik*, xxxiv (*Die Lüneburger Orgeltabulatur KN 208¹*). See the article 'Scheidemann' in *Die Musik in Geschichte und Gegenwart*, xi, for a complete list of chorale compositions.

chorales, chorale motets, or chorale fantasias. The two chorale motets ('In dich hab ich gehoffet' and 'Vater unser' II) differ from Scheidt's fantasia on 'Ich ruf zu Dir' by their more colourful treatment, the various lines appearing not only in their simple forms but also adorned with figuration. Very often the figuration closes with a boldly rising scale, a dramatic gesture used time and again by the later North German organ composers:

Ex.332

Although he was a pupil of Sweelinck, Scheidemann shows the influence of the Dutch master to a much lesser degree than Scheidt, who, so far as we know, did not come into personal contact with Sweelinck. This also applies to Jacob Praetorius as well as other pupils of Sweelinck such as Paul Siefert (1586–1666), Andreas Düben (*c.* 1590–1662), and Melchior Schildt (*c.* 1592–1667), of whom the last named—organist at Wolfenbüttel, Copenhagen, and Hanover—is the most important.[1]

JEAN TITELOUZE

Almost one hundred years of French keyboard music, after Attaignant's publications of 1531 (see Vol. III, p. 449), remain obscure owing to the destruction of sources. Apart from a few scattered pieces—such as two tiny fantasies by Nicolas de La Grotte and Costeley—it is not until 1623 that we find ourselves again on solid ground, with the *Hymnes de l'Eglise pour toucher sur l'orgue avec les Fugues et Recherches sur leur Plain-chant*, by Jean Titelouze (1563–1633), organist at Rouen. This publication[2] contains organ elaborations of twelve hymns, each of which is presented in three or

---

[1] The thirteen fantasias published in *Organum IV*, no. 20, are probably not by Siefert. Compositions by Schildt are printed in ibid., no. 2; Gerdes, op. cit.; *Monatshefte für Musikgeschichte*, xx (1888), pp. 35 ff.; *Vierteljahrsschrift für Musikwissenschaft*, vii (1891), pp. 252 ff.

[2] New edition by Alexandre Guilmant in *Archives des maîtres de l'orgue*, i (Paris, 1898). On Titelouze generally, see Ernst von Werra, 'Beiträge zur Geschichte des französischen Orgelspiels', *Kirchenmusikalisches Jahrbuch*, xxiii (1910), p. 37. The *fantaisies* by Charles Guillet (1610) and Eustache du Caurroy (1610) which are briefly

four versets, i.e. chorale variations, as in Scheidt's *Tabulatura nova*. The first setting is invariably in *cantus planus* style, with the melody in the bass, one note to each bar, and with imitative treatment of the three upper parts. The other variations are either in four-part motet style or in *cantus planus* style, which, however, is often less strictly used here than in the initial variation. This lessening of rigidity may be observed in the use of imitative passages preceding the various lines of chorale, in the distribution of the *canto fermo* among several parts ('migrant' *canto fermo*), and occasionally in the employment of short rapid baroque motives rather than the quiet subjects of the sixteenth century. Three pieces, 'Veni creator' (verset 3), 'Conditor alme' (verset 2), and 'Ave maris stella' (verset 3), are particularly remarkable examples of contrapuntal mastery, since they combine the *cantus planus* with a skilfully written two-part canon, either at the octave or at the fifth. The following table is a structural analysis of the first four hymns from Titelouze's book (*cpl.* indicates *cantus planus* style, *ant. im.*, anticipatory imitation):

	I	II	III	IV
Ad coenam:	*cpl.* bass	motet	motet	*cpl.* migrant, *ant. im.*
Veni creator:	*cpl.* bass	*cpl.* sopr. *ant. im.*	*cpl.* tenor canon	motet
Pange lingua:	*cpl.* bass	motet	*cpl.* migrant *ant. im.*	
Ut queant:	*cpl.* bass	*cpl.* alto *ant. im.*	motet	

A common trait of the versets in *cantus planus* style is the use of motives derived from the hymn melody for the imitative counterpoint. The initial point of imitation is nearly always based on a motive from the beginning of a hymn, and a similar method is occasionally used in the further course of the composition. The first verset of 'Iste confessor' begins as follows:

Ex. 333

discussed in Frotscher's *Geschichte des Orgelspiels*, ii, p. 667, can be played on the organ or by an ensemble of viols.

In the variations in motet style, in which there is no *cantus planus*, the connexion with the hymn melody is effected by the use of themes derived from its various lines. Usually the first of these is presented in two expositions (with eight entries), the others in a single exposition. The following example shows two such themes:

Ex. 334

(i) Ve-ni cre - a - tor Spi - ri-tus

(ii) Pan-ge lin-gua glo-ri-o - si

Titelouze's hymns, conservative for the period, represent a late embodiment of the contrapuntal technique of the sixteenth century, particularly that of Gombert with the uninterrupted continuity of its parts. Modern tendencies appear most clearly and most convincingly in some of the closing versets, in which the *cantus planus* method is combined with freer elements such as extended preludes, interludes, and postludes written in figurative counterpoint. The final variation of 'Ad coenam' is the most impressive example of this type.

In 1626 Titelouze published *Le Magnificat, ou cantique de la Vierge pour toucher sur l'orgue*, a collection of versets for the *Magnificat*, seven for each of the eight *toni*. In the preface he remarks that, the *Hymnes* having been found too difficult for many, technical demands are less exacting in the present publication. Nearly all the versets show the binary division of the plainsong melody, the first section closing with the medial cadence, the second with the final; and for those who might find the versets too long, Titelouze suggests using the latter instead of the former, although it is not always easy to see how this could be accomplished, unless by omission of the first section altogether. Each cycle includes an alternative setting of the verse 'Deposuit', thus bringing the number of versets up to seven, instead of the six required for the *Magnificat*. This, Titelouze tells us, has been done in order to make the pieces available also for the canticle of Zacharias ('Benedictus Dominus') which, consisting of fourteen verses, requires seven organ versets.

Most of the versets are written in imitative *ricercar* style. Occasionally the second section makes use of more lively figurations, and in some cases the first section is in *cantus planus* style, as, for instance, in the 'Gloria patri' of the third *tonus* or in the 'Magnificat' of the fourth. The general style of the Magnificats is somewhat more modern than that of the hymns.

The conservatism of Titelouze's compositions is underlined by a comparison with those of his contemporary, Sweelinck. There is little in them to suggest the innovations of the early baroque period, except perhaps in some of the hymn versets where the introduction of quick motives for the final point of imitation indicates a feeling for climactic effect unusual in the organ music of the Renaissance. On the other hand, the devices of sixteeenth-century counterpoint are handled with the skill of a late master.

MINOR FRENCH COMPOSERS

To fill out the picture of French organ music in the first half of the seventeenth century we must draw on a few pieces preserved in manuscripts. A *fantaisie* by Charles Raquet,[1] organist at Notre-Dame in Paris from 1618 to 1643, is an extended composition obviously written under the influence of Sweelinck, a single theme being presented in a number of sections and in a variety of styles such as augmentation and *bicinium duplici contrapuncto*; nothing else similar was ever written in France. Two preludes by Étienne Richard (organist at St. Jacques in Paris; d. 1669)[2] are among the most beautiful examples of this genre. Particularly noteworthy is a tendency toward a melodious style, a tendency which becomes more and more pronounced in the French organ music of a later period.

Ex. 335

RICHARD: Prelude No. 2

---

[1] Published in Félix Raugel, *Les Maîtres français de l'orgue*, ii, p. 6; the *duos* reproduced on p. 5 are taken from a collection of twelve didactic pieces which Racquet contributed to Mersenne's *Harmonie universelle* (Paris, 1636).

[2] Published in *Les Pré-Classiques français* (G. Litaize and J. Bonfils, *L'Organiste liturgique*, xviii), pp. 8 and 16, the first of these also by Pirro in Lavignac, op. cit. 2e partie, ii, p. 1272.

In addition to these compositions by Racquet and Richard, a number of anonymous pieces are or were preserved in manuscripts at Ste. Geneviève, Paris, and in the City Library of Tours.[1] Some of them adumbrate another typical aspect of later French organ music: the careful specification of organ stops. Thus an 'Ave maris stella' is designated as '*à 3 jeux différents; Plain chant en taille*' (for three different registers; plainsong in the middle); the top part is to be played on '*Positiv, Fluste, Tremblant doux*', the bass on '*Grand corps*', the middle part (*cantus planus*) on '*Pédale*'. The Tours manuscript, which unfortunately was destroyed in 1940, contained numerous versets for the psalmody and the Office chants, some with indications such as '*Le gros jeu de nazard avec le tremblant*', also some *Dialogues* requiring change of registration,—a type frequently used by all the later French organ composers, from Nivers to Grigny.

In addition to these organ compositions we have a number of early pieces for the *clavecin* or harpsichord, written by such composers as René Mézangeau (d. *c.* 1638), Pinel (Pierre or Germain?), Pierre Ballard (d. 1639), Ennemond Gautier (*c.* 1580–1651), Pierre

Ex.336

---

[1] Cf. *Les Pré-Classiques*, nos. 23–30; Lavignac, op. cit., pp. 1269 ff.

La Barre (1592–1656), Nicolas Monnard (d. 1646?), and Étienne Richard (d. 1669).[1] They were the predecessors of the first great clavecinist, Jacques Champion de Chambonnières (*c.* 1605–1672). Some of these musicians were also lutenists, and it is not impossible that their pieces, although preserved in keyboard notation, were originally written for the lute. An example in point is an *Allamande de Mr. Meschanson* (= Mézangeau)[2] which shows the typically loose texture, the *style brisé*, of French lute music. Ex. 336 (opposite) shows the beginning, with the original fingering and signs of ornamentation.

SPANISH COMPOSERS AFTER CABEZÓN

Very little is known about the development of Spanish keyboard music after Cabezón. When his son, Hernando (d. 1602), published his father's works, he included five pieces of his own—though only one, an 'Ave maris stella', is an original composition, the others being intabulations, albeit very interesting ones, of *chansons* by Créquillon, Lassus, and others. A contemporary of Hernando, although probably somewhat younger, was Bernardo Clavijo del Castillo, who in 1588 became organist of the viceregal court at Naples, in 1593 professor of music at the university of Salamanca, and in 1619 court organist at Madrid, where he died in 1626. Only one organ piece of his, a *Tiento de segundo tono*,[3] has been preserved, but this is of great interest because it employs that novel harmonic language which the Italians called *durezze e ligature*, the Spanish, *falsas*:

Ex. 337

---

[1] Reprints in Raugel, *Les Maîtres*, i, and in *Les Pré-Classiques*.

[2] In Copenhagen, Gl. kgl. Saml. 376 2°. Cf. Povl Hamburger, 'Ein handschriftliches Klavierbuch aus der ersten Hälfte des 17. Jahrhunderts', *Zeitschrift für Musikwissenschaft*, xiii (1930–1), p. 133; also Lavignac, op. cit., p. 1232.

[3] In a manuscript of the Archivo de El Escorial which is the main manuscript source of Spanish keyboard music before 1650. Reprints in Pedrell, *Antología de organistas clásicos españoles*, i (Madrid, 1908), Luis de Villalba Muñoz, *Antología de organistas clásicos* (Madrid, 1914), and Apel, *Spanish Organ Masters after Antonio de Cabezón* (American Institute of Musicology, 1965). See also Apel, 'Spanish Organ Music of the early 17th century', *Journal of the American Musicological Society*, xv (1962), p. 62.

Equally remarkable, though from another point of view, is a composition by Francesco Peraza (1564–98), the only surviving work of an organist so famous in his day that it was said 'an angel resided in each of his fingers'. He is reported to have been the inventor of the *medio registro*, the most characteristic device of Spanish organ building, organ playing, and organ composition. Spanish organs of the seventeenth century had only one manual, but this was divided in such a way that different stops could be used for its upper and lower halves. In a *medio registro alto* (or *de tiple*) the right hand had the prominent part to be played with solo stops, the left hand the accompaniment to be played with a softer registration; in a *medio registro baxo* (or *de baxon*) the roles were reversed. Later we also find *tientos de dos tiples* or *de dos baxones*, in which the right or left hand plays two parts. The composition by Peraza is a *medio registro alto*.[1] It begins with an imitation of a simple theme (D F E D in semibreves), but this is soon abandoned, giving way to a variety of playful figurations, to a '*variedad de flores*' which, we are told, 'had never been seen in Europe' (*hasta él nunca vistas en Europa*). Occasionally a certain figure is restated several times in adaptation to the changing harmonies, a device which plays an important role in the works of some later Spanish organ composers:

Ex. 338

[1] Reproduced in Villalba, op. cit., p. 27.

AGUILERA DE HEREDIA

Much better known to us than Clavijo and Peraza is Aguilera de
Heredia (b. 1570), who in 1583 was appointed organist at the cathedral of Huesca (Aragon) and in 1603 went to Saragossa, where he is
mentioned as *portionarius et organis praeceptor*. Seventeen organ
compositions of his are preserved, most of them in the Escorial manuscript, among them settings of 'Salve regina' and 'Pange lingua', and
a number of *tientos*, some of which are called *obra*. The 'Pange
lingua' are based on the Mozarabic melody that had been used by
Cabezón (the earliest known setting is a vocal one by Urrede) and
was used later by Coelho, Jimenez, and others. In all these works the
hymn melody appears complete as a *cantus planus*. In his two settings
of 'Salve regina', however, Aguilera uses only the beginning of the
melody (A G sharp A D) as a theme for a fairly extended fugue (as
in a German chorale fugue), a procedure which is very rare in Spanish
organ music. The motive used contrapuntally in the following passage
from his *Salbe de 1º tono*:

Ex. 339

shows the rhythm 3+3+2 which occurs time and again in the works
of Spanish organ composers.[1]

Among the *tientos* of Aguilera are three *falsas*, similar to Clavijo's
although more 'modern' in their harmonic language. Others employ
a single theme treated in various sections differing from each other
by the use of different figurative motives or by change from duple to
triple metre. An exceptional work is the *Obra de 8º tono* (*Ensalada*), an

[1] Cf. Apel, 'Drei plus Drei plus Zwei = Vier plus Vier', *Acta musicologica*, xxxii
(1960), p. 29.

extended composition divided into five sections which are not thematically related but contain a mixture (= *ensalada*) of free and playful
formations, somewhat like a fantasia by Byrd or an Italian instrumental *canzone*. One passage is obviously written for the trumpet stop so
characteristic of Spanish organs:

Ex. 340

In Aguilera's four *medio registro de baxo* the left hand has a solo
part; of particular interest and historical importance is the *Vajo*
(= *baxo*) *de 1° tono*, because of its extended use of modulatory
passages. A figurative formula of two, three, or more bars recurs in
four subdominant modulations (e.g. E–A–D–G), followed by another
formula restated in four dominant modulations (e.g. C–G–D–A), and
so on. This method, adumbrated in Peraza's *Medio registro alto* (cf.
Ex. 338), plays an even more important role in the works of later
Spanish organ composers such as Jimenez, Bruna, and Cabanilles.

COELHO

With the Portuguese Manuel Rodrigues Coelho we come to the
first Iberian organ master after Cabezón whose complete works are
preserved in a publication. Born *c.* 1555 at Elvas, he was organist at
the cathedrals of Badajoz, Elvas, and Lisbon, later (1603–22) court
organist of Philip III; he died in 1635. In 1620 he published his *Flores
de musica*,[1] containing *tentos*, intabulations of Lassus's 'Susanna',
and numerous settings of hymns ('Pange lingua' and 'Ave maris
stella'), Magnificats, and Kyries.

[1] Modern edition by M. S. Kastner, *Portugaliae musica*, i and iii (Lisbon, 1959
and 1961).

The twenty-four *tentos* (three for each church mode) take a decisive step away from the restrained Renaissance style toward the vividness and picturesque imagery of the early Spanish baroque. These compositions are extended polythematic *ricercari*, but the thematic material, instead of being the substance, is often hardly more than the soil for a luxuriant growth of playful motives and lively figurations.

The four settings of 'Pange lingua' (like those of 'Ave maris stella') are *cantus planus* compositions each having the hymn melody in a different part, surrounded by variegated motives and figurations. The versets for the *Magnificat* are composed in five parts, with the upper part bearing the inscription: '*pera se cantarem ao organo, esta voz nao se tango, as quatro abaixo se tangen*' (to be sung to the organ; this part not to be played, the four below to be played).[1] They are, therefore, examples of the organ concertato of the early baroque period (cf. Viadana's *Concerti ecclesiastici*),[2] a practice which is also reflected in Frescobaldi's ricercar *con obligo di cantare la quinta parte senza toccarla* and in some of Steigleder's chorales on 'Vater unser' (see pp. 656 and 661). Very likely the vocal part was sung by the organist himself.

CORREA DE ARAUXO

Six years after Coelho's *Flores de musica* there appeared another, even more important publication of Iberian organ music, the *Libro de tientos . . . intitulado Facultad organica* by the Spaniard Francisco Correa de Arauxo,[3] who was born *c.* 1575 and served as organist at San Salvador, Seville, from 1598 to 1633. His publication includes 62 *tientos*, three sets of variations, and a few other compositions. In the list of contents the *tientos* are arranged according to difficulty, from *Primer grado, y el mas facil* to the *Quinto y ultimo grado superior a todos*. The terms *ocho* (eight), *diez y seys* (sixteen), or *treinta y dos* (thirty-two), which appear regularly as a part of the title, indicate the quickest motion in the composition: quavers, semiquavers, or demi-semiquavers. The first twenty-four *tientos* are for *registro entero*, the others for *registro medio de tiple, de baxon, de dos tiples*, or *de dos baxones*.

Arauxo represents the culmination of early baroque Spanish organ music. Even more than Coelho he revels in colourful treatment, bold

---

[1] A *verso do primeiro tom* is reprinted in Davison and Apel, op. cit. ii, p. 32.

[2] See pp. 533 ff.

[3] Modern edition by Kastner, *Monumentos de la música española*, vi and xii (Barcelona, 1948 and 1952).

play with erratic figurations, and rapid change of design. After a short imitative presentation of the theme he turns to toccata-like figurations or to figurative treatment and other free methods, occasionally touching again upon the subject, as if to remind us that he has not completely forgotten it during the course of his improvisation. The affective character of his compositions is heightened by a bold use of sustained dissonances, as in the two following excerpts showing what he calls *punto intenso contra remisso* (C against C sharp).

SPANISH LUTE MUSIC

The importance of the lute as a medium for music-making throughout Europe during the sixteenth and seventeenth centuries is clearly reflected in the great quantity of sources which have come down to us, in manuscript as well as in printed form. Only the briefest survey of this material (of which no more than a fraction has as yet been made available in transcription) can be given here. Lute arrangements of vocal music, motets, and *chansons*, which in many cases make up the major part of the contents of a collection, must be disregarded here completely; they are interesting mainly from the sociological point of view, illustrating, as they do, the tastes of a large class of musical amateurs.[1]

The remaining portion of the European lute repertory falls into three main categories: contrapuntal compositions (fantasias, *ricercari*,

[1] See, for example, Vol. III, p. 420.

&c.), variations, and dances. The variations are represented only in the Spanish sources, and it is to these that we turn first, because of their very high artistic quality.

The earliest Spanish source of lute music[1] that has reached us (undoubtedly preceded by many others now lost) is Luis Milán's *Libro de música de vihuela de mano intitulado El Maestro* (Valencia, 1535).[2] This book contains forty 'fantasias', that is, compositions in a free idiomatic lute style consisting of chords, figurations (mostly scale passages), and pseudo-polyphonic elements.

Some of these fantasias belong to a special type which Milán characterizes by the terms *tentar de vihuela* or *fantasias de tentos*. Repeatedly he admonishes the player to perform these fantasias in a flexible tempo, 'es redobles apriesa y la consonancia a espacio' (the ornamented passages fast, and the harmonies slowly), adding that 'este musica no tiene mucho respecto al compas'. In general, these *tentos* are distinguished from the other fantasias by the extended use of running passages and by the absence of imitation.[3] One of the most beautiful examples is no. 16, an almost ceremonial composition which evokes a vivid picture of the famous *maestro* (as he was wont to hear himself called) surrounded by the grandees and ladies of the court society of Valencia or Madrid.[4]

Three years after the publication of Milán's book there appeared *Los seys libros del Delphin de música* by Luis de Narváez (Valladolid, 1538).[5] In addition to arrangements of vocal pieces (by Josquin, Gombert, Richafort) and lute songs (*romances* and *villancicos*) this collection contains fourteen fantasias, four sets of variations, and a *basse danse*, called *Baja de contrapunto*. The fantasias are more clearly and purely contrapuntal than Milán's. With the exceptions of one, called *Fantasía de consonancia* (no. 5), they are free from homophonic elements, and the scale passages so frequently encountered in the fantasias of Milán are completely absent. Narváez's fantasias are modelled after the motet or the imitative organ *ricercar*. Imitative treatment of two or three themes takes up the major part

[1] The word 'lute' is used in this section conveniently, but not quite accurately, to denote a related instrument: the *vihuela de mano* (cf. pp. 127 and 724.)

[2] New edition by Leo Schrade in *Publikationen älterer Musik*, ii (Leipzig, 1927). See also Guillermo de Morphy, *Les Luthistes espagnols du XVIe siècle* (Leipzig, 1902; mostly lute songs; many errors in the transcriptions). For a general account see Willi Apel, 'Early Spanish Music for Lute and Keyboard Instruments', *Musical Quarterly*, xx (1934), p. 289. Selections from Milán, Narváez, Valderrábano, and Fuenllana in Apel, *Musik aus früher Zeit*, ii.

[3] See, for instance, no. 17 (Schrade's edition, p. 42), Davison and Apel, op. cit. i, p. 129.

[4] See J. B. Trend, *Luis Milan and the Vihuelistas* (Oxford, 1925).

[5] Complete edition by Pujol, *Monumentos de la música española*, iii (Barcelona, 1945).

of the piece, while the closing section is (or, at least, gives the impression of being) written in free counterpoint. While the initial theme is usually well characterized (in some cases it is indicated by solmization syllables, e.g. *fa ut mi re*, no. 6), the later ones are of the nondescript type well known from Gombert's motets (e.g. E–F–D–E or F–E–C–D), a fact which often makes exact identification difficult. The final section often includes a repeat of a four- to six-bar passage, an echo effect derived from Josquin's 'paired imitation'. Three such echoes occur in the Fantasia no. 11 (p. 24 of Pujol's edition). Nos. 5 and 6, both based on subjects indicated by solmization syllables, seem to be intended as monothematic, since the main theme is not only used at the beginning but also recurs sporadically throughout the remaining portion in which new themes are introduced.

LUTE VARIATIONS

The *Delphin de música* is particularly interesting and important as one of the earliest extant sources of variations. There can be no doubt that the variation form was cultivated in Spain long before the time of Narváez, whose works in this genre seem to represent a first culmination rather than a beginning. The 'Seys diferencias de contrapunto sobre . . . O gloriosa Domina'[1] are a particularly impressive example of this highly developed art. Inspired by the devotional character and the intrinsic beauty of the church hymn, Narváez has created here an outstanding masterpiece of variation form. Together with a set of five variations on another church hymn, 'Sacris solemniis', this is the earliest known example of variations proper, that is, of variations based on a complete melody which comes to a full stop at the end (sectional variations). Another type, in which a short thematic idea is repeated without interruption (continuous variations) is represented in Narváez by two examples, 'Conde claros' and 'Guardame las vacas'.[2] Variations of this kind are usually called *basso ostinato* or ground, although there is occasionally room for doubt whether the originating idea lies in the bass, in the soprano melody, or simply in the harmonic scheme. Three countries have been claimed as the birthplace of this type of variation: Italy, Spain, and England, the last on the basis of such harpsichord pieces as Aston's 'Hornepype' or the 'Dompe', both found in Brit. Mus. Royal App. 58 (*c.* 1525).[3] Without reopening this question, one may point out a line of

---

[1] Pujol, op. cit., p. 44; also in Davison and Apel, op. cit. i, p. 130.
[2] Pujol, op. cit., pp. 82 and 85; 'Guardame las vacas' also in Apel, *Musik aus früher Zeit*, ii, p. 14.   [3] See Vol. III, p. 458.

development (a term which should be understood here primarily in the technical sense, without necessarily implying a chronological sequence), leading from extremely short thematic ideas to more extended schemes. At the beginning of this sequence stands a very interesting composition for two lutes in Enrique de Valderrábano's *Libro de música de vihuela intitulado Silva de Sirenas* (Valladolid, 1547),[1] described in a prefatory remark as 'a discantar sobre un punto o consonancia que es un compas que communemente llaman el atanbor' (descant over a point or harmony which consists of one bar and is commonly known as the *atanbor*).[2] In this composition the second lute constantly repeats a G major triad in a one-bar broken-chord pattern of a strong rhythmic pulse strikingly reminiscent of oriental dance accompaniments. Against this monotonous background the first lute performs a strongly contrasting music of Western derivation:

Ex. 342

Although this composition, considered *per se*, can hardly be called a variation, it serves as a convenient point of departure, for it exemplifies the simplest realization of the principle of uninterrupted repetition which forms the basis of all continuous variations. Proceeding from the one-harmony basis of this example, we come next to *ostinato* schemes in which two chords (I–V) alternate, as in the English 'Hornepype' and 'Dompe'. In 'Conde claros' the harmonic substance consists of a full cadence, I–IV–V, in an interesting rhythm

---

[1] Reprinted by Pujol, ibid., xxii and xxiii (1965).
[2] On the instrument known as *atanbor* or *atambor*, see Vol. I, p. 468; cf. in that volume also *tambura* and *tambur*.

alternating between $\frac{3}{2}$ and $\frac{6}{4}$, as shown in the examples reproduced in Ex. 343, the first from Alonso de Mudarra's *Tres libros de música en cifras para vihuela* (Seville, 1546), the other, for two lutes, from Valderrábano's *Silva de Sirenas*:

Ex.343

The theme of 'Guardame las vacas' more clearly foreshadows the later grounds in its greater extension, in its phrase structure (two phrases of four bars each), and in its slow triple metre, typical of all the passacaglias and chaconnes. This theme, easily recognizable by its tetrachordal design: A G F E, A G F–E D, recurs in numerous sources, Italian, Spanish, and German, under various names such as 'Romanesca', 'Romanesca O Guardame', or 'Passamezzo antico' (see pp. 614, 645).[1]

ALONSO DE MUDARRA

Mudarra's above-mentioned *Tres Libros de música*[2] contain a repertory similar to Narváez's: fantasias, arrangements, lute songs,

---

[1] Valderrábano's variations on this theme are printed in Davison and Apel, op. cit. i, p. 133.

[2] Complete edition by Pujol, *Monumentos de la música española*, vii (Barcelona, 1949).

and dances. The fantasias are considerably less contrapuntal and imitative than those of Narváez, showing traits similar to those found in Milán. Repetition of passages (echoes), which Narváez uses only in the closing sections, frequently occurs at the very beginning, e.g. in nos. 1, 3, and 6, and imitation is seldom carried out in a systematic manner. Four fantasias, a pavana, and a 'Romanesca' (nos. 18–23) are written for the guitar, which differs from the *vihuela de mano* (which is also a guitar rather than a lute) by having four, instead of six courses of strings. The second of Mudarra's three books (nos. 24–49) consists of pieces arranged in the eight church modes, each group being formed by a *tiento* and two fantasias, or by a *tiento*, a fantasia, and an arrangement (*glosa*) of a *Kyrie* or *Benedictus* from a Mass by Josquin or Févin. Obviously, these groups were intended to represent musical units consisting of several 'movements' somewhat in the manner of a suite or sonata. The *tientos* are short introductory pieces, even less polyphonic than the fantasias, and completely lacking the elaborate treatment characteristic of the organ *tiento* by Cabezón and the later Spanish organ composers. It is interesting to notice that the Spanish *tiento* had an evolutionary life identical with that of the Italian *ricercar*, leading from a short prelude for lute to a lengthy composition in imitative counterpoint for organ.

The variation form is represented by the previously mentioned 'Conde claros' and 'Romanesca, o Guárdame las vacas', the dance literature by two pavanes (nos. 15 and 16) the first of which is based on a melody:

Ex.344

that recurs in Cabezón's 'Pavana italiana',[1] Bull's 'The Spanish Paven',[2] in a 'Pavaniglia' in Fabrizio Caroso's *Nobiltà di Dame* (Venice, 1605),[3] and in the 'Pavana Hispanica' by Sweelinck and Samuel Scheidt.[4]

VALDERRÁBANO

Valderrábano's already mentioned *Silva de Sirenas* of 1547 is a compendious volume of over two hundred pages, divided into seven

[1] Pedrell, op. cit. vii, p. 73.
[2] *Fitzwilliam Virginal Book*, ii, p. 131, and *Musica Britannica*, xix, p. 31.
[3] Oscar Chilesotti, *Danze del secolo XVI* (Milan, n.d.), p. 21.
[4] Sweelinck, *Werken voor Orgel*, p. 248; Scheidt, *Werke*, v, p. 47.

libros. The first three of these contain pieces for lute and voice; the fourth, compositions for two lutes, mostly arrangements of vocal compositions by Willaert, Josquin, Gombert, and others, and also the previously mentioned 'Conde claros'; the fifth, fantasias; the sixth, 'partes de Misas, Duos, Canciones, y Sonetos'; the seventh, variations. The fantasias,[1] thirty-three in number, are 'assi sueltas como acomposturadas' (either free or measured), the latter term obviously referring to those that are based on other compositions, such as the 'Fantasia en el tercero grado remedando [imitating] al motete de Gombert Inviolata', or the 'Fantasia sobre un benedictus de la misa de Mouton Tua est potentia'. Probably these fantasias are not mere arrangements, but compositions based on motives from the vocal models, as is the case in the earliest Italian organ *canzoni* (by Cavazzoni). Valderrábano's original fantasias show a more integrated style than those of Milán, because of the absence of chordal and figurative elements, but seem to be less fully imitative than those of Narváez. They are among the most impressive examples of lute polyphony, their intimate grace and reserved expressiveness forming an interesting contrast to the courtly grandeur of those by Milán.

Among Valderrábano's variations the 'Pavana con diferencias' is of particular interest because the theme is the 'Folia' of seventeenth-century fame, the only difference being that it starts with the dominant chord instead of the tonic, and that it continues with a section in slower triple metre (originally notated in duple metre), which disappeared in later compositions. The following example shows the outline of this pavane; the letters indicate the bass:

Ex.345

The 'Conde claros' theme (Ex. 343) is treated by Valderrábano in two sets numbering respectively forty-six and seventy-two variations, an eloquent testimony to the popularity of this little motive.

Concerning Valderrábano's personality and life we know practically nothing. But perhaps of more weight than dates and facts is the

---

[1] One fantasia is transcribed in Apel, *Musik aus früher Zeit*, ii, p. 15.

motto that appears at the end of his book, under a vignette showing a symbolical figure laden with fetters: 'Ne ingenium volitet, paupertas deprimit ipsum' (Lest genius should soar upward, poverty holds it down).

DIEGO PISADOR

Pisador's *Libro de música de vihuela* (Salamanca, 1552) is divided into seven books (*libros*) which contain mostly lute songs (*Libro I*: *Romances, Sonetos*; *II*: *Villancicos*) or arrangements of vocal music (*Libro IV, V*: eight complete Masses by Josquin; *VI*: Motets, for lute and voice; *VII*: *Villanescas* and *Canciones* [Italian madrigals and French *chansons*], also for lute and voice). The first book opens with thirty-seven variations on 'Conde claros', twelve variations on 'Las Vacas', and a 'Pavana llana' which is essentially identical with the above-mentioned 'Folia' pavane by Valderrábano. In addition to these, the only purely instrumental pieces are two fantasias found at the end of the first book, and twenty-four fantasias which make up the contents of the third. Several of these are noteworthy for the use of red letters to indicate the theme whenever it occurs during the course of the fantasia. Apparently these red signs had not only a demonstrative or didactic function, but also a practical significance, for Pisador says that they should be (or could be?) sung: 'va la boz que se canta señalada de colorado' (the part to be sung is indicated in colour).[1]

In addition to the imitative fantasias or, as Pisador calls them, 'sobre passos remedados' (on imitated themes) there are others 'sin passos remedados' which continue the tradition of Milán's *tañer de gala,* but also foreshadow later tendencies in lute style by their frequent use of full, strumming chords connected by quick running figures, as in this example:

Ex.346

---

[1] Cf. p. 129.

MIGUEL DE FUENLLANA

Miguel de Fuenllana published at Seville, in 1554, his *Orphénica lyra* which, in addition to compositions for the six-stringed vihuela, contains a few pieces for the *vihuela de cinco ordines* (five courses) and the four-stringed guitar.[1] The purely instrumental repertory is represented mainly by twenty-three fantasias included in the first two books together with arranged Mass pieces and motets (by Morales, Lupus, Gombert),[2] each vocal piece being followed by a fantasia, sometimes marked 'Fantasia de l'author' or 'Fantasia que se sigue'. This unusual arrangement suggests that the fantasias are musically related to the pieces preceding them; such a relationship is clearly indicated in a few cases where the fantasia is marked 'que le remeda' (which imitates it, i.e. the preceding piece).

The great tradition of sixteenth-century Spanish lute music came to its end with Esteban Daza's *Libro de música en cifras para vihuela intitulado el Parnaso* (Valladolid, 1576), about which, unfortunately, nothing is known apart from a number of lute songs published in Morphy's *Les Luthistes espagnols du XVIe siècle*. Towards the end of the sixteenth century the *vihuela* began to be displaced in popularity by the guitar,[3] which failed to inspire a repertoire of comparable interest and value.

ITALIAN LUTE MUSIC

In Italy the early lute books by Petrucci (see Vol. III, pp. 418–21) were followed by a great number of publications which cover the period from 1536 to 1600 in fairly close succession.[4] The most important representative of the early Italian lute school is Francesco da Milano (1497–c. 1543), called *il divino*, who was employed at the ducal court of Mantua as well as by Ippolito de' Medici. Eight books of

[1] Cf. Hugo Riemann, 'Das Lautenwerk des Miguel Fuenllana', *Monatshefte für Musikgeschichte*, xxvii (1895), p. 81; A. Koczirz, 'Die Gitarrekompositionen in Miguel de Fuenllana's Orphénica lyra', *Archiv für Musikwissenschaft*, iv (1922), p. 241; J. Bal, 'Fuenllana and the transcription of Spanish lute-music', *Acta Musicologica*, xi (1939), p. 16.

[2] Wolf (*Handbuch der Notationskunde*, ii, p. 113) gives a facsimile of the transcription of part of the *Credo* from Morales' Mass 'Tu es vas electionis'. A two-part fantasia is printed in Apel, *Musik aus früher Zeit*, ii, p. 16.

[3] See Emilio Pujol, 'Les Resources instrumentales et leur rôle dans la musique pour vihuela et pour guitare aux XVIe siècle et au XVIIe', *La Musique instrumentale de la Renaissance*, p. 205.

[4] The gap between Petrucci's publications and 1536 is broken only by the manuscript collection (c. 1517) of the Brescian nobleman Vincenzo Capirola, which has been edited by Otto Gombosi (Neuilly-sur-Seine, 1955); on this collection see Geneviève Thibault, 'Un manuscrit italien pour luth des premières années du XVIe siècle', in *Le Luth et as musique* (ed. Jacquot) (Paris, 1958), p. 43.

Intavolatura di liuto by him, containing mostly *ricercari* and fantasias, appeared at Venice from 1536 to 1563.[1] The *ricercari*, similar to those in Petrucci's books, are free studies in lute style, consisting mainly of chords and scale fragments, as in the following example:

Ex.347

The fantasias, on the other hand, are essentially imitative[2] and therefore correspond to the organ *ricercar* of the same period. Usually two themes are introduced in separate sections, as in the following fantasia from Francesco's *Libro primo* (1546) (cf. pl. I (b)).

Ex.348
(i)

(ii)

Among Francesco's contemporaries and successors were Antonio Castcliono (*Intabolatura* published 1536), Francesco Marcolini (1536), Marcantonio del Pifaro (1546), Giovanni Maria da Crema (1546),[3] Antonio Rotta (1546), Domenico Bianchini (1546),[4] Paolo Borrono

---

[1] Reprints in Chilesotti, *Lautenspieler des 16. Jahrhunderts* (Leipzig, 1891); H. D. Bruger, *Alte Lautenkunst aus drei Jahrhunderten* (Berlin, 1923); J. W. von Wasielewski, *Geschichte der Instrumentalmusik im 16. Jahrhundert* (Berlin, 1878); and Chilesotti, 'Francesco da Milano', *Sammelbände der internationalen Musikgesellschaft*, iv (1903), p. 382. Part of Francesco's arrangement of Janequin's 'Chant des oiseaux' is printed by Andrea della Corte, *Scelta di musiche* (Milan, 1949), p. 104. For biographical details, see H. Colin Slim, 'Francesco da Milano: a bio-bibliographical study', *Musica Disciplina*, xviii (1964), p. 63.

[2] However, a piece described as *ricercar* in one publication may appear as *fantasia* in another: cf. the example analysed by Otto Gombosi, 'A la recherche de la forme dans la musique de la Renaissance: Francesco da Milano', *La Musique instrumentale de la Renaissance*, p. 165.

[3] Transcription by Giuseppe Gullino (Florence, 1955).

[4] On Bianchini's book see Chilesotti, 'Note circa alcuni liutisti italiani', *Rivista musicale italiana*, ix (1902), p. 36, and R. de Morcourt, 'Le Livre de tablature de luth de Domenico Bianchini (1546)', *La Musique instrumentale de la Renaissance*, p. 177.

(1546, 1548, 1549, 1563), Giacomo Gorzanis (1561, 1563, 1564, 1565, 1579),[1] Vincenzo Galilei (1563), Giulio Cesare Barbetta (1569, 1603), Fabrizio Caroso (1581), Giovanni Maria Radino (1592), Giovanni Antonio Terzi (1593, 1599), Simone Molinaro (1599), Giovanni Battista della Gostena (1599), and Cesare Negri (1602, 1604).[2] While Casteliono and d'Aquila preferred to cultivate the fantasia, dance music seems to prevail (side by side with arrangements of vocal pieces) in the later publications. Pifaro's *Intabulatura de lauto* (1546) contains various *chiarenzane*, each followed by a *saltarello* which presents the same tune in triple metre. They are examples of the familiar dance-pair.[3] The German lutenists called such a rhythmic modification of a dance *Proportz*, since it resulted from the application of *proportio tripla*. The following is the beginning of Pifaro's 'Chiarenzana De Magio' as well as of 'Il suo saltarello':

Ex.349

The stylistic characteristics of this example—full, 'strummed' chords and interlacing passage work—remained the stock-in-trade of the Italian composers of lute dances during the second half of the sixteenth century.

In addition to pairs of dances, several lutenists developed fixed combinations of three or more dance types, and these are interesting as predecessors of the seventeenth-century suite. The following is a survey of such combinations, the bracketed figures indicating the number of examples found in each source:

    1508: Dalza   Pavana–Saltarello–Piva[4] (2).
    1529: Attaingnant Basse danse–Recoupe–Tordion (9).

---

[1] See Chilesotti, 'Jacomo Gorzanis, liutista del Cinquecento', *Rivista musicale italiana*, xxi (1914), p. 86.

[2] A fantasia by Marco d'Aquila, published in Casteliono's book, in Schering, *Geschichte der Musik in Beispielen*, p. 89; a sonata by Gorzanis in della Corte, op. cit., p. 101; various pieces in Chilesotti's 'Notes sur les tablatures de luth et de guitare', Lavignac, *Encyclopédie de la musique*, Ire partie, ii, pp. 651–68.

[3] See Vol. III, p. 429.　　　　　　　　　　[4] See Vol. III, pp. 420–1.

1536: Casteliono	Pavana–3 Saltarelli (with variations [*alio modo*] and extensions [*ripresa*])–Tochada (6).
1546: Francesco	Pavana–3 Saltarelli (8).
1546: Rotta	Passamezzo–Gagliarda–Padovano (5).
1563: Gorzanis	Passamezzo–Padovano–Saltarello (?).
1573: Waissel	Passamezzo–Padovano–Saltarello (8).
1577: Caroso	Passamezzo–Gagliarda–Saltarello (or Rotta)–Canario (optional) (8).

Very likely these embryonic suites reflect, to a certain extent, the dance fashions in the various decades of the sixteenth century. In this connexion the emergence of the *passamezzo* about 1550 is worth noticing, as well as the numerical prevalence, in the books of Casteliono and Francesco, of the *saltarello*, a dance which enjoyed the greatest popularity.

Among the later Italian lutenists, Vincenzo Galilei (1520?–91), a prominent member of the Florentine *camerata*,[1] is the most noteworthy.[2] The *ricercari* inserted in his dialogue *Fronimo* (Venice, 1568, second edition 1584) are mostly short studies in chords and passages, as, for instance:

Ex. 350[3]

Another example, considerably more extended,[4] opens with a point of imitation but continues after this in free lute style. Of special interest is a 'Fuga a l'unisono, dopo sei tempi' for two lutes,[5] that is, a group canon in which a complete fabric of chordal and melodic elements is imitated by another lute at a distance of six bars.

Galilei's *Intavolatura de lauto* (Rome, 1563) contains, in addition to twenty-eight arranged madrigals, six *ricercari* of the type described above, while a manuscript *Libro d'intavolatura di liuto* of 1584 con-

[1] See pp. 151 ff.
[2] Complete edition by Fabio Fano in *Istituzioni e monumenti dell'arte musicale italiana*, iv (Milan, 1934). See also Chilesotti, 'Il primo Libro di liuto di Vicenzo Galilei', *Rivista musicale italiana*, xv (1908), p. 753.
[3] Fano, p. 9.   [4] Ibid., p. 10.
[5] Ibid., p. 12

tains numerous galliards with dedicatory titles such as 'Terpsichore', 'Tiresia', and 'Fillide', probably the earliest examples of a practice which became common in the dance music of the seventeenth century.[1]

BACFARC AND GINTZLER

Another interesting lutenist is the Hungarian Valentinus Bacfarc or Bakfark (1507–76), who sometimes styled himself Greff.[2] One of the most renowned musicians of his day, he spent his life at the courts of Hungary, France, Poland, and Austria, but his music is closely related to the Italian tradition. His lute books, the *Intabulatura Valentini Bacfarc* (Lyons, 1552; partly reprinted in *Premier livre de tabelature . . . par Vallentin Bacfarc*, Paris, 1564) and the compendious *Harmoniae musicae . . . prima pars* (Cracow, 1565), as well as the collective publications by Phalèse (*Theatrum musicum*, Louvain, 1571; *Thesaurus musicus*, Louvain, 1574), contain, in addition to numerous arrangements of motets, *chansons*, and madrigals, only four *recercate* and three fantasias. All these are extremely long pieces (one consists of more than 200 bars), written almost completely in three- or four-part imitative polyphony. Together with similar compositions by Simon Gintzler, a German lutenist of Italian leanings, whose *Intabolatura de lauto, Libro primo*[3] appeared at Venice in 1547, they represent the technical highpoint of the imitative lute *ricercar* of the sixteenth century, indicating a tendency to make the lute compete with the organ. The most important Flemish lutenist was Emmanuel Adrianssen, who published his *Pratum Musicum* and *Novum Pratum* at Antwerp in 1584 and 1592.[4]

Brief mention may finally be made of the lute books published by two famous dancing masters of the late sixteenth century, Fabrizio Caroso's *Il Ballarino* (Venice, 1581) and Cesare Negri's *Le Gratie d'amore* (Milan, 1602) and *Nuove Inventioni di Balli* (Milan, 1604).[5] They contain exclusively dances for practical purposes and (perhaps consequently) of very slight musical interest. A 'Bassa imperiale' in Negri's *Le Gratie d'amore* is identical with a 'Pavana alla venetiana' in Dalza's lute-book of 1508[6] as well as with a 'Bassa imperiale'

---

[1] Three late Italian lute books, by Radino (Venice, 1592), Molinaro (Venice, 1599), and Gostena (Venice, 1599) have been published by G. Gullino in *I classici musicali italiani* (Florence, 1949–63).

[2] Reprints in *Denkmäler der Tonkunst in Österreich*, xviii. 2.

[3] Reprints ibid.

[4] See Godelieve Spiessens, 'Emmanuel Adriaenssen et son Pratum Musicum', *Acta Musicologica*, xxxvi (1964), p. 142.

[5] Reprints in Chilesotti's *Danze del secolo XVI*.　　　　[6] See Vol. III, p. 420.

in the *Klavierbuch der Regina Clara im Hoff* (Vienna, Staatsbibl.
MS. 18491) of *c*. 1625[1]—an interesting example of longevity in dance
music.

FRENCH LUTE MUSIC

The French lute music after Attaingnant (see Vol. III, pp. 450 ff.)
is hardly less in quantity than that in Italy after Petrucci. The main
representatives of French lute music were Albert de Rippe (d. 1551),
an Italian in the employ of François I and Henry II, his pupil Guillaume Morlaye who published his teacher's works as well as his own
(Paris, 1552–8), Antoine Francisque with his compendious *Le Trésor
d'Orphée* (Paris, 1600), and Jean-Baptiste Besard with his equally
voluminous *Thesaurus harmonicus* (Cologne, 1603) and its sequel, the
Novus partus (Augsburg, 1617). In addition, such publishers as
Phalèse and Le Roy continued to cater for the demands of the musical
amateurs as Attaingnant had done.

The contents of these books consist of *fantaisies*, dances, and
arrangements of *chansons* and motets, the last-named category far
outnumbering the others, as may be seen from the contents of the
various lute books of de Rippe and Morlaye, issued as *Premier
(Second . . .) livre de tabelature de luth*:

de Rippe   I (1562): 9 fantasias
„   II (1562): 15 *chansons*
„   III (1562): 16 *chansons*
„   IV (1553): 6 fantasias, 2 *chansons*, 3 pavanes, 'La Romanesca'
„   V (1562): 4 fantasias, 5 motets
Morlaye   I (1552): 6 fantasias, 12 *chansons*, 6 *paduanes*, 8 *gaillardes*
„   II (1558): 2 fantasias, 2 motets, 6 *chansons*, 2 pavanes, 4 *gail-
                       lardes*
„   III (1558): 3 fantasias, 2 motets, 5 *chansons*, 1 pavane, 1 *gail-
                       larde*.

Up to now practically nothing of this large repertory has been made
available for study.

An important landmark in the development of lute music is represented by two previously mentioned publications dating from the
turn of the century: Francisque's *Trésor* and Besard's *Thesaurus*.[2]

[1] See Apel, *Musik aus früher Zeit*, i, pp. 20 and 15.
[2] Piano transcription of Francisque by Henri Quittard (Paris, 1906). Numerous
transcriptions from Besard are included in J. N. Garton, *The Thesaurus Harmonicus of
J. B. Besard* (typescript dissertation, Indiana University, 1952); separate pieces in Apel,
Musik aus früher Zeit, ii, p. 24, Adler, *Handbuch der Musikgeschichte*, i, p. 402, Bruger,
Alte Lautenkunst, and above all in Chilesotti's publications—*Biblioteca di rarità*

Both are comprehensive collections in several *livres*, each of which contains a special genre of lute music. Thus, the *Trésor* presents in successive chapters: (1) *préludes et fantaisies*; (2) *passemèzes et pavanes*; (3) *gaillards*; (4) *branles et gavottes*; (5) *courantes*; (6) *voltes*; (7) *ballets*. The *Thesaurus* is even more inclusive, containing (1) 38 *praeludia* (by Laurencinus, Diomedes, Besardus, Bocquet); (2) 42 fantasias (by Laurencinus, Długoraj,[1] Dowland, and others); (3) 16 madrigals and 25 *villanelle*; (4) 17 *cantiones gallicae* and 21 *airs de court* (for voice and lute); (5) 18 *passamezzi*, 1 *pavana hispanica*, and 1 *bergamasco*; (6) 51 *galliardae*; (7) 34 *choreae quas Allemande vocant*; also 8 *choreae polonicae* and 1 *chorea anglica Doolandi* (that is, by John Dowland); (8) 29 *bransles* and 17 *ballets*; (9) 30 *courantes* and 34 *voltes*; (10) various items, such as *batailles, canaries*, &c.

It is in these two books that, for the first time, we find large collections of two dance types which were to become standard movements of the baroque suite: the allemande and the courante. The appearance of the gavotte—previously mentioned in Arbeau's *Orchésographie* (Langres, 1588)—is also worth noticing. Even more important is the fact that these two books give the first evidence of an imminent change of lute style, a change which was to be of fundamental importance not only for lute music but also for the harpsichord music of the seventeenth century. As we have seen previously, the lutenists, near the end of the sixteenth century, had arrived at a luxuriant style of full, pompous chords and rapid, virtuoso passage work. A typical example is the following 'Passo e mezzo bellissimo' by Gorzanis (from the *Secondo Libro*, Venice, 1563):

Ex. 351

musicali, vii and ix, *Lautenspieler des 16. Jahrhunderts*, and 'Notes sur les tablatures' (Lavignoc, *Encyclopédie*, Ire partie, ii, pp. 670–2).

[1] Długoraj was a Polish pupil of Bakfark; a fantasia, finale and six *villanelle*, ed. Piotr Poźniak, *Wydawnictwo dawnej muzyki polskiej* (Cracow, 2nd ed. 1964), xxiii. Another Pole whose work appeared in Besard's publications was Jacob Polak or Polonois, lutenist at the French court; seventeen pieces, ed. Maria Szczepańska, ibid. xxii (1951).

Although pieces written in this style are still to be found in the *Trésor* as well as in the *Thesaurus*, there are others which clearly indicate a break with this tradition. The 'Volte' by Francisque quoted in Ex. 352, i, shows a new type of melody, remarkable for its graceful, charming, and popular simplicity, and his 'Les Favorites d'Angélique' (named after Angélique Paulet, a woman famous for her grace, beauty, and musical talent) is an early example of the seventeenth-century *style brisé* with its characteristic texture of notes alternating in the high and low registers, suggesting two-part writing (Ex. 352, ii):

Ex.352

Besard's *Thesaurus* contains a great number of compositions by other lute composers, particularly Laurencinus Romanus and Diomedes Cato. Laurencinus was Besard's teacher and is probably identical with Lorenzini da Liuto, who served as lutenist to Cardinal d'Este at Tivoli during 1570 and afterwards at Ferrara. Diomedes, also known as Diomedes Venetus or Diomedes Sarmata, was born in Venice and worked at Cracow.[1] By far the most interesting part of the *Thesaurus* is its first book, with its large collection of *praeludia*. As the name suggests, these are free pieces in idiomatic lute style, the seventeenth-century successors to the early Italian *ricercari* and Spanish *tientos* for the lute. Naturally they have more variety and greater fullness of sound, and this, together with an expressive quality reflecting the then fashionable mood of melancholy, makes them truly admirable examples of lute music. Particularly attractive are the relatively short preludes by Besard, such as this:

[1] Thirty pieces, ed. Szczepańska, ibid. xxiv (1953).

Ex.353

Little of importance has come down to us from the three or four decades between the *Thesaurus* and the appearance of the greatest French lutenist of the seventeenth century, Denis Gaultier (see Vol. VI).[1] The chief contribution of this period is the *air de cour* with lute accompaniment, as represented in the eight books of *Airs de différents autheurs mis en tablature de luth* by Gabriel Bataille (Paris, 1608–18), Antoine Boësset's *Airs de Cour* (Paris, 1621), and others.[2]

GERMAN LUTE MUSIC

The earliest extant examples of German lute music are some lute songs contained in Schlick's *Tabulaturen etlicher Lobgesangk und Lidlein* of 1512.[3] The most important of the later lutenists were Hans Judenkünig (*c.* 1450–1526; Vienna), Hans Gerle (*c.* 1500–70; Nuremberg), Hans Neusiedler (1508–63; Nuremberg); his brother Melchior (1507–90; Nuremberg, Augsburg, Italy), Wolff Heckel (Strasbourg), Sebastian Ochsenkun (1521–74; Heidelberg), Sixtus Kargel (died after 1586; Strasbourg, Saverne), and Mattheus Waissel (died after 1573; East Prussia).

Judenkünig's *Ain schone kunstliche Underweisung*[4] appeared at Vienna in 1523, three years before he died 'senex admo[dum]' (a rather old man), as we learn from a comment written in the copy

---

[1] Robert Ballard's lute music (1611 and 1614) has been re-published by André Souris, Sylvie Spycket, and Jacques Veyrier (Paris, two vols., 1963–4).

[2] See p. 189.

[3] See Vol. III, p. 410.

[4] Reprints in *Denkmäler der Tonkunst in Österreich*, xviii. 2; on the composer's life, see Adolf Koczirz, 'Der Lautenist Hans Judenkünig', *Sammelbände der internationalen Musikgesellschaft*, vi (1905), p. 237.

in the Vienna Nationalbibliothek. He was a contemporary of Hofhaimer, and his connexion with the humanistic movement, in which
Hofhaimer played a central role, appears from the fact that, in his
slightly earlier *Utilis et compendiaria Introductio* (Vienna, *c.* 1515),
he included settings of Horatian odes.[1]

The *Underweisung* contains five *priamell* (preambles), short preludes
written in the pseudo-polyphonic and, occasionally, imitative style of
the Italian lute *ricercari*. It also contains several dances, among which
'Der Hoff Dantz' and 'Der ander Hoff Dantz' are of particular
interest, being among the earliest examples of a German dance type,
the *Hoftanz*, which is frequently encountered in German sixteenth-
century sources.[2] Many of these examples are based on a traditional
melody, 'Der schwarze Knab',[3] a reconstruction of which is given
in Ex. 354 (i), together with Judenkünig's 'Der Hoffdantz' (ii), and
a more elaborate version by Neusiedler (iii).[4]

Ex.354

---

[1] See *Denkmäler der Tonkunst in Österreich*, xviii. 2, p. 1.

[2] See Otto Gombosi, 'Der Hoftanz', *Acta musicologica*, vii (1935), p. 50.

[3] See, for instance, Weck's 'Tancz der schwarcz knab' in Merian, op. cit., p. 52.
Here the melody is in the tenor.

[4] Neusiedler's 'Hoftanz' is printed in Davison and Apel, op. cit. i, p. 107.

Hans Neusiedler published *Ein newgeordnet künstlich Lautenbuch* (Nuremberg, 1536), *Ein newes Lautenbüchlein* (Nuremberg, 1540), and *Das Erst Buch. Ein newes Lautenbüchlein—Das Ander Buch. Ein New künstlich Lautten Buch* (Nuremberg, two parts, 1544), containing, in addition to a great number of arrangements of songs, motets, and *chansons* (Janequin's 'L'Alouette' appears under the title 'Lalafete'), eight 'preambels' and about forty dances.[1] Most of the preludes are written in a fairly complete three-part texture, as in the passage shown in Ex. 355.[2] One 'Preambel oder Fantasy' has a fair claim to be the most extended piece ever written for the lute.

Ex. 355

Among the dances we find Italian dances under titles such as 'Welscher Tanz', 'Welischer Tanz', or 'Wascha mesa' (that is, passamezzo), several examples of the 'Hoftanz', and some particularly interesting character dances, such as 'Der Zeuner Tantz' ('Zeuner' probably means *Zigeuner*, gypsy).[3]

Hans Gerle published, under the title of *Musica Teusch* ('German Music'), a collection of pieces for violins (including 'string quartets') and for the lute (Nuremberg, 1532, and later editions). In 1552

---

[1] Reprints in *Denkmäler der Tonkunst in Österreich*, xviii. 2; Oswald Körte, *Laute und Lautenmusik bis zur Mitte des 16. Jahrhunderts* (Leipzig, 1901), and Schering, op. cit., p. 88.

[2] *Denkmäler der Tonkunst in Österreich*, xviii. 2, p. 15.

[3] Transcribed in Apel, *Musik aus früher Zeit*, i, p. 9.

appeared his *Ein newes sehr künstlichs Lautenbuch*, containing numerous preludes and dances, mostly by Italian lutenists such as Francesco
da Milano, Antonio Rotta, Marco d'Aquila, Rosseto, and 'Joan
Maria'[1] (i.e. Giovanni Maria da Crema).

Mention must also be made of some later German lute books:
Wolff Heckel's *Discant (Tenor) Lautten Buch* (i.e. duets for two lutes)
(Strasbourg, 1556), Sebastian Ochsenkun's *Tabulaturbuch auff die
Lautten* (Heidelberg, 1558), Bernhard Jobin's *Das erste (Das ander)
Buch newerlessner Lautenstück* (Strasbourg, 1572 and 1573), Mattheus
Waissel's several *Tabulatura* (Frankfurt-am-Oder, 1573, 1591, and
1592), Melchior Neusiedler's *Teutsch Lautenbuch* (Strasbourg, 1574),
and Sixtus Kargel's *Lautenbuch* (Strasbourg, 1586). Many of the
dances contained in these publications[2] consist of a main dance in
even metre, followed by another in triple metre, the latter being called
Nachtanz (after dance), *Sprungk* (jump), *Hupfauf* (jump up), *Tripla*,
or *Proportz*. Often these second dances are rhythmic variations of
the first dance, particularly if they are called *Tripla* or *Proportz*, both
abbreviations of *proportio tripla*. In Waissel's lute books we find
several examples of suite-like combinations, such as *passamezzo-
padovano-saltarello* (see p. 693).

Waissel's lute book of 1592 is the last printed publication of
German lute music, not only in the sixteenth century but almost
throughout the seventeenth. There exist some fairly compendious
manuscript collections from the early seventeenth century,[3] but even
these cease with the beginning of the Thirty Years War. Not until the
third quarter of the seventeenth century did German lute music reach
a new period of flowering, under Esaias Reusner (1636–79).

ENGLISH LUTE MUSIC[4]

It is not yet possible to discuss the role played by the lute in the
development of English music before 1540 or so. Scattered references
show that the instrument was popular among professional musicians

---

[1] Reprints in Wasielewski, Körte, and Bruger, op. cit. Closely related to the publications of Gerle and Neusiedler is the manuscript Bay. Staatsbibl. Mus. 1512, from which
Heinz Bischoff and Heinz Zirnbauer have published a selection of transcriptions (Mainz,
1938).

[2] See J. Dieckmann, *Die in deutscher Lautentabulatur überlieferten Tänze des 16.
Jahrhunderts* (Kassel, 1931).

[3] Dresden, Staatsbibl. MS. Mus. B. 1030 (Lute Book of Joachim von Loss, early
seventeenth century); Copenhagen, Royal Library, MS. Thott 841 4° (Lute Book of
Petrus Fabricius, 1605 ff.); Leipzig, City Library MS. II. 6. 15 (Lute Book of Adalbert
Długoraj, 1619).

[4] By Thurston Dart.

and amateurs alike. Peter Carmelianus the Luter was one of Henry
VIII's favourites for many years. When Princess Margaret made her
progress to Scotland in 1503 she was visited by her future husband,
James IV: 'Incountenynt the Kynge begonne before hyr to play of the
clarycordes, and after of the lute. . . .' The earliest English lute tablature (Brit. Mus. Royal App. 58), which seems to have been compiled
over a number of years (c. 1530–c. 1550), confirms the idea of the
repertory of the lute which may be deduced from continental sources
of the time: improvisation, arrangements of vocal music, and dance
music.

The arrangements of vocal or ensemble music found in this and in
many subsequent manuscripts do not differ in style from the hundreds
of similar ones found in continental sources. The music is transcribed
either as it stands or else with a number of somewhat stereotyped
embellishments, and the polyphony is often treated rather cavalierly.
Some of the arrangements are for solo voice and lute accompaniment,
and in the expressive power of songs like Johnson's 'Benedicam
Domino' and the anonymous 'Willow Song' may be seen the seeds
of the later ayre. The dance music in Royal App. 58 and in many
later manuscripts is of far greater importance, however, in the
development of idiomatic writing for the lute. 'The dance was the
main source of inspiration to every lutenist composer, and even in the
most florid and idealized examples the basic nature and pulse of the
dance are never lost.'[1]

'During the reigns of Elizabeth, James I, and Charles I, the lute
was the most popular domestic instrument of music in England.'[2]
English lute music of the period 1540 to 1620 is represented by some
2,000 surviving compositions (excluding songs, consort music, and
arrangements of vocal music); the majority of these are dances, the
pavane and galliard standing at the head of the list. In the earlier years
the three component strains of each dance were often unequal in
length, but by the classical period (1585–1610) the strains had become
uniformly eight, twelve, or sixteen bars long, and it was customary to
provide each strain with an elaborate written-out variation. Thematic
connexions between pavanes and galliards are rather rare. Almans,
jigs, corants, and volts were also popular, and in the earlier sources
there are a number of settings of such international harmonic grounds
as the *quadro* and passamezzo pavanes and the hornpipe.

[1] David Lumsden, 'The Sources of English Lute Music (1540–1620)', *Galpin Society
Journal*, vi (1953), p. 14.
[2] Peter Warlock, preface to his edition of some of *The Lute Music of John Dowland*
(London, 1927).

Of the non-dance forms, the most important are variations and the fancy. The themes for variations are those found in such collections as the *Fitzwilliam Virginal Book*: 'Go from my window', 'The carman's whistle', 'Walsingham', 'Bonny sweet Robin'. The variations, like the fancies, often attain great heights of musical and technical complexity.

Most English lute-music survives only in manuscript sources; in general these are similar in layout and contents, and it is clear that most of them were the personal books of good professional or amateur players, compiled over a long period of time, constantly replenished with new music, and primarily intended for use. It is difficult to establish an orderly chronology for them, and the scholar's task is further complicated by the very high proportion of anonymous compositions they contain—about three-quarters of the entire repertory. Many of the best lute-composers are hardly known elsewhere: Bacheler, Cutting, Brewster, Newman, Collarde, Bulman, Robinson[1] are names that occur in few reference books, if any, and little or nothing is known of these composers' lives. Byrd wrote only nine lute pieces, Morley only one or two, and men so renowned as Tye, Gibbons, Weelkes, and Wilbye none at all. Among the more familiar names found in the lute sources are those of Holborne, the Johnsons, Pilkington, Rosseter, 'Phillips',[2] the younger Ferrabosco, and John Dowland. Dowland's music for solo lute includes dances, fancies, and variations; masterly in technique and inspiration, it was famous throughout Europe. In his preface to *A Pilgrimes Solace* (London, 1612), the composer was able to point out with justifiable pride that 'some part of my poore labours have found favour in the greatest part of Europe, and been printed in eight most famous Cities beyond the seas, viz.: Paris, Antwerpe, Collein, Nurenberge, Franckfort, Leipsig, Amsterdam, and Hamburge'. No other English composer of his time could say as much. His music is to be found in one English source after another; there are more than twenty extant versions of his famous 'Lacrimae' pavane, for instance. The melancholy power of this pavane and of such fancies as 'Forlorn Hope', the infectious gaiety of 'My Lady Hunsdon's Puffe',[3] the rich texture of his setting of 'Fortune my Foe' for two lutes: these are typical of Dowland. Yet they can be readily matched in the music of his English contemporaries, both named and unnamed, and they give some indication of the wealth and variety of the English school as a whole.

[1] Cutting, Brewster, Newman, and Bulman are represented in David Lumsden, *An Anthology of English Lute Music* (London, 1954).

[2] More probably Philippe Van Wilder than Peter Philips.

[3] Lumsden, *An Anthology*, pp. 36 and 29.

Many English lute manuscripts include duets for two lutes (often with the supplementary part missing altogether), duets for lute and viol (the viol part again being usually missing), music for bandora, cittern, lyra viol or virginals, lute music by foreign composers (notably Francesco da Milano), and music for broken consort. The instrument's tuning (*Gcfadg'*) remained fairly constant throughout the whole period; in about 1595 a seventh course (tuned to *D*) was added, and diapasons running clear of the fingerboard were added at about the same date. Before 1570 or so, the lower strings were tuned in octaves; after 1596, in unison; but the transition from the one to the other is difficult to trace.

The printed sources are comparatively few in number, and it is curious to note how very few of the pieces from these turn up in the manuscripts. Books like those of Le Roy (London, 1568), Barley (London, 1596), and—above all—Robinson (London, 1603) are important not so much for the music they contain as for their practical instructions in lute-playing; Le Roy's book, translated from the French, includes a number of French *chansons* and dances, and Robert Dowland's *Variety of Lute Lessons* (London, 1610)[1] tends to emphasize foreign composers at the expense of the English school. About fifteen pieces of lute music are included in the printed song-books of Dowland, Maynard, and others.

To judge from the surviving sources, the golden years of English lute music were from 1580 to 1620, and many of the pieces may not unfairly be ranked among the finest compositions of their age. This is the period of the English ayre for voice(s), lute, and viol(s); the decline in its popularity coincides with the decline in the old style of solo lute music in 1620 or so. Thereafter the new and rather precious style introduced by the French lutenist Jacques Gaultier and his compatriots increasingly eclipsed the native English tradition. By 1630 the lute, though still very much in favour, had become utterly Frenchified, and the manuscripts of the time record only new and foreign names and a new and foreign idiom.

SOLO MUSIC FOR OTHER INSTRUMENTS[2]

During the first forty years of the sixteenth century a number of books dealing with the practice of instrumental music were published in the chief cities of Europe. Their contents usually fall into three categories: anthologies of music for such solo harmony instruments

---

[1] Facsimile and transcription by Edgar Hunt (London, 1957).
[2] By Thurston Dart.

as the lute or the organ, these anthologies often being preceded by a rudimentary tutor for the instrument; simple directions for the learner of such consort instruments as the recorder or the viol, primarily designed to show him how to keep his instrument in good order and how to take his place in polyphonic ensemble music; and manuals of extemporized ornamentation, mainly for the more advanced ensemble player. Manuscripts such as Trent 1947–4 show further how a polyphonic *chanson* of the period could be adapted for solo viol with keyboard accompaniment, or for recorder and lute; but in all this repertory there are few traces of an autonomous style for a solo melody instrument. With the publication of Silvestro Ganassi's *Regola Rubertina* (Venice, 1542) and its sequel, his *Lettione Seconda* (Venice, 1543), the development of solo instrumental music took a decisive step forward; and it was the viol that led the way.

Ganassi's books constitute the earliest comprehensive tutor for the viol ever published, and their author dealt with every aspect of the instrument's technique (though the historian may justly deplore Ganassi's tortuous prose, which so often obscures his meaning). His earlier book, *La Fontegara* (Venice, 1535),[1] is a treatise on extemporized ornamentation for the recorder-player, and the bulk of it consists of page after page of musical examples, many of them quite impracticable in performance. The *Regola Rubertina* and its sequel, however, take the learner through every stage of handling his instrument, including such subjects as tuning, testing strings, fretting, bowing, fingering, reading from tablature and from notes, scale-practice, cadenzas, arranging a madrigal for voice and solo viol, and the invention of improvised solo *ricercari*. It is in these *ricercari* that Ganassi's abilities are displayed at their best; their ingenious mixture of melody and harmony and their wide-ranging themes well illustrate the skill in extemporization that he expected of his pupils. Such music as this contains the seeds of two quite separate forms of instrumental music that developed during the later years of the century: music for *viola bastarda* and for division viol, and music for lyra viol. In the first of these the melodic and improvisatory elements in Ganassi's style have taken command; in the second, the harmonic elements.

Diego Ortiz's *Tratado de glosas* (Rome, 1553)[2] marks the next stage. The first book of this important treatise is concerned with the improvised embellishment of polyphonic lines in ensemble music at

---

[1] Edited by Hildemarie Peter (Berlin, 1956); English translation by Dorothy Swainson (Berlin, 1959).
[2] See also p. 560.

cadence points and elsewhere—with cadenzas, in fact. The second book is of greater interest, for it shows the player how to improvise *ricercari* for solo viol, how to embellish an individual polyphonic line to the accompaniment of a keyboard instrument, how to extemporize a fifth part to a four-part madrigal or *chanson*, and how to play 'divisions on a ground'. All these are melody-making techniques. Ortiz's musical style is less rhapsodic and more mature than Ganassi's, his tastes more international, his exposition more orderly. His chosen instrument was the bass viol—here he accurately foresaw the dominant taste of viol-players during the next two centuries—and, like his instrument, Ortiz was by birth a Spaniard. In all probability many of the techniques he describes originated in Spain and were perfected in Italy, more particularly in Naples—then, and for many years to come, part of the Spanish Empire. Such virtuosos as Giovanni Bassano, Orazio and Alfonso della Viola, Riccardo and Francesco Rogniono (or Rognoni), Giovanni Luca Conforto, and Angelo Notari carried Ortiz's techniques of elaborating upon the text of a polyphonic composition to their culmination in the bastard art of the aptly named *viola bastarda*; under the hands and fingers of these men the whole polyphonic fabric of a madrigal became dissolved into a flurry of extemporized skips and runs for a small bass viol, accompanied by a continuo part played upon a harpsichord, organ, or large lute. So parasitic a style could not outlive the carcass upon which it fed; having spread to the greater part of Europe, it expired together with its host during the later 1620's. As for Ortiz's other techniques, the *ricercar* and 'divisions on a ground' led to the English division-playing of the seventeenth century; and since 'cadenzas' were as apt for voice or violin as for viol, their vocabulary of ornament enriched the style of the singers and violinists of the early baroque period.

The harmonic element in Ganassi's music similarly branched off into a style of its own, represented first by the *lira da gamba* and a little later by the lyra viol. The Italian *lira da gamba*,[1] a rather cumbrous bowed instrument with a dozen or more strings tuned in a sequence of rising fifths and falling fourths, was cultivated by only a few virtuosos. Since common chords were extremely easy to play on the *lira*, it could be used either for *continuo*-playing or for sketching the music of a polyphonic madrigal or *chanson*. The lyra viol[2] probably developed as a hybrid between the *lira da gamba* and the small bass viol; it borrowed its notation (tablature) from the lute, its technique and form from the viol, its variable tunings (see Ex. 358)

[1] See also p. 716.   [2] See also pp. 714–15.

from the *lira*, and its tessitura from the tenor viol. Like its probable inventor, the younger Alfonso Ferrabosco, it seems to have been conceived in England of Italian parentage; and he appears to have been the pioneer in developing its elaborate and distinctive style.[1] During much of the seventeenth century the lyra viol was the chosen solo instrument of English violists, and such composers as Hume, Coperario, Corkine, Jenkins, and William Lawes wrote much fine music for one, two, and three lyras as well as for lyra viol and violins. Outside England, however, the instrument seems to have been virtually unknown.

Few countries other than Italy and England and few melody instruments other than the viol can claim much of a share in the development of solo instrumental music during this period. If a true repertory for the *lira da braccio* or for the solo violin ever existed during the sixteenth century, nothing is known of it today. The same is true of such treble wind instruments as the recorder, flute, crumhorn, and shawm, for all these were used either in consort or else merely for playing tunes and dances. Of the brass instruments, the sackbut or trombone was not a solo instrument, though it was customarily used for doubling the bass line in a work for cornett and *continuo*. The horn was for the hunting field alone, and by the late sixteenth century it had evolved an elaborate code of solo calls. The trumpet served another field, war, and its solo music was little more than another code of military and ceremonial signals. The rebec was for beggars, the bagpipe for shepherds, and neither instrument contributed to the growth of solo instrumental music. In the early years of the seventeenth century pairs of solo treble instruments such as violins or cornetts made their appearance at the Mantuan court and elsewhere,[2] but their history, like the history of ensemble music for trumpets and drums, lies outside the scope of this discussion.

During the same period a certain amount of solo music for treble instrument and *continuo* made a rather apologetic appearance in Italy, often appended to collections of vocal monody; this repertory includes the solo *canzoni* of Riccio (Venice, 1614 and 1620), the *esercitii* of Brunelli (Venice, 1614; suitable for cornett, flute, recorder, viol, violin, and similar instruments), the *correnti* of Radesca da Foggia (Venice, 1616), the dances of Marini (Venice, 1617 and 1618: for violin or cornett), the *canzoni* of Rossi (Venice, 1620), and the

---

[1] Some examples may be found in *Jacobean Consort Music* (*Musica Britannica*, ix) (London, 1955), pp. 200 ff.

[2] For instance, in Monteverdi's *Orfeo*, in the trios of Salomone Rossi and Biagio Marini, and in the suites of Coperario and his English and Polish imitators.

violin sonatas of Vivarino (Venice, 1620). Too little of this music has been reprinted for the scholar to reach firm conclusions about the way in which it developed; but from the forms alone it is possible to discern how the sonata seems to have grown out of a blend of the *canzon*, the dance and the instrumental ritornello.

In conclusion, a word or two must be said about such harmony instruments as the harp, the gittern, and the cittern. During the early decades of the sixteenth century the harp had fallen into such low esteem that it was regarded as little more than an instrument fit for jesters or for blind *improvvisatori*. But in the later years of the century it returned to fashion among connoisseurs, first of all perhaps in Spain, and its medieval outlines yielded to the neo-classic form that it has more or less retained ever since. Some idea of its solo style may be obtained from such pieces as Trabaci's *Toccata seconda . . . per l'Arpa, Partite . . . sopra . . . Zefiro . . . appropriate per l'Arpa* and *Ancidetemi pur per l'Arpa*, and Mayone's *Recercare sopra il canto fermo di Constantio Festa per sonare all'Arpa*, to be found in their keyboard books published in Naples in 1615 and 1609;[1] from the printed works of Luys Venegas de Henestrosa, Cabezón, and Coelho, published between 1557 and 1620 and stated to be suitable for keyboard or harp; from the splendid obbligato for double harp in Monteverdi's *Orfeo*, undoubtedly composed for a local virtuoso of Mantua; and from the music written for harp in consort by such Englishmen as Lawes and Porter during the 1620's and 1630's. In sharp contrast to this elaborate style is the surviving music for cittern and gittern.[2] The sudden rise to popularity of these instruments in the 1540's is as hard to explain as the somewhat later rise of the harp. To judge from the musical publications, archives, and literary references of the time, the impulse would seem to have originated in France and to have spread thence to the Low Countries, Spain, West Germany, and England.[3] Like the instruments themselves, music for cittern and gittern is unpretentious and at its best when closest to the dance and to improvisation. In the cities of Europe the upstart guitar, with its five strings and its ingenious 'alphabet' of symbols for the common chords, speedily triumphed during the first decades of the seventeenth century; but the cittern and gittern lingered on in musical backwaters for many years afterwards.

[1] See p. 642.
[2] Cf. the pieces from the Mulliner Book transcribed by Denis Stevens in *The Mulliner Book: a commentary* (London, 1952), p. 78 ff.
[3] See Dart, 'The Cittern and its English Music' *Galpin Society Journal*, i (1948), p. 46.

XIII

INSTRUMENTS
AND INSTRUMENTAL NOTATION

By GERALD HAYES

INTRODUCTORY

THROUGHOUT the Middle Ages the nature of instrumental music is revealed mainly by the record of poem, carving, and picture. Soon after the beginning of the sixteenth century a great number of instrumental texts began to appear and, with this music, instruction books (mostly for the lute) soon began to be published.[1] By the mid-century the instruments in use foreshadowed nearly all the members of the modern orchestra, though most of them were still far removed from their later forms. These are the types that lived on. But for a century and more pride of place was taken by instruments that had become obsolete curiosities by the end of the eighteenth century at latest. Viol, lute, cittern, recorder, cornett, clavichord, and harpsichord were passed by, after all their primacy of importance to performer and composer; their music was forgotten, their techniques lost, and their true nature gradually confused and distorted by historians. It is to these instruments that most of our attention must be given.

THE VIOLS

Of all the instruments that came out of the obscurity of the early Renaissance into full musical use in the sixteenth century, none has so great a value as the viol, both for its music and for its influence on musical development. Early in the sixteenth century the viol is found well established in the field of instrumentally conceived music; for two centuries this music extended its modes of expression to achievements as remarkable as those of contemporary vocal music. This was not a continuous European development, for the viol awoke to maturity in some countries only as it was set aside in others; but at last even France, which had evolved a brilliant school of violists when other peoples were beginning to forget the instrument, turned away

---

[1] Vol. III, p. 450, n. 3, and *supra*, pp. 616, 698 (Judenkünig's *Underweisung*), 704-6.

from it. This neglect was not because of any defect in the instrument or its music, but because the more facile and more powerful voice of the violin had then come to maturity and had found in a changing social world a too ready ear for its appeal.

For two hundred years men forgot that viol and violin had been the bitterest of rivals and, misled by some superficial resemblance, they fell into the fatal error of assuming that one was the ancestor of the other. From that it was a natural step to conclude that the music of the viol was but a nursery for that of the violin.

Four elements are fundamental to the character of the viol. It has six strings: this is the standard for all viols, notwithstanding that instruments with five, or with seven, strings were not uncommon at certain periods. The six strings are tuned in an invariable sequence: a fourth, a fourth, a major third, a fourth, a fourth. This gives a compass of two octaves over the open strings. When for a time departures from this are found, these are always for a specialized form of solo use and have no influence on the unchanging standard. On the fingerboard of the viol there are tied gut frets, set a semitone apart. All sizes of viols, from high-treble to double bass, are bowed in the same manner: the bow is above the hand, which is held with the palm upwards. Consequently all the viols, even the smallest, must be held downwards, resting on, or between, the knees.

Differences of outline between viol and violin are of no importance, but there are differences in structure that are radical in the two instruments. The wood of the viol is much thinner throughout than that of the violin; its strings are lighter, longer, and less tense, and the ribs, especially in the smaller forms, alto and treble, are deeper. The neck of the viol, broad to accommodate its many strings, is almost flat on the under side. From this structure comes the characteristic tone-quality of the viol, clear and resonant with a touch of reediness, lacking the volume and penetrating power of the violin, but speaking readily to the lightest touch of the bow, even upon the double-bass of the family.

A majority of viols, it is true, have sloping shoulders, C-shaped sound-holes, flat backs, and square corners at the bouts, but in any or all of these features a viol may, and sometimes does, resemble the violin without any loss of character. In the sixteenth century the body was often smooth-waisted, guitar fashion. There was, however, a general tendency to adhere to the long tail-piece: this overhangs the base of the instrument and is slotted for attachment by a hook-headed peg, glued to the body.

The sequence of intervals by which the standard tuning is formed is attested by a long line of writers extending from Agricola[1] in 1529 to Jean Rousseau[2] in 1687 and on into the eighteenth century. English authorities invariably, and those of other countries most frequently, define this tuning with the highest string of the treble viol in ♭♮ : this is found consonant with the optimum tone-quality of existing instruments. At this pitch, the varying sizes of viols should be tuned thus:

with the alternative, for what Mersenne[3] calls 'the Italian manner':

The absolute pitch of these notes varied considerably with both period and place; it will be found a safe rule for instruments to regard it as a semitone lower than the standard pitch of today, an approximation for which a comparison of organ pipes provides some justification.

[1] Martin Agricola, *Musica instrumentalis deudsch* (Wittenberg, 1529; reprinted Leipzig 1896). [2] Jean Rousseau, *Traité de la viole* (Paris, 1687).
[3] Marin Mersenne, *Harmonie universelle* (Paris, 1636–7; facsimile edition, Paris, 1963; English translation by Roger Chapman, The Hague, 1957).

While it is of no importance that some earlier authorities[1] give a pitch a whole tone lower throughout than those quoted above, the student of contemporary textbooks may well be puzzled to find that certain writers,[2] often of the same period and country, define the consort so differently that it would appear to have been used by some players a fifth lower throughout: in effect, the treble becomes the tenor and the bass the double bass. Notwithstanding searching investigations,[3] no satisfactory solution of this has yet been discovered; there are no texts of consort music set in such a low pitch.

The frets give to every note the clear sound of an open string. The structure of body, with lightness of strings, gives a ready response to the bow. A steady note is the characteristic of the viol, especially in consort music, and the close shake is appropriate only for emotional moments. These factors, and above all the results of the method of bowing, determined the whole nature of music for viols; it is this, and not mere antiquarianism, that has led to the modern insistence on the use of the correct instruments and correct technique for the interpretation of early instrumental music.

With the bow held above the supine hand, the accented stroke is forward and the impact is made near the peak of the bow where pressure is lightest: the unaccented backward stroke begins with the weightier part of the bow, near the nut. All combines to an evenness of tone. As Mersenne aptly observed, in the strokes of the viol bow everything goes 'tout au contraire' to those of the violin.

Even more conclusive than contemporary instructions,[4] is a remark by a French writer made long after the viol had been submerged in the popularity of the violin. The last surviving viol in France was a small high-treble with five strings known as the *par-dessus de viole* and in 1780 de Laborde[5] describes this instrument, with frets on its fingerboard. He adds: 'pour jouer du Par-dessus, on l'appuie droit sur ses genoux, et on tient l'archet avec la main droite renversée.'

Frets offer no impediment to perfect intonation: the pitch of a note can be adjusted when necessary in consort playing by pulling or pushing with the stopping finger. The sixteenth century was familiar with this practice.[6]

[1] e.g. Hans Gerle, *Musica teusch* (Nuremberg, 1532).

[2] e.g. compare Cerreto, *Della prattica Musica* (Naples, 1601) with Cerone, *El melopeo* (Naples, 1613).

[3] Nicolas Bessaraboff, *Ancient European Musical Instruments* (Boston, 1941) (Appendix B).   [4] e.g. Jean Rousseau, op. cit.

[5] *Essai sur la musique* (Paris, 1780).

[6] See Bottrigari, *Il desiderio* (Venice, 1594; trs. Carol MacClintock, American Institute of Musicology, 1962).

THE VIOLONE

The double-bass, or violone, lies outside the normal consort, but appears occasionally as in the set of Fantasias à 3 'with the double-bass'[1] by Orlando Gibbons. The instrument corresponds in every respect with the other viols and is proportioned throughout to a register an octave below that of the bass viol. The violone 'speaks' with such ease that a child can play it without fatigue; its equivalent in the violin family was so coarse in tone and so tiring to play that it was seldom used. In consequence, the violone survived as the foundation of the *concerto grosso* and, later, of the full orchestra, long after the other viols had been discarded. About 1800, owing to the passion for power, it began to be strengthened; it shed some of its strings and then its frets, but the old method of bowing was much slower to die. The violone is, in fact, the familiar double-bass of the modern orchestra, though the latter is no longer recognizable as the direct descendant of its aristocratic ancestor.

BOWS AND BOWING

Throughout this period the bow, for viol and violin alike, presents one unchanging feature: the tension on the hair is produced by an outward curving of the stick, for the inward camber, so familiar in modern bows, did not appear until the mid-eighteenth century. There is a technical value, especially in music for the solo viol, in the greater space between hair and stick that comes with greater tension. Although long enough to allow some 23 inches of free hair, the viol bow is very light and the spread of the hair is not much more than one-third of an inch. Weight is saved by thinning the wood as it nears the peak and also by the device of fluting the cylindrical stick.

There is no hatchet-head; the stick flows gracefully into a long peak. In early forms the hair is held to the peak by binding, but the plug was devised before the seventeenth century was well advanced. The method of holding the bow demands that the nut be deep so as to allow the necessary space between stick and hair.

Precise instructions for bowing were given in the textbooks of the period[2] and essential passages have been reproduced in modern works: these should be consulted for details. Every delicacy of phrasing and change of tone is readily possible and texts, especially

[1] See p. 586.

[2] e.g. Silvestro Ganassi, *Regola Rubertina* (two parts, Venice, 1542–3), facsimile edition (Leipzig, 1924); Christopher Simpson, *The Division Violist* (London, 1659) (facsimile edition, London, 1956); Jean Rousseau, op. cit.

those of that last great school of violists in the France of Louis XIV, abound in markings of accent and colour.

THE VIOL AS SOLO INSTRUMENT

The story of the viol as a solo instrument is, in the main, that of its music which has been discussed in an earlier chapter.[1] There are two broad divisions of this solo use; firstly, there is a wealth of very diverse music, over more than two centuries, for the normal viol alone in both treble and bass forms and of this, the 'divisions on a ground',[2] the glory of this country's seventeenth century, formed the most important aspect; secondly, there is the use of the viol, for perhaps seventy or eighty years at most, in the form known as 'lyra-way', a name that indicates a special, though variable, system of tuning.

The division-viol was a bass viol, a little smaller than the full consort bass, upon which 'divisions' of short notes between each note of the 'ground' were played, always returning to the note of the ground or to one concordant with it. The ground was played on a full-sized bass. Sometimes the divisions were played on a treble viol.

At the close of the sixteenth century a new conception of tuning of both viols and lutes came to the minds of musicians. The composer had a dual task; not only were his artistic gifts engaged, but he had the technical problem of so arranging his music that it fell to the best advantage of the hand on the finger-board, and the tablature notation enabled him to express his intentions with precision. The innovation was that, instead of adapting the music to a fixed tuning, the tuning was adapted to suit the music. Whether this was done first for the viol, or whether the lutenists showed the way is uncertain, but just at that time the violists greatly developed the use of the solo viol for contrapuntal music akin to that of the lute, and their works, in tablature, began to appear around the year 1600; they can have had no opposition of traditional usage to overcome, as lutenists had, and it is at least possible that they led the way. If they did, the lutenists quickly followed, and printed works for the newly tuned lute slightly antedate the earliest printed works for the lyra viol.

Although 'lyra-way' was applicable to any viol, this type of music was usually played on a bass, smaller than the division-viol, that became known as the lyra viol. The following are typical of a large variety of the tunings:

[1] See pp. 704 ff.
[2] This form dates at least from 1553 when Diego Ortiz published his *Tratado*.

Ex. 358

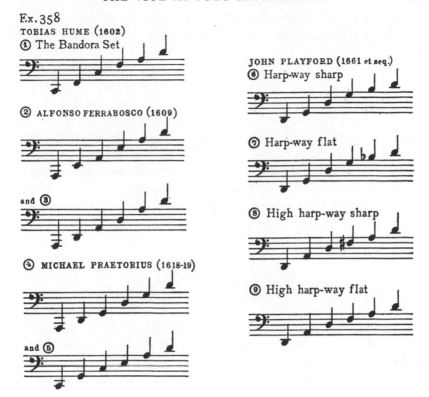

All these tunings are translated from tablature and are irrespective of pitch.

Praetorius[1] calls the viol used in this manner *viola bastarda*,[2] a name that has caused needless confusion to some writers. The early seventeenth century experimented with the effects of sympathetic wire strings inside the lyra viol,[3] but Playford remarks half a century later, 'Of this sort of Viols, I have seen many, but Time and Disuse has set them aside'.[4]

Music for the lyra viol is extremely difficult and is only for advanced violists.

THE LYRAS

In the background of this period there were several bowed instruments, at best but distant relatives of the principal figures; some were

---

[1] *Syntagma Musicum*, II (Wolfenbüttel, 1618–19), p. 47; facsimile edition, *Publikationen der Hist. Sektion des deutschen Orgelrats* (Kassel, 1929); also reprinted in *Publikationen der Gesellschaft für Musikforschung*, xiii.   [2] See p. 706.

[3] Francis Bacon, *Sylva Sylvarum* (London, 1626), Century III, no. 280.

[4] John Playford, *Musick's Recreation on the Viol, Lyra-way*, Preface to the edition of 1661.

about to leave the stage while others were only on the point of entering. None was of serious import in the development of instrumental music.

The *lira da braccio*, so shadowy in musical use, so familiar in the hands of the heavenly choirs of Renaissance art, had begun to pass out of use before 1550, but references to it as late as the early seventeenth century suggest that it lingered on; from it, the name lyra viol was undoubtedly adopted about the year 1600. The lyra had a large shallow body and was played violin-wise, held against the breast; the bridge was only slightly arched and there were three to five strings on the finger-board, with bourdon strings unstopped. Various works[1] give tunings for the lyra; that of Lanfranco may be taken as typical (the pitch is arbitrary, as he gives only the intervals):

Ex. 359

Although often depicted with frets, the evidence of writers such as Lanfranco and Bottrigari suggests that it was played without them in the sixteenth century.

About 1550 a bass lyra was evolved, with from eleven to sixteen strings; these were tuned in a large variety of ways to suit the player's needs but always with the idea that concords could be formed by stopping several strings at once with a finger laid across the frets. Some idea of the general effect of the tunings may be obtained by imagining two descending diatonic scales, pitched a fifth apart, and formed by the alternate strings. Like the small lyra, it had bourdons.[2] The French form was small enough to be held on the knees, but the more usual Italian instrument was large enough to rest on the ground.[3]

There are many references to the astonishing performances of virtuosos on this instrument, for its use was not limited to the playing of full chords in accompaniment. Madrigals were transcribed for the *lira da gamba*, as it was called,[4] and its great exponents, many of whose names have been preserved for us, performed prodigies of extemporization. As late as 1639, the great French violist André

---

[1] e.g. Giovanni Maria Lanfranco, *Scintille di Musica* (Brescia, 1533); Pedro Cerone *El Melopeo* (Naples, 1613); Michael Praetorius, *Syntagma Musicum*, II.
[2] See especially Cerreto, op. cit., for details of this instrument.
[3] Mersenne, op. cit.
[4] Also *archiviola da lira* and *lirone*.

PLATE IV

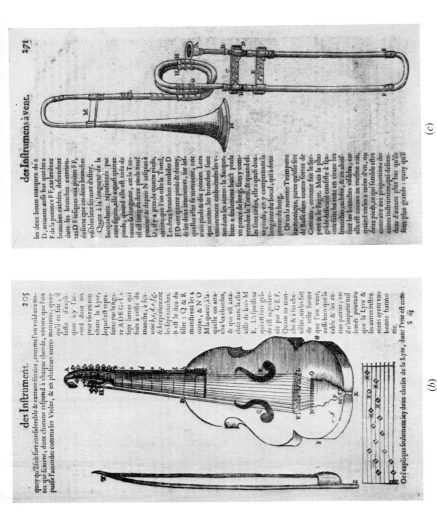

INSTRUMENTS FROM MERSENNE: *HARMONIE UNIVERSELLE* (Paris, 1636)

(*a*) Spinet. (*b*) Bass Lyra. (*c*) Sackbut

Maugars heard it played with remarkable effect in Rome[1], and Mersenne's contemporary, Le Bailly, who specialized on this instrument, was known as 'l'Orphée de France'.

THE TROMBA MARINA

The *tromba marina*, marine trumpet or *Trumscheit* had been fully developed in the fifteenth century and although it had only the smallest place in the musical life of the following three hundred years, it was vigorous enough in this background sphere. Yet how it changed from the small *Trumscheit* that Hans Memling's angel at Antwerp holds with one hand so confidently above her head! It became a seven-foot instrument only to be played resting on the ground or against a wall. Later, the long triangular body was filled with sympathetic strings that gave an echo by which Mr. Pepys was greatly puzzled.[2] The long single string, 'of beast's gutts . . . the thickness of a two-peny cord',[3] required a ratchet-wheel to hold it in tension, but the strange trembling bridge was unchanged and the string was touched by the thumb, as before, between bow and bridge to produce harmonics. When adjusted to the one suitable position—no easy task—this bridge produces from the body sounds that are so similar in their ringing clarity to those of the true trumpet that they must be heard to be believed.

REBEC, HURDY-GURDY, AND CRWTH

From the fecundity of the Middle Ages, a few other bowed instruments strayed into this period with varying fortunes; none was of direct musical importance and all may be dismissed with a brief mention.

The rebec, once so familiar to celestial musicians in fourteenth- and fifteenth-century art, fell from its high estate and passed almost from sight in the later sixteenth century, though doubtless it long maintained an active life in the countryside. Many references in contemporary literature show that its name, at least, was not forgotten, and Shakespeare's rustic player in *Romeo and Juliet* was aptly named Hugh Rebeck. From its half-pear-shaped body came a penetrating brilliance, a product of its tense strings and the highly arched bridge on a sound-board lacking the qualifying presence of sound-post and flat back. The three strings had an age-long tradition of tuning by

[1] Ernest Thoinan, *Maugars . . . son biographie . . .* (Paris, 1865; facsimile reprint, London, 1965).   [2] *Diary*, 24 October 1667.
[3] Brit. Mus., Harl. 2034, fo. 209.

fifths. For those occasions when celebration and merriment demanded sharply accentuated music, a new voice, more flexible and more appealing, was found in the violin and the ancient rebec was set aside.

The two-man organistrum that emerged at the end of the Dark Ages developed into the hurdy-gurdy, symphony, or *vielle àroue* and, like the rebec, may be seen in the hands of angels in Renaissance art. It is a true member of the family of bowed instruments, though the bow is of infinite length: the strings are brought into contact with the circumference of a turning wheel. It lived through the seventeenth century though we know nothing of its musical use during that period; it bloomed into a vigorous and aristocratic life in the France of Louis XV.

Of the crowd, perhaps the oldest of all European bowed instruments, only the name remained and was sometimes applied to any small bowed instrument; yet we know that this bowed descendant of the old north European plucked chrotta or rote lived on at least in Wales and, under the name *crwth*, it was found there in not uncommon use in the eighteenth century.

THE VIOLIN FAMILY

It was not until the first quarter of the sixteenth century was well advanced that anything indicates the existence of such an instrument as the violin; the first clear reference to it seems to be Agricola's description of his third type of 'small *Geigen*' in 1529.[1] Lanfranco's *Violetta da Arco senza tasti* or *Violetta da Braccio e da Arco* (1533)[2] are also almost certainly violins: but Philibert Jambe de Fer gave the earliest decisive picture of the new instrument in relation to the long established viols: 'On appelle violes celles des quelles les gentilhommes, marchands et autres gens de vertu passent leur temps. Le violin est celui duquel on use en danserie communement . . .'[3], and records show that when Henry II visited Lyons in 1548 *violons* were engaged for the open-air celebrations but were never used for the serious music within the buildings.

The earlier writers give three strings tuned a fifth apart; but most of the authorities towards the end of the century[4] allow four strings. The result is the same throughout, even as late as Praetorius:[5]

---

[1] Op. cit. The edition of 1545 considerably expands the description and calls them 'Polish'.
[2] Op. cit. (1533). Ganassi, op. cit., gives a very similar account.
[3] *Epitome musical de tons*, &c. (Lyons, 1556).
[4] e.g. Zacconi, *Prattica di Musica* (Venice, 1592).
[5] Except for the bass, which Praetorius, in advance of his time, sets one tone higher.

Ex.360

and later writers add another instrument called *rebecchino, rebequin, fidicula,* or *violino* that is tuned:

Ex.361

This, of course, is the violin as we know it.

The body of a treble viol corresponds roughly in size to that of an alto violin (our 'viola'). It seems highly probable that the new family of violins reflected the dominant family of viols, from which it became distinguished by the epithet *da braccio* (of the arm), while the older instrument was *da gamba* (of the leg). After the family became fixed, possibly quite early, it may have been found that a higher voice was peculiarly suited to this structure; we do not know what happened, or when, or where. It is clear that something led to the exclusion of our 'violin' from the family tree, and our alto continued to be regarded as the soprano voice of the family. Thus, when Monteverdi bestowed respectability on the violin family with its inclusion in the score of *Orfeo,* his *soprano de viola da braccio* is our alto, while his *violino ordinario da braccio* is our modern violin. 'Ordinario' is probably a direction not to confuse this with the *violino piccolo alla francese* which was also scored for in *Orfeo* and which, as Praetorius confirms, was tuned a fourth higher than the *violino*. It may be mentioned, in passing, that this 'little descant' was not the highest pitched member of the family; Praetorius shows that the kit or pochette was well established in his day.

Of the shape of the violin family in the sixteenth century we know very little, except that in the few representations in which it appears with certainty the form differs noticeably from the later standard pattern.[1] There is an archaic instrument in the Vienna collection that seems to belong to the early part of the century;[2] the body is not unlike that of what is probably the earliest appearance of a *viola da braccio* in a painting;[3] this is the only example with any claim to authenticity until the last years of the century. Coutagne, it is true, gave a dubious acceptance of 'deux ou trois instruments de Gaspar da Salo' in his sweeping condemnations,[4] but over half a century later we feel grave doubts even of these, as the design looks so suspiciously final for their alleged dates, and the size is usually so small; they are more probably the work of his immediate successors. It is quite uncertain how late was the addition to the *viola da braccio* family of that sopranino voice, the *violino*, that we know as the violin. Around the year 1600 the *viola da braccio* was also called the *violetta*.[5] Late in the seventeenth century the name *viola da braccio* became restricted to the alto instrument, with *violetta* as a synonym: and from it comes the English 'viola' and the German *Bratsche* for the alto violin.

The familiar form of the violin became defined at some uncertain period towards the end of the sixteenth century; although we suspect the instruments attributed to him, Gasparo da Salò of Brescia (d. 1609) may have been responsible for the design, as tradition tells. Most of the work of the first two generations of the Cremonese Amatis—Andrea (d. *c.* 1611) and his sons Antonio (d. *c.* 1640) and Geronimo (d. 1630)—was completed by the end of the first third of the seventeenth century. But changes that began in the late eighteenth century resulted in important differences between our modern instruments and those of earlier times. First, the bridge became higher and more arched; this required that the end of the finger-board should be raised, with the consequence that the neck had to be thrown back. As a result of the altered angles a larger component of the tension bore vertically on the belly, and the subsequent rise in the generally used pitch increased this pressure. The neck was slightly lengthened,

---

[1] See, e.g., the Duiffoprugcar portrait by Woeiriot of 1562. Henri Coutagne has confused the violin with the viol in his analysis of this engraving in *Gaspard Duiffopraucart et les luthiers lyonnais du XVIe siècle* (Paris, 1893).

[2] Julius Schlosser, *Die Sammlung alter Musikinstrumenten im Kunsthistorischen Museum* (Vienna, 1920).

[3] By Gaudenzio Ferrari (d. 1546). It is played by one of the *putti* in the Accademia Carrara at Bergamo.

[4] Coutagne, op. cit.

[5] e.g. by Cerone, op. cit.

and notwithstanding a use of thinner strings throughout, the old bass bars were insufficient to reinforce the bellies against the pressure on them; in all old violins the bass bars had to be replaced. Violins bearing the most honoured names of the seventeenth century have been modified greatly since they left their makers' hands.

Until the mid-eighteenth century the violin bow was similar to that already described for the viols, though a little shorter. Such a bow, light yet firm, is helpful in playing rapid detached notes and staccato effects, and in phrasing: added to the flatter bridge, it makes the performance of contrapuntal music for the violin much more natural than with the modern instrument and bow.

THE LUTE

Like the viol, the lute came to maturity long before the beginning of the sixteenth century; there had been a very close affinity between the two families and in Spain the viol form of body was retained for the plucked instrument, while that with the more familiar 'half-pear' body was regarded as a stranger, the *vihuela de Flandres*. However, outside the Iberian Peninsula the lute maintained its traditional shape.

The tuning, irrespective of pitch which varied with the size of instrument, was identical with that of the viol; the normal lute for solo music was tuned approximately to:

Ex.362

A seventh string, tuned one tone below the bass string, appeared in Virdung's time (1511) and later in the century it became a standard part of the lute used by Dowland and his contemporaries.

The rounded body of the lute is built of strips of wafer-thinness; the flat table, of straight-grained pine, is also very thin and the whole body of even a large lute is so light that it can be balanced upon one finger. The late sixteenth century tended to increase the number of strips of which the body was built, but the high esteem in which the craftsmanship of earlier makers was held found practical evidence in the high prices paid in the seventeenth century for lutes by makers such as the Tyrolese Laux Maler who had flourished 150 years before.

In common with nearly all plucked instruments, other than those of the harp type, each string of the lute was double and was known as a 'rank' or 'course'. In the lower pairs the strings were usually an octave apart, though the higher pairs were invariably in unison. Sometimes and especially in England around the year 1600, the pairs were in unison throughout;[1] John Dowland expressed his decided preference for this method,[2] but the octave tuning of the lower ranks persisted into the eighteenth century and Mace[3] shows that the Elizabethans' unisons did not prevail for long in England. Doubtless the original intention was to brighten the tone-colour of the heavy gut string, but it made an extra demand on an already severe technique to produce the sound of the deeper note in contrapuntal music and its purpose passed with the invention of gimping, that is to say, of coated strings, in the latter half of the seventeenth century.

The strings lie close to the table and are attached to a string holder glued on to it; they pass over a finger-board that follows the plane of the table, on a neck broad and thin, to a rectangular peg-box that falls from the neck almost at a right angle. On the neck are tied gut frets similar to those on a viol. To enable the delicate table to withstand the tension of the strings a number of small bars, of varying length, are glued to its underside at right angles to the longer axis: on the placing and size of these bars, the sound quality of each instrument greatly depends. Under the strings, and in a position between the neck and the plucking area, is a circular sound-hole, carved with fine tracery out of the wood of the table; interlacing geometrical patterns of great beauty display the taste and skill of the craftsman. This is the lute for which all the music of its classical period was written, before the changes of the early seventeenth century overtook it.

Shortly before 1600 the traditional tuning of the lute was modified and after a period of conservative resistance it was abandoned altogether in favour of a considerable variety of tunings from which the composer selected that which offered the best fingering for each piece. The lute itself became changed by the addition of bass pairs of strings until twelve ranks or courses replaced the older seven as the standard. These basses were accommodated in different ways: in what became so popular under the name of 'the French lute', the rectangular peg-box was displaced by one somewhat akin to that of

---

[1] Thomas Robinson, *The Schoole of Musicke* (London, 1603).
[2] Robert Dowland, *A Varietie of Lute Lessons* (London, 1610).
[3] Thomas Mace, *Musick's Monument* (London, 1676).

the viol, from which sprang a second, and even a third, peg-box to carry the basses. As the basses below the seventh rank were always played open, they had no need to lie on the finger-board and the device of the extra peg-box not only carried them aside from the neck but also gave them an added length. But the old lute was not discarded; many of the finest lutes of the seventeenth century and even later retain the former type of peg-box with all the ranks of strings lying over a broad finger-board. There is a tendency in these late lutes for the finger-board to acquire a slight rounding.

Something of the purpose of these new tunings has been said in connexion with the lyra viol. A few typical examples of the lute tunings are:

Ex.363
(i) CHANCY[1]

(ii) PIERRE GAULTIER[2]

(iii) RICHARD MATHEW[3]

(iv) JOHN ROGERS[4]

[1] Quoted by Mersenne, op. cit.
[2] *Œuvres de Pierre Gaultier, Orléanais* (Rome, 1638).
[3] *The Lute's Apology for her Excellence* (London, 1652).
[4] *An Essay to the Advancement of Musick* (London, 1672).

These are, of course, irrespective of actual pitch as they are invariably given in tablature. But as the century advanced, the original purpose of variety seemed forgotten and two tunings only survived in an unequal struggle for existence: notwithstanding Mace's enthusiastic support for the 'French Flat Tuning'[1] (Ex. 363, i) it gave way to the so-called 'new' tuning (Ex. 363, iii), which survived as the tuning in which nearly all lute music was written.[2]

Beside all these changes, made desirable by the complexity and brilliance of the lute's music, the old lute lived on; but it was relegated to the sole business of accompaniment. The early tuning was retained, though the extra bass strings were present, and the body became larger to give fullness of tone: in this state it acquired the names of *liuto attiorbato*, *tiorba*, or theorbo, for which no satisfactory explanation has been forthcoming. With the French type of double peg-box, it was also known as the arch-lute. One result of its increased size was a length of string that forbade the highest string to be strained to its proper pitch and it had to be tuned an octave lower; sometimes, even, the second rank was also tuned to its lower octave. Despite the obvious complication thus caused, complex accompaniments were played on such instruments at sight from figured-bass parts.

In the search for deeper volume, the lute acquired one strange form in the late sixteenth century; beyond the peg-box carrying the usual stopped ranks of strings, the neck was extended for several feet to a second peg-box for the bass strings, which had to be of wire on so great a length. This was the *chitarrone*, sometimes miscalled the arch-lute. Its body, unlike that of the theorbo, was usually of normal lute size but it was similar to the theorbo in retaining the old tuning.

The *chitarrone* has a certain amount of serious music of its own and it lived, chiefly for accompaniment, until the middle of the eighteenth century.

VIHUELA AND GUITAR

The Spanish *vihuela*, for which a great quantity of important music exists,[3] was in reality identical with the lute save in its body, which maintained the guitar-like shape of early viols with a flat, or slightly rounded, back. Strictly it should be called the *vihuela da mano* to distinguish it from the bowed viol or *vihuela da arco*. With five

---

[1] Op. cit.
[2] Cf. Ernst Gottlieb Baron, *Untersuchung des Instrumentes der Lauten* (Nuremberg, 1727).
[3] See pp. 682 ff.

ranks only it became the familiar guitar, while a smaller form, with only three ranks, was called *bandurria* and was popular for lighter music.

The guitar has suffered a process of coarsening during the past 150 years; until after the middle of the eighteenth century it retained its lightness of structure and was strung with ranks of double gut strings which were carried to a flat peg-head into which the pegs entered from beneath. The waist was slight and the carved rose of the sound-hole was even more elaborate than that of the lute. Its tone-colour was far nearer to that of the lute than is that of its modern descendant.

There is an immense body of music for the guitar, often of great technical difficulty, and it has two forms: some follows the contra-puntal manner of the lute, but much of it is in a brilliant and vigorous style of batteries of chords.

THE CITTERN FAMILY

The cittern (*cithren, citharen, cetula, citole, sittron, cistre, cetra*) came into the sixteenth century with a long and honourable history through the Middle Ages.[1] So far as it is possible, or even desirable, to assign origins, it seems to have been of purely European descent. From the cittern came a family of other wire-strung instruments, some of which played a prominent part in the half century centred on 1600.

The characteristics of the cittern are a flat back to an almost circular body, four ranks of double wire strings and curious tuning:

Ex. 364

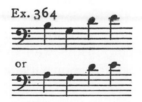

or

The first of these is associated more with England,[2] Italy, and Germany, the second more with France.[3] Two additional strings are recorded as early as 1533:[4]

---

[1] See Vol. III, pp. 467–8.
[2] Anthony Holborne, *The Cittharne School* (London, 1597).
[3] Mersenne, op. cit.
[4] Lanfranco, op. cit.

Ex. 365

and later in the century large citterns with as many as fourteen ranks of strings became popular, though the original instrument continued in unchanged use. The frets are always made with metal strips let into the finger-board.

English tutors for the cittern, from Elizabethan times to Playford's book of 1666, are unanimous that it should be sounded with the finger, though there is abundant evidence that a plectrum was widely used on the Continent. The tone, when half-plucked and half-stroked by the side (and not the point) of the finger is singularly sweet, and free from that tinny jangle so hard to avoid with a plectrum. The circular outline sustained much modification in the hands of craftsmen who delighted to show their skill in flourished corners, as well as in elaborate ornament for the head and neck. In a form known as the Hamburg cittern the body became almost triangular, though fully rounded at the corners.

If a reference to *bandores* among the instruments used in the interludes to Gascoigne's play *Jocasta*, when it was produced in 1566, really indicates the bandora, then that instrument must be the eldest of the cittern's children; specimens are extant dated from 1580 onwards. It is attributed to England by Praetorius, and Pepys refers to it as something quite familiar in 1662, so that it may claim at least a century of active life. The bandora was a bass instrument and is familiar in music titles as a substitute instrument, as in Martin Peerson's *Mottects* (London, 1630): 'with an Organ Part, which for want of Organs may be performed on Virginals, Base-Lute, Bandora or Irish Harp'.

The bandora is no more than a large cittern with six ranks of double wire strings tuned to intervals represented by:

Ex. 366

with similar variations in the lowest string.

The 'stately Orpharion', as William Barley[1] aptly names it, was the most elegant offspring of the cittern. The body was slightly smaller than that of the bandora and with a length greater than the width; it usually departs from the simplicity of the cittern's outline into waves and corners. The purpose of the orpharion was to provide an inexpensive substitute for the lute, but this gave a possibility of new tone-colour to lute music. The tuning of its six ranks of double wire strings followed exactly the standard of viol and lute.

The orpharion had one freak feature: the string holder was set aslant, no doubt to give extra length to the bass ranks, and this meant that all the frets fixed in the finger-board had also to be set aslant. Like the bandora, it figures as a substitute instrument, usually for the lute, in music titles, but it has some music of its own.

The *penorcon*, smaller than the orpharion, is described and pictured by Praetorius[2] but has no other existence. The *orphion*, another variant, is recorded as a name. The *stump* can boast at least one piece of music,[3] from which it is inferred that it had nine bass ranks below the ordinary six, though of its form we are quite ignorant. Playford attributes the invention of both the *stump* and the *polyphant* to Daniel Farrant; elsewhere he records that Queen Elizabeth 'did often re-create her self on an Excellent Instrument called the Poliphant, not much unlike a Lute, but strung with Wire'.[4] But the drawing of the polyphant given in Randle Holmes's *Academy of Armory* suggests a flat bandora-body surmounted by a harp-like frame. Many other references, some with descriptions, convince us that this vanished instrument had an existence by no means negligible.

THE HARP

Harps had acquired a full chromatic compass before the six-teenth century, but these treble-strung instruments, covering four octaves with some eighty strings, were for experts and great occasions. A smaller harp that could be set upon the knee was more common in household music; this had from twenty-five to thirty strings tuned to a diatonic scale, with some additional semitones. But there was no rigid limitation to these sizes, and intermediate forms were made. The diatonic harp was not so restricted as might appear; skilled players could vary the pitch, to produce chromatics, by pressing the strings against the cross-bar with the free hand.

[1] *A new Booke of Tabliture* . . . (London, 1596). See p. 200, n. 5.
[2] Op. cit. [3] Oxford, Ch. Ch. 532.
[4] *An Introduction to the Skill of Musick* (London, edition of 1674).

In the treble-strung harp, the semitones were given by the middle strings; the two outer banks of strings were in unison. On the Continent the sixteenth century produced a large 'double-harp' to achieve the same full chromatic compass; this had two banks of strings with the semitones in consecutive order:

Ex. 367

Praetorius[1] indicates a sound-box between the two banks of strings. To the contemporary mind, the principal distinction among harps was that between the gut-strung and the wire-strung, or Irish, instruments; the seventeenth century preferred the tone-colour of the latter, though good players were becoming rare in Evelyn's day. Some title-pages specify the Irish harp as a substitute for the bandora and theorbo, and Bacon remarks upon its satisfactory consonance with the viols.[2]

Apart from its use in the mixed consort, and for accompaniment, the harp was adequate to interpret the music of many other instruments: 'Quant aux pieces qui se iouent sur la Harpe, elles ne sont point differentes de celles qui se iouent sure le Luth et sure l'Epinette';[3] but a certain amount of music composed specially for the harp exists.

The various mechanical devices for altering the tuning did not emerge until the opening of the eighteenth century.

TYPES OF ORGAN

The basic improvements, from which came the perfected organ of the 'classical' period, had all been devised by 1500 and only refinements resulting from experience, opportunity, and craftsmanship, remained for the sixteenth century to achieve.

The first great step was the introduction of the small portative organ and the almost equally small but stationary 'positive' organ at the end of the thirteenth century or beginning of the fourteenth,[4] instruments which had keyboards that lay comfortably under the hand. The church organ proper remained a cumbersome affair even

---

[1] Op. cit.   [2] Op. cit.
[3] Mersenne, op. cit.   [4] See Vol. III, p. 487.

in the early fifteenth century and the keys were still so large, owing to the wind pressure, that they required a fist action.[1] The keys for the semitones were separate from the diatonic keys. At first the smaller positive organ was used in the church quite apart from the large organ, but during the fifteenth century makers began to incorporate it in the main organ, thus giving the 'great' organ and the 'choir' organ in one instrument. The keyboard of the 'great' organ was much improved and began to resemble the ordinary fingered keyboard. An engraving in a book published in 1492 shows a player at an organ with a keyboard very like that of a harpsichord[2]; and in an organ made in 1499 by Heinrich Cranz at Brunswick the keyboard had seven keys within the space occupied by eight today and had its semitones on the same keyboard.[3] By the early sixteenth century the keyboard of the great organ had been made as convenient as that of the choir organ.

ORGAN PEDALS

The date of the introduction of the pedals on the organ cannot be ascertained with any certainty, but they had appeared before the end of the fifteenth century. For example, Praetorius[4] gives a very thorough description, with pictures of details, of the great Halberstadt organ (finished in 1361) that was still in use in his day, and this included a full pedal keyboard added in 1495. Rimbault[5] quotes the case of an old organ at Beeskow, near Frankfurt am Oder, in which the date 1418 was found engraved on two large pipes that, from their measurements, he concluded must have been pedal pipes; unfortunately, this is hardly precise enough evidence to satisfy modern requirements. There are various unsupported traditions attributing to individuals the honour of inventing the pedals and it is interesting to observe that most of them relate to workers in the last third of the fifteenth century.

What is remarkable is the fate of pedals in other countries. While they became a normal part of all important organs in Germany, pedals were also in use in Italy, as a dialogue of the mid-sixteenth

[1] See Praetorius, op. cit. 'Schiagraphia', for pictures of keyboards of old organs still in use in his day.

[2] Franchinus Gafurius, *Theorica Musice* (Milan, 1492): reproduced in *Grove's Dictionary of Music and Musicians* (5th ed., London, 1954), vi, p. 292, and elsewhere. Although the keys look wide in the engraving, the player is quite clearly fingering them.

[3] C. F. Abdy Williams, *The Story of the Organ* (London, 1903), p. 53.

[4] Op. cit., p. 181; 'Schiagraphia', pls. xxiv and xxv. There are many passing references, e.g. pp. 97, '107' (for 103), 105, &c.

[5] Op. cit., p. 42; see also W. L. Sumner, *The Organ* (London, 1952), p. 70.

century shows; Fronimo has been discussing, somewhat sarcastically, the contemporary additions to the lute which, he says, will soon require a hand as large as that of Artaxerxes:

Eumatio: Dite per fede vostra quello rispose.
Fronimo: Mi disse esser si ritrouate, per hauere nel Liuto come nell organo, il pedale.
Eumatio: Ha, ha, ha![1]

Yet pedals do not seem to have been used on French organs until the mid-seventeenth century and it was long believed that in England they were introduced only about the middle of the eighteenth century.[2]

During the sixteenth century couplers came into general use, and a less creditable invention of that period was the tremulant. The motive power in the organ proved irresistible to the inventiveness of the times and many references attest the exuberant embellishments with which the serious organist had to contend. The following description, given by a traveller in obviously unqualified admiration, indicates what was going on: 'In the Churche of saint Andreus at Burdiouse [Bordeaux] is the fairist and gretest player of Orgyns in al Crystendome, in the whyche Orgins be many instruments and vyces, as Giants heds and sterres, the whych doth moue and wagge with their jawes and eyes as fast as the player playeth.'[3]

One problem that faced the organ builder was the escape from the wolf notes that came in certain places by tuning in just temperament; the worst of these notes were avoided by the provision of separate keys for $d\sharp$ and $e\flat$ and for $g\sharp$ and $a\flat$. Mersenne, who devotes the whole of his sixth book to the organ, shows several diagrams of keyboards designed to give far more elaborate intervals, but these seem largely theoretical.[4] The practice of painting the letter of the note on the keys had persisted from the tenth century even after its practical purpose had been passed by; from this the German system of alphabetical notation for the organ developed in the early fifteenth century (see p. 780). Although staff notation for the organ was used in Germany before the end of that century, German organists for the

---

[1] Vincenzo Galilei, *Il Fronimo* (Venice, 2nd ed. 1584), p. 104.

[2] Yet Praetorius seems to have assumed that pedals were used in England in his day: op. cit., p. 96. And see Benjamin G. Maslen, 'The Earliest English Organ Pedals', *Musical Times*, ci (1960), p. 578, and the subsequent correspondence, which suggest that English organs had pedals in the sixteenth century but not for many years after the Restoration. —Ed.

[3] Andrew Borde, *The Fyrst Boke of the Introduction of Knowledge* (London, 1548), cap. xxxvii.

[4] Op. cit., Livre Sixiesme, Props. xxii and xxiii.

most part clung to the alphabetical or partly alphabetical notation well into the seventeenth century, long after the music had become both rapid and complex.[1]

PITCH

We are fortunate in possessing an early work on organ construction by an outstanding expert of his day. This is Arnolt Schlick's *Spiegel der Orgelmacher und Organisten* which was published at Heidelberg in 1511; Ornithoparcus called the author 'musicus consummatissimus ac Palatini Principis organiste probatissimus'. The book is a rich mine of practical information.[2] The writer bitterly reproves those who made organ cases with moving figures that caused the congregation alarm or laughter, so the Bordeaux organ mentioned above must have had predecessors. But Schlick gives us one quite priceless piece of knowledge; he has been discussing the question of the pitch of the organ, which, he says, must be one that best suits priests as well as choirs, and he gives an engraved line on the page that is one-sixteenth of the length of the 'eight-foot' pipe to give the note F. From this, Ellis computed that the pitch of Arnolt Schlick's organ would be $a' = 377$ vibrations per second.[3] This is a low pitch compared with the modern standard of $a' = 439$ but it is consistent with Praetorius's statement[4] that pitch had risen steadily before his day until it had reached a stage in Italy, and to a lesser degree in England, at which stringed instruments were endangered, and a reaction had set in.

The whole question of the many different pitches in use is far too complex for full treatment here, but a brief reference is essential to the understanding not only of the organs of that period but of all instrumental usage. Even recent standard works of reference are misleading on the relations between the pitches, largely through a failure to recognize the important fact that the meaning of names was different in different periods. The second chapter in Praetorius, to which

---

[1] e.g. Berlin, Deutsche Bibl. Mus. MS. 40147, fo. 108J.

[2] The text, edited by Robert Eitner, appeared in *Monatshefte für Musikgeschichte*, i (1869), and an important study of the book by Raymund Schlecht, ibid. ii (1870), p. 165. A version of the text in modern German was published by Ernst Flade (Mainz, 1932) and the original text (with facsimile) was reprinted by Paul Smets (Mainz, 1937).

[3] Alexander J. Ellis, *The History of Musical Pitch* (London, 1880), p. 371, the *locus classicus* on the subject. But A. J. Hipkins, *Encyclopaedia Britannica* (11th ed.), xxi, p. 660 ('Pitch, Musical') augments and in some cases amends Ellis's results. The question of early pitches has been re-examined by Arthur Mendel, 'Pitch in the 16th and Early 17th Centuries, *Musical Quarterly*, xxxiv (1948), pp. 28–45, 199–221, 336–57, 575–93.

[4] Op. cit., pp. 14 ff.

reference has just been made, is a valuable contribution to our knowledge of pitch in his day; after saying that he considers *Cammerton* (chamber tone) the most suitable for general instrumental work, he adds, '*Der Chor-Thon, aber welcher umb einen ganzen thon tieffer ist, wird allein in den Kirchen gebraucht*' (the *Chorton*, which is about a full tone lower, is used only in churches). Hence his *Chorton* was lower than the *Cammerton*: but even in his day, he says, some used the words the other way round, and by the end of the century the reversal was fully established.

Later, other pitches were used for special purposes, such as *Cornett-Ton*, a minor third above *Cammerton* (when defined as a whole tone *below Chorton*) and Lower *Cammerton*, a semitone below that *Cammerton*. But the former (*Cornett-Ton*) corresponds to a high pitch mentioned by Schlick as necessary for very large organs, and Lower *Cammerton* corresponds to an unnamed pitch on which Praetorius lays stress[1] as being a minor third below *his Cammerton* and which, he says, had been used before his day in England and the Netherlands for keyboard instruments.

Of the forty-four organs that Praetorius describes in detail only five have a 32-foot pipe; the remainder have 16-foot as the longest pipe, though in half a dozen cases the pipe sizes are either omitted or are very incomplete.[2] The best way to describe a typical organ of the end of the sixteenth century is to quote one of the forty-odd elaborate descriptions of German organs that make the fifth section of Praetorius's second volume such a treasure to us; as an example, the organ of the church of St. Lambert in Lüneburg, with its sixty stops and three manuals, is selected as typifying the organ built at the focal point of our period.[3]

Mittel oder Gross Werck: zum Mitlern Clavier
(Great Organ: Middle Keyboard)

1. Principal	16'	5. Querpfeiff	8'	10. Octava	2'
2. Gedact	16'	6. Octava	4'	11. Russpfeiff	
3. Octava	8'	7. Spillpfeiff	4'	12. Zimbel	
4. Jula, oder Spitzflöit	8'	8. Flöite	4'	13. Mixtur	
		9. Spitz Quinta	3'		

[1] Op. cit., p. 14.

[2] The 'foot' of Praetorius is the Brunswick foot, equivalent to 285·36 mm. (11·23 in.).

[3] Michael Praetorius, *Syntagma Musicum*, II, p. 233. More than half this volume is devoted to the organ and the third and fourth sections are full of invaluable information. For specifications of other organs of this period (German, Spanish, Italian, &c.), see Sumner, op. cit., pp. 353–6, and Gotthold Frotscher, *Geschichte des Orgelspiels*, i (Berlin, 1935), pp. 321 ff.

Ober Werk: zum Obern Clavier
(Upper Organ: Upper Keyboard)

14. Principal	8′	19. Gedact	2′	24. Trummet	8′
15. Hellpfeiff	8′	20. Gemshorn	1′	25. Regal	8′
16. Querpfeiff	5½′	21. Waldflöitlin	1′	26. Krumbhorn	8′
17. Quintflöit	3′	22. Feldpfeiff	½′	27. Zinck halbirt	8′
18. Nasat	3′	23. Zimbel			

Rückpositieff
(Choir Organ)

28. Principal	8′	33. Quintflöit	3′	38. Scharp
29. Quintadehna	8′	34. Octava	2′	39. Mixtur
30. Gedact	8′	35. Sedetzen Quint	1½′	40. Regal
31. Blockflöit	4′	36. Seiflöit	1′	41. Schalmey
32. Holflöit	4′	37. Repetirend Zimbel		42. Baarpfeiff

Pedal—Basse

43. Principal = Bass	16′	52. Rauschpfeiff		
44. Untersatz	16′	53. Zimbel		
45. Octava	8′	54. Mixtur		
46. Gedact	8′	55. Posaunen	16′
47. Super-Octava	4′	56. Krumhorn	16′
48. Nachthorn	4′	57. Trommetten	8′
49. Spitz-Quint	3′	58. Schalmey	4′
50. Gemshorn	2′	59. Cornet	2′
51. Bawr Flöit	1′		

Tremulant

1. ⎫
2. ⎬ Ventiël zum ⎰ Oberwerck
3. ⎭ ⎱ Mittelwerck
Pedael

1. Coppel zu beyden Manualen (Coupler—the two manuals)
2. Coppel/Pedal zū Rückpositiff (Coupler—Pedal to choir organ)

The various names of the stops will be recognizable by, even when not familiar to, organists and it would take far too much space to describe them here; the uninitiated can find descriptions in standard works of reference.[1]

POSITIVE AND REGALS

The 'positive' was often made in a completely enclosed case for use in the household as a chamber organ;[2] it had five or six stops and the pure and sweet tone formed an ideal background for stringed

[1] e.g. Curt Sachs, *Real-Lexikon der Musikinstrumente* (Berlin, 1913), and Christhard Mahrenholz, *Die Orgelregister* (Kassel, 1928). No. 38, *Scharp*, is more readily found as *Scharf* (Ger.) or *Scherp* (Dutch). They are all described in detail by Praetorius, op. cit., pp. 126 ff.   [2] Mace describes and illustrates a typical example, op. cit., pp. 242–5.

instruments. In the seventeenth century, consorts of viols 'to the organ' are only less numerous than the consorts for viols alone, 'And *These Things* were *Performed*, upon so many *Equal, and Truly-Sciz'd Viols, . . . The Organ Evenly, Softly, and Sweetly Acchording to All.'[1]

In the fifteenth century, a small positive was sometimes built into the same case as a harpsichord, thus creating that hybrid instrument known as the claviorganum which had over two centuries of life.[2]

Reed stops were introduced in the second half of the fifteenth century and very soon[3] a small transportable organ was developed consisting of pipes only; this was called the 'regals' and became popular for home use. The reed is of the single-beating type and so the regals bears no resemblance to the harmonium of the nineteenth century, which had free reeds. When the pipes have sufficient length the tone of the regals is pleasant, but very small sizes, such as the folding book type (Bible regals), are not attractive to hear.

THE CLAVICHORD

The clavichord (in Romance languages, *manichord*) is one of the most simple in construction of keyboard instruments, yet perhaps the most difficult to play. Its invention dates back to the fourteenth century[4] and the only development in later times was the multiplication of the number of strings. By the sixteenth century the clavichord was as fully equipped as the virginals, with a compass of about four and a half octaves. For that compass only four octaves of keys were required, as the lowest eight keys did duty for more than an octave compass by the omission of some semitones rarely used in that register. This 'short octave' was frequently retained for small keyboard instruments into the eighteenth century.

VIRGINALS

The virginals[5] came into full flower in the sixteenth century. Early in Henry VIII's reign we hear of an Italian finding great favour at Court through his performance on a clavicembalo that he had brought from Venice; another followed him, but with results so much less fortunate that he hanged himself. This long, wing-shaped instrument had appeared early in the century, but the rectangular and pentagonal 'table' virginals continued in popularity in both small and large sizes.

---

[1] Mace, op. cit., p. 234. A number of fantasies and dances for strings and organ by Coperario are printed in *Musica Britannica*, ix (London, 1955), pp. 174–91.

[2] A claviorganum, made in 1712 for the future George I, is in the Metropolitan Museum, New York.   [3] It was familiar to Virdung in 1511.

[4] See Vol. III, pp. 420, n. 3, and 483.   [5] See Vol. III, pp. 484–5.

The Antwerp family of Ruckers, whose famous instruments cover a century from about 1550, are credited with the introduction of the double manual about the end of the sixteenth century, but the description of an instrument in Henry VIII's collection[1] seems to antedate this by fifty years. These manuals were probably tuned a fourth apart in pitch at first,[2] but in the next century the lower keyboard was raised to the same pitch as the upper. The two keyboards, now aided by stops to give variation of tonal effects, extended the resources of the instrument, but the full development of the harpsichord in range of colour belongs to the eighteenth century.

By greatly reducing the size of the wing-shaped harpsichord and omitting all the means of varying tone, the mid-seventeenth century produced the spinet, which was, in essence, merely a return to the simpler virginals of a hundred years earlier: some later spinets have one or two stops, and even a few with two manuals are known.

A form with the strings in a vertical plane was known as the clavicytherium and was useful where space was limited.[3] Sometimes a small organ was combined with larger virginals or cembalo, as mentioned above. Although the usual name was claviorganum, the term clavicymbal, often used for early harpsichords, was also applied to this combination: a 'Lekingfelde proverb' of about 1520 illustrates this:

He that couytithe in clarisymballis to make goode concordaunce
Ought to fynger the keyes with discrete temperannce
To myche wyndinge of the pipis is not the best
Whiche may cause them to sypher wher armoney shulde rest.[4]

The use of 'clari' for 'clavi' is common throughout the sixteenth century, and even later, in all words formed on that basis; in English literature 'clarichord' is probably more frequent than 'clavichord'.

The action of the virginals has already been described in Vol. III.[5] Metal plectra were abandoned early in favour of quills, usually from the raven's wing, but leather was substituted in the best instruments in the sixteenth century, and this not only produces the finest tone but is far more durable than quill. The simple mechanism was greatly elaborated in practice; there were usually two strings, beneath which

---

[1] Brit. Mus., Harl. 1419.
[2] The evidence is late, and therefore weak: see Quirinus Blankenburg, *Elementa musica*, (The Hague, 1739).
[3] As it was pictured and described by Virdung, it must have been an early development.
[4] Brit. Mus. Royal 18 D. II: ed. by Philip Wilson (Oxford, 1924).
[5] See p. 485.

a third, tuned an octave higher, was added, and two jacks were used with each key. The slotted guide bars could be moved slightly so that seven combinations were possible. With the addition of a second manual, different sets of strings could be contrasted.[1]

At first sight it would seem that the player's touch could have had no effect whatever on the note produced, but this is not quite so; there is a very decided sense of touch in harpsichord playing, though the effect on each individual note is, of course, slight. The finger technique is totally different from that of piano playing.

A loose distinction between virginals and clavicembalo or harpsichord might be found in the feature that the strings of the former are parallel with the keyboard, while in the latter they are at right angles to it; thus the clavicytherium and the spinet are both more akin to the harpsichord than to the virginals. Save that the virginals form imposed a limitation on the length of the strings, it is a distinction without much difference.

THE SHAWM

The great impulse given to instrumental development in the sixteenth century was especially remarkable among the woodwind families. While the shawms, krummhorns, and cornetts shared in this advance, the most signal achievement of the inventive genius of the century was the production of the re-curved tube which, after many interesting and sometimes exuberant experiments, left its direct descendant in the bassoon of our own day.[2]

The shawm, although to some degree stabilized in the preceding century, received some minor improvements, but it was not until the middle of the seventeenth century that its offspring, our modern oboe, appeared, in spite of the fact that the two names 'hautbois' and 'shawm' are used together occasionally in Elizabethan literature:

> The cornet and the fife
> The hoboy, sagbut deep, recorder and the flute:
> Even from the shrillest shawm unto the cornamute.[3]

It would be difficult to draft a definition that would sharply distinguish the oboe from the shawm, but the difference is musically

---

[1] Details of harpsichord mechanism should be studied in specialist works, such as Philip James, *Early Keyboard Instruments* (London, 1930); Bessaraboff, op. cit., gives excellent diagrams.

[2] For the results of most recent research, consult Anthony Baines, *Woodwind Instruments and their History* (London, 1957).

[3] Michael Drayton, *Polyolbion*, Song IV, (London, 1622): cf. Charles Butler, *The Principles of Musik* (London, 1636), p. 93, 'Pipe, Organ, Shalm, Sagbut, Cornet, Recorder, Fluit, Waits or Hobois, Trumpet, &c.'

positive and the oboe must not be regarded merely as the shawm refined and perfected, but as a fresh line of evolution of the shawm-principle that superseded, without replacing, its ancient parent. The first great advance, however, was the appearance, soon after 1500, of the bass shawm, a long-needed addition to instrumental resources of which the lowest registers had been weak.

A characteristic of the shawm was its intense, almost strident, tone which made it specially suitable for occasions of outdoor festival; perhaps it is hardly a compliment to our most revered of instruments when Mersenne tells us that in his day a substitute for such use was found in the violin. It might be thought that a version of the shawm some ten feet long would make a noise well-nigh intolerable, but this was not the case; an example of the bass shawm greatly pleased the late Sir Frederick Bridge—no great friend of the older instruments— and its tone is described as 'soft and velvety, quite unlike that of the bassoon'.[1] By the time of Praetorius this size of shawm was regarded as a contrabass, with a 'bass' of about 6 feet in length,[2] but this was a later refinement: an example survives in the Berlin collection (no. 289) which is 9 feet long.

The old German name *pumhart* for the shawm became, in the forms of *pommer* and *bombardt*, restricted to the larger sizes, and in Virdung in 1511 we find the descant called *schalmey*. The key or keys on the alto, tenor, and bass instruments had a protective covering, perforated with great delicacy, known as a *fontanelle*, a word that occurs as early as Praetorius in 1618. The reed of the tenor and smaller forms was controlled by a device called a *pirouette* which gave a half-way stage between the reed not touched by the lips but set in motion by wind pressure in a containing capsule, as in a bagpipe chanter, and the lip-control at the end of the reed as used today. The purpose of the pirouette has been rather misunderstood; only recently acquired knowledge has revealed its true purpose.[3]

In essentials, the pirouette is a cylindrical block of wood, fitted on the top of the instrument, pierced by a cylindrical hole through which the staple passes: it is a defining feature that the end of the staple is always *below* the upper surface of the pirouette. As might be expected, the pirouette is seldom found or depicted in so simple a shape, and much happy design was usually expended on it. European instruments have been served from time out of mind with reeds made from

---

[1] Nicholas Bessaraboff, op. cit., p. 117.
[2] Michael Praetorius, op. cit., pls. vi and xi.
[3] See Baines, op. cit., pp. 114 and 230.

the *arundo donax* which grows in the marshes of southern France and Spain: this provides a reed much stiffer than the soft straw-like reeds of Eastern instruments and analogy cannot be drawn from eastern usage. The eastern reed has to be taken right inside the mouth, which then acts as a capsule, but the European reed will not work in that position and there is no evidence that it was ever used in the Eastern manner. Today precision instruments can cut the cane to one-hundredth of an inch before the scraping knife comes into use; this was beyond the reach of the sixteenth century, hence its reeds, though remarkable examples of what could be achieved with the knife alone, were thicker than those of our time and therefore had more resistance to the flat position.[1]

The reed of the shawm was a good deal wider than the reed of the modern oboe and also rather shorter,[2] though there is some controversy on the latter point; it did not sit very firmly on the staple and to a limited extent the pirouette may have served as a protection. The main purpose of the pirouette, however, was to act as a guide, if not an actual rest, for the lips. In reed playing, the soft lips are drawn in against the teeth and the control is exercised by the firmer outer part of the lips on the lower part of the reed, just as by a bassoon player today. The pirouette prevented the player from taking the reed too far into the mouth, where it would produce only a raucous sound, and the surface, slightly hollowed saucer-fashion, saved fatigue of the lips. The larger size of the reed on the bass pommer made the use of a pirouette unnecessary and no contemporary illustration or description indicates the presence of such a device on that instrument.[3]

This is not an academic matter; it has been stated far too often that the shawm reed was taken into the mouth and that therefore the player could have had no control over the tone. Actually, the very reverse is now known to have been the case. It was said above that the oboe superseded, without replacing, the shawm; but happily the shawm has survived as a living instrument in certain places where it is still used for its original purpose, for which there is no substitute. When the oboe proper became fashionable at the end of the seven-

---

[1] On the use of reeds in the sixteenth century, see Josef Marx, 'The Tone of the Baroque Oboe', *Galpin Society Journal*, iv (1951), pp. 7 and 8. An engraving by Tobias Stimmer, *c.* 1560, shows a small bass pommer played with a reed, at the end of a long crook, held with the end just between the lips.

[2] See, for example, the woodcuts and engravings in Mersenne, op. cit., Liv. Vme. des Instruments, pp. 295, 302, and 306, and Athanasius Kircher, *Musurgia Universalis* (Rome 1650), Iconismus ix, facing p. 500. The slightly less precise woodcuts in Praetorius all confirm this shape of the reed.

[3] See Marx, op. cit.

teenth century, the shawms went out of use, but the oboe in the open air was barely audible.

In Catalonia the true shawm is still used for outdoor music of a festive nature such as marches, dances, and the like, in combination with trumpets, trombone, and flugelhorn, and it shows what brilliance has been lost by its disuse elsewhere; this is a fully developed modern instrument, not to be confused with more primitive shawm-like instruments that survive for folk-use in various corners of Europe. From the players of these instruments we can learn much of the usage of the sixteenth- and seventeenth-century shawms.[1]

HAUTBOIS AND TREBLE SHAWM

The middle of the seventeenth century saw many changes in the construction of woodwind instruments, not only those played with a reed, but also recorders and transverse flutes. The outstanding advance was the introduction of sectional tubes to replace the single piece that had been the rule up to then, so that the true oboe is always a jointed instrument. With this construction came the use of the lathe for boring the sections, as well as turning the close-fitting tenon joints; hence a more perfect bore was obtained than by the older method of hand boring and reaming the single block.[2]

From the Talbot manuscript,[3] which must be dated between 1690 and 1700, we learn that 'the present Hautbois [is] not 40 years old and an improvement of the great French hautbois which is like our Weights [= waits, i.e. shawms] . . . with a good reed and skillful hand it sounds as easy and soft as the Flute'. This was the new 'French' hautbois; but improvements had been made to the shawm—which Talbot calls 'Schalmey', 'Chalmie', 'English Hautbois', and 'Waits' —for there was a late type of schalmey that Talbot describes as 'used Much in German Army . . . Sweeter than Hautbois [i.e. waits]'. This improved treble shawm, of which examples exist in several museums,[4] has a tone not unlike that of the oboe, but it remains a true shawm; there was a tenor form which is not mentioned by Talbot.

[1] For a full musical and technical description, with references to parallel usage elsewhere, see Baines, 'Shawms of the Sardana Coblas', *Galpin Society Journal*, v (1952), pp. 9 ff. For a full classification of the shawm family, based on contemporary authorities, the reader should consult Bessaraboff, op. cit., pp. 113 ff.

[2] Eric Halfpenny, 'The English 2- and 3-Keyed Hautboy', *Galpin Society Journal*, ii (1949), p. 11.

[3] Oxford, Ch. Ch., Music MS. 1187. An invaluable contemporary record analysed, by types of instruments in *Galpin Society Journal*, i (1948), and succeeding issues.

[4] e.g. Basle and Brussels. It is illustrated in Galpin, *Old English Instruments of Music* (London, 1910; 4th, rev., edition by Thurston Dart, 1965), pl. xxxii.

Praetorius mentions and illustrates[1] a small bass or bassett type of shawm which he calls a *nicolo*; this, however, had an uncontrolled reed in a full capsule and therefore should not be regarded as a shawm proper. Another poor relation of the shawm was the *schryari*; according to Praetorius this was made in a complete family and its distinguishing feature was the inverted conical bore of the tube, so that the instrument appeared to taper off at the lower end. The reed was enclosed in a capsule and the tone is described as 'strong and lively'. Doubtless they well merited their German name of *Schreierpfeiffen*.[2]

By a generous interpretation of 'the middle of the seventeenth century', which is the terminal limit of this chapter, we may just see the appearance of the modern oboe. It is usual to accept the date 19 March 1671 for the first public appearance of the true oboe, in Robert Cambert's *Pomone*,[3] so that Talbot's 'not 40 years old' may be approximately correct. The oboe was probably brought to England by James Paisible in 1674 when Cambert directed the Court masque of *Calisto*.[4] The oboe must be regarded as a new instrument, not merely as an advanced form of shawm, yet it is true to say that it derived from the shawm in so far as it was clearly the indoor version of the shawm's outdoor tone-colour. It differs from the shawm in the relative narrowness and less wide angle of its bore and in the absence of a flared bell; the reed approximated more to that in use today. From the first, the oboe was a jointed instrument. The alto and tenor forms soon appeared, but the story of the oboe family lies outside our period.[5] The clarinet, of course, did not appear until the eighteenth century.

THE KRUMMHORN

Although the conical bore had such a long and valuable history, the special properties of the cylindrical bore had been exploited in the fifteenth century, when the *krummhorn* came into general use, or perhaps earlier.[6] The krummhorn is a long tube with the lower end

[1] Op. cit., p. 36 (sig. Eii verso) and Schiagraphia, Pl. xiii.

[2] Ibid., p. 42, and 'Schiagraphia', Pl. xii.

[3] Sanford Terry, *Bach's Orchestra* (London, 1932), pp. 95 and 113. Galpin, in *European Musical Instruments* (London, 1937), p. 199, and Curt Sachs, *Real-Lexikon der Musikinstrumente* (Berlin, 1913), p. 136, give the date as 1659; 1671 is correct.

[4] Halfpenny, 'The French Hautboy: a technical survey', *Galpin Society Journal*, vi (1953), pp. 23 ff.

[5] In addition to works cited above, see Halfpenny, 'The "Tenner Hoboy" ', *Galpin Society Journal*, v (1952), p. 17.

[6] Large krummhorns, with a bladder below the mouthpiece like a bladder-pipe, are depicted in the Spanish *Cantigas de Santa Maria*, of the late thirteenth century, but the instrument does not seem to be shown elsewhere in Europe until the fifteenth century.

turned like the letter J, and was sounded with a double-beating reed enclosed in a capsule; the curved end was a trifle expanded. The krumm-horn was made in a complete family from descant to bass and the larger instruments had one key to operate the lowest hole.

In the art and literature of a century and a half the krummhorn was one of the most common of instruments and all the contemporary treatises accept it as such; yet it is one of the rarest of old instruments to be found today and no music written specifically for it has so far come to light.

It lived on in the seventeenth century. Sir William Leighton wrote: 'With Crouncormes musicke laud the King of Kings with one accord.'[1] Records show that the corps of 'les cromornes et les trom-pettes marines' which formed part of the Grande Écurie of the French Court continued throughout the reign of Louis XIV and it has been said that the instruments were used there as late as 1730;[2] but the posts may have been merely a sinecure, like that of the court lutenist of England in the same century. Mersenne, who had no high opinion of the krummhorns, says that they 'se font en Angleterre',[3] which rather suggests that the instrument, which he names *tournebout*, was obsole-scent in France in 1636.

Experiments with surviving specimens show that the tone was soft and veiled, though not muffled; if the word had not nowadays acquired other associations, one might have said that the krumm-horns crooned. The resemblance of the shape of the tube to that of the Roman military trumpet led to the alternative name *lituus* for the krummhorn; but the 'litui' in Bach's Cantata No. 118 were wald-horns.[4]

THE BASSANELLO

About 1600 Giovanni Bassano, a member of the famous Venetian family of that name which served the English royal music for nearly a century,[5] is said to have invented a variant of the krummhorn known as the *bassanello*. It was perfectly straight, and wider in diameter than the krummhorn, but, like that instrument, it was used with a reed covered with a capsule, except in the bass form on which there was a long curved crook. It is described as having a tone as soft as that of

[1] *Teares or Lamentations of a Sorrowful Soule* (London, 1613), p. 70.
[2] See Marx, op. cit., p. 10.
[3] Op. cit., p. 290.
[4] Sachs, 'Die Litui in Bachs Motette "O Jesu Christ"'; *Bach Jahrbuch*, xviii (1921), p. 96.
[5] H. C. de Lafontaine, *The King's Musick* (London, 1909).

a flute, but we know it only from the account and pictures given by Praetorius.[1] It is sometimes stated that the capsule rendered the player incapable of any control over the reed, but this is not strictly true, as proper breath pressure can have a marked effect. All instruments with a cylindrical bore have the disadvantage that the first overblown tone of their natural scale is the twelfth, and this interval was not spanned satisfactorily until the clarinet was developed; hence the krummhorns and bassanelli had limitations. But it is quite wrong to assert, as many writers have done, that the capsule arrangement made overblowing impossible in any case;[2] it can be done with a rather sudden increase in velocity and pressure of the air. Since Praetorius mentions[3] that these instruments with the reed in a capsule gave only as many notes as there were fingerholes, we must assume that overblowing was not general, but it is unlikely that the virtuosi of those days had failed to develop their technique beyond the possibilities described in textbooks.

THE CORNAMUSE

Closely allied to the krummhorns and the bassanelli was a curiously elusive instrument called the *cornamuse*. This name is, of course, very familiar as applied to the rustic type of bagpipes, but this other cornamuse must have been something quite different. We find many passing references to it, such as Cerone's comparison of the tone of the *sordoni* with 'that of the cornamuse'.[4] The nearest we have to a description comes from Praetorius, although he gives no picture of it, in spite of a specific reference to his 'Schiagraphia'. From the few lines of his text[5] we may gather that it had a single cylindrical tube with no keys and that its tone was 'more gentle than that of a krummhorn'. His table of ranges and tunings indicates a family of cantus, alto, tenor, and bass,[6] and the name occurs in various other parts of his work as something familiar. It is the more confusing that the krummhorns were often called *cornamuti*.

BAGPIPES

Also related to the shawms and krummhorns are the many types of bagpipes that were in general use during one period. There were at least seven different sorts of pipe at the turn of the sixteenth

---

[1] Op. cit., pp. 41 and 42: 'Schiagraphia', pl. xii.
[2] See Bessaraboff, op. cit., n. 169 and n. 179 on p. 393, for an expansion of this statement.
[3] Op. cit., p. 40.   [4] Cerone, op. cit., p. 1063.
[5] Op. cit., p. 41.   [6] Ibid., p. 24.

century, ranging from the great *bock*, with a breath-inflated windbag
operating a single-chanter and a single drone (each with a sort of
megaphone attached to its open end), to the delicate *musette*, with
bellows to fill the windbag and four drones with slide regulators. It
must be remembered that for a long while the bagpipes had existed
as an indoor instrument and that our modern associations, derived
from the powerful Highland pipes, have somewhat distorted our
outlook on this instrument. 'March 1502. Item, to a Mynstrell that
played upon a droon before the Queen at Richemount in reward
iijs. iiijd.'[1] The *dudey*, not unlike the musette, but with a breath-filled
windbag, was equally quiet and sweet. An elaborate form was the
Italian *sordellina*,[2] as perfected by the 'Duc de Brasehane', in which
there were two chanters, and two drones one of which was a long
recurved tube. The drones were fitted with a complex key mechanism
worked by finger plates on long extensions so that, as Mersenne tells
us, it was possible to play 'toutes sortes de chansons à quatre parties'.
The windbag of the sordellina was inflated by a bellows.

The name *corna-musa* or *cornemuse*, also *chalemie*, was given to a
large pastoral pipe, breath inflated, with one chanter and two drones,
one of which was very small;[3] but this name, as we have seen earlier,
was also used for something that seems to have been quite a different
type of instrument.

THE PHAGOTUM

It is not possible to date the application of the recurved tube to the
reed instruments more precisely than late in the first half of the sixteenth century, but there is a good deal of information about what
seems to have been the first use of the doubled tube, when it was
employed for a very different sort of thing as early as 1532. This was
the famous *phagotum* of Canon Afranio. We owe our knowledge of
this instrument principally to Afranio's nephew, Theseo Ambrosio,
who dragged it into his textbook on certain near-Eastern languages;[4]
some manuscript instructions for playing the phagotum, dated 1565,
nearly thirty years later, are known.[5]

---

[1] *Privy Purse Expenses of Elizabeth of York, wife of Henry VII*, ed. Nicolas Harris
Nicolas (London 1830).   [2] Mersenne, op. cit., p. 293.
 [3] Mersenne, op. cit., pp. 282 ff; he has a second type of cornemuse, with only one
drone and this type, he tells us (p. 305), was used in consort with the *hautbois de Poictou*.
The *hautbois de Poictou* was a shawm, with a capsule-covered reed instead of the more
usual pirouette.
 [4] Theseo Ambrosio Albonensis, *Introductio in Chaldaicam Linguā, Syriacā, atq̃
Armenicā, & decē alias linguas* (Pavia, 1539), ff. 33 to 36ᵛ: the diagrams are on ff. 178ᵛ
and 179.   [5] Galpin, *Textbook*, p. 207.

The use of a bellows-inflated windbag allies the phagotum to the bagpipes, but there the resemblance ceases; it had two cylindrical tubes, each doubled, and each was controlled by finger holes and an elaborate key work. The sound was produced by the use of the single beating reed. It was a comparatively small instrument resting on the player's knees and supported by a band round his neck. The results in complex music obtained on it appear to have been remarkable and its inventor must have had a mind in advance of his time. It has nothing to do with the history of the bassoon, but, in a sense, it seems to anticipate something of that of the clarinet.

FAGOTTO AND CURTAL

Once the principle of the recurved tube was accepted, it was developed with enthusiasm during the succeeding half-century, so that by 1600 the number and variety of instruments of this type become almost bewildering. Some confusion in the use of names does not help one to sort out the different structures.[1] *Fagotto, basson, tarot, courtaut, dolzian* or *sordone* (which may not be the same thing as a *dolcesuono* or *dolcian*), *doppiono* or *doblado, kortholt* or *curtal,* and *rackett* or *cervelat,* with some extravagances such as the *tartölde,* are the chief names to be explained.

In the main, the difference is between instruments with a conical bore and those with a cylindrical bore; a small group has a cylindrical bore recurved many times. Which came first is hard to say; if the thirteen 'dulceuses' in the inventory of instruments left by Henry VIII[2] are really fagotti, as is sometimes assumed, then almost certainly the conical bore led the way; but it is very uncertain what these instruments were, as they are described as 'short instruments caulled Dulceuses . . . covered with blacke leather . . . some of them havinge tippinges of silver'. Praetorius[3] confounds confusion with his twin definitions

Fagotten und Dolcianen (Italis Fagotto and Dolcesuono)
Sordun (Italis Sordoni, etliche nennen es Dolzianen)

for whatever the sordone was it was not a *fagott,* since Cerone[4] tells us 'there are other instruments called Sordones that have a sound like the Cornamuses and can go as low as the *fagotto chorista*' (i.e.

---

[1] In addition to the recent works on wind instruments referred to above, the following should be consulted: Adam Carse, *Musical Wind Instruments* (London, 1939); Wilhelm Heckel, *Der Fagott* (Leipzig, 1931); Lyndesay G. Langwill, 'The Curtal (1550–1750)', *Musical Times,* lxxviii (1937).

[2] Gerald Hayes, *King's Music* (London, 1937), p. 87.

[3] Op. cit., pp. 38 and 39.   [4] Op. cit., p. 1063.

to C), which is, as we always expect from Cerone, very much what Zacconi had written twenty years earlier.[1] Fortunately we are in no doubt about the sordoni or *sourdines*, for a complete set exists in the Vienna collection[2] and they have cylindrical bores. It is, moreover, clear from Zacconi and his follower Cerone that the *dolcaine* or *dulcayne* was the conical-bored *fagott*, corresponding to our bassoon.

Whether the first idea was to fit one of Afranio's double cylindrical tubes with a double-beating reed, or whether someone hit on the idea of recurving the long tube of the bass shawm quite independently, we shall probably never know. When, however, the conical-bore tube was doubled back on itself, it was found not that a convenient form of bass shawm had been achieved, but that an entirely new instrument had been discovered. True to the period, this new instrument was made in a complete family from descant to double bass: this was the *fagott*, which was known in England as the curtal as early as 1574 and probably earlier.[3] Mersenne's names, *basson* and *tarot*, are applied to only very slight variations of his *fagot*;[4] the modern name, bassoon, was unknown in this period.

We may then define the fagott, dolcain, or curtal[5] as similar in its fundamentals to our bassoon, but made in a variety of sizes, ranging from a small descant sounding notes from a to c″ to a great *Doppel-Fagott* going down to FF.[6] In England the normal curtal was the instrument with a range of G to g′, and the 'double curtal' usually meant an instrument descending to a note a fifth lower, i.e. C:[7] but Randle Holmes[8] just after the mid-seventeenth century says: 'A double curtaile is double the bigness of the single . . . and in playing is 8 notes deeper'. The double curtal was a favourite instrument for ceremonial occasions; for example, in the coronation procession of William and Mary the royal group was followed by 'two sackbutts and a Double Courtall in Scarlet Cloth Mantles', just before the most important subjects.

---

[1] Zacconi, *Prattica di musica* (Venice, 1592), p. 218.
[2] Nos. 226 to 229.
[3] *Household Accounts of Sir Thomas Kytson of Hengrave* (quoted by Galpin, *Old English Instruments*, p. 166).
[4] Op. cit., p. 299.
[5] Praetorius has applied the name kortholt to two quite different instruments, one of which is the ordinary curtal (pl. x) and the other (pl. xii) has a capsule-covered reed: in his text (p. 39) he suggests that this second kortholt may be something like the *doppioni* that he was unable to see.
[6] Praetorius, op. cit., 'Schiagraphia', pl. x; for a complete analysis see Bessaraboff, op. cit., p. 126.
[7] Galpin, *European Instruments*, p. 199, and Bessaraboff, op. cit., p. 126.
[8] Brit. Mus. Harl. 2034; Harl. 2027 also says 'the double goeth 8 notes lower'.

All the fagotti, even to the small descant, were played, as the bassoon is today, with a reed on a curved crook, so that full lip control could have been used; but they differed in construction from the later instruments since the two tubes were bored in a solid block. The connexion at the lower end was effected by removing a portion of the dividing wall and then closing the open end of the block with a cap.

It may be noted that while the lowest note of the deepest fagott recorded by Praetorius is FF, the largest bass shawm reached a fourth lower to CC.

SORDONE, DOPPIONE, AND COURTAUT

We have seen that the sordoni were the counterpart of the fagotti, in the cylindrical tube class; there were five sizes and all had an uncovered reed on a crook. The normal bass sordone descended to BB♭, but there was a double-bass that had its lowest note on FF; the descant had a range B♭ to g.[1] The tone, as might be forecast from the bore, was soft after the manner of the krummhorn. It is clear from the many references during some forty years from the late sixteenth century, that the sordoni had a wide use, probably chiefly abroad, for there does not seem to be any direct record of the name in England; but it fades from the musical scene before the end of our period. Another form, about which we know very little, was the *doppione*; it is mentioned by Zacconi as made in three sizes and his authority is justification for assuming that it had serious use in his day in Italy. Cerone converts the name into *doblado*, but otherwise follows Zacconi in the main. Praetorius had tried in vain to find an example but has to confess that he knows very little about the instrument: Galpin thought that it probably had an even softer tone than the doppione.

Finally there is the *courtaut* (not to be confused with the curtal or kortholt) which might well have passed out of remembrance if Mersenne had not given it a detailed description with two pictures. We have no idea what distinguishing quality, if any, its tone had, but it possessed a unique feature in the way the sound-holes in the back tube were brought to the front by means of projecting tubes called *tetines*: there were six of these tetines, but only three were used, the duplicates being closed with wax or plugs when not wanted.[2] No other reference to this instrument has come to light.

[1] Praetorius, op. cit., 'Tabella Universalis', xii.
[2] Mersenne, op. cit., pp. 298–303. See also p. 252.

TABLE OF REED NOMENCLATURE

At this stage it will be helpful to tabulate the reed instruments described above.

Single tube: conical bore

Shawms: descant, alto, tenor with pirouette
Shawms: bass, without pirouette

Schalmey ⎱
Hautbois ⎰ names for descant shawms

Pommer ⎱
Bombard ⎰ names for larger shawms

Nicolo (? same as *Hautbois de Poictou*): with capsule-covered reed.

Single tube: inverted conical bore

Schryari: with capsule-covered reed.

Single tube: cylindrical bore

Krummhorn: curved at lower end like letter J: capsule-covered reed

Cornemuti ⎱
Storte ⎰ names for krummhorns

Bassanello: straight, reed on crook
Cornamuse: straight, no information about reed, no keys.

Double tube: conical bore

Fagott or *Curtal*: reed on crook
Dolcian: name for curtal

Basson ⎱
Tarot ⎰ slight variations of curtal

Kortholt: German form of curtal (but also used for an instrument more like a sordone).

Double tube: cylindrical bore

Sordone or *Sourdine*: reed on crook
Doppione or *Doblado*: no information (? reed capsule-covered) (possibly the *Kurz-Pfeiff* or second *Kortholt* of Praetorius)
Courtaut: reed on crook, projecting 'holes' (*tetines*) from back tube.

RACKETT

Not content with the new effects produced by the doubled tube, makers at the end of the sixteenth century experimented with a tube recurved many times and evolved a strange instrument called the *rackett,* in France the *cervelat,* and in Germany the *wurstfagott* (sausage fagotto). In this, a cylindrical tube was recurved nine times[1] and then enclosed in a cylindrical canister around the surface of which the finger holes were placed. A double reed, fixed on a staple protruding through the top of the canister, was lipped by aid of a pirouette, as in the shawms. The effect is quite extraordinary in relation to the size of the instrument; the tube acts as a stopped pipe and so sounds an octave lower than an open tube, hence the largest rackett, which stood barely eleven inches in height, sounded, as Praetorius tells us, 'as deep as a Great Bass-Bombard, CC, with 16-foot tone'.[2] The rackett was made in a complete family of four or five sizes, of which the descant was a small instrument about four inches high, sounding G to d. As these instruments were not overblown, the variety of sizes was necessary to provide a complete tonal range. Praetorius considered that the rackett gave most satisfaction when heard in combination with other instruments such as the viols.[3] There is no record of the use of the rackett in England, nor does it seem to have been widely known in Italy.

A long cylindrical tube was also brought into manageable shape by bending it into the form of a helical spring of nine coils, with finger holes arranged more or less in line on the respective coils; the only survivors of this type are five instruments in the Vienna collection, in three sizes, all in their original wooden cabinet.[4] The inventory, dated 1596, of the collection from which these came names them *tartölde* (= kortholte?) 'in the form of dragons'—an allusion to the fact that these instruments are covered with leather with a dragon's head at the end, which suggests some processional or carnival occasion. The reed was fixed, in some way not now known, to a long flexible tube that formed the tail. Perhaps these tartölde, which may have been as unique when made as they are today, need not be taken too seriously, but they remain a valuable example of the inventiveness and resource of that period.

TONE-QUALITY OF REED INSTRUMENTS

This variety of reed instruments imposes the consideration of a most serious problem, a problem that will be intensified when the cornetti are described; for the long abandoned, recently revived cornett

[1] A diagram of the construction, showing the arrangement of the finger holes and the 'diamond' pattern of the tubes can be seen in Schlosser, op. cit., p. 86.

[2] Op. cit. 'Schiagraphia', pl. x.   [3] Op. cit., p. 40.

[4] Nos. 219 to 223: see Schlosser, op. cit., p. 85, for a full description and analytical diagram.

with its unique tone-colour was used extensively by musicians of the Elizabethan age, who found three variations of its tone necessary for their needs. With the possible exception of the tartölde, these various reed instruments were not freaks or passing fancies; they were clearly well known and widely used in Europe for half a century at least. What was the difference in tone-quality between the shawms and the schryari, or between the krummhorns and bassanelli and cornamuse, or between the sordoni and doppioni and courtaut? We may assume, not unreasonably, that these variations would not have been made and used if they had not been wanted. If they were wanted then, why were they abandoned later on and never recovered? Had the musicians of that age some special feeling for shades of tone-quality that has since been lost, or have the effects at which they aimed been produced by other means?

An extreme sensitivity to intonation in instruments is proved by numerous passages in writers of all countries in the sixteenth and seventeenth centuries. If some authors, such as Zarlino, seem to the weary reader to be theorizing in an abstract way, they were dealing, nevertheless, with problems of temperament that were real enough to them; but such men as Cerreto, Zacconi, Cerone, Praetorius, and Mersenne, to whom we owe so much for our knowledge of the instruments and their use, were practical musicians concerned with day-to-day usage. It is impossible to read a discussion such as that in Bottrigari's *Desiderio*, or to follow the description of the music in Rome by Maugars,[1] without being impressed by the almost exaggerated delicacy of reception to instrumental colour, not only of the trained professional but also of the educated music-lover of those days.

It may be thought that the emergence of the orchestra, with its kaleidoscope of colour, and light and shade, made all the subtle variations of the same types of instruments obsolete, but this explanation does not fit the facts; most of them had faded away before the end of the seventeenth century and in the earlier eighteenth century Bach's use of instrumental combination still followed the fixed pattern of his ancestors, that is to say, a combination once determined for a piece remained unchanged until the conclusion of that piece. Some other explanation must be sought. This question underlies all study of the instruments of the period 1500 to 1650, for in the answer to it there is something basic to the musical mentality of that age.

[1] André Maugars, *Response faite à un Curieux sur le Sentiment de la Musique d'Italie, escrite à Rome le premier Octobre, 1639* (Rome, 1640?): see also Thoinan, op. cit.

THE FLUTE FAMILY

In general, the flute family underwent no radical development in the sixteenth century, though there were some additions to the registers and some minor changes in structure. The next century, however, saw marked advances. The oldest of all, blown across the open end of a cylindrical tube, survived as it had done for so long only in the panpipes, the *frestel* of the early Middle Ages.[1] It was made with twelve pipes of varied lengths adjusted to give a diatonic scale, but there is no indication of its use in serious music and we must suppose that it remained a country instrument, recorded by the learned for the sake of completeness.[2]

At first the fipple-flutes continued in their old forms of the recorder and the *galoubet* or three-holed flute. The principle was the impact of an air-stream on a sharp edge near the end of a tube; the edge, or fipple, was set in a notch cut in the side of the tube and the player breathed into a mouthpiece set just above the notch. The tube of a recorder has a rather complex bore mainly of an inverted conoid, but ending at the lower part almost cylindrically, and, with seven holes in front and one at the back, a considerable range can be obtained which a skilled player can extend a few notes beyond the second octave. When made with the exact bore (which is not always the case with modern recorders) the correct fingering and breathing will give a chromatic scale in perfect intonation: the tone is sweet and slightly reedy, but not as penetrating as the more rounded tone of the transverse flute.

RECORDERS

Of all the dormant instruments of the past, the recorder has had the most remarkable awakening; when Arnold Dolmetsch began to revive it and its music, about 1920, it was unknown except to musical antiquaries.

The bass recorder, descending to F, with one key, had been developed by 1500, for it is shown in Virdung's book of 1511, but without the crook that became necessary on account of its great length. Henry VIII possessed 68 recorders, among them 'twoo base Recorders of waulnuttre . . . one greate base Recorder of woode . . .'[3] which suggests the classification found later in Praetorius by whom the 'greate base' in F is regarded as a contra-bass and the recorder in C as the ordinary bass.

[1] See Vol. III, pp. 479–80.   [2] Mersehne, op. cit., pp. 227 ff.
[3] Hayes, op. cit., p. 87.

Until the middle of the seventeenth century, all recorders were made from a solid block of wood and some specialists prefer the tone of this type to that of the more familiar sectional instrument; the German name *Blockflöte* is derived from this construction. The classic treatise on recorder playing appeared in Venice in 1535,[1] from the same masterly hand that seven years later gave us the definitive work on the viols, but so closely did the recorder become associated with England that one of its French names was *fluste d'Angleterre*.[2] It was also called the *flûte douce*, for obvious reasons, and the *flûte à neuf trous*, which is puzzling at first sight: the explanation is that the lowest hole, for the little finger and therefore rather to the side, was always duplicated on the other side, the unused hole being stopped with wax. This duplication is usually explained as a convenience for left-handed players, but its real purpose was more practical. A similar duplication is found on certain other wind instruments, and all keys on recorders, shawms, fagotti, and their kindred have the finger-plate ends bifurcated to give a surface on both sides; this was because there was no established position of the hands and players placed the left or the right hand uppermost as suited their fancy. Virdung gives a double diagram for the recorder, showing both positions.[3]

The recorder was a consort instrument, in which the various sizes played together. The treble, in f', may be regarded as the standard and there was a tenor in c'. Altos and small basses were sometimes made. Above the treble there was a descant in c'' and a sopranino an octave above the treble, but the tone of these two high recorders lacks something of the round reediness of the familiar treble and is more whistle-like.[4]

Praetorius includes with his large family of recorders a very small fipple-flute 'only three or four inches long'[5] with four holes; this is an old instrument, depicted and described by Agricola as the *Russpfeif* (= reed-pipe) in 1528. In the 1545 edition of Agricola's book there is a new engraving, closely resembling that in Praetorius, and the name is changed to 'Klein Flötlein mit vier löchern', but the text about its technique is the same as in the earlier issue;[6] unlike Praetorius,

[1] Ganassi, *La Fontegara*; see *supra*, p. 705.

[2] Mersenne, op. cit.

[3] Sebastian Virdung, *Musica getutscht* (Basel, 1511), sig. M^v.

[4] A useful modern work on the recorder and its technique is Edgar Hunt and Robert Donington, *Practical Method for the Recorder*, 2 vols. (London, 1935). The internal structure of the recorder is well shown by Bessaraboff, op. cit., p. 61.

[5] Op. cit., p. 34.

[6] Martin Agricola, *Musica instrumentalis deudsch* (Wittenberg, 1528), fos. x^v and xv; edition of 1545, fos. 22^v and 23^v.

Agricola does not include it as a recorder and modern opinion would account him right in this.

OTHER FIPPLE-FLUTES

There were other forms of the fipple-flute that had an importance in our period but which must be considered as outside the recorder class. The first was the age-old *galoubet*, or three-holed vertical flute, the pipe of the 'pipe and tabor' man. The origins of the galoubet are lost in the early Middle Ages and its associations were always with the lowly strolling players, yet it calls for a quite remarkable technique. The bore is narrow and cylindrical and two holes are in front, near the lower end, and one behind; it is played with one hand, the other hand beating the tabor or small drum. A considerable range of nearly two octaves was obtainable but it necessitated skilful use of over-blowing, as most of the notes were harmonics. As might be expected, the pipe and tabor were the favourite instruments for accompanying rustic dancing in the open air and have been specially linked with the morris dance.

A more important application of the fipple principle was the intro-duction of the flageolet at the end of the sixteenth century, from which date the instrument enjoyed a century and more of wide popularity, especially in England and France. The flageolet differs from the recorder in its bore, which is much narrower, and its finger-holes, which are six in number, four in front and two behind. Like the recorder, it was made in sections after the middle of the seventeenth century and Pepys found this form very convenient to carry with him so that he could play on his flageolet while riding in his coach. Instruction books for the flageolet appeared in the second half of the seventeenth century[1] and its serious rivalry with the recorder may be judged from the discussion on the two instruments prefaced to a tutor for the recorder published in that period.[2] The so-called flageolets that were popular in the early nineteenth century, sometimes with double, or even treble, pipes, were in reality much modified recorders lacking any tonal resemblance to their originals.

There was another type of fipple-flute about which many writers, both of the period and of more recent times, are curiously silent. It is depicted by, and receives a brief passing reference from, Prae-

---

[1] e.g. Thomas Greeting, *The Pleasant Companion, or New Lessons and Instructions for the Flagelet* (London, 1661).

[2] See the Introduction to *A Vade Mecum. . . . shewing the Excellency of the Rechorder*, anon. (London, 1679).

torius[1] who calls it *dolzflött*—rather confusingly, as we usually associate such a name with the recorder. It is identical in every respect, save one, with the normal transverse flute, the difference being that the air stream is set in motion by breath acting through a fipple instead of across an open hole. It may be conjectured that it was devised to meet the needs of occasions when recorder players were available, as they were fairly certain to be, and there were no transverse-flautists, who were probably always rather rare; whatever the reason, this instrument is no isolated freak, for it continued to be made, as existing specimens show, as late as the nineteenth century.[2]

TRANSVERSE FLUTE

Although there is no positive evidence for the appearance of the transverse flute in England before 1500, that instrument was so much in use elsewhere in Europe from the eleventh century onwards that it is difficult to think that this country alone rejected it. The inventory of Henry VIII's instruments offers fairly conclusive proof that in the mid-sixteenth century it was known in England as the 'flute' in distinction from the 'recorder', and if this is reflected back to Henry VII's Privy Purse Expenses, then the neighbouring entries for 'recorders' and 'flutes'[3] indicate that the transverse flute was in use at the English Court in 1492. On the other hand, Zacconi mentions only one *fifaro* but has three *flauti* and the latter are obviously recorders;[4] his *fifaro*, then, is not the fife but the ordinary soprano flute sounding d' as its lowest note.[5] Virdung in 1511 had shown only one size of transverse flute, but Agricola had the complete family in his first edition of 1528, the soprano sounding e' as its lowest note, the alto and tenor a and the bass d. By the 1545 edition, Agricola had come into line with what was to become the standard, the soprano d', the alto and tenor g and the bass c; in this edition, too, he makes considerable changes in his instructions for breath pressure.[6]

---

[1] Op. cit., p. 35, and 'Schiagraphia', pl. ix.
[2] Bessaraboff, op. cit., pp. 62–65.
[3] See Vol. III, p. 481.
[4] Op. cit., fo. 218. 'I fifari non passano di sotto da *D sol re*, & sopra il soprano non passa la quinta decima. Il soprano di Flauti ascende da *G sol re ut* primo, sino in *F fa ut* sopr'acuto; & gli tenori da *C fa ut* sino in *A la mi re*; & il basso da *F fa ut* basso basso sino in *B fa b mi*.'
[5] Known then as the 'flute in D': the true tonality, by modern nomenclature, is that in C, as it was not a transposing instrument.
[6] Op. cit., ed. 1528, fos. xiii and xiv; ed. 1545, fos. 25–28.

In Germany the flute had several names; Virdung calls it *zwerch-pfeiff* (cross-pipe) and Agricola calls it *schweitzerpfeiff*, from the close association of the small form with the Swiss military, and as a contraction of this name the more familiar 'fife' became current. But as the sixteenth century advanced these names were set aside and *quer-flött* became the German name for the transverse flute. In France it was known as the *fluste d'Allemagne* until the later seventeenth century, when *flûte traversière* took its place. A curious reversal of usage happened in England, where for a century and a half 'flute' and 'recorder' had identified the two types: the use of 'recorder' began to fade and by the eighteenth century 'flute' in English music invariably means the recorder, while the transverse flute is always specially designated as the 'German flute'.

The flute remained throughout our period very much as it had been for long before: it had a cylindrical bore and six finger-holes and it was, of course, made from a single piece of wood, though Henry VIII's inventory includes 'Item iii fflutes of glasse and one of woode painted like glasse', while there were some others made of ivory.[1] It was not until the middle of the seventeenth century that the great changes were made; with the coming of the sectional construction the bore was made slightly conoidal, inverted, although the head joint remained cylindrical, at all events nominally. At first there were three sections, but the foot joint was very soon divided, with a short section forming the true 'foot': in this foot a seventh hole, covered by a key, was bored to give the first semitone, $d'\sharp$, above the lowest note of the flute. Thus came the famous one-keyed flute upon which such a wealth of musical ability was to be lavished in the following seventy or eighty years.

The transverse flute is a more sensitive instrument than the recorder, as the player has control over the air stream by modifying the impact of the breath across the hole with slight turns of the flute. Probably no instrument has been played with such elaborate delicacy of tone-colour and purity of intonation as the one-keyed flute and it is by the known technique of the late seventeenth century that we must judge the playing of the preceding half-century. Jacques Hotteterre, to whom the above changes in construction are somewhat doubtfully attributed, was a fine flautist at Louis XIV's court and his book, published in many editions,[2] gives complete details of his

---

[1] Hayes, op. cit., p. 87.

[2] *Principes de la Flûte Traversière* (Paris, 1707; facsimile of the 1728 ed., Kassel, 1941).

technique. Mersenne,[1] who does not record any Court use in his day, gives tabulatures for a range of nineteen notes on the flute and fifteen on the fife. Entries in the Lord Chamberlain's records include 'flute players' from the middle of the sixteenth century, but as none of these is found in company with recorders until 1603, this evidence should be received with caution; in the accounts for liveries of the musicians at the funeral of Queen Elizabeth, however, seven recorder players and seven flute players are listed by name and, as several of these 'flutes' can be traced among the 'flutes' of the previous twenty years, it is probable that the earlier 'flutes' were transverse flutes.[2]

The name *pilgrims' staves*, with which we occasionally meet in the sixteenth century, has been associated by some writers with the flute, on an analogy with the 'walking-stick flutes' that had a small vogue at the opening of the nineteenth century; but that explanation is at best incomplete. It seems that pilgrims did carry some sort of long wooden musical instrument, for when Mersenne is describing his *courtaut* (see p. 746) he adds

Il est fait d'vn seul morceau de bois cylindrique, & ressemble à vn gros baston; de la vient que quelques-vns en font de grands Bourdons semblables à ceux des Pelerins de sainct Jacques.

(It is made from a single cylindrical block of wood and resembles a large bâton: for this reason some people make of it large bourdons similar to those of the pilgrims to St. James [of Compostella].[3]

Unfortunately this does not carry us very far, as we do not know what precisely he means by bourdons. It seems probable that the name indicates a shape and not any special instrument, for in the inventory of King Henry VIII's instruments[4] two closely neighbouring entries read: 'Item one case w[t] tenne flutes in it the same are caulled pilgrim Staves and the same case furnisshed conteinethe butt vi hole pipes. Item a case w[t] vij Shalmes in it the same case furnished conteineth but v whole pipes caulled pilgrim Staves.'

TRUMPETS AND HORNS[5]

The classification of what modern organography calls 'lip-vibrated aerophones' is very complicated and by no means generally agreed; here we must be content to describe the more important musical

[1] Op. cit. Livre cinquiesme, pp. 241–4.
[2] Lafontaine, op. cit., p. 45.
[3] Op. cit. v, p. 299.
[4] Hayes, op. cit., loc. cit.
[5] Gerald Hayes had left this section unwritten at his death; it has been contributed by Thurston Dart.

aspects of instruments of this broad type used in our period.[1] Our division will be simply that between cylindrical and conical tubes, taken in a general sense.

Pride of place must be given to the lordly trumpet, the instrument of war and royal pomp. As early as the fifteenth century a distinction had been established between the *trompette des ménéstrels* (a slide trumpet) and the *trompette de guerre*, the heraldic trumpet bent into a flattened loop, with a fixed mouthpiece and consequently an invariable tube-length. Illustrations of both kinds of instrument may be found in Virdung. By the middle of the sixteenth century the *trompette des ménéstrels* had developed into the trombone family; but the *trompette de guerre* survived unchanged as the instrument of state and power, King Henry VIII employing no fewer than fourteen of them among his court musicians. Members of the knightly profession of military trumpeters were among the best-paid musicians in Europe, and the German fraternity of trumpeters formed in 1623 claimed pride of place among all musical guilds. Admission to this fraternity was closely restricted, its members were hierarchically classified in accordance with the ranges of the music they had to play, and its very stylized repertory had its own archaic nomenclature, its own laws of construction, and its own artificial notation. From the information given by such writers and composers as Monteverdi, Praetorius, Mersenne, Fantini, Speer, and Altenburg,[2] it is possible to draw up a list of registers and their names as used by the trumpeters of our period:

Flatter: C
Grob or *Basso*: c (g)
Mittelstimme, Faul, Fulgant, Vulgano, or *Tenor*: g c' (e')
Toccato, Striano or *Prinzipal* (used for marches and alarms): c' e' g' (c")
Prinzipal or *Quinta*: e' g' c" (d" e")
Secundarius, Clarino Secundo, Contraclarino, or *Alto*: g' c" d" e" f" g"
Primarius or *Clarino*: c" d" e" f" g" a" b" c'"

The best trumpeters in Europe at this time came from Germany and the Low Countries, and the earliest surviving trumpet music is to be found in two manuscripts now in the Royal Library, Copenhagen; these were written by German trumpeters in the service of King Christian IV of Denmark, the earlier being dated 1598, its com-

---

[1] Bessaraboff, op. cit., pp. 135–55, develops and defends the 'whole-tube' and 'half-tube' system of Karl Schafhäutl (*Bericht über die Musikinstrumente auf der Münchener Industrieausstellung*, 1854) based on the pedal note, with his usual scientific acumen. (It should be explained that 'Ancient' in the title of his book, means, very roughly, 1600–1830.) Galpin, *European Instruments*, p. 220, had questioned the basis of this system.
[2] See Werner Menke, *History of the Trumpet of Bach and Handel* (London, 1934).

panion volume from about 1615. Nearly all the music consists of no more than a single line of notes for one player, and from the titles of the pieces and the ranges of harmonics used we may conclude that it was intended for *Prinzipal, Quinta,* and (exceptionally) *Clarino* registers; in performance simple lower parts were no doubt improvised by the *Fulgant* and *Grob* players. The repertory contained in these manuscripts[1] is international in character; here are 'Sonaden' from Spain, Spanish Italy, and Pomerania, 'Siegnate' from France, 'Auffzuge' from Moravia and Dresden, military signals from France and Italy (often most curiously spelt: 'Monttacawalla'—*sc.* 'Mont' a cavallo'; 'Alles dandäre'—*sc.* 'à l'estandart'; 'Potesella'—*sc.* 'butta sella', corrupted in English to 'Boots and Saddles'). Here, too, are musical fossils as well as fossils-to-be. Thus each sonata ends with a 'rotta', a term found in the fourteenth-century dance; another group of pieces is called 'Serssenaden', which is to say 'sarrazinades' or music of the Saracens; and the French 'Siegnate' (Shakespeare's 'sennets') consist of sections called 'Posts', the origins of the traditional military bugle-calls of today. Other pieces in the manuscripts are adaptations of popular songs (for instance 'In dulci jubilo'), though these have been almost unrecognizably deformed to fit the harmonic series. The 'Tocceden'—Shakespeare's 'tuckets'—are characterized by overblown thirds (c' to e') in the *Toccato* register, the 'Serssenaden' by dramatic leaps from c' to e'', the 'Auffzuge' by short repeated sections.

The very fact that by the end of the sixteenth century it was thought necessary to write trumpet music down on paper shows that an age was coming to an end. The trumpet made its appearance in the opera-house and the church as an occasional instrument of the orchestra in the opening fanfares of Monteverdi's *Orfeo* (1607) and his *Vespers* (1610), and the publications of Mersenne (1636) and the Italian trumpet virtuoso Fantini (Frankfurt, 1638) laid bare to the world at large the long-guarded secrets of its technique.

With this great change of function and of surroundings came a great advance in technique; in this respect the history of the trumpet during the early years of the seventeenth century is a parallel to the history of the horn seventy or eighty years later. By the middle of the sixteenth century the trumpeter had already lost most of his military duties; by the middle of the following century even his courtly duties had been reduced to mere formalities and in consequence he had

---

[1] Printed in part by Georg Schünemann in *Das Erbe deutscher Musik* (*Reichsdenk-male*, vii).

leisure to develop the technique of his instrument—mutes, hand-stopping, overblowing, and so on. Hence the rise of the new school of *clarino*-playing: its extraordinary command of the upper register of harmonics was to reach its height in the music of Bach and the playing of such virtuosi as Reiche, and the technique itself did not outlive these men. Hence, too, the use of 'artificial' notes described by Fantini and later used in Lully's trumpet music. By 1650 or so the trumpet had left the field of war and was free to take its place in the orchestra as a regular member. The careful distinctions between the various registers and their special nomenclature passed out of use at about this time, though certain national characteristics of the instrument were to persist into the eighteenth century. Thus the German trumpet of the mid-seventeenth century still retained its heraldic shape, its tube being the length of the eight-foot pipe of an organ principal (whence its name) and sounding at about D of chamber pitch (whence its orchestral treatment as a transposing instrument pitched in D). The French trumpet was smaller and clearer in tone, pitched in F (as in Bach's Brandenburg Concerto no. 2). The so-called 'English' trumpet was smaller still, pitched in G; it was known in Italy as the *tromba piccola* or *trombetta* (compare the *Toccata a modo di trombette* by Giovanni Macque,[1] who died in 1614). The Italian trumpet proper was of the same size as the German instrument, but for convenience of handling, the tube was wound in three or four helical coils; such an instrument was called a *tromba da caccia*.

The *corno da caccia* of the late sixteenth and early seventeenth centuries seems to have been a very similar instrument, though we may safely assume that the bores of its tube and mouthpiece were conical. The tube-length was comparable to that of the trumpet; indeed, until the earlier years of the eighteenth century both orchestral instruments were pitched in unison, in D, and used the same range of notes. The horns in F used by Bach supposedly came from France, where they had been invented about 1660; they consequently fall outside the scope of the present section. The music of the early horn seems to have been entirely confined to the traditional hunting calls,[2] and the isolated use of horns in the orchestra of Cavalli's *Le nozze di Teti e di Peleo* (Venice, 1639) is too late to warrant a fuller discussion of the instrument here.

---

[1] Brit. Mus. Add. 30491, fo. 30ᵛ: opening printed by Suzanne Clercx, 'La Toccata, principe du style symphonique', *La Musique instrumentale de la Renaissance* (ed. Jean Jacquot) (Paris, 1955), p. 316.

[2] See Eric Halfpenny, 'Tantivy: an Exposition of the "Ancient Hunting Notes"', *Proceedings of the Royal Musical Association*, lxxx (1953–4), pp. 43–58.

SACKBUT

There is little to be said of the sackbut (which later centuries decided to call by its Italian name of *trombone*) that cannot be said of the modern instrument; its basic design achieved finality at an early stage and has, perforce, remained static ever since. The instrument had been developed from the old *buisine* or *buzine*[1] in the fifteenth century and its origins are reflected in the German name of *Posaune*. *Sackbut* is usually held to represent a Spanish name, *sacabuche* (*sacar*, to draw: *bucha*, a tube),[2] and the sixteenth century took a long time to arrive at a satisfactory English form of this name; *shakbusshe* and *shagbolt* are examples of the earlier efforts.

As with the trumpet, the principal difference in the old sackbut was the mouthpiece. Galpin had a fine tenor instrument made in 1557 with which were two mouthpieces, both apparently original; one of these was the ordinary cup shape while the other was deeply conical, with a broad rim, and different effects could be produced with them. The cup mouthpiece of the trombone around the turn of the sixteenth century was shaped, as in the trumpet, for *clarino* playing and Praetorius records the high notes obtained on the tenor instrument by certain players of his day: Phileno of Munich ascended to e″, while Erhardus Borussus of Dresden could go as high as the cornett, to g″. By the use of *falset-Stimme* (blowing the second harmonic with slack embouchure) such players could also extend the compass downwards below the normal;[3] all these special tricks of technique were obtained by lip work alone.

There was a complete family of sackbuts from descant to deep bass and most of these are scored for in Monteverdi's *Orfeo*,[4] but the tenor was the instrument most used and it is often found as a bass to other wind instruments. Mersenne,[5] after describing the imitations of the trumpet in range and agility that can be produced on the sackbut, says that this tone is esteemed *vitieux et inepte* for concerted work and that there is another method of lipping the sackbut (*une autre maniere pour emboucher la Sacquebute*) which the student must learn practically as it cannot very well be explained in writing. In the Latin

[1] See Vol. III, pp. 408 and 476.
[2] Galpin, *Old English Instruments*, p. 208. Galpin's paper,'The Sackbut, its Evolution and History', *Proceedings of the Musical Association*, xxxiii (1906–7), p. 1, is still the best account.
[3] Praetorius, op. cit., p. 31. By 'the cornett' he apparently means the ordinary top register, as experts could carry the standard cornett a whole octave higher.
[4] The descant does not seem to have been used.
[5] Op. cit. v, p. 272.

version of his book he expresses this rather differently by saying that the skilful musician will avoid imitating the trumpet and will make the sackbut sound closer to the smoothness of the human voice.[1]

Praetorius[2] describes four sizes of the sackbut and mentions a fifth; these are as follows:

Alto or Descant *Posaun*: range B to c" (tonality F).

Standard *Posaun* (Tenor): range E to a' with extensions by *Clarinblasen* and *Falset-stimme* upwards to g" and downwards to AA (tonality B♭).

Quart Posaun (a fourth below the standard (tenor) and an octave below the alto): range AA to c', with extensions upwards to g' and downwards to FF (tonality F). (Another form of the *Quart Posaun* was a fifth below the tenor.)

Octave *Posaun* (two forms are mentioned, the second with a wider tube and so not of the unwieldy length—about 8 feet—of the ordinary form): range GG to a with extensions upwards to c' and downwards to CC.

These instruments had crooks and straight extension pieces (polettes) to alter the pitch when necessary.

THE CORNETT FAMILY

As we have seen,[3] the horn proper, as a serious musical instrument, lies outside the period of this volume. We are concerned here with an ancient instrument much nearer to the animal prototype. This is the cornett, with which we have met in centuries long anterior.[4] The cornett (German *Zinck*) was curved after the fashion of the natural horn and had six finger-holes (and, usually, a thumb-hole at the back) by which a chromatic scale could be produced; it was blown by a cup-shaped mouthpiece. At some stage, probably in the mid-fifteenth century,[5] a straight version of the cornett was invented and this had two forms of mouthpiece to give different tone-colours. The cornett was usually made of wood, and in order to cut the conical bore correctly in the curved form, two pieces were shaped and then bound together with leather.[6] Sometimes cornetts were made of ivory.

---

[1] Mersenne, *Harmonicorum Instrumentorum libri* (Paris, 1636), Lib. ii, prop. xxi, p. 111: '*sed a perito Musico ita debet inspirari, ut Tubae militaris sonos non imitetur, magisque accedat ad vocis suavitatem, ne reliquorum Instrumentorum, ipsarumque vocum humanarum concentibus officiat, et sonum potius militarem quam pacificum edat.*'

[2] Op. cit., pp. 31 and 32: and 'Tabella universalis' on p. 20.

[3] See *supra*, p. 758.

[4] Vol. III, p. 476.

[5] It was known to early writers such as Virdung and Agricola, who do not depict the more normal curved form.

[6] The wood was very delicate and the leather helped to preserve it: cf. Mersenne, *Harmonie universelle*, v, p. 274.

The standard size had a normal range of two octaves from a to a″, but expert players, using a lip technique corresponding to the *clarinblasen* of the trumpeters on a small mouthpiece, could ascent to g‴ in florid passages of great rapidity and with a soft quality that consorted perfectly with, and sometimes imitated, the human voice.[1]

The cornett has a unique tone quality and no modern instrument can give any approximation to it. Mersenne's love of the cornetts' tone can be gathered from his description of their sound: 'il est semble à l'esclat d'un rayon de Soleil, qui paroit dans l'ombre ou dans les tenebres, lors qu'on l'entend parmi les voix dans les Eglises Cathedrales, ou dans les Chapelles'.[2] (It seems like the brilliance of a shaft of sunlight appearing in shadow or in darkness, when one hears it among the voices in cathedrals or in chapels.)

While some writers, in its declining days, thought that the strain on lips and lungs was too great for effective use of the cornett,[3] Mersenne speaks of the ease with which good players could sustain long notes or whole songs without taking breath[4]—what they can do 'surpasse toute sorte de creance'—and he records that the player Sourin d'Avignon could carry on for a hundred measures 'sans respirer, ou reprendre vent'. These apparently contradictory statements are both correct: the cornett is fatiguing when played loudly and with heavy wind pressure on the lips, but soft notes demand no strain.

The straight cornett (*cornetto diritto*) had a softer quality than the curved type and, since the bore could be reamed out of the solid as with other wind instruments, it was easier to make and probably more durable.[5] Like the older type it had a separate mouthpiece of ivory or metal, but it was also made with a mouthpiece carved directly out of the wood of the instrument, and this had a curiously veiling effect on the tone; this type was known as the mute cornett. It is important evidence of the instrumental sensibility of the late sixteenth and early seventeenth centuries that musicians then felt that three varieties of

---

[1] After the loss of trained choristers, the cornett was used in Restoration days in churches in place of boys' voices. See Matthew Locke, *Present Practice of Music Vindicated* (London, 1673).

[2] Op. cit. v, p. 274. Elsewhere on that page he calls the sound of the *dessus* 'ravissant'.

[3] See examples quoted by Terry, *Bach's Orchestra*, pp. 37–38.

[4] Op. cit., p. 276, '. . . qu'ils mesnagent si dextrement qu'ils sonnent une chanson de 80 mesures sans reprendre leur vent ou leur haleine'.

[5] Because the straight type had no need of leather binding, it is often described as the 'white' or 'yellow' cornett, while the curved type was called the 'black' cornett.

the cornett tone-quality were necessary. After the mid-seventeenth century these straight types seem to have faded out gradually, but the older type lived on, especially in Germany, till the mid-eighteenth century, though it became largely restricted to the town bands and bands for playing chorales.

Praetorius lists and illustrates a small curved cornett (*klein zinck*) with a standard compass of e′ to e″, and there was a large type with double curvature, rather like a shallow S, that formed the tenor; this tenor had seven holes, with a key for the lowest hole, and it was pitched a fifth below the standard cornett.[1] He had no very good opinion of the tone of this tenor, which he describes as '*unlieblich und horn-hafftig*', but it is frequently represented pictorially in the late sixteenth and early seventeenth centuries and must have had some good use; Mersenne, who also shows a tenor, does not make any adverse comments. This tenor was also called *corno-torto* or *cornon*[2] and had a range from a (or e) to d″; at least two examples have survived in England[3] and there are several in continental collections.

This 'tenor' or corno-torto might well be considered as the bass of the true cornett family; Mersenne, indeed, refers to his corresponding instrument as the 'basse'; but he points out that 'la vraye Basse du Cornet se fait avec le Serpent, de sorte que l'on peut dire que l'un sans l'autre est un corps sans ame . . .'.[4] (The real bass of the cornett family is the serpent, so much so that the one without the other is body without soul. . . .)

The French use of the cornetto, if we may judge by Mersenne, differed slightly from that in Germany and (so far as our evidence enables us to judge) in England. Praetorius obviously regards his *recht chor zinck* as the principal member of the family; this is what is usually called the treble and is about 26 inches long with a as its lowest note. Seventeenth-century engravings suggest that this was the normal instrument in England. The high descant (*klein zinck*) of Praetorius was about 18 inches long and had for its lowest note e′, but he does not show any extension beyond the normal two-octave range for this size: his S-shaped *cornon* was about 40 inches long and had as its lowest note d or c.[5] In addition he has, in the treble size, the straight cornett and the mute cornett.[6]

---

[1] Op. cit., pp. 35–36.

[2] Thus Praetorius: the name 'cornon' does not occur elsewhere.

[3] In Norwich Museum.   [4] *Harmonie universelle*, v, p. 279.

[5] Praetorius, op. cit., 'Tabella universalis' (p. 22): text pp. 35 and 36: 'Schiagraphia' pl. viii.

[6] i.e. straight, with normal separate mouthpiece: straight, with mouthpiece part of the tube.

The enthusiasm shown by Mersenne for the cornett, which is remarkable even in a book rich in superlatives, was mainly the result of the beauty of its *dessus*; this was, he says, '1¾ pieds' in length precisely,[1] which is roughly 22 inches.[2] His diagram of its range shows the lowest note as c'; the *taille* is the same shape as the *dessus*, but has an additional hole in front, operated by a covered key, and its length was about 28 or 29 inches.[3] The *basse* is shaped like a reversed S with the upper limb thrown sharply back; he tells us it is 'quatre pieds de long'[4] which becomes '4, vel 5 pedes longus' on p. 98 of the Latin version, from which a length of 50 inches as a minimum may be deduced. Like the *taille*, the *basse* had a seventh hole covered by a key: it is to be noted that the serpent, for all its great length, had only six finger holes until well into the eighteenth century when a key was added.

While the above comparison suggests a rather different usage in France from that general elsewhere, there are indications of a considerable variety of sizes in the concerted piece for five cornetts by Henri Le Jeune that he prints on p. 277:

Premier Dessus	*A la mi re tout fermé, G re sol tout ouvert.*
Second Dessus	(the same)
Haute-Contre	*G re sol tout fermé, F ut fa tout ouvert.*
Taille	*D la re sol tout fermé, C sol ut tout ouvert.*
Basse	*G re sol tout fermé, F ut fa tout ouvert.*

Mersenne makes a passing mention of the straight cornett; and he associates the thumb hole at the back with Spain,[4] suggesting that the French cornetts did not use the hole which one regards as normal in this instrument.

SERPENT

The serpent is made of wood, covered with leather, and consists of a conical tube nearly eight feet long, expanding to a diameter of about six inches at the foot; it is folded several times, ending in almost a circle, and its appearance well justifies its name. It is blown with a cup mouthpiece and has the six finger-holes in the middle section. Although a true horn and constructed on principles analogous to those

---

[1] Op. cit., p. 274.

[2] Mersenne's 'pied' is not exactly defined, but it seems to have been not far off the official pre-Revolutionary 'pied' of about 12¾ inches.

[3] This length has to be estimated from that of the *basse* in the engraving on p. 276: 28 inches is a minimum, assuming a '4 pied' bass.

[4] Op. cit., p. 274.

of the cornett, it differs from that family in the relation between the length and size of bore, and also in the relative thinness of the wood; the resulting tone is consequently not quite that of a true cornett. Perhaps we should be more correct to say, with the philosophers, that it is a distinction rather than a difference; but it seems to place the serpent outside the strict family of cornetts and to justify the separate existence to which its truly remarkable capabilities entitle it.

The origin of the serpent is obscure, but it undoubtedly appeared sometime in the late sixteenth century. Most authorities say, without reference, that it was invented by a priest of Auxerre about 1590. The basis for this seems to be the following passage, printed in 1780: 'L'Abbé Lebeuf, *Histoire d'Auxerre*, tome I, page 643, dit que vers l'an 1590, un Chanoine d'Auxerre, nomme Edmé Guillaume, trouva le secret de tourner un cornet en forme de serpent . . .',[1] but Lebeuf wrote in 1743 and, as well as being late, his authority is weak.[2] Mersenne knew nothing of this, for he writes, in another connexion, of 'les Sacquebutts, qu'on croid estre plus anciennes que les Serpens'.[3] The serpent was unknown to Praetorius and seems to have had little or no life in Germany, though an entry in the 1596 inventory of the Ambras Castle instruments, now in Vienna, has been quoted against that view: 'Instrument zu plasen, genannt schlangen, 5 stuckh, als ain pasz, 2 tenor, 2 discanten.'[4] (Wind instruments, called serpents, 5 items, a bass, 2 tenor, 2 descants.) *Schlangen* certainly means 'serpents', but in a collection that also contained the tartölde (see p. 748) these might be anything.

France and England were the real homes of the serpent, though a few early Italian examples are known. For want of anything better, it has become customary to regard the mysterious 'Lysarden' of the Hengrave Hall inventory of 1603 as representing either the S-shaped tenor cornett or the serpent; but this is only a guess.

The music that can be produced from a good instrument by an accomplished performer is something that must be heard to be believed. There is a range of four full octaves, and even higher notes can be produced by a real expert; at the bottom there is a rich bass, vibrant and booming, with a curious woody quality, while in the top register *presto* passages can be played very softly with an almost flute-like purity.

[1] J. B. de Laborde, op. cit., p. 274.

[2] 'An antiquarian whose name is happily characteristic of his capability' (Gibbon, *Decline and Fall*).

[3] *Harmonie universelle*, liv. v, p. 281.

[4] Schlosser, op. cit., p. 13.

DRUMS

The small double-headed drum, known as the tabor, that had come down from the early Middle Ages, was not discarded in the period covered by the present volume but held its place as the associate of the galoubet or three-holed vertical flute; when used alone, it was slung horizontally and played with the hands alone, or with sticks, on both ends. Under Swiss influence, the tabor had developed a much larger form in the fifteenth century and this became the big side drum, slung vertically and played on one head only. In the sixteenth century it was made with a head two feet in diameter,[1] a size that later times found too unwieldy. The famous Swiss association of this large drum with the fife was soon copied by other armies, and the English had their drums and fifes at least by 1540.[2] About that date, too, the old words *tabor* and *tabrett* had become replaced by the Dutch *drum* and players were known as *drumslades*. The Lord Chamberlain's records show 'Tabretts' in the funeral procession of Henry VII (1509),[3] but a 'drume player' at the coronation of Edward VI (1547);[4] and there are instances of the use of the word 'drumslades' in England soon after 1530. These drums had detachable snares and their use was almost entirely processional and military. The official march-rhythm was reformed by the ill-fated Prince Henry two years before his death in 1612, and this version was issued as a Royal Command by Charles I in 1632.[5] It may be noted that Virdung associated the Netherlands and France especially with the use of the small tabor with the galoubet.[6]

The modern bass drum does not appear to have come into general European use before the eighteenth century, yet something rather like it is depicted once or twice in the art of the Middle Ages; it was widely used in the East from early times.

The small single-headed drum with a hemispherical body, known as the *nakers*,[7] also appeared in a large form, though this was less a development than an importation from the near East, where the effects of loud percussion instruments had had a terrifying effect on the armies of the early Crusaders.[8]

Timpani or kettledrums seem to have been adopted first in Hungary, though whether because of the close contact with the Turks

[1] This was still the size of military drums when Praetorius wrote in 1618: see 'Schiagraphia', pl. xxiii. The illustrations in Virdung (1511) show that Germany had adopted the large Swiss size early.
[2] Brit. Mus., Augustus A. iii.
[3] Lafontaine, op. cit., p. 3.   [4] Ibid., p. 8.
[5] The original manuscript is reproduced in Hayes, op. cit., p. 59.
[6] Op. cit., sig. C.4ᵛ.   [7] See Vol. III, p. 492.   [8] Ibid., p. 414.

or whether an inheritance from far-off Asiatic ancestors is not known. Virdung (1511)[1] and Praetorius (1618)[2] both show the kettledrums (*Pauken*) in pairs but it is uncertain whether these were in unison or whether the later tuning, usually a fourth apart, had been introduced. Mersenne,[3] who seems to regard this type of drum as an eastern curiosity, shows two sizes and says they can be used an octave, a fifth, or a fourth apart; but this seems to depend on size, for his instruments look crude and have no keys. Virdung shows ten keys and Praetorius six; clearly no rapid changes could be made and these keys must have been mainly, if not only, for keeping the drums up to pitch.

Kettledrums were essentially military and were used on horseback; in 1541 Henry VIII wrote to Vienna asking for a pair so that they could be played on horseback 'after the Hungarian manner', which suggests that this form of drum had not then reached England. When played in this way, Virdung says that they sounded very alarming.[4]

BELLS

The rows of bells, struck with a mallet, that are so often depicted in art throughout the Middle Ages, fell from favour in the fifteenth century and were little, if at all, used after 1500; in their place the tunes of the carillon became increasingly popular in Europe, especially in France and the Low Countries. Usually the carillon was worked by hand from a keyboard[5] but in the seventeenth century clockwork carillons were made in which the tunes were operated by pins on a revolving drum.[6] England, however, would have none of these things and went on that highly individual road of its own, the ringing of changes on a peal of bells. This mathematical practice had an enthusiastic following and societies began to be formed as early as 1637;[7] in 1668 that great classic of the science, Fabian Stedman's *Tintinnalogia*, was published.

Records of travel show that several foreigners were puzzled by this English use of bells, but in 1598 one visitor at least was under no illusions about it; Paul Hentzner of Brandenburg wrote of the

---

[1] Op. cit., sig. D.1.

[2] Op. cit., 'Schiagraphia', pl. xxiii.

[3] *Harmonicorum Instrumentorum* (Paris, 1636), lib. iv. De Campanis [!], p. 165.

[4] 'gar ungeheur': op. cit., sig E. 4ᵛ.

[5] Mersenne illustrates the mechanism of his day in *Harmonicorum Instrumentorum*, lib. iv, p. 160.

[6] See the elaborate examples in Kircher, op. cit., tom. ii, lib. ix, Iconismus xix.

[7] The first was called 'The Society of College Youths'.

Londoners of that day: 'They are vastly fond of great noises that fill the air, such as the firing of cannon, drums and the ringing of bells, so that in London it is common for a number of them when drunk to go into some belfrey and ring the bells for hours together.'[1]

CYMBALS

Of the other percussion instruments little need be said. Cymbals had come down from ancient times and have continued little changed to our own day, though a small, cup-like variety[2] that was also in general use up to the mid-seventeenth century, if not later, is not seen so much. This small type was used in a manner resembling that of castanets, which were also familiar in this period.[3] The triangle, once known as the 'stirrup' (*Stegreif*),[4] maintained its old form but dropped that name;[5] the only difference between it and our modern type was the use of a number of loose rings on the horizontal bar, which were given up in the eighteenth century. The timbrel—our tambourine—had persisted from antiquity and is practically the same today.

MINOR INSTRUMENTS

There were several very minor instruments hovering in the background of our period and although these have no real musical importance, their names sometimes occur. One example is the *mirliton* or eunuch flute, of which Mersenne gives a detailed description and tells of concerted use with four or five of these bogus flutes played together.[6] The *mirliton* is shaped like a vertical flute, but the player hums the tune which is reinforced by a very thin membrane, 'delice comme la peau d'un oignon', stretched over the top of the tube; there was a genuine hole just below the membrane and, often, three or four dummy 'holes' painted lower on the tube.

Another toy that seems quite ageless is the Jew's harp or Jew's trump which, like the mirliton, has no voice of its own. It is found

[1] Quoted from William Brenchley Rye, *England as Seen by Foreigners in the Days of Elizabeth and James the First* (London, 1865).

[2] Praetorius calls them *Schellen*; Virdung seems to apply this name to the clappers (sig. D. 3ᵛ).

[3] Mersenne, op. cit., lib. iv, prop. xvi, gives details of all these.

[4] See Vol. III, p. 493.

[5] Cf. Praetorius, op. cit, 'Schiagraphia', pl. xxii, where it is called *Triangel*; and Mersenne, op. et loc. cit.

[6] *Harmonie universelle*, liv. v, p. 230. On this page there is a vague passage which suggests that the *mirliton* was then fairly recent ('des jeux noveaux'), but it may have a more general reference.

all over the world at least as far back as the thirteenth century. It is depicted among the French enamels on the crozier of William of Wykeham or Wickwane of about 1280 and it can be detected, though not so clearly, in the fourteenth-century sculpture in Exeter Cathedral;[1] it appears unchanged in Virdung (1511), Praetorius (1618), and Mersenne (1636). In France it was known as the *guimbarde* and in Germany as the *Judenharfe* and *Maultrommel*; the origin of the name is a mystery as it had no connexion with the Jewish race.

One or two instruments, of no musical value in themselves, are worth recording as they left their names to organ stops. Both Virdung and Agricola (who, indeed, helped himself liberally to Virdung's woodcuts) show the *Gemshorn*.[2] This is a short natural chamois horn with four finger-holes, three in a line and the fourth, nearest to the large end of the horn, set a little to one side; there is a fipple notch cut just below the large end, which is closed with a block in which there appears to be a circular hole for the breath. These writers[3] also show another natural horn, rather longer and with a slight double curvature, with four finger-holes, but in this the hole on one side is that nearest the small end; the large end is open and a normal cup mouthpiece is fitted in the small end. This instrument both writers name, rather confusingly, *Krumhorn*, which is strange as it is shown on the same plates as the true krummhorns, to which they also apply that name. This is clearly only a rather limited pastoral horn but its mechanics are at least more comprehensible than those of the *Gemshorn*. The *Russpfeif*, also found as the name of an organ stop, is shown by these two writers as the diminutive recorder already mentioned, with four finger-holes; in fact, in his 1545 edition, Agricola drops the name *Russpfeif* and calls it simply 'Klein Flötlein mit vier löchern' (small flute with four finger-holes).

The aeolian harp was thought by Kircher to be a new invention,[4] but many centuries before his day St. Dunstan had narrowly escaped the charge of sorcery when he made such an instrument and placed it in a draughty aperture in a wall.[5] Kircher's instrument is in the normal form of wires stretched over a sound-box, like a psaltery, but he characteristically proposed various devices of cones and passages to

---

[1] Galpin, *Old English Instruments of Music*, p. 268, and Georg Kinsky, *Geschichte der Musik in Bilder* (Leipzig, 1929), p. 51, pl. 1.

[2] Virdung, op. cit., sig. B. 4; Agricola, op. cit., edn. 1528, fo. xi^v: it is not shown in the edition of 1545.

[3] Virdung, on same page as above; Agricola on the preceding page, and in edition of 1545, fo. 23^v.

[4] 'Est hoc machinamentum uti novum . . .', op. cit., tom. ii, p. 352.

[5] Galpin, op. cit., p. 72.

increase the flow of air. Although not to be compared with Mersenne, Kircher had a considerable knowledge of the science and mechanics of his age and he showed great ingenuity in devising mechanical organs as well as complicated echo-chambers: these curiosities need not detain us except to remark that his diagrams for 'pricking' the cylinders for such instruments anticipate by more than a century the elaborate works of Dom Bedos de Celles and Le Père Engrammelle. His diagrams, like those of later writers, are valuable and definitive evidence for the interpretation of contemporary notated music, with its ornaments.[1]

Another vain search of the early seventeenth century was for a mechanical 'bowed' instrument, for which the ancient *symphony*,[2] later known as the hurdy-gurdy, had pointed the way. The principle of these attempts is basically the same: in the instrument, which looks rather like a harpsichord, the keys bring the required strings in contact with the resined edge of a wheel that is kept rotating by pedals. A specimen made by the Spaniard, Truchado, in 1625 still exists in the Brussels Conservatoire; it is on much the same lines as the famous *Geigenwerck* of Hans Hayden of Nuremberg that Praetorius describes.[3] Kircher describes a machine of the same sort, and in another he includes a set of organ pipes;[4] as the pedals had to operate both the wheel and the bellows, it must have needed heavy foot-work. It is sometimes thought that Henry VIII's collection anticipated all these, since one entry reads 'An Instrumente that goethe wt a whele withoute playinge uppon . . .', but, as this is included among the virginals, it rather suggests mechanical plucking by means of a cylinder.

One other very old instrument to which mechanism was also applied was the xylophone: Virdung (1511), Agricola (1528, 1545), and Praetorius (1618) show the wooden pallets or rods much as we have them today. The Germans called it the *Strohfidel*, from the straw on which the wood was originally laid; in France it was the *claquebois*. Both Mersenne and Kircher[5] show a form in which each wooden pallet is struck by a wooden block operated by a pivoted lever ending in a finger plate; each pallet has its own lever and there is an adjusting device apparently to raise or lower the pallets to alter the tone. Whether this keyed xylophone had any effective life is not known.

[1] Kircher, op. cit. ii, pp. 312 ff.
[2] See Vol. III, p. 486.
[3] Praetorius, op. cit., p. 67: and 'Schiagraphia', pl. iii.
[4] Op. cit. ii, pp. 339 ff.
[5] Mersenne, *Harmonicorum*, p. 163; Kircher, op. cit. i, p. 518.

INSTRUMENTAL COMBINATIONS

It does not fall within the province of this chapter to say anything of the music of the instruments that have been described, or even to comment on those 'broken consorts' of seventeenth-century chamber music in which five or six instruments of different kinds were used.[1] It is, however, pertinent to give an example of how the mid-sixteenth century grouped its instruments for particular effects in the less intimate music that was then developing; this is not only valuable evidence of the appreciation of instrumental tone-colour, for which claims have been made above, but it indicates the foundations of the type of orchestra employed in Monteverdi's *Orfeo*.

In the mid-sixteenth century there was a type of stage performance known as *intermedio*, given between the acts of comedies.[2] The elaborate scenarios of *intermedii*—usually on mythological subjects—were often published; the action and setting of each scene are described and the words of the songs are interpolated in their appropriate places. The scenario sometimes ends with a list of the groupings of instruments that were used in each of the scenes; most unfortunately, it has been the habit of authorities to lump all the instruments together in one comprehensive list that tells nothing of their musical use.[3] One of these entertainments, Francesco d'Ambra's comedy *La cofanaria*, contrived for the wedding of Francesco de' Medici and Johanna of Austria in 1565, was printed at Florence in the following year, with a description of the *intermedii* by Giovambattista Cini, and reprinted in 1593.[4] Cini's *intermedii* are based on Apuleius's story of Cupid and Psyche, and the music of the first, second, and fifth was written by Alessandro Striggio, that for the third, fourth, and last by Francesco Corteccia.[5]

The following is a translation of the end of the 'description':

In order to satisfy those enquiring musicians who may find this work in their hands, it must be explained that, because the hall was of such excep-

---

[1] See p. 583.   [2] See pp. 787 ff.

[3] Kiesewetter started this practice in his *Schicksale und Beschaffenheit des weltlichen Gesanges* (Leipzig, 1841) and has been followed by many writers since.

[4] See O. G. Sonneck, 'A Description of Alessandro Striggio and Francesco Corteccia's Intermedii "Psyche and Amor" 1565', *The Musical Antiquary*, iii (1911), p. 40, for the original text of the *descrizione*, and the same writer's *Miscellaneous Studies in the History of Music* (New York, 1921), p. 276, for a complete translation by Theodore Baker. See also Federico Ghisi, *Feste musicali della Firenze Medicea, 1480–1589* (Florence, 1939).

[5] There is a possibility that the actual music may be recovered as it seems to have been in the press in 1565. Analogous but more limited information is available for instrumental usage in Bibbiena's *La calandria* (1513), Ariosto's *I suppositi* (1518), and Landi's *Il commodo* (1539) among the earlier *intermedii*.

tional beauty, size, and height, it was necessary to make the concerted music very full, and therefore

At the opening the sweetest harmony that came from the [stage scene of] widespread heavens was produced by—

> four double Harpsichords
> four *Viole d'Arco*
> two Trombones
> two *Tenori di Flauti*
> a *Cornetto muto* (soft-toned cornett)
> a transverse Flute (*Traversa*)
> and two Lutes.

Thus one sees the remarkable art with which the musicians contrived the proper settings of the Chariot and the Hours and the Graces which were to be found in their correct places.

The music of the first two stanzas of Venus's ballata was for eight voices; only the singers were on the stage and the accompaniment was off-stage, but with considerable difficulty and artifice, by

> two Harpsichords
> four double-bass Viols (*Violoni*)
> a medium Lute (*Leuto Mezano*)
> a *Cornetto muto*
> a Trombone
> and two Recorders (*Flauti diritti*).

Cupid's last stanza was sung by five voices also on the stage with the accompaniment off-stage of

> two Harpsichords
> a large Lute
> a bass Viol added above the parts (*un sotto basso di Viola aggiunto sopra le parti*)
> a treble Viol (*soprano di Viola*) also added
> a Recorder (*Flauto*) similarly added
> four transverse Flutes
> and a Trombone.

This was during the first *intermedio.*

The second was a quartet, sung by four voices on the stage, and played by

> four Lutes
> a *Viola d'Arco*
> a *Lirone* (*Lyra da gamba*);

and off-stage by

> three Harpsichords
> a large Lute
> a treble Viol (*Viola soprano*)

a contralto transverse Flute (*Traversa contr'alto*)
a large tenor Recorder (*Flauto grande Tenore*)
a bass Trombone
a *Cornetto muto*, which played a fifth part added above.

In the third *intermedio* six [instruments] played and the whole of the music was on the stage, thus—

five *Storte* (krummhorns)
a *Cornetto muto*
and eight voices, doubling the sopranos and basses.

The music of the fourth *intermedio* was similarly à 6 and it was performed entirely on the stage, the voices doubling all the parts and adding thereto—

two Trombones
a *Dolzaina* (perhaps a fagotto)
two ordinary Cornetts
a large Cornett
and two drums (*Tamburi*).

In the fifth *intermedio* [the music was] à 5, one soprano voice solo was accompanied on the stage by—

four double-bass Viols (*Violoni*)
and off-stage by
a *Lirone*
and four Trombones.

The last was a quartet, very lively and very full (*pienissimo*), with all the voices quadruplicated. And adding thereto—

two *Cornetti muti*
two Trombones
a *Dolzaina*
a *Stortina* (small krummhorn)
a *Lirone*
a *Lyra* [*da braccio*]
a *Ribechino* (violin?)
and two Lutes

playing in the first Canzonetta, and all singing.

In the second scene where there was a ballet, eight solo voices sang the stanzas, and the Lyra [da braccio] and *Lirone* played by way of a ritornello which refreshed the minds of the audience; but after this, as it were refreshing the minds of the audience, one heard with a certain new gladness all the performers most joyously singing and playing.

The above lengthy quotation is merely an illustration of what was being done with instruments in combination in the mid-sixteenth century. Two points must be made before leaving the subject: one is that there were highly accomplished players on all these instruments, and Striggio himself was a virtuoso performer on the *lyra da gamba*, an instrument of extraordinary difficulty; the other is that even now we cannot be quite sure of the exact meaning of all the names used. *Viola d'arco* probably meant viol in 1565, but a slight doubt that it may have been a loose expression for the newly developed violin intrudes; *dolzaina* certainly meant *fagotto* in Praetorius's day (1618), but was the *fagotto* so well established in 1565 and may the name not refer to some other type? *Ribechino* ought to mean a *treble rebec* and the setting is just one in which a rebec would be useful, but writers at the end of the century use the word in a very ambiguous manner.[1] *Violone* was a standard name for a double-bass viol later; can we be sure that it meant the same at that date? The answer is almost, but not quite, certainly that it did. We have still much to learn.

TABLATURE

The name 'tablature' originally denoted any 'tabulation' of vocal or instrumental parts in such a way that they could be read and played by a soloist (cf. Scheidt's *Tabulatura nova*),[2] but it is commonly confined to those systems of notation by which the attainment of a certain musical result is indicated by a graphical description of the manner in which fingers must be placed on an instrument. Tablatures were devised for wind instruments such as recorder and oboe, though chiefly for instructional purposes. For a certain group of instruments, viols, lutes, and their kindred, it is infinitely more appropriate than any system of musical notes. Tablature is unambiguous and so free from doubts of the sharpening or flattening of notes by *musica ficta* that beset early texts in staff notation. It has no musical meaning until the tuning of the strings is defined; it operates entirely by intervals and hence is independent of pitch.

The earliest known 'tablature' in this sense of the word is Petrucci's *Intabulatura de Lauto. Libro primo*,[3] and it is remarkable that this utterly novel concept of notation appears first not tentatively in manuscripts, but fully developed in printed books as something in general use. It is hard to believe that no manuscripts exist of a date before 1507, when Petrucci's first volume appeared, and some will surely be found sooner or later. The Venetian lute-tablature was followed closely by Virdung's general treatise on instruments in 1511. But Virdung's system, though fundamentally the same in principle

---

[1] e.g. Bottrigari, op. cit.; see Hayes, *Viols and other Bowed Instruments*, pp. 176 ff.
[2] See pp. 666–7.   [3] See Vol. III, p. 440.

as Petrucci's, yet has so marked a difference in application that one can hardly have developed from the other. If tablature had not existed earlier, we should have to believe that two men invented this completely new type of musical notation not only independently but at the same date. The principle of lute-tablature is easily explained.

Ex. 368
(i)   (ii)

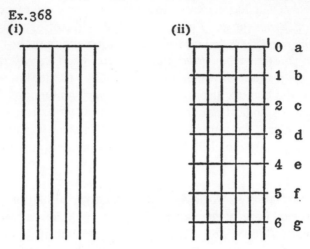

Let the vertical lines in (i) represent the six double 'strings' of a lute and let (ii) represent these same strings with the fretted neck beneath them. In (ii) the frets have been numbered as they recede from the nut, to which the zero sign is given: there is thus a means of identifying the intersection of any one string with the line of a fret. Suppose now that (i) is turned through a right angle so that the lines representing the strings are horizontal: immediately the question arises—which line represents the highest string? With the position of the lute when held by a player in mind, some answered at once, 'The lowest'; others said 'Naturally, the topmost line', and these, too, preferred to letter, rather than to number, the frets, calling the nut 'a'.

Ex. 369

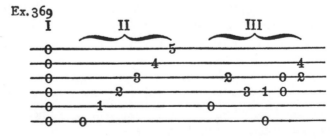

In Ex. 369 the lines represent the strings with the highest string at the bottom; the numbers under I clearly show that all the strings are

plucked together, open; II shows that the strings are plucked successively, the highest open, the second stopped on the first fret, and so
on until the sixth stopped on the fifth fret; III shows the second string
plucked open, then the fourth string stopped on the second fret,
followed by the third string stopped on the third fret, next the first
and third strings plucked together, the first open and the other stopped
on the first fret, followed by the third and fourth plucked open
together and, finally, the fourth string stopped on the second fret and
the fifth string stopped on the fourth fret plucked together. Using
letters instead of numbers, and reversing the order of the lines representing the strings, this same set of groups would appear as in Ex. 370.

Ex.370

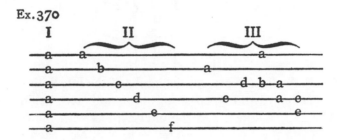

Ex. 369 represents the system adopted by Italy and Spain, while
England and France used the system shown by Ex. 370.

It will be apparent that, as they stand, these diagrams have no
musical meaning, for we do not know the intervals between the open
strings and there is nothing to indicate the duration of each note.

The basis of this method of writing music is a graphical identification of each intersection of the lines of strings and frets: clearly the
result can equally be achieved by applying a different symbol to each
point over the whole neck, rather than having one symbol common
throughout the line of each fret. This was the German method, first
described by Virdung in 1511, by whom its invention is attributed to
Conrad Paumann, the blind organist of Nuremberg;[1] Agricola in
1528 was also well acquainted with this story. The system must have
been devised when the lute normally had only five courses or ranks,
but it was verging into the six-rank instrument in Paumann's lifetime.
It is tempting to guess that this indicates a priority for the German
system, but there is no definite evidence; nor are we even justified in
suggesting that the Italian system was an adaptation of a German
prototype to suit the added strings.

[1] See Vol. III, p. 428.

Ex. 371

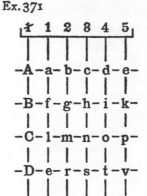

In Ex. 371 the lines represent five ranks of the lute with seven frets on the finger board: the open strings are numbered, beginning with the bass 1, 2, 3, 4, and 5, and the intersections with the frets, again beginning from the bass, are lettered a, b, c, d, &c., each fret beginning from the bass so that they read as do the lines of a printed page.

The three groups of Ex. 369 will appear, in this German system, thus:

Ex. 372

ʇ	5 d h m e E	4 g n 5 ʒ g
1		c z a
2		
3		
4		
5		

When the sixth string was added, each writer devised his own system of symbols and there are at least twenty variations in the century following the publication of Virdung's book: a favourite device was that of denoting the open string by ʇ and the succeeding frets by capital letters A, B, C, D, &c.

Despite its greater tax upon memory, this system had a decided advantage in legibility.

TUNING

Tuning can be represented by denoting on which fret each string must be stopped that it may sound a unison with that next above it.

The standard intervals of the tuning of lute and viol were: fourth, fourth, major third, fourth, fourth. In the three tablature systems this is shown thus:

Ex. 373

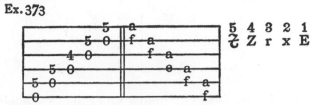

When the tuning of the lute became changeable, around the year 1600, the practice grew of prefacing each piece with its tuning in tablature.

Pitch is undefined and the tablature serves equally well any size of instrument tuned with the defined intervals. With the tuning of Ex. 373 and assuming the highest string to be tuned to the groups I, II, and III of Exs. 369, 370, and 372 will sound:

Ex. 374

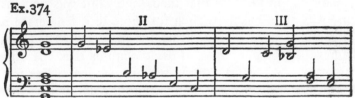

The duration of each note was shown by a sign placed above it; later, the notes of the ordinary stave were used, but for a long while symbols derived from the tails of notes were used:

Ex. 375

(i)   (ii)   (iii)

Only the earlier German tablature repeated a sign for notes of equal duration and these were joined so that (ii) became (iii). In all other tablatures a sign once placed held good for every succeeding note or rest until another sign appeared to change the value.

Ex. 376

Under the hands of hasty scribes these time-value symbols often became sadly corrupted:

Ex. 377

The signs were subject to the usual prolongation of value by dots; a sign over a blank represents a rest of equivalent duration.

For a single line of melody this is plain enough; but the music for which tablature was needed was seldom simple and normally had internal parts that demanded clarification in this notation. Tablature was adapted for this by the introduction of bars, but these must not be read for accent and rhythm, which often bear little relation to such rigid divisions. Printed and carefully written tablature so placed the symbols within the bars that their time value was obvious. But tablature was often hastily written for those too well versed in this type of music to need exact instructions for every part. Dolmetsch has summed up the concept of those tablatures thus: 'If a note or chord is to be held whilst other parts are moving, a line is drawn under the letter, which shows by its length the duration of the hold. These lines are only useful in special cases, for it is a rule that all notes must be held until their vibrations naturally die, whenever possible, or until their prolongation becomes undesirable for melodic or harmonic reasons.'[1] But a study of a typical passage, such as the fantasia from Francesco da Milano's First Book quoted on p. 691 (Ex. 348, (i)), with its original notation (pl. I (b)), will give a more satisfactory understanding of these principles than lengthy explanation.

As time passed, it became evident that it would be much clearer if the signs were placed above, instead of on, the lines and all later tablature is written in this manner; but the origin of the lines was a diagram of the strings. When the extra strings were added the signs were placed outside the base line of the original six: normally only the seventh was stopped and the remainder were off the finger-board. The vestigial remains of leger lines are seen in the symbols for the eighth, ninth, and tenth strings. To avoid confusion the eleventh and twelfth strings were shown by the figures 4 and 5, from the number of leger lines that should have been used.

[1] *The Interpretation of the Music of the XVII and XVIII Centuries* (2nd ed., London, 1944), p. 440.

Ex. 378

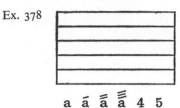

a á a̅ a̿ 4 5

In England the letters look a little strange at first sight owing to their derivation from the so-called 'court hand'.

a β rc ɔ ʋ ʃ g ß ıy ʄ l m

Signs for ornaments abound in later texts; and some composers were particular to indicate with which fingers a string should be plucked, for tone quality, by a system of dots over the symbols.

GUITAR AND WIND TABLATURES

At the opening of the seventeenth century the technique of guitar playing underwent a marked change: lute-like music was replaced by batteries of full chords struck across the whole of the strings. This led to a development of tablature for the guitar that transformed its whole appearance. In the following hundred and fifty years guitar literature became most prolific and rivalled, if it did not exceed, in quantity that for the lute itself. The tablature became both varied and complex and is the most troublesome of all tablatures to decipher, so attenuated did the shorthand of the virtuosi become; it would be far beyond the purpose of this chapter to give even the most brief description of all the forms.[1]

Although the tablature for wind instruments such as the recorder, flageolet, and *galoubet* was intended for instructional purposes, for which indeed it is still in use today, a certain amount of music exists in it. The principle is exceedingly simple: a column of circles represented the finger holes and those stopped were solid black while the open holes were left white. A series of such columns represented a series of notes and for convenience horizontal lines were ruled through them. The first modification was the omission of the open circles from the lines: a second, sometimes adopted mixed with circles and sometimes in entire substitution, was the use of a short vertical line across the horizontal line, instead of a black circle for a stopped hole. Half-stopped holes were shown by half the vertical line or half a

[1] On guitar tablature see Johannes Wolf, *Handbuch der Notationskunde*, ii (Leipzig, 1919), pp. 157–218.

circle, 'pinched' holes by such devices as a circle with a dot in the middle. Time-values of the notes, and signs for ornaments, were added in the ordinary manner of lute tablature.

Mersenne's example for a tenor recorder illustrates a mixed system: the top line is the thumb hole at the back of the instrument and the almost continuously open state of the bottom hole is indicated by the omission of the eighth line except as a leger-line. In his use of the eighth hole Mersenne differs slightly from modern fingering.

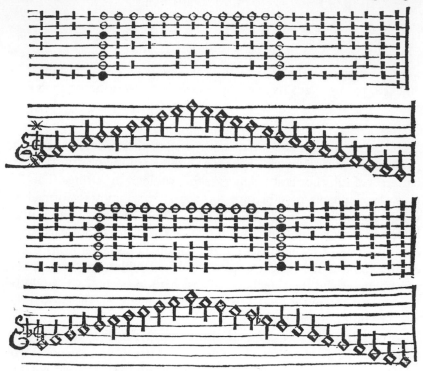

KEYBOARD TABLATURES

So unwieldy do some of the keyboard notations seem that it is hard to understand why sixteenth-century executants sometimes preferred to play from them rather than from staff notation in score. Yet Scheidt, in a note 'To Organists' prefixed to the first part of his *Tabulatura nova* (Hamburg, 1624), points out that they can translate his staff-score into 'the ordinary letter-tablature' (*in die gewöhnliche Buchstaben Tabulatur*) just as easily as they could transcribe into tablature from separate parts.

The so-called 'German' notation for the keyboard—by no means confined to Germany—is the commonest. Its origins can be traced back to the fourteenth-century Robertsbridge Codex.[1] It had a vigorous life for three or four centuries and was abandoned with reluctance, so habituated had players become to its use. It was constructed with one line in ordinary staff notation, underneath which the other parts were written as separate lines of notes in the ordinary letter—'a' to 'g'—notation, with marks for rests and, as in the lute tablature, for time-values. On page 782 are shown the last twelve bars of 'O haylige, onbeflecte' from Virdung, with a transcription underneath.

The most elaborate music was written in this form and after about 1570 many composers wrote all the parts in the alphabet system, dispensing with the staff altogether.[2]

Spanish writers devised systems based on figures. The method advocated by Bermudo in his *Declaración* of 1555[3] accepts a range extending from ◠ to ◠ and numbers each note consecutively from the bass, 1 to 42. There should, of course, be 46 units but four are missing on account of the 'short octave' in the bass, so common in keyboards of the period. A line is ruled for each part and the numbers of the notes are placed on these lines.

Ex. 380

Bermudo's system numbered every semitone, but he refers to a modification of this system which reduced the quantity of numbers to be memorized by numbering only the white notes and introducing signs for flats or sharps (which applied also to the 'short octave') and so on, with numbers from 1 to 27; this extended the range up to ◠. Picchi's *Intavolatura* of 1620[4] employs this notation.

[1] See Vol. III, pp. 420 ff., and pl. IV (a).
[2] See Wolf's list of published works and manuscripts, op. cit. ii, pp. 32 ff.
[3] See p. 641.
[4] See p. 646.

Hie hatt ein endt das lidlin
O haylige: onbeflecte: zart
iunckfrauschafft marie.

Ex. 379

A use of numbers that seems far more practical to our eyes was introduced by Henestrosa in his *Libro de cifra nueva* of 1557[1] and is perhaps best known from its employment by Hernando de Cabezón in the edition of his father's *Obras de música* which he published in 1578.[1] The seven notes of the diatonic scale are numbered 1 to 7 and each octave is distinguished by some modification of the digits:

Ex. 381[2]

Sharp and flat signs are used for chromatic intervals and, when specially needed, the usual lute-tablature signs mark the time-values. Each had a line, as in Bermudo's system, and the works vary from two to six parts.

Ex. 382[3]

The system was still used by Francisco Correa de Arauxo in his *Libro de tientos* published at Alcalá in 1626.[4]

[1] See p. 612.
[2] A sign, ♮ or B, at the head of each piece indicates whether '4' is B♮ or B♭.
[3] Cabezón, *Obras de música* (Madrid, 1578), fo. 84, line 6.   [4] See page 681.

XIV

MUSIC AND DRAMA

By EDWARD J. DENT[1]

THE NEW STYLE

THE creation of opera at the end of the sixteenth century was such
a complete novelty in the world of music that subsequent historians
have racked their brains to find some sort of ancestry for it. It is true
enough that music has been associated with dance and drama from
the days of remote antiquity; but so far as the arts of the Renaissance
are concerned, the integration of drama and music by Ottavio
Rinuccini and Jacopo Peri was something that had never been
achieved or even tentatively approached before. The full history of
that achievement will be described in the next chapter, but before
we discuss the subject of 'opera before opera', as it has been called,
we must form some basic idea of what the fundamental idea of opera
really was.

A modern opera-goer, confronted with the scores—and the scores
only—of Peri's *Euridice*, Caccini's *Euridice*, and Cavalieri's *Rappresentazione di Anima e di Corpo* (all of the year 1600) would probably
find them so intolerably dull from a musical point of view that he
would need some determination and perseverance to read more than
a few pages of any of them. Few musical works require so much concentrated effort of imagination, auditive, visual, and emotional, to
bring them to life. For the visual effort there are indeed available a
few contemporary drawings and prints; the actual words and notes
are easily readable. What we cannot evoke, and what must have made
the deepest impression on their first audiences, is the way in which the
words were declaimed and the music sung—the emotional values of
actual performance. The key to this will be found in a passage from
Pietro della Valle's *Discorso della musica dell'età nostra* (1640):[2]

However, all those [singers of the sixteenth century] had hardly any
other technique of singing apart from trills and florid passages and a good

---

[1] Revised, with additional matter, by Frederick Sternfeld.
[2] Quoted by Angelo Solerti, *Le origini del melodramma* (Milan, 1903), p. 162.

voice-production. As to *piano* and *forte*, gradual *crescendo* and graceful *diminuendo*, expression of feelings, judicious bringing out of the sense of the words, of making the voice sound cheerful or melancholy, tender or courageous, and of other similar *galanterie*[1] which modern singers do supremely well—all such things were never so much as talked about in those days.

Della Valle goes on to say that this new style was introduced to Rome by Emilio de' Cavalieri. What we may deduce from it is that the madrigal singers of the previous century did no more than sing their words and notes, however accurately and intelligently, just as they were written, with nothing like the individual personality of a great actor. Music in the theatre had been no more than an accessory to spoken drama and spectacle. The 'new music' was drama itself.

RENAISSANCE DRAMA

At this point it may be useful to summarize briefly the history of drama during the Renaissance. The religious drama of the Middle Ages, the *sacra rappresentazione*, performed originally by religious confraternities on religious occasions, had by this time become so elaborate and so little devotional that ecclesiastical authorities sometimes forbade such works to be acted in public, though they continued to be printed. The 'revival of learning' led to the performance of the comedies of Plautus and Terence in Latin, followed very soon by Italian translations and Italian imitations of them by Ariosto, Aretino, Machiavelli, and others. These were acted largely by amateurs, chiefly university students, especially at the courts of Ferrara and Mantua. A professional theatre began when the itinerant entertainers of the streets formed themselves into organized companies known as the *commedia dell'arte* (*arte* meaning craft or trade) and in English as the 'comedy of masks'.[2]

The main characteristic of the mask actors was that they improvised their parts, for the simple reason that they were mostly illiterate. So far as we can ascertain (for naturally no complete play of theirs was ever written down), their dialogue originated in the back-chat, naturally in dialect, of local types representing the eternal conflict between rich and poor, learned and ignorant, old and young—the

---

[1] *Galanterie* is hard to translate exactly; it seems to mean the indefinable manners and graces of a singer with a fine intelligence and a distinguished personality.

[2] On the Comedy of Masks see Kathleen M. Lea, *Italian Popular Comedy*, 2 vols. (Oxford, 1934; reprinted New York, 1962) and 'Italy' in *The Oxford Companion to the Theatre* (ed. Phyllis Hartnoll) (London, 1961); also the introduction to Gozzi's *The Blue Monster*, tr. Edward J. Dent (Cambridge, 1951), and Allardyce Nicoll, *The World of the Harlequin* (Cambridge, 1963).

sympathies of the audience being always with the inferior party. When they formed companies they took over skeleton plots from the 'learned' comedy and thus came to include a conventional pair of young lovers who spoke more or less literary Italian. But it must be clearly understood that the *commedia dell'arte* was not a definite play or even a definite type of play; it was simply a system of acting based on conventional types of local character, the chief masks being Pantalone, the rich old man (Venetian), the Doctor, more often of Law than of Medicine (Bolognese), and the servants, knave and fool or both (Bergamask), generally called Zanni (zany), Venetian diminutive of Giovanni (John). Later on we meet with the *miles gloriosus* of Plautus in the shape of a Spanish captain or a German *Landsknecht*.

Tragedy plays a comparatively small part in the Italian theatre. Modern Italian scholars have said that their countrymen are by nature 'anti-tragic'; the tragedy of the Renaissance was too self-consciously literary and erudite to have any appeal outside a very small circle of highly educated people who were influenced by Seneca.[1] Into the history of music it does not enter at all, apart from a few madrigals composed as entr'actes; tragic opera is a creation of much later date. On the literary side the first operas were derived from the *favola pastorale* or pastoral play, of which literary critics have often said that its very language was half-way to music. The classic examples of the pastoral are Tasso's *Aminta* (1573) and Guarini's *Il pastor fido* (1598). The first steps towards the pastoral had been taken before the close of the fifteenth century: in Angelo Poliziano's *Orfeo* at Mantua (1471?, 1480?) and in Nicolo Correggio's *Cefalo* at Ferrara (1487), both of which works devote some time to instrumental interludes and dances. Poliziano's *Orfeo* is one of the first Italian plays to employ the methods of the *sacra rappresentazione* for secular drama. It included a few songs and choruses which were set to music long misattributed to one Germi; unfortunately it has not been preserved.[2]

Music both vocal and instrumental was considered indispensable in all the theatrical entertainments of the courts, but although we often have copious information about the scenery and the spectacle,[3]

---

[1] Concerning the influence of Seneca on Cinzio's *Orbecche* (Ferrara, 1541), with musical entr'actes, and Trissino's *Sofonisba* (Vicenza, 1562), see Heinz Kindermann, *Theatergeschichte Europas*, 5 vols (Salzburg, 1957–62), ii, pp. 64 ff.

[2] See Kindermann, op. cit. ii, pp. 43 ff.; also D. P. Walker, ed., *Les Fêtes du mariage de Ferdinand de Médicis et de Christine de Lorraine . . . Intermèdes de Pellegrina* (Paris, 1963), p. xi.

[3] See *Les Fêtes de la Renaissance* (ed. Jean Jacquot) (Paris, 1956).

details about the music are very scanty and hardly any of the actual music has been preserved. Comedies always had incidental music in the shape of madrigals as prologues and entr'actes; some of these have already been mentioned in Chapter II.[1] As their primary purpose was information about the play, they are extremely simple, in order that the words might be clearly heard; later on they sometimes show more musical interest and a sense of appropriate choral colour, using deep voices and harsh effects for serious situations. None of the instrumental music has survived, although it is frequently mentioned in descriptions. Quite early in the century the practice began of performing *intermedii* between the acts; these soon became more and more elaborate in scenery and machinery until the poets began to complain that their plays were regarded as no more than mere accessories to the *intermedii*.[2]

THE *INTERMEDII*

The *intermedii* seem to have been mainly *tableaux vivants* and dumb shows with or without dances; the most wonderful and the most admired contributions to them were the transformation scenes designed by eminent architects and painters. We note in the descriptions that the musicans were almost invariably concealed; the sudden entry of invisible music was a notable factor in the general effect of magic and mystery. When the music was instrumental it was distributed in different parts of the theatre in groups of different tone-qualities, high and low, loud and soft. The large orchestra of *Orfeo* was nothing new. On rare occasions a group of instrumentalists would be brought on to the stage in sight of the audience, sometimes rising from below on a 'machine'; in such cases they were always in costume, and we may be quite sure that they did not play their parts from sheets of music laid out on desks. How they learned and rehearsed it we do not know. All these court entertainments were given in rooms of palaces, some of which can still be seen, and they were all large oblong halls, not theatres with a more or less semicircular auditorium. A stage would be erected at one end, generally with steps and a slope leading into the central floor; the audience sat in tiers ranged along the back and side walls so that no one turned his back on the duke and duchess seated on separate raised chairs about one-third of the way from the back wall of the audience to the back of the

---

[1] See pp. 41 and 74.

[2] For the comments of Castiglione, Grazzini, and Trissino, see Kindermann, op. cit., pp. 70 ff.; also Walker, op. cit., p. xii.

stage. Where exactly the invisible musicians were placed is uncertain, but we have evidence that the trumpets which announced the arrival of gods and heroes were generally on an elevated platform. This arrangement had its own acoustic problems, of which the stage directors were quite well aware; thus we are told that care must be taken about the music so that it should not sound too noisy in a narrow room and drown the words, or sound thin and dull in a large space. The resonance of these halls must have been very great even when they were well filled, and that probably accounts for the simple harmonies and slow pace of Monteverdi's movements for brass. In any case it was the general sonority of the music which impressed audiences rather than the intricacies of counterpoint.

The only real theatres in Italy built during the sixteenth century were the Teatro Olimpico at Vicenza, begun by Palladio in 1579 and completed by his pupil Scamozzi in 1584 (see pl. V), and the theatre at Sabbioneta by Scamozzi, 1588–90, both of which are comparatively small buildings.

We have a complete description of the festivities at Florence for the marriage of Cosimo I de' Medici to Eleonora da Toledo in 1539 which may be summarized here.[1]

The bride entered Florence on Sunday, 29 June, by the Porta al Prato, while a madrigal by Francesco Corteccia was sung in eight parts by a chorus of 24 voices accompanied by 4 *cornetti* and 4 trombones, all placed on the top of the gate. This was 'Ingredere', followed by 'Sacro e santo Imeneo' (nine parts). The wedding banquet was on the next Sunday morning (6 July), after which a pageant was shown in front of the tables, representing Florence, the Tiber, and various towns near Florence, with seven madrigals by Corteccia and others. On Wednesday evening (9 July) after supper there was a play, *Il commodo*, by Antonio Landi, with *intermedii* invented by Giovambattista Strozzi. The scenery represented the city of Pisa; the music for the prologue and *intermedii* was by Corteccia; some numbers were for solo voices, although printed in four, five, and six parts. (1) 'Vatten' almo riposo', sung by Aurora to a harpsichord and little organs. (2) After Act I, 'Guardane almo pastore', sung by six shepherds, first unaccompanied, then repeated with six more shepherds playing *storte*.[2]

---

[1] These festivities have been described fragmentarily by many scholars, beginning with Kiesewetter in his *Schicksale und Beschaffenheit des weltlichen Gesanges* (Leipzig, 1841), but the first complete account is that of Federico Ghisi, *Feste musicali della Firenze Medicea (1480–1589)* (Florence, 1939). The *intermedii* performed at the marriage of Francesco de' Medici and Johanna of Austria in 1565 have been described in the previous chapter (see pp. 770 ff.).   [2] i.e. krummhorns.

PLATE V

THE TEATRO OLIMPICO AT VICENZA

(3) After Act II, 'Chi ne l'ha tolt' ohimè', sung by three sirens and three sea-nymphs to three lutes. (4) After Act III, 'O begli anni d'oro', sung by Silenus (soprano) with a *violone* playing all the parts. (The singer at that date can hardly have been a castrato but may have been a falsetto alto.) (5) After Act IV, 'Hor chi mai canterà', sung by eight hunting nymphs. (6) At the end of the play, 'Vatten', almo riposo', sung by Night with four trombones. Finally (7) 'Bacco, Bacco evoè', sung and danced by four Bacchantes and four Satyrs with various instruments all together.[1]

The prologue madrigal (no. 1) is so short—two lines of verse only, one repeated—that it may perhaps have had more stanzas; it is rather in the style of a *frottola*. The choruses of shepherds and nymphs are in the early madrigal style and look rather stiff on paper; but we must consider the acoustic conditions and also the visual conditions. The general effect may have been more lively and spirited than the score suggests. In any case the arrangement of the madrigals for solo voices and contrasted groups of men and women, with different kinds of instruments, shows a sense of variety and design.

The madrigals and even the play were but transitory items in the course of perhaps a week's continuous festivities. The first object of a princely wedding was to secure the continuance of the dynasty; the second was the glorification of the dynasty in the most sumptuous way. The bridal pair enjoyed only the barest necessary minimum of privacy; otherwise they were the central figures of continuous publicity. One may say that the general idea of the festivities was to surround them with a realization of the 'golden age', Tasso's 'bell'età dell'oro'. From the detailed descriptions—far too long even to summarize here—we can see that the vast saloons were transformed by the scenic architects into a vision of Arcadia in which all the divinities of classical mythology, some on the stage, some sculptured and painted on the windowsills, had arrived in person as invited guests to the wedding. The whole room, from stage to auditorium, became, thanks to the stairs and slopes, one complete unity, as we can see from the pictures, and the whole week was a continuous homage. In Monteverdi's *Ballo delle ingrate*, produced at Mantua in 1608,[2] Venus calls on Pluto to admire what he sees before him, the palace of Mantua

---

[1] All these *Musiche fatte nelle nozze* were printed at once by Gardano (Venice, 1539). Nos. 2 and 5 are printed in full by Ghisi, op. cit.; no. 1 by Einstein, *The Italian Madrigal*, iii (Princeton, 1949), p. 321; see also p. 148, n. 5. On the *frottola* style of performing a madrigal as a solo with accompaniment, see pp. 36 and 125, and Walker, op. cit., p. xii.

[2] Reprinted by Torchi, *L'arte musicale italiana*, vi (Milan, n.d.) and Malipiero, *Le opere di Claudio Monteverdi*, viii (Asolo, 1929).

and its distinguished company, a sight far more wonderful than
ancient Rome or Athens. These lines illuminate the essential difference
between the *intermedii* (and similar entertainments) and the first real
operas; the operas ignored the audience and concentrated all attention on the actual drama itself. Homage appeared later on, but only
after opera had established itself successfully as a court entertainment
and began to assimilate decorative elements which it had dogmatically
repudiated in its first ascetic and austere beginnings.

The earliest stage music, i.e. music integral to the action of a play,
which has survived[1] is a scene of religious ritual in Agostino Beccari's
pastoral *Il sacrificio* (Ferrara, 1554), composed by Alfonso dalla
Viola; it is a series of versicles and responses sung by a priest of Pan
and the chorus. There is also a *canzone finale* at the end of the play.

Ex. 383
(Note-values halved)
(i) SACERDOTE

You that have Pan's horns pointing towards heaven, fixed in your broad
and aspcious forehead. . . .)

(ii) CHORUS
(a)

(The priest sings two more stanzas in the same style, followed by choral
responses which are different.)

(b)

[1] Printed in full by Solerti in *Gli albori del melodramma*, i (Milan, 1904), between
pp. 12 and 13, but in separate parts, with several misprints.

(iii) CANZONE FINALE

(O ye woodland gods, if anyone near has been listening to our living flames on the coolest shores. . . .)

Some scholars have called the priest's invocations a 'monody', seeing in them a precursor of opera. Although they look more like what the composer might have heard in some more contemporary place of worship, we must note that they were sung by the composer's brother Andrea *con la lira,* with a viola da gamba, on which he must surely have harmonized the obvious cadences with upper parts. Solo music for a bass voice was on principle regarded mainly as a harmonic bass, as indeed often by Purcell and Handel. The three different responses are interesting, and they too suggest a religion more modern than that of Arcadia. The final chorus may look dull to the reader of today, but it follows the rhythm of the words very exactly and indeed expressively. It was not meant to be an operatic finale; it is the end of a poetic drama.

VENETIAN FESTIVE MUSIC

From 1571, when the victory of Lepanto was celebrated, onwards there was a continuous succession of festivities of various kinds, with scenic performance and music, both sacred and secular, at Venice.[1] Practically nothing of the music has survived. Under the Doge Marco Grimani (1595–1605) the Ducal Palace became 'a continuous theatre of musical dramas, performed by the academies'.[2]

We cannot call these 'operas'; it is evident from the printed librettos that they were either oratorios or 'homages' of some sort. The great occasion was when Henry III of France was entertained at Venice in 1574 on his way from Poland to Paris. It was after seeing these various shows that Henry commanded performances of the same kind in his own capital. The so-called *Tragedia* of Cornelio Frangipani, with music by Claudio Merulo, was probably the model for the famous *Balet comique de la Royne*.[3] The poet called it a 'tragedy' because the interlocutors are gods and goddesses, but it has nothing tragic or even dramatic about it; the characters appeared in costume and no doubt made use of gesture and movement, but it is nothing but a series of speeches, songs, and choruses in praise of the heroic King of France. Nothing of Merulo's music has survived, but the poet tells us that: 'Tutti li recitanti hanno cantato in suavissimi concenti, quando soli, quando accompagnati; & in fin il coro di Mercurio era di sonatori, che haueano quanti varij istrumenti che si sonarono giamai'.

His words are given in the original Italian because the interpretation of them is doubtful. Frangipani talks very enthusiastically about the whole work, and his phrase 'as many different instruments as were ever played' does not suggest the accuracy of a scientific historian. Some numbers, a few solos, a duet and the choruses were certainly sung, but the sentence quoted above is no proof that the whole was sung; it would rather seem to mean that 'all the actors sang very well' when required to do so. Einstein[4] suggests that as the speeches were largely in *ottave* the actors improvised melody to them on one of the standard basses; all this is very conjectural, and even if they did so, the result cannot have been anything like the music of Peri's *Euridice*, except possibly the strophic prologue.

---

[1] See Solerti, 'Le rappresentazioni musicali di Venezia, 1571–1605', *Rivista musicale italiana*, ix (1902), p. 503.

[2] Quoted by Solerti from Francesco Caffi, *Storia della musica sacra nella già Cappella Ducale di San Marco* (Venice, 1854–5).

[3] See *infra*, p. 806.

[4] Op. cit. ii, p. 550.

THE *CAMERATA* IN AN *INTERMEDIO*

In 1589, at the wedding of Ferdinando de' Medici and Cristina of Lorraine in Florence,[1] there were *intermedii* on the most magnificent scale with music by Marenzio, Malvezzi, Cavalieri, Peri, Caccini, Bardi, and Antonio Archilei. Several of these, took part also as singers and instrumentalists; some of them afterwards became famous in connexion with the first operas. One of Marenzio's contributions was the *Combattimento d'Apolline col serpente*.[2] As always, the music consisted mainly of madrigals, but on this occasion the *intermedii* were so elaborate that each required four or five madrigals as well as an instrumental *sinfonia* to begin with. The orchestra is enumerated in detail[3] and as usual includes 'all the instruments that were ever played'. Music for the fourth *intermedio*, the 'Comparsa di demoni', was composed by Caccini; it is preserved at Florence (Bibl. Naz. Magl. XIX. 66) where it was discovered by Federico Ghisi. It was sung by a female magician descending on a cloud and accompanying herself on the lute:

Ex. 384

(I who would make the moon fall from the heavens for you. . . .)

while other instruments played off-stage: arch-lyras, basses, viols,

---

[1] See Solerti, *Gli albori*, i, p. 42, where full references to sources are given; D. P. Walker, 'La Musique des intermèdes florentins de 1589 et l'Humanisme', *Les Fêtes de la Renaissance*, p. 133; Federico Ghisi, 'Un aspect inédit des intermèdes de 1589 à la cour médicéenne', ibid., p. 145. Scenes from these famous *intermedii* are reproduced ibid., pl. xxxvi (fig. 2) and xxxix (fig. 7); the music has been edited by Walker, *Les Fêtes du mariage*; long excerpts are printed in Max Schneider, *Die Anfänge der Basso Continuo* (Leipzig, 1918), pp. 116 ff.

[2] The text was by Rinuccini and is therefore, as Gustave Reese says, 'the kernel from which the *Dafne* libretto of 1594 evolved', the libretto composed in turn by Peri, Marco da Gagliano, and (in Opitz's translation) by Schütz.

[3] See Robert L. Weaver, 'Sixteenth Century Instrumentation', *Musical Quarterly*, xlvii (1961), p. 363.

lutes, a violin (*un violino*), double-harps, trombones (*bassi di tromboni*), and *organi di legno*. As one would expect, an orchestra accompanying a supernatural being who commands the blessed spirits (demons) to appear is predominantly composed of strings, with a reinforcement of the bass line by trombones. The *organo di legno*, as we know from Monteverdi's *Orfeo*, was often associated with good or 'white' magic. The blessed spirits themselves perform a madrigal *à* 6 to the accompaniment of another ensemble, predominantly strings: harp, chitarrone, 2 arch-lutes, 2 small lutes, 2 lyres, psaltery, sopranino viol (*una violina*), transverse flute, *viola bastarda*. On the other hand, the spirits of the infernal region are clothed in a sound in which trombones—'quattro tromboni', not 'bassi di tromboni'—dominate the strings; in addition to the five vocal parts, four trombones, four viols, and one lyre are prescribed. Again, the instrumentation anticipates Monteverdi's in the infernal scenes of *Orfeo*.[1]

Monteverdi's masterpiece, performed at Mantua in 1607,[2] also shares with the earlier court interludes the mythological subject matter so characteristic of late humanism. In Mantua, the prologue and the final act with the ascent of Apollo must have reminded some listeners of the Florentine *intermedii* whose six subdivisions were: I. The Harmony of the Spheres; II. The Contest of Muses and Pierides; III. The Victory of Apollo over the Serpent; IV. The Appearance of good and evil Demons; V. The Deliverance of Arion by the Dolphin; VI. The Descent of Apollo [and other deities] with [the spirits of] Harmony and Rhythm.

The descent of Apollo who brings rhythm and harmony to enrich and adorn the world ('per arrichir, per adornar il mondo') is, of course, reminiscent of Jupiter's descent on an eagle in the *Balet comique* of 1581, discussed *infra*. In view of the many intermarriages between the houses of Valois, Lorraine and Medici and the great influence of Catherine de' Medici, who lived in France from the time of her marriage in 1533 until her death in 1589, these similarities are more than coincidence. The harmony of the spheres which is so elaborately represented in the first and sixth of the Florentine *intermedii* has its direct ancestor in the chorus emanating from the *voûte dorée* accompanying the descent of Jupiter. Similarly, the *ballo*, an elaborate piece of 250 bars which concludes the sixth *intermedio*, and in which a full choir alternates with a *concertino* of three soloists who sing and dance,

---

[1] On the polychromatic orchestra of the *intermedii*, and of early Monteverdi, and the monochromatic orchestra of later Venetian opera, see Robert L. Weaver, 'Orchestra in Early Italian Opera', *Journal of the American Musicological Society*, xvii (1964), pp. 83–89.   [2] See pp. 832 ff.

is reminiscent of the *grand balet* with which dryads and naiads bring the *Balet comique* to its close. Since both the *Intermedii* of 1589 and the *Balet* of 1581 were printed, it is not surprising that they were imitated in the sumptuous court masques under James I and Charles I. A good example is *Tempe Restored*, enacted in London on 14 February, 1632, the general idea and the décor by Inigo Jones, the verse by Aurelian Townshend.[1] There the appearance of 'Harmony . . . attended by a chorus of music', succeeded by the appearance of 'the eight spheres . . . seated on a cloud . . . To the music of these spheres there appeared two other clouds descending . . . The highest sphere represented by Mr. [Nicholas] Laniere', leading to the final stage remark, 'Pallas and Circe return into the scene with the nymphs and chorus; and so concluded the last *Intermedium*. After which the Queen and her Ladies began the revels, with the King and his Lords', traces a design obviously indebted to continental models.

Musically, the *intermedii* of 1589 are an important milestone in the development of the new baroque style, to appear in the *Euridice* of 1600 and the *Orfeo* of 1607. It is true that the proportion of choral music is higher than in the early operas. But by and large the texture is homophonic and the style *al fresco*, as one would expect in such sumptuous entertainments addressed primarily to courtiers. The same is true of purely instrumental pieces: the *sinfonia* by Marenzio which opens the second *intermedio* anticipates the brevity and homophony of Monteverdi's preludes to *Orfeo* and *Poppea*; Marenzio's orchestra plays the melody twice, first in duple, then in triple time, and thus provides Monteverdi and Cavalli with one of their favourite designs. The solo arias by Peri, Caccini and Cavalieri with their fanciful melismas (printed in full rather than left to the discretion of the performer) are obvious precursors of the *Nuove musiche* and of Orfeo's 'Possente spirto' in Monteverdi. Certainly, Peri's aria from the fifth *intermedio*, where the elaborate vocal ornaments are echoed twice (*ecco con due risposte*), is an ancestor of the echo-technique of Monteverdi and the Baroque era in general. Yet, it would be an exaggeration to claim that these and other melismas were particularly expressive or placed upon the most suitable syllables. To assist the birth of the *stile nuovo* was one thing, to develop it to perfection another. Probably the most lasting contribution of the 1589 *intermedii* to the development of music was the prominent employment of ritornello

[1] A. Townshend, *Poems and Masks*, ed. E. K. Chambers (Oxford, 1912), pp. 88, 90, 92, 122; Enid Welsford, *The Court Masque* (Cambridge, 1927), pp. 106, 225; W. W. Greg, *Bibliography of Printed English Drama*, 4 vols. (London, 1939–59), ii, p. 602.

and concertato techniques. Malvezzi's chorus of the blessed spirits from the fourth *intermedio* emphasizes the phrase 'e felice ritorna eterno canto' in clear ritornello fashion (bars 27, 33) and sets it off from the rest of the music by a conspicuous suspended seventh, accompanied at the lower third; what is more, the phrase serves also as an effective conclusion. But even more important is the patterning of the *ballo* by Cavalieri, which brings the entire work to a close. It must be remembered that when the music was printed in 1591 it was entitled *Intermedii et concerti*. Obviously, the concertato technique which organizes the 21 sub-sections of this *ballo* applies to sonority, vocal and instrumental, as well as to thematic technique. Throughout a massive vocal tutti, accompanied by the entire orchestra, is contrasted with a trio of female voices, accompanied by two guitars and a tambourine. Thematically the ritornello technique of the tutti sections reminds modern listeners of a Vivaldi concerto: the entire tutti does not reappear until the end, but whenever the full chorus sounds, which happens nine times, apart from the two corner sections, it sings fragments of the opening ritornello. Here the music comes first, *dopo le parole*, which is not in conformity with the precepts of the Florentine *camerata* but an apt analogy to the discrepancy between theory and practice to be observed later with Gluck and Wagner. It is not surprising to read in the printed score of 1591: 'il ballo stesso fù del Sig. Emilio de Cavalieri e le parole furno fatte dopo l'aria del ballo', for the metrical complexity of the *ballo* demands a libretto tailored to musical strains, employing lines of 11 syllables here, 7 syllables there, and 8 syllables in the opening and closing tutti.

FESTIVE MUSIC IN GERMANY

The festivities for the wedding of Duke Wilhelm V of Bavaria with Renata of Lorraine in 1568 have already been mentioned in connexion with the impromptu 'comedy of masks' in which Lassus took part.[1] They lasted from the arrival of the bride on 21 February until 9 March. Every day Mass was celebrated and naturally there was a banquet every day to the accompaniment of music, as well as masquerades and tournaments. Much of the music was by Lassus and a good deal also by Annibale Padovano. At one of the banquets the preliminaries were introduced with trumpets and drums followed by a *battaglia* by Padovano for eight voices with *cornetti* and trombones;[2] then came the

---

[1] See p. 57.

[2] Perhaps the piece published by the Gabrielis in their *Dialoghi musicali de div. ecc. autori* (Venice, 1590) and reprinted by Benvenuti, *Istituzioni e monumenti dell'arte musicale italiana*, i, p. 177.

first course with a motet by Lassus, also with brass, this no doubt by way of grace; and each successive course had its music, sometimes a madrigal with various instruments, sometimes a purely instrumental piece. The instruments were grouped in various ways. It is interesting to note that two female composers were represented, Maddalena Casulana and Caterina Willaert, daughter of Adrian. On 27 February a tragedy on the subject of Samson was presented by the Jesuits, but music seems to have been required only in two of the *intermedii* to present the nine Muses and twelve nymphs.

We note that none of this music was German; the Jesuit play was almost certainly in Latin. We note further that none of the music was really dramatic. The situation seems to have been much the same at the other German courts, at any rate in those which were Catholic by religion. The Netherlanders appeared later in Germany than in Italy, but by the end of the fifteenth century they were firmly established at Munich, Vienna, and Prague. The musical establishments of the princes, which date back well into the fifteenth century and were always a source of great pride to their rulers, began as ecclesiastical and military bodies. Trumpets and drums are always the mark of royalty and indeed were often forbidden to be employed (e.g. at weddings) by anyone not of noble birth. The dance music for social gatherings was generally wind-music, as we can see from contemporary pictures; if the chapel choir was called in to sing, its repertory seems to have been mainly sacred, even on secular occasions. Even in the southernmost courts the imitation of Italian pageantry showed little appreciation of drama until Italian opera had become a well-established form and could be imported with Italian singers (including of course *castrati*) and Italian scenery. Such accounts of festivities as are available give the impression that the German princes, however susceptible to the charms of music, were much more interested in fighting and feasting.

JESUIT AND PROTESTANT SCHOOL DRAMAS

The Germans were always keenly interested in education, and under the influence of humanism drama played a very important part in schools and universities, both Protestant and Catholic. The Jesuits first established themselves in Vienna in 1551 and within four years they had started a long series of school plays; for a long time these were in Latin, but that did not prevent their becoming highly elaborate and indeed vigorously theatrical. They included a certain amount of music, though of a very simple type, and it was not until many years later that the Jesuits undertook performances of opera.

From Vienna the Jesuits spread to Ingolstadt, Munich, and as far as Cologne, as well as southwards to Klagenfurt and Gorizia. Their playwrights were largely influenced by the Spanish theatre and had no hesitation in making use of tragedy, spectacle, and low comedy in a single drama. All these plays were performed by amateurs, school-boys and university students, acting female parts as well as male; they had no contact with the professional theatre, which seems to have been much more like the early Italian *commedia dell'arte* in its methods. The Protestant schools were no less active in drama, though apparently less spectacular, and they very soon began acting their plays in German. The subjects treated, both by Protestants and Catholics, were of course designed for moral edification and derived from the Old Testament and from classical history. It was the systematic practice of the humanists to combine classical and Christian mythology whenever possible; they saw nothing incongruous in the simultaneous appearance of the nine Muses and the four Christian virtues.

Classical prosody was taught by setting such things as the Odes of Horace to music,[1] and the school plays generally ended with a Latin chorus in some classical metre, often intended for dancing as well. A good many of these have been preserved. The earliest, for Reuchlin's *Scenica Progymnasmata* (or *Henno*), goes back as far as 1497; each act ended with a chorus, no doubt sung in unison, in the style of plainsong; the composer was Daniel Megel. Later on we find these tunes harmonized in three and four parts, sometimes in the style of the *frottole*, which seems to point to a lute accompaniment; in every case the music is extremely simple and in the character of a folksong or a chorale melody.[2]

SCHÜTZ'S *DAPHNE*

The first real German opera was the *Daphne* of Heinrich Schütz, performed on 13 April 1627 at Schloss Hartenfels, near Torgau, for the marriage of Princess Sophia of Saxony to George II of Hesse-Darmstadt.[3] The libretto was a translation by Martin Opitz of the

---

[1] See Vol. III, pp. 370–1.

[2] For a full account of the plays see Joseph Gregor, *Weltgeschichte des Theaters* (Zürich, 1933), and Kindermann, op. cit. ii, p. 250. Several examples of the music are printed in Liliencron, 'Die Chorgesänge des lateinisch-deutschen Schuldramas im XVI. Jahrhundert', *Vierteljahrsschrift für Musikwissenschaft*, vi (1890), p. 309.

[3] On the Saxon court festivities of this period generally, see G. Pietzsch, 'Dresdener Hoffeste vom 16.–18. Jh.', *Musik und Bild* (*Festschrift* for Max Seiffert) (Kassel, 1938),

already mentioned *Dafne* written by Rinuccini for Peri in 1594. The music is entirely lost. The work is described in the German libretto as *Pastoral-Tragödie*, and a court diary of the time reports: 'den 13 agirten die Musicanten musicaliter eine Pastoral-Tragi-Comödie von der Daphne'.

Martin Opitz (1597–1639) was a poet of distinction. He was a schoolmaster by profession and perhaps influenced by the humanistic school plays. But *Daphne* as a German opera had no successors, unless we count a number of works performed later at the court of Stuttgart, evidently derived from French models, mixtures of drama, singing, and ballet on mythological subjects. None of their music has survived and the names of the composers are not mentioned either in the manuscripts of the dramas or in the court archives. It seems that the actors were professional; one performed in 1673, apparently without music, has a dedication signed by Christian Janetzky, Pickelhäring, which at once suggests an itinerant troupe of comedians. In the ballets the performers were mostly amateurs, including members of the ducal family.

SEELEWIG

The school drama is also the origin of *Seelewig, ein geistliches Waldgedicht* (religious pastoral), words by Philipp Harsdörffer, music by Siegmund Theophil Staden,[1] which was printed at Nuremberg in 1644 in a periodical called *Frauenzimmergesprächspiele*, apparently the first example of a popular German 'family magazine'.[2] No performance of this work has been traced and it seems to have been intended for domestic entertainment, though it requires considerable resources both vocal and instrumental. Seelewig represents the human soul; she is tempted by various other symbolic figures and finally saved by Understanding and Conscience, as in *Everyman* and in Cavalieri's *Anima e corpo*. The background, however, is that of an Italian pastoral with nymphs and shepherds; it is all on a very small scale. The text, like those of the Stuttgart plays, is mostly in German 'alexandrines', rhymed couplets of six feet, but rhythmically more like the *versi martelliani* in which Goldoni and other Italian dramatists of the eighteenth century sometimes wrote.

p. 83, and Irmgard Becker-Glauch, *Die Bedeutung der Musik für die Dresdener Hoffeste* (Kassel, 1951).

[1] Reprinted by Eitner, *Monatshefte für Musikgeschichte*, xiii (1881), p. 53; long excerpt in Schering, *Geschichte der Musik in Beispielen* (Leipzig, 1931), p. 236.

[2] See Eugen Schmitz, 'Zur musikgeschichtlichen Bedeutung der Harsdörfferschen "Frauenzimmergesprächspiele" ', *Liliencron-Festschrift* (Leipzig, 1910), p. 254.

The lines sometimes rhyme internally (third and sixth foot), which adds to the monotony, as Staden made little difference between recitative and aria; the recitative is too regularly metrical owing to the regular rhymes, and the arias, generally strophic with several verses, too declamatory to sound like songs, though they are sometimes genuinely expressive.

ENGLISH COMEDIANS IN GERMANY

Mention must also be made of the so-called 'English Comedians' (*Englische Komödianten*) who toured Germany from 1592 to the middle of the following century and appeared at several of the German courts. To what extent they were really English is very uncertain; several of the actors bore unmistakably English names, and they undoubtedly acted plays of English origin, but German authorities[1] are inclined to suppose that they were mainly young Germans who had spent some time in London in the service of the Hansa and had visited the London theatres. A collection of their plays (in German) was published in 1620, containing strange travesties of Shakespeare and other English dramatists with additional matter, obviously improvised in the first instance and outrageously filthy; this is supposed to be due to the influence of the Italian comedians who had already appeared in London. The plays were diversified by dancing, acrobatics, and music, and they have a certain interest for the history of opera because they included Elizabethan 'jigs' or comic interludes which were in ballad metres and sung to English ballad tunes such as 'Brave Lord Willoughby', and 'Fortune my foe';[2] these perhaps anticipate the eighteenth-century ballad operas, English and German.

RELIGIOUS AND SECULAR DRAMA IN SPAIN

The Spanish (and Portuguese) drama of the Renaissance originated from the liturgical drama of the Middle Ages as in other countries and was acted by amateurs. Italian influences soon made their appearance through Juan del Encina (1468–1534), who was not only a playwright and actor but a composer of notable eminence. He wrote both sacred and secular *representaciones* or dialogues, the former being in the tradition of the medieval religious dramas. Of his secular pastorals two are outstanding: *Del escudero que se tornó pastor* (The squire who turned shepherd) and its sequel, *De los pastores que se*

---

[1] e.g. Johannes Bolte, *Die Singspiele der englischen Komödianten und ihre Nachfolger— Deutschland, Holland und Skandinavien* (Hamburg and Leipzig, 1893), and J. Tittmann, *Die Schauspiele der englischen Komoedianten in Deutschland* (Leipzig, 1880).

[2] Both, significantly, known to Scheidt who wrote on them respectively a *Canzon a 5* ('O Nachbar Roland'), *Werke*, ii–iii, p. 47, and keyboard variations, ibid. vi (2), p. 56.

tornaron palaciegos (The shepherds who turned courtiers). Nearly all Encina's *representaciones*, sacred or secular, end with a *villancico* composed by Encina himself, sung by all the characters.[1] The one which concludes *Los pastores* is typical:

Ex. 385

(Let no one close the doors if love comes to knock, for it is of no avail. Let us obey love willingly since we must, let us make a virtue of necessity. Let us not resist love, let no one lock it out, for to do so is of no avail.)

[1] Perhaps doubled by instruments: see Ann Livermore, 'The Spanish Dramatists and their Use of Music', *Music and Letters*, xxv (1944), p. 142.

In the middle of the same pastoral the characters sing another *villancico*, 'Gasajémonos de hucía', the opening of which has been quoted as Ex. 164 in Vol. III.[1]

Encina's rival Lucas Fernández (1474–1544), professor of music in the University of Salamanca, published in 1514 a *dialogo para cantar*[2] consisting of twenty-two seven-line stanzas all sung to the tune of 'Quién te hizo, Juan Pastor?' (There is a three-part setting of this tune in the *Cancionero de Palacio*, attributed to one Badajoz: see Anglès, *Monumentos de la música española*, v, p. 218.) Fernández also wrote a religious *Auto de la Pasión*, performed in the cathedral at Salamanca, which not only ends with a *villancico*[3] but has songs interpolated in the spoken text.

The religious drama lasted much longer in Spain than in Italy; the *autos sacramentales* were acted up to 1765. Professional companies did not exist until about 1530, and these were travelling companies acting in innyards and wherever convenient; the first permanent theatres were built about 1580. Music was always an important feature and we find an orchestra of strings as soon as the public theatres came into being. Yet the music was never more than incidental— songs, dances, choruses, but no traces of the declamatory recitative which was the foundation-stone of the first Italian operas.

There is, however, one example at least of a sacred drama which was sung all through, the *Mystery of Elche* representing the Assumption of the Virgin, which is still performed every year at Elche on 14 and 15 August. It has sometimes been compared with the Oberammergau Passion Play but differs in being an annual production and in the fact that it is set to continuous music mostly by Encina and contemporaries of his.[4]

The copy of the play and its music examined by Pedrell is dated 1639, but the original is traditionally ascribed to 1266, when at the end of December an ark is said to have arrived miraculously at Elche

---

[1] Most of Encina's compositions are preserved in the *Cancionero musical de Palacio* (Madrid, Bibl. Pal. Real, 2–1–5), which was first published by F. A. Barbieri (Madrid, 1890); new edition by Anglès in *Monumentos de la música española*, v and x (Barcelona, 1947, 1951). On Encina see further the article by Anglès in *Die Musik in Geschichte und Gegenwart*, iii, col. 1329; Gilbert Chase, 'Juan del Encina: Poet and Musician', *Music and Letters*, xx (1939), p. 420; Emilio Cotarelo y Mori, 'Juan del Encina y los orígenes del teatro español', *Estudios de historia literaria de España*, i (Madrid, 1901).

[2] In *Farsas y églogas al modo y estilo pastoril y castellano* (Salamanca, 1514); reprinted by the Real Academia Española (Madrid, 1867).

[3] Also in the *Cancionero de Palacio*: see Anglès, *Monumentos*, x, p. 169.

[4] It is described in detail and most of the music printed by Felipe Pedrell, 'La Festa d'Elche', *Sammelbände der internationalen Musikgesellschaft*, ii, 1900–1, p. 203, and also J. B. Trend, *A Picture of Modern Spain* (London, 1921).

by sea, containing an image of the Virgin and the book of the ceremonial for the play. Pedrell, on linguistic grounds, concluded that
whatever the date of the original, the present version is based on one
of 1566; but this is later than the death of Encina and he most probably wrote his music for a version of 1492. The language of the play
is Catalan. Some of the music is for one voice without harmony, sung
by the Virgin and other characters; it seems to be a variant of plainsong hymns such as 'Vexilla regis', which is actually mentioned in
the book. Pedrell also obtained copies of two other songs sung by the
Virgin but never written down until his time; they were handed down
orally and apparently well known to every child in Elche. He was
unable to conjecture their source, which he seems to have thought
might be some oriental or Mozarabic liturgy, and he does not seem to
have noticed that the traditional music is (to some extent at any rate)
a variation of the already varied plainsong hymn mentioned above.

Ex. 386

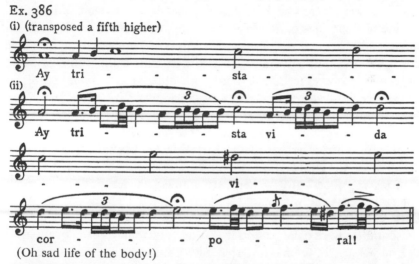

(Oh sad life of the body!)

The choruses are in the early madrigal style with very little use of
imitation, but as they are well contrasted in pitch and grouping of
voices they would make a good effect in performance as long as the
whole action was seen. In the following example the Virgin is received
into Heaven and welcomed by the Trinity:

Ex. 387

The staging of the play was elaborate and the machinery probably dates from the rebuilding of the church in 1673.

THE *MASCARADE* IN FRANCE

Both French and English writers agree that the *mascarades* and masques were introduced from Italy,[1] but in these two countries the course of their development followed very different lines. The fundamental idea was a 'disguising'—a party of gentlemen in fantastic costumes and masks would ride in procession to the house of some nobleman to be entertained there with dancing and banqueting; in the earlier days some form of gaming was always included. In France the word for these 'disguisings' was *momeries*. In the fifteenth century they became very elaborate on the occasion of royal weddings and similar festivities; the masquers generally were brought in on a decorated car in the shape of a castle or a ship or other device. This led to a mock siege or battle. There are numerous descriptions of such entertainments and we are told that music played a large part in them, but we do not learn the names of any composers. The schemes of presentation were chaotic, and it was not until the Italians brought in the new spirit of humanism that any consistent or quasi-dramatic plan was conceived. Italy gave to France two types of spectacle which it is not always easy to distinguish: the *mascherate*, which are partially outdoor shows with a procession and a decorated car, and the *intermedii*, which took place indoors with the accessories of the stationary theatre.[2] It is obvious that music of an elaborate and artistic nature could only be performed adequately within doors.

[1] See, for instance, Marlowe, *Edward II*, Act I, sc. 1, and Ronsard:
            Mascarade et cartels ont prins leur nouriture
            L'un des Italiens, l'autre des vieux François.
[2] See Lionel de La Laurencie, *Le, Créateurs de l'opéra français* (Paris, new ed., 1930); Howard M. Brown, *Music in the French Secular Theater, 1400–1550* (Cambridge, Mass., 1963); *Theatrical Chansons* (Cambridge, Mass., 1963).

PLATE VI

A FRENCH *BALLET DE COUR*

Taken from Dorat: *Magnificentissimi spectaculi . . . a regina . . . descriptio* (1573).

Francis I, after seeing the Italian entertainments in their own country, the culture of which at that time was far in advance of his own, summoned numerous Italian painters, dancers and musicians to Fontainebleau; the records of the actual performances are scanty, but the court archives give copious account of the expenditure involved. Towards the middle of the century there are abundant descriptions in detail, and it is characteristic that both classical and Christian mythology are represented simultaneously. The procession of triumphal cars is always the main feature, and it is at this time that we find the French poets of the court providing words to be recited and sung in explanation of the show. As in Italy, all these spectacles are in the nature of homages. Catherine de' Medici was an accomplished dancer and inventor of dances; her ladies were mostly Italian, and in all these entertainments the dancers were drawn from the nobility. The most magnificent of her ballets was one given in 1573 in honour of the Polish Ambassadors.[1] Sixteen nymphs representing the provinces of France danced a long and intricate ballet designed by Beaujoyeulx, who was to function also as the choreographer of the famous *Balet comique* of 1581. Dorat's description of the *Ballet Polonais* refers to a 'Dialogus ad numeros musicos Orlandi', indicating that the music for the occasion, which included vocal pieces as well, was composed by Lassus. Some scholars think that the music survives as a *contrafactum*, others believe it to be lost.[2] The success of the ballet, which Brantôme named 'le plus beau ballet qui fust jamais faict au monde', is beyond doubt.

INFLUENCE OF BAÏF'S ACADEMY

In 1570 Jean-Antoine de Baïf founded his *Académie de Poésie et de Musique*; one of its objects was to achieve a closer union of music and poetry in what he and his friends believed to be the spirit of the ancients, chiefly by applying to French poetry the metrical rules of the Greek and Latin poets and by setting their verses to music with the same regard for classical prosody.[3] According to Sauval[4] they extended their influence to dramatic representation and there were no more 'de Ballets ni de Mascarades que sous la conduite de Baïf et de Mauduit'. They were also interested in the recovery of classical

[1] Probably represented in one of the Valois tapestries now at the Uffizi: cf. Frances Yates, *The Valois Tapestries* (London, 1959), pp. 67–72, and frontispiece of this volume See also pl. VI.

[2] See Grove (5th edition) v, p. 66; *Die Musik in Geschichte und Gegenwart*, viii, p. 256; Gustave Reese, *Music in the Renaissance* (New York, 1954), p. 571; Wolfgang Boetticher, *Orlando di Lasso* (Kassel, 1958), p. 384.

[3] Cf. p. 29.   [4] *Antiquités de la ville de Paris*, ii (Paris, 1724).

dancing based on classical prosody; here it is a matter of uncertainty whether the French poets derived this idea from the Italian choreographers such as Fabrizio Caroso, who talked much of dactyls and spondees in their treatises,[1] or whether the Italians were borrowers from the French.

In 1572 Henry of Navarre was married to Marguérite de Valois and it was hoped that this union would bring about a reconciliation between the Catholics and the Protestants. An elaborate ballet, entitled *Paradis d'Amour*, for which Ronsard wrote the words, was staged in the Salle de Bourbon on 20 August. The scene showed the Elysian Fields on the right and Hell on the left with the river Styx flowing between them. A number of knights made an assault on the *Paradis* and tried to carry off the nymphs in the garden, but the King (Charles IX) and his brothers repulsed them and drove them into Hell. This caused some comment, as the defeated knights were represented by the King of Navarre and his Huguenot gentlemen. However, Mercury and Cupid came down from Heaven, singing and dancing, to harangue the three knights, who then fetched the twelve nymphs down to the middle of the hall where they danced for an hour, after which they released the other knights from Hell. The ballet ended with a display of arms and fireworks.

'LE BALET COMIQUE DE LA ROYNE'

There was a long interval between this ballet and the *Balet comique de la Royne* of 1581, but it has been necessary to discuss it and the *Ballet Polonais* because they anticipate some of the notable features of their more famous successor. The *Balet comique*, which ought more properly to be called *Circé*, was produced on 15 October 1581 after the marriage of the Queen's sister Mademoiselle de Vaudemont to the Duc de Joyeuse. Queen Louise herself commanded the ballet and discussed it beforehand with the choreographer Baldassarino da Belgioioso, known in France as Balthasar de Beaujoyeulx, who had come to France about 1555 and had been in the service of several royal personages. Between the *Paradis* and the *Balet comique* the new King Henry III had paid his visit to Venice, as described earlier in this chapter.

The leading poets and musicians of the time were so much occupied with other commissions that they were unable to collaborate in *Circé*, and it is not certain who did provide either the words or the music. It seems probable that the words were by a Sieur de Chesnaye, the

---

[1] e.g. Caroso's *Il ballarino* (Venice, 1581).

songs by Lambert de Beaulieu, a bass singer with a very fine voice, and the dances by Salmon, a violinist in the King's service. It is not known who composed the choral music.[1] The title *Balet comique* was as puzzling to contemporaries as it is to us; Beaujoyeulx explains that it did not mean 'comic' in the modern sense, but that the ballet was in the nature of a play, which it is, and in that way a step towards opera.

The stage showed Circe's garden at the back with an enclosure for the animals into which she had transformed her victims. A gentle slope leads down to the main floor; on the right of the audience is the grotto of Pan and opposite to it the *voûte dorée*, a 'golden vault' composed of clouds large enough to contain a choir of singers. After wind music behind the scenes a gentleman (the only human being who appears in the ballet) runs down from the garden, presents himself to the King and explains (in spoken verse) how Circe has taken him prisoner. He begs the King to attack the enchantress, who appears herself in a great rage to look for the fugitive. There follows an entry of tritons and sirens, singing, with a car representing a fountain on which are Thetis and Glaucus attended by naiads; the naiads were the Queen and her ladies, followed by a chorus of tritons with various instruments. The procession advances to the middle of the hall; after a sung dialogue between Peleus and Thetis the naiads descend and dance. Circe reappears and reduces them to immobility; Mercury descends in a cloud and releases them, but Circe again immobilizes them and Mercury too. After a long spoken monologue she takes them all as prisoners into the garden. Satyrs and dryads come to the rescue, joined by Pan and the Four Virtues—a strange alliance. Minerva enters on a car drawn by a dragon, and summons Jupiter who comes down seated on his eagle and accompanied by voices in the *voûte dorée*. They all attack the palace of Circe, take her prisoner and hand her over to the King, presenting also Minerva and Mercury. The dryads dance and fetch the naiads from the garden to perform the *grand balet*, which is very long, on the floor level. They give presents to the King and his party, and the ballet ends with general dancing.

The novelty of *Circé* was that it had a definite plot in which speech, song, and dance were combined into a connected whole. Performed at a concert without the visual spectacle it is a very dull affair, like most of these entertainments, whatever their nationality. The spoken

---

[1] The music was published in a not altogether reliable vocal score by Weckerlin in the series *Chefs d'œuvre classiques de l'opéra français* (Paris, 1881). A facsimile edition has been edited by Giacomo Caula (Turin, 1965).

verse is heavy and uninteresting; the musical monologues are a mixture
of recitative and air with neither the charm of melody nor the interest
of declamation. The choral numbers are homophonic and heavy-
footed, the dances all harmonized in five parts note against note.
A few specimens will give an idea of the music; it is unnecessary to
print the *son de la clochette* as it has been printed by Burney[1] and
Parry[2] and has since then become well known and popular in modern
arrangements which considerably alter both the rhythm and the harmony. The Sirens begin, answered by the *voûte dorée*:

Ex. 388

(Six stanzas, after each of which the singers in the *voûte dorée* reply.)

[1] *A General History of Music*, ed. Frank Mercer (London, 1935), ii, p. 229.
[2] *Oxford History of Music* (Oxford, 1902), iii, p. 220.

Glaucus asks Thetis who is the nymph at the fountain; she tells him that it is the Queen of France. These solos are printed without any accompaniment and without bar-lines; the singers probably improvised their own accompaniments on their lutes. Bar-lines have been added here as a rough guide to the modern reader, since both Burney and Parry seem to have found this music hardly intelligible:

Ex. 389
(note values halved)

Lastly, here is the beginning of the first entry of the dancers;

Ex. 390

There is a great deal more of it, and the *grand balet* after the rescue of the captives, which had forty geometrical figures, is longer still. The whole of *Circé* is full of intricate political and humanistic symbolism, and, significantly, the connexions with the earlier entertainments offered by Catherine de' Medici and her sons (such as the *Paradis d'Amour* and the *Ballet Polonais*) have been stressed by several scholars.[1] There was the common endeavour to reach a compromise between Huguenots and Catholics, and there were the commonplaces of humanist symbolism, such as the harmony of the spheres (perhaps audibly symbolized by the choir in the *voûte dorée*). But, above all, there were the poets, composers, and choreographers working in harmony with both Baïf's Academy and the traditions of the Valois Court. The chief composer of the 1581 festivities was Beaulieu, a pupil of Courville. It was the latter who had joined with Baïf to found the Academy in 1570. It is not surprising, therefore, to find that the choral pieces are very much like *musique mesurée à l'antique*, that is: syllabic, homophonic, and with a tendency to differentiate between long and short syllables. In this connexion, it is worth pointing out that the 'divine Orlando', the composer of the *Ballet Polonais*, has left a specimen of *musique mesurée*—his composition of 'Une puce', first printed in the *Mélange de Chansons* of 1576. When referring to the eloquent effects of *musique mesurée*, the partisans of the Academy invariably coupled the name of Lassus with Claude Le Jeune. In their deliberate and demonstrative avoidance of polyphony and their careful attention to the metrical nature of the libretto, the choruses of the *Balet comique* are of some historical importance.

LATER BALLETS DE COUR

Circé set a new fashion, but for a long time its successors were on a much less costly scale. At first the tendency was to emphasize the literary side of ballet at the expense of the musical, but this vogue was short-lived. The *mascarades*, however, increased in popularity, as they did not need so much preparation or so much outlay, and this led to a great development of the comic ballet, the 'noble' costumes being reserved for royal occasions. We see here the anticipations of the *comédies-ballets* of Molière and Lully.[2] Between 1601 and 1605 both Rinuccini and Caccini spent some time at the French court, and the fruits of this visit in Italy may be seen in the *Ballo delle ingrate* of Monteverdi. From about 1608 onwards there was a return to elaborate ballets in France with much more employment of singing instead of speaking. The most important production was *La Délivrance de*

---

[1] See Yates, op. cit., and her earlier book, *The French Academies of the Sixteenth Century* (London, 1947). See also A. Verchaly, 'Air de Cour et Ballet de Cour', *Histoire de la musique*, ed. Roland-Manuel (Paris, 1960), pp. 1529–60, particularly pp. 1547–8.

[2] Several of these are described in detail by P. Lacroix, *Ballets et mascarades de cour de Henri III à Louis XIV* (Geneva, 1868), and Henry Prunières, *Le Ballet de Cour en France* (Paris, 1914). A more recent study is Margaret M. McGowan, *L'Art du Ballet de Cour en France (1581–1643)* (Paris, 1963).

Renaud in 1617 with music by Guédron, Bataille, Boesset, and Mauduit; Mauduit was the last survivor of Baïf's Academy.[1] Italian influence is shown in the choice of a subject from Tasso's *Gerusalemme liberata*, which was followed by a ballet on the *Orlando furioso* of Ariosto in 1618 and one on Tancredi in 1619. The young King Louis XIII himself danced in these. *La Délivrance* was sung all the way through; the music does not show any great advance on that of *Circé*, except that the solos are much more in the nature of regular songs, and there is none of the rambling quasi-recitative of the earlier ballet. During this period Italian influences came in gradually in the development of stage machinery; the medieval dispersed scenery of *Circé* gave way (though not all at once) to the proscenium stage with its curtain and its successive scenes and transformations. But once again there was a sudden reaction, due no doubt to reasons of economy, and after about 1620 there were only a succession of *ballets à entrées*, mainly comic and grotesque, with no particular story, which could be danced within a single scene if necessary. These are of some interest as setting the example for the late English masques with their endless series of anti-masques, but they led the French stage still farther away from the idea of opera.

CONTINENTAL INFLUENCES IN ENGLAND

The English theatre, like all other forms of culture, owed much to France and Italy in the sixteenth century, but it preserved an individuality of its own, the reasons for which are not always easy to trace. The modern traveller soon discovers that in many aspects of life, some quite trivial, the whole continent of Europe seems to present a unity as contrasted with England. Our theatres—the buildings and the machinery—still preserve characteristics of their own that are quite different from such as are common to practically all continental playhouses. So far as the sixteenth and seventeenth centuries are concerned, we must bear in mind that for geographical reasons Italy was less easily accessible than France. Our poets and musicians could obtain books and scores from Italy, but very few could afford the journey and make really professional contacts with their colleagues there. Those who did travel were generally amateurs, often keenly appreciative of what they saw and heard, but with no opportunity of going behind the scenes and obtaining professional knowledge. Professional contacts were much easier with Paris, although in many ways Italian culture was much more sympathetic to our countrymen than French. We

[1] The whole of this ballet is printed by Prunières, op. cit., p. 251.

shall see later on that as regards opera the English willingly absorbed the music, because it could be read and studied, but for the stage arrangements and dramatic construction they were more dependent on France, because they could go over to Paris and see the theatre at work with their own eyes.

THE MASQUE

The masque, as a court entertainment, was first introduced into England in 1513. Hall's chronicle (1547) records that 'on the daie of the Epiphanie at night the kyng with xi other wer disguised, after the manner of Italie, called a maske, a thing not seen afore in Englande'. We have already seen that Marlowe and Ronsard acknowledged that the masque was of Italian origin. Yet despite Hall's statement it is certain that 'mummings' and 'disguisings' took place much earlier, and the first record of them goes back to 1377.[1] What exactly was Italian in the masque of 1513 has never been clearly explained; it seems possible that the only Italian novelty was the costume.

The masque developed in England on much the same lines as in France, the main idea being always the group of noble masquers in strange disguises who went through characteristic dances of their own and finally took off their masks and danced the ordinary social dances with the ladies of the house where they were received. In England this principle is strictly maintained throughout all the masques, even down to *Cupid and Death* of 1653, and the scheme of the masque can be understood only if it is borne in mind that, whatever other distractions may be presented, the group of noble masquers (sometimes ladies) with their formal dance is always the centre of the entertainment.

About the early masques we have very little information, but it is certain that music played an essential part in them, if only for dancing. The mere fact that the authors and, as we should say, producers of the pageants and 'interludys' at the Tudor court were usually musicians—Banester and Newark under Henry VII, Redford and the younger Cornysh under Henry VIII, Edwards and Richard Farrant under Elizabeth I—indicates the importance of the role of music;

[1] Complete account in Paul Reyher, *Les Masques anglais* (Paris, 1909); see also Otto Gombosi, 'Some Musical Aspects of the English Court Masque', *Journal of the American Musicological Society*, i (1948), no. 3, p. 3, Denis Stevens, 'Pièces de théâtre et "pageants" à l'époque des Tudor', *Les Fêtes de la Renaissance*, i, p. 259, W. J. Lawrence, 'Notes on a Collection of Masque Music', *Music and Letters*, iii (1922), p. 49, and John P. Cutts, 'Jacobean Masque and Stage Music', ibid. xxv (1954), p. 185, and 'Le Rôle de la musique dans les masques de Ben Jonson et notamment dans *Oberon* (1610–1611)', *Les Fêtes de la Renaissance*, i, p. 285 (with two of the dances written for *Oberon* by Robert Johnson and two of Ferrabosco's songs).

most of them were Masters of the Chapel Royal, the members of which could be employed as actors as well as singers. We have stage-directions indicating inserted songs: for instance, an interlude by Redford ends 'Here they syng "hey nony nonye" & so go furth sing-ing' and at the end of his *Wyt and Science* 'Heere cumeth in fowre wyth violes & syng "remembreance" & at the last quere [chorus] all make curtsye & so go forth syngyng'. But unfortunately none of the songs themselves has been preserved, though no doubt some of Cornysh's songs in Brit. Mus. Add. 31922 were written for his pageants.[1]

It was not until the reign of James I that the full texts of masques were printed and some at least of the music preserved. By that time the masque had evidently been modelled on the *Balet comique de la Royne*, and a standard form evolved, chiefly by Ben Jonson on the literary side and Inigo Jones for the spectacle. Inigo Jones studied architecture in Italy and returned to England in 1605. Up till then the masques had continued the system of dispersed scenery as in *Circé*; Jones introduced the perspective system of Serlio and the architec-tural proscenium a few years later in 1612. These innovations borrowed from Italy soon led to the predominance of spectacle over poetry; after *Chloridia* (1631) Jonson, finding his name put second to Jones's on the title-page, broke entirely with Jones and wrote no more words for masques. This was a severe loss to the masque as an artistic achieve-ment, for it was the skilful and attractive verse of the poet which had given the English masque a distinction of its own far superior to any-thing which had been designed in France. After Jonson's retreat the masque came more and more under the influence of the French *ballet de cour*; the anti-masques increased so much in number that they became the principal attraction and the form lost all coherence.

A great deal of the music of the masques has survived,[2] but scattered in so many different places that it is impossible to reconstruct any one of the masques in its musical entirety. The music was very seldom printed in any of the books and descriptions, apart from a few songs. We can see from the accounts of expenditure that the musicians were paid very little in proportion to the other collaborators, though their names have become famous in English musical history for other reasons. As with the Italian and French entertainments we must regard the masques as complete wholes and on no account as anti-cipations of opera, despite the fact that English opera of the Restora-

---

[1] Denis Stevens, op. cit., p. 261. This manuscript has been edited by John Stevens as *Musica Britannica*, xviii (London, 1962).

[2] The best modern collection is Andrew J. Sabol's *Songs and Dances for the Stuart Masque* (Providence, Rhode Island, 1959).

tion did absorb many ingredients of the masque. The musical elements were always much the same: instrumental movements accompanying the entrance of important characters, songs and duets sung by subsidiary characters, choruses, often to accompany ceremonial movements such as processions, and of course large quantities of dance music. As in France and Italy, the instrumentalists and sometimes the chorus too were dispersed in different places and concealed; this was an important factor. We may almost compare this with the lighting arrangements of modern opera and ballet. The music was thought of not as an organic whole in its own right, but simply as a series of patches of musical colour; the groups of strings or brass, even the voices, would impress the spectators more by their mere sonorities than by the actual notes they played. Concealment added to the effect of magic and mystery.

In *Lovers made Men* Jonson tells us that 'the whole Maske was sung (after the Italian manner) *Stylo recitativo*, by Master Nicholas Lanier; who ordered and made both the Scene, and the Musicke' though this passage occurs not in the original edition of 1617 but only in that of 1640.[1] Unfortunately none of this music has survived, though we have an ornamented version of a song, probably Lanier's, from Jonson's other masque of 1617, *The Vision of Delight*.[2] In any case *Lovers made Men* was exceptional, having been given privately by Lord Hay, and it was short and simple in comparison with the court masques. There had been a previous *Masque in Honour of the Lord Hays marriage* (1607) written and composed by Thomas Campion, poet and musician, of which two songs and three dances have survived,[3] as have songs from Campion's *The Lords Masque* (1613) and *Masque in honour of the Marriage of the Earl of Somerset* (1614).[4] The general scheme of the 1607 masque, with its dispersed orchestras, follows the usual conventions derived from *Circé*. The music is simple and very attractive; the description shows that Campion had a clever sense of theatrical effect in the use of his musical resources. The number of musicians is given as forty-two, but there must have been a good many more.

---

[1] McD. Emslie, 'Nicholas Lanier's Innovations in English Song', *Music and Letters*, xli (1960), p. 13.

[2] Ibid., p. 23. See also Cutts, 'Ben Jonson's Masque, "The Vision of Delight" ', *Notes and Queries*, iii. N.S. (1956), p. 64.

[3] Printed by G. E. P. Arkwright in *The Old English Edition*, i (London, 1889). One is printed in *The Oxford History of Music*, iii, p. 201. The whole masque is described in E. J. Dent, *Foundations of English Opera* (Cambridge, 1928), pp. 21 ff.

[4] See Cutts, 'Jacobean Masque and Stage Music', p. 194, and F. W. Sternfeld, 'A Song from Campion's *Lord's Masque*', *Journal of the Warburg and Courtauld Institutes*, xx (1957), p. 373.

In the later masques, such as Shirley's *Triumph of Peace* (1633)[1] with music by Simon Ives and William Lawes, we find the music much more systematically organized. By this time the general technique of composition had made great advances, and the masque is held together musically by a strong sense of a main key (C major) and its nearly related keys.[2] We see here the declamatory 'recitative' style imitated from the Italians but very English in its treatment of English words. It differs conspicuously from the Italian recitative because the words are in rhymed verse, almost always with masculine endings; this gives the music much more metrical regularity, as well as a swifter movement in general, due perhaps to the fact that the English singers were not so much inclined to display their voices as the Italians are by nature. Lawes also shows much ingenuity and literary sense in avoiding a cadence and break where the sense of the poetry overruns the line and its rhyme. Parry and others have commented on the fact that English 'recitative music' always seems to have been written for amateurs with more literary intelligence than sonority of voice. But in all the masques the poetry is never really dramatic; it never calls for vehemence of musical setting and never points the way towards opera. This masque ends with the appearance of Amphiluche (Dawn) whose song may be printed here; it is very characteristic of Lawes's style, though it makes a rather melancholy conclusion to a night of revelry.

Ex. 391

In En-vye of the night That keeps her Revells here, With my un-

-wel-come Light Thus I in-vade her sphere, Pro - claim - ing Warre to

---

[1] Whitelocke's account of this masque is printed in Burney, op. cit. ii, pp. 294 ff.
[2] Long extracts from the music are printed in Dent, op. cit., pp. 30–37.

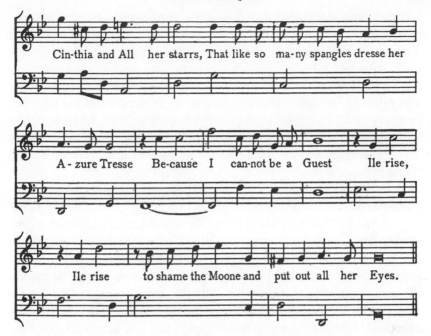

Cin-thia and All   her starrs, That like so ma-ny spangles dresse her

A-zure Tresse   Be-cause I   can-not be a Guest   Ile rise,

Ile rise   to shame the Moone and   put out all   her   Eyes.

The Civil War and the Commonwealth put an end to the court masques, but there are a number of plays, going down even to 1795, in which masques are introduced.[1] The closure of the theatres by the Puritans did not destroy the masque by any means, for it continued in a modified form in schools as an educational instrument; the most notable example is *Cupid and Death* (1653 and 1659) with words by James Shirley and music by Christopher Gibbons and Matthew Locke,[2] which will be described in Vol. V.

MUSIC IN THE ENGLISH THEATRE

From the earliest times music was an essential feature of the English theatre, as may be seen from stage-directions and much other evidence. Practically none of this music has survived in notes, though a few songs sung in plays of Shakespeare and others have been identified,[3] including Richard Farrant's 'Alas, ye salt sea gods' from his *Panthea and Abradatas* (c. 1578), a play with which an instrumental piece by Byrd marked 'Abradate'[4] may be connected, and songs by Byrd himself.[5] In the pre-Shakespearean plays such as *Gorboduc* (1562) there are

[1] A list is given by Reyher, op. cit., appendix iv.
[2] *Musica Britannica*, ii (London, 1951).
[3] See pp. 196 ff.
[4] Of which only two parts survive, one in Tenbury 389, fo. 101, the other in Brit. Mus. Add. 29472, fo. 101.   [5] See p. 198.

many examples of dumb-shows more or less imitated from the Italian *intermedii* and these are always accompanied by music; the stage directions frequently specify the instruments employed, as in the adaptation of Lodovico Dolce's *Giocasta* made by George Gascoigne and Francis Kinwelmersh (1566) where 'before the beginning of the first Acte: did sounde a dolefull and straunge noyse of violles, Cythren, Bandurion, and such like'. It is difficult to determine to what extent Sackville's *Gorboduc* and Gascoigne's *Jocasta* were derived from a native tradition or, on the other hand, were influenced by Italian *intermedii* and French *entremets*. The custom of enlivening plays with music between the acts was fairly international and was still in vogue when Beaumont and Fletcher wrote their *Knight of the Burning Pestle* (before 1613).[1] The musicians in the Elizabethan theatres were generally hidden in a balcony or a music-room over the stage, a position which does not strike one as very favourable to the acoustic effect.[2] Sometimes they had to play under the stage for special dramatic effect. In *Antony and Cleopatra*, Act IV, sc. iii, supernatural strains presage that the gods are about to forsake the hero. The famous stage direction, 'Music of the oboes under the stage', is a reminder that the 'hautbois' of the early seventeenth century was different from the modern instrument. A consort of oboes, probably augmented by sackbuts, is frequently called for in Elizabethan and Jacobean drama. Trumpets, too, were eloquently employed, notably in the duel scene at the end of *King Lear*. Trumpets and drums frequently had to appear on the stage for flourishes and marches; funeral marches were often played by muffled drums alone. Trumpets and drums have always stood apart, socially as well as musically, from other instruments, and this in all countries, because of their association with royalty and ceremonial occasions. Music, whenever employed, is nearly always mentioned as 'above' or 'within', and one wonders how the players can have had light enough to read their notes; very probably they played from memory and played whatever they had in their repertory. Songs would probably have been accompanied on the lute, or even on the regals, and sometimes by the singer himself. Most of the songs seem to have been sung by boys, and they take no further part in the play. A part with many songs, such as the Clown in *Twelfth Night*, would have depended on the engagement of some special singing actor, and

---

[1] On the tradition of instrumental interludes in blank-verse tragedy and the symbolism associated with various families of instruments, see Sternfeld, *Music in Shakespearean Tragedy* (London, 1963), pp. 2–4, 216–17.

[2] A good general survey of the whole field is given by John Stevens, 'Music of the Elizabethan Stage', in *Shakespeare in Music*, ed. Phyllis Hartnoll (London, 1964).

actors who could sing seem to have been as rare in those days as they are now. The extant text of *Twelfth Night* may have been revised as late as 1606, by which time Shakespeare's company had acquired as a regular member Robert Armin, an adult clown equally adept at acting and singing.

Those who sing on the stage are in most cases supposed to be drunk, mad, or supernatural;[1] music is not regarded as a 'normal' way of expressing oneself. Old Merrythought, in *The Knight of the Burning Pestle*, who sings on every possible occasion is certainly an eccentric. Here we are faced with the problem of the accompaniment; it is inconceivable that Old Merrythought played the lute to every one of his sometimes quite fragmentary songs. Audiences of those days must have been quite accustomed to hearing songs without any accompaniment, and even Handel's operas and oratorios sometimes show long stretches of quite unaccompanied melody, even if violins play in unison with the voice. The solo songs in the *Balet comique* of 1581 were published without accompaniment. In any event, Merrythought's repertoire reaches far and wide. He knows his popular ballads, as does Ophelia;[2] his catches, such as 'Three merry men' and 'Troll the bowl' rival those of Toby and Feste in *Twelfth Night*; nor is he ignorant of the melodies of lute ayres, as he hums Morley and Rosseter, among others.

The Elizabethans certainly had a strong sense of the value of unseen music as a background for romantic and highly emotional effects, such as the return to life of Hermione in *The Winter's Tale*, but we have no record of music being specially composed for such occasions; incidental music must have been anything that was available at the moment.

There was, however, a short period and a specialized environment when stage music became very nearly operatic. From the beginning of Elizabeth I's reign to 1585 plays were regularly acted under her immediate patronage by the boys of the Chapel Royal, the Chapel at Windsor, and St. Paul's; their usual theatre was the Blackfriars. The style of their plays can be judged from the play of *Pyramus and Thisbe* in *A Midsummer Night's Dream*, which is a parody of their alliterative doggerel verse. The history of the boy players had been known for a long time, but their music was first discovered by G. E. P.

---

[1] Cf. Sternfeld, 'The Use of Song in Shakespeare's Tragedies', *Proceedings of the Royal Musical Association*, lxxxvi (1959–60), p. 45.

[2] Concerning his 'As you came from Walsingham', and the use made of the famous lyric by Raleigh and Beaumont, see Sternfeld, *Songs from Shakespeare's Tragedies* (London, 1964), s.v. 'How should I your true love know'.

Arkwright in 1914.[1] Several of these songs are anonymous, but others (as we have already seen) are ascribed to Richard Farrant, Robert Parsons, and William Byrd. Most of them have contrapuntal accompaniments for four viols,[2] like Byrd's *Songs of Sadness and Piety*. In the plays they are generally associated with death scenes at the end of the play, and are often extremely poignant and genuinely dramatic. They are not incidental songs like Shakespeare's, but are sung by principal characters at the climax of the dramatic action, as the expression of some deeply felt personal emotion. We can thus regard them as definitely operatic in spirit, and if circumstances had been more favourable they might eventually have led to real English opera. The boy companies suffered from a variety of setbacks, unfortunately. Their main patronage was that of the Court, and in the last decade of the sixteenth century they were not acting at Court or in any theatre, for that matter. When they resumed their dramatic activities around 1600—probably the time from which the passage about the 'little eyases' in *Hamlet* dates—they soon lost their best theatre, the Blackfriars, and they never recovered from the closing of the theatres in 1642. It was not until 1689 that Purcell's *Dido* exhibited in full perfection what these Elizabethan composers were anticipating.

[1] 'Elizabethan Choirboy Plays and their Music', *Proceedings of the Musical Association*, xl (1913–14), p. 117, and 'Early Elizabethan Stage Music', *The Musical Antiquary*, i (1909), p. 30, and iv (1913), p. 112.

[2] See Philip Brett, 'The English Consort Song, 1570–1625', *Proceedings of the Royal Musical Association*, lxxxviii (1961–2), p. 73.

XV

EARLY ITALIAN OPERA

By SIMON TOWNELEY

ARCHITECTURE AND STAGE-DESIGN

The Italian historian Sismondi considered that 'the rise of the opera may, perhaps, be considered as the only literary event of the seventeenth century of which Italy can justly boast',[1] while Evelyn, a contemporary witness of the early Venetian operas, was amazed more at the scenery than at anything else, although he was struck by the new recitative music.[2] It is important, then, to judge early opera with no preconceived views as to what an opera should be. The libretto and the production in the early days had an even more vital part to play than the music; if the history of early opera seems to pay undue attention to the two former, it is because of their greater importance to the contemporary audience.

Vitruvius is not usually connected with the development of opera. But the eager acceptance of his books on architecture by the Renaissance public had a marked effect on its history. His works were the source to which producers of stage entertainment looked for guidance, and the three sets to be found in Serlio's *Secondo Libro d'Architettura* (Paris, 1545)[3] are the basis for the early opera productions as they had been for the masques, comedies, and dramatic entertainments generally. Sebastiano Serlio collated the various interpretations of Vitruvius; his book containing rules for the stage was at once translated into French by Jehan Martin under his own supervision; it was followed by a Dutch translation, in turn put into English in 1611. The *deus ex machina* of classical drama was the point of departure for the elaborate machines characteristic of opera during the seventeenth century. In fact, the little Vitruvius and his contemporaries say of classical music is a reminder to us of the relative unimportance of music in early opera. For, during the seventeenth century, the balance between poet, designer, machine-maker, and musician shifted until

---

[1] *Historical View of the Literature of the South of Europe*, trs. Roscoe (London, 1833), ii, p. 289.   [2] *Memoirs of John Evelyn*, ed. W. Bray (London, 1819), i, pp. 203 ff.
[3] See pl. VII.

the composer had exclusive right to command in the *opera seria* of the eighteenth century.

The permanent theatre was a novelty in 1600. The Teatro Olimpico at Vicenza, perhaps the most perfect theatre still existing and in use, opened only in 1585; its remarkable perspective made from fixed sets[1] was an inspiration to future designers in the countless opera-houses that sprang up like mushrooms in many Italian towns from 1637 onwards. It was natural, therefore, that at the opening of each new theatre public interest should be concentrated on the building itself, the inventions of the designers and machine-makers, rather than on the music. The *intermedii* had instilled into the audiences a taste for the exotic, the sumptuous, and the ingenious; but these performances were, as a rule, part of the entertainment for some special event connected with court life for which no expense was too great. The splendour of their presentation left its mark on the production of later operas. But the music must be traced to another source, although composers had reason to be grateful to the scene-makers and engineers upon whose skill they largely depended for the enthusiasm of the audience.

THE FLORENTINE *CAMERATA*

The initial interest in the *dramma per musica* shown by a group—or, rather, two groups—of Florentine antiquarians and *cognoscenti*[2] resulted in the composition of the first operas. These men were convinced that Greek drama had been set to music and declaimed; their aim was to discover exactly how this was done. They did not rediscover Greek music, but they were convinced that the lines were sung to some kind of monody, and they intended to experiment. In a letter to the theorist G. B. Doni in 1634, Pietro de' Bardi describes his father's experiments 'to extract the essence of the Greek, the Latin, and the more modern writers, and by this means to become a thorough master of the theory of every sort of music. . . . Besides restoring ancient music in so far as so obscure a subject permitted, one of the chief aims of the academy was to improve modern music.'[3]

Experiments in monody, which was to become the essential musical technique for opera, continued alongside the search for means to infuse greater expression into the polyphonic idiom. Caccini (*c.* 1545–1618) urged what he calls 'una nobile sprezzatura'[4] in declaiming the

---

[1] See pl. V.　　　　　　　　　　　　　　　　　　　　[2] See p. 151.

[3] Oliver Strunk, *Source Readings in Music History* (New York, 1950), p. 363; original text in Angelo Solerti, *Le origini del melodramma* (Turin, 1903), p. 143.

[4] See p. 157.

PLATE VII

(a)

(b)

(c)

STAGE SETS FROM *ARCHITETTURA DI SEBASTIANO SERLIO:*
LIBRO SECONDO

(a) Comedy. (b) Tragedy. (c) Pastoral

Reproduced from the Venice edition of 1551

poetry he sets, while Peri (1561–1633) describes his search after what was soon to be called recitative music thus:

I judged that the ancient Greeks and Romans (who, in the opinion of many, sang their tragedies throughout in representing them upon the stage) had used a harmony surpassing that of ordinary speech, but falling so far below the melody of song as to take an intermediate form. . . . And I considered that the kind of speech that the ancients assigned to singing and that they called 'diastematica' (that is, sustained or suspended) could in part be hastened and made to take an intermediate course, lying between the slow and suspended movements of song and the swift and rapid movements of speech, and that it could be adapted to my purpose. . . .[1]

Many composers during the sixteenth century had inserted short monodies into longer polyphonic pieces written to accompany dramatic performances: of particular significance in the early history of opera were the entertainments given in Venice[2] to celebrate the victory of Lepanto in 1571, for the visit of Henry III on his way from Poland to assume the French crown in 1574, and annually from 1578 on the feasts of St. Stephen, St. Mark, and the Ascension. The music for these entertainments is lost, but it is clear from the texts that 'these pieces differ from the later operas only in that they are not yet so called. They anticipate every conceivable type of opera: there are mythological and Christian-mythological scenes . . . allegories, pastorals, and burlesques.'[3] This is perhaps overstating the case, since the essence of the *dramma in musica* was only partly present. A work that contains only a few lines of monody can scarcely be considered more than a forerunner of opera. Merulo's music for Frangipani's *Tragedia* has been mentioned in the previous chapter;[4] it must have been similar to that written by Andrea Gabrieli for the Italian translation of *Oedipus Rex*[5] with which the Teatro Olimpico at Vicenza opened in 1585. These performances had precedents in such works as Cinzio's tragedy *Orbecche* (1541) and Beccari's pastoral *Il sacrificio* (1554);[6] in both these cases the music was by Alfonso della Viola. Such entertainments played their part in the foundations of opera. They show that the *Camerata* had no monopoly, not even priority, in the experiments. But their work had a difference. The earlier pieces were simply plays set to music as an additional attraction; in theirs, the music was to imitate speech so that the language of drama and the gamut of human emotions should be reflected in the accents of the singers.

---

[1] Foreword to *Euridice* translated by Strunk, op. cit., p. 373.   [2] See p. 792.
[3] Alfred Einstein, *The Italian Madrigal* (Princeton, 1949), ii, p. 549.   [4] See p. 792.
[5] See Leo Schrade, *La Représentation d'Edipo Tiranno au Teatro Olimpico* (Paris, 1960), which contains Gabrieli's choruses.   [6] See pp. 790–1.

DAFNE

Various texts were used by members of the *Camerata* in the search for an effective declamatory style: Ugolino's lament from the *Inferno* and part of the Lamentations in the Holy Week services, both set by Galilei,[1] are examples. But the first poem to be used as a libretto was *La Dafne* by Rinuccini.[2] Peri set it. (Practically all his score is lost.) The first performance of the opera took place in Florence at the Palazzo Corsi during the Carnival of 1597 in the presence of a distinguished audience. 'Il piacere e lo stupore che partorì negli animi degl'uditori questo nuovo spettacolo non si può esprimere, basta solo che per molte volte ch'ella s'è recitata, ha generato la stessa ammirazione e lo stesso diletto.'[3] The work was performed in a small room with few instruments and little change of scenery. But Peri had taken considerable pains to compose in the new style, setting the poem in the '"Greek manner", making the words stand out more than in ordinary speech, but less regularly than in music'.

Peri's setting of *La Dafne* now ranks as the first recorded opera. But from the confused contemporary accounts of it and of the events leading up to its composition[4] it is clear that other versions were being prepared some years before. Emilio de' Cavalieri had written music for a semi-dramatic piece, *Il giuoco della cieca*, and after a performance of this in 1594–5 it had been suggested that Peri might try his hand at something similar. It was then that the dilettante Jacopo Corsi and the poet Ottavio Rinuccini considered that the *Dafne* poem might be suitable. Corsi himself wrote music for parts of it; in fact it is possible that parts of his setting were used in the first 1597 performance, for, by a curious chance, although most of Peri's score is lost,[5] some fragments bearing the heading 'del Sr. Jacopo Corsi' are now to be found in the Library of the Conservatoire in Brussels. They include an aria for Apollo 'Non curi la mia piant"', and the final chorus, 'Bella ninfa fuggitiva'.[6]

[1] See pp. 153–4.

[2] Printed by Solerti, *Gli albori del melodramma* (three vols., Milan, 1905), ii, p. 75.

[3] Marco da Gagliano, preface to his own setting of the same libretto (1608).

[4] See O. G. Sonneck, ' "Dafne", the First Opera: a chronological study', *Sammelbände der internationalen Musikgesellschaft*, xv (1913–14), p. 102, and William V. Porter, 'Peri and Corsi's *Dafne*: some new discoveries and observations', *Journal of the American Musicological Society*, xviii (1965), p. 170.

[5] The prologue and a canzonetta, 'Chi da lacci d'amor', have been found by Federico Ghisi, who published them in *Alle fonti della monodia* (Milan, 1940), 48.

[6] Facsimile in Wotquenne, *Catalogue de la Bibliothèque du Conservatoire Royal de Musique* (Brussels, 1901), Annexe I between pp. 46–47; transcribed in Max Schneider, *Die Anfänge des Basso Continuo* (Leipzig, 1918), p. 109, and earlier by Hortense Panum, *Musikalisches Wochenblatt*, xix (1888), p. 346.

Ex. 392

(i) ARIA D'APOLLO

(Let not my plant be touched by flame or frost, let it be evergreen like the emerald, let the wrath of heaven never injure it.)

(ii) CORO FINALE

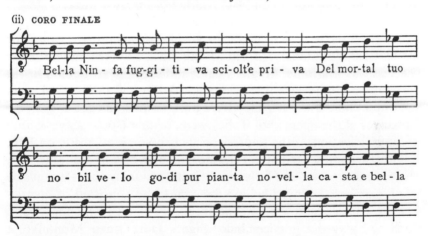

(Beautiful, fugitive nymph, free from and deprived of your mortal, noble veil, enjoying now your new chaste and beautiful life as a plant....)

As mentioned on pp. 798–9, a partial translation of Rinuccini's text provided the libretto for the first German opera: Schütz's *Daphne*. (Incidentally, this was not—as is commonly supposed—the first opera to be produced outside Italy, a distinction which belongs to an *Andromeda* performed at Salzburg in 1618, perhaps that by the Bolognese composer Giacobbi, given originally during the Carnival of 1610 at Bologna 'per disporto delle sue bellissime Dame'.)[1]

PERI'S AND CACCINI'S *EURIDICE*

A number of people must have seen *La Dafne* before the turn of the century. There are several recorded performances with slight variations to the score, and it is likely that there were more. Thus, many distinguished patrons of music visiting Florence, such as the Duke of Parma and the French courtiers who had come to Florence for the betrothal of Maria de' Medici to Henry IV of France in 1600, had an opportunity to carry away impressions of the new art to other parts of Europe. They may even have heard a second setting of this work by Caccini, but this score, too, is lost. However, both composers set a further libretto by Rinuccini;[2] his *L'Euridice*—with a happy ending—was chosen as the text for the opera written specially to celebrate the great wedding in 1600 and both their scores are extant.[3] Peri's work was heard for the first time on 6 October 1600, and can thus claim to be the first extant opera, although, according to the preface to his score published in 1601, parts of Caccini's music also were used for that particular performance. Actually Caccini had to wait until 1602 for a complete hearing of his own work.

Rubens was present at the marriage ceremony and has left a picture[4] of the scene which might, in an idle moment, give cause for speculation. He came over from Mantua in the Duke's suite, for the Duchess was Maria de' Medici's sister and she appears behind her in the picture. Monteverdi was also employed by the Duke of Mantua and one wonders whether they were both in the audience at the performances of the opera; but if they were, neither (so far as we know) left any indication of the impression that these events made on him.

Both Peri and Caccini treat the story of Euridice in the same way. There is no overture and little purely instrumental music. Peri tells us that his orchestra played behind the scenes and consisted of 'gentlemen illustrious by noble blood and excellence in music: Signor Jacopo Corsi . . . played a gravicembalo; Signor Don Grazia Montalvo, a theorbo; Messer Giovan Battista dal Violino, a *lira grande*; and

---

[1] Alfred Loewenberg, *Annals of Opera* (Cambridge, 1943).

[2] In Solerti, *Gli albori*, ii, p. 115.

[3] Modern edition of Peri's by Torchi, *L'arte musicale in Italia*, vi (Milan, n.d.); miniature score of original text (Milan, n.d.); facsimile of first edition (Rome, 1934). Incomplete edition of Caccini's *Euridice* in Robert Eitner, *Publikation älterer praktischer und theoretischer Musikwerk* (Leipzig, 1881); miniature score of original text (Milan, n.d.)   [4] In the Marquess of Cholmondeley's collection.

Messer Giovanni Lapi, a large lute'.[1] He included, it seems, no sustaining instrument for the bass. Theorbos, however, continued to be popular instruments in opera orchestras throughout the century, and their large necks were the subject of complaint from the stalls of the Venetian opera houses where the orchestra had taken its modern place before the stage, for these large necks obscured the view. Peri himself took the part of Orpheus and the celebrated Vittoria Archilei that of Euridice. Peri comments on her musicianship and beauty of voice. But it is clear that the scores that have come down to us from this time give only a bare outline of the sounds heard by a contemporary audience. For 'this lady', he says, 'who has always made my compositions seem worthy of her singing, adorns them, not only with those groups and those long windings of the voice, simple and double, which the liveliness of her talent can invent at any moment (more to comply with the usage of our times than because she considers the beauty and force of her singing to lie in them), but also with those elegances and graces that cannot be written or, if written, cannot be learned from writing'.[1]

Of the two composers Grout considers Peri to be 'perhaps somewhat more forceful in tragic expression, whereas Caccini is more tuneful, excels in elegiac moods and gives more occasion for virtuoso singing'.[2] But there is often little difference between their settings of the same words; consider, for instance, the opening of the Prologue in each:

Ex. 393
(i) PERI

---

[1] Foreword to *Euridice*, trans. Strunk, op. cit., p. 375.
[2] *A Short History of Opera* (London, 1947) p. 52.

(ii) CACCINI

Io che d'al - ti so - spir va - ga e di pian - ti
Spar - s'or di do - glia or di mi - nac - cie il vol - to

(I that desire the deep sighs and weeping, have a face now full of agony, now of threats.)

Both are at their best, naturally, in their settings of Orfeo's lament, 'Non piango e non sospiro', which have more than once been quoted in parallel:[1] Peri's the better calculated for dramatic effect, Caccini's the more melodious. Neither score is entirely recitative; there are a few rudimentary strophic arias, mostly at the ends of scenes; there is some showy coloratura in Caccini; and there are unison or note-against-note choruses, some of them intended to be danced to. Even imitative counterpoint is not entirely absent, witness this little trio for two nymphs and a shepherd in Peri's score:

Ex. 394

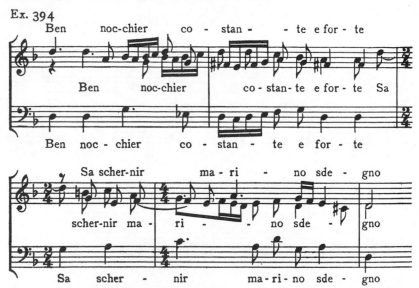

Ben noc-chier co - stan - - te e for - te
Ben noc-chier co - stan - te e for - te Sa
Ben noc - chier co - stan - te e for - te

Sa scher-nir ma - ri - no sde - gno
scher-nir ma - ri - - no sde - gno
Sa scher - nir ma - ri - no sde - gno

[1] Hugo Riemann, *Handbuch der Musikgeschichte*, ii. 2 (Leipzig, 1912), p. 189; Dénes Bartha, *A zenetörténet antológiája* (Budapest, 1948), p. 100.

though the polyphony forecasts that of the trio sonata more than it reminds one of the madrigalists. Setting the same words for two voices with instrumental bass, Caccini actually arrives at the primitive trio-sonata layout.[1]

Ex.395

(A Strong and experienced pilot can scorn the wrath of the sea.)

Caccini was principally a song writer and, even in his own day, as a writer of operas he did not compare with Peri. But curiously enough, in spite of the great success of both *Dafne* and *Euridice*, Peri did not continue with work in the new genre. He wrote other operas, notably *Tetide* for Mantua in 1608, and *Adone* in 1620 for the same court. But neither was performed. He also wrote the part of Clori in Marco da Gagliano's 'favola . . . rappresentata in musica', *Flora*. But his time was spent largely in composing music for the ballets and similar entertainments demanded from him as 'principale direttore della musica e dei musici' at the Medici court. Caccini, on the other hand, was really better known in Europe at large for his attractive songs. Yet his *Euridice* was in fact the first opera to be printed, although it had to wait until 1602 for a performance. His first opera seen on the stage was *Il rapimento di Cefalo*, written, like so many things, for the great wedding festivities of 1600 in Florence and produced three days after Peri's *Euridice*. Actually three other composers had a share in the score, although Caccini made no reference to them when he published parts of the music in *Le Nuove musiche*. In passing, it is worth mentioning that this libretto was translated into French by Chrétien des Croix in 1608. *Le Ravissement de Céfale* is the first known instance of a libretto being translated; it was dedicated to the

---

[1] Cf. Ex. 252 on p. 575.

newly born son of the marriage for which the original had been written.

MARCO DA GAGLIANO

The third name of importance among the Florentine composers is that of Marco da Gagliano (*c.* 1575–1642). He was of a younger generation than Caccini and Peri, and his first opera,[1] once again a setting of Rinuccini's *Dafne*, was not written until 1607 and was first performed, not in Florence, where it was repeated in 1610, but in Mantua in January 1608. However, the preface to it as well as his letters provide us with interesting details, not only of his own but of many other early productions.[2] He was against the pointless addition of 'gruppi, trilli, passaggi ed esclamazioni' by the singers. 'I do not propose to deprive myself of these adornments, but I wish them to be used in the proper time and place', as, for instance, in 'Non curi la mia pianta':[3]

Ex. 396

Non cu - ri la mia pian - ta ò fiam - - - - - - ma o ge - lo, sian' dal vi - vo sme-

---

[1] Partial reprint in Eitner, op. cit.; excerpt in Schering, *Geschichte der Musik in Bei-spielen* (Leipzig, 1931), p. 198, though Gagliano says part of it, Apollo's 'Pur giacque estinto', was composed by another master.

[2] See Emil Vogel, 'Marco da Gagliano. Zur Geschichte des florentiner Musiklebens von 1570–1650', *Vierteljahrsschrift für Musikwissenschaft*, v (1889), pp. 396 ff. and 509 ff.; the letters and preface, etc. are printed in full at the end, pp. 550 ff. The preface is also printed in Solerti, *Le origini*, p. 78.

[3] For a translation of the text see p. 825.

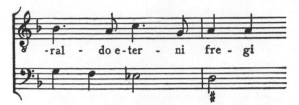

-ral - do e-ter - ni fre - gi

'where a good singer can deploy all the graces that the song demands, which Francesco Rasi's voice displays to the full' ('dove può il buon cantore spiegar tutte quelle maggiori leggiadrie, che richiegga il canto, le quali tutte s'udirono dalla voce del Sig. Francesco Rasi'). (In comparing Gagliano's setting with Corsi's, Ex. 392, one should remember that Corsi may have expected his Apollo to *improvise* ornamentation.) But where the story does not need it, says Gagliano, it is much better to leave out ornaments altogether and instead to pronounce the syllables distinctly ('scolpir le sillabe') so as to make the words clearly understood. The preface also gives detailed suggestions for stage-production. For instance, Apollo's 'Non curi', quoted above, is preceded—and closed—by three chords which are used 'to make it appear in the theatre that Apollo's lyre gives forth some more than ordinary melody'. When he clasps his lyre to his breast, 'which he should do with a fine attitude', four players upon the viol, 'whether a *braccio* or *gamba* matters little', placed nearby where the audience cannot see them, 'watch Apollo and when he puts his bow to his lyre they are to sound the three notes written, taking care to bow equally so that it sounds like a single bow: this deception cannot be recognised, except by the fancy of some particularly attentive person, and causes no little pleasure'.

Gagliano's later works include two operas on sacred themes for performance in Florence in 1625 and 1626: *La Regina Sant' Orsola* and *Istoria di Iudit*. His last opera, *La Flora, o vero Il Natal de' fiori*,[1] was written for the wedding festivities of Margherita de' Medici to the Duke of Parma in 1628. The part of Clori in *La Flora* was composed by Peri, who had already contributed to Gagliano's *Il Medoro* in 1619. Incidentally, Andrea Salvadori's text for *Medoro*, based on an episode from *Orlando furioso*, was used in 1626 by the celebrated group of players known as 'I Comici' and performed presumably as a straight play: an indication that text was more important than music at the time.

The historical importance of the *Camerata* is so great that it is

---

[1] Five excerpts printed in Hugo Goldschmidt, *Studien zur Geschichte der italienischen Oper im 17. Jahrhundert*, i (Leipzig, 1901), pp. 180 ff.

almost beside the point to assess the aesthetic value of these early operas. They certainly enjoyed a *succès d'estime* at the time, though they were not often repeated and their success cannot be compared even in terms of contemporary popularity with that enjoyed by Monteverdi's *Orfeo* or *Arianna*. Peri understands the drama but Caccini's melody is sweeter. Gagliano was a better composer than either, and his *Dafne* surpassed theirs, as Peri handsomely acknowledged,[1] but it had the misfortune to be produced at Mantua between two operas by a far greater master: the *Orfeo* and *Arianna* of Monteverdi.

MONTEVERDI

Monteverdi had gone to Mantua about 1590. With the Duke he had an opportunity of seeing Europe. We have already speculated on the possibility of his presence at the performance of *Euridice* in 1600. Be that as it may, Peri's score was published in 1601 and Monteverdi was certainly conversant with the new developments. He did not work on an opera until 1607, doubtless because there was no occasion for him to do so. But by then he was clear in his own mind that the hearing of an opera must be for the audience an experience. A successful work should involve the listener also in the feelings and emotions of the story. He chose for his first work a text on the Orpheus legend by Alessandro Striggio, altering it to produce a happy ending, and the first performance was given privately some time during the 1607 Carnival by the Accademia degl'Invaghiti at Mantua; it was repeated 'in the hall of the Duchess's apartment' in the Palace (see pl. VIII) on 24 February and again on 1 March 1607. These productions were followed by performances in other towns. The score was printed at Venice in 1609 and 1615,[2] though only eight copies altogether are known to survive. On hearing the work, a contemporary remarked that the music served the poetry so fittingly that it could not be replaced by any better composition. And today few would dispute the opinion that Monteverdi's *Orfeo* is a dramatic work of the highest quality, the first example of an opera with an appeal beyond that for the historian.

It is not merely that Monteverdi uses the new Florentine type of recitative with far more musical power and flexibility than Peri, Caccini, or Gagliano; he combines it much more richly and skilfully

---

[1] Vogel, op. cit., p. 426, n. 4.

[2] A facsimile of the first edition was published by Adolf Sandberger (Augsburg, 1927). There are a number of modern editions, beginning with Eitner's of 1881. *Orfeo* is printed as vol. xi of Malipiero's complete edition of Monteverdi's works, and Malipiero had previously published a vocal score (London, 1923).

PLATE VIII

THE HALL OF MIRRORS IN THE DUCAL PALACE AT MANTUA

with the other resources of contemporary music: madrigal-like choruses such as 'Lasciate i monti' in the First Act, strophic solos of the most varied kinds—Orfeo's simple, lilting 'Vi ricordo o bosch' ombrosi' in Act II, the great virtuoso piece 'Possente spirto' (with *concertante* accompaniment for pairs of instrumental virtuosi) with which he softens Charon's heart in Act III, the triumphant 'Qual honor' with its marching *basso ostinato* to which he brings back Euridice from the underworld in Act IV[1]—and an extraordinarily large and varied orchestra[2] employed not only in purely instrumental *sinfonie* and *ritornelli*[3] but in accompanying combinations carefully planned to emphasize the mood and character of the situation: for instance, the sudden change of colour—the entrance of the *organo di legno*—when Orpheus fatally turns round. However, these combinations are usually of *continuo* instruments, not *concertante* instruments. As an illustration of Monteverdi's (and Striggio's) dramatic insight one instance must suffice: Orfeo's reception of the news of Euridice's death. As Schrade says,[4] 'Orfeo is silent throughout the report; it is the Pastori who first react to the "amara novella". This holding Orfeo back from any spontaneous reaction to the story makes the sudden shock convincing; he was totally unaware and is now stunned. It is as though he had not even heard what the Messagiera recited at great length. For after the report has been sung and the two Pastori have expressed their reactions, Orfeo continues from the last words he heard, "La tua diletta sposa è morta", and begins with "Tu se' morta, se' morta mia vita", his final song of the act, in which he bids farewell to earth, sky and sun.' And there is nothing in the parallel laments of Peri and Caccini to compare with its final bars:

Ex. 397

(Farewell, earth; farewell heaven and sun. Farewell.)

[1] The whole of this scene—'Qual honor', the preceding chorus, and the tragic sequel —is recorded in *The History of Music in Sound*, iv.

[2] See particularly J. A. Westrup, 'Monteverdi and the Orchestra', *Music and Letters*, xxi (1940), p. 230, and Paul Collaer, 'L'orchestre di Claudio Monteverdi', *Musica*, ii (Florence, 1943), p. 86.

[3] See Alfred Heuss, 'Die Instrumental-Stücke des "Orfeo"', *Sammelbände der internationalen Musikgesellschaft*, iv (1902–3), p. 175.

[4] Leo Schrade, *Monteverdi: Creator of Modern Music* (New York, 1950), p. 233. The

Another famous lament is all that survives of Monteverdi's second opera, *Arianna*, which—like Marco da Gagliano's *Dafne*—was composed for the wedding of Francesco Gonzaga, the heir to the Duchy, the following year on a libretto by Rinuccini.[1] *Arianna* was famous in Italy for many years. The first performance was an outstanding success in spite of the death of the great singer Caterina Martinelli who had been cast for the title role; his rival Gagliano tells us in the preface to *Dafne* that the whole audience was visibly moved to tears.

The orchestra in *Arianna* was still placed behind the scenes, and as in *Orfeo*, the orchestration is said to have been such that the timbre and quality of the instruments underlined every nuance of the text. But all that is left of the score is Ariadne's lament 'Lasciatemi morire'[2] which served as a model for laments in countless operas. A five-part arrangement of it was published in the Sixth Book of madrigals (Venice, 1614) and this version, adapted to religious words as a 'Pianta della Madonna', appeared again later in the composer's life (*Selva morale*, Venice, 1640).

These marriage festivities called for quantities of music. Much of it was written for ballets such as Monteverdi's *Ballo delle ingrate*,[3] performed a week after *Arianna* and including a touching farewell to sky and sun and stars, akin to Orfeo's; these were dramatic entertainments in a sense, but not operas. Another dramatic work of Monteverdi's must be mentioned here, though it is not an opera: *Il Combattimento di Tancredi e Clorinda*,[4] a setting of a passage in Tasso's *Gerusalemme liberata* (Canto XII, v. 52–68) performed in the Palazzo Mocenigo, Venice, in 1624. The preface to the first edition describes the method of performance: Tancred, mounted on a hobby-horse, and Clorinda are to act and to sing the direct speech, while Tasso's narrative passages are to be sung by 'il Testo' who stands apart. The orchestra consists of four *viole da brazzo*, with written-out parts, in addition to the harpsichord and *contrabasso da gamba* playing the *continuo*, and

---

literature on Monteverdi's stage-works is considerable; the most exhaustive study is Anna Amalie Abert's *Claudio Monteverdi und das musikalische Drama* (Lippstadt, 1954); the English reader may be referred to the relevant chapters in Schrade's book, in H. F. Redlich, *Claudio Monteverdi: Life and Works* (tr. Kathleen Dale) (London, 1952), and in Denis Arnold, *Monteverdi* (London, 1963).

[1] Printed by Solerti, *Gli albori*, ii, p. 147.

[2] One of the surviving versions was printed by Emil Vogel, *Vierteljahrsschrift für Musikwissenschaft*, iii (1887), p. 443. On the variant readings, see Westrup, 'Monteverdi's "Lamento d'Arianna" ', *Music Review*, i (1940), p. 144.

[3] Reprinted in Torchi, op. cit. vi, and Malipiero's complete edition, viii.

[4] Originally published in the Eighth Book of madrigals (1638); modern editions by Torchi, op. cit., vi, Malipiero (London, 1931), and complete edition, viii, Denis Stevens (London, 1962), and others.

sometimes it has frankly descriptive passages: the 'motto del cavallo' (the movement of Tancred's horse) and the sword-play of the duel, sometimes using tremolo (rapid note-repetition) and pizzicato.

On the other hand, the several real operas that Monteverdi wrote subsequently are mostly lost. Luckily we are left with two great works: *Il Ritorno d'Ulisse in patria* and *L'Incoronazione di Poppea*, written in the last years of his life in Venice. These, unlike *Orfeo*, were entirely free from the influence of the *Camerata* and written in the style that was evolving from the new experiment in public opera that is associated with Venice from 1637 onwards; they will be discussed in the next volume. On the other hand, we must consider here the flowering of another branch of the *Camerata*'s activity, not in Florence, Mantua, or Venice, but in Rome.

CAVALIERI'S *RAPPRESENTAZIONE*

The Oratorian movement founded in Rome by St. Philip Neri[1] had naturally made full use of those century-old aids to popular devotion, the *laudi spirituali*,[2] and called into being a great quantity of new *laudi*: notably the two volumes by Giovanni Animuccia (1563 and 1570), the five compiled by Francisco Soto (1583–98), and Giovenale Ancina's *Tempio armonico della Beatissima Vergine* (1599). The great majority of these newly composed or arranged Oratorian *laudi* maintain the tradition of extreme simplicity, more or less popular melody supported by note-against-note counterpoint, but occasionally other elements begin to intrude: on the one hand, livelier polyphony with points of imitation,[3] on the other the element of dialogue. This may or may not have been a distant reflection of the now decadent *rappresentazioni sacre* or, as Alaleona suggests,[4] of the madrigal comedy; but such pieces as the 'Dialogo di Christo e della Samaritana' and 'Dialogo del Figliuol Prodigo' from G. F. Anerio's *Teatro armonico spirituale* (1619)[5] are unquestionably the prototypes of the form which took its name from the place where they were given: the 'oratorio'. They consist of alternations of narrative or reflective choruses, usually in six parts with organ *continuo*, with monodic dialogue; Christ and the father are basses, the Samaritan woman and the Prodigal sopranos. And the monodic passages are not so very different from those of the Florentines; the Prodigal's first solo is essentially a miniature 'recitative and air':

[1] See p. 363. [2] See Vols. II, pp. 266 ff., and III, pp. 389–90.
[3] See the examples printed by Domenico Alaleona, *Storia dell'oratorio musicale in Italia* (Milan, 1945), pp. 66 ff.
[4] Ibid., p. 81. [5] Printed ibid., pp. 260 and 270.

Ex. 398

Dam-mi la par-te mia   che   più non vo - glio

Gio - vi-net-to star sog-get - to   Ma con-ten - to

Pien d'ar-gen - to   Vo' go-de - re,   Vo' te-ne - re,

Vi - ta quie - ta, Vi - ta lie - ta

(Give me my portion so that I shall no longer be subject to you while I am young, but shall be content and wealthy, and enjoy a peaceful happy life.)

while his second one has Caccini-like *colorature* on 'allegri' and ' ridendo'. The way for quasi-dramatic *laudi* must have been paved by the performance in the Oratorio della Vallicella in February 1600 of a dramatic work by a former member of the *Camerata*, a work that was neither *laude*—though its text by Agostino Manni was essentially an elaboration of an older *laude* text incorporated in it (Act I, scene iv: 'Anima mia, che pensi? . . .')—nor an oratorio: Emilio de' Cavalieri's *Rappresentazione di Anima e di Corpo*.[1]

Cavalieri (*c.* 1550–1602) was a Roman. But from 1588 till 1596 he

[1] Facsimile of the original edition (Rome, 1600), edited by F. Mantica (Rome, 1912); modern editions by F. Vatielli (Leipzig, 1906) and in *I classici della musica italiana*, x (Milan, 1919); extended excerpts in Goldschmidt, op. cit., p. 153; Schering, op. cit., p. 168; Davison and Apel, op. cit. ii, p. 2.

held the post of Inspector-General of Art and Artists in Florence, was a leading member of the Bardi circle and, as we have seen in the previous chapter,[1] had collaborated with them in composing for the wedding festivities of 1589; his music for *Il giuoco della cieca* and its role as a precursor of *Dafne* have already been mentioned. Bianca Becherini[2] has suggested that his *Rappresentazione* is indebted to the tradition of the Florentine *sacre rappresentazioni*. In his preface[3] to the original edition Alessandro Guidotti gives the composer's full instructions as to how he intended the *Rappresentazione* to be performed. The theatre or hall should not seat more than a thousand spectators, the actors on the stage should be beautifully dressed, and the orchestra should be placed behind the scenes. Its size and composition could be adapted to suit the needs of each performance. He suggests 'una lira doppia, un clavicembalo, un Chitarrone, o Teorba', an ensemble similar to that used by the *Camerata* in other performances. And here likewise no mention is made of any sustaining instruments, except that he adds as optional 'un Organo soave con Chitarrone' and two flutes (*tibie all'antica*) for the finale. A violin, he suggests, might double the voice. In the preface he explains the shorthand method he has used to indicate the required harmonies, a practice later to develop into the figured bass. The participants in the drama are allegorical personifications of Time, Life, the World, Pleasure, the Intellect, the Soul, and the Body. Its purpose is didactic, conforming to the ideas of the Counter-Reformation, whereby the senses are used as a means to achieve moral and ethical ends. The recitative is punctuated by many cadences which give the music a monotony found in most of the early works in *stile rappresentativo*. Unlike his contemporaries, but like the later opera composers in Venice, Cavalieri divides the work into three acts. And he suggests that *intermedii* should intersperse them—a practice which a century later helped in the creation of *opera buffa*.

LATER ROMAN OPERAS

Cavalieri died in Rome in 1602, but works of this kind continued to be written. One of his successors, Stefano Landi (*c*. 1590–*c*. 1655), developed the genre into an elaborate entertainment needing hundreds of actors and singers, sumptuous architectural scenery, scores of machines, and an audience with sufficient patience to sit through

[1] See pp. 795–6.
[2] 'La musica nelle "Sacre rappresentazioni" Fiorentine', *Rivista musicale italiana*, liii (1951), p. 193, particularly pp. 233 ff.
[3] Reprinted by Solerti, *Le origini*, p. 1.

a series of loosely connected tableaux illustrating the life of a saint or a biblical story, lasting sometimes as much as eight or nine hours. But Roman opera did not develop quickly. The *dramma pastorale, Eumelio* (1606), of Agostino Agazzari (1578–1640) was only a 'school drama' composed for the pupils of the Seminario Romano but interesting in that it contains instances of melodically varied strophes over a repeated bass in opera earlier than Monteverdi's *Orfeo*.[1] And even this was an isolated work. The heyday of Roman opera opened in 1619 with Landi's 'pastoral tragi-comedy' *La morte d'Orfeo*. (Orpheus has always been a popular operatic subject; the monodist Domenico Belli produced a *Pianto d'Orfeo* or *Orfeo dolente*, five *intermedii* for Tasso's *Aminta*, at Florence in 1616.)[2] The chief productions of its earlier period were Domenico Mazzocchi's *La catena d'Adone* (based on an episode from Giambattista Marino's epic *Adone*) (1626), Landi's *Sant'Alessio* (1632), and Michel Angelo Rossi's *Erminia sul Giordano* (on Cantos VI and VII of *Gerusalemme liberata*) (1633). The two last were performed in the palace of the Barberini, a family which was then reaching the zenith of its influence in Rome. Maffei Barberini ruled as Pope Urban VIII from 1623 to 1642, and his three nephews, Cardinals Francesco and Antonio, and Don Taddeo, Prefect of Rome, built a theatre in the Palazzo Barberini in which a series of such entertainments was inaugurated with *Sant' Alessio*, a *dramma musicale* by Giulio Rospigliosi, later Pope Clement IX. The sets for *Erminia*[3] were designed by Bernini.

Musically these operas are characterized by a number of features that were to become increasingly important in the later history of opera. The treatment of recitative tends to become sometimes more melodious, sometimes more perfunctory, with a good deal of simple note-repetition (such as, indeed, one finds even in Monteverdi's *Combattimento*) and consequent speeding-up of the pace. Mazzocchi significantly speaks in the preface to his *Catena*[4] of 'arias . . . to relieve the tedium of the recitative', and he gives his audience a number of short melodious pieces such as the song Adonis sings before he goes to sleep in the enchanted wood or the one the enchantress Falsirena sings to him when he wakes:

[1] On *Emilio*, see Ambros-Leichtentritt, *Geschichte der Musik*, iv (Leipzig, 1909), pp. 383 ff.; Goldschmidt, op. cit., pp. 6 ff.; A. A. Abert, op. cit., pp. 164 ff.

[2] See Antonio Tirabassi, 'The Oldest Opera: Belli's *Orfeo dolente*', *Musical Quarterly*, xxv (1939), p. 26, though the claim implied in the title was easily refuted by Alfred Loewenberg, ibid. xxvi (1940), pp. 315–17.   [3] See pl. IX.

[4] There is a description of this opera in Goldschmidt, op. cit., pp. 8 ff. with long excerpts from the music, pp. 155 ff. See also Stuart Reiner, 'Vi sono molt' altre mezz' Arie . . .', in *Studies in Music History* (ed. Harold Powers) (Princeton, 1968), p. 241.

PLATE IX

STAGE SET BY BERNINI FROM ROSSI'S *ERMINIA*

Reproduced from the score of 1637

Ex. 399

Ri - de l'au-ret - ta a - man - - te Al bel se

ren - - de'l tuo di - vin sem-bian - te

(7) (6) (6)

, (Let the loving gentle breezes smile on your beautiful, serene, divine countenance.)

Mazzocchi's choruses also are numerous and melodious, more or less
homophonic when they are dances but often characterized by a lighter
texture of decidedly harmonic counterpoint, as in this passage from
a chorus (without *continuo*) which occurs twice in Act I:

Ex. 400

Go - di, go - di fe - sto - -

Go - di, go - di fe - sto - - - so

Go - di, go - di fe-sto -

Go - di, go - di fe - sto - so, go - di fe - sto -

-so fe - sto - so, fe - - sto -

Go - di, go - di fe - sto - - - so

-so fe - sto -

Go - di, go - di, fe - sto - so, fe - sto - - - -

-so fe - sto - - - -

fe - sto - - - -

(Enjoy your happiness)

Landi had anticipated all these features in his *Morte d'Orfeo*,[1] even the dotted rhythms of choral coloratura in *his* chorus of shepherds at the end of his First Act. And Charon's strophic song, 'Bevi, bevi', is perhaps the earliest of all *buffo* arias. This note of humour is typical of Landi; humorous touches and episodes relieve the tedium of *Sant'Alessio*[2]—not only the duet of the two pages, 'Poca voglia di far bene',[3] but also perhaps such points as Demonio's low Es in Act II, scene viii, and Act III, scene i. There are not many arias in *Sant'Alessio* but the score is notable for its vocal ensembles and also for its orchestral pieces, the *sinfonia per introduzione del prologo* (slow introduction followed by a contrapuntal *canzone*) and the *canzone*-like *sinfonia*[4] before Act II.

Rossi's *Erminia*[5] is on similar lines. Tancred's short aria from Act II may be quoted as an example of Rossi's melodic style:

Ex. 401
ARIA A UNA VOCE SOLA

(O valleys, O woods, O nymphs, O noble nymphs, sweet sirens, tell me where is my love.)

---

[1] Excerpts in Goldschmidt, op. cit., p. 188; Charon's 'Bevi, bevi' is recorded in *The History of Music in Sound*, iv. Landi's operas are described in Goldschmidt, p. 39.

[2] Excerpts in Torchi, op. cit. v, p. 43, and Goldschmidt, op. cit., p. 202. See also Ambros-Leichtentritt, op. cit., p. 496, and Abert, op. cit., p. 176.

[3] Also reprinted in Davison and Apel, op. cit. ii, p. 50.

[4] In Goldschmidt, op. cit., p. 252, and Davison and Apel, op. cit. ii, p. 47.

[5] Description in Goldschmidt, op. cit., p. 64, and excerpts, p. 258. See also Ambros-Leichtentritt, op. cit., p. 508, and Abert, op. cit., p. 180.

but the best of the music is to be found in the ensembles. The preface
contains vivid descriptions of the first performance. A brief extract
gives a picture of the kind of thing an audience enjoyed. 'I piacevoli
inganni delle macchine e delle volubili scene, impercettibilmente fecero
apparire, hora annichilarsi una gran rupe e comparirse una grotta,
et un fiumme . . . hora da non sa qual voragine di Averno far sortita
piacevolmente horribile i Demonii in compagnia di Furie, le quali
insieme danzando et assise poscia in carri infernali per l'aria se ne
sparissero.' (The pleasant deceptions of the machines and of the
changing scenes imperceptibly made now a great cliff seem to disappear and a grotto to appear, and a river . . now from some vortex
of Avernus to emerge in pleasing horror Demons in company with
Furies, dancing together, who, seated afterwards in infernal chariots,
disappeared through the air.) Armida, the pagan enchantress, sends
Furies to plague the encamped Christians with a hailstorm at which
's'oscura il cielo e cade horribil piogge con grandine, e con vento'
(the sky darkens and horrid rain falls, with hail and wind):

Ex. 402

(Come, come, let us fly.)

The wind machine, the tin sheet for thunder and rain, the dipping lights, the emphasis on the bizarre and extravagant are, even in these early days, the *sine qua non* of opera production. The effects may have been crude, but from all accounts the stage designers, architects, and machine-makers were skilled and imaginative workmen-artists. Indeed, the descriptions of the scenic marvels in librettos and diaries are not figments of the imagination. One of the best known artists, Niccolo Sabbatini, gives advice for most conceivable possibilities in his guide to making scenery and machinery for the theatre.[1]

THE AESTHETICS OF OPERA

It must be emphasized that, in spite of such exceptions as Monteverdi, composers, like the public, cared little for the dramatic and poetic qualities of a libretto, provided that it contained a sufficient number of improbable situations and occasions for the use of wonderful machines. That is not to say that the poem went unread. In fact each libretto was devoured like some salacious French novel. For it stood not on its poetry, construction, or depiction of character, but on the number, variety, and oddness of the situations. Monteverdi almost alone saw that a phrase of music was able to create character and that by changes of harmony the listener could be swept up into the action on the stage. At this date we seldom meet with views such as those he expressed in a well-known letter to Alessandro Striggio, in which he objects to Scipione Agnelli's libretto *Peleo e Theti* on the grounds that the characters are not sufficiently real. Orpheus and Arianna are real, he says, and for them he could write moving music. But for the 'winds' and such like he cannot find the inspiration or interest to compose.[2] In fact Monteverdi's operas are entirely different from the lavish productions of the Roman school. He was interested in the *dramma per musica*; they enjoyed a wonderful display for which a series of connected tableaux gave greater scope.

It cannot be said that by 1630 the opera had crystallized into its classical shape. The aims of the *Camerata* had been achieved. It had been found possible to set a whole poem in *stile rappresentativo*. The declamatory style had been successful and the music was able to enhance the meaning of the text. But these operas are, on the whole, monotonous; the form is loose and discursive. Looking back, we can

[1] *La pratica di fabricar scene e machine ne' teatri* (Ravenna, 1638; German translation, Weimar, 1926; French translation, Neuchâtel, 1942).

[2] Letter of 9 December 1616: cf. Prunières *La Vie et l'Œuvre de Claudio Monteverdi* (Paris, 1926), letter XIV; Domenico de' Paoli, *Claudio Monteverdi* (Milan, 1945), p. 210.

see that this difficulty was to be overcome by the formal use of recitative and aria: the *recitativo secco* that carried forward the action, and the aria, the point of repose, the catharsis, as it were, in which the musician released his melodic invention. An audience seems to need this contrast; nature demands that where there is tension there must be a release also. But it needed many performances to countless audiences before the balance could be achieved. The insatiable demand for opera in the public theatres enabled poets to invent libretti divided into scenes with lines in blank verse culminating in short lyrical stanzas, which the composer could turn as he wished, to suit the free outpourings of his melodic invention. The early opera writers at Florence, Rome, and Mantua scarcely touched on the problems that were to confront the singers, producers, and architects during the rest of the century. However, they had laid the foundations of an artistic medium that would absorb the skill and inspiration of musicians and poets exclusively until well into the eighteenth century 'di maniera che', as Marco da Gagliano[1] himself wrote, 'con l'intelletto, vien lusingato in uno stesso tempo ogni sentimento più nobile dalle più dilettevoli arti ch'abbia ritrovato l'ingegno umano' (So that, beside the intellect, at the same time every fine feeling is flattered by the most delightful arts invented by the human mind). The early opera composers did not rediscover Greek drama, but they began to develop a form the significance of which has not been exceeded in the history of music.

[1] Preface to *Dafne*.

BIBLIOGRAPHY

Edited by JOHN D. BERGSAGEL

GENERAL

ADLER, GUIDO: *Handbuch der Musikgeschichte.* 2nd ed., 2 vols. (Berlin, 1930).

ALBRECHT, HANS: 'Musik und Dichtkunst im 16. Jahrhundert', *Die Musikforschung,* viii (1955).

AMBROS, A. W., and KADE, O.: *Geschichte der Musik.* 3rd ed., iii–v. (Leipzig, 1887–1911).

APEL, WILLI: *The Notation of Polyphonic Music, 900–1600.* 4th ed. (Cambridge, Mass., 1950).

BESSELER, HEINRICH: *Die Musik des Mittelalters und der Renaissance* (Potsdam, 1931–5).

BIRTNER, HERBERT: *Studien zur ndl.-humanistischen Musikanschauung* (Heidelberg, 1930).

BLUME, FRIEDRICH: *Die evangelische Kirchenmusik* (Potsdam, 1931; new edition, Kassel and Basle, 1965).

BUKOFZER, MANFRED: *Music in the Baroque Era* (New York, 1947).

BURNEY, CHARLES: *A General History of Music from the Earliest Ages to the Present Period* (1776–89). 2nd ed., 2 vols., ed. Frank Mercer (New York, 1935), reprinted (New York, 1957).

CARPENTER, NAN COOKE: *Music in Medieval and Renaissance Universities* (Norman, Oklahoma, 1958).

CLERCX, SUZANNE: *Le Baroque et la musique* (Bruxelles, 1948).

COMBARIEU, JULES: *Histoire de la musique,* 3 vols. (Paris, 1946–8 [c. 1913–20]).

CREVEL, M. VAN: *Adrianus Petit Coclico, Leben und Beziehungen eines nach Deutschland emigrierten Josquinschülers* (The Hague, 1940).

DAHLHAUS, CARL: 'Zur Theorie des Tactus im 16. Jahrhundert', *Archiv für Musikwissenschaft,* xvii (1960).

DUFOURCQ, NORBERT: *La Musique des origines à nos jours* (Paris, 1946).

EINSTEIN, ALFRED: *A Short History of Music.* 5th ed. (London, 1948). The illustrated edition (London, 1953) is without the valuable appendix of music examples.

EISENRING, GEORG: *Zur Geschichte des mehrstimmigen Proprium Missae bis um 1560* (Düsseldorf, 1913).

FERAND, ERNST: *Die Improvisation in der Musik* (Zürich, 1938).

—— *Die Improvisation in Beispielen aus neun Jahrhunderten abendländischer Musik* (Cologne, 1956).

GROUT, DONALD J.: *A History of Western Music* (New York, 1960).

HAAS, ROBERT: *Aufführungspraxis der Musik* (Potsdam, 1931).

—— *Die Musik des Barocks* (Potsdam, 1928).

HANDSCHIN, JACQUES: *Musikgeschichte im Überblick* (Lucerne, 1948).

HAWKINS, SIR JOHN: *A General History of the Science and Practice of Music* (1776). 2nd ed., 2 vols. (London, 1853), reprinted (New York, 1963).

HUIZINGA, JOHAN: 'The Problem of the Renaissance', *Men and Ideas* (London, 1960).

ILLING, CARL-HEINZ: *Zur Technik der Magnificat-Komposition des 16. Jahrhunderts* (Wolfenbüttel and Berlin, 1936).

KADE, OTTO: *Die ältere Passionkomposition bis zum Jahre 1631* (Gütersloh, 1893).

KAHL, WILLI: 'Das Geschichtsbewußtsein in der Musikanschauung der italienischen Renaissance und des deutschen Humanismus', *Hans Albrecht in Memoriam* (Kassel, 1962).

KINSKY, GEORG: *A History of Music in Pictures* (London, 1930).

KROYER, THEODOR: 'Von der Musica Reservata', *Festschrift für Heinrich Wölfflin* (Dresden, 1934).

LARUE, JAN, ed.: *Aspects of Medieval and Renaissance Music. A Birthday Offering to Gustave Reese* (New York, 1966; London, 1967).

LEICHTENTRITT, HUGO: *Geschichte der Motette* (Leipzig, 1908).

LESURE, FRANÇOIS, ed.: *La Renaissance dans les provinces du Nord* (Paris, 1956).

—— *Répertoire international des sources musicales*, i. *Recueils imprimés, XVIe–XVIIe siècles*, i: Liste chronologique (Munich and Duisburg, 1960).

LIPPHARDT, WALTHER: *Die Geschichte des mehrstimmigen Proprium Missae* (Heidelberg, 1950).

LOWINSKY, EDWARD E.: 'The Concept of Physical and Musical Space in the Renaissance', *Papers of the American Musicological Society for 1941* (New York, 1946).

—— 'Early Scores in Manuscript', *Journal of the American Musicological Society*, xiii (1960).

—— 'The Medici Codex: A Document of Music, Art and Politics in the Renaissance', *Annales musicologiques*, v (1957).

—— *Nicola Vicentino: L'antica musica, ridotta alla moderna prattica* (1555). Facs. ed. (Basle, 1959).

—— *Tonality and Atonality in Sixteenth-Century Music* (Berkeley, California, 1916).

MEIER, BERNHARD: 'Reservata-Probleme. Ein Bericht', *Acta Musicologica*, xxx (1958).

MENDEL, ARTHUR: 'Pitch in the 16th and Early 17th Centuries', *Musical Quarterly*, xxiv (1948).

MERSENNE, MARIN: *Harmonie Universelle (1636)*. Facs. ed., 3 vols. (Paris, 1963).

MILLER, CLEMENT A.: 'The "Dodecachordon": Its Origins and Influence on Renaissance Musical Thought', *Musica Disciplina*, xv (1961).

—— ed.: *Heinrich Glareanus: Dodecachordon*, 2 vols. (American Institute of Musicology, 1965).

MÜLLER-BLATTAU, J.: *Das Verhältnis von Wort und Ton in der Geschichte der Musik* (Stuttgart, 1952).

PALISCA, CLAUDE V.: 'Scientific Empiricism in Musical Thought', *Seventeenth Century Science and the Arts* (Princeton, 1961).

PIRRO, ANDRÉ: *Histoire de la musique de la fin du XIVe siècle à la fin du XVIe* (Paris, 1940).

REESE, GUSTAVE: *Music in the Renaissance*. Rev. ed. (New York, 1959).

RIEMANN, HUGO: *Geschichte der Musiktheorie im IX–XIX Jahrhundert*. 2nd ed. (Leipzig, 1921). English translation by Raymond Haggh (Lincoln, Nebraska, 1962).

—— *Handbuch der Musikgeschichte*. 2nd ed., vol. ii, 1 and 2 (Leipzig, 1920).

SCHERING, ARNOLD: *Geschichte des Oratoriums* (Leipzig, 1911).

SCHRADE, LEO: 'Renaissance. The Historical Conception of an Epoch', *Kongress-Bericht: Utrecht 1952* (Amsterdam, 1953).

STRUNK, OLIVER: *Source Readings in Music History* (New York, [1950]).

URSPRUNG, OTTO: *Die katholische Kirchenmusik* (Potsdam, 1931–3).

WAGNER, PETER: 'Aus der Musik-Geschichte des deutschen Humanismus', *Zeitschrift für Musikwissenschaft*, iii (1920–1).

—— *Geschichte der Messe*, i (Leipzig, 1913).

WALKER, D. P.: 'Musical Humanism in the 16th and early 17th Centuries', *Music Review*, ii–iii (1941–2).

WOLF, JOHANNES: *Geschichte der Musik in allgemeinverständlicher Form*. 3 vols. 2nd ed. (Leipzig, 1934).

WOLF, R. E.: 'The Aesthetic Problem of the "Renaissance" ', *Revue belge de musicologie*, ix (1955).

WOLFF, H. CHR.: 'Die geistlichen Oden des Georg Tranoscius und die Oden-komposition des Humanismus', *Die Musikforschung*, vi (1953).

CHAPTER I

THE FRENCH POLYPHONIC CHANSON

(i) *Sources*

ALBRECHT, HANS: *Das Chorwerk*, xv. *Johannes Lupi: Zehn weltliche Lieder zu vier Stimmen* (Wolfenbüttel, 1932); lxi. *Zwölf französische Lieder aus Jacques Moderne: Le Parangon des chansons* (Wolfenbüttel, 1957).

BERNET KEMPERS, K. PH.: *Corpus mensurabilis musicae*, iv. *Jacobus Clemens non Papa: Opera Omnia*, x, xi. *Chansons* (American Institute of Musicology, 1962, 1965).

BESSELER, HEINRICH: *Das Chorwerk*, xiii. *Orlando di Lasso, Madrigale und Chansons* (Wolfenbüttel, 1931).

BOETTICHER, WOLFGANG: *Orlando di Lasso: Sämtliche Werke. Neue Reihe*, i (Kassel and Basle, 1956).

CAUCHIE, MAURICE: *Quinze chansons françaises du XVIᵉ siècle* (Paris, 1926).

—— *Trente chansons de Clément Janequin* (Paris, 1928).

COMMER, FRANZ: *Collectio operum musicorum Batavorum saeculi XVI*, xii (Berlin, 1858).

EITNER, ROBERT: *Publikation älterer praktischer und theoretischer Musik-werke*. Jg. 27 (Bd. xxiii). *60 Chansons* (Leipzig, 1899).

EXPERT, HENRY: *Florilège du concert vocal de la Renaissance*, i–vi and viii (Paris, 1928–9).

—— *La Fleur des musiciens de P. de Ronsard* (Paris, 1923).

—— *Les Maîtres musiciens de la Renaissance française*, iii, v, vii, x, xii–xix (Paris, 1896–1904).

—— *Les Monuments de la musique française au temps de la Renaissance*, i, iii, iv–v (Paris, 1924–6).

HELM, E. B.: *Smith College Music Archives*, v. *The Chansons of J. Arcadelt*, i (Northampton, Mass., 1942).

LESURE, F. et al.: *Anthologie de la chanson parisienne au XVIᵉ siècle* (Monaco, 1953).

MAIRY, L., LA LAURENCIE, L. DE, and THIBAULT, G.: *Chansons au luth et airs de cour français du XVIᵉ siècle* (Paris, 1934).

MALDEGHEM, R. VAN: *Trésor musical. Musique profane*, 29 vols. (Brussels, 1865–93). See annotated index by Gustave Reese in Music Library Association, *Notes* (Washington, D.C.), ser. 2, vol. vi (December, 1948).

SANDBERGER, A.: *Orlando di Lasso: Sämmtliche Werke*, xii, xiv, xvi (Leipzig, 1894–1927).

SEAY, ALBERT: *Das Chorwerk*, lxxiii. *Clément Janequin: Zehn Chansons* (Wolfenbüttel, 1959); lxxxii. *Pierre Certon: Zehn Chansons* (Wolfenbüttel, 1962).

SEIFFERT, MAX: *J. P. Sweelinck: Werken*, vii–ix (The Hague and Leipzig, 1899–1900).

VAN DOORSLAER, G.: *Philippe de Monte: Opera*, xx. *Collectio decem carminum gallicorum alias Chansons françaises* (Malines, 1932).

WALKER, D. P.: *Claude Le Jeune: Airs*, i (1608) (American Institute of Musicology, 1951).

(ii) *Books and Articles*

BARTHA DÉNES: 'Probleme der Chansongeschichte im 16. Jahrhundert', *Zeitschrift für Musikwissenschaft*, xiii (1931).

BERNET KEMPERS, K. PH.: 'Die wallonische und die französische Chanson in der ersten Hälfte des 16. Jahrhunderts', *International Society for Musical Research: First Congress* (*Liège, 1930*) *Report* (Burnham, 1931).

BERNSTEIN, LAWRENCE F.: 'Claude Gervaise as Chanson Composer', *Journal of the American Musicological Society*, xviii (1965).

BOETTICHER, WOLFGANG: 'Die französische Chansonkomposition Orlando di Lassos', *Bericht über den internationalen musikwissenschaftlichen Kongress Wien, Mozartjahr 1956* (1959). ·

—— *Orlando di Lasso und seine Zeit* (Kassel and Basle, 1958).

BRENET, MICHEL: *Musique et musiciens de la vieille France* (Paris, 1911).

BROWN, HOWARD: 'The Chanson rustique: Popular Elements in the 15th, and 16th-century Chanson', *Journal of the American Musicological Society*, xii (1959).

CAUCHIE, MAURICE: 'Clément Janequin: recherches sur sa famille et sur lui-même', *Revue de musicologie*, iv (1923).

—— 'Documents pour servir à une biographie de Guillaume Costeley', *Revue de musicologie*, vii (1926).

—— 'Les Chansons à trois voix de Pierre Cléreau', *Revue de musicologie*, viii (1927).

—— 'Les deux plus anciens recueils de chansons polyphoniques imprimés en France', *Revue de musicologie*, v (1924).

DROZ, E.: 'Les Chansons de Nicolas de la Grotte', *Revue de musicologie*, viii (1927).

—— 'Guillaume Boni de Saint-Flour en Auvergne, musicien de Ronsard', *Mélanges offerts à M. Abel Lefranc* (Paris, 1936).

EITNER, ROBERT: 'Jacob Arcadelt', *Monatshefte für Musikgeschichte*, xix (1887).

GLÄSEL, RUDOLF: *Zur Geschichte der Battaglia* (Diss. Leipzig, 1931).

HAAR, JAMES, ed.: *Chanson and Madrigal, 1480–1530* (Cambridge, Mass., 1964).

HELM, E. B.: 'The Sixteenth-Century French Chanson', *Proceedings of the Music Teachers National Association*, xxxvi (1942).

HERTZMANN, ERICH: *Adrian Willaert in der weltlichen Vokalmusik seiner Zeit* (Leipzig, 1931).

—— 'Trends in the Development of the Chanson in the early 16th Century', *Papers of the American Musicological Society, 1940* (1946).

JACQUOT, JEAN, ed.: *Fêtes et cérémonies au temps de Charles Quint* (Paris, 1960).

—— *Musique et poésie au XVIe siècle* (Paris, 1954).

LALOY, L.: 'La Chanson au XVIe siècle', *Revue musicale*, i (1901).

LESURE, FRANÇOIS: 'Autour de Clément Marot et de ses musiciens', *Revue de musicologie*, xxxiii (1951).

—— 'Les Chansons à trois voix de Clément Janequin', *Revue de musicologie*, xliv (1959).

—— 'Clément Janequin: Recherches sur sa vie et ses œuvres', *Musica Disciplina*, v (1951).

—— 'Pierre Attaingnant: notes et documents', *Musica Disciplina*, iii (1949).

—— *Poets and Musicians of the French Renaissance* (New York, 1955).

LEVRON, JACQUES: *Clément Janequin, musicien de la Renaissance* (Grenoble and Paris, 1948).

LEVY, KENNETH J.: '"Susanne un jour". The History of a 16th-Century Chanson'
Annales musicologiques, i (1953).

—— 'Costeley's Chromatic Chanson', *Annales musicologiques*, iii (1955).

MASSON, PAUL-MARIE: 'L'Humanisme musical en France au XVIe siècle: Essai
sur la musique " mesurée à l antique " ', *R.I.M.: Revue musicale mensuelle*,
iii (1907).

MORÇAY, R.: 'L'Avènément du lyrisme au temps de la Renaissance', *Humanisme
et Renaissance*, iii (Paris, 1936).

OEBEL, M.: *Beiträge zu einer Monographie über Jean de Castro* (Bonn, 1928).

PARKINSON, J. A.: 'A Chanson by Claudin de Sermisy', *Music and Letters*, xxxix
(1958).

POULAILLE, H.: *La Fleur des chansons d'amour au XVIe siècle* (Paris, 1943).

QUITTARD, HENRI: '"L'Hortus Musarum" de 1552–53 et les arrangements de
pièces polyphoniques pour voix seule et luth', *Sammelbände der internationalen Musikgesellschaft*, viii (1906–7).

SCHMIDT-GÖRG, J.: *Nicolas Gombert, Kapellmeister Karls V: Leben und Werk*
(Bonn, 1938).

SEAY, ALBERT: 'Poetry and Music in the French Chanson of the Renaissance',
The Consort, No. 20 (1963).

SILLIMAN, A. C.: '"Responce" and "Replique" in Chansons published by
Tylman Susato, 1543–1550', *Revue belge de musicologie*, xvi (1962).

THIBAULT, G.: 'Les Amours de P. de Ronsard, mises en musique par Jean de
Maletty (1578)', *Mélanges de musicologie offerts à M. Lionel de la Laurencie*
(Paris, 1933).

—— and PERCEAU, L.: *Bibliographie des poésies de P. de Ronsard mises en
musique au XVIe siècle* (Paris, 1941).

TIERSOT, JULIEN: 'Ronsard et la musique de son temps', *Sammelbände der internationalen Musikgesellschaft*, iv (1902–3).

TROTTER, ROBERT MOORE: 'The Chansons of Thomas Crecquillon: Texts and
Forms', *Revue belge de musicologie*, xiv (1960).

VAN DEN BORREN, CHARLES: *Orlande de Lassus* (Paris, 1920).

—— 'Quelques notes sur les chansons françaises et les madrigaux italiens de
J. P. Sweelinck', *Gedenkboek aangeboden aan Dr. D. F. Scheurleer* (The
Hague, 1925).

—— *Roland de Lassus* (Brussels, 1943).

VAN DEN SIGTENHORST MEYER, B.: *De vocale Muziek van Jan P. Sweelinck* (The
Hague, 1948).

VAN DOORSLAER, G.: *La Vie et les œuvres de Philippe de Monte* (Brussels, 1921).

VERCHALY, ANDRÉ: 'Desportes et la musique', *Annales musicologiques*, ii (1954).

WALKER, D. P.: 'The Aims of Baïf's *Académie de Poésie et de Musique*',
Journal of Renaissance and Baroque Music, i (1946).

—— 'The Influence of *Musique mesurée à l'antique*, particularly on the *Airs de
cour* of the early Seventeenth Century', *Musica Disciplina*, ii (1948).

—— 'Musical Humanism in the 16th and early 17th Centuries', *Music Review*,
ii (1941) and iii (1942).

—— 'Some Aspects and Problems of *Musique mesurée à l'antique*', *Musica
Disciplina*, iv (1950).

—— and LESURE, F.: 'Claude Le Jeune and *Musique mesurée*', *Musica Disciplina*,
iii (1949).

WAUTERS, E.: *Jean Guyot de Châtelet, musicien de la Renaissance: sa vie et son
œuvre* (Brussels, 1944).

YATES, F. A.: *The French Academies of the Sixteenth Century* (London,
1947).

CHAPTER II

THE SIXTEENTH–CENTURY MADRIGAL

(i) *Sources*

ANGLÈS, HIGINI: *Monumentos de la música española*, iv. *Vásquez, Recopilación de Sonetos y Villancicos, 1560* (Barcelona, 1946).

ARKWRIGHT, G. E. P.: *Old English Edition*, xi–xii. *Ferrabosco, Madrigals from 'Musica Transalpina'* (London, 1894).

ARNOLD, DENIS: *Luca Marenzio: Ten Madrigals for mixed voices* (London, 1966).

AROCA, D. J.: *Cancionero musical y poético del siglo XVII* (Madrid, 1916).

BENVENUTI, G.: *Istituzioni e monumenti dell'arte musicale italiana*, i (Milan, 1931).

BOALCH, D. H.: *Thomas Morley: Two-part canzonets* (Oxford, 1950).

CASIMIRI, R.: *G. P. da Palestrina: Le opere complete*, ix and xxix (Rome, 1940 and 1957).

EINSTEIN, ALFRED: *The Golden Age of the Madrigal* (New York, 1942).

—— *The Italian Madrigal*, iii (Princeton, 1949).

—— *Publikationen älterer Musik*, iv, vi. *Luca Marenzio: Sämtliche Werke*, i, ii (Leipzig, 1929 and 1931).

ENGEL, HANS: *Anthology of Music*, iii. *The Sixteenth-Century Part Song in Italy, France, England and Spain* (Cologne, 1961).

—— *Marenzio, Villanellen* (Kassel, 1928).

FELLOWES, E. H.: *The Collected Vocal Works of William Byrd*, xii–xvi (London, 1948–9).

—— *The English Madrigal School*, 36 vols. (London, 1914–24); revised edition, *The English Madrigalists*, by Thurston Dart and others (1958–).

HABERL, F. X.: *Giovanni Pierluigi da Palestrinas Werke*, xxviii and xxix (Leipzig, 1883 and 1884).

HERMANN, W.: *Gastoldis Balletti a tre voci*, 3 vols. (Berlin, 1927).

HERTZMANN, ERICH: *Das Chorwerk*, viii. *Adrian Willaert und andere Meister, Volkstümliche italienische Lieder* (Wolfenbüttel, 1930).

HESELTINE, PHILIP: *Whythorne, Eleven 'Songes of fower and five voyces'* (London, 1927).

D'INDY, VINCENT: *Salomone Rossi (Ebreo), Choix de 22 madrigaux* (Paris, 1877).

KAUFMANN, HENRY W.: *Corpus mensurabilis musicae*, xxvi. *Nicola Vicentino: Collected Works* (American Institute of Musicology, 1963).

MACCLINTOCK, CAROL: *Corpus mensurabilis musicae*, xxiv. *Giaches de Wert: Opera Omnia*, i–iii (American Institute of Musicology, 1961–).

MALDEGHEM, R. VAN: *Trésor musical. Musique profane*, 29 vols. (Brussels, 1865–93).

MALIPIERO, G. F.: *Tutte le opere di Claudio Monteverdi*, i–x (Vienna, 1926–9).

MEIER, BERNHARD: *Das Chorwerk*, lviii. *Jakob Arcadelt und andere Meister, Sechs italienische Madrigale* (Wolfenbüttel, 1956).

—— *Das Chorwerk*, lxxxviii. *Giovan Nasco und andere Meister, Fünf (Petrarca) Madrigale* (Wolfenbüttel, 1962).

MITJANA, RAFAEL: *Cancionero de Uppsala* (Uppsala, 1909). New edition by Jesús Bal y Gay (Mexico, 1944).

MOMPELLIO, F.: *L. Marenzio, Madrigali a 5 e 6 v.* (Milan, 1953).

NOSKE, FRITS: *Monumenta Musica Neerlandica*, v. *Cornelis Thymanszoon Padbrue. Nederlandse madrigalen* (Amsterdam, 1962).

PEDRELL, F., and ANGLÈS, H.: *Els Madrigals i la Missa de Difunts d'En Brudieu* (Barcelona, 1921).

Pizzetti, I.: *I classici della musica italiana*, xiv. *Gesualdo da Venosa, Madrigali* (Milan, 1919).

Querol Gavaldá, Miguel: *Romances y letras a tres vozes* (Barcelona, 1956).

Sandberger, Adolf: *Orlando di Lasso: Sämtliche Werke*, ii, iv, vi, viii, x (Leipzig, 1895–9).

Smith, G. P.: *Smith College Music Archives*, vi. *The Madrigals of Cipriano de Rore for 3 and 4 voices* (Northampton, Mass., 1943).

Squire, Barclay: *Ausgewählte Madrigale*, 3 vols. (Leipzig, 1903–13).

Therstappen, J.: *Das Chorwerk*, xxxiv, xxxvii, xli. *Orlando Lasso, Busstränen des Heiligen Petrus* (Wolfenbüttel, 1935–6).

Torchi, Luigi: *L'arte musicale in Italia*, i, ii (Milan, 1897–   ).

Van Doorslaer, G.: *Philippi de Monte Opera*, vi, xix, xxv (Bruges, 1927–39).

Vatielli, Francesco: *Madrigali di Carlo Gesualdo, Principe di Venosa* (Rome, 1942).

Vergili, L.: *Madrigalisti italiani*, i–   (Rome, 1952–   ).

Weismann, W.: *Gesualdo da Venosa, Sechs Madrigale* (Leipzig, 1931).

—— *Gesualdo di Venosa, Madrigale*, i–vi (Leipzig and Hamburg, 1957–62).

Wiora, Walter: *Das Chorwerk*, v. *Adrian Willaert und andere Meister, Italienische Madrigale* (Wolfenbüttel, 1930).

(ii) *Books and Articles*

Arnold, Denis: 'Thomas Weelkes and the Madrigal', *Music and Letters*, xxxi (1950).

—— 'Croce and the English Madrigal', *Music and Letters*, xxxv (1954).

—— 'Gastoldi and the English Ballett', *Monthly Musical Record*, lxxxvi (1956).

—— '"Seconda Pratica": a Background to Monteverdi's Madrigals', *Music and Letters*, xxxviii (1957).

—— *Marenzio* (London, 1965).

Boetticher, W.: *Orlando di Lasso und seine Zeit* (Kassel and Basle, 1958).

—— 'Über einige neue Werke aus Orlando di Lassos mittlerer Madrigal- und Motettenkomposition (1567–1569)', *Archiv für Musikwissenschaft*, xxii (1965).

Bontoux, G.: *La Chanson en Angleterre au temps d'Elisabeth* (Oxford, 1936).

Brown, David: 'William Byrd's 1588 Volume', *Music and Letters*, xxxviii (1957).

Carapetyan, Armen: 'The Concept of the "Imitazione della natura" in the Sixteenth Century', *Journal of Renaissance and Baroque Music*, i (1946).

—— 'The "Musica Nova" of Adriano Willaert', *Journal of Renaissance and Baroque Music*, i (1946).

Cesari, G.: *Die Entstehung des Madrigals im 16. Jahrhundert* (Cremona, 1908). Revised as 'Le origini del madrigale cinquecentesco', *Rivista musicale italiana*, xix (1912).

Cimbro, A.: 'I madrigali di Cl. Monteverdi', *Musica*, ii (Florence, 1943).

Clercx, Suzanne: 'Jean de Macque et l'évolution du madrigalisme à la fin du XVIᵉ siècle', *Festschrift für Schmidt-Görg* (Bonn, 1957).

Collet, Robert: 'John Wilbye: Some Aspects of his Music', *The Score*, no. 4 (1951).

Della Corte, A.: *Le relazioni storiche della poesia e della musica italiana* (Turin, 1936).

Dent, E. J.: 'Notes on the "Amfiparnasso" of Orazio Vecchi', *Sammelbände der internationalen Musikgesellschaft*, xii (1911).

—— 'The "Laudi spirituali" in the XVIth and XVIIth Centuries', *Proceedings of the Musical Association*, xliii (1917).

DENT, E. J.: 'William Byrd and the Madrigal', *Festschrift für Johannes Wolf* (Berlin, 1929).
—— 'The Musical Form of the Madrigal', *Music and Letters*, xi (1930).
DOHRN, ELLINOR: *Marc'Antonio Ingegneri als Madrigalkomponist* (Hanover, 1936).
EINSTEIN, ALFRED: 'Claudio Merulos Ausgabe der Madrigale des Verdelot', *Sammelbände der internationalen Musikgesellschaft*, viii (1907).
—— 'Augenmusik im Madrigal', *Zeitschrift der internationalen Musikgesellschaft*, xiv (1912).
—— 'Die Parodie in der Villanella', *Zeitschrift für Musikwissenschaft*, ii (1920).
—— 'Dante im Madrigal', *Archiv für Musikwissenschaft*, iii (1921).
—— 'Filippo di Monte als Madrigalkomponist', *International Society for Musical Research. First Congress (Liège, 1930) Report* (Burnham, 1931).
—— 'Italian Madrigal Verse, 1500–1600', *Proceedings of the Musical Association*, lxiii (1937).
—— 'Narrative Rhythm in the Madrigal', *Musical Quarterly*, xxix (1943).
—— 'The Elizabethan Madrigal and "Musica Transalpina"', *Music and Letters*, xxv (1944).
—— 'Bibliography of Italian Secular Vocal Music' (a revision of Vogel's book, q.v.), *Music Library Association Notes*, ii–v (1945–8).
—— *The Italian Madrigal*, 3 vols. (Princeton, 1949).
EITNER, ROBERT: 'Adrian Willaert', *Monatshefte für Musikgeschichte*, xix (1887).
—— 'Jacob Arcadelt', *Monatshefte für Musikgeschichte*, xix (1887).
—— 'Cipriano de Rore', *Monatshefte für Musikgeschichte*, xxi (1889).
ENGEL, HANS: 'Marenzios Madrigale', *Zeitschrift für Musikwissenschaft*, vii (1935).
—— 'Marenzios Madrigale und ihre dichterischen Grundlagen', *Acta Musicologica*, viii (1936) and ix (1937).
—— 'Die Entstehung des italienischen Madrigals und die Niederländer', *Kongress-Bericht: Utrecht 1952* (Amsterdam, 1953).
—— *Luca Marenzio* (Florence, 1957).
—— 'Werden und Wesen des Madrigals', *Kongress-Bericht Köln 1958* (Kassel and Basle, 1959).
FELLERER, K. G.: 'Beziehungen zwischen geistlicher und weltlicher Musik im 16. Jahrhundert', *International Musicological Society, Report of the Eighth Congress, New York, 1961*, 2 vols. (Kassel, 1961–2).
FELLOWES, E. H.: *English Madrigal Composers* (Oxford, 1921).
—— *English Madrigal Verse* (Oxford, 1920).
—— *Orlando Gibbons and his Family* (London, 2nd. ed. 1951).
—— *William Byrd* (London, 2nd. ed. 1948).
FERAND, E.: 'Die "Motetti, Madrigali et Canzoni Francese. . . . Diminuiti . . ." des Giovanni Bassano (1591)', *Festschrift Helmuth Osthoff zum 65. Geburtstag* (Tutzing, 1961).
—— '"Anchor che col partire": Die Schicksale eines berühmten Madrigals', *Festschrift Karl Gustav Fellerer* (Ratisbon, 1962).
VON FICKER, RUDOLF: 'Beiträge zur Chromatik des 14. bis 16. Jahrhunderts', *Studien zur Musikwissenschaft*, ii (Leipzig and Vienna, 1914).
FREY, HERMAN-WALTHER: 'Michelagniolo und die Komponisten seiner Madrigale', *Acta Musicologica*, xxiv (1952).
GALLICO, CLAUDIO: *Un canzoniere musicale italiano del cinquecento* (Florence, 1961).
GÉROLD, THÉODORE: *L'Art du chant en France au XVIIe siècle* (Strasbourg, 1921).
GLÄSEL, RUDOLF: *Zur Geschichte der Battaglia* (Diss. Leipzig, 1931).

GRAY, C., and HESELTINE, P.: *Carlo Gesualdo, Prince of Venosa: Musician and Murderer* (Oxford, 1926).

HAAR, JAMES: 'The "Note Nere" Madrigal', *Journal of the American Musicological Society*, xviii (1965).

HELM, EVERETT: 'Italian Traits in the English Madrigal', *Music Review*, vii (1946).

HERTZMANN, ERICH: *Adrian Willaert in der weltlichen Vokalmusik seiner Zeit* (Leipzig, 1931).

HEURICH, HUGO: *John Wilbye in seinen Madrigalen* (Augsburg, 1931).

HEUSS, ALFRED: 'Ein Beitrag zu dem Thema: Monteverdi als Charakteristiker in seinen Madrigalen', *Festschrift: Rochus Freiherr von Liliencron* (Leipzig, 1910).

HOL, J. C.: 'Cipriano de Rore', *Festschrift für Karl Nef* (Zürich and Leipzig, 1933).

—— *Horatio Vecchis weltliche Werke* (Strasbourg, 1934).

HORSLEY, IMOGENE: 'Improvised Embellishment in the Performance of Renaissance Polyphonic Music', *Journal of the American Musicological Society*, iv (1951).

HUBER, K.: *Ivo de Vento* (Munich, 1917).

KAUFMANN, HENRY W.: *Nicola Vicentino (1511–1576): Life and Works* (American Institute of Musicology, 1965).

KEINER, F.: *Die Madrigale des Gesualdo di Venosa* (Leipzig, 1914).

KERMAN, JOSEPH: 'Elizabethan Anthologies of Italian Madrigals', *Journal of the American Musicological Society*, iv (1951).

—— 'Master Alfonso and the English Madrigal', *Musical Quarterly*, xxxviii (1952).

—— 'Morley and the "Triumphs of Oriana"', *Music and Letters*, xxxiv (1953).

—— *The Elizabethan Madrigal* (New York, 1962).

KINKELDEY, OTTO: 'Luzzasco Luzzaschis Solo-Madrigale mit Klavierbegleitung', *Sammelbände der internationalen Musikgesellschaft*, ix (1908).

KIWI, EDITH: *Studien zur Geschichte des italienischen Liedmadrigals im XVI. Jahrhundert* (Würzburg, 1937).

KLEFISCH, W.: *Arcadelt als Madrigalist* (Cologne, 1938).

KROYER, THEODOR: *Die Anfänge der Chromatik im italienischen Madrigal des XVI. Jahrhunderts (1535–1560)* (Leipzig, 1902).

LEICHTENTRITT, HUGO: 'Claudio Monteverdi als Madrigalkomponist', *Sammelbände der internationalen Musikgesellschaft*, xi (1910).

MANGEOT, ANDRÉ: 'The Madrigals of Joan Brudieu', *The Score*, no. 7 (1952).

MITJANA, RAFAEL: *Estudios sobre algunos músicos españoles del siglo XVI* (Madrid, 1918).

MONTI, G. M.: *Le villanelle alla napoletana e l'antica lirica dialettale a Napoli* (Città di Castello, 1925).

MUSIOL, JOSEF: *Cyprian de Rore, ein Meister der venezianischen Schule* (Halle, 1932).

NUTEN, PIET: *De 'Madrigali spirituali' van Filip de Monte, 1521–1603* (Brussels, 1958).

OBERTELLO, ALFREDO: *Madrigali italiani in Inghilterra* (Milan, 1949).

PALISCA, CLAUDE V.: 'Vicenzo Galilei and some Links between "Pseudo-Monody" and Monody', *Musical Quarterly*, xlvi (1960).

PANNAIN, GUIDO: 'Note sulle madrigali di Monteverdi', *Rassegna musicale*, iv (1931).

PATTISON, BRUCE: *Music and Poetry of the English Renaissance* (London, 1948).

PRUNIÈRES, HENRY: *La Vie et l'œuvre de Claudio Monteverdi* (Paris, 1924). Trs. M. D. Mackie (London, 1926).

REDLICH, H. F.: *Claudio Monteverdi: Life and Works.* Trs. Kathleen Dale (London, 1952).

—— *Claudio Monteverdi,* i. *Das Madrigalwerk* (Berlin, 1932).

—— 'The Italian Madrigal: a Bibliographical Contribution', *Music and Letters,* xxxii (1951).

RONCAGLIA, GINO: 'Orazio Vecchi e il "madrigale drammatico"', *Orazio Vecchi (1550–1605): Contributi di studio nel 4° centenario della nascita* (Modena, 1950).

ROSE, BERNARD: 'Thomas Tomkins', *Proceedings of the Royal Musical Association,* lxxxii (1955–6).

ROSE, GLORIA: 'Polyphonic Italian Madrigals of the Seventeenth Century', *Music and Letters,* xlvii (1966).

RUBSAMEN, WALTER H: 'Sebastian Festa and the Early Madrigal', *Kongress-Bericht, Kassel 1962* (Kassel and Basle, 1963).

SCHMITZ, EUGEN: 'Zur Geschichte des italienischen Continuo-Madrigals im 17. Jahrhundert', *Sammelbände der internationalen Musikgesellschaft,* x (1909–10).

SCHOFIELD, B., and DART, T.: 'Tregian's Anthology', *Music and Letters,* xxxii (1951).

SCHRADE, LEO: *Monteverdi, Creator of Modern Music* (New York, 1950).

SCHULZ, H.: *Das Madrigal als Formideal* (Leipzig, 1939).

SPRINGER, HERMANN: 'Zu Leonardo Giustiniani und den Giustinianen', *Sammelbände der internationalen Musikgesellschaft,* xi (1909–10).

STEVENS, DENIS: *Thomas Tomkins: 1572–1656* (London, 1957).

TADLOCK, RAY J.: 'Alessandro Striggio, Madrigalist', *Journal of the American Musicological Society,* xi (1958).

TESSIER, A.: 'Les deux styles de Monteverde', *Revue musicale,* iii (1922).

TRADE, H.: *Manierismus und Barock im italienischen Madrigal des 16. Jahrhunderts* (Erlangen, 1928).

TREND, J. B.: 'Spanish Madrigals', *Proceedings of the Musical Association,* lii (1926).

—— 'Spanish Madrigals and Madrigal-Texts', *Festschrift für Guido Adler* (Vienna, 1930).

UHLER, J. E.: 'Thomas Morley's Madrigals for Four Voices', *Music and Letters,* xxxvi (1955).

VAN DEN BORREN, C.: 'The Aesthetic Value of the English Madrigal', *Proceedings of the Musical Association,* lii (1926).

—— 'Les Madrigaux de Jean Brudieu', *Revue musicale,* vi (1925).

—— *Orlande de Lassus* (Paris, 1920).

VOGEL, EMIL: *Bibliothek der gedruckten weltlichen Vocalmusik Italiens aus den Jahren 1500–1700,* 2 vols. (Berlin, 1892): reprint revised by Alfred Einstein (Hildesheim, 1962).

—— 'Claudio Monteverdi', *Vierteljahrsschrift für Musikwissenschaft,* iii (1887).

WAGNER, PETER: 'Das Madrigal und Palestrina', *Vierteljahrsschrift für Musikwissenschaft,* viii (1892).

WARLOCK, PETER: *Thomas Whythorne: an Unknown Elizabethan Composer* (Oxford, 1927).

WEISMANN, WILHELM: 'Die Madrigale des Carlo Gesualdo', *Deutsches Jahrbuch der Musikwissenschaft,* v (1960).

WESTRUP, J. A.: 'Monteverdi and the Madrigal', *The Score,* no. 1 (1949).

ZIMMERMAN, FRANKLIN B.: 'Italian and English Traits in the Music of Thomas Morley', *Anuario musical*, xiv (1959).

CHAPTER III

GERMAN POLYPHONIC SECULAR SONG

(i) *Sources*

AMELN, KONRAD: *Leonhard Lechner-Werke*. Vorabdruck aus vol. v, *Italienische Madrigale, 1579–88* (Kassel, 1956).

BLUME, FRIEDRICH: *Das Chorwerk*, li. *Lambert de Sayve und Michael Praetorius, Teutsche Liedlein* (Wolfenbüttel, 1938).

BÖHME, FRANZ MAGNUS: *Altdeutsches Liederbuch* (Leipzig, 1877).

BOHN, EMIL: *50 historische Konzerte in Breslau 1881–92. Nebst einer bibliographischen Beigabe: Bibliothek des gedruckten mehrstimmigen weltlichen deutschen Liedes vom Anfang des 16. Jahrhunderts bis ca. 1640* (Breslau, 1893).

BOSE, FRITZ: *Nicolaus Zangius, Geistliche und weltliche Lieder mit fünf Stimmen, Köln 1597* (Berlin, 1960).

EITNER, ROBERT: *Das deutsche Lied des XV. und XVI. Jahrhunderts*, 2 vols. (Berlin, 1876–80).

EITNER, ROBERT, ERK, LUDWIG, and KADE, OTTO: *Publikation älterer praktischer und theoretischer Musikwerke*, i–iii. *Johann Ott, 115 guter newer Liedlein, Nürnberg 1544* (Berlin, 1873–5); iv. *Einleitung, Biographieen, Melodieen und Gedichte zu Johann Ott's Liedersammlung von 1544* (Berlin, 1876).

EITNER, ROBERT: Ibid., viii. *Heinrich und Hermann Finck, Auswahl von geistlichen und weltlichen Liedern, Hymnen und Motetten* (Leipzig, 1879); xxix. *Georg Forster, Der Zweite Teil der kurtzweiligen guten frischen teutschen Liedlein* (Leipzig, 1905); xix. *Jakob Regnart's Deutsche dreistimmige Lieder nach Art der Neapolitanen nebst Leonhard Lechner's fünfstimmiger Bearbeitung* (Leipzig, 1895); xxi. *Johann Eccard, Newe teutsche Lieder mit fünf und vier Stimmen, Königsberg 1589* (Leipzig, 1897).

ENGEL, HANS: *Paul Kugelmann, Sieben teutsche Liedlein, 1558* (Kassel, 1954).

FELLERER, KARL GUSTAV: *Das Chorwerk*, lxxv. *Anton Gosswin, Newe teutsche Lieder mit dreyen Stimmen, 1581* (Wolfenbüttel, 1960).

FOCK, GUSTAV: *Das Erbe deutscher Musik, xxix. Johann Steffens, Neue teutsche weltliche Madrigalia und Balletten* (Wolfenbüttel, 1958).

GEERING, ARNOLD, and ALTWEGG, WILHELM: *Das Erbe deutscher Musik, Reichsdenkmale*, x, xv. *Ludwig Senfl, Deutsche Lieder*, i, ii (*Sämtliche Werke*, ii, iv) (Wolfenbüttel, 1938–40); ibid. iii (*Sämtliche Werke*, v), (Wolfenbüttel, 1949).

GERBER, RUDOLF: *Das Erbe deutscher Musik*, xxix. *Johann Jeep, Studentengärtlein* (Wolfenbüttel, 1958).

GOEDEKE, KARL: *Grundriß zur Geschichte der deutschen Dichtung*, ii (Dresden, 1886).

GRUSNICK, BRUNO: *Das Chorwerk*, xxxviii. *Melchior Franck, Musikalische Bergreihen* (Wolfenbüttel, 1936).

GUDEWILL, K.: *Das Chorwerk*, liii. *Melchior Franck, Drei Quodlibets* (Wolfenbüttel, 1956); lxiii. *Zehn weltliche Lieder aus Georg Forster: Frische teutsche Liedlein III–V* (Wolfenbüttel, 1957).

—— and HEISKE, WILHELM: *Das Erbe deutscher Musik, Reichsdenkmale*, xx. *Georg Forster, Frische teutsche Liedlein (1539–56)*, i. *Ein Außzug guter alter und neuer teutscher Liedlein, 1539* (Wolfenbüttel, 1942).

LILIENCRON, ROCHUS VON: *Deutsches Leben im Volkslied um 1530* (Berlin, 1884).

MARRIAGE, M. ELIZABETH: *Georg Forsters Frische Teutsche Liedlein in fünf Teilen. Neudrucke deutscher Litteraturwerke des XVI. und XVII. Jahrhunderts* Nr. 203-6 (Halle, 1903).

MARTIN, UWE: *Leonhard Lechner-Werke*, iii. *Newe teutsche Lieder mit vier und fünf Stimmen, 1577* (Kassel, 1954).

MOSER, HANS JOACHIM: *Gassenhawerlin und Reutterliedlein zu Franckenfurt am Meyn, bei Christian Egenolf 1535*. Facs. ed. (Augsburg, 1927).

—— *Corydon, das ist: Geschichte des mehrstimmigen Generalbaßliedes und des Quodlibets im deutschen Barock*, ii (Brunswick, 1933).

NOWAK, LEOPOLD: *Denkmäler der Tonkunst in Österreich*, xxxvii, 2. *Das deutsche Gesellschaftslied in Österreich von 1480–1550* (Vienna, 1930).

OSTHOFF, HELMUTH: *Jacob Regnart, Deutsche Lieder mit fünf Stimmen vom Jahre 1580* (Kassel, 1928).

—— *Das Musikwerk*, x. *Das deutsche Chorlied vom 16. Jahrhundert bis zur Gegenwart* (Cologne, n.d.).

PIERSIG, FRITZ: *Reutterische und Jegerische Liedlein durch M. Caspar Othmayr mit vier Stimmen componirt, Nürnberg 1549*, 2 vols. (Wolfenbüttel, 1928–33).

PRÜFER, ARTHUR: *Johann Hermann Scheins Werke*, i. *Venuskränzlein, Wittenberg 1609 und Banchetto musicale, Leipzig 1617;* ii. *Musica boscareccia oder Waldliederlein, 3 Teile, 1621–1628;* iii. *Diletti pastorali (Hirtenlust), Leipzig 1624 und Studentenschmauß à 5, Leipzig 1626* (Leipzig, 1901 ff.).

REICHERT, GEORG: *Das Erbe deutscher Musik, Sonderreihe* iii. *Erasmus Widmann, Ausgewählte Werke* (Mainz, 1959).

SACHS, HANS, and PFALZ, ANTON: *Denkmäler der Tonkunst in Österreich*, lxxxvii. *Nicolaus Zangius, Geistliche und weltliche Gesänge* (Vienna, 1951).

SANDBERGER, ADOLF: *Orlando di Lasso: Sämtliche Werke*, xviii, xx. *Kompositionen mit deutschem Text* (Leipzig, 1909–10).

SCHMID, ERNST FRITZ: *Leonhard Lechner, Newe teutsche Lieder mit fünff und vier Stimmen, 1582* (Augsburg, 1926).

—— *Leonhard Lechner-Werke*, ix. *Neue lustige teutsche Lieder nach Art der Welschen Canzonen mit vier Stimmen, 1586–88* (Kassel, 1958).

SCHMITZ, EUGEN: *Denkmäler der Tonkunst in Bayern*, viii, 1. *Johann Staden, Ausgewählte Werke*, ii (Leipzig, 1907).

SCHWARTZ, RUDOLF: *Denkmäler der Tonkunst in Bayern*, v, 2. *Werke Hans Leo Hasslers*, ii. *Canzonette von 1590 und Neue teutsche Gesang von 1596* (Leipzig, 1904).

—— *Ibid.*, xi, 1. *Werke Hans Leo Hasslers*, iii. *Madrigale zu 5, 6, 7 und 8 Stimmen von 1596* (Leipzig, 1910).

SPITTA, PHILIPP: *Heinrich Schütz, Sämmtliche Werke*, ix. *Italiänische Madrigale* (Leipzig, 1890); xv. *Gesammelte Motetten, Concerte, Madrigale und Arien* (Leipzig, 1893).

STANGL, KURT: *Das Erbe deutscher Musik, Sonderreihe* i. *Christoph Demantius, Neue Teutsche Weltliche Lieder, 1595. Convivalium Concentuum Farrago, 1609* (Kassel, 1954).

VETTER, WALTHER: *Das frühdeutsche Lied*, ii (Münster, 1928).

ZELLE, FRIEDRICH: *Publikation älterer praktischer und theoretischer Musikwerke*, xv. *Hans Leo Hassler, Lustgarten Neuer Teutscher Gesäng, Nürnberg 1601* (Leipzig, 1887).

ZENCK, HERMANN: *Das Erbe deutscher Musik, Landschaftsdenkmale Niedersachsen*, i. *Johannes Schultz, Musikalischer Lüstgarte, 1622* (Wolfenbüttel, 1937).

(ii) *Books and Articles*

ABERT, HERMANN: 'Entstehung und Wurzeln des begleiteten deutschen Sololiedes', *Gesammelte Schriften und Vorträge*, ed. F. Blume (Halle, 1929).

ALBRECHT, HANS: *Caspar Othmayr. Leben und Werk* (Kassel, 1950).

BAUMANN, A.: *Das deutsche Lied und seine Bearbeitung in den frühen Orgeltabulaturen* (Kassel, 1934).

BEHR, LUDWIG: *Die deutschen Gesänge Orlando di Lassos* (Diss. Würzburg, 1935).

BIENENFELD, ELSA: 'Wolfgang Schmeltzl, sein Liederbuch (1544) und das Quodlibet des 16. Jahrhunderts', *Sammelbände der internationalen Musikgesellschaft*, vi (1904).

DAHMEN, ELISABETH: *Die Wandlungen des weltlichen deutschen Liedstils im Zeitraum des 16. Jahrhunderts* (Botropp i. W., 1934).

EITNER, ROBERT: 'Das ältere deutsche mehrstimmige Lied und seine Meister', *Monatshefte für Musikgeschichte*, xxv–xxvi (1893–4).

—— 'Das deutsche Lied im mehrstimmigen Tonsätze aus der ersten Hälfte des 16. Jahrhunderts', ibid., xxxvii (1905).

ENGEL, HANS: 'Etliche Teutsche Liedlein geistlich und weltlich. Paul Kugelmanns Königsberger Sammlung von 1558, ein Spätling deutschen Gesellschaftsliedes', *Ostpreußische Musik* (Königsberg, 1937).

GEERING, ARNOLD: 'Die Vokalmusik in der Schweiz zur Zeit der Reformation', *Schweizerisches Jahrbuch für Musikwissenschaft*, vi (1933).

—— 'Textierung und Besetzung in Senfls Liedern', *Archiv für Musikforschung*, iv (1939).

GUDEWILL, KURT: 'Die deutschen Liedersammlungen des 15. und 16. Jahrhunderts als Zeugnisse bürgerlicher Musikkultur', *Deutsche Musikkultur*, vii (1942–3).

—— 'Zur Frage der Formstrukturen deutscher Liedtenores', *Die Musikforschung*, i (1948).

—— 'Identifizierungen von anonymen und mehrfach zugewiesenen Kompositionen in deutschen Liederdrucken aus der 1. Hälfte des 16. Jahrhunderts', *Fontes Artis Musicae*, iv (1957).

—— 'Beziehungen zwischen Modus und Melodiebildung in deutschen Liedtenores', *Archiv für Musikwissenschaft*, xv (1958).

—— 'Ursprünge und nationale Aspekte des Quodlibets', *International Musicological Society: Report of the Eighth Congress New York 1961*, vol. 1 (Kassel, 1961).

KALLENBACH, HANS: *Georg Forsters Frische teutsche Liedlein* (Diss. Gießen, 1931).

MOSER, HANS JOACHIM: 'Renaissancelyrik deutscher Musiker um 1500', *Deutsche Vierteljahrsschrift für Litteraturwissenschaft und Geistesgeschichte*, v (1927).

—— 'Hans Ott's erstes Liederbuch', *Acta Musicologica*, vii (1935).

—— 'Das Chorlied zwischen Senfl und Hassler', *Jahrbuch der Musikbibliothek Peters* (1928).

—— *Corydon, das ist: Geschichte des mehrstimmigen Generalbaßliedes und des Quodlibets im deutschen Barock*, i (Brunswick, 1933).

MÜLLER, GÜNTHER: *Geschichte des deutschen Liedes vom Zeitalter des Barock bis zur Gegenwart* (Munich, 1925).

NOWAK, LEOPOLD: 'Das deutsche Gesellschaftslied in Österreich von 1480 bis 1550', *Studien zur Musikwissenschaft*, xvii (1930).

OBRIST, ALOYS: *Melchior Franck. Ein Beitrag zur Geschichte der weltlichen Composition in Deutschland in der Zeit vor dem dreißigjährigen Kriege* (Diss. Berlin, 1892).

OSTHOFF, HELMUTH: *Die Niederländer und das deutsche Lied (1400–1640)* (Berlin, 1938).

PRÜFER, ARTHUR: *Johann Hermann Schein und das weltliche deutsche Lied des 17. Jahrhunderts* (Leipzig, 1908).

RADECKE, ERNST: 'Das deutsche weltliche Lied in der Lautenmusik des 16. Jahrhunderts', *Vierteljahrsschrift für Musikwissenschaft*, vii (1891).

REICHERT, GEORG: *Erasmus Widmann (1572–1634). Leben, Wirken und Werke eines württembergisch-fränkischen Musikers* (Stuttgart, 1951).

REICHMANN, G.: *Johann Eccards weltliche Werke* (Diss. Heidelberg, 1923).

REINHARDT, CARL PHILIPP: *Die Heidelberger Liedmeister des 16. Jahrhunderts* (Kassel, 1939).

ROSENBERG, HERBERT: 'Frottola und deutsches Lied um 1500', *Acta Musicologica*, xviii–xix (1946–7).

SCHWARTZ, RUDOLF: 'Hans Leo Hassler unter dem Einfluß der italienischen Madrigalisten', *Vierteljahrsschrift für Musikwissenschaft*, ix (1893).

SOWA, GEORG: 'Eine neuaufgefundene Liederhandschrift mit Noten und Text aus dem Jahre 1544', *Bericht über den internationalen musikwissenschaftlichen Kongreß, Hamburg 1956* (Kassel, 1957).

URSPRUNG, OTTO: 'Der Weg von den Gelegenheitsgesängen und dem Chorlied über die Frühmonodisten zum neueren deutschen Lied', *Archiv für Musikwissenschaft*, vi (1924).

VELTEN, RUDOLF: *Das ältere deutsche Gesellschaftslied unter dem Einfluß der italienischen Musik* (Heidelberg, 1914).

VETTER, WALTHER: *Das frühdeutsche Lied. Ausgewählte Kapitel aus der Entwicklungsgeschichte und Ästhetik des ein- und mehrstimmigen Kunstliedes im 17. Jahrhundert*, i (Münster, 1928).

WIORA, WALTER: *Europäische Volksmusik und abendländische Tonkunst* (Kassel, 1957).

CHAPTER IV

SOLO SONG AND CANTATA

(i) *Sources*

BRUGER, H. D.: *Alte Lautenkunst aus drei Jahrhunderten*, i (Berlin and Leipzig, 1923).

—— *Schule des Lautenspiels*, i (Wolfenbüttel, 1925).

CHILESOTTI, OSCAR: *Lautenspieler des XVI. Jahrhunderts* (Leipzig, [1891]).

FERAND, ERNEST T.: *Improvisation in Nine Centuries of Western Music* (Cologne, 1961).

NOSKE, FRITS: *The Solo Song outside German-speaking Countries* (Cologne, 1958).

(ii) *Books and Articles*

FERAND, ERNEST: *Die Improvisation in der Musik* (Zürich, 1938).

KUHN, MAX: *Die Verzierungs-Kunst in der Gesangs-Musik des 16–17. Jahrhunderts (1535–1650)* (Leipzig, 1902).

LA LAURENCIE, LIONEL DE: *Les Luthistes* (Paris, 1928).

STEVENS, DENIS, ed.: *A History of Song* (London, 1960).

WOLF, JOHANNES: *Handbuch der Notationskunde*, ii (Leipzig, 1919).

SPAIN

(i) *Sources*

ASENJO BARBIERI, FRANCISCO: *Cancionero musical de los siglos XV y XVI* (Madrid, 1890; reprinted Buenos Aires, 1945).

BAL Y GAY, JESÚS: *Romances y villancicos españoles del siglo XVI* (Mexico, 1939).
MARTÍNEZ TORNER, EDUARDO: *Collección de vihuelistas españoles del siglo XVI* (Madrid, 1923).
MORPHY, G.: *Les Luthistes espagnols du XVIᵉ siècle*, 2 vols. (Leipzig, 1902).
PEDRELL, FELIPE: *Cancionero musical popular español*, iii (Barcelona, 1920).
PUJOL, EMILIO: *Monumentos de la música española*, iii. *Luys de Narváez: Los seys libros del Delphin de música* (Barcelona, 1945); vii. *Alonso Mudarra: Tres libros de música* (Barcelona, 1949).
SCHRADE, LEO: *Publikationen älterer Musik . . . der deutschen Musikgesellschaft*, ii. *Luis Milán: Musikalische Werke* (Leipzig, 1927).
VILLALBA MUÑOZ, LUIS DE: *Diez canciones españolas de los siglos XV y XVI* (Madrid, n.d.).

(ii) *Books and Articles*

BAL, J.: 'Fuenllana and the Transcription of Spanish Lute-music', *Acta Musicologica*, xi (1939).
DEVOTO, DANIEL: 'La Canción traditional y la música culta', *Revista de la Universidad de Buenos Aires*, 3rd series, ii (1944).
—— 'La música vocal de los vihuelistas españoles', *Dos clases públicas de historia de la música* (Mendoza, 1945).
—— 'Noticia sobre los vihuelistas españoles', *Correo literario* [Buenos Aires] (15 Feb. 1944).
—— 'Poésie et musique dans l'œuvre des Vihuelistes', *Annales musicologiques*, iv (1956).
KOCZIRZ, ADOLF: 'Die Gitarrenkompositionen in Miguel de Fuenllana's *Orphenica lyra* (1554)', *Archiv für Musikwissenschaft*, iv (1922).
PEDRELL, FELIPE: *Catàlech de la Biblioteca Musical de Diputació de Barcelona*, ii (Barcelona, 1909).
QUEROL GAVALDÁ, MIGUEL: 'Importance historique et nationale du romance', *Musique et poésie au XVIᵉ siècle* (Paris, 1954).
RIEMANN, HUGO: 'Das Lautenwerk des Miguel de Fuenllana (1554)', *Monatshefte für Musikgeschichte*, xxvii (1895).
ROBERTS, JOHN: 'Some Notes on the Music of the Vihuelistas', *The Lute Society Journal*, vii (1965).
ST. AMOUR, SISTER M. P.: *A Study of the Villancico up to Lope de Vega* (Washington, D.C., 1940).
TREND, J. B.: *Luis Milan and the Vihuelistas* ([London], 1925).
—— *The Music of Spanish History to 1600* ([London], 1926).
VINDEL, FRANCISCO: *Solaces bibliográficos* (Madrid, 1942) (for the chapter 'Libros españoles sobre la vihuela y ghitarra de los siglos XVI al XVIII').

ITALY

(i) *Sources*

BEDFORD, HERBERT: *Giulio Caccini: 'Deh, dove son fuggiti'* (London, 1924).
BENVENUTI, GIACOMO: *35 arie di vari autori del secolo XVII* (Milan, 1922).
—— *Andrea Falconieri: 17 arie a una voce* (Milan, 1921).
—— *Carlo Milanuzzi: 22 arie a una voce* (Milan, 1922).
BOGHEN, F.: *Girolamo Frescobaldi: Primo libro d'arie musicali* (Rome, 1933).
BONAVENTURA, ARNALDO: *Ariette di Francesca Caccini e Barbara Strozzi* (Rome, 1930).
CACCINI, GIULIO: *Le nuove musiche*. Facs. ed. (Rome, 1934).
CHIGI-SARACINI, COUNT GUIDO: *Claudio Saracini: Le seconde musiche*. Facs. ed. (Siena, 1933).

CHILESOTTI, O.: *Biblioteca di rarità musicali*, iii. *Giovanni Stefani: Affetti amorosi* (Milan, 1886).

DISERTORI, B.: *Istituzioni e monumenti dell' arte musicale italiana, nuova serie*, iii. *Le Frottole per Canto e liuto intabulate da Franciscus Bossinensis* (Milan, 1964).

FANO, FABIO: *Istituzioni e monumenti dell'arte musicale italiana*, iv. *La Camerata fiorentina: Vincenzo Galilei* (Milan, 1934).

FELLER, M.: 'The New Style of Giulio Caccini', *Kongress-Bericht Köln 1958* (Kassel and Basle, 1959).

GEVAERT, F. A.: *Les Gloires d'Italie*, 2 vols. (Paris, [1868]).

GOTWALS, V., and KEPPLER, P.: *Smith College Music Archives*, xiii. *Paolo Quagliati: La sfera armoniosa* and *Il carro di fedeltà d'Amore* (Northampton, Mass., 1957).

JEPPESEN, KNUD: *La Flora*, 3 vols. (Copenhagen, 1949).

MacCLINTOCK, C.: *The Wellesley Edition*, viii. *The Bottegari Lutebook* (Wellesley, Mass., 1965).

MALIPIERO, G. F.: *Claudio Monteverdi: Tutte le opere*, vii, ix–x ([Bologna], 1928, n.d.).

MANTICA, F.: *Prime fioriture del melodramma italiano*, ii. *Giulio Caccini: Le nuove musiche*. Facs. ed. (Rome, 1930).

PARISOTTI, ALESSANDRO: *Arie antiche ad una voce*, ii–iii (Milan, [1890–1900]).
—— *Piccolo album di musica antica* (Milan, n.d.).

PERINELLO, C.: *Raccolta nazionale delle musiche italiane*, ix–xii. *Giulio Caccini: Le nuove musiche* (Milan, 1919).

RICCI, VITTORIO: *Antiche gemme italiane* (Milan, [1910?]).

SPOHR, H.: *Musikalische Denkmäler*, iv. *Girolamo Frescobaldi: Arie musicali* (Mainz, 1960).

WALKER, D. P. *et al.*: *Les Fêtes du Mariage de Ferdinand de Medicis et de Christine de Lorraine, Florence, 1589*, i. *Musique des Intermèdes de 'La Pellegrina'* (Paris, 1963).

(ii) *Books and Articles*

ARNOLD, DENIS: *Monteverdi* (London, 1963).

ARNOLD, F. T.: *The Art of Accompaniment from a Thorough-Bass* (Oxford, 1931).

BONAVENTURA, ARNALDO: 'Di un'opera di Girolamo Frescobaldi stampata a Firenze', *Ferrara a Girolamo Frescobaldi*, ed. N. Bennati (Ferrara, 1908).

BOYER, FERDINAND: 'Giulio Caccini à la cour d'Henri IV (1604–1605) d'après des lettres inédites', *Revue musicale*, vii (1926).

BRIDGMAN, NANIE: 'Giovanni Camillo Maffei et sa lettre sur le chant', *Revue de musicologie*, xxxviii (1956).

CALCATERRA, CARLO: *Poesia e canto* (Bologna, 1951).

CHILESOTTI, OSCAR: 'Canzonette del seicento con la chitarra', *Rivista musicale italiana*, xvi (1909).

DENT, EDWARD J.: 'Italian Chamber Cantatas', *Musical Antiquary*, ii (1910–11).

DONI, G. B.: *Compendio del trattato de' generi e de' modi della musica* (Rome, 1635).
—— *De' trattati di musica*, ed. A. F. Gori, ii (Florence, 1763).

EHRICHS, ALFRED: *Giulio Caccini* (Leipzig, 1908).

EINSTEIN, ALFRED: 'Die Arie di Ruggiero', *Sammelbände der internationalen Musikgesellschaft*, xiii (1911–12).
—— 'Ein Emissär der Monodie in Deutschland: Francesco Rasi', *Festschrift für Johannes Wolf* (Berlin, 1929).
—— *The Italian Madrigal*, 3 vols. (Princeton, 1949).

—— 'Orlando Furioso and La Gerusalemme Liberata as set to music during the 16th and 17th Centuries', Music Library Association Notes, viii (1951).

—— 'Vincenzo Galilei and the Instructive Duo', Music and Letters, xviii (1937).

FORTUNE, NIGEL: 'Continuo Instruments in Italian Monodies', Galpin Society Journal, vi (1953).

—— 'A Florentine Manuscript and its Place in Italian Song', Acta Musicologica, xxiii (1951).

—— 'A Handlist of Printed Italian Secular Monody Books, 1602–1635', R.M.A. Research Chronicle, iii (1963).

—— 'Italian Secular Monody from 1600 to 1635: an Introductory Survey', Musical Quarterly, xxxix (1953).

—— 'Italian Seventeenth-Century Singing', Music and Letters, xxxv (1954).

—— 'Sigismondo d'India. An Introduction to his Life and Works', Proceedings of the Royal Musical Association, lxxxi (1954–5).

GALILEI, VINCENZO: Dialogo della musica antica e moderna (Venice, 1581). Facs. eds. (Rome, 1934, and Milan, 1946).

GANDOLFI, RICCARDO: 'Alcune considerazioni intorno alla riforma melodrammatica a proposito di Giulio Caccini detto Romano', Rivista musicale italiana, iii (1896).

GHISI, FEDERICO: Alle fonti della monodia (Milan, 1940).

—— Del Fuggilotio musicale di Giulio Romano (Rome, 1934). Revised version in Alle fonti della monodia.

—— 'An Early Seventeenth-Century MS. with Unpublished Italian Monodic Music by Peri, Giulio Romano and Marco da Gagliano', Acta Musicologica, xx (1948).

—— Feste musicali della Firenze medicea (1480–1589) (Florence, 1939).

GOLDSCHMIDT, HUGO: Die italienische Gesangsmethode des XVII. Jahrhunderts (Breslau, 1890).

GOMBOSI, OTTO: 'Italia, patria del basso ostinato', Rassegna musicale, vii (1934).

KINKELDEY, OTTO: 'Luzzasco Luzzaschi's Solo-Madrigale mit Klavierbegleitung', Sammelbände der internationalen Musikgesellschaft, ix (1907–8).

—— Orgel und Klavier in der Musik des 16. Jahrunderts (Leipzig, 1910).

LEICHTENTRITT, HUGO: 'Der monodische Kammermusikstil in Italien bis gegen 1650', in A. W. Ambros, Geschichte der Musik, iv. 3rd ed. (Leipzig, 1909).

MACCLINTOCK, CAROL: 'A Court Musician's Songbook: Modena MS. C311', Journal of the American Musicological Society, ix (1956).

—— 'The Monodies of Francesco Rasi', abstract in Journal of the American Musicological Society, ix (1956).

—— 'The Monodies of Francesco Rasi', ibid., xiv (1961).

MARCHAL, ROBERT: 'Giulio Caccini', Revue musicale, vi (1925).

MARTIN, HENRIETTE: 'La "Camerata" du Comte Bardi et la musique florentine du XVIe siècle', Revue de musicologie, xiii–xiv (1932–3).

MASERA, M. G.: 'La famiglia Caccini alla corte di Maria de' Medici', Rassegna musicale, xiii (1940).

MAZE, NANCY: 'Tenbury MS. 1018: a Key to Caccini's Art of Embellishment', abstract in Journal of the American Musicological Society, ix (1956).

MEI, GIROLAMO: Discorso sopra la musica antica e moderna (Venice, 1602). Facsimile ed. (Milan, 1933).

MOMPELLIO, FEDERICO: Sigismondo d'India (Milan, 1956).

—— 'Sigismondo d'India e il suo primo libro di Musiche da cantar solo', Collectanea Historiae Musicae, i (1953).

NETTL, PAUL: 'Über ein handschriftliches Sammelwerk von Gesängen italienischer Frühmonodie', Zeitschrift für Musikwissenschaft, ii (1919–20).

PALISCA, CLAUDE V.: *Girolamo Mei, Letters on Ancient and Modern Music to Vincenzo Galilei and Giovanni Bardi: a study with annotated texts* (*Musicological Studies and Documents*, iii) (American Institute of Musicology, 1960).

—— 'Girolamo Mei, mentor to the Florentine Camerata', *Musical Quarterly*, xl (1954).

—— 'Vincenzo Galilei and some links between "Pseudo-Monody" and monody', *Musical Quarterly*, xlvi (1960).

PAOLI, DOMENICO DE': *Claudio Monteverdi* (Milan, 1945).

PIRROTTA, NINO: 'Temperamenti e tendenze nella Camerata fiorentina', *Le manifestazioni culturali dell'Accademia Nazionale di Santa Cecilia* (Rome, 1953). Annotated English translation, 'Temperaments and Tendencies in the Florentine Camerata', *Musical Quarterly*, xl (1954).

—— 'Tragédie et comédie dans la Camerata fiorentina', *Musique et poésie au XVIe siècle* (Paris, 1954).

PORTER, W. V.: 'Peri and Corsi's *Dafne*: some new discoveries and observations', *Journal of the American Musicological Society*, xviii (1965).

PRUNIÈRES, HENRY: 'The Italian Cantata of the XVIIth Century', *Music and Letters*, vii (1926).

—— *Monteverdi: his life and work*. Trans. M. D. Mackie (London, 1926).

RACEK, JAN: *Stilprobleme der italienischen Monodie* (Prague, 1965).

REDLICH, HANS FERDINAND: *Claudio Monteverdi* (London, 1952).

RONGA, LUIGI: *Gerolamo Frescobaldi* (Turin, 1930).

SCHERING, ARNOLD: 'Zur Geschichte des begleiteten Sologesanges im 16. Jahrhundert', *Zeitschrift der internationalen Musikgesellschaft*, xiii (1912).

SCHMITZ, EUGEN: 'Antonio Brunelli als Monodist', *Zeitschrift der internationalen Musikgesellschaft*, xi (1910).

—— *Geschichte der weltlichen Solokantate* (Leipzig, 2nd ed. 1955).

—— 'Zur Frühgeschichte der lyrischen Monodie Italiens im 17. Jahrhundert', *Jahrbuch der Musikbibliothek Peters*, xviii (1911).

SCHNEIDER, MAX: *Die Anfänge des Basso Continuo und seiner Bezifferung* (Leipzig, 1918).

SCHRADE, LEO: *Monteverdi: Creator of Modern Music* (London, 1951).

SOLERTI, ANGELO: *Musica, ballo e drammatica alla corte medicea, 1600–1637* (Florence, 1905).

—— *Le origini del melodramma* (Turin, 1903).

—— 'Un viaggio in Francia di Giulio Caccini (1604–1605)', *Rivista musicale italiana*, x (1903).

VOGEL, EMIL: *Bibliothek der gedruckten weltlichen Vocalmusik Italiens aus den Jahren 1500–1700, mit Nachträgen von A. Einstein*, 2 vols., reprint (Hildesheim, 1962).

WILLETTS, PAMELA J.: 'A Neglected Source of Monody and Madrigal', *Music and Letters*, xliii (1962).

WOTQUENNE, ALFRED: 'Notice sur le manuscrit 704 (ancien 8750) de la Bibliothèque du Conservatoire', *Annuaire du Conservatoire Royal de Musique de Bruxelles*, xxiv (1900).

GERMANY

(i) *Sources*

PRÜFER, A.: *Johann Hermann Scheins Sämtliche Werke*, ii (Leipzig, 1904).

(ii) *Books and Articles*

BÜCKEN, ERNST: *Das deutsche Lied* (Hamburg, 1939).

EINSTEIN, ALFRED: 'Ein unbekannter Druck aus der Frühzeit der deutschen Monodie', *Sammelbände der internationalen Musikgesellschaft*, xiii (1911–12).

KRETZSCHMAR, HERMANN: *Geschichte des neuen deutschen Liedes*, i (Leipzig, 1911).

MÜLLER, GÜNTHER: *Geschichte des deutschen Liedes* (Munich, 1925).

PRÜFER, ARTHUR: *Johann Hermann Schein und das weltliche deutsche Lied des 17. Jahrhunderts* (Leipzig, 1908).

STEVENS, D.: 'German Lute-songs of the early sixteenth century', *Besseler Festschrift* (Leipzig, 1961).

THOMAS, R. HINTON: *Poetry and Song in the German Baroque* (Oxford, 1963).

URSPRUNG, OTTO: 'Der Weg von den Gelegenheitsgesängen und dem Chorlied über die Frühmonodisten zum neueren deutschen Lied', *Archiv für Musikwissenschaft*, vi (1924).

VOLKMANN, HANS: 'Johann Nauwachs Leben', *Zeitschrift für Musikwissenschaft*, iv (1921–2).

FRANCE

(i) *Sources*

CHILESOTTI, O: *Biblioteca di rarità musicali*, vii. *J. B. Besard: Airs de court . . . dal 'Thesaurus Harmonicus'* (Milan, [1914]).

EXPERT, HENRY: *La Fleur des musiciens de P. de Ronsard* (Paris, 1923).

LA LAURENCIE, L. DE, MAIRY, A., and THIBAULT, G.: *Chansons au luth et airs de cour français du XVIᵉ siècle*. Publications de la Société Française de Musicologie, iii–iv (misprinted iv–v) (Paris, 1934).

MORCOURT, R. DE: *Guillaume Morlaye: Psaumes de Pierre Certon réduits pour chant et luth*. Introduction historique par F. Lesure (Paris, 1957).

VERCHALY, ANDRÉ: *Airs de cour pour voix et luth (1603–1643)* (Paris, 1961). (And review by Daniel Heartz in *Journal of the American Musicological Society*, xv (1962).)

WARLOCK, PETER: *French Ayres from Gabriel Bataille's Airs de différents autheurs (1608–1618)* (London, [1926]).

(ii) *Books and Articles*

ARNHEIM, AMALIE: 'Ein Beitrag zur Geschichte des einstimmigen weltlichen Kunstliedes in Frankreich im 17. Jahrhundert', *Sammelbände der internationalen Musikgesellschaft*, x (1908–9).

CHILESOTTI, OSCAR: 'Gli airs de cour di Besard', *Atti del Congresso Internazionale di Scienze Storiche*, viii for 1903 (1905).

DODGE, JANET: 'Les Airs de cour d'Adrian le Roy', *Mercure musical et bulletin de la S.I.M.*, iii (1907).

FRISSARD, CLAUDE: 'A propos d'un recueil de "chansons" de Jehan Chardavoine', *Revue de musicologie*, xxx (1948).

GÉROLD, THÉODORE: *L'Art du chant en France au XVIIᵉ siècle* (Strasbourg, 1921).

KÖRTE, OSWALD: *Laute und Lautenmusik bis zur Mitte des 16. Jahrhunderts* (Leipzig, 1901).

LE ROY, ADRIAN: *Instruction de partir toute musique facilement en tablature de luth* (lost). Translated into English 'by F. Ke. Gentleman' as *A briefe and plaine Instruction to set all Musicke of eight divers tunes in Tableture for the Lute* (London, 1574). Translation of second part only 'by J. Alford Londenor' as *A briefe and easye instruction to learne the tableture to conducte and dispose thy hande unto the Lute* (London, 1568).

LEVY, KENNETH JAY: 'Vaudeville, vers mesuré et airs de cour', *Musique et poésie au XVIᵉ siècle* (Paris, 1954).

MERSENNE, MARIN: *Harmonie universelle*, ii (Paris, 1636). Facs. ed. and translation by Roger Chapman (The Hague, 1957).

MORCOURT, RICHARD DE: 'Adrian le Roy et les psaumes pour luth', *Annales musicologiques*, iii (1955).

PRUNIÈRES, HENRY: 'Ronsard et les fêtes de cour', *Revue musicale, numéro spécial: Ronsard et la musique* (May, 1924).

QUITTARD, HENRI: 'L'*Hortus Musarum* de 1552–53 et les arrangements de pièces polyphoniques pour voix seule et luth', *Sammelbände der internationalen Musikgesellschaft*, viii (1906–7).

TIERSOT, JULIEN: 'Ronsard et la musique de son temps', *Sammelbände der internationalen Musikgesellschaft*, iv (1902–3).

VERCHALY, ANDRÉ: 'Les Airs italiens mis en tablature de luth dans les recueils français du début du XVIIe siècle', *Revue de musicologie*, xxxv (1953).

—— 'Gabriel Bataille et son œuvre personnelle pour chant et luth', ibid. xxix (1947).

—— 'La tablature dans les recueils français pour chant et luth (1603–1643), *Le Luth et sa musique* (Paris, 1958).

—— 'Poésie et air de cour en France jusqu'à 1620', *Musique et poésie au XVIe siècle* (Paris, 1954).

WALKER, D. P.: 'The Influence of *musique mesurée à l'antique*, particularly on the *airs de cour* of the early seventeenth century', *Musica Disciplina*, ii (1948).

WOTQUENNE, ALFRED: 'Étude sur L'*Hortus Musarum* de Pierre Phalèse', *Revue des bibliothèques et archives de Belgique*, i (1903).

ENGLAND

(i) *Sources* (Separate editions of songs edited by E. H. Fellowes in *The English School of Lutenist Song Writers* are not listed here.)

AUDEN, W. H., KALLMAN, C., and GREENBERG, N.: *An Elizabethan Song Book* (London, 1957).

COOPER, GERALD M.: *Robert Dowland: Two Songs* [by Caccini] *from A Musical Banquet. (Tudor Edition of Old Music*, Series B, 2) (London, 1924).

—— *Three Songs* [by Thomas Bateson, Thomas Greaves, and Richard Nicholson]. (*Tudor Edition of Old Music*, Series B, 1) (London, 1924).

DART, T.: *William Byrd: 'Out of the Orient Crystal Skies'* (London, 1960).

DODGE, JANET: *Twelve Elizabethan Songs, 1601–1610* (London, 1902).

DOLMETSCH, ARNOLD: *Select English Songs and Dialogues of the 16th and 17th Centuries*, 2 vols. (London, 1898–1912).

DUPRÉ, D.: *John Dowland: Six Songs* (arr. for voice and guitar) (London, 1954).

FELLOWES, E. H.: *William Byrd: The Collected Vocal Works*, xv (London, 1948).

—— *John Dowland: Fifty Songs*, 2 vols. (London, 1925).

—— *The English Madrigal School*, 36 vols. (London, 1913–24). A few volumes in the revised edition by T. Dart and others as *The English Madrigalists* contain a few solo songs with strings.

—— *The English School of Lutenist Song Writers*, 32 vols. (London, 1920–32). Revised edition by T. Dart and others as *The English Lute-Songs* (1959–) includes additional volumes of songs by Giovanni Coperario and others.

—— DART, T., and FORTUNE, N.: *Musica Britannica*, vi. *John Dowland: Ayres for four voices* (London, 2nd ed. 1963).

OBOUSSIER, P.: *Anon.: 'Miserere my Maker'* (London, 1954).

POTTER, FRANK HUNTER: *Reliquary of English Song* (New York, [1915]).

SABOL, ANDREW J.: *Songs and Dances for the Stuart Masque: an Edition of Sixty-three Items of Music for the English Court Masque from 1604 to 1641, with an Introductory Essay* (Providence, Rhode Island, 1959).

SOURIS, ANDRÉ, and JACQUOT, JEAN: *Poèmes de Donne, Herbert et Crashaw mis en musique par leurs contemporains*. Transcription et réalisation par A. Souris. Introduction par J. Jacquot (Paris, 1961).

WARLOCK, PETER: *The First (Second, Third) Book of Elizabethan Songs that were Originally Composed for One Voice to Sing and Four Stringed Instruments to Accompany* (London, 1926).
—— *Giovanni Coperario: 'How like a golden dream'* (London, 1929).
—— *Two Songs from A Pilgrim's Solace* (London, 1923).
—— and WILSON, PHILIP: *English Ayres, Elizabethan and Jacobean*, 6 vols. (London, 1927–31).

(ii) *Books and Articles*

[ARKWRIGHT, G. E. P.]: 'Early Elizabethan Stage Music', *Musical Antiquary*, i (1909–10) and iv (1912–13).
—— 'Elizabethan Choirboy Plays and their Music', *Proceedings of the Musical Association*, xl (1913–14).
—— 'Robert Douland's *Musicall Banquet*, 1610', *Musical Antiquary*, i (1909–10).
BONTOUX, GERMAINE: *La Chanson en Angleterre au temps d'Elisabeth* (Oxford, 1936).
BOYD, MORRISON COMEGYS: *Elizabethan Music and Musical Criticism*. (Philadelphia, 2nd. ed., 1962).
BRETT, PHILIP: 'The English Consort Song, 1570–1625', *Proceedings of the Royal Musical Association*, lxxxviii (1961–2).
—— and DART, THURSTON: 'Songs by William Byrd in Manuscripts at Harvard', *Harvard Library Bulletin*, xiv (1960).
BROWN, DAVID: 'William Byrd's 1588 volume', *Music and Letters*, xxxviii (1957).
CUTTS, JOHN P.: 'Early Seventeenth-century lyrics at St. Michael's College, Tenbury', *Music and Letters*, xxxvii (1956).
—— 'A Reconstruction of the *Willow Song*', *Journal of the American Musicological Society*, x (1957).
—— *Seventeenth-Century Songs and Lyrics* (Columbia, Missouri, 1959).
—— 'Songs Vnto the Violl and Lute', *Musica Disciplina*, xvi (1962).
DART, THURSTON: 'Rôle de la danse dans l'"ayre" anglais', *Musique et poésie au XVIᵉ siècle* (Paris, 1954).
DOWLING, MARGARET: 'The Printing of John Dowland's *Second Booke of Songs or Ayres*', *The Library*, 4th. series, xii (1932–3).
DUCKLES, VINCENT: 'Florid Embellishment in English Song of the Late 16th and Early 17th Centuries', *Annales musicologiques*, v (1957).
—— 'The Gamble Manuscript as a Source of continuo Song in England', *Journal of the American Musicological Society*, i (1948).
—— 'The Lyrics of John Donne as Set by his Contemporaries', *Seventh International Musicological Congress, Cologne: Bericht* (Kassel, 1959).
EMSLIE, McD.: 'Nicholas Lanier's Innovations in English Song', *Music and Letters*, xli (1960).
FELLOWES, EDMUND H.: *English Madrigal Verse, 1588–1632* (Oxford, 2nd ed. 1929).
—— 'The Songs of Dowland', *Proceedings of the Musical Association*, lvi (1929–30).
—— 'The Text of the Song-books of Robert Jones', *Music and Letters*, viii (1927).
—— *William Byrd* (London, 2nd ed. 1948).
FORTUNE, NIGEL: 'Philip Rosseter and his Songs', *The Lute Society Journal*, vii (1965).
GREER, DAVID: 'The Lute Songs of Thomas Morley', *The Lute Society Journal*, viii (1966).
—— '"What if a Day"—an Examination of the Words and Music', *Music and Letters*, xliii (1962).
JUDD, PERCY: 'The Songs of John Danyel', *Music and Letters*, xvii (1936).

KASTENDIECK, M. M.: *England's Musical Poet: Thomas Campion* (New York, 1936).

KERMAN, JOSEPH: *The Elizabethan Madrigal: a Comparative Study* (*American Musicological Society: Studies and Documents,* iv) (New York, 1962).

MANNING, ROSEMARY J.: 'Lachrymae: a Study of Dowland', *Music and Letters,* xxv (1944).

MELLERS, WILFRID: *Harmonious Meeting* (London, 1963).

OBOUSSIER, PHILIPPE: 'Turpyn's Book of Lute-songs', *Music and Letters,* xxxiv (1953).

OLSHAUSEN, ULRICH: *Das Lautenbegleitete Sololied in England um 1600* (Frankfurt/M., 1963).

PATTISON, BRUCE: *Music and Poetry of the English Renaissance* (London, 1948).

—— 'Philip Rosseter, Poet and Musician', *Musical Times,* lxxii (1931).

—— 'Sir Philip Sidney and Music', *Music and Letters,* xv (1934).

POULTON, DIANA: 'Dowland's Songs and their Instrumental Forms', *Monthly Musical Record,* lxxxi (1951).

—— 'John Dowland, Doctor of Musick', *The Consort,* xx (1963).

—— 'Was John Dowland a Singer?' *The Lute Society Journal,* vii (1965).

RAYNOR, HENRY: 'Framed to the Life of the Words', *Music Review,* xix (1958).

SPINK, IAN: 'Angelo Notari and his "Prime Musiche Nuove"', *Monthly Musical Record,* lxxxvii (1957).

—— 'English Cavalier Songs, 1620–1660', *Proceedings of the Royal Musical Association,* lxxxvi (1959–60).

STERNFELD, F. W.: *Music in Shakespearean Tragedy* (London, 1963).

STEVENS, DENIS: 'La Chanson anglaise avant l'école madrigaliste', *Musique et poésie au XVIᵉ siècle* (Paris, 1954).

—— 'Plays and Pageants in Tudor Times', *Monthly Musical Record,* lxxxvii (1957).

—— 'Tudor Part-songs', *Musical Times,* xcvi (1955).

STEVENS, JOHN: *Music and Poetry at the Early Tudor Court* (London, 1961).

WARLOCK, PETER: *The English Ayre* (London, 1926).

—— *English Ayres, Elizabethan and Jacobean* (London, 1932).

—— *Thomas Whythorne: An Unknown Elizabethan Composer* (London, 1925).

WHYTHORNE, THOMAS: *Autobiography,* ed. J. M. Osborn (Oxford, 1961).

WOODFILL, WALTER L.: *Musicians in English Society* (Princeton, 1953).

CHAPTER V

LATIN CHURCH MUSIC ON THE CONTINENT–I

(a) THE FRANCO-FLEMINGS IN THE NORTH

(i) *Sources*

BERNET KEMPERS, K. PH.: *Corpus mensurabilis musicae,* iv. *Jacobus Clemens non Papa: Opera Omnia* (American Institute of Musicology, 1951–).

LENAERTS, R. B.: *Monumenta Musicae Belgicae,* ix. *Nederlandse Polyfonie uit Spaanse Bronnen* (Antwerp, 1963).

MALDEGHEM, R. VAN: *Trésor musical. Musique sacrée,* 29 vols. (Brussels, 1865–93). See annotated index by Gustave Reese in *Music Library Association Notes* (Washington, D.C.), ser. 2, vol. vi (December, 1948).

MEIER, BERNHARD: *Das Chorwerk*, lxxii. *Jacobus Clemens non Papa: Drei Motetten* (Wolfenbüttel, 1959).

MERRITT, A. TILLMAN: *Quatorzième Livre de motets composés par Pierre de Manchicourt, parus chez Pierre d'Attaingnant (1539)* (Monaco, 1964).

SCHMIDT-GÖRG, J.: *Corpus mensurabilis musicae*, vi. *Nicolas Gombert: Opera Omnia* (American Institute of Musicology, 1951–   ).

SEIFFERT, MAX: *Werken van Jan Pieterszn. Sweelinck*, vi. *Cantiones sacrae (1619)* (Leipzig and The Hague, 1899).

VAN DEN SIGTENHORST MEYER, B.: *Jan Pieterszn. Sweelinck: Opera Omnia, editio altera*, vi. *Cantiones sacrae* (Amsterdam, 1957).

(ii) *Books and Articles*

BERNET KEMPERS, K. PH.: 'Bibliography of the Sacred Works of Jacobus Clemens non Papa: A Classified List with a Notice on his Life', *Musica Disciplina*, xviii (1964).

—— *Jacobus Clemens non Papa und seine Motetten* (Augsburg, 1928).

—— 'Die Souterliedekens des Jacobus Clemens non Papa', *Tijdschrift der Vereeniging voor Nederlandsche Muziekgeschiedenis*, xii (1928); xiii (1929).

BRIDGMAN, N.: 'Les Échanges musicaux entre l'Espagne et les Pays-Bas au temps de Philippe le Beau et de Charles-Quint', *La Renaissance dans les provinces du nord* (Arras, 1955).

DELPORTE, J.: '*L'Ave virgo Cecilia* de Pierre de Manchicourt', *Revue liturgique et musicale* (1936–7).

EPPSTEIN, HANS: *Nicolas Gombert als Motettenkomponist* (Würzburg, 1935).

LENAERTS, R. B.: 'The 16th-Century Parody Mass in the Netherlands', *Musical Quarterly*, xxxvi (1950).

—— 'Voor de biographie van Clemens non Papa', *Tijdschrift der Vereeniging voor Nederlandsche Muziekgeschiedenis*, xiii (1929).

LOWINSKY, EDWARD E.: *Secret Chromatic Art in the Netherlands Motet* (New York, 1946).

PAAP, WOUTER: 'Jacobus Clemens non Papa en zijn Souterliedekens', *Mens en Melodie*, xvii (1962).

SCHMIDT-GÖRG, JOSEPH: *Nicolas Gombert, Kapellmeister Karls V: Leben und Werk* (Bonn, 1938).

—— 'Die Messen des Clemens non Papa', *Zeitschrift für Musikwissenschaft*, ix (1926–7).

VAN DEN BORREN, CHARLES: *Geschiedenis van de muziek in de Nederlanden*, 2 vols. (Antwerp, 1948–51).

—— *La Musique en Belgique* (Brussels, 1950).

—— 'Quelques réflexions à propos du style imitatif syntaxique', *Revue belge de musicologie*, i (1946).

VAN DOORSLAER, G.: *Jean Lestainnier, organiste-compositeur* (Malines, 1921).

—— *Jean Richafort, maître de chapelle-compositeur* (Antwerp, 1930).

VENTE, M. A.: 'Sweelinckiana', *Tijdschrift der Vereniging voor Nederlandse Muziekgeschiedenis*, xix (1960–3).

(b) FRANCE IN THE SIXTEENTH CENTURY (1520–1610)

(i) *Sources*

BORDES, CH.: *Anthologie des maîtres religieux ... Livre des messes* (Paris, [1894]).

EXPERT, H.: *Anthologie chorale des maîtres musiciens de la Renaissance française* (Paris, 1938).

—— *Monuments de la musique française au temps de la Renaissance,* ii, ix (Paris, 1925, 1928).

MARTIN, E., and BURALD, J.: *E. Du Caurroy: Missa pro defunctis* (Paris, 1951).

SMIJERS, A., and MERRITT, A. T.: *Treize Livres de motets parus chez Pierre Attaingnant en 1534 et 1535* (Paris and Monaco, 1934–63).

(ii) *Books and Articles*

AUDA, A.: *B. Beaulaigue, poète et musicien prodige* (Woluwé St-Pierre, 1957).

BRENET, M.: *Musique et musiciens de la vieille France* (Paris, 1911).

LESURE, FRANÇOIS: 'La Musique religieuse en France au XVIᵉ siècle', *Revue musicale,* no. 222 (1953–4).

—— 'Notes pour une biographie de J. Lhéritier', *Revue de musicologie,* xli (1958).

—— and THIBAULT, GENEVIÈVE: 'Bibliographie des éditions musicales publiées par N. du Chemin', *Annales musicologiques,* i (1953).

—— *Bibliographie des ouvrages publiés par A. le Roy et R. Ballard* (Paris, 1954).

PIRRO, ANDRÉ: 'L'Enseignement de la musique aux universités françaises', *Acta Musicologica,* ii (1930).

RIGSBY, LEE: 'Elzéar Genet: A Renaissance Composer', *Studies in Music History and Theory* (Florida State University Studies, xviii) (Tallahassee, Florida, 1955).

TRICOU, G.: 'Les deux Layolle et les organistes lyonnais du XVIᵉ siècle', *Mémoires de la Soc. litt., hist. et archéol. de Lyon* (1896–7).

(c) CENTRAL EUROPE

(i) *Sources*

ALBRECHT, H.: *Das Erbe deutscher Musik,* xvi, xxvi. *Caspar Othmayr: Ausgewählte Werke,* 1. Teil (1941), 2. Teil (1956); xxii. *Thomas Stoltzer: Ausgewählte Werke* (1942).

—— *et al.*: *Georg Rhau: Musikdrucke aus den Jahren 1538 bis 1545* (Kassel and St. Louis, 1955–).

—— *Musik alter Meister,* vi. *Benedictus Ducis: Zwei Psalmmotetten* (Graz, 1957); xi. *Benedictus Ducis: Missa de Beate Virgine* (Graz, 1959).

BEZECNY, E., and RABL, W.: *Denkmäler der Tonkunst in Österreich,* x, Jg. v (1). *Heinrich Isaac: Choralis Constantinus liber 1 (1550)* (Vienna, 1898).

BLUME, F., and SCHULZE, W.: *Das Chorwerk,* xliv. *Galliculus: Mass 4* (Wolfenbüttel, 1936).

—— *Das Chorwerk,* xlvii. *Resinarius (Harzer): Passion* (Wolfenbüttel, 1937).

COMMER, FRANZ: *Collectio operum musicorum Batavorum (Saeculi xvi)* (Berlin, 1844–58).

CUYLER, LOUISE: *H. Isaac: Choralis Constantinus, Book III* (Ann Arbor, Mich., 1950).

CVETKO, DRAGOTIN: *Gallus, Plantzius, Dolar et leur œuvre* (Ljubljana, 1963).

FUNK, JOSEPH: *Musica orans,* xxiv. *Gregor Aichinger: Maria uns tröst*; xxviii. *Gregor Aichinger: Missa paschalis* (München–Gladbach, n.d.).

GERSTENBERG, W.: *Das Chorwerk,* lxii. *Ludwig Senfl: Ave rosa sine spinis* and *Mater digna Dei* (Wolfenbüttel, 1957).

—— *Ludwig Senfl: Sämtliche Werke,* viii. *Motetten II, Kompositionen des Proprium Missae* (Wolfenbüttel and Zurich, 1964).

HOFFMANN-ERBRECHT, L.: *Das Chorwerk,* lxxiv. *Thomas Stoltzer: Missa paschalis* (Wolfenbüttel, 1958).

KROYER, T.: *Denkmäler der Tonkunst in Bayern*, iii (2). *Ludwig Senfl: Werke*, i (Leipzig, 1903).

LÖHRER, E., URSPRUNG, O., and GERSTENBERG, W.: *Das Erbe deutscher Musik*, v, xiii. *Ludwig Senfl: Sämtliche Werke*, i. *Sieben Messen zu vier bis sechs Stimmen* (1936); iii. *Motetten I* (1939).

MEYER, E. H.: *Das Chorwerk*, ii. *Jacob Vaet: Sechs Motetten* (Wolfenbüttel, 1929).

PARKER, ROBERT L.: *Adam Rener: Collected Works*, i. *The Motets* (Brooklyn, 1964).

PISK, P.: *Denkmäler der Tonkunst in Österreich*, lxxviii, Jg. xlii (1). *Jakob Handl (Gallus): Sechs Messen* (Vienna, 1935).

SCHMITZ, ARNOLD: *Musikalische Denkmäler*, i. *Oberitalienische Figuralpassionen des 16. Jahrhunderts* (Mainz, 1955).

STEINHARDT, MILTON: *Denkmäler der Tonkunst in Österreich*, cviii/cix. *Jacobus Vaet: Sämtliche Werke*, iv. *Messen I* (Graz and Vienna, 1964).

WEBERN, A. VON: *Denkmäler der Tonkunst in Österreich*, xxxii, Jg. xvi (1). *Heinrich Isaac: Choralis Constantinus liber II* (Vienna, 1909).

ZENCK, H.: *Das Erbe deutscher Musik*, xxiii. *Sixt Dietrich: Ausgewählte Werke: Hymnen (1545), erste Abteilung* (1942); complete ed. of *Novum opus musicum (1545)* (St. Louis, Missouri, 1960).

—— *Publikationen älterer Musik*. Jg. iii, 2. *Sixtus Dietrich* (Leipzig, 1928).

—— *Publikationen älterer Musik*. Jg. ix. *Adrian Willaert: Sämtliche Werke: Motetten 1539, 1545*, i (Leipzig, 1937).

(ii) *Books and Articles*

BARTHA, DÉNES: *Benedictus Ducis und Appenzeller* (Wolfenbüttel, 1930).

BECK, F. A., ed.: *Dr. M. Luther's Gedanken über die Musik* (Berlin, 1825).

BIRTNER, H.: 'Sieben Messen von Ludwig Senfl', *Archiv für Musikforschung*, vii (1940).

BLASCHKE, H.: 'Heinrich Isaaks Choralis Constantinus', *Kirchenmusikalisches Jahrbuch*, xxvi (1931).

BROWN, HOWARD: 'The "Chanson spirituelle", Jacques Buus, and Parody Technique', *Journal of the American Musicological Society*, xv (1962).

CUYLER, LOUISE: 'The Sequences of Isaac's *Choralis Constantinus*', *Journal of the American Musicological Society*, iii (1950).

DREHER, CARL: 'Die Lamentationen des Stephan Mahu', *Monatshefte für Musikgeschichte*, vi (1874).

FALVY, ZOLTÁN: 'Thomas Stoltzers Anstellungsurkunde aus dem Jahre 1522', *Studia Musicologica*, i (1961).

FEDERHOFER, HELLMUT: 'Biographische Beiträge zu Erasmus Lapicida und Stephan Mahu', *Die Musikforschung*, v (1952).

HAMPE, KARL-LUDWIG: 'Über zwei deutsche Psalmen Thomas Stoltzers', *Musik des Ostens*, i (1962).

HOFFMANN-ERBRECHT, LOTHAR: 'Thomas Stoltzer in Schlesien. Neue Beiträge zu seiner Biographie', *Musik des Ostens*, i (Kassel, 1962).

—— *Thomas Stoltzer: Leben und Schaffen* (Kassel, 1964).

HUIGENS, P. C.: 'Blasius Amon', *Studien zur Musikwissenschaft*, xviii (Vienna, 1931).

KADE, REINHARD: 'Antonius Scandellus (1517–1580): ein Beitrag zur Geschichte der Dresdener Hofkantorei', *Sammelbände der internationalen Musikgesellschaft*, xv (1914).

KRAUS, HEDWIG: 'Jacob Buus, Leben und Werke', *Tijdschrift der Vereeniging voor Nederlandsche Muziekgeschiedenis*, xii–xiv (1926–8).

LÖHRER, E.: *Die Messen von Senfl: Beiträge zur Geschichte des polyphonen Messordinariums um 1500* (Lichtensteig, 1938).

NAYLOR, E. W.: 'Jacob Handl (Gallus)', *Proceedings of the Musical Association*, xxxv (1908).

—— 'Jacob Handl (Gallus) as Romanticist', *Sammelbände der internationalen Musikgesellschaft*, xi (1909).

PISK, PAUL: 'Das Parodieverfahren in den Messen des Jacobus Gallus', *Studien zur Musikwissenschaft*, v (Leipzig and Vienna, 1918).

SCHMITZ, ARNOLD: 'Zur motettischen Passion des 16. Jahrhunderts', *Archiv für Musikwissenschaft*, xvi (1959).

SCHRÖDER, INGE-MARIE: *Die Responsorienvertonungen des Balthasar Resinarius* (Kassel, 1953).

SCHULZE, WILLI: *Die mehrstimmige Messe im frühprotestantischen Gottesdienst* (Wolfenbüttel, 1940).

SMIJERS, ALBERT: *Karl Luython als Motettenkomponist* (Amsterdam, 1923).

STEINHARDT, MILTON: *Jacobus Vaet and his Motets* (East Lansing, Michigan, 1951).

TORCHI, LUIGI: *L'arte musicale in Italia*, i. *Composizioni sacre e profane a più voci, secolo XIV, XV e XVI*; ii. Ibid., *secolo XVI* (Milan, 1897–).

URSPRUNG, OTTO: *Jacobus de Kerle. Sein Leben und seine Werke* (Munich, 1913).

WERNER, T. W.: 'Die Magnificat-Kompositionen Adam Reners', *Archiv für Musikwissenschaft*, ii (1920).

(d) THE VENETIAN SCHOOL

(i) *Sources*

ARNOLD, DENIS: *Corpus mensurabilis musicae*, xii. *Giovanni Gabrieli: Opera omnia* (American Institute of Musicology, 1956–).

AVERKAMP, ANTON: *Adrian Willaert: Missa 'Benedicta es'* (Amsterdam, 1915).

BENVENUTI, GIACOMO: *Istituzioni e monumenti dell'arte musicale italiana*, i. *Andrea e Giovanni Gabrieli e la musica strumentale in San Marco* (Milan, 1931).

FLURY, ROMAN: *Das Chorwerk*, lxxvii. *Gioseffo Zarlino: Drei Motetten und ein geistliches Madrigal* (Wolfenbüttel, 1961).

MEIER, BERNHARD: *Corpus mensurabilis musicae*, xiv. *Cipriano di Rore: Opera omnia* (American Institute of Musicology, 1959–).

ZENCK, H., and GERSTENBERG, W.: *Corpus mensurabilis musicae*, iii. *Adriano Willaert: Opera omnia* (American Institute of Musicology, 1950–).

(ii) *Books and Articles*

ALESSI, GIOVANNI d': 'Precursors of Adriano Willaert in the Practice of *Coro Spezzato*', *Journal of the American Musicological Society*, v (1952).

ANTONOWYTSCH, MYROSLAW: *Die Motette 'Benedicta es' von Josquin des Prez und die Messen 'super Benedicta' von Willaert, Palestrina, de la Hêle und de Monte* (Utrecht, 1951).

ARNOLD, DENIS: 'Andrea Gabrieli und die Entwicklung der "cori-spezzati"-Technik', *Die Musikforschung*, xii (1959).

—— 'The Significance of "Cori spezzati"', *Music and Letters*, xl (1959).

BECK, HERMANN: 'Adrian Willaerts Messen', *Archiv für Musikwissenschaft*, xvii (1960).

—— 'Adrian Willaerts Motette "Mittit ad Virginem" und seine gleichnamige Parodiemesse', *Archiv für Musikwissenschaft*, xviii (1961).

—— 'Probleme der venezianischen Messkomposition im 16. Jahrhundert', *Bericht über den internationalen musikwissenschaftlichen Kongress Wien, Mozartjahr 1956* (1959).

CAFFI, FRANCESCO: *Storia della musica sacra nella già Cappella ducale di San Marco in Venezia dal 1318 al 1797*, 2 vols. (Venice, 1854–5; facs. reprint Milan, 1931).

CARAPETYAN, ARMEN: 'The *Musica Nova* of Adriano Willaert', *Journal of Renaissance and Baroque Music*, i (1946).

FLURY, ROMAN: *Gioseffo Zarlino als Komponist* (Winterthur, 1962).

HABERL, F. X.: 'Messen Adrian Willaerts, gedruckt von Francesco Marcolini da Forlì', *Monatshefte für Musikgeschichte*, iii (1871).

HERTZMANN, ERICH: *Adrian Willaert in der weltlichen Vokalmusik seiner Zeit* (Leipzig, 1931). See also review by Otto Gombosi in *Zeitschrift für Musikwissenschaft*, xvi (1934).

JEPPESEN, KNUD: 'Marcellus-Probleme', *Acta Musicologica*, xvi–xvii (1944–5).

JOHNSON, ALVIN H.: 'The Masses of Cipriano de Rore', *Journal of the American Musicological Society*, vi (1953).

KENTON, EGON F.: 'The Late Style of Giovanni Gabrieli', *Musical Quarterly*, xlviii (1962).

LENAERTS, R. B.: 'De zesstimmige mis "Mente tota" von Adriaen Willaert' *Musica Sacra*, lxii (1935).

MUSIOL, JOSEF: *Cyprian de Rore, ein Meister der venezianischen Schule* (Halle, 1932).

SMIJERS, ALBERT: 'Hesdin of Willaert', *Tijdschrift der Vereeniging voor Nederlandsche Muziekgeschiedenis*, x (1915).

WINTERFELD, CARL VON: *Johannes Gabrieli und sein Zeitalter*, 3 vols. (Berlin, 1834, reprinted 1965).

ZENCK, HERMANN: 'Adrian Willaerts "Salmi spezzati" (1550)', *Die Musikforschung*, ii (1949).

—— *Sixtus Dietrich* (Leipzig, 1928).

—— 'Über Willaerts Motetten. Zum Motettenbegriff des 16. Jahrhunderts', in *Zenck, H.: Numerus und Affectus* (1959).

(e) EASTERN EUROPE

(i) *Sources*

CHOMIŃSKI, JÓZEF, and LISSA, ZOFIA: *Music of the Polish Renaissance* (Cracow, 1955).

CHYBIŃSKI, A. et al.: *Wydawnictwo dawnej muzyki polskiej* (Warsaw and Cracow, 1928–).

GIEBUROWSKI, W., ed.: *Cantica selecta musices sacrae in Polonia* (Poznań, 1928).

MALINOWSKI, WŁADYSŁAW: *Zieleński: Opera omnia* (Warsaw, (1966–)

POHANKA, JAROSLAV: *Dějiny české hudby v přikladech* (Prague, 1958).

SNÍŽKOVA, JITKA: *Musica Polyphonica Bohemiae* (Prague, 1958).

SURZYŃSKI, JÓZEF, ed.: *Monumenta musices sacrae in Polonia*, i–iv (Poznań, 1885–96).

(ii) *Books and Articles*

CHYBIŃSKI, ADOLF: *Słownik muzyków dawnej Polski* (Cracow, 1949).

—— *Materiały do dziejów królewskiej kapeli rorantystów na Wawelu*, i (Cracow, 1910).

—— 'Wacław z Szamotuł', *Kwartalnik Muzyczny*, xxi–xxiv (1948).

—— 'O motetach Wacława z Szamotuł', *Przegląd Muzyczny*, iii (Poznań, 1929).

—— 'O koncertach wokalno-instrumentalnych Marcina Mielczewskiego', *Kwartalnik Muzyczny*, i (1928), ii (1929), iii (1929), v (1929), viii (1930).

DUNICZ, J. J.: 'Do biografji Mikołaja Zieleńskiego', *Polski Rocznik Muzykologiczny*, ii (1936).

FEICHT, HIERONIM: 'O myszy wielkanocnej Marcina Leopolity', *Kwartalnik Muzyczny*, vi–vii (1930).

FINSCHER, LUDWIG: 'Deutsch-polnische Beziehungen in der Musikgeschichte des 16. Jahrhunderts', *Musik des Ostens*, ii (1963).

JACHIMECKI, ZDZISŁAW: *Historja muzyki polskiej* (Warsaw, 1920).

—— *Wpływy włoskie w muzyce polskiej—I: 1540–1640* (Cracow, 1911).

KONRÁD, KAREL: *Dějiny posvátneho zpěvu staročeského od 15. věku do zrušeni literátskych bratrstev* (Prague, 1893).

QUOIKA, RUDOLF: 'Christoph Harant von Polschitz und seine Zeit', *Die Musikforschung*, vii (1954).

RACEK, JAN: *Česká hudba* (Prague, 1958).

SURZYŃSKI, JÓZEF: 'Über alte polnische Kirchenkomponisten und deren Werke', *Kirchenmusikalisches Jahrbuch*, v (1890).

SZCZEPAŃSKA, MARIA: 'O dwunastogłosowem "Magnificat" Mikołaja Zieleńskiego z r. 1611', *Polski Rocznik Muzykologiczny*, i (1935).

SZWEYKOWSKI, ZYGMUNT, ed.: *Z dziejów polskiej kultury muzycznej—I: Kultura staropolska* (Cracow, 1957).

CHAPTER VI

LATIN CHURCH MUSIC ON THE CONTINENT–II

(i) *Sources*

CASIMIRI, R.: *Monumenta Polyphoniae Italicae*, i. *Missa cantantibus organis* [*Palestrina, Stabile, Soriano, Dragoni, Giovanelli, Manicini, Santini*], (Rome, 1930).

CISILINO, SIR°: *Costanzo Porta: Opera Omnia, I: Motecta quatuor vocum* (Padua, 1964).

CROSBY, C. RUSSEL: *Hans Leo Hassler: Sämtliche Werke* (Wiesbaden, 1961–).

DAGNINO, E.: *Monumenta Polyphoniae Italicae*, ii. *Constantius Festa: Sacrae Cantiones 3, 4, 5, 6 vocibus* (Rome, 1936).

FOUSE, DONALD M.: *Giammateo Asola: Sixteen Liturgical Works* (New Haven, Conn., 1964).

HAYDON, GLEN: *Francesco Corteccia: Hinnario secondo l'uso della chiesa romana et fiorentina*, 2 vols. (Cincinnati, 1958–60).

—— *Monumenta Polyphoniae Italicae*, iii. *Constantius Festa: Hymni per totum annum 3, 4, 6 vocibus* (Rome, 1958).

JEPPESEN, KNUD: *Italia Sacra Musica*, 3 vols. (Copenhagen, 1962).

MAIN, ALEXANDER: *Corpus mensurabilis musicae*, xxv. *Costanzo Festa: Opera Omnia* (American Institute of Musicology, 1962–).

SEAY, ALBERT: *Corpus mensurabilis musicae*, xxxi. *Jacobus Arcadelt: Opera Omnia* (American Institute of Musicology, 1965–).

SMIJERS, A.: *Van Ockeghem tot Sweelinck* (Amsterdam, 1939–).

SNOW, ROBERT J.: *Costanzo Porta: Musica in introitus missarum*, 2 vols. (Cincinnati, 1958–61).

VAN DEN BORREN, C., VAN DOORSLAER, G., and NUFFEL, J. VAN: *Philippe de Monte: Opera*, 31 vols. (Düsseldorf, 1927–39).

(ii) *Books and Articles*

AMANN, J. J.: *Allegris Miserere und die Aufführungspraxis in der Sixtina* (Ratisbon, 1935).

ANTONOWYTSCH, M.: *Die Motette 'Benedicta es' von Josquin und die Messen 'super Benedicta' von Willaert, Palestrina, de La Hêle und de Monte* (Utrecht, 1951).

BECK, HERMANN: 'Das Konzil von Trent und die Probleme der Kirchenmusik', *Kirchenmusikalisches Jahrbuch*, xlviii (1964).

CAMETTI, ALBERTO: 'Nuovi contributi alle biografie di Maurizio e Felice Anerio', *Rivista musicale italiana*, xxii (1915).

CASIMIRI, R.: 'Maurizio, Felice e Giov. Franc. Anerio', *Rivista musicale italiana*, xxvii (1920).

ELDERS, WILLEM: 'Enkele aspecten van de parodie-techniek in de madrigaal-missen van Philippus de Monte', *Tijdschrift der Vereeniging voor Neder-landsche Muziekgeschiedenis*, xix (1960–3).

ENGEL, HANS: *Luca Marenzio* (Florence, 1956).

FEDERHOFER, HELLMUT: 'Ein Beitrag zur Biographie von G. F. Anerio', *Die Musikforschung*, ii (1949).

FELLERER, KARL GUSTAV: 'Church Music and the Council of Trent', *Musical Quarterly*, xxxix (1953).

FERAND, ERNEST T.: '"Anchor che col partire": Die Schicksale eines berühmten Madrigals', *Festschrift Karl Gustav Fellerer* (Ratisbon, 1962).

FREY, H. W.: 'Ruggiero Giovannelli: eine biographische Studie', *Kirchenmusika-lisches Jahrbuch*, xxii (1909).

GABRIELLI, A.: *Ruggiero Giovannelli nella vita e nelle opere* (Velletri, 1926).

HABERL, F. X.: 'Felici Anerio', *Kirchenmusikalisches Jahrbuch*, xviii (1903).

—— 'Francesco Soriano', *Kirchenmusikalisches Jahrbuch*, x (1895).

—— 'Giovanni Francesco Anerio', *Kirchenmusikalisches Jahrbuch*, i (1886).

—— 'Giovanni Maria Nanino', *Kirchenmusikalisches Jahrbuch*, vi (1891).

—— 'Marcantonio Ingegneri. Eine bio-bibliographische Studie', *Kirchen-musikalisches Jahrbuch*, xiii (1898).

—— 'Die römische "schola cantorum" und die päpstlichen Kapellsänger bis zur Mitte des 16. Jahrhunderts', *Vierteljahrsschrift für Musikwissenschaft*, iii (1887).

HAYDON, GLEN: 'The Hymns of Costanzo Festa. A Style Study', *Journal of the American Musicological Society*, xii (1959).

LEICHTENTRITT, HUGO: 'The Reform of Trent and its Effect on Music', *Musical Quarterly*, xxx (1944).

LOCKWOOD, LEWIS H.: 'Vincenzo Ruffo and Musical Reform after the Council of Trent', *Musical Quarterly*, xliii (1957).

MOLITOR, RAFFAEL: *Die Nach-Tridentinische Choralreform zu Rom*, 2 vols. (Leipzig, 1901–2).

MOSER, H. J.: 'Vestiva i colli', *Archiv für Musikforschung*, iv (1939).

NUTEN, PIET: 'De "geestelijke Madrigalen" van Filip de Monte (1521–1603)', *Vereeniging voor Muziekgeschiedenis, Antwerpen. Jaarboek* (1959).

PALISCA, C. V.: 'A Clarification of "Musica Reservata" in Jean Faisnier's "Astrologiae [indiciarae ysagogica]", 1559', *Acta Musicologica*, xxxi (1959).

PIRRO, ANDRÉ, 'Leo X and Music', *Musical Quarterly*, xxi (1935).

RADICIOTTI, G.: *Giovanni Maria Nanino* (Pesaro, 1909).

SCHMIDT, GÜNTHER: 'Grundsätzliche Bemerkungen zur Geschichte der Passions-historie', *Archiv für Musikwissenschaft*, xvii (1960).

SCHMITZ, ARNOLD: 'Bemerkungen zu Vincenzo Ruffo's Passionkompositionen', *Miscelánea en homenaje a Monseñor Higinio Anglés*, ii (Barcelona, 1961).

TORRI, LUIGI: 'Nei parentali di Felice Anerio e di Carlo Gesualdo', *Rivista musicale italiana*, xxi (1914).

—— 'Vincenzo Ruffo, madrigalista e compositore di musica sacra del sec. XVI', *Rivista musicale italiana*, iii–iv (1896–7).

VAN CREVEL, M.: *Adrianus Petit Coclico* (The Hague, 1940).

VAN DOORSLAER, GEORGES: *La Vie et les œuvres de Philippe de Monte* (Brussels, 1921).

WEINMANN, KARL: *Das Konzil von Trient und die Kirchenmusik* (Leipzig, 1919).

WINTER, CARL: *Ruggiero Giovannelli* (Munich, 1935).

WOLFF, HELMUTH CHRISTIAN: 'Die ästhetische Auffassung der Parodiemesse des 16. Jahrhunderts', *Miscelánea en homenaje a Monseñor Higinio Anglés*, ii (Barcelona, 1961).

LASSUS

(i) *Sources*

BOETTICHER, WOLFGANG: *Orlando di Lasso: Sämtliche Werke: Neue Reihe* (Kassel and Basle, 1956–).

HABERL, F. X., and SANDBERGER, A.: *Orlando di Lasso: Sämmtliche Werke*, 21 vols. (Leipzig, 1894–1927).

(ii) *Books and Articles*

BALMER, LUCIE: *Orlando di Lassos Motetten* (Berne, 1938).

BOETTICHER, WOLFGANG: *Aus Orlando di Lassos Wirkungskreis* (Kassel, 1963).

—— *Orlando di Lasso und seine Zeit* (Kassel and Basle, 1958).

—— 'Zum Spätstilproblem im Schaffen Orlando di Lassos', *Bericht über den 7. Internat. Musikwiss. Kongress Köln, 1958*.

CASIMIRI, RAFFAELE: *Orlando di Lasso, maestro di cappella al Laterano nel 1553* (Rome, 1920).

HUSCHKE, JOACHIM: 'Orlando di Lassos Messen', *Archiv für Musikforschung*, v (1940).

LEUCHTMANN, HORST: *Die musikalischen Wortausdeutungen in den Motetten des Magnum opus musicum von Orlando di Lasso* (Strasbourg, 1959).

LOWINSKY, EDWARD E.: *Das Antwerpener Motettenbuch Orlando di Lassos und seine Beziehungen zum Motettenschaffen der niederländischen Zeitgenossen* (The Hague, 1937).

MEIER, BERNHARD: 'Wortausdeutung und Tonalität bei Orlando di Lasso', *Kirchenmusikalisches Jahrbuch*, xlvii (1963).

SANDBERGER, ADOLF: *Beiträge zur Geschichte der bayrischen Hofkapelle unter Orlando di Lasso*, i and iii (Leipzig, 1894–5).

VAN DEN BORREN, C.: 'En quelle année Rol. de Lattre est-il né?', *Bulletin de la société Union musicologique*, vi (1925).

—— *Orlande de Lassus* (Paris, 1920).

—— *Roland de Lassus* (Brussels, 1943).

PALESTRINA

(i) *Sources*

CASIMIRI, R., VIRGILI, L., JEPPESEN, K., and BIANCHI, L.: *Giovanni Pierluigi da Palestrina: Le opere complete* (Rome, 1939–).

ESPAGNE, F., HABERL, F. X. et al.: *Giovanni Pierluigi da Palestrina: Werke*, 33 vols. (Leipzig, 1862–1907).

(ii) *Books and Articles*

ANDREWS, H. K.: *An Introduction to the Technique of Palestrina* (London, 1958).

FELLERER, KARL GUSTAV: *Der Palestrinastil und seine Bedeutung in der vokalen Kirchenmusik des 18. Jahrhunderts* (Augsburg, 1929).

—— *Palestrina* (Ratisbon, 1930; rev. and enlarged ed., Düsseldorf, 1960).

HABERL, F. X.: 'Die ersten drei Bände der Motetten Palestrinas', *Kirchenmusikalisches Jahrbuch*, v (1890).

—— 'Die Kardinalskommission von 1564 und Palestrina's Missa Papae Marcelli', *Kirchenmusikalisches Jahrbuch*, vii (1892).

HALLER, MICHAEL: 'Analyse der Missa "O admirabile commercium" von G. P. da Palestrina', *Kirchenmusikalisches Jahrbuch*, ix (1894).

HAMBURGER, POUL: 'The Ornamentations in the Works of Palestrina', *Acta Musicologica*, xxii (1950).

JEPPESEN, KNUD: 'Marcellus-Probleme, einige Bemerkungen über die Missa Papae Marcelli', *Acta Musicologica*, xvi–xvii (1944–5).

—— *Der Palestrinastil und die Dissonanz* (Leipzig, 1925; 2nd Eng. ed., rev., *The Style of Palestrina and the Dissonance*, Copenhagen and London, 1946).

—— 'Pierluigi da Palestrina, Herzog Guglielmo Gonzaga und die neugefundenen Mantovaner-Messen Palestrinas', *Acta Musicologica*, xxv (1953).

—— 'The Recently Discovered Mantova Masses of Palestrina', *Acta Musicologica*, xxii (1950).

—— 'Some Remarks to "The Ornamentations in the Works of Palestrina" by Poul Hamburger', *Acta Musicologica*, xxii (1950).

KLASSEN, JOSEPH: 'Die Parodieverfahren in der Messe Palestrinas', *Kirchenmusikalisches Jahrbuch*, xxxviii (1954).

—— 'Untersuchungen zur Parodiemesse Palestrinas', *Kirchenmusikalisches Jahrbuch*, xxxvii (1953).

—— 'Zur Modellbehandlung in Palestrinas Parodiemessen', *Kirchenmusikalisches Jahrbuch*, xxxix (1955).

MARSHALL, ROBERT L.: 'The Paraphrase Technique of Palestrina in his Masses based on Hymns', *Journal of the American Musicological Society*, xvi (1963).

RAHE, HEINRICH: 'Der Aufbau der Motetten Palestrinas', *Kirchenmusikalisches Jahrbuch*, xxxv (1951).

—— 'Theme und Melodiebildung der Motette Palestrinas', *Kirchenmusikalisches Jahrbuch*, xxxiv (1950).

SAMSON, JOSEPH: *Palestrina ou la poésie de l'exactitude* (Geneva, 1940).

SCHNÜRL, K.: 'Die Variationstechnik in den Choral-Cantus firmus-Werken Palestrinas', *Studien zur Musikwissenschaft*, xxiii (1956).

WIDMANN, WILHELM: 'Motette und Messe "Dies sanctificatus" von Palestrina', *Kirchenmusikalisches Jahrbuch*, xxi (1908).

—— 'Sechsstimmige Messen Palestrinas', *Kirchenmusikalisches Jahrbuch*, xxv–xxviii (1930–3).

CHAPTER VII

LATIN CHURCH MUSIC ON THE CONTINENT—III

(i) *Sources*

ALEGRIA, JOSÉ AUGUSTO: *Polyphonia, Série A, No. 2* (Lisbon, 1955).

—— *Portugaliae Musica*, v, vi. *Frei Manuel Cardoso: Liber primus missarum*, 2 vols. (Lisbon, 1962).

ANGLÈS, HIGINI: *Mateo Flecha, Las Ensaladas* (Barcelona, 1955).

—— *Monumentos de la música española*, xi, xiii, xv, xvii, xx, xxi, xxiv. *Cristóbal de Morales: Opera Omnia* (Barcelona, 1952–   ).

Anglès Higini: *Monumentos de la música española,* iv. *Juan Vasquez. Recopilación de Sonetos y Villancicos a Quatro y a Cinco* (*Sevilla, 1560*) (Barcelona, 1946).

—— *Monumentos de la música española,* ii. *La música en la corte de Carlos V* (Barcelona, 1944).

Aroca, J., ed.: *Cancionero musical y poético del siglo XVII* (Madrid, 1916).

Bal y Gay, Jesús: *Tesoro de la música polifónica en México: El Códice del Convento del Carmen* (Mexico, 1952).

Calo, José Lopez: *La musica en la catedral de Granada en el siglo XVI,* 2 vols. (Granada, 1963).

Elústiza, J. B. de, and Castrillo Hernández, G.: *Antología musical* (Barcelona, 1933).

Eslava, Miguel Hilarión: *Lira sacro-hispana* (Madrid, 1869).

Gerber, Rudolf: *Das Chorwerk,* lx. *Spanisches Hymnar um 1500* (Wolfenbüttel, 1957).

Guzmán, J. B.: *Obras musicales de J. B. Comes,* 2 vols. (Madrid, 1888).

Joaquim, Manuel: *Composições polifónicas de Duarte Lôbo* (Lisbon, 1945–   ).

—— *Portugaliae Musica, Série A,* iv. *Estevão Lopes Morago: Várias obras de música religiosa, a cappella* (Lisbon, 1961).

Ortiz, Diego: *Tratado de glosas, 1553* (Berlin, 1913; 2nd ed. Kassel, 1936).

Pedrell, Felipe: *Cancionero musical popular español,* 4 vols. (Valls, 1918–22).

—— *Hispaniae Schola Musica Sacra,* 8 vols. (Barcelona and Leipzig, 1894–8).

—— *Tomás Luis de Victoria: Opera Omnia,* 8 vols. (Leipzig, 1902–13).

—— and Anglès, Higini: *Joan Brudieu: Els Madrigals i la Missa de Difunts* (Barcelona, 1921).

Proske, Karl: *Musica Divina,* ii, iii, iv (Ratisbon, 1854, 1859, 1862).

Querol Gavaldá, Miguel, ed.: *Monumentos de la música española,* viii, ix. *Cancionero musical de la Casa de Medinaceli siglo XVI,* 2 vols. (Barcelona, 1949–50).

—— and Garcia, V.: *Monumentos de la música española,* xvi, xix. *Francisco Guerrero: Opera Omnia* (Barcelona, 1955–   ).

Rubio, Samuel: *Antología polifónica sacra,* 2 vols. (Madrid, 1956).

Sampayo Ribeiro, Mario de: *Polyphonia, no. 3* (Lisbon, 1956).

Santos, Júlio Eduardo dos: *A polifonia clássica portuguesa,* i (Lisbon, 1937).

(ii) *Books and Articles*

Alvarez Pérez, José M.: 'La polifonia sagrada y sus maestros en la catedral de Léon (siglos XV y XVI)', *Anuario musical,* xiv (1959); '(durante el siglo XVII)', ibid., xv (1960).

Anglès, Higini: 'Cristóbal de Morales en España', *Anuario musical,* viii (1953).

—— 'Cristóbal de Morales y Francisco Guerrero', *Anuario musical,* ix (1954).

—— 'Els cantors i organistes franco-flamencs i alemanys a Catalunya els segles XIV–XVI', *Scheurleer-Gedenkboek* (The Hague, 1925).

—— 'Historia de la música española', in Johannes Wolf, *Historia de la música* (Barcelona, 1934).

—— *La música española desde la Edad Media hasta nuestros dias* (Barcelona, 1941).

—— 'La música sagrada de la Capilla Pontificia de Avignon en la Capilla real Aragonesa', *Anuario musical,* xii (1957).

—— 'Les Musiciens flamands en Espagne et leur influence sur la polyphonie espagnole', *Kongress-Bericht Utrecht 1952* (Amsterdam, 1953).

—— 'Musikalische Beziehungen zwischen Österreich und Spanien in der Zeit vom 14. bis zum 18. Jahrhundert', *Festschrift für Erich Schenk* (Vienna, 1962).

—— 'Palestrina y los "Magnificat" de Morales', *Anuario musical*, viii (1953).

—— 'La Polyphonie religieuse péninsulaire antérieure à la venue des musiciens flamands en Espagne', *Report Congrès Liège, 1930* (Burnham, 1931).

—— 'Das sakrale Charakter der Kirchenmusik von Cristóbal de Morales', *Festschrift für Theobald Schrems* (Ratisbon, 1963).

—— 'Tomás Luis de Victoria und Deutschland', in *Festschrift Wilhelm Neuss* (*Spanische Forschungen der Görresgesellschaft*, erste Reihe, xvi, 1960).

ARÁIZ MARTIÑEZ, A.: *Historia de la música religiosa en España* (Barcelona and Madrid, 1942).

BARWICK, STEVEN: 'Sacred Vocal Polyphony in Colonial Mexico' (Diss. Harvard, 1949).

BECQUART, PAUL: 'Musiciens néerlandais en Espagne (XVIᵉ–XVIIᵉ siècles)', *Revue belge de musicologie*, xiv (1960).

—— 'Trois documents inédits relatifs à la Chapelle flamande de Philippe II et Philippe III', *Anuario musical*, xiv (1959).

—— 'Un Compositeur néerlandais à la Cour de Philippe II et de Philippe III, Nicolas Dupont (1575–1623)', *Anuario musical*, xvi (1961).

BRIDGMAN, NANIE: 'Charles-Quint et la musique espagnole', *Revue de musicologie*, xliii (1959).

CASIMIRI, RAFFAELE: *Il Vittoria: nuovi documenti per una biografia sincera di Tommaso Ludovico de Victoria* (Rome, 1934).

CHASE, GILBERT: 'Juan Navarro *Hispalensis* and Juan Navarro *Gaditanus*', *Musical Quarterly*, xxxi (1945).

CIVIL, FRANCESCO: 'La música en la catedral de Gerona durante el siglo XVII', *Anuario musical*, xv (1960).

COLLET, HENRI: *Le Mysticisme musical espagnol du XVIᵉ siècle* (Paris, 1913).

—— *Victoria* (Paris, 1914).

FEDERHOFER, HELLMUT: 'États de la chapelle musicale de Charles V (1528) et de Maximilien (1554)', *Revue belge de musicologie*, iv (1950).

FIGUERAS, J. ROMEU: 'Mateo Flecha el Viejo, la Corte literario-musical del duque de Calabria y el Cancionero llamado de Upsala', *Anuario musical*, xiii (1958).

FISCHER, KURT VON: 'Ein singulärer Typus portugiesischer Passionen des 16. Jahrhunderts', *Archiv für Musikwissenschaft*, xix/xx (1962/3).

FREITAS BRANCO J., *Historia de música portuguesa* (Lisbon, 1959).

FREITAS BRANCO, L.: 'Les Contrepointistes del 'école d'Évora', *Actes du Congrès d'histoire d'art, Paris, 1921*, iii (Paris, 1924).

—— *D. João IV, músico* (Lisbon, 1956).

GEIGER, ALBERT: 'Juan Esquivel: ein unbekannter spanischer Meister des 16. Jahrhunderts', *Festschrift zum 50. Geburtstag Adolf Sandberger* (Munich, 1918).

HOWELL, ALMONTE C., JR.: 'Cabezón: An Essay in Structural Analysis', *Musical Quarterly*, l (1964).

JACQUOT, JEAN, ed.: *Fêtes et cérémonies au temps de Charles Quint* (Paris, 1960).

JACOBS, CHARLES: *Tempo Notation in Renaissance Spain* (Brooklyn, N.Y., 1964).

LIMA CRUZ, M. A. DE: *Duarte Lôbo* (Lisbon, 1937).

—— *Historia de música portuguesa* (Lisbon, 1935).

LLORENS, J. M.: 'Juan Escribano, cantor pontificio y compositor', *Anuario musical*, xii (1957).

LOZANO, ANTONIO: *La música popular, religiosa y dramática en Zaragoza* (Saragossa, 1895).

LUPER, ALBERT T.: 'Portuguese Polyphony in the Sixteenth and Early Seventeenth Centuries', *Journal of the American Musicological Society*, iii (1950).

MAY, HANS VON: *Die Kompositionstechnik T. L. de Victorias* (Berne, 1943).

MITJANA Y GORDÓN, RAFAEL: *Estudios sobre algunos músicos españoles del siglo XVI* (Madrid, 1918).

—— *Don Fernando de las Infantas: teólogo y músico* (Madrid, 1918).

—— *Francisco Guerrero: estudio critico-biográfico* (Madrid, 1922).

MOLITOR, RAPHAEL: *Die Nach-Tridentinische Choral-Reform zu Rom*, 2 vols. (Leipzig, 1901–2).

MOLL, JAIME: 'Músicos de la corte del Cardinal Juan Tavera (1523–45): Luis Venegas de Henestrosa', *Anuario musical*, vi (1951).

PALAU, MANUEL: *La obra del músico valenciano Juan Bautista Comes* (Madrid, 1944).

PEDRELL, FELIPE: *Tomás Luis de Victoria Abulense* (Valencia, 1918).

POPE, ISABEL: 'The "Spanish Chapel" of Philip II', *Renaissance News*, v, (1952).

REVELLA, JOSÉ TORRE: 'Algunos libros de música traídos a América en el siglo XVI', *Boletín interamericano de música* (November, 1957).

RUBIO, SAMUEL: 'La capilla de música del monasterio de El Escorial', *La Ciudad de Dios*, clxiii (1951).

RUIZ DE LIHORI, J., BARÓN DE ALCAHALI: *Diccionario biográfico de músicos valencianos* (Valencia, 1903).

SAMPAYO RIBEIRO, MARIO DE: 'A música em Coimbra', *Biblos*, xv (1939).

—— *Achegas para a Historia de Música em Portugal*, ii. *Damião de Goes na Livraria Real de Música* (Lisbon, 1935).

—— *Frei Manuel Cardoso* (Lisbon, 1961).

SOLAR-QUINTES, NICOLAS ALVAREZ: 'Nuevas noticias de músicos de Felipe II, de su época . . .' *Anuario musical*, xv (1960).

STEVENSON, ROBERT: 'The Bogotá Music Archive', *Journal of the American Musicological Society*, xv (1962).

—— 'Cristóbal de Morales: a Fourth-Centenary Biography', *Journal of the American Musicological Society*, vi (1953).

—— 'European Music in 16th-Century Guatemala', *Musical Quarterly*, l (1964).

—— *Juan Bermudo* (The Hague, 1960).

—— *Music in Mexico* (New York, 1952).

—— *The Music of Peru* (Washington, 1959).

—— *Spanish Music in the Age of Columbus* (The Hague, 1960).

—— *Spanish Cathedral Music in the Golden Age* (Berkeley and Los Angeles, 1961).

TREND, J. B.: 'Cristóbal Morales', *Music and Letters*, vi (1925).

TRUMPFF, G. A.: 'Die Messen des Cristóbal de Morales', *Anuario musical*, viii (1953).

VAN DER STRAETEN, EDMOND: *Charles Quint Musicien* (Ghent, 1894).

—— 'Les Musiciens néerlandais en Espagne', *La Musique aux Pays-Bas avant le XIXᵉ siècle*, vii–viii (Brussels, 1884–8).

VAN DOORSLAER, GEORGES: 'La Chapelle musicale de Charles Quint en 1552', *Musica Sacra* (Malines, 1933).

CHAPTER VIII

PROTESTANT MUSIC ON THE CONTINENT

(*a*) LUTHERAN MUSIC

(i) *Sources*

ABERT, A. A.: *Das Chorwerk*, xxiv. *Melchior Franck: Fünf Hohelied-Motetten* (Wolfenbüttel, 1933); xxxix. *Christoph Demantius: Vier Motetten* (Wolfenbüttel, 1936).

ADRIO, ADAM: *Das Chorwerk*, xii. *Johann Hermann Schein: Sechs deutsche Motetten* (Wolfenbüttel, 1931); xxxvi. *Joh. Hermann Schein und Christoph Demantius: Der 116. Psalm* (Wolfenbüttel, 1935).

—— *Johann Hermann Schein: Neue Ausgabe sämtlicher Werke* (Kassel and Basle, 1963–).

ALBRECHT, HANS: *Das Erbe deutscher Musik*, xvi, xxvi. *Caspar Othmayr: Ausgewählte Werke*, i. *Symbola* (Leipzig, 1941); ii. *Cantilenae ..., Epitaphium ... Lutheri ..., Bicinia ..., Tricinia .... Einzelne Werke aus verstreuten Quellen* (Frankfurt/M., 1956).

—— *Georg Rhau: Musikdrucke aus den Jahren 1538 bis 1545* (Kassel and Basle, 1955–), i, ii. *B. Resinarius: Responsorien*, ed. J. Schröder (1955, 1957); iii. *Symphoniae iucundae*, ed. H. Albrecht (1959); iv. *Vesperorum precum officia*, ed. H. J. Moser (1960).

AMELN, KONRAD: *Das Achtliederbuch* (*Nürnberg 1523/4*). Facs. ed. (Kassel and Basle, 1957).

—— *Das Babstsche Gesangbuch* (*Leipzig, 1545*). *Geystliche Lieder. Mit einer newen vorrhede D. Mart. Luth.* Facs. ed. (Kassel, 1929).

—— *Gesangbuch, darinn begriffen sind die aller fürnemisten und besten Psalmen, geistliche Lieder und Chorgeseng* (*Strasbourg, 1541*). Facs. ed. (Stuttgart, 1953).

—— *Das Klug'sche Gesangbuch* (*1533*). *Geistliche lieder, auffs new gebessert. ...* Facs. ed. (Kassel and Basle, 1955).

—— *Kaspar Othmayr: Geistliche Lieder zu vier Stimmen, 1546* (Kassel, 1935).

—— *Leonhard Lechner: Das Leiden unsers Herren Jesu Christi aus dem Evangelisten Johannes, 1594* (Kassel, 1934).

—— *Leonhard Lechner. Werke* (Kassel and Basle, 1954–).

—— *Luthers Kirchenlieder in Tonsätzen seiner Zeit* (Kassel, 1934).

—— *Melchior Franck: Deutsche Evangeliensprüche für das Kirchenjahr* (Kassel, 1937).

—— *Michael Weisse: Gesangbuch der Böhmischen Brüder 1531.* Facs. ed. (Kassel, 1957).

—— *et al.: Heinrich Schütz: Neue Ausgabe sämtlicher Werke* (Kassel and Basle, 1955–).

—— and LIPPHARDT, W.: *Leonhard Lechner: Deutsche Sprüche von Leben und Tod* (Kassel and Basle, 1929).

—— MAHRENHOLZ, CHR., and THOMAS, W., eds.: *Handbuch der deutschen evangelischen Kirchenmusik* (Göttingen, 1932–).

—— and THOMAS, W.: *Das deutsche Kirchenlied mit seinen Weisen*, 3 vols. (Kassel, 1925–32), i. *Das Morgenlied* (1926); ii. *Das Abendlied* (1929); iii. *Das Weihnachtslied* (1932).

AUER, JOSEPH: *Denkmäler deutscher Tonkunst*, xxiv–xxv. *H. Leo Hassler's Sacri Concentus* (Leipzig, 1906).

BAUSSNERN, F. VON: *Joh. Eccard: Geistliche Lieder auf den Choral* (*1597*), I. Teil (Wolfenbüttel, 1928); II. Teil: *Geistliche Lieder zu fünf Stimmen* (Wolfenbüttel, 1963).

BLUME, FRIEDRICH: *Das Chorwerk*, xiv. *Lasso, Hassler, Hieronymus Praetorius, Sweelinck und Schein: Sieben chromatische Motetten* (Wolfenbüttel, 1931); xxvii. *Christoph Demantius: Deutsche Johannes-Passion* (Wolfenbüttel, 1933).

—— MENDELSSOHN, A., and GURLITT, W.: *Michael Praetorius: Gesamtausgabe der musikalischen Werke*, 21 vols. (Wolfenbüttel, 1928–42, 1959).

CLEMEN, O.: *Das älteste Zwickauer Gesangbuch von 1525* (Zwickau, 1935).

EITNER, ROBERT: *Publikation älterer praktischer und theoretischer Musikwerke*, Jg. 24. *Martin Agricola's Musica instrumentalis deudsch* (Leipzig, 1896); Jg. 25. *Joh. Eccard's Neue geistliche und weltliche Lieder* (Leipzig, 1897); Jg. 26. *Joachim von Burck: Lieder und Passionen* (Leipzig, 1898). *Eyn Enchiridion oder Handbüchlein eynem ytzlichen Christen fast nützlich bey sich zu haben* (*Erfurt, 1524*). Facs. ed. (Kassel, 1929).

FISCHER, A., and TÜMPEL, W.: *Das deutsche evangelische Kirchenlied des 17. Jahrhunderts*, 6 vols. (Gütersloh, 1904–16, reprinted 1964).

GEHRMANN, H.: *Denkmäler deutscher Tonkunst*, ii. *H. L. Hassler's 'Cantiones Sacrae'* (Leipzig, 1894).

GERBER, RUDOLF: *Das Erbe deutscher Musik*, xxi, xxv. *Georg Rhaw: Sacrorum Hymnorum Liber Primus*, Teil 1: *Proprium de Tempore* (1942); Teil 2: *Proprium et Commune Sanctorum* (1943).

HARMS, G., MAHRENHOLZ, CHR., and ADRIO, A.: *Samuel Scheidts Werke* (Hamburg, 1923–).

HOFMANN, HANS: *Michael Blum: Das erste Leipziger Gesangbuch* (*Leipzig, 1530*) (Leipzig, 1914).

KADE, OTTO: *Publikation älterer praktischer und theoretischer Musikwerke*, Jg. 6. *Johann Walther's Wittenbergisch Gesangbuch von 1524* (Leipzig, 1878).

LEICHTENTRITT, HUGO: *Denkmäler deutscher Tonkunst*, xxiii. *Hieronymus Praetorius: Ausgewählte Werke* (Leipzig, 1905).

LEUPOLD, ULRICH S.: *Luther's Works*, liii. *Liturgy and Hymns* (Philadelphia, 1965).

LIPPHARDT, W.: *Kaspar Othmayr: Geistliche Zweigesänge, 1547*, 2 vols. (Kassel, 1928–9).

LÖHRER, E., URSPRUNG, O., and GEERING, A.: *Ludwig Senfl: Sämtliche Werke* (Basle and Wolfenbüttel, 1937–).

MAYR, O.: *Denkmäler deutscher Tonkunst, 2. Folge: Denkmäler der Tonkunst in Bayern*, x (2). *A. Gumpelzhaimer: Ausgewählte Werke* (Leipzig, 1909).

MÜLLER-BLATTAU, J.: *Die zwei ältesten Königsberger Gesangbücher von 1527: Etliche gesang dadurch Got . . . gelobt wirt; Etliche newe verdeutschte . . . Christliche Hymnus*. Facs. ed. (Kassel, 1933).

OSTHOFF, HELMUTH: *Das Chorwerk*, xxx. *Josquin Desprez, Le Maistre, Regnart, de Vento, Utendal und Hollander: Acht Motetten* (Wolfenbüttel, 1934).

OVERATH, JOHANNES: *Denkmäler rheinischer Musik*, iii. *Cunradus Hagius Rinteleus: Die Psalmen Davids nach Kaspar Ulenberg* (*Köln, 1582*) (Kassel and Basle, 1955).

PRÜFER, ARTHUR: *Johann Hermann Scheins Sämtliche Werke*, 7 vols. (Leipzig, 1901–23).

ROSELIUS, LUDWIG: *Denkmäler deutscher Tonkunst, 2. Folge: Denkmäler der Tonkunst in Bayern*, xxix–xxx. *Andreas Raselius: Cantiones sacrae* (Leipzig, 1931).

SAALFELD, R. VON: *H. L. Hassler: Kirchengesänge, Psalmen und geistliche Lieder . . . simpliciter* (Kassel, 1927).

SCHMITZ, EUGEN: *Denkmäler deutscher Tonkunst, 2. Folge: Denkmäler der Tonkunst in Bayern*, vii (1), viii (1). *Johann Staden: Ausgewählte Werke* (Leipzig, 1906).

SCHÖBERLEIN, LUDWIG: *Schatz des liturgischen Chor- und Gemeindegesanges*, 2 vols. (Göttingen, 1865–72).

SCHRÖDER, OTTO: *Johann Walther: Sämtliche Werke* (Kassel and St. Louis, Missouri, 1953–).

SPITTA, P., SCHERING, A., and SPITTA, H: *Heinrich Schütz: Sämtliche Werke*, 18 vols. (Leipzig, 1885–1927).

STERN, H., and NITSCHE, H.: *Melchior Franck: Ausgewählte Kirchenlieder* (*Das Chorwerk alter Meister, Reihe IV*, Nr. 14) (Stuttgart, 1963).

TESCHNER, G. W.: *Joh. Eccard: Geistliche Lieder auf den Choral* (Leipzig, 1860).

—— *Joh. Eccard: Preussische Festlieder* (Leipzig, 1858).

—— *H. L. Hassler: Kirchengesänge, vierstimmig simpliciter* (Leipzig, 1865).

THOMAS, WILHELM: *Gesangbuch der Böhmischen Brüder vom Jahre 1531 von M. Weisse*. Facs. ed. (Kassel, 1931).

—— *Singen wir heut mit gleichem Mund* [20 tunes for congregational singing from the repertory of the Bohemian Brethren] (Kassel, 1929).

TUCHER, GOTTLIEB: *Schatz des evangelischen Kirchengesanges im ersten Jahrhundert der Reformation*, 2 vols. (Leipzig, 1848).

WOLF, JOHANNES: *Denkmäler deutscher Tonkunst*, xxxiv. *Newe deudsche geistliche Gesänge für die gemeinen Schulen* (*Rhaw, 1544*) (Leipzig, 1908).

—— *Martin Luther: Deudsche Messe* (*1526*). Facs. ed. (Kassel, 1934).

ZAHN, JOHANNES: *Die Melodien der deutschen evangelischen Kirchenlieder*, 6 vols. (Gütersloh, 1888–93; reprinted Hildesheim, 1963).

ZELLE, FRIEDRICH: *Die Singweisen der ältesten evangelischen Lieder*, 3 vols. (Berlin, 1899–1910).

—— *Das älteste lutherische Hausgesangbuch: 'Färbefass'-Enchiridion* (*Erfurt, 1524*) (Göttingen, 1903).

—— *Das erste evangelische Gesangbuch*. [*Fünfftzig Geistliche Lieder und Psalmen von Lucas Osiander, 1586*] (Berlin, 1903).

ZENCK, HERMANN: *Das Erbe deutscher Musik*, xxiii. *Sixtus Dietrich: Ausgewählte Werke*, i. *Hymnen* (*1545*) (Leipzig, 1942).

(ii) *Books and Articles*

ADRIO, ADAM: *Die Anfänge des geistlichen Konzerts* (Berlin, 1935).

ALBRECHT, HANS: *Caspar Othmayr* (Kassel and Basle, 1950).

ALLERUP, ALBERT: *Die 'Musica practica' des Johann Andreas Herbst und ihre entwicklungsgeschichtliche Bedeutung* (Münster, 1931).

AMELN, KONRAD: 'Leonhard Lechner. Kapellmeister und Komponist. Um 1553–1606', *Lebensbilder aus Schwaben und Franken*, vii (1960).

—— 'Luthers Liedauswahl', *Jahrbuch für Liturgik und Hymnologie*, v (1960).

—— MAHRENHOLZ, C., and MÜLLER, K. F., eds.: *Jahrbuch für Liturgik und Hymnologie* (Kassel and Basle, 1955–).

AUER, JOSEPH: 'M. Andreas Raselius Ambergensis: sein Leben und seine Werke', *Monatshefte für Musikgeschichte*, xxiv (Supplement) (1892).

BARTHA, DÉNES: *Benedictus Ducis und Appenzeller: ein Beitrag zur Stilgeschichte des 16. Jahrhunderts* (Wolfenbüttel, 1930).

BIRTNER, HERBERT: 'Ein Beitrag zur Geschichte der protestantischen Musik im 16. Jh. dargestellt an Joachim à Burck (1546–1610)', *Zeitschrift für Musikwissenschaft*, x (1928).

BLANKENBURG, WALTER: 'Zur Frage nach der Herkunft der Weisen des Gesangbuchs der Böhmischen Brüder von 1531', *Musik und Kirche*, xxi (1951).

BLUME, FRIEDRICH: *Das monodische Prinzip in der protestantischen Kirchenmusik* (Leipzig, 1925).
—— *Die evangelische Kirchenmusik* (Potsdam, 1931; 2nd rev. ed. Kassel and Basle, 1965).
—— *Michael Praetorius Creuzburgensis* (Wolfenbüttel, 1929).
BOËS, ADOLF: 'Die reformatorischen Gottesdienste in der Wittenberger Pfarrkirche von 1523 an', *Jahrbuch für Liturgik und Hymnologie*, iv (1958–9)–vi (1961).
BRAUN, WERNER: 'Samuel Scheidts Bearbeitungen alter Motetten', *Archiv für Musikwissenschaft*, xix–xx (1962–3).
BUSZIN, WALTER: 'Luther on Music', *Musical Quarterly*, xxxii (1946).
CLEMEN, OTTO: 'Zur Musikgeschichte der Reformationszeit', *Die Musikforschung*, ii (1949).
EINSTEIN, ALFRED: *Heinrich Schütz* (Kassel, 1928).
EITNER, ROBERT: 'Johann Walther: Biographisches und Bibliographisches'. *Monatshefte für Musikgeschichte*, x (1878).
—— 'Leonhard Lechner', *Monatshefte für Musikgeschichte*, x (1878).
EPSTEIN, PETER: *Die Frankfurter Kapellmusik zur Zeit J. A. Herbsts* (Frankfurt/M., 1924).
FLECHSIG, WERNER: *Thomas Mancinus [Mencken]* (Wolfenbüttel, 1933).
FORCHERT, A.: *Das Spätwerk des M. Praetorius: italienische und deutsche Stilbegegnung* (Berlin, 1959).
FRIEDERICH, BRUNO: *Der Vokalstil des Hieronymus Praetorius* (Hamburg, 1932).
GEBHARDT, FRIEDRICH: 'Die musikalischen Grundlagen zu Luthers deutscher Messe', *Luther-Jahrbuch*, x (1928).
GERHARDT, CARL: *Die Torgauer Walter-Handschriften. Eine Studie zur Quellenkunde der Musikgeschichte der deutschen Reformationszeit* (Kassel and Basle, 1949).
GÉROLD, THÉODORE: *Les plus anciennes mélodies de l'Église Protestante de Strasbourg* (Paris, 1928).
—— 'Les premiers recueils de mélodies religieuses protestantes à Strasbourg', *Revue de musicologie*, vi (1925).
GERSTENBERG, WALTER: *Beiträge zur Problemgeschichte der evangelischen Kirchenmusik* (Cologne, 1935).
—— 'Von Luther zu Schütz', *Jahrbuch der Musikbibliothek Peters*, xlii (1936).
GESSNER, ERIKA: *Samuel Scheidts geistliche Konzerte* (Berlin, 1961).
GLAHN, HENRIK: *Melodiestudier til den Lutherske Salmesangs Historie fra 1524 til ca. 1600*, 2 vols. (Copenhagen, 1954).
GOSSLAU, WERNER: *Die religiöse Haltung in der Reformationsmusik* (Kassel, 1933).
GOTTWALD, CLYTUS: 'Eine neuentdeckte Quelle zur Musik der Reformationszeit', *Archiv für Musikwissenschaft*, xix/xx (1962–3).
GRÖSSEL, HEINRICH: *Georgius Otto. Ein Motettenkomponist des 16. Jhs. (1550–1618)* (Kassel, 1935).
GÜNTHER, SIEGFRIED: *Die geistliche Konzertmusik Thomas Selles nebst einer Biographie* (Giessen, 1935).
GURLITT, WILIBALD: *Michael Praetorius (Creuzburgensis). Sein Leben und seine Werke* (Leipzig, 1915).
—— 'Johann Walther und die Musik der Reformationszeit', *Luther-Jahrbuch*, xv (1933); reprinted separately (Munich, 1933).
HAAS, ROBERT: 'Zu Walthers Choralpassion nach Matthäus', *Archiv für Musikwissenschaft*, iv (1922).
HASSE, KARL: 'Johann Hermann Schein', *Zeitschrift für Musikwissenschaft*, ii (1920).

HERMELINK, SIEGFRIED: 'Rhythmische Struktur in der Musik von Heinrich Schütz', *Archiv für Musikwissenschaft*, xvi (1959).

HEYDT, JOHANN VON DER: *Geschichte der evangelischen Kirchenmusik in Deutschland* (Berlin, 1926; 2nd ed. 1932).

HOFMANN, GERTRUD: 'Die freien Kompositionen Leonhart Schröters', *Zeitschrift für Musikwissenschaft*, xvi (1934).

HUBER, KURT: *Ivo de Vento* (ca. *1514–1575*) (Munich, 1918).

HUBER, WALTER SIMON: *Motivsymbolik bei Heinrich Schütz; Versuch einer morphologischen Systematik der Schützschen Melodik* (Basle, 1961).

HÜNICKEN, ROLF: *Samuel Scheidt: ein althallischer Musikus* (Halle, 1934).

ILLING, KARL-HEINZ: *Zur Technik der Magnificatkomposition des 16. Jahrhunderts* (Wolfenbüttel, 1936).

JENNY, MARKUS, and AMELN, KONRAD: 'Zur Entstehungszeit und Herkunft der Strassburger Lutherweisen', *Jahrbuch für Liturgik und Hymnologie*, iv (1958–9).

KADE, OTTO: *Die ältere Passionskomposition bis zum Jahre 1631* (Gütersloh, 1893).

——— 'Ein bisher unbekanntes protestantisches Gesangbuch vom Jahre 1531', *Monatshefte für Musikgeschichte*, iv (1872).

——— *Matthäus Le Maistre* (Mainz, 1862).

KADE, REINHARD: 'Christoph Demant', *Vierteljahrsschrift für Musikwissenschaft*, vi (1890).

——— 'Antonius Scandellus (1517–1580): ein Beitrag zur Geschichte der Dresdener Hofkantorei', *Sammelbände der internationalen Musikgesellschaft*, xv (1914).

KEMPFF, GEORG: *Der Kirchengesang im lutherischen Gottesdienst und seine Erneuerung* (Leipzig, 1937).

KIRSCH, WINFRIED: 'Die Verbindung von Magnificat und Weihnachtsliedern im 16. Jahrhundert', *Festschrift Helmuth Osthoff zum 65. Geburtstag* (Tutzing, 1961).

KOSEL, ALFRED: *Sebald Heyden* (*1494–1561*) (Würzburg, 1940).

KRAFT, GÜNTHER: 'Die Chorbücher der Lutherstube zu Schmalkalden', *Zeitschrift für Musikwissenschaft*, xii–xiii (1930).

——— 'Johann Steuerlein (1546–1613)', *Zeitschrift für Musikwissenschaft*, xiii (1931).

KRETZSCHMAR, HERMANN: 'Luther und die Musik', *Jahrbuch der Musikbibliothek Peters*, xxiv (1918).

KRICKENBERG, D.: *Das protestantische Kantorat im 17. Jahrhundert* (Berlin, 1965).

LILIENCRON, R. VON: *Chorordnung für die Sonn- und Festtage des evangelischen Kirchenjahres* (Gütersloh, 1900; new ed. Kassel, 1929).

——— *Liturgisch-musikalische Geschichte der evangelischen Gottesdienste von 1523–1700* (Schleswig, 1893).

LUCKE, W., and MOSER, H. J.: articles in *Dr. Martin Luther's Werke. Kritische Gesamtausgabe*, xxxv (Weimar, 1923).

LUTHER, WILHELM MARTIN: *Gallus Dressler: ein Beitrag zur Geschichte des protestantischen Schulkantorats im 16. Jh.* (Kassel, 1941).

LYRA, JUSTUS W.: *Andreas Ornithoparcus aus Meiningen, der Zeitgenosse Luthers und dessen Lehre von den Kirchenaccenten* (Gütersloh, 1877).

——— *Die liturgischen Altarweisen* (Göttingen, 1873).

——— and HEROLD, M.: *D. M. Luthers Deutsche Messe und Ordnung des Gottesdienstes* (Gütersloh, 1904).

MAHRENHOLZ, CHRISTHARD: 'Die deutsche Psalmodie', *Musik und Kirche*, xii (1940).

MAHRENHOLZ, CHRISTHARD: *Das evangelische Kirchengesangbuch. Ein Bericht über seine Vorgeschichte* (Kassel and Basle, 1950).
—— *Luther und die Kirchenmusik* (Kassel, 1937).
—— *Samuel Scheidt: sein Leben und sein Werk* (Leipzig, 1924).
—— 'Zur musikalische Gestaltung von Luthers Gottesdienstreform', *Musik und Kirche*, v (1933).
MARTIN, UWE: 'Bemerkungen zum deutschen geistlichen Madrigal im 16. Jahrhundert', *Jahrbuch für Liturgik und Hymnologie*, iv (1958–9).
MESSERSCHMID, FELIX: *Das Kirchenlied Luthers* (Würzburg, 1937).
MOBERG, CARL-ALLAN: *Kyrkomusikens Historia* (Stockholm, 1932).
MOSER, HANS JOACHIM: *Die evangelische Kirchenmusik in Deutschland* (Berlin, 1954).
—— *Heinrich Schütz: Sein Leben und Werk* (Kassel, 1936); English ed., trans. by Carl F. Pfatteicher from the 2nd rev. ed. (St. Louis, Missouri, 1959).
—— *Die mehrstimmige Vertonung des Evangeliums* (Leipzig, 1932).
—— *Die Melodien der Lutherlieder* (*Welt des Gesangbuchs*, iv) (Leipzig, 1935).
MÜLLER, E. H.: *Heinrich Schütz: Gesammelte Briefe und Schriften* (Ratisbon, 1931).
NELLE, WILHELM: *Geschichte des deutschen evangelischen Kirchenliedes* (Hamburg, 1904; 3rd ed. 1928, reprinted Hildesheim, 1962).
NETTL, PAUL: *Luther and Music* (Philadelphia, 1948).
OBRIST, ALOYS: *Melchior Franck* (Berlin, 1892).
OVERATH, JOHANNES: *Untersuchungen über die Melodien des Liedpsalters von Kaspar Ulenberg (Köln, 1582) (Beiträge zur rheinischen Musikgeschichte,* xxxiii) (Cologne, 1960).
PIRRO, ANDRÉ: *Schütz* (Paris, 1913).
PRÜFER, ARTHUR: *Johann Hermann Schein* (Leipzig, 1895).
—— 'Scheins *Cymbalum Sionium*', *Festschrift für R. von Liliencron* (Leipzig, 1910).
RAMBACH, AUGUST JAKOB: *Über Martin Luthers Verdienste um den Kirchengesang* (Hamburg, 1813).
RAUTENSTRAUCH, JOHANNES: *Luther und die Pflege der kirchlichen Musik in Sachsen* (Leipzig, 1907).
RECKZIEGEL, WALTER: *Das Cantional von J. H. Schein* (Berlin, 1963).
REINDELL, WALTER: *Das De-tempore-Lied des ersten Halbjahrhunderts der reformatorischen Kirche* (Würzburg, 1942).
RIEMER, OTTO: *Erhard Bodenschatz und sein 'Florilegium Portense' [Leipzig, 1603–21]* (Leipzig, 1928).
ROTH, ILSE: *Leonhard Paminger* (Munich, 1935).
RUBSAMEN, WALTER H.: 'The International "Catholic" Repertoire of a Lutheran Church in Nürnberg (1574–1597)', *Annales musicologiques*, v (1957).
SANDBERGER, ADOLF: *Denkmäler deutscher Tonkunst*, 2. Folge: *Denkmäler der Tonkunst in Bayern*, v (1). *Hans Leo Hassler: Werke*, II. Teil: *Bemerkungen zur Biographie H. L. Hasslers und seiner Brüder sowie zur Musikgeschichte der Städte Nürnberg und Augsburg* (Leipzig, 1904).
SANDVIK, OLE MORK: *Norsk Koral-historie* (Oslo, 1930).
Samuel Scheidt: Festschrift aus Anlass des 350. Geburtstages (Wolfenbüttel, 1937).
—— *Eine Gedenkschrift zu seinem 300. Todestag am 24. März 1954* (Leipzig, 1954).
SCHERING, ARNOLD: *Die metrisch-rhythmische Grundgestalt unserer Choralmelodie* (2nd ed. Halle, 1927).
SCHILD, EMILIE: *Geschichte der protestantischen Messenkomposition des 17. und 18. Jahrhunderts* (Leipzig, 1934).

SCHMID, ERNST FRITZ: 'Hans Leo Hassler und seine Brüder', *Zeitschrift des historischen Vereins für Schwaben*, liv (1941).

SCHNEIDER, CHARLES: *Luther poète et musicien et les Enchiridiens de 1524* (Geneva, 1942).

SCHREIBER, MAXIMILIAN: *Die Kirchenmusik des Kapellmeisters Leonhard Lechner Athesinus (1553–1606)* (Ratisbon, 1935).

SCHREMS, THEOBALD: *Die Geschichte des gregorianischen Gesanges in den protestantischen Gottesdiensten* (Freiburg i. Schw., 1930).

SCHRÖDER, I.-M.: *Die Responsorienvertonungen des Balthasar Resinarius* (Kassel and Basle, 1954).

SCHULZ, WALTHER: *Studien über das deutsche protestantische monodische Kirchenlied des 17. Jahrhunderts* (Breslau, 1934).

SCHULZE, WILLI: *Die mehrstimmige Messe im frühprotestantischen Gottesdienst* (Wolfenbüttel, 1940).

SEHLING, EMIL: *Die evangelischen Kirchenordnungen des 16. Jahrhunderts*, 5 vols. (Leipzig, 1902–13).

SMALLMAN, BASIL: *The Background of Passion Music* (London, 1957).

SMEND, JULIUS: 'Zur Wortbetonung des Lutherischen Bibeltextes bei Heinrich Schütz', *Zeitschrift für Musikwissenschaft*, v (1922).

SPITTA, FRIEDRICH: *Die Passionen nach den vier Evangelisten von Heinrich Schütz* (Leipzig, 1886).

STERNFELD, FREDERICK W.: 'Music in the Schools of the Reformation', *Musica Disciplina*, ii (1948).

THOMAS, WILHELM: 'Deutscher Brüdergesang in Böhmen vor 400 Jahren', *Musik und Kirche*, ii (1930).

WACKERNAGEL, PHILIPP: *Das deutsche Kirchenlied von der ältesten Zeit bis zum Anfang des 17. Jahrhunderts*, 5 vols. (Leipzig, 1864–77; reprinted Hildesheim, 1964).

WERNER, A.: 'Samuel und Gottfried Scheidt', *Sammelbände der internationalen Musikgesellschaft*, i (1899–1900).

—— 'Neue Beiträge zur Scheidt-Biographie', *Sammelbände der internationalen Musikgesellschaft*, xiii (1911–12).

WESTPHAL, JOHANNES: *Das evangelische Kirchenlied nach seiner geschichtlichen Entwicklung* (Leipzig, 1901; 6th ed. Berlin, 1925).

WIDDING, S.: *Dansk messe, tide- og psalmesang 1528–1573*, 2 vols. (Copenhagen, 1933).

WINTERFELD, CARL VON: *Der evangelische Kirchengesang und sein Verhältnis zur Kunst des Tonsatzes*, 3 vols. (Leipzig, 1843–7; reprinted Hildesheim, 1965).

WIORA, WALTER: 'Die Melodien der "Souterliedekens" und ihre deutschen Parallelen', *Kongress-Bericht (Utrecht, 1952)* (Amsterdam, 1953).

WOLF, E.: *Der vierstimmige homophone Satz. Die stilistischen Merkmale des Kantional-satzes zwischen 1590 und 1630* (Wiesbaden, 1965).

WOLF, JOHANNES: 'Das evangelische Gesangbuch in Vergangenheit und Zukunft: ein Beitrag zur Vierjahrhundertfeier', *Jahrbuch der Musikbibliothek Peters*, xxxi (1925).

—— 'Lieder aus der Reformationszeit', *Archiv für Musikwissenschaft*, vii (1925).

—— 'Luther und die musikalische Liturgie des evangelischen Hauptgottesdienstes', *Sammelbände der internationalen Musikgesellschaft*, iii–iv (1902).

WOLFRUM, PHILIPP: *Die Entstehung und erste Entwicklung des deutschen evangelischen Kirchenliedes in musikalischer Beziehung* (Leipzig, 1890).

ZENCK, HERMANN: *Sixtus Dietrich: ein Beitrag zur Musik und Musikanschauung im Zeitalter der Reformation* (Leipzig, 1928).

(b) Calvinist Music

(i) *Sources*

Bernet Kempers, K. Ph.: *Corpus mensurabilis musicae*, iv. *Jacobus Clemens non Papa: Opera Omnia*, ii. *The Four Books of Psalms* (*Souterliedekens*) (American Institute of Musicology, 1953).

—— *37 Psalmen en vierstemmige bewerking van Louis Bourgeois uit 1547* (Delft, 1937).

Delétra, D.: *Aulcuns pseaulmes et cantiques mys en chant* (*Strasbourg, 1539*). Facs. ed. (Geneva, 1919).

Expert, Henry: *Florilège du concert vocal de la Renaissance*, vii. *Jacques Mauduit: Psaumes mesurés à l'antique de J.-A. de Baïf* (Paris, 1928).

—— *Les Maîtres musiciens de la Renaissance française*, ii, iv, vi. *Claude Goudimel: Les 150 Psaumes de David* (Paris, 1895–7); xi. *Claude Le Jeune: Dodecacorde*, fasc. 1 (Paris, 1900); xx–xxii. *Claude Le Jeune: Pseaumes en vers mesurez* (Paris, 1905–6).

—— *Le Pseautier huguenot du XVIe siècle, publié sur un plan nouveau* (Paris, 1902).

Gaillard, Paul-André: *Schweizerische Musikdenkmäler*, iii. *Loys Bourgeois: Vingt-quatre Pseaulmes à 4 voix* (Basle, 1961).

Gérold, Théodore: *Psaumes de Clément Marot avec les mélodies* (Strasbourg, 1919).

Lagas, R.: *Jan Pieterszoon Sweelinck: Opera Omnia, editio altera*, ii. *Cinquante Pseaumes de David* (*Premier Livre des Pseaumes de David*) (Amsterdam, 1965).

Mincoff-Marriage, E.: *Souterliedekens: Een nederlandsch psalmboek van 1540* (The Hague, 1922).

Pidoux, Pierre: *La Forme des prières et chants ecclésiastiques* (*Geneva, 1542*). Facs. ed. (Kassel and Basle, 1959).

—— *Le Pseautier huguenot du 16e siècle*, 2 vols. (Kassel and Basle, 1962).

—— and Ameln, K.: *Claude Goudimel: Les Pseaumes mis en rime francoise* (*Geneva, 1565*). Facs. ed. (Kassel and Basle, 1935).

—— and Holliger, H.: *L'Estocart: Les cent cinquante Pseaumes de David*. Facs. ed. (Kassel and Basle, 1954).

Riggenbach, C. J., and Löw, R.: *Ausgewählte Psalmen Goudimels* (Basle, 1868).

Seiffert, Max: *Werken van Jan Pieterszn. Sweelinck*, ii–v. *Psalmen* (Leipzig and The Hague, 1897–8).

Terry, R. R.: *Calvin's First Psalter* [*1539*]. Facs. ed. (London, 1932).

(ii) *Books and Articles*

Ameln, K., Mahrenholz, C., and Müller, K. F., eds.: *Jahrbuch für Liturgik und Hymnodie* (Kassel and Basle, 1955–).

Becker, Georg: 'Chronologische Reihenfolge der ältesten bekannten Psalmenausgaben von Cl. Marot und Th. de Bèze', *Monatshefte für Musikgeschichte*, ii (1870).

—— 'Nochmals die französischen Psalmenmelodien', *Monatshefte für Musikgeschichte*, iv (1872).

Bovet, Félix: *Histoire du psautier des églises réformées* (Neuchâtel, 1872).

Brenet, Michel: *Claude Goudimel: essai bibliographique* (Besançon, 1898).

Cauchie, Maurice: 'Les Psaumes de Janequin', *Société Internationale de Musicologie, Premier congrès, Liège: compte rendu* (1930), (Burnham, 1931).

Clive, H. P.: 'The Calvinist Attitude to Music, and its Literary Aspects and Sources', *Bibliothèque d'humanisme et renaissance*, xix (1957) and xx (1958).

Douen, O.: *Clément Marot et le psautier huguenot*, 2 vols. (Paris, 1878–9).

DROZ, E.: 'Notes sur Théodore de Bèze', *Bibliothèque d'humanisme et renaissance*, xxiv (1962).

EITNER, ROBERT: 'Die ältesten französischen Psalmen-Melodien', *Monatshefte für Musikgeschichte*, vi (1874).

FORNACON, SIEGFRIED: 'L'Estocart und sein Psalter', *Die Musikforschung*, xiii (1960).

GAILLARD, PAUL-ANDRÉ: 'Essai sur le rapport des sources mélodiques des "Pseaulmes cinquantes" de Jean Louis (Anvers, 1555) et des "Souterliedekens" (Anvers, 1540)', *Kongress-Bericht* (*Utrecht, 1952*) (Amsterdam, 1953).

—— 'Le Matériel mélodique employé par Loys Bourgeois dans son Premier Livre des Pseaulmes, Lyon 1547', *Schweizerische Musikzeitung*, xlii (1952).

—— *Loys Bourgeoys: sa vie, son œuvre comme pédagogue et compositeur* (Lausanne, 1948).

GARSIDE, CHARLES, JR.: 'Calvin's Preface to the Psalter: A Re-appraisal', *Musical Quarterly*, xxxvii (1951).

—— *Zwingli and the Arts* (New Haven, Conn., 1966).

GEERING, ARNOLD: 'Die Vokalmusik in der Schweiz zur Zeit der Reformation', *Schweizerisches Jahrbuch für Musikwissenschaft*, i (1933).

GÉROLD, THÉODORE: *Les plus anciennes mélodies de l'Église Protestante de Strasbourg* (Paris, 1928).

—— 'Les Premiers Recueils de mélodies religieuses protestantes à Strasbourg', *Revue de musicologie*, vi (1925).

JENNY, MARKUS: 'Das erste offizielle Zürcher Gesangbuch von 1598', *Jahrbuch für Liturgik und Hymnologie*, vii (1962).

KAT, ALOYSIUS: *De geschiedenis der kerkmuziek in'de Nederlanden* (Hilversum, 1939).

NIEVERGELT, EDWIN: *Die Tonsätze der deutsch-schweizerischen reformierten Kirchengesangbücher im 17. Jahrhundert* (Zürich, 1944).

ODINGA, TH.: *Das deutsche Kirchenlied der Schweiz im Reformationszeitalter* (Frauenfeld, 1889).

PIDOUX, PIERRE: 'Notes sur quelques éditions des psaumes de Claude Goudimel', *Revue de musicologie*, xlii (1958).

—— 'Les Psaumes d'Antoine de Mornable, Guillaume Morlaye et Pierre Certon (1546, 1554, 1555). Étude comparative', *Annales musicologiques*, v (1957).

PRATT, WALDO S.: 'The Importance of the Early French Psalter', *Musical Quarterly*, xxi (1935).

—— *The Music of the French Psalter of 1562* (New York, 1939).

REIMANN, HANNES: *Die Einführung des Kirchengesangs in der Zürcher Kirche nach der Reformation* (Zürich, 1959).

—— 'Huldrych Zwingli—der Musiker', *Archiv für Musikwissenschaft*, xvii (1960).

—— 'Johannes Calvin und der Huguenottenpsalter', *Der evangelische Kirchenchor*, lxix (1964).

RIGGENBACH, C. J.: 'Die französischen Psalmenmelodien', *Monatshefte für Musikgeschichte*, iii (1871).

—— *Der Kirchengesang in Basel seit der Reformation* (Basle, 1870).

ROKSETH, YVONNE: 'Les Premiers chants de l'église calviniste', *Revue de musicologie*, xxxvi (1954).

SCHEUERLEER, D. F.: *De Souterliedekens. Bijdrage tot de geschiedenis der oudste nederlandsche psalmberijming* (Leyden, 1898).

SCHILD, EMILIE: 'Calvins Vermächtnis an die evangelische Kirchenmusik', *Musik und Kirche*, xiv (1942).

SCHILD, EMILIE: 'Die Ordnung der reformierten Gottesdienste', *Musik und Kirche*, xiv (1942).

SCHOLES, PERCY A.: *The Puritans and Music in England and New England* (London, 1934; 2nd ed. New York, 1962).

TEUBER, ULRICH: 'Notes sur la rédaction musicale du psaultier genevois (1542–1562)', *Annales musicologiques*, iv (1956).

THÜRLINGS, ADOLF: *Die schweizerischen Tonmeister im Zeitalter der Reformation* (Berne, 1903).

VAN DEN SIGTENHORST MEYER, B.: *De vocale muziek van Jan P. Sweelinck* (The Hague, 1948).

WEBER, G.: *Huldrych Zwingli: Seine Stellung zur Musik und seine Lieder* (Zürich, 1884).

WIORA, WALTER: 'Die Melodien der "Souterliedekens" und ihre deutschen Parallelen', *Kongress-Bericht (Utrecht, 1952)* (Amsterdam, 1953).

WOODWARD, G. R.: 'The Genevan Psalter of 1562, set in Four-part Harmony by Claude Goudimel in 1565', *Proceedings of the Musical Association*, xliv (1918).

CHAPTER IX

CHURCH MUSIC IN ENGLAND

(i) *Sources*

ANDREWS, H. K., and DART, T.: *Thomas Morley, Collected Motets* (London, 1959).

ARKWRIGHT, G. E. P.: *Old English Edition*, x. *Christopher Tye, Mass Euge Bone*; xxi. *R. White, G. Kirbye, J. Wilbye and W. Daman, Anthems and Motets*; xxii. *John Milton, Six Anthems* (London, 1893–1900).

BERGSAGEL, J. D.: *Early English Church Music*, i. *Early Tudor Masses: I* (London, 1963).

BROWN, D., COLLINS, W., and LE HURAY, P.: *Musica Britannica*, xxiii. *Thomas Weelkes: Collected Anthems* (London, 1966).

ELLIOTT, K., and SHIRE, H. M.: *Musica Britannica*, xv. *Music of Scotland 1500–1700* (London, 1957; rev. ed., 1965).

FELLOWES, E. H.: *The Collected Works of William Byrd*, i–vii and xii–xv (London, 1937–49).

FROST, M.: *English and Scottish Psalm and Hymn Tunes c. 1543–1677* (London, 1953).

HARRISON, F. LL.: *Das Chorwerk*, lxxxiv. *John Sheppard, Sechs Responsorien* (Wolfenbüttel, 1960).

—— *Early English Church Music*, ii. *William Mundy, Latin Antiphons and Psalms* (London, 1963).

HUNT, J. E.: *Cranmer's First Litany, 1544, and Merbecke's Book of Common Prayer Noted, 1550* (London, 1939).

LE HURAY, P.: *John Weelkes, Evening Service for Trebles* (London, 1962).

ROSE, BERNARD: *Early English Church Music*, v. *Thomas Tomkins, Musica Deo Sacra: I* (London, 1965).

STEVENS, DENIS: *Musica Britannica*, i. *The Mulliner Book* (London, 1951).

TERRY, R. R.: *The Scottish Psalter of 1635* (London, 1935).

Tudor Church Music, ii; iv–x (London, 1922–9); Appendix with Supplementary Notes by E. H. Fellowes (London, 1948).

WULSTAN, D.: *Early English Church Music*, iii. *Orlando Gibbons, Verse Anthems* (London, 1964).

(ii) *Books and Articles*

ATKINS, I.: *The Early Occupants of the Office of Organist and Master of the Choristers . . . of Worcester* (London, 1918).

ARKWRIGHT G. E. P.: 'Notes on the Ferrabosco Family', *Musical Antiquary*, iv (1912–13).

—— *Catalogue of the Manuscripts in Christ Church, Oxford*, 2 vols. (Oxford, 1915–23).

BAILLIE, HUGH: 'Some Biographical Notes on English Church Musicians, Chiefly Working in London (1485–1560)', *R.M.A. Research Chronicle*, no. 2 (1962).

—— 'Squares', *Acta Musicologica*, xxxii (1960).

BERGSAGEL, J. D.: 'The Date and Provenance of the Forrest–Heyther Collection of Early Tudor Masses', *Music and Letters*, xliv (1963).

BROWN, DAVID: 'The Anthems of Thomas Weelkes', *Proceedings of the Royal Musical Association*, xci (1964–5).

—— 'Thomas Morley and the Catholics: Some Speculations', *Monthly Musical Record*, lxxxix (1959).

—— 'The Styles and Chronology of Thomas Morley's Motets', *Music and Letters*, xli (1960).

BUTTREY, J.: 'William Smith of Durham', *Music and Letters*, xliii (1962).

CLULOW, PETER: 'Publication Dates for Byrd's Latin Masses', *Music and Letters*, xlvii (1966).

DART, R. THURSTON.: 'Morley and the Catholics: Some Further Speculations', *Monthly Musical Record*, lxxxix (1959).

—— 'Music and Musicians at Chichester Cathedral, 1545–1642', *Music and Letters*, xlii (1961).

—— 'Two New Documents Relating to the Royal Music, 1584–1605', *Music and Letters*, xlv (1964).

DUCKLES, VINCENT: 'Florid Embellishment in English Song of the Late 16th and Early 17th Centuries', *Annales musicologiques*, v (1957).

ELLINWOOD, L.: 'Tallis' Tunes and Tudor Psalmody', *Musica Disciplina*, ii (1948).

FELLOWES, E. H.: *The Catalogue of Manuscripts in the Library of St. Michael's College, Tenbury* (Paris, 1934).

—— *English Cathedral Music* (London, 1941).

—— *Orlando Gibbons and his Family: the Last of the Tudor School of Musicians* (London, 2nd ed. 1951).

—— *William Byrd* (London, 2nd ed., 1948).

FOWLER, J. T.: *Durham Account Rolls* (Durham, 1898).

FRERE, W. H.: 'Edwardine Vernacular Services before the First Prayer Book', *Walter Howard Frere: A Collection of his Papers* (London, 1940).

GEE, H.: *The Elizabethan Prayer-Book and Ornaments* (London, 1902).

HARRISON, F. LL.: *Music in Medieval Britain* (London, 1958).

HISCOCK, W. G.: *A Christ Church Miscellany* (Oxford, 1946).

HISTORICAL MANUSCRIPTS COMMISSION: *Appendix to the 4th Report* (London, 1874).

HUGHES, DOM ANSELM: *Catalogue of the Musical Manuscripts at Peterhouse* (Cambridge, 1953).

HUGHES, P.: *The Reformation in England*, 3 vols. (London, 1950–4).

JACKMAN, J. L.: 'Liturgical Aspects of Byrd's *Gradualia*', *Musical Quarterly*, xlix (1963).

KERMAN, J.: 'An Elizabethan Edition of Lassus', *Acta Musicologica*, xxvii (1955).

—— 'Byrd's Motets: Chronology and Canon', *Journal of the American Musicological Society*, xiv (1961).

KERMAN, J.: 'The Elizabethan Motet: a Study of Texts for Music', *Studies in the Renaissance*, ix (1962).

LAFONTAINE, H. C. DE: *The King's Musick* (London, 1909).

LEGG, J. W.: *English Orders for Consecrating Churches* (London, 1911).

LE HURAY, PETER: 'The English Anthem 1580–1640', *Proceedings of the Royal Musical Association*, lxxxvi (1959/60).

—— 'Towards a definitive study of pre-Restoration Anglican service music', *Musica Disciplina*, xiv (1960).

MORLEY, THOMAS: *A Plaine and Easie Introduction to Practicall Musicke*, ed. R. A. Harman (London, 1952).

PETTI, A. G.: 'New Light on Peter Philips', *Monthly Musical Record*, lxxxvii (1957).

—— 'Peter Philips, Composer and Organist: 1561–1628', *Recusant History*, iv, 2 (Bognor Regis, 1958).

PINE, E.: *The Westminster Abbey Singers* (London, 1953).

PROCTER, F., and FRERE, W. H.: *A New History of the Book of Common Prayer* (London, 1932).

RAINE, J.: *Depositions and other Ecclesiastical Proceedings from the Courts of Durham* (London and Edinburgh, 1845).

REYNOLDS, H.: *Use of Exeter Cathedral* (London, 1891).

RIMBAULT, E. F.: *The Old Cheque-Book . . . of the Chapel Royal* (London, 1872; reprinted New York, 1966).

ROGERS, C.: *History of the Chapel Royal of Scotland* (Edinburgh, 1882).

ROSE, BERNARD: 'Thomas Tomkins, 1575?–1656', *Proceedings of the Royal Musical Association*, lxxxii (1955–6).

SCHOFIELD, B., and DART, T.: 'Tregian's Anthology', *Music and Letters*, xxxii (1951).

SHAW, H. W.: 'Thomas Morley of Norwich', *Musical Times*, cvi (1965).

SPINK, IAN: 'The Musicians of Queen Henrietta-Maria: Some Notes and References in the English State Papers', *Acta Musicologica*, xxxvi (1964).

STEVENS, DENIS: *Thomas Tomkins* (London, 1957).

—— *Tudor Church Music* (London, 1961).

STEVENSON, R.: 'John Marbeck's "Noted Booke" of 1550', *Musical Quarterly*, xxxvii (1951).

SUMNER, W. L.: *The Organ* (London, 1952).

TERRY, R. R.: *A Forgotten Psalter and Other Essays* (Oxford, 1929).

THOMPSON, EDWARD: 'Robert Ramsey', *Musical Quarterly*, xlix (1963).

WAILES, MARYLIN: 'Martin Peerson', *Proceedings of the Royal Musical Association*, lxxx (1953–4).

CHAPTER X

EARLY BAROQUE CHURCH MUSIC

(i) *Sources*

ABERT, A. A.: *Das Chorwerk*, xxiv. *Melchior Franck: Fünf Hoheliedmotetten* (from the *Geystliche Gesäng und Melodeyen, Coburg, 1608*) (Wolfenbüttel, 1933).

ADLER, GUIDO: *Denkmäler der Tonkunst in Österreich*, xx, Jg. x (1). *Orazio Benevoli: Festmesse und Hymnus* (Vienna, 1903).

AGAZZARI, AGOSTINO: *Del sonare sopra il basso*. Facs. ed. (Milan, 1933).

AMELN, KONRAD *et al.*: *Heinrich Schütz: Neue Ausgabe sämtlicher Werke* (Kassel and Basle, 1955–).

ARNOLD, DENIS: *Corpus mensurabilis musicae*, xii. *Giovanni Gabrieli: Opera Omnia* (American Institute of Musicology, 1956–).

BENVENUTI, GIACOMO: *Istituzioni e monumenti dell'arte musicale italiana*, i–ii. *Andrea e Giovanni Gabrieli e la musica strumentale in San Marco*, 2 vols. (Milan, 1931–2).

BEZECNY, E., and MANTUANI, J.: *Denkmäler der Tonkunst in Österreich*, xii, Jg. vi (1). *Jacob Handl's (Gallus) 'Opus musicum'*, I. Teil (Vienna, 1899); xxiv, Jg. xii (1). II. Teil (Vienna, 1905); xxx, Jg. xv (1). III. Teil (Vienna, 1908); xl, Jg. xx (1). IV. Teil (Vienna, 1913); xlviii, Jg. xxiv. V. Teil (Vienna, 1917); li–lii, Jg. xxvi. VI. Teil (Vienna, 1919).

BLUME, F., MENDELSSOHN, A., and GURLITT, W.: *Michael Praetorius: Gesamtausgabe der musikalischen Werke*, 21 vols. (Wolfenbüttel, 1928–42, 1959).

FEININGER, LAURENCE: *Monumenta Liturgiae Polychoralis*, i–ix (Rome, 1950–4).

GALLICO, CLAUDIO: *Viadana: Cento concerti ecclesiastici (prima parte)* (Kassel and Basle, 1964).

GURLITT, WILIBALD: *Michael Praetorius: Syntagma musicum, III.: Termini musici (Wolfenbüttel, 1619)*. Facs. ed. (Kassel and Basle, 1958).

HUIGENS, P. C.: *Denkmäler der Tonkunst in Österreich*, lxxiii, Jg. xxxviii (2). *Blasius Amon: Kirchenwerke* (Vienna, 1931).

KROYER, THEODORE: *Denkmäler deutscher Tonkunst*, 2. Folge: *Denkmäler der Tonkunst in Bayern*, x (1). *G. Aichinger: Ausgewählte Werke* (Leipzig, 1909).

MALIPIERO, G. F.: *Claudio Monteverdi: Tutte le opere*, 16 vols. (Asolo, 1926–42).

MAYR, O.: *Denkmäler deutscher Tonkunst*, 2. Folge: *Denkmäler der Tonkunst in Bayern*, x (2). *A. Gumpelzhaimer: Ausgewählte Werke* (Leipzig, 1909).

SCHARNAGL, AUGUST: *Musica Divina* (new series), x. *Viadana: Missa Dominicalis* (Ratisbon, 1954).

SCHMITZ, EUGEN: *Denkmäler deutscher Tonkunst*, 2. Folge: *Denkmäler der Tonkunst in Bayern*, vii (1), viii (1). *Johann Staden: Ausgewählte Werke* (Leipzig, 1906).

SPITTA, P., SCHERING, A., and SPITTA, H.: *Heinrich Schütz: Sämtliche Werke*, 18 vols. (Leipzig, 1885–1927).

(ii) *Books and Articles*

ABERT, ANNA AMALIE: *Die stilistischen Voraussetzungen der 'Cantiones sacrae' von Heinrich Schütz* (Wolfenbüttel, 1935).

ABRAHAM, LARS ULRICH: *Der Generalbass im Schaffen des Michael Praetorius und seine harmonischen Voraussetzungen* (Berlin, 1961).

ADRIO, ADAM: *Die Anfänge des geistlichen Konzerts* (Berlin, 1935).

AMANN, J.: *Allegris Miserere und die Aufführungspraxis in der Sixtina* (Ratisbon, 1935).

ARNOLD, DENIS: 'Alessandro Grandi, a Disciple of Monteverdi', *Musical Quarterly*, xliii (1957).

—— 'Ceremonial Music in Venice at the Time of the Gabrielis', *Proceedings of the Royal Musical Association*, lxxxii (1955–6).

—— 'Giovanni Croce and the *Concertato* style', *Musical Quarterly*, xxxix (1953).

—— 'Instruments in Church: Some Facts and Figures', *Monthly Musical Record*, lxxxv (1955).

—— *Monteverdi* (London, 1963).

—— 'Monteverdi's Church Music: Some Venetian Traits', *Monthly Musical Record*, lxxxviii (1958).

—— 'The Monteverdian Succession at St. Mark's', *Music and Letters*, xlii (1961).

—— 'Notes on Two Movements of the Monteverdi "Vespers"', *Monthly Musical Record*, lxxxiv (1954).

BARBLAN, G.: 'Contributo a una biografia critica di Agostino Agazzari', *Collectanea historiae musicae*, ii (1957).

BLANKENBURG, WALTER: 'Der Harmonie-Begriff in der lutherisch-barocken Musikanschauung', *Archiv für Musikwissenschaft*, xvi (1959).

BLUME, FRIEDRICH: *Das monodische Prinzip in der protestantischen Kirchenmusik* (Leipzig, 1925).

BRIGIDI, A.: *Cenni sulla vita e sulle opere di Giulio Belli* (Modena, 1865).

BUKOFZER, MANFRED: *Music in the Baroque Era, from Monteverdi to Bach* (London, 1948).

CHIGI SARACINI, COUNT GUIDO: *Claudio Saracini: Le seconde musiche (Venice, 1620)*. Facs. ed. (Siena, 1933).

CLERCX, SUZANNE: *Le Baroque et la musique* (Brussels, 1948).

CORADINI, F.: *Antonio Maria Abbatini* (Arezzo, 1922).

FORCHERT, ARNO: *Das Spätwerk des Michael Praetorius* (Berlin, 1959).

GERBER, RUDOLF: *Das Passionsrezitativ bei Heinrich Schütz und seine stilgeschichtlichen Grundlagen* (Gütersloh, 1929).

HAAS, ROBERT: *Aufführungspraxis der Musik* (Potsdam, 1930–2).

—— *Die Musik des Barocks* (Potsdam, 1928).

HABERL, F. X.: 'Felice Anerio, Lebensgang und Werke', *Kirchenmusikalisches Jahrbuch*, xviii (1903).

—— 'Giovanni Francesco Anerio . . .', *Kirchenmusikalisches Jahrbuch*, i (1886).

—— 'Giovanni Croce. Eine bio-bibliographische Skizze', *Kirchenmusikalisches Jahrbuch*, iii (1888).

—— 'Giovanni Maria Nanino', *Kirchenmusikalisches Jahrbuch*, vi (1891).

—— 'Francesco Soriano', *Kirchenmusikalisches Jahrbuch*, x (1895).

—— 'Lodovico Grossi da Viadana', *Kirchenmusikalisches Jahrbuch*, iv (1889).

HIEKEL, HANS OTTO: 'Der Madrigal- und Motettentypus in der Mensurallehre des Michael Praetorius', *Archiv für Musikwissenschaft*, xix/xx (1962/3).

HUDSON, FREDERICK: 'Giovanni Gabrieli's Motet *a* 15, "In ecclesiis"', *Music Review*, xxiv (1963).

HUIGENS, P. C.: 'Blasius Amon', *Studien zur Musikwissenschaft*, xviii (1931).

KENTON, EGON F.: 'The Late Style of Giovanni Gabrieli', *Musical Quarterly*, xlviii (1962).

KIRCHNER, GERHARD: *Der Generalbass bei Heinrich Schütz* (Kassel and Basle, 1960).

KREIDLER, WALTER: *Heinrich Schütz und der Stile concitato von Claudio Monteverdi* (Kassel, 1934).

LEICHTENTRITT, HUGO: *Geschichte der Motette* (Leipzig, 1908).

—— 'Was lehren uns die Bilderwerke des 14.–17. Jahrhunderts über die Instrumentalmusik ihrer Zeit?', *Sammelbände der internationalen Musikgesellschaft*, vii (1906).

MALIPIERO, GIAN FRANCESCO: *Claudio Monteverdi* (Milan, 1929).

MOLITOR, R.: *Die nach-tridentinische Choralreform in Rom*, 2 vols. (Leipzig, 1901–2).

MÜLLER-BLATTAU, J. M.: *Die Kompositionslehre Heinrich Schützens in der Fassung seines Schülers Christoph Bernhard* (Leipzig, 1926).

PAOLI, DOMENICO DE: *Claudio Monteverdi* (Milan, 1945).

PARAZZI, A.: *Della vita e delle opere musicali di L. Grossi-Viadana* (Milan, 1876).

PASQUETTI, GUIDO: *L'oratorio musicale in Italia* (Florence, 1906).

REDLICH, HANS FERDINAND: 'Aufgaben und Ziele der Monteverdi-Forschung', *Die Musikforschung*, iv (1951).

—— *Claudio Monteverdi* (Olten, 1949; augmented English ed., trans. K. Dale, London, 1952).

—— 'Monteverdi's Religious Music', *Music and Letters*, xxvii (1946).

—— 'New Editions of Monteverdi and Schütz', *Music Review*, xix (1958).

REITTER, LUMIR: *Doppelchörigkeit bei H. Schütz* (Zürich, 1937).

RIEMER, OTTO: *Erhard Bodenschatz und sein 'Florilegium Portense'* (Leipzig, 1928).

SCHERING, ARNOLD: *Aufführungspraxis alter Musik* (Leipzig, 1931).

—— *Die niederländische Orgelmesse im Zeitalter des Josquin* (Leipzig, 1912).

SCHNEIDER, MAX: *Die Anfänge des Basso Continuo und seiner Bezifferung* (Leipzig, 1918).

SCHRADE, LEO: *Monteverdi: Creator of Modern Music* (London, 1951).

SCHUH, WILLI: *Formprobleme bei Heinrich Schütz* (Leipzig, 1928).

WAGNER, PETER: *Geschichte der Messe.* (Leipzig, 1913).

WINTERFELD, CARL VON: *Johannes Gabrieli und sein Zeitalter*, 3 vols. (Berlin, 1834; reprinted Hildesheim, 1965).

CHAPTER XI

CONCERTED INSTRUMENTAL MUSIC

(i) *Sources*

BECK, SYDNEY: *Thomas Morley: The first book of consort lessons 1599 and 1611* (New York, 1959).

BENVENUTI, G.: *Istituzioni e monumenti dell'arte musicale italiana*, i, ii. *Andrea e Giovanni Gabrieli e la musica strumentale in San Marco* (Milan, 1931–2).

BERNOULLI, E.: *M. Praetorius: Syntagma Musicum, Teil III* (*Wolfenbüttel, 1619*) (Leipzig, 1916).

BLUME, FRIEDRICH: *M. Praetorius: Gesamtausgabe*, xv. *Terpsichore (1612)*, ed. G. Oberst (Wolfenbüttel, 1929).

DART, R. THURSTON: *Parthenia In-Violata* (*London, c. 1625*). Facs. and practical ed. (New York, 1961).

—— and COATES, WILLIAM: *Musica Britannica*, ix. *Jacobean Consort Music* (London, 1955).

DUYSE, F. VAN: *Vereeniging voor Nederlandsche Muziekgeschiedenis*, xxix. *Tielman Susato: Het ierste musyck boexken* (*Antwerp, 1551*) (Amsterdam, 1908).

EINSTEIN, ALFRED: *Giovanni Gabrieli: Canzoni per sonare . . . a Quattro* (*Venice, 1608*) (Mainz, 1933).

ENGELKE, BERNHARD: *Musik und Musiker am Gottorfer Hofe, I. Die Zeit der englischen Komödianten* (*1590–1627*) (Breslau, 1930).

EXPERT, HENRY: *Les Maîtres musiciens de la Renaissance française*, xxiii. *Claude Gervaise, Estienne du Tertre, et Anonymes: Danseries*, Part I (Paris, 1908).

FELLOWES, E. H.: *The Collected Works of William Byrd*, xvii. *String Fantasies*, etc. (London, 1948).

—— *Nine Fantasies for Two Viols* (London, 1928).

—— *Orlando Gibbons: Nine Fantasies for Three and Two for Four Instruments*, 3 vols. (London, 1924–5).

—— *Orlando Gibbons: Pavane a 6* (London, 1925).

—— *Thomas Tomkins: Fantasia a 6* (London, 1939).

GEIRINGER, KARL: *Denkmäler der Tonkunst in Österreich*, Jg. xxxvi/2 (vol. lxx). *P. Peuerl and J. Posch: Instrumental and Vocal Compositions* (Vienna, 1929).

GIESBERT, F. J.: *Pierre Attaingnant: Pariser Tanzbuch aus dem Jahre 1530* (Mainz, [1950]).

—— *Salomone Rossi: Sinfonie a 3* (*Venice, 1608*) (Mainz, 1956).

—— *Tielman Susato: Het derde musyck boexken* (*Antwerp, 1551*) (Mainz, 1936).

KELLER, HERMANN: *S. Scheidt: 15 Symphonien* (*Leipzig, 1644*) (Mainz, 1939).

LEFKOWITZ, MURRAY: *Musica Britannica*, xxi. *William Lawes: Select Consort Music* (London, 1963).

MEYER, ERNST HERMANN: *Englische Fantasien aus dem 17. Jahrhundert* (Kassel, 1949).

PRÜFER, ARTHUR: *Johann Hermann Scheins Sämtliche Werke*, i. *Venuskränzlein und Banchetto musicale* (Leipzig, 1901).

RIKKE, FRITZ, and NEWMAN, JOEL: *Salomon Rossi: Sinfonie, Gagliarde, Canzone 1607–1608* (New York, n.d.).

SCHNEIDER, MAX: *Diego Ortiz: Tratado de glosas . . . (Rome, 1553)* (Kassel, 1913; 2nd ed. 1936).

SLIM, H. COLIN: *Monuments of Renaissance Music*, i. *Musica nova (Venice, 1540)* (Chicago, 1965).

STEVENS, JOHN: *Musica Britannica*, xviii. *Music at the Court of Henry VIII* (London, 1962).

TORCHI, LUIGI: *L'arte musicale in Italia*, vii. *Musica istrumentale, secolo XVII* (Milan, [1908]).

WIRTH, H. F.: *Vereeniging voor Nederlandsche Muziekgeschiedenis*, xxxiv. *Orchestral Compositions by Dutch Masters of the early 17th Century: Paduanen and Galliarden by Melchior Borchgreving, Benedictus Grep and Nicolaus Gistow* (Amsterdam, 1913).

ZENCK, H.: *A. Willaert: Neun Ricercari für drei beliebige Instrumente* (Mainz, 1933).

(ii) *Books and Articles*

ARNOLD, CECILY, and JOHNSON, MARSHALL: 'The English Fantasy Suite', *Proceedings of the Royal Musical Association*, lxxxii (1955–6).

ARNOLD, DENIS: 'Ceremonial Music in Venice at the Time of the Gabrielis', *Proceedings of the Royal Musical Association*, lxxxii (1955–6).

ARNOLD, F. T.: *The Art of Accompaniment from a Thorough-Bass* (London, 1931, reprinted 1961).

BACHMANN, W.: *Die Anfänge des Streichinstrumentenspiels* (Leipzig, 1964).

BARBOUR, J. M.: *Trumpets, Horns and Music* (East Lansing, Mich., 1964).

BLUME, FRIEDRICH: *Studien zur Vorgeschichte der Orchestersuite im 15. und 16. Jahrhundert* (Leipzig, 1925).

BOYDEN, DAVID D.: *The History of Violin Playing from its Origins to 1761 and its Relationship to the Violin and Violin Music* (London, 1965).

BRENNECKE, WILFRIED: 'Musique instrumentale d'après un manuscrit allemand (Ratisbonne, MS. A.R. 940/41)', *La Musique instrumentale de la Renaissance* (Paris, 1955).

COATES, WILLIAM: 'English Two-Part Viol Music 1590–1640', *Music and Letters*, xxxiii (1952).

COLE, ELIZABETH: 'L'Anthologie de madrigaux et de musique instrumentale pour ensembles de Francis Tregian', *La Musique instrumentale de la Renaissance* (Paris, 1955).

COLLAER, PAUL: 'L'orchestra di Claudio Monteverdi', *Musica*, ii (Florence, 1943).

DART, R. THURSTON: 'Morley's Consort Lessons of 1599', *Proceedings of the Royal Musical Association*, lxxiv (1947–8).

—— 'The Printed Fantasies of Orlando Gibbons', *Music and Letters*, xxxvii (1956).

DONINGTON, R., and DART, R. T.: 'The Origin of the "In nomine"', *Music and Letters*, xxx (1949).

FELLOWES, E. H.: *Orlando Gibbons and his Family* (London, 2nd ed. 1951).

GEIRINGER, KARL: 'Paul Peuerl', *Studien zur Musikwissenschaft*, xvi (1929).

GLÄSEL, RUDOLF: *Zur Geschichte der Battaglia* (Leipzig, 1931).

HABERL, F. X.: 'Giovanni Francesco Anerio', *Kirchenmusikalisches Jahrbuch*, i (1886).

HAYES, GERALD: *King's Music* (London, 1937).

JACQUOT, JEAN, ed.: *La Musique instrumentale de la Renaissance* (Paris, 1955).

KUNZE, STEFAN: *Die Instrumentalmusik Giovanni Gabrielis*, 2 vols. (Tutzing, 1963).

LAFONTAINE, H. C. DE: *The King's Musick* (London, 1909).

LAUNAY, DENISE: 'La Fantaisie en France jusqu'au milieu du XVIIᵉ siècle', *La Musique instrumentale de la Renaissance* (Paris, 1955).

LUCIANI, S. A.: 'Agostino Agazzari e l'orchestrazione del seicento', *Musica d'oggi* (1931).

MEYER, ERNST HERMANN: 'L'Élément populaire dans les danses instrumentales allemandes jusqu'à la Guerre de Trente Ans', *La Musique instrumentale de la Renaissance* (Paris, 1955).

—— *English Chamber Music* (London, 1946).

—— *Die mehrstimmige Spielmusik des 17. Jahrhunderts in Nord- und Mitteleuropa* (Kassel, 1934).

——'La Musique légère et la musique à danser du Moyen Âge à la fin du XVIIᵉ siècle', *Revue musicale*, numéro spécial no. 255 (Paris, 1962).

NAGEL, W.: *Annalen der englischen Hofmusik 1509–1649* (Leipzig, 1894).

NEF, KARL: *Geschichte der Sinfonie und Suite für Orchester* (Leipzig, 1921).

NOBLE, JEREMY: 'Le Répertoire instrumental anglais (1550–1585)', *La Musique instrumentale de la Renaissance* (Paris, 1955).

OBERST, GÜNTHER: *Englische Orchestersuiten um 1600* (Wolfenbüttel, 1929).

PRÜFER, ARTHUR: *Johann Hermann Schein* (Leipzig, 1895).

—— *Johann Hermann Schein und das weltliche deutsche Lied des 17. Jahrhunderts. Anhang: Scheins Stellung zur Instrumentalmusik* (Leipzig, 1908).

REESE, GUSTAVE: 'The Origin of the English "In nomine"', *Journal of the American Musicological Society*, ii (1949).

ROSE, GLORIA: 'Agazzari and the Improvising Orchestra', *Journal of the American Musicological Society*, xviii (1965).

SCHLOSSBERG, A.: *Die italienische Sonate für mehrere Instrumente im 17. Jahrhundert* (Diss. Heidelberg, 1932).

SCHNEIDER, MAX: *Die Anfänge des Basso Continuo und seiner Bezifferung* (Leipzig, 1918).

STEVENS, DENIS: 'The Background of the "In nomine"', *Monthly Musical Record*, lxxxiv (1954).

TORCHI, LUIGI: 'L'accompagnamento degl'istrumenti nei melodrammi italiani della prima metà del seicento', *Rivista musicale italiana*, i (1894).

WALKER, ERNEST: 'An Oxford Book of Fancies', *Musical Antiquary*, iii (1911–12).

WASIELEWSKI, JOSEF WILHELM VON: *Geschichte der Instrumentalmusik im 16. Jahrhundert* (Berlin, 1878).

—— *Die Violine im XVII. Jahrhundert und die Anfänge der Instrumentalcomposition* (with separate musical supplement: *Instrumentalsätze vom Ende des XVI. bis Ende des XVII. Jahrhunderts*) (Bonn, 1874).

WEAVER, R. L.: 'The Orchestra in Early Italian Opera', *Journal of the American Musicological Society*, xvii (1964).

—— 'Sixteenth Century Instrumentation', *Musical Quarterly*, xlvii (1961).

WESTRUP, J. A.: 'Domestic Music under the Stuarts', *Proceedings of the Musical Association*, lxviii (1941–2).

—— 'Monteverdi and the Orchestra', *Music and Letters*, xxi (1940).

WILSON, JOHN: *Roger North on Music* (London, 1959).

CHAPTER XII

SOLO INSTRUMENTAL MUSIC

(i) *Sources*

ANDREWS, HILDA: *William Byrd: My Ladye Nevells Booke* (London, 1926).

ANGLÈS, HIGINI: *Monumentos de la música española*, ii. *La Música en la Corte de Carlo V. Con la transcripción del 'Libro de Cifra Nueva para tecla, harpa y vilhuela' de Luys Venegas de Henestrosa (1557)* (Barcelona, 1944).

APEL, WILLI: *Corpus of Early Keyboard Music*, ii. *Marco Facoli: Collected Works* (American Institute of Musicology, 1963).

—— *Musik aus früher Zeit für Klavier (1350–1650)*, 2 vols. (Mainz, [1934]).

AULER, WOLFGANG: *Spielbuch für Kleinorgel oder andere Tasteninstrumente* (Leipzig, 1942).

BEDBROOK, G. S.: *G. Gabrieli: Works for Keyboard Instruments* (Kassel and Basle, 1957).

BENVENUTI, GIACOMO: *I classici della musica italiana*, vi. *Girolamo Cavazzoni: Musica sacra, ricercari e canzoni* (Milan, 1919).

—— *I classici musicali italiani*, i. *M. A. Cavazzoni, J. Fogliano, J. Segni ed Anonimi: Composizioni per organo* (Milan, 1941).

—— *Istituzioni e monumenti dell'arte musicale italiana*, i–ii. *Andrea e Giovanni Gabrieli e la musica strumentale in San Marco* (Milan, 1931-2).

BRUGER, H. D.: *Alte Lautenkunst aus drei Jahrhunderten*, 2 vols. in one (Berlin and Leipzig, 1923).

—— *Schule des Lautenspiels* (Berlin, 1925-8).

BYRD, W., BULL, J., and GIBBONS, O.: *Parthenia, or the Maydenhead of the First Musicke that ever was printed for the Virginals (1611)*. Facs. ed. (*The Harrow Replicas*, iii) (London, 1942).

CALDWELL, JOHN: *Early English Church Music*, vi. *Early Tudor Organ Music: I. Music for the Office* (London, 1966).

CASIMIRI, RAFFAELE: *Musica Veterum*, iii. *G. Frescobaldi: XIV composizioni inedite* (Rome, n.d.).

CHILESOTTI, OSCAR: *Biblioteca di rarità musicali*, ii. *G. Picchi: Balli d'Arpicordo* (Milan, [1884?]), vi. *G. Frescobaldi: Partite sopra la Romanesca, la Monicha, Ruggiero e la Follia* (Milan, [1908]).

—— *Danze del secolo XVI* (Milan, n.d.).

—— *Lautenspieler des 16. Jahrhunderts* (Leipzig, 1891).

CURTIS, ALAN: *Monumenta Musicae Neerlandicae*, iii. *Nederlandse Klaviermuziek uit de 16ᵉ en 17ᵉ eeuw* (Amsterdam, 1961).

DALLA LIBERA, SANDRO: *Antologia organistica italiana* (Milan, 1957).

—— *A. Gabrieli: Tre messe per organo* (Milan, 1958).

—— *G. Gabrieli: Composizioni per organo*, 2 vols. (Milan, 1957).

—— *Toccate per organo*, 3 vols. (Milan, 1958-9).

DART, THURSTON: *Matthew Locke: Keyboard Suites* (London, 1959).

—— *Byrd, Bull, Gibbons: Parthenia* (London, 1960; 2nd rev. ed. 1962).

—— *Thomas Morley: Keyboard Works*, 2 vols. (London, 1959).

DAWES, FRANK: *Schott's Anthology of Early Keyboard Music. English Virginalists*, 5 vols. (London, 1951).

DELLA CORTE, ANDREA: *Scelta di musiche* (Milan, 1949).

DISERTORI, BENVENUTO: *C. Merulo: Sei Canzoni da sonar a 4* (Milan, 1950).

EITNER, R.: *Vereniging voor Nederlandsche Muziekgeschiedenis*, iii. *Organ Compositions by Sweelinck and Scheidt* (Amsterdam, 1871).

EMSHEIMER, ERNST: *J. U. Steigleder: Vier Ricercare für Orgel* (Kassel, 1928).

FANO, FABIO: *Istituzioni e monumenti dell'arte musicale italiana*, iv. *La Camerata fiorentina: Vincenzo Galilei* (Milan, 1934).

FROIDEBISE, PIERRE: *Orgue et liturgie*, xlvii. *Juan Bermudo: Œuvres d'orgue (1555)* (Paris, 1960); xlix. *Tomás de Santa Maria: Arte de tañer fantasia (1565)* (Paris, 1961).

FROTSCHER, GOTTHOLD: *L'organo italiano, 1567–1619* (Copenhagen, [1960]).

FULLER MAITLAND, J. A., and SQUIRE, W. B.: *The Fitzwilliam Virginal Book*, 2 vols. (London, 1894–9; reprinted New York, 1964).

FUSER, IRENEO: *Classici italiani dell'organo* (Padua, 1955).

—— *A. Valente: Versi spirituali* (Padua, 1957).

GERDES, GISELA: *Musikalische Denkmäler*, iii: *46 Choräle für Orgel von J. P. Sweelinck und seinen deutschen Schülern* (Mainz, 1957).

GOMBOSI, OTTO: *Compositione di meser Vincenzo Capirola* (Lutebook, c. 1517) (Neuilly-sur-Seine, 1955).

GUILMANT, ALEXANDRE: *Archives des maîtres de l'orgue des XVIe, XVIIe et XVIIIe siècles*, i. *J. Titelouze: Œuvres complètes* (Paris, 1898); x. *Liber fratrum cruciferorum Leodiensium (A. Gabrieli, P. Philippi, J. P. Sweelinck, C. Merulo, Fr. G. Scroux, R. Cornet, F. Fontana, G. M. Casini, etc.)* (Paris, 1910).

—— BONNET, J., and GUILMANT, M. A.: *Les Grands Maîtres anciens de l'orgue*, i. *G. Frescobaldi: Fiori musicali* (Paris, 1922).

GULLINO, G.: *G. B. della Gostena: Intavolatura di Liuto (1599)* (Florence, 1949).

—— *S. Molinaro: Intavolatura di Liuto, Libro primo (1599)* (Florence, 1940).

—— *G. M. Radino: Intavolatura di Balli per sonar di Liuto (1592)* (Florence, 1949).

GURLITT, WILIBALD: 'Michael Praetorius: Orgelwerke', *Archiv für Musikwissenschaft*, iii (1921).

HALBIG, HERMANN: *Klaviertänze des 16. Jahrhunderts* (Stuttgart, 1928).

HARDING, ROSAMOND E. M.: *G. M. Radino: Il primo libro d'Intavolatura di Balli d'Arpicordo (1592)*. Facs. ed. and transcription (Cambridge, 1949).

HARMS, G., and MAHRENHOLZ, C.: *Samuel Scheidts Werke*, i. *Tabulaturbuch vom Jahre 1650* (Kleckens, 1923); v. *Unedierte Kompositionen für Tasteninstrumente* (Hamburg, 1937); vi–vii. *Tabulatura nova* (Hamburg and Leipzig, 1953).

HAYNES, M. B.: *Corpus of Early Keyboard Music*, v. *Bernardo Pasquini: Collected Works for Keyboard* (American Institute of Musicology, 1964).

HENDRIE, GERALD: *Musica Britannica*, xx. *Orlando Gibbons: Keyboard Music* (London, 1962).

HUDSON, B.: *Corpus of Early Keyboard Music*, iii. *Giovanni Salvatore: Collected Keyboard Works* (American Institute of Musicology, 1964).

HUNT, EDGAR: *Robert Dowland: Variety of Lute Lessons (1610)*. Facs. ed. and transcription (London, 1957).

KALLER, ERNST: *Liber organi*, 9 vols. (Mainz, 1931–54).

KASTNER, MACARIO SANTIAGO: *Altitalienische Versetten für Orgel oder andre Tasteninstrumente* (Mainz, 1957).

Monumentos de la música española, vi and xii. *Francisco Correa de Arauxo:*
—— *Libro de tientos y discursos de música practica y theorica de organo intitulado facultad orgánica (1628)* (Barcelona, 1948 and 1952).

—— *Obras de Música para Tecla, Arpa y Vihuela* (Mainz, 1951).

—— *Portugaliae Musica*, i and iii. *Manuel Rodrigues Coelho: Flores de Musica para o instrumento de tecla e harpa (1620)* (Lisbon, 1959 and 1961).

—— *Rocco Rodio: Cinque ricercate, una fantasia* (Padua, 1958).

—— *Silva iberica* (Mainz, 1954).

KELLER, HERMANN: *G. Frescobaldi: Fiori musicali* (Leipzig, 1943).
—— *Samuel Scheidt: Ausgewählte Werke für Orgel und Klavier* (Leipzig, [1939]).
KOCZIRZ, A.: *Denkmäler der Tonkunst in Österreich*, Jg. xviii/2 (vol. xxxvii). *Österreichische Lautenmusik im XVI. Jahrhundert* (Vienna, 1911).
LEFKOFF, GERALD: *Five Sixteenth-Century Venetian Lute Books* (Washington, D.C., 1960).
LUMSDEN, DAVID: *An Anthology of English Lute Music* (London, 1954).
MAHRENHOLZ, C.: *Samuel Scheidt: Das Görlitzer Tabulaturbuch vom Jahre 1650* (Leipzig, [1941]).
MARLOW, RICHARD: *Musica Britannica*, xxiv. *Giles and Richard Farnaby: Keyboard Music* (London, 1965).
MATTHÄI, KARL: *Michael Praetorius: Sämtliche Orgelwerke* (Wolfenbüttel, 1930).
MERIAN, WILHELM: *Der Tanz in den deutschen Tabulaturbüchern des 16. Jahrhunderts* (Leipzig, 1927).
MISCHIATI, OSCAR: *G. Cavazzoni: Orgelwerke* (Mainz, 1958).
MORCOURT, RICHARD DE: *Adrian Le Roy: Psaumes. Tiers livre de tablature de luth (1552); Instruction (1574)* (Paris, 1962).
MORPHY, GUILLERMO DE: *Les Luthistes espagnols du XVIᵉ siècle*, 2 vols. (Leipzig, 1902).
NEWCOMB, WILBURN: *Lute Music of Shakespeare's Time* (London, 1966).
OXENBURY, WILLIAM, and DART, THURSTON: *Intabolatura nova di balli (Venice, 1551)* (London, 1965).
PEDRELL, FELIPE: *Antología de organistas clásicos españoles*, 2 vols. in 1 (Madrid, 1908).
—— *Hispaniae Schola Musica Sacra*, iii–iv. *Antonius a Cabezón: Composiciones-Fabordones-Salmodia-Intermedios-Tiento* (Leipzig, 1895); vii–viii. *Antonius a Cabezón: Composiciones à cinco y seis, Parte I, II* (Leipzig, 1898).
PETER, HILDEMARIE: *Silvestro Ganassi: La Fontegara (Venice, 1535)* (Berlin, 1956). English trans. by D. Swainson (Berlin, 1959).
PIDOUX, PIERRE: *Andrea Gabrieli: Orgelwerke*, 5 vols. (Kassel, 1941–53).
—— *Girolamo Frescobaldi: Orgel- und Klavierwerke*, 5 vols. (Kassel and Basle, 1949–54).
—— *Claudio Merulo: Canzonen (1592)* (Kassel, 1941).
PIERRONT, N., and HENNEBAINS, J. P.: *Annibale Padovano: Ricercari* (Paris, 1934).
PUJOL, E.: *Monumentos de la música española*, iii. *Luys de Narváez: Los seys libros del Delphin de música de cifra para tañer vihuela (1538)* (Barcelona, 1945); vii. *Alonso Mudarra: Tres libros de música en cifra para vihuela (1546)* (Barcelona, 1949).
RAUGEL FÉLIX: *Les Maîtres français de l'orgue*, 2 vols. (Paris, 1925).
RAYNER, CLARE G.: *Corpus of Early Keyboard Music*, iv. *Hieronymus Praetorius: Organ Magnificats on the Eight Tones* (American Institute of Musicology, 1963).
REIMANN, MARGARETE: *Das Erbe deutscher Musik*, xxxvi. *Die Lüneberger Orgeltabulatur KN 208a* (Frankfurt a/M., 1957).
REISS, CARL: *Old Spanish Organ Music* (Copenhagen, 1960).
SCHNEIDER, MAX: *Diego Ortiz: Tratado de glosas . . . (Rome, 1553)* (Kassel, 1913; 2nd ed. 1936).
SCHRADE, LEO: *Publikationen älterer Musik*, ii. *Luis Milán: Libro de música de vihuela de mano* (Leipzig, 1927).
—— 'Tänze aus einer anonymen italienischen Tabulatur', *Zeitschrift für Musikwissenschaft*, x (1928).
SEIFFERT, MAX: *Denkmäler deutscher Tonkunst*, i. *Samuel Scheidt: Tabulatura nova* (Leipzig, 1892).

—— *Jan Pieterszoon Sweelinck: Werken voor Orgel en Clavecimbel* (Amsterdam, 1943). Supplement (1958), ed. A. Annegarn.

—— *Organum*, 4. Reihe: *Orgelmusik*, i. *H. Scheidemann: 15 Präludien und Fugen* (Leipzig, 1925); ii. *Orgelmeister, I (J. Praetorius, M. Schildt, J. Decker, D. Mayer, M. Olter, C. Flor)* (Leipzig, 1925).

SOURIS, A., SPYCKET, S., VEYRIER, J., and ROLLIN, M.: *Robert Ballard: Premier Livre (1611)* and *Deuxième Livre (1614) et pièces diverses*, 2 vols. (Paris, 1963 and 1964).

STEELE, J., CAMERON, F., and DART, T.: *Musica Britannica*, xiv, xix. *John Bull: Keyboard Music*, 2 vols. (London, 1960, 1963).

STEVENS, DENIS: *Musica Britannica*, i. *The Mulliner Book* (London, 1951).

—— *Thomas Tallis: Complete Keyboard Works* (London, 1953).

STONE, KURT: *Parthenia* (New York, 1951).

TAGLIAPIETRA, GINO: *Antologia di musica antica e moderna per pianoforte*, 14 vols. (Milan, 1931–2).

TORCHI, LUIGI: *L'arte musicale in Italia*, iii. *Composizioni per organo o cembalo, secoli XVI, XVII e XVIII* (Milan, 1898).

TUTTLE, STEPHEN D.: *William Byrd: Forty-five Pieces for Keyboard Instruments* (Paris, 1939).

VILLALBA MUÑOZ, LUIS DE: *Antología de organistas clásicos españoles*, 2 vols. (Madrid, 1914).

WARD, JOHN: *The Dublin Virginal Manuscript (The Wellesley Edition*, iii) (Wellesley, Mass., 1954).

WARLOCK, PETER: *The Lute Music of John Dowland* (London, 1927).

WATELET, J.: *Monumenta Musicae Belgicae*, iv. *Charles Guillet, Giovanni Macque, Carolus Luython: Werken voor Orgel of vier Speeltuigen* (Antwerp, 1938).

WERRA, ERNST VON: *Denkmäler deutscher Tonkunst*, 2. Folge: *Denkmäler der Tonkunst in Bayern*, iv (2). *Christian Erbach: Ausgewählte Werke* (i) and *H. L. Hassler: Werke für Orgel und Klavier* (i) (Leipzig, 1903).

(ii) *Books and Articles*

ANGLÈS, HIGINI: 'Die Instrumentalmusik bis zum 16. Jahrhundert in Spanien', *Natalicia musicologica Knud Jeppesen* (Copenhagen, 1962).

APEL, WILLI: 'Drei plus Drei plus Zwei = Vier plus Vier', *Acta Musicologica*, xxxii (1960).

—— 'Du nouveau sur la musique française pour l'orgue au XVIᵉ siècle', *Revue musicale*, xviii (1937).

—— 'The Early Development of the Organ Ricercar', *Musica Disciplina*, iii (1949).

—— 'Early Spanish Music for Lute and Keyboard Instruments', *Musical Quarterly*, xx (1934).

—— 'Die handschriftliche Überlieferung der Klavierwerke Frescobaldis', *Festschrift Karl Gustav Fellerer* (Ratisbon, 1962).

—— 'Neapolitan Links between Cabezón and Frescobaldi', *Musical Quarterly*, xxiv (1938).

—— 'Spanish Organ Music of the Early 17th Century', *Journal of the American Musicological Society*, xv (1962).

—— 'Tänze und Arien für Klavier aus dem Jahre 1588', *Archiv für Musikwissenschaft*, xvii (1960).

APFEL, ERNST: 'Ostinato und Kompositionstechnik bei den englischen Virginalisten der elisabethanischen Zeit', *Archiv für Musikwissenschaft*, xix–xx (1962–3).

BAL, J.: 'Fuenllana and the Transcription of Spanish Lute-music', *Acta Musicologica*, xi (1939).

BASSO, ALBERTO: 'La musica strumentale del rinascimento polacco', *Rassegna musicale*, xxviii (1958).

BECKMANN, GUSTAV: *Das Violinspiel in Deutschland vor 1700* (Leipzig, 1918).

BEDBROOK, G. S.: *Keyboard Music from the Middle Ages to the Beginnings of the Baroque* (London, 1949).

BENVENUTI, GIACOMO: 'Noterella circa tre fughe attribuite al Frescobaldi', *Rivista musicale italiana*, xxvii (1920).

BIRKNER, GÜNTER: 'La Tablature de luth de Charles, duc de Croy et d'Arschot (1560–1612)', *Revue de musicologie*, xlix (1963).

BLUMENFELD, HAROLD: *Syntagma musicum of Michael Praetorius, Volume Two, De organographia, First and Second Parts*. English translation (St. Louis, Miss., 1949).

BOETTICHER, WOLFGANG: *Bibliographie des sources de la musique pour luth* (Paris, c. 1957).

BREIG, WERNER: 'Der Umfang des choralgebundenen Orgelwerkes von Jan Pieterszoon Sweelinck', *Archiv für Musikwissenschaft*, xvii (1960).

BURNS, JOSEPH A.: 'Antonio Valente, Neapolitan Keyboard Primitive', *Journal of the American Musicological Society*, xii (1959).

CALDWELL, JOHN: 'Keyboard Plainsong Settings in England, 1500–1660', *Musica Disciplina*, xix (1965).

CHILESOTTI, OSCAR: 'Francesco da Milano', *Sammelbände der internationalen Musikgesellschaft*, iv (1903).

—— 'Jacomo Gorzanis, liutista del Cinquecento', *Rivista musicale italiana*, xxi (1914).

—— 'Il primo Libro di liuto di Vicenzo Galilei', *Rivista musicale italiana*, xv (1908).

—— 'Note circa alcuni liutisti italiani della prima metà del Cinquecento', *Rivista musicale italiana*, ix (1902).

DART, THURSTON: 'The Cittern and its English Music', *Galpin Society Journal*, i (1948).

—— 'Elizabeth Eysbock's Keyboard Book', *Svensk tidskrift för musikforskning*, xliv (1962); also in *Hans Albrecht in Memoriam* (Kassel, 1962).

—— 'Simone Molinaro's Lute-Book of 1599', *Music and Letters*, xxviii (1947).

DEFFNER, OSKAR: *Über die Entwicklung der Fantasie für Tasteninstrumente bis Sweelinck* (Diss. Kiel, 1927).

DIETRICH, FRITZ: *Geschichte des deutschen Orgelchorals im 17. Jahrhundert* (Kassel, 1932).

FELLERER, K. G.: *Orgel und Orgelmusik, ihre Geschichte* (Augsburg, 1929).

FLADE, E.: 'J. H. Schein und die Orgel', *Musik und Kirche*, ix (1936).

FROTSCHER, GOTTHOLD: *Geschichte des Orgelspiels und der Orgelkomposition*, 2 vols. (Berlin, 1935; 2nd ed. 1959).

GEORGII, WALTER: *Klaviermusik. Geschichte der Musik für Klavier zu zwei Händen von den Anfängen bis zur Gegenwart* (Zürich, 1941; 4th ed. 1965).

GOMBOSI, OTTO: 'Der Hoftanz', *Acta Musicologica*, vii (1935).

GOOL, A. VAN: 'Once more: Sweelinck's Keyboard Music: Organ or Harpsichord?', *Tijdschrift der Vereniging voor Nederlandse Muziekgeschiedenis*, xix (1960–3).

HAMBURGER, POUL: 'Die Fantasien in Emmanuel Adrianssens *Pratum Musicum* (1600)', *Zeitschrift für Musikwissenschaft*, xii (1929–30).

—— 'Ein handschriftliches Klavierbuch aus der ersten Hälfte des 17. Jahrhunderts', *Zeitschrift für Musikwissenschaft*, xiii (1930–1).

HARWOOD, IAN: 'The Origins of the Cambridge Lute Manuscripts', *The Lute Society Journal*, v (1963).

HEARTZ, DANIEL: 'An Elizabethan Tutor for the Guitar', *The Galpin Society Journal*, xvi (Paris, 1963).

—— 'Les Premières "Instructions" pour le luth (jusque vers 1550)', *Le Luth et sa musique* (Paris, 1958).

HENDRIE, GERALD: 'The Keyboard Music of Orlando Gibbons (1583–1625)', *Proceedings of the Royal Musical Association*, lxxxix (1962–3).

HORSLEY, IMOGENE: 'The 16th-Century Variation. A New Historical Survey', *Journal of the American Musicological Society*, xii (1959).

—— 'The Solo Ricercar in Diminution Manuals: New Light on Early Wind and String Techniques', *Acta Musicologica*, xxxiii (1961).

HOWELL, ALMONTE C., JR.: 'Cabezón: An Essay in Structural Analysis', *Musical Quarterly*, l (1964).

JACHIMECKI, ZDZISŁAW: 'Eine polnische Orgeltabulatur aus dem Jahre 1548', *Zeitschrift für Musikwissenschaft*, ii (1920).

JACQUOT, JEAN, ed.: *Le Luth et sa musique* (Paris, 1958).

—— *La Musique instrumentale de la Renaissance* (Paris, 1955).

—— 'La Musique pour luth', *International Musicological Society Report of the Eighth Congress, New York, 1961*, 2 vols. (Kassel, 1961–2).

JEPPESEN, KNUD: 'Eine frühe Orgelmesse aus Castell' Arquato, *Archiv für Musikwissenschaft*, xii (1955).

—— *Die italienische Orgelmusik am Anfang des Cinquecento* (Copenhagen, 1943).

KASTNER, MARCARIO SANTIAGO: *Contribución al estudio de la música española y portuguesa* (Lisbon, 1941).

—— 'Los manuscritos musicales ns. 48 y 242 de la Biblioteca General de la Universidad de Coimbra', *Anuario musical*, v (1950).

—— *Música hispánica: O Estilo musical de Padre Manual R. Coelho* (Lisbon, 1936).

—— 'Parallels and Discrepancies between English and Spanish Keyboard Music of the Sixteenth and Seventeenth Century', *Anuario musical*, vii (1952).

—— 'Rapports entre Schlick et Cabezón', *La Musique instrumentale de la Renaissance* (Paris, 1955).

—— 'Relations entre la musique instrumentale française et espagnole au XVIᵉ siècle', *Anuario musical*, x–xi (1955–6).

—— 'Una intavolatura d'organo italiana del 1598', *Collectanea historiae musicae*, ii (1956).

KINKELDEY, OTTO: *Orgel und Klavier in der Musik des 16. Jahrhunderts* (Leipzig, 1910).

KITTLER, G.: *Geschichte des protestantischen Orgelchorals* (Ückermünde, 1931).

KOCZIRZ, A.: 'Die Gitarrekompositionen in Miguel de Fuenllana's Orphenica lyra', *Archiv für Musikwissenschaft*, iv (1922).

—— 'Der Lautenist Hans Judenkünig', *Sammelbände der internationalen Musikgesellschaft*, vi (1905).

KÖRTE, OSWALD: *Laute und Lautenmusik bis zur Mitte des 16. Jahrhunderts* (Leipzig, 1901).

KRAUS, H.: 'Jacob Buus, Leben und Werke', *Tijdschrift der Vereeniging voor Nederlandsche Muziekgeschiedenis*, xii (1926–8).

KREBS, CARL: 'Girolamo Diruta's Transilvano', *Vierteljahrsschrift für Musikwissenschaft*, viii (1892).

KUNZE, STEFAN: *Die Instrumentalmusik Giovanni Gabrielis*, 2 vols. (Tutzing, 1963).

LÖWENFELD, HANS KARL: *Leonhard Kleber und seine Orgeltabulatur* (Berlin, 1897).

LOWINSKY, E.: 'English Organ Music of the Renaissance', *Musical Quarterly*, xxxix (1953).

LUMSDEN, DAVID: 'The Sources of English Lute Music (1540–1620)', *Galpin Society Journal*, vi (1953).

LUNELLI, RENATO: *L'arte organaria del Rinascimento in Roma* (Florence, 1958).

MACHABEY, ARMAND: *Girolamo Frescobaldi Ferrarensis* (Paris, 1952).

MAHRENHOLZ, CHRISTHARD: 'Aufgabe und Bedeutung der *Tabulatura Nova*', *Musica*, viii (1954).

—— 'Samuel Scheidt und die Orgel', *Musik und Kirche*, xxv (1955).

MARLOW, RICHARD: 'The Keyboard Music of Giles Farnaby', *Proceedings of the Royal Musical Association*, xcii (1965–66).

MELLERS, WILFRID: 'John Bull and English Keyboard Music', *Musical Quarterly*, xl (1954).

MERIAN, WILHELM: *Die Tabulatur des Hans Kotter* (Leipzig, 1916).

—— *Der Tanz in den deutschen Tabulaturbüchern* (Leipzig, 1927).

MOHR, ERNST: *Die Allemande*, 2 vols. (Zürich *and* Leipzig, 1932).

MORCOURT, R. DE: 'Le Livre de tablature de luth de Domenico Bianchini (1546)', *La Musique instrumentale de la Renaissance* (Paris, 1955).

MOREL, FRITZ: *Gerolamo Frescobaldi* (Winterthur, 1945).

MOSER, HANS JOACHIM: *Paul Hofhaimer. Ein Lied- und Orgelmeister des deutschen Humanismus* (Stuttgart and Berlin, 1929).

MÜLLER-BLATTAU, JOSEPH: *Grundzüge einer Geschichte der Fuge* (Königsberg, 1923; 2nd ed. Kassel, 1931).

NELSON, ROBERT U.: *The Technique of Variation* (Berkeley, 1948).

NEUDENBERGER, LUCIA: *Die Variationstechnik der Virginalisten im Fitzwilliam Virginal Book* (Berlin, 1937).

NOSKE, FRITS: 'Sweelinck's Keyboard Music: Organ or Harpsichord?', *Tijdschrift der Vereniging voor Nederlandse Muziekgeschiedenis*, xix (1960–3).

PANNAIN, GUIDO: *Le origini e lo sviluppo dell'arte pianistica in Italia dal 1500 al 1730 circa* (Naples, 1919).

PANUM, HORTENSE: 'Melchior Schild oder Schildt', *Monatshefte für Musikgeschichte*, xx (1888).

PFATTEICHER, C. F.: *John Redford, Organist and Almoner of St. Paul's Cathedral* (Kassel, 1934).

PIETZSCH, GERHARD: 'Orgelbauer, Organisten und Orgelspiel in Deutschland bis zum Ende des 16. Jahrhunderts', *Die Musikforschung*, xii (1959).

PUJOL, E.: 'Les Ressources instrumentales et leur rôle dans la musique pour vihuela et pour guitare au XVIᵉ siècle et au XVIIᵉ', *La Musique instrumentale de la Renaissance* (Paris, 1955).

RIEMANN, HUGO: 'Das Lautenwerk des Miguel Fuenllana', *Monatshefte für Musikgeschichte*, xxvii (1895).

RITTER, A. G.: *Zur Geschichte des Orgelspiels, vornehmlich des deutschen, im 14. bis zum Anfange des 18. Jahrhunderts*, 2 vols. (Leipzig, 1884).

RONGA, LUIGI: *Gerolamo Frescobaldi, organista vaticano, 1583–1643* (Turin, 1930).

ROQUETA, JAIME MOLL: 'Músicos de la corte dal Cardenal Juan Tavera (1523–1545): Luis Venegas de Henestrosa', *Anuario musical*, vi (1951).

SCHEIDE, AUGUST: *Zur Geschichte des Choralvorspiels* (Hildburghausen, 1930).

SCHIERNING, LYDIA: *Quellengeschichtliche Studien zur Orgel- und Klaviermusik in Deutschland aus der I. Hälfte des 17. Jahrhunderts* (Kassel and Basle, 1962).

—— *Die Überlieferung der deutschen Orgel- und Klaviermusik aus der ersten Hälfte des 17. Jahrhunderts* (Kassel and Basle 1961).

SCHRADE, LEO: 'Ein Beitrag zur Geschichte der Tokkata', *Zeitschrift für Musikwissenschaft*, viii (1925–6).

SCHÜNEMANN, GEORG: *Geschichte der Klaviermusik* (Berlin, 1940).

SEIFFERT, MAX: 'J. P. Sweelinck und seine direkten deutschen Schüler', *Vierteljahrsschrift für Musikwissenschaft*, vii (1891).

SLIM, H. COLIN: 'Francesco da Milano: a Bio-Bibliographical Study', *Musica Disciplina*, xviii–xix (1964–5).

SPEER, KLAUS: 'The Organ *Verso* in Iberian Music to 1700', *Journal of the American Musicological Society*, xi (1958).

SPIESSENS, GODELIEVE: 'Emmanuel Adriaenssen et son *Pratum Musicum*', *Acta Musicologica*, xxxvi (1964).

STEVENS, DENIS: 'The Keyboard Music of Thomas Tallis', *Musical Times*, xciii (1952).

—— *The Mulliner Book: A Commentary* (London, 1952).

STEVENSON, ROBERT: *Juan Bermudo* (The Hague, 1960).

SUTHERLAND, GORDON: 'The Ricercari of Jacques Buus', *Musical Quarterly*, xxxi (1945).

TORCHI, LUIGI: *La musica strumentale in Italia nei secoli XVI, XVII e XVIII* (Turin, 1901).

TREND, J. B.: *Luis Milan and the Vihuelistas* (Oxford, 1925).

TUSLER, ROBERT L.: *The Organ Music of Jan Pieterszoon Sweelinck* (Bilthoven, 1958).

VALENTIN, ERICH: *Die Entwicklung der Tokkata im 17. und 18. Jahrhundert (bis J. S. Bach)* (Münster, 1930).

VALLE DE PAZ, GIACOMO DEL: *Annibale Padovano* (Turin, 1933).

VAN DEN BORREN, CHARLES: *Les Origines de la musique de clavier dans les Pays-Bas jusque vers 1630* (Brussels, 1914).

—— *The Sources of Keyboard Music in England* (London, 1913).

VAN DEN SIGTENHORST MEYER, B.: *Jan P. Sweelinck en zijn instrumentale muziek* (The Hague, 1934; 2nd ed. 1946).

WARD, JOHN: 'The Editorial Methods of Venegas de Henestrosa', *Musica Disciplina*, vi (1952).

WASIELEWSKI, JOSEF WILHELM VON: *Geschichte der Instrumentalmusik im 16. Jahrhundert* (Berlin, 1878).

WERRA, ERNST VON: 'Beiträge zur Geschichte des französischen Orgelspiels', *Kirchenmusikalisches Jahrbuch*, xxiii (1910).

YOUNG, WILLIAM: 'Keyboard Music to 1600', *Musica Disciplina*, xvi–xvii (1962–3).

CHAPTER XIII

INSTRUMENTS AND INSTRUMENTAL NOTATION

(i) *Sources*

CHAPMAN, ROGER: *Marin Mersenne: Harmonie universelle* (Paris, 1636–7). Facs. ed. and English translation (The Hague, 1957).

DOLMETSCH, N.: *Christopher Simpson: The Division Violist* (London, 1659). Facs. of 2nd ed., 1667 (London, 1956).

EITNER, ROBERT: 'Arnolt Schlick: Spiegel der Orgelmacher und Organisten (Heidelberg, 1511)', *Monatshefte für Musikgeschichte*, i (1869).

—— *Publikation älterer praktischer und theoretischer Musikwerke*, xi (Jg. 10). *Sebastian Virdung: Musica getutscht (Basel, 1511)* (Leipzig, 1896); xiii (Jg. 12). *Michael Praetorius: Syntagmatis musici Tom. II de Organographia (Wolfenbüttel, 1618–20)* (Leipzig, 1884); xx (Jg. 24). *Martin Agricola: Musica instrumentalis deudsch, erste und vierte Ausgabe (Wittenberg, 1528 und 1545)* (Leipzig, 1896).

FLADE, ERNST: *Arnolt Schlick: Spiegel der Orgelmacher und Organisten* (*Heidelberg, 1511*). Edition in modern German (Mainz, 1932).

GURLITT, WILIBALD: *Michael Praetorius: Syntagma musicum*, ii. *De organographia*. Facs. ed. (Kassel, 1929).

HELLWIG, H. J.: *Jacques Hotteterre: Principes de la Flûte Traversière* (*1707*). Facs. of 1728 ed. with German translation (Kassel, 1941).

JACQUOT, JEAN: *Thomas Mace: Musick's Monument* (*London, 1676*). Facs. of 1686 ed. (Paris, 1958).

KINSKY, GEORG: *Geschichte der Musik in Bilder* (Leipzig, 1929).

LESURE, F.: *P. Trichet: Traité des instruments de musique* (*c. 1640*) (Neuilly-sur-Seine, 1957).

MEYER, KATHI: *Ercole Bottrigari: Il Desiderio, ovvero de' concerti di vari stromenti musicali, dialogo di musica* (*1594*). Facs. ed. (Berlin, 1924).

SCHNEIDER, MAX: *Silvestro Ganassi: Regola Rubertina* (*Venice, 1542-3*). Facs. ed. (Leipzig, 1924).

SCHÜNEMANN, GEORG: *Das Erbe deutscher Musik*, vii. *Trompeterfanfaren, Sonaten und Feldstücke nach Aufzeichnungen deutscher Hoftrompeter des 16./17. Jahrhunderts* (Leipzig, 1936).

SMETS, PAUL: *Arnolt Schlick: Spiegel der Orgelmacher und Organisten* (*Heidelberg, 1511*). Original text with facs. (Mainz, 1937).

(ii) *Books and Articles*

BACHMANN, WERNER: *Die Anfänge des Streichinstrumentenspiels* (Leipzig, 1964).

BAINES, ANTHONY, ed.: *Musical Instruments through the Ages* (Harmondsworth, 2nd ed. 1966).

—— *Woodwind Instruments and their History* (London, 1957).

BATE, PHILIP: *The Oboe* (London, 1956; 2nd rev. ed. 1962).

BESSARABOFF, NICHOLAS: *Ancient European Musical Instruments* (Boston, 1941).

BOALCH, DONALD H.: *Makers of the Harpsichord and Clavichord, 1440-1840* (London, 1956).

BOYDEN, DAVID D.: *The History of Violin Playing from its Origins to 1761 and its Relationship to the Violin and Violin Music* (London, 1965).

BUCHNER, A.: *Musical Instruments through the Ages* (London, 1956).

CARSE, ADAM: *Musical Wind Instruments* (London, 1939).

COUTAGNE, HENRI: *Gaspard Duiffopraucart et les luthiers lyonnais du XVIe siècle* (Paris, 1893).

DONINGTON, ROBERT: *The Instruments of Music* (London, 1949; 3rd ed., rev., 1962).

DUFOURCQ, NORBERT: *Esquisse d'une histoire de l'orgue en France du XIIIe au XVIIIe siècle* (Paris, 1935).

ELLIS, ALEXANDER J.: *The History of Musical Pitch* (London, 1880).

FROTSCHER, G.: *Geschichte des Orgelspiels*, 2 vols. (Berlin, 1935; 2nd ed. 1959).

GALPIN, FRANCIS W.: *Old English Instruments of Music* (London, 1910; new ed. with supplementary notes by Thurston Dart, 1965).

—— 'The Sackbut, its Evolution and History', *Proceedings of the Musical Association*, xxxiii (1906).

—— *A Textbook of European Musical Instruments* (London, 1937).

GEIRINGER, KARL: *Musical Instruments* (London, 1943).

GILL, DONALD: 'The Elizabethan Lute', *Galpin Society Journal*, xii (1959).

—— 'The Orpharion and Bandora', *Galpin Society Journal*, xiii (1960).

HALFPENNY, ERIC: 'The English 2- and 3-Keyed Hautboy', *Galpin Society Journal*, ii (1949).

—— 'Tantivy: an Exposition of the "Ancient Hunting Notes"', *Proceedings of the Royal Musical Association*, lxxx (1954).

—— 'The "Tenner Hoboy"', *Galpin Society Journal*, v (1952).

HARRISON, F., and RIMMER, J.: *European Musical Instruments* (London, 1964).

HAYES, GERALD: *King's Music* (London, 1937).

—— *Musical Instruments and their Music, 1500–1750*, i. *The Treatment of Instrumental Music* (Oxford, 1928); ii. *Viols and other Bowed Instruments* (Oxford, 1930).

HEARTZ, DANIEL: 'An Elizabethan Tutor for the Guitar', *Galpin Society Journal*, xvi (1963).

HECKEL, WILHELM: *Der Fagott* (Leipzig, 1931).

HIPKINS, A. J. and GIBB, W.: *Musical Instruments, Historic, Rare and Unique* (Edinburgh, 1888).

HUBBARD, FRANK: *Three Centuries of Harpsichord Making* (Cambridge, Mass., 1965).

HUNT, EDGAR, and DONINGTON, ROBERT: *Practical Method for the Recorder*, 2 vols. (London, 1935).

JAMES, PHILIP: *Early Keyboard Instruments* (London, 1930).

KENDALL, RAYMOND: 'Notes on Arnold Schlick', *Acta Musicologica*, xi (1939).

KÖRTE, OSWALD: *Laute und Lautenmusik bis zur Mitte des 16. Jahrhunderts* (Leipzig, 1901).

LANGWILL, LYNDESAY G.: *The Bassoon and Contrabassoon* (London, 1965).

—— 'The Curtal (1550–1750)', *Musical Times*, lxxviii (1937).

LA LAURENCIE, LIONEL DE: *Les Luthistes* (Paris, 1928).

LEFÈVRE, JEAN: *La Vielle* (Paris, 1861).

LEICHTENTRITT, HUGO: 'Was lehren uns die Bilderwerke des 14.–17. Jahrhunderts über die Instrumentalmusik ihrer Zeit?', *Sammelbände der internationalen Musikgesellschaft*, vii (1906).

MAHRENHOLZ, CHRISTHARD: *Die Orgelregister* (Kassel, 1928).

MARCUSE, SYBIL: *Musical Instruments. A Comprehensive Dictionary* (New York, 1964).

MARX, JOSEF: 'The Tone of the Baroque Oboe', *Galpin Society Journal*, iv (1951)

MASLEN, BENJAMIN G.: 'The Earliest English Organ Pedals', *Musical Times*, ci (1960). See also subsequent correspondence, ibid. (Nov., 1960; Feb., April, 1961).

MENDEL, ARTHUR: 'Pitch in the 16th and Early 17th Centuries', *Musical Quarterly*, xxxiv (1948).

MENKE, WERNER: *History of the Trumpet of Bach and Handel* (London, 1934).

NEUPERT, HANS: *Das Klavichord* (Kassel, 1950).

NORLIND, TOBIAS: *Musikinstrumentens Historia* (Stockholm, 1941).

RUSSELL, RAYMOND: *The Harpsichord and Clavichord: an Introductory Study* (London, 1959).

SACHS, CURT: 'Chromatic Trumpets in the Renaissance', *Musical Quarterly*, xxxvi (1950).

—— *Handbuch der Musikinstrumentenkunde* (Leipzig, 1920).

—— *History of Musical Instruments* (London, 1940).

—— *Real-Lexikon der Musikinstrumente* (Berlin, 1913).

SCHLESINGER, KATHLEEN: *The Instruments of the Modern Orchestra and Early Records of the Precursors of the Violin Family*, 2 vols. (London, 1910).

SCHLOSSER, JULIUS: *Die Sammlung alter Musikinstrumente im Kunsthistorischen Museum* (Vienna, 1920).

SUMNER, W. L.: *The Organ* (London, 1952).

THOINAN, ERNEST: *André Maugars* (Paris, 1865).

VALENTIN, ERICH: *Handbuch der Instrumentenkunde* (Ratisbon, 1954).

WILLIAMS, C. F. ABDY: *The Story of the Organ* (London, 1903).
WOLF, JOHANNES: *Handbuch der Notationskunde*, ii (Leipzig, 1919).
WORSCHING, J.: *Die historischen Saitenklaviere* (Mainz, 1946).

CHAPTER XIV

MUSIC AND DRAMA

(i) *Sources*

BROWN, HOWARD M.: *Theatrical Chansons* (Cambridge, Mass., 1963).
CAULA, GIACOMO ALESSANDRO: *Beaujoyeulx: Balet Comique de la Royne.* Facs. ed. with introduction (Turin, 1965).
CUTTS, JOHN P.: *La Musique de scène de la troupe de Shakespeare* (Paris, 1959).
DENT, EDWARD J.: *Musica Britannica*, ii. *Locke and Gibbons: Cupid and Death* (London, 1951).
EITNER, ROBERT: '*Seelewig* von S. T. Staden', *Monatshefte für Musikgeschichte*, xiii (1881).
GHISI, FEDERICO: *Feste musicali della Firenze Medicea, 1480–1589* (Florence, 1939).
PEDRELL, FELIPE: 'La Festa d'Elche', *Sammelbände der internationalen Musikgesellschaft*, ii (1900–1).
SABOL, ANDREW J.: *Songs and Dances for the Stuart Masque* (Providence, Rhode Island, 1959).
SOLERTI, ANGELO, ed.: 3 vols. (Palermo and Milan, 1905).
—— ed.: *Gli albori del melodramma, Le origini del melodramma* (Turin, 1903).
STERNFELD, F. W.: *Songs from Shakespeare's Tragedies* (London, 1964).
STEVENS, JOHN: *Musica Britannica*, xviii. *Music at the Court of Henry VIII* (London, 1962).
WALKER, D. P.: *Les Fêtes . . . Médicis et . . . Lorraine, Florence 1589 . . . Intermèdes de Pellegrina* (Paris, 1963).
WECKERLIN, JEAN-BAPTISTE: *Beaujoyeulx: Balet Comique de la Royne* (*Chefs d'œuvres de l'opéra français*) (Paris, n.d. [1881]).

(ii) *Books and Articles*

ARKWRIGHT, G. E. P.: 'Elizabethan Choirboy Play and their Music', *Proceedings of the Royal Musical Association*, xl (1914).
BOLTE, JOHANNES: *Die Singspiele der englischen Komödianten* (Leipzig, 1893).
BRENNECKE, ERNEST and HENRY: *Shakespeare in Germany: 1590–1700* (Chicago, 1964).
CHAMBERS, E. K.: *The Elizabethan Stage*, 4 vols. (Oxford, 1923).
CHASE, GILBERT: 'Juan del Encina', *Music and Letters*, xx (1939).
CUTTS, JOHN P.: 'Jacobean Masque and Stage Music', *Music and Letters*, xxxv (1954).
BRETT, PHILIP: 'The English Consort Song, 1570–1625', *Proceedings of the Royal Musical Association*, lxxxviii (1961–2).
DENT, EDWARD J.: *Foundations of English Opera* (Cambridge, 1928).
EMSLIE, McDONALD: 'Nicholas Lanier's Innovations in English Song', *Music and Letters*, xli (1960).
GOMBOSI, OTTO: 'Some Musical Aspects of the English Court Masque', *Journal of the American Musicological Society*, i (1948).
GREG, W. W.: *Bibliography of Printed English Drama*, 4 vols. (London, 1939–59).
GREGOR, JOSEPH: *Weltgeschichte des Theaters* (Zürich, 1933).

HARTNOLL, PHYLLIS, ed.: *Oxford Companion to the Theatre* (London, 1961).
—— *Shakespeare in Music* (London, 1964).
JACQUOT, JEAN, ed.: *Les Fêtes de la Renaissance*, i (Paris, 1956).
KIESEWETTER, R. G.: *Schicksale und Beschaffenheit des weltlichen Gesanges* (Leipzig, 1841).
KINDERMANN, HEINZ: *Theatergeschichte Europas*, 5 vols. (Salzburg, 1957–62).
LEA, KATHLEEN M.: *Italian Popular Comedy*, 2 vols. (Oxford, 1934).
LEFKOWITZ, MURRAY: 'The Longleat Papers of Bulstrode Whitelocke; New Light on Shirley's *Triumph of Peace*', *Journal of the American Musicological Society*, xviii (1965).
LILIENCRON, ROCHUS VON: 'Die Chorgesänge des lateinisch-deutschen Schuldramas . . .', *Vierteljahrsschrift für Musikwissenschaft*, vi (1890).
LIVERMORE, ANN: 'The Spanish Dramatists and their Use of Music', *Music and Letters*, xxv (1944).
McGOWAN, MARGARET M.: *L'Art du Ballet de Cour en France* (*1581–1643*) (Paris, 1963).
NICOLL, ALLARDYCE: *The World of the Harlequin* (Cambridge, 1963).
PIETZSCH, GERHARD: 'Dresdener Hoffeste vom 16.–18. Jahrhundert', *Festschrift für Max Seiffert* (Kassel, 1938).
POPE, ISABEL: 'El villancico polifonico', *Cancionero de Upsala*, ed. J. Bal y Gay (Mexico City, 1944).
PRUNIÈRES, HENRY: *Le Ballet de cour en France* (Paris, 1914).
REYHER, PAUL: *Les Masques Anglais* (Paris, 1909).
SABOL, ANDREW J.: 'New Documents on Shirley's Masque "The Triumph of Peace"', *Music and Letters*, xlvii (1966).
SCHNEIDER, MAX: *Die Anfänge des Basso Continuo* (Leipzig, 1918).
SOLERTI, ANGELO: 'Le rappresentazioni musicali di Venezia 1571–1605', *Rivista musicale italiana*, ix (1902).
SONNECK, O. G.: 'A Description of Alessandro Striggio and Francesco Corteccia's Intermedii "Psyche and Amor" 1565', *Musical Antiquary*, iii (1911).
—— *Miscellaneous Studies in the History of Music* (New York, 1921).
STERNFELD, F. W.: 'Music in the Schools of the Reformation', *Musica Disciplina*, ii (1948).
—— *Music in Shakespearean Tragedy* (London, 1963).
WEAVER, ROBERT L.: 'Sixteenth-century Instrumentation', *Musical Quarterly*, xlvii (1961).
—— 'The Orchestra in Early Italian Opera', *Journal of the American Musicological Society*, xvii (1964).
WELSFORD, ENID: *The Court Masque* (Cambridge, 1927).

CHAPTER XV

EARLY ITALIAN OPERA

(i) *Sources*

EITNER, ROBERT: *Publikation älterer praktischer und theoretischer Musikwerke*, x (Jg. 9). *Die Oper von ihren ersten Anfängen bis zur Mitte des 18. Jahrhunderts: Caccini: Euridice; Gagliano: Dafne; Monteverdi: Orfeo* (Leipzig, 1881).
FANO, FABIO: *Istituzioni e monumenti dell'arte musicale italiana*, iv. *La Camerata fiorentina: Vincenzo Galilei* (Milan, 1934).

FLEMMING, WILLI: *Nicola Sabbatini: Pratica di fabricar scene e machine ne' teatri* (*Ravenna, 1638*). German edition as *Anleitung Dekorationen und Theatermaschinen herzustellen* (Weimar, 1926). French translation (Neuchâtel, 1942).

GUBITOSI, E.: *E. de' Cavalieri: Rappresentazione di anima e di corpo* (Milan, c. 1956).

LOEWENBERG, ALFRED: *Annals of Opera, 1597–1940.* 2nd ed., 2 vols. (Geneva, 1955).

MALIPIERO, G. FRANCESCO: *Claudio Monteverdi: Orfeo.* Vocal score (London, 1923).

—— *I classici della musica italiana*, x. *E. del Cavaliere: Rappresentazione di anima e di corpo* (Milan, 1919); xix. *C. Monteverdi: Il combattimento di Tancredi e Clorinda* (Milan, 1919); xxiv. *J. Peri: L'Euridice* (Milan, 1919).

—— *Tutte le opere di Claudio Monteverdi*, viii. *Madrigali guerrieri et amorosi, con alcuni opuscoli in genere rappresentativo . . . (Libro ottavo, 1638)* (Leipzig, 1929); xi. *L'Orfeo: Favola in musica (1609)* (Leipzig, 1930).

MANTICA, F.: *Prime fioriture del melodramma italiano*, i. *E. de' Cavalieri: Rappresentazione di anima e di corpo (Rome, 1600)*. Facs. ed. (Rome, 1912).

PERI, JACOPO.: *L'Euridice* (1600). Facs. ed. (Rome, 1934).

SANDBERGER, ADOLF: *C. Monteverdi: L'Orfeo.* Facs. of 1609 ed. (Augsburg, 1927).

SOLERTI, ANGELO: *Gli albori del melodramma*, 3 vols. (Palermo and Milan, 1905).

—— *Le origini del melodramma* (Turin, 1903).

STEVENS, DENIS: *C. Monteverdi: Il ballo delle ingrate* (London, 1960).

—— *C. Monteverdi: Il combattimento di Tancredi e Clorinda* (London, 1962).

TORCHI, LUIGI: *L'arte musicale in Italia*, v. *Composizioni ad una e più voci, secolo XVII* (Milan, n.d.); vi. *La musica scenica, secolo XVII: Jacopo Peri, Claudio Monteverdi* (Milan, n.d.).

VATIELLI, F.: *E. de' Cavalieri: Rappresentazione di anima e di corpo* (Leipzig, 1906).

(ii) *Books and Articles*

ABERT, ANNA AMALIE: *Claudio Monteverdi und das musikalische Drama* (Lippstadt, 1954).

ALALEONA, DOMENICO: *Studi su la storia dell'oratorio musicale in Italia* (Milan, 1945).

—— 'Su Emilio de Cavalieri', *La nuova musica*, Nos. 113–14 (1905).

ARNOLD, DENIS: *Monteverdi* (London, 1963).

BECHERINI, BIANCA: 'La musica nelle "Sacre rappresentazioni" Fiorentine', *Rivista musicale italiana*, liii (1951).

CIVITA, A.: *Ottavio Rinuccini e il sorgere del melodramma in Italia* (Mantua, 1900).

COLLAER, PAUL: 'L'orchestra di Claudio Monteverdi', *Musica*, ii (Florence, 1943).

DELLA CORTE, ANDREA: *Drammi per musica dal Rinuccini allo Zeno*, 2 vols. (Turin, [1958]).

EHRICHS, ALFRED: *Giulio Caccini* (Leipzig, 1908).

EINSTEIN, ALFRED: 'Firenze prima della monodia', *Rassegna musicale*, vii (1934).

GHISI, FEDERICO: *Alle fonti della monodia: Due nuovi brani della 'Dafne': il 'Fuggilotio musicale', di G. Caccini* (Milan, 1940).

—— 'An Early seventeenth Century MS. with Unpublished Italian Monodic Music by Peri, Giulio Romano, and Marco da Gagliano', *Acta Musicologica*, xx (1948).

GHISLANZONI, ALBERTO: *Luigi Rossi (Aloysius de Rubeis), biografia e analisi delle composizioni* (Milan and Rome, [1954]).

GOLDSCHMIDT, HUGO: *Die italienische Gesangmethode des XVII. Jahrhunderts* (Breslau, 1890).

—— *Studien zur Geschichte der italienischen Oper im 17. Jahrhundert*, 2 vols. (Leipzig, 1901–4).

GROUT, DONALD JAY: 'The Chorus in Early Opera', in *Festschrift Friedrich Blume* (Kassel and Basle, 1963).

—— *A Short History of Opera* (New York, 1947; 2nd rev. ed. 1965).

HEUSS, ALFRED: 'Die Instrumental-Stücke des *Orfeo*', *Sammelbände der internationalen Musikgesellschaft*, iv (1902–3).

PALISCA, CLAUDE V.: *Girolamo Mei: Letters on Ancient and Modern Music to Vincenzo Galilei and Giovanni Bardi* (American Institute of Musicology, 1960).

—— 'Girolamo Mei: Mentor to the Florentine Camerata', *Musical Quarterly*, xl (1954).

—— 'The First Performance of *Euridice*', *Queen's College (New York): Twenty-fifth Anniversary Festschrift* (New York, 1964).

—— 'Vincenzo Galilei and Some Links between "Pseudo-Monody" and Monody', *Musical Quarterly*, xlvi (1960).

PAOLI, DOMENICO DE': *Claudio Monteverdi* (Milan, 1945).

PIRROTTA, NINO: 'Temperaments and Tendencies in the Florentine Camerata', *Musical Quarterly*, xl (1954).

PORTER, WILLIAM V.: 'Peri and Corsi's *Dafne*: Some New Discoveries and Observations', *Journal of the American Musicological Society*, xviii (1965).

PRUNIÈRES, HENRY: *L'Opéra italien en France avant Lulli* (Paris, 1913).

—— *La Vie et l'œuvre de Claudio Monteverdi* (Paris, 1924).

REDLICH, H. F.: *Claudio Monteverdi: Life and Works*. Trans. Kathleen Dale (London, 1952).

ROBINSON, M. F.: *Opera before Mozart* (London, 1966).

ROLLAND, ROMAIN: *Histoire de l'opéra en Europe avant Lully et Scarlatti* (Paris, 1895).

—— 'La Première Représentation du *Alessio* de Stefano Landi en 1632', *Revue d'histoire et de critique musicales* (Paris, 1902).

SCHILD, MARION: *Die Musikdramen Ottavio Rinuccinis* (Munich, 1933).

SCHRADE, LEO: *Monteverdi: Creator of Modern Music* (London, 1951).

—— *La Représentation d'Edipo Tiranno au Teatro Olimpico* (Paris, 1960).

SOLERTI, ANGELO: *Musica, ballo e drammatica alla Corte Medicea de 1600 al 1637* (Florence, 1905).

SONNECK, O. G.: '"Dafne", the First Opera: A Chronological Study', *Sammelbände der internationalen Musikgesellschaft*, xv (1913–14).

TIRABASSI, ANTONIO: 'The Oldest Opera: Belli's *Orfeo dolente*', *Musical Quarterly*, xxv (1939).

TOWNELEY WORSTHORNE, S.: *Venetian Opera in the Seventeenth Century* (Oxford, 1954).

VOGEL, EMIL: 'Claudio Monteverdi: Leben, Werken im Licht der zeitgenössischen Kritik', *Vierteljahrsschrift für Musikwissenschaft*, iii (1887).

—— 'Marco da Gagliano. Zur Geschichte des florentiner Musiklebens von 1570–1650', *Vierteljahrsschrift für Musikwissenschaft*, v (1889).

WESTRUP, J. A.: 'Monteverdi and the Orchestra', *Music and Letters*, xxi (1940).

—— 'Monteverdi's "Lamento d'Arianna"', *Music Review*, i (1940).

LIST OF CONTENTS OF
THE HISTORY OF MUSIC IN SOUND
VOLUME IV

The History of Music in Sound is a series of volumes of gramophone records, with explanatory booklets, designed as a companion series to the *New Oxford History of Music*. Each volume covers the same ground as the corresponding volume in the *New Oxford History of Music* and is designed as far as possible to illustrate the music discussed therein. The records are issued in England by E.M.I. Records Ltd. (H.M.V.) and in the United States by R.C.A. Victor, and the booklets are published by the Oxford University Press. The editor of Volume IV of *The History of Music in Sound* is Sir Jack Westrup.

The History of Music in Sound is available on LP records, and the side numbers are given below.

LUTHERAN CHURCH MUSIC
>   Band 5   *Wie schön leuchtet der Morgenstern* (Praetorius)

GIOVANNI GABRIELI (1557–1612)
>   Band 6   *In ecclesiis*

SOLO SONG: French, Spanish, and English
Side IV   Band 1   *Vivray-je tousjours en soucy?* (Claudin de Sermisy)
>   Band 2   *Toda mi vida os amé* (Luis Milán)
>   Band 3   *Thyrsis and Milla* (Morley)
>   Band 4   *Sleep, wayward thoughts* (Dowland)

INSTRUMENTAL ENSEMBLE
>   Band 5   Ricercar no. 7 (Willaert)
>   Band 6   Padouan and Intrada from Suite no. 3 (Peuerl)
>   Band 7   3-part Fantasia, no. 3 (Gibbons)
>   Band 8   4-part Fantasia (Coperario)

KEYBOARD MUSIC
Virginals
>   Band 9   *My lady Carey's Dompe* (anon.)
>   *My Selfe* (Bull)
>   *His Humour* (Farnaby)
>   *The King's Juell* (Gibbons)

Harpsichord
Side v   Band 1   *Capriccio sopra un soggetto* (Frescobaldi)

Organ
>   Band 2   *Ricercar arioso*, no. 1 (Andrea Gabrieli)
>   Band 3   Chorale Variations: *Ach Gott, vom Himmel sieh'*
>   *darein* (Sweelinck)

EARLY OPERA
>   Band 4   Scene from *Orfeo*, Act IV (Monteverdi)
>   Band 5   *Bevi, bevi* from *La Morte d'Orfeo* (Landi)

INDEX

The general plan of the Index follows that of Vol. III, except for the treatment of substantial works, which are now arranged under the names of their composers or author, as they will be in all subsequent volumes. Such items as *chansons*, madrigals, motets, and psalm-paraphrases continue to be indexed by title in the general alphabet.

3 R